Proceedings

The 16th Annual International Symposium on
COMPUTER ARCHITECTURE

 IEEE Computer Society Press

Washington ● **Los Alamitos** ● **Brussels** ● **Tokyo**

The 16th Annual
International Symposium on

COMPUTER ARCHITECTURE

Published by

IEEE Computer Society Press
1730 Massachusetts Avenue, N.W.
Washington, D.C. 20036-1903

Cover design by Jack I. Ballestero

IEEE Computer Society Order Number 1948
Library of Congress Number 85-642899
IEEE Catalog Number 89CH2705-2
ISBN 0-8186-1948-1 (paper)
ISBN 0-8186-5948-3 (microfiche)
ISBN 0-8186-8948-X (case)
ACM Order Number 415890
ISBN 0-89791-319-1
ISSN 0884-7495

Additional copies of the 1989 Proceedings may be ordered from:

| ACM Order Department P.O. Box 64145 Baltimore, MD 21264 | IEEE Computer Society Order Department 10662 Los Vaqueros Circle Los Alamitos, CA 90720-2578 | IEEE Service Center 445 Hoes Lane P.O. Box 1331 Piscataway, NJ 08855-1331 | IEEE Computer Society 13, Avenue de l'Aquilon B-1200 Brussels BELGIUM | IEEE Computer Society Ooshima Building 2-19-1 Minami-Aoyama Minato-ku, Tokyo 107, JAPAN |

THE INSTITUTE OF ELECTRICAL AND ELECTRONICS ENGINEERS, INC.

IEEE

iv

General Co-Chairmen's Message

Welcome to the 16th Annual International Symposium on Computer Architecture, taking place in the historic city of Jerusalem, holy to Jews, Christians, and Moslems all over the world. This year's venue has attracted a truly international field of participants, as evidenced by the number of contributed papers from the US, Europe, and the Far-East. We hope that the interaction among the Symposium participants from abroad, and their Israeli colleagues, will lead to more international cooperation in the computer architecture field, both in academia and industry.

Highlights of this Symposium include an opening address on "Trends in Technology and Systems," by John A. Darringer, and a keynote address on "The Evolution to Post-RISC Architectures," by Michael W. Blasgen, both from IBM Research, Yorktown Heights, as well as an invited talk by Mario Tokoro from Sony Corporation and Keio University, on "Concurrent Objects: A Way to Efficiently Utilize Hardware Parallelism." Also, two panel sessions have been organized, one on "Choosing a Parallel Paradigm: SIMD or MIMD?" chaired by Andre M. van Tilborg, ONR, and the other on "Hardware and Software Architectures for Real-Time Computing" chaired by Abraham Waksman, AFOSR.

The main component of the technical program is made up of 46 carefully selected, high quality contributed papers, presented in two parallel streams of sessions. As in the past, the Symposium Banquet will serve as the forum for the Eckert-Mauchly Award ceremony, as well as the site of the annual SIGARCH Business Meeting. In addition, and for the first time in its history, the Symposium will feature a poster session.

Also, in what we hope will become the beginning of a tradition for future Symposia, a number of workshops on computer architecture will be held in Eilat preceding the Symposium. Two full-day, and four half-day tutorials complete a week of activities associated with the Symposium.

We thank Jean-Claude Syre, the Program Chairman, for his devotion and excellent world-wide organization, leading to a very careful selection of the most suitable papers. Our thanks also go to the Program Vice-Chairs Arvind, John Gurd, and Masaru Kitsuregawa, to all the other members of the Program Committee and the reviewers, whose combined efforts contributed so much to the high standard of papers selected.

Our thanks also go to the Vice-Chairs Gideon Frieder, Zeev Barzilai, Ulrich Trottenberg, Yoshihiro Tohma, to Uri Weiser (Publicity and Publications), Ran Ginosar (Finance), Ilan Spillinger (Travel Grants), Danny Tabak (Tutorials), Benny Atlas (Posters) and Helnye Azaria (Exhibits). Special thanks go to Trevor Mudge for coordinating the Eilat workshops.

As in years past, the Symposium is co-sponsored by ACM's Special Interest Group on Computer Architecture (SIGARCH), and the Technical Committee on Computer Architecture (TCCA) of the IEEE Computer Society. We are most grateful to Doug DeGroot, SIGARCH Chairman, for his efforts in making this Symposium and its associated workshops possible, and to Zary Segall for his initiative to hold the Symposium in Israel.

We thank Nehama Yoeli for her relentless efforts as the Symposium coordinator in Israel, and we appreciate the assistance of Donna Baglio (ACM), Lee Blue (IEEE), and Sara Wohlfeiler (Unitours).

Michael Yoeli
Technion

Gabriel (Gabby) Silberman
CMU & Technion

Program Chairman's Message

When time comes to write the Program Chairman's Message, it means that his job is nearly finished. Let me take this opportunity to trace a teamwork of more than twelve months full of rich times and fruitful contacts.

When I was contacted by Zary Segall, on behalf of the ISCA89 Steering Committee, I accepted the challenge, and decided that a teamwork with Arvind (MIT), John Gurd (U. Manchester), and Masaru Kitsuregawa (U. Tokyo) would do better than a single headed Chair. I gratefully acknowledge them for their splendid work. The task of forming the Program Committee was considerably eased because they all spontaneously accepted the task with great pleasure. Our special thanks to all of them for what can be considered one of the most difficult parts of the paper selection process.

The submittals arrived only later. We received 170 drafts, partitioned into 96 from America, 50 from Europe, and 24 from Far East. They were immediately sent to the PC members, who dispatched them to referees selected for their expertise in the field. Around 180 referees contributed to the reviews process (and we apologize if some names are missing in the list printed in the next pages), each paper being reviewed by three of them.

The reviews were really excellent and provided an invaluable input to the three Regional PC Meetings respectively held in Cambridge, Manchester, and Tokyo. After the regional PC meetings, a PC meeting was held on January 26th and 27th at ECRC in Munich. Arvind, John, Chriss Jesshope, myself, and Gabriel Silberman, the General Chairman, have spent these two days with the definite objective of building a high quality technical program. If the task was eased by the first order filter some days before, the job was far from being done. Besides the 32 first very good, no-comment papers already selected, we had to cross-compare all the remaining ones still competing for acceptance. Their quality was high enough to generate very long discussions, comparisons, and re-evaluations. For the sake of the high standards required for the conference, only 46 papers were accepted altogether. The remaining ones had to be left, but we are sure that many of them were very valuable, and we hope that their authors will have found another forum to express their ideas. I believe that the end result, which is offered now in the Proceedings, reflects very much on the real value of the submissions.

So far I have been talking of the noble work, implying a good technical expertise. However, beside each of us, many persons have been working very hard to make it possible. Natalie Tarbet, Arvind's secretary, took over a quantity of problems that Arvind could not have solved alone. This remark applies equally well to Jane James in Manchester, and Nobuko Serizawa in Tokyo. Astrid Maerkl, at ECRC, did a tremendous job and spent many hours to make the whole thing possible and on time. And last but not least, Uri Weiser and his team in Haifa were given the remaining task of supervising the Proceedings, also a generator of headaches and hectic times I believe.

To conclude, it has been a great honor and pleasure to act as ISCA89 Program Chairman together with Arvind, John, and Masaru. The Program Committee, all the referees, and people behind the scenes think that their respective tasks have been carefully completed. We all hope that you will find the conference enjoyable and of excellent quality.

Jean-Claude Syre
ECRC, Computer Architecture Group

Organizing Committee for the
16th Annual International Symposium on Computer Architecture

Steering Committee

Doug DeGroot, Texas Instruments, USA
Zary Segall, Carnegie Mellon University, USA
Yale N. Patt, University of Michigan at Ann Arbor, USA

Symposium Committee

General Co-Chairs
Michael Yoeli, Technion, ISRAEL
Gabriel M. Silberman, Technion, ISRAEL, and Carnegie Mellon University, USA
Vice-Chairs, USA
Gideon Frieder, Syracuse University, USA
Zeev Barzilai, IBM T.J. Watson Research Center, USA

Vice-Chair, Europe
Ulrich Trottenberg, SUPRENUM GmbH and GMD, FRG

Vice-Chair, Far-East
Yoshihiro Tohma, Tokyo Institute of Technology, JAPAN
Program Chair
Jean-Claude Syre, European Computer-Industry Research Center GmbH, FRG

Program Vice-Chair, USA
Arvind, Massachusetts Institute of Technology, USA

Program Vice-Chair, Europe
John R. Gurd, University of Manchester, UK

Program Vice-Chair, Far-East
Masaru Kitsuregawa, University of Tokyo, JAPAN

Posters Chair
Benny Atlas, Technion, ISRAEL

Finance & Local Arrangements Chair
Ran Ginosar, Technion, ISRAEL

Registration & Travel Grants Chair
Ilan Spillinger, Technion, ISRAEL

Publicity & Publications Chair
Uri Weiser, INTEL, ISRAEL

Tutorials Chair
Daniel Tabak, George Mason University, USA

Exhibits Chair
Helnye Azaria, Ben-Gurion University, ISRAEL

Program Committee

ISCA89 List of Referees

Abraham, S.
Adelantado, M.
Agarwal, A.
Agrawal, D.P.
Akers, S.B.
Amamiya, M.
Amano, H.
Appiani, E.
Arvind
Banatre, J.P.
Baru, C.
Bassett, P.
Batcher, K.E.
Benker, H.
Berry, M.W.
Birmingham, W.P.
Bohm, A.P.W.
Boku, T.
Boyle, P.D.
Bribst, S.A.
Bronnenberg, W.
Caccia, F.
Capon, P.C.
Carpenter, A.F.
Cecinati, R.
Cheong, H.
Colla, A.M.
Comte, D.
Culler, D.E.
Dally, W.J.
Davidson, E.S.
Davis, A.
Davis, T.
Dennison, L.
Derbyshire, M.
Dijkstra, H.
Dixon, R.N.
Dorochevski, M.
Durrieu, G.
Dyer, C.R.
Edwards, D.A.
Eggers, S.
Eshagian, M.M.
Farmwald, M.
Feo, J.
Foley, J.F.
Fortes, J.A.B.
Fraboul, C.
Ganz, A.
Garner, R.

Gerritsen, M.
Goodman, J.
Goosen, H.A.
Goto, A.
Gottlieb, A.
Granara, M.
Greenlaw, R.
Grunwald, D.
Gupta, S.A.
Gurd, J.
Haney, M.
Hattori, A.
Hifdi, N.
Higuchi, T.
Hill, M.D.
Hopkins, T.P.
Hornick, S.
Howard, T.L.J.
Hsu, P.Y.-T.
Hsu, W.T.
Hubbold, R.J.
Iannucci, R.A.
Ibbett, R.N.
Irani, K.B.
Jajszczyk, A.
Jaxon, G.
Jesshope, C.
Kai, M.
Kagan, M.
Kelly, E.
Kessaci, K.
Kimura, Y.
Kirkham, C.C.
Kishimoto, M.
Kitsuregawa, M.
Knight, T.
Knowles, A.E.
Kodama, Y.
Koike, N.
Konicek, J.
Koren, I.
Koren, Z.
Krishnamurthy, B.
Kudo, T.
Kuszmaul, B.C.
Lawrie, D.H.
Lécussan, B.
Leighton, F.T.
Lin, J.J.
Lipovski, J.

Litaize, D.
Maa, G.
Maggs, B.
Maresca, M.
Mazumder, P.
McNally, I.
Mendelson, A.
Mendelson, B.
Miller, P.
Morrison, J.P.
Mudge, T.
Muller, G.
Musicus, B.
Mustaffa, S.
Nagashima, S.
Nakagawa, Takayuki
Nakagawa, Tohru
Nation, W.
Nishida, K.
Noyé, J
Nuth, P.R.
Odijk, E.
Padmanabhan, K.
Palmer, S.
Papadopoulos, G.M.
Park, K.H.
Patel, J.
Patel, M.B.
Patt, Y.
Perlmutter, D.
Pierotti, D.
Pleszkun, A.R.
Poluchronopoulos, C.
Quinton, P.
Rau, B.R.
Ravishankar, C.V.
Rawsthorne, A.
Reddy, U.
Rettberg, R.D.
Robinson, J.
Rochat, B.
Roncarolo, L.
Rossi, G.
Roten, S.
Rousselot, J.Y.
Ruhman, S.
Sakai, S.
Sanchez, P.
Schlanker. M.
Schreiber, R.

Sharma, M.
Shen, X.
Shibayama, K.
Skedzielewski, S.
Smith, B.J.
Smith, J.E.
Smith, S.D.
Sohi, G.S.
Sorkin, A.
Stankovic, J.
Su, H.-M.
Sugumar, R.
Sunahara, H.
Syre, J.C.
Tanaka, H.
Tang, P.

Taylor, C.J.
Thomas, R.
Thompson, B.C.
Tiao, J.
Tick, E.
Toda, K.
Tomita, S.
Tomlinson, R.
Tsakogiannis, G.
Upfal, E.
VanEssen, H.A
VanTwist, R.
Veidenbaum, A.
Vernon, M.K.
Vlot, M.C.
Walden, D.C.

Watson, I.
Watson, P.
Weiser, U.
White, J.
Wijshoff, H.
Woest, P.J.
Wolczko, M.
Woods, J.V.
Xu, L.
Yamaguchi, Y.
Yantchev, J.
Yarkoni, E.
Yen, D.
Yen, W.
Yuba, T.
Zobel, R.N.

The 16th Annual International Symposium on Computer Architecture

Table of Contents

Cache Coherence and Synchronization I
Chair: M. Dubois, USC

Evaluating the Performance of Four Snooping Cache Coherency Protocols 2
    S.J. Eggers and R.H. Katz
Multi-level Shared Caching Techniques for Scalability in VMP-MC 16
    D.R. Cheriton, H.A. Goosen, and P.D. Boyle
Design and Performance of a Coherent Cache for Parallel Logic Programming
Architectures 25
    A. Goto, A. Matsumoto, and E. Tick

Dataflow
Chair: I. Koren, UMASS Amherst

The Epsilon Dataflow Processor 36
    V.G. Grafe, G.S. Davidson, J.E. Hoch, and V.P. Holmes
An Architecture of a Dataflow Single Chip Processor 46
    S. Sakai, Y. Yamaguchi, K. Hiraki, Y. Kodama, and T. Yuba
Exploiting Data Parallelism in Signal Processing on a Dataflow Machine 54
    P. Nitezki

Pipeline Architectures
Chair: A. Gottlieb, NYU

Architectural Mechanisms to Support Sparse Vector Processing 64
    R.N. Ibbett, T.M. Hopkins, amd K.I.M. McKinnon
A Dynamic Storage Scheme for Conflict-Free Vector Access 72
    D.T. Harper III and D.A. Linebarger
SIMP (Single Instruction stream/Multiple instruction Pipelining): A Novel High-Speed
Single-Processor Architecture 78
    K. Murakami, N. Irie, M. Kuga, and S.Tomita

Mapping Algorithms
Chair: A.L. Davis, HP

2-D SIMD Algorithms in the Perfect Shuffle Networks 88
    Y. Ben-Asher, D. Egozi, and A. Schuster
Systematic Hardware Adaptation of Systolic Algorithms 96
    M. Valero-Garcia, J.J. Navarro, J.M. Llaberia, and M. Valero
Task Migration in Hypercube Multiprocessors 105
    M.-S. Chen and K.G. Shin

Uniprocessor Caches
Chair: D. Alpert, INTEL

Characteristics of Performance-Optimal Multi-Level Cache Hierarchies 114
    S. Przybylski, M. Horowitz, and J. Hennessy
Supporting Reference and Dirty Bits in SPUR's Virtual Address Cache 122
    D.A. Wood and R.H. Katz
Inexpensive Implementations of Set-Associativity 131
    R.E. Kessler, R. Jooss, A. Lebeck, and M.D. Hill
Organization and Performance of a Two-Level Virtual-Real Cache Hierarchy 140
    W.-H. Wang, J.-L. Baer, and H.M. Levy

Networks

Chair: H.J. Siegel, Purdue University

High Performance Communications in Processor Networks 150
  C.R. Jesshope, P.R. Miller, and J.T. Yantchev

Introducing Memory into the Switch Elements of Multiprocessor Interconnection Networks 158
  H.E. Mizrahi, J.-L. Baer, E.D. Lazowska, and J. Zahorjan

Using Feedback to Control Tree Saturation in Multistage Interconnection Networks 167
  S.L. Scott and G.S. Sohi

Constructing Replicated Systems with Point-to-Point Communication Links 177
  P.D. Ezhilchelvan, S.K. Shrivastava, and A. Tully

Prolog Architectures

Chair: R. Ginosar, Technion

KCM: A Knowledge Crunching Machine 186
  H. Benker, J.M. Beacco, S. Bescos, M. Dorochevsky, Th. Jeffré, A. Pöhlmann, J. Noyé,
  B. Poterie, A. Sexton, J.C. Syre, O. Thibault, and G. Watzlawik

A High Performance Prolog Processor with Multiple Function Units 195
  A. Singhal and Y.N. Patt

Evaluation of Memory System for Integrated Prolog Processor IPP 203
  M. Morioka, S. Yamaguchi, and T. Bandoh

A Type Driven Hardware Engine for Prolog Clause Retrieval over a Large Knowledge Base 211
  K.-F. Wong and M.H. Williams

Instruction Fetching

Chair: I. Spillinger, Technion

Comparing Software and Hardware Schemes for Reducing the Cost of Branches 224
  W.W. Hwu, T.M. Conte, and P.P. Chang

Improving Performance of Small On-Chip Instruction Caches 234
  M.K. Farrens and A.R. Pleszkun

Achieving High Instruction Cache Performance with an Optimizing Compiler 242
  W.W. Hwu and P.P. Chang

The Impact of Code Density on Instruction Cache Performance 252
  P. Steenkiste

Parallel Architectures

Chair: H. Mühlenbein, GMD

Can Dataflow Subsume von Neumann Computing? 262
  R.S. Nikhil and Arvind

Exploring the Benefits of Multiple Hardware Contexts in a Multiprocessor Architecture:
Preliminary Results 273
  W.-D. Weber and A. Gupta

Architectural and Organizational Tradeoffs in the Design of the MultiTitan CPU 281
  N.P. Jouppi

Run-Time Checking in Lisp by Integrating Memory Addressing and Range Checking 290
  M. Sato, S. Ichikawa, and E. Goto

Perfomance Evaluation

Chair: D. Siewiorek, CMU

Multiple vs. Wide Shared Bus Multiprocessors 300
  A. Hopper, A. Jones, and D. Lioupis

Performance Measurements on a Commercial Multiprocessor Running Parallel Code 307
  M. Annaratone and R. Rühl

Interprocessor Communication Speed and Performance in Distributed-Memory Parallel
Processors 315
  M. Annaratone, C. Pommerell, and R. Rühl

Analysis of Computation-Communication Issues in Dynamic Dataflow Architectures 325
  D. Ghosal, S.K. Tripathi, L.N. Bhuyan, and H. Jiang

Logic Simulation Systems
Chair: E. Kronstadt, IBM

Logic Simulation on Massively Parallel Architectures 336
  S. Kravitz, R.E. Bryant, and R. Rutenbar
R256: A Research Parallel Processor for Scientific Computation 344
  T. Fukazawa, T. Kimura, M. Tomizawa, K. Takeda, and Y. Itoh

Special Purpose Architectures
Chair: S. Ruhman, Weizmann Institute

A Three-Port/Three-Access Register File for Concurrent Processing and I/O
Communication in a RISC-Like Graphics Engine 354
  M.L. Anido, D.J. Allerton, and E.J. Zaluska
An Architecture Framework for Application-Specific and Scalable Architectures 362
  J.M. Mulder, R.J. Portier, A. Srivastava, and R. in't Velt

Memory Systems
Chair: G. Frieder, Syracuse University

Perfect Latin Squares and Parallel Array Access 372
  K. Kim and V.K. Prasanna Kumar
An Aperiodic Storage Scheme to Reduce Memory Conflicts in Vector Processors 380
  S. Weiss
Analysis of Vector Access Performance on Skewed Interleaved Memory 387
  C.-L. Chen and C.-K. Liao

Cache Coherence and Synchronization II
Chair: J. Goodman, University of Wisconsin, Madison

Adaptive Backoff Synchronization Techniques 396
  A. Agarwal and M. Cherian
A Cache Consistency Protocol for Multiprocessors with Multistage Networks 407
  P. Stenström
On Data Synchronizations for Multiprocessors 416
  H.-M. Su and P.-C. Yew

Author Index 425

EVALUATING THE PERFORMANCE OF
FOUR SNOOPING CACHE COHERENCY PROTOCOLS

Susan J. Eggers

Department of Computer Science, FR-35
University of Washington
Seattle, WA 98195

Randy H. Katz

Computer Science Division
Dept. of Electrical Engineering & Computer Science
University of California
Berkeley, California 94720

Abstract

Write-invalidate and write-broadcast coherency protocols have been criticized for being unable to achieve good bus performance across all cache configurations. In particular, write-invalidate performance can suffer as block size increases; and large cache sizes will hurt write-broadcast. Read-broadcast and competitive snooping extensions to the protocols have been proposed to solve each problem.

Our results indicate that the benefits of the extensions are limited. Read-broadcast reduces the number of invalidation misses, but at a high cost in processor lockout from the cache. The net effect can be an increase in total execution cycles. Competitive snooping benefits only those programs with high per-processor locality of reference to shared data. For programs characterized by inter-processor contention for shared addresses, competitive snooping can degrade performance by causing a slight increase in bus utilization and total execution time.

1. Introduction

Snooping cache coherency protocols [Arch86] are a good match for bus-based, shared memory multiprocessors, because they take advantage of the broadcast capabilities of the single interconnect. Within the snooping coherency category, two techniques, *write-invalidate* and *write-broadcast*, have been developed. In write-invalidate a processor invalidates all other cached copies of shared data and can then update its own without further bus operations. Under write-broadcast, a processor broadcasts updates to shared data to other caches, so that all copies are the same.

Both techniques have been criticized for being unable to achieve good bus performance across all cache

configurations. In particular, write-invalidate performance can suffer as block size increases because of inter-processor contention for addresses within the cache block; and large cache sizes will hurt write-broadcast, because of continued bus updates to data that remains in the cache but is no longer actively shared.

Enhancements to the original protocols have been proposed to solve each problem. A read-broadcast extension [Good88, Karl88, Sega84] to write-invalidate reduces the number of misses for invalidated data by allowing all caches with invalidated blocks to receive new data when any of them issues a read request. It should therefore improve both the miss ratio and bus utilization of write-invalidate. A competitive snooping protocol, introduced in [Karl86, Karl88], was designed to limit the number of broadcasts in write-broadcast. It therefore puts a cap on the performance loss caused by large caches.

The goal of this paper is twofold: first, to measure the performance problems in the write-invalidate and write-broadcast protocols, as block or cache size increases; and second, to gauge the extent to which the read-broadcast and competitive snooping extensions solve each problem. All studies were done via trace-driven simulation of parallel applications. Our results indicate that read-broadcast reduces the number of invalidation misses, but at a high cost in processor lockout from the cache. The net effect can be an *increase* in total execution cycles. Competitive snooping benefits only those programs with high per-processor locality of reference (sequential sharing) to shared data. For programs characterized by inter-processor contention (fine-grain sharing) for shared addresses, competitive snooping can degrade performance by causing a slight increase in bus utilization and total execution time.

We have used trace-driven simulation of parallel programs in two other studies. In [Egge88] trace-driven analysis verified a model of coherency overhead in write-invalidate and write-broadcast protocols. [Egge89b] studied the effects of increasing block and cache size on the cache and bus behavior of parallel programs running under write-invalidate protocols. A summary of the block size results from that paper is the basis for the evaluation of write-invalidate protocols in this work.

The remainder of this paper begins with a brief description of the methodology. The two companion protocol studies follow. Each begins with a description of the original protocol and empirical evidence of the performance loss caused by increasing block or cache size. Then the protocol extensions are described, and the extent to which they improve performance is measured. Section 3 reviews write-invalidate protocols and the effects of increasing block size on miss ratio and bus utilization studied in [Egge89b]. Section 4 presents the read-broadcast extension and its benefits and costs to both performance and cache controller implementation. Write-broadcast and the effects of increasing cache size on bus traffic is covered in section 5. Section 6 discusses the competitive snooping alternative and its performance relative to write-broadcast. The last section integrates the results of both studies.

2. Methodology and Workload

We used trace-driven simulation in our analysis. Our simulator emulates a simple shared memory architecture, in which a modest number of processors (five to twelve) are connected on a single bus. The CPU architecture is RISC-like [Patt85], assuming one-cycle per instruction execution. Not all instructions follow this model; therefore the bus utilization results will be slightly overestimated and throughput underestimated, because the simulation processors return to use the bus more quickly than in a real machine. However, the studies in this paper rely only on the *relative* values of these metrics between coherency mechanisms; absolute figures are not germane to the analysis and conclusions. All other metrics used in the studies, for example, cache miss rates and numbers of bus operations, should be unaffected.

With the exception of those cache parameters that are varied in the studies (cache size, block size and coherency protocol), the memory system architecture is roughly that of the SPUR multiprocessor [Hill86]. The simulator's board-level cache is direct mapped, with one-cycle reads and two-cycle writes. Its cache controller implements a test-and-test-and-set sequence for securing locks [Wood87], processor lockout from the cache during snoop activity, and many of the timing constraints of the actual SPUR implementation. Bus activity is implemented using a modified NuBus arbitration protocol [Gibs88], and bus contention is accurately modeled.

The inputs to the simulator are traces gathered from four parallel CAD programs, developed for single-bus, shared memory multiprocessors (Table 2-1). The choice of application area was deliberate, so that the workload being analyzed was appropriate for a small-scale machine. One program is production quality (SPICE); the others are research prototypes. Two of the programs are based on simulated annealing algorithms. CELL [Caso86] uses a modified simulated annealing algorithm for IC design cell placement, and placed twenty-three cells in our trace. TOPOPT [Deva87] does topological compaction of MOS circuits, using dynamic windowing and partitioning techniques. Its input was a technology independent multi-level logic circuit. VERIFY [Ma87] is a combinational logic verification program, which compares two different circuit implementations to determine whether they are functionally (Boolean) equivalent. The circuits used for the trace were combinational benchmarks for evaluating test generation algorithms. The final program, SPICE [McGr86], is a circuit simulator; it is a parallel version of the original direct method approach, and its input was a chain of 64 inverters.

All applications use a coarse-grain programming paradigm for carrying out parallel activities. The granularity of parallelism is a process, in this case one for each processor in the simulation. The model of execution is single-program-multiple-data, with each process independently executing identical code on a different portion of

Parallel Applications			
Trace Name	Architecture, Operating System	Program Description	Number of Processors
CELL	Sequent Balance, Unix	simulated annealing algorithm for cell placement	12
TOPOPT	Sequent Balance, Unix	simulated annealing algorithm for topological optimization	11
VERIFY	Sequent Balance, Unix	logic verification	12
SPICE	ELXSI 6400, Embos	direct method circuit simulator	5

Table 2-1: Traces Used in the Simulations. The traces used in the sharing simulations were gathered from parallel programs that were written for shared memory multiprocessors. The programs are all "real", being either production quality (SPICE) or research prototypes.

shared data. The shared data is divided into units that are placed on a logical queue in shared memory. Each process takes a unit of work from the queue, computes on it, writes results, and then returns the unit of work to the end of the queue.

The traces were generated on a per-processor basis. The number of processors in the simulations is identical to the number of processors used in trace generation. For SPICE this number is 5, and for the Sequent traces either 11 or 12. Each per-processor trace is a separate input stream to the simulator. Synchronization among the streams depends on the use of locks and barriers in the programs, and is handled directly by the simulator. Statistics are generated from approximately 300,000 references per processor, after cache steady state has been reached. (See [Egge89a] for a more detailed discussion of the methodology.)

3. The Write-Invalidate Protocols

3.1. Protocol Description

Write-invalidate protocols maintain coherency by requiring a writing processor to invalidate all other cached copies of the data before updating its own. It can then perform the current update, and any subsequent updates (provided there are no intervening accesses by other processors) without either violating coherency or further utilizing the bus. The invalidation is carried out via an invalidating bus operation. Caches of other processors monitor the bus through the snoop portion of their cache controllers. When they detect an address match, they invalidate the entire cache block containing the address.

Berkeley Ownership [Katz85] is a write-invalidate protocol that has been implemented in the SPUR multiprocessor [Hill86]. It is based on the concept of cache block ownership. A cache obtains exclusive ownership of a block via two invalidating bus transactions. One is used on cache write misses and obtains the block for the requesting processor, at the same time it invalidates copies in other caches. The second is an invalidation signal that is used on cache write hits. Once ownership has been obtained, a cache can update a block locally without initiating additional bus transfers. A block owner also updates main memory on block replacement and provides data to other caches upon request. Cache-to-cache transfers are done in one bus transfer, with no memory update.

Write-invalidate protocols have two sources of bus-related coherency overhead. The first is the *invalidation signal* mentioned above. The second is the cache misses that occur when processors need to rereference invalidated data. These misses, called *invalidation misses*, would not have occurred had there been no sharing. They are present because the shared data had previously been written, and therefore invalidated, by another processor. They are additional to the customary, uniprocessor misses (for example, first-reference misses and those necessitated by block replacements).

3.2. The Write-Invalidate Trouble Spot

Because they create a data writer that can access a shared block without using the bus, write-invalidate protocols minimize the overhead of maintaining cache coherency in two cases: when there are multiple consecutive writes to a block by a single processor (sequential sharing), and when there is little inter-processor contention (fine-grain sharing) for the shared data. Periods of severe contention, however, cause coherency overhead to rise. Inter-processor contention for an address produces more invalidations; the invalidations interrupt all processors' use of the data and increase the number of invalidation misses to get it back. The result is that shared data pingpongs among the caches, with each processor's references causing additional coherency-related bus operations. The greater the number of processors contending for an address, the more frequent the pingponging.

The problem is exacerbated by a large block size, because contention can occur for *any* of the addresses in the block. Therefore the probability that the block will be actively shared increases. An invalidation to one word in a block causes all other words to be invalidated. When other processors subsequently reread these addresses, additional read misses are incurred. The overhead is paid even when a processor reads an address that was not updated. With small block sizes, particularly those of only one word, a write to one address has less effect on reads to another.

3.3. Empirical Evidence for the Trouble Spot Analysis

In [Egge89b] we studied the effect on both miss ratio and bus utilization of increasing block size and cache size under write-invalidate protocols. (The write-invalidate protocol used in the simulations was also Berkeley Ownership.) The results quantify the loss in performance due to invalidations and invalidation misses. In particular, they support the above analysis concerning the adverse effects of fine-grain sharing, as block size increases.

Parallel programs with both types of sharing behavior suffer from coherency overhead. Unlike uniprocessor misses [Agar88, Alex86, Good87, Hill87, Smit87], invalidation misses react less favorably to increasing block size. [Egge89b] found that the proportion of invalidation misses to total misses increased with larger block sizes, and for three of the traces was significant. (The proportions grew from .32 to .37 for CELL, .14 to .30 for SPICE, .06 to .51 for VERIFY and .39 to .94 for TOPOPT, as block size was increased from 4 to 32 bytes.) For programs with sequential sharing (CELL and SPICE), (total) miss ratios were higher than for comparable uniprocessor programs and declined with increasing block size at a slower rate.

The effect on programs with fine-grain sharing (TOPOPT and VERIFY) was more severe. Here invalidation misses increased with increasing block size, not only in proportion to total misses, but in absolute numbers as well. (The proportion of invalidation misses for TOPOPT and VERIFY is stated above; the percentage increase in number of misses was 511 and 840 percent, respectively.) Their dominance was so complete that they caused miss ratios to rise with block size, rather than fall, as is normally the case with uniprocessor programs in caches of this size (128K bytes).

The additional cache misses increased bus utilization. Moreover, sharing under write-invalidate protocols introduces another type of bus operation, the invalidation signal, which further increased bus utilization. Bus utilization rose 407 and 94 percent for TOPOPT and VERIFY, as block size increased from 4 to 32 bytes. Even for the small-scale multiprocessors studied (12 processors at most), the bus was well utilized, with bus utilization figures of 45 and 97 percent, respectively, at the 32 byte block size. Bus utilization for CELL and SPICE was midrange, higher than for uniprocessor programs, and declined over the block size spectrum.

4. The Read-Broadcast Extension

4.1. Protocol Description

Since invalidation misses play such a large role in the cache and bus performance of parallel programs at large block sizes, coherency protocols that can reduce them are desirable. *Read-broadcast* [Good88, Sega84] is an enhancement to write-invalidate protocols designed explicitly for this purpose. Under read-broadcast snoops update an invalidated block with data from the bus, whenever they detect a read bus operation for the block's address. Detection is positive whenever the tag of the snooped address matches that of a cached block, and the block state is invalid. The read-broadcast extension adds little complexity to the cache controller hardware. An examination of the SPUR cache controller implementation indicates that one additional minterm is required in the snoop PLA for the detection. Assuming that the snoop can have access to the cache in a short and bounded amount of time, a buffer large enough to hold the data as it comes from the bus is also needed. If timely snoop access to the cache cannot be guaranteed, an extra bus line is necessary to delay transmission of the data. Finally, control to implement read-interference[1] is

---

[1] Read-interference occurs when a processor has queued a bus read request for an address that is read-broadcast before the requesting processor obtains the bus. During the read-broadcast the requesting processor updates its cache with data from the bus. Therefore it can satisfy its read reference directly from the cache and no longer requires the bus operation. Control is needed to detect this interference and cancel the requesting processor's pending read bus operation.

required to meet the invalidation miss limit, described below.

The technique improves the performance of write-invalidate by limiting the number of invalidation misses to one per invalidation signal. One invalidation miss occurs if the bus operation is a read issued by a cache with a previously invalidated block. No invalidation misses result when the bus read is a first-reference or replacement miss. Subsequent rereads by processors that have received data on a read-broadcast will be a cache hits rather than invalidation misses.

4.2. Read-Broadcast Results

4.2.1. The Benefits to Miss Ratio and Bus Utilization

Read-broadcast reduced the number of invalidation misses (see Table 4-1). For three of the traces (CELL, TOPOPT and VERIFY) the drop ranged from 13 to 51 percent, over all block sizes. The decrease for SPICE was much lower. SPICE data structures had been explicitly sized to the ELXSI 6400 64-byte cache block to avoid inter-processor contention for addresses within a block. Therefore, for block sizes considered in this study, up to 32 bytes, little contention was observed; and read-broadcast consequently brought less benefit.

Because of the decrease in invalidation misses, the proportion of invalidation misses within total misses was less than for write-invalidate (Figure 4-1). This is important, because increases in block and cache size produce steeper reductions in uniprocessor misses than invalidation misses. Therefore, to the extent that misses in parallel programs are caused by normal cache accesses rather than sharing activity, cache performance will improve as block and cache sizes increase. At larger block sizes invalidation misses for CELL, TOPOPT and VERIFY dropped to between a quarter and a third of the total. (Under Berkeley Ownership they had ranged from thirty to over forty percent.) But for TOPOPT invalidation misses still dominated miss ratio behavior at most block sizes (90 percent at 32 bytes at maximum). As with the original write-invalidate protocol, the ratio of invalidation to total misses for all traces rose with increasing block size.

For the most part the consequence of the drop in invalidation misses was a decline in the total miss ratio (see Table 4-1). CELL and TOPOPT had moderate decreases (13.7 to 15.6 percent and 17.2 to 33.8 percent, respectively); VERIFY had a wider range of decrease (1.0 to 19.3 percent). The miss ratio for SPICE did not decline across all block sizes, and, when it did, the decrease was small. The small increases occured because the samples in comparative (Berkeley Ownership vs. read-broadcast) simulations covered a slightly different set of references. The difference in samples was caused by the elimination of invalidation misses from the read-broadcast simulations. Changing invalidation misses to cache hits allows processors to process references more

Comparison of Berkeley Ownership & Read-Broadcast							
Trace	Block Size (bytes)	Invalidation Misses			Miss Ratio		
		Berkeley Ownership	Read Broadcast	Decrease (percent)	Berkeley Ownership	Read Broadcast	Decrease (percent)
CELL	4	22649	13566	40.1	1.93	1.67	13.7
CELL	8	18823	11264	40.2	1.49	1.28	14.1
CELL	16	15040	8942	40.5	1.10	0.93	15.6
CELL	32	11748	7325	37.6	0.86	0.73	14.4
SPICE	4	6918	6663	3.7	2.90	2.97	-2.2
SPICE	8	4143	3870	6.6	1.64	1.65	-0.2
SPICE	16	3607	3447	4.4	1.09	1.10	-0.4
SPICE	32	3726	3009	19.2	0.77	0.74	3.4
TOPOPT	4	1890	922	51.2	0.15	0.12	20.1
TOPOPT	8	6117	4706	23.1	0.25	0.20	17.2
TOPOPT	16	8835	6459	26.9	0.30	0.23	23.2
TOPOPT	32	11556	7385	36.1	0.37	0.25	33.8
VERIFY	4	2441	2062	15.5	1.42	1.41	1.0
VERIFY	8	8921	7786	12.7	1.38	1.34	2.6
VERIFY	16	15371	11497	25.2	1.40	1.28	9.1
VERIFY	32	22957	13717	40.2	1.45	1.17	19.4

Table 4-1: Comparison of Invalidation Misses and Miss Ratios for Berkeley Ownership and Read-Broadcast. This table depicts the decline in the number of invalidation misses and the miss ratio that occured with read-broadcast. The drop in invalidation misses was less pronounced for SPICE, because its shared data had been optimized for a block size larger than the maximum studied here. This small decline, coupled with a slight rise in uniprocessor misses, produced rising miss ratios (negative decreases) for some block sizes. (All simulations were run with a 128K byte cache; miss ratios are the geometric mean across all processors.)

quickly than under Berkeley Ownership. The effect is to slightly alter the set of references executed and the global order in which they are processed under the two protocols. For SPICE the consequence was a slight rise in the uniprocessor component of the miss ratio for read-broadcast (relative to Berkeley Ownership), which offset the small decline in the number of invalidation misses. For the other traces the sample discrepancy was considerably less, the uniprocessor misses were almost identical, and the reduction in the number of invalidation misses was also greater. Therefore the drop in invalidation misses produced a corresponding decline in the miss ratio.

The critical system bottleneck in a single-bus, shared memory multiprocessor is the bandwidth of the system bus. Therefore the most important consequence of read-broadcast is the effect of its lower miss ratios on bus utilization. The improvement (i.e., drop in bus utilization) ranged from 8.7 to 10.9 percent for CELL, .8 to 5.1 percent for SPICE, 14.3 to 22.6 percent for TOPOPT and .8 to 11.5 percent for VERIFY. (Details appear in Table 4-2.) To put the read-broadcast benefit in perspective, the change was large enough to allow an additional two processors for TOPOPT, and one each for CELL and VERIFY, and still maintain the same level of bus utilization. (SPICE had lower bus utilization for the block sizes that had a slight rise in the miss ratio, because the total

cycles in the simulation were higher with read-broadcast. The cycle increase was due to a greater delay in obtaining the bus and several other read-broadcast-related factors that are discussed below.)

The magnitude of the drop in both miss ratio and bus utilization was moderate. The performance gain was less than expected because of the extremely sequential nature of sharing in the programs. Sequential sharing can be measured by several metrics. The most pertinent for a study of invalidation misses is the average number of processors that reread an address between writes by different processors. For all traces this figure averaged around one (1.1 for CELL, .7 for SPICE, .8 for TOPOPT and 1.0 for VERIFY), with the distribution heavily weighted by zeros and ones. (CELL had the most evenly spread distribution, with 2 or more processors rereading between 25 and 21 percent of the time. This accounts for its greater decline in invalidation misses. SPICE had the most skewed distribution, with between 91 and 98 percent of the writes followed by zero or one rereads. Its improvement was the least of the traces.) In actual practice the number of invalidation misses was quite close to the read-broadcast limit of one. This was true even for the traces characterized by fine-grain sharing (TOPOPT and VERIFY). If there had been more processors involved in the contention, read-broadcast would have provided greater benefit.

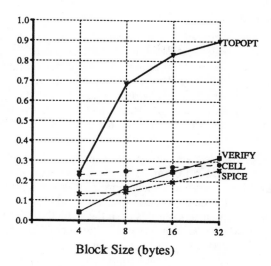

Figure 4-1: Ratio of Invalidation Misses to Total Misses for Read-Broadcast. Under read-broadcast the ratio of invalidation misses to total misses still increases with block size, although the proportions are lower than with Berkeley Ownership. At larger block sizes the invalidation misses for three of the traces have dropped to between a quarter and a third of the total; for TOPOPT they still dominate miss ratio behavior. (The numbers are the geometric mean of the ratio of invalidation to total misses, across all processors.)

Comparison of Berkeley Ownership & Read Broadcast				
Trace	Block Size (bytes)	Bus Utilization		
		Berk. Own.	Read Bdcast.	Change (percent)
CELL	4	42.155	38.470	8.743
CELL	8	39.798	35.849	9.924
CELL	16	38.592	34.383	10.906
CELL	32	42.559	38.042	10.614
SPICE	4	59.546	59.070	0.798
SPICE	8	44.821	44.159	1.477
SPICE	16	40.298	39.948	0.870
SPICE	32	42.221	40.061	5.117
TOPOPT	4	8.925	6.979	21.806
TOPOPT	8	21.289	18.247	14.288
TOPOPT	16	30.972	25.656	17.165
TOPOPT	32	45.108	34.895	22.640
VERIFY	4	49.738	49.346	0.788
VERIFY	8	68.380	66.802	2.307
VERIFY	16	84.760	79.215	6.543
VERIFY	32	96.566	85.491	11.469

Table 4-2: Comparision of Bus Utilization for Berkeley Ownership and Read-Broadcast. This table depicts the decline in bus utilization that occured with read-broadcast over Berkeley Ownership. (All simulations were run with a 128K byte cache; bus utilization figures are the geometric mean across all processors.)

4.2.2. The Cost in Per Processor and System Throughput

The reduction in invalidation misses did not come for free. Read-broadcast has two side effects that contribute to processor execution time: an increase in processor lockout from the cache and an increase in the average number of cycles per bus transfer. Their consequence for three of the traces was an increase in total execution cycles over the Berkeley Ownership simulations.

The more important of the two factors is the increase in processor lockout from the cache. Cache lockout occurs because of CPU and snoop contention over the shared cache resource. The CPU must use the cache for fetching the current instruction (on a miss in the on-chip instruction cache or for all instructions if there is no on-chip cache), obtaining data referenced by the current instruction, and prefetching subsequent instructions. In machines like the one being simulated, with a RISC-based architecture, no on-chip instruction cache and a cache access time that matches the cycle time of the CPU, the CPU needs to access the cache each cycle.[2] At the same time, the snoop also needs access to the cache for maintaining coherency. Read-broadcast requires more snoop-related cache activity than Berkeley Ownership, because snoops must deposit data into the cache on some bus reads and more snoops must update the processor's cache state on subsequent invalidations. The first operation does not occur under Berkeley Ownership, and the latter occurs less frequently. Both activities divert the CPU from its normal instruction execution and contribute to program slowdown.

The increase in lockout with read-broadcast was substantial (278 to 305 percent for CELL, 147 to 191 percent for SPICE, 35 to 87 percent for TOPOPT and 143 to 329 percent for VERIFY). On the average 42 percent of total lockout cycles was attributable to taking data on read-broadcasts, and 40 percent to the state updates. (Cache-to-cache transfers account for the remainder.) The increase due to these factors was softened somewhat by the lockout savings from a decline in cache-to-cache transfers that had satisfied invalidation misses under Berkeley Ownership.

However, in terms of total execution cycles, processor lockout was a minor cost. The ratio of lockout to total cycles averaged 5.8 percent for all traces, across most block sizes. The lone exception was VERIFY's 32 byte block simulation, in which processor lockout accounted for an appalling 21 percent of total cycles. The importance of processor lockout is that for three of the traces (CELL, SPICE and VERIFY), its increase *wiped out the benefit to total execution cycles gained by the decrease in invalidation misses.* The consequence was a slight increase in total execution cycles, ranging from .9 to 3.6 percent. The lone exception was TOPOPT,

---

[2] In CPUs with instruction caches on-chip, prefetching accesses would replace many of the instruction accesses.

in which the benefit from declining invalidation misses was greater than the cost of processor lockout; here the improvement in total execution cycles varied from .1 to 7.7 percent, as block size increased from 4 to 32 bytes.

The negative effect of processor lockout would not be as severe with a more optimized cache controller implementation. In the SPUR implementation, the priority for using the cache belongs to the processor rather than the snoop, and the two run on asynchronous clocks. Therefore the snoop must negotiate to obtain use of the cache (via separate request and grant cycles), and acknowledge that it has finished. A more optimized implementation would eliminate the handshaking cycles by using a single clock for the entire system.

A lower bound can be placed on processor lockout by eliminating the extra cycles from the above results: read-broadcast is then assumed to cost only the number of cycles needed to fill the cache. The results indicate that, even under these best case assumptions, the increase in processor lockout cycles is greater than the decrease in invalidation miss cycles for more than half the simulations. For these simulations read-broadcast still causes a net gain in total execution cycles. (The major exception was TOPOPT. Since it had fewer execution cycles under read-broadcast even with the less optimized implementation, it is not surprising that the lower bound assumptions would bring further improvement.)

The second factor that contributed to an increase in processor execution time was a rise in the average number of cycles per bus transaction. The increases ranged from .3 to 3.1 percent, for all traces and over all block sizes, and averaged around one. There are two causes. The first is the additional cycle required in the read-broadcast implementation for the snoops to acknowledge that they have completed the operation. Under write-invalidate the same snoops are not actively involved in the bus operation; they merely do a lookup and decide to take no action. The lookup can easily be subsumed in the time required for either the cache-to-cache or memory transfer that satisfies the invalidation miss. The second is the need to update the processor's state on both read-broadcasts and simple state invalidations. For both operations more caches are involved than with invalidation misses and state invalidations under Berkeley Ownership. Therefore there is a greater probability that the update will be delayed, because the processor is using the cache to service a memory request.

4.3. Write-Invalidate/Read-Broadcast Summary

The criticism of write-invalidate, that multiple-processor contention within the block would cause excessive invalidation misses as block size is increased, was not born out by the analysis of these traces. It is true that the number of invalidation misses rose with increasing block size, and for the traces with fine-grain sharing this caused an adverse effect on miss ratios and bus utilization. However, most of these misses were caused by a reread by a *single* processor. Therefore the read-broadcast solution had less impact than was originally postulated.

Still, at first glance it appears that read-broadcast is a good extension to the write-invalidate protocols, primarily because it is an extremely low cost solution (in terms of additional cache controller complexity) for the moderate benefit it provides. However, when the increase in both processor lockout and average cycles per bus transaction are considered, for most of the simulations the result is a net *gain* in total execution cycles.

Read-broadcast would be more beneficial if two conditions were different. The most important is if the workload were one in which more processors were contending for the data (for example a one producer/several consumers situation). In this case the reduction in invalidation misses would be greater. The second condition, which is a second order effect, is a more optimized cache controller implementation, designed to minimize the cycles consumed during processor lockout.

5. The Write-Broadcast Protocols

5.1. Protocol Description

Write-broadcast protocols broadcast updates to shared addresses, so that all caches and memory have access to the most current value. Blocks are known to be shared through the use of a special bus line. Snoops assert this signal whenever they address match on an operation for a block that resides in their caches. When a writing processor detects an active shared line, it issues a broadcast. In the absence of an active shared signal, the processor completes the write locally. Thus, the signal provides write-through for shared data, but allows a copy-back memory update policy to be used for private data.

Write-broadcast protocols have potential performance benefits for both private and actively shared blocks. First, an inactive shared line prevents needless bus operations to data that reside only in the cache of the writing processor. In addition, because it broadcasts all shared updates, write-broadcast avoids the pingponging of shared data that occurs in programs with inter-processor data contention under write-invalidate. However, for data that is shared in a sequential fashion, with each processor accessing the data many times before another processor begins, the write-through policy for shared data may degrade bus performance.

In the write-broadcast protocols coherency overhead stems entirely from the bus broadcasts to shared data. They occur for all updates to data that is contained in more than one cache, and for the first update to an address after the writing processor has the only copy. (In this case the block has been replaced in the other caches.)

The particular write-broadcast protocol that has been used in this study is the Firefly protocol, implemented on the DEC SRC Firefly [Thac88]. It differs from other write-broadcast protocols in that it updates memory simultaneously with each write to shared data.

5.2. The Write-Broadcast Trouble Spot

[Egge89b] demonstrated that sharing-related bus traffic will require multiprocessors to have larger or more complex caches than uniprocessors to obtain comparable performance. The requirement is particularly troublesome for the write-broadcast protocols, because larger cache sizes can cause an increase in broadcast operations. As cache size grows, the lifetime of cache blocks increases, because of a decline in block replacements. Shared data tends to remain in a cache for longer periods of time, long past the point when its processor has finished accessing it. However, its presence in the cache drives the shared bus line, giving the illusion of sharing. Therefore write-broadcasts continue for data that is no longer being actively shared.

5.3. Empirical Support for the Trouble Spot

The traces confirm this analysis. For all traces, the number of write-broadcasts rises with increasing cache size (see Figure 5-1). CELL and SPICE have a much larger increase than TOPOPT and VERIFY (84.2 and 100.3 percent over the entire cache size range, versus 3.7 and 15.2 percent). The steepness of their rise correlates with several factors, the most important of which is the pattern of inter-processor references to shared data. For CELL and SPICE this pattern is characterized by good per processor locality (sequential sharing) for shared data within a coherency block. Sequential sharing is indicated by long average write run lengths[3] for the blocks. (The exact figures are 4.9 for CELL and 6.2 for SPICE.) In small caches not all the writes in a long write run result in write-broadcasts. First, shared data is replaced more frequently than in larger caches, and, secondly, in these traces only two processors are involved in the sharing the vast majority of the time. The combined effect is that data may reside in only one cache for the final writes in a write run, allowing these writes to take place locally. In an infinite cache, *all* writes become write-broadcasts, because blocks remain in the cache indefinitely. Therefore, as cache size increases, more writes in a long write run will result in bus broadcasts; and the greater the average write run length, the greater the increase in write-broadcasts. TOPOPT and VERIFY, on the other hand, had short average write run lengths, 1.21 and 2.2, respectively. The smaller length was one of the factors responsible for the more level write broadcast curves, as cache size increased.

A second factor contributing to the shape of the curves is the rate of block replacement. Within a particular trace, the increase in write-broadcasts (with cache size) is most pronounced for smaller caches, where the drop in block replacements is also greatest. Thirdly, at large cache sizes the working sets of TOPOPT and VERIFY fit into the cache. The number of block replacements drops to zero and the level of write-broadcasts remains constant.

Despite the rise in write-broadcasts, bus utilization fell for all traces (see Figure 5-2).[4] The decrease is due to the positive effects of increasing cache size on the uniprocessor component of bus utilization, which dropped an average of 84 percent over the cache size range. It is offset somewhat by the increase in write-broadcast cycles (see a representative trace in Figure 5-3).

For all traces, the proportion of write-broadcast cycles within total cycles increased dramatically with increasing cache size (see Figure 5-4). The increase only leveled off at the point at which the working set of the program fit into the cache. At the largest cache sizes the write-broadcast cycles dominated bus activity for all traces. The high ratio of sharing cycles to total cycles means that with large cache sizes, sharing bus traffic will

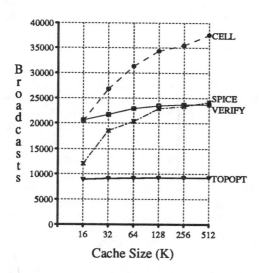

Figure 5-1: Write Broadcasts to Shared Data under Firefly. In the Firefly protocol the number of write-broadcasts increases with increasing cache size for all traces, giving credence to the "illusion of sharing" hypothesis.

---

[3] A write run is a sequence of write references to the shared addresses in a coherency block by a single processor, uninterrupted by any accesses by other processors. The length of a write run is the number of writes it contains. The average write run length is that figure, averaged over all coherency blocks [Egge88]. In other words the average write run length is the average number of writes that are issued for the addresses within a particular block, each time a new processor writes to them.

[4] The only exception is the transition to a 512K byte cache for SPICE.

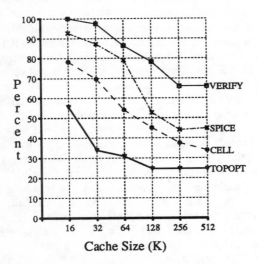

Figure 5-2: Bus Utilization under Firefly. Despite the rise in write-broadcasts, bus utilization fell because of the benefits of large caches on uniprocessor misses.

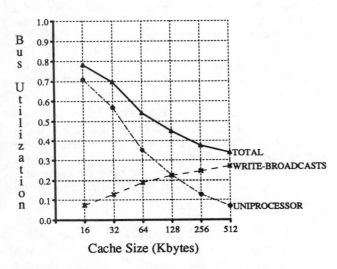

Figure 5-3: Bus Cycles for CELL under Firefly. This classification of bus cycles for CELL illustrates the effect of write-broadcast cycles on total bus cycles, using the Firefly protocol. Write-broadcast cycles rise with increasing cache size; uniprocessor bus cycles tend to fall. The two effects produce bus utilization that still declines, but less steeply than for uniprocessor programs.

be the cause of the bus bottleneck. Therefore a protocol that limits the number of write-broadcasts is desirable.

6. Competitive Snooping

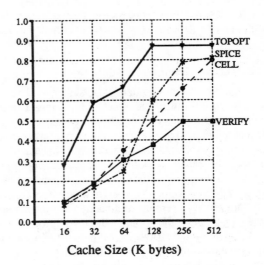

Figure 5-4: Ratio of Broadcast Cycles to Total Bus Cycles. The ratio of write-broadcast cycles to total bus cycles increases with increasing cache size under Firefly. The rise is much steeper for the traces with longer average write run lengths, CELL and SPICE.

6.1. Protocol Description

Competitive snooping [Karl86, Karl88] is a write-broadcast protocol that switches to write-invalidate when the breakeven point in bus-related coherency overhead between the two approaches is reached. The breakeven point for a particular address occurs when the sum of the write broadcast cycles issued for the address equals the number of cycles that would be needed for rereading the data had it been invalidated. Competitive snooping thus limits coherency overhead to twice that of optimal.[5]

The first algorithm proposed in [Karl86] (called "Standard-Snoopy-Caching") assumes that an adversary can choose any processor to either write or reread a shared address. A counter, whose initial value is the cost in cycles of a data transfer, is assigned to each cache block in every cache. On a write broadcast, a cache that contains the address of the broadcast is (arbitrarily)[6]

---

[5] Larry Rudolph makes a very apt analogy between the rationale behind competitive snooping and the dilemma faced by any novice skier. The beginning skier is hesitant to buy skis immediately for fear that his/her interest in skiing might be a passing fancy. On the other hand renting week after week can be costly. The pivotal question is therefore *when* to stop renting and make the purchase. Not knowing ahead of time which will be his or her preference, the budding skier should rent until he or she has spent an amount equivalent to the purchase price of new skis; and then buy the skis. Like competitive snooping, this course of action limits the total cost to twice that of optimal.

[6] The particular choice of cache does not affect the worst-case bound.

chosen, and its counter is decremented. When a counter value reaches zero, the cache block is invalidated. When all counters for an address, other than that of the writer, are zero, write-broadcasts for it cease. Any reaccess by a processor to an address resets its cache's counter to the initial value. The algorithm's lower bound proof demonstrates that the total costs of invalidating are in balance with the total costs of rereading.

In an alternate algorithm (called "Snoopy-Reading") the adversary is allowed to read-broadcast on rereads. In order to obtain the lower bound of the previous algorithm, the coherency algorithm is given the same capability. All other caches with invalidated copies take the data, and reset their counters. As in the original scheme, when a cache's counter reaches zero, it invalidates the block containing the address; and write broadcasts are discontinued, when all caches but that of the writer have been invalidated.

Read-broadcasting by the adversary also prompts other changes in the coherency algorithm. For example, on a write-broadcast *all* caches that contain the updated address decrement their counters rather than only one; and the decrementing is done on consecutive write broadcasts *by a particular processor*, rather than any processor. The simultaneous decrements complement the simultaneous cache updates on read-broadcasts, i.e., they reduce the costs of broadcasting to match the cheaper rereads. The single writer requirement corresponds to all counters being reset on an access by another processor. More than one processor referencing the data indicates (obviously) that there is sharing. As long as data is shared, a good competitive coherency algorithm will broadcast rather than invalidate. Broadcasting occurs as long as counter values are greater than zero. Therefore when a processor other than the current writer accesses the data, all counters are reset to force broadcasting.

The advantages of the alternate scheme over the original are that (1) it is well suited for a workload in which there are few rereads (as is the case with these traces) and (2) its implementation doesn't require hardware to "arbitrarily" choose a cache for counter decrementing. When there are few rereads, a competitive coherency algorithm should make the data private sooner rather than later, in order to avoid unnecessary broadcasts. By requiring all processors to decrement their counters simultaneously, Snoopy-Reading can invalidate more quickly than Standard-Snoopy-Caching.

In the simulator's implementation of Snoopy-Reading, a writing processor keeps track of the number of its consecutive writes to each address (through cache state values). When the breakeven point for broadcasts has been reached, it signals to the other caches to invalidate. The breakeven point was defined to be the maximum of the ratio of data transfer to write-broadcast cycles that is used in the algorithm and the value three. The constant insures that write-broadcasts will continue long enough to prevent busywaiting over the bus. A processor uses the first of the three broadcasts for setting the

lock, and the second for clearing it. At this point the lock is still present in other caches, and processors can detect locally that it has been freed. On the third broadcast (which, if it occurs, demonstrates that the address is not a lock), the data is invalidated. This implementation requires a six-value coherency state, and a correspondingly larger PLA for both the snoop and the portion of the cache controller that services memory requests for the CPU.

6.2. Competitive Snooping Results

Competitive snooping decreased the number of write-broadcasts issued for all traces (see Table 6-1). The benefit was greater for those traces with sequential sharing (CELL and SPICE). (Recall that their average write run lengths were 4.9 and 6.2.) Given the breakeven

Write-Broadcasts				
Trace	Cache Size (Kbytes)	Firefly	Comp. Snoop.	% Change
CELL	16	20402	13199	35.31
CELL	32	26841	15507	42.23
CELL	64	31300	15514	50.43
CELL	128	34287	15212	55.63
CELL	256	35444	15192	57.14
CELL	512	37579	15338	59.18
SPICE	16	12076	4510	62.65
SPICE	32	18555	5900	68.20
SPICE	64	20362	6373	68.70
SPICE	128	22925	7045	69.27
SPICE	256	23344	7251	68.94
SPICE	512	24184	7412	69.35
TOPOPT	16	8918	8218	7.85
TOPOPT	32	9111	8352	8.33
TOPOPT	64	9190	8410	8.49
TOPOPT	128	9244	8458	8.50
TOPOPT	256	9244	8458	8.50
TOPOPT	512	9244	8458	8.50
VERIFY	16	20589	18091	12.13
VERIFY	32	21726	18835	13.31
VERIFY	64	22914	19097	16.66
VERIFY	128	23476	19107	18.61
VERIFY	256	23719	19330	18.50
VERIFY	512	23719	19330	18.50

Table 6-1: Comparison of Write-Broadcasts for Firefly and Competitive Snooping. This table depicts the decline in the number of write-broadcasts that occured with competitive snooping. The drop was most pronounced for CELL and SPICE, which had the longest average write run lengths. Identical values across cache sizes for TOPOPT and VERIFY indicate that their working sets fit into the caches. (All simulations were run with a 32 byte block.)

Sharing Cycles							
Trace	Cache	Firefly	Competitive Snooping				Percentage
	Size (Kbytes)	Write Broadcasts	Write Broadcasts	Invalidations	Invalidation Misses	Total	Change
CELL	16	167122	108850	24489	17820	151159	9.55
CELL	32	221925	129716	33051	28706	191473	13.72
CELL	64	259327	130740	37395	39140	207275	20.07
CELL	128	285430	129361	40597	51286	221244	22.49
CELL	256	295069	129527	41450	55567	226544	23.22
CELL	512	312668	130360	42849	57944	231153	26.07
SPICE	16	102645	39190	7912	2236	49338	51.93
SPICE	32	158119	51491	13660	12786	77937	50.71
SPICE	64	172139	55384	15115	15168	85667	50.23
SPICE	128	191106	60515	18126	18068	96709	49.40
SPICE	256	193971	61880	18491	18262	98633	49.15
SPICE	512	200782	63020	19076	18907	101003	49.70
TOPOPT	16	75828	74927	1603	2655	79185	-4.43
TOPOPT	32	77214	76249	1916	3366	81531	-5.59
TOPOPT	64	77936	76821	1920	3238	81979	-5.19
TOPOPT	128	78256	77120	1942	3380	82442	-5.35
TOPOPT	256	78256	77120	1942	3380	82442	-5.35
TOPOPT	512	78256	77120	1942	3380	82442	-5.35
VERIFY	16	170952	155223	9228	8679	173130	-1.27
VERIFY	32	183516	165910	10798	12157	188865	-2.91
VERIFY	64	194813	170477	12007	15809	198293	-1.79
VERIFY	128	199733	171116	12744	18125	201985	-1.13
VERIFY	256	200341	171961	13323	19132	204416	-2.03
VERIFY	512	200341	171961	13323	19132	204416	-2.03

Table 6-2: Comparison of Sharing Cycles for Firefly and Competitive Snooping. This table depicts the difference in the number of cycles for the sharing-related bus operations for Firefly and competitive snooping. The decline in write-broadcast cycles is offset by cycles for invalidation signals and invalidation misses. For TOPOPT and VERIFY the combination of a smaller cycle savings in write-broadcasts and the additional cycles related to invalidations produced a net increase in sharing-related cycles. (All simulations were run with a 32 byte block.)

point in the simulations, each trace saved on the average, 2 or 3 broadcasts each time a different processor wrote to a shared address.[7] The average write run lengths for TOPOPT and VERIFY were below the simulator's breakeven point (1.2 and 2.2, respectively). Therefore no broadcast savings was accrued in most cases.

The corresponding decrease in the number of write-broadcast cycles was offset to varying extents by the additional cycles for invalidation signals and invalidation misses (see Table 6-2). For CELL and SPICE the effect was to reduce the percentage improvement in cycles consumed in sharing-related bus operations to 10 to 26 percent for CELL and 49 to 52 percent for SPICE. However, the savings was still substantial enough to

cause a drop in bus utilization relative to write-broadcast. The decline in bus utilization for CELL ranged as high as 19 percent; for SPICE as high as 30 percent. For all simulations but two (CELL with 16K and 32K byte caches) the lower bus utilization produced fewer total execution cycles.

For TOPOPT and VERIFY the smaller decline in write-broadcasts, coupled with the additional cycles for invalidation signals and invalidation misses, produced an *increase* in sharing-related bus cycles. This increase was responsible for a slight rise in bus utilization over write-broadcast (1.6 to 4.5 percent for TOPOPT and .8 percent at most for VERIFY). Higher bus utilization brought an increase in total execution cycles. (Details on bus utilization and total execution cycles appear in Table 6-5.)

6.3. Write-Broadcast/Competitive Snooping Summary

---

[7] Technically this is true only for the larger caches. At smaller cache sizes the savings would be less. See the discussion on the effect of average write run length on write-broadcast protocols in section 5.3.

Bus Utilization & Total Execution Cycles							
Trace	Cache Size (Kbytes)	Bus Utilization			Total Execution Cycles		
		Firefly	Competitive Snooping	Percentage Change	Firefly	Competitive Snooping	Percentage Change
CELL	16	78.21	78.24	-0.04	2251417	2275472	-1.07
CELL	32	69.65	69.41	0.34	1722507	1726670	-0.24
CELL	64	54.07	51.94	3.95	1367997	1358706	0.68
CELL	128	45.13	41.29	8.49	1267754	1246316	1.69
CELL	256	37.52	32.68	12.90	1196530	1170737	2.16
CELL	512	33.88	27.56	18.67	1156534	1128079	2.46
SPICE	16	92.66	92.24	0.46	1385228	1344603	2.93
SPICE	32	87.17	86.09	1.24	1078916	1007891	6.58
SPICE	64	79.10	77.34	2.22	886776	795919	10.25
SPICE	128	52.80	43.43	17.74	603795	517028	14.37
SPICE	256	44.06	31.98	27.42	559356	474377	15.19
SPICE	512	44.88	31.38	30.08	553071	474123	14.27
TOPOPT	16	55.55	56.42	-1.56	491294	495603	-0.88
TOPOPT	32	33.89	34.96	-3.13	389304	391695	-0.61
TOPOPT	64	30.76	31.82	-3.43	381349	382676	-0.35
TOPOPT	128	24.68	25.79	-4.51	364345	364798	-0.12
TOPOPT	256	24.68	25.79	-4.51	364345	364798	-0.12
TOPOPT	512	24.68	25.79	-4.51	364345	364798	-0.12
VERIFY	16	99.97	99.97	0.00	1760674	1786211	-1.45
VERIFY	32	97.41	97.58	-0.17	1002740	1017567	-1.48
VERIFY	64	86.24	86.58	-0.39	744443	749358	-0.66
VERIFY	128	78.18	78.25	-0.08	677634	682098	-0.66
VERIFY	256	65.99	66.08	-0.14	617141	622265	-0.83
VERIFY	512	65.99	66.08	-0.14	617141	622265	-0.83

Table 6-5: Comparison of Bus Utilization & Total Execution Cycles for Firefly and Competitive Snooping. This table depicts the change in the bus utilization and total execution cycles that occured with competitive snooping. The decrease in sharing-related cycles for CELL and SPICE resulted in a decline in both. And, conversely, the increase in sharing cycles for TOPOPT and VERIFY produced a rise. (All simulations were run with a 32 byte block.)

The extent to which competitive snooping improves the performance of write-broadcast depends on the pattern of references to shared data. When sharing is sequential, as exhibited by relatively longer average write run lengths, the benefit is greatest. Here the savings in write-broadcast cycles decreases bus utilization and total execution time. As inter-processor contention for the shared addresses rises, competitive snooping becomes less attractive. The decrease in write-broadcasts diminishes, and in some cases can be offset by the rise in invalidations and the more expensive (in numbers of cycles) invalidation misses. The result is an increase in bus utilization and total execution time. (An alternative argument is that programs with fine-grain-sharing for shared addresses are a good match for write-broadcast protocols. Therefore, they have less need for competitive snooping, and it consequently provides less benefit.)

7. Summary of the Paper

This paper contains two companion studies of bus-based, shared memory cache coherency protocols. The purpose of each is twofold: first, to measure the performance loss of changing particular cache parameter values on well-known snooping coherency techniques; second, to determine to what extent extensions, designed specifically to eliminate deficiencies in the original protocols, achieve performance improvements. In the first study, read-broadcast was proposed to eliminate the rise in invalidation misses in write-invalidate protocols that occur with increasing block size. In the second, competitive snooping was intended to limit the increase in bus broadcasts caused by increasing cache size in write-broadcast coherency protocols.

Our results have found that neither extension produces a savings in coherency overhead across all workloads studied. In those cases in which there was a performance loss, the original protocol, write-invalidate or write-broadcast, was a good match for the program. Therefore there was not much room for improvement;

and the extension often introduced secondary costs which outweighed the small savings in coherency overhead. Furthermore, both extensions required some additional hardware complexity.

Our particular workload is characterized by sequential sharing, i.e., data is shared by very few processors at a time. Therefore read-broadcast reduced the number of invalidation misses only moderately, and at a high cost in processor lockout from the cache. In some cases, the net effect was an increase in total execution cycles. These results clearly indicate that read-broadcast is inappropriate for programs with sequential sharing. However, if more processors had been involved in the sharing, for example, a single-producer, multiple-consumer situation, read-broadcast would have provided more benefit for a similar cost in processor lockout.

Competitive snooping benefitted only those programs in which the reference pattern to shared data was very sequential. In this case the decline in the number of write-broadcast cycles was greater than the additional cycles introduced by invalidations and invalidation misses; the net effect was a drop in bus utilization. However, for programs characterized by inter-processor contention (fine-grain sharing) for shared addresses, competitive snooping degraded performance by causing a slight increase in bus utilization and total execution time. Competitive snooping works well in programs that would have incurred less coherency overhead with write-invalidate protocols (rather than write-broadcast). The reason is that it uses invalidations to terminate broadcasts to shared data.

Acknowledgements.

We wish to acknowledge the efforts of several others who contributed to the work in this paper. Garth Gibson and Dave Ditzel gave valuable comments on an earlier draft. Mark Manasse consulted on competitive snooping issues. Dominico Ferrari and Yale Patt provided resources for running many of the simulations. Andrea Casotto (CELL), Steve McGrogan (SPICE), Srinivas Devadas (TOPOPT) and Hi-Keung Tony Ma (VERIFY) donated the parallel programs and a considerable portion of their time discussing them. John Sanguinetti wrote the ELXSI trace generator; Dianne DeSousa helped with the generation of the ELXSI trace; Sequent provided the software on which the Sequent trace generator was based; and Frank Lacy generated and postprocessed the Sequent traces. This work was supported by an IBM Predoctoral Fellowship, SPUR/DARPA contract No. N00039-85-C-0269, NSF Grant No. MIP-8352227, Digital Equipment Corporation, and California MICRO (in conjunction with Texas Instruments, Xerox, Honeywell, and Philips/Signetics).

References

[Agar88]   A. Agarwal, J. Hennessy and M. Horowitz, "Cache Performance of Operation System and Multiprogramming Workloads", *ACM Transactions on Computer Systems*, 6, 4 (November 1988), 393-431.

[Alex86]   C. Alexander, W. Keshlear, F. Cooper and F. Briggs, "Cache Memory Performance in a UNIX Environment", *Computer Architecture News*, 14, 3 (June 1986), 14-70.

[Arch86]   J. Archibald and J. Baer, "An Evaluation of Cache Coherence Solutions in Shared-Bus Multiprocessors", *ACM Transactions on Computer Systems*, 4, 4 (November 1986), 273-298.

[Caso86]   A. Casotto, F. Romeo and A. Sangiovanni-Vincentelli, "A Parallel Simulated Annealing Algorithm for the Placement of Macro-Cells", *Proceedings of the IEEE International Conference on Computer-Aided Design*, Santa Clara, CA (November 1986), 30-33.

[Deva87]   S. Devadas and A. R. Newton, "Topological Optimization of Multiple Level Array Logic", *IEEE Transactions on Computer-Aided Design* (November 1987).

[Egge88]   S. J. Eggers and R. H. Katz, "A Characterization of Sharing in Parallel Programs and its Application to Coherency Protocol Evaluation", *Proceedings of the 15th Annual International Symposium on Computer Architecture*, Honolulu HA (May 1988), 373-383.

[Egge89a] S. J. Eggers, "Simulation Analysis of Data Sharing in Shared Memory Multiprocessors", Ph.D. thesis, University of California, Berkeley (March 1989).

[Egge89b] S. J. Eggers and R. H. Katz, "The Effect of Sharing on the Cache and Bus Performance of Parallel Programs", *Proceedings of the 3rd International Conference on Architectural Support for Programming Languages and Operating Systems*, Boston MA (April 1989).

[Gibs88]   G. A. Gibson, "SpurBus Specification", to appear as Computer Science Division Technical Report, University of California, Berkeley (December 1988).

[Good87]   J. R. Goodman, "Cache Memory Optimization to Reduce Processor/Memory Traffic", *Journal of VLSI and Computer Systems*, 2, 1 & 2 (1987), 61-86.

[Good88]   J. R. Goodman and P. J. Woest, "The Wisconsin Multicube: A New Large-Scale Cache-Coherent Multiprocessor", *Proceedings 15th Annual International Symposium on Computer Architecture*, Honolulu HA (May 1988), 422-431.

[Hill86]   M. D. Hill, S. J. Eggers, J. R. Larus, G. S. Taylor, G. Adams, B. K. Bose, G. A. Gibson,

P. M. Hansen, J. Keller, S. I. Kong, C. G. Lee, D. Lee, J. M. Pendleton, S. A. Ritchie, D. A. Wood, B. G. Zorn, P. N. Hilfinger, D. Hodges, R. H. Katz, J. Ousterhout and D. A. Patterson, "SPUR: A VLSI Multiprocessor Workstation", *IEEE Computer*, 19, 11 (November 1986), 8-22.

[Hill87]   M. D. Hill, "Aspects of Cache Memory and Instruction Buffer Performance", Technical Report No. UCB/Computer Science Dpt. 87/381, University of California, Berkeley (November 1987).

[Karl86]   A. R. Karlin, M. S. Manasse, L. Rudolph and D. D. Sleator, "Competitive Snoopy Caching", *Proceedings of the 27th Annual Symposium on Foundations of Computer Science*, Toronto, Canada (October 1986), 244-254.

[Karl88]   A. R. Karlin, M. S. Manasse, L. Rudolph and D. D. Sleator, "Competitive Snoopy Caching", *Algorithmica*, 3 (1988), 79-119.

[Katz85]   R. Katz, S. Eggers, D. Wood, C. L. Perkins and R. Sheldon, "Implementing a Cache Consistency Protocol", *Proceedings of the 12th Annual International Symposium on Computer Architecture*, 13, 3 (June 1985), 276-283.

[Ma87]   H. T. Ma, S. Devadas, R. Wei and A. Sangiovanni-Vincentelli, "Logic Verification Algorithms and their Parallel Implementation", *Proceedings of the 24th Design Automation Conference* (July 1987), 283-290.

[McGr86]   S. McGrogan, R. Olson and N. Toda, "Parallelizing Large Existing Programs - Methodology and Experiences", *Proceedings of Spring COMPCON* (March 1986), 458-466.

[Patt85]   D. A. Patterson, "Reduced Instruction Computers", *Communications of the ACM*, 28, 1 (January 1985), 8-21.

[Sega84]   Z. Segall and L. Rudolph, "Dynamic Decentralized Cache Schemes for an MIMD Parallel Processor", *Proceedings of the 11th International Symposium on Computer Architecture*, 12, 3 (June 1984), 340-347.

[Smit87]   A. J. Smith, "Line (Block) Size Choice for CPU Caches", *IEEE Trans. on Computers*, C-36, 9 (September 1987), 1063-1075.

[Thac88]   C. P. Thacker, L. C. Stewart and E. H. Satterthwaite, Jr., "Firefly: A Multiprocessor Workstation", *IEEE Transactions on Computers*, 37, 8 (August 1988), 909-920.

[Wood87]   D. A. Wood, S. J. Eggers and G. A. Gibson, "SPUR Memory System Architecture", Technical Report No. UCB/Computer Science Dpt./87/394, University of California, Berkeley (December 1987).

Multi-Level Shared Caching Techniques
for Scalability in VMP-MC

David R. Cheriton, Hendrik A. Goosen and Patrick D. Boyle
Computer Science Department
Stanford University

Abstract

The problem of building a scalable shared memory multiprocessor can be reduced to that of building a scalable memory hierarchy, assuming interprocessor communication is handled by the memory system. In this paper, we describe the VMP-MC design, a distributed parallel multi-computer based on the VMP multiprocessor design, that is intended to provide a set of building blocks for configuring machines from one to several thousand processors. VMP-MC uses a memory hierarchy based on shared caches, ranging from on-chip caches to board-level caches connected by busses to, at the bottom, a high-speed fiber optic ring. In addition to describing the building block components of this architecture, we identify the key performance issues associated with the design and provide performance evaluation of these issues using trace-drive simulation and measurements from the VMP.

This work was sponsored in part by the Defense Advanced Research Projects Agency under Contract N00014-88-K-0619.

1 Introduction

Our goal is to develop a *building block* technology from which components made from workstation-class hardware can be composed into a spectrum of machines, ranging from single-processor personal computers to supercomputer configurations with thousands of processors. All configurations should run the same software and be incrementally upgradeable from the smallest to the largest configurations. The availability of high-performance low-cost microprocessors makes this feasible from the standpoint of raw processing power. The problem lies in the interconnection. To address this, we propose a scalable shared memory multiprocessor based on characteristics of the VMP architecture [8, 7], extended by using multi-level, shared caches.

In this paper we present the overall design of VMP-MC, a distributed parallel multi-computer, focusing on the design of the building block components and the novel techniques which support scalability. We also identify the key performance issues with this design and investigate them using trace-driven simulation and experience from the original VMP design. We argue that VMP-MC provides a credible approach to a highly scalable architecture.

Novel aspects of the design include: (1) limited sharing of secondary caches to reduce miss rates and cost; (2) a hierarchically structured, directory-based consistency mechanism; and (3) locking and message exchange explicitly supported by the memory hierarchy.

The next section describes the function and interconnection of the VMP-MC components. Section 3 investigates and evaluates the critical performance issues. Section 4 describes the current status of the VMP-MC hardware and software. Section 5 compares our work to other relevant projects. We close with a summary of our results, identification of the significant open issues, and our plans for the future.

2 VMP-MC Design

The basic VMP-MC design is shown in Figure 1.

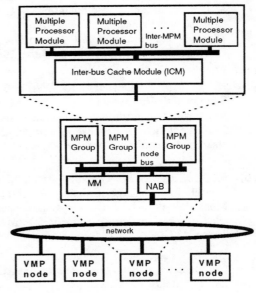

Figure 1: VMP-MC Overview

A VMP-MC configuration consists of one or more network nodes connected by a high-speed network. The V kernel and its virtual memory system manage the caching of data at each node and maintain consistency among nodes, relying on network file servers for non-volatile storage. The *Network Adapter Board* (NAB) provides high-performance communication between the *Memory Modules* (MMs) and the network. Consistency among *Multiple Processor Modules* (MPMs), *Inter-bus Caching Modules* (ICMs) and NABs on the node bus is ensured by the MM. An ICM connects a *Multiple Processor Module Group* (MPMG) to the node bus, providing caching and consistency within the MPMG. The MPM recursively provides the same caching and consistency for the multiple processors sharing the on-board cache.

The following sections describe these modules and their interaction in greater detail.

2.1 Memory Module (MM)

The memory module (MM) provides the bulk memory for the system, and is a physically-addressed slave module on the node bus. It includes a directory, the *Memory Module Directory* (MMD), that records the consistency state of each *cache block* (an aligned 128 byte unit of memory) that it stores. Rapid data exchanges with the MPMs are achieved by block transfers using a sequential access bus protocol and interleaved fast-page mode DRAMs.

For each 128 byte block of memory in the MM, the MMD has a 16-bit entry indicating the block's state:

CC	L	P_{12}	P_{11}	...	P_0

where CC is a two bit code, and L is the LOCK bit used for locking and message exchange (described below). Each P_i corresponds to one MPM or ICM, allowing up to 13 MPMs and ICMs to share this memory board[1]. The meaning of the CC and P fields is summarized in Figure 2.

CC	Meaning if P_i set
00	undefined
01	MPMs/ICMs with a shared copy of block
10	MPM/ICM with private copy of block
11	MPMs/ICMs requesting notification

Figure 2: CC Bit Interpretation

If the P_i are all clear, then the block is neither cached nor in use for message exchange. Directory entries can be written and read directly, but they are normally modified as a side effect of bus operations. The MMD is designed to support the implementation of consistent cached shared memory, memory-based locking and a memory-based multicast message facility, as described below.

2.1.1 Consistent Shared Memory Mode

The consistency protocol follows the same *invalidation* protocol used in VMP, ensuring either a single writable (*private*) copy or multiple read-only (*shared*) copies of a block.

If the block is uncached, the P field of its MMD entry will contain zeros. A read-shared or read-private bus operation by module i on an uncached block returns the block of data. As a side-effect, P_i is set, and the CC bits are set to 01 (shared) or 10 (private). A read-shared operation on a shared block returns the data and sets P_i. A read-private or assert-ownership operation by module i on a shared block changes the CC to 10 (private), interrupts all modules j for which P_j is set, clears all P_j, and sets P_i. When a block is private, the MM aborts read-shared and read-private operations and interrupts the owner. A writeback operation by the owner i sets the CC to 01 (shared). Depending on the type of writeback, P_i is either reset or left unchanged.

Using this MMD entry format, the MM requesting a block of memory knows exactly which modules to interrupt, if any, to allow it to acquire a copy of the block in the desired mode. This attribute of the design is important to its scalability.

2.1.2 Memory-Based Locking

The unit of locking in VMP-MC is the cache block (128 bytes). A *lock bus* operation by module i on an unlocked block (the L bit in the MMD entry is clear) succeeds and sets the L bit and P_i. Otherwise, the bus operation fails and P_i is set. (Variants of the read-shared and read-private bus operations include the locking action, and fail if the lock is already set.)

An *unlock bus* operation by module i clears the MMD entry's lock bit, and all modules j for which P_j is set, where $j \neq i$, are

---

[1]An MPM and an ICM appear identical to the MM on the node bus. We use MPM in the exposition for brevity.

signalled that the lock has been released. This mechanism allows different processes to set and clear the lock, as is required in some applications. Variants of the write-back bus operation include the unlock action.

Read-shared and read-private operations without the lock action succeed independently of the lock setting and do not change the lock setting. This behavior allows the application process that sets a lock to migrate between processors.

The expected use of this facility is for the application to first attempt to lock a block corresponding to some shared data. Once the block is locked, the application updates the logically locked data structures and then releases the lock. Other waiting caches are notified of unlocking, relying on the P field for notification.

The provision of locking as part of the consistency mechanism provides several optimizations over a conventional lock mechanism using test-and-set operations and memory consistency. In our scheme, a processor needing to acquire a lock is forced to wait until it is unlocked, rather than steal the block containing the lock away from the lock holder, as would occur in the original VMP architecture. Thus, the locking mechanism serves as *contention control* on data structures. Used in combination with the read operations that specify locking, this facility allows one to acquire both the lock and the data in one bus operation, but not until the lock is free. In contrast, the conventional approach may induce a high level of contention when, for example, processors spin on locks while the lock holder is updating data in the same cache block.

2.1.3 Memory-Based Message Exchange Protocol

The message exchange protocol uses blocks of shared memory as message buffers. A separate protocol is needed since the semantics of message exchange differs from that of consistent shared memory. A receiving processor wants to be notified after a block (message buffer) has been written, and not before it is read, as in consistent shared memory mode. A sending processor wants to be able to write a block without having read it.

A *Notify* bus operation (i.e., notify me when the block is written) by module i on a given block places the block in message exchange mode by setting the CC field in the corresponding MMD to 11, and setting P_i. A subsequent writeback to that block causes every module specified in the P field to be interrupted and the L bit to be set. The L bit indicates that the block has been written, but not yet read. A read-shared operation then causes the L bit to be cleared and returns the data.

One use of this facility is for interprocessor messages, as part of the operating system kernel implementation. A kernel operation on one processor that affects a process on another processor sends a message to that processor. Each processor has one or more message buffers for which it requests notification when they are written. One communicates with a processor by simply writing to one of its message buffers. For synchronization, the write is aborted if the L bit of the block is set (i.e., the block has been written and not subsequently read).

Another use is notification of memory mapping changes. A memory block is associated with each portion of the kernel memory mapping information (e.g., one MM cache block per address space). If an MPM is caching data from some virtual memory space, it requests notification of writes to the corresponding message block. When a kernel memory management operation modifies the virtual memory mapping, the changes are written to the associated message blocks. The affected modules are notified and update their caches and memory mapping information. Gap-free sequence numbers on the updates are used so a processor can detect that it missed an update (i.e., it failed to read the message block before the block was overwritten), without requiring the hardware to provide this level of synchronization. When a processor does miss an update, it invalidates all of the cache data associated with that portion of virtual memory.

This scheme builds upon the memory coherency mechanism to provide interprocessor interrupts and message data transfer, eliminating the need for a separate facility. It requires only two extra bits in each directory entry and one additional type of bus operation.

In contrast, interprocessor communication implemented purely in terms of message buffers in conventional shared memory would result in considerable extra cache and bus traffic for locking and coherency, imposing unnecessary overhead on key system resources, and limiting scalability.

2.2 Multiple Processor Module (MPM)

The Multiple Processor Module (MPM) occupies a single printed circuit board, and is shown in Figure 3. Multiple CPUs (micro-

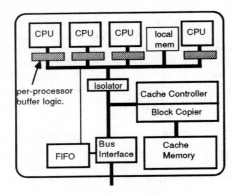

Figure 3: MPM Board Layout

processors) are attached by an on-board bus to a large virtually addressed cache and a small amount of local memory. The cache lines are large, and the cache is managed under software control, as in VMP [8]. The local memory contains cache management code and data structures used by a processor incurring an on-board cache miss. A FIFO buffer queues requests from the node-bus for actions required to maintain cache consistency, and to support the locking and message exchange protocols. One of the processors is interrupted to handle each such request as it arrives.

Each CPU is a high-speed RISC processor with a large (16K or more) virtually addressed on-chip cache with a moderate cache line size (32 bytes). Interference between processors is reduced by transferring data (in 2 cycles) from the on-board cache to a wide per-processor holding register[2], which then transfers the line to the on-chip cache in burst-mode. With each on-chip cache line, in addition to the usual flags such as *valid*, *modified* and *writable*, we require *locked*, *held* and *requested*[3]. Encodings of the extra flags are summarized in Figure 4.

The processor has a *lock* and an *unlock* instruction. The lock instruction specifies an address aligned to a cache block. If the lock is held and not requested (LHR=110 or 010), lock and unlock instructions execute locally (i.e., lock acquisition is done entirely in the cache, and locking has low latency if the lock is held and

---

[2]This is an aggressive requirement. Slower transfers would degrade the MPM performance through increased interference between processors, and further study is required to evaluate the cost/performance tradeoff.

[3]We also require a *privileged* tag bit so that kernel and user data can reside in the cache together. This eliminates the need to flush the cache on return from a kernel call.

LHR	meaning
000	on-chip cache does not hold the lock
001	on-chip cache has requested lock from on-board cache
110	on-chip cache holds the lock and it is locked
010	on-chip cache holds the lock but it is unlocked
111	on-chip cache holds the lock, it is locked, and the on-board cache has requested the lock

Figure 4: LHR Flags Encoding

unlocked). If the *requested* flag is set for a held lock, the lock instruction returns a failure indication. If the lock is not held, the lock instruction causes the request of the lock from the on-board cache (like a cache miss), which either returns the lock (110), indicates the lock should be marked as requested (001) or causes the processor to handle an on-board cache miss, as described below. The unlock instruction simply clears the lock flag unless the requested flag is set, in which case it releases the lock to the on-board cache and clears the held flag[4]. Finally, the on-board cache can signal the processor to writeback and invalidate a specific cache line, that a lock on a cache line has been granted, or that a particular lock has been requested.

The on-board cache implements the same consistency, locking and message exchange protocols as the MM. The cache flag entry per cache line is the same as that of the MM except that it includes 4 additional control bits (replacing 4 P bits). An *exclusively held* bit indicates whether or not the cache holds exclusive ownership of the block. This allows a block to be shared by processors within the MPM, while it is exclusively owned by the MPM relative to the rest of the system. A *dirty* bit indicates whether the entry has been modified since last being written to its MM. Finally, there are the *requested* and *held* bits associated with the locking. The *held* bit allows the cache to hold the lock even if no processor in the MPM has the lock set. The *requested* bit indicates that the lock should be released to the lower level when it is released, rather than just held within the on-board cache (in anticipation of a processor in the MPM requesting the lock).

Upon on-board cache miss, the faulting processor behaves like a VMP processor. It traps to a software miss-handling routine, determines the physical address of the missing data and a cache slot to use (writing out the data if modified), initiates a block transfer of the data into the cache slot by the cache controller, and resumes execution when the block transfer completes. The cache software is synchronized to allow multiple processors to incur cache misses at the same time. Cache access from other processors may also proceed concurrently with miss handling except for when actual bus transfers are taking place.

The block transfer can fail if the block is not available immediately, either because it is not up-to-date in memory, it is not cached in the local ICM, or it is locked and a lock bus operation was invoked. In the first two cases, the cache management software retries the transfer (perhaps after a short delay to allow writebacks and the ICM to acquire the data) until it succeeds, up to some maximum number of retries. The memory system takes the necessary actions to make the requested block available. In the lock case, the processor marks the block as requested in the on-chip cache, signals to the lock instruction that the instruction failed to acquire the lock and resumes execution. If the processor spins on the lock, the instruction is handled entirely by the on-chip cache until the on-board cache notifies the processor that the lock has been released.

---

[4]A cache line may be removed from the cache even if the lock flag has been set. An unlock instruction then incurs a cache miss, which causes the lock bit to be cleared at the memory module level, or some cache level in between.

The design of the MPM has several significant advantages. First, it recognizes and exploits the trend of the increasing sizes of on-chip caches on microprocessors. The large line size of the on-board cache is compatible with increasing on-chip line sizes. The inclusion of the locked, requested and held cache flag bits in both the on-chip and on-board caches effectively improves the cache and bus behavior by reducing latency, coherence interference, and contention. The bits impose a modest space overhead which decreases with increasing cache line size. The virtually addressed on-board cache eliminates the need for memory management on chip, thereby freeing chip area for a larger cache. Absence of mapping on chip also simplifies the invalidation of on-chip cache lines. The value of large cache blocks has been demonstrated by the VMP design.

Sharing the on-board cache has three major advantages. First, it results in a higher on-board cache hit ratio due to the sharing of code and data in the on-board cache and by localizing access to some shared data to the on-board cache. Compared to per-processor on-board caches, the sharing reduces the total bus traffic imposed by the processors. The reduction in bus traffic contributes to scalability, and hence performance[5]. Second, sharing the on-board cache reduces the total hardware cost for supporting N processors, since only N/K MPM boards (and on-board caches) are required if K processors share each on-board cache[6]. Finally, the increased hit ratio of the on-board cache reduces the average memory access time of the processor, resulting in a higher instruction execution rate. However, this effect is relatively small since the on-chip cache will typically have a high hit ratio, limiting the possible improvement in the memory access time.

The on-board cache exploits a number of ideas of the original VMP processor cache. First, the cache is virtually addressed so there is a direct connection between the on-chip cache and the on-board cache, i.e., no MMU. Thus, miss handling is fast and the complexity of virtual-to-physical mapping is placed (in software) between the MPM and the inter-MPM bus, simplifying both the processor chip and the on-board logic, and reducing the translation frequency. For example, with an on-chip TLB one expects 0.004 TLB faults per memory reference [15] whereas we have measured 0.00004 translation misses [7] using the VMP cache, an improvement of a factor of 100. Also, the cache miss software uses compact data structures to replace conventional page tables, thereby reducing the memory space overhead of virtual memory implementations.

Second, the on-board cache minimizes replacements and flushing by using set-associative mapping and an address space identifier as part of the virtually addressed cache mechanism. Thus, the cache can hold data from multiple address spaces and need not be flushed on context switch. The on-board cache provides one address space identifier register per processor. Each off-chip reference by a processor (cache miss) is presented to the on-board cache prepended with the address space identifier. Thus, the on-board cache knows about separate address spaces but the processor chip need not.

Third, the large cache block size makes it feasible for the on-board cache to be quite large (i.e., .5 megabytes or more), reducing the replacement interference and thereby permitting multiple processors to share the on-board cache even when running programs in separate address spaces.

With 8 processors per MPM, it is possible to configure up to 104 processors on a single bus as 13 MPMs and one or more MMs. To scale larger, we introduce extra levels of caching and busses using the ICM and the NAB.

2.3 Inter-bus Cache Module (ICM)

The inter-bus cache module (ICM) is a cache, shared by the MPMs on an inter-MPM bus (an MPM group or MPMG), which connects such an MPMG to a next level bus. It appears as an MPM on the node bus and an MM on the inter-MPM bus. It caches memory blocks from the MMs, implementing the same consistency, locking and message exchange protocols as the MPMs. These blocks are cached in response to requests from MPMs on its inter-MPM bus. The MMD entry per block in the ICM is the same as that of the MPM, limiting the P field to 9 bits[7].

When an ICM receives a read transfer request for a block[8], it determines whether it has the block cached. If so, it responds in the same manner as an MM to the request. However, if the operation is a read-private request, it may have to gain exclusive ownership of the block on the node bus before responding. If the ICM does not contain the referenced block, it aborts the transfer and then attempts to acquire the block from the MM on the node bus, in the same way an MPM would.

To accommodate device access and uncached references, the ICM also provides direct uncached references to the node bus. In particular, an MPM can write a block directly through to the node bus, allowing it, for example, to transfer data to the NAB control register.

The ICM supports the message exchange facility by implementing the same states for its cached entries as the MPM cache. In addition, the exclusive flag is used to indicate when the message receivers are entirely local to the MPMG, automatically allowing the message activity to be localized to the group when appropriate.

Several merits of the ICM are of note. First, as a shared cache, the ICM makes commonly shared blocks, such as operating system code and application code available to an MPMG without repeated access across the node bus. This contrasts with the *cluster controller* approach described by Wilson [18][9], where repeated reads by MPM's in one group would result in repeated read requests to another group if the block is not in a memory module local to the requesting group. The ICM shared cache is important for scalability, for the same reasons identified for the MPM on-board cache. Second, the ICM supports the hierarchical directory-based consistency, providing a complete record of cache page residency, thereby minimizing consistency bus traffic and interprocessor interrupt overhead. Finally, because the ICM appears the same as an MPM, one can mix MPM's and ICM's on the node bus without change to the MMs.

A maximal configuration of 8-processor MPMs, ICMs and MMs would produce a 936-processor machine. Even larger configurations can be achieved using multiple levels of ICMs and busses. The address range switches on the ICM allow the memory load to be split below the MPM bus level between two or more separate ICMs and separate node-level busses and MMs, as illustrated in Figure 5. However, we see a more common configuration being a group of more modestly configured machines, connected by a high-speed network using the NAB.

2.4 Network Adapter Board (NAB)

The NAB [11] provides reliable transport-level communication between network nodes connected by a high-performance network.

---

[5]For example, if the bus traffic is decreased by 50%, the number of processors on the bus may be doubled. For an application with linear speedup, this will result in a doubling of performance.

[6]Because sharing on-board cache significantly reduces the parts count and the number of connectors and thus presumably improves the reliability, the sharing also contributes to scaling through improved reliability.

[7]The restriction of the entry to 16 bits is primarily to minimize the chip count for the board.

[8]The ICM has switches to indicate the range of physical addresses it should cover.

[9]Wilson also mentions the caching approach as used by the ICM.

19

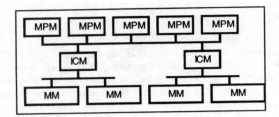

Figure 5: Partitioned Memory Hierarchy

Thus, the NAB performs all packetizing, checksumming and encryption required as part of transport-level transmission, and the reverse on reception. Several aspects of the NAB are specifically relevant to multiprocessors. First, on-board processing and "intelligent" DMA provided by the NAB imposes the minimal load on the node bus and MPMs by performing a single block transfer to memory on reception and from memory on transmission. Data is delivered page-aligned with headers removed, allowing the data to be mapped directly to application memory without copying. Second, because the NAB performs the protocol processing, the MPM caches are not polluted by packetizing and checksumming data to be transmitted or received. It also reduces the network-related interrupt activity at the MPMs because the NAB handles multi-packet segments on transmission and reception. Finally, the NAB transfers to and from physical memory using the same bus operations used by the MPMs and ICMs so these block transfers can be aborted by an MM to cause an ICM or MPM to writeback exclusively-owned blocks. This approach avoids the cost of brute-force techniques to ensure that none of the data being read or overwritten is cached, as would otherwise be required.

A NAB-style network interface is also required for pure performance reasons, now that networks are available in the gigabit range. The serial, pipelined nature of protocol processing is not well-suited to the multi-level cache architecture supporting the general-purpose processors in VMP-MC.

The VMP-MC building blocks described above allow a large parallel machine to be configured. However, the feasible scale of configuration depends significantly on the actual speeds of the busses and memories and the program performance characteristics. The following section provides an initial evaluation of the design with a focus on identifying realistic parameters for this design using hardware technology we see available in the foreseeable future.

3 Design Evaluation

This section describes the results of several studies undertaken to provide a preliminary evaluation of key aspects of the design and aid in choosing certain design parameters. An important assumption is that on-chip processor caches can reduce on-board cache misses to the extent that the performance benefits of sharing the on-board cache, in terms of reduced bus traffic and reduced memory access time, overwhelms the interference cost of multiple processors sharing the cache. We evaluated this approach using trace-driven simulation.

3.1 Primary/Secondary Cache Parameters

In the simulations, each processor chip is assumed to have a virtually-addressed 16 kilobyte unified cache with a cache block size of 32 bytes[10]. Caches of this size will be feasible on microprocessors in the near future.

---

[10]The actual processor chip will probably have split instruction and data caches to increase the available bandwidth.

The on-board cache is a 4-way set associative virtually addressed cache of .5 megabytes using a 128 byte cache block size, the same as previous VMP on-board caches [7]. Upon a hit to the on-board cache, the data is transferred to a 16 byte wide by 2 deep per-processor FIFO in 2 processor cycles[11]. The data is then transferred to the processor in 8 cycles. Similarly, a FIFO (16 bytes wide, 8 deep) is used to reduce the cache busy time on a read and writeback on the inter-MPM bus. An on-board cache block (128 bytes) is moved over the 64-bit wide inter-MPM bus into this FIFO in 16 cycles (250 Mbytes/sec if the cycle time is 30 ns). Using this approach, we can write 16 bytes in parallel from the FIFO into the on-board cache, and fill the cache in 8 cycles.

On a miss in the on-board cache, the cache is busy for 1 cycle signalling the miss and then another 8 cycles transferring data from the latch. During the software cache miss handling by the faulting processor, the cache is busy only during the bus transfer, not during the entire processing of the miss. The cache is also made busy by invalidations and writebacks that occur as part of consistency interrupts. A slot invalidation makes the cache busy for 2 cycles (invalidation time plus arbitration time). A writeback makes the cache busy for 8 cycles. The on-board cache signals the affected processors to write-back or invalidate blocks as required by the ownership and locking protocol that we use.

3.2 Cache Behavior

In this section we examine the tradeoff between the benefits of sharing the on-board cache (decreased traffic on the inter-MPM bus), and the interference introduced by having more than one processor share the on-board cache. We will refer to an on-chip cache as an *L1 cache*, and to an on-board cache as an *L2 cache*.

Simulations were run using several multiprocessor traces. The traces were collected using a combined hardware/software method, using the VAX T-bit mechanism to single-step the processor through each process in round-robin fashion. The traces do not include operating system references, and all the traces are of 16-processor parallel executions. The characteristics of the following traces are summarized in Table 1 [17]:

Locusroute: This is a global router for VLSI standard cells. Each processor removes a wire from the task queue and selects the best route for that wire. No locks are used in the cost data structure.

Mp3d: This is a three-dimensional particle simulator for rarefied flow. During each time step, the particles are moved one at a time. One lock protects an index into the global particle array.

Distributed Csim: This is a distributed logic simulator which does not rely on a global time during simulation. The trace does not include references to locks.

Name	references in trace ($\times 10^6$)	i-fetches (%)	reads (%)	writes (%)
mp3d	7.05	61	33	6
dcsim	7.09	50	39	11
locusroute	7.70	50	38	12

Table 1: Trace characteristics

The 16-processor traces were run against different MPM configurations, obtained by varying the number of processors sharing the L2 cache. The L1 and L2 cache sizes were the same for all the simulations. We compensate for start-up effects by keeping track of the blocks that a cache has accessed, and ignoring the first ac-

---

[11]In this discussion, time is expressed in terms of processor cycles, which will be 20–30 ns for the processors we consider.

cess to a block when calculating miss ratios and bus traffic. This approximates the stationary behavior of a cache.

Table 2 shows the L1 miss ratio for different numbers of processors sharing each L2 cache. The miss ratios for *locusroute* are comparable to those reported in [16] for a similar size cache, considering that we compensate for start-up effects. The higher miss ratios for the other applications reflect a higher degree of coherence activity. Significantly, the L1 miss ratios stay almost constant as we increase the degree of sharing. This means that we can optimize the degree of sharing without impacting the L1 cache performance.

Name	Processors per MPM				
	1	2	4	6	8
mp3d	7.6	7.6	7.6	7.6	7.6
dcsim	2.5	2.5	2.5	2.6	2.5
locusroute	.80	.80	.79	.82	.79

Table 2: L1 miss ratio (% of references)

Table 3 shows the decrease in the L2 miss ratio as we increase the number of processors sharing an L2 cache from 1 to 8. The improvements are 55% for *dcsim*, 57% for *mp3d*, and 61% for *locusroute*. The lower miss ratios imply a reduction in the average memory access time. For the system we described, this improvement in L2 miss ratio will double the instruction execution rate for *mp3d* and *dcsim*, but result only in a 3% increase for *locusroute*. This is because the high L1 hit ratio measured for *locusroute* makes it difficult to further decrease the average memory access time.

Name	Processors per MPM				
	1	2	4	6	8
mp3d	77	67	54	43	33
dcsim	20	17	14	11	9.3
locusroute	3.3	3.1	2.2	1.7	1.3

Table 3: L2 miss ratio (% of L2 references)

Table 4 shows how the number of L2 cache coherence actions per processor decreases as we increase the amount of sharing. The coherence actions consist of block invalidations, changes in ownership mode from private to shared, and writeback transactions if an invalidated or downgraded block was dirty.

The simulations show a decrease in the number of coherence actions of 50% for *mp3d*, 65% for *dcsim*, and 67% for *locusroute* as we move from no sharing to 8 processors sharing an L2 cache. This supports our claim that L2 cache sharing reduces coherence activity. The shared L2 cache allows fewer invalidations to propagate beyond the MPM.

Name	Processors per MPM				
	1	2	4	6	8
mp3d	7.8	7.1	5.9	4.9	3.9
dcsim	.88	.72	.54	.43	.31
locusroute	.06	.05	.04	.03	.02

Table 4: Number of coherence actions (% of processor references)

The decrease in the L2 miss ratio (shown in Table 3) should directly result in sharply lower traffic on the inter-MPM bus. This is supported by Table 5, which shows how the number of block move transactions (read and writeback) on the inter-MPM bus change as we increase the sharing. The reduction in block move traffic is 44% for *mp3d*, 46% for *dcsim*, and 59% for *locusroute*. The block move transactions constitute more than 90% of the traffic on the inter-MPM bus. This reduction in traffic on the inter-MPM bus means

that we can put roughly twice as many processors on the inter-MPM busses when sharing the L2 caches by 8 processors, compared to the case where we do not share the L2 caches. This enables us to double the performance of an MPM group, while reducing the cost of the system at the same time.

Name	Processors per MPM				
	1	2	4	6	8
mp3d	7.2	6.9	5.9	5.3	4.0
dcsim	.81	.75	.60	.61	.44
locusroute	.005	.005	.004	.004	.002

Table 5: Block move transactions (% of references in trace)

3.3 Loading of shared resources

The on-board cache and the on-board bus are the two bottlenecks in the MPM. The utilization of these resources limit the number of processors that can share the L2 cache: if they are too busy, a processor may have to wait when handling an L1 cache miss. In the following evaluation, the utilization is approximated by counting the total number of processor cycles that the resource is occupied, and dividing that by the number of cycles that the processors will take to execute the trace.

Table 6 shows the utilization of the on-board bus. We see that the utilization starts out low and increases linearly as the number of processors is increased. *Mp3d* shows a slight superlinearity due to the increased on-board bus traffic caused by the coherence traffic confined to the L2 cache. For all three traces, the on-board bus utilization is fairly low up to 8 processors sharing the L2 cache. This suggests that the on-board bus will probably not be a bottleneck in the system.

Name	Processors per MPM				
	1	2	4	6	8
mp3d	2.8	5.6	13	22	34
dcsim	2.6	5.5	11	18	25
locusroute	1.1	2.2	4.3	6.8	8.5

Table 6: On-board bus utilization (% of available cycles)

Next we look at the on-board cache utilization, shown in Table 7. The cache is occupied by the following: cache hits (2 cycles), reads from the inter-MPM bus (8 cycles), writebacks (8 cycles), and invalidations (2 cycles), as explained earlier. Requests to the cache are handled on a FCFS basis. The cache management software is not a bottleneck since it is executed in parallel by the on-board processors. We assume that contention for the cache data structures can be minimized by fine-grain locking. The cache utilization is reasonably low for all the traces up to four processors sharing the L2 cache. After that, the cache is very busy for both *dcsim* and *mp3d*.

Name	Processors per MPM				
	1	2	4	6	8
mp3d	9.3	19	40	59	78
dcsim	6.9	14	27	41	51
locusroute	2.2	4.3	8.3	12	16

Table 7: On-board cache utilization (% of available cycles)

A first order estimate of the average length of the request queues at the cache can be obtained by approximating the cache as an M/M/1 queueing system [12]. For the organization outlined above, and using the measurements of utilization given in Table 7, this yields average queue lengths of 0.2 for *locusroute* (with 8 processors per MPM). For the other two applications it seems that 4 processors per MPM would be more appropriate. This organization yields queue lengths of 0.4 for *dcsim*, and 0.7 for *mp3d*.

From these results we make the following conclusions:

1. The traffic on the inter-MPM bus is sharply reduced when the L2 cache is shared by 8 processors, each with its own L1 cache. We observe a 50% reduction in inter-MPM bus traffic when we share an L2 cache among 8 processors. We speculate that it may be possible to reduce the traffic even further by software techniques which attempt to localize interprocess communication to an MPM.

2. The hardware cost of the system decreases significantly while increasing the scalability, and therefore also the performance of the system.

3. The instruction execution rate of a single processor increases because of the decrease in the L2 cache miss ratio. This effect is more pronounced when the L1 cache hit ratio is low.

4. The figures show that, for *locusroute*, 8 is reasonable number of processors to share an on-board cache, given the constraints on board real estate and the interference level introduced by higher degrees of sharing. Programs with poorer cache behavior (*dcsim* and *mp3d*) will not perform well if more than 4 processors share an L2 cache.

The traces deal only with running one single address space parallel program. If the processor runs different applications in separate address spaces, replacement interference is not a problem because the on-board cache is large and set associative. We conjecture that separate applications will run with a higher miss ratio primarily because of lack of *miss sharing*, rather than replacement interference.

3.4 Inter-MPM Bus Loading

On the inter-MPM bus, each MPM used approximately 3% of the available bus bandwidth with our preferred configuration of 8 processors per board, executing *locusroute*. Thus, it may well be feasible to configure up to 16 or more MPMs per bus, yielding an 128-processor configuration. However, it is optimistic to extrapolate our results to larger processor configurations. Further evaluation requires either traces for larger-scale parallel applications, or the realization of VMP-MC on that scale.

The use of an ICM and another level of bus allows an even larger configuration, potentially up to 1000 processors or more. Given our lack of data on this scale of system, we limit ourselves to a few comments. First, the ICM allows one to (largely) isolate a computation node as part of an extended workstation. It will share the MM, network adapter, and possibly local disks with the workstation, but with only slightly greater loading than a single additional processor. For example, an engineer might add such an expansion cabinet to his multiprocessor workstation, allowing him to run compute-intensive simulations on the ICM-connected module while running normal CAD software on the rest of the machine.

Second, if one can partition the application sufficiently well, these very large configurations of VMP-MC would work well. This partitioning problems seems easier than that imposed by distributed memory systems, such as the Cosmic Cube [13], since it is only an optimization. *Most* of the references should be to data that is locally cached, although this is not required for correctness.

3.5 Hierarchical Latency

We estimate that it will cost the MPM 20 cycles to access a 128-byte block from the ICM. The extra delay for accessing a block MPM-to-MM in this design (going through an ICM) is estimated as another 20 cycles. This is assuming a copy into the ICM cache while

passing it through to the inter-MPM bus, with no consistency or bus contention at the MM or inter-MPM bus level. Using measured cache miss ratios of less than 0.05 percent (*locusroute*), the extra delay is about 1% of the cycle time per memory reference on average. Thus, the extra delay is not significant in the absence of contention.

With consistency contention, the faulting MPM must force a write-back in another MPMG. This cost is estimated as an extra 65 cycles. Again, with the low expected frequency of these events, the incremental cost on the average memory reference time is not significant.

The limited size of the ICM memory (compared to the total number of MMs) makes it feasible to provide faster memory in the ICM than in the MMs. Thus, with a good ICM hit ratio, the lower delay for ICM hits should compensate for the higher cost of the ICM misses. (This point was also made by Wilson [18].)

Latency for page faults and contention with other networks nodes is significantly higher than for MPMs within a single network node. For example, with a 100 Mb network and NAB, we expect roughly 1.1 milliseconds for a 1 kilobyte page fault from a file server without contention. With file server contention, we expect the page fault time to be approximately 2.2 milliseconds in the absence of packet loss.

Investigation is required to understand the trade-offs between the "height" and "width" of the memory hierarchy. In particular, placing more MPMs on the same bus reduces the latency of interaction between these MPMs as compared to placing them on separate busses and possibly separate VMP-MC nodes. However, placing them on a common MPM bus imposes more load on this bus. In essence, this says that sharing MPMs should be on the same MPM bus or at least the same node, whereas non-sharing ones should be separated at the highest levels of the hierarchy.

3.6 Locking Performance Effects

To directly evaluate the benefits of the VMP-MC locking mechanism would require designing applications specifically for this architecture. While we plan to do this eventually, we approximate the behavior by identifying memory locations used for locking, and ignoring these references in the simulation.

Previously, we reported a 40% reduction in bus traffic when locks were ignored in a trace [7]. For the traces used here, only one (*mp3d*) contains access to locks. Although only 3.4% of the accesses in *mp3d* is to the lock, we observe substantial reductions in bus traffic when lock access is ignored. There is a reduction of 20% in cycles on the inter-MPM bus, a reduction of 21% in cycles on the on-board bus, and an increase of 18% in the L1 cache hit ratio. This substantial reduction in the traffic supports the notion of a specialized locking mechanism that will reduce memory contention for locks.

3.7 Message Exchange and Mapping Performance

A message send takes roughly 50 cycles, including the cost of a *Notify* and a *Writeback*. Message reading time varies depending on the processor activity at the time of the message write. However, if there is no miss or consistency handling active at the time the message is sent, the processor receives the message in the time required to interrupt, transfer the block and continue, roughly 100 cycles.

If the action occurs between processors in the same MPM, no bus action is generated. If the action is local to an MPMG, the ICM ensures that it does not result in traffic on the node bus.

The primary use at present for the inter-processor communication is to allow efficient notification of processors when aspects of the memory mapping is changed, affecting the implicit mapping represented in the caches. We draw on measurements done of Accent [9] to argue the acceptability of this mechanism.

Measurements of Accent indicate a rather low level of mapping changes. Although no memory reference counts were given, we estimate there to be roughly 2600 million references in the measurements (assuming an average instruction time of 3 microseconds for the Perq). Using these measurements as a rough guide, there was approximately 1 memory mapping change per 3 million memory references. Thus, remapping imposes an overhead of .003 percent on each processor, assuming one processor performs the remapping and the rest are interrupted. This figure does not incorporate the cost of additional misses resulting from the remapping. Note that VMP-MC normally remaps the memory when copy-on-write is performed, rather than simply invalidating the cache entry. This technique reduces the number of cache misses resulting from mapping changes.

4 Status

The VMP-MC represents (and requires) the cumulation and focus of several projects with the V software and VMP hardware. It would be very costly (in terms of time and money) to build a full-scale VMP-MC configuration, so we are progressing incrementally in the development, evaluation and construction of hardware.

The MM design and layout is complete. The transfer speed in the prototype (using the VME bus) is approximately 40 megabytes per second. (Our board utilizes a two-edge handshake protocol, not the VME standard block transfer protocol.) We expect to have working boards in mid-1989. We plan to use existing VMP processor boards initially, since it will require only minor modifications to work with the MM. The MPM is still in design as we evaluate the possible choices of microprocessor. The ICM, combining the logic of the MM and MPM, is still at the initial design stage.

A NAB prototype (wire-wrap) board has been completed and we are now doing a PC board version for FDDI. To get a prototype VMP-MC working quickly and build on our prior work, we are using the VMEbus as the bus. However, future wide bus standards with more support for block transfers will clearly be a better long-term choice.

The V distributed system has been ported and runs on the VMP. It is planned to be the operating system for VMP-MC. V supports light-weight processes, symmetric multiprocessing, distributed shared memory and high-performance interprocess communication. We are currently reworking the V kernel to provide cleaner and faster parallel execution within the kernel. In related work on distributed operating systems, we have been investigating a distributed virtual memory system [6] that provides memory consistency of virtual memory segments shared across a cluster of workstations.

5 Related Work

Most work on scalable architectures to date has resulted in machines that do not support shared memory or that require a high initial investment, machines with limited general computation flexibility, and machines with large numbers of relatively slow or limited processors. For example, the Connection Machine [10] provides a large number of processors of limited power and is unable to run a conventional operating system. Similarly, the Cosmic Cube [13] does not run a general-purpose operating system and thus is not usable as a workstation or general-purpose computing node. From our experience, we view the shared memory multiprocessor as the most desireable form of general-purpose machine.

The extension of the VMP design to a hierarchically structured memory system is similar to the design described by Wilson [18] with the ICM corresponding to his *cluster cache*. However, we have provided a detailed design for handling coherency and caching

that was lacking in his description. Also, we focus on using a cache module to interconnect busses rather than a simple bus interconnect (*routing switch* in his terminology). All the VMP-MC memory is attached to the lowest level bus, the node bus, rather than distributed across the clusters, or bus groups. We believe that the ICM caching eliminates the extra bus traffic one might otherwise expect from locating all the memory on the node bus and in fact leads to a lower level of traffic on non-local MPM busses.

In general, we believe that the caching approach to bus interconnect is superior to using *routing switches* and distributing the physical memory among the MPMGs (as suggested by Wilson). First, the caching approach avoids the need to optimize the allocation of physical memory relative to processors on a bus. Memory effectively migrates to an MPMG based on demand. Thus, the system must concern itself only with locating interacting processes within the same MPMG. Allocating physical memory for these processes from within their MPMG is not required. Second, it avoids multiple transfers by the MPMG to move a given data block into several MPMs. Third, the ICM knowledge of data blocks in its MPMG allows it to selectively filter out irrelevant invalidation operations from the bus.

We argue that sharing the on-board cache is necessary given the low hit ratio, and the resulting low hardware utilization, also predicted by other studies [14].

Merits of software control and additional performance evaluation for VMP have been described elsewhere [7]. In summary, the three major changes to the MPM from the original VMP design are:

- Multiple processors share the on-board cache, rather than a single processor, assuming sizeable on-chip caches.
- The bus monitor and action table of VMP have been replaced by the MM directories (and the equivalent on the ICMs). The elimination of the action table makes the MPM configuration independent of the amount of physical memory in the system.
- Support for locking and message exchange has been added.

These changes do not detract from the relative simplicity of the VMP design.

The memory-directory based consistency scheme has been described and studied in various forms by a number of researchers [4, 1, 2]. The use of large cache line size in VMP-MC makes it feasible to store a processor bitmask per directory entry while keeping the space overhead around 2 percent. (This corresponds roughly to the *DirallB* scheme of Agarwal et al. [1].) The hierarchical distribution of the cache directory information minimizes space cost while avoiding unnecessary broadcasting of coherency-induced traffic. Our approach contrasts with that of Archibald and Baer [2], who use 4 bits per directory entry to keep the space overhead reasonable, using 32-bit cache line sizes. Their scheme leads to a nodewide broadcast whenever a cache page frame appears to be shared with another processor node.

The locking scheme bears some similarity to that proposed by Bitar and Despain [3]. Although our scheme also uses cache flags, we are free to discard locked cache blocks from the cache, relying on the memory module to record locking. Since they do not use a directory scheme, they require a separate lock bit that has to be written to memory. We view our scheme as more consistent with uses of locks at the application level, especially when processes may migrate between different processors.

VMP-MC is designed to work well with the virtual memory and transaction management system that we are developing for the V distributed system. VMP-MC appears well suited to support the Mach virtual memory system [19] as well as the 801 transaction software [5], both of which reflect current directions in operating system design.

6 Concluding Remarks

The VMP-MC design is a simple but powerful extension of the basic VMP design we have been investigating for a number of years. We propose it as a building block technology for configuring workstations and parallel machines with 1 to several thousand powerful (50 or more MIPS) processors.

Several aspects of the VMP-MC design are of particular interest. First, secondary-level cache sharing is exploited to reduce the miss ratios of these caches, the hardware costs of these caches, and the contention between caches. Our simulation results indicate that the reduced miss and contention activity from cache sharing allows more than twice as many modules loading the next level bus. This sharing also significantly reduces the amount of hardware required to support a large-scale configuration, particularly at the MPM level. The reduction in cost and reliability problems makes the architecture practically scalable. The sharing also reduces the average memory reference cost.

Second, the hierarchical directory-based consistency scheme allows coherency, locking and message traffic to be selectively broadcast, if not unicast, to just the affected processor(s). In contrast to the original VMP design, the memory directory-based consistency scheme eliminates the per-processor action table from each processor module, making this module independent of the physical memory size. The large cache line size of VMP allows this scheme to be implemented with less than 2 percent space overhead. The hierarchical extension of VMP is transparent to the software except for various scheduling controls and heuristics that we are introducing to improve the inter-MPM cluster behavior.

Finally, VMP-MC provides explicit support for locking and message exchange, reducing the cost of these operations, particularly for large-scale configurations. The locking facility essentially provides a *contention control* mechanism, allowing the software to synchronize with little contention. The message facility allows the operating system to avoid contention as part of implementing interprocess and memory management operations.

Our work to date has developed the design and implemented several of the components of VMP-MC as well as provided an initial performance evaluation of the design based on trace-driven simulation. Further work is required to fully evaluate the feasibility of this design, including construction of the multiple processor board. This is the next focus of our hardware effort. Considerable software effort will be required along the way to properly exploit this architecture.

Overall, we see the VMP-MC as providing a credible approach to building a scalable multiprocessor without using costly technology or giving up the availability of shared memory, an important facility for many parallel applications. As a building block technology, it provides a means of configuring a wide range of general-purpose parallel machines, ranging from a moderate scale multiprocessor to a teraop multi-computer configuration. This approach offers a lower entry cost, greater generality and easier extensibility than the approaches to large-scale parallel machines proposed by many other research projects. We hope to further substantiate these conclusions by the construction and experimentation evaluation of a VMP-MC configuration following the design described in this paper.

7 Acknowledgements

We are grateful to Anoop Gupta and Wolf Weber for making the trace data used in this paper available to us. This paper has benefited from comments and criticisms of members of the Distributed Systems Group at Stanford.

References

[1] A. Agarwal, R. Simoni, J. Hennessy, and M. Horowitz. Scalable directory schemes for cache coherence. In *Proc. 15th Int. Symp. on Computer Architecture*, pages 280–289. ACM SIGARCH, IEEE Computer Society, June 1988.

[2] J. Archibald and J.L. Baer. An economical solution to the cache coherence problem. In *Proc. 12th Int. Symp. on Computer Architecture*, pages 355–362. ACM SIGARCH, June 1985. Also SIGARCH Newsletter, Volume 13, Issue 3, 1985.

[3] P. Bitar and A.M. Despain. Multiprocessor cache synchronization issues, innovations, evolution. In *13th Int. Symp. on Computer Architecture*, pages 424–433. ACM SIGARCH, IEEE Computer Society, June 1986.

[4] M. Censier and P. Feautier. A new solution to coherence problems in multicache systems. *IEEE TC*, C-27(12):1112–1118, December 1978.

[5] A. Chang and M. Mergen. 801 Storage: Architecture and Programming. In *11th Symp. on Operating Systems Principles*. ACM, November 1987.

[6] D.R. Cheriton. Unified management of memory and file caching using the V virtual memory system. Submitted for publication, 1989.

[7] D.R. Cheriton, A. Gupta, P. Boyle, and H.A. Goosen. The VMP multiprocessor: Initial experience, refinements and performance evaluation. In *Proc. 15th Int. Symp. on Computer Architecture*, pages 410–421. ACM SIGARCH, IEEE Computer Society, June 1988.

[8] D.R. Cheriton, G. Slavenburg, and P. Boyle. Software-controlled caches in the VMP multiprocessor. In *13th Int. Conf. on Computer Architectures*. ACM SIGARCH, IEEE Computer Society, June 1986.

[9] R. Fitzgerald and R.F. Rashid. The integration of virtual memory management and interprocess communication in accent. *ACM Transaction on Computer Systems*, 4(2):147–177, May 1986.

[10] W.D. Hillis. *The Connection Machine*. MIT Press, 1985.

[11] H. Kanakia and D.R. Cheriton. The VMP network adapter board (NAB): High-performance network communication for multiprocessors. In *SIGCOMM '88 Symposium*, pages 175–187. ACM SIGCOM, IEEE Computer Society, August 1988.

[12] Leonard Kleinrock. *Queueing Systems, Volume 1: Theory*. Wiley Interscience, 1975.

[13] C.L. Seitz. The Cosmic Cube. *CACM*, 28(1):22–33, January 1985.

[14] R.T. Short and H.M. Levy. A simulation study of two-level caches. In *Proc. 15th Int. Symp. on Computer Architecture*, pages 81–88. ACM SIGARCH, IEEE Computer Society, June 1988.

[15] A.J. Smith. Cache Memories. *Computing Surveys*, 14(3), September 1982.

[16] A.J. Smith. Line (block) size choice for cpu cache memories. *IEEE Transactions on Computers*, C-36(9):1063–1075, September 1987.

[17] W. Weber and A. Gupta. Analysis of cache invalidation patterns in multiprocessors. To appear, ASPLOS 1989.

[18] A.W. Wilson, Jr. Hierarchical cache/bus architecture for shared memory multiprocessors. In *14th Int. Conf. on Computer Architectures*, pages 244–253. ACM SIGARCH, IEEE Computer Society, June 1987.

[19] M. Young et al. The duality of memory and communication in the implementation of a multiprocessor operating system. In *11th Symp. on Operating Systems Principles*. ACM, November 1987.

Design and Performance of a Coherent Cache
for Parallel Logic Programming Architectures

Atsuhiro Goto*   Akira Matsumoto†   Evan Tick‡

Institute for New Generation Computer Technology (ICOT)§

Abstract

This paper describes the design and performance of a tightly-coupled shared-memory coherent cache optimized for the execution of parallel logic programming architectures. The cache utilizes a copy-back write-allocation protocol having five states and a hardware lock mechanism. Optimizations for logic programming are introduced in four software-controlled memory access commands: direct-write, exclusive-read, read-purge, and read-invalidate. In this paper we describe these operations and present simulated measurements showing their performance advantage for an architecture of the committed-choice language KL1. The cache optimizations also improve the performance of non-committed-choice languages, such as OR-parallel Prolog. A version of the cache design described here is currently being implemented for ICOT's Parallel Inference Machine (PIM).

1   Introduction

Current interest in parallel logic programming stems from its declarative semantics which facilitate writing and debugging programs and remove most of the need for explicit uncovering and control of parallelism. Parallel logic programming languages, many based on Prolog, are high-level in the sense that destructive assignment is forbidden and programs often appear as many small recursive procedures instead of fewer, large iterative ones. In addition, some languages retain Prolog's nondeterminacy, resulting in backtracking over assignment. Another important difference is the granularity size of processes. In general, logic programming languages have much smaller tasks than explicitly controlled proce-

---

*E-Mail: goto%icot.jp@relay.cs.net

†Currently at Mitsubishi Electric Corporation, MIEL, 5-1-1 Ofuna Kamakura-city, Kanagawa 247

‡Currently at University of Tokyo, RCAST, 4-6-1 Komaba, Meguro-ku, Tokyo 153

§Mita Kokusai Bldg 21F, 1-4-28 Mita, Minato-ku, Tokyo 108

dural languages. These attributes result in a significantly higher memory bandwidth requirement than for procedural languages [19]. There are various means of reducing the bandwidth requirement, and certainly both compiler optimization and hardware support are necessary to attain high performance. This paper discusses shared-memory multiprocessor hardware support in the form a cache design [10] optimized for the memory accessing characteristics of parallel logic programming languages.

Several cache protocols have been proposed, e.g., [1, 2, 5, 7, 13, 18], each aiming to solve the cache coherency problem and reduce common bus traffic. The cache protocol described here, called the PIM (Parallel Inference Machine) cache, is similar to the Illinois protocol [13]; however, the PIM protocol has an additional state, distinguishing between SM (shared modified) and S (shared). The new features added for logic programming architectures are the direct write (**DW**), read purge (**RP**), read invalidate (**RI**), and exclusive read (**ER**) commands, described in detail in Section 3.2.

In summary, parallel logic programming languages display different (more severe) memory referencing and process control characteristics than do procedural languages such as C in a multi-user UNIX environment. Considering shared memory multiprocessors, such as the Sequent [15], these different characteristics translate to a general requirement for higher memory bandwidth, an efficient locking mechanism for short intervals, and an efficient communication mechanism necessary for balancing the load of many small tasks.

This paper is organized as follows. Motivation for the PIM cache design is given in Section 2, with a description of the memory referencing characteristics of the parallel KL1 architecture. Section 3 describes the cache protocol. Section 4 presents the results of a performance evaluation of the cache with a software KL1 emulator and cache simulator. Finally conclusions are presented.

2   Motivation for Cache Design

To motivate the coherent cache design presented later in this paper, it is beneficial to review the KL1 language based on FGHC, and its corresponding architecture. KL1 [3] is designed for ICOT's PIM [1] [6] by adding system programming support features to FGHC. Other similar languages and architectures based on the Warren Abstract Machine

---

[1]Figure 4 shows the PIM pilot machine.

(WAM) [22] are surprisingly similar in their requirements, and can therefore also advantageously utilize the cache optimizations. See Tick [20] for a performance analysis of one such architecture, Aurora [9], on the PIM cache.

2.1 FGHC: Base of KL1

Flat Guarded Horn Clauses (FGHC) [21] is a language based on Horn clauses of the form: $H :- G_1, ...G_m | B_1, ..., B_n$. where H is the head of the clause, G_i are guards, "|" is the commit, and B_j are the body goals. In FGHC, as in Prolog, procedures are composed of sets of clauses with the same name and arity. Unlike Prolog, there are no nondeterminate procedures. Execution proceeds by attempting unification between a goal (the caller) and a clause head (the callee). If unification succeeds, execution of the guard goals are attempted. These goals can only be system-defined builtin procedures, e.g., arithmetic comparison. If the guard succeeds, the procedure call "commits" to that clause, i.e., any other possibly good candidate clauses are dismissed. If the head or guard fails, another candidate clause in the procedure is attempted (if all clauses fail, the program fails). There is a third possibility however: that the call *suspends*. This is described in detail below.

FGHC restricts unification in the head and guard (the "passive part" of the clause) to be input unification only, i.e., bindings are not exported. Output unification can be performed only in the body part (the "active part"). These restrictions allow AND-parallel execution of body goals and even OR-parallel execution of passive parts during a procedure call (the implementation discussed herein executes passive parts sequentially and executes body goals in a depth-first manner). Synchronization between processes is inherently performed by the requirement that no output bindings can be made in the passive part. If a binding is attempted, the call *potentially* suspends. If none of the clauses succeeds, and one or more potentially suspend, then the procedure call suspends (possibly on multiple variables).

When any of the variables to which an export binding was attempted are in fact bound (by another process), the suspended call is resumed. These semantics permit stream AND-parallel execution of the program, i.e., incomplete lists of data can be streamed from one parallel process to another in a producer/consumer relationship. For example, when a stream runs dry, the consumer receives the unbound tail of a list and suspends. When the producer generates more data, the consumer is resumed and continues processing the transmitted data.

2.2 KL1 Architecture

The current KL1 system [14] uses the five main (shared-memory) storage areas: heap, instruction, goal, communication, and suspension. Unlike similar Prolog architectures, the goal and heap areas *cannot* be managed in a stack-like fashion. The goal, suspension and communication areas are managed with free-lists. The heap is allocated from the top, like an ever-growing stack, and can only be reclaimed with a general garbage collection (GC) mechanism.

The KL1 execution model is a reduction mechanism wherein the initial user query (a set of goals) is reduced to the empty set. A goal is represented by a goal record, similar to a Prolog environment [22]. Reducible goal records are stored as a linked list (goal list), one per processing element (PE), and reduction proceeds in a depth-first manner. However, unlike a Prolog environment, KL1 goal arguments consisting of unbound variables and structures are both indirectly stored in the heap.

A single goal is reduced in the following manner [8]. The goal is dequeued from the goal list and its arguments are loaded into a register set. The compiled code sequence corresponding to the goal is executed, attempting to commit to one of the clauses of its procedure. If a clause commits, the body instructions cause body goals to be created and pushed onto the front of the goal list. Otherwise, if all clauses fail, the program fails. Otherwise, if no clause commits, but one or more can suspend, the goal is recreated from registers to the goal area, and the synchronizing variables are hooked to the goal, each via a suspension record. The goal is now floating, i.e., not linked to the goal list. A single variable may be hooked to multiple waiting goals, thus suspension records can be linked. When a hooked variable is bound at some point, a resumption routine is executed which relinks the floating goal(s) to the goal list and reclaims the suspension record(s).

The current KL1 system uses an on-demand scheduler, i.e., idle PEs request a goal from busy PEs [14]. The communication area is used primarily for passing these goal request and reply messages. Message records are only two words and are usually written once and read once. Goals are similar: goal records are always created in the register file. However, when enqueued/dequeued onto/from the goal list, memory is always written once and read once. Suspension has the same effect as enqueue.

When binding a variable in KL1, the variable must be locked to prevent other PEs from concurrently attempting an inconsistent binding. When actively unifying two variables, substructures must be locked in a careful manner to prevent races. Sending messages (to and from idle and working PEs during load balancing) must be also locked.

2.3 Optimizing Cache Performance

As discussed above, each PE in a KL1 system executes goal reductions of a relatively small granularity (compared to procedural languages). Thus there are significant differences in KL1 memory referencing characteristics from the characteristics of conventional multiprocessor systems like the Symmetry [15]. First, the PEs communicate more often with each other, through logical variables, than the usual parallel processing on the Symmetry system, because parallel goals share logical variables. Thus it is important for a locally parallel cache to have an efficient cache-to-cache data transfer mechanism as well as to work as a shared global memory cache. Second, there are many exclusive accesses to communicate through shared logical variables. The frequency of locking shared data during KL1 execution is relatively high. However, we can expect that exclusive memory accesses seldom conflict with each other [14]. Therefore, we require a high-speed lock mechanism that uses hardware support and works efficiently, at least when one lock does not conflict with other locks. Third, because of the single-assignment feature of KL1, data write frequency is higher than in conventional languages [16]. Hence, it is necessary to reduce the number of copyback operations from cache to shared global memory.

In normal write operations, a fetch-on-write strategy is used, i.e., a cache block is allocated in the cache for both read and write misses. As previously stated, in KL1, new data structures are created dynamically in the heap and goal areas. Thus it is not necessary to fetch-on-write when a new cache block is allocated for a new data structure. A PE can write data in a cache block without fetching the contents from shared memory. This is the motivation for the *direct write* command. Similar optimizations have been, for instance, suggested by Tick [19], and implemented in the PSI machine [11].

As stated in Section 2.2, KL1 goal records are referenced with a strict write-once, read-once rule. When KL1 goals are distributed during load balancing from one PE to another, the goal records both in the sender's cache and in the receiver's cache are useless after the receiver PE reads the contents. Thus meaningless swap-in and swap-out can be avoided by invalidating the sender's cache block after cache-to-cache transfer and by purging the receiver's cache block after the receiver finishes reading. This is the motivation of the *exclusive read* command. Exclusive read is used in conjunction with direct write. For example, the sender PE creates a goal record in the goal area with the direct write command (i.e., without fetching the contents from shared global memory). Then the receiver PE reads the goal record with exclusive read. This idea can also be applied to general inter-PE communication via a strict write-once and read-once communication buffer. Although exclusive read must be used carefully so as not to confuse cache coherency, it can reduce common bus traffic by avoiding useless swap-in and swap-out operations.

Lock operations are essential in shared global memory architectures. The KL1 language processor uses lock operations for heap and communication area accesses [14]. The frequency of locking shared data is high; however, actual lock conflicts seldom occur [14]. Therefore, it is effective to introduce a hardware lock mechanism that has less overhead when there are no lock conflicts.

3 PIM Cache Protocol

Copyback cache protocols have been proved effective for reducing common bus traffic in shared-memory multiprocessors for procedural languages, as shown by Goodman [5] and Archibald [1], among others. For logic programming languages, Tick [19] shows that AND-parallel Prolog benefits from copyback even more than procedural languages because of Prolog's high write bandwidth requirement. Thus the basis for the PIM cache is a copyback protocol.

Common shared-memory coherent cache protocols, e.g., [1, 2, 13, 17], use both invalidation and broadcast to ensure all caches are consistent. Both types of protocols have been compared in the literature [1, 4]. Invalidation reduces common bus traffic when the frequency of shared block write accesses is low. Broadcast is better when many PEs frequently write data to the same shared blocks. Considering the single-assignment feature of FGHC, the base language of KL1, most logical variables are shared by only two KL1 goals. In other words, most PE communication has a one-to-one correspondence with regard to heap and goal record accesses. Thus broadcasting is not necessary for most programs, and invalidation suffices.

KL1 write frequency is higher than that of procedural languages, and in addition, cache-to-cache data transfer occurs often. Therefore, when transferring a dirty block on the shared bus, avoiding the update of shared global memory can reduce the busy ratio of memory modules, more so than for a procedural architecture.

3.1 Cache and Lock Directories

The PIM cache has five states: EM (Exclusive modified—The block is exclusive and modified. It is necessary to swap out), EC (Exclusive clean—The block is exclusive and unmodified. It is not necessary to swap out), SM (Shared modified—The block is modified and perhaps shared. It is necessary to swap out), S (Shared—The block is perhaps shared. It is not necessary to swap out), INV (Invalid—The block is invalid). This protocol is similar to the Illinois protocol [13]; however, the PIM protocol has an additional state, distinguishing between SM and S. The SM state is not necessary in the Illinois protocol because modified blocks are always copied-back to shared memory when transferring between PEs, and thus the blocks become unmodified. This reduction in modified blocks likewise reduces swap-out bus traffic. On the other hand, such a protocol will cause the busy ratio of shared-memory modules to increase if the cache-to-cache data transfer rate is relatively high as in the KL1 system. Therefore, the shared modified state (SM) was included in the PIM cache.

In addition to the cache directory, there is a separate lock directory, with three states [2]: LCK (Lock—The address is locked by an **LR** operation of the PE, and other PEs are not waiting to be unlocked), LWAIT (Lock waiter—The address is locked by this PE. In addition, one or more PEs are waiting to be unlocked), EMP (Not locked—empty). When a PE locks an address, the address is registered in the LCK state in the lock directory at first. Subsequently if the cache block is referenced by another PE, the state of the lock directory changes from LCK to LWAIT. In this case, the requester enters the busy wait state, and retries the operation after receiving the unlock (**UL**) bus command.

Three standard lock operations, **LR** (lock and read), **UW** (write and unlock), and **U** (unlock), are offered. The PIM cache uses busy-wait locking because it usually allows locking and unlocking to occur in zero time [2]. The hardware locks reduce bus traffic in two key ways. **LR** operations do not require bus commands when they hit in exclusive cache blocks (EC or EM). Also, **UW** and **U** operations use the bus only when other PEs are waiting to be unlocked, i.e., in the LWAIT status. In the KL1 architecture, actual lock conflicts seldom occur because the locking periods are short [14].

The lock and cache directories are separated because if the lock information is held in the cache directory (such as in cache-state locking [2]), there are three major difficulties. First, it is difficult to distinguish every locked word in the same cache block. Second, it is difficult to swap out the block that contains the locked address. Third, it is costly to add lock states for each cache tag. These problems can all be solved by introducing a separate lock directory. The lock directory contains the locked word address and state to enable word-by-word locking. The lock directory controller snoops the common bus to detect and inhibit access to the locked address even if the locked address is swapped out. Therefore, multiple locks in the same cache block can be distinguished. We think only one or two lock entry per directory is needed in most parallel logic programming architectures.

3.2 Memory Operations

Memory operations include read (**R**) and write (**W**) in addition to the following optimizations.

(1) DW (address): Direct write—To avoid swap-in overhead, the **DW** command writes data to an unused memory area without fetching a cache block. The **DW** command acts in two different ways according to the relative position of a cache block, as follows:

(i) When the memory address is on a cache block boundary and a cache miss occurs, a new cache block is allocated and the data is written to the block without fetching the original data from shared global memory. In this case, it must be clear that remote caches do not have a corresponding cache block.

(ii) When the memory address is not a cache block boundary, the cache controller automatically replaces **DW** with **W**.

The **DW** command can be applied locally only when the target cache block entry does not exist in a remote cache. This restriction is necessary to guarantee cache coherency when the corresponding cache block is swapped out. Depending on the precise definition of "cache block boundary," **DW** will work either for upward-growing or downward-growing stacks. To optimize both, two commands are necessary.

(2) ER (address): Exclusive read—This command reads data and invalidates or purges a cache block to avoid swap-out overhead (the word "purge" is used when purging its own cache entry). The **ER** command acts in three different ways according to the relative position of a cache block:

(i) When the target address misses but the block resides on another PE, and the address is not the last word of a block, a cache-to-cache transfer from a supplier PE occurs. In this case, the supplier cache block is invalidated after the cache block transfer. This operation is called read invalidate (**RI**).

(ii) When the target address hits and *is the last word in a block*, the block in the receiver cache is forcibly purged, after the last word of the block is read. This is the same as read purge (**RP**), described below.

(iii) Otherwise the cache controller automatically replaces **ER** with read **R**.

The **ER** command is used when the contents of a cache block are not required (in cache) after the PE reads the contents (into registers).

(3) RP (address): Read purge—This command, like **ER**, reads data by invalidating or purging a cache block to avoid swap-out overhead. The **RP** command acts in two different ways according to a cache hit or miss, as follows:

(i) When the target address hits, the cache block is forcibly purged after the **RP** operation.

(ii) When the target address misses and the cache block resides on another PE, the supplier cache block is invalidated after the data block transfer, and the fetched cache block is also forcibly purged after the **RP** operation.

The **RP** command is used when a cache block cannot be purged by **ER**, i.e., when the number of words of the reading area is not a multiple of the cache block word size. In this case, the last word of the reading area is read by **RP**.

(4) RI (address): Read invalidate—This command is effective for avoiding invalidate bus commands when the data is rewritten just after it is read from other PE cache.

3.3 Specifications of Bus Commands and Responses

There are three bus commands and one response to implement the locally-parallel cache mechanism for the PIM. Additional bus commands or responses are not necessary for the optimized memory operations.

(1) F (address): Fetch—The fetch command is a request to fetch a cache block from other PEs or shared global memory.

(2) FI (address): Fetch and invalidate—The fetch and invalidate command is a request to fetch a cache block from other PEs or shared global memory, and to invalidate the cache blocks of all other PEs, including the supplier PE of a cache-to-cache transfer.

(3) I (address): Invalidate—The invalidate command is a request to invalidate the cache blocks of all other PEs.

(4) H: Hit—response for **F** and **FI** requests.

Two additional bus commands and one response are necessary for lock operations.

(1) LK (address): Lock—This is a broadcast message to report that a specified address will be locked. The **LK** bus command is always used together with the **FI** or **I** bus commands. Note that the **LK** bus command is used only when the **LR** memory operation misses or hits to shared blocks.

(2) UL (address): Unlock—This is a broadcast message that a specified address has been unlocked, in the LWAIT state. If the locked address is not in the LWAIT state, in other words, another PE does not refer to the address, then the **UL** bus command is not broadcast. This is an optimization to reduce the common bus traffic.

(3) LH: Lock hit—This is a response to the **F**, **FI**, or **LK** bus commands. The **LH** response shows that the referred address is locked. The requester PE which received the **LH** response starts busy waiting. The requester PE retries a memory reference after it receives the **UL** bus command. The common bus is not used during busy waiting cycles [2].

In summary, the PIM cache protocol is a copyback locally parallel cache with invalidation (of other caches when writing to shared blocks) and no copyback to shared memory (during a cache-to-cache transfer). Optimizations include the direct write, exclusive read, read invalidate, and read purge memory commands. A busy wait lock mechanism with a separate lock directory is implemented. Refer to Matsumoto [10] for the complete state transition tables of the PIM cache protocol.

4   Cache Performance Evaluation

The cache design was evaluated with a parallel simulator written by A. Matsumoto. The simulator executes in cooperation with an abstract machine emulator—in this paper, we only discuss the parallel KL1 emulator written by M. Sato. These tools currently run on the Sequent Symmetry multiprocessor (refer to Tick [20] for a detailed description of these tools). Each PE runs a reduction engine for the abstract machine, dynamically feeding memory requests to a local cache simulator. The cache simulators artificially synchronize among themselves at each simulated bus request. This synchronization retains the accuracy of the model's parallelism without overly impacting simulation speed. These tools represent an improvement in accuracy over previous studies [10] which used a pseudo-parallel emulator, synchronizing only on each reduction.

Modeling a real architecture on a target host, with an emulated architecture on a partially mapped host, requires creating a correspondence between emulator variables and target machine registers and memory. In the measurements presented here, we assume a very liberal correspondence of architecture state to registers. Most emulator variables are considered either not necessary for the target architecture, or able to be allocated to temporary registers. In addition, the state and argument registers of the architectures, based on the WAM [22], are also mapped onto registers. For KL1, this means that references to goal queue pointers, processor

bench	lines	sec.	su	reduct	susp	instr	ref
Tri	182	49.3	5.8	666233	1	13.0M	28.9M
Semi	104	87.5	4.8	268820	23487	4.8M	23.1M
Puzzle	151	55.3	6.5	849539	3069	15.6M	29.1M
Pascal	310	16.6	6.1	302432	17681	5.0M	10.5M

Table 1: Short Summary of Benchmarks on Eight PEs

Mem Ref	inst	data	heap	goal	susp	comm
$E(inst + data)$	42.87	57.13	34.31	20.71	0.26	1.86
$\sigma(inst + data)$	13.17	13.17	23.86	11.82	0.37	1.23
$E(data)$	—	—	60.06	36.25	0.46	3.26
Bus Cyc.	inst	data	heap	goal	susp	comm
$E(inst + data)$	4.52	95.48	65.70	11.16	1.14	17.49
$\sigma(inst + data)$	3.45	3.45	15.74	7.15	1.22	9.20
$E(data)$	—	—	68.81	11.69	1.19	18.31
Tri	7.15	92.85	43.00	22.68	0.00	27.16
Semi	0.93	99.07	79.66	4.80	1.17	13.45
Puzzle	8.69	91.31	81.10	5.59	0.26	4.36
Pascal	1.30	98.70	59.03	11.57	3.12	24.98

Table 2: % Memory References and Bus Cycles by Area

status, communication buffer pointers, interrupt status, suspension stack pointers, meta-counts, and GC pointers are *not* counted as memory references. This is of course a best case assumption. Memory references to the major storage areas of the architecture (for KL1: heap, goal, instruction, suspension, and communication) are instrumented as target architecture memory references. Note that the system measured uses stop-and-copy GC, and that inclusion of incremental GC will significantly affect heap referencing characteristics [12].

In the following sections, the performance of the PIM cache design is evaluated with respect to the KL1 architecture, the target architecture for which the cache was designed.

4.1   Characteristics of the Benchmarks

Measurements of four KL1 benchmarks (written in pure FGHC) are analyzed in this paper. High-level characteristics of the benchmarks are given in Table 1 (for discussion and code listings of these programs, see Tick [20]). Lines of static code, execution time (sec.) and relative speedup (su) on eight PEs, reductions, suspensions, (millions of) KL1 instructions executed, and (millions of) emulated memory references (both instruction and data), are given. For some benchmarks, these high-level statistics are sensitive to emulator timing, but the accuracy is sufficient for our needs.

Table 2 shows the memory access and bus traffic characteristics, averaged over the benchmarks. Means (E) and standard deviations (σ) for instructions plus data and data only are calculated. The simulation assumed an eight cycle memory access, a one word bus, and eight PEs, each with a four-word block, four-way set-associative, four Kword I+D cache (with *no* optimized commands). These statistics are useful to gain insight into the relative bandwidth requirements of the different storage areas.

Table 2 shows 43% of the memory references are used for fetching instructions. In subsequent sections, the various

operation	R	LR	W	UW+U
$E(inst + data)$	78.95	2.66	15.71	2.70
$\sigma(inst + data)$	8.01	0.82	6.57	0.91
$E(data)$	58.91	5.14	30.73	5.22
$\sigma(data)$	18.61	2.23	14.47	2.38
$E(heap)$	57.64	10.39	21.38	10.60
$\sigma(heap)$	21.22	5.26	11.35	5.48
Tri	54.62	12.06	21.27	12.06
Semi	93.17	1.70	3.42	1.71
Puzzle	41.88	11.90	34.26	11.96
Pascal	40.87	15.88	26.57	16.68

Table 3: Percentage of Memory References by Operation

cache parameters are examined in more detail. Here we see that 95% of all bus cycles are devoted to data indicating that the cache is very successful at reducing the instruction bandwidth requirement. Larger benchmarks are anticipated to offer less instruction locality and therefore generate a larger percentage of instruction bus traffic. In general however, it is most important to reduce the data bandwidth requirement further with cache optimizations.

Heap access frequency is 34%, yet the heap accounts for 66% of all bus cycles, significantly greater than the other areas. The dynamic heap area size is very large (e.g., over 80% of all shared memory for the **BUP** benchmark as reported in [10]) and access locality low. The communication and goal area management, based on free-lists, helps to reclaim space and retain locality; however, still these areas account for 29% of all bus cycles. Note that the shared communication area is particularly troublesome: less than 2% of all memory requests require more than 17% of all bus cycles.

Table 3 shows the memory references by operations. Data write frequency is 36% (**W + UW**), somewhat lower than 47% for Prolog [19]. This statistic is highly variant however: **Semi** with only 7% data writes lowers the average. Locking (**LR**) and unlocking (**U, UW**) frequency is more than 5%. Examining heap accesses in more detail, we find that for these benchmarks, heap write frequency varies from 5–46%. Heap lock/unlock reference frequency (**LR + UW + U**) varies from 3–33%. The high variance is again due to **Semi**. In any case, these statistics show that logic programs generate significant heap write traffic because of dynamic structure creation. In addition, dependent AND-parallel programs generate significant heap lock/unlock traffic to protect bindings. The cache design introduced helps mollify and alleviate much of these overheads (see Section 4.7).

4.2 Cache Simulation Parameters

There are many complex tradeoffs made in cache design. We choose to concentrate, in this paper, on the reduction of common bus traffic, which is of critical importance in the design of tightly-coupled shared-memory multiprocessors. In the following sections, we discuss the organization of relatively small caches (16K words and less), always with bus bandwidth reduction as our primary figure of merit. Unless otherwise

stated, the simulations were run for eight PEs, where each PE's cache memory is four Kwords, four-way set-associative with 256 columns and four-word blocks. Perturbations of this base model are examined in subsequent sections. The simulator models a common bus used for swap-in from shared memory, swap-out to shared memory, cache-to-cache transfer between PEs, and invalidation. Additional assumptions are:

(1) The width of the common bus is one word, which consists of tag and data parts. Separate address and data buses are not distinguished. Therefore, it is assumed that an address cannot be sent with data during the same cycle.

(2) It takes eight cycles to access shared memory. However, a swap-out write operation to shared memory is hidden by a subsequent memory operation.

(3) The common bus is not freed until one memory operation is completed.

Given the above assumptions, there are six common bus access patterns: swap-in from shared memory with swap-out (13 cycles), swap-in from shared memory without swap-out (13 cycles), cache-to-cache transfer with swap-out (10 cycles), cache-to-cache transfer without swap-out (7 cycles), swap-out only (5 cycles—this access pattern appears only in **DW**), invalidation of other PEs' cache blocks (2 cycles).

This model produces a raw bus cycle count. We refrain from introducing a ratio statistic (as in [10, 20]) to avoid confusion. When the above bus width and memory access time assumptions are modified, the bus access cycle times change as does the raw cycle count. Experiments [20] indicate that bus traffic is insensitive to memory access time because most bus traffic is cache-to-cache. Increasing bus width, however, more significantly decreases bus traffic, as shown in Section 4.4.

4.3 Effects of Cache Block Size

Figure 1 shows the relationship between cache block size (in words), miss ratio and bus traffic, for four-way set-associative, four Kword I+D caches (with all optimized commands). Whereas miss ratio improves significantly with increasing block size, the difference in bus traffic for two and four word blocks is relatively small. Above four words, bus traffic is restrictive. Since two-word blocks require about twice the cache address array size as four-word blocks, the latter is most suitable for the PIM cache. Note that in sequential Prolog studies, Tick [19] also found four-word blocks to be optimal. Essentially, logic programming languages, without arrays and with more procedure calls (and suspensions, failures, etc.) than procedural languages, can make less efficient use of large block sizes because there is less spatial locality. Matsumoto [10] found that two-way set-associative PIM caches produce 18% more bus traffic than four-way (for the **BUP** benchmark), whereas direct-mapped caches create significantly greater bus traffic.

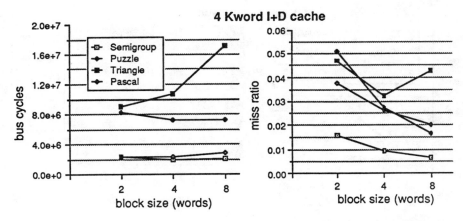

Figure 1: Cache Block Size vs. Cache Miss Ratio and Bus Traffic

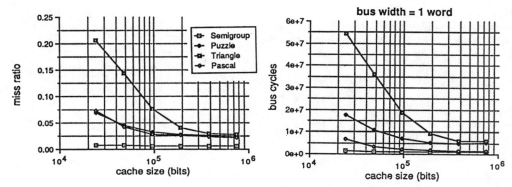

Figure 2: Cache Capacity vs. Bus Traffic

4.4 Effects of Cache Capacity

Figure 2 shows the relationship between cache size, miss ratio and bus traffic, for four-word block I+D caches (with all optimized commands) of sizes 512–16K data words. The plots assume a 5 byte data word and account for directory size, e.g., a "four-Kword cache" is 190000 bits. In **BUP**, if the block size is increased above eight words, bus traffic increases in spite of the increased capacity of the data array [10], thus we limit our measurements to four-word blocks. The knee of both the miss ratio and bus traffic curves is at 4×10^5 bits (8 Kword data cache). **Semi** is seen to have a small working-set that is captured in even the smallest cache. **Puzzle** generates a constant 5×10^6 more bus cycles than **Pascal**, although they both achieve the same miss ratio. **Puzzle**, with more touched code and larger data structures than **Pascal**, generates a great deal of swap in/out and cache-to-cache traffic to achieve an equal miss ratio. **Tri** has the most touched code of the benchmarks, causing poor code locality on small caches and thus excessive bus traffic. In fact, much of the I+D cache benefit is due to instruction bandwidth reduction. Analyzing data-only caches (not shown), bus traffic is about twice that of I+D caches for the largest caches. Considering a two-word bus width, the benchmarks exhibit a decrease in traffic, to 62–75% of the one-word bus traffic (both assuming an eight cycle memory access and non-overlapped bus). This percentage decrease is insensitive to the benchmark and

increases slightly with decreasing cache size.

4.5 Effects of the Number of PEs

Figure 3 shows the relationship between the number of PEs and bus traffic. **Tri** creates a search tree of height 12 with a branch factor of 36 at each node. The inability of the simple KL1 scheduler to balance this load causes excessive bus traffic due to task distribution. **Pascal** shows similar, but less radical, characteristics. Analyzing the separate areas contributing to bus traffic, we find that by percentage of total bus traffic, communication increases from 0–29% and suspension increases from 0.8–2.1% (average from all benchmarks) when increasing from one to eight PEs. At the same time, heap bus traffic decreases from 71–45%, and other areas remain approximately the same. Thus inter-PE communication becomes a dominant factor in parallel processing for more than four or eight PEs. It is likely that about eight high-performance PEs will be connected for one common bus of current specifications in the PIM [10, 6].

4.6 Effects of Cache Optimizations

The effects of the cache optimizations at reducing the bus bandwidth requirement are summarized in this section. Recall from Section 3.2 that direct write (**DW**) reduces swap-in overhead, exclusive read (**ER**) and read purge (**RP**) (in con-

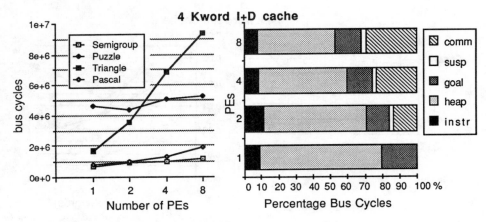

Figure 3: Number of PEs vs. Bus Traffic

junction with **DW**) reduce swap-out overhead, and read invalidate (**RI**) reduces bus invalidations (**I**). Table 4 shows, for each benchmark. the number of bus cycles relative to a non-optimized cache ("None"), for several different optimizations (in each column). The "Heap" optimization is **DW** used only in the heap area. "Goal" is **ER**, **RP** and **DW** used only in goal area. "Comm" is **RI** used only in the communication area. "All" uses all optimizations. As can be seen, **DW** contributes almost all of the savings, with the other optimizations most effective for **Tri**.

More precisely, the **DW** commands for the heap area reduce the swap-in from global shared memory to 10% in **Tri** and 55% in **Puzzle**. The **DW** commands are very effective not only for reducing bus traffic but also for avoiding the CPU waits for fetching from memory. The **ER**, **RP** and **DW** commands for the goal area decrease meaningless swap-out by about 2–10%. The **RI** commands for the communication area can avoid about 60–70% of invalidate (**I**) bus commands. As shown in Figure 3. **Tri** bus traffic increases with the number of PEs because load balancing of many small tasks is a dominant factor. The **ER**, **RP** and **RI** commands are effective in reducing bus traffic for precisely this situation: when many goals are distributed within PEs for load balancing and when the inter-PE communication is a dominant factor of the bus traffic. The **RI** commands avoid only unnecessary **I** bus commands. Thus **RI**, while not reducing the bus traffic in Table 4. becomes more effective in reducing bus traffic as bus width increases or memory access time decreases.

4.7 Effects of Lock Protocol

As stated in Section 3. the lock mechanism reduces the bandwidth requirement because the **LR** operation does not require bus commands when it hits in an exclusive cache block (Ec or Em). and the **UW** and **U** operations use the bus only when other PEs are waiting to be unlocked. which is rare. Table 5 shows the hit ratios of the **LR** operations in general, **LR** directed to exclusive cache blocks, and **UW** and **U** operations directed to non-waiting locks (Lck directory state). As shown, the proposed lock protocol avoids most of the bus traffic for these lock/unlock operations.

	bus cycles relative to no-opt.				
benchmark	None	Heap	Goal	Comm	All
Tri	1.00	0.62	0.80	0.83	0.52
Semi	1.00	0.65	1.00	0.99	0.62
Puzzle	1.00	0.55	0.98	0.98	0.51
Pascal	1.00	0.64	0.94	0.96	0.60

Table 4: Effect of Optimized Cache Commands in Reducing Bus Traffic

	Tri	Semi	Puzzle	Pascal
LR hit-ratio	0.743	0.912	0.959	0.847
LR hit-to-Exclusive	0.658	0.910	0.954	0.816
U, UW hit-to-No-waiter	0.999	0.993	0.997	0.976

Table 5: Hit Ratios of No Cost Lock Operations

5 Conclusions

This paper describes the design and estimated performance of a coherent cache for parallel logic programming architectures. The cache is optimized around the KL1 execution model; however, it is general enough to execute other architectures. Memory access characteristics of KL1 benchmarks, gathered by emulation, indicate that data write frequency is 36%. This value is slightly lower than Prolog (because KL1 does not backtrack), but higher than in conventional languages. Therefore the PIM cache is based on a copyback protocol. In normal write operations, a fetch-on-write strategy is used. However, in KL1, and other WAM-based architectures, new data structures are created dynamically on the top of the heap area. Therefore, it is not necessary to fetch the contents of shared global memory when a cache block is allocated for a new data structure. In addition, writing goal records also need not fetch their contents. To accomplish this, the *direct write* command was introduced.

In KL1 and other parallel architectures, PE communication (for goal distribution, etc.) uses a shared message buffer. In this case, swap-in and swap-out of meaningless data can be avoided by invalidating the sender's cache block after a

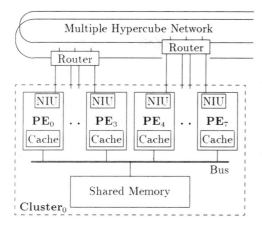

Figure 4: The PIM Pilot Machine: PIM/p (part)

cache-to-cache transfer and by purging the receiver's cache block after the receiver finishes reading. To accomplish this, the *exclusive read* and *read purge* commands were introduced.

These new commands can reduce common bus traffic by avoiding useless swap-in and swap-out operations. Cache simulations indicate that these optimizations reduce bus traffic by 40–50% with respect to an unoptimized system. Direct write affords 35–45% reduction and other optimizations only 5% reduction. From our preliminary data on the Aurora system [20], we believe these optimizations will prove effective on other parallel logic programming architectures as well.

The PIM cache three-state lock protocol was shown to be effective at reducing the bus traffic of lock/unlock operations: for KL1, no bus cycles are needed for the high percentage of lock reads hitting in exclusive blocks and unlocks to non-waiting locks. Locking efficiency aside, we feel however that the most critical bottleneck of parallel logic programming architectures is the high communication cost of load balancing. We have illustrated this with the KL1 **Tri** benchmark, but the problem extends to non-committed choice architectures as well [20].

A version of the PIM cache described here is currently being implemented for ICOT's Parallel Inference Machine (PIM). See Figure 4, and Goto [6] for the PIM architecture overview.

Acknowledgements

We wish to thank Mr. M. Sato for developing the parallel KL1 emulator. We also wish to thank all research members of the PIM R&D project for their fruitful discussions. Finally, we would like to thank ICOT Director, Dr. K. Fuchi, and the chief of the fourth research section, Dr. S. Uchida, for their valuable suggestions and guidance. E. Tick was supported by NSF Grant No. IRI-8704576.

References

[1] J. Archibald and J. Baer. Cache Coherence Protocols: Evaluation Using a Multiprocessor Simulation Model. *ACM Transactions of Computer Systems*, 4(4):273–298, 1986.

[2] P. Bitar and A. M. Despain. Multiprocessor Cache Synchronization. In *13th ISCA*, pages 424–433, June 1986.

[3] T. Chikayama et. al. Overview of the Parallel Inference Machine Operating System PIMOS. In *Int. Conf. on 5th Gen. Comp. Sys.*, Tokyo, November 1988.

[4] S.J. Eggers and R.H. Katz. A Characterization of Sharing in Parallel Programs and its Application to Coherency Protocol Evaluation. In *15th ISCA*, pages 373–382, June 1988.

[5] J. R. Goodman. Using Cache Memory to Reduce Processor-Memory Traffic. In *10th ISCA*, pages 124–131, 1983.

[6] A. Goto et. al. Overview of the Parallel Inference Machine Architecture PIM. In *Int. Conf. on 5th Gen. Comp. Sys.*, Tokyo, November 1988.

[7] R. H. Katz et. al. Implementing a Cache Consistency Protocol. In *12th ISCA*, pages 276–283, June 1985.

[8] Y. Kimura and T. Chikayama. An Abstract KL1 Machine and its Instruction Set. In *Int. Symp. on Logic Prog.*, pages 468–477, August 1987.

[9] E. Lusk et. al. The Aurora Or-Parallel Prolog System. In *Int. Conf. on 5th Gen. Comp. Sys.*, Tokyo, November 1988.

[10] A. Matsumoto et. al. Locally Parallel Cache Design Based on KL1 Memory Access Characteristics. Technical Report 327, ICOT, 1987.

[11] H. Nakashima and K. Nakajima. Hardware Architecture of the Sequential Inference Machine: PSI-II. In *Int. Symp. on Logic Prog.*, pages 104–113, August 1987.

[12] K. Nishida et. al. Evaluation of the Effect of Incremental Garbage Collection by MRB on FGHC Parallel Execution Performance. Technical Report 394, ICOT, 1988.

[13] M. S. Papamarcos and J. H. Patel. A Low-Overhead Coherence Solution for Multiprocessors with Private Cache Memories. In *11th ISCA*, pages 348–354, 1984.

[14] M. Sato et al. KL1 Execution Model for PIM Cluster with Shared Memory. In *4th Int. Conf. on Logic Prog.*, pages 338–355. MIT Press, May 1987.

[15] Sequent Computer Systems, Inc. *Sequent Guide to Parallel Programming*, 1987.

[16] A. J. Smith. Cache Memories. *ACM Computing Surveys*, 14(3):473–530, September 1982.

[17] L.C. Stewart et. al. Firefly: A Multiprocessor Workstation. *IEEE Transactions on Computers*, 37(8), August 1988.

[18] P. Sweazey and A. J. Smith. A Class of Compatible Cache Consistency Protocols and Their Support by the IEEE Futurebus. In *13th ISCA*, pages 414–423, June 1986.

[19] E. Tick. Data Buffer Performance for Sequential Prolog Architectures. In *15th ISCA*, May 1988.

[20] E. Tick. Performance of Parallel Logic Programming Architectures. Technical Report TR-421, ICOT, September 1988.

[21] K. Ueda. Guarded Horn Clauses. In E.Y. Shapiro, editor, *Concurrent Prolog: Collected Papers*, pages 140–156. MIT Press, Cambridge MA, 1987.

[22] D. H. D. Warren. An Abstract Prolog Instruction Set. Technical Report 309, SRI International, 1983.

Dataflow
Chair: I. Koren, UMASS Amherst

The εpsilon Dataflow Processor *

V.G. Grafe

G.S. Davidson

J.E. Hoch

V.P. Holmes

Sandia National Laboratories

Albuquerque, New Mexico

Abstract

The εpsilon dataflow architecture is designed for high speed uniprocessor execution as well as for parallel operation in a multiprocessor system. The εpsilon architecture directly matches ready operands, thus eliminating the need for associative matching stores. εpsilon also supports low cost data fan out and critical sections. A 10 MFLOPS CMOS/TTL processor prototype is running and its performance has been measured with several benchmarks. The prototype processor has demonstrated sustained performance exceeding that of comparable control flow processors running at higher clock rates (three times faster than a 20 MHz transputer and 24 times faster than a Sun on a suite of arithmetic tests, for example).

1   Introduction

The dataflow model of computation has been the subject of study for over twenty years. Although much progress has been made, only a handful of dataflow computers have actually been built [1].

In the dataflow model of computation, operations proceed on the availability of data rather than the action of a program counter as in the von Neumann model of computers. Dataflow research began in the late 1960's as a study of models of parallel computation by Karp and Miller [2] and by Rodriguez [3]. As

the dataflow model was further explored, researchers began to see that hardware and computer languages could be developed to directly execute computations as specified by the model. The earliest machines executed graphs that did not change as the computations developed, ie., they did not dynamically unfold loops or procedure calls. Dennis and Misunas [4] proposed such a static model, together with a dataflow language VAL [5] and the MIT engineering model, an experimental architecture [4]. Two other static machines were developed, one in the U.S.A by Texas Instruments [6] and the LAU in France [7].

Arvind and Gostelow developed the dynamic model and proposed a new language, Id, and the Tagged Token Dataflow Architecture for executing dynamic dataflow graphs [8]. The dynamic model extends the concept of data token matching for an instruction by including a portion of the matching tag that dynamically changes for each loop instance. Several dynamic dataflow machines have been built, most notably the Manchester computer in England [9] and more recently the Sigma-1 in Japan [10]. In the United States, the research at MIT continues with the development and construction of the Monsoon computer [11]. While these dynamic machines, and the languages that support them, can potentially uncover more parallel work than the static machines, they have the difficult task of managing their finite collection of tags to avoid resource allocation deadlocks.

Davidson and Pierce used strictly software approaches [12] and special purpose hardware accelerators (DFAM [13]) to apply static dataflow principles to high performance, real-time embedded multiprocessor computing for aerospace applications. This early work utilized the SANDAC multiprocessing computer [14].

These early Sandia research efforts utilized the static dataflow model by coupling it to an existing traditional processor. The knowledge gained from this approach was later incorporated into a much more powerful and general purpose family of pure dataflow supercomputer elements, the εpsilon processors. The first of these processors have continued the DFAM tra-

*This work supported by the U.S. Department of Energy at Sandia National Laboratories under Contract DE-AC04-76DP00789.

dition of extremely fast firing rules by means of the direct matching approach, while incorporating dynamic binding mechanisms and abandoning the earlier reliance on von Neumann processors.

While the overall research scope of our effort includes processors and languages for parallel computation systems, the focus of this paper will be on one part of that system, the εpsilon processor. The εpsilon architecture is described in Sections 2 and 3. Detailed descriptions of the characteristics and features of the prototype processor are first presented, followed by performance measurements. Section 4 describes some of the current work being done with the εpsilon architecture given the lessons learned from the prototype. The principal advances in εpsilon are then summarized in Section 5.

2   The Prototype Processor

The εpsilon prototype was designed with several principles in mind. Chief among these were scalability and design simplicity. Each processor in a multiprocessor system will have its own tagged memory, sharing only network resources with other processors. The performance required of each block in a processor therefore does not increase as the number of processors increase. The design philosophy followed some RISC-like ideas, such as simple control hardware, single clock instruction execution (where possible), and the availability of ways in which to combine simple functions into more complicated ones. The goal of the development was a high speed dataflow processing element, suitable for use in a parallel processing supercomputer.

The processor architecture couples a fast ALU with a tagged memory. Results are routed either back to the local tagged memory or to an external target. The external target could be the tagged memory of another processor, a peripheral, or the host processor. A block diagram of the prototype processor is shown in Figure 1. The tagged memory contains idle or partially enabled instructions, only one of which may become enabled during a given clock cycle. An instruction may be the recipient of up to two data operands, the A and B fields, whose arrival enables the instruction. The result of performing the operation can then be routed back to the local memory through the local feedback FIFO, or to the external network through the external output FIFO, or both. The addresses for this routing come from the LOCAL and GLOBAL fields of the instruction. The instruction tags serve to indicate the presence of data operands.

There is a single, FIFO buffered port from the host into the processor and another from the processor to the host. Communication with the host (and eventually other processors and peripherals) is accomplished with memory-mapped transfers through these two ports. Another FIFO buffered path is provided for local feedback of intermediate results, allowing the εpsilon processor to take advantage of locality in a computation. Both the feedback and external input data are passed through an input stage and written into εpsilon's tagged memory. The writing of data into the tagged memory causes the matching tags to be checked and updated (in a single clock), and may fire an instruction. The data from the memory is sent to the arithmetic and address calculation units, where it is processed. Results are then written to one, both, or neither of the output ports based on the action of the conditional unit.

The prototype processor is constructed as a five stage, non-blocking pipeline (five clock cycles are required from the arrival of a data value until the result of the instruction it fires is returned to the tagged memory). It requires about 1 square foot of board space and consumes approximately 65 watts. It is built entirely with standard, off-the-shelf TTL and CMOS integrated circuits. The pipeline is guaranteed to be non-blocking by the dataflow model of execution. The pipeline is kept completely full as long as there is at least five-fold parallelism, making εpsilon efficient even with low degrees of parallelism. This is a marked departure from many of the earlier dataflow computers that required hundreds of ready instructions to keep their pipelines full [15].

2.1   Tagged Memory

Each word of the **TAGGED MEMORY** has several independently addressable fields. They are:

A input parameter data field.

B input parameter data field.

OP operation code, made of various sub-fields that control the operation of the ALU, the ADDRESS calculation, and the CONDitional section.

LOCAL destination address for feedback results, made of sub-fields that select destination word and field, and control the repeat function.

GLOB. L destination address for external results, made of sub-fields that select destination word and field, and control the repeat function.

TAGS monitor the state of the input parameter slots, fires instructions when both have arrived.

The two one bit TAGS associated with each word of the memory track the arrival and presence of data in the two parameter slots. Writing the opcode of a word causes the two tags to be cleared, ie., no data has arrived. Writes to the input data slots modify the tags and can fire instructions, according to the following rule:

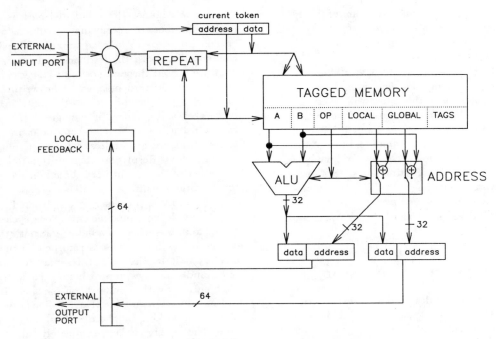

Figure 1. The εpsilon processor prototype.

if (other tag is set)
    then fire op and clear both tags
    else set this tag

In this way, writes to an instruction may fire it, but the instruction need only be checked when one of its operands is written (this is the only time its status is changed). The tag manipulation is performed in a single clock, so the dataflow overhead is no greater than the program counter manipulation of a control flow machine.

Constant values are handled with a slight modification to the scheme described above. Two bits of the opcode are used as *sticky* tags, one for each data field. A sticky data item is defined to be one that, once written, is always available (eg., constants). The tag rule is then modified to replace the tags with the sticky tags rather than clearing them. Sticky tags thus remain set once initialized, and non-constant values behave just as before. Constant values do not have to circulate or be regenerated, another departure from previous dataflow machines.

2.2 Arithmetic operations

The prototype εpsilon processor supports a full complement of arithmetic and logic operations in its ALU section. These include floating point ADD, SUBTRACT, MULTIPLY, DIVIDE, SQUARE ROOT, ABSolute value, NEGATE, MIN/MAX, COMPARE, and SCALEing. Similar arithmetic functions are available for integer data types. Logical operations include NAND, NOR, AND, OR, XOR, XNOR, SET, CLEAR,

and a full set of SHIFTs and ROTATEs. Conversions between data types are also supported. Identity operations are also allowed (denoted PASSA), and are used to build many forms of control constructs. The operations supported are determined by the implementation of the arithmetic execution unit, and were chosen to support the needs of scientific computing. Other types of operations could be implemented if needed to support different types of computing.

2.3 Address Calculation

Destination addresses are computed in the ADDRESS calculation section. This operation proceeds in parallel with the arithmetic execution, similar to control flow machines with separate address calculation units. There are two sections to the address calculation unit, one for LOCAL FEEDBACK destinations and one for the EXTERNAL port. Each section is similar in operation with two inputs and three possible modes of address calculation. One mode is for static addresses known at load time and the other two are for run-time calculation of destination addresses. All three modes execute at the same rate. Selection of a particular mode is by a sub-field of the opcode.

One input is the hardcoded target (address) that is loaded with the code. This allows for destinations known at load time, as shown in Figure 2 where $z = (w * x) + y$ is being computed. The arc from the multiplication to the addition is known at load time, so the target destination is loaded with the appropriate address. This is also shown in loader notation on

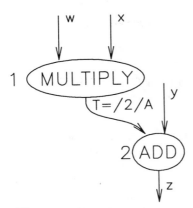

Figure 2. Use of static target.

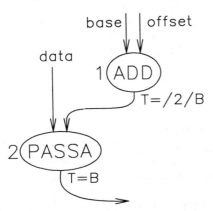

Figure 3. Run-time address computation.

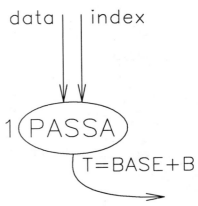

Figure 4. Run-time indexed address computation.

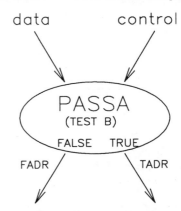

Figure 5. Switch operation in εpsilon

the figure, where the /2 signifies instruction number 2, and the /A signifies the A parameter. The multiply executes when both w and x have arrived, and writes the product to the first parameter location of the subsequent add instruction.

The second mode allows run-time computation of a destination address. The second input to each side of the address calculation section is a data value from the tagged memory, the A data value for local feedback and the B value for external addresses. This data value can be used as the destination address. An example of this is shown in Figure 3, where the PASSA instruction passes the input data value in the A field to the address written to the input B field. The T=B notation specifies that the target address is taken from the B input field. In this example, a data value, data, is to be written to some address computed by adding an **offset** to a **base** address. The result of the addition is written to the B parameter of the PASSA instruction, where it is used as the destination. Thus, this instruction writes **data** to address **base** + **offset**.

The third mode of address calculation is used when one of the addends to an address is known at load time, but the other is not. An example of this is shown in Figure 4. In this case, **data** is written to the data

structure element **index** away from the structure start address BASE. BASE is written into the destination field at load time. At run-time, when **data** and **index** have both arrived the instruction will fire and pass **data** to the address formed by adding the B parameter (**index**) to the constant BASE. This mode allows traditional accesses such as arrays to proceed with no address calculation overhead.

2.4 Conditionals

Conditional constructs — **if-then-else**, **while**, etc. — are implemented by controlling the writes to the EXTERNAL and FEEDBACK FIFOs. The status flags from the arithmetic unit and the sign bits (used as boolean values) of the two input parameters, as well as a sub-field of the opcode are used to select which of the two ports to write (LOCAL, GLOBAL, both, or none). Traditional SWITCHes may be built as shown in Figure 5. In this example, a data value, data, is to be written to FADR if the control signal, control, is false, and to TADR if it is true. This is accomplished in εpsilon by using a PASSA instruction to pass **data** and making the outputs conditional on control. When this instruction fires **data** will be written to one of the

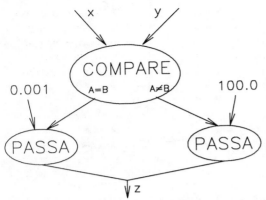

Figure 6. Conditional used as enable to computation graph.

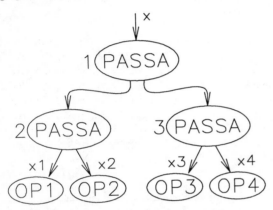

Figure 7. Additional instructions required for data fanout to multiple instructions.

2.5 Input Handling and Data Fanout

The dataflow scheduling mechanism used in εpsilon requires that each instruction have its data written into the tagged memory associated with the opcode. This allows high speed scheduling and execution, but requires that data be duplicated if it is needed by several instructions. The straightforward approach is shown in Figure 7. Here three extra instructions are needed to write the value x to four locations. This duplication requires extra instructions to generate additional copies of the data, and adds additional pipeline transit

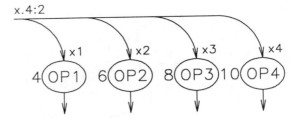

Figure 8. The previous data fanout example using repeats, repeat count equals four and repeat step equals two.

times to the latency of the computation. We have observed this overhead to be as much as 30 to 40 percent of the instructions executed in some codes.

This problem is addressed in εpsilon through a *repeat-on-input* [16] implemented with the REPEAT section. Address/data pairs are read out of the FIFOs, and written to the location specified by the address. The address contains fields specifying a repeat count and a repeat step, as well as selecting a word and field in the tagged memory. If the count is zero, the next address/data pair is read from the FIFO. If it is nonzero, the step is added to the address, the repeat count is decremented, the same data is written to the new address, and the cycle repeated. The fanout shown in Figure 7 is shown again in Figure 8 using this repeat feature with a repeat step of two words. The .4:2 after the x signifies that x is to be written to four words with a step between words of two. The overhead of data fanout is now reduced to the four clocks required to write the data. No additional instructions are required, and nothing is added to the latency of the computation. The restriction that instructions in a repeat chain must be loaded fixed steps apart is easily satisfied since the dataflow execution model makes no assumptions about instruction location.

The repeat-on-input's exploitation of the locality inherent in parameter duplication gives it advantages over both trees of instructions to duplicate parameters, as required in some dataflow machines [11,15], and destination lists, another proposed approach. With destination lists the execution pipeline must be stopped while the list of destinations is serially traversed, degrading performance. Alternatively, the execution pipeline may be insulated from the list processing with buffers. This incurs extra hardware cost, and adds latency to the computation because of the transfers from the execution pipeline to the list hardware. εpsilon's repeat-on-input does not add anything to the computation's latency, and does not force the processor pipeline to idle while data is written to multiple instructions.

two destinations based on the value of control.

The status flags from the arithmetic unit may be used to implement a different sort of conditional graph as illustrated in Figure 6. In this example the values of two parameters x and y are compared. If they are equal, z will be set to 0.001. If they are not equal, z will be set to 100.0. This implementation of conditionals can result in lower cost conditional graphs than the typical SWITCH-based implementations for **case**-like constructs.

Static critical path scheduling information can be exploited with the repeat-on-input. The order of instructions in a repeat chain gives control over the or-

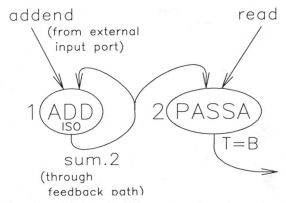

addend (from external input port)

read

1 ADD ISO

2 PASSA

sum.2 (through feedback path)

T=B

Figure 9. Computing the sum of an arbitrary input stream using isolate and repeat.

der of instruction firing. Operations on critical paths are placed at the front of a repeat chain, ensuring that they will execute before any of the other operations in the chain.

2.6 Critical Sections

Computers' limited resources are often managed through *critical sections*, code that must be executed without interruption from other resource requesters. The synchronization mechanisms required to limit access to these critical sections in control flow computers have received much attention. While dataflow computers have built in synchronization, the problem of uninterruptible instruction streams has not been addressed in previous dataflow designs.

Uninterruptible streams of instructions are supported in εpsilon through a mechanism called *isolate* [17]. Any εpsilon instruction may be declared to be *isolated*. No inputs are read from the EXTERNAL input FIFO as long as the processor is isolated. The processor becomes isolated when it fires an isolated instruction, and remains isolated until the result of that instruction passes through the FEEDBACK FIFO and is written into the tagged memory. If that result immediately fires another isolated operation, the processor will remain isolated, allowing chains of isolated operations to be executed.

An example of the utility of this function is shown in Figure 9, where the sum of an arbitrary input stream is computed. The running sum is initialized to zero. Addends are written to the A input of instruction 1. Each addend fires the add, causing the processor to add the addend to the sum in isolation. The processor remains isolated until the new sum is written back to the B parameter of the add. The sum is also repeated to another memory location for later use (by writing the **read** parameter). The addition in isolation ensures that no addends are lost or overwritten. Other local feedback data may still fire instructions

when the processor is isolated. The isolated operation therefore may not incur any performance penalty. In the worst case, it will incur the single pipeline transit required to feedback the new value of the sum.

The isolation mechanism gives the programmer more explicit control over the execution of a program graph. It can be used for controlling asynchronous access to code segments as in the previous example, and for dictating the relative order of instruction execution. Instructions that enable many other instructions can be isolated, thus guaranteeing that their results are generated before any external inputs are allowed into the instruction stream.

3 Measured Performance of εpsilon

Several benchmark codes have been implemented in εpsilon's native graph representation and run on the prototype processor. The measured performances are compared here to several control flow processors. The codes included simple arithmetic diagnostics, random number generators, and scientific computing benchmarks. The performance measurements provide experimental evidence that a dataflow computer's performance can rival or better that of comparable control flow computers. This demonstration relegates many architectural arguments to second order effects.

Since it is difficult to precisely define what characteristics would make a control flow processor *comparable* to the εpsilon dataflow processor, two approaches were taken here. The first two sets of benchmarks compared εpsilon's performance to that of control flow processors performing the same function. The control flow implementations are comparable to the εpsilon implementation in that single board computers built with these architectures are available and require about the same amount of board space as εpsilon, cost about the same amount, and are built with the same level of technology. This comparison therefore gives a demonstration of the εpsilon dataflow processor's performance relative to control flow processors built with similar resources.

The last set of benchmarks are representative of scientific problems, so comparable processors were chosen to be those with similar performance goals as εpsilon. This set of comparisons gives a demonstration of εpsilon's *absolute* performance compared with control flow processors optimized for scientific computing. The inherent imprecision in defining comparable dataflow and control flow processors makes the performance comparisons less precise than would be the case in comparing control flow vector processors, for example.

There is a long held belief that dataflow computers require more instructions than comparable con-

```
#define MAX 1000000
#define MAXERR 0.1
main()
{ int i;
  float error=0,j,jsqd1,jsqd2,
  oneoverj,shouldbej,shouldbe0;

  for (i=0;i<MAX;i++)
  { j        = (float)i;
    jsqd1    = j * j;
    jsqd2    = j * j;
    oneoverj = j / jsqd2;
    shouldbej = jsqd1 * oneoverj;
    shouldbe0 = shouldbej - j;
    if (shouldbe0>MAXERR)
       printf("\nERR,i=%d",i);
    if (shouldbe0>error)
       error = shouldbe0;           }
  printf("max error = %f",error);}
```

Figure 10. Sample arithmetic diagnostic loop.

trol flow computers. Much of this has been shown to be an artifact of parallel processing, rather than dataflow processing [18]. In the benchmarks implemented for the εpsilon uniprocessor prototype, the number of εpsilon instructions required was similar to the number required for the control flow processors. Most of the differences, when present, were due to the CISC nature of the control flow processor being compared. Memory indirection and other multi-cycle instructions count as only one instruction, but actually cost many clocks of latency. Counting clocks, as the execution timings do, shows that the εpsilon dataflow uniprocessor requires *fewer* primitive (one clock) operations than the control flow uniprocessors. The primitive operations allowed on εpsilon make use of parallel computation and address calculation, and all fit this same model. In this way, the processing hardware is completely utilized with each instruction.

3.1 Arithmetic Diagnostic Benchmark

The first benchmark is a set of simple arithmetic diagnostics originally developed for testing the floating point units of control flow processors. These are tight loops that compute a complicated function of the loop index. The function algebraically reduces to a known value (typically zero or one), so the result of the computation can be checked in each iteration. An example of such a loop is shown in Figure 10. The performance on this type of diagnostic is presented to demonstrate εpsilon's high speed execution on problems with low parallelism, and to show that the εpsilon dataflow pro-

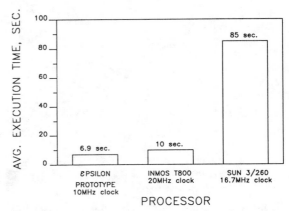

Figure 11. Average execution times on four arithmetic diagnostics.

cessor executes *faster* than comparable control flow machines. The diagnostic also demonstrates the ability of a single εpsilon processor to exploit available parallelism.

Four of these diagnostic codes were run. They emphasized different arithmetic operations: square root, multiply and divide, add and subtract, and a mix of these. They were coded in C for the control flow processors, and directly translated to εpsilon's native graph representation. In fairness to the control flow processors, εpsilon was restrained by the cross-iteration antidependencies [19] to execute only one iteration at a time. As the execution times in Figure 11 show, εpsilon at 10 MHz is faster than the control flow computers. This speed advantage is apparent even on essentially serial codes, even though the control flow processors were running at higher clock rates (the Sun at 16.67 MHz and the T800 at 20 MHz). These results suggest that dataflow uniprocessor computers are not inherently *slower* than comparable control flow computers, especially on problems with low degrees of parallelism.

The dataflow processor's ability to exploit parallelism, even in a uniprocessor configuration, is evident when the four diagnostic loops were run together. The execution times shown in Figure 12 demonstrate that the control flow machines must execute the independent loops in sequence. εpsilon is able to execute them in parallel, exploiting the parallelism to keep its pipelines completely full. εpsilon's speed advantage is now even more apparent. The εpsilon dataflow processor is able to exploit any degree of available parallelism, unlike the control flow processors.

3.2 Bit Manipulation Benchmark

The second benchmark, like the first, was originally developed for control flow processors. It uses various bit manipulations to generate a sequence of random

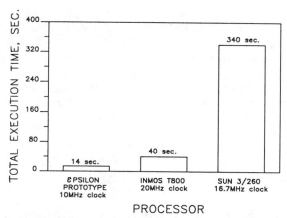

Figure 12. Total execution times for executing all four diagnostics together.

```
float rand()
{#define M 13    /* # of bits to shift */
 #define NmM 18 /* 31 - M = 18 */
 #define MAXrange 2147483647.0
                 /* 2**(31)-1*/
 static int a=524287;
 register int b;
  b = a >> M;
  a = a ^ 1;
  b = a << NmM;
  a = abs(a ^ b);
  return (float) a / MAXrange;}
```

Figure 13. Random number generator used as a benchmark.

numbers. The algorithm is shown in Figure 13. The benchmark results are presented in Figure 14 as the time to generate one million random numbers. Again εpsilon is *faster* than the control flow processor, even on a code with a low degree of parallelism. This benchmark demonstrates that εpsilon's performance benefits over comparable control flow processors are present on bit manipulation operations as well as the floating point functions used in the first set of benchmarks.

3.3 Scientific Computing Benchmark

The other set of benchmarks presented are some of the Livermore FORTRAN Kernels [20]. These are a series of FORTRAN kernels taken to be representative of a scientific computing workload. The specific kernels used were chosen for the simplicity of the function performed, with no attempt to either avoid or favor vectorizable codes. In these benchmarks, εpsilon was allowed to execute several iterations in parallel as long as the data dependencies were observed. εpsilon's per-

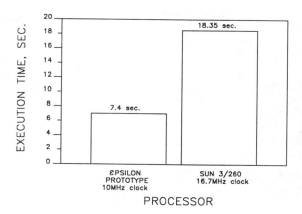

Figure 14. Time to generate one million random numbers.

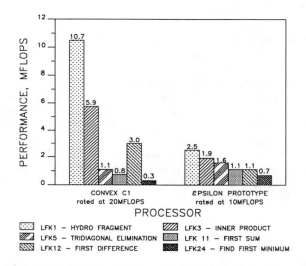

Figure 15. Measured performance on selected Livermore FORTRAN Kernels.

formance on six of these kernels is shown in Figure 15, along with that of the Convex-C1. The control flow vector computer is significantly faster than εpsilon on the kernels where the algorithm vectorizes well, but its performance falls drastically when vector parallelism is not available. εpsilon's performance is similar on all the kernels since it is determined by the ratio of floating point operations to integer and control operations. The control flow vector computer demonstrates much *more* sensitivity to the type (vector) and amount of parallelism present.

The sustained performance of these two machines on these kernels gives a better indication of what might be expected on a typical workload. Figure 16 shows the harmonic mean of the performances in Figure 15, along with that of the Cray-1S on the same kernels. From these results we would expect that one εpsilon processor would sustain higher through-

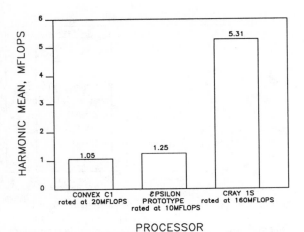

Figure 16. Harmonic mean of performance on FOR-TRAN Kernels.

put than the Convex-C1 and about one-fourth the throughput of the Cray-1S for a work load accurately represented by these kernels. It is important to note that the εpsilon processor is a single board, wire-wrap, 10 MHz CMOS prototype. The vector machines are multi-board, high speed computers constructed with advanced technology and custom chips. The εpsilon dataflow processor is able to exploit more types of parallelism than the control flow machines. Its performance is therefore determined by the total parallelism in the algorithm rather than how that parallelism is expressed.

4   Current Work

The εpsilon processor prototype described above demonstrates that this architecture points to a promising direction for future supercomputers. Continuing in this direction requires an overall system approach that addresses data structure storage, input/output facilities, network interconnections, and programming tools. All of these issues are currently being addressed.

The static nature of the εpsilon prototype was not conducive to recursive programming, and dynamic parallelization of loops was more cumbersome than desired. A new version of the εpsilon architecture is being developed. This new architecture, currently called εps'88 [21], retains the high performance features of the εpsilon prototype, including direct matching, pipelined processing, and local feedback paths. It abandons the static dataflow model in favor of a dynamic frame-based scheme to better support recursion and looping, and allow a straightforward port of the Id language. The repeat-on-input function has been expanded and generalized in εps'88. Combining the repeat feature with a general frame access capability

allows large portions of a dataflow graph to be coalesced into a single node. This combination of features has prompted work on a FORTRAN compiler that has greatly increased the appeal of the εpsilon project to the application programming community.

The design of the εps'88 system is also addressing the network interconnections between the processors, and the associated structure memory units. The design of these elements is nearing completion, and a fully functional multiprocessor system with high level language support should be available within the next year.

5   Summary and Conclusions

The performance measurements suggest that a dataflow computer's performance under even a low degree of parallelism can be competitive with comparable control flow computers. They also show the dataflow computer's ability to exploit parallelism, even in a uniprocessor configuration.

εpsilon's execution pipeline is only five stages. It has the additional benefit of being guaranteed to be non-blocking — once an instruction has fired its required operands are, by definition, ready. Interlocks often required to ensure correct operation of pipelined computer are not required in a dataflow computer such as εpsilon. Because of this, the design of the εpsilon prototype processor is in fact simpler than the design required to build a conventional five-stage, pipelined processor with optimal pipeline control.

Pipelining along the critical path is inherent in εpsilon. The latency between instructions is five clocks. Pipelined computers must have some latency between instructions along a strictly serial thread, but conventional architectures have much greater difficulty finding other ready operations to cover that latency.

The principal result of this work has been the demonstration of a dataflow processor whose sustained performance exceeds that of comparable conventional processors. This comparison of measured performances shows that εpsilon is more efficient than the other processors. The comparison was done in the realm where conventional computers were previously believed to have an architectural advantage over dataflow computers — uniprocessor systems, running codes with low degrees of parallelism.

The εpsilon architecture benchmarks illustrate that a dataflow processor can take advantage of locality in a code, previously thought to be an exclusive property of control flow machines. The prototype processor exploited locality through its local feedback path and the repeat function. Intermediate results may be routed through the FEEDBACK FIFO, decreasing network traffic and latency between instructions. The repeat feature is also used to exploit locality by allowing fanout with strictly local feedback and by allowing multiple uses of the same data to be satisfied in the minimum time.

The performance measurements on the Livermore FORTRAN Kernels demonstrated the dataflow computer's ability to find and exploit any parallelism in the code. This is a distinct difference from traditional computers which require that the parallelism be in a specific form in order to be useful to the processor. Difficult programming practices and time-consuming algorithm changes are made to adapt the parallelism to a particular control flow machine's mold. These practices greatly complicate the task of obtaining acceptable sustained performance from the machine, and are often not portable to the next generation of computers.

References

[1] V.P. Srini. An architectural comparison of dataflow systems. *Computer*, March 1986.

[2] R.M. Karp and R.E. Miller. Properties of a model for parallel conventions: determinacy, termination, queueing. *SIAM journal of applied math*, 1390–1411, November 1966.

[3] J.E. Rodriguez. *A graph model for parallel computations*. Technical Report TR-64, Dept. of Elect. Engr., Project MAC, MIT, September 1967.

[4] J.B. Dennis and D.P. Misunas. A preliminary architecture for a basic data-flow processor. In *Proceedings of the Second Symposium on Computer Architecture*, December 1974.

[5] W.B. Ackerman and J.B. Dennis. *VAL — a value-oriented algorithmic language: preliminary reference manual*. Technical Report TR-218, MIT Laboratory for Computer Scicnce, June 1979.

[6] M. Cornish, D.W. Hogan, and J.C. Jensen. The Texas Instruments distributed data processor. In *Proceedings of the Louisiana Computer Exposition*, pages 189–193, March 1979.

[7] A. Plas et al. LAU system architecture: a parallel data-driven processor based on single assignment. In *Proceedings of 1976 International Conference on Parallel Processing*, pages 293–302, 1976.

[8] Arvind, K.P. Gostelow, and W. Plouffe. *an asynchronous programming language and computing machine*. Technical Report TR 114a, Dept. of Information and Computer Science, Univ. of California, Irbine, September 1978.

[9] J. Gurd and I. Watson. Data driven system for high speed parallel computing — part 2: hardware design. *Computer Design*, 97–106, July 1980.

[10] T. Shimada, K. Hiraki, K. Nishida, and S. Sekiguchi. Evaluation of a prototype data flow processor of the SIGMA-1 for scientific computations. In *13th Annual International Symposium on Computer Architecture*, June 1986.

[11] G.M. Papadopoulos. The Monsoon architecture. notes for MIT summer course 6.83s, March 1988.

[12] G.S. Davidson. *A practical paradigm for parallel processing problems*. Technical Report SAND85-2389, Sandia National Laboratories, March 1986.

[13] G.S. Davidson and P.E. Pierce. A multiprocessor data flow accelerator module. In *Military Computing Conference, Conference Proceedings*, 1988.

[14] C.R. Borgman and P.E. Pierce. A hardware/software system for advanced development guidance and control experiments. In *Proceedings AIAA Computers in Aerospace Conference*, pages 377–384, October 1983.

[15] J.R. Gurd, C.C. Kirkham, and I. Watson. The Manchester prototype dataflow computer. *Communications of the ACM*, January 1985.

[16] V.G. Grafe and J.E. Hoch. *Repeat on Input: a New Approach to Data Fanout in Dataflow Computers*. Technical Report SD-4621, Sandia National Laboratories, 1988.

[17] V.G. Grafe and G.S. Davidson. *Uninterruptible Groups of Instructions in Dataflow Computers*. Technical Report SD-4592, Sandia National Laboratories, 1988.

[18] K. Ekanadham, Arvind, and D.E. Culler. *the price of parallelism*. Computation Structures Group Memo 278, MIT Laboratory for Computer Science, 1987.

[19] D.A. Padua and M.J. Wolfe. Advanced compiler optimizations for supercomputers. *Communications of the ACM*, December 1986.

[20] F. H. McMahon. *The Livermore Fortran Kernels: A Computer Test of the Numerical Performance Range*. Technical Report, Lawrence Livermore National Laboratory, December 1986.

[21] V.G. Grafe, J.E. Hoch, and G.S. Davidson. εps'88:Combining the Best Features of von Neumann and Dataflow Computing. Technical Report SAND88-3128, Sandia National Laboratories, 1988.

An Architecture of a Dataflow Single Chip Processor

Shuichi SAKAI, Yoshinori YAMAGUCHI, Kei HIRAKI,

Yuetsu KODAMA and Toshitsugu YUBA

Electrotechnical Laboratory

1-1-4 Umezono, Tsukuba, Ibaraki 305, JAPAN

ABSTRACT

A highly parallel (more than a thousand) dataflow machine **EM-4** *is now under development. The* **EM-4** *design principle is to construct a high performance computer using a compact architecture by overcoming several defects of dataflow machines. Constructing the* **EM-4**, *it is essential to fabricate a processing element (PE) on a single chip for reducing operation speed, system size, design complexity and cost. In the* **EM-4**, *the PE , called* **EMC-R**, *has been specially designed using a 50,000-gate gate array chip. This paper focuses on an architecture of the* **EMC-R**. *The distinctive features of it are: a strongly connected arc dataflow model; a direct matching scheme; a RISC-based design; a deadlock-free on-chip packet switch; and an integration of a packet-based circular pipeline and a register-based advanced control pipeline. These features are intensively examined, and the instruction set architecture and the configuration architecture which exploit them are described.*

1. Introduction

A dataflow architecture is supposed to be the most suitable architecture for highly parallel computers. The reasons are: it can naturally extract the maximum available concurrency in a computation; it is suitable for VLSI implementation since a large number of identical processing elements (PEs) and repetitive data networks can be used in its construction; and dataflow languages provide an elegant solution for writing concurrent programs. There are, however, many technical problems involved in realizing a practical dataflow computer. Feasibility studies in the practical use of dataflow computers are essential.

Several architectures based on the dataflow concept have been proposed[1,2,3,4,5,8,9], some of which have been implemented in experimental machines. Among them the **SIGMA-1** [5], which is a large-scale dataflow supercomputer for numerical computations, shows the possibility to surpass the conventional von Neumann computers. It consists of 128 PEs and has a processing performance of more than 100 MFLOPS. A **SIGMA-1** PE is implemented by several gate array chips and a large memory. To construct a highly parallel machine, direct extension by merely adding more **SIGMA-1** PEs is not practical because the architectural design is complicated and too much hardware is required to implement all the PEs and the network. To realize a highly parallel machine, one or more PEs should be implemented on a single chip and the network structure must be simplified. The total architecture including computation model must be reconsidered.

The EM-4[10], whose target structure is more than 1000 PEs, is also being developed at the Electrotechnical Laboratory on the basis of the **SIGMA-1** project. The design principles of the **EM-4** are as follows.

1. Simplify the total architecture of a dataflow machine, e.g. interconnection network with O(N) hardware, a RISC-based single-chip PE design, and a direct matching scheme.
2. Improve machine performance by integrating a packet-based circular pipeline and a register-based advanced control pipeline.
3. Afford versatile resource management facilities, which current dataflow machines do not have, by introducing a strongly connected arc dataflow model.

The EM-4's single-chip processor, called the **EMC-R**, realizes these principles. This paper focuses on the architecture of the **EMC-R**.

Section 2 describes design features of the **EMC-R**. Defects of current dataflow architectures are listed and distinctive features of the **EMC-R** (or the **EM-4**) for conquering them are shown. In section 3, the instruction set architecture of the **EMC-R** which reflects the above principles is described. Features of an instruction set, instruction formats and a packet format are shown there. Section 4 describes the configuration architecture of the **EMC-R** which realizes all of the above.

2. Design Features of the EMC-R

2.1. Defects of Current Dataflow Architectures

In order to design an efficient parallel machine, we closely examined the defects of current dataflow architectures. They are summarized as follows.

D1. A circular pipeline [4] does not work well as a "pipeline" for less parallel execution.

This is because current dataflow execution models have no advanced control mechanism. In the case of highly parallel execution ($\geq N \times S$, where N is the number of PEs and S is the number of pipeline stages in each PE), all the stages of a circular pipeline can be filled with tokens. In other cases, it may occur that only one token is going round the pipeline cycle, and that PE throughput is less than one per a pipeline circulation time.

D2. Simple packet-based architecture cannot exploit registers or a register file efficiently.

If you always realize a token as a packet, and if you make each of the packets enter a PE whenever possible, it is nonsense to reserve tokens in registers for the future node operation. This is one of the main reasons why a fine pitch pipeline is difficult to implement in a dataflow machine.

D3. Time complexity and hardware complexity for matching are heavy if you adopt the colored token style.

© 1989 ACM 0884-7495/89/0000/0046$01.50

Color matching needs special hardware like associative memory or hashing hardware. They both require complex control logics and matching takes considerable time.

D4. Packet flow traffic is too heavy.

With a simple packet architecture, packet flow traffic is too heavy and a high-bandwidth low-delay interconnection network must be implemented. However, network performance is limited by current device technology.

D5. Current dataflow concepts cannot provide flexible and efficient resource management mechanisms.

If you realize mutual exclusion for resource management in a dataflow machine, you should provide some serialization mechanism (e.g. waiting queue). Its implementation is difficult, however, because the access to a concerned section can be violated by anyone else.

D6. It takes much time to eliminate garbage tokens.

If a program uses switch operations for conditional computations, there may occur a lot of garbage tokens. At the end of the execution, they must be collected to allow the working space to be reused. Time overhead for such operations is usually considerably large.

To overcome these defects, several novel facilities and mechanisms are introduced in the **EMC-R**, which are described in the following subsections.

2.2. Strongly Connected Arc Model

Although the basic **EM-4** architecture is based on the dataflow model, a new model called a *strongly connected arc model* [7] has been introduced to compensate for the pure dataflow architecture. The strongly connected arc model can solve all the problems described in the previous subsection.

In this model, dataflow graph arcs are divided into two categories: the normal arcs and the strongly connected arcs. A dataflow subgraph whose nodes are connected by strongly connected arcs is called a strongly connected block. The control strategy of the modified dataflow model in which this model is introduced is that the operation nodes are executed exclusively in a strongly connected block. Figure 1 shows an example of strongly connected blocks. In this figure, there are two strongly connected blocks, A and B. When node 5 or node 6 is fired, block A or block B is executed exclusively. This has the effect of giving the nodes in a strongly connected block the highest priorities if nodes are executed depending on priorities. A strongly connected block acts as a macro node which includes several instructions and is executed as if it were a single basic node. In the **EM-4**, each strongly connected bock is executed by a single PE.

There are several advantages in the strongly connected arc model, which are shown below.

A1. This model makes it easy to introduce an advanced control pipeline to dataflow architecture, because the exclusion of the outer block instructions causes more deterministic execution of codes. This solves the problem of **D1**.

A2. Instruction execution cycles can be reduced by introducing a strongly connected register file which is used for storing tokens in a strongly connected block. This is possible as the registered data in the concerned block are not violated by any other data. This overcomes the defect **D2**.

A3. In an intra-block execution, matching can be realized much more easily and efficiently because it is not necessary to match function identifiers (i.e. colors) if the block is included in the function. This solves the inefficiency problem of **D3**.

These **A1**, **A2** and **A3** enable the **EMC-R** to have a fine pitch execution pipeline.

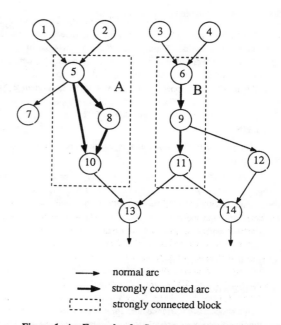

normal arc
strongly connected arc
strongly connected block

Figure 1 An Example of a Strongly Connected Block.

A4. There are no packet transfers in a strongly connected block. This reduces the defect **D4**.

A5. It can provide flexible resource management facilities by constructing an indivisible instruction sequence (e.g. test and set). This overcomes the defect **D5**.

A6. It can simplify the problem of remaining garbage tokens. This is because only the flag resets of a strongly connected register file are needed for eliminating the garbage tokens. The operation can be performed simultaneously with the result data transfer, i.e. with no overhead. This reduces the defect **D6**.

2.3. Direct Matching Scheme

To remove the defect **D3**, a fast and simple data matching scheme is needed. A strongly connected model solves this problem within a block but matching overhead on a normal dataflow node is not solved. We have designed a simple new data matching scheme, called a *direct matching scheme*. This scheme is implemented using ordinary memories. Since the logic for realizing the scheme is fairly simple, it can be easily implemented by wired logic on the **EMC-R**.

When a function is invoked, an instance of storage is allocated to a group of PEs. This instance is called an *operand segment*. It is used for waiting and matching of operands. An operand segment has memory words whose number is equal to or larger than that of two operand instructions in the concerned function. The compiled codes for the function are stored in another area, which is called a *template segment*. The address of the instruction in the template segment has a one-to-one simple correspondence with that of the matching. Binding of an operand segment and a template segment is also performed at the function invocation time.

The matching is executed by checking the stored data in an operand segment and by storing new data if its partner is absent. The matching location for each dataflow node is uniquely given as an absolute memory address in an operand segment. Thus matching can be carried out without using the associative memory or a hashing mechanism.

2.4. Processor Connected Omega Network

The **EM-4** uses a processor connected omega network as its interconnection network. Figure 2 illustrates an example of its topology. The advantages of this network are: the average distance from any PE to any other PE is order log(N), while N is the total number of PEs; the number of connection links from a PE is a small constant even if there are many PEs; and total number of switching elements is O(N) which is smaller than that of a multi-stage network (O(Nlog(N))).

The precise routing algorithm of the network will be reported in another paper.

The **EMC-R** contains an element of the processor connected omega network. One reason for this is to reduce the packet transfer time between a switch and a PE. The other reasons are the low hardware cost and the design simplicity. This element and processing function can work independently and concurrently.

3. Instruction Set Architecture

3.1. RISC Architecture

We adopt a RISC architecture for the **EMC-R** for simplicity and execution efficiency. Current dataflow architectures are not suited to RISC because defects **D2**, **D3**, and **D4** in 2.1 obstruct its implementation. The **EMC-R** is suited to RISC for its features in 2.2 and 2.3. It can exploit a fine pitch pipeline, each stage of which is simple. It has a register file whose member is the strongly connected register described in 2.2.

The **EMC-R** is a dataflow RISC chip due to the following features: it has only 26 instructions; there are only four kinds of instruction formats; it has only two memory addressing modes; it has a register file; it uses no microprograms; its packet size is fixed; there are only a few packet types; and it has simple synchronization mechanisms (direct matching and a register-based sequencing).

Among them, the latter three should be regarded as the features of a *RISC PE for a parallel computer*.

In the following subsections, the features of **EMC-R** instruction set architecture are described.

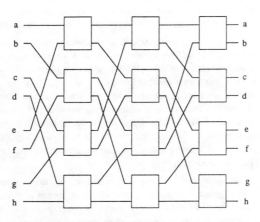

Figure 2 Processor Connected Omega Network.

3.2. Instruction Set

Table 1 shows an instruction set of the **EMC-R**. It has twenty-six kinds of instructions, each of which is executed in a single clock cycle (except continuous-memory-word-access instructions).

Details of an operation are afforded by the **AUX** field. For instance, the **SHF** instruction left or right shifts according to the contents of the **AUX** field.

In the **EMC-R**, a complex instruction can be performed by a strongly connected bock which contains simpler instructions. This is called a *macro instruction*. For instance, an integer division operation, a function call operation and complex structure operations are provided as macro instructions.

The following instructions are the characteristic instructions of the **EMC-R**.

(1) Branch Instructions

In the **EMC-R**, an action of a data switch operation in a strongly connected block is to fire one of the adequate nodes of its destination, without flowing any data. For this reason, the word **BRANCH** is used instead of **SWITCH** in the **EMC-R** for representing a data switch. There are six **BRANCH** instructions as shown in the Table 1. In order to simplify sequencing, they are implemented in a delayed branch style.

The **EMC-R** can provide a normal dataflow switch by strongly connecting the **BRANCH** instruction and the **MKPKT** instructions described below. In a good program, however, almost all of the switches are realized in a strongly connected block, because a packet flow overhead and a garbage token collection overhead are removed with this method (see 2.2).

(2) MKPKT

In the **EMC-R**, all of the instructions, except those of memory access and branch instructions, can make a packet for sending their results. In addition, it has a **MKPKT** instruction dedicated to packet

Table 1 Instruction Set

CATEGORY	INSTRUCTION	ACTION
Arithmetic and Logic	ADD	integer add
	SUB	integer subtract
	MUL	integer multiply
	DIV0	preparation of division
	DIV1	element of division
	DIV2	correction of division 0
	DIVR	remainder of division 0
	DIVQ	quotient of division 0
	SHF	shift
	AND	bitwise AND
	OR	bitwise OR
	EOR	bitwise exclusive OR
	NOT	bitwise NOT
	ALUTST	ALU test
Branch	BEQ	branch by equality
	BGT	branch by greatness
	BGE	branch by greatness or equality
	BTYPE	branch by data type
	BTYPE2	branch by 2 data types
	BOVF	branch by overflow
Memory or Register Read or Write	L	load from memory
	S	store to memory
	LS	load and store from/to memory
	LDR	load from register
Others	GET	send packet for remote operation
	MKPKT	make packet by two operands

48

generation. The **MKPKT** sends a packet whose address part is its first operand and whose data part is its second operand. Continuous **MKPKT**s perform the efficient distribution of the same data. Moreover, **MKPKT** supplies two special operations: an inter-function data transfer and a global data transfer such as a structure data transfer.

(3) GET

GET is an instruction for remote operations. It sends a return address to the address represented as its operand. For instance, CAR, CDR and sending a return address of a function are performed by the **GET**.

3.3. Instruction Format

The **EMC-R** has four types of instruction formats. Two of them are shown in Figure 3 (the other two are the immediate attached ones). Both of them are stored in a single memory word where each memory word is 38 bits long.

The **OP** field holds an operation code. **AUX** is a secondary field of the **OP**. If the concerned strongly connected block ends with the next instruction execution, then the **M** field (mode field) contains zero. **R0** and **R1** are the strongly connected registers used for the *next* instruction, if this instruction is strongly connected to other instructions. In this way, register-based advanced control is implemented in the **EMC-R**.

OUT is a tag field indicating whether the instruction generates a packet or not. If **OUT** is zero (Figure 3 (a)), then no packets are generated and the result is stored in **R2**. In this case, **BC** is a branch condition field which describes a branching style and **DPL** contains the displacement of a branching address. The latter two fields are used only in branch instructions.

If the **OUT** field contains one (Figure 3 (b)), then a packet is generated. The address part of the output packet is made up of the **WCF, M2, CA,** and **DPL** fields, and the operand segment identifier of the concerned function. The data part of the packet is the operation result.

A typical instruction execution is illustrated in more detail in 4.1 and 4.2.

3.4. Packet Format

A typical packet format is illustrated in Figure 4. Each packet consists of an address part and a data part, both of which have 39 bits.

(1) Address Part

HST field indicates whether this packet is bound for a normal destination or a host. **PT** is a packet type field. **WCF** is a waiting condition flag field, which indicates a type of matching. **M** is also a flag which indicates a type of dataflow arc. If it is zero, then the packet will fire a normal node; otherwise it will fire a strongly connected block. (GA, CA, MA) are the destination address fields. **GA** is a destination PE group address, **CA** is its column (i.e. member) address, and **MA** is a memory address. If this is a normal data packet, then **MA** is the matching address.

(2) Data Part

C is a cancel bit field indicating that the packet is a nonsense packet. **DT** and **D** are the data type and the data, respectively, which this packet carries.

3.5. Special Packets

A normal data packet has a NORM packet type, but packets for function control, structure access, remote memory access, etc. have special types. These special packets have no operand segment number, i.e. they are colorless. A special packet is generated by a **MKPKT** instruction or by a **GET** instruction. It is executed by a special strongly connected block named **SP Monitor**. A system manager can set the **SP Monitor** in any way desired during the system initialization, so the effect of a special packet can be properly determined by the manager. Thus the special packet execution in the **EMC-R** is completely flexible.

3.6. Program Examples

Figure 5 illustrates two FIBONACCI programs. Figure 5 (a) is a pure dataflow program and Figure 5 (b) is a program with strongly connected blocks. In the latter one, type checking and data switching

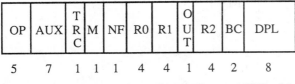

5 7 1 1 1 4 4 1 4 2 8

(a) Without Immediate, without Packet Output (OUT = 0)

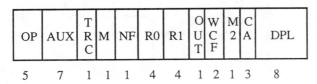

5 7 1 1 1 4 4 1 2 1 3 8

(b) Without Immediate, with Packet Output (OUT = 1)

Each figure is the field size.

Figure 3 Two Typical Types of Instruction Format.

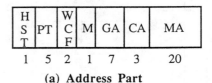

1 5 2 1 7 3 20

(a) Address Part

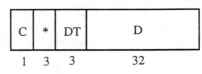

1 3 3 32

(b) Data Part

Each figure is the field size.

Figure 4 Typical Packet Format.

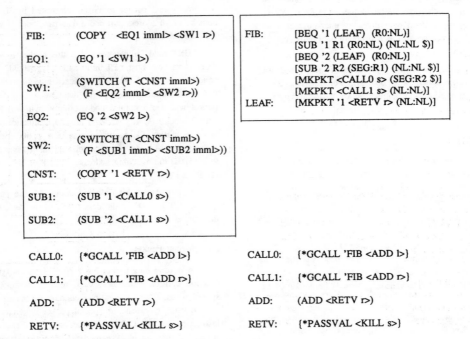

FIB:	(COPY <EQ1 imml> <SW1 r>)		FIB:	[BEQ '1 (LEAF) (R0:NL)]
				[SUB '1 R1 (R0:NL) (NL:NL $)]
EQ1:	(EQ '1 <SW1 l>)			[BEQ '2 (LEAF) (R0:NL)]
SW1:	(SWITCH (T <CNST imml>)			[SUB '2 R2 (SEG:R1) (NL:NL $)]
	(F <EQ2 imml> <SW2 r>))			[MKPKT <CALL0 s> (SEG:R2 $)]
EQ2:	(EQ '2 <SW2 l>)			[MKPKT <CALL1 s> (NL:NL)]
			LEAF:	[MKPKT '1 <RETV r> (NL:NL)]

FIB: (COPY   <EQ1 imml> <SW1 r>)

EQ1:   (EQ '1 <SW1 l>)

SW1:   (SWITCH (T <CNST imml>)
            (F <EQ2 imml> <SW2 r>))

EQ2:   (EQ '2 <SW2 l>)

SW2:   (SWITCH (T <CNST imml>)
            (F <SUB1 imml> <SUB2 imml>))

CNST: (COPY '1 <RETV r>)

SUB1:   (SUB '1 <CALL0 s>)

SUB2:   (SUB '2 <CALL1 s>)

FIB: [BEQ '1 (LEAF) (R0:NL)]
          [SUB '1 R1 (R0:NL) (NL:NL $)]
          [BEQ '2 (LEAF) (R0:NL)]
          [SUB '2 R2 (SEG:R1) (NL:NL $)]
          [MKPKT <CALL0 s> (SEG:R2 $)]
          [MKPKT <CALL1 s> (NL:NL)]
LEAF: [MKPKT '1 <RETV r> (NL:NL)]

CALL0:   {*GCALL 'FIB <ADD l>}   CALL0:   {*GCALL 'FIB <ADD l>}

CALL1:   {*GCALL 'FIB <ADD r>}   CALL1:   {*GCALL 'FIB <ADD r>}

ADD: (ADD <RETV r>)   ADD: (ADD <RETV r>)

RETV: {*PASSVAL <KILL s>}   RETV: {*PASSVAL <KILL s>}

KILL: {*KILL}   KILL: {*KILL}

    (a) A Normal Dataflow Program   **(b) A Strongly Connected Dataflow Program**

Figure 5 FIBONACCI Program.

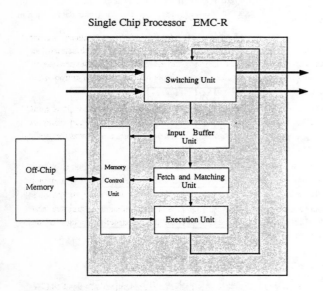

Figure 6 Block Diagram of the EMC-R.

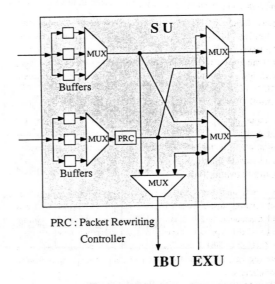

PRC : Packet Rewriting
Controller

Figure 7 Switching Unit Organization.

are strongly connected to a single block illustrated as a rectangle in Figure 5 (b). It takes twenty-three clocks to execute the rectangular part if you select the former program (in the case of occurring recursive calls). If you select the latter program, it only takes nine clocks. This means that the strongly connected method can execute this subprogram about two and half times as fast as the pure dataflow method.

Remark that, in the above comparison, a **SWITCH** instruction and a **COPY** instruction were supposed to exist in the EMC-R. And remark that all the normal nodes of the EMC-R are executed in the same clock cycles with the pure dataflow machine **SIGMA-1**.

4. Configuration Architecture

4.1. EMC-R Architecture

Figure 6 shows a block diagram of the EMC-R which realizes all of the features described in the previous sections. The **EMC-R** consists of a Switching Unit (SU), an Input Buffer Unit (IBU), a Fetch and Matching Unit (FMU), an Execution Unit (EXU), a Memory Control Unit (MCU), and Maintenance Circuits.

(1) Switching Unit

The Switching Unit (SU) is a three-by-three packet switch which is an element of a processor connected omega network. It switches data independently of and concurrently with the other units. Each input port of the network has structured buffers. Organization of the **SU** is illustrated in Figure 7.

When a processor connected omega network is used in a buffered manner, store-and-forward deadlock prevention facilities must be supplied. In the EMC-R, a three bank buffer is provided in each input port. Firstly, a packet is buffered in the least level bank. When the packet arrives at the zeroth stage of the network, it is pushed into the one-upper-level bank. Because of the topological property of the processor connected omega network, any packet never covers three rounds of this network, so the logical structure of a packet transfer cannot make loops. This three bank strategy thus removes all store-and-forward deadlocks from the network.

Another feature of the SU is the function level dynamic load balancing facility. In the EM-4, special packets which monitor the load of PEs travel through the network. The SU rewrites these packets within the time period required by a normal packet transfer, i.e. with no overhead, and performs the load balancing. This rewriting is made by the **PRC** in Figure 7.

(2) Input Buffer Unit

The Input Buffer Unit (IBU) is a buffer for packets waiting for execution. A 32-word FIFO type buffer is implemented using a dual port RAM on chip. If this buffer is full, a part of the off-chip memory is used as a secondary buffer.

(3) Fetch and Matching Unit

The Fetch and Matching Unit (FMU) is used for matching tokens and fetching instructions. It performs a direct matching for a packet and a sequencing for a strongly connected block. It controls the pipelines of the processor, especially integrating two types of pipelines (see 4.2). The FMU contains an instruction address register, a packet data register, a register for matching data, several multiplexers, and control circuits.

(4) Execution Unit

The Execution Unit (EXU) is an instruction executor. Figure 8 illustrates its organization. The EXU contains an instruction register, two operand registers, a register file, an ALU, a barrel shifter, a multiplier, a versatile comparator, packet generation circuits, and control

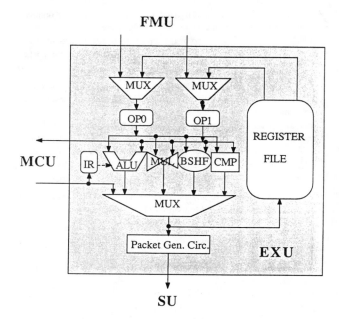

IR : Instruction Register   OPi : Operand Register i

Figure 8 Execution Unit Organization.

circuits.

In an execution cycle, the contents of operand registers are sent to the ALU, etc. Then the operation is carried out according to the **OP** and **AUX** fields of the instruction register. The result is sent in a packet or stored in a register file. All of these actions are made in a single clock, and, in the same clock, fetch and decode of the next instruction and data load from the **FMU** or a register file are performed (see 4.2).

(5) Memory Control Unit and Off-Chip Memory

The Memory Control Unit (MCU) arbitrates memory access requests from the IBU, the FMU, and the EXU, and sends data between the off-chip memory and the EMC-R. The MCU consists of a data multiplexer, an address multiplexer, and an arbitration controller.

The off-chip memory size can be up to 5 megabytes. It is used for a secondary packet buffer, a matching store, an instruction store, an area for the SP monitor (see 3.5), a structure store, and a working area.

(6) Maintenance Circuits

The Maintenance Circuits make initialization of the chip and memory words, handle many kinds of errors and provide the dynamic monitor which reports a system performance and the system status such as processor load, an active function number and structure area used. We will report the concept and the construction method of the Maintenance Circuits in another paper.

4.2. Pipeline Organization

Figure 9 illustrates the pipeline organization of the **EMC-R**. Basically, the pipeline has four stages, some of which have two substages. Each stage has a rectangle which represents a single clock action, or a bypass line which means no clock action. A small rectangle represents a half clock action.

51

Each packet from a network is buffered in the **IBU** if necessary (the far left side of the figure). Then the concerned template segment number (see 2.3) is fetched from the off-chip memory in the first stage (**TNF**). The number is stored at the top of the operand segment at the function invocation time. The first stage is bypassed when the packet is not a normal data packet.

The second stage is the matching stage. In the case of matching with the immediate, an immediate fetch (**IMF**) occurs. In the case of matching with data in the matching store, data at the concerned address is read in the former half clock (**RD**). If a partner exists, the flag at the address is eliminated in the latter half clock (**EL**); else a new packet data is written in the latter half clock (**WR**). This read-modify-write action is completed in a single clock cycle. The second stage is omitted if a new token fires a single operand instruction.

The third stage is an instruction fetch (**IF**) and decode (**DC**) stage. Each operation is performed in a half clock.

The fourth stage is an execution stage. Transfer of the result packet can be overlapped with the execution. If the next instruction is strongly connected with the current instruction, instruction fetch and data load of the next instruction are overlapped with the execution. The third stage and the fourth stage are repeated in the overlapped manner until there are no executable instructions in the concerned strongly connected block. If the instruction is a normal mode instruction or the last instruction of the strongly connected block, its execution can be overlapped with the instruction fetch and decode of a next packet processing. Thus, an integration of two types of pipelines, a packet-based circular pipeline (illustrated as thin lines in Figure 9) and a register-based advanced control pipeline (illustrated as thick lines in Figure 9), is realized.

During each stage, the **TNF**, the **IMF**, the **RD**, the **WR**, the **EL** and the **IF** are performed by the **FMU** with the assistance of the **MCU**. The **DC** and the **EX** are performed by the **EXU**.

The register-based advanced control pipeline is a fast and simple pipeline exploited by strongly connected blocks. Its throughput is at most six times as high as that of the packet-based circular pipeline.

Each PE has a peak processing performance of more than 12 MIPS.

4.3. Implementation

The **EMC-R** is a real processor chip, so its implementation is limited by current chip fabrication technology. Our chip contains 50,000 CMOS gates and 256 signal lines.

Table 2 shows the gate usage and pin usage of each **EMC-R** unit. The Switching Unit is complex as it has three bank buffers and their multiplexer at each port. The Execution Unit is also complex because it has many large modules such as a register file, a multiplier, a barrel shifter, and a packet generator. The Fetch and Matching Unit requires a little hardware, because the direct matching reduces the hardware cost of it.

As for pins, almost all of them are used for data buses of the network and the off-chip memory.

The **EMC-R** will be fabricated by June 1989. Then the **EM-4** prototype which has 80 PEs will be constructed. It will consist of 16 processor boards, each of which will have five PEs and a mother board which the network will be implemented on. The **EM-4** prototype hardware will be operational in 1990. Peak performance of this prototype is expected to be more than 1 GIPS. Construction of an efficient real machine of 1,000 PEs is the next program, which is the goal of the **EM-4** project.

Table 2   Hardware Complexity

UNIT	Gates	Pins
Switching Unit	10,112	176
Input Buffer Unit	9,238	-
Fetch and Matching Unit	3,504	-
Execution Unit	19,692	-
Memory Control Unit	1,518	67
Maintenance Circuits	1,589	12
Total	45,653	255

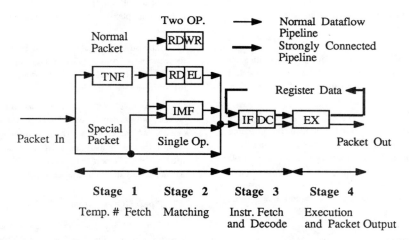

Figure 9 Pipeline Organization of the EMC-R.

5. Conclusion

This paper describes the architecture of the **EMC-R**, a single-chip dataflow processor which is a PE of the **EM-4**. The distinctive features of the **EMC-R** are:

(1) a strongly connected arc dataflow model;
(2) a direct matching scheme;
(3) a RISC-based design;
(4) a deadlock-free on-chip packet switch; and
(5) an integration of a packet-based circular pipeline and a register-based advanced control pipeline.

These features were examined, and the instruction set architecture and configuration architecture which exploit them were described.

The schedule of the hardware implementation is written in 4.3. As for softwares, a high level language and an optimizing compiler are currently under development. The latter has a node labeling scheduler for the intra-function load balancing [6] and a block constructor for automatically making strongly connected blocks. The optimization schemes and algorithms will be reported in another paper.

Future problems are as follows.
(1) Close consideration and expansion of a strongly connected arc dataflow model.
(2) Consideration of a chip design using much highly-integrated VLSI.

Acknowledgement

We wish to thank Dr. Hiroshi Kashiwagi, Deputy Director-General of the Electrotechnical Laboratory, Dr. Akio Tojo, Director of the Computer Science Division and Mr. Toshio Shimada, Chief of the Computer Architecture Section for supporting this research, and the staff of the Computer Architecture Section for the fruitful discussions.

References

[1] Amamiya,M., Takesue,M., Hasegawa,R. and Mikami,H.: Implementation and Evaluation of a List-Processing-Oriented Data Flow Machine, Proc. the 13th Annu. Symp. on Computer Architecture, pp.10-19 (June 1986).

[2] Arvind, Dertouzos,M.L. and Iannucci,R.A.: A Multiprocessor Emulation Facility, MIT-LCS Technical Report 302 (Sep. 1983).

[3] Dennis,J.B., Lim,W.Y.P. and Ackerman,W.B.: The MIT Dataflow Engineering Model, Proc. IFIP Congress 83, 553-560 (1983).

[4] Gurd,J., Kirkham,C.C. and Watson,I.: The Manchester Prototype Dataflow Computer, Commun. ACM, 21, 1, pp.34-52 (1985).

[5] Hiraki,K., Sekiguti,S. and Shimada,T.: System Architecture of a Dataflow Supercomputer, TENCON87, Seoul (1987).

[6] Otsuka,Y., Sakai,S. and Yuba,T.: Static Load Allocation in Dataflow Machines, Proc. of Technical Group on Computer Architecture, IECE Japan, CAS86-136, in Japanese (1986).

[7] Sakai,S., Yamaguchi,Y., Hiraki,K. and Yuba,T.: Introduction of a Strongly-Connected-Arc Model in a Data Driven Single Chip Processor EMC-R, Proc. Dataflow Workshop 1987, IECE Japan, pp.231-238, in Japanese (1987).

[8] Shimada,T., Hiraki,K., Nishida,K. and Sekiguchi,S.: Evaluation of a Prototype Data Flow Processor of the SIGMA-1 for Scientific Computations, Inf. Process. Lett.,16, 3, pp.139-143 (1983).

[9] Yamaguchi,Y., Toda,K. and Yuba,T.: A Performance Evaluation of a Lisp-Based Data-Driven Machine(EM-3), Proc. 10th Annual Symposium on Computer Architecture, pp.163-169 (1983).

[10] Yamaguchi,Y., Sakai,S., An Architectural Design of a Highly Parallel Dataflow Machine, to appear in IFIP'89 (1989).

Exploiting Data Parallelism in Signal Processing on a Data Flow Machine

Peter Nitezki

Forschungszentrum Informatik
Technische Expertensysteme und Robotik
Haid-und-Neu-Str. 10-14
Karlsruhe 1
West Germany
Prof. U. Rembold
NITEZKI%FIX@IRA.UKA.DE

ABSTRACT

This paper will show that the massive data parallelism inherent to most signal processing tasks may be easily mapped onto the parallel structure of a data flow machine. A special system called STRUCTFLOW has been designed to optimize the static data flow model for hardware efficiency and low latency. The same abstractions from the general purpose data flow model that lead to a quasi systolic operation of the processing elements make explicit flow control of the data tokens as they pass through the arcs of the flow graph obsolete. We will describe the architecture of the system and discuss the restrictions on the structure of the flow graphs.

1 INTRODUCTION

Nearly all signal processing tasks show an algorithmic structure of extreme regularity both in the computing structure and the access pattern of their data. This inspired a variety of architectures that exploit this parallelity to provide the necessary computing power for real time operation. Some examples are processor arrays, systolic arrays and hard wired algorithms. Unfortunately their flexibility and programmability is quite low and the burden to parallelize an algorithm is completely put on the programmer.

Data flow computers that automatically exploit the fine grain parallelism of a program seemed to be very attractive to avoid these restrictions. In the last ten years several data flow systems have been proposed for signal processing applications /CHEN, HOGE, SAWA, SEAL, TEMM, VEDD/. However, pure data flow mechanisms turned out to be quite inefficient in processing large data structures and have a tendency to large overheads in data storage and flow control. Dynamic data flow systems need to enumerate any atomic data element in order to provide correct pairing of the operands. This makes a huge name space necessary which is only sparsely occupied. Static data flow schemes do not provide easy mechanisms for recursion and procedure calls and are therefore not much used. Most of the designs tried to overcome the problems by either restricting the parallelism of their machines to relatively low rates /HOGE, TEMM/ or by using data flow only for high level runtime scheduling of conventional computing resources /HONG, SEAL/. Another approach abandons some of the principles of pure data flow to gain efficiency and parallelism /LEIE, CHAS/. This is a step back to user controlled parallelism and brings back the problem of efficient programming of the individual tasks.

Some recent designs use the static principle together with static scheduling of the graphs. The massive use of parallelism is guaranteed by compilers, which make efficient use of the parallelism in the application and map it automatically onto the hardware /VEDD, HONG, CAMP/.

2 THE STRUCTFLOW APPROACH

The design of STRUCTFLOW is guided by the fact that most signal processing algorithms show a very regular structure with nearly no conditional expressions. Furthermore the computational structure of the algorithm is relatively small containing typically less than about twenty nodes. The parallelity in the data structure is far more important. A 3x3 convolution on an image has for instance a computational structure of 16 nodes that has to be applied to 512x512 images. Therefore STRUCTFLOW has been adapted to the processing of streams, a concept first used in data flow machines by Dennis /DEN1/ and nowadays included in many modern single assignment languages /SISA/.

Streams can be looked at as one-dimensional data structures mapped onto an ordered sequence in time. Signals therefore may be directly be modeled as streams. By introducing separator symbols to structure such sequences, arbitrary data structures can be represented by streams. STRUCTFLOW provides means to handle both infinite and structured streams and exploits their inherent parallelity by dividing single streams into multiple streams and mapping those multiple streams onto multiple identical processing elements (PE) that execute a copy of the same graph. That kind of parallel data structures results in an order both in time and space. These multiple sequences of data elements may be automatically mapped onto the hardware structure. As signal processing is a task that does not require frequent activation and deactivation of a multitude of activities, the mapping may be statically scheduled and determined offline. The generation of the multiple streams from input signals and the synchronisation with the outer world is done by separate I/O-Modules. The handling of data items within the systems is purely asynchronous. Intermediate storage of data structures for restructuring and storage of large amount of input data is provided by structure memory (SM) modules (Fig. 1).

Tasks like image sequence analysis and algorithms with runtime dependent access patterns require intermediate storage. The individual modules are connected through a global network providing stream routing. The term stream routing refers to the property that individual streams traveling on the network maintain their sequence in time although then may share a particular physical link with other streams. STRUCTFLOW is designed to use a packet switching cube connected cycles network due to its fixed degree and logarithmic growth. The routing elements implement a static deterministic routing algorithm that preserves the integrity of streams and enables the scheduler to determine throughput offline.

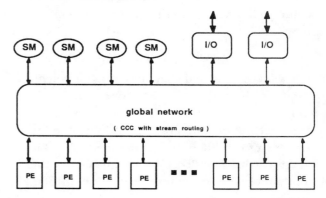

Fig. 1: The global structure of STRUCTFLOW

2.1 ABSTRACTIONS FROM PURE DATA FLOW

STRUCTFLOW uses the special features of streams to ease the design of the PEs. By restricting the data flow principle a very efficient hardware utilization can be achieved.

First if the sequence of data elements in time and space is strictly kept the elements of a stream don't have to be enumerated. The global network and the PE´s are designed to keep the sequence in time in all cases. That means a token that enters a module first will be processed first and its resulting token will also exit first. Therefore only the name of the stream has to be attached to a data element, so the position of an element in a data structure is not explicitly accessible except in storage modules where structures can be arbitrarily addressed. Storage modules contain simple address generators to generate frequently used access patterns to form the streams. All other patterns have to be generated in PEs to form a stream of addresses for the SMs.

Second, all data flow graphs will be processed serially in a pseudo systolic mode of data flow. All operands on the inbound arcs of the graph will be input in one wave, so the first data token of the second wave will only enter the processor if the first wave has been completely consumed. This quasi systolic operation allows the elimination of flow control within the PEs. As a consequence only the links across the network need to store an acknowledge arc that allow to implement a flow control protocol. The wavefront operation within the PEs avoids token clash without any special acknowledgement of the token consumption.

These two features ease the design of the PEs as we will see later and they have a lot of potential to reduce latency in the processing of the streams. There are of course some restrictions on the structure of the graphs and on the programming of conditionals and iterations, but most of them can be handled by a compiler, and there is not much use of general recursion in signal processing applications anyhow.

3 THE ARCHITECTURE OF A STRUCTFLOW PROCESSING ELEMENT

The PEs in STRUCTFLOW consist of three units (Fig. 2). Two of them, the matching unit (MU) and the processing unit (PU) form the classical data flow ring. The communication unit (CU) handles the flow control of the inbound and outbound arcs and forms the wavefronts for the quasi systolic processing of the graphs. Online loading of programs is also handled by this Unit.

3.1 STRUCTFLOW INSTRUCTION SET AND ITS IMPLEMENTATION

For the ease of implementation the current version of STRUCTFLOW PEs use 16 bit integer arithmetic. The integer operators implemented today are addition, subtraction, multiplication, division, modulo function, supremum, infimum, and all relational operators on the ordered set of integers. Furthermore all 16 functions on two boolean operands are implemented.

Data items are endowed with a 3 bit type tag. It distinguishes integers and Booleans and allows the coding of special tokens for stream structuring and arithmetic exceptions. For the handling of arithmetic exceptions the set of integers is augmented by a *positive* and a *negative infinity value* which denotes overflow in the respective direction. All operators are functionally extended to allow arithmetic operations on these infinity values. Type mismatches or undefined value combinations like multiplying infinity by zero result a *bottom* -token. These extensions allow exception handling without any context sensitive elements.

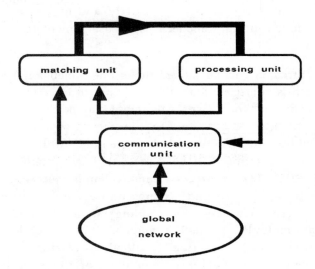

Fig. 2: Overview of the Processing Element

Iteration and conditional constructs are supported by special control operators. The **watch**-operator selects a data element of its input stream by the control of a boolean input. In case of a *True* the data input is copied to the output, in case of a *False* the result is a *bottom* -token. The **select**-operator chooses among its input operands that one, that is non-*bottom*. In case of two *bottom*-inputs *bottom* is the result. In case of two non-*bottom* values one is chosen arbitrarily. These operators have two non-stream-preserving counterparts, **guard** and **choice**, that suppress the output of a *bottom* token and therefore allow nondeterministic behaviour. Although those nondeterministic are important in the efficient programming of conditionals and iterations they are not safe in any case. The correct propagation of wavefronts and the correctness of the streams must be ensured by the compiler.

Two instructions provide flow control and duplication of streams. The **identity**-operator may serve as pipeline buffer element or as a semaphore or gate mechanism using the regular matching mechanism. The **copy**-operator interprets its second operand as the destination name of the second outgoing arc and provides stream copying and switching. The same interpretation of the second operand shows the **switch**-operator that does not duplicate its left operand but sends it to the port specified by the right one. In case of a *bottom* token in the right operand the destination field specifies the default destination. Additional output operators may be used to partition graphs and sharing them among several PEs, or for transmission of a stream to the I/O or structure memories.

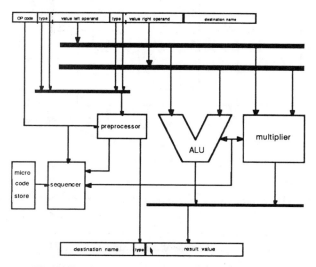

Fig. 3: The Processing Unit of a SRUCTFLOW PE

In the current first version of the STRUCTFLOW PU /AUGE/ (Fig. 3) all operators are processed by a microprogrammed ALU with an attached multiplier chip. Microprogramming has been chosen for the flexibility of the design in this phase of research and evaluation. The processing of the type tag together with the sign bit which also holds the boolean values is done by a function table preprocessor. This preprocessing needs no extra time as it is done in parallel with the ALU operation and speeds up microprograms

as they do not have to examine the operands explicitly.

3.2 THE MATCHING OPERATION IN THE STRUCTFLOW PROCESSOR

Previous designs of data flow machines show matching as the major time consuming factor. Our intention was to keep matching as easy and fast as possible. The work of Dennis et al. /DEN2/ was the most encouraging influence. STRUCTFLOW uses static dataflow on nodes with exactly two inbound edges and exactly one destination. The **copy**-operator fits fully into this scheme as copying is done by a microprogram in the PU that interprets the second operand in a special way. Matching is strict so every operation will only be enabled when both operands are present. Modern memory technology makes direct storage of the data tokens feasible. This eliminates the need of an associative mechanism which needs extra time and hardware. Matching is achieved in a single read-modify-write cycle on the node store, where the node name in the data token directly addresses the memory.

Since all flow graphs are executed in a systolic pipelining of streams, no local flow control on the edges of the graph is needed. This frees the node or matching store of the need of backlink pointers for the acknowledge arcs and makes extra flow control steps obsolete. In addition to the effect of simplification of the matching outlined above, the speed of matching is at least doubled by this mode of operation. The matching unit /GALL/ therefore needs only a small finite state machine as matching controller. Only two transitions are needed per matching of one token: In the first step a token is selected from two input registers where the source is determined by the state of the token queue (Fig. 4). In the second step the node store is accessed and the three match control bits are examined. If there is no match, the token is stored. Otherwise, the token and the stored operand together with the instruction code are forwarded to the node formation unit. In this unit the different fields of the node are suitably arranged and sent to the PU as an instruction packet.

The matching control is driven by three bits of the node store. The first bit determines whether a token has yet been stored in this location in a prior operation. The second bit determines whether the present operand is a constant which is not to be deleted after a successful match. The third bit is set if the stored operand is on the left port of that node.

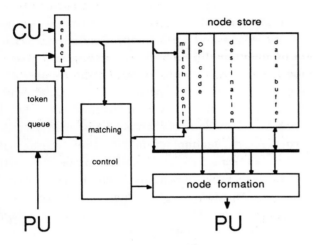

Fig. 4: The Matching Unit of a STRUCTFLOW PE

The quasi systolic wavefront processing frees the MU from flow control on the internal data path. The traffic of tokens on the input arcs however is influenced by the global network and the external timing of the I/O. STRUCTFLOW thus has to provide an acknowledge mechanism on the inbound edges of the flow graphs to prevent so-called token clash - two data items on the same arc at the same time. The interface of MU and CU is designed to work in lockstep and allows rejection of tokens to prevent that situation.

3.3 FLOW CONTROL AND THE ROLE OF THE COMMUNICATION UNIT

The CU performs mainly two tasks. First is the flow control of the in- and outbound arcs and the formation of the input wavefronts. Second is the online loading of program information in the node store of the MU and in its I/O control store.

Flow control is implemented through the input and output module /SCAR/ (Fig. 5). The input module maintains a hardware queue for any of the input arcs which form a fixed subset of the name space of the MU. The state of the queues controls an X-On/X-Off protocol on acknowledge arcs that are stored in the CU's control memory. That control store also contains information which arcs belong to a wavefront and therefore controls the information of input wave fronts. The input module scans that control store to form a sequence of input tokens for the MU. In case that every token is accepted the wavefronts of the active graphs are scanned sequentially. If a token is rejected or a queue is empty that wavefront is suspended and the next one will be processed. In the next scan the suspended wavefront will be resumed with the suspended arc quite like an interrupt in a von Neumann machine.

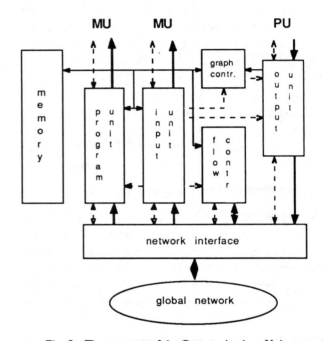

Fig. 5: The structure of the Communications Unit

The graph control module scans the streams for start or end tokens to enable or disable the wavefront formation and controls the use of particular graphs.

Program loading consists mainly of the task of scanning the network input for program tokens and storing of the information in the appropriate store. The program stream is therefore structured by special control tokens and has a particular structure to determine the different parts of the program eg. node information and wavefront information.

4 PROGRAMMING ISSUES

Some of the design decisions of this system affect the programming of the machine. The most important issue is that all graphs are executed in a quasi systolic fashion. The consequence is that all possible paths that lead to a node have to be of equal length. The finite depth of the queues in the CU also places an upper bound on the depth of a graph as there is no means to stop wavefronts that entered the MU. In case of acyclic flow graphs these graphs have to be balanced with respect to the root and with an upper bound on their depth. All these restrictions may be met automatically at compile time by inserting identity operations forming a pipeline delay of appropriate length. In case of the commutativity and distributivity of certain operators the graphs may be automatically restructured to their maximally broad equivalents. These problems are all covered by a paper of Montz /MONT/ who investigated these issues for the MIT static data flow project.

4.1 THE PROGRAMMING OF CONDITIONALS

The programming of conditional expressions has to deal with the same restrictions as other acyclic graphs. The most straightforward solution is to evaluate both branches in parallel and to select the desired result at the end with a selector node (a merge in terms of Dennis who gave an example for this style in /DEN2/). This solution shows all desired properties like cleanliness (no tokens remain in the graph after execution of the conditional), safety (no deadlock may occur), and strictness (the result will only produced when all input tokens have been supplied) in a very straightforward manner, but wastes a lot of the necessary computing power as only one of the results will be used.

The particular properties of the STRUCTFLOW PE help to overcome this problem. Any token will be processed as soon as it enters the MU and neither the MU nor the PU does some reordering on the packets they act on. So, if two different

subgraphs of equal depth are fed with two consecutive wavefronts, the graph that got the first wave will produce the first result. If now the condition is evaluated, a switch might distribute the wavefronts and a nonstrict merge may form the correct result stream. STRUCTFLOW does not provide nonstrict operators. This dilemma is a fake, as only one wavefront can arrive at a time and a knot /VEE1/ can be employed. The term knot refers to an extension of flow graphs to flow nets where two arcs of the net point at the some port of an operator. It is easy to show that in our case of conditional wavefront processing no token clash or violation of strictness and cleanliness can occur.

Let us look at the example depicted in Fig. 6. For comparison it is the same small conditional that can be found in the paper of Dennis /DEN2/.

```
if C[i] then (A[i] + B[i])
else 5 * (A[i] * B[i] + 2)
endif
```

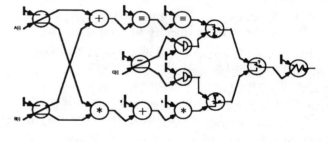

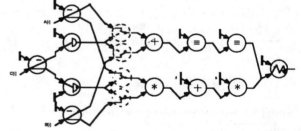

Fig. 6:   Two structural variants of a conditional expression

In first graph we see a strictly deterministic implementation. The rightmost node provides the name of an external arc where the result will be used. The switches and logic gates to its left provide the conditional selection of the results of the two branches. The two copy nodes on the left distribute copies of the input to the two branches (not depicted in the example of Dennis). In the upper branch the pipeline buffers can be found in the chaining of the two identity nodes. Please note that both branches execute wether the result will be used or discarded. The input arcs of the graph provide flow control so the arc named C needs no pipeline buffers.

The second graph shows the same conditional expression in an implementation with nondeterministic switches. Only in case that the branch will be chosen an input will be routed to it. The other branch will be inactive. Note the necessity for pipeline buffering to keep the wavefronts intact even in this case.

4.2 ITERATION AND RECURSION

As all data structures are already mapped onto streams, the classical loop for scanning of data structures is obsolete. Iterations are only needed for recurrence relations, where the computation of a value requires previously computed ones. Dennis /DEN2/ gives a complete solution for that case of iteration. The only concern of the compiler or the programmer is to supply the number of initial values that matches the depth of the iteration cycle for that the wavefronts will be correctly formed and to control the switches that feedback the previous values. The problem with a ´do while´ kind of iteration is that the nett consumption resp. production of tokens by the loop may vary and thus the wavefront processing gets out of step. As a consequence the input of the graph has to be gated to synchronize the loop. Input arcs are the only arcs that provide acknowledgement of tokens, so every gate has to be coded as an operation with an input arc for the wavefront element and a control arc that gets tokens from the termination test of the loop.

The example in Fig. 7 shows an implementation of a *forall* expression in VAL (also found in /DEN2/). Due to the stream processing no explicit control of iterations as in implicit languages occurs. The non-deterministic switches on the left provide an efficient construct to choose the elements of the input stream and saves the pipeline buffers necessary elseway. The control stream denoted through a sequence of boolean

values can be formed quite easily and can be derived from the elements of the input stream. In this case a non-deterministic implementation of the conditional expression can be seen. The deterministic version would also be possible but much less effective.

In the implementation of the MU the problem of general recursion was also considered. Gallinat /GALL/ could show that linear recursion could be programmed without changes to the hardware or the set of operators. The token queue in the MU takes the role of buffer memory where the tokens of a software controlled stack will reside. Although this kind of recursion is not very efficient, because all the tokens in the stack will pass the MU and the PU many times as they all travel around the data flow ring, it still proved feasible even on a data flow machine designed for stream processing.

4.3 THE EFFICIENCY OF STRUCTFLOW PARALLELISM

The basic mechanism of procedure call and recurrence execution in STRUCTFLOW is graph locking. Most designers /VEE2/ abandoned this kind of control in data flow machines because it reduces the available parallelism and thus causes idle times due to uncompletely filled pipelines. STRUCTFLOW however has only very few stages in the data flow ring, so 5 to 10 tokens are enough to keep both MU and PU busy. Only pathological graphs might show less usable parallelism. Due to the sequential execution of the individual flow graphs more available parallelism only causes more tokens to wait in the queue. All of the massively parallel execution in STRUCTFLOW comes from the consequent parallelization of streams.

5 PROJECT STATE

The present project is to bee seen in a as an academic enterprise in a restricted university research environment. It has been performed by one assistant and an a handful of students working on their theses. Up to now one PE has been built and undergos test. The design of the CU has lead to a prototype to be redesigned for proper integration into a network of processors. In some parts of the design the lack of tailored ICs restricted the size and performance of the PE. Some activities in the direction of custom VLSI have been started.

6 ACKNOWLEDGEMENT

This research has been done in the context of the research programme "Physics and Application of Novel Sensors" and has been funded by the state of Baden-Württemberg. Also many thanks to Karl Kleine who helped to improve my poor English.

7 REFERENCES

/AUGE/ Augenstein, R.; *Entwurf und Realisierung einer Verarbeitungseinheit*; Masters Thesis, Fak. Electrical Eng., Universität Karlsruhe, 1987(in German)

/CAMP/ Campbell, M. L.; *Static Allocation for a Data Flow Multiprocessor*; IEEE Int. Conf. Parallel Processing, p. 511ff, 1985

/CHAS/ Chase, M.; *A Pipelined Data Flow Architecture for Digital Signal Processing*, VLSI Signal Processing, Sect. 18, IEEE Press, 1984

/CHEN/ Chen, S.; Ritter, G.X.; *A Reconfigurable Architecture for Image Processing*; IEEE, Int. Conf. Computer Design, p. 516ff, 1984

/DEN1/ Dennis, J. B.; *Data Flow Ideas for Supercomputers*, IEEE COMPCON Spring, p. 15ff, 1984

/DEN2/ Dennis, J.B.; Rong, G.G.; *Maximum Pipelining of Array Operations on Static Data Flow Machine*, IEEE, Int. Conf. Parallel Processing, p. 331ff, 1983

/GALL/ Gallinat, J.; *Entwurf und Aufbau einer Matching-Einheit*, Masters Thesis, Fak. Computer Science, Universität Karlsruhe, 1987 (in German)

/HOGE/ Hogenauer, E.B.; Newbold, R.F.; Inn, Y.J.; *DDSP - A Data Flow Computer for Signal Processing*, IEEE Int. Conf Parallel Processing, p. 126ff, 1982

/HONG/ Hong, Y.-C.; Payne, T. H.; Ferguson, L. O.; *An Architecture for a Dataflow Multiprocessor*, IEEE Int. Conf. Parallel Processing, p. 349ff, 1986

/LEIE/ Leier, W.; *A Small, High-Speed Data Flow Processor*, IEEE Int. Conf. Parallel Processing, p. 341ff, 1983

/MONT/ Montz, L.B.; *Safety and Optimization Transformations for Data Flow Programs*; TR 240, LCS, MIT, 1980

/SAWA/ Sawakar, P.S.; Forquer, T.J.; Derry, R.P.; *Programmable Modular Signal Processor - A Data Flow Computer for Real Time Signal Processing*, IEEE Int. Conf. Parallel Processing, p. 344ff, 1985

/SCAR/ Scarchillo, A.; *Entwurf und Aufbau einer Kommunikationseinheit*; Masters-Thesis, Fak. Electrical Eng., Universität Karlsruhe, 1987 (in German)

/SEAL/ Seals, J.D.; Shively, R.R.; *EMSP: A Data Flow Computer for Signal Processing Applications*, VLSI Signal Processing, Sect. 6, IEEE Press, 1984

/SISA/ McGraw, J., et al.; *SISAL: Streams and Iteration in a Single-Assignment Language*; Lawrence Livermore Ntnl. Labs, 1983

/TEMM/ Temma, T., Mizoguchi, M.; Hanaki, S.; *Template-Controlled Image Processor TIP-1 Performance Evaluation*, IJCAI,1983

/VEDD/ Vedder, R.; Finn, D.; *The Huges Data Flow Multiprocessor: Architecture for Efficient Signal and Data Processing*, IEEE 12th Ann. Int. Symp. Computer Architecture, p. 324ff, 1985

/VEE1/ Veen, A.; *A Formal Model for Data Flow Programs with Token Coloring*; internal report, MC, Asterdam, 1981

/VEE2/ Veen, A.; *The Misconstrued Semicolon: Reconciling Imperative Languages and Dataflow Machines*; CWI Tract, MC, Amsterdam, 1986

```
A : array(integer) :=
  forall
          i in [0, m+1]      % range specification
          P : integer :=     % definition
              if (i = 0) | (i = m+1) then
              else 25 * (C[i-1] + 2 * C[i] + C[i+1])
              endif;
  construct B[i] * (P *P)     % accumulation
  endall
```

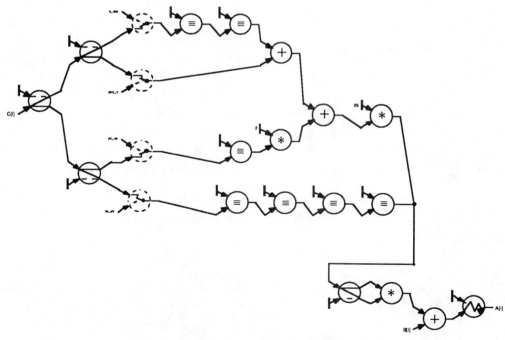

Fig. 7:   Implementation of a forall construct

61

Session 3A
Pipeline Architectures
Chair: A. Gottlieb, NYU

Architectural Mechanisms To Support Sparse Vector Processing

R.N. Ibbett, T.M. Hopkins and K.I.M. McKinnon

Departments of Computer Science and Mathematics
University of Edinburgh
James Clerk Maxwell Building, King's Buildings
Mayfield Road, Edinburgh, EH9 3JZ

Abstract

We discuss the algorithmic steps involved in common sparse matrix problems, with particular emphasis on linear programming by the revised simplex method. We then propose new architectural mechanisms which are being built into an experimental machine, the Edinburgh Sparse Processor, and which enable vector instructions to operate efficiently on sparse vectors stored in compressed form. Finally, we review the use of these new mechanisms on the linear programming problem.

1 Introduction

Sparse vectors are an important feature of a number of computer applications. Their distinguishing characteristic is the occurrence of large numbers of zero elements in vectors and arrays, and in mapping sparse applications on to existing computers a variety of software techniques have been employed to reduce the storage and processing required for the zero elements. Most sparse codes run on *scalar* machines, or the scalar processors of vector computers, and make no use of standard vector processing facilities. A few computers, notably the CDC CYBER 205, have provided architectural support for sparse vectors in the form of addressing modes and special orders [7], but these orders have proved difficult to use in practice, mainly because of the *fill-in* problem. Fill-in occurs when, for example, two sparse vectors are added and the positions of the non-zero elements in the two vectors do not match, so that the result vector contains more elements than either of the source vectors. Since the extent of fill-in cannot be predicted at compile time, the compiler cannot know how much space to allocate to sparse vectors which are created during the running of a program.

2 Sparse Matrix Computation

Computation with sparse matrices whose pattern of sparsity is regular (*eg* matrices arising from partial differential equation solution by finite difference or finite element methods) can often be carried out efficiently on standard vector processor machines. Computation on matrices with irregular sparsity pattern is not amenable to these techniques, and so it is problems of this nature in particular that the proposed new architectural mechanisms address.

Irregular sparsity patterns arise from irregularity in the real-world problem being modelled, typical examples being found in engineering design simulations of physical structures or electrical circuits, and in Linear Programming (LP) problems. As examples of the type of vector and matrix calculation steps a sparse vector processor must support, we examine the steps of the *Product Form of Inverse (PFI) simplex* algorithm for Linear Programming, which include (in the re-invert step), the more general problem of the direct solution of a system of sparse linear equations.

2.1 Linear Programming

LP problems are typically very sparse. A large LP problem might involve a matrix of several thousand rows and 3 times as many columns, but with only 6 or so non-zeroes in each column. The four most computationally intensive steps of the PFI simplex algorithm are the so-called **BTRAN, pricing, FTRAN**, and **re-invert** steps, which typically take 30%, 35%, 20%, and 7% respectively of the total solution time. In the PFI method, the current inverse of the basis matrix is held as a series of *PFI matrices*, of special form, the product of which is the basis inverse. Each pivot step in the solution adds another PFI matrix to the series, so the series will usually contain many hundreds of matrices. Each of these has the same number of rows as the original problem matrix, and has the form of the unit matrix plus a single non-zero column, which may typically have a density between 1% and 20%. For each PFI matrix, only the non-zero column, plus a record of its position in the matrix, need be stored; these column vectors are generally known as the η (eta-) vectors.

2.1.1 BTRAN

This involves the post-multiplication of a vector by each of the PFI matrices in turn. Because of the special form of the PFI matrices, each multiplication step reduces to the replacement of one element of the vector being updated with the scalar product of that vector and the η vector of the relevant PFI matrix:

$$v_k \leftarrow \mathbf{v}.\eta$$

where k is the column position of the η vector in its PFI matrix.

2.1.2 Pricing

The result of the BTRAN operations is a *price vector*, and the pricing step involves the formation of the scalar product of this vector with each of the columns of the original problem matrix. The price vector will typically be 40% dense, while the original columns are very sparse - less than 0.1%.

2.1.3 FTRAN

This step involves the pre-multiplication of a vector (a column of the original problem matrix) by each of the PFI matrices in turn. Each multiplication step reduces to the summation of the vector with the relevant η vector, first scaled by a single element of the vector being updated:

$$\mathbf{v} \leftarrow \mathbf{v} + v_k * \eta$$

As above, k is the column position of η in the PFI matrix.

The vector being updated starts very sparse ($< 0.1\%$) and typically reaches 20% density at the end.

2.1.4 Re-invert

For reasons of numerical stability, it is necessary from time to time during the solution to replace the accumulated series of PFI matrices with an equivalent series of matrices of the same form derived by direct Gaussian Elimination on the current basis matrix. That matrix is a portion of the original problem matrix, and is therefore less than 0.1% dense. Each pivot step in the elimination will consist of the subtraction of a multiple of the pivot row from rows of the (updated) matrix with a non-zero in the pivot column:

$$B_{n*} \leftarrow B_{n*} - S * B_{p*}$$

where B_{n*} is a row of the matrix B with a non-zero in the pivot column, B_{p*} is the pivot row, and S is a scalar equal to the element of B_{n*} in the pivot column, divided by the pivot element.

Here, both vectors are of roughly equal sparsity (although if the Markowitz criterion *(see below)* is used to choose the pivot, the pivot row will tend to be somewhat sparser than the other). When the matrix is very sparse, the subtraction is fast, and it is crucial that one can rapidly determine which rows have a non-zero in the pivot column, and access the value of that non-zero, or this operation will dominate.

As the elimination proceeds, the part of the matrix remaining to be eliminated becomes more dense. This can lead to a drastic increase in the number of floating point operations required, both to complete the elimination, and in the remainder of the LP solution. It is therefore vital to minimize fill-in by careful choice of pivot at each step. However, except in the special case of a matrix which is symmetric positive definite, it is also necessary to consider numerical stability in choosing the pivots. The usual compromise is known as *threshold pivoting* [2]. A potential pivot is chosen by selecting an element whose row and column are both very sparse (the *Markowitz* criterion [9]), but the potential pivot is rejected if it is too much smaller than the largest element in its column. Operation of this method requires knowledge at each pivot step of the number of non-zeroes in each row and column of the updated matrix. It also requires that the each non-zero in the proposed pivot column be accessible in reasonable time.

3 ESP Sparse Vector Mechanisms

ESP is a vector processing system consisting of a scalar control processor and a separate vector processing pipeline, in a manner similar to the CYBER 205. However, ESP is not designed as a stand-alone computer, but rather as a high-performance back-end co-processor which executes routines to complete critical core sections of numerical programs, under control of a main program running on the host computer. These main programs may be compiled on the host, and a range of optimised ESP routines will be available as a library. The prototype is being designed as a co-processor for an ORION [6] minicomputer, but it is intended that the design be easily adaptable to operate with commonly available workstations as host machines.

The routines executed by the ESP co-processor consist of a mix of vector instructions, and more conventional scalar and control instructions. A typical vector instruction involves two source vectors and one destination vector. As in the CYBER 205 [7], each vector is accessed via a descriptor, but in ESP the descriptors contain more information about the vector, and are more reminiscent of those used in MU5 [10]. In order to support the kinds of operation required for efficient execution of LP and other sparse problems, two different storage mechanisms for vectors are provided in ESP and many instructions do not specify the storage mechanism used for their operands (this information is in the descriptor) but will work on vectors stored in either form. The descriptor also contains the necessary information for the storage controller to find the vector elements, and information on the type of the vector elements (single or double precision etc.).

The first storage mechanism is the **full** vector. Here a vector is stored in standard form as a sequence of values in store, so that an n-element vector occupies n storage locations, and the element of a vector with a specified index is found by offsetting from the vector base address specified in the descriptor. While efficient for access to any element from its index, this mechanism does not support fast access to the non-zero elements only, and of course wastes enormous amounts of store if vectors are very sparse. For sparse vectors, the **list** vector storage mechanism is used.

3.1 The List Vector Mechanism

3.1.1 Linked List Methods - General Strategy

Storing a sparse vector as a list of non-zero values, plus a corresponding list of the indices of the non-zeroes within the vector is attractive, as it incurs *no* storage or access overhead for the zeroes, and thus remains efficient even for very sparse vectors. Standard vector/vector operations, such as add, subtract and scalar product, can be performed directly on vectors stored in this form if *both* the index list and the value list of each operand are simultaneously accessible by the processor, with the lists maintained in order of ascending index.

This ordering of the lists is necessary for efficient implementation of vector/vector operations such as $C \leftarrow A + B$. These are implemented by streaming the lists A and B into the vector processor's arithmetic unit (AU), using additional hardware in the AU input stage to align A and B elements with equal indices. Thus in the example of the add instruction, illustrated in figure 1, if the first index in the A list is n, and that in the B list is m, then if $n < m$ the first element output is the first index/value pair from A. This element is discarded from the list A, while the list B is unchanged. Similarly for $m < n$, while if $n = m$, the output element is the sum of the elements at the front of the A and B queues, both of which are then discarded. Input vector index matching is also required for vector/vector multiplication

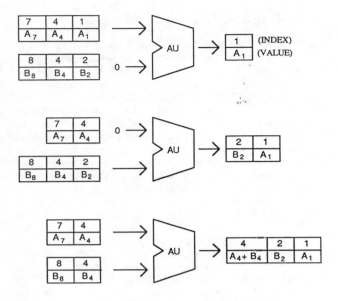

Figure 1: An ADD operation on list vectors

operations, but in this case a multiply step is only required if non-zeroes appear at the same index position in *both* input streams. If either or both of the vector lists were not in ascending index order, vector/vector arithmetic would involve searching for matching indices, and would be very inefficient.

As has already been noted, the amount of space needed to store a sparse vector in compressed form is not usually known at compile time. Nor is it in general known at run-time, even at the start of the operation producing the vector. In the add example above, the output list C may be as short as the longer input list or as long as the sum of the input list lengths, depending on the extent to which the postions of non-zeroes in the input vectors coincide. In some operations (*eg* the run-time compression of a vector from full storage format to list format) the resulting list length may be anywhere within much wider bounds. For the list storage format to be useful therefore, the amount of memory space allocated to a vector must be dynamically and automatically variable. The hardware must maintain a pool of free memory space, allocating extra space from the pool to vectors as required. Because it is impossible tell at the start of a vector operation how long the result list will be, it is not feasible to allocate at the start a single free block of store guaranteed to be large enough to hold the result. The solution adopted is to allow the index/value list comprising a single vector to reside in one or more *linked blocks* of memory locations. If the block allocated to hold the result at the start of an operation turns out to be too small, another block can be linked onto it. The unused portion of the last block allocated may be returned to the free pool.

Space may be freed by explicit de-allocation (under program control) of the memory used by temporary vectors which are no longer required. However, more often, it will become free automatically. To see why this is so, consider an operation of the type $A \leftarrow A + B$, and suppose vector A has non-zeroes at index positions 100 - 199, while B has non-zeroes at index positions 0 - 99. If the result vector is written into the memory blocks already occupied by A, then the first 100 output elements will overwrite the 100 non-zeroes of the original A. The first few of these will be in the arithmetic unit input pipe, but most will not yet have been read from memory, as the AU must deal with all 100 non-

zeroes of B before using up any from A. As a result, most of the required input elements will have been corrupted before they are read. To avoid this, when a vector appears as both an input and result of an operation, the result vector must be allocated new space, and the original space used by that vector automatically returned to the free pool at the end of the operation.

3.1.2 Implementing Linked Lists in a Single-level Memory Environment

These list structures can be implemented in a simple way by treating memory as a pool of fixed size (small) blocks, each with a single link field. The free space is a linked list of unused blocks. As a vector operation produces its result, that result is written into the first locations on the free list, following links as required. The result vector's descriptor is updated to hold a pointer to the start of the vector list. The unused part of the final block in the result vector is wasted; this is the reason for small blocks. Reclaimed space is linked onto the start or end of the free list. The hardware required to support these operations is simple, and the operations of allocating new space and reclaiming old space are both very fast, each requiring only the updating of processor pointer registers, and the alteration of two links in memory.

Matrix codes tend to use many operations of the type $A \leftarrow B \text{ op } A$. For example, every elimination step in Gaussian Elimination causes a vector to be re-written, usually with a small increase in density, and for reasons in explained section 3.1.1 above, these re-writing steps involve the allocation of new space for the updated vector, and the reclaiming of space previously used. As space from vectors is reclaimed and later used again by vectors of different length, the blocks on the free list will become thoroughly mixed. As a result, the blocks used to store any vector will be randomly distributed throughout the whole memory space. In a single-level memory environment this may not matter, but in a hierarchical memory environment it is very likely to lead to thrashing of the paging/cacheing system. We believe that to restrict ESP to problems which will fit into a restricted single-level memory space (or which can be explicitly partitioned into smaller problems which fit) would be a mistake. We have therefore rejected this simple implementation in favour of mechanisms which retain more locality of reference.

3.1.3 Implementing Linked Lists in a Hierarchical Memory Environment

In this implementation, the free list remains a linked list of blocks of free memory, and allocation of new space for a result vector proceeds as above, except that blocks may now be of any length. Any space in the last block allocated (to a result vector) which remains unused at the end of the operation is left, as a smaller block, on the front of the free list. The key to maximising locality of reference lies in ensuring that the blocks on the free list remain as large as possible, so that the space allocated to a new vector consists of a small number of large blocks; this requires a more complex de-allocation algorithm. In general, a vector to be de-allocated itself consists of a list of blocks, and the de-allocation algorithm must check, for each of these blocks, whether is is *adjacent in memory* to a block (or blocks) already on the free list, and if it is, must merge the blocks. A simple way of achieving this merging de-allocation is to maintain the blocks in the vector lists and in the free list in order of ascending memory address (*ie* links from block to block are always *forward* through the memory address space). The de-allocation algorithm may then merge the two sorted lists of blocks in a straightforward way.

In ESP, this mechanism is supported by hardware interposed

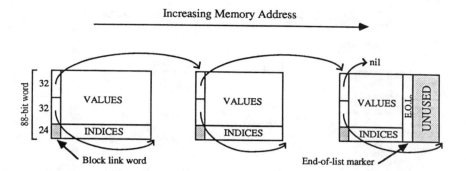

Figure 2: Structure of linked list vector

between the arithmetic unit and the memory. Vector elements are held in memory as an index/value pair, in a single memory word of 88 bits (64 bits for the value, and at 24 for the index). In addition to straight index/value pairs, memory words may hold an *end-of-list marker*, or they may hold *block link* words. A list vector is held in a series of blocks of consecutive memory words, the final word in the list being an end-of-list marker (see Fig. 2). The first word of each block is a block link word, and these words contain *two* pointers, each of which is a 32 bit (or larger) virtual memory address, known as the *external* pointer and the *internal* pointer. The external pointer holds the address of the first word (*ie* the word containing the block link) of the next block in the list, and is there to maintain the list linkage. The external pointer in the last block of a list holds the special value **nil**. The internal pointer holds the address of the first word *after* the end of the current block, and is there because the de-allocation algorithm needs to know the size of blocks to perform concatenation of adjacent blocks. Because the blocks are in order of increasing memory address, all pointers point forwards. Vector descriptors contain, in addition to other information about vector type and size, a pointer to the current position of the first word of the first block in the vector list. The free list is of identical structure, and a pointer to the start of it is maintained in a register.

As the AU produces index/value pairs as the results of a vector operation, these are written into the free list. The hardware for performing this contains a small number of pointer registers to keep track of the position in the free list currently being written to, and the block linkage. Eventually, the AU will signal the end of the result vector, by producing an element with the form of the special end-of-list marker. This is written out in the normal way, and a check is performed to determine how much free space remains in the block currently being written to. If this space is less than the minimum block size, it is left on the end of the result vector, otherwise it is reclaimed (by writing new block link words), and left at the front of the free list.

The de-allocation hardware, which reclaims vector space for the free list, requires two pointer registers (**A** and **B**), plus a small number of working registers. The algorithm merges two ordered lists of blocks - the free list, and the vector list being de-allocated. At the start, the free list pointer register is updated to point to the lower of the two list starting addresses. **A** also points to this address; **B** points to the other list. During the algorithm, the pointers **A** and **B** proceed along the two lists. The external pointers in the block link words are adjusted to merge the two lists, while the internal pointers are examined to check for contiguous blocks, and updated to merge such blocks.

The algorithm terminates when one list is exhausted, and at this point, all blocks are linked, in order of increasing memory address, onto the list pointed to by the free list pointer. The maximum number of algorithm iterations will equal the total number of blocks on both lists which occupy memory locations between the lower starting address and the lower end address of the two lists.

3.1.4 Efficiency Considerations

The transfer of operand elements between memory and the arithmetic unit can be made as efficient for list structured vectors as it is for vectors stored in the usual full form. Because the link word is at the *start* of the block, if blocks are above a certain minimum size, there is time to emit the start address of the next block to the memory sufficiently far in advance to avoid a gap in the address generator→memory→AU pipeline. The writing of result elements back to memory may also be effectively pipelined.

Many vector processing systems use interleaved banks of memory to achieve the memory bandwidth required to run the arithmetic unit at full speed and in ESP, within a block of a list vector, interleaving will work effectively. However, even though the link address is known well in advance, if the first word of the next block falls into the wrong bank, there will be a hiatus in the interleaving. To avoid this, it is sensible to restrict all blocks to starting in a particular bank, and all pointers are thus multiples of the number of banks. For example, in an eight-way interleaved memory, to allow full use of interleaving and pipelining, pointers should be restricted to be a multiple of 16.

A potential performance limitation in the system so far described is the de-allocation operation (a de-allocate must be performed after most vector operations). How long this takes depends on the number of blocks on the free list and on the vector list being disposed, and on the start and end positions of both lists; in the worst case, the algorithm must examine every block on both lists to complete the de-allocation. However, there are several ways of mitigating the delays caused by this operation.

Firstly, note that the list restructuring remaining to be performed at any time during de-allocation takes place *beyond* the locations pointed to by **A** and **B**. Since the new free list pointer is set up at the *start* of the de-allocate, writing the result of the next vector operation into the free list can commence almost immediately after any pending de-allocate has started, and can continue concurrently with the de-allocate, subject to the condition that each free block used by the write must start at a memory address *less than* the value of pointer **A** (which in the particular algorithm used, is itself always less than **B**). If this condition fails, the write must be delayed until it is again satisfied. In this way, so long as

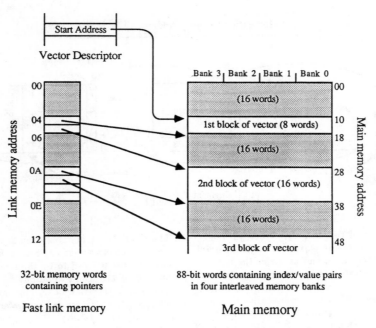

Figure 3: List vector storage with separate link memory

the de-allocation of vectors normally takes less time than writing them, de-allocation need not necessarily delay the processor.

For de-allocation to work concurrently with writing (which is also often concurrent with the reading of one or two streams of input operands *into* the arithmetic unit), there must be plenty of memory bandwidth, and since all pointers are restricted to one bank of memory (all blocks start in the same bank), the band-width requirement is considerably greater for that bank than for the other banks. One way of providing this extra bandwidth is to provide a completely separate memory to hold the block link words, as illustrated in figure 3. Here, the words in the link memory are 32 bits wide, which is large enough to hold one pointer only. There is one word of link memory per four words of main memory, and the internal and external pointers of a list vector block which starts at main memory address a are at link memory addresses $a/4$ and $a/4+1$ respectively. Since every block uses two link memory words, the minimum block size is 8 words. Virtual to real mappings must be maintained in parallel on both mem-ories, but the link memory need not be accessible by the vector or scalar processors, only by the memory controller. Of course, if blocks are large, large amounts of the link memory will be un-used, and so the dual memory system introduces an overhead of wasted memory area. However, this overhead is more than com-pensated for by the main memory bus bandwidth gained, and by the simpler bus arrangements which result from the separation of the two memory types.

Finally, alternative deallocation strategies have been consid-ered. By linking lists in both directions, and tagging the block link words in free blocks, it is possible to deallocate a list of blocks in a time proportional to the number of blocks in the list being deallocated, independent of the number of free list blocks (see for example, memory management algorithms in [8]). Because, as described above, deallocation can be overlapped with vector writing, we do not think that the extra complexity of dealloca-tion hardware would be justified. However, simulations of ESP's mechanisms, and we hope, the prototype hardware itself, will be flexible enough to experiment with alternatives in this respect.

3.2 The LP problem on ESP

List vectors do not waste store, and they provide immediate and implicit identification of the non-zero positions of the vector. An operation like the Gaussian Elimination step $B_{n*} \leftarrow B_{n*} - S * B_{p*}$, where both vectors are of roughly equal sparsity, will execute efficiently using list vector storage and a single ESP vector in-struction, which operates by streaming operand elements into the arithmetic unit in the manner described in section 3.1.1 above. This is also true of other vector/vector operations on vectors in list form, where both vectors are of roughly equal sparsity. In the *pricing* step of LP (section 2.1 above), however, the price vector is much denser than the column vectors it is multiplied into. To execute the multiplication by streaming in two list vectors would be inefficient, as most of the elements of the price vector would be discarded because there is a zero in the corresponding position of the column vector.

If one vector is several times denser than the other, the scalar product operation is more efficient with the denser vector stored in *full* form. The sparser vector (stored in list form) moves into the vector unit element by element, and the index fields of the elements are used to offset into the denser vector, using normal indexed addressing (this is similar to the *gather* operation sup-ported in hardware in several vector supercomputers [7]). Obvi-ously, access to the elements of the denser vector is slower than streaming a vector out of memory, because the elements accessed are in non-consecutive locations, and memory bank interleaving will be interrupted, and so this method of access is only prefer-able where the sparsity of the two vectors differs by a factor of four or more.

Performance on list vector/full vector operations can be fur-ther increased, if the same full vector is to be operated on many times over, by providing a fast access vector register near the arithmetic unit, to hold the full vector operand. This reduces memory bandwidth use, and circumvents the problem of failure of interleaving.

The usefulness of a vector register is even clearer in the case of the *BTRAN* and *FTRAN* steps. BTRAN also requires a scalar product of a sparse η vector with a vector which is (for most of the BTRAN steps) less sparse, and then requires that one element of that less sparse vector be replaced with the result of the product. This final step requires access to an element of the vector with specified index, and is clearly *very* inefficient on a list vector. However, it can be carried out with ease if the vector is stored in full form in a register. The result of the complete series of BTRAN steps is the price vector, which is thus conveniently in the register ready for the pricing step.

FTRAN requires a summation of a sparse η vector (scaled) with a vector which for most of the FTRAN steps is denser than the η vector. The scaling factor to be applied to the η vector is an element of the denser vector, specified by its index value. It is therefore useful to store the vector being updated in full form in the register, to allow indexed access to these scaling elements.

Finally, the *re-invert* step provides special problems. These cannot be overlooked, as it is intended that ESP should be generally useful on a wide range of sparse matrix problems, including the solution of large sparse linear systems of equations by Gaussian Elimination, which corresponds to the re-invert step of LP.

3.3 Sparse Gaussian Elimination on ESP

In some cases, in particular when the matrix to be factorised is symmetric positive definite, it is possible to decide which elements to use as pivots on sparsity grounds only, before the elimination starts [2]. The matrix may be permuted so that pivoting proceeds down the diagonal, and it is possible to work out in advance (ignoring cancellation during the subtraction steps) the positions of non-zeroes in each pivot column. Elimination will then be very efficient on ESP with the rows of the matrix stored as list vectors. Many Gaussian Elimination implementations on standard computers need to switch over from 'sparse code' to 'dense code' when the density of the filling matrix reaches a critical value. This is not necessary on ESP - operations on list vectors, such as that illustrated in figure 1, remain more efficient than equivalent operations on full vectors, however much the vectors fill in.

As described in section 2.1.4 above, Gaussian Elimination on matrices which are not symmetric positive definite requires knowledge of the number of non-zeroes in each row and column of the partially eliminated matrix, and also requires rapid access to the non-zeroes in each column. In this case, the number and position of non-zeroes in each row and column of the matrix as elimination proceeds cannot be determined in advance. If the matrix is stored within ESP as row vectors in list form, then the elimination steps themselves are efficient, but choosing the pivot is very inefficient. This is because the number and positions of the non-zeroes in each *row* are available (vector descriptors include a field specifying the number of non-zeroes in the vector), but not the corresponding information for each *column*. It is also not possible to access directly the non-zeroes in a specified column - one must search down the row vectors to find them. To support the pivot choosing algorithm, codes for Gaussian Elimination of sparse indefinite matrices which run on *scalar* machines normally store the matrix as a linked structure linked in two directions, along both rows and columns. However, to provide links to matrix elements by column is directly at variance with the dynamic nature of list vector storage in ESP - if a row of the matrix is operated on by a vector instruction, it will move in memory, invalidating any pointers to its elements. An extra facility has therefore been added to the vector processor in ESP, known as the *sideways list unit (SLU)*, which supports maintenance of lists of non-zero *indices* (but not values) by column as the elimination proceeds (ignoring cancellation during subtractions).

3.4 The Sideways List Unit

The SLU keeps updated counts of the *number* of non-zeroes per column of a matrix, and their positions, throughout Gaussian Elimination by rows. The list of non-zero positions in each column is kept in main memory as a linked list of single memory locations each holding a non-zero position (24 bits) and a link to the next word on the list (32 bits), as illustrated in figure 4. These 56-bit pairs are held in the 64-bit value field of locations of a vector which is itself stored in the ESP list format described in section 3.1.3 above. Many such lists of non-zero positions can be stored inside a single ESP list vector and, since the non-zero position lists do *not* have to be linked forwards in memory, a single non-zero position list can extend through several ESP list vectors. The reason for storing the non-zero position lists *inside* ESP list vectors is that memory space for extending the non-zero position vectors can then be allocated using the standard list vector allocation mechanism, and when elimination is complete, all the space can be de-allocated by de-allocating all the list vectors used for this purpose.

After the first pivot is chosen, but before the elimination steps using that pivot row are executed, a list vector is produced (using a vector instruction which generates a vector of specified length) with number of non-zeroes equal to the maximum number of new non-zeroes that the elimination with that pivot row can possibly produce. (That number is the multiple of the number of non-zeroes in the pivot row and the number of non-zeroes in the pivot column, and has already been calculated during pivot choice using the Markowitz criterion.) The descriptor of this list vector is passed to the SLU, so that the vector can be used as space into which to expand the lists of non-zeroes in the matrix columns, during the elimination steps with the first pivot row. The vector is known as the *SLU space vector*.

A single elimination step consists of the operation $B_{n*} \leftarrow B_{n*} - S * B_{p*}$. Whenever the arithmetic unit produces a non-zero in an index position in the result vector B_{n*} which contained a zero in the left-hand input operand, that element is a new non-zero, and its index, i, (its column position in the matrix) is passed to the SLU. The SLU contains a register holding the row number n, and three vector registers, one (the *count register*) holding a count of the number of non-zeroes in each column of the matrix, the second (the *base register*) holding the address of the start of the list of non-zero positions for each column, and the third (the *address register*) holding, for each column, a pointer to the address of the next free location in the list of non-zeroes in that column. On receiving an index i from the AU, the SLU increments the non-zero count for column i, and adds the row number n of the new non-zero onto the non-zero list for column i, by writing it, togther with a link to the next free location in the SLU space vector, to the address pointed to by the ith entry in the address register. It then updates that entry in the address register, loading into it the address of the next free location in the space vector. Since the space vector is an ESP list vector, determining the next free location may involve following a link to the next block of the space vector.

When all the elimination steps with the first pivot row are complete, the SLU space vector may still contain some unused locations, as the real amount of fill-in may have been less than the possible maximum calculated at the start. The SLU maintains a count of the number of locations remaining in the space vector. After the second pivot is chosen, the maximum possible fill-in during elimination with *that* pivot may be calculated, and a new list vector generated and queued for use by the SLU, to replace the current SLU space vector when it is full. This is repeated for

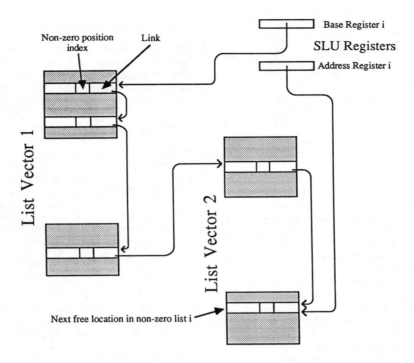

Figure 4: The structure of non-zero position lists

each new pivot, and ensures that the SLU will never run out of space.

The information maintained by the SLU is accessed by ESP's scalar/control processor during pivot choice. The new non-zero counts for all the columns in which there were non-zeroes in the previous pivot row (these are the only columns which can have had extra non-zeroes added during the elimination steps with that pivot row) are read from the SLU to enable pivot choice by the Markowitz criterion. The positions of the non-zeroes in the chosen pivot column are then read from the SLU, which itself reads them direct from main memory, following the links. The *values* of the non-zeroes must be found by using the vector pipeline to search down the relevant rows until the correct column index is reached (using a vector instruction which extracts from a vector the element with a specified index). Depending on sparsity, these operations are likely to involve an overhead of perhaps 100% on top of the time for the subtraction steps of the elimination, and this compares very favourably with the total time required for pivot choice (compared with elimination time) in scalar Gaussian Elimination codes for sparse indefinite matrices [2].

Before the elimination steps start, the SLU must be fed the positions of the non-zeroes in the original matrix, and this is achieved by first allocating a space vector large enough to contain all the non-zeroes in that matrix. The SLU registers are then initialized by loading zeroes into the count register, and loading the base and address registers with locations taken from the space vector. The operation $B_{n*} \leftarrow 0 + B_{n*}$ is then performed on each row of the matrix. Here, the left-hand operand is always zero, so every non-zero position in B_{n*} is passed to the SLU to be added to the relevant column non-zero position list.

4 Performance

Mechanisms similar to those described above for operating directly on compressed sparse vectors have been implemented in the *software* of sparse matrix programs for many years [1, 3, 11, 2]. Such programs run on scalar processors and do not use vector instructions. By providing hardware to implement the vector loops in these programs as single vector instructions, with separate hardware units operating in parallel on the subfunctions which scalar implementations control with separate instructions, we expect to achieve an order of magnitude improvement in the arithmetic rate of these codes.

More recently, there has been interest in the use of the hardware vector indirect addressing facilities (*scatter/gather*) provided in some vector machines (eg CYBER 205, IBM 3090VF), to support sparse vector operations. Because of the bank conflict problem (see section 3.2 above), such operations will always be several times slower than ESP's sparse vector instructions, if the vectors concerned are of roughly equal sparsity. Where the sparsity of the two operand vectors differs markedly, indirect addressing is relatively more efficient, and ESP's provision of a large vector register allows such operations to proceed at the full rate of the arithmetic pipeline.

A further problem (on existing machines) with vector instructions involving indirection into one of the operand vectors is the long instruction startup time, due to the long effective pipeline length. Because LP problems involve sparse vectors with a very small number of non-zeroes, we have been concerned to keep vector startup times to a minimum, and have therefore decided to implement the vector pipeline as several short, independently controlled, sections. A queue is provided for vector instructions which have been issued by the control processor, but not yet executed, and there is a mechanism for the control processor to determine whether a particular vector instruction has completed.

Together, these provisions allow us to have several vector instructions flowing through the pipeline at once, substantially reducing effective start-up times. Simulations are underway to quantify the resulting speed-up on representative problems, and to determine the optimum number of pipeline sections.

The detailed design of the prototype ESP is now underway. This will be built in slow technology (clock speed 100-200ns), using standard VLSI arithmetic components, and will achieve peak speeds of up to 20 MFLOPs. The prototype will allow us to make a thorough investigation of the new mechanisms on real, large, sparse matrix problems.

5 Conclusions

Pipelined vector processors achieve their high performance in part by taking advantage of the storage of vector elements in sequential memory locations. The mechanisms developed for ESP allow this advantage to be maintained in the case of sparse vectors, by providing a new form of vector storage, the *list* vector. The list form wastes no space for the zeroes in a vector, and unlike compressed sparse vector storage mechanisms in other machines, solves the problem of fill-in.

ESP supports all the normally found vector/vector operations, including two operator functions such as scalar product and the Gaussian Elimination step $B_{n*} \leftarrow B_{n*} - S * B_{p*}$, as single vector instructions which will operate directly and efficiently on full form vectors, list form vectors, or a combination of the two. The operations work efficiently over the whole range of non-zero densities. This allows the advantages of vector processing to be extended to the case of sparse vectors.

However, some particular computations commonly performed on sparse matrices, such as the Gaussian Elimination of an indefinite matrix, require that information be maintained about the matrix as a two-dimensional object, rather than simply as a set of one-dimensional vectors, throughout the program's execution. Although it is possible to write algorithms which treat the matrix symmetrically, allowing it to be viewed both by row and by column, fully symmetrical treatment is not possible without sacrificing the fundamental advantage of sequential vector element storage. A compromise solution to this particular problem has therefore been developed, which retains the full advantages of the *one-dimensional* list vector system described above, but in addition allows information about the non-zero distribution in the *two-dimensional* matrix to be maintained in easily accessible form. The mechanism which supports this, the *sideways list unit*, has been developed with the specific requirements of Gaussian Elimination codes in mind, but it is expected to prove useful in other sparse matrix computations.

There has recently been interest in putting sparse problems on to *parallel* processors [4, 5]. We believe that, whilst coarse grain parallelism will clearly enable the solution of very much larger problems, the increasing scale of silicon circuit integration will mean that individual processors can cost-effectively incorporate extra hardware to exploit parallelism at the level of single vector or matrix operations. This is the level of parallelism at which ESP derives its advantages. Such individual processors may then be connected to work in parallel on larger problems.

Acknowledgements

The ESP project is a collaborative project between the Departments of Computer Science and Mathematics at the University of Edinburgh, and High Level Hardware Ltd., of Oxford. The authors would like to acknowledge the support of High Level Hardware, and of the UK Science and Engineering Research Council.

References

[1] James R. Bunch and Donald J. Rose, editors. *Sparse Matrix Computations*. Academic Press, 1976.

[2] Thomas F. Coleman. *Large Sparse Numerical Optimization*. Lecture Notes in Computer Science. Springer Verlag, 1984.

[3] Iain S. Duff and G.W. Stewart, editors. *Sparse Matrix Proceedings 1978*. SIAM, Philadelphia, 1979.

[4] H. Amano et al. (SM)^2 : Sparse matrix solving machine. In *ACM Proc. 10th Symposium on Computer Architecture*, pages 213–220. ACM, 1983.

[5] H. Amano et al. (SM)^2-II : A new version of the sparse matrix solving machine. In *ACM Proc. 12th Symposium on Computer Architecture*, pages 100–107. ACM, 1985.

[6] High Level Hardware Ltd., Headington, Oxford, UK. *ORION Time Sharing Manual*, 1986.

[7] R.N. Ibbett and N.P. Topham. *Architecture of High Performance Computers*, volume 1. Macmillan, Basingstoke, Hampshire, UK, 1989.

[8] D.E. Knuth. *The Art of Computer Programming*, volume 1 - Fundamental Algorithms. Addison-Wesley, 2 edition, 1973.

[9] H.M. Markowitz. The elimination form of the inverse and its application to linear programming. *Management Science*, 3:255–269, 1957.

[10] D. Morris and R.N. Ibbett. *The MU5 Computer System*. Macmillan, London, 1979.

[11] Ole Østerby and Zahari Zlatev. *Direct Methods for Sparse Matrices*. Lecture Notes in Computer Science. Springer-Verlag, 1983.

A Dynamic Storage Scheme for Conflict-Free Vector Access

D. T. Harper III* and D. A. Linebarger

Erik Jonsson School of Engineering and Computer Science
The University of Texas at Dallas, Mail Stop MP-32
Richardson, Texas 75083 USA
(214) 690–2893
dth@engc1.dal.utexas.edu

Abstract

Previous investigations into data storage schemes have focused on finding a storage scheme that permits conflict-free access for a set of frequently encountered access patterns. This paper considers an alternative approach. Rather than forcing a single storage scheme to be used for all access patterns, conflict-free accesses of any constant stride can be made by selecting a storage scheme for each vector based on the accessing patterns used with that vector.

By factoring the stride into two components, one a power of 2 and the other relatively prime to 2, a storage scheme can be synthesized which allows conflict-free access to the vector using the specified stride. All such schemes are based on a variation of the row rotation mechanism proposed by Budnik and Kuck[1]. Each storage scheme is based on two parameters, one describes the type of rotation to perform and the other describes the amount of memory to be rotated as a single block. Hardware required to implement this storage scheme is efficient.

The performance of the memory under access strides other than the stride used to specify the storage scheme is also considered. This models a vector being accessed with multiple strides, in particular the row/column access of a matrix, and situations when the stride can not be determined prior to initializing the vector. Simulation results show that if a single buffer is added to each memory port then the average performance of the dynamic scheme surpasses that of the interleaved scheme for arbitrary stride accesses.

For dynamic storage schemes to be effective, the compiler must be able to detect information about the stride of vector accesses. In general, this is within the capabilities of current vectorizing compilers. Dynamic storage schemes also may allow more flexibility in program transformations performed by vectorizing compilers during optimization.

Introduction

The performance of heavily pipelined vector supercomputers is highly dependent upon the architecture's ability to rapidly move data in and out of main memory. Because processor speeds are substantially higher than memory speeds, it has been necessary to develop architectural features to support parallelism in the memory subsystems. These

* This work was supported by Texas Advanced Research Program grant number 10897–701.

features include superword accesses and parallel memory modules. This paper considers a problem associated with the use of parallel memory modules.

The topic of vector accesses in parallel memory systems has been studied by many previous investigators. Most have centered their investigation on the question of the mapping between addresses and physical storage locations in the memory. The algorithm used to describe this mapping is often referred to as the *storage scheme* of the system. The simplest storage scheme is the low-order interleaved (also referred to simply as interleaved) scheme which maps address a into memory module $a \bmod N$, where N is the number of memory modules in the system. This scheme, shown in figure 1, has been successfully implemented in many high-performance systems. In the following discussion, memory is viewed as a two dimensional matrix consisting of *rows* and *modules*. The term *module address* refers to the module number into which the address is mapped and the term *row address* refers to the position of the storage location relative to the beginning of the module. For example, in figure 1 the row address of element 9 is 2 (addressing begins at 0) and the module address of 9 is 1.

M_0	M_1	M_2	M_3
0	1	2	3
4	5	6	7
8	9	10	11
12	13	14	15
16	17	18	19
20	21	22	23
24	25	26	27
28	29	30	31

Figure 1: Low-order interleaved storage scheme.

The rationale for using the interleaved scheme is two-fold:

1. A parallel memory system allows concurrent access to multiple data items by placing items which can be used in parallel in different modules. If this can be done such that N items can be accessed in a single memory cycle, a *conflict-free* access is said to have occurred. The assumption is made that addresses can be presented to all of the modules in parallel and that, after a delay equal to the cycle time of the memory, data can be removed in parallel from all of the modules. Previous work discussing features of interconnection networks capable of this has been presented by several authors [2] [3][4]. One of the most common accessing patterns, particularly in vector operations, is sequential access, in which the first datum needed is found at address a, the next at address $a + 1$, *etc*. In this case, the interleaved scheme permits conflict-free access.

2. The interleaved scheme is a simple mapping. Parallel memory systems usually use an address composed of two fields. One field,

72

the module address, determines which module contains the physical storage location and the other field, the row address, determines the offset of the storage location within the module. Each of these fields must be computed from the original address. When N is of the form $N = 2^n$, for some non-negative integer n, this computation is trivial for the interleaved scheme. The n low-order bits of the address form the module address field and the remaining high-order bits form the row address.

Unfortunately, interleaved schemes do not perform as well when other accessing patterns are encountered. The *stride* of an access is defined to be the distance between successive addresses; this paper only considers access patterns with constant strides. The sequential access pattern is said to be a stride 1 access. A stride 2 access references alternate addresses, stride 3 accesses reference every third address, *etc.* The interleaved scheme provides conflict-free access as long as the stride, S, is relatively prime to N. If S and N are not relatively prime, *collisions* occur in the memory when a reference is mapped to a module which is busy processing (reading or writing) a previous reference. This can cause substantial degradation in the performance of the system [5].

One solution to this problem is to *skew* the storage scheme of the system. This was proposed by Budnik and Kuck [1] and maps addresses to physical locations as shown in figure 2. Several authors have proposed storage schemes which are variants on figure 2. These schemes are collectively referred to as skewing schemes in the literature. Shapiro [6] presents a classification of these schemes and several investigations have considered properties of such schemes [7] [8]. In this paper, the term skewed storage scheme refers to the scheme shown in figure 2.

M_0	M_1	M_2	M_3
0	1	2	3
7	4	5	6
10	11	8	9
13	14	15	12
16	17	18	19
23	20	21	22
26	27	24	25
29	30	31	28

Figure 2: Skewed storage scheme

In figure 2, address a is mapped to module $(a + \lfloor \frac{a}{N} \rfloor) \bmod N$. As noted in [1], this mapping allows conflict-free access for strides which were not conflict-free in the interleaved scheme. If N is prime, a larger set of conflict-free patterns results than when N is composite. This fact was used in the design of the Burroughs Scientific Processor [9]. However, the use of a prime number of modules has several disadvantages, the primary one being that the address to storage location mapping becomes computationally expensive [10][11]. To deal with these problems a different approach to achieving conflict-free accesses is proposed.

Dynamic Storage Schemes

To date, investigations into storage schemes have discussed the use of a single scheme for all memory accesses. For a system where the number of memory modules in the system is given by $N = 2^n$, no single scheme has been found which allows conflict-free access to vectors for all strides. For this reason, it is proposed that multiple storage schemes be used within a single system. The scheme to be used with each vector is chosen dynamically, and is based on the system's perception of the vector's access patterns. Deciding what stride will be used to access a vector can be done by current vectorizing compilers. The following sections show how to synthesize a storage scheme for conflict-free accesses to the vector once the access stride is known.

To achieve this goal, several problems must be solved. A family of storage schemes, which collectively permit a vector to be accessed with both stride 1 (to initially load the vector) and the stride required to operate on the specified subset of the vector, must be identified. Second, a mapping must be found which determines the appropriate storage scheme to use for each stride. Finally, hardware support must be provided for the use of multiple storage schemes. In concept, the use of multiple storage schemes should not be seen as a disadvantage. Several vector architectures force the stride of an access to be defined in a processor register before a vector reference occurs. The specification of a storage scheme, discussed in detail later, is compact and can be done concurrently.

Conflict-Free Storage Schemes

The goal of this section is to develop a family of stride-dependent or dynamic storage schemes which allow conflict-free access to a vector using any predetermined stride. Let S be the stride used to access the vector and let $N = 2^n$ be the number of memory modules in the system.

Development of the storage scheme begins by considering the interleaved scheme as shown in figure 1. It was seen that the performance of the interleaved scheme degraded when S was not relatively prime to N. In order to see the relationship between S and N, it is useful to consider a particular factorization of S.

Let $S = \sigma 2^s$ for $(\sigma, 2) = 1$; the notation $(\sigma, 2)$ represents the greatest common factor of σ and 2. This factorization exists and is unique for all integers $S > 0$. For the moment, assume that $\sigma = 1$. This means that S is of the form $S = 2^s$. The situation for $\sigma > 1$ will be discussed later.

If $S = 2^s$, it is useful to partition the set of strides into two categories; strides which have at least one access per row and strides which have fewer than one access per row (accesses do not occur in every row). The first case occurs when $S \leq N$, or when $s \leq n$. The second case occurs when $s > n$.

Case 1, $s \leq n$:

The following discussion assumes an initial access to the first element of a vector. This element is stored in module 0. No loss of generality results from this assumption.

Assuming an interleaved scheme, the sequence of module addresses is: $0, 2^s, ..., 2^{n-s-1}2^s$. After 2^{n-s} references the sequence repeats since $2^{n-s}2^s$ is congruent modulo N to 0. In the interleaved scheme the $(2^{n-s})^{th}$ access falls in module 0 of the row following the initial row. This causes a collision with the 0th access. However, if the second row is skewed relative to the initial row then rather than referencing module 0, the $(2^{n-s})^{th}$ access references module 1. Skewing the second row relative to the first allows $2 \cdot 2^{n-s}$ accesses to be made before a conflict occurs. Each reference in the second 2^{n-s} accesses goes to the module adjacent to the module of the corresponding reference in the first 2^{n-s} accesses. To permit N accesses to occur before a conflict occurs (the condition for conflict-free accesses), it is necessary to skew 2^s rows relative to each other. Therefore, a conflict-free storage scheme for any stride $S = 2^s$, $s \leq n$, can be generated by circularly rotating each row. Row r should be rotated $r \bmod 2^s$ places relative to its state in the interleaved scheme. Figure 3 shows an example of a dynamic storage scheme for $N = 8$ and $S = 4$.

Case 2, $s > n$:

In this case the situation is somewhat different: there is a maximum of one access per row. For convenience and without loss of generality, it is assumed that the initial module address is again 0. The sequence of modules referenced is: $0, 2^s, 2 \cdot 2^s, ...$ Since $2^s = k2^n = kN$, it is clear that all references fall in the same module and maximum performance degradation occurs. Again, the technique of row rotation is used to distribute references over all of the modules so that conflict-free accesses can be made. However, the rotation pattern is different from the previous case. This time, blocks of contiguous rows will be rotated relative to preceding blocks. In particular, blocks of 2^{s-n} rows are rotated as single entities. Note that 2^{s-n} is exactly the number of rows between consecutive elements required in the stride S access. This rotation pattern serves to place consecutive accesses in adjacent modules. Over a period

73

M_0	M_1	M_2	M_3	M_4	M_5	M_6	M_7
0	1	2	3	4	5	6	7
15	8	9	10	11	12	13	14
22	23	16	17	18	19	20	21
29	30	31	24	25	26	27	28
32	33	34	35	36	37	38	39
47	40	41	42	43	44	45	46
54	55	48	49	50	51	52	53

Figure 3: Dynamic storage scheme for $N = 8$ and $S = 4$.

M_0	M_1	M_2	M_3
0	1	2	3
4	5	6	7
11	8	9	10
15	12	13	14
18	19	16	17
22	23	20	21
25	26	27	24
29	30	31	28
32	33	34	35

Figure 4: Dynamic storage scheme for $N = 4$ and $S = 8$.

of N accesses each module is referenced exactly once and conflict-free access is obtained. An example of a 4 memory scheme configured for a stride 8 access is shown in figure 4.

The schemes described in cases 1 and 2 provide for conflict-free accessing for any stride of the form $S = 2^s$.

Now the restriction placed on σ is removed and strides of the form $S = \sigma 2^s, (\sigma, 2) = 1$, are discussed. Assuming the schemes described in cases 1 and 2 have been applied, consider the sequence of module addresses generated by an access of stride $\hat{S} = 2^s$. Let this sequence be indicated by $\hat{M} = \hat{a_0}, \hat{a_1}, \ldots$ This sequence is periodic with a period of length N and each period contains exactly one address equal to i, $0 \leq i < N$. If an access is made from the same initial address but with a stride $S = \sigma \hat{S} = \sigma 2^s$, then the sequence of module addresses for this access, M, is formed by selecting every σ^{th} element from $\hat{M}$. That is, the ith element of M is given by $a_i = \hat{a}_{i_\sigma}$. Because σ is relatively prime to N, any N consecutive elements of M will reference N different memory modules. Therefore, stride S accesses are conflict-free.

Stride to Storage Scheme Mapping

The solution to the problem of finding an algorithm which maps each stride into a storage scheme has been outlined in the previous section. In the cases above, the proposed storage schemes can be characterized using two parameters

The first parameter, w_{max}, indicates the maximum rotation a row can have relative to the first row. For the $s \geq n$ case, this parameter is always N. For the $s < n$ case, w_{max} is given by 2^s. Another way to view this parameter is that rotations are always performed modulo w_{max}.

$$w_{max} = min(2^s, N) \qquad (1)$$

The second parameter, B, specifies the number of rows to rotate as a single block. When $s < n$, B is always 1; when $s \geq n$, B is equal to 2^{s-n}.

$$B = \lceil 2^{s-n} \rceil \qquad (2)$$

Knowledge of these two parameters is sufficient to generate a conflict-free storage scheme for any constant stride vector access. Because both of the parameters are functions only of n and s, determination of n and s is also sufficient to generate the appropriate storage scheme.

Hardware Support

Providing hardware support so that a dynamic storage scheme can be implemented efficiently requires a mechanism to transform addresses into physical storage locations. To perform this transformation, the relationship of s to n must be known. Since n, the base 2 logarithm of the number of memory modules, is generally considered fixed and known, it is only necessary to compute s. This computation is simple when it is noted that s is merely the exponent of the largest power of 2 which is a factor of the stride; s can be found by dividing S by 2 until the remainder is non-zero. The hardware required to do this is a shift register which is initially loaded with the stride and performs right shifts. Shifting is continued until a 1 bit is shifted out of the register. At this point the number of shifts performed is $s + 1$.

To design hardware which implements the proper address transformation, it is useful to consider equations which describe the mappings. The notation $x_{i:j}$ indicates a bit-field of x which begins with bit position i and continues through bit position j. Bit 0 is the least significant position and bit $l - 1$ is the most significant. Equation (3) computes the module address in the case where $s < n$.

$$\begin{aligned} m(a) &= \left(a \bmod N + \left\lfloor \frac{a}{N} \right\rfloor \bmod 2^s \right) \bmod N \\ &= \left(a \bmod 2^n + \left\lfloor \frac{a}{2^n} \right\rfloor \bmod 2^s \right) \bmod 2^n \\ &= (a_{0:n-1} + a_{n:l-1} \bmod 2^s) \bmod 2^n \\ &= (a_{0:n-1} + a_{n:n+s-1}) \bmod 2^n \end{aligned} \qquad (3)$$

Because the modulo and division operations involve only power of two divisors, they can be implemented inexpensively by masking and shifting operations. If these operations are combined and reduced, the hardware required to evaluate equation (3) is simply an n-bit adder, as shown in figure 5.

Equation (4) computes the module address when $s \geq n$. Again, the hardware required to implement this equation is simply an n-bit adder as shown in figure 5 combined with a circuit to extract the $s : s+n-1$ field from a. Unfortunately, the field selection circuit introduces some hardware complexity. Because the address bits used to compute the address are determined by the storage scheme of the vector being referenced, provision must be made to gate any n bit field of the address to the adder. This can be implemented using an array of pass transistors $(n \times l)$ so that the address delay is minimized. Note that the field selection hardware is required for any dynamic address calculations based on the stride of the access.

$$\begin{aligned} m(a) &= \left(a \bmod N + \left\lfloor \frac{\lfloor \frac{a}{N} \rfloor}{2^{s-n}} \right\rfloor \bmod N \right) \bmod N \\ &= \left(a_{0:n-1} + \left\lfloor \frac{a_{n:l-1}}{2^{s-n}} \right\rfloor \bmod 2^n \right) \bmod 2^n \\ &= (a_{0:n-1} + a_{n+(s-n):l-1} \bmod 2^n) \bmod 2^n \\ &= (a_{0:n-1} + a_{s:s+n-1}) \bmod 2^n \end{aligned} \qquad (4)$$

The efficiency of the mapping hardware allows it to be used in high-performance architectures. An alternative implementation when n and s are small is to use a ROM to perform a table lookup similar to the address mapping circuit used in the IBM RP3 architecture [12].

Multiple Stride Accesses

To this point, it has been tacitly assumed that a vector is only accessed with a single stride. Examination of applications programs from a variety of disciplines has shown that while vectors are not

74

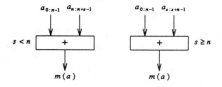

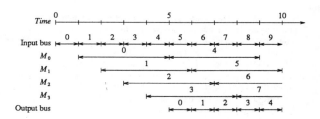

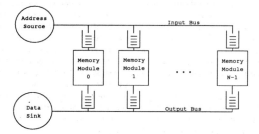

Figure 5: Address mapping hardware.

Figure 6: Architectural model.

Figure 7: Memory system timing.

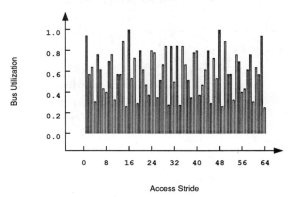

Figure 8: Memory system performance, $N = 8$, $S_{stored} = 16$.

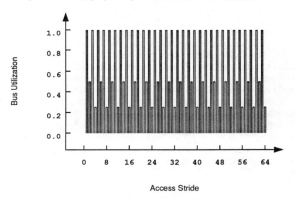

Figure 9: Memory system performance, $N = 8$, Interleaved.

always accessed with a single stride, single stride accesses are by far the most common case. The primary exception to this is the row/column accessing patterns found in matrix manipulation routines. However, since operations on matrices compose a substantial portion of numerical computing it is important to determine how dynamic storage schemes perform on multiple stride accesses. Three questions are considered.

1. What form should the storage scheme take when a vector is accessed with more than one stride?
2. How well does the memory system perform under multiple stride accesses?
3. Array reshaping is a simpler way of reducing conflicts. Why should dynamic storage schemes be used instead?

Consider the first and second questions which are closely related. Let a vector be accessed with two strides, $S_1 = \sigma_1 2^{s_1}$ and $S_2 = \sigma_2 2^{s_2}$. The vector should be stored as if it were to be accessed with a stride of $S_{stored} = 2^{max(s_1,s_2)}$. The argument for this is straight-forward. Assume, without loss of generality that $2^{s_1} < 2^{s_2}$. In this case, the vector should be stored so conflict-free accesses can be made for S_2. Although conflict-free access for S_1 does not occur, all modules are referenced during the S_1 access and buffers, to be discussed, can be used to maintain system throughput. Suppose instead, the vector is stored using stride $S_{stored} = 2^{s_1}$. S_2 is now an even multiple of S_{stored}; this means that not all memory modules will be referenced. The number of modules referenced is given by $N/2^{s_2-s_1}$. Reducing the number of modules referenced may severely degrade the performance of the memory system.

More quantitative results have been obtained using simulation. Figure 6 shows the architectural model used in the simulations.

Addresses are presented to the memory system sequentially on the input bus. If the referenced module is not busy, the address is latched and the bus is released for subsequent address transfers. If the memory is busy, the bus blocks until the module becomes available. Data read from the module is transferred to the processor over the output bus. Data is guaranteed to return to the processor in the order requested by tagging addresses as they cross the input bus and then ordering access to the output bus based on these tags. This technique is simple and avoids the need for centralized bus control. Time is normalized to the bus transfer time and it is assumed that the memory cycle time is equal to the N. If the elements of the vector are distributed optimally over the modules then the cycle time of each module is overlapped with address transfers to the other modules and the memory system as a whole operates with an effective cycle time of 1.0. This is shown for $N = 4$ and $S = 1$ in figure 7.

Figure 8 shows the performance of an $N = 8$ module system in which the vector has been stored to optimize stride 16 accesses ($S_{stored} = 16$). The figure shows the performance of accesses as the

stride is varied from 1 to $N \cdot S_{stored}$; the periodic nature of the storage scheme causes all strides to be congruent modulo $N \cdot S_{stored}$. Utilization of the data bus is used as the measure of memory system performance. Data bus utilization is calculated by:

$$U_{data\,bus} = \frac{L}{t_{stop} - t_{start}} \qquad (5)$$

where L is the number of elements accessed in the vector, t_{start} is the time the address of the first element is loaded onto the address bus, and t_{stop} is the time the last element is removed from the data bus. This measure reflects both memory throughput and latency. Because the bus speed is matched to the memory, $1/U_{databus}$ is the effective cycle time of the memory. The effective cycle time is a measure of the memory throughput. By measuring time from the initial address bus cycle to the final data bus cycle, increased latency introduced by buffering (to be discussed later) is also measured.

Comparison of figure 8 with similar data for an interleaved storage scheme (figure 9) shows the interleaved scheme performs 16% better if a uniform distribution of strides is assumed.

75

A more detailed investigation finds that this is due to transient non-uniformities in the address sequence. In these cases, the number of references to each module is uniform, but the references to a given module are not spaced evenly in time. This effect was noted by Harper and Jump [10] who proposed the use of queues at the input and output of the memory modules to buffer the transients in the address stream. Figure 10 shows the performance of the dynamic scheme if one additional register is added to the input and output of each module (the parameter q indicates the number of buffers on each memory port).

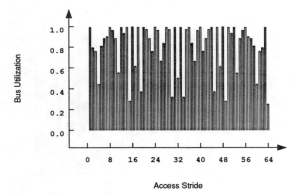

Figure 10: Memory system performance, $N = 8$, $S_{stored} = 16$, $q = 2$.

The dynamic scheme now outperforms the interleaved scheme by 18% and additional performance can be gained by adding more buffers as shown in table A, however only small performance gains are realized by adding buffers beyond two or three. The left column of table A is the number of buffers present at each memory port. The next column to the right shows memory performance averaged over all strides. Next is the change in performance due to the addition of another buffer. The right column shows the performance change as a percentage. Simulation data indicates that the performance gain per additional buffer is relatively insensitive to both N and S_{stored}. It should be noted that the relative performances are dependent on S_{stored} and the particular strides used. The dynamic scheme takes advantage of the fact that the stride of the access is known and optimizes performance for that access. This means that the assumption of uniform stride distribution produces a very conservative estimate of the performance of the dynamic storage scheme.

# Buffers	$\overline{U}_{databus}$	$\Delta\overline{U}$	% Δ
Interleaved	0.685	-	-
1	0.592	-	-
2	0.808	0.216	36.5
3	0.891	0.083	10.3
4	0.923	0.032	3.3
5	0.938	0.015	1.6
∞	0.968	-	-

Table A: Data bus utilization vs. buffer length, $S_{stored} = 16$.

Using dynamic storage schemes is a better alternative than array reshaping for several reasons. First, array reshaping by embedding an array inside a larger array wastes space and may not be possible for large data structures. Also, the "gaps" in the new matrix which do not contain data from the original matrix may inhibit vectorization due to non-constant stride considerations. Second, using a dynamic storage scheme permits *run-time* decisions to be made about access strides. The choice of storage scheme to be used may be deferred until the data in the vector is defined. For loop structures which have data dependent indices, this can be a major advantage.

An alternative storage scheme might also be considered which, rather than adding the two address fields together to compute the module

address, the module address is computed simply by using different bits of the address to determine the module number. The storage scheme achieved using this technique suffers when multiple stride accesses are made to a vector, particularly in the common row/column type access. Figure 11 shows simulation data obtained to compare the two schemes in two multiple stride cases. The first type of access assumes that all strides are equally likely and performance is measured as an unweighted average of the performance over all strides. This data is labeled using a $\times$ and is equal for both schemes. The second case models the row/column access of a matrix where the strides used are 1 and 2^s (the size of the matrix). This data is labeled with a $+$ for the proposed scheme with the adder and a $\triangle$ for the scheme without the adder. The dotted line indicates buffering of size 1, the solid line is for size two buffers. The figure plots bus utilization as a function of the access stride used. It is assumed that both storage schemes are optimized for the matrix being accessed.

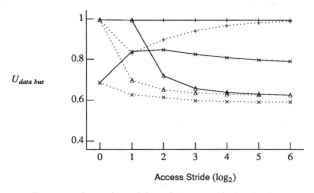

Figure 11: Comparison of dynamic storage schemes, $N = 4$.

When a single buffer is used, the performance of the averaged case is equal for both schemes. However, when row and column accesses are considered, the proposed scheme is far superior due to its increased performance on stride 1 accesses. If a single additional buffer is added, the performance of the proposed scheme is substantially improved while the performance of the simple scheme remains constant.

Compiler - Architecture Interaction

One premise of this work is that a vectorizing compiler can determine the stride of a vector access. Discussions with several people actively involved with vectorizing compiler projects have indicated that determination of the access stride is generally within the capabilities of the compiler. Because the factorization of stride and the mapping configuration are done in hardware, there is little program overhead in initiating a vector access.

The dynamic storage scheme also provides advantages to vectorizing compilers performing loop optimization. Cowell and Thompson [13] and others have described methods of transforming loop structures in programs into vector operations. In the process of doing so the stride of the vector access may change from the stride specified by the programmer. If the dynamic storage scheme is used in the memory system then the transformation will not cause memory conflicts to occur because the storage scheme is simply optimized for the new stride. This can be particularly advantageous when transformations such as loop interchange and strip mining are used. The fact that any stride can be conflict-free also frees the applications programmer from coding information about the memory architecture into the program. Instead the programmer is able to concentrate on a natural expression of the algorithm. For example, FORTRAN programmers do not need to force column-major matrix accesses into their algorithms. Row-major accesses will perform equally well.

Conclusions

Results presented in this paper show how memory conflicts can be eliminated during vector accesses if the stride of the access is known. This is achieved by designing a dynamic storage scheme. The scheme does not rely on having a prime number of memory modules in the system as do many other proposed schemes.

Previous investigations into storage schemes have identified a set of commonly used vector access patterns and then attempted to synthesize a storage scheme which permitted conflict-free access to these patterns. The dynamic storage scheme presented here is a departure from the previous approach. Rather than design a single scheme for all access patterns, the storage scheme for each vector is adapted to the pattern which will be used with that vector. Taking this approach allows any vector to be accessed conflict-free.

To synthesize a storage scheme which allows conflict-free access to a vector, the stride of the access is factored into two components. One of the factors is a power of 2, the other is relatively prime to 2. Based on the value of the first factor, two parameters are chosen. These parameters are sufficient to specify the storage scheme. Hardware was presented to implement the stride factoring and the address transformation. The expense of the hardware was shown to be small.

Accesses with multiple strides to the same vector were also considered. Through the use of one or two additional buffers at each memory port it was shown that the dynamic storage scheme performs substantially better than interleaved memory. This is true even when accesses are made with strides other than those for which the memory scheme has been optimized.

Finally, it was noted that the use of dynamic storage schemes relies on the compiler to determine the stride of the vector access. This is within the capabilities of current compilers. It was also noted that the use of dynamic storage schemes will allow a compiler more flexibility in its choice of program transformations for code optimization because it no longer must maintain stride 1 access patterns or face memory performance degradation.

Because the additional hardware cost of dynamic storage schemes is so small, the use of dynamic storage schemes is an attractive method of boosting memory bandwidth during vector accesses. The hardware implementation is a simple extension of memory architectures found on current high-performance machines but memory performance is significantly improved relative to conventional interleaving.

References

[1] P. Budnik and D. Kuck, "The organization and use of parallel memories," *IEEE Trans. Computers*, vol. C-20, no. 12, pp. 1566–1569, December 1971.

[2] D. Lawrie, "Access and alignment of data in an array processor," *IEEE Trans. Computers*, vol. C-24, no. 12, pp. 1145–1155, December 1975.

[3] K. Batcher, "The multidimensional access memory in STARAN," *IEEE Trans. Computers*, vol. C-26, pp. 174–177, February 1977.

[4] R. Swanson, "Interconnections for parallel memories to unscramble p-ordered vectors," *IEEE Trans. Computers*, vol. C-23, pp. 1105–1115, November 1974.

[5] W. Oed and O. Lange, "On the effective bandwidth of interleaved memories in vector processing systems," *IEEE Trans. Computers*, vol. C-34, no. 10, pp. 949–957, October 1985.

[6] H. Shapiro, "Theoretical limitations on the efficient use of parallel memories," *IEEE Trans. Computers*, vol. C-27, no. 5, pp. 421–428, May 1978.

[7] H. Wijshoff and J. van Leeuwen, "The structure of periodic storage schemes for parallel memories," *IEEE Trans. Computers*, vol. C-34, no. 6, pp. 501–505, June 1985.

[8] H. Wijshoff and J. van Leeuwen, "On linear skewing schemes and d-ordered vectors," *IEEE Trans. Computers*, vol. C-36, no. 2, pp. 233–239, February 1987.

[9] D. Lawrie and C. Vora, "The prime memory system for array access," *IEEE Trans. Computers*, vol. C-31, no. 5, pp. 435–442, May 1982.

[10] D. T. Harper III and J. R. Jump, "Vector access performance in parallel memories using a skewed storage scheme," *IEEE Trans. Computers*, vol. C-36, no. 12, pp. 1440–1449, 1987.

[11] A. Ranade, "Interconnection networks and parallel memory organizations for array processing," *Int. Conf. on Parallel. Proc.*, pp. 41–47, August 1985.

[12] A. Norton and E. Melton, "A class of boolean linear transformations for conflict-free power-of-two stride access," *Int. Conf. on Parallel. Proc.*, pp. 247–254, 1987.

[13] W. R. Cowell and C. P. Thompson, "Transforming Fortran DO Loops to Improve Performance on Vector Architectures," *ACM Transactions on Mathematical Software*, vol. 12, pp. 324–353, December 1986.

SIMP (Single Instruction stream/Multiple instruction Pipelining): A Novel High-Speed Single-Processor Architecture

Kazuaki Murakami, Naohiko Irie, Morihiro Kuga, and Shinji Tomita

Department of Information Systems
Interdisciplinary Graduate School of Engineering Sciences
Kyushu University
Fukuoka, 816 JAPAN

Abstract

SIMP is a novel multiple instruction-pipeline parallel architecture. It is targeted for enhancing the performance of SISD processors drastically by exploiting both temporal and spatial parallelisms, and for keeping program compatibility as well. Degree of performance enhancement achieved by SIMP depends on; i) how to supply multiple instructions continuously, and ii) how to resolve data and control dependencies effectively. We have devised the outstanding techniques for instruction fetch and dependency resolution. The instruction fetch mechanism employs unique schemes of; i) prefetching multiple instructions with the help of branch prediction, ii) squashing instructions selectively, and iii) providing *multiple conditional modes* as a result. The dependency resolution mechanism permits *out-of-order execution* of sequential instruction stream. Our out-of-order execution model is based on *Tomasulo's algorithm* which has been used in single instruction-pipeline processors. However, it is greatly extended and accommodated to multiple instruction pipelining with; i) detecting and identifying multiple dependencies simultaneously, ii) alleviating the effects of control dependencies with both *eager execution* and *advance execution*, and iii) ensuring a precise machine state against branches and interrupts. By taking advantage of these techniques, SIMP is one of the most promising architectures toward the coming generation of high-speed single processors.

1. Introduction

The demand for high-speed single-processors forces more sophisticated instruction pipelines to be implemented in SISD (Single Instruction stream/Single Data stream) processors of a wide range from microprocessors to supercomputers. These conventional pipelined SISD processors exploit temporal parallelism in the process of instruction execution; i.e., the process is segmented into consecutive subprocesses (stages of a pipeline). The performance of these processors can be expressed as the program execution time;

$$E = N \times C \times T,$$

where N is the number of instructions that must be executed, C is the average number of cycles per instruction, and T is the cycle

time. N and C depend on processor architectures; e.g., CISC architectures decrease N but increase C by improving functionality of instructions, while RISC architectures reduce C to nearly 1 but increase N by simplifying the instruction set. Although processor architectures may influence T in some degree, semiconductor technology mostly determines T. Since T has been decreasing constantly with advances in VLSI technology, conventional pipelined SISD processors have enjoyed speedups regardless of their architectures: CISC or RISC.

However, the physical lower limit of T obviously exists in any semiconductor technology, and therefore some architectural changes must be considered for SISD processors.

Some innovative approaches of such challenges are VLIW (Very Long Instruction Word) architectures [Fisher83], which are derivatives of SISD and exploit spatial parallelism (low-level parallelism). VLIW architecture decreases N by specifying two or more independent operations in an instruction, without increasing C by having each operation be a RISC-style instruction. We have already developed two VLIW processors: the QA-series (QA-1 and QA-2) [Hagiwara80; Tomita83,86]. To exploit spatial parallelism, the QA-series provide multiple functional units such as quadruple ALUs, quadruple memory access units, and a sequencer. QA-1 and QA-2 employ very long instruction formats of 160-bits and 256-bits respectively, for controlling every functional unit independently. However, VLIW architectures have a serious drawback; i.e., it is difficult to keep program compatibility, because their hardware architectures are exposed to compilers.

Other, somewhat old, approaches are found in single instruction-pipeline processors with multiple functional-units (called MFU processors), such as the CDC 6600 and the IBM 360/91. MFU processors have potential of reducing C to nearly 1 by having multiple pipelined-functional units busy, and keep N comparable to CISC processors. Unlike VLIW, program compatibility is preserved very easily. Nevertheless, the limit exists to performance enhancement because the instruction issue rate ($= 1/C$) can not exceed one instruction per cycle.

All these approaches attempt to exploit low-level fine-grained parallelism by utilizing multiple functional units. Key problems in the exploitation of low-level parallelism are; i) to detect data dependencies and control dependencies, ii) to resolve these hazards, and iii) to schedule the order of instruction execution. VLIW architectures rely solely on clever compilers which solve the problems by means of static code scheduling, such as trace scheduling [Fisher81] and software pipelining [Lam88]. MFU processors also solve the problems at run time by implementing dynamic code scheduling in hardware. Static and dynamic code scheduling methods differ in their domain; i.e., static code scheduling is done with a broad overview of program codes, but dynamic code scheduling is done with a peephole. However, these code scheduling methods are not mutually exclusive.

After evaluating the QA-series, we have studied the feasibility for enhancing the performance of SISD processors drastically by combining both temporal and spatial parallelisms, and for preserving program compatibility as well. As a result of this study, we have introduced the multiple instruction-pipeline parallel architecture: SIMP [Murakami88]. Given that P instruction pipelines are provided, SIMP processors ideally reduce C to $1/P$ by fetching P instructions per cycle, and keep N comparable to conventional single-pipelined SISD processors as well. As the first implementation of SIMP, we are now developing the SIMP processor prototype: 「 新 風 」 (in Japanese), whose English pronunciation is [ʃimpu：]. It implies "new streamline" processor.

The paper is organized in 6 sections. The following two sections present the rationale of SIMP architecture (section 2), and give some background regarding instruction-pipelining techniques (section 3). In section 4, we introduce the SIMP processor prototype and discuss its pipeline flow and instruction-set architecture. In section 5, we describe the instruction fetch mechanism and the out-of-order execution model, both of which are devised for the SIMP prototype. Section 6 offers a few concluding remarks.

2. Principles of SIMP Pipelined Instruction Execution

There are various models of pipelined instruction execution. They apply temporal parallelism (i.e., pipelining) and/or spatial parallelism (i.e., low-level parallelism) to a single instruction stream, as schematically depicted in Figure 1. We clarify SIMP architecture by comparing its instruction pipelining model with those of its counterparts such as linear-pipeline, MFU, and pipelined VLIW. In the discussion here, we assume that the process of instruction execution is decomposed into 5 stages: IF (instruction fetch), D (instruction decode), OF (operand fetch), E (execute), and W (result write).

2.1 Linear-Pipelined Processor

Most of conventional pipelined SISD processors employ single pipeline structure shown in Figure 1-a. Instructions are sequentially processed one by one from preceding stages to succeeding stages. Instructions should enter and leave each stage in-order with respect to the compiled code sequence. This pipeline structure is referred to as a *linear pipeline*.

Linear-pipelined processors exploit only temporal parallelism. *Pipeline interlock logic* is usually placed between critical stages to detect and resolve data and control dependencies; otherwise, the interlock logic is imposed on a compiler.

The maximum throughput of instruction execution is at most one instruction per cycle; i.e., C (the average number of cycles per instruction) cannot be less than 1. Thus, the ideal program execution time of linear-pipelined processors results in;
$$E = N \times 1 \times T.$$

2.2 MFU processor

Some pipelined SISD processors such as the CDC 6600, the IBM 360/91 floating-point unit, and the CRAY-1 scalar unit, provide multiple functional units (MFUs) in E-stage (Figure 1-b). Each functional unit may or may not be pipelined. Although not shown in Figure 1-b, W-stage can be multiplied by the number of MFUs.

MFU processors can exploit both temporal and spatial parallelisms. To increase MFU utilization, most of pipeline interlock logic is localized to the stages prior to E-stage. It is referred to as *instruction issue logic* [Weiss84]. Simple instruction issue logic issues an instruction to an MFU sequentially. Complex issue logic such as *Tomasulo's algorithm* [Tomasulo67] is capable of dynamic code scheduling by allowing instructions to begin and/or complete execution nonsequentially.

Even if any instruction issue logic is employed, however, at most one instruction can be issued per cycle. Thus, the maximum throughput of instruction execution is the same as in linear-pipelined SISD processors; i.e., C cannot be less than 1. The ideal

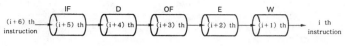

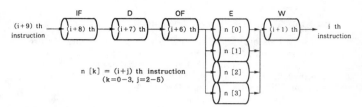

(a) Linear-pipelined processor

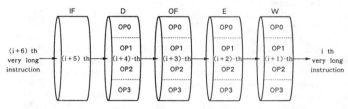

$$n[k] = (i+j) \text{ th instruction}$$
$$(k = 0-3, \ j = 2-5)$$

(b) MFU processor (case of 4 functional units)

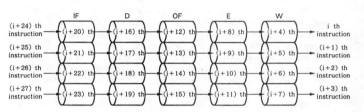

(c) Pipelined VLIW processor (case of 4 operations/VLIW)

(d) SIMP processor (case of 4 instruction pipelines)

Figure 1. Pipelined Instruction Execution Models

program execution time of MFU processors results in;
$$E = N \times 1 \times T.$$

More complex issue logic capable of issuing multiple instructions per cycle are studied so as to reduce C less than 1 [Tjaden70; Acosta86; Pleszkun88]. If F functional units are provided and the same number of instructions can be issued each cycle, the ideal program execution time now results in;
$$E = N \times (1/F) \times T.$$

2.3 Pipelined VLIW Processor

VLIW processors also provide multiple functional units. Unlike MFU processors, however, VLIW processors attempt to utilize functional units by specifying multiple independent operations in a single very long instruction. Original, non-pipelined, VLIW processors such as the QA-series have exploited only spatial parallelism. Since each operation can be pipelined, pipelined VLIW processors such as the Multiflow TRACE [Colwell87] and the Cydrome Cydra 5 [Rau89] can now exploit both temporal and spatial parallelisms (Figure 1-c).

A very long instruction is fetched each cycle, each operation field of the instruction is decoded in parallel, and each decoded operation is processed simultaneously and independently at the corresponding functional unit. A clever compiler is well aware of the architecture (e.g., the number of functional units, the number of pipeline stages, etc.), and is responsible for scheduling the order of operations strictly to prevent any hazard from causing incorrect results at run time. Therefore, no pipeline interlock logic or complex instruction issue logic need be implemented in hardware.

Given that F functional units are provided (e.g., $F=4$ in Figure 1-c), pipelined VLIW processors can reduce N' (the number of very long instructions to be executed) to N/F, where N is the number of short instructions to be executed, by compacting F operations into one very long instruction. The ideal program execution time of pipelined VLIW processors results in;

$$E = (N/F) \times 1 \times T.$$

2.4 SIMP Processor

SIMP processors employ multiple instruction-pipeline structure shown in Figure 1-d, and exploit both temporal and spatial parallelisms. All pipelines should be identical. Each pipeline may be either the linear pipeline shown in Figure 1-a, or the MFU-processor-like pipeline shown in Figure 1-b.

Regardless of the number of instruction pipelines provided, a single program counter (PC) controls the flow of instruction execution; i.e., a single instruction stream. Given that P instruction pipelines are provided (e.g., $P=4$ in Figure 1-d), instructions can be processed in blocks of P. We refer to this block as an *"instruction block"*, which consists of successive P instructions in an object program. An instruction block starting with the instruction specified by c(PC) and ending with the instruction specified by $c(PC)+P-1$ is fetched each cycle, where c(PC) indicates the contents of PC. Each instruction of an instruction block is decoded and processed simultaneously, but *dependently*, at the corresponding instruction pipeline.

SIMP processors would appreciate the advantages of static code scheduling, but they should exploit spatial parallelism by scheduling instructions at run time. It is because, unlike VLIWs, SIMP processors should not expose their hardware architectures (e.g., the number of instruction pipelines) to such clever compilers as used for VLIW processors. In such a case, even if an ordinary compiler could increase the dependency distance, some dependencies may still remain in the compiled code until run time. As linear-pipelined and MFU processors do, SIMP processors must provide a way to resolve these remaining dependencies at run time.

From a standpoint of program compatibility, the above is a major difference between SIMP and VLIW. For VLIW, it is not impossible but difficult to have compiled codes portable among VLIW processors with the various number of functional units, because the instruction size reflects the number of functional units directly. On the other hand, in SIMP, one instruction corresponds to one instruction pipeline, and therefore the number of instruction pipelines installed is transparent to its ISP (Instruction-Set Processor) architecture.

The maximum throughput of instruction execution is at most one instruction block of P instructions per cycle; i.e., C can be reduced to $1/P$. Thus, the ideal program execution time of SIMP processors results in;

$$E = N \times (1/P) \times T.$$

3. Critical Issues Regarding SIMP

There are several critical issues to be resolved before implementing SIMP architecture, which issues are also common to most pipelined processors. We identify those issues by giving some background regarding instruction-pipelining techniques.

3.1 Branch Problem

The detrimental effects of branch instructions are severe, because fetching the next instruction is postponed until a branch decision (i.e., taken or not-taken) is resolved and a branch target address is generated. As a result, a lot of "bubbles" are forced into a pipeline, and the pipeline stalls. There are some techniques to reduce the branch penalty: delayed branch, branch prediction, multiple prefetching, and so on [Lee84]. A popular technique is *branch prediction*. By means of branch prediction, instructions fetched from a predicted branch path can be executed in a *conditional mode*. If the predicted path is incorrect, however, some prediction-miss handling should be done to nullify or squash the conditionally executed instructions.

SIMP processors also can adopt branch prediction with prediction-miss handling. However, branch prediction involves other critical issues unique to SIMP;

"How to determine predicted paths inside an instruction block which substantially consists of multiple instructions to be fetched simultaneously, and how to recover if one of the paths is incorrect."

3.2 Data Dependency

There are 3 types of data dependencies: flow (RAW: Read-After-Write), anti (WAR: Write-After-Read), and output (WAW: Write-After-Write). Two popular hardware solutions exist to the data dependency problem: *pipeline interlock logic* in linear-pipelined processors, and *instruction issue logic* in MFU processors.

Pipeline interlock logic is so simple and straightforward that, if it detects data dependencies, it just interlocks pipeline until the dependencies are resolved. The detrimental effects of data dependencies, however, can not be alleviated.

Simple instruction issue logic can issue an instruction to an MFU, only if its data dependencies are resolved; otherwise, the instruction and subsequent instructions are blocked from issuing. Complex issue logic such as Tomasulo's algorithm permits an instruction to be issued even when its dependencies are not resolved. Flow dependencies can be resolved by waiting and monitoring instruction results, and anti/output dependencies can be eliminated by renaming registers with tags. In addition, Tomasulo's algorithm allows subsequent instructions to bypass the instruction issued previously, while it waits until its dependencies have been resolved. Thus instructions can begin and/or complete their execution out-of-order with respect to the compiled code sequence. This scheme of instruction execution is referred to as *out-of-order execution* model [Weiss84; Patt85], and can minimize the effects of flow dependencies.

To utilize multiple instruction pipelines as well as multiple functional units, SIMP processors also can employ the out-of-order execution model. In such a case, there are critical issues unique to SIMP;

"How to detect data dependencies among multiple instructions simultaneously, and how to represent them."

3.3 Control Dependency

Even if above-mentioned techniques such as conditional-mode execution and out-of-order execution are employed, control dependencies still impede the execution of instructions. It is because the domain of out-of-order execution may be affected by the size of a *basic block* (in which only one control dependency occurs at the bottom). There are two schemes of the out-of-order execution model: *lazy* (or normal) *execution* and *eager execution*.

Lazy execution scheme disallows out-of-order execution to proceed beyond any branch instruction; i.e., the domain of out-of-order execution is limited to the basic block whose execution is certainly needed. Although the scheme is simple, the effect of out-of-order execution is diminished by small basic blocks.

On the other hand, eager execution scheme causes instructions to be executed out-of-order regardless of basic blocks they belong to. The scheme applies out-of-order execution to instructions fetched from a predicted path, and it therefore requires more sophisticated prediction-miss handling mechanisms, such as the *reorder buffer* of the RUU (Register Update Unit) [Sohi87] and the checkpoint repair mechanism [Hwu87], in order to avoid an imprecise machine state (described in section 3.4).

3.4 Imprecise Machine State

When instructions may finish out-of-order, an imprecise machine state can be introduced by branches and instruction-generated traps (e.g., an exception and a page fault). It is because, when a branch or trap occurs, out-of-order execution can modify a machine state (such as register file and memory) inconsistently with the sequential architectural specification. The problem caused by traps is well-known as *imprecise interrupt*, and there are many solutions to the problem [Smith85]. Also, there are common solutions to both the imprecise interrupt problem and the problem caused by branches [Hwu87; Sohi87].

4. SIMP Processor Prototype

The SIMP processor prototype, the first implementation of SIMP, is a quadruple instruction-pipeline processor composed of 4 identical instruction pipelines. It is an ideal SIMP processor, in the sense that it is equipped with rich hardware mechanisms to resolve the issues discussed in section 3; i.e., branch prediction, conditional-mode execution, out-of-order execution, and reorder buffer. Note that its design never limits other implementations of SIMP architecture, especially on the number of instruction pipelines.

4.1 Processor Organization

Block diagram of the SIMP processor prototype is shown in Figure 2. Each instruction pipeline comprises 5 stages: IF (Instruction-block Fetch), D (Decode), I (register-read and Issue), E (Execute), and R (register-write and Retire). The prototype will be implemented in off-the-shelf TTL/CMOS chips, with a machine cycle time of 60 ns, or a pipeline cycle time of 120 ns (i.e., 2-cycle pipeline). Hereafter cycles refer to pipeline cycles. The SIMP processor prototype consists of the following main components.

(a) MBIC (Multiple-Bank Instruction Cache):

The MBIC is an instruction cache consisting of 4 independent banks of RAMs, where a bank width equals to an instruction size (4 bytes). A cache line contains 16 contiguous instructions from a *static instruction stream* (i.e.;object program) in memory. The MBIC also includes a BTB (Branch Target Buffer) for purpose of branch prediction.

(b) IBSU (Instruction-Block Supply Unit):

The IBSU is common to all instruction pipelines, and it plays a role of IF-stage. At each cycle, the IBSU fetches 4 successive instructions from the MBIC with the help of branch prediction and distributes them to all the IPUs.

(c) IPUs (Instruction Pipeline Units):

Four identical IPUs are installed. For an instruction received from the IBSU, each IPU performs a pipeline sequence from D-stage to R-stage individually. E-stage is equipped with 5 pipelined functional units: IALU (Integer ALU), IMUL (Integer MULtiplier), FALU (Floating-point ALU), FMUL (Floating-point MULtiplier), and DCAR (Data Cache Access Requester). They are constructed with 32-bit building blocks such as Advanced Micro Devices Am29323/32 and Weitek WTL2264/65.

To allow out-of-order execution and to ensure the precise machine state, E-stage provides a queue of 4 entries, called *WRB (Waiting and Reorder Buffer)*, which comprises a pair of WB (Waiting Buffer) and RB (Reorder Buffer). The WB corresponds to the *reservation stations* in the IBM 360/91 [Tomasulo67], and the RB corresponds to the *reorder buffer* proposed in [Smith85; Sohi87].

(d) DHRF (Dependency-Handling Register-File):

The DHRF is a register file with 8 read-ports and 4 write-ports. The DHRF is shared by all the IPUs, and is accessed three times (i.e., two source-register accesses at I-stage and one destination-register access at R-stage) per cycle by every IPU. The DHRF maintains a *WRT (Write Reservation Table)*, each entry of which is associated with a register, to detect flow dependencies. It also maintains a *CDT (Control Dependency Table)* to detect control dependencies. The DHRF provides 4 *BBs (Bypass Buffers)*, each of which contains a copy of the RB in each IPU.

(e) MPDC (Multiple-Port Data Cache):

The MPDC is a data cache with 4 load-ports and 4 store-ports. The MPDC is shared by all the IPUs, and is accessed twice (i.e., one LOAD access at E-stage and one STORE access at R-stage) per cycle by every IPU, if executing a LOAD/STORE instruction.

(f) IPCN (IPU Chaining Network):

The IPCN is an interconnection network among all the WRBs.

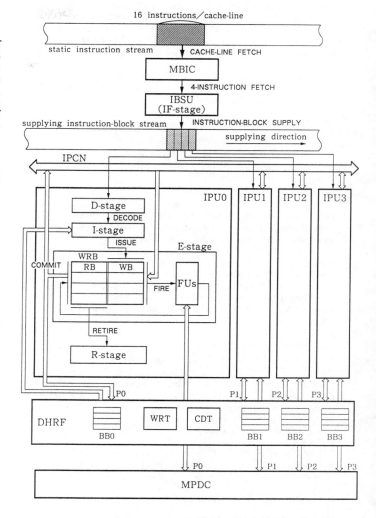

Figure2. Block Diagram of the SIMP Processor Prototype

It consists of 4 broadcast buses, where every IPU is the bus master of the corresponding bus. When one IPU places an execution result on its own bus, all the IPUs (including the sender itself) can catch the result from the bus. Thus the IPCN works like the common data bus used in the IBM 360/91 [Tomasulo67].

4.2 Pipeline Flow

During IF-stage, the IBSU fetches an instruction block of 4 successive instructions from a static instruction stream cached in the MBIC, and then supplies it for all the IPUs, one instruction per IPU. The instruction stream being supplied by the IBSU is called *"supplying instruction-block stream"*. Hereafter, the instruction block is a unit of management until it retires from the supplying instruction-block stream. At most 7 instruction blocks can reside in the stream; i.e., 1/D-stage, 1/I-stage, 4/E-stage, and 1/R-stage.

Once each IPU takes the corresponding instruction in an instruction block, it can accomplish pipelined processing for the instruction individually. All the 4 instructions in the same instruction block, however, should flow through D, I, and R-stages on a lockstep basis, and in-order with respect to the instruction-block sequence. Only one slack exists in E-stage, where instructions can wait requisite operands and begin the execution when the operands become available. Instructions can begin and complete the execution out-of-order with respect to both the instruction sequence in the instruction block and the instruction-block sequence. The out-of-order execution model is also referred to as "*local dataflow execution*", because instructions are executed in a dataflow-execution fashion and the scope is localized in E-stage.

A general pipeline flow following IF-stage is summarized below. A brief description of out-of-order execution, which involves I, E, and R-stages, follows in section 5.

(a) D (Decode) stage:

In each IPU, the decoder accepts an instruction from the IBSU and decodes an operation field of the instruction. It then forwards identifiers of requisite registers (up to 3: 2 sources and 1 destination) and an operation type (i.e., BRANCH, or not) of the decoded instruction to the DHRF.

(b) I (register-read and Issue) stage:

The DHRF receives the register identifiers and the operation type from every IPU. The DHRF updates the entries in the WRT, each of which is indexed by a destination-register identifier. It also updates the CDT, according to the operation types.

The DHRF then transmits the current contents of source registers, which are fetched from the register file or bypassed from BBs, to the IPU requesting the source operands. It appends some control information representing flow and control dependencies .

Each IPU accepts them and "*issues*" the instruction by forwarding them to the tail entry of the WRB, if the WRB is not full.

(c) E (Execute) stage:

At each machine cycle, every instruction in the WRB is checked to see if it can be executed. If an instruction has no "probable" flow dependency (which is defined in section 5.3), then the IPU can "*fire*" the instruction by dispatching it to one of functional units. Otherwise, the instruction must wait in the WRB until its probable flow dependencies have been resolved. An instruction can resolve its dependencies by monitoring the IPCN. When the firing instruction completes its execution, the result is stored in the WRB.

At the same time, if no control dependency exists to the instruction which has completed its execution, the IPU can "*commit*" the instruction by broadcasting the execution result to all the IPUs via the IPCN. Otherwise, the instruction must wait in the WRB until its control dependencies have been resolved.

(d) R (register-write and Retire) stage:

Each IPU forwards a committed result, if any, from the WRB to the associated BB in the DHRF. The DHRF updates the WRT and CDT, according to the committed results. For the instruction block at the head of the WRBs, if all 4 instructions are committed, then the instruction block can be "*retired*" from the IPUs. The retirement has the DHRF update the destination registers with the contents of the head entries of the BBs.

4.3 Balanced Instruction Set Computer

The SIMP architecture itself is not an ISP architecture but a vehicle useful for implementing several different target ISP architectures. We believe, however, that there is a class of ISPs most suitable for SIMP in a wide spectrum of ISPs from RISC to CISC. We refer to it as "*BISC (Balanced Instruction Set Computer)*", and apply it to the SIMP processor prototype. In order to utilize strengths of SIMP, we place the following constraints on the BISC architecture;

(1) Single-sized instructions: Single-sized instructions allow fetching and decoding multiple instructions simultaneously.
(2) LOAD/STORE architecture: Register-register operations relieve some of the burden to detect and resolve data dependencies.
(3) Fixed-cycle operations: Unlike RISCs emphasizing single-cycle operations, operations need not be completed in one cycle, but in some fixed cycles. If E-stage is pipelined by

means of multiple arithmetic pipelines, it is no longer necessary to limit all instructions to single-cycle operations. Also, from a viewpoint of code scheduling, it is sufficient to fix the number of operation cycles for every instruction. Thus BISC can include some complex instructions requiring fixed multiple cycles, such as integer MULTIPLY/DIVIDE and floating-point instructions, which are usually excluded from RISCs. However, the other complex instructions, whose operations spend the variable number of cycles, are still excluded from BISC.

(4) Balanced execution time: Though the fixed-cycle operations can loosen RISCs' constraint of single-cycle operations, the unbalance of execution time of every instruction introduces problems of large pipeline latency and low pipeline throughput. The pipeline stall due to the unbalance is severe in SIMP, because all instructions in an instruction block had better flow through pipelines on a lockstep basis so as to avoid the imprecise machine state problem. It means that an instruction with the longest execution time in an instruction block determines the pipeline elapsed time for the instruction block. Therefore the execution time, especially the number of operation cycles in E-stage, of every instruction should be balanced within limits.

The ISP architecture for the SIMP processor prototype is a representative of BISC; i.e., 32-bit single-sized instructions, LOAD/STORE architecture, register-register operations specified by 3-operand formats, and balanced fixed-cycle operations ranging from 2 to 6 machine-cycles in E-stage. From a standpoint of the balanced execution time, DIVIDE instructions (which would require over 13 machine-cycles) are not provided, but MULTIPLY instructions, for both integer and floating-point (which require 2 and 6 machine-cycles respectively), are provided.

5 Resolution Algorithms

To resolve the critical issues discussed in section 3, we have already developed algorithms for branch problem resolution, data dependency resolution [Kuga89], control dependency resolution, and so on. Details of all the algorithms cannot be presented here due to insufficient space, however, and they will be reported elsewhere. We describe the outline of these algorithms below.

5.1 Branch Problem Resolution

During IF (Instruction-block Fetch) stage, the IBSU (Instruction-Block Supply Unit) supplies an instruction block of 4 successive instructions. Because of the presence of branch instructions, the supplying instruction-block stream is somewhat different from a *dynamic instruction stream*, which is a sequential execution order of instructions in a static instruction stream. The supplying instruction-block stream has the following characteristics;

(1) To fetch and distribute 4 instructions simultaneously, the IBSU simply makes an instruction block of 4 successive instructions in the static instruction stream. Thus the instruction block may include some instructions not to be executed (i.e., to be excluded from the dynamic instruction stream).
(2) The instruction block to be prefetched is determined with the help of branch prediction using a BTB (Branch Target Buffer). Thus the supplying instruction-block stream may contain some instruction blocks fetched from incorrectly predicted branch paths.

Conventional prediction-miss handling techniques nullify all the instructions executed in a conditional mode (i.e., flush the pipeline), if (and only if) a branch prediction is wrong. Such a *pipeline flushing scheme* is, however, inadequate to the supplying instruction-block stream because of the following reasons;

(1) Even if a prediction is accurate, some instructions must be nullified due to the above-mentioned characteristics 1.
(2) Although a prediction is wrong, it is not efficient to flush the pipeline regardless of whether or not the instruction to be refetched already exists in the pipeline. The inefficiency is

82

more severe in the SIMP processor prototype, because as many as 23 instructions can be executed in a conditional mode.

Hence, instead of the pipeline flushing scheme, we have introduced the selective instruction-squashing scheme, which squashes only the instructions to be excluded from the dynamic instruction stream whenever a branch decision is resolved [Murakami88]. The selective instruction-squashing scheme results in allowing the instructions fetched from multiple branch paths to be execute in *multiple conditional modes*.

The selective instruction-squashing scheme forces the IBSU to select instructions to be squashed. For that purpose, the IBSU maintains a queue, called *IBAT (Instruction-Block Address Table)*, each of whose entries is associated with an instruction block under pipelined execution. There are the following 4 patterns of squashing instructions selectively, as shown in Figure 3;

(1) Predict-Not-taken/Not-taken (Figure 3-a): When a prediction is "Not-taken" and found to be accurate, no squashing occurs.

(2) Predict-Taken/Taken (Figure 3-b) and Predict-Not-taken/Taken (Figure 3-c): When a branch is taken, the IBAT is associatively searched to see if the branch target instruction has already been supplied. If the target is present, all the instructions between the branch and the target must be squashed. In such a case, it is not necessary to refetch the target; otherwise, the pipeline must be flushed and the target refetched.

(3) Predict-Taken/Not-taken (Figure 3-d): When a prediction is "Taken" and found to be wrong, the IBAT is associatively searched to see if the sequential target instruction, which is incidentally fetched from the sequential stream, has already been supplied. The succeeding process is the same as that stated above.

5.2 Data Dependency Resolution

Our data-dependency resolution algorithm is an extension to Tomasulo's algorithm [Tomasulo67]. We describe the outline of our algorithm by comparing it with original Tomasulo's algorithm and the other extensions.

(a) Flow Dependency Detection and Representation:

(1) Tomasulo's algorithm: Instructions are sequentially issued one by one. Each register is assigned a busy bit which indicates if it is the destination register of an instruction in execution. Each register is also assigned a tag which identifies the instruction that must write the result into the register. When an instruction is issued, the source registers are checked to see if they are busy. An instruction whose source registers are busy obtains tags for the busy source registers.

(2) Our algorithm: We adopt a bitmap scheme, called *"multiple-dependency representation scheme"*, rather than Tomasulo's tag scheme, because the tagging substantially needs to be carried out in sequential. Four instructions are issued simultaneously. Each register is assigned an entry of the WRT (Write Reservation Table), which entry is a bitmap and identifies *all* the instructions that must write the results into the register. When an instruction is issued, it always obtains the bitmaps for its source registers. Thus every instruction is capable of recognizing its multiple flow dependencies caused by up to 3 preceding instructions in the same instruction block and by up to 3 preceding instruction blocks (i.e., up to 15 dependencies per source-register). It is another reason for the bitmap scheme, and detailed in section 5.3.

(b) Flow Dependency Resolution:

(1) Tomasulo's algorithm: An instruction whose source registers are busy is forwarded to a reservation station (RS). The instruction must wait in the RS until its flow dependencies have been resolved. It can resolve its dependencies by monitoring the common data bus (CDB) and by performing the

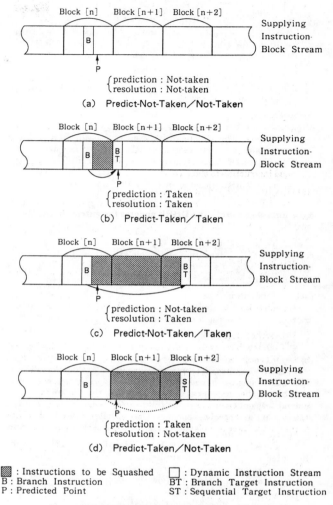

supplying direction

(a) Predict-Not-Taken/Not-Taken

(b) Predict-Taken/Taken

(c) Predict-Not-Taken/Taken

(d) Predict-Taken/Not-Taken

▨ : Instructions to be Squashed   ☐ : Dynamic Instruction Stream
B : Branch Instruction   BT : Branch Target Instruction
P : Predicted Point   ST : Sequential Target Instruction

Figure 3. Selective Instruction-Squashing Scheme

tag-matching process. If a matching tag is found, the data on the CDB is the requisite source operand.

(2) Our algorithm: Every instruction is forwarded to the tail entry of the WRB (Waiting and Reorder Buffer) in the corresponding IPU (Instruction Pipeline Unit). The WB (Waiting Buffer) part of the WRB corresponds to reservation stations. If an instruction has any "probable" flow dependency (which is defined in section 5.3), then it must wait in the WRB until its probable flow dependencies have been resolved. Flow dependencies can be resolved by monitoring the IPCN (IPU Chaining Network) and by clearing bits in bitmaps representing dependencies. No tag-matching logic is needed. If a bit associated with a probable flow dependency is cleared, the data on the IPCN is the requisite source operand.

(c) Anti/Output Dependency Resolution:

(1) Tomasulo's algorithm: If the destination register is busy at issuing an instruction, the instruction renames its destination register by updating the tag of the destination register with a new tag. Every register as well as the RS monitors the CDB, and updates its contents and clears its busy bit if a matching tag is found. The direct register renaming scheme introduces imprecise interrupts, because the instruction that completes its execution is allowed to write the result into the destination

register directly if a tag match occurs. In other words, the result disappears if no tag match occurs.

(2) Patt's and Sohi's algorithms: The registers are not renamed directly, but done indirectly through a buffer such as the result buffer [Patt85] or the reorder buffer of the RUU (Register Update Unit) [Sohi87]. That is, an instruction result is not written into the destination register straightforward, but stored in the buffer temporarily. The indirect register renaming scheme allows recovery from wrong branch predictions and traps, and therefore implements precise interrupts.

(3) Our algorithm: Basically the same as Patt's and Sohi's algorithms. The scheme of interest to us is the RUU, which acts as a queue and merges the RSs with the reorder buffer [Sohi87]. The WRB (Waiting and Reorder Buffer) in our algorithm corresponds to the RUU. Unlike the RUU, a separate WRB is located in every IPU and a set of all the WRBs acts as a queue.

5.3 Control Dependency Resolution

As stated briefly in section 3.3, there have been two hardware solutions of the basic block problem caused by control dependencies: lazy execution and eager execution. In addition to the eager execution scheme, we attempt a more eager execution scheme, called *"advance execution scheme"*.

(a) Lazy Execution:
When a branch instruction is present, subsequent instructions are blocked from firing (or dispatching) their executions until the control dependency due to the branch has been resolved [Tomasulo67].

(b) Eager Execution:
In the above case, subsequent instructions are allowed to fire their executions as soon as their flow dependencies are resolved, even before the control dependency has not been resolved. The scheme does not commit the instructions (i.e., update the machine state) until the control dependencies have been resolved [Sohi87].

(c) Advance Execution:
To take advantage of multiple conditional modes derived from the selective instruction-squashing scheme, the advance execution scheme allows an instruction to fire its execution (called *pre-execution*) even before its flow dependencies have not been definitely resolved because of the presence of control dependencies. It also allows the instruction to *re-execute* (or *backtrack*) when the pre-execution result is found invalid.

We first introduce two types into flow dependencies: *PFD (Probable Flow Dependency)* and *UFD (Uncertain Flow Dependency)*. As shown in Figure 4, a PFD occurs when the instruction A is going to write to the register *Rn* from which the instruction D is going to read, and when no control dependency covers A. On the other hand, a UFD occurs when the instruction C is going to write to *Rn* and some control dependencies covers C. From the viewpoint of the instruction D, at most 1 PFD and more than 1 UFD may be present per source operand at a time. To identify all the PFD and UFDs, we employ the multiple-dependency representation scheme mentioned in 5.2.

For this example, Tomasulo's tag scheme represents that D is flow-dependent on C, with a single tag to identify C which will supply D with the latest version of *Rn*. However, whether C is executed or not depends on the conditional branch instruction B. If the branch is taken and the branch target falls between C and D, then C is never executed, and therefore the tag identifying C has no meaning. The instruction D should access the correct version of *Rn*, which was generated by A and may be already written into the register file. In such a case, conventional pipeline flushing schemes recover from the incorrect sequence by squashing all the instructions following B, and by refetching instructions starting from the branch target. Then the instruction D is refetched, and now can obtain the correct version of *Rn* from the register file.

Since the selective instruction-squashing scheme need not refetch the instruction D, however, D cannot obtain the correct source operand with the tag. The tag scheme is inadequate to the selective instruction-squashing scheme consequently. The multiple-dependency representation scheme has just resulted from the selective instruction-squashing scheme.

Now an instruction can fire its pre-execution as soon as its PFDs are resolved, regardless of whether or not its control dependencies have been resolved. Resolution of its control dependencies may uncover any new PFD (which was one of UFDs), even after the instruction completed its pre-execution. In such a case, the instruction must backtrack and wait in a WRB until its PFDs have been resolved again. There is no limit to the number of the backtrack. The WRB commits the instruction when its PFDs and control dependencies have been resolved. The committed result is then forwarded, via the IPCN, to all the instructions waiting for it.

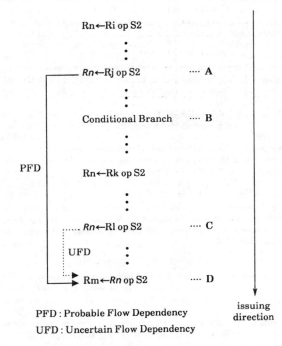

PFD : Probable Flow Dependency
UFD : Uncertain Flow Dependency

Figure 4. Probable and Uncertain Flow Dependencies

6. Conclusions

In this paper, we have introduced a novel multiple instruction-pipeline parallel architecture: SIMP. Our goal is to enhance the performance of SISD processors drastically by exploiting both temporal and spatial parallelisms, and to keep program compatibility as well. Key techniques to achieving high performance are the mechanisms of fetching multiple instructions simultaneously and continuously, and of resolving instruction dependencies effectively at run time. We have devised these mechanisms for the SIMP processor prototype which is a quadruple instruction-pipeline processor under development.

The dependency resolution mechanism permits out-of-order execution of sequential instruction stream. Our out-of-order execution model is based on Tomasulo's algorithm, but is greatly extended and accommodated to multiple instruction pipelining. The instruction fetch mechanism cooperates with the out-of-order execution model by supplying it with multiple instructions continuously with the help of branch prediction. In this paper, we have introduced several unique schemes such as selective instruction squashing, multiple conditional modes, multiple-dependency representation, advance execution, and so on.

Although SIMP does not limit the target ISP architectures, we have suggested a class of ISP architectures most suitable for SIMP: BISC. BISC is a LOAD/STORE architecture with single-sized instructions, but it loosens RISCs' constraint of single-cycle operations. We apply BISC to the SIMP processor prototype.

Currently we have several projects in progress regarding SIMP; the development of the SIMP processor prototype, the design of an optimizing C compiler capable of static code scheduling for the prototype, and the evaluation of SIMP architecture via software simulations.

Since we have not yet completed a software simulator of the SIMP processor prototype, we cannot report the performance estimate for the prototype here. The measurements obtained by a simple trace-driven simulator (see Table 1), however, show that a quadruple instruction-pipeline processor can achieve a performance of about 200-270% of a single instruction-pipeline processor [Irie88].

Table 1. Relative Speedups over Single Instruction Pipeline

Execution Model	Functional Unit	Number of Instruction-Pipelines			
		1	2	4	6
In-Order	Not Pipelined	1	1.45-1.58	2.04-2.23	2.36-2.62
	Pipelined	1.02-1.28	1.52-2.03	2.10-2.60	2.37-2.64
Out-of-Order	Not Pipelined	1	1.60-1.62	2.21-2.37	2.53-2.76
	Pipelined	1.03-1.33	1.71-2.27	2.39-2.72	2.59-2.98

We would like to emphasize that the results are very preliminary and the benchmarks are not optimized by static code scheduling. The results therefore encourage us to expect more performance enhancement in the SIMP processor prototype.

As our future work, we are planning a VLSI implementation of SIMP architecture. It will be done by implementing one or more instruction pipelines on a single-chip VLSI, and by constructing an SIMP processor using the chips as building blocks. We refer to the single-chip VLSI as *"pipeline-slice microprocessor"* on the analogy of bit-slice microprocessor. The processor organization using pipeline-slice microprocessors will support scalability toward more instruction pipelines. As bit-slice microprocessors can achieve a wide range of data width, pipeline-slice microprocessors will be able to achieve a wide range of performance.

We believe that SIMP architecture is one of the most promising architectures toward the coming generation of high-speed single processors.

Acknowledgements

We would like to thank the following students who have contributed or are now contributing to the project: T.Goto (currently with Toshiba Corp.), O.-B.Gwun, T.Hara, and T.Hironaka. We would also like to acknowledge the considerable contributions from A. Fukuda and T.Sueyoshi.

References

[Acosta86] R.D.Acosta, J.Kjelstrup, and H.C.Torng, "An Instruction Issuing Approach to Enhancing Performance in Multiple Functional Unit Processors," *IEEE Trans. Comput.*, vol.C-35, no.9, pp.815-828, Sept. 1986.

[Colwell87] R.P.Colwell, R.P.Nix, J.J.O'Donnell, D.B.Papworth, and P.K.Rodman, "A VLIW Architecture for a Trace Scheduling Compiler," *Proc. 2nd Int. Conf. Architectural Support for Programming Languages and Operating Systems (ASPLOS II)*, pp.180-192, Oct. 1987.

[Fisher81] J.A.Fisher, "Trace Scheduling: A Technique for Global Microcode Compaction," *IEEE Trans. Comput.*, vol. C-30, no.7, pp.478-490, July 1981.

[Fisher83] J.A.Fisher, "Very Long Instruction Word Architectures and the ELI-512," *Proc. 10th Ann. Int. Symp. Computer Architecture*, pp.140-150, June 1983.

[Hagiwara80] H.Hagiwara, S.Tomita, S.Oyanagi, and K.Shibayama, "A Dynamically Microprogrammable Computer with Low-Level Parallelism," *IEEE Trans. Comput.*, vol.C-29, no.7, pp.577-595, July 1980.

[Hwu87] W.W.Hwu and Y.N.Patt, "Checkpoint Repair for Out-of-order Execution Machines," *Proc. 14th Ann. Int. Symp. Computer Architecture*, pp.18-26, June 1987; also *IEEE Trans. Comput.*, vol.C-36, no.12, pp.1496-1514, Dec. 1987.

[Irie88] N.Irie, M.Kuga, K.Murakami, and S.Tomita, "Speedup Mechanisms and Performance Estimate for the SIMP Processor Prototype (in Japanese)," *IPSJ WGARC report* 73-11, Nov. 1988.

[Kuga89] M.Kuga, K.Murakami, and S.Tomita, "Low-level Parallel Processing Algorithms for the SIMP Processor Prototype (in Japanese)," *Proc. IPSJ Joint Symp. Parallel Processing'89*, pp.163-170, Feb. 1989.

[Lam88] M.Lam, "Software Pipelining: An Effective Scheduling Technique for VLIW Machines," *Proc. SIGPLAN'88 Conf. Programming Language Design and Implementation*, pp.318-328, June 1988.

[Lee84] J.K.F.Lee and A.J.Smith, "Branch Prediction Strategies and Branch Target Buffer Design," *IEEE Computer*, vol.17, no.1, pp.6-22, Jan. 1984.

[Murakami88] K.Murakami, A.Fukuda, T.Sueyoshi, and S.Tomita, "SIMP: Single Instruction stream/Multiple instruction Pipelining (in Japanese)," *IPSJ WGARC report* 69-4, Jan. 1988.

[Patt85] Y.N.Patt, W-M.Hwu, and M.Shebanow, "HPS, A New Microarchitecture: Rationale and Introduction," *Proc. 18th Ann. Workshop on Microprogramming*, pp.103-108, Dec. 1985.

[Pleszkun88] A.R.Pleszkun and G.S.Sohi, "The Performance Potential of Multiple Functional Unit Processors," *Proc. 15th Ann. Int. Symp. Computer Architecture*, pp.37-44, May 1988.

[Rau89] B.R.Rau, D.W.L.Yen, W.Yen and R.A.Towle, "The Cydra 5 Departmental Supercomputer," *IEEE Computer*, vol.22, no.1, Jan. 1989.

[Smith85] J.E.Smith and A.R.Pleszkun, "Implementation of Precise Interrupts in Pipelined Processors," *Proc. 12th Ann. Int. Symp. Computer Architecture*, pp.36-44, June 1985; also *IEEE Trans. Comput.*, vol.C-37, no.5, pp.562-573, May 1988.

[Sohi87] G.S.Sohi and S.Vajapeyam, "Instruction Issue Logic for High-Performance, Interruptable Pipelined Processors," *Proc. 14th Ann. Int. Symp. Computer Architecture*, pp.27-34, June 1987.

[Tjaden70] G.S.Tjaden and M.J.Flynn, "Detection and Parallel Execution of Independent Instructions," *IEEE Trans. Comput.*, vol.C-19, no.10, pp.889-895, Oct. 1970.

[Tomasulo67] R.M.Tomasulo, "An Efficient Algorithm for Exploiting Multiple Arithmetic Units," *IBM J. Res. Develop.*, vol.11, pp.25-33, Jan. 1967.

[Tomita83] S.Tomita, K.Shibayama, T.Kitamura, T.Nakata, and H.Hagiwara, "A User-Microprogrammable, Local Host Computer with Low-Level Parallelism," *Proc. 10th Ann. Int. Symp. Computer Architecture*, pp.151-157, June 1983.

[Tomita86] S.Tomita, K.Shibayama, T.Nakata, S.Yuasa, and H.Hagiwara, "A Computer with Low-Level Parallelism QA-2 - Its Applications to 3-D Graphics and Prolog/Lisp Machines -," *Proc. 13th Ann. Int. Symp. Computer Architecture*, pp.280-289, June 1986.

[Weiss84] S.Weiss and J.E.Smith, "Instruction Issue Logic for Pipelined Supercomputers," *Proc. 11th Ann. Int. Symp. Computer Architecture*, pp.110-118, June 1984; also *IEEE Trans. Comput.*, vol.C-33, no.11, pp.1013-1022, Nov. 1984.

Mapping Algorithms

2-D SIMD Algorithms in the Perfect Shuffle Networks

Yosi Ben-Asher, David Egozi & Assaf Schuster

The Hebrew University

Abstract

This paper studies a set of basic algorithms for SIMD Perfect Shuffle networks. These algorithms where studied in several papers, but for the 1-D case, where the size of the problem N is the same as the number of processors P. For the 2-D case of $N = L * P$, studied by [GK-80] and [Kr-81], we improve several algorithms, achieving run time $O(L + \log P)$ rather than $O(L * \log P)$, as N exceeds P. We give non-trivial algorithms for the following 2-D operations: Row-Reduction, Parallel-Prefix, Transpose, Smoothing and Cartesian-Product.

KEYWORDS: Perfect Shuffle, Networks, SIMD.

1 Introduction

Schwartz [Sc-80] introduced the idea of a parallel processor based on the *Perfect Shuffle* connections [St-71], reviewed various basic SIMD algorithms for such an ensemble of processors, and analyzed their asymptotic time complexities. These algorithms are designed for the 1-D case, where N, the size of the problem, is restricted to be P, the number of processors. In reallity, the general case where $N > P$ is much more likely to appear. In this case each processor stores $L = N/P$ data elements in its local memory. This data structure is referred to as a *2-D array* of P columns and L rows, where the i'th column corresponds to the local memory of the pro-

cessor PE_i. Algorithms for the 2-D case were introduced in [Kr-81] and [GK-80], where they are called *supersaturated*. Here we improve several of the algorithms presented there and proceed to complete the list of efficient 2-D algorithms.

We present algorithms for the following problems (in section order):

2) Row-reduction - apply some operation on all elements of each row and collect the results in first processor.

3) Parallel prefix by rows - same as row reduction, except that all partial results are also generated.

4) Transpose rows to columns and vice versa.

5) Smoothing - move elements to make all columns heights the same.

6) Cartesian product of groups of elements.

1.1 The Model

Our model is a SIMD multicomputer with shuffle-exchange interconnections. More formally, we have a set of P processors numbered $0, ..., P - 1$. The j'th processor will be denoted PE_j. For simplicity, we assume that P is a power of 2. Subgroups of processors are referred to in a "natural" manner: left half, right half, odd, even etc. Each processor is connected to 3 other processors. it is easiest to describe the topology of these connections by the relations between the IDs of the connected PEs. Given the ID of a certain PE,

- the shuffle (σ) connects to the PE whose ID is a cyclic left shift of one bit,

- the unshuffle (σ^{-1}) connects to the PE whose ID is a cyclic right shift of one bit,

- the exchange (EX) connects to the PE whose ID is the complement of the least significant bit.

© 1989 ACM 0884-7495/89/0000/0088$01.50

Note that for PE_0 and PE_{P-1} the shuffle and unshuffle connect to itself. All other processors have in and out degree 3.

At every step of the computation, all the processors perform the same operation. This can either be a send or receive on one of the interconnections lines (same one for all processors), or a (fixed size) local computation. Of course, each processor uses its own local data.

Rounds	PE_0	PE_1	PE_2	PE_3	PE_4	PE_5	PE_6	PE_7	PE_8	PE_9	PE_{10}	PE_{11}	PE_{12}	PE_{13}	PE_{14}	PE_{15}
round 8	5	5														
round 7	4	4	5	5												
round 6	3	3	4	4	5	5	5	5								
round 5	2	2	3	3	4	4	4	4	5	5	5	5	5	5	5	5
round 4	1	1	2	2	3	3	3	3	4	4	4	4	4	4	4	4
round 3			1	1	2	2	2	2	3	3	3	3	3	3	3	3
round 2					1	1	1	1	2	2	2	2	2	2	2	2
round 1									1	1	1	1	1	1	1	1

Fig. 1. 2-D Row-Reduction on 16-Processors.

2 Row-Reduction Operation

The 2-D reduction operation calculates the result of some binary associative operation bop (such as $+$, min, etc) for each row of the $L \times P$ array. The results are stored in the first processor, thus we refer to this operation as "all-rows to one-column" operation.

In [GK-80] this operation is referred to as "summing by columns" (pp. 23) and the naive way of summing the rows sequentially, using a 1-D algorithm for each row, is used, resulting in $O(L * \log P)$ steps run time. In order to get an efficient 2-D algorithm we process the rows in a pipelined fashion. The algorithm advances in $L + \log P - 1$ rounds. The rounds are equivalent except for the following:

- The first round is a short one and consists of steps (3) and (4) only, to be described next.

- At the i'th round, $i = 1, ..., \log P$, processors $0, ..., 2^{\log P - i} - 1$ are inactive.

- At the i'th round, $L < i < L + \log P$, processors $2^{\log P + L - i}, ..., P - 1$ are inactive.

The i'th round, $i > 1$, consists of four steps:

(1) Every even processor sends the step (4) result to its σ^{-1} neighbor.

(2) Every processor which got a new value at step (1), computes bop for this value with its own value of the i'th row. For the next round the result is its new value of the i'th row.

(3) For every odd processor, PE_j, PE_j moves the value of the i'th row to PE_{j-1} using the EX connection. (Note that for each individual processor the round number (i) is the number of rounds it has been active so far.)

(4) For every even processor compute bop for its i'th row value, and the value it received at step (3).

At each round a new row becomes "active", and its remaining number of elements starts to decrease. Consider a row, k, which is currently being processed.

Note that the set of processors still containing elements of k is consecutive and starts from PE_0. Let K_l (K_r) denote the left (right) half of this set. At steps (3) and (4) of each round, K_r is decreased by half, with the remaining half stored at the even processors. At steps (1) and (2) (of the following round) this half is folded on and bop'ed with the right half of K_l, so K_r is "free" to proceed with the next line.

This pipeline process is demonstrated in Fig. 1, the numbers denote the row number which a PE is currently processing. The table is for sixteen processors, $L = 5$. Note the results accumulating in PE_0, starting with the first row at round 4.

The reduction operation requires $4(L+\log P)$ steps. The reverse sequence of steps can be used for broadcasting a column stored at PE_0 to the "rest of the world". This is a 2-D column broadcast operation which is useful for many algorithms.

The reverse operation is handy not only for duplication but also for generating different values. Note that 2-D reduction spans a binary tree for each row. By reversing its steps we are actually traversing the tree topdown. We name rop some function $rop(x, y) \longmapsto (l, r)$ of a local value x and an inherited value y to create two different values l, r, for the left and the right sons.

Let each processor store L elements in its local memory. The multiple-broadcast operation is defined as the distribution all elements to all processors. The following is an $O(L * P)$ steps multiple broadcast algorithm (Clearly $\Omega(L * P)$ steps are required): In $L * (P - 1)$ steps all elements arrive at PE_0. Then, using reverse 2-D reduction, PE_0 broadcasts all $L * P$ elements to the rest of the world in $4(L * P + \log P)$ steps.

3 Parallel Prefix by Rows

There is a trivial $O(L + \log P)$ PP by columns algorithm but the best known algorithm for PP by rows requires $O(L * \log P)$ steps [Kr-81]. We close this gap with a PP by rows algorithm which requires only $O(L + \log P)$ steps.

The algorithm uses a variant of the 2-D reduction (see section 2). Observe that the reduction algorithm virtually constructs a binary tree above the right half of the row of processors. Skipping step (4) of the reduction iterations, i.e. avoiding adding the local values of the internal nodes of that tree, we get a binary tree containing all partial sums of the right half. For the i'th row we denote that tree as T_i^R. We denote by T_i^L the tree obtained by executing the symmetric algorithm for the left half, note that the root value is stored at PE_{P-1} rather than PE_0. It is important that both trees preserve the processor order in the following sense: if an internal node contains the sum of the values of $PE_n, ..., PE_m$ then its left son contains the corresponding sum of $PE_n, ..., PE_{(n+m-1)/2}$ and the right son contains that sum for $PE_{(n+m+1)/2}, ..., PE_m$.

The algorithm (and its validity) is based on the following easy observations:

(i) If we have such an ordered binary tree for the complete row, we could easily get 1-D PP for the i'th row. This is done by traversing the tree top down, where each father hands its inherited value to its left son and its inherited value plus its left son's value to its right son.

(ii) The same idea of (i) is correct when the two halves of the tree are available separately, and the root of the right half gets the value of the root of the left half.

(iii) Finally, note that given the sum of the lower indexed rows, the i'th row 2-D PP can be achieved by the same idea of (i) and (ii).

The algorithm advances as follows:

(1) Use the variant of 2-D reduction to compute T_i^L for all i in $4(L + \log P)$. Repeat the same computation for T_i^R. All processors save up to $2L$ partial sums to use at phase (5) of the algorithm below.

(2) In $L + 2\log P$ steps move the column of step-(1)'s results, stored in PE_{P-1}, to PE_0.

(3) PE_0 computes the total sum of each row and PP for the column of sums. This takes $2L$ steps.

(4) In $L + 2\log P$ steps move the resulted column at step (3) to PE_{P-1}.

(5) Reverse the tree constructions made at step (1), computing 2-D PP for each row, as described in the above observations.

4 The Transpose Operation

The transpose operation transposes the elements of a 2-D array $L \times P$ from row order into column order (T_{rc}) or from column order into row order (T_{cr}). Suppose we have $L * P$ array elements numbered $1, ..., L * P$. Row order means that the numbering of elements increases first by rows and then by columns, i.e. PE_i contains the following elements $\{i + p * j + 1\}_{j=0,...,L-1}$. In column order PE_i contains $\{i * L + 1, ..., i * L + L\}$. Note that unless $L = P$, $T_{rc} \neq T_{cr}$.

We present a general algorithm for the 2-D case in $O(L * \log P)$ steps. When $L \geq P$ we could use the 2-D sorting operation, as described in [GK-80]. However we would get the same order of time for the transpose operation. Our algorithm holds for any L and is far better in terms of constants.

We first describe the Transpose Rows to Columns operation, T_{rc}.

We denote the location of an element by $[i, j]$, where j is the processor location and i is its local memory location. The new location is $[i', j']$ where :

$$j' = \left\lfloor \frac{i * P + j}{L} \right\rfloor \quad i' = i * P + j - (j' - 1) * L \quad (1)$$

Assume for simplicity that L is a power of two. Let $< i, j >$ denote the binary representation of $i * P + j$. From (1) j' is equal to $< i, j >$ shifted right $\log L$ bits. Thus j' is equal to the $\log P$ most significant bits of $< i, j >$.

Moving from j to j' is done by $\log P$ iterations of updating the least significant bit of j (EX step), followed by a σ^{-1} step to cyclically shift the bits to the right. Moving elements between columns, without careful selection may cause collisions and congestion while correcting the bits.

Partition the L elements of each processor into P groups of L/P elements each, such that the elements of each group have the same leftmost $\log P$ address bits. The i'th group at the j'th processor is destined to $j \oplus i$, where $\oplus$ denotes the binary xor operation.

The elements in the first group are destined for the current processor, therefore only local transformations are required. For the second group in each processor we need to correct one bit, so one step is sufficient. In general, for the i'th group we need to correct up to $\lceil \log i \rceil$ bits, so $2 * \lceil \log i \rceil - 1$ steps are required. In every even step σ connection is used and in every odd step either EX connection is used or the element stays in place. We say that a *collision* occurs when in some step some processors use EX and others do not. That is, when collision do not occur during some odd step, the number of elements in all processors do not change.

The algorithm advances in phases. In a single phase every processor sends one element of the same group i to its destination. The following phase starts when all of these elements arrive. The key observation is that all of these elements need to correct address bits at the same locations. We conclude that there can be no collisions during a phase, since all elements originate at different processors and since in odd steps either *all* of them use EX to complement the right bit or *none* of them does.

The complete algorithm sends elements by the group order. The i'th group completes after L/P phases, each phase takes at most $2 * \lceil \log i \rceil - 1$ steps. Note that an "odd" step in which no EX connection is taken may be skipped.

For $L \geq P$ the algorithm is optimal since at each step P edge traversals are taken and shortest paths are used. Counting the required address bit changes show that the algorithm terminates after $\frac{3}{2} * L * \log P$ steps.

The Transpose Columns to Rows operation, T_{cr}, can be used to scatter local results of every processor to all other processors. We use the same method as for T_{rc} with the following differences:

$$ i' = \left\lfloor \frac{j * L + i}{P} \right\rfloor \quad j' = \frac{j * L + i}{P} - i' $$

Recall that j is the processor number and i is the row number. j' is the reminder $< j, i > /P$, thus j' is the $\log P$ rightmost bits of $< j, i >$.

We would like to show a lower bound of $\Omega(L * \log P)$ for the transpose operation. We call two processors *far* when at least $\log P - 3$ edge traversals are necessary to reach one from the other. Since the network degree is at most 3, each processor has more than $P/4$ of the other processors far from it. If $L = P$ the transpose is a 2-D permutation, where every processor sends an element to all other processors. In such a case a total of at least $P * P/4 * \log P$ edge traversals are necessary for the completion of the transpose operation. Hence the operation terminates after at least $P/4 * \log P$ steps, since at most P such edge traversals are possible at a single step. Thus the lower bound follows for $L \geq P$.

5 The Smoothing Operation

This operation moves elements among columns, to make the height of each column the same. It can serve as a load-balancing operation. Denote by $L = L_{max}$ the length of the highest column, L_{min} the length of the lowest one. Denote by D_{max} the biggest difference of all column size differences at odd-even pairs (i.e. pairs connected by an EX). An $O(L + \log L * \log P)$ approximate smoothing algorithm for certain families of expanders was presented in [UP-87].

Smoothing is also packing, so smoothing can be completed in $O(L * \log P)$ using the packing algorithm from [GK-80]. However, since the preservation of order is not necessary, we hope to do better. First, a rather straightforward $O(L * \log P)$ algorithm is presented.

5.1 Simple Smoothing Algorithm

The algorithm incorporates (at most) $\log P$ iterations. At the i'th iteration:

(i) Find D_{max}, broadcast to all processors. Use EX connections to move elements such that every pair of odd-even processors has an equal size column. This takes $D_{max}/2$ steps.

(ii) Find L_{min} and L_{max} and broadcast these to all processors. If $L_{min} = L_{max}$ then stop. Each processor now recomputes its column size to be the actual current value minus L_{min}. L_{max} is updated accordingly. In L_{max} steps each processor uses the σ^{-1} connection to send his column.

The correctness of the algorithm is due to the fact that the σ^{-1} connections "unshuffles" 2 consecutive odd-even pairs onto new 2 odd-even pairs. Hence the number of equal height columns doubles at each iteration.

Suppose only one column is of size L and the rest are zero's. Then after $2 * L + 4 * \log^2 P$ steps the size of each column is L/P. At the other extreme case, let the left half of the processors have columns of size L and the right half has columns of size zero. It is easy to see that at every phase there exist columns of size L and columns of size zero, so in this case the algorithm takes $L * \log P + 4 * \log^2 P$ steps.

This algorithm is subject to several "small" improvements. However it has a fundamental characteristic which makes it slow: it is nonadaptive in the sense that elements move in one direction only on σ^{-1} edges, full columns are being moved in cases where this may be superfluous and local information only is taken into account.

5.2 The Support Algorithm

The following "Support" algorithm seems to be free of the Simple smoothing algorithm flaws. We had no success in proving its optimality, so we present simulation results (see section 5.3). All the cases that we checked were smoothed by the Support algorithm (up to 3 times) faster than by the Simple algorithm. For any reasonable scope of P, Support proves to be very efficient.

Let L_{AV} denote the final column height. The algorithm consists of $\log L_{AV}$ identical phases, each involving $\log P$ rounds. After the first phase every processor has at least half ($L_{AV}/2$) of its final set of elements. In every subsequent phase, the number of elements missing at the lowest column processor is decreased by half. Moreover, the height of the highest column is also decreased by half at the termination of each phase, so in terms of the highest column size, the Support algorithm performance is twice the performance of the first phase. We describe in details the first phase.

At the beginning of the phase, the EX connections are used for equalizing the sizes of "pairs" of odd-even columns. Now each column is split into two halves. We call one collection of all halves of all columns H_1 and the other H_2. Note that

$$|H_1| = |H_2| \qquad (1)$$

and that is how it is going to stay throughout the phase. Note also that, for both sets

The total number of elements residing at odd processors is equal to that of even processors. $\qquad (2)$

Although the actual set of elements of H_j change during the run of algorithm, the notion of which elements belong to H_1 at each step and which to H_2 will be obvious.

Let i' denote $\log P - i$. Let S_i denote the collection of all sequences of $2^{i'}$ consecutive processors. By a "sequence" of processors of length 2^m, we always mean that counting starts at one of the processors $0, 2^m, ..., P - 2^m$. The phase advances in rounds: at the end of the i'th round $H_{i(2)}$ ($H_{i \bmod 2}$) is evenly distributed among the elements of S_i. In other words, if $L_{l,i(2)}$ denotes the number of elements in PE_l belonging to $H_{i(2)}$, then for all $k = 0, 2^{i'}, ..., P - 2^{i'}$ (zero-sum for sequence starting at PE_k)

$$\sum_{l=0}^{2^{i'}-1} (L_{k+l,i(2)} - L_{AV}/2) = 0. \qquad (3)$$

Clearly after $\log P$ rounds smoothing of one of the H sets is completed.

During the i'th round we use elements of $H_{i-1(2)}$ to "support" $H_{i(2)}$ such that (3) holds. Note that (3) implies (1). Then $H_{i(2)}$ uses the EX connections so that (2) holds. Thus, at the end of the i'th round, both (3) and (2) hold for $H_{i(2)}$. This implies a strengthened

versions of (3): for all $k = 0, 2^{i'}, ..., P - 2^{i'}$ (zero-sum for even processors in the sequence starting at PE_k)

$$\sum_{l=0}^{2^{i'}/2-1} (L_{k+2l,i(2)} - L_{AV}/2) = 0, \qquad (4)$$

and (zero-sum for odd processors in the sequence starting at PE_k)

$$\sum_{l=0}^{2^{i'}/2-1} (L_{k+2l+1,i(2)} - L_{AV}/2) = 0. \qquad (5)$$

Finally observe that, using σ^{-1} connections, a subsequence of odd (or even) processors of some sequence in S_i is connected to a single sequence of S_{i+1}. Also every sequence in S_{i+1} is "covered" by such subsequence. At the beginning of round $i+1$ this property is used so $H_{i(2)}$ "supports" $H_{i+1(2)}$ such that (3) holds for $i + 1$, and so on and so forth.

We now describe how $H_{i(2)}$, obeying (5) and (4) at the beginning of the $i + 1$'th round, "supports" $H_{i+1(2)}$ so that (3) holds. Consider a forest which is all subtrees of height i' of a complete tree of height $\log P$. Each subtree calculates the difference between the total number of elements of $H_{i+1(2)}$ in a sequence of S_{i+1} to its corresponding total number of elements of $H_{i(2)}$ in the corresponding odd (or even) subsequence of S_i. This difference determines how many elements should $H_{i(2)}$ move to $H_{i+1(2)}$ (or vice versa) through the σ^{-1} connections. Going "back", down the tree, each father splits the work of moving elements between its children and according to their partial sums. This procedure of "control" takes at most $\sim 8i'$ steps. The total time spent in the control procedure throughout the run of the algorithm is $O(\log^2 P * \log L_{max})$.

Our last observation is that the control procedure may run independent of moving the elements. It is actually performing a simulation of the algorithm itself, given the initial number of elements at each processor as input and giving the total flow and direction of flow at every edge as output. Thus, to improve the total run time, we first perform the control procedure, saving the data about the movement of elements on every edge. Then, for each edge, a number which is the total sum of elements traversing it is calculated, where two opposite traversals cancel each other. Only then the flow of elements starts: a processor sends an element using an out-edge if (and only if) it has an element and the edge "control number" is positive. The intuition motivating this two parts separation is to let the control procedure gather global information which pays in optimizing the flow part.

5.3 Simulation Results

We know the control procedure takes $O(\log^2 P * \log L_{max})$ steps. The question remaining is: how fast is the flow part? The flow is carried out in an optimal pipeline, what about the involved paths? To gain more information we ran simulations of the algorithm, measuring the time of the flow part only. Early results showed that the worst initial distributions consist of $P/2$ columns of height $L = L_{max}$ and the rest of height 0. Since we are interested in worst case analysis, these are the initial distributions we have chosen, where the location of the full/empty columns is randomly chosen.

The scope of P, achievable by our Sun-3 workstation, is limited to 2^{17}. However, this range turned out sufficient in getting a clear tendency of the results which, if does not hold for all P, is probably kept up to at least $P = 2^{25}$. We tried 2 sizes of L: 1024 and 4096. To normalize, the total number of steps was divided by L. For each value of $\log P = 8, ..., 17$ the average of 10 experiments is presented. Most deviations from the averages presented are small: the highest of them, 0.55, is a real exception.

The results suggest a linear growth of the flow part run-time and $\log P$, so the algorithm behaves asymptotically as $L * \log P$. Note, however, that the constants make the algorithm competitive with a $5 * L$ algorithm at the feasible range of P (taking the control part into account). Moreover, when the number of columns is much less or much more then $P/2$ or when it is not a zero/full-column distribution then the performance is a lot better. Results of the simulations are presented in figure 2.

5.4 A Smoothing Lower Bound

To achieve a smoothing lower bound one needs a better insight of the Perfect Shuffle structure. This can be done as follows: the $P = 2^n$ nodes of the network are split into $n+1$ disjoint sets: $PS_0, ..., PS_n$. PS_i is the set of processors having exactly i set address bits. The relative size of the sets follows the binomial distribution. The links between the sets PS_i and PS_{i+1} are exactly all the EX edges originating at nodes in PS_i having a "0" rightmost address bit. Analogously, the PS_i to PS_{i-1} links originate at nodes in PS_i having a set rightmost address bit. σ edges always connect processors in the same PS-set. Clearly, to move from a processor in PS_i to a processor in PS_j ($i < j$), one has to visit at least two processors at each of $PS_{i+1}, ..., PS_{j-1}$ in that order.

Suppose half of the processors, say, all the processors having at most $n/2$ set address bits, have a full column size L_{max} and the other half are "empty".

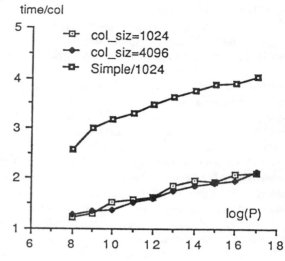

Figure 2: Simulation Results

Then smoothing requires $L_{max}/2 * P$ elements be moved through $PS_{n/2}$. However, there are only

$$\binom{n-1}{n/2} \approx \frac{1}{2} * \frac{1}{\sqrt{2\pi n}} * 2^n = \frac{1}{2\sqrt{2\pi n}} * P$$

edges connecting $PS_{n/2}$ to $PS_{n/2-1}$, a bottleneck of factor $\frac{1}{\sqrt{\log P}}$. Hence $\Omega(L * \sqrt{\log P})$ steps are necessary to complete the smoothing operation.

Consider a node of the PS network and all the nodes it can reach using σ connections only. This defines a "ring" of processors which we call a *necklace*. The internal structure of the PS-sets consists of disjoint, disconnected necklaces. Suppose bits are moving through a necklace in the following fashion: a necklace edge can carry 1 bit per second, an even necklace node is the exit of 1 bps and an odd necklace node is the entrance of 1 bps. Then the number of bps moving through the necklace is exactly the number of all the odd-even pairs of necklace processors which are neighbors. This observation, however, applied to the total flow through $PS_{n/2}$, does not change the asymptotics of the previous estimate.

5.5 The Dup Operation

The 2-D dup operation duplicates each element, e, producing extra copies according to a tag number ($e.c$) associated with e. The resulting total number of elements is $D = \sum_{\text{all } e} e.c$. Note that there is no requirement on the final distribution of the copies. Let $D_i = \sum_{e \text{ in } PE_i} e.c$ and L_i the number of elements in PE_i before duplication.

For the 1-D case Schwartz [Sc-80] suggested to use PP to determine the place of each element in the new array, then use sorting to move each element to its place, and finally PP by groups to duplicate each element in the space between every two original elements.

For the 2-D case smoothing is used to equally distribute the duplication work among the processors. Then D/P more steps are required to complete the duplication at each processor locally. Note that in the course of the smoothing operation it may be necessary to duplicate e, tagged $e.c$, to e_1 and e_2 and assign them with new tags $e_1.c'$ and $e_2.(e.c - e_1.c')$. This duplication might cause the size of (real) columns, L_i, to increase which might increase the smoothing runtime too. However, in the next subsection a way is shown how to equalize D_i and D_j for two adjacent columns, where L_i and L_j increase by at most 1. Hence the real column size increases by at most $\log P$ so the total dup algorithm runtime is $O(\text{Smooth}(L) + D/P)$, where L is the size of the highest column *before* duplication and $\text{Smooth}(L)$ is the cost of the smoothing operation. When $D/P > L$, this algorithm performs better than the minimum of $O(D/P * \log P + \log^2 P)$ steps required by adopting the 1-D algorithm to the 2-D case.

5.6 Dup - Smoothing

Given two adjacent processors, PE_i and PE_j, it remains to show that their "D-heights" can be equalized such that their "L-heights" increase by at most 1. It is easier to see for the Simple smoothing algorithm (section 5.1). Before the beginning of the algorithm each column is sorted by tags. The columns are kept sorted from this point on, throughout the algorithm. Consider step (i) where all odd-even pairs of processors equalize their column D-heights. Let PE_i, PE_{i+1} be such a pair.

- While the L-heights are different, move elements from the higher column to the lower one, preserving the internal column order sorted by tags.

- W.l.o.g. $D_i > D_{i+1}$. Denote $Top(i)$ the element with the largest tag in PE_i's column and $Bottom(i + 1)$ the element with smallest tag in PE_{i+1}'s column. Obviously $Top(i) > Bottom(i + 1)$. Preserving the internal column order sorted, PE_i and PE_{i+1} exchange these two elements. Keep exchanging until D_{i+1} becomes larger then or equal to D_i. If $D_{i+1} > D_i$, then the last element moved from PE_i to PE_{i+1} can be split into two, such that the return of one of them to PE_i makes the D-heights equal.

For the new step (i) of the simple smoothing algorithm, the final L-heights are at most the average of the L-heights of initial columns plus one. Moreover, the preservation of order is easily kept, using a merge-like scan of the columns, in $O(L)$ steps. The overall algorithm runtime is $O(L * \log L + L * \log P + \log^2 P)$, regardless of the D-heights.

6 Cartesian Product

Assume that the elements in the 2-D array are divided into two groups: A and B. Then the Cartesian product (CP) $A \times B$ operation produces all pairs a, b, such that a belongs to A and b belongs to B. There is no restriction on the final distribution of pairs.

In [Sc-80] there is an algorithm for 1-D CP for groups of size at most $P^{\frac{1}{2}}$. A naive adaptation of this algorithm to the 2-D case requires at least $O(\frac{|A| * |B|}{P} * \log P)$ steps. Suppose $|A| > |B|$ and $|A| > P$, and assume A is smoothed, i.e. each processor has $\frac{|A|}{P}$ of A's elements. The following algorithm achieve 2-D CP of A and B in $O(\frac{|A|*|B|}{P} + |B|)$ steps:

(i) Use 2-D broadcast to produce a copy of each element of B in each processor. This takes at most $2 * (|B| + \log P)$ steps.

(ii) Locally, each processor creates a, b for every a which belongs to A's elements stored in it and every b in B. This takes $\frac{|A|*|B|}{P}$ steps.

6.1 Cartesian Product by Groups

Given list of CPs CPBG= $\{A_1 \times B_1, ..., A_r \times B_r\}$, the Cartesian product by group (CPBG) operation produces all pairs of all the products in CPBG. The following assumptions are natural for many cases:

- r is "sufficiently" small, i.e. $r \ll P$ and $r \ll L$.

- The CPBG is initially known for all processors, including group sizes. Here we also assume that CPBG is given such that all processors discriminate groups appearing at the "B-side" from those appearing at the "A-side". The CPBG is stored in the following data structure: for every "A-group" A_j there is an ordered list L_j containing all "B-groups" that are "taken product" with A_j in CPBG, i.e. G is in L_j if and only if $A_j \times G$ belongs to CPBG.

- The groups are mutually disjoint, i.e. elements of different groups may have same value but always different "id"s.

Operation	Perfect Shuffle Time	Lower Bound
Row-Reduction	$4(L + \log P)$	
Parallel-Prefix	$20(L + \log P)$	
Transpose (T_{rc} and T_{cr})	$1.5 * L * \log P$	$\Omega(L * \log P)$
Smoothing	$L * \log P$	$\Omega(L * \sqrt{\log P})$
Dup	$D/P + O(L * \log P)$	D/P
Cartesian Product of A and B	$\frac{|A| * |B|}{P} + 5 * |B|$	$\frac{|A| * |B|}{P}$
Cartesian Product by Groups	$L * \log P + \sum(|B_i| + \frac{|B_i| * |A_i|}{P})$	$\sum \frac{|B_i| * |A_i|}{P}$

Figure 3: Table of Results

The following CPBG algorithm is a close variant of the CP algorithm:

(i) All groups at the "B-side" are broadcasted to all processors, not repeating the same group-broadcast twice. Note that this enables an ordering of the elements of each "B-group" consecutively, which is equivalent at all processors.

(ii) Let e be an element of a group A_j where A_j is at the "A-side". Let $|L_j|$ denote the total number of elements of all groups in L_j. e is associated with a label containing its group id and a range: $e.A_j. < 1, ..., |L_j| >$. The range of e corresponds to the (ordered) elements from the (ordered) groups of L_j with which it is to be paired.

(iii) The labeled elements are "smoothed" by a variant of the smoothing incorporated in the dup operation (section 5.6). Whenever the smooth operation requires a splitting of $e.A_j. < x, ..., y >$ into e_1 and e_2, the range of e is split into disjoint "segments": $e_1.A_j. < x, ..., z >$ and $e_2.A_j. < z + 1, ..., y >$. The result of this step is an even distribution of the "pairing" work among all processors.

(iv) Each processor generates all pairs of "A-elements" with their "B-partners", specified by their labels.

The total number of steps required is at most $L_A * \log P + \sum_{i=1}^{r}(|B_i| + \frac{|B_i| * |A_i|}{P})$ where L_A is the highest column at the "A-side".

7   Discussion and Summary

Figure 3 summarizes performance of 2-D algorithms presented in this work. Only dominating terms are given. It turned out that the efficient 2-D algorithms are those related to problems which may involve some computation of values but do not involve (sets of) permutations. On the other hand, problems for which the best algorithm is provably inefficient, such as the packing or transpose operations, clearly are special cases of 2-D permutations. It is interesting to refer to smoothing not as a specific 2-D permutation, but rather as a collection of such, from which one has to be chosen. The question remains open wether smoothing can be done more efficiently.

References

[Sc-80] J. T. Schwartz: *Ultracomputers*, ACM TOPLAS 2, pp. 484-521, 1980.

[St-71] Harold S. Stone: *Parallel Processing with the Perfect Shuffle*, IEEE Trans. C-20, pp. 153-161, 1971.

[Kr-81] Clyde P. Kruskal: *Upper and Lower Bounds on the Performance of Parallel Algorithms*, Ph.D. Dissertation, Courant Inst., NYU, 1981.

[GK-80] A. Gottlieb and C. Kruskal: *Supersaturated Ultracomputer Algorithms*, Ultracomputer note #11.

[Be-88] Y. Ben-Asher: *M&P A Non Procedural Parallel programming Language Based on Set Theory*, Ph.D. dissertation, Hebrew University 1988.

[UP-87] E. Upfal and D. Peleg: *The Generalized Packet Routing Problem*, IBM Research Report, RJ 5529 (56428), 1987.

SYSTEMATIC HARDWARE ADAPTATION OF SYSTOLIC ALGORITHMS

Miguel Valero-Garcia, Juan J. Navarro
Jose M. Llaberia and Mateo Valero

Dept. Arquitectura de Computadores
Facultad de Informática (UPC) Pau Gargallo 5
08028 BARCELONA (SPAIN)

ABSTRACT

In this paper we propose a methodology to adapt Systolic Algorithms to the hardware selected for their implementation. Systolic Algorithms obtained can be efficiently implemented using Pipelined Functional Units. The methodology is based on two transformation rules. These rules are applied to an initial Systolic Algorithm, possibly obtained through one of the design methodologies proposed by other autors. Parameters for these transformations are obtained from the specification of the hardware to be used. The methodology has been particularized in the case of one-dimensional Systolic Algorithms with data contraflow.

1. INTRODUCTION

Systolic Algorithms (SAs) exhibit some features that make them suitable for a direct hardware implementation (VLSI/WSI). Specifically, SAs are highly parallel/pipelined algorithms, specified on the basis of simple operations (fine granularity), with an high degree of homogeneity in the operations and regularity in the communication pattern. When an SA is implemented in hardware, then a *Systolic Array Processor* (SAP) is obtained [1].

The early SAs were obtained, probably, in an heuristic way [2]. They are SAs oriented to matrix problems (matrix multiplication, LU decomposition, etc). Later, automatic methodologies to design SAs have been proposed. The benefits of a design methodology are, among others, a savings in design time, the correctness of designs, and the possibility to obtain several solutions and choose the best according to a given criterium.

Any methodology uses some representation of the computation to be performed (signal flow graphs [3], [4], algorithms with loops [5], recurrences [6], [7], parallel programming languages [8], or data dependency graphs [9]). SAs are obtained through systematic manipulations of the chosen representation. In [10] a survey of proposed methodologies can be found. An up-to-date version of this paper appears in [11].

This work was supported by CAICYT under contract PA85-0314.

In general, SAs obtained through these methodologies show some features which trouble their direct and efficient hardware implementation. Among them, we point out the following:

a) SAs are *problem-size-dependent*, that is, the number of cells of the SAs depends on the size of the problem to be solved.

b) SAs have *simple synchronization*, that is, it is assumed that any cell spends the same time (a systolic cycle) to perform any operation, in spite of the fact that some operations can be more complex than others.

Feature (a) represents an evident drawback, because the number of processing elements (PEs) in an SAP is fixed and the size of the problems can be variable. This problem can be solved by *partitioning* the SA. Particular solutions to the partitioning problem have been presented in [12], [13] and [14], and more general solutions in [15], [16] and [17].

An SA with simple synchronization may exhibit two mayor drawbacks:

1) For a given implementation, some operations (square roots, divisions,etc) may require more time to be performed than others (multiplications, additions, etc), due to its complexity. If the SA is directly implemented, then the time required to perform the slowest operation becomes the cycle time. In this case, cells that perform simpler operations will be idle during a part of every cycle. We have not found, up to the present, any report dealing with this problem that we call *cycle-level unbalanced load*.

2) The SA can not be efficiently implemented using *Pipelined Functional Units* (PFUs). This kind of units can be used to increase the throughput of the system. Two-level pipelined SAs, that can be efficiently implemented using PFUs, are described in [18] and [19]. In [20] a technique is proposed to transform SAs with simple synchronization into two-level pipelined SAs. This technique was applied only to SAs without *data contraflow*.

In this paper we present a technique which permits to solve systematically, any of the above mentioned problems. Some previous results appear in [21]. This technique uses two transformations. The first one is based on the *retiming* and *slowdown* concepts [3], [22]. The second one is based on *coalescing* [23]. We propose a model to represent SAs in order to permit the formalization of these transformations. This model improves the one proposed in [22]. Algorithms are proposed to determine the transformations that allow us to obtain cycle-level balanced SAs efficiently implementable using PFUs. More precisely, the model and transformations are particularized in the case of one-dimensional (1D) band SAs with data contraflow.

1D band SAs with data contraflow are efficient for solving problems such as: band triangular systems of linear equations [1], LU decomposition [1] or QR decomposition [24]. For any of these problems, dense SAs without data contraflow can also be found.

In 1D dense SAs without contraflow for the above problems, matrices involved in the computation enter the cells by rows or columns. Every cell must perform complex operations (square roots, divisions) in some cycles, and simpler operations (multiplications and additions) in other cycles. Dense SAs are easily partitioned. Typically, matrices are partitioned into square blocks and partial results are combined to produce the final result. SAs without data contraflow can be easily modified to use efficiently a second level of pipeline if the cells are implemented using PFUs.

On the other hand, in 1D band SAs with data contraflow, matrices enter the cells by diagonals. In this case only one cell performs complex operations. So, band SAs with data contraflow require less hardware to be implemented. However, partitioning the SA is not intuitively simple and the use of PFUs is more difficult due to the existence of feedback cycles. Efficient solutions to the partitioning problem can be found in [24], [25] and [26]. In this paper, automatic techniques are given to solve the problems associated with the use of PFUs in the design of the PEs.

This paper is structured as follows: Section 2 presents the model proposed for the description of SAs. In section 3, transformations applied to SAs are enunciated. In section 4, we propose an algorithm to adapt an SA to the hardware used to implement its cells. This algorithm uses transformations described in section 3. In this section, some restrictions are imposed to the hardware in order to facilitate the use of transformations. In section 5 an improvement is proposed to obtain more efficient algorithms. In section 6, restrictions imposed in section 4 are eliminated. In section 7, a final improvement is proposed which will permit to apply our methodology to a wide set of SAs.

2. MODELLING OF SYSTOLIC ALGORITHMS

An SA is a set of cells interconnected through unidirectional links. Each cell is also possibly communicated with the outside world through I/O unidirectional links. The cells perform operations on data arriving every cycle through input links. Every cell is busy during each cycle in which it performs an operation. In the proposed model for SAs, we assign these cycles to communication links, and it is assumed that any operation is performed in zero time. Results of operations are sent to other cells, or to the outside, through output links in every cell. To synchronize the whole computation performed by the SA, a time delay is associated with each link. The value of this delay is the number of cycles required to traverse the link. We assume that every cell performs the same operation each cycle (time__homogeneous SAs). Furthermore, we suppose that only one link, at most, in each direction exists between any pair of cells is the SA. These restrictions are imposed here just in order to simplify notation, and they could be easily eliminated.

Any SA, and in particular, an 1D band SA with data contraflow, can be modelled by the tuple:

$$A = (w, I, O, R, E, S, k)$$

and by the definition of operations performed in each cycle by every cell. The meaning of each element in the tuple is the following:

w is the number of cells of SA A.

I is the set $\{I_1..I_p\}$, with p being the number of links entering into the SA from the outside. I_j is the data sequence $\{I_j(1), I_j(2),..\}$ which inputs to the SA through the j-th input link.

O is the set $\{O_1..O_q\}$, with q being the number of links leaving the SA. O_j is the data sequence $\{O_j(1), O_j(2),..\}$ which outputs the SA through the j-th output link.

R and E are matrices with elements in the form of : $X(i,j) = Z^{-x(i,j)}$ or $X(i,j) = 0$ [22]. Matrix R has w-by-w elements. The value

$r(i,j)$ is the delay associated with the link from cell j to cell i. If such link does not exist, then $R(i,j) = 0$. Matrix E has w-by-p elements. The value $e(i,j)$ is the number of cycles from the beginning of the SA operation until cell i receives the first data item in the I_j sequence. If cell i receives no data from I_j then $E(i,j) = 0$.

Matrix S has w-by-q elements in the form of $S(i,j) = Z^{s(i,j)}$ or $S(i,j) = 0$. The value $s(i,j)$ is the number of cycles until cell i produces the first data item in O_j. If cell i produces no data for O_j, then $S(i,j) = 0$.

k is the *slow* [3] of the SA. A k-slow SA can solve k equal and independent problems in an interleaved way.

In most cases, the SA has a *regular I/O structure*, that is, only data $\{I_j(1), I_j(k+1), I_j(2k+1)...\}$ are valid data (data which influence the final result). Analogously, only data $\{O_j(1), O_j(k+1), O_j(2k+1) ...\}$ are valid results.

Operations performed by every cell in each cycle can be described in several ways (algorithmically, graphically, etc). In our case, we use a graphic notation, but this decision does not affect the methodology at all.

As an example, we show the model for an 1D band SA with data contraflow to solve the band triangular system of linear equations $Lx = b$. This SA is shown in figure 1.a. The model is:

$$w = bandwidth\ of\ matrix\ L\ (8\ in\ the\ example)$$

$$k = 2$$

$$e(i,i) = i + 6 \quad i \in [1..8]$$

$$e(8,9) = 14$$

$$E(i,j) = 0 \quad i \in [1..8], j \in [1..9], i \neq j\ and\ (i,j) \neq (8,9)$$

$$s(8,1) = 14$$

$$S(i,1) = 0 \quad i \in [1..8]\ and\ i \neq 8$$

$$r(i,i+1) = 1 \quad and\ r(i+1,i) = 1 \quad i \in [1..7]$$

$$R(i,j) = 0 \quad i,j \in [1..8], i \neq j+1\ and\ j \neq i+1$$

$$I_i(kt+1) = l_{t+i,t+1} \quad t \geq 0\ ;\ I_i(t) = 0\ otherwise \quad i \in [1..8]$$

$$I_9(kt+1) = b_{t+1} \quad t \geq 0\ ;\ I_9(t) = 0\ otherwise$$

$$O_1(kt+1) = x_{t+1} \quad t \geq 0\ ;\ O_1(t) = 0\ otherwise$$

$$cell\ 1\ performs\ a\ division\ in\ every\ cycle$$

$$cell\ i\ (i \neq 1)\ performs\ an\ inner\ product\ step\ in\ every\ cycle$$

This SA, proposed in [1], can also be obtained through any design methodology. It exhibits the drawbacks mentioned in section 1:

a) The number of cells ($w=8$) is equal to the bandwidth of matriz L. In a practical case, the number of PEs of an SAP is fixed and, likely lesser than w.

b) It is assumed that any operation requires one cycle to be performed. In this case, divisions, performed in cell 1, are more time consuming than inner product steps, performed in the rest of cells. In a direct implementation of the algorithm, the cycle time would be fixed by the time required to perform a division.

3. TRANSFORMATION RULES FOR SYSTOLIC ALGORITHMS

In this section we describe two transformation rules which will permit to obtain SAs efficiently implementable in hardware. The formulation of these rules is based on the model presented in the previous section. The rules have been particularized in the case of 1D SAs.

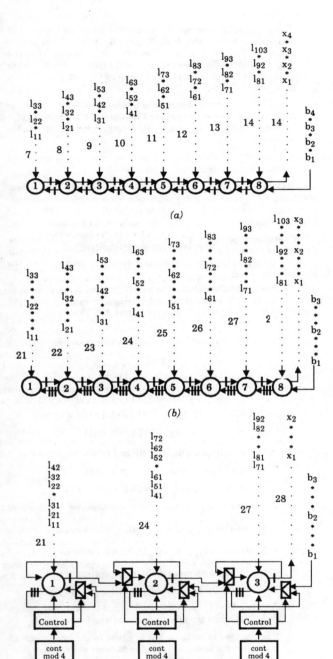

Figure 1. (a) 1D SA for band triangular system of linear equations, (b) SA after applying rule 1, and (c) SA after applying rule 2.

Rule 1:

Rule 1 is equivalent to transformations presented in [22]. It is based on the concepts of retiming and slowdown [3]. The rule allows to obtain an equivalent SA by resynchronizing the original one. In this new SA, cycles in which data arrive to cells and delays between cells have been modified. These new delays will serve to model the time needed to perform every operation for a given hardware to implement the cells. The rule is:

SA $A' = (w', I', O', R', E', S', k')$ performs the same computation as $A = (w, I, O, R, E, S, k)$ if:

A has a regular I/O structure

$$w' = w$$

$$k' = ck$$

$$E' = DE^c$$

$$S' = S^c D^{-1}$$

$$R' = DR^c D^{-1}$$

$$I'_i(k't+1) = I_i(kt+1) \quad i \in [1..p] \text{ and } t \geq 0$$

$$O'_i(k't+1) = O_i(kt+1) \quad i \in [1..q] \text{ and } t \geq 0$$

Any matrix of the form X^c is defined as: $X^c(i,j) = Z^{-cx(i,j)}$ if $X(i,j) = Z^{-x(i,j)}$ or $X^c(i,j) = 0$ if $X(i,j) = 0$. D is a diagonal matrix with w-by-w elements in the form of $D(i,i) = Z^{-d_i}$. The values c and d_i can be any of those belonging to the set of rationals. Values c and d_i ($i \in [1..w]$) are the parameters of rule 1.

Rule 2:

This rule is based on coalescing. Its objective is to eliminate the inefficiency of a k-slow SA, with a regular I/O structure, in which every cell performs one valid operation only one out of every k cycles. The rule allows to transform an SA $A'(k'$-slow) into an SA A^*, which performs the same computation, requiring the same number of cycles, but using a lesser number of cells (w^*). Cell q of A^* will perform operations assigned to $p(q)$ adjacent cells of A'. That will be possible if the $p(q)$ adjacent cells of A' perform their operations in different cycles. The values of $p(q)$ ($q \in [1..w^*]$) are the parameters of rule 2. These values must satisfy the following condition:

$$\sum_{q=1}^{w^*} p(q) = w'$$

Cell q of A^* will perform operations assigned to cells $a(q)..b(q)$ of A', where:

$$a(q) = 1 + \sum_{i=1}^{q-1} p(i) \quad \text{and} \quad b(q) = a(q) + p(q) - 1 \quad q \in [1..w^*]$$

Rule 2 can be formulated as follows:

Let A' be an SA represented by $A' = (w', I', O', R', E', S', k')$. We define $T(i)$ as the number of cycles a data item requires to travel from cell 1 to cell i in SA A':

$$T(i) = \sum_{j=1}^{i-1} r'(j+1,j) \quad i \in [1..w']$$

If A' satisfies condition:

$$T(i) \bmod k' \neq T(j) \bmod k' \quad i,j \in [a(q)..b(q)], i \neq j \text{ and } q \in [1..w^*] \quad (1)$$

then applying rule 2, with parametres $p(q)$ to A' we obtain a new SA $A^* = (w^*, I^*, O^*, R^*, E^*, S^*, k^*)$ which performs the same computation as A'. Elements in the tuple modelling A^* are obtained by the following expressions:

$$e^*(q,q) = \min_{i=a(q)}^{b(q)} e'(i,i) \quad q \in [1..w^*]$$

$$e^*(w^*, w^*+1) = e'(w', w'+1)$$

$$s^*(w^*, 1) = s'(w', 1)$$

$$r^*(q+1,q) = r'(a(q+1),b(q)) \; ; \; r^*(q,q+1) = r'(b(q),a(q+1))$$

$$q \in [1..w^*-1]$$

$$I^*_q(t+1) = I'_i(hk'+1) \; if \; t+e^*(q,q)-e'(i,i) = hk'$$

$$i \in [a(q)..b(q)], q \in [1..w^*] \; and \; t \geq 0$$

$$I^*_{w^*+1} = I'_{w'+1}$$

$$O^*_1 = O'_1$$

k^* is the number of different problems that can be solved by SA A^* in an interleaved way. An algorithm to obtain k^* is described in [27]. This value is not necessary to achieve our goal.

Figure 1.b shows the SA obtained by applying rule 1 with parameters $c=2$ and $d_i = -(i-1)$ $(i \in [1..8])$ to the SA shown in figure 1.a. The new SA is 4-slow. Delays between cells and the structure of input data sequences have been changed according with expressions described in this section. Now, applying rule 2 with parameters $p(1)=3$, $p(2)=3$ and $p(3)=2$ we obtain a new SA A^* shown in figure 1.c. This SA has only 3 cells. Using a counter module $k'=4$, initialized to zero, it is possible to determine, in every cycle, the operation to be performed by each cell as well as the data involved. These data can arrive from the neighbour cells or from operations performed by the cell in previous cycles. That is the reason for the feedback links. These links represent communications between cells of A', assigned by coalescing, to the same cell of A^*. The input data sequences to each cell of A^* have been obtained by interleaving data sequences in SA A'. A more detailed description of the procedure to obtain this structure can be found in [27].

Note that, in the previous example, rule 2 could have been applied with parameters $p(q) = k'=4$. For these values of the parameters $p(q)$, the number of cells of A^* is minimum $(w^* = w'/k')$ and the utilization of every cell is maximum (each cell performs one valid operations every cycle).

4. ADAPTING SYSTOLIC ALGORITHMS TO THE HARDWARE

Transformation rules presented in the previous section can be used with different goals in mind (automatic SA partitioning, SA adaptation for its execution in Distributed Memory Multiprocessor Systems, etc). In this section we show how to use these rules to adapt SAs to the hardware selected to implement their cells. Specifically, a method is proposed to implement 1D band SAs with data contraflow using PFUs efficiently.

Figure 2 synthesizes graphically the proposed methodology. Using a description of the hardware, parameters for rules 1 and 2 are obtained. These rules are then applied to the initial SA A. Using the resulting models for A' and A^* and the description of the hardware, the structure and control of the SAP is automatically obtained. In this section we will see how to obtain an SA A^* with a minimum number of cells $(w^* = w'/k')$. So, parameters for rule 2 are: $p(q) = k'$ $(q \in [1..w'/k'])$ and it will be necessary to find the parameters for rule 1.

We define OP_i as the operation performed by cell i of the initial SA A. This operation produces two results. One of them is sent to cell $i+1$ (or to the outside) and the other is sent to cell $i-1$ (or to the outside). We need some kind of representation of the hardware to be used in order to implement each cell. We propose a couple as a model of the hardware:

$$H = (RT, L)$$

RT is a vector of w reservation tables. Reservation table RT_i describes how the stages of a pipelined multifunctional unit (PMU) are used to perform OP_i. We suppose that the PMU is able to perform any of the w operations $OP_1 .. OP_w$.

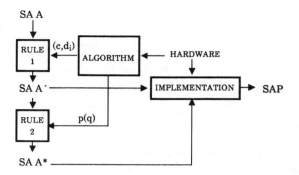

Figure 2. Use of transformation rules to adapt systolic algorithms to the hardware selected to implement their cells

L is a matrix with w-by-w elements in the form of $L(i,j) = Z^{-l(i,j)}$ or $L(i,j) = 0$. The value $l(i,j)$ is the number of cycles required by the PMU to obtain, by performing OP_j, the value to be sent to cell i. If cell j produces no values for cell i then $L(i,j) = 0$.

To apply rule 2, it is necessary to fulfil condition (1) described in section 3. But, if PMUs are used to implement each cell, this condition is not sufficient. It is necessary also to guarantee that there will not be conflicts in the use of the stages of the PMUs. In our case, $p(q) = k'$ $(q \in [1..w^*])$. So, reservation tables for the k' operations assigned to each cell of A^* must allow that any two operations can be initiated, in successive cycles, without conflicts. This restriction obviously influences the design of the PMUs to be used. Henceforth, we will call this restriction as R1.

As an example, figure 3 shows the hardware selected to implement SA in figure 1.a. To perform divisions required in cell 1, the division inversion algorithm [28] is applied, as shown in the following expression:

$$Q = \frac{A}{B} \simeq -AR(2+RB)$$

where R is an approximation of value $-1/B$ obtained by indexing a lookup table with some bits of B. If we use two 3-stages pipelined multipliers and one 2-stages pipelined adder then a division requires 8 cycles, if we disregard the time to access the lookup table. Reservation table in figure 3.a shows how this operation is performed. Using the same kind of multipliers and adders, an inner product step can be performed in 5 cycles as shown in figure 3.b. Note that reservation tables in figure 3 satisfy restriction R1.

The model for the hardware to be used is completed by giving the following values:

$$l(2,1) = 8$$

$$l(i+1,i) = 0 \; i \in [2..w-1]; \quad l(i,i+1) = 5 \; i \in [1..w-1]$$

$$L(i,j) = 0 \; otherwise$$

Now, we need to obtain the parameters of rule 1 which is necessary to adapt SA A to the hardware. These parameters must satisfy the following conditions:

condition (a):

In the resulting SA A', the delay associated with a link from a cell to any of its neighbours must be, at least, equal to the number of cycles required by the former to produce a value to be sent to the later. Moreover, this value must be, at least 1 to avoid data broadcasting. For the case of 1D band SAs with data contraflow, this condition can be enunciated as follows:

$(a.1) \quad r'(i,i+1) = d_i + cr(i,i+1) - d_{i+1} \geq max(1, l(i,i+1)) \quad i \in [1..w-1]$

$(a.2) \quad r'(i+1,i) = d_{i+1} + cr(i+1,i) - d_i \geq max(1, l(i+1,i)) \quad i \in [1..w-1]$

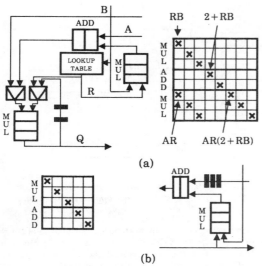

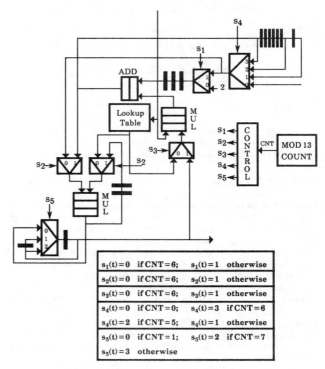

(a)

(b)

Figure 3. A possible hardware to implement: (a) divisions, (b) inner product steps.

	$s_1(t)=0$ if CNT$=6$;	$s_1(t)=1$ otherwise
	$s_2(t)=0$ if CNT$=6$;	$s_2(t)=1$ otherwise
	$s_3(t)=0$ if CNT$=6$;	$s_3(t)=1$ otherwise
	$s_4(t)=0$ if CNT$=0$;	$s_4(t)=3$ if CNT$=6$
	$s_4(t)=2$ if CNT$=5$;	$s_4(t)=1$ otherwise
	$s_5(t)=0$ if CNT$=1$;	$s_5(t)=2$ if CNT$=7$
	$s_5(t)=3$ otherwise	

Figure 4. Internal structure and control for PE 1 of SAP to solve a band triangular system of equations.

condition (b):

The first data item in any input sequence to A' must not arrive to the cells before the SA computation starts. In our case, this condition can be expressed as follows:

$(b.1)$ $e'(i,i) = d_i + ce(i,i) \geq 0$ $i \in [1..w]$

$(b.2)$ $e'(w,w+1) = d_w + ce(w,w+1) \geq 0$

condition (c):

This condition is derived from the particularization of condition (1) described in section 3, for the case of 1D band SAs with data contraflow, and assuming $p(q) = k'$. In this case:

$$T(i) = \sum_{j=1}^{i-1} r'(j+1,j) = \sum_{j=1}^{i-1} (d_{j+1} + cr(j+1,j) - d_j) \quad i \in [1..w]$$

The condition is:

(c) $T(i) \bmod k' \neq T(j) \bmod k'$

$i,j \in [(q-1)k'+1..qk'], i \neq j$ and $q \in [1..\frac{w'}{k'}]$

Algorithm 1 can be used to find a set of values (c, d_i) which satisfy conditions (a), (b) and (c). In the obtained solution, c has the minumum possible value. There can be different valid solutions. It is possible also that no solution exists, if we use the minimum value for c. In this case, solutions must be found by increasing the value of c. This increase represents a loss of parallelism, and consequently, the resulting SA A^* will require more cycles than A' to obtain the same final result.

Once values (c, d_i) are obtained, then rule 1 and rule 2 are applied to A. From the models of A', A^* and the hardware used, a simple algorithm presented in [27] obtains the SAP structure and control. Figure 4 shows the internal structure and control for PE 1 abtained by applying the method to SA in figure 1.a and using the hardware described in figure 3.This PE initiates divisions when the CNT is 6 and inner product steps otherwise.

5. TRANSMITTENT DATA FLOWS

SAs obtained by applying rule 2 (as the one shown in figure 1.c) allow high hardware utilization, which tends to *1*, when the initiation phase has been completed (and all the cells begin to perform valid operations). However, the initiation phase requires many cycles. Most of these cycles are the result of the unnecessary retention suffered by some data items inside the cells. For instance, in figure 1.c, each element of vector x computed in cell 1 is held in this cell during $k'=4$ cycles before it is sent to cell 2. This value could be sent to cell 2 as soon as it is computed. Thus, the initiation phase could become shorter.

This innefficiency appears when, in the initial SA A, there is a transmittent data flow. Data in a transmittent data flow do not suffer any change during its travel through the cells. This problem can be solved by appropriately applying rule 1 to A.

In this section we consider the case of an 1D band SA with data contraflow in which there is a transmittent data flow. Data in this flow are generated at one end of the SA and travel to the other end without modifications. If data in the transmittent data flow go from cell *1* to cell w then, in the model of the hardware to be used, we have:

$$l(i+1,i) = 0 \quad i \in [2..w-1]$$

If data in the transmittent data flow go from cell w to cell *1* then we have:

$$l(i,i+1) = 0 \quad i \in [1..w-2]$$

We will show how to solve the first case. The second one can be solved in a similar way. We will assume also, as in the previous section, that $p(q) = k'$ $(q \in [1..w^*])$. Now, the parameters of rule 1 must satisfy the following conditions:

$(a.1)$ $d_i + cr(i,i+1) - d_{i+1} \geq max(1,l(i,i+1))$ $i \in [1..w-1]$

$(a.2)$ $d_{i+1} + cr(i+1,i) - d_i \geq max(1,l(i+1,i))$

$i \in [1..w-1]$ and i is not a multiple of k'

$(a.3)$ $d_{qk'+1} + \sum_{j=(q-1)k'+1}^{qk'} cr(j+1,j) - d_{(q-1)k'+1} \geq$

$\geq max(1,l((q-1)k'+2,(q-1)k'+1))$

$q \in [1.. \dfrac{w'}{k'}-1]$

Conditions (a.1) and (a.2) are similar to those appearing in section 4. Condition (a.3) indicates that the minimum delay associated to the path from cell *(q-1)k' +1* to cell *qk' +1* in *A'(q ∈ [1..w*-1])* is equal to the number of cycles needed by the former to produce a value which will be sent through this path. So, after applying, cell *q-1* of *A** will send data to cell *q* as soon as possible. On the other hand, parameters d_i must satisfy conditions (b) and (c) as described in section 4.

The algorithm to obtain parameters for rule 1 is a slightly different version of algorithm 1. Sentences (3) and (4) in procedure *find__initial__parameters* of algorithm 1 must be replaced now by the following ones:

for $i := 1$ **to** *w-1* **do**
  if i is not a multiple of k'
    then $d_{i+1} := max(1,l(i+1,i))-cr(i+1,i)+d_i$

for $q := 1$ **to** *w'/k'-1* **do**
  $d_{k'q+1} := max(1,l((q-1)k'+2,(q-1)k'+1))+d_{(q-1)k'+1} -$
    $- \sum_{j=(q-1)k'+1}^{qk'} cr(j+1,j)$

This set of values are obtained by replacing the sign $\geq$ for $=$ in expressions (a.2) and (a.3). Sentences (16), (17) and (18) in procedure *find-new-parameters* must be replaced by:

if not *impossible*
  then for $m := i$ **to** *r(q)-1* **do**
    $d_{m+1} := d_m + max(1,l(m+1,m))-cr(m+1,m)$

As an example, applying rule 1 with parameters $c=2$, $d_1=0$, $d_2 = -1$, $d_3 = -2$, $d_4 = -5$, $d_5 = -6$, $d_6 = -7$, $d_7 = -10$, and $d_8 = -11$, to the SA shown in figure 1.a we obtain SA in figure 5. A delay of *-1* cycle is associated with link from cell *3* to cell *4* and link from cell *6* to cell *7*. This delay is represented by means of a white rectangle. A negative delay does not make any physical sense. However, SA in figure 5 must be understood in the following way: a value sent to the right by cell *1* is received at the same time, one cycle later, by cells *2* and *4*, and 2 cycles later by cells *3*, *5* and *8*. Applying now rule 2 with parameters *p(1)=3*, *p(2)=3* and *p(3)=2* we obtain an SA similar to that shown in figure 1.c. However, in this case, cells *2* and *3* receive the first value from the North *2* and *3* cycles sonner respectively.

There is another source of innefficiency when applying rule 2. With reference to figure 1.c, cell *1* can not perform the first valid operation until it receives b_1. This value requires *21* cycles to reach cell *1* from cell *8* in spite of the fact that it is not modified during its travel. This problem can be solved bypassing the firsts values of *B* so that the cells can initiate operations as soon as possible.

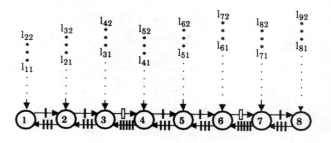

Figure 5. *Applying rule 1 when there is a transmittent data flow*

6. IMPLEMENTATION WITH MINIMUM HARDWARE

Restriction R1, described in section 4, can force to use more hardware than is strictly necessary to implement each operation. For example, as figure 6 shows, a division can be implemented with just one multiplier and one adder, in the same number of cycles as if two multipliers and one adder were used. However, if this implementation were used, then restriction R1 would not be satisfied and rule 2 could not be applied as described in section 4. In this section we propose an algorithm to determine the parameters of rule 1 when the used hardware does not satisfy restriction R1. In this case, it will not be generally possible to assign k' cells of *A'* to every *A** cell . The proposed algorithm also obtains the parameters *p(q)* for rule 2.

Solutions to this problem can be found by adapting results of previous works [29], [30]. In these works, methods are proposed to optimize the execution of a given set of operations in a PMU. In our case we know that:

a) the order in which operations must be initiated is fixed by the SA.

b) the initiation sequence must be periodically repeated, depending on the slow of the SA.

c) due to data dependencies, the initiation of operations must be separated in time by a minimum number of cycles.

On the other hand, an additional restriction is imposed to the solution of our problem. We will not allow a PMU to initiate more than one operation per cycle. The objective of this restriction is to limit the required bandwidth when implementing each cell.

Our first step is to evaluate the number of adjacent cells of *A'* that can be assigned to each *A** cell , that is, the parameters of rule 2. Then, the cycles in which every operation must be initiated are obtained. These values will serve to determine the parameters of rule 1. Without any lack of generality, we describe the method by applying it to cell *1* of *A**. This cell will execute OP_1, OP_2,...

Suppose that c is evaluated as described in algorithm 1. So, $k' = kc$. Suppose also that every PMU has p stages and that it is able to perform any of the w operations of SA *A*. Let RT_i be the reservation table to execute OP_i, using the PMU.

We define $MU(i,m)$ as the number of marks in the m-th row of RT_i. It is possible to assign, at most, s operations to cell *1* of *A** if, for any of the p stages of the PMU, the number of marks in reservation tables of these operations is not greater than k'. So, s satisfies the following condition:

$$max_{m=1}^p \sum_{i=1}^{s} MU(i,m) \leq k' \quad and \quad max_{m=1}^p \sum_{i=1}^{s+1} MU(i,m) > k'$$

Value s is a maximum for parameter *p(1)* fixed from the reservation tables. A maximum for the MAL (minimum average latency) [30] of the PMU is s/k'.

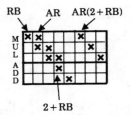

Figure 6. *Reservation table to implement a division using just one multiplier and one adder*

It is possible that not all of these s operations can be assigned to cell 1 of A^*. To determine the real value of $p(1)$ we use the reservation tables and the static collision matrices. Suffice it to apply the theory described in [30], taking into account features (a), (b) and (c) of our problem.

Let CM_i be the static collision matrix associated to OP_i. To obtain this matrix it is necessary to consider feature (b), that is, OP_i must be initiated every k' cycles. Moreover, all the elements in the first column of every CM will be TRUE to avoid the initiation of more than one operation in the same cycle.

Suppose that OP_i has been initiated in a given cycle and the dynamic collision matrix (DCM) of the PMU for this cycle, has been obtained. Now, we decide when OP_{i+1} can be initiated. Due to (c), this operation can be initiated x-1 cycles after OP_i if:

$$(1)\ x-1 \geq l(i+1,i)$$

$$(2)\ x-1 + l(i,i+1) \leq k'$$

$$(3)\ DCM\ (i+1,x) = 0$$

Conditions (1) and (2) are due to data dependencies between OP_i and OP_{i+1} and between OP_{i+1} and OP_i, respectively. Condition (3) must be satisfied to avoid conflicts in the use of the stages of the PFU.

If we decide to initiate OP_{i+1} x-1 cycles after OP_i then the new DCM must be obtained by ORing , bit-by-bit, CM_{i+1} with the DCM associated to the PMU when OP_i was initiated, rotated x-1 columns left. This rotation in necessary to take into account feature (b).

Due to the fact that the initiation sequence is finite and periodical, the typical modified state diagram appearing in [30], which represent states of the PMU (nodes) and transitions (edges), becomes, in our case, a tree. Each node at level i in the tree represents a possible initiation of OP_i. From every node at level i there are as many edges to nodes at level $i+1$ as valid initiations exist for OP_{i+1}. The number of levels of the tree is the value of $p(1)$, the number of A' cells assigned to cell 1 of A^*. Any path in the tree with size $p(1)$ gives a possible initiation sequence for the $p(1)$ operations.

In order to improve the PMU efficiency it is possible to modify the reservation tables by using the method of delay insertion [30]. Moreover, in our case, a little increase of value c (which implies an increase of k') can result in an increase of the number of cells assigned to each A^* cell.

Figure 7 shows a simple example of this procedure. Figure 7.a shows the reservation tables to implement the 4 cells of an SA. Values of matrix L, needed to complete the hardware model, are also shown. Suppose that $k' = 8$. Then only 3 cells, at most, can be assigned to cell 1 of A^*. Figure 7.b shows the static collision matrices for these 3 operations and figure 7.c shows the resulting tree. In this case, the 3 operations can be assigned to cell 1 of A^*. OP_2 must be initiated 5 cycles after OP_1 and OP_3 2 cycles after OP_2.

Algorithm 2 synthesizes the proposed procedure. It can be used to obtain the parameters for rules 1 and 2 that must be used to adapt SA A to the hardware.

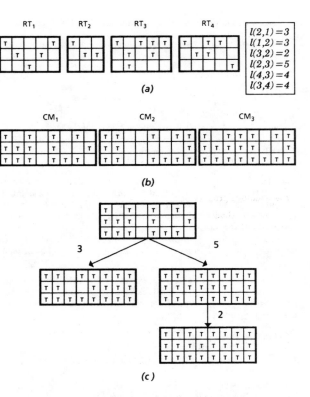

Figure 7. *Example of procedure described in section 6: (a) model for the hardware to be used, (b) collision matrices, (c) state obtained.*

7. NON_TIME_HOMOGENEOUS SYSTOLIC ALGORITHMS

The methodoly presented in previous sections can be applied to SAs in which each cell must perform always the same operation (time__homogeneous SAs), though different cells can perform different operations (non__spatial__ homogeneous SAs).

Non__time__homogeneous SAs appear frecuently in the literature. For instance, in the systolic ring for triangular system of equations proposed in [20], every cell must perform divisions in some cycles and inner product step in others. Non__time homogeneity appears also is most cases when applying DBT patitioning [14].

Non__time__homogeneous SAs can be easily treated by the proposed methodology. Let $OP_{i,1},..,OP_{i,n_i}$ be the n_i different operations performed by cell i during the SA computation. Let $RT_{i,j}$ be the reservation table to implement $OP_{i,j}$. We define RT_i as the reservation table obtained by ORing the n_i reservation tables associatted with cell i. Now, using RT_i as the reservation table for cell i, algorithms presented in previous sections can be used. This simple procedure can be successfully applied, specially if reservation tables associated with a cell are similar. This fact can be easily achieved for typical operations appearing in non__time__homogeneous SAs.

8. CONCLUSIONS

Generally, SAs Design Methodologies proposed in the literature start working from a specification of the problem to be solved, but do not take into account any implementation restriction.

In this paper we have proposed a technique that can be used to adapt automatically an SA to the hardware used to implement it. This technique permits to obtain SAs with any of the following features:

a) number of cells independent of the problem size,

b) different time consuming operations,

c) two_level pipelined

The technique is based on two transformation rules and a set of algorithms that use these transformations. Specifically, algorithms have been particularized to obtain efficiently implementable, two-level pipelined 1D band SAs with data contraflow. As an example, an SA to solve band triangular system of equations is presented. This kind of SAs can not be obtained through any other design methodology proposed up to now.

The methodology is generalizable to any other kind of 1D SAs as well as 2D SAs.

Transformation rules described in this paper can also be used for automatic partitioning of SAs. The basic idea consists on applying rule 1 with parameter:

$$c = \frac{1}{k} \lceil \frac{N}{w} \rceil$$

where N and k are, respectively, the number of cells and the slow of the original SA and w is the number of cells of the target one. Rule 2 is then applied with parameters:

$$p(q) = \lceil \frac{N}{w} \rceil \quad q \in [1..w]$$

At present, we are developing software tools based on the results of this work. These tools will permit to design automatically efficient SAPs.

REFERENCES

[1] H.T. Kung and C.E. Leiserson, "Systolic Arrays (for VLSI), " *Sparse Matrix Proc. 1978*, 1979, Society for Industrial and Applied Mathematics (SIAM), pp. 256-282. (A slightly different version appears in the text *Introduction to VLSI Systems*, Section 8.3. C.A. Mead and L.A. Conway, eds.,1980, Addison-Wesley, Reading, Mass.).

[2] H.T. Kung, "Why Systolic Architectures?," *Computer*, Vol. 15, No. 1, Jan. 1982, pp. 37-46.

[3] C.E. Leiserson and J.B. Saxe, "Optimizing Synchronous Systems," *Proc. 22nd Annual Symp. on Foundations of Computer Science*, Oct. 1981, pp. 23-36.

[4] S.Y. Kung, "On Supercomputing with Systolic/Wavefront Array Processors," *Proc. IEEE* Vol. 72, No. 7, July 1984.

[5] D.I. Moldovan, "On the Design of Algorithms for VLSI Systolic Arrays," *Proc. IEEE*, Vol. 71, No. 1, pp. 113-120, 1983.

[6] P. Quinton, "Automatic Synthesis of Systolic Arrays form Uniform Recurrent Equations," *11th Int' l Symp. Computer Architecture*, pp. 208-214, IEEE & ACM, June 1984.

[7] G.J. Li, B.W. Wah, "The Design of Optimal Systolic Arrays," *IEEE Trans. on Computers*, Vol. C-34, No. 10, Jan. 1985, pp. 66-77.

[8] M. Chen, "Synthesizing VLSI Architectures: Dynamic Programming Solver," *Int' l Conf. on Parallel Processing*, 1986, pp. 776-784.

[9] I.V. Ramakrishnan and D.S. Fussell, "On Mapping Homogeneous Graphs on a Linear Array-Processor Model," *Int'l Conf. Parallel Processing 1983* pp. 440-447.

[10] J.A.B. Fortes, K.S. Fu and B.W. Wah, "Systematic Approaches to the Design of Algorithmically Specified Systolic Arrays," *Proc. Int'l Conf. Acoustic, Speech and Signal Processing, 1985*, pp. 8.9.1-8.9.5.

[11] J.A.B. Fortes, K.S. Fu and B.W. Wah, "Systematic Design Approaches to Algorithmically Specified Systolic Arrays," *Computer Architecture Concepts and Systems*, North Holland 1988, pp. 455-494.

[12] D. Heller, "Partitioning Big Matrices for Small Systolic Arrays," *Chapiter 11 of VLSI and Modern Signal Processing*, S.Y. Kung, H.J. Whitehouse and T. Kailath eds. 1985, Prentice-Hall, Englewood Cliffs, N.J., pp. 185-199.

[13] R. Schreiber and P.J. Kucks, "Systolic Linear Algebra Machines in Digital Signal Processing," *Chapter 22 of VLSI and Modern Signal Processing*, S.Y. Kung, H.J. Whitehouse and T. Kailath eds. 1985, Prentice-Hall, Englewood Cliffs, N.J., pp.389-405.

[14] J.J. Navarro, J.M. LLaberia and M. Valero, "Partitioning: An Essential Step in Mapping Algorithms Into Systolic Array Processors," *Computer*, Vol. 20, No. 7, July 1987, pp. 77-89.

[15] D.I. Moldovan and J.A.B. Fortes, "Partitioning and Mapping Algorithms Into Fixed Size Systolic Arrays," *IEEE Trans. on Computers*, Vol. C-35, No. 1, Jan. 1986, pp. 1-12.

[16] H.W. Neils and E.F. Deprettere, "Automatic Design and Partitioning of Systolic/Wavefront Arrays for VLSI," *Circuits Systems Signal Process*, Vol. 7, No. 2, 1988, pp. 235-252.

[17] H. Moreno and T. Lang, "Graph-based Partitioning of Matrix Algorithms for Systolic Arrays: Application to Transitive Closure," *1988 Int'l Conf. on Parallel Processing*.

[18] H.T. Kung, L.M. Ruane and D.W.L. Yen, "Two-Level Pipelined Systolic Array for Multidimensional Convolution," *Image and Vision Computing*, Vol. 1, No. 1, Febr. 1983 pp. 30-36

[19] D.W.L. Yen and A.V. Kulkarni, "Systolic Processing and an Implementation for Signal and Image Processing," *IEEE Trans. on Computers*, Vol. C-31, No. 10, Oct. 1982, pp. 1000-1009.

[20] H.T. Kung and M.S. Lam, "Wafer-Scale Integration and Two-Level Pipelined Implementation of Systolic Arrays," *Journal of Parallel and Distributed Processing*, Vol. 1, No, 1, 1984.

[21] M. Valero-Garcia, J.J. Navarro, J.M. LLaberia and M. Valero, "Systematic Design of Two-Level Pipelined Systolic Arrays with Data Contraflow," *Proc. IEEE Int'l Conf. on Circuits and Systems 1988*, pp. 2521-2525.

[22] H.T. Kung and W.T. Lin, "An Algebra for Systolic Computation," *Elliptic Problem Solvers II*, Academic Press 1984, pp. 32-63.

[23] C.E. Leiserson, "Area-Efficient VLSI Computations," *PhD dissertation*, Departament of Computer Science, Carnegie-Mellon University, OCt. 1981, Published in book form as part of the *ACM Doctoral Dissertation Award Series* by the MIT Press, Cambridge, Massachusetts, 1983.

[24] N. Torralba and J.J. Navarro, "A One-Dimensional Systolic Arrays for Solving Arbitrarily Large Least Mean Square Problems, " *Proc. Int'l Conf. on Systolic Arrays*. May 1988 pp. 103-112.

[25] J.J. Navarro, J.M. LLaberia and M. Valero, "Computing Size-Independent Matrix Problems on Systolic Array Processors," *13th Int'l Symp. Computer Architecture*, 1986, pp. 271-279

[26] J.J. Navarro, J.M. LLaberia and M. Valero, "Solving Matrix Problems with No Size Restriction on a Systolic Array Processor," *Int'l Conf. Parallel Processing, Aug. 1986*, pp. 676-683.

[27] M. Valero-Garcia, J.M. Llaberia and J.J. Navarro, "Considering Implementation Features in the Design of Systolic Array Processors," *Internal Report*, RR 88/01, Facultad de Informatica Barcelona, Spain.

[28] Floating Point Division/ Square Root/ IEEE Arithmetic WTL 1032/1033, Application Note, *Weitek*, 1983.

[29] C.V. Ramamoorthy, "Pipeline Architecture," *Computing Surveys*, Vol. 9, No. 1, March 1977, pp 61-102.

[30] P.M. Kogge, "The Architecture of Pipelined Computers," *Hemisphere Publishing Corporation*, 1981.

ALGORITHM 1

/* Algorithm 1 finds parameters c and d_i for rule 1 assuming that parameters for rule 2 are $p(q) = k'$ $(q \in [1..w*])$. First, the algorithm finds a set of values which satisfies condition (a) described in section 4. Then, these values are successively modified until they satisfy condition (c). Finaly, a simple correction of the values is applied to fulfil condition (b). */

Procedure *find_initial_parameters*

/* This procedure find a set of values which satisfy condition (a) */

begin

/* Adding expressions (a.1) and (a.2) we obtain the minimum possible value for c */

(1) $$c := \max_{i=1}^{w-1} \left(\frac{\max(1,l(i,i+1)) + \max(1,l(i+1,i))}{r(i,i+1) + r(i+1,i)} \right)$$

(2) $d_1 := 0$

/* We assign values to d_i by replacing the sign $\geq$ for $=$ in expression (a.2) */

(3)   **for** $i := 1$ **to** w-1 **do**
(4) $d_{i+1} := \max(1,l(i+1,i)) - cr(i+1,i) + d_i$

/* This solution represents the assignation of the necessary delays to the links going from right to left of the SA. Similary, delays can be assigned to the links going from left to right */

end

Procedure *check_condition(p, ok)*

begin

/* This procedure, not shown here, checks condition (c). If it is not satisfied then p takes the value of the index of the cell which causes conflicts */

end

Procedure *find_new_parameters (p,impossible)*

begin

(1) $k' := ck$
(2) $q := (p-1)$ **div** $k' + 1$

/* Cell p of A' will be assigned to cell q of A* */

(3) $a(q) := (q-1)k + 1$
(4) $b(q) := a(q) + k' - 1$
(5) $i := p$
(6) $stop := $ **FALSE**
(7)   **while not** *stop* **do**
      begin
(8) $d_i := d_i + 1$

/* This increment of d_i represents the transfer of one delay unit from the link going from cell i to cell i-1 to the link going from cell i-1 to cell i. It is necessary to check if this transfer is possible, that is, if this delay unit exists */

(9)   **if** $d_i + cr(i,i-1) - d_{i-1} + \max(1,l(i-1,i)) \leq k'$
          then   begin
(10) $stop := $ **TRUE**
(11) $impossible := $ **FALSE**
          end
          else   begin
(12) $i := i-1$
(13)   **if** $i = a(q)$
              then   begin

/* It is not possible to avoid conflicts between operations assigned to cell q of A* */

(14) $stop := $ **TRUE**
(15) $impossible := $ **TRUE**
              end
          end
(16) **if not** *impossible*
(17)   **then for** $m := i$ **to** w-1 **do**
(18) $d_{m+1} := d_m + \max(1,l(m+1,m)) - cr(m+1,m)$

end

Procedure *fit_parameters*

/* This procedure modifies parameters in order to satisfy condition (b) */

begin

(1) $$d := \min \left(\min_{i=1}^{w} (d_i + ce(i,i)), d_w + ce(w,w+1) \right)$$

(2)   **for** $i := 1$ **to** w **do**
(3) $d_i := d_i - d$

end

begin   /* Algorithm 1 */

(1)   *find_initial_parameters*
(2)   **repeat**
(3)   *check_condition (p, ok)*
(4)   **if not** *ok*
(5)   **then** *find_new_parameters (p, impossible)*
(6)   **until** *ok* **or** *impossible*
(7)   **if** *ok*
(8)   **then** *fit_parameters*

end

ALGORITHM 2

/* This algorithm obtains parameters for rules 1 and 2 if restriction R1 is not satisfied by the hardware. */

begin /* Algorithm 2 */

(1) $$c := \max_{i=1}^{w-1} \left(\frac{\max(1,l(i,i+1)) + \max(1,l(i+1,i))}{r(i,i+1) + r(i+1,i)} \right)$$

(2) $k' := kc$
(3) $q := 1$
(4) $a(q) := 1$
(5) $stop := $ **FALSE**
(6)   **while not** *stop* **do**
      begin
(7)   Select $b(q)$ which satisfies

$$\max_{m=1}^{p} \sum_{i=a(q)}^{b(q)} MU(i.m) \leq k' \text{ and}$$
$$(\max_{m=1}^{p} \sum_{i=a(q)}^{b(q)+1} MU(i,m) > k' \text{ or } b(q) = w)$$

(8)   Obtain the tree for cell q of A* and select a maximum size path. Let $p(q)$ be the number of operations in the initiation sequence associated with the selected path

(9) $b(q) := a(q) + p(q) - 1$

(10)   Let $r'(a(q)+i, a(q)+i-1)$ be the label of edge from node at level i to node at level $i+1$ in the selected path $(i \in [1..p(q)-1])$

(11)   **if** $b(q) = w$
          then   begin
(12) $stop := $ **TRUE**
(13) $w^* := q$
              end
          else   begin
(14) $a(q+1) := b(q) + 1$
(15) $r'(a(q+1), b(q)) := l(a(q+1), b(q))$
(16) $q := q + 1$
              end
          end
(17) $d_1 := 0$
(18) **for** $i := 1$ **to** w-1 **do**
(19) $d_{i+1} := r'(i+1,i) + d_i - cr(i+1,i)$
(20) **for** $i := 1$ **to** w **do**
(21) $d_i := d_i - d$

/* The value of d is defined in algorithm 1 */
/* Cell q of A* will perform operations assigned to cells a(q)..b(q) of A* */

end

TASK MIGRATION IN HYPERCUBE MULTIPROCESSORS

Ming-Syan Chen[‡] and Kang G. Shin[†]

† Real-Time Computing Laboratory
Department of Electrical Engineering and Computer Science
The University of Michigan
Ann Arbor, Michigan 48109-2122

‡ IBM Thomas J. Watson Research Center
P.O. Box 704
Yorktown Heights, New York 10598

ABSTRACT

Allocation and deallocation of subcubes usually result in a fragmented hypercube where even if a sufficient number of hypercube nodes are available, they do not form a subcube large enough to execute an incoming task. As the fragmentation in conventional memory allocation can be handled by memory compaction, the fragmentation problem in a hypercube can be solved by *task migration*, i.e., relocating tasks within the hypercube to remove the fragmentation. The procedure for task migration closely depends on the subcube allocation strategy used, since active tasks must be relocated in such a way that the availability of subcubes can be detected by that allocation strategy.

In this paper, we develop a task migration strategy for the subcube allocation policy based on the binary reflected Gray code. A goal configuration (of destination subcubes) without fragmentation is determined first. Then, the node-mapping between the source and destination subcubes is derived. Finally, a routing procedure to achieve shortest deadlock-free paths for relocating tasks is developed.

1. INTRODUCTION

Owing to their structural regularity and high potential for the parallel execution of various algorithms, hypercube computers have drawn considerable attention in recent years from both academic and industrial communities [1-6].

Each task arriving at the hypercube multiprocessor must be allocated to an unoccupied subcube for execution. Upon completion of a task, the subcube used for the task is released and made available to other tasks. In [3], we proposed a subcube allocation[1] strategy based on the binary reflected Gray code (BRGC), called the *GC strategy*, as opposed to the one based on the binary encoding scheme, called the *buddy strategy* [7]. The former is shown to outperform the latter due mainly to its superiority in recognizing the existence of available subcubes within a hypercube.

---

[1]In view of the fact that each task is allocated to a subcube, we use the term *subcube allocation* in this paper, instead of processor allocation which was used in [3].

Similarly to conventional memory management, allocation and deallocation of subcubes usually results in a fragmented hypercube, where even if a sufficient number of nodes are available, they do not form a subcube large enough to accommodate an incoming task. Fig. 1 shows an example of a fragmented hypercube where four available nodes cannot form a 2 dimensional cube, or Q_2, to be used; thus, if a task requiring a Q_2 arrives, it has to be either queued or rejected.

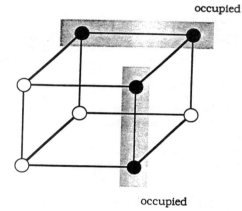

Figure 1. An example of hypercube fragmentation.

As shown in the simulation results in [3], such fragmentation leads to poor utilization of hypercube nodes, and the improvement achieved by the GC strategy is thus limited. As the fragmentation problem in conventional memory allocation can be handled by memory compaction, the fragmentation problem in a hypercube can be solved by *task migration*, i.e., relocating and compacting active tasks[2] within the hypercube at one end so as to make large subcubes available at the other end. Note that there is a strong dependence of task migration on the subcube allocation strategy used, since active tasks must be relocated in such a way that the availability of subcubes can be detected by that allocation strategy.

We shall in this paper focus on the development of a task migration strategy under the GC strategy of subcube allocation. A collection of occupied subcubes is called a *configuration*. We first determine the goal configuration to which a given fragmented hypercube must change by relocating active tasks. Since the GC strategy is proved in [3] to be optimal for static allocation[3], fragmentation can definitely be removed by task migration. When a

---

[2]Those tasks which are allocated to subcubes but not completed yet.

[3]By static allocation, we mean the allocation of subcubes to a sequence of incoming tasks without considering the deallocation of subcubes.

task is allocated to a subcube, the portion of the task located at each hypercube node of this subcube is called a *task module*. The action for a hypercube node to move its task module to one of its neighboring nodes is called a *moving step*. The cost of each task migration is then measured in terms of the number of moving steps required while task migrations between different pairs of source and destination subcubes are allowed to be performed *in parallel*. Note that to move tasks in parallel, it is very important to avoid deadlocks during task migration. We not only formulate the node-mapping between each pair of source and destination subcubes in such a way that the number of moving steps required is minimized, but also develop a routing procedure to use shortest deadlock-free paths for task migration.

The paper is organized as follows. Section 2 introduces the necessary definitions and notation first, and then describes the operation of the GC strategy. Our main results on task migration are given in Section 3. In three subsections are respectively presented the three steps for task migration under the GC strategy: (i) determination of a goal configuration, (ii) determination of the node-mapping between the source and destination subcubes, and (iii) determination of shortest deadlock-free routing for moving task modules. Several illustrative examples are also given. The paper concludes with Section 4.

2. PRELIMINARIES

2.1. Notation and Definitions

An n-dimensional hypercube is defined as $Q_n = K_2 \times Q_{n-1}$, where K_2 is the complete graph with two nodes, Q_0 is a trivial graph with one node and $\times$ is the product operation on two graphs [8]. Let $\sum$ be the ternary symbol set $\{0, 1, *\}$, where $*$ is a *don't care* symbol. Every subcube in a Q_n can then be uniquely represented by a string of symbols in $\sum$. For example, the address of the subcube Q_2 formed by nodes 0010, 0011, 0110 and 0111 in a Q_4 is 0*1*. Also, the *Hamming distance* between two hypercube nodes is defined as follows.

Definition 1: The Hamming distance between two nodes with addresses $u = u_n u_{n-1} \cdots u_1$ and $w = w_n w_{n-1} \cdots w_1$ in a Q_n is defined as

$$H(u,w) = \sum_{i=1}^{n} h(u_i,w_i), \text{ where } h(u_i,w_i) = \begin{cases} 1, & \text{if } u_i \neq w_i, \\ 0, & \text{if } u_i = w_i. \end{cases}$$

For convenience, the rightmost coordinate in the address of a subcube or a node will be referred to as *dimension 1*, the second to the rightmost coordinate as *dimension 2*, and so on. A *coding scheme* with n bits, denoted by C_n, is defined as a one-to-one mapping from an integer number between 0 and 2^n-1 to a binary representation with n bits, and $C_n(m)$ denotes the representation of a number m with n bits under a given coding scheme. For convenience, let B_n and G_n denote n-bit coding schemes associated with the binary encoding scheme and the BRGC, respectively. For example, $B_3(5)=101$, $G_3(5)=111$, while $C_4(7)=1110$ for the coding scheme in Fig. 2.

In addition, a *path* is defined as an ordered sequence of hypercube nodes in which any two consecutive nodes are physically adjacent to each other in the hypercube. Also, we assume that the hardware of the hypercube system under consideration is so designed that each hypercube node has separate input and output ports. Thus, each node can receive a task module while sending another task module to its next hop. Each moving step is assumed to take the same amount of time, which is defined as one time unit.

0.	0000	8.	1100
1.	0001	9.	1000
2.	0011	10.	1010
3.	0010	11.	1011
4.	0110	12.	1001
5.	0111	13.	1101
6.	1111	14.	0101
7.	1110	15.	0100

Figure 2. A coding scheme with 4 bits.

2.2. Descriptions of the GC Strategy

Note that the GC strategy is based on a first-fit sequential search. Node addresses under the GC strategy are ordered in a list according to the BRGC. Such a list is called an *allocation list*. Under the GC strategy, the availability of hypercube nodes is then kept track of by its allocation list. Suppose $k = |I_i|$ is the dimension of a subcube required to execute an incoming task I_i. The GC strategy will search for a set of 2^k consecutive unoccupied nodes in its allocation list, say $G_n(p)$, $G_n(p+1)$, $\cdots$, $G_n(p+2^k-1)$, under the constraint that p has to be a multiple of 2^{k-1}. A formal description of the GC strategy and the buddy strategy can be found in [3]. For a comparison purpose, examples for the operation under both strategies are given in Fig. 3.

$$|I_1| = 0 \qquad |I_3| = 0 \qquad |I_5| = 1$$

$$|I_2| = 2 \qquad |I_4| = 0$$

0.	0000 — I_1
1.	0001 — I_3
2.	0011 ⎤
3.	0010
4.	0110 I_2
5.	0111 ⎦
6.	0101 — I_4
7.	0100 ⎤
8.	1100 ⎦ I_5
9.	1101
10.	1111
11.	1110
12.	1010
13.	1011
14.	1001
15.	1000

0.	0000 — I_1
1.	0001 — I_3
2.	0010 — I_4
3.	0011
4.	0100 ⎤
5.	0101 I_2
6.	0110
7.	0111 ⎦
8.	1000 ⎤
9.	1001 ⎦ I_5
10.	1010
11.	1011
12.	1100
13.	1101
14.	1110
15.	1111

(a) GC strategy   **(b) Buddy strategy**

Figure 3. Example operations of both strategies.

3. TASK MIGRATION UNDER THE GC STRATEGY

Due to a similar reason for the memory fragmentation in conventional memory allocation, allocation and deallocation of subcubes may result in a fragmented hypercube. Although the GC strategy outperforms the buddy strategy, the improvement achieved by using multiple codes is rather limited [3]. This fact in turn implies that poor utilization of hypercube nodes is due mainly to system fragmentation, rather than the subcube recognition ability of an allocation strategy. Consequently, it is very important to develop an efficient procedure for task migration under the GC strategy, which relocates active tasks to eliminate the fragmentation. In the following three subsections we shall determine, respectively, the goal configuration, the node-mapping between the source and destination subcubes, and shortest deadlock-free paths for task migration.

3.1. Determination of Goal Configuration

There are usually many ways to relocate active tasks and compact occupied subcubes. However, since it is desirable to perform the task migration between each pair of subcubes in parallel, it is very important to avoid any deadlock during the migration. Clearly, a deadlock might occur if there is a circular wait among nodes. To prevent this, a linear ordering of hypercube nodes is established in such a way that each node can only move its task module to a node with a lower address, i.e., a node with address $G_n(p)$ sends its task module to another node with address $G_n(q)$, if and only if $p > q$. Since a node with a lower address never sends its task module to a node with a higher address, it is easy to see that the condition for any circular wait can be avoided by the above method. Thus, given a configuration of occupied subcubes, the goal configuration without fragmentation can be determined by the algorithm below.

Algorithm A_1: Determination of the goal configuration

Step 1.   Label each task in the availability list with a distinct number in such a way that each task allocated to a subcube with a lower address is labeled with a smaller number.

Step 2.   Relocate all tasks according to an increasing order of their labels.

For example, the goal configuration in Fig. 4b can be derived from the initial fragmented configuration in Fig. 4a. It can be easily verified that by using algorithm A_1, each task will always be moved from a subcube with a higher address to a subcube with a lower address, while a task with a smaller label is not necessarily ahead of a task with a larger label in the goal configuration. An allocation strategy is said to be *statically optimal* if a Q_n using the strategy can accommodate any input request sequence $\{I_i\}_{i=1}^{k}$ iff $\sum_{i=1}^{k} 2^{|I_i|} \leq 2^n$, where $|I_i|$ is the subcube dimension required by request I_i. As it was proved in [3], the GC allocation strategy is statically optimal. This fact implies that fragmentation will definitely be removed by A_1.

3.2. Node-Mapping Between Source and Destination Subcubes

Once the goal configuration is determined, each active task will be moved from its current or source subcube to the destination subcube. The action for a node to move its task module to one of its neighboring nodes is called a moving step. To determine the number of moving steps for a task migration, we first define the *moving distance* of a task between two subcube locations as follows. As it will be shown in Theorem 1 below, the minimal number of moving steps required to move a task from one subcube location to another can be determined by the moving distance between the two subcube locations. Furthermore, as it will become clear later, when modules of a task are migrated in parallel, the moving distance

0.	0000		0.	0000	— task 1
1.	0001		1.	0001	— task 4
2.	0011	— task 1	2.	0011	
3.	0010		3.	0010	
4.	0110		4.	0110	task 2
5.	0111		5.	0111	
6.	0101		6.	0101	
7.	0100	task 2	7.	0100	task 3
8.	1100		8.	1100	
9.	1101		9.	1101	
10.	1111		10.	1111	
11.	1110	task 3	11.	1110	
12.	1010		12.	1010	
13.	1011		13.	1011	
14.	1001	— task 4	14.	1001	
15.	1000		15.	1000	

(a). Before   (b). After

Figure 4. Task migration under the GC Strategy.

between two subcube locations is equal to the number of moving steps required to move a task module from the source node to its destination node under the node mapping scheme described in Corollary 1.1.

Definition 2 : The moving distance of a task between two subcube locations with addresses $\alpha = a_n a_{n-1} \cdots a_1$ and $\beta = b_n b_{n-1} \cdots b_1$ in a Q_n, $M : \sum^n \times \sum^n \to I^+$, is defined as

$$M(\alpha, \beta) = \sum_{i=1}^{n} m(a_i, b_i), \text{ where } m(a_i, b_i) = \begin{cases} 1, & \text{if } \{a_i, b_i\} = \{0, 1\}, \\ 0, & \text{if } a_i = b_i, \\ \frac{1}{2}, & \text{otherwise.} \end{cases}$$

Then, we have the following theorem for the minimal number of moving steps required to move a task from one subcube location to another.

Theorem 1 : Let $T(\alpha, \beta)$ be the minimal number of moving steps from a subcube location α to another location β. Then, $T(\alpha, \beta) = M(\alpha, \beta) 2^{|\alpha|}$, where $|\alpha| = |\beta|$ is the dimension of the subcube.

To facilitate the proof of Theorem 1, it is necessary to introduce the following proposition whose proof can be found in [9].

Proposition 1 : Given a node $u \in Q_n$, $\sum_{w \in Q_n} H(u, w) = n2^{n-1}$.

Proof of Theorem 1: We shall prove $T(\alpha, \beta) \geq M(\alpha, \beta) 2^{|\alpha|}$ first. Suppose $\alpha = a_n a_{n-1} \cdots a_1$ and $\beta = b_n b_{n-1} \cdots b_1$. We define the *frontier subcube* of α towards β, denoted by $\sigma_{\alpha \to \beta}(\alpha) = f_n f_{n-1} \cdots f_1$, in such a way that, $\forall i$, $f_i = b_i$ if $a_i = *$ and $b_i \in \{0, 1\}$, and $f_i = a_i$ otherwise. For example, if $\alpha = 00**$ and $\beta = 1*1*$, then $\sigma_{\alpha \to \beta}(\alpha) = 001*$ and $\sigma_{\beta \to \alpha}(\beta) = 101*$. Clearly, $\sigma_{\alpha \to \beta}(\alpha)$ contains all the nodes in α which are closest to β. Besides, we define the Hamming distance between two subcubes as the shortest distance between any two nodes which respectively belong to the two subcubes, i.e., $H^*(\alpha, \beta) = \min_{u \in \alpha, w \in \beta} H(u, w)$. Since we align some bits of α with their corresponding bits of β to obtain $\sigma_{\alpha \to \beta}(\alpha)$, it is easy to see that $\forall u \in \alpha$ and $w \in \beta$, $H(u, w) \geq H^*(u, \sigma_{\alpha \to \beta}(\alpha))$ $+ H^*(\sigma_{\alpha \to \beta}(\alpha), \sigma_{\beta \to \alpha}(\beta)) + H^*(\sigma_{\beta \to \alpha}(\beta), w)$.

Let $u' \in \beta$ denote the node to which the task module originally located at $u \in \alpha$ is to be moved. Notice that the number of moving steps required to move a task module from u to u' is greater than or equal to the Hamming distance between them, $H(u, u')$. Then, $T(\alpha, \beta) \geq \sum_{u \in \alpha} H(u, u')$. Moreover, from the above reasoning, we obtain:

$$T(\alpha, \beta) \geq \sum_{u \in \alpha} H(u, u')$$

$$\geq \sum_{u \in \alpha} \{ H^*(u, \sigma_{\alpha \to \beta}(\alpha)) + H^*(\sigma_{\alpha \to \beta}(\alpha), \sigma_{\beta \to \alpha}(\beta))$$

$$+ H^*(\sigma_{\beta \to \alpha}(\beta), u') \}$$

$$= \sum_{u \in \alpha} H^*(u, \sigma_{\alpha \to \beta}(\alpha)) + 2^{|\alpha|} H^*(\sigma_{\alpha \to \beta}(\alpha), \sigma_{\beta \to \alpha}(\beta))$$

$$+ \sum_{u \in \alpha} H^*(\sigma_{\alpha \to \beta}(\alpha), u').$$

Let r_1 be the number of dimensions in which $\{a_i, b_i\} = \{0, 1\}$, r_2 the number of dimensions in which $a_i = b_i = *$, r_3 the number of dimensions in which $a_i = *$ and $b_i \in \{0, 1\}$, and r_4 the number of dimensions in which $b_i = *$ and $a_i \in \{0, 1\}$. Clearly, $r_1 = H^*(\sigma_{\alpha \to \beta}(\alpha), \sigma_{\beta \to \alpha}(\beta))$, $r_2 + r_3 = |\alpha|$, $r_1 + r_3 = M(\alpha, \beta)$, and $r_3 = r_4$, because the addresses of α and β have the same number of *'s. Therefore,

$$T(\alpha, \beta) \geq \sum_{u \in \alpha} H^*(u, \sigma_{\alpha \to \beta}(\alpha)) + 2^{|\alpha|} H^*(\sigma_{\alpha \to \beta}(\alpha), \sigma_{\beta \to \alpha}(\beta))$$

$$+ \sum_{u \in \alpha} H^*(\sigma_{\alpha \to \beta}(\alpha), u')$$

$$= 2^{|\alpha|} H^*(\sigma_{\alpha \to \beta}(\alpha), \sigma_{\beta \to \alpha}(\beta)) + 2 \sum_{u \in \alpha} H^*(u, \sigma_{\alpha \to \beta}(\alpha))$$

$$= 2^{|\alpha|} r_1 + 2(2^{r_2} 2^{r_3 - 1} r_3)$$

(From Proposition 1 and $r_2 = |\sigma_{\alpha \to \beta}(\alpha)|$.)

$$= 2^{|\alpha|} (r_1 + r_3) = M(\alpha, \beta) 2^{|\alpha|}.$$

Next, we prove the inequality $T(\alpha, \beta) \leq M(\alpha, \beta) 2^{|\alpha|}$ by showing the existence of a one-to-one mapping between nodes in α and β, and that the Hamming distance between each pair of mapping and mapped nodes is $M(\alpha, \beta)$. Suppose $p_1, p_2, \cdots, p_{r_3}$ are those dimensions in which $a_{p_i} \in \{0, 1\}$ and $b_{p_i} = *$, and $q_1, q_2, \cdots, q_{r_4}$ are those dimensions in which $a_{q_i} = *$ and $b_{q_i} \in \{0, 1\}$. Note that $r_3 = r_4$. Each node $u = u_n u_{n-1} \cdots u_1 \in \alpha$ can then be mapped to a node $w = w_n w_{n-1} \cdots w_1 \in \beta$ in such a way that when $i \neq p_j$ for any $1 \leq j \leq r_3$,

$$w_i = \begin{cases} b_i, & \text{if } b_i \in \{0, 1\}, \\ u_i, & \text{if } a_i = b_i = *, \end{cases}$$

and when $i = p_j$ for some j, $1 \leq j \leq r_3$,

$$w_{p_j} = \begin{cases} \overline{u_{p_j}}, & \text{if } w_{q_j} = u_{q_j}, \\ u_{p_j}, & \text{if } w_{q_j} \neq u_{q_j}. \end{cases}$$

This is a one-to-one mapping, since the possibility of a many-to-one mapping is eliminated by different assignments of bits in the p_j-th dimension, $1 \leq j \leq r_3$. Moreover, we have $H(u, w) = r_1 + r_3 = M(\alpha, \beta)$. By the above node-mapping, we can determine, for each source node in α, the corresponding mapped node in β, and the total number of moving steps is $M(\alpha, \beta) 2^{|\alpha|}$, thus satisfying $T(\alpha, \beta) \leq M(\alpha, \beta) 2^{|\alpha|}$. Q.E.D.

The above theorem proves that the minimal number of moving steps required to move a task from a subcube location α to another subcube location β is $M(\alpha, \beta) 2^{|\alpha|}$. There may be many ways to move a task from one subcube to another, each having the same total number of moving steps. For example, we can move an active task from 10*1 to 000* by either (a). 1011 $\to$ 0000 (3 hops) and 1001 $\to$ 0001 (1 hop), or (b). 1011 $\to$ 0001 (2 hops) and 1001 $\to$ 0000 (2 hops). The total number of moving steps in either case is 4. However, in order to exploit the inherent parallelism, we naturally want the total $M(\alpha, \beta) 2^{|\alpha|}$ moving steps to be equally distributed among all pairs of source and destination nodes such that every node u in α requires exactly $M(\alpha, \beta)$ moving steps to transfer its task module to the corresponding node in β. Clearly, this can be accomplished by the node-mapping scheme introduced in the proof of Theorem 1. Notice that the source and destination subcubes for tasks being migrated under a strategy must be recognizable by that strategy. In light of this fact, a simplified node-mapping scheme will be introduced in Corollary 1.1. However, it is necessary to introduce the following proposition first.

Proposition 2: Suppose $\alpha = a_n a_{n-1} \cdots a_1$ and $\beta = b_n b_{n-1} \cdots b_1$ are two k-dimensional subcubes recognizable by the GC strategy. Then, there is at most one dimension, say p, in which $a_p \in \{0, 1\}$ and $b_p = *$.

Proof: From Theorem 3 of [3] and the fact that $g_i = i$, $1 \leq i \leq n$, for the BRGC, we know $a_i = *$ and $b_i = *$ for $1 \leq i \leq k-1$. Since there are exactly k *'s in the address of a Q_k, this proposition follows. Q.E.D.

The node-mapping between two subcubes recognizable by the GC strategy can be determined as follows. Suppose $\alpha = a_n a_{n-1} \cdots a_1$ is the source subcube and $\beta = b_n b_{n-1} \cdots b_1$ the destination subcube. Let p and q be the dimensions in which $a_p \in \{0, 1\}$ and $b_p = *$, and $a_q = *$ and $b_q \in \{0, 1\}$.

Corollary 1.1: Each source node $u = u_n u_{n-1} \cdots u_1 \in \alpha$ can be one-to-one mapped to a destination node $w = w_n w_{n-1} \cdots w_1 \in \beta$ in such a way that when $i \neq p$,

$$w_i = \begin{cases} b_i, & \text{if } b_i \in \{0, 1\}, \\ u_i, & \text{if } a_i = b_i = *, \end{cases}$$

when $i = p$,

$$w_p = \begin{cases} \overline{u_p}, & \text{if } w_q = u_q, \\ u_p, & \text{if } w_q \neq u_q, \end{cases}$$

and $H(u, w) = M(\alpha, \beta)$.

For example, when $\alpha = 1*1*$, $\beta = 00**$ and $u = 1110$, we have $p = 3$ and then $w = 0010$. It can be verified that every node in 1*1* will need exactly 2 moving steps to relocate its task module to the corresponding node in 00**, i.e., 1010 (12) $\to$ 0000 (0), 1011 (13) $\to$ 0001 (1), 1110 (11) $\to$ 0010 (3) and 1111 (10) $\to$ 0011 (2). It is worth mentioning that the order of source nodes in the BRGC is not necessarily the same as that of their corresponding destination nodes after the node-mapping (see Fig. 4).

3.3. Determination of Shortest Deadlock-Free Routing

After the determination of the node-mapping, we now want to develop a routing method to move each task module from its source node to its destination node. As mentioned earlier, in order to avoid deadlocks, a linear ordering among hypercube nodes is enforced such that each node can only move its task module to a node with a lower address. More formally, we need the following definition.

Definition 3: A path is said to be *shortest deadlock-free* (SDF) with respect to a coding scheme if it is a shortest path from the source node to the destination node and the reverse order of nodes in that coding scheme is preserved in the node sequence of that path.

In other words, if $C_n(i)$ and $C_n(j)$ are two nodes in a SDF path, then $C_n(i)$ is ahead of $C_n(j)$ in the path iff $i > j$. For example, the path [110, 010, 011] is a SDF path in G_3, whereas [110, 111, 011] is not. A coding scheme, C_n, is said to be *SDF path preserving* if $\forall$ p < q there exists a SDF path from $C_n(q)$ to $C_n(p)$, i.e., there exists $[C_n(q), C_n(r_1), C_n(r_2), \cdots, C_n(r_{d-1}), C_n(p)]$, such that $q > r_1 > \cdots > r_{d-1} > p$.

Once the node-mapping between each pair of source and destination subcubes is determined, each source node appends to its task module the address of its destination node. Each node can then determine the next hop on which to route a task module by the algorithm below.

Algorithm A_2: Determination of a SDF path

Step 1.   Each node compares the destination address $d = d_n d_{n-1} \cdots d_1$ with its own address $s = s_n s_{n-1} \cdots s_1$ from left to right. Let the j-th and k-th dimensions be respectively the first and second dimensions in which they differ, i.e., $s_i = d_i$ for $j+1 \leq i \leq n$ and $k+1 \leq i \leq j-1$, and $s_j \neq d_j$, $s_k \neq d_k$.

Step 2.   If $\sum_{i=k}^{j-1} s_i$ is even **then** send the task module to a neighboring node along the k-th dimension **else** send the task module to a neighboring node along the j-th dimension.

For example, suppose the source node is $G_4(12) = 1010$ and the destination node d is $G_4(1) = 0001$, then j=4 and k=2. The next node determined by A_2 is $G_4(3) = 0010$ since $\sum_{i=2}^{3} s_i$ is odd, and thus, the 4-th dimension of 1010 is changed. Then, the next hop determined by the intermediate node $G_4(3) = 0010$ is $G_4(2) = 0011$, since we get j=2 and k=1 for s=0010 and d=0001. It can be verified that [1010 (12), 0010 (3), 0011 (2), 0001 (1)] is a SDF path. Actually, this is not a coincidence. As it will be proved later, the paths determined by A_2 must be SDF. To facilitate the proof, it is necessary to introduce the following lemma which compares the order of two BRGC numbers.

Lemma 1: Let $G_n(p) = a_n a_{n-1} \cdots a_1$ and $G_n(q) = b_n b_{n-1} \cdots b_1$ be two BRGC numbers. Suppose the i-th dimension is the first dimension in which $G_n(p)$ and $G_n(q)$ differ, when they are compared from left to right, i.e., $a_j = b_j$ for $n \geq j > i$ and $a_i \neq b_i$. Without loss of generality, we can assume $a_i = 1$ and $b_i = 0$. Then, p > q iff $\sum_{j=i+1}^{n} a_j$ is even.

Proof: Consider the following procedure to generate the BRGC. Let $G_1 = \{0, 1\}$. Given a k-bit BRGC $G_k = \{d_0, d_1, \cdots, d_{2^k-1}\}$, a (k+1)-bit BRGC can be generated by:

$$G_{k+1} = \{d_0 0, d_0 1, d_1 1, d_1 0, d_2 0, d_2 1, \cdots, d_{2^k-1} 1, d_{2^k-1} 0\}.$$

It is proved in [10] that this procedure indeed generates the BRGC. This procedure can be described by the complete binary tree in Fig. 5. As the number of bits in the BRGC increases, the corresponding tree grows. The address of every external node (leaf) is determined by the coded bits in the path from the root to the external node, and the BRGC is then obtained by the addresses of external nodes from left to right. It can be verified that every node which is reached from the root via an even number of links labeled with 1 has a 0 left-child and a 1 right-child. Note that an external node further to the right is associated with a larger number in the BRGC. Thus, it is proved that p > q if $\sum_{j=i+1}^{n} a_j$ is even, and the fact that p < q if $\sum_{j=i+1}^{n} a_j$ is odd follows similarly.   **Q.E.D.**

For example, in the 3-bit BRGC, $G_3(3) = 010$ appears after $G_3(1) = 001$, since the number of 1's in the left of their first different bit position in $G_3(3)$ is zero which is even, whereas $G_3(4) = 110$ appears before $G_3(6) = 101$ since the number of 1's in the left of their first different bit position in $G_3(4)$ is one. With the aid of Lemma 1, the following important theorem can be derived.

Theorem 2: The path determined by A_2 is SDF.

Proof: Let f(m) denote the number mapped into the binary string m in the BRGC, i.e., p = f(m) iff $m = G_n(p)$. Since f(s) > f(d), from Lemma 1 we know that $\sum_{i=j}^{n} s_i$ is odd. Let $u = u_n \cdots u_1$ denote the address of the next hop determined by A_2. Consider the case when $\sum_{i=k}^{j-1} s_i$ is even. Clearly, from Step 2 of A_2, H(u,s)=1 and H(u,d) = H(s,d) − 1, since $u_i = s_i$ if $i \neq k$, and $u_k = \overline{s_k} = d_k$. Besides, we have f(u) > f(d) since $\sum_{i=j}^{n} u_i = \sum_{i=j}^{n} s_i$ is odd, and f(s) > f(u) since $\sum_{i=j}^{n} s_i + \sum_{i=k}^{j-1} s_i$ is odd.

On the other hand, in the case when $\sum_{i=k}^{j-1} s_i$ is odd, H(u,s)=1 and H(u,d) = H(s,d) − 1, since $u_i = s_i$ if $i \neq j$, and $u_j = \overline{s_j} = d_j$. Also, f(s) > f(u) since $\sum_{i=j}^{n} s_i$ is odd, and f(u) > f(d) since $\sum_{i=k}^{n} u_i = \sum_{i=k}^{j-1} u_i + \sum_{i=j}^{n} u_i = \sum_{i=k}^{j-1} s_i + \overline{s_j} + \sum_{i=j+1}^{n} s_i$ is odd. Therefore, in both cases, H(u,d) = H(s,d) − 1, f(s) > f(u) and f(u) > f(d). Since the above results hold for every intermediate node, this theorem follows.   **Q.E.D.**

The above theorem shows that task migration under the GC strategy can be accomplished via SDF paths. Also, the following corollary results from Theorem 2.

Corollary 2.1: The BRGC is SDF path preserving.

Note that the binary encoding scheme is not SDF path preserving, neither is the coding scheme given in Fig. 2. For example, no SDF path exists from $B_3(2) = 010$ to $B_3(1) = 001$, and nor does from $C_4(9) = 1000$ to $C_4(1) = 0001$. This fact demonstrate another advantage of the GC strategy.

Furthermore, as it will be proved below, A_2 will not send any two modules of a task to the same next hop, implying that task migration can be done in parallel. It was assumed in Section 2 that a hypercube node can send and receive task modules at the same time and each moving step takes one time unit. Let α be the source subcube and $S_1, S_2, \cdots, S_{2^{|\alpha|}}$ be the nodes of α. Suppose β is the destination subcube and $S_i(t)$ is the hypercube node which receives, via the path determined by A_2, the task module originally residing at S_i after t time units under the node-mapping scheme in Corollary 1.1. Thus, $S_i = S_i(0)$, $1 \leq i \leq 2^{|\alpha|}$, are the nodes of α, $S_i(M(\alpha,\beta))$, $1 \leq i \leq 2^{|\alpha|}$, are the nodes of β, and $[S_i(0), S_i(1), \cdots, S_i(M(\alpha,\beta))]$ is the path for moving a task module from S_i to its destination. Two paths $[S_i(0), S_i(1), \cdots, S_i(M(\alpha,\beta))]$ and $[S_j(0), S_j(1), \cdots, S_j(M(\alpha,\beta))]$ are said to be *stepwise disjoint*, if at any time t, the two corresponding

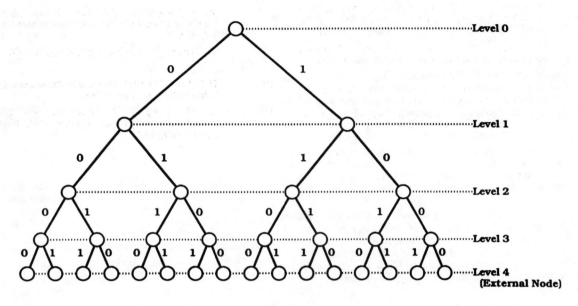

Figure 5. The labeled complete binary tree for a BRGC.

task modules will not be sent to the same next hop, i.e., $S_i(t) \neq S_j(t)$, $\forall\, t \in [0, M(\alpha,\beta)]$. Then, we have the following corollary which states the impossibility for two task modules to compete for the same next hop during task migration, another advantage of using the GC strategy.

Corollary 2.2: Under the node-mapping scheme in Corollary 1.1, the paths determined by A_2 are stepwise disjoint.

Proof: Suppose $\alpha = a_n a_{n-1} \cdots a_1$ and $\beta = b_n b_{n-1} \cdots b_1$ are respectively the source and destination subcubes, and $|\alpha| = |\beta| = k$. From Proposition 2, we get $a_k = a_{k-1} = \cdots = a_1 = b_k = b_{k-1} = \cdots = b_1 = *$. From the node-mapping scheme in Corollary 1.1, it follows that for any pair of source node $u = u_n u_{n-1} \cdots u_1$ and destination node $w = w_n w_{n-1} \cdots w_1$, we have $u_{k-1} \cdots u_1 = w_{k-1} \cdots w_1$. This in turn implies that the path from u to w must be within subcube $*^{n-k+1} u_{k-1} \cdots u_1$.

Divide a Q_n into 2^{k-1} Q_{n-k+1}'s, whose addresses are $*^{n-k+1} d_{k-1} \cdots d_1$, $d_i \in \{0,1\}$, $1 \leq i \leq k-1$. Call each of these Q_{n-k+1}'s a *partition*. From Proposition 2, it can be seen that each partition contains exactly two adjacent nodes in α. The entire paths for moving two task modules in a partition to their destination nodes will remain within the same partition. This means that task modules from different partitions will not collide with one another at any time. Moreover, since there is no cycle of an odd length in a Q_n, two task modules originally residing at two adjacent nodes in the source subcube will not collide with each other at any time. This corollary thus follows. **Q.E.D.**

To illustrate the entire process of task migration, consider the fragmented configuration in Fig. 4a. From A_1, we obtain the goal configuration in Fig 4b. By the node-mapping scheme developed in Section 3.2, we have $0011 \rightarrow 0000$ for task 1, $0101 \rightarrow 0011$, $0100 \rightarrow 0010$, $1100 \rightarrow 0110$ and $1101 \rightarrow 0111$ for task 2 ($*10* \rightarrow 0*1*$), $1010 \rightarrow 0100$ and $1011 \rightarrow 0101$ for task 3 ($101* \rightarrow 010*$), and $1001 \rightarrow 0001$ for task 4. (Note that the relative order of source nodes is changed during the node-mapping for task 3.) The SDF routing can then be determined by A_2 as follows:

Task 1: $0011 \rightarrow 0001 \rightarrow 0000$;

Task 2: $0101 \rightarrow 0111 \rightarrow 0011$, $0100 \rightarrow 0110 \rightarrow 0010$, $1100 \rightarrow 0100 \rightarrow 0110$ and $1101 \rightarrow 0101 \rightarrow 0111$;

Task 3: $1010 \rightarrow 1110 \rightarrow 1100 \rightarrow 0100$ and $1011 \rightarrow 1111 \rightarrow 1101 \rightarrow 0101$, and

Task 4: $1001 \rightarrow 0001$.

4. CONCLUSION

In this paper, we have developed a procedure for task migration under the GC strategy to eliminate the system fragmentation, which consists of three steps. First, a goal configuration without fragmentation is determined in light of the static optimality of the GC strategy. Second, the node-mapping between the source and destination subcubes is formulated. Finally, a routing procedure for obtaining shortest deadlock-free paths for task migration is derived. Moreover, the migration paths determined by A_2 are proved to be stepwise disjoint, thus allowing for the full parallelism in task migration. Our results confirm the inherent superiority of the GC strategy over others.

ACKNOWLEDGEMENT

The authors would like to thank Andre van Tilborg for his support and encouragement of this work.

This work was supported in part by the Office of Naval Research under contracts N00014-85-K-0122 and N00014-85-K-0531. Any opinions, findings, and conclusions or recommendations expressed in this publication are those of the authors and do not necessarily reflect the view of the ONR.

REFERENCES

[1]   T. F. Chan and Y. Saad, "Multigrid Algorithms on the Hypercube Multiprocessor", *IEEE Trans. on Comput.* C-35, 11 (Nov. 1986), 969-977.

[2]   Y. Saad and M. H. Schultz, "Topological Properties of Hypercubes", *IEEE Trans. on Comput.* C-37, 7 (July, 1988), 867-872.

[3]   M. S. Chen and K. G. Shin, "Processor Allocation in an N-Cube Multiprocessor Using Gray Codes", *IEEE Trans. on Comput. C-36*, 12 (Dec. 1987), 1396-1407.

[4]   M. S. Chen and K. G. Shin, "On the Relaxed Squashed Embedding of Graphs a into Hypercube", *SIAM J. Computing*, 1989 (in press).

[5]   C. L. Seitz, "The Cosmic Cube", *Commun. of the Assoc. Comp. Mach. 28*, 1 (Jan. 1985), 22-33.

[6]   N. Corp., NCUBE/ten: an overview, Nov. 1985.

[7]   K. C. Knowlton, "A Fast Storage Allocator", *Commun. of the Assoc. Comp. Mach. 8*, 10 (Oct. 1965), 623-625.

[8]   F. Harary, *Graph Theory*, Addison-Wesley, Mass., 1969.

[9]   D. E. Knuth, *The Art of Computer Programming, vol. 1*, Addison-Wesley, Mass., 1968.

[10]   E. M. Reingold, J. Nievergelt and N. Deo, *Combinatorial Algorithm*, Prentice Hall, Englewood Cliffs, Mass., 1977.

Characteristics of Performance-Optimal
Multi-Level Cache Hierarchies

Steven Przybylski, Mark Horowitz, John Hennessy

Computer Systems Laboratory, Stanford University,
Stanford University, CA., 94305

Abstract

The increasing speed of new generation processors will exacerbate the already large difference between CPU cycle times and main memory access times. As this difference grows, it will be increasingly difficult to build single-level caches that are both fast enough to match these fast cycle times and large enough to effectively hide the slow main memory access times. One solution to this problem is to use a multi-level cache hierarchy. This paper examines the relationship between cache organization and program execution time for multi-level caches. We show that a first-level cache dramatically reduces the number of references seen by a second-level cache, without having a large effect on the number of second-level cache misses. This reduction in the number of second-level cache hits changes the optimal design point by decreasing the importance of the cycle-time of the second-level cache relative to its size. The lower the first-level cache miss rate, the less important the second-level cycle time becomes. This change in relative importance of cycle time and miss rate makes associativity more attractive and increases the optimal cache size for second-level caches over what they would be for an equivalent single-level cache system.

1. Introduction

Multi-level cache hierarchies are memory systems in which there are two or more levels of caching between the CPU and main memory. It is widely accepted that the large difference between CPU cycle times and main memory access times will continue to grow, and that computer implementors will have to use multi-level memory hierarchies to get the best system performance [3, 12, 13]. Several studies have shown that in many situations there is substantial opportunity for performance improvement by increasing the depth of the memory hierarchy [4, 5, 10, 11, 15]. This paper presents empirical and analytical results regarding the behaviour of caches within multi-level hierarchies.

Recent work has shown how the tradeoffs inherent in cache design change when the metric used for evaluating cache performance is shifted from cache miss rates to overall system performance [6, 8]. This earlier work showed that a designer needs to pay close attention to cache organizational changes that affect cycle time, and that the best overall performance is obtained when the designer balances the conflicting goals of a short cycle time and a low miss ratio. A change in the cache organization that decreases the miss ratio can decrease performance if an accompanying increase in the cycle time results in a greater increase in the time spent handling cache hits than the reduction in the time spent handling cache misses. This paper extends the use of system performance as the key metric to the analysis of multi-level cache hierarchies. The goal is to find the multi-level hierarchy that maximizes the overall performance while satisfying all the implementation constraints.

Two unavoidable conclusions made in an earlier paper motivate the use of multi-level cache hierarchies [8]. First, there is an upper bound on the performance that can be achieved through the use of a single level of caching; after a certain point, the performance cannot be improved by changing any of the cache's parameters (including the cache size). Second, the difference between the optimal CPU cycle time and the minimum realizable cycle time is potentially very large. By reducing the cache miss penalty of the cache closest to the CPU, multi-level cache hierarchies can simultaneously break the single-level performance barrier and help a designer strive towards the dual performance goals of a low mean cycles per instruction (CPI) and a short CPU cycle time.

One step towards finding the best realizable hierarchy is understanding how the different levels of caching in a multi-level hierarchy interact with, and influence, one another. The interaction between levels of caching is presented in two ways. Section 3 shows that if the miss ratio is appropriately defined then a cache's miss ratio is independent of the presence of the other caches in the hierarchy. This important result allows us to transfer our

114

experience and intuition about the relationship between a cache's organizational parameters (size, associativity, block size) and its miss rate from the single-level domain to the multi-level design problem. Sections 4 and 5 then look specifically at the important cache design tradeoffs between a cache's cycle time and both its size and associativity. These sections closely parallel the two sections in our earlier paper on single-level cache design [8]. A comparison between these and the previously reported results helps illuminate the differences between the single-level design problem and the design of a cache within a multi-level hierarchy. Section 6 summarizes the results and predicts some characteristics of future multi-level cache hierarchies.

2. Terminology and Method

We will use Smith's terminology for cache organizations [12], with a few extensions. In particular, we define several terms for a multi-level hierarchy. We call the cache nearest the CPU the first level cache; level $i+1$ is further from the CPU than level i. An upstream (or predecessor) cache is closer to the CPU, while a downstream (or successor) cache is closer to main memory (and further from the CPU). In multi-level hierarchies, there are three sets of miss ratios of interest. A *local miss ratio* of a particular cache is the number of misses experienced by the cache as a fraction of its incoming references. The *global miss ratio* of a cache is the number of misses incurred by that cache divided by the number of references made by the CPU. Finally, the *solo miss ratio* of a cache is defined as the miss ratio that we are familiar with in computer systems with a single-level cache hierarchy. It is the miss ratio of a cache would have if it were the only cache in the system. We define miss ratios in terms of read requests (loads and instruction fetches) only. Combining read and write requests can lead to confusing results since the mechanisms by which reads and writes affect the overall performance are quite different.

Two complementary techniques will be used to investigate the performance implications of multi-level cache hierarchies: trace-driven simulation and analytical modelling. The former gives precise answers for the set of caches simulated, while the latter provides a means of explaining the trends shown by simulation, and of generalizing the results to a larger set of cache designs.

To properly measure the performance impact of a multi-level hierarchy using trace-driven simulation, one needs both a simulator that accurately keeps track of time within each level of the hierarchy and a set of representative traces to run through the simulator. For the results to be credible, the simulator must be able to model realistic systems, including write buffering, prefetching, and multiple simultaneous events at the various levels of caching. The simulation environment and empirical method used in this study is an extension of the one used,

and described in detail, in an earlier paper [8]. The simulation system reads a file that specifies the depth of the cache hierarchy and the configuration of each cache. The user has control of the latency of cache operations as well as the organization (total size, set size, block size, fetch size, write strategy, write buffering) of each cache.

Our CPU model is a high performance, RISC-like CPU. It executes one instruction fetch and either zero or one data accesses on every clock cycle in which it is not waiting on the memory system. In our traces, about 50% of non-stall cycles contain a data reference and roughly 35% of those are reads. The base machine for this study is a hypothetical single chip processor that runs at a 10ns cycle time. The chip contains split 4KB (2KB each I and D) on-chip first-level cache (L1). Both caches are direct-mapped, with a block size of 4 words. The data cache is write-back, with write hits taking two cycles. Both caches cycle at the same rate as the CPU. There also is a much larger second-level (L2) external cache. Though its size and associativity are varied in the experiments presented here, the default is a 512KB direct-mapped cache with a block size of 8 words. The basic cycle time of the external cache is 3 CPU cycles. It too is a write-back cache, with write hits taking 2 L2 cycles. An L1 cache miss stalls the processor until all of the L1 block is received from the L2 cache. The bus between the integrated processor and the L2 cache is assumed to be 4 words wide, and cycles at the same rate as the L2 cache. Thus, a read request that misses in L1 but hits in L2 suffers a nominal cache miss penalty of 3 CPU cycles. If the request misses in L2 as well, the processor is stalled until the entire L2 block is fetched from main memory.

The memory model used in the simulations decomposes main memory access time into three components. Read operations (from address available to 8 words of data available) take 180 ns. Write operations (from address and data available to write complete) take 100 ns, and at least 120 ns of refresh and cycle time must elapse between successive data operations. The bus between main memory and the L2 cache is also 4 words wide, so that in addition to the main memory operation time, one bus cycle is needed to transmit the address to memory, and two are needed to retrieve the data. The backplane cycle time is set to be the same as the L2 cycle time. The net result is that the L2 cache miss penalty for fetching an 8 word block is between 270ns and 370ns, depending on the elapsed time since the previous operation. Between each of the levels of the hierarchy are write buffers that are 4 entries deep, each entry being the width of a block in the upstream cache.

We use a set of eight large multiprogramming traces for our cache simulations. Four of the traces were generated using ATUM [1] running on a VAX 8200. These traces contain system references and have captured actual multiprogramming behavior. Three of these traces are VMS traces and one is an Ultrix trace. The other four traces were generated by interleaving uniprocessor traces from a MIPS Computer System's R2000 processor. These traces do not contain system references, but were randomly interleaved to match the context switch intervals seen in the VAX traces. Care was taken to collect data only after the caches had left the cold start region. The traces are described in detail in other publications [2, 9].

3. Independence of Cache Layers

The multi-level hierarchy design problem is substantially more complex than the single-level case. Not only is there an additional set of design decisions introduced for each level in the hierarchy, but the optimal choices at each level depend on the characteristics of the adjacent caches. The direct influence of upstream caches can be seen in the miss ratio. Figure 3-1 shows the L2 miss ratios for the base machine described above as the L2 cache size is varied. To reiterate, local metrics refer to parameters measured relative to the input stream to a given level, while global metrics are measured with respect to the CPU reference stream. Thus, the L2 local read miss ratio is the number of L2 misses divided by the number of read requests reaching the second-level cache, or alternatively, the ratio of the number of L2 misses to the number of L1 misses. The global miss ratio is the same number of misses divided by the number of reads in the input stream. The L2 solo miss rates result when the L1 cache is removed entirely, and the larger cache is the only one in the system.

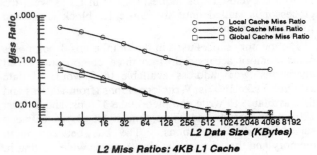

L2 Miss Ratios: 4KB L1 Cache

Figure 3-1

The local miss ratio for any cache is always dependent on its predecessor's miss ratio. However, Figure 3-1 shows that if the L1 cache is small, and the second cache is significantly larger than the first, then the L2 global miss ratio is the same as its solo cache miss ratio. In this case, the global miss ratio for the L2 cache is completely independent of L1's parameters. This independence means that the overall hierarchy design problem can be decomposed to some extent into the design of the individual layers.

For larger first level caches, the independence of the layers still applies. Figure 3-2 shows the L2 miss ratios for a substantially larger L1 cache (32KB total). Again, until a size increment of a factor of 8 is reached, the presence of the upstream cache disturbs the characteristics

of the reference stream reaching the subsequent level sufficiently to noticeably perturb the L2 global miss ratio from the solo miss ratio even for very large caches.

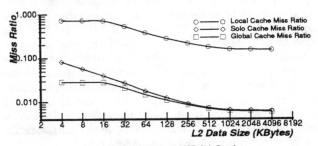

L2 Miss Ratios: 32KB L1 Cache

Figure 3-2

The following sections discuss the tradeoffs between a cache's cycle time and two important organizational parameters: its size and associativity. Though an upstream cache does not necessarily change the global miss ratios, it does affect the local miss ratios and changes the optimum balance between the conflicting goals of a short cache cycle time and a large cache size and associativity.

4. Speed – Size Tradeoffs

The tradeoff between a temporal and an organizational parameter is investigated experimentally by varying the two design variables simultaneously and comparing their relative effects on performance.[1] Figure 4-1 shows the relative execution time for the base two-level system as the L2 size is varied from 4KB to 4MB and the L2 cycle time is varied from 1 through 10 CPU cycles. The L2 cycle time represents the basic SRAM access time: reads that tag hit are completed in this time, while writes take two such cycles. The main memory access portion of the second-level cache miss penalty is kept constant.

These curves are very similar to the curves generated for a single-level cache [8]. They show that as caches get larger, the benefit to performance of further increasing cache size decreases. In contrast, the effect on performance of a change in cache cycle time is nearly independent of cache size. For small caches, a change in size is more important than a change in cycle time, while for large caches the reverse is true. The interaction between the two levels of caches causes the curves to be somewhat straighter for small caches than in the single-level model.

Taking horizontal slices through the curves exposes classes of machines with the same performance level. These sets of machines can be mapped on a graph with L2 size on one axis and L2 cycle time on the other. All of the

---

[1]Since the CPU cycle time is not being varied, the total cycle count is equivalent to the total execution time.

machines in each set lie on a single line of constant performance across the design space (see Figure 4-2). The slopes of the lines of constant performance are crucial, since they represent the equivalence between changes in cache size and changes in cache cycle time. Increasing slope means each change in cache size is worth a larger change in cycle time.

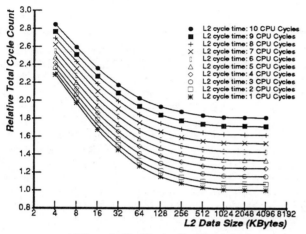

L2 Speed - Size Tradeoff: 4KB L1 Cache

Figure 4-1

The boundaries between the shaded regions follow the contours of equal slope, and delimit regions where the speed – size tradeoff is comparable. The unshaded region contains slopes less than 0.75 CPU cycles per L2 size doubling. The rightmost shaded region is the area in which the lines of constant performance have slopes between 0.75 and 1.5 CPU cycles per doubling, and so on. Since the CPU cycle time is 10ns, in the leftmost region, where the slopes are at least 3 CPU cycles per doubling, quadrupling of the L2 size is beneficial if the total access time degradation is less than 60ns – a very substantial change. Even the rightmost shaded region represents a guaranteed improvement in performance if the L2 cycle time degrades by less than 15ns with a quadrupling of the cache size. The large slopes represent a strong pull towards caches greater than 128KB. Though the basic shape of these curves and the locations of the tradeoff regions are similar to those for the single-level cache case [8], these curves are not as flat for very large caches. This difference implies that given an identical set of implementation technologies, the optimal L2 cache would be significantly larger than the optimal single-level cache.

Figure 3-2 showed the L2 miss ratios for a larger first-level cache (32KB) and Figure 4-3 gives the corresponding lines of constant performance across the L2 design space. The low cache miss ratio of the 32KB L1 cache dramatically decreases the performance impact of the second-level cache. Despite the increased separation between the lines of constant performance in Figure 4-3, the individual lines of constant performance have roughly the same shape and slope. Increasing the L1 size by a

factor of 8 shifted the lines of constant performance to the right by slightly less than one factor of two. This shift would result in a slight increase in the optimal L2 size. The more pronounced effect of a larger L1 cache is to limit the maximum slope of the lines and to dramatically cut the magnitude of the performance improvement possible.

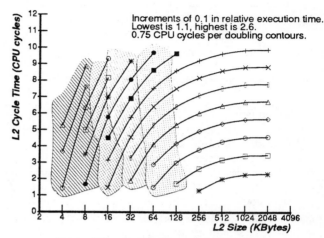

Lines of Constant Performance: 4KB L1 Cache

Figure 4-2

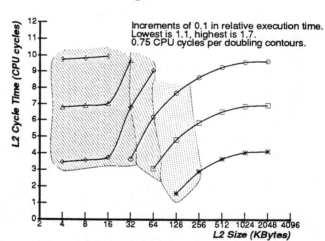

Lines of Constant Performance: 32KB L1 Cache

Figure 4-3

A slower main memory increases the L2 cache miss penalty, which in turn increases the slope of the lines of constant performance. Figure 4-4 shows the L2 design space for the default 4KB L1 cache, given a main memory that is twice as slow as in the base system. Since memory times are measured in CPU cycles, this graph looks much like a graph for the original memory but with a CPU cycle time of 5ns. The only substantial difference is the scale of the Y-axis and, correspondingly, the magnitude of the slopes. The effect of doubling memory latency is to shift the shaded regions (which denote regions of different slope) to the right by approximately a factor of two in cache size.

An analytical exploration of the L2 speed – size tradeoffs begins with the general equation relating the total cycle count to the global miss rates and cycle times in a multi-level cache hierarchy. For a two-level hierarchy with negligible write effects[2], the total execution time becomes the sum of the time spent doing reads at each of the three layers of the hierarchy plus the cycles spent doing writes into the first-level cache:

$$N_{Total} = N_{Read} n_{L1} + N_{Read} M_{L1} n_{L2}$$
$$+ N_{Read} M_{L2} n_{MMread} + N_{Store} \overline{n}_{L1write} \qquad (1)$$

In this equation, N_{Total} is the total cycle count for the execution of a program with N_{Read} reads (including loads and instruction fetches) and N_{Store} stores, n_{L1} and n_{L2} are the number of CPU cycles needed to do a read of the first- and second-level caches, M_{L1} and M_{L2} are the global read miss ratios of the two caches, n_{MMread} is the number of CPU cycles to complete a fetch from main memory into the L2 cache, and $\overline{n}_{L1write}$ is the mean number of write and write stall cycles per store in the program.

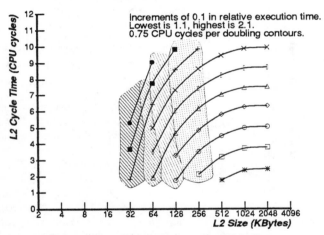

Increments of 0.1 in relative execution time. Lowest is 1.1, highest is 2.1. 0.75 CPU cycles per doubling contours.

Lines of Constant Performance: Slow Main Memory

Figure 4-4

Since the performance is a well behaved function of the cache parameters and the cycle time, the minimum execution time can be found by setting its derivative to zero. When the derivative of the cycle count with respect to the L2 cache size is set to zero, the tradeoff between the second-level cache's size and cycle time, t_{L2}, is exposed. The performance optimal configuration is obtained when the change in the cycle count caused by increasing the time L2 cycle time balances the decrease in the mean time

---

[2]The write effects are small because we are using write-back caches with a large amount of write buffering. The writes are mostly hidden between the read requests.

for a miss:

$$\frac{1}{\overline{t}_{MMRead}} \frac{\partial t_{L2}}{\partial C_{L2}} = -\frac{1}{M_{L1}} \frac{\partial M_{L2}}{\partial C_{L2}} \qquad (2)$$

This equation is similar to the one for a single-level cache except for the presence of the L1 (global) miss ratio on the right hand side of the equation – a potentially large factor. For instance, for the 4KB L1 cache used in the base machine, $\frac{1}{M_{L1}}$ equals about 10. The reason for this factor is easy to understand. The upstream cache filters most of the references, but does not, to first order, change the misses of the second-level cache. Because there are fewer hits, the cost of handling hits (the L2 cache cycle time) has a smaller effect on the total system performance. The marginal advantage of decreasing the cycle time has been decreased. Yet since the L1 cache does not noticeably affect the total cost of L2 misses, the marginal advantage of decreasing the L2 miss rate remains unchanged. Since an optimal cache matches these two marginal costs, the net effect of the additional factor is to shift the balance towards larger, slower caches.

To be more definitive about characteristics of the optimal cache size we need a model that describes how the miss rate and cycle time depend on the cache size. Figure 3-1 verifies that for the range of caches under investigation, the previously reported result that a doubling of the cache size decreases the solo miss rate by a constant factor is true, and the factor for these traces is about 0.69. To first order then, the miss rate is roughly proportional to the one over the square-root of the cache size. One finds that the lines of constant performance for a second-level cache shift to the left by about a third of a binary order of magnitude in cache size for each doubling of the L1 size. Thus, assuming that the marginal cycle time cost of increasing the cache is independent of cache size, the L1 cache would have to increase sixteen fold for the optimal L2 size to double. Across Figures 4-2 and 4-3, the L1 size increased by a factor of 8, and the lines of constant performance shifted by a factor of 1.74 – close to the 2.04 predicted by this model. Any changes in the L2 cycle time due to this increase in the L2 size would naturally affect the speed half of the speed – size tradeoff and would either incrementally increase or decrease the optimal cache size, depending on the local characteristics of the function linking the L2 speed and L2 size.

As was noted earlier, the miss rate reaches a plateau for very large caches. For these caches, the presence of the other levels in the cache hierarchy does not change the tradeoff; further increases in the cache size are never worthwhile, regardless of how small the cycle time penalty is.

The presence of a L1 cache does not change the influence of the main memory access time, $\overline{t}_{MMRead}$, on the design tradeoffs. Specifically, a change in the cache miss penalty inversely modifies the cycle time half of the balancing equation (Equation 2), thereby reducing the cost of increasing the cache cycle time. Thus, increasing the L2 cache miss penalty again linearly skews the speed – size tradeoff towards larger caches, as it does for the single-level case.

5. Set Size Tradeoffs

This section examines the costs and benefits of set associativity for caches within a multi-level hierarchy. Following the methodology used previously, the benefits associated with the improved miss ratio due to increased set associativity can be translated into equivalent cycle time changes [6, 7, 8].

Figure 4-1 showed the execution time of a direct-mapped, second-level cache as a function of its size cycle time. When it is compared with similar graphs for 2-way, 4-way and 8-way set associative caches, we can determine the cycle times for equivalently performing machines with the same cache sizes but different associativities. The difference between the cycle times of the two caches is the amount of time available for the implementation of set associativity. If the implementation of set associativity degrades the cycle time over the direct-mapped case by an amount greater than this break-even implementation time, then there is a net decrease in performance. The break-even times for large, single-level caches are consistently too low to warrant a set-associative implementation: generally less than 4 ns for caches greater than 16KB. Within a multi-level hierarchy, however, the break-even times can be substantially larger depending on the effectiveness of the upstream cache. Figures 5-1 through 5-3 show the cumulative break-even implementation times for the base 4KB L1 cache. In this case, we represent the break-even implementation times in terms of nanoseconds instead of CPU cycles. The shaded regions are bounded by the 10 ns through 40 ns contours.

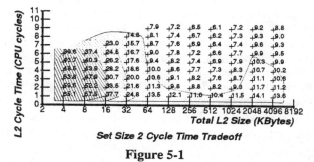

Set Size 2 Cycle Time Tradeoff

Figure 5-1

For the base two-level system, and for most of the L2 sizes and cycle times of interest, a designer has between 10 ns and 20 ns available for the implementation of eight-way set associativity. These times, which correspond to between one and two CPU cycles, are larger for small L2 sizes. When the two caches are of similar size, the direct-mapped L2 local cache miss ratio is close to one and so

the addition of set associativity causes a large relative decrease in the effective L1 cache miss penalty. Given a 4KB L1 cache, an eight-way set-associative 8KB L2 caches is substantially better at reducing the memory traffic than a direct-mapped cache of the same size.

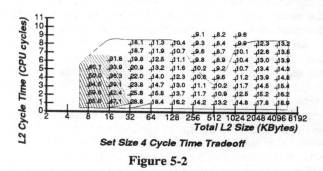

Set Size 4 Cycle Time Tradeoff

Figure 5-2

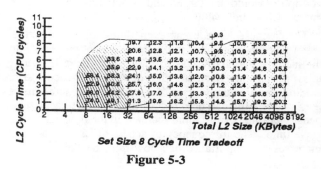

Set Size 8 Cycle Time Tradeoff

Figure 5-3

Analytically, the L1 cache miss ratio also appears in the equations for the incremental break-even times for the implementation of set associativity. The incremental break-even time, Δt_{BE}, is the cycle time degradation that is allowed across a doubling of associativity, for instance from 4 to 8, as opposed to across a larger span, such as from a set size of 1 to a set size of 8. Starting with the same simple execution time model used in the previous section, it follows that this break-even increase in cycle time which exactly balances the performance improvement due to doubling the associativity is equal to the product of the change in the global miss ratio, the mean main memory access time, and the inverse of the L1 miss ratio:

$$\Delta t_{BE} = -\frac{1}{M_{L1}} \overline{t}_{MMread} \Delta M_{L2}$$

Therefore, as the upstream cache increases in size, the downstream break-even implementation times also dramatically increase. With each doubling of the upstream cache size, the incremental and cumulative break-even times are multiplied by a factor of 1.45 across the entire L2 design space. Just as in the single-level case, the break-even times increase linearly with the main memory access times.

A likely scenario for multi-level hierarchies involves

building the larger second-level cache out of discrete TTL parts. Realistically, in this environment, the minimum implementation cycle time overhead for associativity is about the 11ns *select* to *data-out* time for a two-to-one Advanced-Schottky multiplexor [14]. In the above figures, a large portion of the design space has break-even times less than this cutoff. However, recall that a 4KB L1 size was used. Since each doubling in the L1 size decreases its miss ratio by about 28%, the L2 break-even times will increase in the same proportion. As the size of the upstream cache increases, the benefit of set associativity also increases. If the size increments between levels of the hierarchy are small, on the order of four or eight, then the cumulative break-even times are uniformly greater than 17ns, and reach as high as 45ns. If the caches are small, then the L2 cache break-even implementation times are substantially greater than their minimum. Keeping the same cache size ratio, a large second-level cache implies a larger first-level cache, so the L1 miss rate multiplier would be larger and a set associative cache might still be preferable.

To put these large break-even times into perspective, recall that the motivation for introducing more levels into the memory hierarchy was to reduce the mean L1 cache miss penalty to decrease the optimal L1 cache size. Adding set-associativity to the second and subsequent levels of caching can help reduce the mean L1 cache miss penalty despite a substantial increase in the deeper cache's cycle time. The infrequency of access of L2 dramatically increases the importance of a low miss rate over a short cycle time.

6. Conclusions

Multi-level caches provide one means of dealing with the large difference between the CPU cycle time and the access time of the main memory. By providing a second level of caching, one can reduce the cost of the first level misses, which in turn improves the overall system performance. Furthermore, by reducing the L1 cache miss penalty, the optimal L1 size is also reduced, increasing the viability of high-performance RISC CPUs coupled with small, short cycle time L1 caches. As with single-level cache design, to optimize system performance the designer must carefully weigh the tradeoff between increased hit rates and faster cache cycle times throughout the memory hierarchy. For a multi-level cache, the optimization becomes slightly more complex, since an upstream cache affects the reference pattern seen by the next cache, and hence changes its optimal design point.

One way to partially decouple the caches is to measure the global miss ratios of the caches – the ratio of the number of cache misses to the number of CPU references. This ratio is relatively independent of the upstream caches and is close to the miss ratio that results if all the upstream caches were removed. Although the number of misses that leave a cache is relatively unaffected by upstream caches, the upstream caches reduce the number of references that are sent to the cache. The resulting large change in the local miss rate modifies the balance between the change in cycle time and the change in the miss ratio that exists at the optimal design point. The reduction in the number of cache hits dramatically increases the importance of a low miss rate in comparison to a short cycle time for downstream caches.

Equating the effect of the upstream cache to a change in cache size is straightforward. The addition of a 4KB L1 cache, with a 10% miss rate, shifts the lines of constant performance to the right by about seven binary orders of magnitude from the single-level case, all things being equal. Locally, a doubling in the L1 cache size is shown to shift the curves of constant performance about 0.24 powers of two to the right. Thus, the presence of an L1 cache moves the optimal design point for the second-level cache toward larger, slower caches.

Improving the miss rate of the upstream cache increases the viability of set-associative second-level caches. Break-even implementation times are multiplied by the inverse of the previous cache's global cache miss ratio. Increasing the set associativity, even at the expense of a significant increment in the L2 cycle time, minimizes the mean L1 cache miss penalty, and therefore helps reduce the optimal L1 speed and size, as desired.

Unfortunately, but not unexpectedly, the empirical and analytical results indicate that the strong motivation to increase the L2 cache size at the expense of its cycle time remains relatively unchanged from the analysis of a single-level hierarchy. However, as the L2 cycle time gets much above 4 CPU cycles, the optimal L1 cache size is significantly increased above its minimum. The magnitude slopes of lines of constant performance, and the optimal L2 speeds and sizes that they forebode, indicate that even with two-level hierarchies the optimal L1 caches will be somewhat larger and slower than computer implementors might desire.

References

1. Agarwal, A., Sites, R., Horowitz, M. ATUM: A New Technique for Capturing Address Traces Using Microcode. Proceedings of the 13th Annual International Symposium on Computer Architecture, Tokyo, Japan, June, 1986, pp. 119-129.

2. Agarwal, A. *Analysis of Cache Performance for Operating Systems and Multiprogramming.* Ph.D. Th., Stanford University, May 1987. Available as Technical Report CSL-TR-87-332.

3. Baer, J.-L., Wang W.-H. Architectural Choices for Multi-Level Cache Hierarchies. Tech. Rept. TR-87-01-04, Department of Computer Science, University of Washington, January, 1987.

4. Colglazier, D.J. A Performance Analysis of Multiprocessors using Two-Level Caches. Tech. Rept. CSG-36, Computer Systems Group, University of Illinios, Urbana – Champaign, August, 1984.

5. Gecsei, J. "Determining Hit Ratios for Multilevel Hierarchies". *IBM Journal of Research and Development 18*, 4 (July 1974), 316-327.

6. Hill, M.D. *Aspects of Cache Memory and Instruction Buffer Performance*. Ph.D. Th., University of California, Berkeley, November 1987. Available as Technical Report UCB/CSD 87/381.

7. Hill, M.D. "The Case for Direct-Mapped Caches". *IEEE Computer 21*, 12 (December 1988), 25-41.

8. Przybylski, S., Horowitz, M., Hennessy J. Performance Tradeoffs in Cache Design. Proceedings of the 15th Annual International Symposium on Computer Architecture, June, 1988, pp. 290-298.

9. Przybylski, S. *Performance-Directed Memory Hierarchy Design*. Ph.D. Th., Stanford University, September 1988. Available as Technical Report CSL-TR-88-366.

10. Short, R.T. A Simulation Study of Multilevel Cache Memories. Department of Computer Science, University of Washington, January, 1987.

11. Short, R.T., Levy, H.M. A Simulation Study of Two-Level Caches. Proceedings of the 15th Annual International Symposium on Computer Architecture, June, 1988, pp. 81-89.

12. Smith, A.J. "Cache Memories". *ACM Computing Surveys 14*, 3 (September 1982), 473-530.

13. Smith, A.J. Problems, Directions and Issues in Memory Hierarchies. Proceedings of the 18th Annual Hawaii Conference on System Sciences, 1985, pp. 468-476.

14. *ALS/AS Logic Data Book*. Texas Instruments, Dallas, TE., 1986.

15. Wilson, A.W. Jr. Hierarchical Cache/Bus Architecture for Shared Memory Multiprocessors. Proceedings of the 14th Annual International Symposium on Computer Architecture, June, 1987, pp. 244-252.

Supporting Reference and Dirty Bits in SPUR's Virtual Address Cache

David A. Wood
Randy H. Katz

Computer Science Division
Electrical Engineering and Computer Science Department
University of California, Berkeley
Berkeley, CA 94720

ABSTRACT

Virtual address caches can provide faster access times than physical address caches, because translation is only required on cache misses. However, because we don't check the translation information on each cache access, maintaining reference and dirty bits is more difficult. In this paper we examine the trade-offs in supporting reference and dirty bits in a virtual address cache. We use measurements from a uniprocessor SPUR prototype to evaluate different alternatives. The prototype's built-in performance counters make it easy to determine the frequency of important events and to calculate performance metrics.

Our results indicate that dirty bits can be efficiently emulated with protection, and thus require no special hardware support. Although this can lead to *excess faults* when previously cached blocks are written, these account for only 19% of the total faults, on average. For reference bits, a *miss bit approximation*, which checks the references bits only on cache misses, leads to more page faults at smaller memory sizes. However, the additional overhead required to maintain true reference bits far exceeds the benefits of a lower fault rate.

1. Introduction

Virtual address caches generally provide faster access times than physical address caches because they eliminate address translation from the critical path. Given this fundamental performance advantage, we might expect to find virtual address caches in most high-performance systems. Unfortunately, several problems have kept virtual address caches from wide spread use. The most serious of these, virtual address *synonyms*, has received considerable attention [Knap85, Smit82]. The simplest solutions restrict the virtual address mapping and require only minimal hardware support. In SPUR, the operating system prevents synonyms by restricting processes that share memory to use the same global virtual address [Hill86]. The hardware supports a simple segment mapping from the process virtual space to the global virtual space. The Sun-3 architecture prevents synonyms by restricting the cache to be direct-mapped, and restricting virtual address synonyms (aliases) to be equal modulo the cache size [Sun85].

While these solutions make large virtual address caches more attractive, maintaining reference and dirty bits is difficult.

Most systems use them as hints to help optimize page replacement policies. A page's reference bit is set on the first reference to the page, and its dirty bit is set on the first write to the page. Systems with physical address caches usually use a translation lookaside buffer (TLB) to translate virtual addresses to physical addresses. The TLB provides a convenient place to cache the reference and dirty bits, along with the translation information. Since the TLB must be accessed on each reference, checking the bits incurs no additional overhead.

Systems with virtual address caches generally do not have this luxury. Since the cache is accessed with virtual addresses, the TLB is only accessed on cache misses. Thus these systems require additional hardware support to maintain reference and dirty bits. For example, the Sun-3 hardware checks the dirty bit in the memory management unit (in place of a TLB) on the first write to a cache block.

There are several different approaches to maintaining reference and dirty bits in systems with virtual address caches, requiring different levels of hardware and software support. In this paper we examine the most promising schemes and use measurements from the SPUR prototype to evaluate them.

In the remainder of this section, we briefly summarize the relevant background of SPUR and introduce some terminology. In Section 2, we describe the methodology used to evaluate the design alternatives. In Section 3, we examine and evaluate different implementations of dirty bits. In Section 4, we discuss reference bits, and evaluate the alternatives. Finally, in Section 5 we summarize the results and present our conclusions.

1.1. Background

SPUR is a shared-memory multiprocessor workstation developed at U.C. Berkeley [Hill86]. Each workstation can contain up to 12 processor boards (the prototype used in these studies was a uniprocessor system), each with three custom chips: a CPU, a floating point unit (FPU), and a cache controller (CC). A 128 Kilobyte direct-mapped unified cache reduces the load each processor demands of the single shared bus. The cache controller implements the Berkeley Ownership coherency protocol [Katz85] to maintain a consistent image across all the caches.

The cache is accessed with virtual addresses, so cache hits proceed without translation. Cache misses require the virtual address to be translated into a physical address before accessing main memory. The cache controller implements in-cache address translation [Wood86], an algorithm unique to SPUR.

In-cache translation does not use a TLB; instead, page table entries (PTEs) compete with instructions and data for space in the unified cache. When a reference misses in the cache, the controller computes the virtual address of the corresponding PTE, using a simple shift-and-concatenate circuit. Then the controller looks for the PTE in the cache, essentially using it as a very large TLB. If the PTE is found, then translation is complete. If not, the cache controller looks for the second-level PTE, which contains the physical address of the first-level PTE. If the second-level PTE is not in the cache either, the cache controller gets it directly from memory; this is possible because second-level page tables are "wired down" at well known addresses. The SPUR cache controller also implements reference and dirty bits, but we defer this discussion until the later sections.

Throughout the rest of this paper we discuss the interactions of virtual memory with the cache. It is important to distinguish between the 4 Kbyte virtual memory *pages* and the 32 byte cache memory *blocks*. When we discuss dirty bits, we are concerned with the *page dirty bits*, used for virtual memory replacement, not the *block dirty bits*, used for cache replacement.

2. Methodology

We usually use trace-driven simulation to evaluate memory system designs, such as cache memory organizations and paging algorithms. Trace-driven simulation provides precise repeatability using an accurate representation of a real workload. It is more accurate than analytic models, but still allows evaluation of systems which do not exist. Unfortunately, trace-driven simulation is limited by the length of the traces. In this study, we want to look at the interactions of the cache memory and the paging algorithm. However, for a trace to include a significant number of paging events it must contain 100's of millions of references. Traces of this length are well beyond our abilities to obtain, store, and simulate.

Because we could not fully evaluate the alternatives before we built SPUR, we were forced to use back-of-the-envelope calculations and small scale simulations to make our design decisions. However, we included a set of performance counters on the cache controller chip to count important events. These on-chip counters give us the opportunity to re-evaluate our decisions with more complete information.

The SPUR cache controller [Wood87] contains 16 32-bit performance counters. A mode register selects one of 4 possible sets of events to be measured. Events include the number of instruction fetches, processor reads and writes, and the number of times each type of reference misses in the cache. The counters also measure the performance of the SPUR in-cache translation algorithm and the Berkeley Ownership coherency protocol.

The measurements reported in this paper were taken on a prototype SPUR system. Because of noise problems on this system's processor board, it runs at 1.5 times the design cycle time. In addition, the processor chip's instruction buffer was disabled, further slowing the performance by nearly a factor of 3. These factors combine to make the system run at approximately 1.5 MIPS. However, since the relative speed of the processor and I/O is a second order effect to our measurements, we believe our results scale to faster processors.

The Sprite operating system [Oust88] runs on the SPUR hardware. Sprite is UNIX compatible at the system call level,

Table 2.1: SPUR System Configuration	
Processor Information	
Cache Size	128 Kbytes
Associativity	Direct Mapped
Block Size	32 bytes
Page Size	4 Kbytes
Instruction Buffer	Disabled
Processor cycle time	150ns
Backplane cycle time	125ns
Memory Information	
Time to first word	3 cycles
Time to next word	1 cycle

but is completely rewritten with an emphasis on network services and multiprocessors. Because Sprite was developed at Berkeley, as part of the larger SPUR project, it was easy to modify the kernel as described later.

To evaluate the different alternatives, we needed synthetic workloads that could be repeated with different paging policies and memory sizes. We designed a workload (called *WORKLOAD1*) to reflect a moderately heavy load for a CAD tool developer. This script includes the compilation of several modules plus the link and debug of a 12000 line CAD tool (espresso). The same CAD tool runs in the background optimizing a large PLA. Other edit, compile, and miscellaneous commands manipulate files and directories. In addition, two performance monitor programs periodically report status of the virtual memory system and CPU performance[1]. For a second workload (called *SLC*), we used the SPUR Common Lisp [Zorn87] system and the SPUR lisp compiler compiling a set of benchmark programs. These two workloads are representative of the types of applications originally intended to run on SPUR.

3. Dirty Bit Alternatives

3.1. Dirty Bit Implementation Trade-offs

In this section, we examine the performance of several dirty bit implementations. Since maintaining dirty bits is a small component of total system performance, we are not interested in finding the optimal approach. Rather, our goal is to determine the simplest implementation that yields acceptable performance.

One of the lessons we have learned from RISC processor designs [Patt85] is to implement frequent cases in hardware and trap to software for the infrequent ones. We can apply this lesson to dirty bits. A page's dirty bit must be checked frequently, perhaps as often as every processor write, but only needs to be set infrequently, on the first write to each page. Thus while we must dedicate some hardware to check the bit, we can trap (or, in SPUR nomenclature, *fault*) to software to update the bit. Moving infrequent functions from hardware into software reduces the hardware complexity and may improve performance by reducing the cycle time.

Setting the dirty bit in software is very desirable in shared-memory multiprocessors. Because page table entries (PTEs) are shared between processors, updates must either be atomic or controlled by some higher level synchronization

---

[1] This workload lacks any window activity, a major deficiency for a workstation environment. Unfortunately, no window system currently runs on SPUR, so it is not possible to include this behavior.

Page Table Entry

Page A	RO

RW

Virtual Cache Tags, Protection and State

VirtTag(Page A)	RO	
VirtTag(Page A)	RO	

Figure 3.1: Example of Multiple Cache Blocks

In a virtual address cache, the protection is cached along with each block. In this example, two blocks from Page A were brought into the cache while the page protection was read-only. Changing the protection in the page table entry does not directly affect the protection of the two previously cached blocks. If these blocks are left unchanged, subsequent writes will result in protection faults.

---

mechanism, such as a semaphore. Performing the PTE updates in software can therefore substantially simplify the memory management unit design. Throughout the rest of the paper we assume this hardware/software partitioning.

Since we are going to update the dirty bit using a software fault handler, it is natural to consider combining the dirty bit checking mechanism with the protection checking mechanism. After all, both functions cause a fault to software on the first write to a page. To emulate dirty bits with protection, the operating system initially marks writable pages as read-only, then when the first write causes a fault, it sets a software dirty bit and increases the protection level to read-write. This approach requires no special hardware support, and only minor changes to the operating system.

This approach, which we will refer to as the *FAULT* alternative, is very promising, and is used in several commercial machines, e.g., the MIPS R2000 [DeMo86]. However, there is a drawback to using it in systems with virtual address caches. In a virtual address cache like SPUR's, a copy of the protection information is stored with each cache block. Thus there may be several blocks from a particular page in the cache, each with its own copy of the protection level. Changing the protection in the page table entry does not affect blocks already brought into the cache, as illustrated in Figure 3.1. Thus, even though the first write to a page results in a fault, making the page writable, subsequent writes to other resident cache blocks will also fault. If these *excess faults* occur frequently, they could significantly degrade performance.

One approach to eliminating excess faults is to flush the page from the cache when the first fault occurs. This guarantees that no blocks from the page remain in the cache with the old protection level. This alternative, called *FLUSH*, incurs less overhead if the time to flush the page is less than the expected overhead due to excess faults. On the other hand, if flushing a page from the cache is inefficient, or excess faults are infrequent, then this alternative could be slower.

In the design of SPUR, we took another approach to reducing the performance penalty of previously cached blocks. Rather than emulate the dirty bit with protection, the PTE con-

tains an explicit, hardware-defined dirty bit. And just as we cache the page's protection with each cache block, we also cache the page's dirty bit. Note that this bit is distinct from the *block dirty bit* that indicates that a particular cache block has been modified (this difference is illustrated in Figure 3.2). When a block is brought into the cache, both the protection and dirty bit are copied from the PTE into the cache. Thus if the page has already been modified, the cached page dirty bit will be a one.

Each time a processor writes to a cache block, the hardware checks the cached copy of the page dirty bit. The first time a page is written, the cached copy indicates that the page is clean. To verify that this is the first write to a page, the hardware checks the PTE. If the PTE dirty bit indicates that the page is still clean, then this is the first write to the page and the hardware generates a "dirty bit fault" to a software handler which sets the bit. If a write finds that the cached copy of the dirty bit indicates the page is clean, but the PTE is marked dirty, then we have already faulted on another cache block and don't need to fault again. Instead, the hardware merely updates the cached copy of the page dirty bit, and the write proceeds normally. All subsequent writes to that block find the cached copy of the page dirty bit set, and proceed without delay. In the SPUR implementation, updating the cached copy of the page dirty bit is implemented by forcing a cache miss; this leads to the name *dirty bit miss*, which we use for the rest of the paper.

It is important to emphasize the similarities and differences between the SPUR scheme and emulating dirty bits with protection (the FAULT alternative). In both approaches, the "dirty bit information" (dirty bit or protection) is cached with each block on a cache miss, and the first write to a page results in a fault to a software routine that actually modifies the PTE. The key difference is that any subsequent writes to other cache blocks (from the same page) that were brought in while the page was still clean cause faults when emulating with protection, but only dirty bit misses in the SPUR scheme. Since a fault takes at least one order of magnitude longer than a dirty bit miss (as discussed in the next section), the SPUR scheme performs significantly better under certain workload conditions.

Note that while SPUR implements an explicit dirty bit, the same idea could be applied directly to the protection. Instead of immediately faulting to software when the cached copy of the protection indicates an access violation, the hardware first checks the PTE. If the cached copy is out of date, the hardware refreshes it (with a "protection bit miss") and permits the access to proceed. Since the performance of this scheme is identical to what we implemented in SPUR, we will not discuss it separately.

Finally, we also consider a fourth alternative, called WRITE, that is similar to the approach used in the Sun-3 architecture [Sun85]. In this scheme, the hardware checks the PTE dirty bit on the first write to a cache block. There are two cases to consider. First, when a write misses in the cache, the controller must examine the PTE to obtain the physical address, so checking the dirty bit incurs no additional penalty. In the second case, a write hits on a clean cache block. In this case, some additional overhead is needed to access the PTE and check the dirty bit. Unlike the Sun-3, we assume that the hardware generates a fault if the page is clean, and that software performs the update. This assumption makes the comparison unbiased, by using the mechanisms available in SPUR. Since this scheme always checks the PTE before faulting it never generates excess faults.

---

a) SPUR Page Table Entry Format

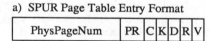

PR = Protection (2 bits)
C = Coherency
K = Cacheable
D = Page Dirty Bit
R = Page Referenced Bit
V = Page Valid Bit

b) SPUR Cache Tag Format

VirtAddrTag	PR	P	B	CS

PR = Protection (2 bits)
P = Page Dirty Bit
B = Block Dirty Bit
CS = Coherency State (2 Bits)

Figure 3.2: SPUR Page Table and Cache Line Format

This figure illustrates the page table entry format and cache line (block frame) format in the SPUR prototype. Note that the cache line contains two dirty bits: a *block dirty bit*, that indicates that the cache block has been modified while in the cache, and a *page dirty bit*, that indicates that the page has been modified. When a block is brought into the cache, the page dirty bit and protection are copied from the PTE into the cache line. Since the PTE may change while a block is in the cache, the cached copies of the page dirty bit and protection may become inconsistent with respect to the PTE.

3.2. Analysis

The goal of this analysis is to determine which alternative is superior under different workload conditions. Emulating dirty bits with protection makes the least demands upon the hardware, and is therefore the most attractive to implement. But do the excess faults present a performance problem? If so, is flushing the page an efficient alternative? Does the performance gain from SPUR's dirty bit miss mechanism justify the implementation complexity? Our inability to answer these questions to our satisfaction led us to choose a conservative alternative for SPUR (i.e., the dirty bit miss mechanism). Now that the SPUR prototype is operational, we can use the built-in performance counters to evaluate the trade-offs.

We evaluate the different approaches by comparing simple models of their overhead. We use measurements from SPUR to determine the frequency of different events, and, in some cases, measure their duration in the SPUR implementation. We also consider some alternatives to what was actually built in SPUR.

The performance overhead of the four alternatives

$$O\ (policy\ ) = overhead\ of\ dirty\ bit\ policy$$

can be expressed in terms of the following parameters:

N_{ds}	Number of necessary dirty bit faults.
$N_{ef} = N_{dm}$	Number of previously cached blocks that cause *excess faults* or *dirty bit misses*.
N_{zfod}	Number of zero-filled page faults.
N_{w-hit}	Number of blocks brought into cache by a read that are later modified.
N_{w-miss}	Number of blocks brought into cache by a write miss.
t_{ds}	Time required to handle a dirty bit fault.
t_{dm}	Time required to handle a dirty bit miss.
t_{flush}	Time to flush a page from the cache. Assumes 10% of blocks from the page are in cache and are clean.
t_{dc}	Time to check the dirty bit when writing to a clean block in the cache.

In the first alternative (FAULT), the hardware faults when it is necessary to set the dirty bit (i.e., on the first write to a page) and also on previously cached blocks. In the SPUR implementation, the fault handler must switch to the kernel stack, read a cache controller status register to determine the type of fault, then decode the instruction to determine the address of the page table entry. Because of the high overhead incurred on a fault, roughly 1000 cycles[2], the actual time to update the PTE is a small fraction of the total time.

$$O\ (FAULT\ ) = (N_{ds} + N_{ef}\ )\ t_{ds}$$

Thus we assume there is no difference in the time to handle necessary and excess faults.

The second alternative (FLUSH) calls for flushing the page from the cache on a fault, preventing the excess faults from occurring.

$$O\ (FLUSH\ ) = N_{ds}\ (t_{ds} + t_{flush}\ )$$

---

[2] The current implementation of the fault handler has not been tuned. We believe that it can be improved, but doing so will not affect our conclusions.

SPUR's flush mechanism flushes a single cache block regardless of its virtual address tag. Thus flushing a page from the cache requires 128 flush operations, one for each block. Since the hardware does not check the address tag, blocks from other pages may be unnecessarily flushed, substantially increasing the bus traffic and the total overhead. Assuming one-fifth of the blocks must actually be written back to memory, the flush would cost nearly 2000 cycles.

However, a flush operation that checks the address tag could easily be implemented, and we assume this operation exists for a more generic comparison. Even with this operation, flushing a page from the cache will still take approximately 500 cycles (128 blocks to check, two instructions for loop overhead, 90% of blocks at 1 cycle per block, 10% must be flushed at 10 cycles per block). This is approximately half the overhead of an excess fault, not counting the time to reread blocks that are accessed again. Therefore, FAULT is superior to FLUSH if there are at least twice as many necessary faults as excess faults.

The SPUR alternative greatly reduces the overhead of writes to previously cached blocks. A dirty bit miss takes 25 cycles, on average, compared to 1000 cycles for an excess fault.

$$O(SPUR) = N_{ds}(t_{ds} + t_{dm}) + N_{dm} t_{dm}$$

If a large fraction of the blocks in a page are read before they are written, then this scheme will greatly reduce the overhead to maintain dirty bits.

The last alternative (WRITE) checks the PTE on the first write to a cache block.

$$O(WRITE) = N_{ds} t_{ds} + N_{w-hit} t_{dc}$$

We assume that translation is done using SPUR's in-cache translation algorithm, and that the probability the PTE is in the cache is the average across all PTE references. This assumption is pessimistic, but, as we shall see below, does not affect our conclusions. It takes 3 cycles to check the PTE if it is in the cache, plus a weighted miss penalty of about 2 cycles. Thus t_{dc} is approximately 5 cycles.

Finally, we also consider the minimal policy (MIN) for comparison.

$$O(MIN) = N_{ds} t_{ds}$$

This alternative includes only the overhead to update the dirty bit in software, and is optimal in the sense that it incurs no

Table 3.2: Time Parameters		
Parameter	Cycle Count	Description
t_{ds}	1000	Time for handler to set dirty bit
t_{flush}	500	Time to flush page from cache
t_{dm}	25	Time to update cached dirty bit
t_{dc}	5	Time to check PTE dirty bit

additional overhead to check the dirty bit or to handle excess faults.

Table 3.1 summarizes the implementation alternatives. Table 3.2 summarizes the time parameters discussed above; we assume the faster flush operation for a more balanced comparison. Table 3.3 summarizes the event frequencies, measured on the SPUR prototype. It is immediately clear from this table that *excess faults occur very infrequently*. At 6 and 8 megabytes of main memory, both workloads cause less than 8% as many excess faults as necessary faults. At 5 megabytes, the fraction climbs to 16% for WORKLOAD1 and 10% for SLC. However, in all cases excess faults are infrequent, suggesting that pages that will be modified are modified quickly. The ratio of N_{w-hit} to N_{w-miss} supports this hypothesis: roughly one-fifth (from 16% to 24%) of the modified cache blocks are read before they are written. Based on this ratio, a simple probability model[3] predicts less than 20% as many excess faults as modified faults. The model provides some intuition why the number of excess faults is low.

However, further investigation uncovered another reason for the low percentage of excess faults. Like UNIX, the Sprite operating system initializes newly allocated stack and heap pages to zero. The kernel maps the initialized page into the process's address space with the dirty bit turned off. But since programs rarely want to read stack and heap pages before they are written (i.e., read a zero), the first operation to these pages is almost always a write, resulting in a dirty bit fault. If we exclude these zero-fill pages from from the necessary dirty bit faults, the fraction of excess faults increases, ranging from 15% to 34%. While still a small percentage, this range is closer to our model's prediction.

Table 3.4 summarizes the overhead for the implementation alternatives. Because they are not intrinsic, we exclude the zero-fill pages from the calculations[4] (i.e., the difference $N_{ds} - N_{zfod}$ is substituted for N_{ds} in the models). Because excess faults occur infrequently, we expect the FAULT policy to perform well. Flushing the page from the cache, the FLUSH policy, increases the overhead by 26% over FAULT on average. Only for WORKLOAD1 at 5 megabytes does FLUSH start to come close, dropping to only 12% worse. The SPUR scheme has the best performance, requiring only 3% more than the minimum (MIN). But since excess faults are rare, SPUR's overhead is only 16% less than FAULT's; this difference amounts to only a small fraction of total system performance. In addition, the SPUR scheme requires one additional state bit

Table 3.1: Dirty Bit Implementation Alternatives	
FAULT	Emulate dirty bits with protection. Writes to previously cached blocks cause excess faults.
FLUSH	Emulate dirty bits with protection. When a fault occurs, flush all blocks in that page from the cache, preventing excess faults.
SPUR	Store a copy of the dirty bit with each cache block. Check the PTE before faulting; if the cached copy is merely out of date, update it with a dirty bit miss.
WRITE	Check the PTE on the first write to each cache block.
MIN	Minimal policy. Includes only overhead intrinsic to all policies.

---

[3] The model assumes a) a uniform distribution of read and write misses, b) infinitely large pages, and c) that necessary faults occur only on write misses. With these assumptions, the number of excess faults has a geometric distribution with parameter $p_w = \dfrac{N_{w-miss}}{N_{w-hit} + N_{w-miss}}$. Relaxing assumptions b) and c) only reduces the expected number of excess faults.

[4] Note that Sprite will always write a zero-filled page to swap the first time it is replaced, even if the program has not modified it.

	Table 3.3: Event Frequencies						
Workload	Memory Size (megabytes)	N_{ds}	N_{zfod}	$N_{ef}=N_{dm}$	N_{w-hit} (million)	N_{w-miss} (million)	$t_{elapsed}$ (seconds)
SLC	5	2349	905	237	1.27	7.38	948
	6	1838	905	143	0.839	5.11	502
	8	1661	905	120	0.612	3.68	341
WORKLOAD1	5	9860	5286	1534	6.15	34.0	3016
	6	7843	5181	456	4.92	20.4	2535
	8	7471	5182	364	4.10	17.3	2555

	Table 3.4: Overhead of Dirty Bit Alternatives (Excluding Zero-Fills)					
Workload	Memory Size (megabytes)	MIN	FAULT	FLUSH	SPUR	WRITE
		millions of cycles (relative to MIN)				
SLC	5	1.44 (1.00)	1.68 (1.16)	2.17 (1.50)	1.49 (1.03)	7.81 (5.41)
	6	0.933 (1.00)	1.08 (1.15)	1.40 (1.50)	0.960 (1.03)	5.13 (5.50)
	8	0.756 (1.00)	0.876 (1.16)	1.13 (1.50)	0.778 (1.03)	3.82 (5.05)
WORKLOAD1	5	4.57 (1.00)	6.11 (1.34)	6.86 (1.50)	4.73 (1.03)	35.3 (7.72)
	6	2.66 (1.00)	3.12 (1.17)	3.99 (1.50)	2.74 (1.03)	27.3 (10.2)
	8	2.29 (1.00)	2.65 (1.16)	3.43 (1.50)	2.36 (1.03)	22.8 (9.95)

per cache block[5], plus an additional 14 product terms in the controller's main PLA (193 vs 207, or 7%). We believe the minor performance improvement does not justify the increase in chip and board complexity.

Not surprisingly, the WRITE policy performed worst of all by a large margin. Roughly one fifth of all cache blocks are read before they are written. Therefore, even though checking the PTE is relatively fast, the frequency it must be done makes the total overhead higher than the other schemes. Even if the time to check the PTE dirty bit is reduced to only 1 cycle, this alternative still has the worst performance. Since this policy has higher overhead despite special hardware support, it is clearly inferior to the FAULT policy.

To summarize the results of this section, it is clear that dirty bits can be efficiently emulated using protection even when using a large virtual address cache. Based on our synthetic benchmarks and measured events on the SPUR hardware, the frequency of excess faults ranges from 16% to 34% the frequency of necessary faults. Additional hardware support can improve dirty bit performance by at most 34%, which amounts to much less than 1% of overall system performance. Simply tuning the fault handler would probably

achieve a larger improvement. This is good news to hardware designers because it further simplifies the logic they must support. Had these results been available during the design of SPUR, we could have eliminated the dirty bit support, reducing the number of product terms in the sequencer PLA by 7%.

3.3. Benefits of Dirty Bits

In the first half of this section, we looked at the cost and performance impact of different implementations of dirty bits. In the remainder of the section, we take a step back and look at what we gain from implementing dirty bits. Although we have shown that dirty bits require no special hardware support, they do add some complexity to the operating system.

Dirty bits improve system performance by eliminating unnecessary page-outs; clean pages need not be written back to secondary storage when displaced from main memory. Dirty bits only help for pages which can be modified; since most systems disallow direct updates of code, dirty bits provide no information for code pages. During times of heavy paging, pages do not stay in memory long and thus are unlikely to be modified. Under these conditions dirty bits can greatly reduce the page-out traffic. However, memory prices have dropped by a factor of 100 over the last 10 years [Myer86] prompting a rapid increase in main memory sizes[6]. Workstations are now commonly sold with at least 8 megabytes of memory. With the relatively low price of memory, most users will increase their memory size rather than sustain consistently high paging rates. Many computing environments also provide compute servers in addition to workstations; jobs which page heavily on a workstation are usually moved to these larger machines.

In conjunction with the increase in memory size, many workstations have gone to large page sizes: the Sun-3's pages are 8 kbytes, the MIPS R2000's and SPUR's are 4K bytes.

---

[5] The generalized version, using the protection field, eliminates the need for an extra bit.

[6] We believe the recent DRAM shortage is only a short-term aberration resulting from protectionist trade policies.

Table 3.5: Page-Out Results from Sprite Development Systems

Hostname	Memory Size	Uptime (hours)	Number of Page-Ins	Potentially Modified Pages	Not Modified Pages	Percent (%) Not Modified	Percent (%) Additional Paging I/O
mace	8 MB	70	15203	2681	488	18%	2.8%
sloth	8 MB	37	10566	2146	129	6%	1.0%
mace	8 MB	46	48722	5198	814	16%	1.4%
sage	12MB	45	5246	544	14	3%	0.2%
fenugreek	12MB	36	8556	1154	58	5%	0.6%
murder	16 MB	119	23302	12944	895	7%	2.5%

Both factors, large memories and large pages, suggest that most modifiable pages will be modified while in memory. Thus dirty bits may be of marginal utility, and perhaps could be excluded from future operating systems. To examine this hypothesis, we looked at the page-out performance of our Sun-3's running Sprite. The Sprite developers use these systems to enhance and maintain the Sprite operating system, as well as other tasks such as reading mail, and writing papers and dissertations. The workload on these machines is similar to many other software development environments.

All the systems have at least 8 megabytes of memory, so the paging rates are relatively low. There is also a certain amount of self-scheduling; users tend to run programs with very large memory demands on the systems with more physical memory.

Table 3.5 displays the measurements from the development machines. The second to last column holds the main result: with 8 megabytes of memory at least 80% of all modifiable pages are modified. With 12 megabytes or more, the fraction is at least 90%. Also, as shown in the last column, the total number of additional pages that would be written out without dirty bits only increases the total number of paging I/Os by at most 3%. Since the paging rate is already low, a 3% increase will have a negligible impact on the total system performance.

These results support our hypothesis, indicating that dirty bits provide only negligible performance improvement for this class of workload. While these results may not apply to all applications, it is clear that for an important class of workloads dirty bits provide little benefit, which will decline further with increasing memory size.

4. Reference Bits

4.1. Reference Bit Policies

In this section, we examine the trade-offs in reference bit implementations. Reference bits are used to maintain a pseudo-LRU ordering of resident pages. A *page daemon* periodically clears the reference bits and reclaims unreferenced pages.

As with dirty bits, the approach generally taken in systems with TLBs is not directly applicable to systems with virtual address caches. In traditional implementations, the reference bits are cached in the TLB and checked on each processor reference. However, in a system like SPUR, it is impractical to check the bits this frequently. Instead, SPUR only checks the reference bit on cache misses; since the hardware must access the PTE on a cache miss, there is no additional penalty to check the reference bit. As with dirty bits, SPUR generates a fault to a software handler when the bit must be set. While SPUR supports an explicit reference bit, we could just as easily emulate them with the valid bit, as done in BSD Unix [Baba81].

Checking the reference bit on cache misses reduces the overhead, but it does not provide exactly the same functionality. When the page daemon, or allocate procedure, clears the

							Table 4.1: Reference Bit Results			

Workload	Memory Size (megabytes)	Policy	Page-Ins		Elapsed Time (seconds)	
SLC	5	MISS	4647	(100%)	948	(100%)
		REF	4738	(102%)	1020	(108%)
		NOREF	8230	(177%)	1341	(141%)
	6	MISS	1833	(100%)	502	(100%)
		REF	1866	(102%)	534	(106%)
		NOREF	3465	(189%)	703	(140%)
	8	MISS	1056	(100%)	341	(100%)
		REF	1062	(101%)	342	(101%)
		NOREF	1512	(143%)	382	(112%)
WORKLOAD1	5	MISS	11959	(100%)	3016	(100%)
		REF	11119	(93%)	3153	(105%)
		NOREF	16045	(134%)	3214	(107%)
	6	MISS	3556	(100%)	2535	(100%)
		REF	3617	(102%)	2677	(106%)
		NOREF	5073	(143%)	2555	(101%)
	8	MISS	1837	(100%)	2555	(100%)
		REF	1790	(97%)	2701	(106%)
		NOREF	1926	(105%)	2505	(98%)

reference bit, it does not affect blocks from that page that are already in the cache. Thus the processor can continue to reference those blocks without setting the reference bit. Under this policy, which we call the *MISS bit approximation*, or simply the *MISS* policy, the page daemon may incorrectly replace pages that have actually been recently referenced, but have not recently caused a cache miss.

We can eliminate these incorrect replacements if the page daemon flushes the page from the cache when it clears its reference bit. This guarantees that the next reference to the page will cause a cache miss, setting the reference bit. Under this policy, called *true reference bits* or simply the *REF* policy, the reference bits are accurately maintained and should result in fewer page faults than the MISS policy. However, the REF policy does not come for free. Flushing a page from the cache is an expensive operation, relative to the cost of clearing the reference bit. This is especially true in a multiprocessor, which must flush the page from all the caches. Not only does the flush take a long time, but it disrupts the cache, forcing additional cache misses to refetch some of the blocks.

For small caches, the MISS policy is probably a good approximation to true reference bits. When the cache miss rate is high then the average residency of a block is short, and the reference bit for active pages will be set fairly soon after it is cleared. But as caches increase in size, we expect the approximation to become worse. Consider a cache of infinite capacity. Once a block is brought into the cache it never leaves without being explicitly flushed. Thus the MISS policy never sets the reference bit once the entire page is resident in the cache. At this extreme, the MISS bit approximation provides no benefit; eliminating reference bits all together, the *NOREF* policy, would be superior since it eliminates the overhead of checking, setting and clearing them.

The NOREF policy should also be superior with large memory sizes. It has been observed that large systems spend lots of time searching for unreferenced pages [McKu85]. With large enough main memories, the overhead to maintain pseudo-LRU ordering may exceed the overhead of additional faults incurred by not maintaining reference bits.

We consider a very simple NOREF policy, primarily to minimize changes to the Sprite virtual memory system [Nels86]. Under this policy, the basic replacement algorithm is unchanged, however the machine dependent routine that reads the hardware reference bit always returns false. Conversely, the routine that clears the hardware reference bit has no effect, leaving the hardware bit always set (thus preventing reference faults). While we consider this policy to be reasonable, we believe there may be better replacement algorithms that do not support reference bits. Nonetheless, if we get acceptable results under this policy, then it supports the proposition that we can eliminate reference bits.

4.2. Reference Bit Evaluation

To evaluate these three policies, we modified Sprite to use each of the them, under control of run-time flags. We ran our synthetic workloads on the SPUR prototype, with 5, 6, and 8 megabytes of memory. We ran five repetitions of each data point, using a randomized experiment design to minimize bias. The main results are summarized in Table 4.1.

Running WORKLOAD1 at 8 megabytes of main memory generates only a small amount of paging activity, so the overhead of maintaining reference information exceeds the benefits. The REF policy requires 3% fewer page-ins than the MISS policy, but takes 6% longer to execute due to the flush overhead. The NOREF policy generates 5% more page-ins than MISS, but because it spends no time maintaining reference bits runs 2% faster.

As we would expect, the reference bits provide more benefit as memory becomes more scarce. At both 5 and 6 megabytes, the NOREF policy generates significantly more page-in traffic, 134% and 143% respectively. Note, however, that at 6 megabytes, the performance degradation is still only 1%. Finally, at 5 megabytes paging becomes heavy and the REF policy results in 7% fewer page-ins than MISS. Nonetheless, MISS still requires 5% less time to execute because of its lower overhead.

The SLC workload displays much more uniform behavior. The MISS policy always results in the fewest page-ins and the shortest elapsed time. For this workload, the NOREF policy never comes closer than 12% slower; for the two smaller memory sizes, it is 40% slower. The REF policy has comparable performance to MISS at 8 megabytes, when there is little paging. But at smaller memory sizes, despite selective cache flushing on reference bit clears, it still generates more page-ins than MISS; consequently, REF has a longer execution time than MISS.

In summary, implementing true reference bits may reduce the number of page-ins at low memory sizes, but the cpu overhead required always exceeds the benefit of the lower fault rate. The MISS bit approximation has the best overall performance, generating significantly fewer page-ins than the NOREF policy but without the high overhead of true reference bits. For WORKLOAD1, however, eliminating reference bits altogether (NOREF) has the best performance at 8 megabytes, and only slightly worse performance at 6 megabytes. Clearly these results do not apply to all systems, but certainly for this workload reference bits provide at best a small increase in performance. As memory sizes increase, this benefit will tend to decrease and may eventually become a hindrance.

5. Summary and Conclusions

In this paper, we have examined alternative implementations of reference and dirty bits for virtual address caches. Virtual address caches provide faster access times than physical address caches, but by eliminating the TLB they make maintaining reference and dirty bits more difficult.

We have shown that simpler is better; dirty bits may be efficiently emulated with protection. The excess faults that occur when multiple blocks from a clean page are brought into the cache and then modified account for only 19% of all dirty bit faults, on average. Thus hardware alternatives like SPUR's dirty bit miss mechanism and the Sun-3's first-write mechanism are not justified. No special hardware is necessary to efficiently support dirty bits.

Approximating reference bits by checking only on cache misses can result in more page faults at smaller memory sizes. However, the overhead of maintaining true reference bits, by flushing a page when clearing the reference bit, far exceeds the benefit of a lower fault rate.

We also examined the possibility of eliminating reference and dirty bits entirely. In measurements on machines used for software development, more than 80% of all writable pages are dirty when replaced; eliminating dirty bits would have increased the total paging activity by at most 3%. Similarly, for some workloads maintaining reference bits, even with the miss bit approximation, may become a liability at larger memory sizes. At 8 megabytes, not a large memory for today's workstations, the overhead to maintain reference bits exceeds the benefits for one of the two workloads presented. These results strongly suggest that the benefits of reference and dirty bits decline as memory size increases, and may eventually degrade rather than improve performance. We are conducting further studies to evaluate the performance of larger applications and larger memory sizes.

6. Acknowledgements

We are very grateful to Mendel Rosenblum who sacrificed progress on his own research to debug the Sprite virtual memory system; without his generous efforts the SPUR measurements would have been impossible. Mike Nelson also provided earlier assistance with Sprite. Alan Smith suggested the probabilistic model in Section 3. Jane Doughty, Garth Gibson and Doug Johnson provided useful comments on earlier drafts of this paper. This work was supported by SPUR/DARPA contract No. N00039-85-C-0269, NSF MIP-8352227, the California MICRO program (together with Texas Instruments, National Semiconductor, Xerox, Honeywell, and Philips/Signetics), and the IBM Predoctoral Fellowship program.

7. References

[Baba81] Babaoglu, O., "Virtual Storage Management in the Absence of Reference Bits", U.C. Berkeley, Electronic Research Laboratory, Memo. No. UCB/Electronics Research Lab. M81/92, November 1981. Ph.D. Dissertation.

[DeMo86] DeMoney, M., J. Moore and J. Mashey, "Operating System Support on a RISC", *Proceedings 1986 IEEE Compcon*, pp. 138-143, March 1986.

[Hill86] Hill, M. D., S. J. Eggers, J. R. Larus, G. S. Taylor, G. Adams, B. K. Bose, G. A. Gibson, P. M. Hansen, J. Keller, S. I. Kong, C. G. Lee, D. Lee, J. M. Pendleton, S. A. Ritchie, D. A. Wood, B. G. Zorn, P. N. Hilfinger, D. Hodges, R. H. Katz, J. Ousterhout and D. A. Patterson, "Design Decisions in SPUR", *IEEE Computer*, Vol. 19, No. 11 , November 1986.

[Katz85] Katz, R. H., S. J. Eggers, D. A. Wood, C. L. Perkins and R. G. Sheldon, "Implementing a Cache Consistency Protocol", *Proc. 12th International Symposium on Computer Architecture*, Boston, Mass. , pp. 276-283, June 1985.

[Knap85] Knapp, V., "Virtually Addressed Caches for Multiprogramming and Multiprocessing Environments", U. of Washington, Dept. of Computer Science, Technical Report No. 85-06-02, June, 1985.

[McKu85] McKusick, M. K., M. Karels and S. Leffler, "Performance Improvements and Functional Enhancements in 4.3BSD", U.C. Berkeley Computer Science Division Technical Report No. UCB/Computer Science Dpt. 85/245, June 1985.

[Myer86] Myers, G. J., A. Y. C. Yu and D. L. House, "Microprocessor Technology Trends", *Proceedings of the IEEE*, Vol. 74, No. 12 , December 1986.

[Nels86] Nelson, M., "Virtual Memory for the Sprite Operating System", UC Berkeley, Computer Science Division, Technical Report No. UCB/Computer Science Dpt. 86/301, June 1986. M.S. Thesis.

[Oust88] Ousterhout, J. K., A. R. Cherenson, F. Douglis, M. N. Nelson and B. B. Welch, "The Sprite Network Operating System", *IEEE Computer*, Vol. 21, No. 2 , February 1988, pp. 23-36.

[Patt85] Patterson, D. A., "Reduced Instruction Set Computers", *Communications of the ACM*, Vol. 28, No. 1 , January, 1985, pp. 8-21.

[Smit82] Smith, A. J., "Cache Memories", *Computing Surveys*, Vol. 14, No. 3 , Sept. 1982, pp. 473-530.

[Sun85] Sun Microsystems, Inc, Sun-3 Architecture Manual (July 1985).

[Wood86] Wood, D. A., S. J. Eggers, G. A. Gibson, M. D. Hill, J. M. Pendelton, S. A. Ritchie, G. S. Taylor, R. H. Katz and D. A. Patterson, "An In-Cache Address Translation Mechanism", *Proc. Thirteenth International Symposium on Computer Architecture*, Tokyo, Japan , pp. 358-365, June 1986.

[Wood87] Wood, D. A., S. Eggers and G. Gibson, "SPUR Memory System Architecture", Technical Report UCB/Computer Science Dpt. 87/394, University of California, Berkeley , December 1987.

[Zorn87] Zorn, B., P. Hilfinger, K. Ho and J. Larus, "SPUR Lisp: Design and Implementation", Technical Report UCB/Computer Science Dpt. 87/373, U.C. Berkeley, September 1987.

Inexpensive Implementations of Set-Associativity

R. E. Kessler[†], Richard Jooss, Alvin Lebeck and Mark D. Hill[‡]

University of Wisconsin
Computer Sciences Department
Madison, Wisconsin 53706

ABSTRACT

The traditional approach to implementing wide set-associativity is expensive, requiring a wide tag memory (directory) and many comparators. Here we examine alternative implementations of associativity that use hardware similar to that used to implement a direct-mapped cache. One approach scans tags serially from most-recently used to least-recently used. Another uses a partial compare of a few bits from each tag to reduce the number of tags that must be examined serially. The drawback of both approaches is that they increase cache access time by a factor of two or more over the traditional implementation of set-associativity, making them inappropriate for cache designs in which a fast access time is crucial (e.g. level one caches, caches directly servicing processor requests).

These schemes are useful, however, if (1) the low miss ratio of wide set-associative caches is desired, (2) the low cost of a direct-mapped implementation is preferred, and (3) the slower access time of these approaches can be tolerated. We expect these conditions to be true for caches in multiprocessors designed to reduce memory interconnection traffic, caches implemented with large, narrow memory chips, and level two (or higher) caches in a cache hierarchy.

1. Introduction

The selection of associativity has significant impact on cache performance and cost [Smit86] [Smit82] [Hill87] [Przy88a]. The *associativity (degree of associativity, set size)* of a cache is the number of places (*block frames*) in the cache where a block may reside. Increasing associativity reduces the probability that a block is not found in the cache (the *miss ratio*) by decreasing the chance that recently referenced blocks map to the same place [Smit78]. However, increased associativity may nonetheless result in longer effective access times since it can increase the latency to retrieve data on a cache *hit* [Hill88, Przy88a]. When it is important to minimize hit times direct-mapped (associativity of one) caches

[†] This work has been supported by graduate fellowships from the National Science Foundation and the University of Wisconsin-Madison.
[‡] This work was sponsored in part by research initiation grants from the graduate school of the University of Wisconsin-Madison.

may be preferred over caches with higher associativity.

Wide associativity is important when: (1) miss times are very long or (2) memory and memory interconnect contention delay is significant or sensitive to cache miss ratio. These points are likely to be true for shared memory multiprocessors. Multiprocessor caches typically service misses via a multistage interconnect or bus. When a multi-stage interconnect is used the miss latency can be large whether or not contention exists. Bus miss times with low utilizations may be small, but delays due to contention among processors can become large and are sensitive to cache miss ratio. As the cost of a miss increases, the reduced miss ratio of wider associativity will result in better performance when compared to direct-mapped caches.

Associativity is even more useful for *level two caches* in a two-level multiprocessor cache hierarchy. While the *level one cache* must service references from the processor at the speed of the processor, the level two cache can be slower since it services only processor references that miss in the level one cache. The additional hit time delay incurred by associativity in the level two cache is not as important [Przy88b]. Reducing memory and memory interconnect traffic is a larger concern. Wide associativity also simplifies the maintenance of multi-level inclusion [Baer88]. This is the property that all data contained in lower level caches is contained in their corresponding higher level caches. Multi-level inclusion is useful for reducing coherency invalidations to level one caches. Finally, preliminary models indicate that increasing associativity reduces the average number of empty cache block frames when coherency invalidations are frequent[1]. This implies that wider associativity will result in better utilization of the cache.

Unfortunately, increasing associativity is likely to increase the board area and cost of the cache relative to a direct-mapped cache. Traditional implementations of *a*-way set-associative caches read and compare all *a* tags of a set in parallel to determine where (and whether) a given block resides in the cache. With *t*-bit tags, this requires a tag memory that can provide $a \times t$ bits in parallel. A direct-mapped cache can use fewer, narrower, deeper chips since it requires only a *t*-bit wide tag memory. Traditional implementations of associativity also use *a* comparators (each *t*-bits wide) rather than one, wider data memory, more buffers, and more multiplexors as compared to a direct-mapped cache. This adds to the board area needed for wider associativity. As the size of memory chips increases, it becomes more expensive to consume board area with multiplexors and other logic since the same area could hold more cache memory.

While numerous papers have examined associativity [Lipt68] [Kapl73] [Bell74] [Stre76] [Smit78] [Smit82] [Clar83] [Agar88], most have assumed the traditional implementation. One of the few papers describing a cache with a non-traditional implementation of

---

[1] A miss to a set-associative cache can fill any empty block frame in the set, whereas a miss to a direct-mapped cache can fill only a single frame. Increasing associativity increases the chance that an invalidated block frame will be quickly used again by making more empty frames available for reuse on a miss.

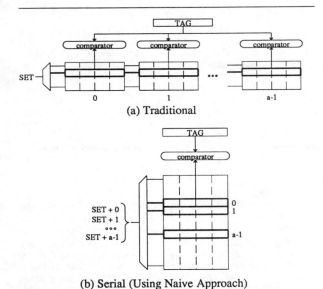

(a) Traditional

(b) Serial (Using Naive Approach)

Figure 1. Implementing Set-Associativity.

Part (a) of this figure (top) shows the traditional implementation of the logic to determine hit/miss in an a-way set-associative cache. This logic uses the "SET" field of the reference to select one t-bit tag from each of a banks. Each stored tag is compared to the incoming tag ("TAG"). A hit is declared if a stored tag matches the incoming tag, a miss otherwise.

Part (b) (bottom) shows a serial implementation of the same cache architecture. Here the a stored tags in a set are read from one bank and compared serially (the tags are addressed with "SET" concatenated with 0 through $a - 1$).

associativity is [Chan87]. It discusses a cache implemented for a System/370 CPU that has a one-cycle hit time to the most-recently-used (MRU) block in each set and a longer access time for other blocks in the set, similar to the Cray-1 instruction buffers [Cray76] and the biased set-associative translation buffer described in [Alex86].

This paper is about lower cost implementations of associativity, implementations other than the traditional. We introduce cache designs which combine the lower miss ratio of associativity and the lower cost of direct-mapped caches. In the new implementations the width of the comparison circuitry and tag memory is t, the width of one tag, instead of the $a \times t$ required by the traditional implementation. Implementations using tag widths of $b \times t$ $(1 < b < a)$ are possible and can result in intermediate costs and performance, but are not considered here. This paper is not about level two caches per se, but we expect these low cost schemes to be applicable to level two caches. We organize this paper as follows. Section 2 introduces the new approaches to implementing associativity, shows how they cost less than the traditional implementation of associativity, and predicts how they will perform. Section 3 analyzes the approaches of Section 2 with trace-driven simulation.

2. Alternative Approaches to Implementing Set-Associativity

Let a, a power of two, be a cache's associativity and let t be the number of bits in each address tag. During a cache reference, an implementation must determine whether any of the a stored tags in the set of a reference match the incoming tag. Since at most one stored tag can match, the search can be terminated when a match is found (a cache hit). All a stored tags, however, must be examined on a cache miss.

Figure 1a illustrates the traditional implementation of the tag memory and comparators for an a-way set-associative cache, which reads and *probes* all tags in parallel. We define a probe as a comparison of the incoming tag and the tag memory. If any one of the stored tags match, a hit is declared. We concentrate only on cache tag memory and comparators, because they are what we propose to implement differently. Additional memory (not shown) is required by any implementation of associativity with a cache replacement policy other than random. A direct-mapped cache does not require this memory. The memory for the cache data (also not shown) is traditionally accessed in parallel with the tag memory.

Figure 1b shows a naive way to do an inexpensive set-associative lookup. It uses hardware similar to a direct-mapped cache, but serially accesses the stored tags of a set until a match is found (a hit) or the tags of the set are exhausted (a miss). Note how it requires only a single comparator and a t-bit wide tag memory, whereas, the traditional implementation requires t comparators and an $a \times t$ wide tag memory.

Unfortunately, the naive approach is slow in comparison to the traditional implementation. For hits, each stored tag is equally likely to hold the data. Half the non-matching tags are examined before finding the tag that matches, making the average number of probes $(a-1)/2 + 1$. For a miss, all a stored tags must be examined in series, resulting in a probes. The traditional implementation requires only a single probe in both cases.

2.1. The MRU Approach

The average number of probes needed for a hit may be reduced from that needed by the naive approach by ordering the stored tags so that the tags most likely to match are examined first. One proposed order [So88] [Matt70] is from most-recently-used (MRU) to least-recently-used (LRU). This order is effective for level one caches because of the temporal locality of processor reference streams [So88] [Chan87]. We find (in Section 3) that it is also effective for level two caches due to the temporal locality in streams of level one cache misses.

One way to enforce an MRU comparison order is to swap blocks to keep the most-recently-used block in block frame 0, the second most-recently-used block in block frame 1, etc. Since tags (and data) would have to be swapped between consecutive cache accesses in order to maintain the MRU order, this is not a viable implementation option for most set-associative caches.[2] A better way to manage an MRU comparison order, illustrated in Figure 2a, is to store information for each set indicating its ordering. Fortunately, information similar to a MRU list per set is likely to be maintained anyway in a set-associative cache implementing a true LRU replacement policy. In this case there is no extra memory requirement to store the MRU information. We will also analyze (in section 3) reducing the length of the MRU list, using approximate rather than full MRU searches, to further decrease memory requirements. Unfortunately, the lookup of MRU information must precede the probes of the tags[3]. This will lead to longer cache lookup times than would the swapping scheme.

If we assume that the initial MRU list lookup takes about the same time as one probe, the average number of probes required on a cache lookup resulting in a hit using the MRU approach is $1 + \sum_{i=1}^{a} i f_i$ where f_i is the probability the i-th MRU tag matches, given that one of them will match[4]. The MRU scheme performs particularly poorly on cache misses, requiring $1 + a$ probes. This

---

[2] While maintaining MRU order using swapping may be feasible for a 2-way set-associative cache, Agarwal's hash-rehash cache [Agar87] can be superior to MRU in this 2-way case.

[3] While it is possible to lookup the MRU information in parallel with the level-one-cache access, it is also possible to start level-two-cache accesses early for any of the other implementation approaches [Bren84].

[4] Each f_i is equal to the probability of a reference to LRU distance i divided by the hit ratio, for a given number of sets [Smit78].

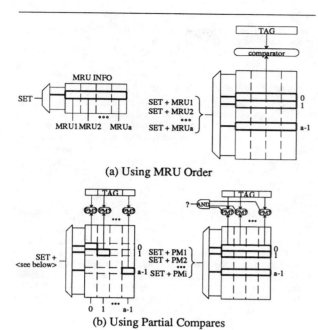

(a) Using MRU Order

(b) Using Partial Compares

Figure 2. Improved Implementations of Serial Set-Associativity.

Part (a) of this figure (top) shows an implementation of serial set-associativity using ordering information. This approach first reads MRU ordering information (left) and then probes the stored tags from the one most-likely to match to the one least-likely to match (right). Note "+" represents concatenate.

Part (b) (bottom) shows an implementation of serial set-associativity using partial compares. This approach first reads k ($k = \lfloor t/a \rfloor$) bits from each stored tag and compares them with the corresponding bits of the incoming tag. The second step of this approach serially compares all stored tags that partially matched ("PM") with the incoming tag until a match is found or the tags are exhausted (right).

---

is one more than the naive implementation on misses since the MRU list is uselessly consulted.

2.2. The Partial Compare Approach

We have carefully defined a probe to be the comparison of the incoming tag and the tag memory, without requiring that all bits of the tag memory come from the same stored tag. We now introduce the *partial compare* approach that uses a two step process to often avoid reading all t bits of each stored tag. In step one, the partial compare approach reads t/a bits from each of a stored tags and compares them with the corresponding bits of the incoming tag. Tags that fail this *partial comparison* cannot hit and need not be examined further on a cache lookup. In step two, all stored tags that passed step one are examined serially with t-bit (full) compares.

The implementation of partial compares is not costly, as it can use the same memory and comparators as the naive approach assuming k, the partial compare width ($k = \lfloor t/a \rfloor$), is a multiple of memory chip and comparator width. Partial compares are done with the help of a few tricks. The first trick, illustrated in Figure 2b, is to provide slightly different addresses to each k-bit wide collection of memory chips, addressing the i-th collection with the address of the set concatenated with $\log_2 i$. The second trick is to divide the t-bit comparator into a separate k-bit comparators[5].

---

[5] If $k \times a$ does not equal t then $\lfloor t/a \rfloor \times a$ bits of the tag can be used for partial compares, with another comparator for the extra bits.

This is straight-forward, since wide comparators are often implemented by logically AND-ing the results of narrow comparators. Note how step two of this partial compare approach uses the same tag memory and comparators as step one, but does full tag compares rather than partial compares.

The performance of this approach depends on how well the partial compares eliminate stored tags from further consideration. For independent tags, the average number of probes will be minimized if each of the values $[0, 2^k - 1]$ is equally likely for each of the k-bit patterns on which partial compares are done. While this condition may be true for physical address tags, it is unlikely to be true for the high order tag bits of virtual addresses. Nevertheless, we can use the randomness of the lower bits of the virtual address tag to make the distribution of the higher ones more uniform and independent. For example, one can transform a tag to a unique other tag by exclusive-oring the low-order k bits of the tag with each of the other k-bit pieces of the tag before it is stored in the tag memory. Incoming tags will go through the same transformation so that the incoming tag and the stored tag will match if the untransformed tags are the same. The original tags can be retrieved from the tag memory for writing back blocks on replacement via the same transformation in which they were stored (i.e. the transformation is its own inverse). This method is used throughout this paper to produce stored tags with better probabilistic characteristics. We will also analyze using no transformation, and using a more sophisticated one in Section 3. We make the assumption in our analysis to follow that each of the values $[0, 2^k - 1]$ is equally likely and independent for each partial compare. Our trace-driven simulation (in Section 3) tests this assumption.

The probability that an incoming tag partially-matches a stored tag is $1/2^k$. A *false match* is a partial tag match which will not lead to a match of the full tag. Given a hit, the expected number of false matches in step one is $(a-1)/2^k$, of which half will be examined in step two before a hit is determined. Thus, the expected number of probes on a hit is $1 + (a-1)/2^{k+1} + 1$, where the terms of the expression are: the probe for the partial comparison (step one), the full tag comparisons (in step two) due to false matches, and the full tag match which produces the hit, respectively. On a miss, the expected number of probes in simply $1 + a/2^k$, the probe for the partial comparison and the number of false matches, respectively.

The partial compare scheme can lead to poor performance if many false matches are encountered in step two. Wider partial compares could eliminate some of these false matches. The partial compare width can be increased by partitioning the a stored tags of a set into s proper *subsets* (each containing a/s tags) and examining the subsets in series[6]. The step one and step two partial compare sequence is performed for each of the subsets to determine if there is a cache hit. The order in which the subsets are examined is arbitrary throughout this paper. Increasing the number of subsets will increase the partial compare width since fewer partial compares are done concurrently. For example, 2 subsets could be used in an 8-way set-associative cache, with 4 entries in each. A lookup in this cache would proceed as two 4-way (single subset) lookups, one after the other. With a 16-bit wide tag memory in this cache, partitioning into 2 subsets would result in 4-bit partial compares. This will result in fewer false matches than with the 2-bit partial compares without subsets. The number of probes per access decreases when using proper subsets if the expected number of false matches is reduced (due to wider partial compares) by more than the number of probes added due to the additional subsets. Subsets may be desirable for implementation considerations in addition to performance considerations if the memory chip or comparator width dictate that the partial compares be wider.

At one extreme (where $s = a$), partial compares with subsets would be implemented as the naive approach, while the other

---

[6] Note that subsets are not useful with the naive and MRU approaches.

	Configuration			Expected Probes	
Method	Assoc-iativity	Number Subsets	Tag Memory Width (bits)	Assume Hit	Assume Miss
Traditional	a	1	$a \times t$	1	1
	4	1	64	1	1
Naive	a	1	t	$(1/2)(a-1)+1$	a
	4	1	16	2.5	4
MRU	a	1	t	$1+\sum_{i=1}^{a} i\, f_i$	$1+a$
	4	1	16	$[2,5]$	5
Partial ($k=4$ bits)	a	1	$\max(t, a \times k)$	$2+(a-1)/2^{k+1}$	$1+a/2^k$
	4	1	16	2.09	1.25
Partial w/Subsets ($k=2$ bits) ($k=4$ bits)	a	s	$\max(t, a/s \times k)$	$2+(1/2)(s-1)$ $+(a-1)/2^{k+1}$	$s+a/2^k$
	8	1	16	2.88	3.00
	8	2	16	2.72	2.5

Table 1. Performance of Set-Associativity Implementations.

For various methods and associativities this table gives the number of subsets, the tag memory width, the number of probes for a hit, and, the number for a miss. The table assumes t-bit tags ($t=16$), k-bit partial compares, and that the i-th most-recently used tag matches with probability f_i on a hit. Note how an increase from 1 to 2 subsets improved the predicted performance of the partial compare approach at an associativity of 8.

($s=1$) can lead to many false matches. An important question to ask is: what number of subsets leads to the best performance (i.e. fewest number of probes per cache lookup) ? The next three answers to this question vary from the most-accurate to the most succinct. (1) One can compute the expected number of probes for each of $s=1,2,4,\ldots,a/2$ and a using the equations for a hit and miss (from Table 1) weighted to reflect your expected miss ratio and choose the minimum. (2) One can ignore misses (which are less common and never require more than twice the probes of hits), assume variables are continuous, and find the optimum partial compare width, $k_{opt}=\log_2 t - 1/2$ for hits only. The optimum number of subsets for hits and misses together is likely to be the value for s resulting from a partial compare width of $\lfloor k_{opt} \rfloor$ or $\lceil k_{opt} \rceil$. (3) Finally, one can observe that many tags in current caches are between 16 and 32 bits wide, implying the number of subsets that

gives at least four-bit partial compares will work well.

Table 1 summarizes our analysis of the expected number of probes required for the traditional, naive, MRU and partial compare approaches to implementing set-associativity. Note that this table as well as most of the trace-driven simulation assumes 16 bit tags are used. We will examine the positive effect of increasing the tag width on the partial compare approach in section 3.

Table 2 summarizes paper implementations of tag memory and comparison logic for a direct-mapped cache, a traditional implementation of set-associativity, and an implementation of set-associativity using MRU and partial compares. We found that the MRU and partial compare implementations have a slower access time than the traditional implementation of associativity but includes no implementation surprises. Most notably, the control logic was found to be of reasonable complexity. The MRU and partial compare implementations use hardware similar to a direct-mapped cache and can make effective use of page-mode dynamic RAMs, as would other serial implementations of set-associativity. Page-mode dynamic RAMs are those in which the access time of multiple probes to the same set can be significantly less than if the probes were to other sets. Subsequent probes take less than half the time of the first probe to the set. Cache cost is reduced in two ways when using one of the alternative implementations of associativity. First, tag memory cost is directly reduced, by 1/3 to 1/2 in our design. Second, cache data memory cost is reduced since only 1, rather than a words, need to be read at a time.

3. Trace-Driven Performance Comparison

This section analyzes the performance of the low-cost schemes to implement set-associativity in level two caches using simulation with relatively short multiprogramming traces. We analyze associativity in the level two cache since the low cost implementations of associativity are more appropriate for level two (or higher) caches than for level one caches. We concentrate on presenting and characterizing the relative performance of the alternatives. We do not demonstrate the absolute utility of these approaches to important future cache configurations (e.g. multiple megabyte level two caches in multiprocessors) since our traces are for a single processor and are not sufficiently long to exercise very large caches.

The makeup of the traces and the assumed cache configurations are indicated in Table 3. We assume a uniprocessor system with a two level cache hierarchy (a level one cache and a level two cache) in our study, largely because the traces were

Cache Tag Memory and Comparator Implementations							
	Using Dynamic RAMs				Using Static RAMs			
	Direct-Mapped	4-Way Set-Associative			Direct-Mapped	4-Way Set-Associative		
		Traditional	MRU	Partial		Traditional	MRU	Partial
Memory Packages								
Basic Access Time (ns)	100	80	100	100	40	40	40	40
Page Mode Access Time (ns)	n/a	n/a	35	35	n/a	n/a	n/a	n/a
Basic Cycle Time (ns)	190	160	190	190	40	40	40	40
Page Mode Cycle Time (ns)	n/a	n/a	35	35	n/a	n/a	n/a	n/a
Size (bits)	1Mx8	256Kx8	1Mx8	1Mx8	1Mx4	256Kx(16,8)	1Mx4	1Mx4
Implementations								
Access Time (ns)	136	132	150+50x	150+50y	61	84	65+55x	65+55y
Cycle Time (ns)	230	190	250+50(x+u)	250+50y	85	100	75+55(x+u)	75+55y
Number of Packages	18	42	22	21	20	37	25	24

Table 2. Trial Set-Associativity Implementations.

This table compares paper implementations of the tag memory and comparison logic for a direct-mapped and four-way set-associative cache holding 1 million 24-bit tags, assuming dynamic or static RAM chips housed in hybrid packages. The top half of the table summarizes the memory packages used to implement tag memory, while the bottom half gives cache implementation numbers. The MRU implementation assumes that the MRU list storage costs nothing extra (as it would if full LRU replacement is used). MRU access and cycles are given assuming "x" is the expected number of probes after reading the MRU information ("x" is between 1 and a for hits, a for misses) and "u" is the probability that MRU information must be updated. Partial compare access and cycles are given assuming "y" probes in step two ("y" is between 1 and a for hits and 0 and a for misses). The number of packages assumes some semi-custom logic and hybrid packages.

Trace-Driven Two-Level Cache Simulation	
Traces	ATUM [Agar86] virtual address traces of a multiprogrammed operating system, described in [Hill87]. Operating system references are included as well as references of user-level processes. One very large trace (over 8 million references) was constructed as a concatenation of 23 individual ATUM traces, each of which is approximately 350,000 references. Cache flushes of the level one and level two caches were inserted between each of the 23 traces, thus each trace starts from a "cold" cache.
Level One Cache	A direct-mapped write-back cache. On misses causing replacement of a dirty block, the new block is first obtained via a *read-in* request, then a *write-back* is issued to the level two cache. Three level one caches are simulated: A 4 Kbyte cache with a 16 byte block size (4K-16); 16 Kbyte with 16 byte blocks (16K-16); and 16 Kbyte with 32 byte blocks (16K-32). The miss ratios corresponding to these level one caches are: 0.1181, 0.0657, and 0.0513, respectively.
Level Two Cache	An *a*-way set-associative write-back cache which services read-ins and write-backs from the level one cache. We compare different implementations of associativity in the level two cache. The least-recently-used entry in a set is replaced on a cache miss. We simulate five different level two caches: a 64 Kbyte cache with 16 byte block size (64K-16); 64 Kbyte with 32 byte blocks (64K-32); 256 Kbyte with 16 byte blocks (256K-16); 256 Kbyte with 32 byte blocks (256K-32); and 256 Kbyte with 64 byte blocks (256K-64). While multi-level inclusion is not enforced in this simulation, by monitoring the number of write-backs which missed when written back to the level two cache we were able to extrapolate that the maintenance of multi-level inclusion would have a very small effect (in most configurations studied, no effect) on the miss ratio of the level two cache (and no effect on the miss ratio of the level one cache).

Table 3. Detailed Information on the Trace-Driven Simulation.

uniprocessor traces. The level one cache is direct-mapped, while the level two cache is of varying associativity. Both caches are write-back caches, with the level two cache servicing *read-in* and *write-back* requests from the level one cache. We chose this write-back configuration to minimize the amount of communication between cache levels. This can be important in a shared memory multiprocessor since the level one cache will be utilized servicing processor references while the level two cache is servicing coherency invalidations, as in [Good88]. Also, it was found in [Shor88] that this configuration has better performance than if either cache is write-through. Cache sizes simulated here (up to 256 Kbytes) are limited by the size of the traces. We expect future level two (and higher) caches to be considerably larger (e.g. 4 Mbytes). Though the results presented are for "cold" caches, limited "warmer" results were found to be similar, except that the miss ratios were smaller.

The graphs in Figure 3 show the average number of probes versus the associativity of the level two cache for a 16K-16 (16 Kbyte capacity with 16 byte block size) level one cache and 256K-32 (256 Kbyte with 32 byte block size) level two cache. The tag width is 16-bits ($t = 16$) and the partial compare width 4-bits ($k = 4$) in all simulations unless otherwise specified. 1, 2, and 4 subsets were used for 4, 8, and 16-way set-associative partial compare implementations, respectively. The graphs indicate the general linearly increasing relationship between the number of probes required per search and the associativity. The number of probes per access is expected to increase for the alternative

implementations of associativity as the associativity increases since there are more places where a given cache block can reside. A cache lookup simply must look in more places on the average. For wider associativity to be preferred, the added delay for these additional probes must be more than offset by the time saved servicing fewer misses. One would also expect the Naive and Partial schemes to have a linear relationship between probes per access and associativity. However, the fact that this relation is linear for MRU came as a surprise. We will examine the MRU and partial schemes more closely in subsequent figures. As will always be the case, the traditional implementation of associativity results in the minimum number of probes. These graphs show that the partial compare approach performs the best of the low cost implementations. The naive scheme performs the worst, with the MRU scheme between them.

Figure 3 also shows the performance benefit of a write-back optimization which can be made when the multi-level inclusion property is maintained with a cache hierarchy. The level one cache can be certain that all write-back requests will hit in the level two cache. It can also be certain that the block will reside in precisely the same position in which it was loaded in the level two cache from memory (if blocks do not change position in the level two cache from the time they are loaded to the time they are replaced). This implies that if the level one cache retains a $\log_2 a$-bit indicator of which position in the set the given cache block occupies (a is the associativity of the level two cache), write-backs can proceed without requiring tag probes. Note that even if multi-level inclusion is not maintained, the indicators in the level one cache can be used as *hints*, not always correct, where the entry resides in the level two cache.

All the methods, Traditional, Naive, MRU, and Partial require no probes to service a write-back request when using the write-back optimization. Since write-backs are approximately 20% of the requests to the level two cache (as shown in Table 4), this can result in significant performance improvements, as indicated in the figure. We feel the cost of implementing this optimization is sufficiently modest (2 bits per level one cache entry for a 4-way set-associative level two cache) to warrant its use when implementing one of the reduced cost implementations of associativity. We assume the write-back optimization is used, and all subsequent figures contain data for read-in requests only, since the different approaches perform the same on write-backs. Write-back requests are still considered references as they update the MRU list, determining the replacement policy of the cache.

Table 4, presented at the end of the paper, lists the number of probes required for various cache configurations when using the naive, MRU, and partial schemes. Note that the data in Table 4 assumes the write-back optimization is being used. Table 4 uses the terms *global miss ratio* and *local miss ratio* [Przy88b]. The global miss ratio is the fraction of processor requests which miss in both the level one and level two cache. The local miss ratio of the level two cache is the fraction of read-ins and write-backs from the level one cache which miss in the level two cache. Note that 8 and 16-way set-associativity did not improve the miss ratios substantially over 4-way in our simulations.

The partial scheme performs best (requires the least number of probes) for most configurations studied. However, MRU did perform best for the configuration with the largest level two cache block size and the largest ratio of level two to level one cache size (4K-16 256K-64). This leads to several key observations regarding the MRU scheme. First, MRU is a better scheme as the block size of the level two cache increases relative to the level one cache block size. MRU can take advantage of the larger block sizes in the level two cache since more data spatially near the latest reference is in the MRU block. Second, its performance improves as the size of the level one cache is decreased relative to the size of the level two cache. The miss stream from a smaller level one cache has more temporal locality than larger level one caches. This locality results more often in hits to the first entry in the MRU list of a set.

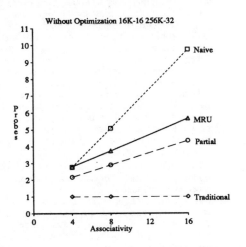
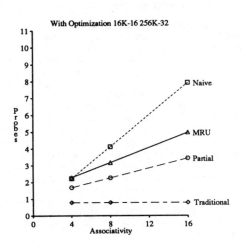

Figure 3. Probes for Read-Ins and Write-Backs.

This figure shows the average number of probes per cache access for the Traditional, Partial, MRU, and Naive implementations of various associativities. It also shows the usefulness of the write-back optimization in which the first level cache retains an indicator which allows it to write-back to the second level cache without any tag comparisons (probes).

The number of probes per cache access increases with associativity for the non-traditional implementations since there are more places for a given block to reside. Lower effective access times may nevertheless result, particularly as miss latencies are increased, since higher associativity results in lower miss ratios.

Figure 4 compares the performance of the schemes on read-in hits and misses separately. It shows how the partial and MRU approach are close in performance on hits, followed by the naive approach. The partial approach is the undeniable winner on misses, dominating the a and $a+1$ probes needed by the naive and MRU approaches, respectively[7]. The rest of the figures in this paper will concentrate on read-in hits for that reason. One should keep in mind, however, that the figures will be biased in favor of the MRU and naive approaches, when compared to the partial approach.

Figure 5 looks more closely at the MRU scheme. It examines the performance impact of shortening the MRU list to less than the total number of entries in a set. An associative lookup with a shortened MRU list proceeds by first searching the entries in the list in order and then searching the rest of the set in an arbitrary order. The examination shows that it is not necessary to retain the entire MRU list to achieve close to the performance of the entire list. It also shows that the length of the shortened MRU list must increase linearly with associativity to achieve near the performance of a full MRU list. For instance, a reduced MRU list of two entries performs well for an associativity of 8, whereas, a reduced list of 4 entries is needed to produce comparable performance with an associativity of 16.

The right graph in figure 5 plots the values of f_i for various associativities in the level two cache. Lower associativities result in a higher probability that a hit is to the first entry of the MRU list. For instance, the probability is 75%, 60%, and 36% for 4, 8, and 16-way associativities, respectively, in the right graph of Figure 5. It was found in [So88] that the probability that a hit is to the first element in the MRU list of a 4-way set-associative level one cache is above 90% for cache sizes greater than 32 Kbytes (block size = 128 bytes). We have not seen this percentage reach 90% for the level two cache in any of our cache configurations. The closest was 89% with the 4K-16 level one cache and the 256K-64 4-way set-associative level two cache.

It was previously noted that the linear relationship between the average number of probes per cache access and the associativity

of the level two cache was unexpected when using the MRU scheme. This relationship can be explained, with some approximations, by examining the right graph of Figure 5. If the lines in the right graph were straight lines, there would be an exponential (more precisely, geometric) relationship between the probability of a hit and the MRU distance. If this were the case and the slope of these lines (ignoring the log scale of the vertical axis and considering it a linear scale) is proportional to $-1/a$, then, (with some approximations) we can say that there will be a linear relationship between probes and associativity. Since both the conditions are roughly true, it can explain the linearity.

Figure 6 examines the partial compare approach in more detail. It shows that wider tags improve the performance of the partial scheme on read-in hits. The larger tag size allows for a reduced number of subsets in the 8 and 16-way set-associative caches and an increase in the partial compare width for the 4-way set-associative cache. Tag widths may be larger because the system supports a large virtual address space or may be artificially increased for better performance. Note that the number of probes required by the naive and MRU schemes do not change as the tag width is changed.

Figure 6 compares the performance of the partial scheme to the predictions of the theory of Section 2. It shows that the simple transformation outlined in Section 2 in which the low order k bits are exclusive-ored with each of the higher order bits performs worse than the prediction of theory (particularly with 32 bit tags). This is not surprising since the theory is a probabilistic lower bound. We considered other transformations which exclusive-or a bit with a subset of the other bits of the tag. This transformation may be required to be efficiently invertible. If we restrict the bits that are exclusive-ored to be from less significant fields, the resulting transformation produces unique and invertible tags[8]. The improved transformation passes the least significant k-bit field unchanged, exclusive-ors the second least significant field with the

---

[7] Note that the local miss ratio of large level two caches is not vanishingly small, especially with a large level one cache [Przy88b].

[8] Taking "exclusive-or" as addition and "and" as multiplication, the set {0,1} forms a finite field, denoted by GF(2). Our hash function is a linear transformation T from $GF(2)^t$ to itself, given by a lower-triangular matrix with 1's on the diagonal. It can be shown using Gaussian elimination that T is invertible, and its inverse is lower-triangular as well. See [Pete72] for an introduction to finite fields and linear transformations.

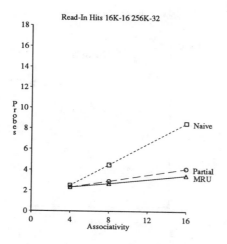

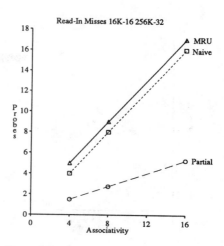

Figure 4. Probes for Read-In Hits and Misses.

This figure separates the performance of the Naive, Partial, and MRU algorithms for read-in hits (on the left) and misses. For hits, the Partial and MRU algorithms perform well, with Naive considerably worse. On misses, the Partial algorithm is superior, followed by the Naive and MRU algorithms. Both the Naive and MRU algorithms cycle through the entire set on a miss, with MRU charged an extra probe for the look-up of the ordered list.

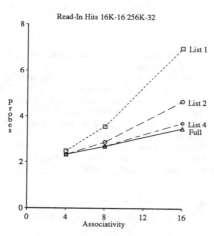

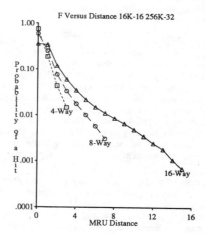

Figure 5. Reduced MRU Lists and Distance Distribution.

This figure demonstrates the performance of the MRU scheme on read-in hits in more detail. The left graph compares the performance of reduced MRU lists. The right graph shows the MRU distance distributions for hits.

first, and exclusive-ors all other fields with both the first and the second fields. The new transformation can be implemented with one two-input exclusive-or gate per higher order bit, the same number required for the original transformation. Unfortunately, the new transformation is not its own inverse, but, the inverse also requires the same number of exclusive-or gates. The left graph of Figure 6 shows that the new transformation results in better performance, particularly for 32-bit tags. This indicates that the transformation should be carefully chosen. We also investigated a transformation in which the bits of the tag are swapped so that the low order bits of the incoming tag are always compared with the low order bits of the stored tag. Its performance was good, near the theory lines in Figure 6, but it is more expensive to implement.

4. Conclusions

We have described and analyzed three methods for implementing set-associative caches which retain many of the implementation advantages of direct-mapped caches while providing the reduced miss ratio of associative cache lookups. These implementations are less expensive than the traditional approach since they eliminate comparators and obviate the need to access cache tags and data within the same set in parallel. Our trace-driven analysis of these schemes for use in level two caches was done using various level one and level two cache configurations. This allowed us to examine the trends of the various schemes as the cache parameters were varied. This is important since the traces were inadequate to simulate the multi-megabyte level two caches we expect will be useful in future systems.

The three low cost schemes explained in this paper are the naive, MRU, and partial compare implementations of set-associativity. The naive scheme uses a linear scan over all the stored tags in a set during a cache lookup. The MRU list scheme

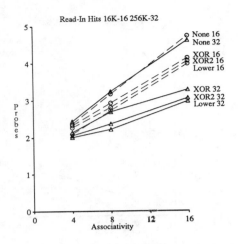
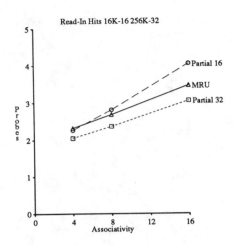

Figure 6. Partial Algorithm With Larger Tags and Different Transformation.

This figure analyzes the performance of the partial scheme on read-in hits in more detail. The left graph compares its performance versus the prediction of theory outlined in Section 2 for 16-bit (dashed lines) and 32-bit tags (solid lines). There are four lines for each tag width: the top line is the results when using no transform (None), the next lower line is the simple transformation of Section 2 (XOR), the next lower line the more sophisticated transformation outlined in Section 3 (XOR2), and the bottom line is the prediction of the theory, a probabilistic lower bound (Lower).

The right graph compares the performance of the partial scheme using the more sophisticated transformation versus the MRU scheme for 16 and 32 bit tags.

retains an ordered list per set to search the stored tags in an "intelligent" order. The partial compare scheme looks once at small pieces of many of the stored tags of a set. It then decides whether it should do full tag comparisons on the tags depending on the outcome of the partial comparison. Naive and partial lookups require the same memory and comparison logic as a direct-mapped cache, only extra control logic is needed for associativity. The MRU scheme may require the extra memory to hold the ordered search list as well as extra hardware to maintain it, although the same hardware is likely needed to implement an LRU cache replacement policy.

The average number of probes (tag memory reads and compares) per cache lookup was measured. As expected, the naive scheme performed poorly as compared to the MRU and partial compare schemes for associativities of 4 and above. Both the MRU and partial compare schemes perform well on cache hits, with perhaps a slight advantage to MRU. The partial compare scheme achieves superior performance on cache misses since it does not require a probe to examine each and every tag in the set.

Over the widest range of cache configurations considered, the partial compare algorithm required the least number of probes per cache access. However, the partial compare scheme is not the best scheme for all cases. The MRU scheme is better when the local miss ratio of the level two cache is small. This is true when the ratio of level two to level one block sizes is large (4 or more) and when the ratio of level one to level two cache sizes is large (64 or more). The partial compare scheme is better when the tag width is increased and when the local miss ratio of the level two cache is increased. The local miss ratio of the level two cache increases when the above cache and blocksize ratios decrease.

This study does not show either the MRU or partial compare schemes to be the superior low cost implementation of associativity for future level two caches. The optimum scheme depends on all the factors above, in particular: the cache size ratio, block size ratio, and the tag width. Since we expect tag widths to be larger than the 16 bits used in most of our study, we favor the partial compare scheme. However, it may be true that the level two to level one cache size ratio will be larger in the future than our simulation, in which case the MRU scheme is more favorable.

We feel that low cost implementations of associativity are useful, particularly for level two caches. The slower access times of the associativity implementations outlined in this paper are less important in level two caches since the processor sees the latency of the level two cache only on a level one cache miss. The lower cost and board area minimization of the approaches presented in this paper may prove to be more important than speed since we expect future level two caches to be large (megabytes). Some recently proposed multiprocessors [Wils87] [Good88] promise to require many large caches. In this environment, cost can be an extremely important consideration.

5. Acknowledgements

The authors would like to thank Jim Smith for some suggestions inspiring this research, Eric Bach for much needed mathematical assistance, and all those involved with the Multicube project for providing focus and feedback. We would also like to thank Anant Agarwal, Mark Horowitz, Richard Sites, and Digital Equipment Corporation for providing the traces used in our study. Thanks also to those who read and improved drafts of this paper: Tom Bricker, Garth Gibson, Ross Johnson, B. Narendran, Harold Stone, Chuck Thacker, Phil Woest, David Wood, and The University of Washington Architecture Lunch Group.

6. References

[Agar86]   A. Agarwal, R. L. Sites and M. Horowitz, ATUM: A New Technique for Capturing Address Traces Using Microcode, *Proc. Thirteenth International Symposium on Computer Architecture* (June 1986).

[Agar87]   A. Agarwal, Analysis of Cache Performance for Operating Systems and Multiprogramming, Ph.D. Thesis, Technical Report No. CSL-Tech. Rep.-87-332, Stanford University (May 1987).

[Agar88]   A. Agarwal, M. Horowitz and J. Hennessy, Cache Performance of Operating Systems and Multiprogramming Workloads, *ACM Trans. on Computer Systems*, 6, 4 (November 1988).

[Alex86]   C. Alexander, W. Keshlear, F. Cooper and F. Briggs, Cache Memory Performance in a UNIX Environment, *Computer Architecture News*, 14, 3 (June 1986), 14-70.

[Baer88]   J. Baer and W. Wang, On the Inclusion Properties for Multi-Level Cache Hierarchies, *15th Annual International Symposium on Computer Architecture*, Honolulu, Hawaii (June 1988).

4-Way Set-Associative Level Two Cache										
Configuration	Global Miss Ratio	Local Miss Ratio	Fraction Write-Back	Naive Probes		MRU Probes		Partial Probes		
				Hits	Total	Hits	Total	Hits	Misses	Total
16K-16 256K-32	0.0143	0.1721	0.2141	1.85	2.22	**1.72**	2.29	**1.72**	**1.49**	*1.68
16K-16 256K-16	0.0223	0.2665	0.2141	1.77	2.37	1.71	2.59	**1.68**	**1.51**	*1.64
16K-32 256K-32	0.0144	0.2157	0.2302	1.77	2.25	1.72	2.42	**1.64**	**1.49**	*1.61
4K-16 256K-64	0.0097	0.0653	0.2083	1.94	2.08	**1.66**	1.88	1.78	**1.46**	*1.76
4K-16 256K-32	0.0144	0.0964	0.2083	1.92	2.12	**1.66**	1.98	1.81	**1.49**	*1.78
4K-16 256K-16	0.0223	0.1494	0.2083	1.89	2.20	**1.66**	2.16	1.82	**1.51**	*1.77
4K-16 64K-32	0.0195	0.1310	0.2083	1.90	2.18	1.84	2.25	**1.62**	**1.29**	*1.58
4K-16 64K-16	0.0279	0.1870	0.2083	1.86	2.26	1.90	2.48	**1.60**	**1.29**	*1.54

8-Way Set-Associative Level Two Cache										
Configuration	Global Miss Ratio	Local Miss Ratio	Fraction Write-Back	Naive Probes		MRU Probes		Partial Probes		
				Hits	Total	Hits	Total	Hits	Misses	Total
16K-16 256K-32	0.0141	0.1682	0.2141	3.34	4.12	**1.99**	3.17	2.17	2.74	*2.27
16K-16 256K-16	0.0220	0.2629	0.2141	3.19	4.45	**2.04**	3.87	2.12	2.76	*2.28
16K-32 256K-32	0.0141	0.2110	0.2302	3.18	4.20	**2.07**	3.53	2.08	2.74	*2.22
4K-16 256K-64	0.0094	0.0631	0.2083	3.50	3.78	**1.80**	*2.25	2.25	2.72	2.28
4K-16 256K-32	0.0141	0.0943	0.2083	3.47	3.89	**1.80**	2.48	2.27	2.74	*2.32
4K-16 256K-16	0.0220	0.1473	0.2083	3.40	4.08	**1.82**	2.88	2.27	2.76	*2.34
4K-16 64K-32	0.0189	0.1264	0.2083	3.43	4.00	2.25	3.10	**2.08**	2.51	*2.13
4K-16 64K-16	0.0270	0.1808	0.2083	3.36	4.20	2.42	3.61	**2.04**	2.51	*2.12

16-Way Set-Associative Level Two Cache										
Configuration	Global Miss Ratio	Local Miss Ratio	Fraction Write-Back	Naive Probes		MRU Probes		Partial Probes		
				Hits	Total	Hits	Total	Hits	Misses	Total
16K-16 256K-32	0.0139	0.1663	0.2141	6.31	7.93	**2.58**	4.97	3.07	5.27	*3.43
16K-16 256K-16	0.0218	0.2612	0.2141	6.03	8.64	**2.75**	6.47	2.96	5.26	*3.56
16K-32 256K-32	0.0139	0.2086	0.2302	6.03	8.11	**2.81**	5.77	2.95	5.27	*3.43
4K-16 256K-64	0.0092	0.0619	0.2083	6.61	7.19	**2.08**	*3.00	3.22	5.27	3.35
4K-16 256K-32	0.0139	0.0932	0.2083	6.55	7.43	**2.11**	3.50	3.22	5.27	*3.41
4K-16 256K-16	0.0218	0.1464	0.2083	6.43	7.83	**2.18**	4.35	3.19	5.26	*3.49
4K-16 64K-32	0.0185	0.1240	0.2083	6.48	7.66	**3.04**	4.77	**3.04**	5.02	*3.28
4K-16 64K-16	0.0266	0.1780	0.2083	6.35	8.07	3.45	5.87	**2.99**	5.03	*3.35

Table 4. Data for Various Cache Configurations.

These tables show the number of probes for the different schemes in varying cache configurations, as well as the miss ratios for the configurations. The numbers of probes are shown for hits and totals (hits and misses together). Misses are not shown for the MRU and Naive schemes since they require *associativity*+1 and *associativity*, respectively. The bold entries indicate the best method for hits, misses, and in total for the given configurations. The entries with asterisks indicate the best method in total. Write-backs from the level one cache are assumed to require no probes due to the write-back optimization, yet they are counted as a hit and included in the averages. The fraction of write-backs is the fraction of requests from the level one cache which are write-backs.

[Bell74]   J. Bell, D. Casasent and C. G. Bell, An Investigation of Alternative Cache Organizations, *IEEE Trans. on Computers*, C-23, 4 (April 1974), 346-351.

[Bren84]   J. G. Brenza, Second Level Cache Fast Access, *IBM Technical Disclosure Bulletin*, 26, 10B (March 1984), 5488-5490.

[Chan87]   J. H. Chang, H. Chao and K. So, Cache Design of a Sub-Micron CMOS System/370, *14th Annual International Symposium on Computer Architecture*, Pittsburgh, PA (June 1987), 208 - 213.

[Clar83]   D. W. Clark, Cache Performance in the VAX-11/780, *ACM Trans. on Computer Systems*, 1, 1 (February, 1983), 24 - 37.

[Cray76]   Cray Research Inc., The Cray-1 S Series Hardware Reference Manual, Publication No. HR-0808 (1976).

[Good88]   J. R. Goodman and P. J. Woest, The Wisconsin Multicube: A New large-Scale Cache-Coherent Multiprocessor, *Proc. Fifteenth Symposium on Computer Architecture* (June 1988).

[Hill87]   M. D. Hill, Aspects of Cache Memory and Instruction Buffer Performance, Ph.D. Thesis, Computer Science Division Technical Report UCB/Computer Science Dept. 87/381, University of California, Berkeley (November 1987).

[Hill88]   M. D. Hill, A Case for Direct-Mapped Caches, *IEEE Computer*, 21, 12 (December 1988), 25-40.

[Kapl73]   K. R. Kaplan and R. O. Winder, Cache-based Computer Systems, *Computer*, 6, 3 (March, 1973).

[Lipt68]   J. S. Liptay, Structural Aspects of the System/360 Model 85, Part II: The Cache, *IBM Systems Journal*, 7, 1 (1968), 15-21.

[Matt70]   R. L. Mattson, J. Gecsei, D. R. Slutz and I. L. Traiger, Evaluation techniques for storage hierarchies, *IBM Systems Journal*, 9, 2 (1970), 78 - 117.

[Pete72]   W. W. Peterson and E. J. Weldon, Jr., *Error-Correcting Codes*, MIT Press, (1972).

[Przy88a]   S. Przybylski, M. Horowitz and J. Hennessy, Performance Tradeoffs in Cache Design, *15th Annual International Symposium on Computer Architecture*, Honolulu, Hawaii (June 1988).

[Przy88b]   S. A. Przybylski, Performance-Directed Memory Hierarchy Design, Ph.D. Thesis, Technical Report No. CSL-Tech. Rep.-88-366, Stanford University (September 1988).

[Shor88]   R. T. Short and H. M. Levy, A Simulation Study of Two-Level Caches, *15th Annual International Symposium on Computer Architecture*, Honolulu, Hawaii (June 1988).

[Smit78]   A. J. Smith, A Comparative Study of Set Associative Memory Mapping Algorithms and Their Use for Cache and Main Memory, *IEEE Trans. on Software Engineering*, SE-4, 2 (March 1978), 121-130.

[Smit82]   A. J. Smith, Cache Memories, *Computing Surveys*, 14, 3 (September, 1982), 473 - 530.

[Smit86]   A. J. Smith, Bibliography and Readings on CPU Cache Memories and Related Topics, *Computer Architecture News* (January 1986), 22-42.

[So88]   K. So and R. N. Rechtschaffen, Cache Operations by MRU Change, *IEEE Trans. on Computers*, C-37, 6 (June 1988).

[Stre76]   W. D. Strecker, Cache Memories for PDP-11 Family Computers, *Proc. Third International Symposium on Computer Architecture* (January 1976), 155-158.

[Wils87]   A. W. Wilson, Hierarchical Cache/Bus Architecture for Shared Memory Multiprocessors, *14th Annual International Symposium on Computer Architecture*, Pittsburgh, PA (June 1987).

Organization and Performance of a Two-Level Virtual-Real Cache Hierarchy

Wen-Hann Wang, Jean-Loup Baer and Henry M. Levy

Department of Computer Science, FR-35
University of Washington
Seattle, WA 98195

Abstract

We propose and analyze a two-level cache organization that provides high memory bandwidth. The first-level cache is accessed directly by virtual addresses. It is small, fast, and, without the burden of address translation, can easily be optimized to match the processor speed. The virtually-addressed cache is backed up by a large physically-addressed cache; this second-level cache provides a high hit ratio and greatly reduces memory traffic. We show how the second-level cache can be easily extended to solve the synonym problem resulting from the use of a virtually-addressed cache at the first level. Moreover, the second-level cache can be used to shield the virtually-addressed first-level cache from irrelevant cache coherence interference. Finally, simulation results show that this organization has a performance advantage over a hierarchy of physically-addressed caches in a multiprocessor environment.

Keywords: Caches, Virtual Memory, Multiprocessors, Memory Hierarchy, Cache Coherence.

1   Introduction

Virtually-addressed caches are becoming commonplace in high-performance multiprocessors due to the need for rapid cache access [11, 3, 17]. A virtually-addressed cache can be accessed more quickly than a physically-addressed cache because it does not require a preceding virtual-to-physical address translation. However, virtually-addressed caches have several problems as well. For example:

1. They must be capable of handling synonyms, that is, multiple virtual addresses that map to the same physical address.

2. While address translation is not required before a virtual cache lookup, address translation is still needed following a miss.

3. In a multiprocessor system, the use of a virtually-addressed cache may complicate cache coherence because bus addresses are physical, therefore a reverse translation may be required.

4. I/O devices use physical addresses as well, also requiring reverse translation.

5. A virtual cache may need to be invalidated on a context switch because virtual addresses are unique to a single process.

None of these problems is insolvable by itself, and several schemes have been proposed for managing virtual caches. For example, dual tag sets, one virtual and one physical, can be used for each cache entry [7, 6]. As another example, the SPUR system restricts the use of address space, prohibits caching of I/O buffers, and requires bus transmission of both virtual and physical addresses [11]. However, these schemes tend to have performance shortcomings or unpleasant implications for system software. Virtually-addressed caches are fundamentally complicated, and this time or space complexity reduces the ability of the cache to match the ever-increasing needs of modern processors.

To attack this problem, we propose a two-level cache organization involving a virtually-addressed first-level cache and a physically-addressed second-level cache (recent studies of two-level uniprocessor and multiprocessor caches can be found in [4, 5, 12, 13]). The small first-level cache can be fast to meet the requirements of high-speed processors; it is virtually addressed to avoid the need for address translation. The large second-level cache will reduce miss ratios and memory traffic; it is physically addressed to simplify the I/O and multiprocessor coherence problems. Furthermore, we show how the second-level cache can be utilized to solve the synonym problem and to shield the first-level cache from irrelevant cache coherence traffic. Overall, we believe that this two-level virtual-real organization simplifies the design of the first-level, where performance is crucial, while solving some of the difficult problems at the second level, where time and space are more easily available.

Our organization involves the use of pointers in the two caches to keep track of the mappings between virtual cache and physical cache entries [7]. We also provide a translation buffer at the second level which operates in parallel with first-level cache lookups in case a miss requires reverse translation. Trace-driven simulations are used to demonstrate the advantages of a two-level V-R (virtual-real) cache over a hierarchy of real-addressed caches in a multiprocessor environment.

The rest of this paper is organized as follows. Section 2 describes the approaches taken in solving various problems related to virtual address caches and presents some design choices for high performance multiprocessor caches. Section 3 gives the specific organization of a V-R two-level cache hierarchy and its detailed operational description. Section 4 presents performance results from simulations, and conclusions are drawn in section 5.

2 Design issues of two-level V-R caches for high performance multiprocessors

This section addresses some important issues in the design of two level V-R caches and motivates our design choices. A more detailed operational description of our approach is given in the following section. The proposed architecture for this evaluation is a shared-bus multiprocessor where each processor has a private, two-level, V-cache–R-cache hierarchy as shown in Figure 1.

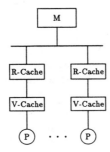

Figure 1: Shared-bus organization

Write policies

For a two-level cache, the write policy can be selected independently at each level. In the literature, write-through has been proposed as the most reasonable write policy for the first-level cache in a two-level hierarchy, while write-back is advocated for the second level [10, 8, 13]. A major motivation for the choice of write-through at the first level is that cache coherence control is simplified. In this case, the first- and second-level caches will always contain identical values.

There are several problems, however, with using a first-level write-through cache. First, assuming no write-allocate, write-through caches will have smaller hit ratios than write-back caches. Second, a write takes longer under write-through because the second-level cache must be updated as well; primary memory may also need to be updated depending on the write policy for the second level.

The reduced write latency with write-through can be greatly hidden by the use of write buffers between the first and second levels, but several write buffers may be needed. Table 1, for example, shows that in the execution of the VAX program *pops* (cf. section 4), 30% of writes are due to procedure calls, each of which typically generates six or more successive writes. Table 2 shows the inter-write interval distribution for a snapshot (411,237 references) of the same trace using a 16K direct-mapped cache with a 16-byte block size. As can be seen, the high percentage of short inter-write intervals confirms the need for several buffers.

Unfortunately, while write buffers can reduce the write latency of the first-level cache, they re-introduce a complexity that write-through was intended to avoid, namely cache coherence. Write buffers can hold modified data for which other processors might encounter a miss. Thus, cache coherency control must be provided for the write buffers on every cache coherence transaction.

These difficulties lead us to favor the write-back policy for our virtually-addressed cache at the first level.

no. of wr. per call	count	total writes
1	3	3
2	2	4
3	0	0
4	2	8
5	2	10
6	4123	24738
7	1266	8862
8	1246	9968
9	2634	23706
10	797	7970
11	539	5929
12	441	5292
13	0	0
14	0	0
15	0	0
16	43	688
no. of wr. due to proc. call		87178
total no. of writes		283057

Table 1: Number of writes due to procedure calls

interval	count
1	4589
2	1015
3	1270
4	786
5	1482
6	687
7	63
8	481
9	735
10 and larger	3245

Table 2: Inter-write intervals (snapshot of 411,237 references)

The synonym problem

As previously noted, a two-level V-R organization can be used to solve the synonym problem. The solution requires the use of a *reverse translation table* [15] for detecting synonyms, and a natural place to put that table is at the second level.

Our two-level organization permits and detects synonyms, but guarantees that at most one copy of a data element exists in the V-cache at any time. Each second-level cache block will have a pointer to its first-level child block, if one exists. If we guarantee an inclusion property, where the R-cache contains a superset of the tags in the V-cache, the reverse translation information can be stored in log(V-cache size/page size) superset bits in each R-cache block. For each entry in the R-cache with a child in the V-cache, these extra bits, together with the page offset, provide the V-cache location of its child.

When a miss occurs in the V-cache, the virtual address is translated (using a second-level translation buffer) and the R-cache is accessed. If an R-cache hit occurs, the R-cache checks whether the data is also in the V-cache under another virtual address (a synonym). If so, it simply invalidates that V-cache copy and moves the data to the new virtual address in the V-cache. Thus, while a data element can have synonyms, it is always stored in the V-cache using the last virtual address with which it was accessed.[1]

---

[1]Note that our approach in dealing with the synonym problem has some similarities to Goodman's approach [7]. One can view our approach as moving Goodman's real directory from being just for snooping to being associated with the level two cache. This move provides two benefits. First, it hides the cost of Goodman's extra, real directory by making it the level two cache directory. Second, it reduces the misses caused by real-address collisions via making the real directory much bigger.

Context switching

In a multiprogramming environment, addresses are unique to each process and therefore the V-cache must be flushed whenever a context switch occurs. This might be costly for a large virtually-addressed cache. For small caches we believe the penalty on hit ratios will be negligible and this is confirmed by our simulation results (cf. Section 4). However, if a write-back policy is used for the V-cache, a substantial number of write-backs may occur at each context switch, which greatly increases context-switch latency.

Another solution to avoid the address mapping conflict is to attach a process identifier to each tag entry of the V-cache. This approach does not improve the hit ratio for a small V-cache [1], but can avoid the large number of write-backs at context switch time. Unfortunately, this approach increases the complexity of a two-level hierarchy because the V-cache needs to be purged or selectively flushed when a TLB entry of an inactive process is replaced by an entry of the active process, or a process-id is reassigned.

We wish to have the benefits of reduced context-switch latency without needing to flush the V-cache when a TLB entry changes. Our approach meets these goals by invalidating all V-cache blocks on a context switch but *not* writing them back at that time. Instead, each block is written back only when it is replaced, that is, when a new block is read into that cache slot. The writes are thus distributed in time where the latency can be hidden using write-back buffers.

To implement this scheme, we add two new fields to each V-cache block. First, we add a *swapped-valid bit*, which is set for each V-cache block on a context switch. Upon a replacement, if the V-cache finds a block with swapped-valid set, it checks whether that block is also marked both dirty and valid; if so, that block must be written back. Second, we add an *r-pointer*, which is the low-order bits of the page number, to each V-cache block. The r-pointer, together with the page offset, is sufficient to link a V-cache entry to its corresponding location in the R-cache. This linkage makes a write-back or a state check efficient, since there is no need for an address translation. This approach uses space comparable to that of the process identifier scheme, but without its disadvantages.

Table 3 shows the effect of the swapped-valid bit; here we see the inter-write interval from the same benchmark as Table 2 when the swapped-valid bit is used. Because swapped write-backs are typically far apart from other (swapped) write-backs, a single write-back buffer is sufficient to overlap swapped write-backs with processor execution. Our simulations show that with a single buffer the amount of stalling on a swapped write-back is indeed negligible. On the other hand, if the incremental write-back is not used we need to write back over a hundred blocks at context switching time for this specific benchmark. Notice that the number of write-backs needed due to context switching is a function of cache size, cache organization, the duration of the running state of a process, and the workload.

Cache coherence

While two-level caches are attractive, cache coherence control is complicated by a two-level scheme. Without special attention to the coherence problem, the first-level cache will be disturbed by every coherency request on the bus. A solution to this problem is to use the second-level cache as a filter to shield the first-level cache from irrelevant interference. In order to achieve this, we need to impose an inclusion property where the tags of the

interval	count
1	2
2	3
3	0
4	2
5	5
6	0
7	1
8	2
9	1
10 and larger	119

Table 3: Write interval with write-back and swapped write-back (snapshot of 411,237 references)

second-level cache are a superset of the tags of its child cache. We say that a multilevel cache hierarchy has the inclusion property if this superset relation holds. Imposing inclusion is also essential for solving the synonym problem as stated above.

In a multiprocessor environment, the inclusion property cannot be held even with a global LRU replacement [4]. In [5] the following replacement algorithm was proposed as one of the conditions to impose the inclusion.

- First level: Any replacement algorithm will do (e.g., LRU). Notify the second level cache of the block being replaced.

- Second level: Replace a block which does not exist in the first level (this is done by checking an inclusion bit; there is one inclusion bit per block to indicate whether the block is present in the first level).

The general problem with inclusion is its implications for a large set size in the second level (i.e., high associativity). By following the same approach as in [5], and letting S_i be the number of sets, B_i be the block size, and $size(i)$ be the cache size of a level i cache, we can show that in order to impose inclusion under the above replacement algorithm, the set-associativity of the second-level cache A_2 must be:

$$A_2 \geq \frac{size(1)}{pagesize} \times \frac{B_2}{B_1}$$

under the usual practical situations where $S_2 > S_1$, $B_2 \geq B_1$, $size(2) > size(1)$ and $B_1 S_1 \geq pagesize^2$.

In practical cases, this constraint can be too strict to be feasible. For example, if the V-cache is 16K bytes, the page size is 4K bytes, and B_2 is 4 times as large as B_1, even with a direct-mapped V-cache we need a 16-way R-cache to achieve the inclusion.

To relax the strict constraint on the set-associativity of the R-cache, we change the replacement rule of the R-cache to operate as follows: replace a block with the inclusion bit clear if there is one; otherwise replace a block according to some predefined replacement algorithm and invalidate the corresponding V-cache block. Note that the latter won't happen very often since the R-cache is much larger than the V-cache. For example, the analysis of the multiprocessor trace, pops (over 3 million memory references), shows that only 21 inclusion invalidations are needed if the V cache is 16K bytes, 2-way set-associative with a 16 byte block size and the R cache is 256K bytes with same set size and block size.

---

[2] if $B_1 S_1 < pagesize$ the results of [5] apply.

3 Organization of a V-R two-level cache

A simplified organizational block diagram of a V-R two-level cache is given in Figure 2. The V-cache is accessed via virtual addresses, which are also forwarded to the TLB at the second level so that address translation can proceed concurrently with the access to the V-cache. This translation and the access to the R-cache are aborted if there is a valid hit in the V-cache. A number of tag and control bits that we call tag entry are associated with data blocks in both caches as shown in Figure 3. Each tag entry in the V-cache contains a tag, an r-pointer, a dirty bit, a valid bit and a swapped-valid bit. The r-pointer contains the lower log(R-cache-size/page-size) bits of the real address page number. Together with the page offset, it can be used to address the related entry in the R-cache. The swapped-valid bit is used to indicate whether the entry belongs to a swapped process. This is needed in order to avoid a large context switch overhead, as previously described.

Each tag entry in the R-cache tag store contains a tag and a number of subentries, one subentry per V-cache block since we allow larger block sizes in the R-cache. A subentry contains an inclusion bit that indicates whether a copy of the data is in the V-cache or not, a buffer bit that indicates if a copy of the data is in a write buffer of the V-cache, a few state bits for sharing status and cache coherence control (with other R-caches), two

dirty bits, one for V-cache dirty and for R-cache dirty, and a v-pointer which contains the lower log(V-cache-size/page-size) bits of the virtual page number. Together with the page offset, the v-pointer can be used to address the entry in the V-cache.

In order to properly provide the data and manage cache coherence and synonyms, we list in Table 4 the communication buses between the V-cache and the R-cache. The following is a detailed operational description of a two-level V-R cache.

For simplicity, let us assume that an invalidation protocol is used at the R-cache level although our scheme will also work for other protocols as well. An invalidation protocol invalidates all other cache copies before updating shared data in the local cache. Write-backs to memory are performed when a dirty block moves from one cache hierarchy to another. A number of existing protocols belong to this category [16].

V-R hierarchy algorithm

1. Read hit in V-cache. Give the data to the processor. The hit signal is sent to the R-cache to abort the R-cache and TLB accesses.

2. Read miss in V-cache. Raise the replacement signal if a V-cache block needs to be replaced to give room to the incoming new data. Give the R-cache both the v-pointer, which is the V-cache location for the new data, and the r-pointer, which is the R-cache location of the block being replaced. If the replaced block in V-cache is clean, the

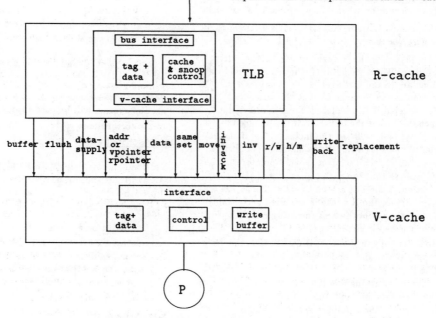

Figure 2: V-R cache organization

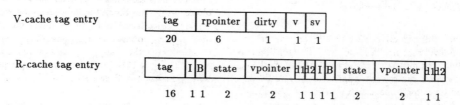

Figure 3: Contents of tag stores (assume page size is 4K, C_1 is 16K and C_2 is 256K, $B_2 = 2 \times B_1$.)

143

From V to R:	
read/write	tells the R-cache whether the current request is a read or a write.
replacement	tells the R-cache that a V-cache block needs to be replaced.
hit/miss(v-pointer, r-pointer)	tells the R-cache whether the current access results in a hit or a miss in the V-cache. If it is a miss, the target v-pointer gives the V-cache slot for the new data and the r-pointer gives the R-cache entry where the inclusion bit is to be erased if the block to be replaced is clean, or where the buffer bit is to be set if the block is dirty. If it is a hit the R-cache access is aborted.
write back(r-pointer)	tells the R-cache that the data in the write buffer will be written back to the place pointed to by the r-pointer.
From R to V:	
sameset(v-pointer)	tells the V-cache that there is a synonym copy in the same set; no need to write back; and the data is available under v-pointer.
move(v-pointer)	tells the V-cache that there is a synonym copy in a different set; the data is available under v-pointer.
data supply(r-pointer)	tells the V-cache that the data is ready to be loaded and gives its location in the R-cache to be stored as part of the tag entry.
invalidation(v-pointer)	tells the V-cache to invalidate the data under v-pointer.
flush(v-pointer)	tells the V-cache to flush the data under v-pointer.
invalidation(buffer)	tells the V-cache to invalidate the data in the buffer.
flush(buffer)	tells the V-cache to flush the data in the buffer.
invack	tells the V-cache that the coherency has been cleared and that it can update the data.

Table 4: V-R interface

R-cache resets the inclusion bit. If the block is dirty, the V-cache copies the block into the write buffer and the R-cache sets the buffer bit to indicate that the block is still in the write buffer of the V-cache. This bit gets reset when the write-back occurs or when the write-back is canceled (see below).

(a) Hit in R-cache.

   i. The data is in the V-cache under another virtual address. The R-cache tests whether the two locations are in the same set. If so, a *sameset* signal is sent to the V-cache so that the write-back can be canceled if the replaced block is dirty; the R-cache will reset the buffer bit if the replaced block is dirty, or it will set the inclusion bit if the replaced block is clean[3]. If the blocks are in different sets, the R-cache sends a move(v-pointer) to the V-cache so that the data can be stored at the new location. Valid bits are set to valid. The v-pointer tag entry of the R-cache is modified accordingly. Notice that in both cases the v-tag is updated to reflect the new virtual address.

   ii. No other copy in V-cache. R-cache raises the data supply signal and sends the block to the V-cache. The R-cache also supplies the r-pointer to the V-cache to set up the link information. R-cache sets the inclusion bit and the v-pointer and the V-cache stores the r-pointer, sets the valid bits, and resets the dirty bit.

(b) Miss in R-cache. Proceeds as described in the cache coherence subsection. Gets a clean copy and then back to (a)ii.

3. Write hit on clean block in V-cache. Wait till the R-cache raises the *invack* signal (cf. the cache coherence subsection); then update the data and set the dirty bit in the V-cache.

4. Write miss in V-cache. The replacement proceeds as in the case of a read miss.

[3]the inclusion bit was reset earlier to reflect the replacement.

(a) Hit in R-cache. Resolve the cache coherency (cf. below); resolve the synonyms as in the case of a read miss; load the block into V-cache; update the data and sets the dirty bit in the V-cache.

(b) Miss in R-cache. Proceed as described in the cache coherence subsection; get a clean copy, load the block into the V-cache and the R-cache and set appropriate pointers and inclusion as in the case for a read; update the data, and set the dirty bit in the V-cache.

It is worth noticing that the cost of handling a synonym is approximately the same as a first-level miss and second-level hit. This observation will be used in our performance evaluations.

Cache coherence

Processor induced:

1. Read miss in the V-cache and in the R-cache. Initiate a read-miss bus transaction and get the block. Set the state of the block as shared if another cache acknowledges having this block; otherwise set the state as private.

2. Write hit on a clean block in the V-cache. Check the state in the R-cache. If private, raises the *invack* to let the V-cache proceed; sets the vdirty bit in the R-cache. Otherwise, the R-cache initiates an invalidation bus transaction and when it is completed, raise the *invack* signal and set the vdirty bit in the R-cache.

3. Write miss in the V-cache.

(a) Hit in the R-cache. Check the state in the R-cache. If shared, initiate an invalidation bus transaction. Supply the block to the V-cache when the transaction is completed and set the vdirty bit in the R-cache.

(b) Miss in the R-cache. Initiate a read-modified-write bus transaction; get the block; reset the rdirty bit in the R-cache and set the vdirty bit in the R-cache.

Bus induced:

1. Read-miss. Acknowledge the sharing status if in possession of the requested block and:

144

(a) If the block is modified in the V-cache, the R-cache sends a flush(v-pointer) to V-cache and gets the block, updates itself, changes its state to shared, resets the vdirty bit, resets the rdirty bit, supplies the block to the requesting cache and updates the memory.

(b) If the block is modified in the write buffer of V-cache, R-cache sends a flush(buffer) to V-cache and gets the block, updates itself, changes its state to shared, resets vdirty bit, resets the rdirty bit, resets the inclusion bit, supplies the block to the requesting cache and updates the memory.

(c) If the block is dirty in the R-cache, the R-cache supplies the block to the requesting cache, updates the memory, changes its state to shared, and resets its dirty bit.

(d) Otherwise, memory supplies the block.

2. Invalidation. The R-cache invalidates its own entry if present and checks the inclusion bit. If it is set, the corresponding entry in the V-cache is invalidated. This is done by issuing invalidate(v-pointer) to the V-cache.

3. Read-modified-write. Treated as a read-miss followed by an invalidation.

Replacement

(a) V-cache: Any replacement algorithm will do (e.g., LRU).

(b) R-cache: Replace a block with all inclusion bits (i.e., for each subentry) reset. If there is none (this might happen if we follow the strategy of the end of section 2), randomly choose one block and invalidate the copy (or copies if $B_2 > B_1$) in the V-cache.

4 Performance

In this section, we compare the relative performance of virtual-real (V-R) and real-real (R-R) two-level caches. We also examine the merits of splitting the first-level virtually-addressed cache into I and D caches. Finally, we measure the effect of the R-cache in shielding the V-cache from irrelevant cache coherence interference.

To gather the performance figures, we use trace-driven simulations and three parallel program traces: pops, thor and abaqus [2, 14]. In pops and thor, context switches occur rarely while they are frequent in abaqus. Table 5 gives a summary of some characteristics of these traces.

Relative performance of V-R and R-R two-level caches

To compare the performance of V-R and R-R two-level caches, we gather the hit ratios at different levels; the hit ratios are then used in generic memory access time equations to predict relative performances. We assume that the inclusion property defined previously also holds for the R-R two-level cache. For simplicity, we consider only direct-mapped caches at both levels.

The generic access time equation of a two-level cache hierarchy is as follows:

T_{acc} = Prob(hit at level 1) × access time at level 1
+ Prob(hit at level 2 & miss at level 1) × access time at level 2
+ Prob(miss at level 1 and 2) × memory access time

that is:

$$T_{acc} = h_1 t_1 + (1 - h_1)h_2 t_2 + (1 - h_1 - (1 - h_1)h_2)t_m$$

where h_1, h_2 are hit ratios at levels 1 and 2, t_1 and t_2 are access times at the two levels, and t_m is the memory access time including the bus overhead.

Because the second-level caches are the same for both V-R and R-R organizations, and because inclusion holds, the number of misses and the traffic from the second-level cache are the same in both organizations. Therefore the third term in the above equation is the same for both V-R and R-R organizations. Assuming that handling a synonym has a cost equivalent of handling a miss in the first-level cache that hits in the second-level cache, the relative performance where there is a hit in the hierarchy can be estimated solely on the first two terms of the above equation.

Table 6 shows the hit ratios at both levels of V-R and R-R organizations for the three traces under three different pairs of first and second-level cache sizes. Figures 4, 5 and 6 depict the relative performance of the two organizations under different degrees of assumed R-cache degradation due to address translation overhead. These figures plot the relative performance of the two hierarchies with $t_2 = 4t_1$ vs. the percentage of slow down due to address translation for various first-level/second-level cache sizes. The points on the y-axis correspond to no slow down at all. From these figures we can draw the following conclusions.

Let us assume that there is no time penalty involved in performing a virtual-real address translation in conjunction with the access to the first level cache. When context switches occur rarely, as is the case for the first two traces (Figures 4 and 5), the performances of the V-R and R-R hierarchies are almost indistinguishable (the points on the y-axis are the same). When context switches are frequent, as in the third trace (Figure 6), the V-R hierarchy is slower by 2 to 6% depending on the size of the V-cache (a larger V-cache seems to imply a larger relative degradation).

Now, let us assume a time penalty for the translation. There are two possible reasons for this penalty. The first is that TLB access and cache access cannot be completely overlapped as soon as the cache size is larger than the page size multiplied by the set associativity. Second, even if there were total overlap, there would still be an extra comparison necessary to check the validity of a cache hit. From the observations of the previous paragraph, it is clear that the V-R hierarchy will perform better in the case of rare context-switches. The relative improvement is approximately equal to the overhead of address translation. What is interesting is to see the cross-over point for the case of frequent context-switches. From Figure 6, we see that the V-R hierarchy will have a better performance when the address translation slows down the first level R-cache access by 6% or more.

Since 6% is a conservative figure for the penalty due to the insertion of a TLB at the first level, it appears that the V-R hierarchy is a better solution. Its performance is as good as that of an R-R hierarchy and its cost is less since the TLB does not have to be

trace	num. of cpus	total refs	instr count	data read	data write	context switch count
thor	4	3283k	1517k	1390k	376k	21
pops	4	3286k	1718k	1285k	283k	7
abaqus	2	1196k	514k	600k	82k	292

Table 5: Characteristics of traces

trace	thor			pops			abaqus		
sizes	4K/64K	8K/128K	16K/256K	4K/64K	8K/128K	16K/256K	4K/64K	8K/128K	16K/256K
h1VR	.925	.957	.968	.928	.943	.954	.852	.873	.888
h1RR	.925	.958	.969	.928	.943	.954	.857	.889	.908
h2VR	.692	.531	.463	.609	.608	.567	.551	.559	.585
h2RR	.691	.526	.449	.608	.608	.563	.536	.493	.498

Table 6: hit ratios

trace	thor			pops			abaqus		
sizes	.5K/64K	1K/128K	2K/256K	.5K/64K	1K/128K	2K/256K	.5K/64K	1K/128K	2K/256K
h1VR	.755	.828	.872	.727	.882	.909	.766	.793	.822
h1RR	.755	.828	.872	.727	.882	.909	.767	.797	.827
h2VR	.905	.883	.867	.897	.810	.781	.716	.728	.739
h2RR	.905	.883	.867	.897	.810	.781	.715	.723	.732

Table 7: Hit ratios for small first-level caches

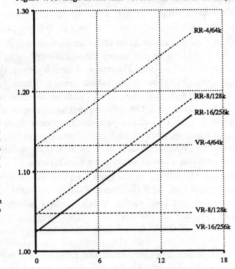

Figure 4: Average access time vs. slow-down of R-cache (thor)

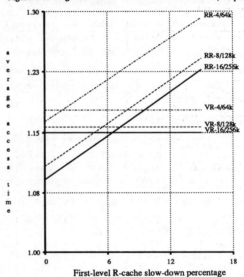

Figure 6: Average access time vs. slow-down of R-cache (abaqus)

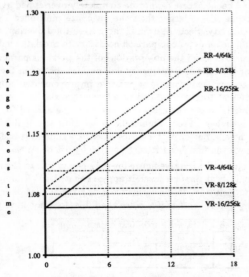

Figure 5: Average access time vs. slow-down of R-cache (pops)

implemented in fast logic. Another advantage is that problems such as TLB coherence can also be handled at the second level.

The results presented above assumed 4K to 16K first-level caches, which may be impractical for some advanced technologies, such as GaAs. However, we believe that the V-R organization is even more attractive for hierarchies with smaller first-level caches. Our results in Table 7 show that for smaller first-level caches (e.g., .5K to 2K), the first-level hit ratios of V-R and R-R organizations are nearly identical. Therefore, performance of a V-R hierarchy will be superior given any penalty for a TLB lookup. In addition, for technologies in which space is at a premium, we can trade the first-level TLB of an R-R hierarchy for a larger first-level cache in a V-R hierarchy. This in turn provides larger hit ratios and hence smaller average access time.

Splitting the first-level virtually-addressed cache

There are a number of reasons why it is advantageous to split the first-level cache into separate I and D caches. First, the bandwidth can almost be doubled for pipelined processors where an instruction fetch can occur at the same time as a data fetch of a previous instruction (e.g., the IBM801 and Motorola 88000). Second, each I and D cache is smaller and has the potential to be optimized for its speed. Third, and this pertains mostly to V-caches, the I cache is simpler than the D cache since it does not need to handle the synonym and the cache coherence problems provided that self-modifying programs are not permitted. A disadvantage, however, is that we need more wirings or pins for the processor and cache module. It is important to assess, however, if splitting the cache into I & D components will improve performance.

Our results in Table 8, 9 and 10 show that the hit ratios of split I&D caches are very close to that of a unified I&D cache and are not necessarily worse. In these tables, the I and D separate caches are of equal sizes (i.e., in the 4K example the I-cache and the D-cache are each 2K). Similar results have been found in [9, 13]. Thus, we would advocate such a split for a V-R hierarchy.

thor	4K/64K	8K/128K	16K/256K
data read split	0.924	0.937	0.945
unified	0.913	0.938	0.950
data write split	0.952	0.962	0.969
unified	0.946	0.966	0.972
instruction split	0.957	0.963	0.989
unified	0.930	0.973	0.984
overall split	0.942	0.952	0.968
unified	0.925	0.957	0.968

Table 8: Hit ratios of level 1 caches for the thor trace

pops	4K/64K	8K/128K	16K/256K
dataread split	0.902	0.912	0.923
unified	0.900	0.915	0.926
data write split	0.936	0.946	0.955
unified	0.937	0.948	0.958
instruction split	0.947	0.966	0.978
unified	0.948	0.963	0.974
overall split	0.928	0.944	0.955
unified	0.928	0.943	0.954

Table 9: Hit ratios of level 1 caches for the pops trace

abaqus	4K/64K	8K/128K	16K/256K
data read split	0.795	0.818	0.837
unified	0.806	0.829	0.845
data write split	0.841	0.861	0.875
unified	0.847	0.857	0.895
instruction split	0.920	0.947	0.949
unified	0.907	0.926	0.938
overall split	0.852	0.876	0.888
unified	0.852	0.873	0.888

Table 10: Hit ratios of level 1 caches for the abaqus trace

Shielding cache coherence interference

An important advantage of the two-level approach is that the R-cache can shield the V-cache from irrelevant cache coherence interference. For example, on a read miss bus request, the R-cache needs to send a flush request to its V-cache only when the V-cache contains a modified copy of the data; otherwise the V-cache will not be disrupted. Note that this shielding effect is achieved because the inclusion property holds in our V-R two-level cache. Imposing inclusion might not seem to be essential for an R-R two-level hierarchy because the synonym problem is not present. However, the results in Tables 11, 12 and 13, which give the number of coherence messages being percolated to each first-level cache, show that a V-R two-level cache has much less coherence interference at the first level than that of an R-R two-level cache without inclusion. The results also show that inclusion is important in an R-R two-level cache since it results in approximately the same savings in coherence messages to the first-level cache.[4]

We believe that the shielding effect on cache coherence will be more prominent as the number of processors increases. This is due to the fact that more bus coherence requests will be generated from a larger number of processors, and without the shielding, a first-level cache will be disrupted more often. Our results in Tables 11, 12 (4 cpus) and 13 (2 cpus) reflect this effect. For example, on the average, the first-level cache of a V-R hierarchy encounters about half the coherence messages than that of the R-R hierarchy without inclusion for the two processor trace (cf. Table 13), whereas for four processor traces the first-level cache of the V-R hierarchy encounters from three to six times fewer coherence messages. We plan to further confirm this observation when we are in possession of larger-scale traces.

5 Conclusions

One of the most challenging issues in computer design is the support of high memory bandwidth. In this paper, we have proposed

---

[4] We notice that RR with inclusion has over 10% fewer coherence messages than that of VR for the abaqus trace. This discrepancy is due to a large amount of inclusion invalidations incurred in this specific trace due to a large number of context switchings.

pops	4K/64K			8K/128K			16K/256K		
cpu	VR	RR(incl)	RR(no incl)	VR	RR(incl)	RR(no incl)	VR	RR(incl)	RR(no incl)
0	6717	7113	23804	7237	7707	20783	8309	8854	19468
1	10015	10351	30523	10606	11027	26128	11771	12357	24258
2	9518	9861	30063	10143	11027	26407	11344	11906	24817
3	9368	9963	31311	10001	10650	27528	11144	12061	25932

Table 11: Number of coherence messages to the first-level cache

thor	4K/64K			8K/128K			16K/256K		
cpu	VR	RR(incl)	RR(no incl)	VR	RR(incl)	RR(no incl)	VR	RR(incl)	RR(no incl)
0	3755	3743	23005	4342	4317	21773	5785	4473	18123
1	4144	4139	27056	4727	4722	23538	5473	5170	18304
2	4229	4229	27005	4810	4820	23915	5561	5229	18776
3	4135	4129	25210	4699	4692	21593	6797	5103	16231

Table 12: Number of coherence messages to the first-level cache

abaqus	4K/64K			8K/128K			16K/256K		
cpu	VR	RR(incl)	RR(no incl)	VR	RR(incl)	RR(no incl)	VR	RR(incl)	RR(no incl)
0	10961	8436	18855	11677	9379	21295	11067	9853	22603
1	10527	8029	20726	10547	9528	24202	10599	10028	26845

Table 13: Number of coherence messages to the first-level cache

a two-level cache hierarchy to address this issue. We have argued that the first level cache is best accessed directly by virtual addresses. We back up the small virtually-addressed cache by a large second-level cache. A virtually-addressed first-level cache does not require address translation and can be optimized to match the processor speed. Through the use of a swapped-valid bit, we avoid the clustering of write-backs at context switching time. The distribution of these write-backs is more evenly spread over time. The large second-level cache provides a high hit ratio and reduces a large amount of memory traffic. We have shown how the second-level cache can be easily extended to solve the synonym problem resulting from the use of a virtually-addressed cache at the first level. Furthermore, the second-level cache can be used effectively to shield the virtually-addressed first-level cache from irrelevant cache coherence interference.

Our simulation results show that when context switches are rare, the virtually-addressed cache option has comparable performance to its physically-addressed counterpart, even assuming no address translation overhead. When context switches occur frequently, the virtually-addressed cache option has a performance edge when a small address translation penalty is taken into account, and the smaller the virtually-addressed cache the larger the relative performance edge. We also advocate splitting the virtually-addressed cache into separated instruction and data caches. This approach has the potential of doubling the memory bandwidth since our results show that the hit ratios of split instruction and data caches are very close to that of a single I&D cache.

As a final remark, we note that cache performance is workload dependent. In this study we have confined ourselves to a limited VAX multiprocessor workload. We plan to enlarge our workload sample as soon as we are in possession of other multiprocessor traces.

Acknowledgment

This work was supported in part by National Science Foundation (Grants No. CCR-8702915 and CCR-8619663), Boeing Computer Services, Digital Equipment Corporation (the System Research Center and the External Research Program) and a GTE fellowship. The experimental part of this study could not have been possible without Dick Sites who made the traces available to us and Anant Agarwal who allowed us to share his postprocessing programs and who patiently answered our many questions. We also thank the members of the "Computer Architecture lunch", especially Tom Anderson, Jon Bertoni, Sanglyul Min and John Zahorjan for their excellent comments and suggestions.

References

[1] Agarwal, A., R. L. Sites and M. Horowitz. ATUM: A new technique for capturing address traces using microcode. In *Proc. 13th Symposium on Computer Architecture*, pages 119–127, 1986.

[2] Agarwal, A., R. Simoni, J. Hennessy and M. Horowitz. An evaluation of directory schemes for cache coherence. In *Proc. 15th Symposium on Computer Architecture*, pages 280–289, 1988.

[3] Atkinson, R. R. and E. M. McCreight. The dragon processor. In *Proc. Architectural Support for Programming Languages and Operating Systems(ASPLOS-II)*, pages 65–69, 1987.

[4] Baer, J.-L. and W.-H. Wang. Architectural choices for multi-level cache hierarchies. In *Proc. 16th International Conference on Parallel Processing*, pages 258–261, 1987.

[5] Baer, J.-L. and W.-H. Wang. On the inclusion property for multi-level cache hierarchies. In *Proc. 15th Symposium on Computer Architecture*, pages 73–80, 1988.

[6] Cheriton, D.R., G. Slavenburg and P. Boyle. Software-controlled caches in the VMP multiprocessor. In *Proc. 13th Symposium on Computer Architecture*, pages 367–374, 1986.

[7] Goodman, J. Coherency for multiprocessor virtual address caches. In *Proc. Architectural Support for Programming Languages and Operating Systems(ASPLOS-II)*, pages 72–81, 1987.

[8] Goodman, J. and P.J. Woest. The Wisconsin multicube: A new large-scale cache-coherent multiprocessor. In *Proc. 15th Symposium on Computer Architecture*, pages 422–431, 1988.

[9] Haikala, I.J. and P.H. Kutvonen. Split cache organizations. In *Proc. Performance '84*, pages 459–472, 1984.

[10] Hattori,A., Koshino,M. and S.Kamimoto. Three-level hierarchical storage system for FACOM M-380/382. In *Proc. Information Processing IFIP*, pages 693–697, 1983.

[11] Hill,M. et al. Design decisions in SPUR. *Computer*, 19(11):8–22, November 1986.

[12] Przybylski, Steven A. *Performance-Directed Memory Hierarchy Design*. Ph.D Dissertation, Stanford University, 1988.

[13] Short R.T. and H.M. Levy. A simulation study of two-level caches. In *Proc. 15th Symposium on Computer Architecture*, pages 81–88, 1988.

[14] Sites, R.L. and A. Agarwal. Multiprocessor cache analysis using ATUM. In *Proc. 15th Symposium on Computer Architecture*, pages 186–195, 1988.

[15] Smith,A.J. Cache memories. *Computing Surveys*, 14(3):473–530, September 1982.

[16] Sweazey, P. and A.J. Smith. A class of compatible cache consistency protocols and their support by the IEEE future-bus. In *Proc. 13th Symposium on Computer Architecture*, pages 414–423, 1986.

[17] Cheng, Ray. Virtual address cache in UNIX. In *Proc. USENIX Conference*, pages 217–224, June 1987.

HIGH PERFORMANCE COMMUNICATIONS IN PROCESSOR NETWORKS

Jesshope CR, Miller PR,Yantchev JT

Dept. of Electronics and Computer Science
The University
Southampton
England

Abstract

In order to provide an arbitrary and fully dynamic connectivity in a network of processors, transport mechanisms must be implemented, which provide the propagation of data from processor to processor, based on addresses contained within a packet of data. Such data transport mechanisms must satisfy a number of requirements - deadlock and livelock freedom, good hot-spot performance, high throughput and low latency. This paper proposes a solution to these problems, which allows deadlock free, adaptive, high throughput packet routing to be implemented on networks of processors. Examples are given which illustrate the technique for 2-D array and toroidal networks. An implementation of this scheme on arrays of transputers is described. The scheme also serves as a basis for a very low latency routing strategy named the *mad postman*, a detailed implementation of which is described here as well.

Keywords: Deadlock-free, packet routing, low latency, routing networks, transputers.

1. Introduction

It has become clear over the last decade, that parallelism in the form of replication has been able to provide cost effective improvements in computer performance. Replication is cost effective, because it allows relatively slow but dense technologies such as MOS to compete with intrinsically faster technologies such as ECL. The technique of replication is most successful if the replication factor is high and the unit of replication is simple. To apply the high density technologies to improving the speed of computer systems, a technique is required to design incrementally extensible architectures so one can increase the processing power of a system by simply plugging in more chips. Message passing computers, collections of processing nodes connected by a communications network, offer a solution to the problem of building extensible computers. These concurrent computers are extended by adding processing nodes and communication channels.

The design of an efficient general communication network is one of the most important issues in architectures that permit any processor to communicate with any other. One choice is a network of reconfigurable topology implemented by configuring a circuit switch between communications links connecting the processors. However, even a fully reconfigurable network has limitations imposed by its static nature, fixed valency and central control; it is also very expensive to implement with the current 2-D (even 3-D) technology for networks with a large number of processors. If the nature of the problem is such that the topology required changes dynamically, then other means must be used in order to realise a dynamic virtual topology.

In order to provide a fully dynamic arbitrary connectivity in a fixed valence network of processors, a transport mechanism must be implemented, which provides the propagation of data from processor to processor, based on addresses contained within a packet of data. In such a network each processor might wish to send a message to any other. Such a data routing mechanism must satisfy a number of requirements depending on the particular application. Among the most demanding ones are:

- the routing protocol must be deadlock free;
- no packet is infinitely delayed in the network;
- a packet always takes the shortest route to its destination;
- the routing mechanism must adapt to traffic conditions and exploit the full available communications bandwidth (no restriction on the routing must be imposed other than the above);
- a node must not be able to refuse the input of a message from its user for ever;
- the highest possible throughput must be achieved (possibly only limited by the bandwidth of the internode links);
- the lowest possible latency must be achieved.

The requirements for high throughput and low latency in communication are extremely important if the ratio of computation/communication costs are to remain well balanced even in the case of fine grain parallelism. This ratio scales rather badly in highly replicated designs because of increases in the network diameter or because of wiring costs. Deadlock freedom is a natural requirement unless one wants the routing network to have the potential of being nondeterministically brought to a complete halt until some external intervention brings it back into life. The requirement for fair allocation of routing resources ensures that no packet is indefinitely delayed in the routing network before being delivered at its destination.

Different schemes have been proposed by others [1,2,3], but none of them seems able to satisfy all the requirements above. Here we discuss some of these schemes and describe a new scheme which meets these requirements and provides for a great deal of design freedom to make compromises in order to achieve a desired cost/performance ratio. This scheme can be applied to arbitrary networks; however, we will restrict our attention to k-ary n-cubes and to 2-D toroidal arrays in particular.

A method [4] is proposed to solve the problems of deadlock and livelock freedom. It provides for a maximum distribution of the processing of packets at each node thus allowing for a maximum throughput to be achieved. It is based on splitting the physical network into a set of independent directed-cycle free *virtual networks*, each one of which can be proved deadlock free and hence the whole set must be deadlock free. The proposed method allows for all available communications bandwidth between the source and destination of a packet to be utilised and an adaptive routing strategy to be implemented. It also serves as a base for the development of a very low latency and high throughput routing strategy which we named the *mad postman* [4,5].

2. Overview of the Existing Packet Routing Algorithms

Many deadlock-free routing algorithms have been developed for *store-and-forward* computer communications networks [2,3]. In store-and-forward, each packet is stored completely in a node and then transmitted to the next node. These algorithms are based on the concept of a *structured buffer pool*. The message buffers in each node of the network are partitioned into classes, and the assignment of buffers to messages is restricted to define a partial order on buffer classes. The main disadvantage of this method of routing is the very high latency in delivering an individual packet; it is proportional to the product of the packet length and the number of channels traversed. It also imposes stringent requirements on the minimum buffer space in each node. We have simulated permutations on a two-dimensional 1024 processor array, where for one packet per processor injected into the network, a maximum buffering requirement was many tens of packets [6]. A node must therefore be able to accommodate a number of full length packets, or it will fail to use its critical resources - the connections to other nodes.

Instead of storing a packet completely in a node and then transmitting it to the next node, *wormhole* routing [7] operates by advancing the head of a packet directly from incoming to outgoing channels. Only a few control digits (flits) are buffered at each node. A *flit* is the smallest unit of information that a queue or a channel can accept or refuse.

As soon as a node examines the header flit (flits) of a message, it selects the next channel on the route and begins forwarding flits down that channel. As flits are forwarded, the message becomes spread out across the channels between the source and the destination. It is possible for the first flit of a message to arrive at its destination node before the last flit of the message has left the source. Because most flits contain no routing information, the flits in a message must not be interleaved with the flits of other messages. Thus, when the header flit of a message is blocked, all of the flits of a message stop advancing and block the progress of any other message requiring the channels they occupy.

A solution to the problem of deadlock freedom in wormhole routing has been proposed in [1]. It is based on preventing cycles in a channel dependency graph. Given an arbitrary network and a routing function, the cycles in the channel dependency graph can be removed by splitting physical channels into groups of virtual channels; each virtual channel having its own queue. The virtual channels approach restricts routing of packets; it reduces the number of possible paths that a packet may take from one which may be very large to a single path, thus disallowing any adaptation to local traffic conditions.

It is claimed that to prevent deadlock in wormhole routing one must restrict the routing of packets [1]. The next section will show that this is not true. The method of *virtual networks* proposed here avoids deadlock by preventing cycles in the directed communications graph; there is no restriction on the number of paths a packet may take, given that it always moves closer to its destination. The method of virtual networks also reduces the required minimum buffer space at each node; instead of each virtual channel having its own queue, now each virtual network only needs its own queue.

Virtual cut-through [8] is a method similar to wormhole routing. It differs from wormhole routing in that it buffers messages when they block, removing them from the network; this improves the hot-spot performance of the network and, in general, increases the throughput. The deadlock properties of cut-through routing are identical to those of store-and-forward routing (i.e. it implements the same deadlock avoidance algorithms).

The method of *double-buffering* [9] is an exotic approach to deadlock avoidance proposed recently. In this method messages start off by being buffered at their sending node. Each then attempts to establish a connection with the destination node by forming an unbroken path across intermittent nodes. If a block or a failure is encountered along the route the message gives up by recoiling back to the sender, thus avoiding deadlock. After non-deterministic delay the message tries again. Once a connection is made the entire message is transferred from source to destination, where it is again buffered before eventual off-loading to the receiving system.

In [8] it is claimed that the method provides a reasonable performance, but it is likely that it may be very expensive in terms of communications costs, which will increase disproportionately as network diameter increases. It is very difficult to imagine this method working efficiently in a network of hundreds or thousands of nodes. It is also difficult to see how, in such large networks, the delivery of a packet may be guaranteed; it seems that a packet may indefinitely try to find its way to the destination node and always fail.

3. Virtual Networks - a Method for Deadlock Avoidance in Packet Routing Networks

A method is outlined here for designing deadlock free packet routing networks, which is described in more detail in [4].

Deadlock occurs in a concurrent network when no further action can take place. This is usually because, even though each component process is in a state in which it can communicate, its potential communications are blocked by its neighbours. This is a common problem in concurrent systems and is unique to them. A very good treatment of the problems of deadlock is given in [10], with methods for deadlock analysis applicable to a large class of networks. One of the most fundamental results of the work described in that paper is given by the following theorem.

Theorem 1 [10] If V is a busy, triple disjoint and strong conflict free network, then any deadlock state contains a cycle of ungranted requests (a cycle of at least three processes, each of which is blocked by the next). #

Not all cycles of ungranted requests lead to deadlock, they are just symptomatic of deadlock; hence, one approach to deadlock avoidance is to avoid cycles of ungranted requests. In packet routing networks comprised of buffer processes, cycles of ungranted requests leading to deadlock arise when all buffers in the cycle are full and each one is trying to output a message along the cycle. These cycles of ungranted requests correspond to cycles in the directed communication graph of the network and therefore, an acyclic network of buffers must be deadlock free. A more formal definition and proof of this is given as theorem 2 in [4].

Now, if a physical network can be split into a set of independent virtual networks, all of which satisfy the conditions of theorem 2, then the whole network will be deadlock free. To illustrate this let us consider the 2-D array case.

The 2-D array. Although each node of the physical grid must route messages in all four directions, this provides for a large amount of unnecessary connectivity, as far as a particular packet is concerned. All packets can be divided into four classes according to the directions they need to be routed. These four classes correspond to the four quadrants of a 2-D plane:

Class I	(+X,+Y)
Class II	(-X,+Y)
Class III	(-X,-Y)
Class IV	(+X,-Y)

Four independent virtual networks, each routing messages in one of the four quadrants, can provide for the necessary routing paths provided each packet is initially injected into the proper network. These virtual networks represent four systolic arrays, as shown in Fig.1. Each node is a buffer process of the type described above. These systolic arrays all satisfy the conditions of the theorem presented in [4], and the whole network is therefore deadlock free by design.

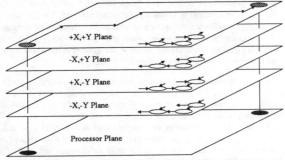

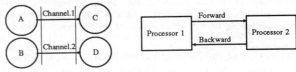

The Set of Virtual Channels and
Processes

The Available Physical Resources

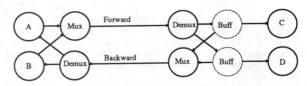

Practical Implementation of Flow Control; n.b. if C and D are themselves buffers, then
there is no need for additional buffers

Fig.1 Virtual Network Topology; showing a message routing in the
+X,+Y Plane

Toroidal networks. For a toroidal network, at a first glance, it seems impossible to close a mesh in such a way so as to allow for communications between opposite ends of the mesh, without introducing any directed cycles in the communication graph. However, by stating the problem in a convenient form, a simple solution which provides the connectivity of a torus among the physical nodes and preserves the deadlock freedom of the whole network is possible.

If the [N x N] array is split into four [N/2 x N/2] subarrays (if N is odd then round off suitably), then the arrangement in Fig.2 provides all the connectivity of a torus. In this case the classes of message have to be further subdivided, so that if the distance travelled by a packet in either direction (d say) is greater than N/2, then it is routed in the opposite direction, by a distance of d-N/2 using the wrap-around connections. In this way a total of 8 message classes or virtual networks may be defined to provide deadlock free packet routing in the 2-D torus.

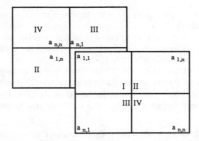

Fig.2 Unwrapping a Torus

This arrangement needs a storage space at each node for eight (8) packets. This though is not a large number and seems a reasonable price to pay for a twofold reduction in the network diameter and a peak performance at each physical node of eight packets in and eight packets out.

Mapping virtual networks onto a physical network. If buffering is not a restriction the nodes of the systolic arrays (the virtual nodes) may be suitably mapped onto the physical nodes of the physical array, so that packets from virtual planes may be interleaved over the same physical links. In this case, to preserve the deadlock freedom, flow control must be used with each output on a virtual channel being immediately followed by a wait for acknowledgement. This scheme is illustrated in Fig.3. In store-and-forward and virtual cut-through schemes, to reduce the overhead of the acknowledgement signals, it is possible to use one acknowledgement per packet rather than per data item. In the case of wormhole routing the acknowledgement must be per data item, otherwise deadlock may result.

Application to arbitrary networks. It is easy to see that this method can be applied to arbitrary networks. In the extreme case, each message class will consist of one message only and the number of virtual subnetworks will be equal to the number of classes. Although possible,

Fig.3 Deadlock Free Mapping of Two Virtual Channels over one Bidirectional Link

in such extreme cases the method may not be of great use. For example, some ill conditioned networks may require excessive storage requirements, but then one can always reduce the packet size or indeed use wormhole routing. In most practical cases, however, the number of virtual networks need not be large.

For arbitrary networks the procedure below must be followed:

    i) subdivide all messages into classes according to their direction of routing;

    ii) split the whole network into directed-cycle free virtual subnetworks, each of which provides all possible paths (if needed) for any of the message classes in (i);

    iii) implement a buffer process at each node of the virtual subnetworks and map them, together with all virtual channels, onto the physical network.

An advantage of this method is the design freedom it offers. The designer can always make a trade-off between storage space, speed, number of possible paths, etc.. For example, a packet routing protocol for a 4-D cube can be designed in at least two different ways. Firstly, the 4-D cube can be split into sixteen 4-D systolic cubes (e.g., a 4-D cube routing chip used), thus utilizing all possible paths the physical network provides. Alternatively, the 4-D cube can be split into two cascaded 2-D subnetworks (say, two cascaded 2-D cube routing chips) each in turn split into four systolic arrays. Each packet is then routed in the first two dimensions and then in the next two. The first network strips off the first two addresses of each packet before passing them to the second subnetwork, which then treats the next two symbols as addresses in the next two dimensions and routes packets accordingly. This reduces the number of possible paths to some extent, but still allows for adaptive routing.

4. An Implementation of Deadlock-Free Packet Routing using Virtual Networks on a 2-D Array of Transputers

The transputer [11] was the first commercially available microprocessor that combined both processing and communication facilities on a single chip. However, it only provides for fixed point-to-point communications, rendering it most useful for embedded systems (its intended application). The more general packet routing mechanism could be implemented by a dedicated software layer. Running this together with applications on a single transputer would result in a poor performance and bandwidth utilisation, due to the internal sequentiality of the transputer.

For maximum performance one may provide a dedicated routing transputer plane, coupled to a processing plane of transputers. Because of its bidirectional links one transputer can implement two virtual planes without any need for channel multiplexing (Sec.3); because of the independence of the two channels within a link the virtual planes remain independent. In this way the four virtual networks for a 2-D array connectivity can be implemented on two dedicated transputer routing planes. Alternatively, the four virtual networks can be incorporated into a single routing plane by using channel multiplexing.

The transputers in the routing plane(s) are fully connected and therefore a fifth link must be added to couple them to the processing plane. This fifth link can be realised by using the memory interface of the routing transputers.

A transputer system that utilises two T414 routing planes and a single T800 processing plane is currently being implemented using surface-mount chiprack technology.

5. The Mad Postman - a Low Latency Routing Strategy

Among our top requirements detailed in the introduction were those for adaptive routing, high throughput and low latency. It is easy to see that the method proposed above provides for a fully adaptive routing strategy. Also, the processing of packets can be fully distributed over all input and output channels and thus all available channel bandwidth may be exploited.

Here a routing strategy, described in [4,5], with the same channel bandwidth, reduces the latency of routing packets by more than one order of magnitude in comparison to the other known present time routing strategies such as store-and-forward, wormhole routing and virtual cut-through. This strategy was named the *mad postman*, which will be seen to be quite an appropriate name.

Latency is defined here, as elsewhere [1], as the delay in delivering a single message in isolation. In the treatment below bit-serial internode communication will be assumed. The latency of the present known routing strategies needs to be defined in order to provide comparison with the *mad postman*. First define:

L is the packet length in words(flits);

W is the word length;

T is the time to transmit one bit;

D is the number of channels traversed;

then,

i) store-and-forward routing, latency = LWTD;

ii) wormhole routing, latency = WTD + LWT;

iii) virtual cut-through, latency = WTD + LWT.

Store-and-forward routing gives a latency that depends on the product of the message length L, and the number of communication channels traversed D. Wormhole routing and virtual cut-through result in a latency which depends on the sum of the two terms. Virtual cut-through provides for the same latency as wormhole but eliminates the deteriorating effect of blocked messages.

Obviously, for minimum latency one must route along the dimension of the leading address flit. Latency will be further reduced if when each packet has been fully routed in a particular dimension then the associated address flit is stripped off. This will also increase the efficiency of transmitting packets. If a packet cannot be routed in the first dimension then it can either be routed in some other dimension or wait till the necessary channel is available.

To summarise, if virtual cut-through routing with all features mentioned above is implemented, then the minimal achievable latency would be WTD + LWT, and accordingly the delay per node would be WT seconds. For example, in case of asynchronous communication with eight data bits, one start bit, one stop bit and T=50 nSec., it means a delay per node of at least 500 nSec. This delay is necessary to accumulate enough information (a full address flit) for a routing decision to be made.

Another important consideration is a dedicated routing hardware. If such is available, then there is nothing inherently wrong in using it for

any purpose if it would otherwise stay idle. Furthermore, there is nothing wrong if some (or even all) of the additional work turns out to be useless, if this helps us achieve a latency far less than the minimum latency achievable otherwise. This is the strategy adopted in *mad postman* routing. In order to reduce latency, without changing any of the terms L,W,D,T, the only choice left is to output every packet along the same dimension it is arriving from, as soon as its first bit arrives and make the routing decisions later. Latency then becomes:

iv) mad postman routing, latency = kTD + LWT

where k is a coefficient between 0 and 1 and is implementation dependent. In the case of synchronous communication k is most likely to be 1, and in the case of asynchronous communication kT will be the time to restore the pulse waveform (usually far less than T). When the whole leading address flit has been examined, one of the following will be true:

- the leading address flit indicates that the packet has to be forwarded further along the same dimension. Then simply continue transmitting the packet, thus achieving minimum latency.

- the leading address flit indicates that the packet has been fully routed in this dimension, and now has to be routed in the next dimension. In this case one must stop the transmission along the first dimension and start transmitting the second flit along the next routing dimension. The second address flit need not be delayed for more than kT time and again minimum latency is achieved! The penalty is that a 'dead' address flit has been transmitted along the first routing dimension.

- the packet has arrived at its destination. Then stop transmission and store the rest of the packet into memory. Again a 'dead' address flit has been transmitted.

Using the figures quoted in the example above, the mad postman will result in a delay per node of less than 50 nSec. which represents an improvement of ten times achieved without any change in the available channel bandwidth. This is indeed a significant step towards reducing the communications cost in a highly parallel computer.

What then, if any, are the costs of this reduction in latency. The *mad postman* only works for the class of directed cycle-free networks described above. However, as it was shown in the previous section, any network can be split into a set of virtual directed cycle free networks which can then be multiplexed onto the physical network. The only additional requirement to obtain this low latency is that the reverse acknowledge signals introducing discipline in the processing of packets be implemented in hardware.

The *mad postman* works properly in any traffic conditions and can be made to adapt to traffic density. Of course, in conditions of increased traffic some blocking is inevitable due to the inevitable contentions for output channels. If, due to blocking at some intermediate node, a packet cannot be routed in the dimension of the leading address flit then it can either wait for the corresponding output channel to be freed or be routed along some other dimension by swapping the first address flit with any other depending on the traffic conditions (i.e. adapting to traffic density). Note that no dead address flit is generated when a packet changes its dimension of routing due to traffic conditions.

In general, in an empty network the maximum number of generated dead address flits will equal the degree of the network. However, they will never reduce the performance beyond that of virtual cut-through or wormhole routing. By comparing it with the local address a dead address flit can always be recognised as such and ignored by the intermediate nodes on its way. It will either quickly reach the boundary of the associated virtual network or will be blocked at some intermediate node. In both cases it will be immediately discarded from the network. Of course, a dead address flit may affect some other packet if there is a contention for the output channel of the associated routing dimension. However, the delay will never be greater than the duration of one address flit and this is precisely the minimum delay introduced at each node by virtual cut-through or wormhole routing. By the time the first address flit has been accumulated the blocking dead address flit will have left the node and the packet may be routed properly. Since normally a whole packet is much larger than an address flit then the probability of a 'good' packet blocking a dead address flit (which will result in discarding the dead flit from the network) is much greater than the probability of a dead address flit blocking a 'good' packet. Simulation results (see later) convince us that 'dead' flits have little or no effect on overall performance. However, although not covered here, an improvement is possible whereby the 'dead' flits can be reduced in size as they propagate thus reducing their effect still further.

As traffic density increases, the number of blocked packets will also increase and correspondingly, the number of dead address flits per packet will decrease and the dead address flits will disappear more quickly from the network. In the extreme case of a maximum traffic density no dead address flits will be generated and packets will propagate in virtual cut-through or wormhole fashion. However, due to the much lower latency of the *mad postman* and hence better relaxation properties of the routing network, it will allow for higher throughput to be achieved as well. The improved latency also increases the channel bandwidth usage by increasing the rate of processing of packets by the communication network.

In general, the *mad postman* is most advantageously used in lower dimension networks, for example 2-D meshes, where latency is usually higher due to higher network diameter. Moreover, such networks best match form to function, and in current implementation technologies (i.e. VLSI chips and PCBs) they will lead to a cheaper hardware, thus allowing for a higher cost/performance ratio to be achieved. It may appear, that in higher dimension networks the efficiency of the *mad postman* routing will be lower due to the higher number of dead address flits generated per packet. However, in such networks the dead address flits will be shorter and (for a given number of nodes N) the total number of dead address bits will be the same - [$\log_2 N$] (the start and stop bits aside).

If well implemented, the *mad postman* will provide a message latency which is the absolute minimum achievable for its class (eg. synchronous or asynchronous networks) In an empty network, the speed of propagation of a packet will only be limited by the physical constraints of propagating a signal pulse (electrical, optical, etc.) between the source and the destination.

6. Hardware Implementation of the Mad Postman Routing Strategy

In this section we present an overview of a prototype hardware design that incorporates many of the ideas presented so far. The objective has been to develop a communications network, with a 4-degree mesh topology, that applies the *mad postman* routing stategy and achieves deadlock freedom through the virtualisation of acyclic routing planes.

Methods for realising the four virtual planes necessary for full interconnection from various hardware configurations have been covered, so it is suffice to say that what follows is a presentation on a hardware realisation of a single virtual plane (ie. it only routes in 2 directions).

The basic configuration. At each node in the network there are two machines, namely X and Y, each with its own datapath, finite-state machine controller and buffers. Each has its own unique data input from the previous node in the corresponding dimension, but they contend for the respective output channels depending on behaviour.

The datapath. Before discussing the datapath organisation, consider the format of packets adopted in the system (Fig.4). There is either one or two leading address flits, followed by the data to be transmitted. Economies of buffer size at each node will dictate the maximum packet length that can be in the system, but within this upper bound variable length packets can exist in the system simultaneously.

The information is segmented into units of eight-bit bytes (or flits), each with its own header bit. The address flits contain a dimension flag indicating whether the address is the first of two, or the second. In the case of only one address flit preceeding the data, the interpretation is that it is the second address. Another interpretation of the flag's

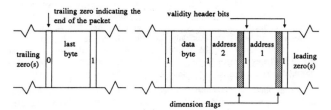

Fig.4 Format of Packets in the Network

meaning is that it indicates whether or not the packet is in its final dimension of routing.

The reader will notice therefore that only seven bits are available in the current scheme for addressing. Thus, at most a 128x128 array can be supported. Furthermore, because of the bit-serial nature of operation, the flit length can easily be increased to theoretically any size by simply *stretching* the datapaths. The machine operation will remain fundamentally unchanged. The end of a message is detected by a zero validity bit following the last databyte of the packet.

In each of the machines at each node therefore, with the current packet format, a 9-bit datapath shift register must be provided so that flits can be held in their entirety for decision and buffering purposes. The essence of the *mad postman* routing strategy is introduced here. Consider the schematic comparison (Fig.5) of an obvious datapath insertion and the one adopted. The communication delay incurred by a message in traversing nodes is dramatically reduced (k=1). Therefore, latency is also minimised, being paid for by eagerly transmitting the data (ie. before any decision can be made concerning its address). By the time a leading address flit is fully into a datapath at say node X, then it will be partially into subsequent datapaths up to node X+8 (assuming no blockage). Hence the generation of dead address flits as discussed earlier.

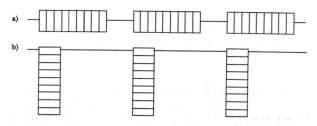

Fig.5 Comparison between   a) conventional datapath (wormhole)
         &   b) mad postman datapath

At a more detailed level of implementation, Fig.6 shows the datapath arrangement. The source and buffer interface registers connect directly to the 8-bit transit buffer for the machine. Having a separate source register, as opposed to directly loading into the datapath register, enables a machine to accept and transmit separate packets simultaneously. Indeed, if sourcing can occur sometime before a message has finished buffering then we are *chaining* the packet through the buffer ensuring maximum throughput at all times. Each time a valid flit sits within the datapath a copy is made to the buffer interface register ready for buffering if required.

Switching occurs at the output rather than the input. The disadvantage of the latter approach being that, in the case of dimension transfer into the complementary datapath (through junctioning or adaption), both input channels are occupied.

Adjacent node interface. Between adjacent machines there are two signals; data transmission forwards and a busy signal in the reverse direction. Because of the exclusivity of the these signals (*if the next node is busy then data o/p from the previous node is not required as it will either have to be re-routed into the other dimension or buffered*)

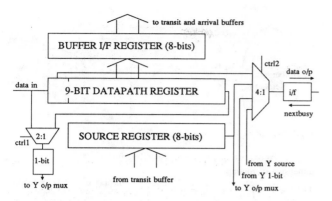

Fig.6 Datapath Organisation

they can share the same physical link as shown in fig.7. The important feature to note here is the symmetry of the circuit. With very simple reconfiguration control the sense of the two signals can be reversed. The implications are of course that, with negligable overheads, the same hardware network can be used to emulate the four virtual networks. Alternatively, two identical hardware networks could be implemented, thus sharing the virtual load, or even one network for each virtual plane (or more!). The trade-off is near-linear and need not stop here. We argue that the independence of virtual planes is a more flexible way of obtaining bandwidth than adopting bit-parallelism.

Fig.7 The Internode Link

The finite-state machine controllers. The controlling machines across the array are not functioning in lockstep as would be the case if the datapath insertions were 9-bits. They have been implemented as autonomous FSM's, activated by the head of an incident packet and deactivated by the tail. The states of the machine, one for X and one for Y, at each node are as follows:

Sourcexx: Output X buffer data onto X output channel;

Sourcexy: Output X buffer data onto Y output channel;

Junctionx: Re-route the 2nd address byte and subsequent data;

Adaptx: Swap the address bytes, incurring a delay of 9 cycles, and re-route into Y;

BFAX: Buffer an arrival in X arrival buffer;

BTHX: Buffer a blocked message in X transit buffer;

BTOX: Buffer a message, that wishes to junction into Y but can't, in X transit buffer.

Fig.8 shows the state diagram (complementary states exist for the Y machine).

In the case of a junction being established, subsequent input data is directed to the complementary output, with the first address flit escaping along the same dimension. Adaption of routing (for a packet with two addresses) occurs if a path is blocked and the complementary output is free. If it is not, or the message is in its final dimension then it must be buffered (BTH). The BTO state is essentially the same as BTH. It differs only in that the buffered data must be output into the complementary dimension upon re-sourcing. Adaptive sourcing can also

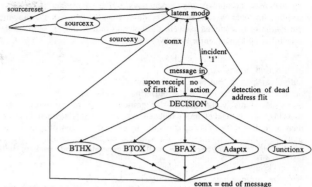

Fig.8 The Finite-State Machine

result in BTH buffered data being output into the other dimension. The conditions for this to occur are that two addresses have been buffered, and only the complementary output is free for sourcing. Otherwise, the buffered packet will be re-sourced into the same dimension it entered the node on.

The reader will note that there are two adaption mechanisms, namely adaptive routing and adaptive sourcing. They are not essential to the correct delivery of packets, but are simply system performance enhancements. This is verified through our simulation results, although one can intuitively realise their benefits. It should also be noted that the hardware expense of their inclusion is negligable.

Buffer Protocol. In the initial development of a suitable buffering protocol for the system, the approach taken was to provide, intuitively, the least performance-limiting solution. The objective being to provide a reference upon which to compare simpler implementations through simulation. This we termed the *ample buffering* strategy.

When a machines buffers are occupied it must generate a *busyback* to the previous node in its dimension to prevent reception of packets that it could potentially not cope with. In the ample buffer case therefore, no *busybacks* are ever generated. In the more realistic case of each machine providing only a single buffer then *busybacks* are generated alot more frequently.

A point worthy of note with minimal buffering systems is that when a region in the array is heavily loaded, *a hot-spot*, the generation of busy signals due to buffer occupation will be more prevalent and will in effect create a protective barrier. The result being that incident 2-dimensional packets will if possible adapt around the area, thus preventing worsening of the situation. This is viewed as an attractive feature that would not occur with ample buffers and occur less often with multiple buffers.

The provision of multiple buffers at a machine, as well as being expensive in chip area, also involves greater complexity in the buffer control hardware. For these reasons, and those stated above, our hardware interests are currently focussed on a minimal one buffer per machine implementation that enables variable length packets to co-exist in the network. This shall now be described briefly. Note that each machine has an arrival buffer, with its own input pointer, that is independent of the transit buffer and whose operation is quite trivial.

The transit buffer has two pointers; one for input (buffering) and the other for output (sourcing). Upon buffering a blocked packet, a flag is set to indicate that the buffer will contain a packet, and the flits are written to the buffer as they arrive, incrementing the pointer each time. When the conditions are satisfied for sourcing, be it adaptive or not, the buffered packet is output in the order in which it arrived (in the case of adaptive sourcing this rule is broken for the two address flits), and the flag reset. This can occur at any time after the first flit is buffered, since the input and output bandwidths are identical, and the output pointer will therefore always remain behind the input pointer for that packet. Furthermore, as soon as sourcing commences, the node can accept another packet (by disasserting its *busyback*, which is the flag set and reset as above) and if necessary buffer this behind the source pointer. In other words, maximum throughput is ensured by allowing the *chaining* of blocked packets through the transit buffer, without the possibility of loosing information.

To enable the co-existance of variable length packets in the network, information needs to be derived that indicates the length of each individual packet buffered. This is readily available from the input pointer value at the end of the buffering process, so all that is required is to latch this value before the pointer needs to be reused, and sourcing of the packet has exceeded its length. This latched value is then compared with the output pointer to indicate the end of sourcing.

Because of the *chaining* ability of the buffer it is in fact necessary to provide two latches which are used alternately for comparison with the output pointer value. Fig.9 shows a schematic of this simple but effective arrangement. The two latches MSLEN1 and MSLEN2 are initialised to maximum (all 1's) and, when their use is over, reset to maximum. They alternately latch the value of PTADDRX at the end of buffering. The source pointer is initially compared to MSLEN1, and then the comparison alternates upon re-sourcing of subsequently buffered packets. The comparison is used to terminate the sourcing and toggle the comparison selection, while the derivation of the latch and reset signals is trivial. Of course, there are issues not discussed here, such as resolution of simultaneous read/write's to the single-port RAM buffer, and the orchestration of reading and writing, but hopefully the principles are clearly conveyed.

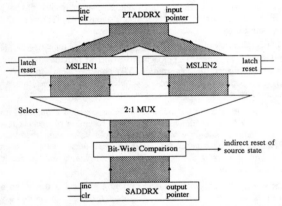

Fig.9 Buffer Pointer Arrangement allowing variable length packets

Processor - communication node interfacing. Here we shall only consider the one-buffer machine, as this is the probable implementation of the family.

There exists a time in the machine's operation, which can be decoded from it's states, when the buffer contents can simply be overwritten by external means. This is how information may be injected into the network, and it can occur at any suitable time during the networks activity. The input pointer can be used by this injection mechanism to write data to the transit buffer. However, this scheme does not decouple the communication network from the processing element very well. A better implementation would employ a separate buffer for the injection/reception of packets, as depicted in Fig.10. Depending on the construction of the node and the injection rates required, it is possible to use many known techniques for interfacing to the communications node. These include DMA or cache-like interfaces, which could even provide hardware addressing across the network.

Hardware simulation. A full logic simulation of a 32x32 array of communication nodes, employing the described buffer strategy has been performed. It runs on the ideally suited AMT Distributed Array Processor with a Sun 3/160 host. The host software, through extensive use of the windows facilities, allows interactive buffer editing and viewing to enable the initialisation and monitoring of different routing

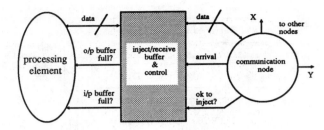

Fig.10 Processor/Communication Node Interface

scenarios. Furthermore it has the ability to display on the DAP monitor the states of the network nodes in real time. The progression of messages through the network can therefore be viewed. Clock cycle time in the simulation program is less than 0.2 seconds, although this is far from being fully optimised.

Performance. Given current technology and bit-serial communications then it is difficult to perceive a more efficient alternative scheme to the *mad postman* implementation. Simulation results are currently being obtained, and comparisons made with other known strategies. The results will be published in full at a later date [12]. However, given below are some figures which may be of interest.

To make comparisons of the mad postman with another strategy, we have also simulated virtual cut-through routing. In this, the forwarding of a packet is delayed until a whole address flit is received, and only then is a routing decision made. The comparison between the two strategies is therefore fair, since the machine behaviour is otherwise the same (adaption is still possible), and the packet format is identical.

Consider the transmission of a packet on a 32x32 node array from node (1,1) to node (32,32) of an 8 bit integer:

Mad Postman : Time taken = 89 clock cycles

Virtual Cut-Through : Time taken = 570 clock cycles

In both cases the packet is of length 27 bits.

As an example that illustrates the performance of the *mad postman* under heavy traffic conditions, we present results for the transposition of a 32x32 8-bit integer matrix, using two hardware planes to emulate the four virtual acyclic planes. The sparsity value refers to the percentage of the permutation actually performed. So, in the case of 25% sparsity, only 1 in 4 of the matrix elements are actually routed. Note also that these figures are for a non-toroidal array:

Sparsity :	100%	50%	33%	25%
Mad Postman :	464	272	191	154
Virtual Cut-Through :	664	570	570	570

It should be noted that the results given for either strategy do not include the minimal overhead of writing the packets into the buffers initially, or the corresponding overhead of reading the arrivals.

We wish to make two comments on the above results. As the traffic density is increased the mad postman latency assymptotically increases towards that of virtual cut-through. In the limiting case of maximum traffic density at all times, the two strategies will be equal. The second comment is that due to its much higher latency, even in medium to light traffic densities, virtual cut-through, unlike the mad postman, cannot utilise the available channel bandwidth and thus yield a proportional reduction in permutation time.

Future work. Currently in progress are simulations of the various arrangements discussed. Furthermore, a full-custom CMOS implementation at a scale of one node per die is underway, the objective being to assess and minimise the silicon area required. It is envisaged however that with current VLSI densities a powerful processor and four hardware networks (one for each virtual plane) could easily be incorporated onto a single chip (ie. a packet routing transputer-like device).

The current version gives k=1 in the latency equation. Before discussing a k=0 version, there exists a method, in theory, of reducing k in discrete steps towards zero. The method involves the application of phased clocks across the array, the result being that k is reduced by the factor 1/(no. of phases). In other words, in one clock cycle a packet can propagate across n nodes, where n is the number of clock phases applied. Clearly, this is a promising area for further optimisation and research is currently focussed here. Another implementation, whereby a packet is received along all or part of a dimension (k=0) in one clock cycle, is both a viable and optimal implementation of the *mad postman*. Optical technology has a place here.

Another promising field of further research is the implementation of the *mad postman* in self-timed logic.

7.Conclusions

A network partitioning has been described for networks of processors, which allows the deadlock free routing of addressed packets of data, provided that the routing algorithm used provides a minimum distance path from a packet's source to its destination. This technique has been proven for a general class of networks and has been demonstrated for a regular 2-dimensional toroidal array.

The scheme has application to concurrent hardware implementation, as it partitions the network into independent virtual networks, in which packets once injected into a virtual network will remain in it until they have been routed to their destination.

The minimum buffering requirement is only one packet of data for each node in each virtual network. In some networks, it is possible to decrease this buffering still further by reducing the number of virtual networks required to partition the network. This may be achieved by allowing packets of data to be passed from one virtual network to another, provided that no cycles are introduced by this relaxation. In such cases, a message will have to be routed to its destination in each virtual network before being transferred to another.

This scheme serves as a basis for a low latency routing strategy named the *mad postman*. The *mad postman* outputs every packet along the same dimension it is arriving from, as soon as its first bit arrives and makes the routing decisions later. A number of 'dead' address flits equal to the network dimension (eg. two in the case of a 2-D array) may be generated in the process but they will quickly disappear from the network.

If well implemented, the *mad postman* will provide a message latency which is the absolute minimum achievable for its class (eg. synchronous or asynchronous networks). In an empty network, the speed of propagation of a packet will only be limited by the physical constraints of propagating a signal pulse (electrical, optical, etc.) between the source and the destination.

Obviously, as network size increases, so do the communication costs. A common solution has been to increase the network dimensionality, thus reducing the logical network diameter and providing more bandwidth per node. This however disproportionately increases the wiring costs, physical size and physical diameter of the system. With the same channel bandwidth per node the *mad postman* achieves the same throughput, and even lower latency.

8.References

[1] Dally WJ and Seitz C 1987 *Deadlock-Free Message Routing in Multiprocessor Interconnection Networks*, IEEE Trans Comp C-36 pp 547-553.

[2] Gelernter D 1981 *A DAG-Based Algorithm for Prevention of Store-and Forward Deadlock in Packet Networks*, IEEE Trans Comp C-30 pp 709-715.

[3] Roscoe AW 1987 *Routing Messages Through Networks: An Exercise in Deadlock Avoidance*, Oxford University Computing Laboratory Report.

[4] Yantchev JT, Jesshope CR 1988 *Adaptive, Low Latency, Deadlock-Free Packet Routing for Networks of Processors*, to be published IEE Proc.E.

[5] Jesshope CR, Miller PR, Yantchev JT 1988 *Programming with Active Data*, Proc. PARCELLA 88, Akademie-Verlag Berlin.

[6] Jesshope CR O'Gorman R, Stewart JM 1988 *A Microprocessor Array*, submitted to IEE Proc E.

[7] Seitz CL 1985 *The Cosmic Cube*, Comm ACM 28(1) pp 22-23.

[8] Kermani, Parviz, Kleinrock L 1979 *Virtual Cut-Through: A New Computer Communication Switching Technique*. Computer Networks 3 pp 267-286.

[9] Whobrey D et al 1988 *A Communications Chip for Multiprocessors*, Proc. CONPAR 88, Cambridge University Press.

[10] Roscoe AW, Dathi N 1986 *The Pursuit of Deadlock Freedom*, Oxford University Computing Laboratory Technical Monograph PRG-57.

[11] INMOS Ltd 1985 *The Occam Programming Manual*, Prentice Hall International.

[12] Miller PR, Yantchev JT, Jesshope CR 1989 *High Performance Packet Routing Based on Systolic Arrays*, Proc. Int. Conf. on Systolic Arrays 1989, Killarney, Ireland.

We would like to acknowledge the SERC for the support of Mr. Miller and the Bulgarian Ministry of Education for the support of Mr. Yantchev, both by Research Studentships.

Introducing Memory into the Switch Elements of Multiprocessor Interconnection Networks

Haim E. Mizrahi, Jean-Loup Baer, Edward D. Lazowska, and John Zahorjan

Department of Computer Science
University of Washington
Seattle, Washington 98195

Abstract

As VLSI technology continues to improve, circuit area is gradually being replaced by pin restrictions as the limiting factor in design. Thus, it is reasonable to anticipate that on-chip memory will become increasingly inexpensive since it is a simple, regular structure than can easily take advantage of higher densities.

In this paper we examine one way in which this trend can be exploited to improve the performance of multistage interconnection networks (MINs). In particular, we consider the performance benefits of placing significant memory in each MIN switch. This memory is used in two ways: to store (the unique copies of) data items and to maintain directories. The data storage function allows data to be placed nearer processors that reference it relatively frequently, at the cost of increased distance to other processors. The directory function allows data items to migrate in reaction to changes in program locality. We call our MIN architecture the Memory Hierarchy Network (MHN).

In a preliminary investigation of the merits of this design [8] we examined the performance of MHNs under the simplifying assumption that an unlimited amount of memory was available in each switch. We found that despite the longer switch processing times of the MHN, system performance is improved over simpler, conventional schemes based on caching.

In this paper we refine the earlier model to account for practical storage limitations. We study ways to reduce the amount of directory storage required by keeping only partial information regarding the current location of data items. The price paid for this reduction in memory requirement is more complicated (and in some circumstances slower) protocols. We obtain comparative performance estimates in an environment containing a single global memory module and a tree-structured MIN. Our results indicate that the MHN organization can have substantial performance benefits and so should be of increasing interest as the enabling technology becomes available.

1 Introduction

In this study a new architecture for shared memory multiprocessors, the Memory Hierarchy Network (MHN), is introduced and analyzed. The systems under study are medium scale multiprocessors where processors are connected to memory modules by a multistage interconnection network. The approach advocated here extends the memory hierarchy into the interconnection network, tailoring it to the specific needs of accessing shared variables. A hierarchy of memory elements is built into the switches of the interconnection network, and dynamic data positioning and routing protocols are introduced. The study focuses on the performance and cost of various realistic implementations of this idea.

The motivation for this study is that there may be a considerable performance penalty in existing systems when shared variables are heavily referenced. This problem will be aggravated by the need for bigger systems. Trends in VLSI technology will allow faster and denser CPUs and memory designs. The inter-chip communication times, however, will not be sped up in the same proportion. Because of these developments, traditional measures of cost, such as total memory space, will be replaced by design constraints such as interconnection costs and pin count. Thus, adding memory and some logic to the interconnection switches will become an attractive way to enhance system performance.

A key observation is that keeping coherent multiple copies of shared variables, in the context of a multistage interconnection network, is very traffic intensive. Therefore, the proposed scheme is based on keeping only a single copy of each shared writable variable in the system, and dynamically moving it in the extended memory hierarchy to adapt to changing access patterns. As there is only one copy of shared writable data, there cannot be any inconsistent data, i.e., the coherency problem does not exist. Therefore, this study does not provide "yet another coherency protocol". Rather, the main questions addressed here are when and where to migrate a data object, as opposed to when to create a new copy or when to invalidate or update an existing one.

The material presented here has two major parts. The first part reviews the background and recent relevant studies, discusses the motivation for a new architecture, and briefly presents the main ideas. In the second part, the performance of a tree network with practical amounts of memory in switches is analyzed in relation to the implementation cost.

2 Architecture Models

In this section the models of the parallel systems used in our study are presented. First, for the purposes of our performance comparisons, we define a baseline system in which shared writable data is not cached. We then present a "standard improvement" to that system that allows caching and uses a single, central directory to maintain coherency. Finally, we present an overview of the general MHN architecture and identify four specific versions of particular interest.

2.1 The baseline Processors-Caches model

The baseline architecture will be referred to as the Processors-Caches (PC) model. It contains N (a power of two) identical processors and associated local caches, a global memory, and a multistage interconnection network of depth log N.

In our model the caches are used exclusively for private and read-only shared data, as well as (non-writable) code. Accesses to local caches always result in hits satisfied in a single processor cycle. In other words, we assume a fast, conflict-free conventional multistage network that is transparent to the architecture.

Global memory is used for shared writable data. It is accessed through the network, and a cache is placed between each memory module and the network to speed accesses. (Note that there is no coherency problem associated with a single cache located at this port.)

To simplify our feasibility study, we decompose the model by assuming that there is only a single memory module. Therefore, our interconnection network is a complete binary tree with the global memory (and its cache) at the root and processors at the leaves. Because the single module case is not preferential to either the MHN or conventional network designs, the comparative results obtained for this model should be applicable to systems with larger numbers of memory modules.

We assume that read requests to global memory are synchronous, that is, the issuing processor waits for the result. The use of the interconnection network, memory access latency time, and potential memory contention cause the processor to remain idle for some period of time during this request. In contrast, write requests are assumed to be asynchronous: the issuing processor immediately resumes computing after the request packet is placed on the network.

We define the processor cycle time to be equal to one. The relatively simple switches in our PC model are also assumed to have unit cycle times. The global memory module has an access time of four.

2.2 The directory-based scheme

A clear weakness of the PC architecture is that all accesses to writable shared data must be sent to the global memory

module. Performance may be improved through the use of "directory schemes" [1]. This involves caching data items at the processors and using a single, central directory located at the root to maintain coherence. In the simplest directory scheme, which we call DIR, only a single copy of each shared data block is kept in the system. (Note that this policy corresponds to policy "Dir1NB" from [1].) As will be seen shortly, the MHN also maintains only a single copy of each data item. Thus, the comparisons between DIR and the MHN serve to isolate the contribution of the dynamic routing capabilities of the latter.

Because the switches required by the DIR scheme are not substantially more complicated than those required by PC, we assume the same cycle times for them. This is a slightly optimistic assumption for DIR, and so serves to understate somewhat the performance advantages of the MHN design demonstrated in Section 4.

2.3 The MHN architecture

As in the DIR scheme, data items in the MHN architecture may move dynamically from one memory to another (although only a single copy of a data item can be present in the system at a time). However, the MHN extends the DIR scheme in two ways. Firstly, switches of the MHN can hold data. Thus, data can be present not only in the global memory module and the caches located at the processors, but also at intermediate stages of the interconnection network. Secondly, MHN switches contain directories indicating the location of items stored in the subtrees for which they are the roots. Thus, the information in the single directory of the DIR scheme is partially replicated and distributed among the interconnection network switches of the MHN.

The exact manner in which data movement takes place in an MHN is controlled by a data migration policy. In the selection of an appropriate migration policy for use in the MHN there are two dimensions to be considered: "when should data be migrated?" and "how far toward the referencing processor should it be migrated?". A family of answers to the question of "when" is given by "each time the last j references are from the same processor" for differing values of j. For example, for j=1 data items are moved on every reference, while for j=2 two successive references to the item must come from the same processor before migration takes place. Similarly, a family of answers to the question of "how far" is given by "k steps" for various values of k. Here obvious choices for k are 1 (one step toward the referencing processor) and ∞ (all the way to the referencing processor). We introduce the notation MHN/j/k to denote the MHN policy that moves a data item k positions after j consecutive references by the same processor.

Intuitively, appropriate values for parameters j and k of the migration policy relate to the assumptions made about the "burstiness" of workload. A workload is considered bursty if it exhibits alternating periods of high and low frequency of access to individual data items. (In contrast, the workload behavior is considered to be "random" if the frequency of access to an individual data item is relatively constant over time.) A workload becomes increasingly bursty when, other factors (in particular, overall average reference rate) held fixed, either the length of the high frequency periods increases or the access rate during the low frequency periods decreases.

Parameter k of the migration policy relates to the assumed length of a burst. The longer a burst is likely to be, the more advantageous it is to move data towards the referencing processor despite the fact that this moves it away from many other processors. Thus, parameter k should be large for bursty workloads and small for random workloads.

Parameter j relates to the low frequency reference rate. It is used to detect when a burst has begun. Some references to a data item are made even during periods of overall low frequency. It is counter-productive to migrate a data item in response to these accesses. For a very bursty workload, however, these low frequency period accesses are rare. Thus, for a bursty workload j can be small, that is, it is safe to assume that (nearly) all references to the data item indicate the beginning of a high access frequency period.

In the work presented here, we have chosen to evaluate four specific policies:

1. MHN/1/1: Move the data one step on each reference. Here a step is one edge in the path from the current location towards the processor that issued the request.

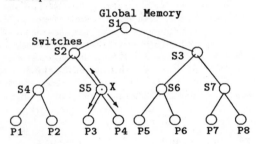

Figure 1: Data Migration in a Tree MHN/1/1 Architecture

Consider the example shown in Figure 1. The data block X, located in switch $S5$, will move to switch $S2$ if the next reference to it is made by a processor in the set $\{P1, P2, P5, P6, P7, P8\}$. If the reference is made from $P3$ or $P4$, it will move to the local cache of the referencing processor.

2. MHN/2/2: Move the data two steps after two successive references from the same processor. This policy has almost the same "speed of migration" as the previous one but is more conservative in its estimate of when a burst has begun.

3. MHN/1/∞: Move the data all the way to the requesting processor on each reference. Note that while a requested data item is never migrated into a switch memory other than at the processors, all switches contain some data storage. This storage is used to "bubble up" replaced data items that arise when a lower level memory is full and a new item must be migrated there.

4. MHN/2/∞: Move the data all the way to the requesting processor on each two successive references from the same processor.

The performance evaluation of these alternatives is presented in Section 4. For brevity in what follows, whenever

a detailed description is needed we will demonstrate the operation of the MHN/1/1 policy.

As will be seen in the next section, implementation of an MHN requires switches that are more complicated than those needed for the PC or DIR designs. Thus, in our performance evaluation of MHN we assume a switch cycle time of two, i.e., twice the cycle time of the switches in the simpler networks. (The one exception is that the MHN switches connected directly to the processors are relatively simple, acting as normal caches. Thus, we keep the unit cycle time assumption for those switches.)

3   The Design of MHN Networks

3.1   Switch protocols

In this section possible designs for MHN switches are discussed and their relative complexity and performance are compared. The complexity of these switches can be substantial, mainly as a result of the dynamic routing capabilities. Therefore, attention is focused on cost/performance tradeoffs in the implementation of the directories.

The basic operation of a switch consists of three tasks. First, as part of the global but distributed shared *memory*, the switch controls accesses to the data currently held in its local store. The switch data memory acts as a conventional memory module in a global memory system. However, because the position of data changes dynamically, the local data memory is accessed associatively, like a cache.

Second, as part of a global but distributed *directory*, the switch performs routing of requests from processors to memory. Arriving request packets are routed according to information on the current location of the requested data. Since routing decisions are made locally, a switch needs to hold enough information to uniquely select an appropriate port to forward the request. In contrast to a global directory approach, the routing information in a switch need not be updated on every movement of the data, but only when there is a change in the port through which the data is accessible, i.e., when the data passes through the switch.

Finally, as part of a conventional multistage interconnection network, the switch performs "static" routing of packets on the return path from memory to processors.

3.2   Switch structure

Figure 2 depicts a schematic block diagram of an MHN switch. The major components are:

1. Input and output buffers, implemented as First In First Out (FIFO) queues. The external inter-switch links can carry only one packet at a time. Whenever a destination buffer at a switch is full, transfers to it are stalled.

2. I/O ports. Each switch has six unidirectional ports, two for each of its neighbors ("Up", "Left" and "Right"), allowing full-duplex communication. The data paths of the inter-switch links are wide enough to handle one packet in a cycle.

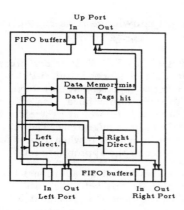

Figure 2: Basic MHN Switch Structure

3. Internal busses. The internal busses and logic can transfer a packet from each input port to any output queue in a switch cycle. Separate parts of the output queue allow insertion of multiple packets into it, thus avoiding contention when more than one packet is routed to the same port. The head of the output queue is one of the heads of its sub-queues, selected randomly by arbitration logic. (Similar assumptions have been made for almost all interconnection network performance evaluations, and a switch design that achieves this degree of parallelism was designed for the NYU architecture [3].)

4. Data memory. This is the part of the global shared memory that is currently located in the switch. It is organized like a cache. The size of the data memory depends on the size of the global memory, the technology used, and the switch's level in the network. The appropriate amount of memory at each level depends on the migration policy. For the MHN/(1 or 2)/∞ policies, for example, it will be reasonable to allocate a substantial portion of the memory to the leaves (processors) and to the levels near the root.

5. Routing directory. This part of the switch holds dynamically updated routing information. As routing is performed locally in each switch, the relative position ("Up", "Left", or "Right") of the data is sufficient. An important aspect of this work is to assess the complexity and the performance implications of various directory implementations. Two possible approaches are valid: (1) a single directory, which is accessed for routing all the packets through the switch, or, (2) separate subdirectories, each holding routing information for the data accessible through a particular external port. (Figure 2 depicts the latter organization.) Note that a separate directory for data stored locally is not necessary, as "hits" or "misses" on the local data store provide this information explicitly.

3.3 Basic switch operation and protocol under optimistic assumptions

The simplest switch protocol is based on two assumptions: that the data memory in each switch is large enough to contain all the shared data, and that the switches' directories hold "full knowledge" (i.e., they include routing information for *all* data blocks that are located in all descendants of the switch). Under these optimistic conditions: (1) data entries are never replaced, (2) routing information is never lost because of lack of space in a directory, (3) broadcasting is not needed, and (4) requests that cannot be serviced locally are forwarded through one port only. The protocol assures that whenever a data block is stored in a switch or transferred through it, the appropriate entry in the directory at the switch is updated. For data blocks that have never been transferred through a switch, the default information ("Up", as initialized) correctly indicates that packets referring to this data should be forwarded upwards.

The "full knowledge directory" switch protocol distinguishes among the following five types of packets: Read (issued when a processor loads a shared writable data item), Write (issued when a processor stores a shared data item), Answer (issued by a switch to forward data in response to a Read request), Answer Migrate (like Answer, but carrying a migration counter to support MHN/j/k policies), and Write Migrate (like Write but carrying a migration counter).

The assumption of unlimited memory space on which this straightforward protocol is based is not tractable for large systems. In practice, only limited memories are available and therefore misses on both the data store and the directory must be addressed. Replacement policies for data and directory entries, and routing in cases when information on the location of the data is not available, need to be specified. These modifications to the basic protocol are discussed in the next section.

3.4 Alternative directory organizations

In this section we discuss possible directory organizations. The possibilities fall into two groups. In the first, the "full knowledge" approach, each directory keeps information sufficient to forward on the correct port an arriving request for any data item. These organizations admit relatively simple routing protocols but require extensive directory memory.

The second approach requires that directories keep information on only some subset of the global data items. Here memory requirements are reduced at the price of more complicated protocols in the event that no information on the requested data item exists in the directory.

3.4.1 Full Knowledge Bit Map directories (FKBM)

A simple way to keep full routing information is to hold in each switch a full bit-map table, with an entry for each block in the shared memory subsystem. For the dynamic routing protocol in a tree network two bits are enough to encode the three possible relative positions of each data block ("Up", "Left", or "Right"). A fourth logical location information, "Local", is not kept explicitly in the directory, but is available to the router by checking the local data memory.

The obvious advantages of this approach are the simplicity of the protocol and the overall performance that all full knowledge schemes exhibit. By keeping a full bit map, the directory entry corresponding to each data block can be directly accessed and there is no need for associative search. By keeping full routing information for every block, no broadcasting is ever needed. The disadvantages of this approach are the size of the directories needed and the lack of scalability. The directory size in each switch grows linearly with the size of the global memory for shared data. Bigger directories will not only increase the cost of the implementation but will also mean slower switches, as the time to perform a memory access is a function of the memory size.

3.4.2 Full Knowledge Set Associative directories (FKSA)

An alternative full knowledge organization can be obtained by observing that each switch need keep track only of those data items that currently reside in the memories of descendant switches. Given this "inclusion property" [2], a very simple protocol suffices to effect correct routing: on a directory "hit", the packet is routed either "Left" or "Right" according to the routing information in the directory; on a "miss", the request is forwarded "Up".

As compared with FKBM, under FKSA the directory memory requirement of each switch is reduced from linear in the total amount of global memory to linear in the amount of memory contained in its descendants. Nonetheless, this still represents a substantial number of directory items in at least some switches (those near the root). To make manageable the task of building hardware to support these directories, a set associative scheme is used.

Let us denote by $A_{dir}(i)$ the associativity of the directories of switch i at the l_i^{th} level in the tree, by $A_{data}(i)$ the associativity of the data memory, and by $S_{dir}(i)$ and $S_{data}(i)$ the number of sets in the directory and data memory respectively. Then it can be proven ([2], [7]) that the inclusion condition requires

$$A_{dir}(i) \geq \sum_{j \in Des(i)} A_{data}(j) * \max(1, \lceil \frac{S_{data}(j)}{S_{dir}(i)} \rceil) \qquad (1)$$

Note that the number of sets in the data memory and the directories need not be fixed over the entire network. The last factor in the equation above takes into account the ratio of the number of data sets to the number of directory sets. If the number of sets in the (parent) directory is bigger than the number of sets in the (descendant) data memory, the ratio is less than 1, and the associativity of the directory "includes" room for all the entries in the data memory. If the directory has fewer sets than a descendant data memory, several sets of the descendant will fall into the same set in the parent directory, and the associativity is increased to reserve enough room for all the data blocks. Note that the maximum in the equation is taken for each level independently, guaranteeing that there is enough room for the routing information of each data block in each descendant level independently, regardless of the organization in other descendant levels.

3.4.3 The full knowledge data replacement protocol

Both the FKBM and FKSA directory organization are based on finite data memories in the switches. This finiteness causes a "data replacement" whenever a migration packet tries to write into a filled data set. Some modifications to the basic protocol are therefore necessary to handle the cases of data migration. The only cases when a directory entry is replaced is when a *local data store* in a switch has no place in the appropriate set.

The protocol makes use of an additional type of packet, labeled "DataMigrate" packets, that will be used to migrate a data block when a replacement occurs. Writing new routing information in an unfilled set of a directory poses no problems. Writing new routing information into a filled set requires more care. To avoid any loss of routing information when the location information of a migrating packet needs to replace an existing entry in the directory, the protocol limits the migration of data blocks into its sub-trees. Since there is always enough room in each directory for all data blocks in its descendant switches, a full directory set implies that the corresponding sets in the data memories in the descendant switches are also full, and local data replacement will take place. In these cases, the data replacement protocol will free a line (an entry in the local data set), making room for the new data entry. The protocol makes use of an "overflow" buffer to temporarily store routing information for added entries. During this time, additional data migrations whose directory entries fall in the same set are disallowed. The overflow buffer holds the routing information for data blocks that are currently being inserted into the sub-tree, until a data block is migrated out of the sub-tree to free a directory entry. When the "overflow" buffer is full, no additional migrations are allowed. (Overflow buffer entries are removed when the replaced data arrives at the switch).

3.4.4 Partial Knowledge Set Associative directories (PKSA)

In this section, the full knowledge conditions are relaxed, allowing switch directories to be smaller at the cost of more complicated request routing protocols. This leads to the design of limited set associative directories, holding only partial routing information.

The organization of PKSA follows that of FKSA, with the difference that the associativity is not required to increase with the level in the tree. This means that a PKSA switch is incapable of keeping directory entries for all data items in descendant switches. When a switch decides to add a new directory entry and the set into which that item falls is full, the switch simply discards one of the existing entries. There is no need for the switch to notify either the parent or descendant nodes of this action.

Clearly, PKSA does not satisfy the inclusion or full knowledge conditions. However, a modified form of the inclusion property does hold: although blocks can be located in the sub-tree and not have a valid entry in the directory, all the (valid) entries in the directories refer to data blocks located in the sub-tree. Therefore, no blocks that are not located in the sub-tree can have a valid entry in the directory.

An additional requirement of PKSA networks needed to make the data location protocol work is that the root directory *is* inclusive, that is, it contains routing information for all data items held by its descendants. In this sense, PKSA resembles the DIR scheme. However, there are two important differences. First, while the number of directory entries at the root under PKSA is the same as that for DIR, the amount of information per item under PKSA is substantially smaller. This is because PKSA stores only *routing* information (i.e., "Left", "Right", or "Up"), while DIR must store *location* information (i.e., a processor address). Second, because DIR stores location information, the root must be notified *every* time a data item changes location. In contrast, the root of a PKSA network needs to update its routing information only when the data item is migrated through the root (from one subtree to the other).

The protocol used to handle directory misses takes advantage of the modified inclusion property of PKSA networks. The protocol has two phases: an initial search up the tree until a directory is located that contains information on the data item, followed by a search down the tree to locate the item itself. The search up the tree is performed using SearchUpRead and SearchUpWrite packets. A switch receiving such a packet and neither storing the data item nor having a directory entry for it simply forwards the packet to its parent. We are guaranteed to reach eventually a directory holding routing information for the data item because of the pure inclusion property of the root directory.

Once routing information has been encountered, a downward search for the data item begins. If the switch with the routing information does not actually contain the data item, it sends a Read or Write packet as appropriate down the port indicated by its directory entry. Each subsequent switch receiving a Read or Write packet (and not containing the data item) interrogates its directory for further routing information. If such information is present, the packet is simply forwarded. If there is no directory entry present for the data item, we cannot know which subtree the data item is in. Thus, in this case the switch sends a BroadcastRead or BroadcastWrite packet down both the Left and the Right port.

The broadcast mechanism assures that the data referred to in the packet will be located so long as it is resident in the sub-tree where the broadcast takes place. A problem may arise when a broadcast packet (*bp*) references a data block that currently is being migrated out of the sub-tree to which *bp* is being sent. This can be solved by searching through a buffer holding recently sent broadcasts (or migration packets). Each broadcast (migrating packet) is placed in the buffer as soon as it is inserted in the output queue, and is removed from this buffer only after an acknowledgement message (BroadcastAck) is received.

4 The Performance of MHN Networks

In this section, the performance of systems built with limited data memories and partial directories is examined. A controlled set of experiments, in which the original assumptions concerning the memories in the systems are gradually relaxed, is conducted. By comparing the performance of the different designs, an assessment of the major consequences of the various organizations is possible:

1. The effect of *data* misses and replacements is evaluated by comparing the performance of the full knowledge MHN network with unlimited memory space to the performance of full knowledge MHN networks with limited data memory.

2. The effect of limited *directory* memory is evaluated by comparing the performance of FKSA to PKSA.

4.1 Workload characterization

It is clear that the workload used in comparing interconnection network architectures can have a strong influence on the results. For example, a (perhaps artificial) workload exhibiting little or no locality of reference will tend to favor a very simple network built out of fast, dumb switches over a network with smarter, slower switches.

Unfortunately, measurement data about the behavior of real workloads is scarce [4], and so it is not possible to make performance comparisons using "a typical, live workload". Because of this, a flexible abstract model of reference patterns is adopted that allows, through varying parameterizations of a single basic workload model, the exploration of the interconnection network performance over a wide spectrum of possible program behaviors.

The analytical workload model is specified by five parameters:

$$< Shared, AverBurst, NoObjects, Contention, Write >$$

The first parameter, *Shared*, is defined as the fraction of a processor's references that are to shared writable data out of the total number of memory references (both private and shared) that it makes. As only shared references are placed on the MHN network, this parameter controls the overall load on the network.

In comparing conventional interconnection networks and the MHN, we are particularly interested in the impact of locality. Our locality measure, *AverBurst*, reflects the tendency of a processor to reference repeatedly shared variables during a relatively short period of time. It specifies the average length of a burst of references (that is, the average number of consecutive shared references to the same data item.) When one burst ends, the next burst to begin is for a data item that is chosen at random among all the shared writable data items. The number of such items is given by *NoObjects*.

The third parameter, *Contention*, is defined as the fraction of memory references generated by a processor to randomly chosen shared data objects. Each processor is considered to have at all times a set of current "burst variables" which it references with probability (1 − *Contention*) on each shared variable reference. With probability *Contention* a shared variable reference is made to some other data item, chosen uniformly. These accesses are not included in the burst produced by this processor, but rather represent occasional references to other global data items which are accessed from within a burst.p

Parameter *Write* is defined as the fraction of accesses to shared data that change the value of the accessed data item.

While it is possible to choose different values for these parameters for each data item and processor (as appropriate), a homogeneous system, in which a single parameter value applies to all processors and data items, is assumed. This simplifies the interpretation of results, as well as the construction and manipulation of the models.

To summarize, we briefly describe the processor behavior in terms of workload model parameters. On each cycle, each processor generates a single reference (provided that it is not waiting for a pending memory request). This reference is either to a private or to a shared data object, in the proportion specified by the *Shared* parameter. Each shared request is either a read or a write, with proportions that are specified by the *Write* parameter. To generate the address of the request, a data item is first selected following the *Contention*, and *AverBurst* parameters. When generating a *Contention* request, this item is picked at random uniformly from the appropriate set of data items. When generating a burst request, the likelihood of continuing the one of the current bursts from the given processor is specified by *AverBurst*.

4.2 Performance evaluation methodology

We have used simulation to obtain performance estimates because of the complexity of the mechanisms being investigated. However, there is a basic limitation to this approach in this domain. So long as we have infinite memory in the switches, the simulation results are insensitive to the number of data objects in the global shared memory. For the infinite memory case, different data objects do not interact and the presence of a data item in a given switch is not affected by references made to other data items. In the finite memory case this is no longer true, since the migration of one data item can cause the replacement of another one. Because of a practical limitation on the simulation run's CPU time, we could not simulate systems with realistic memory sizes. However, it is common practice in studies of this type to run simulations with a limited number of data objects to efficiently produce approximate results. A "scaled down" system is used in the simulation in which the size of the data memory and directory in the simulated system is proportional to the size of real systems. We have checked the sensitivity of our results to the number of data objects in the global shared memory over the range in which it was still feasible to simulate a 128 processors system. The changes in the performance metrics were minor. Unless otherwise stated, the results reported below are a system with 128 processors and 512 shared writable data items.

4.3 The effect of limited data memory

In this section we evaluate the effect of limited data memory. The question to be answered is the extent to which the limitation of the data memory degrades performance due to longer access times (since less data can be stored close to the processors) and the increased network traffic generated by data migrations needed for replacements. We assess this impact by comparing limited data memory versions to unlimited data memory versions, with unlimited directory memory in each case. (The performance of MHN with both limited data and directory memories, as well as

a comparison of MHN performance with the simpler PC and DIR designs, is considered subsequently.)

Figure 3 displays the effect of finite data memories on the four MHN architectures for two locality patterns (*AverBurst*= 2, 20) as a function of memory size. (A memory size of '1' indicates that a total storage equivalent to 1024 data objects is distributed among all the switches in the network.) In our examples there are 512 shared writable data objects (i.e., *NoObjects*=512). Directories are organized as FKSA. The total data memory has been allocated among the MHN switches in an attempt to equalize their utilizations, that is, the ratio of the number of valid entries to the capacity.

The Y-axis of Figure 3 is the ratio of the effective processing power of the system with limited data memory to that of the same system with unlimited data memory. We call this ratio a "speedup gain".

It is interesting to compare the sensitivity of different MHN architectures to the limitation of memory space, as a function of the locality in the access pattern. As can be seen, the MHN/1/1 architecture is the most sensitive to the allocation of memory in the switches, while MHN/2/∞ and MHN/1/∞ are the less sensitive . This is expected, as these latter policies do not allocate data in the memories of the network switches. Thus, data objects which are no longer in use percolate slowly towards the root, becoming more accessible to a new user (processor). In fact, because of this phenomenon the performance of more limited memory space systems can be better than that of less limited ones. This is observed for the unit memory configurations, which outperform configurations richer in memory space. Generally, the degradation in performance due to limited memory unit configuration exhibits a sharp knee. While the 6 memory unit configuration has essentially the same performance as the unlimited memory case, and the degradation due to a 2 memory unit limitation is between about 40% of speedup in the MHN/1/1 case, reducing the data memory further, as 1.0 or 0.1 units, causes a steep degradation.

4.4 The effect of limited directory memory

In this section the effect of limited associativity in the directories is studied.

To assess the relative effect that the restricted directory organization has on performance, we checked the performance under the PKSA protocol, which includes the search, broadcast and broadcast–acknowledgement phases. We measured the degradation relative to the FKSA case. We also recorded the number of broadcast packets, the level at which they were introduced, and the level at which they were consumed.

Figure 4 displays the expected performance of MHN/1/1 and MHN/2/∞ in their PKSA implementation. (Other MHN policies behave similarly.) The speedup is compared to that of the same architectures with full knowledge directories and the same data memory capacity. We note that for small localities (small burst lengths), performance is almost unaffected by limited directory space. This insensitivity is the result of the fact that for both policies data items never migrate very far from the root.

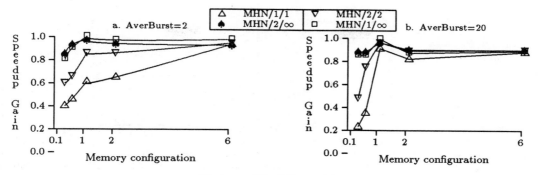

Figure 3: The Effect of Limited Data Memory

For higher localities (longer burst lengths), data is more spread out throughout the MHN. Thus, directory information is more important, resulting in some noticeable differences between the limited and unlimited directory memory schemes. The degradation caused is quite modest, however, never exceeding 20%.

Comparing the different migration policies, we observe that the MHN/1/1 architecture is much more sensitive to the organization of the directories than MHN/2/∞. This is intuitive, as MHN/x/∞ policies make much less usage of the data memories of the network switches. The MHN/2/∞ policy performs well because it is selective about which data objects should be placed in the (limited) data memories. Data blocks that are randomly accessed are not migrated, and therefore, the data memory holds only those objects that have a high probability of being accessed in bursts. So long as the capacity is sufficient to contain this active working set the performance is good.

4.5 The bottom line

We conclude this section by exploring the performance of MHN architectures with limited memory relative to the performance of PC and DIR architectures. This will be the "bottom line" of the expected performance, incorporating the degradation due to all the restrictions implied by limited data memories and practical partial directories. All the sources of overhead discussed above (data replacements, searching and broadcasting) are included in this evaluation.

Figure 5 shows the ratio of the effective processing power under a number of organizations to that obtained by the basic PC scheme. As can be seen, except for workloads exhibiting essentially no locality, the expected performance of MHN/1/1, MHN/2/2, and MHN/2/∞ is very good compared to both PC and DIR. All of the MHN architectures exhibit substantial performance gains, but the MHN/x/∞ schemes are clearly superior. This is an indication that much of the performance benefit of the MHN comes from the dynamic routing capability provided by the switch directories rather than from the ability to store data in intermediate levels of the network. Quantitatively, MHN/2/2 exhibits a factor of 2.2 to 3.2 improvement over PC, and MHN/2/∞ a factor of 2.2 to 4.0 (for the longer burst length). However, the MHN/1/1 scheme presents little advantage (and even a potential degradation at light loads) over the much simpler DIR scheme, making the cost effec-

tiveness of this policy questionable.

5 Conclusions

The main conclusion of the feasibility study is that the MHN approach, based on the inclusion of data memories and dynamic routing capabilities in the switching elements of the interconnection network, is a promising one. The use of sophisticated switches in the implementation of the network for shared data was demonstrated to offer a significant performance improvement.

The price for this performance gain is more complex switches, with a substantial amount of memory. The implementation of such switches requires an ambitious VLSI design. In particular, large and fast memories are required in each switch for directory (and possibly data) storage. Based on the trends in VLSI technology, we believe that such switches will become feasible in the near future.

Specifically for the MHN, an obvious observation is that most of the complexity of the switch structure stems from the directories used to locate the data items. Recall that the dynamic routing capability is the major reason for observed performance gain. Thus, the price paid for implementing the dynamic routing cannot be avoided. The simulation results show that, under the wide set of assumptions made in the workload model, the dynamic routing capability of the switches contributed most of the performance gain, while the introduction of memory in the switches was found to be beneficial in only a limited domain.

Another important result can be inferred from the performance of the deferred migration policies (MHN/2/x), which performs substantially better than the commonly used "copy on the first reference". We claim that this has general applicability in the domain of multistage networks, where the cost of indiscriminate copying is high. Whenever there is only a single copy for each shared variable, its location becomes very important. Therefore, the decisions of whether to migrate a data item, and where to migrate it, should correlate with workload behavior. The workload used in our study exhibits bursts that are reliably indicated by two successive references from the same processor. Mapping this as a decision rule into the migration logic of each switch has little ramification on the hardware, but requires additional memory space for state information. The results show that this additional cost is well rewarded, in terms of improved performance.

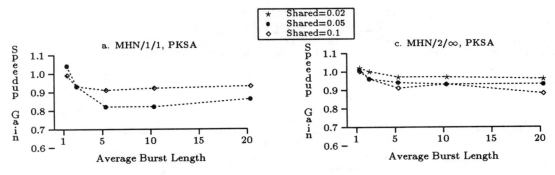

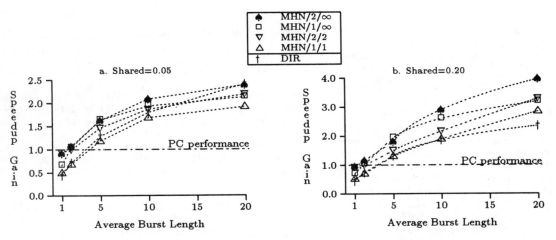

Figure 4: The Effect of Limited Directory Memory

Figure 5: "Bottom line" (PKSA) Performance

Acknowledgements

This material is based on work supported by the National Science Foundation (Grants DCR-8352098, CCR-8619663, CCR-8702915, and CCR-8703049), the Naval Ocean Systems Center, U S WEST Advanced Technologies , The Washington Technology Center, and Digital Equipment Corporation (the External Research Program and the System Research Center). Additional partial support for this work was generously provided by Bell Communications Research, Boeing Computer Services, Tektronix, Inc., the Xerox Corporation, and the Weyerhauser Company. The Centre National de la Recherche Scientifique, France, and Laboratoire MASI, University of Paris 6, provided generous support and resources for Zahorjan for the year sabbatical leave during which this work was performed.

References

[1] Agarwal, A., Simoni, R., Hennessy J. and Horowitz, M. "An Evaluation of Directory Schemes for Cache Coherence". In *Proc. 15th Int. Symp. on Computer Architecture*, pages 280–289, 1988.

[2] Baer,, J.-L. and Wang, W.-H. "On the Inclusion Property for Multi-Level Cache Hierarchies". In *Proc. 15th Int. Symp. on Computer Architecture*, pages 73–80, 1988.

[3] Dickey, S., Kenner, R., Snir, M. and Solworth, J. "A VLSI Combining Network for the NYU Ultracomputer". *Ultracomputer Note 85*, June 1985.

[4] Eggers, J., and Katz, Randy H. "A Charaterization of Sharing in Parallel Programs and its Applicability to Coherency Protocol Evaluation". In *Proc. 15th Int. Symp. on Computer Architecture*, pages 373–382, 1988.

[5] Goodman, J.R., and Woset, P.J. "The Wisconsin Multicube: A New Large-Scale Data-Coherent Multiprocessor". In *Proc. 15th Int. Symp. on Computer Architecture*, pages 422–433, 1988.

[6] Kruskal, C.P. and Snir, M. "The Performance of Multistage Interconnection Networks for Multiprocessors". *IEEE Trans. on Computers*, pages 1091–1098, December 1983.

[7] Mizrahi, E. Haim. *"Extending the Memory Hierarchy into Multiprocessor Interconnection Networks"*. University of Washington, Dept. of Comp. Sci., Ph.D. Dissertation, Technical Report 88-11-03, November 1988.

[8] Mizrahi, H.E., Baer, J.-L., Lazowska, E.D., and Zahorjan, J. *"Extending the Memory Hierarchy into Multiprocessor Interconnection Networks: A Performance Analysis"*. University of Washington, Dept. of Comp. Sci., Tech. Report 88-11-10, November 1988.

USING FEEDBACK TO CONTROL TREE SATURATION IN MULTISTAGE INTERCONNECTION NETWORKS*

Steven L. Scott and Gurindar S. Sohi

Computer Sciences Department
University of Wisconsin-Madison
1210 W. Dayton Street
Madison, WI 53706

Abstract

In this paper, we propose the use of feedback schemes in multiprocessors which use an interconnection network with distributed routing control. We show that by altering system behavior so as to minimize the occurrence of a performance-degrading situation in the network, the overall throughput of the system can be improved.

As an example, we have considered the problem of tree saturation caused by hot spots in multistage interconnection networks. Tree saturation degrades the performance of all processors in a system, including those not participating in the hot spot activity. We see that feedback schemes can be used to control tree saturation, reduce degradation to memory requests that are not to the hot memory module and increase overall system bandwidth. As a companion to feedback schemes, damping schemes are also considered. Simulation studies presented in this paper show that feedback schemes can improve overall system performance significantly in many cases.

1. INTRODUCTION

One of the most important and widely used concepts in the design of engineering control systems is the concept of dynamic *feedback* [3]. Feedback is primarily used to: i) prevent instability in a system and ii) prevent the system from settling down into a stable but undesirable state. Fig. 1 illustrates how feedback works. Without feedback (Fig. 1(a)), the inputs of the system are independent of events that might be occurring in the system. Consequently, an unstable or an undesirable situation could arise. With feedback (Fig. 1(b)), the outputs of the system (and possibly other state values of the system) are fed back to the system input generator. Using the feedback information, the system input generator tries to modify the system inputs and prevent the occurrence of an unstable or an undesirable situation in the system.

Modern computing systems have evolved into large-scale parallel processors that consist of possibly hundreds of processors and memory modules interconnected together in some fashion. Fig. 2 illustrates a typical processing system based on a shared memory

programming paradigm [1, 15]. The processing system consists of a set of processing elements, a set of memory modules and an interconnection network. The interconnection network is logically broken into a forward network and a reverse network though it is possible that the two networks could be the same physical network (for

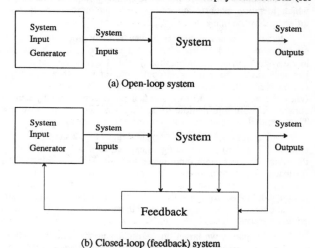

(a) Open-loop system

(b) Closed-loop (feedback) system

Fig. 1: An Engineering Control System.

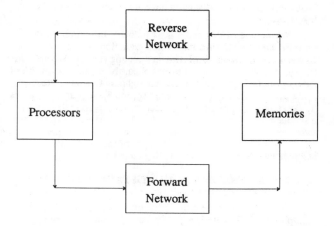

Fig. 2: A Typical Shared Memory Multiprocessing System.

* This work was supported by NSF Grant CCR-8706722.

example, a set of buses). It is important to realize that the overall performance of such a processing system is not determined solely by the performance of the individual components; it is affected by how the components interact dynamically when they are connected together.

Let us compare Figs. 1 and 2. If we assume that the forward interconnection network is the system, then the inputs to the system are the requests generated by the processors and the outputs of the system are the inputs to the memory modules. An example of an undesirable situation in such a system is blockage or congestion that unnecessarily reduces the effective bandwidth of the system (interconnection network). Considering the resemblance between Figs. 1 and 2, we ask ourselves: i) why has explicit feedback not been used thus far in the design of computing systems and ii) why might it be useful now?

Traditionally, a computing system consisted of a single processor (system input generator). In a single processor system, the control mechanism of the processor has sufficient information about the state of the overall system (processor, network and memory) to prevent the occurrence of an undesirable situation. This is because the single processor is generally the only entity generating requests which can alter the state of the system. Moreover, there exists some implicit feedback in the responses to memory requests; the rate at which memory requests are entered into the network is directly influenced by the rate at which responses are received.

In a multiprocessor system, however, many processors are generating requests without knowledge of the state of other components in the system. In such a processing system, it is possible that the collective input of the processors could interact in such a way as to cause undesirable degradation of the network. The implicit feedback (via the reverse network) to individual processors generally cannot convey enough information to correct the anomalous behavior. Thus, explicit feedback mechanisms may be warranted.

One could alter the processing system of Fig. 2 to resemble the system of Fig. 1(b) by providing an explicit feedback from points in the system to the system input generators (see Fig. 3). This explicit feedback could then be used to detect potential undesirable situations and instruct the processors to modify their inputs to the network such that they do not contribute to the undesirable situation. If an undesirable situation is prevented, the overall performance of the system could be enhanced.

In this paper, we target one particular undesirable situation in parallel computer systems that use buffered multistage interconnection networks -- the problem of *tree saturation*. We demonstrate how feedback concepts can be used to instruct the processors to modify their requests to the interconnection network so that the problem is alleviated.

The outline of this paper is as follows. In section 2, we consider the undesirable situation of tree saturation in multistage interconnection networks with a distributed routing control. We point out that, if tree saturation could be controlled, the overall bandwidth of the network (and consequently the throughput of the multiprocessor) could be improved in many cases. In section 3, we propose schemes for controlling tree saturation. In section 4, we present the results of a simulation analysis carried out to test the effectiveness of the tree-saturation-controlling mechanisms. In section 5, we present a discussion of the feedback concept in light of the results of section 4, and in section 6 we present concluding remarks.

2. TREE SATURATION IN MULTISTAGE INTERCONNECTION NETWORKS

A popular interconnection network for medium to large scale multiprocessors is a blocking, buffered $O(N log N)$ multistage interconnection network (ICN) with distributed routing control. An example of such a ICN is the Omega network [10]. An Omega network consists of $log N$ levels of switching elements (or switches). Messages enter the network at the inputs to the first stage and proceed to the outputs of the last stage, one level at a time. Routing

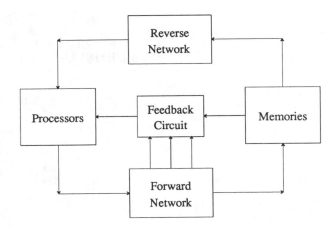

Fig. 3: A Shared Memory Multiprocessing System with Feedback.

decisions are made local to each switch. Since there is no global control mechanism, the state of any particular switch is unknown to other entities (processors, memories, other switches) in the multiprocessor and a particular input request pattern to the network might cause an undesirable situation.

The problem of *tree saturation* is a classic example of what we consider to be an undesirable situation in a multiprocessor system. This problem was first observed by Pfister and Norton in conjunction with requests to a *hot spot* [13]. In their analysis, the hot spot was caused by accesses to a shared lock variable. When the average request rate to a *hot memory module* exceeds the rate at which the module services the requests, the requests will back up in the switch which connects to the hot memory module. When the output queue in this switch is full, it will back up the queues in the switches that feed it. In turn, those switches will back up the switches feeding them. Eventually, a tree of saturated switches results. Depending upon the number of outstanding requests and the reference patterns of the various processors, this tree of saturated queues may extend all the way back to every processor. Any request which must pass through any of the switches in the saturated tree, whether to a hot module or not, must wait until the saturated queues are drained. Thus, even requests whose destinations are idle will be blocked for potentially long periods of times, leading to unnecessary degradation of the network bandwidth.

Since the problem of tree saturation (caused by hot spot activity or otherwise) can be catastrophic to the performance of systems such as the NYU Ultracomputer [5], Cedar[7] and the IBM RP3 [14], considerable effort has been devoted to studying the problem and suggesting solutions to it [1, 5, 11, 13, 17].

When the problem is caused by accesses to synchronization variables (or more generally, by accesses to the same memory location), *combining* can be used. *Hardware combining* uses special hardware in the network switches to combine requests destined to the same memory location. On the return trip, the response for the combined request is broken up into responses for the individual requests. It is estimated that using combining hardware would increase the hardware cost of a multistage interconnection network by a factor of 6 to 32 [13]. *Software combining* uses a tree of variables to effectively spread out access to a single, heavily-accessed variable [4, 17]. It is applicable only to known hot spot locations such as variables used for locking, barrier synchronization, or pointers to shared queues.

Since the overall bandwidth of the network is determined by the number (or equivalently the rate) of requests that have to be serviced by the hot module, combining can improve overall network bandwidth by reducing the number of requests that have to be serviced. Combining also improves the latency of memory requests that do not access the hot memory module since it alleviates tree saturation. Unfortunately, combining cannot alleviate the bandwidth degradation or the tree saturation if the hot requests are to different memory locations in the same memory module, that is, the entire memory module is hot. Such a situation could arise from a larger percentage of shared variables residing in a particular module, stride accesses that result in the non-uniform access of the memory modules or temporal swings where variables stored in a particular module are accessed more heavily. In these cases, one module will receive more requests than its uniform share, just as if it contained a single hot variable. Recognizing this problem, the RP3 researchers have suggested scrambling the memory to distribute memory locations randomly across the memory modules [2, 12]. With a scrambled distribution, it is hoped that non-uniformities will occur less often, though we are unaware of any hard data to support this fact.

Even though processor requests may be distributed uniformly amongst the memory modules, tree saturation can still occur if any of the switches in the network has a higher load (in the short term) than other switches at the same level [9]. Alternate queue designs may improve the latency of memory requests that do not access the hot module, but eventually tree saturation will occur even with alternate queue designs [16].

To alleviate the problem of tree saturation in general, we need a mechanism that detects the possibility of tree saturation and instructs the processors to hold requests that might contribute to the tree saturation. If many of the problem-causing requests can be held outside the network (for example, in the processor queues), the severity of the problem can be reduced.

Before proceeding further, let us convince the reader that alleviating tree saturation can indeed result in an increase in the overall performance of the system. We shall only consider hot requests that cannot be combined in this paper since no solution to the problem of tree saturation is known in this case. We shall also restrict ourselves to $N \times N$ Omega networks.

Bandwidth Degradation Due to Tree Saturation

Consider a situation in which a fraction f of the processors (the hot processors) are making requests to a hot module with a probability of h on top of a background of uniform requests to all memory modules, and the remaining processors (the cold processors) are making only uniform requests (processors may have multiple outstanding requests.) This is a likely scenario if more than one job is run on the multiprocessor. Let r_1 be the rate at which the hot processors can generate requests and let r_2 be the rate at which the cold processors can generate requests. The number of requests per cycle that appear at the hot module is, therefore:

$$R_{hot} = f r_1(hN + (1-h)) + (1-f)r_2 \qquad (1)$$

Since the hot module can service only one request in each memory cycle, the maximum value of R_{hot} is one. Equating the right hand side of equation (1) to 1 and rearranging terms we get:

$$r_1 = \frac{1 - (1-f)r_2}{f(1 + h(N-1))} \qquad (2)$$

To calculate the overall bandwidth of the network, we observe that fN processors have a throughput of r_1 and $(1-f)N$ processors have a throughput of r_2. Therefore, the average peak bandwidth per processor is:

$$BW = \frac{r_1 fN + r_2(1-f)N}{N} = \frac{1 + (1-f)h(N-1)r_2}{1 + h(N-1)} \qquad (3)$$

If there was no tree saturation in the network and the cold processors could proceed without any interference, they could achieve a best-case throughput of 1 request per cycle, i.e., $r_2 = 1$. In this case, the peak (or cutoff) bandwidth of each processor in the system the system is:

$$BW_{cut} = \frac{1 + (1-f)h(N-1)}{1 + h(N-1)} \qquad (4)$$

with r_1 limited to

$$r_1 = \frac{1 - (1-f)r_2}{f(1 + h(N-1))} = \frac{1}{1 + h(N-1)}$$

Unfortunately, tree saturation prevents the cold processors that are generating uniform requests from proceeding without interference. When hot requests block in the network, cold processors as well as hot processors suffer degraded service. It does not matter which processors generated the hot requests, the requests are there causing tree saturation and blocking traffic from all processors. In this case, one can expect the system to behave as if all processors were participating in the hot spot activity, i.e., it appears that all N processors have a smaller hot spot of fh rather than only fN processors having a hot spot of h and the other processors proceeding without interference caused by the hot spot (this observation is empirical and has been verified by simulation). Therefore, the average cutoff bandwidth per processor can be estimated as [13]:

$$BW_{cut} = \frac{1}{1 + hf(N-1)} \qquad (5)$$

Since equation (4) estimates the bandwidth of the system when the cold processors are not degraded by tree saturation and equation (5) estimates the bandwidth when they are, we can estimate the bandwidth improvement (if tree saturation is controlled) by comparing equations (4) and (5). Fig. 4 plots the bandwidths suggested by equations (4) and (5) as a function of f, for $h = 4\%$, and $N = 256$. These are just upper limits but, as we shall see in section 4, simulation results exhibit a similar relationship. As we can see from Fig. 4, the overall bandwidth of the network can be improved significantly if the problem of tree saturation is controlled. The bandwidth improvement is zero at the endpoints, and largest at $f = 1/2$. Our experimental results in section 4 will confirm this.

3. CONTROLLING TREE SATURATION

As mentioned earlier, tree saturation occurs if the rate at which the processors are generating requests to a hot module is greater than the rate at which the memory module can service them. Once requests to a hot module enter the network, they block in the network and eventually lead to tree saturation and when tree saturation is present, even processors that do not participate in the hot spot activity are penalized.

To alleviate the problem of tree saturation, requests that compound the problem must be prevented from entering the network until the problem has subsided. Ideally, requests to the hot module must be made to wait outside the network (at the processor-network interface) until the hot module is ready (or slightly before it is ready) to service them, and then proceed at a rate at which they can be serviced by the hot module. Now, we present two schemes that try to achieve this goal. The two schemes are *limiting* and *feedback*.

3.1. Limiting the Number of Requests

One way of preventing the problem of tree saturation is to limit the number of requests to each memory module that enter the network each cycle to the number of requests that the memory module can service in the same time. Requests that cannot enter the network in a particular cycle must be blocked until a later cycle. Unfortunately, in its complete generality, limiting suffers from two problems.

The first problem is that limiting may unnecessarily constrain the available bandwidth of the system when no hot spots exist (as we shall see in section 4). With limiting, requests issued in the same cycle to the same memory module are constrained to enter the network one at a time. This delays these requests and any requests

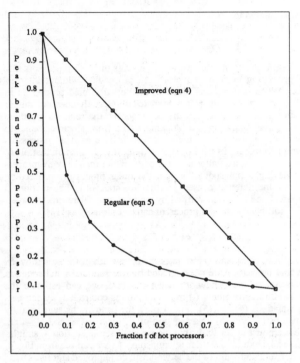

(a) Estimated peak bandwidth per processor
from equations (4) and (5).

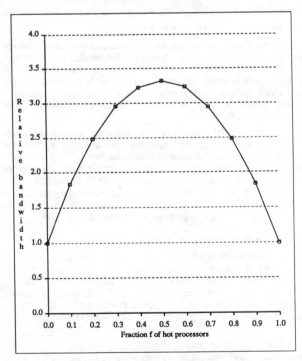

(b) Estimated bandwidth improvement
(eqn. (4) relative to eqn. (5)).

Fig. 4: Estimated Peak Bandwidth per Processor With and Without
Tree Saturation Control ($N=256$, $h=4\%$).

behind them, thereby reducing system bandwidth. When the destination module is cold, this delay is unnecessary as multiple requests could enter the network in the same cycle and proceed to the final stage of the network without hindering requests to other memory modules. In the final stage, they could queue up and be serviced one at a time.

The second problem is the cost of implementing a full-blown limiting scheme. To implement limiting from all N processors to all N memory modules requires a global arbiter that is capable of performing N arbitrations every cycle (one for each memory module) where each arbitration has an input from each of the N processors. The hardware costs of doing so can be prohibitive, *i.e.*, limiting is not scalable. As an alternative to full-blown limiting, limiting could be restricted to a single hot module. This requires only a single arbiter to control access to the memory module currently identified as the hot module. More on this in section 5.

3.2. Use of Feedback

Fig. 3 presents a multiprocessing system with feedback. Select state information is tapped from the ICN and the memory modules and fed back to the processors. The processors use this information to hold back problem-aggravating requests.

The feedback scheme that we use in this paper is very simple. The only state information that we monitor is the size of a queue at the input to each memory module (or output of the network). If the size of the queue exceeds a certain threshold T, we assume that the module is hot and notify the processors. The processors respond by holding back requests to the hot modules. When the size of the queue falls below the threshold T, the module is considered to be cold and the processors can again submit requests to it.

This feedback scheme prevents a module from causing full tree saturation because, as soon as the module becomes hot, requests to that module are stopped from entering the network. However, there are some problems. First, there is a finite delay between the time at which requests enter the network and at which they reach their destination memory module and trigger the feedback to the processors (if need be). At the instant that a module becomes hot, there may be many requests for that module already in transit. These requests may temporarily cause some tree saturation in the network. However, the resulting tree saturation will not be as severe as the tree saturation caused when requests can enter the network arbitrarily. It has been estimated that the onset of full tree saturation occurs as quickly as several network traversal times (the time for a packet to traverse the network in one direction, equivalent to the depth of the network) [8]. The feedback scheme outlined above allows only a single network traversal time before stopping requests to a hot module.

A second problem is that if the threshold value (T) is less than the number of levels in the network, a hot module may become cold and service all its queued requests before any newly released requests arrive, thus laying idle for some number of cycles. A final problem is that when a hot module becomes cold, many hot requests blocked in the processors may be released simultaneously, leading to overflow at the memory module queue when the requests arrive. These problems are very similar to overshoot, undershoot and oscillation in engineering control systems with feedback [3].

To reduce overshoot, undershoot and oscillation, some form of *damping* may be introduced [3]. The damping must allow a systematic release of requests to the hot module into the network. This is precisely what a limiting scheme accomplishes. Limiting could be used to dampen a feedback scheme as follows. When a module is hot, only one request to that module is allowed to enter per cycle. Up to two requests for every cold module are allowed to enter the network each cycle. Allowing one request per cycle to a hot module prevents the module's queue from becoming empty. Allowing only two requests per cycle for each cold module prevents queues from overflowing quickly, keeping any temporary tree saturation to a minimum.

In this paper, we have limited our simulations of feedback schemes to a simple feedback from the memory modules back to the processors and to the same feedback scheme with the limiting-damping discussed above. As we shall see, this strong form of damping is highly effective but quite expensive in hardware. In section 5, we discuss several other aspects of feedback system design which may be used to improve upon simple feedback at a more reasonable cost.

The hardware complexity of implementing a feedback scheme is minimal. To implement the scheme that we have described (without damping), all that we need to do is to monitor the size of the queue at each memory module and notify the processors if it exceeds a threshold. Doing so requires only N wires (one per memory module) that the processors must monitor. Processors decode the destinations of their requests, and issue a request into the network only when the destination module is cold. A simple bus of N wires used to convey per-cycle feedback information scales linearly with the number of memory modules and is relatively inexpensive compared to the ICN.

If we assume that only one module will be hot at a given time, then the necessary information (hot module number) can be conveyed with only $\log_2 N$ wires. Even if multiple modules may be hot at once, we can still get by with $\log_2 N$ wires by maintaining a buffer of hot module numbers at each processor. A module monitor would only acquire this bus to signal a transition from hot to cold or vice versa. Both these feedback schemes clearly scale to large numbers of processors.

4. SIMULATION MODEL AND RESULTS

4.1. Network Model

For all our experiments we considered an N×N Omega network connecting N processors to N memory modules. A forward network carries requests from the processors to the memories and a reverse network is used for responses from the memory modules to the processors.

A 2×2 crossbar switching element (shown in Fig. 5) is used as the basic building block. The size of the queue at each output is Q requests and each queue can accept a request from both inputs simultaneously if it has room for the requests. The order in which multiple inputs are gated to the same output is chosen randomly.

Requests move from one stage of the network to the next in a single network cycle. Each memory module can accept a single request every network cycle and the latency of each memory module is one network cycle. Therefore, the best-case round trip time for a processor request is $2\log_2 N + 2$ network cycles (issue (1) + forward network hops ($\log_2 N$) + memory module service (1) + reverse network hops ($\log_2 N$)).

In each network cycle, a processor makes a request with a probability of r. A fraction f of the processors make a fraction h of their requests to a hot memory module and the remaining $(1-h)$ of their requests are distributed uniformly over all memory modules. The remaining fraction $(1-f)$ of the processors make uniform requests over all memory modules.

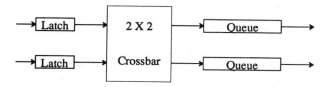

Figure 5: Switch Used in Model and Simulations

4.2. Simulation Results

The results presented in this section are for 256×256 (N=256) Omega networks with queue sizes of 4 elements (Q=4) at each switching element output. We also simulated 64×64, 128×128 and 512×512 Omega networks, each with varying queue sizes and memory latencies. The results follow a similar trend to the results we report for 256×256 networks with queue sizes of 4 and memory latencies of 1, though the magnitude of the results are different. For reasons of brevity, we shall not present those results in this paper.

Four varieties of networks were simulated:

- Regular Omega networks.
- Networks with feedback (threshold T =1,2,3, and 4 queue elements).
- Networks with straight limiting (one request per module per cycle).
- Networks with feedback threshold (T=1), plus limiting-damping.

Fig. 6 plots the peak bandwidth per processor of a regular Omega network (without feedback) as f varies from 0 to 1. Various hot rates h are considered. From Fig. 6 we see that as the fraction of processors making hot requests increases, the overall system bandwidth decreases. The higher the hot rate, h, the faster the bandwidth drops off. When all processors are making hot requests, the bandwidth is severely affected by the hot rate.

The purpose of feedback schemes and limiting schemes is to control tree saturation and consequently improve overall network bandwidth. At the end points of each curve in Fig. 6, i.e., f =0 and f =1, feedback is of little use in improving the bandwidth (but as we shall see, it can still improve memory latency). This is because when all processors are making uniform requests (f =0), little tree saturation occurs, and when all processors are making hot requests (f =1), the bandwidth is limited by the rate at which the hot module can service requests and not by the tree saturation that is present.

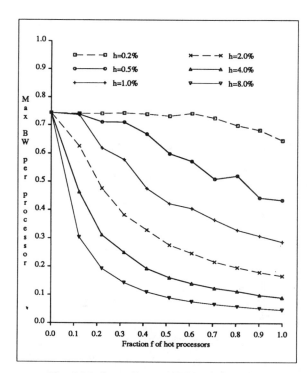

Fig. 6: Maximum Bandwidth per Processor with a Regular Omega Network (*N*=256).

Overall bandwidth of the network can be improved by controlling tree saturation only when the tree saturation is actually limiting the bandwidth, *i.e.*, f is between 0 and 1.

Now we consider the use of our feedback schemes of section 3.2. Figs. 7(a), 7(b), 7(c) and 7(d) plot the bandwidths improvements (relative bandwidth) for networks with feedback thresholds (T) of 1, 2, 3, and 4, respectively. The bandwidth improvement is the bandwidth of the modified network divided by the bandwidth of a regular network with no feedback or limiting. A value of 1 for the improvement indicates that the 2 networks have the same bandwidth; a value greater than 1 indicates that the modified network has a higher bandwidth and a value of less than 1 indicates that the modified network has a lower bandwidth.

From Fig. 7 we see that when f lies between 0 and 1, the use of feedback alleviates the tree saturation caused by the hot requests, allowing the processors making uniform requests to proceed with less interference, and increasing overall system bandwidth. The actual magnitude of the improvement is less than what is possible, since tree saturation has not been eliminated, but rather just alleviated. Note that these figures qualitatively confirm the results that were predicted in section 2.

We can also make two additional observations concerning threshold values for feedback. The first observation is that under high hot rates, lower thresholds give more improvement than higher thresholds. This is due to the fact that lower thresholds prevent hot traffic from entering the network sooner, and thus have less temporary hot module queue overflow. With a threshold of 1, a hot module's queue can accept 3 more requests at the time it becomes hot, without overflowing and causing tree saturation. With a threshold of 4, the queue is already full by the time it becomes hot and further requests to the module that are already in the network will cause partial tree saturation.

The second observation is that using thresholds that are too small can limit bandwidth to less than the bandwidth of a regular

network. The smaller the threshold, the more likely a request is to be blocked at the entrance to the network even though the destination memory module of the request is receiving an average of less than one request per cycle. Networks with larger thresholds are less likely to unnecessarily restrict bandwidth due to temporal fluctuations in the traffic pattern. Another reason that smaller thresholds restrict bandwidth is that they allow the hot module's queue to become empty for longer periods of time (as discussed in section 3.2). Under high hot rates, these problems are offset by the smaller threshold's ability to better control tree saturation.

On closer look at Fig. 7(d), we see that even with a high feedback threshold T of 4, the bandwidth is sometimes slightly less than the bandwidth of a regular network. This can be attributed to the problem of the hot module's queue occasionally becoming idle for a few cycles. When $f = 0$ (no hot spots) the relative bandwidth is unity. This indicates that normal traffic is not being restricted. If the queue sizes permitted a threshold equal to the number of levels in the network, then the problem of a hot module's queues becoming idle could be eliminated. We have simulated larger queue sizes and thresholds and found this to be the case but we do not present the results due to space limitations.

The higher the hot rate, the more the overall network bandwidth is improved by using feedback. With a hot rate of 4 or 8%, significant increases in system bandwidth occur even with a small percentage of processors making hot requests. As systems become larger, the tree saturation caused by a given hot rate will become more severe, and the hot rate needed to cause a given level of tree saturation will decrease. In such cases, the need for feedback is even more compelling.

Now let us examine the results of using limiting (Fig. 7(e)) and feedback with limiting-damping (Fig. 7(f)). From the figures, we see that both techniques are quite effective when the hot rate is high. Tree saturation is not allowed to develop and processors making only uniform requests see much less interference from processors making hot requests. For example, with 50% of the processors making

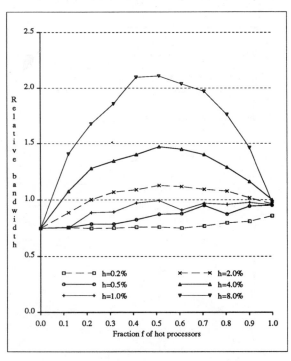

(a) Feedback ($T = 1$)

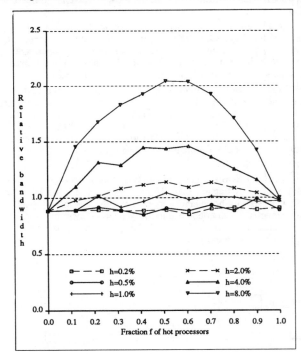

(b) Feedback ($T = 2$)

Fig. 7 (a-b) : Maximum Bandwidth per Processor With Tree Saturation
Control Mechanisms, Relative to a Regular Omega Network (N=256).

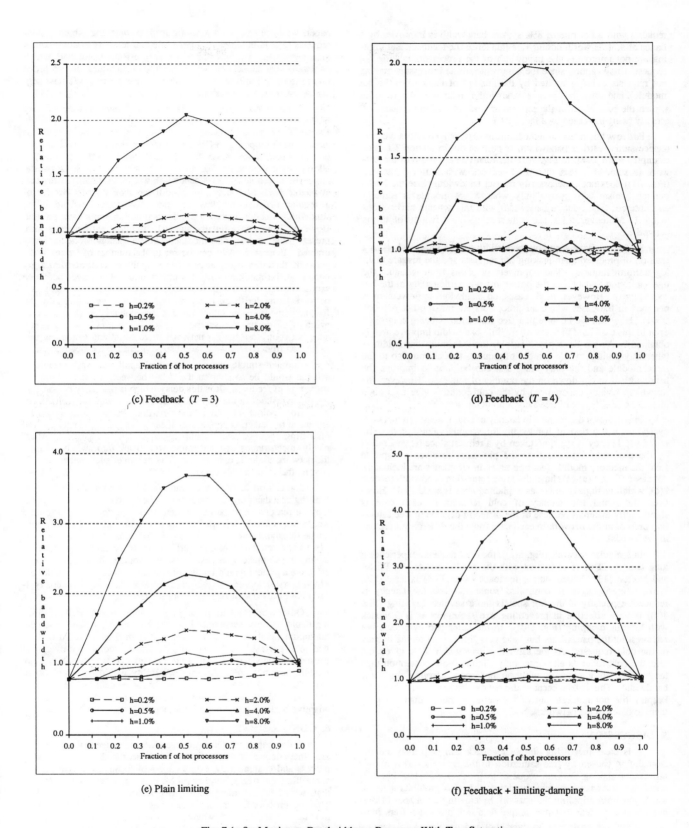

(c) Feedback (T = 3)

(d) Feedback (T = 4)

(e) Plain limiting

(f) Feedback + limiting-damping

Fig. 7 (c-f) : Maximum Bandwidth per Processor With Tree Saturation
Control Mechanisms, Relative to a Regular Omega Network (N=256).

requests with a hot rate of 8%, system bandwidth is improved by a factor of 4. It is worth noting here that since the feedback and limiting are not improving the bandwidth of the processors making hot requests (they cannot, since the bandwidth of the processors making hot requests is being limited by the number of requests to the hot module), and since the *average* bandwidth is increased by a factor of 4, then the bandwidth of the processors making uniform requests is actually being increased by a factor of 7.

For low hot rates, straight limiting is overly conservative and unnecessarily restricts bandwidth, as pointed out in section 3.1. For example, when $f = 0$ in Fig. 7(e), the relative bandwidth of the network is somewhat less than 1. Feedback with limiting-damping (Fig. 7(f)) does not unnecessarily restrict bandwidth since the limiting mechanism is triggered only when a hot module is actually encountered. The relative bandwidth with this scheme never drops below 1. Moreover, it has the highest relative bandwidths of all the networks.

So far, we have seen how bandwidth can be improved when a fraction of processors are making hot requests and the rest are making uniform requests. The improvement stems from reducing the tree saturation that blocks the processors not participating in the hot spot activity. However, in all cases, no bandwidth improvement is obtained in the cases where all processors are making hot requests ($f = 1$). How can we be sure that tree saturation is being controlled even in this case (and in cases where little bandwidth improvement is obtained)? As we have noted before, the maximum bandwidth is inherently limited by the number of requests that all must go to the same module and the only thing that can be done to improve the bandwidth is to cut down on the number of requests. However, the round trip latency experienced by the cold requests give us a good measure of the degree of tree saturation in the network.

Fig. 8 shows the round trip latency of cold requests (in network cycles) as a function of bandwidth for various values of h. The round trip latency is the time taken by a request since its generation by the processor until the time the processor receives a response from the memory module (waiting times in all queues are included). All cases (Figs. 8(a)-(d)) have the same saturation bandwidth (except 8(c), which is slightly lower as explained above) since $f = 1$. However, the round trip latency of cold requests in each case is significantly different because of the different degrees of tree saturation present in the network in each case (note the difference in scales in the Y-axis).

In a regular network (Fig. 8(a)), the cold requests experience a long latency. This is consistent with the results reported by Pfister and Norton [13]. When simple feedback (with $T=4$) is used (Fig. 8(b)), tree saturation is controlled somewhat and the latency is reduced, especially if the hot spot is more severe. Limiting (Fig. 8(c)) is very effective in preventing tree saturation as is feedback with limiting-damping (Fig. 8(d)). In the latter two cases, the hot rates restrict the bandwidth, but have very little effect on the latency of the cold requests. At the saturation bandwidth for a given hot rate, the cold requests encounter only slightly more contention than they would in a network with no hot spots carrying the same bandwidth. This is true because the bandwidth has been reduced by keeping the hot requests out of the network, rather than allowing them to block in the network.

5. DISCUSSION

It is clear that using simple feedback can help alleviate the degradation caused by tree saturation in the network. This allows processors making uniform requests to proceed with less interference, thus increasing system throughput. It also prohibits a single user's job from crippling the network by creating a hot spot. However, it is also clear that this simple feedback method suffers from some problems analogous to overshoot and oscillation in classical control theory. If steps can be taken to reduce these problems, the effectiveness of feedback can be significantly enhanced. In this paper, we have discussed a strong form of damping which limited requests to cold modules to 2 per cycle and requests to hot modules to 1 per cycle. This proved to be very effective, but had a high hardware cost associated with it. Other techniques that improve upon the basic limiting scheme need to be explored. We now suggest a few possible extensions.

One obvious improvement is to use large queues at the memory modules to increase the buffering of temporary tree saturation. Using larger queues toward the memory side of the switch has already been proposed in [15] for general networks. This technique is particularly appropriate for networks with feedback. First, it allows larger thresholds. Recall from the simulation results that the larger the threshold, the less bandwidth was unnecessarily restricted. With thresholds of 1 and 2, bandwidth was reduced to below that of a regular network for low hot rates. With a threshold of 4, bandwidth was not degraded at all when no hot spots were present. However, it was occasionally reduced slightly when hot spots were present, due to the hot module's queue becoming temporarily drained. If the threshold can be set to the number of levels in the network, then this degradation can essentially be eliminated. Larger queues at the modules will also buffer more of the overshoot tree saturation that occurs with feedback. Since the queue overflow in a network using feedback is temporary, and will be stopped by the feedback mechanism, larger queues can potentially absorb all or much of the partial tree saturation, even in the presence of a steady state hot spot. In a regular network, there is nothing to prevent tree saturation from overflowing larger sized queues in the steady state.

Another simple way to improve upon our basic feedback scheme would be to shorten the delay between the inputs and the triggering of feedback. It is this delay which is primarily responsible for the overshoot in the system. Such schemes would involve feedback from points internal to the network. Performance would be enhanced by detecting congestion at earlier stages in the network and restricting requests that would aggravate this congestion. Alternately, mechanisms that fed information back *into* switches within the network could be constructed. The design of such mechanisms is beyond the scope of this paper.

Some form of damping would still be beneficial. Full-blown limiting as a damping mechanism may be impractical to build, but it may be reasonable to build a system which performs limiting on a single hot memory module, as suggested in section 3.1. Memory queue threshold detectors and a single arbiter could be used to identify the hot module. Another arbiter would be used by processors attempting to make a request to the hot module. It is not clear how effective a system would be that only dealt with one hot module, but preliminary experience shows that large scale parallel programs typically have only one or two hot spots at a time [6, 13].

Other weaker forms of damping could be used as well. If limiting could be done separately in k slices of the processors, then the maximum number of requests to a particular module could be limited to k per cycle. This could significantly reduce the overshoot caused by many requests entering the network at once when a hot module becomes cold. Another possibility would be some sort of variable waiting time after a module becomes cold before different requests destined for that module enter the network (similar to the adaptive back off scheme used in Ethernets).

6. CONCLUSIONS

In this paper, we have proposed the use of feedback in multistage interconnection networks as an aid in the distributed routing process and evaluated the effectiveness of feedback mechanisms in controlling the tree saturation problem in such networks. We saw that, with feedback mechanisms, tree saturation can be controlled. That is, processors can avoid sending requests to a hot memory module into the network where they will consume buffer space and block requests that could otherwise proceed. A network with feedback could be used in conjunction with software combining to provide protection against hot spots that are not caused by access to syn-

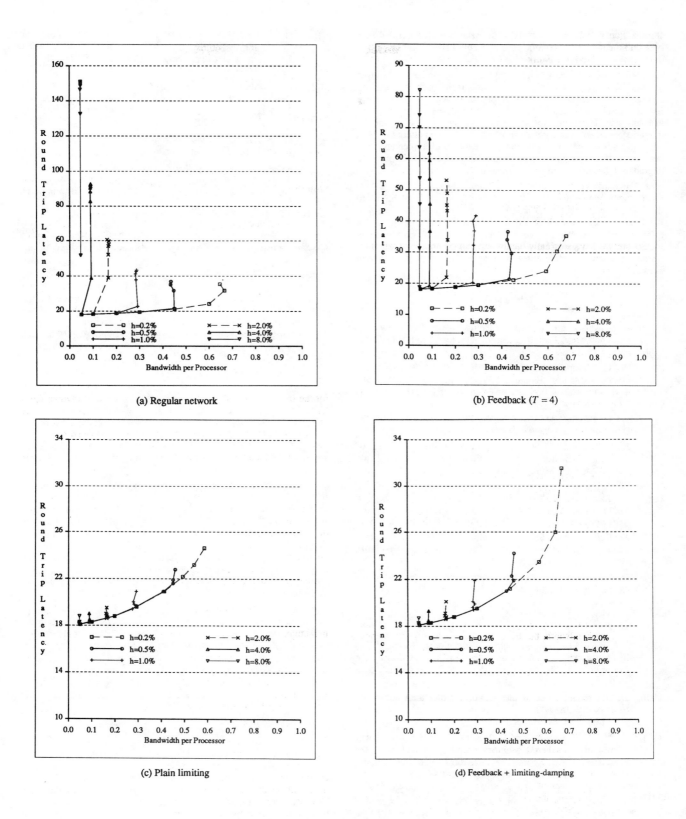

Fig. 8: Latency of Cold Requests vs. Bandwidth ($f = 1$).

chronization variables. Alternately, in systems with a general purpose and a combining network, feedback could be profitably applied to the general purpose network.

While we have only considered the example of tree saturation in multistage interconnections, feedback techniques are general enough to be used in any parallel or distributed system where a resource can be accessed without the use of a global control mechanism and when contention for access to this resource can degrade the overall system. A network with feedback presents an alternative to a network with global control (which is expensive to implement) or a network with only a distributed routing control (which is prone to degradation because of non-uniform access of its resources).

The hardware requirements of feedback are modest. In a multistage interconnection network, feedback from the destinations to the sources requires no alteration of the interconnection network itself, and could thus be added to existing network designs with minimal upheaval. We believe that feedback could be used easily in many systems and specifically recommend its use in large-scale multiprocessors that use distributed routing controlled interconnection networks.

References

[1]   G. S. Almasi and A. Gottlieb, *Highly Parallel Computing*. Redwood City, CA: Benjamin/Cummings Publishing Company, Inc., 1989.

[2]   W. C. Brantley, K. P. McAuliffe, and J. Weiss, "RP3 Processor-Memory Element," *Proceedings 1985 International Conference on Parallel Processing*, pp. 782-789, August 1985.

[3]   W. L. Brogan, *Modern Control Theory*. New York, NY: Quantum Publishers, Inc., 1974.

[4]   J. R. Goodman, M. K. Vernon, and P. J. Woest, "A Set of Efficient Synchronization Primitives for a Large-Scale Shared-Memory Multiprocessor," in *Proc. ASPLOS-III*, Boston, MA, April 1989.

[5]   A. Gottlieb, et al, "The NYU Ultracomputer -- Designing a MIMD, Shared Memory Parallel Machine," *IEEE Transactions on Computers*, vol. C-32, pp. 175-189, February 1983.

[6]   M. Kalos, et al, "Scientific computations on the Ultracomputer," Ultracomputer Note 27, Courant Institute, New York University, New York, NY.

[7]   D. J. Kuck, et al, "Parallel Supercomputing Today and the Cedar Approach," *Science*, vol. 21, pp. 967-974, Feb. 1986.

[8]   M. Kumar and G. F. Pfister, "The Onset of Hot Spot Contention," *Proceedings 1986 International Conference on Parallel Processing*, August 1986.

[9]   T. Lang and L. Kurisaki, "Nonuniform Traffic Spots (NUTS) in Multistage Interconnection Networks," *Proceedings 1988 International Conference on Parallel Processing*, August 1988.

[10]   D. H. Lawrie, "Access and Alignment of Data in an Array Processor," *IEEE Transactions on Computers*, vol. C-24, pp. 1145-1155, December 1975.

[11]   G. Lee, C. P. Kruskal, and D. J. Kuck, "The Effectiveness of Combining in Shared Memory Parallel Computers in the Presence of 'Hot Spots'," *Proceedings 1986 International Conference on Parallel Processing*, August 1986.

[12]   A. Norton and E. Melton, "A Class of Boolean Linear Transformations for Conflict-Free Power-Of-Two Access," *Proceedings 1987 International Conference on Parallel Processing*, pp. 247-254, August 1987.

[13]   G. F. Pfister and V. A. Norton, "'Hot-Spot' Contention and Combining in Multistage Interconnection Networks," *IEEE Transactions on Computers*, vol. C-34, pp. 943-948, October 1985.

[14]   G. F. Pfister, et al, "The IBM Research Parallel Processor Prototype (RP3): introduction and architecture," *Proceedings 1985 International Conference on Parallel Processing*, pp. 764-771, August 1985.

[15]   H. S. Stone, *High-Performance Computer Architecture*. Reading, MA: Addison-Wesley, 1987.

[16]   Y. Tamir and G. L. Frazier, "High-Performance Multi-Queue Buffers for VLSI Communication Switches," in *Proc. 15th Annual Symposium on Computer Architecture*, Honolulu, HI, pp. 343-354, June 1988.

[17]   P.-C. Yew, N.-F. Tzeng, and D. H. Lawrie, "Distributing Hot-Spot Addressing in Large Scale Multiprocessors," *IEEE Transactions on Computers*, vol. C-36, pp. 388-395, April 1987.

CONSTRUCTING REPLICATED SYSTEMS USING PROCESSORS WITH POINT TO POINT COMMUNICATION LINKS

by

Paul D. Ezhilchelvan, Santosh K. Shrivastava and Alan Tully

Computing Laboratory, University of Newcastle Upon Tyne, England, U.K.

Abstract

Replicated processing with majority voting is a well known method of achieving fault tolerance. We consider the problem of constructing a distributed system composed of an arbitrarily large number of N-modular redundant (NMR) nodes, where each node itself is composed of N, $N = 2m + 1$ and $m \geq 1$, processing and voting elements. Advanced microprocessors, such as Inmos Transputers, provide fast serial communication links for inter-processor communication, making it possible to construct large networks of processors. We describe how replicated processing with majority voting can be achieved for such processor networks. This paper will present the overall systems architecture, including voting and NMR synchronization algorithms specially developed to exploit fast point to point communication facilities.

Keywords: Replicated processing, majority voting, N-modular redundancy, sequencing algorithm, fault tolerance

1. Introduction

We consider the problem of making a system of concurrent processes tolerant to a bounded number of processor failures. Given a non-redundant system of C ($C \geq 1$) concurrent processes partitioned to run on P ($P \leq C$) number of processors, we address the problem of constructing a *voted replicated system* of N*C processes ($N = 2m + 1$, $m \geq 1$) partitioned to run on N*P processors and capable of tolerating up to P*m processor failures. Each process $c \in C$ is replaced by a group of processes with N members, and each processor $p \in P$ is replaced by a group of N processors. We assume that processes interact by message passing. This requires that all message interactions must be voted upon in the replicated system. It is our objective to achieve *replication transparency* such that any problems posed by replication and voting are hidden from the application programmer who is then only concerned with the development of a non-redundant system.

Replicated processing with majority voting -N-modular redundant (NMR) processing- is a well known method of achieving fault tolerance. The problem of applying this method to distributed and multicomputer systems has received much attention [1-5]. Many fault tolerant distributed systems have been implemented under a rather restricted fault assumption, which is that processors fail "cleanly" by just stopping [eg. 6]. Such an assumption is hard to justify in computer systems intended for mission and life critical applications where failure probabilities in the range 10^{-6} to 10^{-10} per hour are often specified [3,4]. It is then necessary to design and implement such systems under a highly unrestricted fault assumption, namely, that a failed processor can behave in an arbitrary manner (in the literature this failure mode is often referred to as the *Byzantine failure* mode [7]). While certainly not common, experience has shown that Byzantine failures cannot be ruled out in the design of fault tolerant systems [3-5]. NMR processing, whereby outputs from faulty processors can be masked by voting, provides a practical means of constructing systems capable of tolerating Byzantine processor failures. In this paper we develop a specific architecture necessary for supporting replicated processing. This architecture exploits the following property that we assume for all processors: each processor has a fixed number of communication links through which processes executing on that processor may send or receive messages from processes of other connected processors. In the following we shall present a processor interconnection and communication scheme together with voting and sequencing algorithms necessary for replicated processing.

The overall architecture that we present here is of practical importance. This is borne out of the fact that some current microprocessors such as the Inmos Transputer [8] provide just the kind of communication facilities assumed here (a Transputer has 4 bi-directional 10Mbit/sec serial communication links). Using such links, large multi-Transputer networks can be built for specific applications. A number of these applications make use of *Transputer farms* (either single or two dimensional Transputer arrays) for parallel processing. The architecture developed can be used for such applications. NMR processor networks have also been proposed for realtime control applications such as railway signalling [9]. Thus there is every reason to develop an optimized communications architecture for such systems. From now on we will assume the degree of replication to be three giving us the well known Triple Modular Redundant (TMR) system. The paper is structured as follows. The second section develops a model for replicated processing and describes the voting and sequencing requirements. Section three presents a processor interconnection scheme which meets the TMR criterion of tolerating one processor failure per TMR node. Section four presents the algorithm for voting and sequencing. In section five the design presented here is compared and evaluated with other approaches reported in the literature. Conclusions from our work are presented in section six.

2. Replicated Processing Model

We assume that application programs can be mapped on to a number of processes that interact via messages. Communicating processes have bi-directional links between them. Figure 1a shows a system of five concurrent processes with six links. A link connecting two processes has the property that the messages sent by one process are received by the other process uncorrupted and in the sent order. We also assume that if a process with multiple links (such as c_2 in Figure 1a) simultaneously receives messages on those links then these messages are chosen non-deterministically for processing. Message selection is however assumed to be *fair*, that is, the process will eventually select a message present on a link. We assume that such a system of processes can be configured to run on a given set of processors. Each processor is assumed to possess a fixed number of bi-directional communication links. For example, Figure 1b shows a particular configuration for three processors with c_1 and c_2 mapped onto processor p_1, c_3 mapped onto p_2 and c_4 and c_5 mapped onto p_3. Interprocess links l_i are also mapped onto physical links s_j connecting the host processors (eg. l_2, l_3 mapped onto s_1). A physical link connecting two processors, such as s_1, is composed of a bi-directional link from p_1 and a similar link from p_2 connected electrically to form a single bi-directional link. The model presented here is sufficiently general in that other models, such as clients and servers interacting through remote procedure calls, or objects communicating by messages can be seen as special cases. It is also worth noting that processors such as Transputers directly support a processing model very similar to the one presented here via the Occam programming language [10].

A processor with its links will be treated as a single entity, so a processor with either faulty links or a faulty processing unit or both will be treated as a faulty processor. A failed processor may behave in an arbitrary manner and hence, processes of a failed processor may behave in an arbitrary manner. In the replicated version of the system, each process c_i ($1 \leq i \leq 5$ in Figure 1b) will be replaced by a process triad C_i, such that $C_i \equiv \{C_{i1}, C_{i2}, C_{i3}\}$ and each processor p_j ($1 \leq j \leq 3$ in Figure 1b) will be replaced by a processor triad P_j such that $P_j \equiv \{P_{j1}, P_{j2}, P_{j3}\}$ with C_{i1} mapped onto P_{j1}, C_{i2} onto P_{j2} and C_{i3} onto P_{j3}. Computations performed by a process are assumed to be *deterministic*. In particular this means that if all non-faulty processes of a triad have identical initial states and process identical messages in an identical order, then identical output messages in an identical order will be produced. To simplify subsequent discussions, it will be assumed that the function of a computational process, such as C_{ij}, is simply to remove the selected message from the link and output a message after some processing. Assuming that at most one processor in each triad may fail, at most one process in each triad may be faulty. A non-faulty process must reject inputs from a faulty process; this is achieved by majority voting as shown in Figure 2 which depicts the voters for the jth process triad of C_1 (The replicated version of process c_1 in Figure 1a).

In Figure 2, if C_{1j} receives two voted messages simultaneously then one of them will be chosen non-deterministically for processing. It is however necessary for all the non-faulty members of a process triad to make an identical selection. This is difficult to achieve even if it is assumed that non-deterministic choice is replaced by a fixed priority selection criterion, since voted messages need not arrive at the same time at all processes of the triad. We will convert the problem of identical message selection to

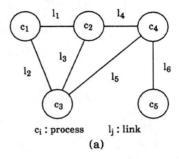

c_i : process l_j : link

(a)

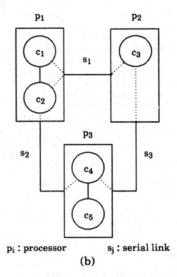

p_i : processor s_j : serial link

(b)

Figure 1: Process-Processor Mapping

that of *identical message ordering* by serializing the inputs to a process as shown in Figure 3. All voted messages are stored for processing in the voted message pool (VMP). The *order processes* of a triad cooperate to select a voted message for processing using a protocol which will be discussed later. The selected message is inserted in the voted message queues (VMQs). Every process C_{ij} has a VMQ$_{ij}$ associated with it. Process C_{ij} picks up the message at the head of its VMQ and processes it. The results are

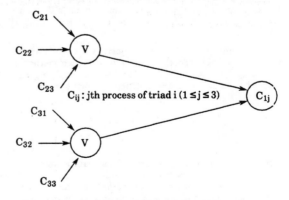

C_{ij} : jth process of triad i ($1 \leq j \leq 3$)

Figure 2: Voting of incoming messages

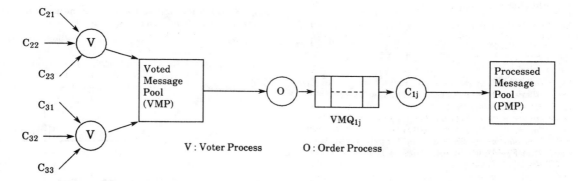

Figure 3: Processing of Voted Messages

stored in the processed message pool (PMP) for transmission to the relevant triad. We now require the following *sequencing condition* to be satisfied by all non-faulty processes of a triad :

SEQ: All the non-faulty computational processes of a triad process voted messages in an identical order.

The order processes ensure that SEQ is met by delivering voted messages to the VMQs in an identical order.

Transforming a system such as shown in Figure 2 to it's equivalent form shown in Figure 3 has several advantages. Communications software can be developed for maintaining the message pools (Figure 3) which can be shared between all the processes mapped onto that processor. Similarly, a single order process per processor can be utilized for delivering messages to all the VMQs of the processes of that processor. Finally, a single voter process per processor can be utilized for voting messages. Voting can be carried out either on *incoming messages* (at the receiver triad) or on *outgoing messages* (at the sender triad, in which case receiver triads receive only voted messages). We will assume that the voter of a processor votes all outgoing messages (the reason for this choice will be explained subsequently after processor interconnections have been discussed). A shortcoming of the scheme shown in Figure 3 is that process C_{1j} has only one incoming link (from VMQ_{1j}) and one outgoing link (to PMP) and hence it no longer communicates like its unreplicated counterpart c_1 which has bidirectional links with c_2 and c_3. This shortcoming can readily be overcome by introducing a *stub process* S_{1j} into the host processor of C_{1j} to emulate the two original links to c_2 and c_3 as illustrated in Figure 4. Process S_{1j} interfaces to VMQ_{1j} and the PMP: it picks up a message

from VMQ_{1j} and sends it to C_{1j}; a message from C_{1j} on the other hand is deposited in the PMP for voting. It can be seen that stub processes are similar to client and server stubs employed in remote procedure call systems [11]. In the subsequent discussions, for the sake of simplicity, we will assign to C_{ij} the role played by the stub process S_{ij} thereby supposing that process C_{ij} interacts directly with VMQ_{ij} and PMP as shown in Figure 3.

To summarize: a processor maintains two pools: VMP and PMP. Each process C_{ij} on that processor processes messages on its VMQ_{ij}. The order process of the processor selects messages from the VMP and inserts them in the appropriate VMQs. The voter process of the processor votes messages from the PMP before transmitting them.

3. Processor Interconnection and Message Diffusion

We will assume that a processor has four bidirectional links. Four links are enough to construct a pipeline (or a ring) of processor triads as shown in Figure 5.

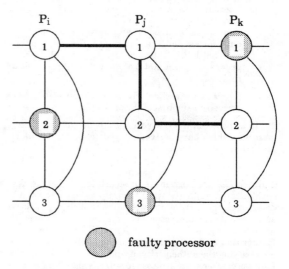

Figure 5: Processor Interconnections

The pipelined nature of interconnection means that a message intended from one processor to some other processor may have to be relayed by intermediate processors. From a TMR system we require the capability of masking at most one processor failure per triad Under

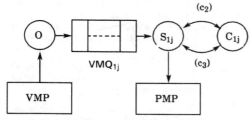

S_{1j} : stub process to emulate c_2 and c_3

C_{1j} : jth replicated version of c_1

Figure 4: A Stub Process

such a failure assumption, the pipelined system possesses the following two properties:

(i) Any non-faulty processor of a triad is directly connected to all other non-faulty processors of the same triad.

(ii) From any non-faulty processor in a triad P_i, there is a non-faulty path connecting that processor to any non-faulty processor of triad P_k. A path between any two non-faulty processors is non-faulty if all the intermediate processors in the path are non-faulty (for example, the path between P_{i1} and P_{k2} drawn in bold lines in Figure 5 is non-faulty).

We will refer to a link connecting processors of a triad as *internal* and a link connecting processors of two adjacent triads as *external*. All the processors of the system as well as processor and process triads will be assumed to possess unique names. We will assume the existence of some name mapping scheme for process triads such that a sender or relayer can determine whether the destination triad is on its 'left' or 'right'. In addition, it will be assumed that a message contains an *ordernumber* (a form of sequence number, see section 4). The following message handling primitives will be assumed (to be provided by the communications software of a processor):

(i) *send(message)* : The message intended for the named destination process triad, where the destination process triad is not on the same triad as the sender, is sent on the appropriate external link.

(ii) *diffuse_internal(message)* : The message is sent over all the internal links of a processor.

(iii) *diffuse_external(message)* : This operation is invoked by a relaying processor if it receives a double signed message on one of its links. If a message is received on an external link, then the processor sends the received message on all internal links as well as the external link which is towards the direction of the destination. If a message is received on an internal link, then it is only forwarded outwards via the appropriate external link. Optimizations are possible, since a processor need not relay a message already relayed.

(iv) *receive(message)* : Receive a message that has arrived on any link of the processor.

It is necessary for a receiver to be able to detect messages which have arrived altered. This is particularly important within the context of a pipelined architecture where messages can be relayed. For this reason, a message must contain enough redundancy. If it is assumed that faulty processors can behave in an arbitrary manner, then sophisticated authentication techniques are required to detect message corruptions with high probability [12]. We assume that each processor has a mechanism to generate a unique unforgeable signature for a given message and further that each processor has an *authentication function* for verifying the authenticity of a signature. Thus if a non-faulty processor sends a message with its signature to some other non-faulty processor, any corruption of this message by a relaying processor can be detected by the receiver by authenticating the signature associated with the message. These assumptions about signatures are identical to those made by other researchers [7,13]. The *send* primitive and the *diffuse_internal* primitive automatically sign the message to be sent. On the other hand, the

diffuse_external primitive does not sign the message (since this operation is invoked for relaying a message).

If more than four links per processor are available, then structures other than a pipeline can be formed. For example, Figure 6 shows a triplicated grid structure which requires six links per processor. If necessary, a six link "processor" can be built using two four link processors as shown in the figure.

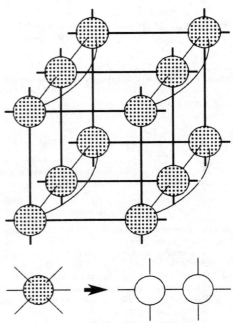

Figure 6: A Triplicated Grid

The above message handling facilities are used by voting and ordering processes as described in the next section.

4. Voting and Ordering

Recall that there is one voter process in every processor and that messages produced by a member process of a triad are voted before being sent to the destination. Assume that a process triad C_m mapped onto processor triad P_i (Figure 5), is sending voted messages to process triad C_n on processor triad P_k. The voting of messages is achieved as follows: any message produced by a member process of C_m is diffused internally to its neighbours. When a member processor of triad P_i accumulates at least two messages which agree, it sends this message on one of its external links depending on the location of the destination triad (signed messages are authenticated as we will see shortly). Figure 7 shows the flow of messages from source triad to destination triad.

For the purpose of sending and receiving voted messages, a processor maintains message pools VMP, PMP and two additional pools:

(i) *Voted Message Pool (VMP)* : Contains voted messages intended for members of process triads (C_{ij}'s) mapped onto this processor.

(ii) *Processed Message Pool (PMP)* : Contains processed messages deposited by $C_{ij}s$. These messages must be voted before transmission

180

(iii) *Received Message Pool (RMP)* : Contains signed messages that are received for voting and found to be authentic.

(iv) *Candidate Message Pool (CMP)* : Contains unsigned messages waiting for a signed message of identical contents to arrive at RMP.

Two operations are defined on these pools:

remove(pl,m): a message is removed from pool pl and assigned to m.

deposit(pl,m): message m is deposited in pl, if m is not already present in pl.

As stated before, each process C_{ij} has a VMQ containing messages to be processed and each message contains an *ordernumber*. Messages in a VMQ are queued such that if m_1 and m_2 are in the VMQ and m_1 is before m_2 then $m_1.\text{ordernumber} < m_2.\text{ordernumber}$. This ordernumber is generated by the *order* process as it deposits a voted message in a given VMQ. As we shall see, the order process composes such a number by taking the current local clock time and concatenating it with the host triad identifier. The ordernumber of a message is a convenient means of determining its "age" within a processor and can be utilized for detecting unwanted messages (see process *flush* below). Messages have the property that their ordernumbers are unique within a given non-faulty processor. The function of a process such as C_{ij} is to process messages in its VMQ:

A result message deposited in the PMP retains its original ordernumber (it is not modified by C_{ij}).

The voter process is composed of four concurrent processes: *sender, receiver, majority* and *flush*. In the algorithms we will make use of the following notation:

m.dest : destination processor triad of message m.
m.destproc : destination process triad of message m.
m.ordernumber : ordernumber of message m.
ordernumber.clockvalue : clock value component of ordernumber

The *sender* process diffuses messages internally for voting. The receiver process collects all the messages sent by member triad processors for voting in the pool RMP. All voted messages contain two signatures from two members of the sending triad. If the received message is signed twice and is not meant for the receiver then the message is relayed by diffusing it using the *diffuse_external* procedure, otherwise the message is deposited, if it is authentic, in the VMP. The majority process tries to vote messages from pools CMP and RMP. If a majority can be formed, the message from RMP is countersigned and the double signed message is sent to the destination if the destination is remote, otherwise the countersigned message is and deposited in the VMP. From then on, double signed local messages in the VMP are treated like any other voted messages received from other triads. In addition to the three processes discussed above, it will be necessary to have another process -*flush*- which occasionally runs to flush out unwanted messages from the RMP (messages are unwanted if their replicas have already been voted upon; in addition, those messages, sent by faulty- possibly malicious- processors, that will never find a matching message from CMP are also unwanted). The constant D_{max} should be based on an extremely generous estimation of the time taken for any message to progress from the instant it is deposited in a VMQ to CMP

```
process C_ij :
    cycle
        pick up the message at the head of VMQ_ij
        process the message
        deposit the result message in PMP
    end
end C_ij

process voter :
    { process sender :
        var m:message
        cycle
            remove(PMP,m)
            deposit(CMP,m)
            diffuse_internal(m)
                /*signed m is sent to neighbours */
        end
    end sender
    //
    process receiver :
        var m:message; me:host_triad_identifier
        cycle
            receive(m)
            if m is signed once & authentic →
                deposit(RMP,m)
            □ m is signed once & not authentic → discard
            □ m is signed twice & m.dest ≠ me →
                diffuse_external(m)
            □ m is signed twice & m.dest = me & authentic
                → deposit(VMP,m)
            □ m is signed twice & m.dest = me
                & not authentic →
                discard /* corrupted message */
            fi
        end
    end receiver
    //
    process majority :
        var m:message; me: host_triad_identifier
        cycle
            m: = a message from RMP identical to a
            message from CMP
            /* such a pair is removed from these pools */
            if m.dest ≠ me → send(m)
            /* double signed voted message
            is sent to its destination */
            □ m.dest = me → countersign and
            deposit(VMP,m) /* local message */
            fi
        end
    end majority
    //
    process flush:
        var T:timestamp
        cycle
            T: = local_clock_time - D_max
            remove any messages from RMP with
                ordernumber.clockvalue ≤ T
            remove any messages from RMP with
                ordernumber.clockvalue >
            local_clock_time
            wait for a while
        end
    end flush
    }
end voter
```

Recall that the ordernumber.clockvalue of a message records the local clock time when that message was put in the VMQ. Thus any message with ordernumber.clockvalue less than the current local clock time minus D_{max} can be deemed to be unwanted. Similarly, any message with ordernumber.clockvalue greater than the current local clock time must also be treated as unwanted (this is because a message must take a finite amount of time to progress from a VMQ to the CMP). The flush process performs an important function as it prevents an overflow of the RMP; in its absence, a faulty processor of a triad can cause non-faulty member processors to fail by creating overflows. It is worth noting that since inter-triad messages are voted and double signed at the senders and accepted only if authenticated at the receivers, a single failed processor of a triad cannot successfully send arbitrary messages to remote triads; so flush processes are required for intra-triad traffic only. The advantages of voting at sender triads can be appreciated given the processor connection schemes shown in Figures 5 and 6: inter-triad message traffic is cut down by a factor of three.

The function of the *order* process is to pick up a message from the VMP and assign it a *new ordernumber* and place it in the appropriate VMQ. The order process of a non-faulty processor must assign ordernumbers that are identical to those assigned by any other order process of a non-faulty member triad processor. We assume the existence of an *atomic broadcast* mechanism [13] between the member processors of a triad. The clocks of non-faulty processors of a triad are also assumed to be synchronized such that the measurable difference between readings of clocks at any instant is bounded by a known constant.

We require the properties of *atomicity, validity, termination* and *order* from the atomic broadcast mechanism. When a sender broadcasts a message m at local clock time T then:

(i) m is delivered to either all non-faulty receivers or to none of them (*atomicity*);

(ii) if the sender is non-faulty then m is delivered to all non-faulty receivers (*validity*);

(iii) m is delivered to all non-faulty receivers at their local clock time $T + \Delta$ (*termination*); and

(iv) all the messages broadcast by non-faulty senders are delivered to non-faulty receivers in an identical order (*order*);

where Δ is some known bounded quantity.

Two primitive operations for atomic broadcasts will be assumed:

(i) *Acast(msg)*: message "msg" is broadcast to member processors of the triad, including itself.

(ii) *Areceive(msg)*: message "msg" is received.

The *order* process is composed of three processes: *broadcaster, receiver* and *sequencer*. A queue of messages named *broadcast message queue* (BMQ) is maintained by the order process. Two standard queue operations -*put* and *get*- are available on a BMQ.

The broadcaster process ensures that every voted (double signed) message is made available to other member triads. Referring to figure 5, it can be seen that only the second processor of P_k will receive a voted message from P_j; local broadcast of this message will thus ensure that the message gets distributed. In general then, a processor can

```
process order:
   {process broadcaster:
      var m:message
      cycle
         remove(VMP, m)
         Acast(m)
      end
   end broadcaster
   //
   process receiver:
      var m:message
      cycle
         Areceive(m)
         if m is signed twice &
         authentic → put(BMQ,m)
            /*put in BMQ*/
         ☐ m is not signed twice & authentic → discard
            /*spurious message*/
         ☐ m is signed twice & not authentic → discard
            /*spurious message*/
         fi
      end
   end receiver
   //
   process sequencer:
      var m:message; T: timestamp;
      var i:process_triad_identifier
      T: = initial start time
      wait until local_clock_time = T
      cycle
         get(BMQ,m)
            /*remove the message at the head of BMQ
            */
         if m ≠ null → i: = m.destproc
            /*get the identifier of source process */
            if Delivered_VMQ(m,i) → discard
               /*replica */
            ☐ not Delivered_VMQ(m,i) →
               m.ordernumber: = T concatenate
               host_triad_identifier
               strip off double signatures from m
               deposit in the VMQ of process i
            fi
         ☐ m = null → skip
         fi
         T: = T + ∂
         wait until local_clock_time = T
      end
   end sequencer
   }
end order
```

receive at most two extra copies of a voted message through broadcasts. The receiver process receives atomically broadcasted messages and deposits them in the BMQ. Because of the use of the atomic broadcast facility, the BMQ of a non-faulty processor possesses the following *stability* property: at any local clock time *t*, the state of the BMQ will be identical to the state of the BMQ of any other non-faulty member processor triad at its local clock time *t*. This property of BMQs is exploited for sequencing and generating new ordernumbers for messages by the sequencer processes. Assume that the initial start time (some value greater than the current local clock time) and the constant ∂ are the same for all the sequencer processes of a triad. Then all the non-faulty sequencer processes of a triad enter the loop at identical local clock times and then

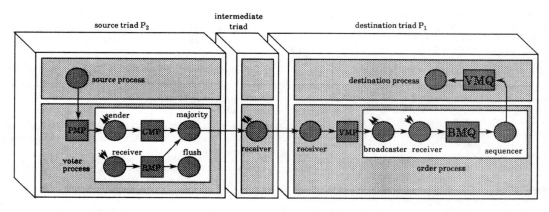

Figure 7: Message Flow

periodically remove identical messages from BMQs. The period ∂ must be chosen to be greater than the maximum processing time within the loop. Since a BMQ can contain replicas of a message, a function *Delivered__VMQ(m,i)* is assumed to exist to determine whether m is a replica of a message that has already been delivered to the VMQ of process i. Clearly, a sequencer process will have to maintain some state information about the messages delivered to the various VMQs, but these details have been omitted here for the sake of simplicity. Some optimizations to the scheme presented here are possible and briefly mentioned here. A protocol can be designed to reduce the number of broadcasts by exploiting the fact that a processor need not broadcast a message if it has already received a similar message from a broadcast from some other member processor. Also it is possible to design an integrated method for broadcasting and synchronization of clocks to reduce the number of messages needed just for clock synchronization [14]. Finally, voted messages whose destinations are local, need not be double signed, and can be treated specially, rather than uniformally as done here, to save processing time.

5. Design Evaluation

Our claim that the architecture presented here is suitable for point to point link based communication systems is based on the observation that while communication between directly connected processors can be fast, communication which involves intermediate processors for relaying can be considerably slower. Thus a good system design should minimize the number of inter-triad messages and eliminate altogether any need for complex protocols between any two processor triads. We achieve this by voting at the source triad, so at most three voted messages are sent by a triad, and by requiring the facilities of clock synchronization and atomic broadcast only for individual triads.

SIFT [3] and DELTA-4 [5] are two well known examples of systems capable of supporting NMR processing; both rely on bus or LAN based communications. SIFT employs a global clock synchronization facility for scheduling of *periodic* tasks only, while DELTA-4 employs special purpose LAN hardware to support atomic broadcasts between any set of communicating entities. Neither of these approaches is suitable to the kind of systems considered here.

There are essentially two classes of solutions to the problem of meeting the sequencing condition. One class of solutions makes use of Byzantine agreement protocols

where no attempt is made to detect faulty processors while the other class of solutions make use of timeouts for detecting possibly faulty processors. The solution adopted in this paper falls in the first class since atomic broadcast algorithms require Byzantine agreement (recall that we are assuming arbitrary behaviour by failed processors). It is possible to perform Byzantine agreement at a higher level than proposed here, for example, by performing agreement on VMQs, as discussed in [15]. In this scheme, voted messages are inserted directly in VMQs, and order processes *periodically* execute a Byzantine agreement algorithm called *join* to agree upon a common ordering for messages present in all VMQs. This solution can be attractive if a reasonable period for executing the algorithm can be determined. There is however no simple means of determining this period. Our solution avoids this problem by making use of atomic broadcast *before* entering messages in VMQs.

A very interesting scheme - which does not make use of Byzantine agreement and thus falls in the second class of solutions - has been proposed in [16]. This scheme optimizes the number of messages that need be exchanged between process triads for voting and sequencing. Here processes at sender and receiver triads are partitioned into primary and secondary groups and a clever *distance voting* scheme is used for sequencing. This scheme appears unattractive in the system proposed here for two reasons. Firstly, it requires accurate assessment of timeouts for detecting absence of messages - this is not easy if messages have to be relayed through intermediate processors; and secondly, the scheme is very much 'process triad based', such that there does not appear to be any means of delegating the task of voting and ordering to 'system processes' that can be shared by all the processes of a processor. This makes the task of achieving replication transparency much harder. A scheme which also makes use of primary and secondary groups has been proposed in [17]; however it assumes a restricted 'fail stop' failure model for processors.

Another approach to solving the sequencing problem is to use another voter between a VMQ and C_{ij} [18]. If such an input voter detects a disagreement or cannot form the majority then this could either be due to a sequencing failure (all three messages being voted are different) or due to processor failures or both. Thus, it is necessary to be able to distinguish sequence failures from processor failures. The paper [18] describes a means of achieving this. A possible shortcoming of this approach is that it makes voting algorithms rather complex. We believe that if atomic broadcast among processor triads can be achieved

183

cheaply then the scheme presented here is more attractive. Input voting has also been suggested in the VOTRICS system [9]. This system employs a processor interconnection scheme which is similar to ours. The description of input voting presented there is however not in sufficient detail to enable us to evaluate the approach.

Finally, we would like to mention the scheme described in [19] where sequence failures are detected as *exceptions* by voters and backward error recovery is performed by processes causing the sequencing failure. In the present paper we have assumed that backward error recovery facility is not available, thus ruling out this solution.

As stated before, the atomic broadcast mechanism requires the properties of termination and atomicity. To achieve termination, it is necessary to have the clocks of all non-faulty processors of a triad to be synchronized such that the measurable difference between the readings of clocks at any instant is bounded by a known constant (say ϵ). To achieve atomicity, each processor is required to relay the message received as a result of a broadcast to both of its neighbours. Let d be the maximum unpredictable message transmission delay, then the lower bound for constant Δ of atomic broadcast can be shown to be equal to $2(d + \epsilon)$ [7]. Clock synchronization error ϵ will be of the order of d [20] thus giving the value of Δ to be of the order of a few d. Since processors of a triad are directly connected to each other, d can be made quite small by employing special low level protocols. With Transputers for example, d for short messages can be of the order of several microseconds, thus Δ is expected to be of the order of a few hundred microseconds. This is not deemed excessive if we realize that tolerance to Byzantine faults is being achieved.

6. Concluding Remarks

We have presented an architecture for triplicated processing of concurrent programs. The architecture has been devised for processors with point to point communication links. Assuming four (six) links per processor, a pipeline (grid) processor interconnection scheme has been proposed. We have developed a model for replicated processing and shown how replication transparency can be achieved. The underlying communications layer is required to support clock synchronization and atomic broadcasts between processor triads and provide a fairly conventional inter-process message passing facilities. A replication layer can then be built on top to perform ordering and voting of all inter-process messages between computational processes. As can be seen, exploiting redundancy in a distributed system to mask the effects of arbitrarily failing processors is a hard task! We are embarking on a project to build a Transputer based system with the characteristics discussed here. At the same time, we are investigating design issues for supporting time critical computations by enabling a process to deterministically select any message from its VMQ rather than just the one at the head . The prototype system will enable us to evaluate the cost of replication.

7. Acknowledgments

The work reported here has been supported in part by grants from the UK Science and Engineering Research Council.

References

[1] F.B. Schneider, "Abstractions for fault tolerance in distributed systems", Proc. of IFIP 86 Congress, 1986, pp. 727-733, North Holland.

[2] S.K. Shrivastava, "Replicated distributed processing", Lecture notes in Computer Science, Vol. 248, 1987, pp. 325-337, Springer Verlag.

[3] J.H. Wensley et al., "SIFT: Design and analysis of a fault-tolerant computer for aircraft control", Proc. of IEEE, 66, 10, October 1978, pp. 1240-1255.

[4] R.E. Harper, J.H. Lala and J.J. Deyst, "Fault tolerant processor architecture overview", Digest of papers, Fault Tol. Comp. Symp-18, Tokyo, June 1988, pp. 252-257.

[5] D. Powell et al., "The Delta-4 approach to dependability in open distributed computing systems", Digest of papers, Fault Tol. Comp. Symp-18, Tokyo, June 1988, pp. 246-251.

[6] K.P. Berman, "Replication and fault tolerance in the ISIS system", Proc. of 10th ACM Symp. on Operating System Principles, Washington, December 1985, pp. 79-86.

[7] L. Lamport, R. Shostak and M. Pease, "The Byzantine Generals problem", ACM Trans. on Prog. Lang. and Systems, 4(2), July 1982, pp. 382-401.

[8] Inmos Ltd, "Transputer Reference Manual", Prentice Hall, 1988.

[9] N. Theuretzbacher, "VOTRICS: Voting triple modular computing system", Digest of papers, Fault Tol. Comp. Symp-16, Vienna, July 1986, pp. 144-150.

[10] Inmos Ltd, "OCCAM 2 Reference Manual", Prentice Hall, 1988.

[11] A.D. Birrell and B.J. Nelson, "Implementing remote procedure calls", ACM Trans. on Computer Systems, 2(1), February 1984, pp. 39-59.

[12] R. Rivest, A. Shamir and L. Adleman, "A method of obtaining digital signatures and public-key cryptosystems", Comm. ACM, February 1978, pp. 120-126.

[13] F. Cristian, H. Aghili, R. Strong and D. Dolev, "Atomic broadcast: from simple message diffusion to Byzantine Agreement", Digest of papers, Fault Tol. Comp. Symp-15, Ann Arbor, June 1985, pp. 200-206.

[14] O. Babaoglu and R. Drummond, "(Almost) no cost clock synchronization (preliminary version)", Digest of papers, Fault Tol. Comp. Symp-17, Michigan, June 1987, pp. 42-47.

[15] L. Mancini, "Modular redundancy in a message passing system", IEEE Trans. on Soft. Eng., January 1986, pp. 79-86.

[16] K. Echtle, "Fault masking and sequencing agreement by a voting protocol with low message number", Proc. of 6th Symp. on reliability in dist. soft. and database systems, Williamsburg, March 1987, pp. 149-160.

[17] N. Natarajan and J. Tang, "Synchronization of redundant computation in a distributed system", Proc. of 6th Symp. on reliability in dist. software and database systems, Williamsburg, March 1987, pp. 139-148.

[18] L. Mancini and S.K. Shrivastava, "Failure detection in replicated systems", Computing Laboratory, University of Newcastle Upon Tyne, Tech. report no. 238, June 1987.

[19] L. Mancini and S.K. Shrivastava. "Exception handling in replicated systems with voting", Digest of papers, Fault Tol. Comp. Symp-16, Vienna, July 1986, pp. 384-389.

[20] J.Y Halpern, B. Simons, R. Strong and D. Dolev, "Fault tolerant clock synchronization", Proc. of 3rd Symp. on Principles of Dist. Computing, Vancouver, August 1984, pp. 89-102.

Prolog Architectures
Chair: R. Ginosar, Technion

KCM: A Knowledge Crunching Machine

H. Benker, J.M. Beacco, S. Bescos, M. Dorochevsky, Th. Jeffré, A. Pöhlmann,
J. Noyé, B. Poterie, A. Sexton, J.C. Syre, O. Thibault, G. Watzlawik

ECRC, Arabellastr. 17, 8000 Muenchen 81, West Germany

E-mail: {hans, jacques, jclaude}@ecrcvax.uucp

ABSTRACT

KCM (Knowledge Crunching Machine) is a high-performance back-end processor which, coupled to a UNIX* desk-top workstation, provides a powerful and user-friendly Prolog environment catering for both development and execution of significant Prolog applications. This paper gives a general overview of the architecture of KCM stressing some new features like a 64-bit tagged architecture, shallow backtracking and an original memory management unit. Some early benchmark results obtained on prototype machines are presented. They show that KCM, which runs at a peak speed of 833 Klips on list concatenation, compares favorably with other dedicated Prolog machines and available commercial systems running on fast general purpose processors.

Keywords: Prolog engine, tagged architecture, memory system

1 Introduction

KCM (Knowledge Crunching Machine) is intended to be a single user, single task high-performance back-end processor which, coupled to a UNIX* desk-top workstation, provides a powerful and user-friendly Prolog environment catering for both development and execution of significant Prolog applications. Conducted at ECRC, this project is a joint effort involving ECRC 's shareholders Bull, ICL and Siemens who intend to build KCM pilot machines in 89. Until now and unlike its predecessors ICM3 [12] and ICM4 [1] which did not go beyond chip level simulations, prototype KCM machines have been built. A complete software environment is currently being written, based on SEPIA [8], a second generation Prolog system also developed at ECRC.

Starting from the ICM3 design the general architecture was simplified and the functionality of the machine was extended (FPU, MMU supporting paging, hardware stack overflow check). Much care has been taken to keep the machine as flexible as possible. Though KCM is dedicated to Prolog, it is not restricted to Prolog and can be seen as a tagged general purpose machine with support for Logic Programming in general.

This paper is organised as follows; section 2 explains the main design decisions. Then section 3 describes the architecture of the machine. In section 4, some early benchmark results are presented. Comparisons are made with other dedicated Prolog machines and Prolog systems running on general purpose computers. We conclude by sketching future work.

We assume some familiarity with the programming language Prolog [16] and its implementation techniques [20, 5].

2 Design Decisions

2.1 System Environment of KCM

The KCM machine is intended to supply a workstation type of machine with high performance for processing logic programming languages. Our first approach to this goal was to design a Prolog co-processor, following the example of existing numerical co-processors. This is the easiest way to connect to existing software written under UNIX*. Unfortunately, as opposed to numerical co-processors, the memory behaviour of Prolog programs is very dynamic and they need random access to all symbol tables and to the entire run-time environment. Therefore either the Prolog co-processor has to share all data with the host or to support its own run-time environment.

Sharing all data between the host and the co-processor means that all data need to be in identical formats on both processors. Due to the architectural differences between the machines such a format can only be a non-optimal compromise for at least one of the machines.

The high memory bandwidth requirement is easier to match if the memory is not shared with another processor.

It is very inefficient to frequently switch the execution of a program between the host and the co-processor. Unlike numerical co-processors it may ask for help from the host, e.g. to execute a built-in predicate in Prolog. In this case the complete internal state of the co-processor has to be sent to the host. This is very costly, since the internal state consists of all internal registers and the dirty entries in the cache (if it is store-in, which is reasonable to assume).

For these reasons KCM was designed as back-end processor with its own private memory. The complete language sub-system runs on KCM which is designed as a single-task machine. It uses the host with its operating system (UNIX) as server for I/O including tasks like e.g. interaction with the user (tty, window system etc.), file management, paging etc.

---

*UNIX is a registered trademark of AT&T.

Figure 1 shows the system environment of KCM and how it is connected to a host machine. Physically the CPU of KCM is implemented on one large printed circuit board. The interface with the communication memory and the main memory of KCM are separate boards of double-euro format. All boards together fit into the cabinet of the diskless desktop workstation that is used as host.

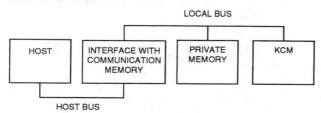

Figure 1: KCM System Environment

2.2 Technology

For the implementation of KCM we choose to use standard TTL and CMOS technology. Although top-of-the-range ASIC technology certainly gives performance advantages over the use of off-the-shelf components, it was not considered worthwhile for a research project. It is easier to experiment with standard components and undertake small design changes if one does not fix the design in silicon. Nevertheless two small ASIC chips are used which make it easier to fulfill the requirement to fit into a workstation.

2.3 Word Format

The model of computation for KCM is derived from the WAM, the abstract machine defined by D.H.D. Warren [20]. This model supposes tagged data words, i.e. a basic entity consists of a value plus an additional tag field that gives information on its type.

Most commercial Prolog systems on general-purpose computers pack tag and value into a 32-bit word, thus reducing the range of virtual addresses and integers. Many tagged architectures are based on a word of 36 - 40 bits to store a 32 bit value together with the tag, causing problems to the communication with standard machines, due to the non-standard word length. Therefore some AI-machines actually use 40 bits internally but 64 bits externally, i.e. in memory and on disc ([7]). There are also software systems using 64 bits to store a Prolog entity. In particular the system developed at ECRC is designed that way, see [8]. This was adopted for KCM which is built as a 64-bit machine, 32 bits for the value part and 32 bits for the tag part (figure 2 shows the KCM data word).

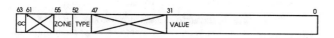

Figure 2: KCM Data Word Format

For simplicity of the design it was decided to use identical size for both code and data words. RISC supporters have proved that a fixed instruction length saves a lot of decoding hardware and also time in the critical path. A 64-bit instruction word allows encoding register addresses etc. always in the same fields of the instruction. The savings in decoding hardware make up for a large amount of the additional memory used. Also a 64-bit instruction width provides room for a lot of flexibility allowing a more regular and simple, but yet powerful instruction set. Figure 3 shows the two basic instruction formats of KCM.

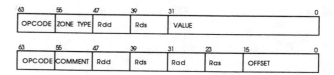

Figure 3: KCM Instruction Word Formats

2.4 Memory System

KCM has two separate access paths to memory, one for code and one for data. There are two independent caches, but the physical memory is shared between instructions and data. KCM shares this property with most RISC architectures as well as some of the recent CISC designs (e.g. 68030).

Both caches of KCM are logical caches, i.e. they operate on the basis of virtual addresses. Logical caches are faster than physical caches, because there is no need to translate addresses for every memory access, but only for cache misses. The main reason why logical caches are rarely used is that they need to be flushed on a context switch. This is no problem to KCM as it is designed as a single-task backend processor.

To improve locality on stacks it was decided to use a version of the WAM known as the split-stack model, i.e. there are two separate stacks for environments and choice points to control execution instead of one.

2.5 Control

The basic operation in unification is a kind of pattern matching which involves the comparison of the type and value parts of two words in parallel. Multiple different reactions may be required, according to the result of the analysis of the two types involved. Due to its microcoded control KCM can quickly change the flow of control. It is equipped with special data paths to calculate entry points into microcode according to the combination of two types.

The semantics of some instructions of KCM are not context-free. According to the value of a number of flags such instructions may be executed in different modes. The mode bits are taken into account when decoding instructions and therfore do not need to be tested explicitly.

KCM is an entirely synchronous machine, controlled by a single central microsequencer. Simulation studies revealed that typically the gain achievable by asynchronous operation of an instruction prefetch unit is compensated by the overhead of synchronisation.

2.6 Top-Level Architecture

Starting from the Harvard architecture the top-level block diagram of the machine is easily developed. The basic parts are the two caches with the data processing units connected to them: the execution unit to the data cache and the instruction prefetch unit to the code cache. These units are controlled by the control unit and the memory management connects the physical memory. The memory management is in between the caches and the main memory, not in between the CPU and the caches, i.e. logical caches are used. The block diagram in figure 4 shows these units with the main buses of KCM.

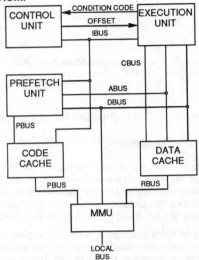

Figure 4: KCM Top Level Architecture

3 Architecture of KCM

According to the design decisions developed in the previous section we can now present the main features of KCM:

- 64-bit tagged architecture
- conventional technology (TTL/CMOS) plus two CMOS-ASICs
- 4-phase clock system, 80 ns cycle time
- separate logical code and data caches, 8K words each
- private memory (32 Mbytes on one board)
- hardware support for unification and backtracking
- verification of access rights to virtual addresses

3.1 The CPU

3.1.1 Basic Data Manipulation

Source and destination for all data manipulation instructions are registers in the 64 x 64 bit register file. The instructions have a four address format; two source and two destination registers. The addresses are supplied to the register file by the Register Address Calculator RAC which is implemented in an 1.5 µm CMOS ASIC.

Using the four address format KCM supports a move instruction that moves the contents of two 64 bit wide registers in one cycle. Figure 5 shows the basic data paths used: the source data are put on the buses ABUS and BBUS. They are transferred via the ALUs ALU_C and ALU_D and written back to the register file on the buses CBUS and DBUS respectively.

For arithmetic and other data manipulation the ALU_D or the FPU are used. Such instructions use only three of the four register address fields in the instruction format: two source and one destination register. Both the ALU and FPU only treat the data part of a word; 32 bit IEEE data format is used. The

tag part of the data word usually just bypasses the ALU or FPU using the Tag-Value-Multiplexer TVM.

For operations on 64 bit words the TVM is used. It can manipulate the garbage collection bits in the data word and swap value and tag parts of a word.

Most data manipulation instructions execute in one cycle. Exceptions to this rule are: floating point operations, integer multiplication and division.

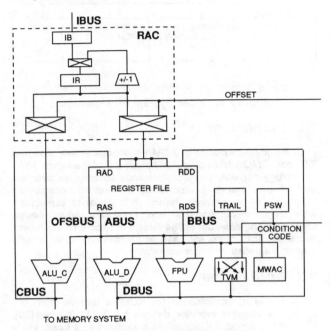

Figure 5: The Execution Unit

3.1.2 Memory Access

KCM supports three address modes: direct, pre-address calculation, post-address calculation.

The direct address mode uses an instruction format that comprises an absolute address and a source or destination register for a store or load instruction respectively.

The pre- and post-address calculation instructions use an instruction format with three register addresses and a 16-bit signed offset. The register addresses are:

- Ras - address source register
- Rad - address destination register
- Rds - data source register for store instructions
- Rdd - data destination register for load instructions

The contents of Ras is put on the ABUS. The ALU_C adds the 16 bit signed offset from OFSBUS to the address and the result of the computation is stored into register Rad via the CBUS.

The data cache can use either ABUS or CBUS as address source, i.e. the address can be taken directly from register Ras or include the offset. The data input/output of the data cache is connected to the DBUS.

The addressing modes allow implementation of stacks that grow in either direction. Pre-increment, post-increment, predecrement, post-decrement, as well as an offset from the top-of-stack are all supported.

3.1.3 Instruction Sequencing

Figure 6 shows a diagram of the instruction prefetch unit of KCM. It is based on a three stage pipeline: the register P contains the address of n+2; the register IB contains the instruction n+1 and SP the address from where it was fetched; the register IR contains the instruction n that is currently executed and TP its address in the code space.

During normal execution P is incremented every cycle and the registers SP, TP, IB, and IR are all clocked. This allows to fetch and execute instructions at a rate of 1 instruction/cycle.

A special instruction predecoding hardware switches the multiplexer for P to use IB as input if the currently fetched instruction is a branch. Thus immediate jump and call instructions take two cycles. All branches in KCM have absolute addresses as branch targets.

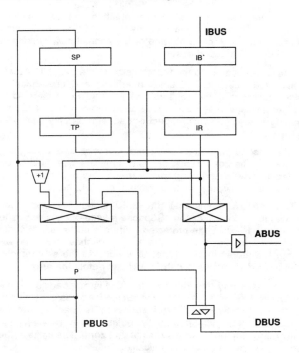

Figure 6: The Prefetch Unit

Conditional branches operate on the status bits of the ALU and FPU as well as other status bits in the machine that are all stored in the Processor Status Word PSW. Conditional branches take only one cycle if the branch is not taken and four cycles if the branch is taken.

The prefetch unit is implemented as two 32-bit slices using 1.5 μm CMOS ASIC technology.

3.1.4 Support for Unification

The basic elements supporting unification in KCM are the Multi-Way-Address-Calculator MWAC together with the microcoded control.

Following the basic ideas of the WAM [20] the compiler splits unification into a number of smaller steps implemented as unification instructions. The corresponding algorithms are to first determine the types of the input parameter(s) and then take appropriate action. In order to implement these unification steps efficiently it is therefore necessary to quickly react, according to the combination of types of the input parameters.

The MWAC is implemented as a PROM. Its inputs are the two type fields of the source operands on ABUS and BBUS. Depending on the current unification instruction it maps the two input types onto a 4 bit offset. The microcode sequencer branches to a microcode address to which it adds this offset, i.e. it does a 16-way branch according to the input types.

The algorithms for the instructions unifying lists or structures are different for the read and write case. The *get_list* and *get_structure* set the read/write mode flag. In KCM this flag is directly used for the decoding of the unification instructions. The appropriate microcode can therefore start immediately and no time is lost for a test.

The register file holds the source operands for unification instructions. These may be the objects to be unified themselves or they may be references to objects in memory. The objects in memory may again be references to other objects. Some hardwired control in addition to microcoded control of the data cache supports the detection of references. It is possible to start a dereferencing operation in the data cache even if the object sent to the data cache is not an address. If it is an address, then the data cache will perform a read, if it is not then it will abort the read (this is important, because random data - like e.g. a floating point number - used as an address may cause a cache-miss and even a page fault which certainly is not tolerable). This allows following reference chains at the rate of one reference per cycle.

3.1.5 Support for Backtracking

In general, Prolog execution relies heavily on backtracking. Each time there are at least two clauses matching the current goal, the state of the computation has to be saved. In case of failure of the first alternative, the execution can then backtrack and try the following alternative.

In the standard WAM, a special frame called choice point has to be pushed onto memory each time such a situation occurs. The size of a choice point varies with the number of arguments but its typical size is about 10 words. Saving and restoring such frames was found to be a major source of memory traffic. According to [17], it amounts to about 50% of all memory references.

In KCM, the creation of choice points is delayed so that in case of shallow backtracking saving and restoring a choice point is avoided. Shallow backtracking is very frequent (see [21] or [17]). It corresponds to a failure in the head or the guard of a clause for which there are still alternatives. The guard is a possibly empty series of goals following the head which is known not to modify the Prolog state of execution (with the exception of the continuation).

The scheme used (inspired by [13]) relies on two flags. In case of failure the *shallow flag* indicates the type of the failure. It is set each time a clause with some remaining alternatives is entered and reset at the neck of the clause (i.e. after the guard). The *choice point flag* indicates whether there is already a choice point for the current clause. If a clause is entered in deep mode, it is set, otherwise it is reset.

When trying the first alternative, only three state registers are saved into shadow registers in the register file. No choice point is generated until the neck of the clause (or the neck of some of its alternatives in case of shallow backtracking) is encountered. The execution of many predicates is then made deterministic, i.e. the head and the guard suffices to select a unique matching clause without any choice point creation.

Both flags are treated as the read/write mode flag at decode time and thus never tested at execution time.

The creation of choice points itself is supported by the Register Address Calculator (RAC). It supplies the register file with addresses. On choice point creation/restoration a number of consecutive registers, depending on the arity of the predicate, need to be stored/loaded. The RAC can increment and decrement register addresses and therefore a microcode loop can store/load one register per cycle.

When unification binds a variable that is older than the last choice point, it has to push an item onto the trail stack in order to unbind the variable upon the next fail. Up to three comparisons of the address of the variable with the contents of special registers are required in order to determine whether trailing is necessary or not. The Trail hardware in the execution unit of KCM performs these comparisons in parallel with dereferencing.

3.2 The Memory System of KCM

3.2.1 Virtual Address Spaces

Code and Data Space
Prolog and other AI languages allow some kind of self modifying code and incremental compilation. To overcome resulting consistency problems between data and code cache KCM has two different address spaces for code and data along with two sets of instructions to access each of them. Incrementally generated code is written directly to the code cache. This however preserves the possibility for a compiler/assembler/linker/loader to run in batch mode and generate large blocks of instructions in the data space (where a write access is more efficient). When the compilation is finished, the memory management system can invalidate the virtual data page and attach the physical page to the code space.

Available Virtual Address Space
All addresses in KCM are word addresses, i.e. they address a 64-bit entity. In the current implementation of the KCM architecture only the 28 least significant bits of the value part of the address are used. Due to the two separate virtual address spaces the total amount of virtual memory is the equivalent of 32 bits, i.e. KCM can address as much virtual space as most 32-bit processors but the address format has room for future extensions.

3.2.2 Semantics of an Address

There are only two different types of words in KCM that need to be distinguished by context: code and data. Instructions are distinguished by opcodes and data contain a type field encoding different types. Data words can be used as addresses. Figure 7 shows the format of a data word used as address.

The bits 31 to 0 are the actual value of the address. These bits correspond to an address in a non-tagged architecture.

The four bits 51 to 48 encode 16 possible types such as *integer*, *floating point*, *variable*, *list*, *data pointer*, or *code pointer*.

The four bits 55 to 52 encode a zone in virtual memory. Stacks, heaps, and other data areas are mapped to zones. Thus the zone bits encode information like e.g. local stack, global stack, heap, and static data area.

The bits 63 to 56 and 47 to 32 are currently not used for addresses.

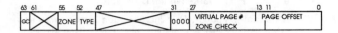

Figure 7: KCM Address Format

3.2.3 Check of Access Rights at the Logical Level

The MMU provides protection mechanisms for physical memory. There are three reasons which led us to introduce an additional protection scheme called zone check, working at the level of virtual addresses.

The first reason is to monitor the size of the multiple stacks. This allows detection of stack overflows and prevention of stack collisions. The monitoring of stack size can be used to trigger garbage collection as well as to implement an adapted paging strategy. In this respect our scheme is very similar to [15].

The second reason is additional security and debugging support. The zone check of KCM uses the type field of an object to prevent the programmer from using e.g. the result of a floating point operation to address a memory cell.

The third reason is that the MMU is not involved when writing to the logical cache. Suppose a write-access occurs to an invalid or write-protected virtual address. Without protection on the level of the logical caches the data will simply be stored in the cache. It is not until the same cache cell is used otherwise that the MMU can detect the error.

Each stack and memory area in KCM is mapped to a zone which is defined by a start and an end address. Using the zone number given with every address it is checked that the value of that address actually points to in between the minimum and maximum address of that zone. The limits of the zones may be changed dynamically.

Each of the different stack pointers has a different zone number. If the stack pointer is incremented or decremented beyond the minimum or maximum address of its zone then the next access using it will cause a trap.

The zone check helps developing system (assembler) programs by forcing and verifying the proper use of addresses: each zone may only allow a limited number of types as addresses and each zone may be write-protected. In the following we give examples of types that are or are not allowed as addresses in different zones. Any number type like *integer* or *floating point* is not allowed as address pointing into any zone. Lists and structures are constructed on the global stack. Therefore the types *list* and *structure* are allowed as addresses into the global stack as well as the types *reference* and *data pointer*. On the local stack, however, only *reference* and *data pointer* are allowed, since lists and structures are not constructed there. Other stacks like the choice point stack allow only *data pointer* to be used as an address, since no *reference* may ever point into that stack.

The zone check operates on virtual addresses when accessing the data cache. It verifies that the most significant 4 address bits not used in the current implementation are zero. Then it checks whether the 16 bits from 27 to 12 (see figure 7) are within the range stored in a special RAM field. This allows the definition of zones with a granularity of 4K words.

3.2.4 The Caches

The Data Cache
Studies of Prolog memory behaviour show that many items get pushed onto the stacks that are never accessed again [17]. This is due to the fact that environments and structures are allocated but never read because of failure. As result the ratio of reads to writes in Prolog is about 1:1 which is much smaller than in conventional programming languages. Therefore the data cache in KCM is a so called store-in or copy-back cache where data is written to memory only when the cache cell is needed otherwise, but not at every single write. The access time for both read and write is 80 ns.

Prolog stacks show a high locality near the top [17]. Thus, a direct-mapped cache works very well for a single stack. For a stack which is only accessed from the top it has exactly the same behaviour as a top-of-stack circular buffer, but it is easier to implement. A direct mapped cache can also cache items deep in the stack, if required, for stacks with random accesses. The problem with direct mapped caches is what happens if accesses to multiple stacks occur and the top-of-stack pointers modulo the cache size are close to each other. We ran a number of small programs in a simulator of a direct mapped cache with two different initialisations: In the first run the top-of-stack pointers were initialised to values such that they used different cache locations. For the second run the top-of-stack pointers were initialised such that they all pointed to the same cache cell. The hit ratios were very good in the first run and dropped quite dramatically in the second.

In a direct mapped cache such collisions between stacks are bound to occur at some stage, because stacks grow at different rates. A set associative cache solves this problem, but at a high cost in hardware - and even worse - a slower cycle time. KCM uses a direct mapped data cache, but it is split into 8 sections of 1K x 64 bits each. The sections are selected by the zone field of the address word.

The line (block) size of the data cache is one.

The Code Cache
Unlike the data cache the instruction cache almost always is accessed to read an instruction, but only very rarely to write. Therefore it is designed as a write-through cache. The read access time is 80ns.

The size of the code cache is 8K x 64 bits.

The line size of the code cache is one. Since it is a write-through cache the line size does not prevent the code cache from using the page mode of the memory and fetching a few words ahead when a miss occurs.

3.2.5 Address Translation and Allocation of Physical Memory

The address translation hardware is designed for speed and simplicity, i.e. a simple RAM is used to hold the entire page table rather than storing the page table in main memory and use an associative cache for fast access to recent translations. This design works because KCM is a single-task machine that does not need to do context switches. There is no need to exchange valid page tables between one process and another and so the size of the page table held in the machine does not matter. There is no need either to swap pages out because another process would need them. Therefore pages can be quite large.

The bits 27 to 14 of an address give the virtual page number and the bits 13 to 0 the offset into one page (see figure 7), i.e. the page size is 16K words.

The address translation is done using a RAM organised as 32K x 16 bit. It contains one entry for each virtual page (16K virtual pages for code and data each). Each entry consists of 5 status bits plus 11 bits physical page number.

3.2.6 Main Memory

The main memory is implemented on a separate board of double-euro format. Using SMD technology with components mounted on both sides one such board holds 32 MBytes. This is using 1 Mbit chips, but the layout of the board allows the use of 4 Mbit chips to obtain 128 MBytes. Two such boards can be plugged into the workstation.

The memory is implemented with a 32 bit wide data bus. A fast page mode is used to access two 32 bit words in order to form a 64 bit KCM word. The page mode is also used to prefetch data for the code cache. The page mode cycle time is 120 ns.

4 Early Results

Since the first prototype started working in July 1988, a number of benchmark programs have been run on KCM in order to verify the correctness and measure the performance of the machine. Currently there are three KCM machines available on which the benchmark programs are run, using a first software environment including:

- code generation tools (Prolog compiler, macro assembler, linker)

- a loader

- an emulator

- monitors (at microcode, macrocode, and Prolog levels)

- a message passing system connecting the tools to the KCM systems (KCM and its driver or the emulator) in a plug-compatible way.

Though many more benchmark programs have been run, we will restrict ourselves to the PLM suite. This suite was gathered by the PLM team at U.C. Berkeley in order to evaluate the performance of the PLM [4]. It is an extension of the initial set of benchmarks written by D.H.D. Warren [19]. It has the advantage of having been widely distributed and used so that there is no ambiguity on the benchmark programs and queries.

The programs were compiled and assembled on the host

with integer arithmetic and static linking*. Each program was linked together with a small runtime library (I/O, timing predicates to control a timer residing on the KCM-host interface card...). Note that this library did not include any assert/retract facilities which made it impossible to run one of the programs of the suite. The programs were finally downloaded and run on KCM.

4.1 Static Code Size Comparisons

Table 1 compares the static code sizes for KCM, PLM and SPUR. SPUR is a general-purpose RISC architecture that supports tagged data developed at U.C. Berkeley [7]. The figures on PLM and SPUR are taken from [2]. Note that in the three cases the values indicated do not include the code of the runtime library which has to be linked with each program.

	PLM		SPUR		KCM			KCM/PLM		SPUR/KCM	
Program	Instr.	Bytes	Instr.	Bytes	Instr.	Words	Bytes	Instr.	Bytes	Instr.	Bytes
con1	28	87	414	1656	33	31	248	1.18	2.85	12.55	6.68
con6	32	106	430	1720	39	41	328	1.22	3.09	11.03	5.24
divide10	213	661	3988	15952	214	234	1872	1.00	2.83	18.64	8.52
hanoi	52	183	385	1540	56	59	472	1.08	2.58	6.88	3.26
log10	207	625	4040	16160	198	208	1664	0.96	2.66	20.40	9.71
mutest	141	468	1703	6812	162	172	1376	1.15	2.94	10.51	4.95
nrev1	71	260	761	3044	64	70	560	0.90	2.15	11.89	5.44
ops8	205	633	3804	15216	206	216	1728	1.00	2.73	18.47	8.81
palin	178	565	2556	10224	230	240	1920	1.29	3.40	11.11	5.32
pri2	132	383	1933	7732	141	151	1208	1.07	3.15	13.71	6.40
qs4	121	456	1230	4920	184	192	1536	1.52	3.37	6.68	3.20
queens	242	723	3636	14544	212	224	1792	0.88	2.48	17.15	8.12
query	273	1138	3942	15768	305	357	2856	1.12	2.51	12.92	5.52
times10	213	661	3988	15952	214	224	1792	1.00	4.68	18.64	8.90
average								1.10	2.96	13.61	6.43

Table 1: Static code size comparison

As expected, the static instruction KCM/PLM ratios are close to 1, though a little bit higher. Both machines rely on the same kind of high-level WAM-like instructions to run Prolog. The main difference is due to the use of cdr-coding in PLM. This allows PLM to compile a statically known list cell in one instruction rather than two in KCM. This notably results in high ratios for nrev1 and qs4 which include long input lists (respectively 30 and 50 elements). However, as discussed in [18], cdr-coding is only effective, as far as code space is concerned, for statically built lists. It does not bring a significant benefit on average.

The static byte KCM/PLM ratio is about 3. The average PLM instruction is 3.3 bytes long, whereas the average KCM instruction is slightly more than 8 bytes long (because of the *switch* instructions which are the only multi-word instructions together with some specialised byte manipulation instructions). This gives an idea of the cost of our instruction encoding in terms of memory space. This cost is quite reasonable compared to the cost of a low level instruction set such as SPUR, which produces, on average, code which is more than 6 times bigger. The code cache is expected to be large enough to keep the incurred traffic ratio low. This however requires further evaluation.

4.2 Benchmark Execution Times

Table 2 compares the PLM machine with KCM. The PLM figures are first evaluation figures extracted from [4]. For each program two timings were given, one for hand compiled code and one for automatically compiled code. The best figure is retained.

Benchmark		PLM		KCM		PLM/KCM
Program	Inferences	ms	Klips	ms	Klips	ms/ms
con1	6	0.023	261	0.007	857	3.29
con6	42	0.137	307	0.059	712	2.32
divide10	22	0.380	58	0.091	242	4.18
hanoi	1787	7.323	244	2.795	639	2.62
log10	14	0.109	128	0.039	359	2.79
mutest	1365	12.407	110	4.644	294	2.67
nrev1	499	2.660	188	0.650	768	4.09
ops8	20	0.214	93	0.059	339	3.63
palin25	325	3.152	103	1.221	266	2.58
pri2	1235	10.000	124	5.240	236	1.91
qs4	612	4.854	126	1.316	465	3.69
queens	687	4.222	163	1.205	570	3.50
query	2893	17.342	167	12.610	229	1.38
times10	22	0.330	67	0.082	268	4.02
average						3.05

Table 2: Comparison with PLM

It is important to note that the PLM timings result from a simulation of the benchmark programs and, as such, rely on some simplifying assumptions. In particular, built-in functions implemented via the escape mechanism (i.e. resorting to the host) were not accurately timed; they were allocated a standard 3 cycles.

To get a fair comparison, the same kind of assumption was made, on KCM side, for write/1 and nl/0 which were compiled as unit clauses, so that a call to these predicates costs only 5 cycles (the minimum for a call/return sequence which creates two prefetch pipeline breaks). We cannot however guarantee that both assumptions match completely. This has however no influence on mutest which does not include any I/O and very small influence on most of the programs for which I/O are used only to report the final result. Exceptions are con1 and con6 because of their very small size as well as hanoi which reports each move executed on the towers.

The Klips (Kilo logical inferences by seconds) figures use our own definition of an inference. A logical inference is taken to be the invocation of a goal at the source level. Independently whether a goal is compiled in line or not, it is counted as an inference. For instance the evaluation of an arithmetic expression (predicate is/2) is counted as one inference whatever the complexity of the expression. More generally, calls to built-in predicates are counted as one inference*. This definition has the advantage of being implementation independent. This is not the case for the definition used in [4].

According to these figures, KCM is between two and four times faster than the initial PLM.

---

*In the final system, compilation will take place on KCM with generic arithmetic and dynamic linking by default

---

*The cut operation is not counted as an inference

Table 3 compares KCM with one of the best commercial systems, QUINTUS 2.0, running on a SUN3/280 workstation (M68020 25MHz, FPU 20MHz, 16Mbytes of main memory).

The benchmark programs are not exactly the same as in the previous paragraph. All the I/O predicates (used to print the solutions) have been removed in order to measure the pure inferencing capabilities of both systems. This gives less inferences as well as less Klips. The Klips were, in the previous table, somehow artificially inflated because of the assumptions made on built-in predicate timings.

The holes in the table correspond to programs which were too small to get significant results. On the remaining programs, some important discrepancies were also sometimes noted between successive runs of the same program. For each program, the figure given here is the best figure obtained on 4 successive runs on a quiet system (benchmarking was the only user activity).

According to these measurements, KCM is on average almost 8 times faster than QUINTUS. The ratios range from 5.08 (nrev1) to 10.17 (query). As expected, the lower ratios are obtained for intrinsically deterministic programs for which no backtracking is required. As soon as the execution backtracks, higher ratios are observed. The highest ratio is actually obtained on query, a small database-like query model, showing the efficiency of KCM indexing.

Note however that these figures are slightly biased since Quintus does not allow the integer arithmetic and static linking optimisations. However we do not expect generic arithmetic and dynamic linking to slow down programs significantly, thanks to the use of multi-way branching for generic arithmetic and fast indirect calls via memory (4 cycles). Actually, some programs, e.g. query, will even be speeded up with generic arithmetic (floating arithmetic is significantly faster than integer arithmetic on multiplications and divisions).

Benchmark		QUINTUS		KCM		Q/KCM
Program	Inferences	ms	Klips	ms	Klips	ms/ms
con1*	4			0.006	666	
con6*	12			0.046	261	
divide10*	20			0.090	222	
hanoi*	767	11.600	66	1.264	607	9.18
log10*	12			0.039	308	
mutest*	1365	41.500	33	4.644	294	8.94
nrev1*	497	3.300	151	0.649	766	5.08
ops8*	18			0.058	310	
palin25*	323	9.330	35	1.220	265	7.65
pri2*	1233	30.500	40	5.239	235	5.82
qs4*	610	11.000	55	1.315	464	8.37
queens*	657	9.010	73	1.182	556	7.62
query*	2888	128.170	23	12.605	229	10.17
times10*	20			0.081	247	
average						7.85

Table 3: Comparison with QUINTUS/SUN

4.3 Comparisons with other Prolog Machines

Let us sacrifice to the Klips tradition (we could not escape it in the abstract either), mainly to say that it has not much sense. Table 4 compares the peak performance of a number of major Prolog machines, CHI-II [6], DLM-1 [14], IPP [10], AIP [9], KCM, PSI-II [11] and the successor of PLM, X-1 [3].

The first figure gives the performance of a con1-like program (concatenation of two lists), the second of a nrev1-like (naive reversal of a list).

Machine	By	Klips	Word	Comment
CHI-II	NEC C&C	490 - ?	40	Back-end - multi-processing
DLM-1	BAe	800? - ?	38	Back-end - physical memory
IPP	Hitachi	1360 - 1197	32	Integrated in super-mini (ECL)
AIP	Toshiba	? - 620	32	Back-end
KCM	ECRC	833 - 760	64	Back-end
PSI-II	ICOT	400 - 320	40	Stand-alone - multi-processing
X-1	Xenologic	400?	32	SUN co-processor

Table 4: Comparison with other dedicated Prolog machines

The problem is that there is no standard way to compute these figures. It is especially noticeable on list concatenation. There are two ways to compute Klips there. Either, the whole execution is taken into account, including the generation of input data, or only the basic inferencing step, i.e. the concatenation of one more element, is taken into account. In the first case, further questions are: What is the length of the lists? Is the top-level goal counted as an inference? In Table 4, we used, as CHI-II, the second method (one concatenation step is 15 cycles). Needless to say, it does not give the worst figure.

In spite of these problems, it is clear that KCM compares favorably with other dedicated machines in terms of peak performance. Not taking into account IPP which is implemented in ECL, DLM-1 is the only machine which is claimed to reach the same level of performance as KCM. It is also clear that first, peak performance is not an accurate measure of the efficiency of a system, and second it does not give any hint on its usability. With respect to these points, we think that KCM has definitive assets over DLM like a much simpler design, virtual memory, support of SEPIA (including modules, coroutining, events...).

In all cases, a fair comparison (outside the scope of this paper) should also take into account such points as the system environment of the machine (back-end, co-processor or stand-alone, single or multi-user, multi-processing), its size (chip, desktop, deskside), its memory system (caches, main memory, paging), its technology, the status of the project (paper design, prototype, product, software available)...

5 Future work

Much work remains to be done. On one hand, pilot machines are to be produced in 1989, as a joint effort of ECRC and its three shareholder companies Siemens, Bull, and ICL. On the other, a complete system is expected to be operational by the second quarter of 1989. This will include full host connection including paging and a complete Sepia environment running on KCM (incremental Prolog compiler, modules, coroutining...). The pilot machines will be delivered to selected customers in Europe.

Further evaluation studies will be conducted in parallel with this work, to get proper figures on the influence of each specialized unit (trail, dereferencing, RAC, double port register file...), on the overall performance and on the behaviour of the system on real-size programs.

In the longer term, addressing the problems of C compilation on KCM and of the implementation of constraints is contemplated.

Acknowledgement

Special thanks are due to the Sepia team at ECRC for its extensive collaboration, and particularly Micha Meier for his time and expertise. We acknowledge the invaluable support of Bill O'Riordan at ICL, Chairman of the KCM Project Board. The KCM Project could not have reached its current state without the strong backing of Peter Mueller-Stoy and Walter Woborschil at Siemens, Francois Salle and Francois Anceau at BULL, and many other people in ECRC's Shareholder companies.

References

1. H. Benker, J. Noye, G. Watzlawik. ICM4. Technical report CA-25, ECRC, February, 1987.

2. Gaetano Borriello, Andrew R. Cherenson, Peter B. Danzig and Michael N. Nelson. RISC vs. CISCs for Prolog: A Case Study. ASPLOS II, IEEE Computer Society, October, 1987, pp. 136-145.

3. Tep Dobry. A Coprocessor for AI; LISP, Prolog and Data Bases. Proceedings of Spring Compcon' 87, IEEE Computer Society, February, 1987, pp. 396-402.

4. T.P. Dobry, A.M. Despain and Y.N. Patt. Performance Studies of a Prolog Machine Architecture. The 12th Annual International Symposium on Computer Architecture, IEEE/ACM, June, 1985, pp. 180 - 190.

5. John Gabriel, Tim Lindholm, E.L. Lusk, R.A. Overbeek. A Tutorial on the Warren Abstract Machine for Computational Logic. ANL--84-84, Argonne National Laboratory, June, 1985.

6. S. Habata, R. Nakazaki, A. Konagaya, A. Atarashi and M. Umemura. Co-Operative High Performance Sequential Inference Machine: CHI. Proceedings of ICCD'87, New York, 1987.

7. M. Hill, S. Eggers, J. Larus, G. Taylor, G. Adams, B.K. Bose, G. Gibson, P. Hansen, J. Keller, S. Kong, C. Lee, D. Lee, J. Pendleton, S. Ritchie, D. Wood, B. Zorn, p. Hilfinger, D. Hodges, R. Kerz, J. Ousterhout and D. Patterson. "Design Decisions in SPUR". Computer 19 (November 1986), 8 - 22.

8. M. Meier, P. Dufresne, A. Herold, D. de Villeneuve. Sepia: An Extendible Prolog System. To appear in the proceedings of IFIP 89.

9. S. Kawakita, M. Saito, Y. Hoshino, Y. Bandai, Y. Kobayashi. An Integrated AI Environment for Industrial Expert Systems. International Workshop on AI for Industrial Applications 1988, IEEE Computer Society, 1988, pp. 258-263.

10. K. Kurosawa/ S. Yamaguchi/ S. Abe/ T. Bandoh. Instruction Architecture for a High Performance Integrated Prolog Processor IPP. Proceedings of the 5th International Conference & Symposium on Logic Programming, Hitachi Research Lab., August, 1988, pp. 1507-1530.

11. Hiroshi Nakashima and Katsuto Nakajima. Hardware architecture of the sequential inference machine: PSI-II. Proceedings - 1987 Symposium on Logic Programming, IEEE Computer Society, September, 1987, pp. 104 - 113.

12. J. Noye, J.C. Syre, et al. ICM3: Design and evaluation of an Inference Crunching Machine. Database Machines and Knowledge Base Machines, October, 1987, pp. p. 3-16.

13. M. Meier. Shallow Backtracking in Prolog Programs. Technical Report TR-LP, ECRC, February, 1987.

14. A. Pudner. DLM - A Powerful AI Computer For Embedded Expert Systems. Frontiers in Computing, December, 1987, pp. 187 - 201.

15. M.L. Ross, K. Rammaohanarao. Paging strategy for Prolog based on dynamic virtual memory. TR 86/8, University of Melbourne, August , 1986.

16. Leon Sterling and Ehud Shapiro. Advanced Programming Techniques. Volume I: The Art of Prolog. The MIT Press, 1986.

17. Evan Tick. Frontiers in Logic Programming Architecture and Machine Design. Volume I: Memory Performance of Prolog Architectures. Kluwer Academic Publishers, 1988.

18. Herve Touati and Alvin Despain. An empirical study of the Warren Abstract Machine. Proceedings - 1987 Symposium on Logic Programming, IEEE Computer Society, September, 1987, pp. 114 - 124.

19. David H.D. Warren. Implementing Prolog. 49 and 50, University of Edinburgh, May, 1977.

20. David H. D. Warren. An abstract prolog instruction set. tn309, SRI, October, 1983.

21. A. Yamamoto, M. Mitsui, M. Yokota, K. Nakajiama. The Program Characteristics in Logic Programming Language ESP. OKI Electric, 1986.

A High Performance Prolog Processor with Multiple Function Units

Ashok Singhal

Computer Science Division
University of California
Berkeley, CA 94720

Yale N. Patt

Department of Electrical Engineering and Computer Science
University of Michigan
Ann Arbor, MI 48109-2110

ABSTRACT

We describe the Parallel Unification Machine (PLUM), a Prolog processor that exploits fine grain parallelism using multiple function units executing in parallel. In most cases the execution of bookkeeping instructions is almost completely overlapped by unification, and the performance of the processor is limited only by the available unification parallelism. We present measurements from a register transfer level simulator of PLUM. These results show that PLUM with 3 Unification Units achieves an average speedup of approximately 3.4 over the Berkeley VLSI-PLM, which is usually regarded as the current highest performance special purpose, pipelined Prolog processor. Measurements that show the effects of multiple Unification Units and memory access time on performance are also presented.

1. Introduction

The growing interest in logic programming and Prolog, has resulted in substantial research towards the design of high performance Prolog systems by taking advantage of parallel hardware. Many research groups are trying to exploit parallelism available in Prolog programs by executing parallel processes on multiple processors [2,5,8-10]. Others have tried to exploit parallelism of a finer grain size by overlapping the execution of instructions of a single Prolog process by means of special purpose, pipelined processors [6,14]. Since the pipelines in these processors are quite short, instructions are overlapped only to a very limited extent. A large fraction of the execution time of such processors is spent on control and bookkeeping instructions, instead of unification (an operation similar to pattern matching that performs most of the "useful work" in a Prolog program). In this paper we demonstrate that a processor with multiple function units can overlap execution of many more instructions, and thus achieve a much larger speedup over

sequential pipelined processors. Bookkeeping operations can overlap almost completely with unification, and several unifications can also execute in parallel. We describe one such processor, the Parallel Unification Machine (PLUM), and present performance measures obtained by register transfer level simulation. Each function unit of PLUM can be implemented by a VLSI chip of moderate complexity with a clock frequency comparable to modern single chip microprocessors.

Before proceeding with the description of PLUM, we provide the necessary background for this paper: a brief description of Prolog, a description of the execution and storage model used by PLUM, an introduction to the sources of parallelism in Prolog programs, and a summary of relevant literature. In section 2 we describe the main principles used in the PLUM design. We describe PLUM's architecture and implementation in section 3. Simulation results and analysis are presented in section 4. Section 5 concludes the paper with a summary of our results and a discussion of work in progress.

1.1. A Brief Description of Prolog

Prolog programs consist of a collection of *clauses* and a *goal*. The first goal is also called a *query*. The program is executed by the Prolog system by trying to satisfy the goal using the clauses in the program. Clauses have a *head* and an optional *body* that consists of one or more goals. Goals and clause heads are represented by *terms*. Terms may be simple or complex. Complex terms are *structures* (a list is a special case of a structure); each consists of a *functor* (name and arity of the term) and one or more *arguments*. The arguments are themselves terms. Simple terms are *atoms* or *variables*. The *unification* of two terms is the process by which the variables in the terms are bound such that the two terms become identical. Prolog finds the smallest such set of bindings (this set is unique). A goal succeeds if it unifies with a clause head and if all the goals in the body of the clause also succeed when executed in sequence. If no such clause exists, the goal fails. In order to execute a goal, Prolog tries each clause in the program in sequence. Since a goal can never unify with a clause whose head has a different functor, only clauses that have the same functor in their heads need be tried. The collection of such clauses is called a *procedure*. Thus, a goal is a procedure call. If a procedure has more than one clause

© 1989 ACM 0884-7495/89/0000/0195$01.50

195

that could potentially satisfy a goal, Prolog tries the candidate clauses in sequence until a clause succeeds or there are no more clauses to try. Before trying one of several candidate clauses, the state of the program must be saved in a *choicepoint* so that the state can be restored if the clause fails and another clause must be tried. The process by which the state is restored on failure is called *backtracking*. Backtracking implements Prolog's left to right, depth first search for a solution to the query.

1.2. PLUM's Prolog Execution Model

PLUM's execution model is based on that of the Warren Abstract Machine (WAM) [17]. Conventional procedural languages, such as C, have a stack on which call frames are stored. A call frame contains information such as the return address and procedure arguments. Values of registers may also be saved in the call frame by the caller so that the registers may be restored when control returns to the caller. PLUM also has a memory area in which call frames (called *environments*) are stored. Although we refer to this area as the "environment stack", it is not really a true stack. In conventional programming languages the call frame could be deallocated from the stack when control returns from the callee, and the stack space is reclaimed. Prolog, however, may have to backtrack to the environment of the procedure to try another clause. This can happen if a choicepoint is created after the environment frame is created, and in that case the memory space occupied by the environment cannot be reclaimed when control returns from the callee. Therefore, the current environment frame is not necessarily on top of the environment area, as required by a true stack.

Prolog also needs to provide storage for choicepoints to implement backtracking. Since backtracking uses a depth first search strategy, the choicepoints may be stored on a stack. Environments and choicepoints may be placed in separate stacks (as in PLUM) or in the same stack (as in the PLM [6]).

Prolog creates it data structures, including unbound variables in a memory area called the heap. The heap space is allocated and deallocated as a stack as a simple means of garbage collection. In addition to state saved in a choicepoint, Prolog needs to keep track of all bindings of variables on the heap made after each choicepoint so that these bindings can be undone when backtracking to the choicepoint. This is accomplished by saving the addresses of the variables that are bound after each choicepoint on another stack called the *trail*. The location of the top of the trail stack at the time the choicepoint is created is saved in the choicepoint. All variables whose addresses are in the trail stack above the location saved in the choicepoint are unbound when Prolog backtracks to the choicepoint. Yet another stack, the *push down list* (PDL), is used by the unification algorithm for nested lists and structures.

Arguments could be passed to procedures either in registers (in which case the argument registers must be saved in choicepoints), or in an environment frame in memory (see [15] for a comparison of the two methods). PLUM uses argument registers for reasons that will be explained in section 2.

1.3. Fine Grain Parallelism in Prolog

Several forms of parallelism can be exploited in Prolog programs [13]. AND parallelism is exploited when several goals of a clause are executed in parallel. OR parallelism is exploited when several clauses of a procedure are tried in parallel. The AND and OR branches of the solution tree are usually exploited by parallel processes. Parallelism of a finer grain is also present in Prolog. Unification parallelism is exploited when several arguments of the goal are unified in parallel with corresponding arguments of a clause head. Bookkeeping and control operations, such as choicepoint creation and environment allocation, can execute in parallel with unification. Since unification, bookkeeping and control operations usually execute in far fewer cycles than an AND or OR process, parallelism among them must be exploited with far less overhead in order to be useful. In PLUM fine grain parallelism is exploited by multiple function units.

1.4. Related Work

PLUM evolved out of experiments with PUP [3], which also used multiple function units to exploit fine grain parallelism in Prolog, and with HPS [12], a restricted data flow architecture that uses the Tomasulo algorithm [16] to control multiple function units. PLUM's register set and pipeline control design benefited from the design of the POPE processor [1]. POPE exploits fine grain parallelism only across procedure boundaries by executing each procedure on a separate processor. PLUM's storage model and abstract machine are based on the Warren Abstract Machine (WAM) [17]. Ito et al [11] and Hasegawa et al [9] have proposed data flow machine for logic programming languages that exploit fine grain parallelism. Citrin [4] proposes a static data dependency analysis to determine which unifications of a clause head are known to be independent at compile time, and can be scheduled to run in parallel.

2. Design Philosophy

PLUM's design is based on three main principles: using multiple function units to execute instructions in parallel, using data driven control of the function units so that operations may execute whenever their operands are available, and partitioning memory to increase available memory bandwidth and reduce the sharing of memory among function units. In this section we justify these principles. In addition to this design philosophy, PLUM is designed to eliminate stalls in instruction dispatch pipeline wherever possible by providing architectural support for static branch prediction. Static branch prediction in PLUM requires very little extra hardware because the mechanism is similar to choicepoint creation and backtracking.

2.1. Multiple Specialized Functional Units

The short pipelines of most processors allow only limited overlap of operations. Figure 2.1 illustrates how multiple function units increase the overlap of operations that require multiple cycles to execute. On an average, the Berkeley PLM instructions execute in about 7 cycles [6], but consecutive instructions are overlapped by only one cycle (microinstruction execution is also overlapped by pipelining in the microen-

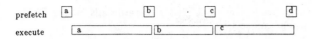

(a) 1 cycle overlap of instructions in the PLM

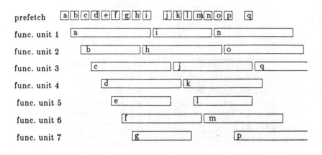

(b) Multiple functional units increase overlap

Figure 2.1: Multiple Functional Units Increase Overlap

gine). Potentially, therefore, a speedup of up to 7 could be achieved by multiple function units. However, because of stalls due to data dependencies and branches in the execution stream, we do not expect to achieve complete overlap of instructions. Each function unit in PLUM has specialized hardware that enables it to execute a particular set of tasks efficiently.

2.2. Data Driven Control

PLUM uses data driven control to resolve data dependencies between instructions. An instruction can execute when its operands are available. Instructions may execute out of order. Instruction dispatch can, therefore, continue beyond a stalled instruction. Additional parallelism is exploited because subsequent instructions may be independent of the stalled instruction and can execute on other function units.

As mentioned earlier, PLUM uses registers to pass arguments to procedures instead of passing them in a call frame. There are two reasons for this choice. First, access to registers is faster than access to memory. Second, data driven control requires some hardware to indicate whether or not an argument is valid, usually a "valid bit" for each datum. Valid bits for the entire memory are expensive and slow (since the valid bits must be reset whenever stack space is reclaimed). Valid bits for a small number of registers are easier to implement. The disadvantage of registers is that they have to be saved in memory in choicepoints and environments. With suitable buffering, and with parallel execution of choicepoint and environment instructions, copying and restoring registers from memory is overlapped with other operations and usually does not slow down execution of a program.

2.3. Partitioned Memory

Since Prolog execution is memory intensive, high performance Prolog processors must provide a high bandwidth access to memory. With multiple function units executing in parallel, PLUM's memory

bandwidth requirement is even greater. In order to provide this bandwidth, each function unit has its own port to memory. A shared memory that can be accessed in parallel through multiple ports is either expensive or slow. In PLUM, the memory is partitioned so that each type of specialized function unit accesses only one partition of memory, and there is no sharing among partitions. This means that the memory can be easily implemented as multiple modules, one for each partition, that can be accessed in parallel.

3. Architecture and Implementation

3.1. Architecture Description

PLUM's architecture is similar to the WAM. Like the WAM, data types are specified by tag fields in data words. A PLUM data word is 32 bits wide. Each data word has a 4-bit type tag and 28-bit value field. The types are listed in table 3.1. List and structure data types contain pointers to lists and structures respectively. Lists consist of elements and links (which have list tags). A list ends with a word in the link position that does not dereference to a list. Although PLUM's storage model is also similar to the WAM, PLUM's memory partitioned as described section 3.1.1. PLUM's registers organization is quite different from the WAM and is described in section 3.1.2. The PLUM instruction set is described in section 3.2.

Table 3.1: Data Types in PLUM

tag (hex)	type
0	unbound variable
1	bound variable (reference)
2	list
3	structure
4	integer
5	atom
6 - E	(currently undefined)
F	nil (special constant)

3.1.1. Memory Organization

The PLUM has 3 separate address spaces (memory partitions): the choicepoint stack, the environment stack, and a global address space. The global address space contains 4 memory areas: code, heap, trail and system memory. The system memory is used by the operating system. The PLUM architecture does not specify a memory area for the *push down list* (PDL), a stack used in the unification of nested lists and structures. A PLUM implementation provides memory space for one or more PDLs either in a separate memory area or in a part of shared memory. Multiple PDLs are useful because several Unification Units could unify nested structures in parallel.

Tick's measurements [15] show that about 50 percent of all data memory accesses in Prolog programs are to the choicepoint stack and about 25 percent to the environment stack. Separate address spaces for the choicepoint and environment areas greatly reduce the memory traffic that would otherwise compete with accesses to the global memory. In our implementation, only the global memory is accessed by multiple function units. Overheads due to cache coherence will only apply to this area which accounts for only about 25 percent of data accesses.

3.1.2. Register Sets

The instruction set of the PLUM is based broadly on the WAM but registers are treated quite differently so that procedure executions are pipelined as in POPE [1]. A procedure has access to two register sets: a source or input register set, and a destination or output register set. A procedure only writes to the output register set. The output register set of one procedure becomes the input register set of the next procedure. The number of register sets is not specified by the architecture. In fact the architecture may assume a very large number of sets and the implementation must ensure that it appears that way.

Table 3.2: PLUM Registers

Name	Register
R0-R7(in,out)	Argument registers(input, output)
CP(in,out)	Continuation pointer
E(in,out)	Environment pointer
TE(in,out)	Top of Environment stack
B(in,out)	Backtrack pointer
TR(in,out)	Trail Pointer
H(in,out)	Heap pointer
L(in,out)	Alternate address
P	Program counter

Table 3.2 lists the registers in each PLUM register set. Apart from the input and output argument registers, there are registers in the input and output set with special functions. The Continuation Pointer (CP) contains the address of the next instruction to execute should the current goal succeed. The Environment Pointer (E) points to the current environment on the environment stack. The TE register points to the top of the environment stack. Note that, unlike the PLM, the PLUM has separate stacks for the environments and choicepoints. The TE register is necessary because the environment stack is not a true stack and the current environment may not be on the top of the environment stack. The backtrack Pointer (B) points to the last choicepoint on the choicepoint stack. The Trail Pointer (TR) points to the top of the trail stack. The Heap Pointer (H) points to the top of the heap. The L register contains the address of the next instruction to execute should the current goal fail. In addition to these registers, there is a Program Counter (P). Memory addresses that appear as arguments in PLUM instructions are offsets from the current value of P.

An important feature of a register set is that it acts as a buffer for the environment and choicepoint because its registers are only written once. Thus, environment and choicepoint instructions can execute after the rest of the instructions for the register set have completed.

3.2. The Instruction Set

Table 3.3 lists the PLUM instructions. They are similar to the Berkeley PLM instructions. We describe them briefly here (see [7] for more details on the PLM instruction set).

Table 3.3. PLUM Instruction Set

Indexing	Load and Save
swot Reg,Lv,Lc,Ll,Ls	load Reg,Y
swoc Reg,Hashtable	save Reg,Y
swos Reg,Hashtable	asave Reg,Y
Get	**Put**
getval(type) R1,R2	putval R1,R2
getconst(type) R,C	putconst R,C
getlist(type) R,L	putlist R,L
getstruct(type) R,S	putstruct R,S
	putvar R
Procedure Control	**Clause Control**
tryelse T,L	proceed
retryelse T,L	execute P
predictelse T,L	dexecute P
trust T	calls P
fail	acalls P
cut	allocate N
cutd	
nocp	
Miscellaneous (incomplete list)	
add R1, R2, Rd	sub R1, R2, Rd
inc R1, Rd	dec R1, Rd
mul R1, R2, Rd	deref R1, R2
cgtz R1	clsz R1
cgtr R1,R2	ceql R1, R2

3.2.1. Indexing, Clause and Procedure Control Instructions

The indexing instructions are used to filter the set of candidate clauses based on the type and value of input argument registers. The procedure control instructions create and manipulate choicepoints. The *predictelse* instruction is used for static branch prediction (to select one of several clauses to try). The branch destination is checked during subsequent head unification of the clause. Whenever possible, a compiler should use static branch prediction instead of indexing instructions, since the indexing instructions cause instruction dispatch to stall (unless the implementation also supports dynamic branch prediction of indexing instructions). The *nocp* (no choicepoint operation) instruction is used if there is no choicepoint or prediction instruction to load the output B register. The clause control instructions deal with environment allocation and deallocation, and control transfer associated with procedure calls and returns. The *acalls* instruction is similar to the *calls* (procedure call) instruction except that it does not transfer the input E and TE registers to the output set like the *calls* instruction. It is used if there is an *allocate* instruction preceding it in the current set which loads new values of the E and TE registers into the output set. The *dexecute* instruction is similar to the *execute* instruction except that it also deallocates the current environment.

3.2.2. Get and Put Instructions

The *get* instructions unify arguments of the clause

head with the arguments of the goal (available in the input argument registers). The *put* instructions are used to load arguments of a goal or procedure. The *get* instructions have two "type" attributes. The "shared" attribute implies that the unification must get exclusive access to every variable that it binds because that variable could be shared with another unification. Static analysis of programs, as proposed by Citrin [4], can be used to determine which unifications could potentially share unbound variables with other unifications, and only these unifications need incur the overhead of synchronization before binding variables. The "check" attribute requires that the instruction first check that the type of the input argument is appropriate. The "check" attribute is used to check if a predicted branch destination is correct.

3.2.3. Get and Put for Lists and Structures

Unlike the WAM and the PLM, the *getlist*, *putlist*, *getstruct* and *putstruct* instructions are not followed by *unify* instructions. Instead, each list and structure unification is treated as a single instruction. Each instruction contains a pointer to a list of words in code space that describe elements of the list or structure. These list and structure descriptions are different from other instructions in that they are not dispatched to Unification Units, but rather they are fetched directly from memory by the Unification Unit that executes the list or structure get or put instruction.

3.2.4. Load and Save Instructions

Unlike the Berkeley PLM, the get and put instructions cannot have permanent variables in the environment as arguments. This allows the environment memory area to be treated as a separate address space inaccessible to the Unification Units. The load instruction loads an argument register with a permanent variable from the environment, and the save instruction saves an argument register in the environment as a permanent variable. The *asave* instruction is similar to the *save* instruction except that it is used if an environment has been allocated in the current set (in which case the input E register does not point to the current environment, but the input TE register does).

3.2.5. Miscellaneous Instructions

The miscellaneous instructions include arithmetic and logic operations, as well as simple general purpose instructions that could be used to implement builtin operations of Prolog. Instructions such as *cgtz* (which succeeds if the argument is greater than zero and fails otherwise) can also be used to check that a particular clause was correctly predicted.

3.3. Implementation

3.3.1. Overview

Figure 3.1 is an overview of a PLUM implementation. A Prefetch Unit fetches, buffers and dispatches instructions to appropriate functional units. The Choicepoint Unit and Environment Unit access and manipulate the choicepoint and environment stacks respectively. Several Unification Units execute

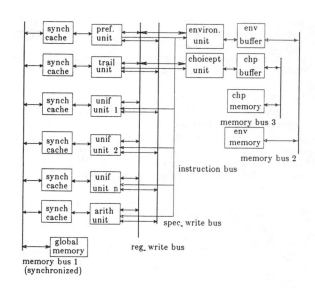

Figure 3.1: Overview of the PLUM microarchitecture.

unification instructions as well as some simple arithmetic instructions. An Arithmetic Unit performs more complicated arithmetic operations (such as floating point instructions). A Trail Unit trails variables bound by the Unification Units and performs the detrail operation during backtracking.

3.3.2. Multiple Register Sets

The PLUM architecture assigns a new register set for the outputs of instructions each time a procedure boundary is crossed. A practical implementation can provide only a limited number of register sets. The microarchitecture described in this section provides a few (we think 4 are sufficient) register sets, simulating a large number of register sets by re-using them. The register set numbers "wrap around", and each register set is reset so that all its registers are marked invalid before it is re-used. The Prefetch Unit appends the physical set number to each instruction that it dispatches to functional units.

3.3.3. Data Driven Control

Each register has a valid bit associated with it, and the valid bits are used to implement the data driven control. An instruction can only execute when its input operands are valid. Some instructions need to wait for implicit operands (that are not specified explicitly in the instruction). For example, a unification cannot allocate space on the heap until all the heap space for the previous goal has been allocated in order to prevent interleaving of data for different goals on the heap. The Unification Unit must wait until the input heap register for its set is valid, and the input heap register is loaded by the previous goal when it requires no more heap space.

Each functional unit contains a shadow copy of all the register sets (we refer to all the register sets together as the register file). The microarchitecture maintains consistent copies of the register file in all the functional units by insisting that registers in the file can only be written over shared buses. The PLUM has two buses: the register_write bus is used to write the argument registers, and the special_write bus is used to write the other registers. The functional units arbitrate for the use of a bus one cycle before they use the bus.

4. Simulation Results and Analysis

We have written a register transfer level simulator for PLUM in order to estimate the performance of the implementation and evaluate various design choices. The measurements described below demonstrate that PLUM achieves an average speedup of 3.4 over the Berkeley VLSI-PLM, a specialized pipelined processor for Prolog.

4.1. Assumptions and Benchmarks

The PLUM simulator accepts the access times of each memory port and the number of Unification Units as inputs. The shared memory (connected to the ports of the Prefetch Unit, Unification Units, and Trail Unit) is treated as a multi-port memory for purposes of simulation. Since a multi-port memory is expensive, an actual implementation would use one of several memory systems, depending on the desired cost and performance, to allow parallel access to a shared memory. For example, one option is to use caches at each port connected to a shared bus. A cache coherence protocol can be used to ensure that shared data are kept consistent. Another option is to have multiple memory modules connected to the processors by an interconnection network such as a cross-bar switch. These and other options have lower performance than a multi-port memory with the same access time, but we believe that the performance degradation is small. Memory traces from the simulator can aid in evaluating performance degradation with various memory system designs, but that is beyond the scope of this paper.

The simulator models a branch target instruction buffer (4 lines, 16 words per line) and a 16 word prefetch buffer in the Prefetch Unit. The Trail Unit contains an 8 word trail buffer and each Unification Unit contains an 8 word prefetch buffer to hold elements of lists and structure unifications from the code space. They have been included in the simulator so that the performance measurements are not degraded by factors that can easily be eliminated by small and simple buffers that are common in modern VLSI processors. At the same time, the simulation models the performance degradation that can be expected due to misses in buffers. Since our simulations are run with cold starts (the buffers are initially empty), the performance of a program with a short execution time is usually degraded more than that of a longer program.

We present measurements on four benchmarks that have commonly been used in comparing the performance of Prolog systems. *Concat* is a small program that concatenates a list of 3 elements to a list of 6 elements. *Hanoi* computes the solution to the "towers of Hanoi" puzzle for 8 disks , *nrev1* reverses a list of 30 elements, and *qs4* sorts a list of 50 integers using the quicksort algorithm.

4.2. Effect of Multiple Unification Units

In figure 4.1 we plot PLUM's performance (rela-

tive to the performance of PLUM with 1 Unification Unit and 1 cycle memory access) for each benchmark, and figure 4.2 is a similar graph for the average of all the benchmarks. Performance is measured as the reciprocal of the number of execution cycles, and the number of cycles for the average is the sum of the cycles for each benchmark. Figures 4.1 and 4.2 show that PLUM's performance improves with additional Unification Units, but the performance improvement is small beyond three Unification Units for the benchmark programs chosen. Programs with more unification parallelism can be expected to benefit more from multiple Unification Units. Such programs usually have a large number of complex argument unifications in each goal.

4.3. Effect of Memory Access Time

Figure 4.3 shows how PLUM's performance (relative to the performance of PLUM with 1 Unification Unit and 1 cycle memory access time) on each benchmark is affected by memory access time. In these measurements we assume that the memory access time on all memory ports is the same. Figure 4.4 shows the effect on the average performance. The figures show that PLUM's performance degrades slowly with increasing memory access time. This suggests that a PLUM implementation will perform quite well even if the memory system's effective memory access time is more than 1 cycle (for example, due to cache misses and synchronization for shared data).

The *hanoi* benchmark behaves differently from the other benchmarks. Unlike the other benchmarks, unification is not the bottleneck to *hanoi*'s performance, and none of the Unification Unit instructions in the benchmark access memory. As memory access time increases, therefore, the performance is determined almost completely by the Choicepoint, Environment and Prefetch Units, and the curves for various numbers of Unification Units merge.

4.4. Comparison with the Berkeley VLSI-PLM

Table 4.1 compares the performance of the VLSI-PLM (using a simulator that assumes a 1 cycle memory access and 100nsec clock cycle) with that of PLUM (using a simulator with 3 Unification Units, 1 cycle memory access and 100nsec clock cycle). On some benchmarks, PLUM's speedup over the VLSI-PLM cannot be attributed only to fine grain parallelism. The VLSI-PLM has little support for arithmetic operations and comparisons. For example, the VLSI-PLM's performance on the *hanoi* benchmark can be improved by approximately 0.7 millisec (13.4 percent) by an improved instruction set for arithmetic. Table 4.1 shows that PLUM achieves a speedup of 3.42 over the VLSI-PLM averaged over the benchmarks chosen.

Table 4.1. Comparison of VLSI-PLM and PLUM

Benchmark	Execution Time (millisec)		Speedup
	VLSI-PLM	PLUM	
concat	0.035	0.015	2.33
hanoi	5.211	1.331	3.91
nrev1	2.116	0.788	2.68
qs4	4.304	1.28	3.36
average	11.67	3.414	3.42

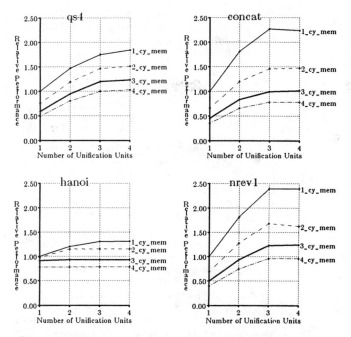

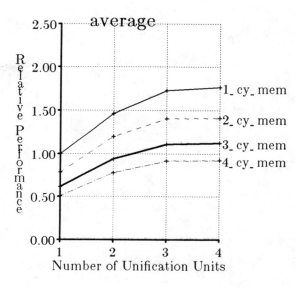

Fig. 4.1: Effect of Multiple Unification Units on Performance

Fig. 4.2: Effect of Multiple Unification Units on Average Performance

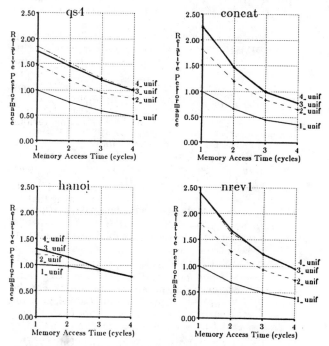

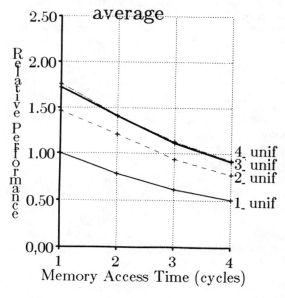

Fig.4.3: Effect of Memory Access Time on Performance

Fig. 4.4: Effect of Memory Access Time on Average Performance

Although we feel that execution times are more appropriate measures of Prolog processor performance, it has unfortunately become customary to report the LIPS (Logical Inferences Per Second) that a processor can achieve. Table 4.2 lists the KLIPS (Kilo LIPS)

that PLUM with 3 Unification Units achieves on the benchmark set using different clock cycle lengths and memory access times. With current CMOS technology and memory speeds, an implementation of PLUM with 50 nsec clock cycle and 1 cycle memory access is feasible. With these assumptions, PLUM achieves **1102 KLIPS**.

Table 4.2. KLIPS Rates for PLUM (with 3 Unif. Units)

Clock Cycle	100nsec		50nsec	
Mem. Access (cycles)	2	1	2	1
Benchmark				
concat	302	470	604	940
hanoi	508	576	1016	1152
nrev1	444	631	888	1262
qs4	399	477	798	954
average	449	551	898	1102

5. Summary and Conclusions

We have described the architecture and implementation of PLUM, a high performance processor for Prolog that exploits fine grain parallelism by executing instructions in parallel on multiple specialized function units, each of which can be implemented on a single VLSI chip. PLUM achieves a speedup of approximately 3.4 over the Berkeley VLSI-PLM averaged over a set of benchmarks. Performance of PLUM improves with additional Unification Units but the performance improvement is small beyond three Unification Units for the benchmarks chosen. The amount of parallelism that can be exploited by multiple Unification Units varies from program to program. However, even programs without sufficient unification parallelism perform well because of parallel execution of choicepoint and environment instructions. PLUM's performance degrades slowly with increasing memory access time, indicating that it will perform well with a wide range of memory systems.

We are currently optimizing the microcode for each function unit and running simulations on a larger and more diverse benchmark set. We are confident that simulations on the larger benchmarks will result in comparable or greater speedup than that observed in this paper.

Acknowledgement

Sponsored by Defense Advanced Research Projects Agency under Contract Nos. N0039-84-C-0089 and N00014-88-K-0579

The authors also wish to thank Zycad Corporation for the use of their Endot N.2 hardware simulation tools that greatly simplified the task of simulating PLUM.

References

1. J. Beer, Concepts, Design, and Performance Analysis of a Parallel Prolog Machine, *PhD thesis, Technical University*, Berlin, .

2. M. Carlton and P. V. Roy, A Distributed Prolog System with AND-Parallelism, *Proceedings of Hawaii International Conference on System Science 88*, Honolulu, Hawaii, January, 1988.

3. C. Chen, A. Singhal and Y. N. Patt, PUP: An Architecture to Exploit Parallel Unification in Prolog, *(submitted for publication)*, 1988.

4. W. Citrin, Parallel Unification Scheduling in Prolog, *PhD thesis, University of California, Berkeley*, Berkeley, California, 1988.

5. J. S. Conery, The AND/OR Model for Parallel Interpretation of Logic Programs, *PhD thesis, Dept. of Information and Computer Science, University of California, Irvine*, 1983.

6. T. Dobry, A High Performance Architecture for Prolog, *PhD thesis, University of California, Berkeley*, Berkeley, California, 1987.

7. B. Fagin and T. Dobry, The Berkeley PLM Intruction Set: An Instruction Set for Prolog, *Report No. UCB/Computer Science Dpt. 86/257, Computer Science Division, University of California, Berkeley*, September 1985.

8. B. S. Fagin, A Parallel Execution Model for Prolog, *PhD thesis, Computer Science Division, Univ. of California, Berkeley*, November, 1987. Available as Tech. Report UCB/Computer Science Dpt./87/380.

9. R. Hasegawa and M. Amamiya, Parallel Execution of Logic Programs based on Dataflow Concept, *Proceedings of the International Conference on Fifth Generation Computer Systems, 1984*, 1984, 507-516.

10. M. V. Hermenegildo, An Abstract Machine for the Restricted AND-Parallelism of Logic Programs, *Third International Conference on Logic Programming*, July, 1986, 25-39.

11. N. Ito, H. Shimizu, M. Kishi, E. Kuno and K. Rokusawa, Data-flow Based Execution Mechanisms of Parallel and Concurrent Prolog, *New Generation Computing 3* (1985), 15-41, OHMSHA, LTD and Springer-Verlag.

12. Y. N. Patt, W. Hwu and M. C. Shebanow, HPS, A New Microarchitecture: Rationale and Introduction, *Proceedings of the 18th International Microprogramming Workshop*, Asilomar, California, December, 1985.

13. J. Syre and H. Westphal, A Review of Parallel Models for Logic Programming Languages, *Technical Report CA-07, European Computer Industry Research Centre, GmbH, Arabellastr, 17, D-8000 Muenchen 81, West Germany*, 10 June 1985.

14. E. Tick and D. Warren, Towards a Pipelined Prolog Processor, *1984 International Symposium on Logic Programming*, February 1984.

15. E. Tick, Studies in Prolog Architectures, *Phd thesis (also Technical Report No. CSL-Tech. Rep.-87-329, Computer Systems Laboratory, Stanford University)*, Stanford, California, June, 1987.

16. R. M. Tomasulo, An Efficient Algorithm for Exploiting Multiple Arithmetic Units, *IBM Journal of Research and Development 11* (1967).

17. D. H. D. Warren, An Abstract Prolog Instruction Set, *Technical Report 309, Artificial Intelligence Center, SRI International*, 1983.

EVALUATION OF MEMORY SYSTEM FOR
INTEGRATED PROLOG PROCESSOR IPP

M. Morioka   S. Yamaguchi   T. Bandoh

Hitachi Research Laboratory, Hitachi, Ltd.

4026 Kuji, Hitachi, Japan

ABSTRACT

This paper discusses an optimal memory system to realize a high performance integrated Prolog processor, the IPP. First, the memory access characteristics of Prolog are analyzed by a simulator, which simulates the execution of a Prolog program at a micro instruction level. The main findings from this analysis are that: the write access ratio of Prolog is larger than that of procedural languages; and performance improvement requires the memory system to process concentrated, large write accesses effectively.

Then the Prolog acceleration strategies for conventional cache memories are discussed. Comparison is made of cache memories (store-swap, store-through) and a stack buffer, regarding not only performance but also reliability, complexity and effects on procedural languages. The advanced store-through cache with a multi-stage write buffer and an interleaved main memory are seen to have the same performance level as the store-swap cache. When considering data reliability, the advanced store-through cache is judged more suitable for the IPP than the store-swap cache. In a comparison between stack buffer and advanced store-through cache, the stack buffer is found to achieve higher peak performance, but this is affected by the program features. On the other hand, the advanced store-through cache constantly gets high performance for Prolog and procedural languages. As a result, it is concluded that the advanced store-through cache is best suited to the IPP.

1. INTRODUCTION

AI systems using Prolog and Lisp are expected to support human intelligent activities. Since Prolog is a declarative language, it is easier to program and maintain than procedural languages like C and Fortran. But to develop actual AI systems (e.g. expert systems using Prolog), it is sometimes necessary to link Prolog programs with procedural languages. Thus, in those systems, high speed execution of both Prolog and procedural languages is required. In order to meet these requirements, we developed an integrated Prolog processor (IPP) based on Warren's instruction set 1), which integrates Prolog acceleration hardware into a general purpose minicomputer 2) 3) 4).

The most characteristic mechanisms in executing Prolog programs are unification and backtracking. Especially for the latter, it is necessary to save and restore processor environments into/from a stack frequently to allow retrying of alternative clauses. Thus memory access behavior of Prolog programs differs from that of procedural languages. Therefore, for efficient execution of Prolog the memory system should guarantee large memory throughput. To do this, existing dedicated Prolog machines have adopted a hardware stack 5) 6) 7). But such an approach is often heavily affected by the locality of memory accesses. And also a dedicated Prolog hardware stack is not effective for speeding up execution of procedural languages.

The contribution of this paper is to clarify the most effective structure of the memory system to achieve high performance for both Prolog and procedural languages. This is done through the investigation of Prolog acceleration strategies for a conventional cache memory and the comparison between the hardware stack and the advanced cache memory, regarding not only performance but also reliability, complexity and effects on procedural languages.

In performance comparison of memory system organizations, the hit ratio and memory traffic of the cache memory and various hardware stack architectures suited to Prolog have been evaluated in 8) 9). However the average memory access time was not included, although it is as important as the hit ratio of the local memory. Therefore, in this paper, we compare the performance of each memory system in the average memory access time. The factor which determines the average access time consists of the hit ratio of the local memory and the recovery time when a miss hit occurs. As for the hardware stack, the overhead of a copy-back operation, which is necessary when overflow of the hardware stack occurs, must be taken into account. In particular, for the store-through cache with a write buffer and an interleaved main memory, the average memory access time is seriously affected by overflow of the write buffer and write processing ability of the interleaved main memory.

Section 2 describes the IPP design approach and topics related to the memory system. Then Section 3 describes a quantitative analysis of the memory access behavior of Prolog. Considering these results, Section

203

4 compares the cache memory and the hardware stack architecture.

2. PROLOG ACCELERATION STRATEGIES IN THE IPP

2.1 Design Targets

When developing actual expert systems, it is sometimes necessary to link Prolog with procedural languages. In these systems, numerical calculations and the tasks which have a fixed algorithm are programmed effectively by procedural languages. On the other hand, for diagnosis or inference according to the obtained results, Prolog is more suitable. Therefore, both Prolog and procedural languages should be run fast with less linkage overhead.

Dedicated Prolog machines, which have tagged architecture, cannot satisfy the requirement, because in general, they have poor ability in processing procedural languages (numerical calculations). While it seems more attractive to implement Prolog processing functions on a general purpose computer, the performance is reduced remarkably for the following two reasons.

(1) Tag manipulation

In Prolog, a tag is indispensable to recognize data types, such as variables, constants, and structures. In the case of Prolog implementation on a general purpose computer, the tag is often packed into a 32-bit datum, because of compatibility with standard I/O devices. This causes frequent tag manipulations such as separating the tag from the datum, evaluating the tag and packing it in the datum. According to our analysis, tag manipulations need 5-18 microprogram steps and as a whole they occupy about half the execution time of the Append program 3).

(2) Memory throughput

Memory accesses occurring in Prolog are mainly for stack manipulation, due to its stack oriented computations. In particular, saving and restoring of environments for backtracking occur frequently, because of the non-deterministic characteristics of Prolog, and that causes a heavy load on the memory system. For example, memory throughput of over 200 MB/s is required to get 1MLIPS 8).

Therefore, we designed the IPP with a focus on acceleration of tag processing and improvement of memory throughput. In the following sections, we discuss the memory system strategies of the IPP.

2.2 The Memory System for Integrated Architecture

In Warren's architecture, three stacks are defined in the memory areas, that is, the local stack, heap stack and trail stack. The local stack contains a frame needed for backtracking called CHOICE-POINT, and a frame for goal calling denoted as ENVIRONMENT. The heap stack contains structures, which are created while executing Prolog programs. The trail stack contains a history of bound variables which must be unbound when backtracking occurs. The local stack and the heap stack accesses are comparatively high among these three stacks. Especially for a non-deterministic program, saving and restoring of CHOICE-POINT (whose size is about 11 words 8)) to/from the local stack impose a heavy load on the memory system. Accordingly it is necessary for performance improvement to support backtracking efficiently.

To realize this, dedicated Prolog machines provide hardware stack architecture such as a specialized stack buffer, or a large size register file. Though these hardware stacks are certainly effective when the access converges to the top of the stacks, they show poor performance for scattered accesses, such as accesses to plural stacks or to the deep stack area, which are characteristics to Prolog. A conventional cache memory is more flexible than a hardware stack, but much time is needed to access it due to the tag comparison. However if it is possible to achieve high performance in saving and restoring CHOICE-POINT, it seems attractive for the IPP to adopt the conventional cache memory, because it can get high performance for both Prolog and procedural languages. Thus the two major points for designing the IPP memory system are:

(1) To clarify the memory system strategies leading to a good processing ability for saving and restoring CHOICE-POINT within the conventional cache memory.
(2) To clarify the most suitable memory system organization for the IPP.

The former is done through a detailed analysis of the Prolog memory access behavior, and the latter is done through a comparative study of various memory systems, such as a cache memory and a hardware stack.

3. PROLOG MEMORY ACCESS CHARACTERISTICS

3.1 The Local and Heap Stacks

This section discusses the memory access characteristics for the local stack and the heap stack, which have higher access frequencies than the trail stack.

(1) Local Stack

CHOICE-POINT and ENVIRONMENT are stacked on the local stack. CHOICE-POINT is created at non-determinate goal calling, and stack control registers and argument registers are saved in it. Almost all accesses are limited to the top portion of the local stack for saving, restoring, and modification of CHOICE-POINT.

ENVIRONMENT is allocated on the local stack, if a selected clause has more than one goal. Access to ENVIRONMENT occurs when head parameters are unified with permanent variables on argument registers, and permanent variables in a goal are loaded for goal calling. Thus, access is not limited to the top portion of the stack, but the deep portion of the stack can be accessed as well. Fig.1 shows an example of local stack access. This result was obtained by executing the Qsort program on the simulator described later. In this case, Prolog creates CHOICE-POINT for backtracking, and if unification fails, a backtrack operation occurs and CHOICE-POINT is restored into the registers. According to this access behavior, the local stack accesses occur at shorter intervals especially for a non-deterministic Prolog program, and the access addresses have a continuous feature.

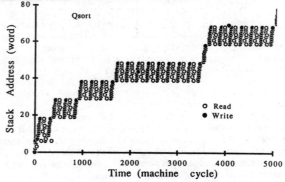

Fig. 1 Example of Local Stack Access

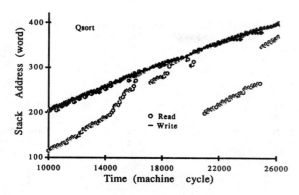

Fig. 2 Example of Heap Stack Access

(2) Heap Stack

The heap stack accesses are divided into two cases. One is stacking structures produced in program execution on the top of the heap stack. The other case is reference and binding to produced structures, which are usually in a deep portion of the heap stack. An example of heap stack accesses for the Qsort program is shown in Fig.2. From this figure, it is clear that almost all write accesses converge to the top of the heap stack, on the other hand read accesses are scattered throughout the stack. These features decrease the locality of the heap stack accesses.

3.2 Simulator Analysis

In order to clarify memory access characteristics, we developed a simulator. which simulates execution of a Prolog program at a micro instruction level. The simulator provides an execution sequence of Prolog instructions and a trace of the executed micro steps, including initiation for read and write requests and their addresses. The simulator is written in the C language, and executes object codes which are generated by our optimizing Prolog compiler 2). The summary of the benchmark programs used in the analysis are shown in Table 1. Details of the first six programs for the Prolog benchmarks are given in 12). Expert is a part of an expert system program written in Prolog. The four programs for C and Fortran are well known benchmarks for procedural languages.

Table 1 Summaries of Benchmark Programs

| Language | Program | Source step | | Dynamic | Data access |
		Rule	Fact	instruction step	frequency
Prolog	Nreverse	2	3	3,657	3,229
	Conslist	1	1	3,250	4,783
	Solve	5	5	7,724	10,288
	Qsort	3	3	4,545	7,820
	Queen	10	2	21,483	20,834
	Shallow	14	1	48,010	99,019
	Expert	36	29	291,263	203,928
C	Dhrystone	345		241,086	173,044
	Prime	26		1,064,871	687,975
Fortran	Whetstone	168		690,232	685,641
	Linpack	562		227,979	179,781

(1) Access ratios for read and write

Table 2 shows the memory access ratios for data read, and data write obtained from simulated executions of Prolog, C and Fortran programs. Instruction fetch is not included, because the local memory for instruction fetch is commonly separated from that for data fetch in recent memory systems. The result shows that the ratios of memory write accesses of Prolog are larger than those of procedural programs, especially for Fortran. On average for the Prolog programs, the write access occupies about 50% of all data accesses.

Table 2 Comparison of Memory Access Ratios

Language	Program	Data read (%)	Data write(%)
Prolog	Nreverse	49.9	50.1
	Conslist	29.3	70.7
	Solve	57.5	42.5
	Qsort	41.2	58.8
	Queen	57.6	42.4
	Shallow	69.7	30.3
	Expert	55.6	44.4
	AVERAGE	51.5	48.5
C	Dhrystone	54.4	45.6
	Prime	55.9	44.0
Fortran	Whetstone	70.1	29.9
	Linpack	70.6	29.4
	AVERAGE	62.8	37.2

(2) Memory access ratios of each stack

Table 3 shows the memory access ratios of the three stacks and other areas, which contain accesses to clause indexing tables and a built-in command area. On average, about 80% of all data accesses are for the local and heap stack. In Nreverse, Conslist and Solve (which form Group 1), accesses to the heap stack occupy about 60% of all data accesses. But for Qsort, Queen, Shallow and Expert (which form Group 2), the local stack accesses occupy about 60% on average, because of frequent allocations of CHOICE-POINT and ENVIRONMENT.

(3) Locality of stack accesses

Table 4 shows the locality of stack accesses. Locality is defined as the hit ratio of the full-associative cache memory, which has a 1-word block size and uses the LRU replacement algorithm. Capacity of the cache memory (window size) is changed from 4 words to 256 words. For a large window size, local stack accesses show higher locality than those of the heap stack, because local stack accesses mainly converge to the top of the stack in contrast with the scattered behavior of heap stack accesses. Heap stack accesses have high locality for a small window size, because read-modify-write accesses occur frequently for the heap stack.

(4) Distribution of write access occurrences

The distribution of write access occurrences for the Prolog programs is shown in Table 5. The first 4 columns represent ratios of write accesses, which occur in the inter-arrival time of 4, 6, 8 and 16 machine cycles, respectively. The last column is the mean inter-arrival time of write accesses. About 55% of the write accesses occur under the inter-arrival time of 6 machine cycles, although the average is 17.6 machine cycles. These features of Prolog are caused by the CHOICE-POINT accesses.

Table 3 Memory Access Ratios of Each Stack

| Program | | Local (%) | | Heap(%) | | Trail(%) | | Others(%) | |
		read	write	read	write	read	write	read	write
Gr.1	Nreverse	4.8	5.0	43.2	45.0	-	0.1	1.9	-
	Conslist	6.7	7.1	21.7	62.7	-	0.9	0.9	-
	Solve	13.2	13.9	31.3	27.9	0.3	0.6	12.8	-
	AVERAGE	8.2	8.7	32.1	45.2	0.1	0.5	5.2	-
Gr.2	Qsort	23.1	36.7	14.8	17.3	1.6	4.7	1.8	-
	Queen	22.1	27.4	25.2	10.7	4.2	4.3	6.1	-
	Shallow	66.7	29.3	1.0	1.0	-	-	2.0	-
	Expert	28.0	30.5	1.0	1.0	-	-	26.6	12.9
	AVERAGE	35.0	31.0	10.4	7.5	1.5	2.3	9.1	3.2

Table 4 Locality of Stack Accesses

| Stack | Program | Locality of Stack Access | | | |
		W *<4word	W<16word	W<64word	W<256word
Local	Group1	13.0%	51.2%	61.4%	72.1%
	Group2	11.8%	71.6%	86.3%	95.0%
	AVERAGE	12.3%	62.8%	75.6%	85.2%
Heap	Group1	38.5%	39.4%	53.7%	61.6%
	Group2	36.4%	45.9%	67.7%	67.8%
	AVERAGE	37.3%	43.1%	61.7%	65.1%

* W : Window Size

Table 5 Distribution of Write Access Occurrences

Program	Distribution of Inter-arrival Time				mean (mc)
	T *<4 mc	T<6 mc*	T<8 mc	T<16 mc	
Nreverse	2.3%	61.8%	63.6%	65.6%	15.6
Conslist	6.3%	39.5%	67.9%	97.5%	8.7
Solve	10.0%	62.9%	63.4%	65.1%	17.6
Qsort	25.7%	68.0%	71.2%	82.8%	11.7
Queen	22.2%	55.4%	67.9%	74.4%	23.3
Shallow	36.7%	46.7%	50.0%	56.7%	26.5
Expert	24.4%	52.2%	56.7%	71.2%	19.8
AVERAGE	18.2%	55.2%	63.0%	73.3%	17.6

* T : Inter-Arrival Time of Write Access
* mc: machine cycle

In summary :

(1) In Prolog, the ratio of memory write accesses occupy 48.5% of all data accesses, and it is larger than the 37.2% value of the procedural languages.

(2) In the case of a non-deterministic Prolog program, write access occurrences have shorter inter-arrival time, and their addresses have a continuous feature.

(3) Local stack accesses have high locality because of the frequent saving and restoring of frames. On the other hand, heap stack accesses have less locality because of their scattered feature.

(4) There are two types of Prolog programs. One has dominant accesses to the heap stack, while the other to the local stack.

Therefore in order to improve the performance of Prolog, it is necessary for the memory system to process large, concentrated write accesses efficiently, and to process multi-stack accesses which are scattered to the local stack and heap stack.

4. MEMORY SYSTEM EVALUATION

Due to multi-stack based ·computations, stack management is the main job in executing a Prolog program. Therefore, a technique for speeding up the stack accesses by using a high speed local memory has a good effect on performance improvement of Prolog. There are two ways to get speed up. One is a conventional cache memory, either a store-swap or store-through strategy, applied to general purpose computers, and the other is a hardware stack mainly applied to dedicated Prolog processors. In this Section, we make a comparative study of these local memory strategies based on the results obtained in Section 3.

4.1 Store-swap Cache vs. Store-through Cache

To compare a store-swap cache and a store-through cache, we considered two issues to be examined for the IPP, that is reliability and memory throughput for Prolog.

4.1.1 Reliability

Data reliability is very important for the high speed local memory, because the local memory is an extension of the main memory. In a store-swap cache, some valid data in it may not exist in the main memory, thus some way is needed to realize high reliability, such as an error correcting code. But this has a bad influence on the critical-path delay. On the other hand, copies of the valid data in the store-through cache always exist in the main memory, thus it has a higher reliability.

4.1.2 Memory Throughput for Prolog

It is said that a store-swap cache works better for Prolog than a store-through cache, because of the high ratio of write accesses. Thus it is implemented in commercial Prolog machines. But from analysis of the memory access characteristics of Prolog, we feel that a store-through cache can perform the memory write accesses of Prolog effectively, if a multi-stage write buffer and an interleaved main memory are provided. That is, the concentrated write accesses caused by saving CHOICE-POINT's are absorbed by the multi-stage write buffer. Furthermore the data stored in the multi-stage write buffer are effectively transferred to the interleaved main memory, because these data have contiguous write addresses. By using these techniques, an advanced store-through cache can provide high memory throughput for Prolog. But in this organization, if the modified data, which are not on the cache memory, are referenced immediately, the read access time becomes long, because the reference must wait until the modification to the main memory is completed. Table 6 shows the accumulated distribution of modified-data references, as an average of all benchmarks. For a 20-machine cycle interval time, which is almost equal to the main memory access time of the IPP, the accumulated distribution is under 11.4%. In addition to this, since most referenced data are on the cache memory, immediate reference to the modified data does not affect the performance of the store-through cache very much.

Table 6 Accumulated Distribution of Modified-Data References

Program	Distribution of Interval Time				
	T *<10mc*	T<15 mc	T<20 mc	T<25 mc	T<30 mc
Average of all	10.5 %	11.1 %	11.4 %	11.5 %	16.0 %

* T : Interval Time of Modified-Data References
*mc : machine cycle

4.1.3 Memory Throughput Evaluation with Simulator

A comparison of the memory throughput for Prolog is important for the choice of the memory system organization, thus we evaluated this with the simulator.

· Method

In order to evaluate the average memory access time for various memory organizations, we developed a memory system simulator. The memory system simulator is driven by memory access timing and memory addresses obtained by the micro level Prolog simulator, which was described earlier. In this memory simulator, the behavior of the write buffer and the interleaved main memory are simulated dynamically.

· Memory System Model

For a store-swap cache, two models are evaluated.

Model 1: if a block to be replaced has been modified when a cache miss occurs, the block is copied back before the required block is loaded in the cache memory.

Model 2: if a block to be replaced has been modified when a cache miss occurs, the block is pushed into a temporary buffer (copy-back buffer) before the required block is loaded in the cache memory. Then the contents of the copy-back buffer are copied back to the main memory in background.

The average access time T of the store-swap cache can be defined as follows:

$$T = (Nr * Tr + Nw * Tw) / (Nr + Nw)$$

where

$$Tr = hcr * Tca + (1 - hcr) * \{dr * (Ts+Tcb+Tbk) + (1 - dr) * (Ts+Tbk)\},$$

$$Tw = hcw * Tca + (1-hcw) * \{dw * (Ts+Tcb+Tbk) + (1-dw) * (Ts+Tbk)\},$$

Nr, Nw : access frequencies for read and write accesses, respectively,

hcr, hcw : cache hit ratios for read and write accesses, respectively,

dr, dw : the ratios that the replaced block is modified for read and write accesses, respectively,

Tca : cache access time,

Tbk : block transfer time from the main memory to the cache,

Tcb : block copy-back time from the cache to the main memory for Model 1, and from the cache to the copy-back buffer for Model 2, and

Ts : busy time of the main memory for Model 2, due to the copy-back operation from the copy-back buffer to the main memory.

The memory system simulator simulates the micro instruction steps taking into account all the above factors and relations that determine the average access time.

As for store-through cache, it is combined with the multi-stage write buffer and an interleaved main memory. If a read miss occurs in the store-through cache, the required block is fetched after the contents of the write buffer are completely copied back to the main memory. The factors and their relationship, incorporated into the simulator, for the average access time Ta of the advanced store-through cache are represented as follows:

$$Ta = (Nr * Tr + Nw * Tw) / (Nr + Nw)$$

where

$$Tr = hcr * Tca + (1 - hcr) * (Twe + Tbk),$$
$$Tw = k * Twb + (1 - k) * (Tws + Twb),$$

k: acceptance ratio of the write buffer,

Twb: write buffer access time,

Twe: wait time until the write buffer becomes empty, and

Tws: wait time until the write buffer has room for write access.

Twe and Tws is affected by the write buffer size, the number of interleaves and the store access time of the main memory.

• Measurement Condition

(1) The values of hcr, hcw, dr, dw, Ts, k, Twe and Tws are obtained by simulation of each memory system. The hit ratio of the cache memory is a function of the cache capacity, block size, the number of associated sets, and the replacement algorithm. In these models, we evaluated the effects of the hit ratio mainly as a function of the cache capacity. We assumed a 16-byte block size, 2-set size for the set-associative cache, and the FIFO replacement algorithm in all the evaluations.

(2) The access time of the cache memory, the store access time of the main memory and the block transfer time from the main memory to the cache memory are in the ratio of 2 : 15 : 20, which is based on the IPP ratio. The access time of the write buffer is equal to that of the cache memory.

(3) The block transfer time Tbk of each cache is equal to 10 times the cache memory access time, irrespective of the main memory interleaves.

(4) The block copy-back time Tcb is equal to 10 times the cache memory access time for Model 1 of the store-swap cache, and is equal to 4 times for Model 2, which is based on the IPP ratio.

(5) In the initial state of the store-swap cache, the ratio of the modified block is 50% 11) in order to take the start up effect into account.

(6) Instruction fetch is not evaluated, because the local memory for instruction fetch is commonly separated from that for data fetch in recent memory systems.

• Result

Fig.3 shows the average access time obtained from the simulation of all benchmarks for the store-swap cache and the store-through cache. In the store-through cache, we evaluated several organizations, which have different write buffer sizes and different

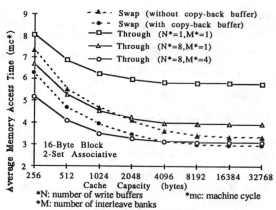

Fig. 3 Comparison of Average Access Time

numbers of interleaves of the main memory. Fig.3 indicates that the advanced store-through cache with the 8-stage write buffer and the 4-way interleaved main memory always has better performance than the store-swap cache without copy-back buffer, and the same performance as the store-swap cache with copy-back buffer. However in a small cache capacity, the advanced store-through cache has better performance than each model of the store-swap cache. This result is mainly due to the hit ratio degradation of the store-swap cache. In executing Prolog programs, the local and the heap stack are accessed simultaneously, and the accesses for each stack are scattered through the top and deep regions of the stack. In the store-swap cache, access conflicts occur more frequently than in the store-through cache, because the block is loaded when both read and write miss hits occur. In addition to this, the overhead to copy back the modified block to the main memory makes the average access time of the store-swap cache worse. On the other hand, in the store-through cache, the write access throughput is improved greatly by the multi-stage write buffer and the interleaved main memory, so concentrated write accesses caused by saving CHOICE-POINT's are processed effectively.

Fig.4 shows the read and write average access time of several organizations of each cache with the 16-Kbyte cache capacity. In the store-through cache with one-stage write buffer and no interleaved main memory, the processing ability of the write access drops remarkably due to overflow of the write buffer. If an 8-stage write buffer is provided to the store-

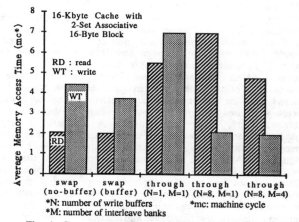

Fig. 4 Comparison of Read and Write Access Times

through cache, the processing ability for the write access is improved, but the average read access time becomes large. This is because the read must wait until the write buffer becomes empty on occurrence of a read miss. When the store-through cache is provided with the 8-stage write buffer and the 4-way interleaved main memory, it has good performance for read and write accesses, because the interleaved main memory provides a high service rate for the write buffer.

By simulator evaluation, it is clear that the advanced store-through cache shows the same performance as the store-swap cache with copy-back buffer. As a result, in consideration with reliability, we concluded the advanced store-through cache is more suited to the IPP than the store-swap cache.

4.2 Stack buffer vs. Store-through Cache

In this comparison, we examined four issues to judge the suited memory system for the IPP, that is effects on procedural languages, reliability, control complexity and memory throughput for Prolog.

4.2.1 Effects on Procedural Languages

To achieve high memory throughput is also necessary to speed up procedural languages like C, which is a stack-oriented language 10). However, if the hardware stack is employed, it needs to be managed explicitly by instructions. Thus, extension of the general purpose instructions and development of a sophisticated compiler are necessary. On the other hand, a cache memory, which is already applied to general purpose computers, can give good performance for both Prolog and procedural languages.

4.2.2 Reliability

As mentioned in the previous Section, a store-through cache has high reliability. On the other hand, in a hardware stack, some valid data in them may not exist in the main memory, thus some way is needed to realize high reliability.

4.2.3 Control Complexity

In general, the hardware stack is accessed via a virtual address, and some valid data in it may not exist in the main memory. Therefore, whenever task switching occurs in the multi-virtual memory, all the data in the hardware stack must be saved in the main memory. A cache memory reduces the task switching overhead, because it can be accessed by a physical address. The task switching overhead is a serious problem for the IPP, because there are many transactions to be processed in the real expert system.

4.2.4 Memory Throughput for Prolog

The most significant advantage of a hardware stack is a high access speed, since there is no need for accessing and comparing an address tag which are indispensable for a cache memory. But performance of the hardware stack depends heavily on the access locality. Namely stack accesses must be concentrated on the top of the stack. The analysis shown in Section 3 shows that the hardware stack is effective for the local stack accesses but not for the heap stack accesses because of the low locality. Therefore, the performance improvement is not expected for the program in which the heap stack accesses are dominant. As for a cache memory, its access time is worse than that of hardware stack. But it can hold the plural stack data or the top and deep portion of the stack data simultaneously. Thus it has high flexibility for scattered accesses.

4.2.5 Memory Throughput Evaluation with Simulator

The method of evaluation, the memory system model of a store-through cache and measurement condition were already mentioned in Section 4.1. Here we describe the hardware stack model and an additional measurement condition.

• Hardware Stack Model

There are several strategies for the Prolog-oriented hardware stack, such as a stack buffer, which holds CHOICE-POINT and ENVIRONMENT, and a choice-point-buffer, which holds only the current CHOICE-POINT 5) 8) 9). We took the more effective stack buffer strategy for evaluation. The stack buffer is combined with a store-through cache memory in the hierarchy as in a commercialized Prolog processor 6). The stack buffer is organized on the wrap around buffer shown in Fig.5, and it holds the top portion of the local stack. The valid data area on the stack buffer is shown with two pointers, the top pointer and the base pointer. The valid flag represents the validity of the whole buffer.

The control algorithm of the stack buffer is based on the algorithm shown in 8). The instructions, which create CHOICE-POINT or ENVIRONMENT, are used to make room in the stack buffer for new frames. If there is not enough space for these new frames, the data pointed by the base pointer are copied back to the combined cache memory until sufficient space is obtained. The instructions discarding frames do nothing but modify the top pointer of the stack buffer. If all the frames on the stack buffer become unnecessary, the valid flag is invalidated. In this case, the valid frames in the stack are not loaded into the stack buffer. The accesses of the local stack which access out of the stack buffer are serviced by the cache memory. Memory accesses to the heap stack, the trail stack, and the other areas are serviced by the cache memory. The factors and their relationship, incorporated into the simulator, for the average access time Ts of the stack buffer are represented as follows:

$$Ts = (Nr * Tr + Nw * Tw + Ncb * Tcb) / (Nr + Nw)$$
where
$$Tr = hbr * Tsb + (1 - hbr) * \{ hcr * Tca + (1 - hcr) * (Twe + Tbk) \},$$
$$Tw = hbw * Tsb + (1 - hbw) * \{ k * Twb + (1 - k) * (Tws + Twb) \},$$
$$Tcb = k * Twb + (1 - k) * (Tws + Twb),$$

Ncb: number of copy-backed words,
hbr, hbw: stack buffer hit ratio for read and write accesses, respectively, and
Tsb: stack buffer access time.

• Additional Measurement Condition

(1) The values of Ncb, hbr, hbw, hcr, k, Twe and Tws are obtained by the memory system simulation.
(2) The access time of the stack buffer, and that of the cache memory are in the ratio of 1 : 2.

• Result

The average memory access time for the stack buffer and the cache memory are plotted in Figs.6 and 7 for the various cache capacities, measured

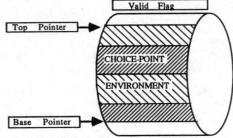

Fig. 5 Structure of Stack Buffer

respectively for Group 2 benchmark, and Group 1 benchmark programs. In this evaluation, the store-through cache was assumed to be combined with the 4-way interleaved main memory for all organizations. The evaluated organizations are as follows:

1. Store-through cache with 1-stage write buffer
2. Advanced store-through cache with 8-stage write buffer
3. Stack buffer combined with store-through cache
4. Advanced stack buffer combined with advanced store-through cache

For the average access time of all accesses for Group 2 shown in Fig.6 (b), the 256-stage stack buffer can give an 80% performance improvement to the store-through cache with 1-stage write buffer. This performance improvement is larger than that of the advanced store-through cache of 40%. This is because the 256-stage stack buffer works well for Group 2 benchmarks due to the high locality of the local stack accesses, as shown in Fig.6 (a). But if the stack buffer size is not sufficient (for example 32-stage in Fig.6 (b)), the effect of the stack buffer is decreased, mainly due to the copy-back operation to the main memory needed to make room for new frames. Then the 32-stage stack buffer with no-multi-stage write buffer only has a performance equal to that of the advanced

store-through cache. If the stack buffer combined with the advanced store-through cache, it can double the performance of the store-through cache with 1-stage write buffer, even if it does not have too large a stack buffer size. The reason for this is that the copy-back operation to the main memory is processed effectively by the multi-stage write buffer.

From Fig.7 (a), the average local stack access time is seen to be improved greatly for the Group 1 benchmarks, if a 256-stage stack buffer is provided. But in the average access time for all accesses shown in Fig.7 (b), the 256-stage stack buffer cannot give much performance improvement to the store-through cache with 1-stage write buffer. This is because heap accesses occupy the main parts of all accesses and the stack buffer cannot give any improvement to heap stack accesses. On the other hand, the advanced store-through cache provides a 35% performance improvement to the store-through cache with 1-stage write buffer, because the multi-stage write buffer can process the heap stack access effectively. The stack buffer can achieve the same performance as that of the advanced store-through cache, when it is combined with the multi-stage write buffer.

Another observation is obtained from the results for Group 1 benchmarks. Performance becomes worse in local stack accesses, if the small size stack buffer is

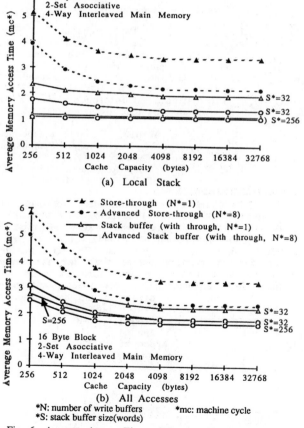

(a) Local Stack

(b) All Accesses

*N: number of write buffers   *mc: machine cycle
*S: stack buffer size(words)

Fig. 6 Average Access Time of Group 2 Benchmarks

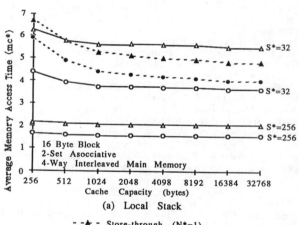

(a) Local Stack

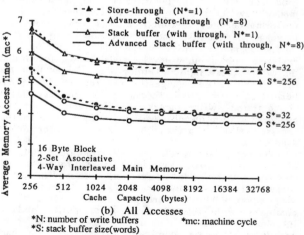

(b) All Accesses

*N: number of write buffers   *mc: machine cycle
*S: stack buffer size(words)

Fig. 7 Average Access Time of Group 1 Benchmarks

combined with a store-through cache with 1-stage write buffer. This is because ENVIRONMENT's are successively stacked on the local stack, and frequent copy-back operations are needed to make room for new ENVIRONMENT's.

A comparison of memory throughput for Prolog between the stack buffer and the store-through cache can be summarized as follows:

(1) For the Group 2 benchmarks, which access mainly the local stack, a stack buffer can give a 50%-80% performance improvement to the store-through cache with 1-stage write buffer. But for the Group 1 benchmarks, which access mainly the heap stack, the stack buffer cannot give as much performance improvement.

(2) An advanced store-through cache with 8-stage write buffer can achieve the 35%-40% performance improvement over the store-through cache with 1-stage write buffer irrespective of the benchmark characteristics.

(3) A stack buffer combined with advanced store-through cache gets the highest performance and flexibility of all organizations. It can give a 50%-100% performance improvement to the store-through cache, independent of the benchmark program features.

Based only on performance, the stack buffer with a store-through cache and a multi-stage write buffer is the best choice. But in consideration of the amount of hardware, reliability and complexity, it takes a great effort to implement this. On the other hand, the advanced store-through cache with the multi-stage write buffer and the interleaved main memory can realize performance improvement both in Prolog and procedural languages with comparatively little hardware, and less effort to implement. Therefore, we concluded that the advanced store-through cache is the most suitable organization for the integrated Prolog processor.

The IPP is composed of 144 ECL LSI's, each of which is a 2000- or 5000- gate gate-array. It achieves a machine cycle time of 23 ns. The store-through cache with the 8-stage write buffer and the 4-way interleaved main memory is adopted to the IPP. The integrated hardware occupies only 2 or 3% of the entire processor hardware. The performance of the IPP measured for Append program is 1.36 MLIPS 4).

5. CONCLUSIONS

To realize a high performance integrated Prolog processor (IPP), we investigated the most suitable memory system strategy for it in consideration of the performance for Prolog, effects on procedural languages, reliability, and control complexity.

The memory access characteristics of Prolog were analyzed with a micro level simulator. We found that: the write access ratio of Prolog was larger than that of procedural languages; in order to improve performance, it was necessary to process large, concentrated write accesses effectively; and the memory system must have flexibility for scattering accesses, such as accesses to plural stacks or to the deep stack area.

We compared stack buffer strategies and the conventional cache memory (store-through and store-swap cache). In comparison between store-swap cache and store-through cache, it was clarified that the advanced store-through cache, which was combined with a multi-stage write buffer and an interleaved main memory, showed the same performance as the store-swap cache with copy-back buffer. From consideration of data reliability, we concluded that the advanced store-through cache was more suitable for the IPP than store-swap cache.

As for a comparison between the stack buffer and advanced store-through cache, it was clarified that the stack buffer could achieve higher peak performance, but it was affected by the features of the benchmark programs. On the other hand, the advanced store-through cache had a high flexibility for scattering access and consistently gave a 35%-40% performance improvement to store-through cache without multi-stage write buffer. It was clarified that a combination of these strategies gave the highest performance.

As a result, in consideration of reliability, effects on procedural languages, control complexity, and the ease of implementation, we concluded that the advanced store-through cache with a multi-stage write buffer and an interleaved main memory is the most suitable organization for the IPP.

REFERENCES

1) D. H. Warren, "An Abstract Prolog Instruction Set," Technical Note 309, Artificial Intelligence Center, SRI International, October 1983.

2) S. Abe et al., "High Performance Integrated Prolog Processor IPP," Proceedings of the 14th International Symposium on Computer Architecture, June 1987, pp 100-107.

3) S. Yamaguchi et al., "Architecture of High Performance Integrated Prolog Processor IPP," Proceedings of 1987 Fall Joint Computer Conference, October 1987.

4) K. Kurosawa et al., "Instruction Architecture for a High Performance Integrated Prolog Processor IPP," Fifth International Conference and Symposium on Logic Programming, August 1988, pp 1506-1530.

5) A. M. Despain and Y. N. Patt, "Aquarius -- A High Performance Computing System for Symbolic/Numeric Applications," Proceedings of Compcon 85 Spring, February 1985, pp 376-382.

6) K. Taki et al., "Hardware Design and Implementation of the Personal Sequential Inference Machine (PSI)," International Conference on Fifth Generation Computer System, November 1984, pp 398-409.

7) E. Tick and D. H. Warren, "Towards a Pipelined Prolog Processor," 1984 International Symposium on Logic Programming, February 1984, pp 29-40.

8) E. Tick, " Prolog Memory Referencing Behavior," Technical Report No.85-281, Stanford University, September 1985.

9) E. Tick, "Data Buffer Performance for Sequential Prolog Architectures," Proceedings of the 15th International Symposium on Computer Architecture, June 1988, pp 434-442.

10) D. R. Ditzel and H. R. McLellan, "Register Allocation for Free : The C Machine Stack Cache," Symposium on Architecture Support for Programming Languages and Operating Systems, 1982, pp 48-56.

11) A. J. Smith, "Cache Evaluation and the Impact of Workload Choice," Proceedings of the 12th International Symposium on Computer Architecture, June 1985, pp 64-73.

12) H. G. Okuno, "The Report of the Third Lisp Contest and the First Prolog Contest," WG SYM 33-4 IJP Japan, Sept. 1985, pp 1-24.

210

A Type Driven Hardware Engine for Prolog Clause
Retrieval over a Large Knowledge Base

Kam-Fai Wong[†] and M. Howard Williams[††]

† Software Engineering Department, Unisys Ltd., Livingston, EH54 7AZ, Scotland.

†† Dept. of Computer Science, Heriot-Watt University, Edinburgh EH1 2HJ, Scotland.

Abstract

Whereas existing Prolog systems are very effective at handling small knowledge bases, they are not very efficient at and often incapable of handling large sets of clauses. Large knowledge bases which may comprise millions of clauses and are shared by a number of users, may need to reside in secondary memory. In such cases exhaustive search is inordinately slow. Various approaches have been put forward for handling the problem, most of which involve *coupled* systems (loosely or tightly coupled). A Prolog data/knowledge based system which provides an *integrated* solution to the problem is being developed. An essential element in this system is the CLAuse Retrieval Engine, CLARE, which is a special purpose hardware engine designed to perform selective retrieval of data from disk in order to identify all potential clauses which will be required for full unification during a query. The engine consists of two separate hardware components, which together form a two-stage filtering configuration. This paper concentrates on the second stage filter which is concerned with partial test unification.

1. Introduction

One of the important application areas of Prolog is knowledge base implementation. Most existing systems for handling large knowledge bases [3,4] are constructed by *coupling*[1] a Prolog translator to a relational database manager. In a coupled knowledge based system, clauses are usually stored in one of two different databases : an Extensional Database (EDB) consisting of ground facts equivalent to tuples in a relational database and an Intensional Database (IDB) consisting of non-ground facts and rules. Such a system is usually based on the following assumptions :

(1) The EDB constitutes the bulk of the knowledge base.

(2) The IDB is small enough to fit into main memory.

(3) Mixed relations consisting of both ground facts and non-ground facts or rules do not occur.

An exception to this is the EDUCE system [1] which stores facts and rules in a relational database which is tightly coupled to a Prolog system. One way to increase the performance of a coupled system is to employ a database machine to provide for rapid searching of disk files. The major role of the database machine is to expedite the data retrieval process by matching the argument terms of the disk resident facts against the argument terms of a query on-the-fly. Term matching in conventional database machines is based on equality testing which is a sufficient test only in the case of clauses which are ground facts whose arguments are purely atomic.

Equality testing is, however, inadequate for handling rules and non-ground facts which may contain variables and possibly also complex structures as their arguments. Evaluation of a Prolog query is based on *resolution* which invokes *unification* - a complex and time consuming term matching process. Compounding this with a low disk transfer rate, unification applied to a large set of disk resident rules would be impractically slow. For this reason, the decision is usually taken to separate rules and non-ground facts and store them separately in the IDB under the management of a Prolog system. On the other hand, retaining the IDB in main memory incurs a serious size restriction to the entire knowledge based system.

Another problem in a coupled knowledge base arises from the fact that in the Prolog system there is an ordering

211

associated with clauses which is used to effect the user in writing Prolog programs, whereas in the database part the ordering of clauses is determined by the system. For this reason mixed relations cannot be catered for in a uniform way and are usually disallowed. This difference in philosophy is quite acceptable for some applications but is a serious problem for a general purpose knowledge base.

In the future an increasing amount of semantic information will be included in knowledge based systems. For example, medium-size knowledge based systems are envisaged by D.H.D. Warren to be ".... of the order of 3000 predicates, 30000 rules, 3000000 facts, and 30 Mbytes total size" [5]. Clauses with rules and structures will not be uncommon. Rules and facts will coexist in the same file. Ordering of clauses, which contributes to the interpretation of the knowledge based system, will be important. For these reasons, the idea of coupling a Prolog system to a relational database will be inadequate, and purpose built systems will be required.

One way of providing a knowledge based system suitable for the future is to adopt the *integrated* implementation approach. In an integrated system, users have a uniform view of the knowledge base : rules and facts of a predicate are kept together in a user-specified order and they are managed by a single Prolog system. Compared with a coupled knowledge base, an integrated knowledge base is more flexible and can be engaged in a much wider scope of applications. However, existing systems are restricted to small applications due to their inefficient way of handling disk resident clauses†. One of the chief problems with Prolog is that when it searches for a clause, it uses the process of unification to match the goal against each clause in turn. This is a complicated process of matching functor and arguments according to certain rules, and takes up a considerable proportion of query processing time. For a large knowledge base stored on disk, the time taken to perform this could well be intolerable.

In order to provide for high-speed retrieval of clauses from large clause sets stored on disk, a special purpose Prolog data/knowledge base machine, CLARE - CLAuse Retrieval Engine, has been designed and is under development. A two-stage filtering process is used by CLARE which employs two pieces of dedicated hardware to search disk resident data on-the-fly. The first stage filter (FS1) is a hardware realisation of index searching based on *superimposed codeword plus mask bits* [2], while the second stage filter (FS2) is responsible for *partial test unification*. In the next section, an overview of the Prolog Data Base Machine (PDBM) project - a project which is aimed at developing the type of system to handle large knowledge bases - is outlined. The architecture of the second stage filter (FS2) of the CLARE hardware is described in detail in section three which also includes the timing calculations of the various hardware operations supported by the FS2.

---

† A set of benchmarks have been devised for evaluating the efficiency of various Prolog systems in handling data bases of different sizes [6]. The benchmark programs were run on a Sun3/160 workstation, equipped with 4MB of main memory, and revealed that the Prolog systems were unable to cope with more than about 60k clauses and even then the overhead of loading these clauses into main memory was very high [7].

2. The PDBM Project - A Brief Overview

The aim of the Prolog Data Base Machine (PDBM) project is to produce a Prolog system which will handle large sets of clauses efficiently [8]. This is achieved by a combination of software and hardware development. The software component is based on a C version of Prolog-X. Prolog-X is a Prolog compiler originally developed by Clocksin[9] and which now runs on ICL3900 and SUN systems. It uses Edinburgh Prolog syntax but with extension to handle modules. Using Prolog-X, clauses are compiled and stored in modules, each module containing one or more procedures. Modules are then classified into two types depending on their size, viz small modules which are loaded into main memory when required, and large modules which are disk resident.

The hardware component of the system consists of a special purpose Clause Retrieval Engine (CLARE) which is designed to increase the performance of the system in retrieval over large clause sets. CLARE selectively retrieves clauses on the fly from a disk. As clauses stream from the disk, they are subjected to a two stage filtering process, as follows :

2.1. Superimposed Code Word plus Mask Bits (SCW+MB)

Predicates with the same functor names and arities are stored in a compiled clause file. For fast searching in large files, codewords are generated for facts and rule heads and these are maintained in a secondary file. The secondary file is effectively an index table associating codewords with clause addresses. When a query is given, the first stage filtering hardware scans through the secondary file and extracts the addresses of those clauses whose codewords successfully match with the codeword corresponding to that query. The size of a secondary file is generally much smaller than that of a compiled clause file [10], thereby enabling quicker retrieval to be achieved by scanning the former than by searching the latter exhaustively. The superimposed codeword plus mask bits indexing scheme (SCW+MB) [11] is an extension of the basic superimposed codeword method which takes account of complex structures and variables which arise in Prolog clauses by the use additional field comprising a set of mask bits. Index matching is performed in parallel, using standard PLAs and MSI components [2], in the first stage of the CLARE engine.

Indexing via SCW+MB is a partial matching technique. Clauses satisfying the matching process are only potential unifiers for a query. Some of these satisfiers are false drops (or 'ghosts') and will fail at the subsequent full unification. False drops are derivable from two main sources [12]:

(1) *Non-unique encoding* in which the same codeword is shared by one or more clauses.

(2) *Restrictive codeword representation* which is caused by truncation of clauses with arities larger than the allowable hardware limit. (In the present system, only 12 arguments of a query is encoded).

Another problem which cannot be handled by the superimposed codeword scheme is that of shared variables. Variables are ignored in the encoding process. This would create no problem if each variable only occurs once in a predicate. However, if a variable occurs more than once in a predicate, a large proportion of false drops could be generated. For example, the query married_couple(Same_surname,Same_surname) would result in the retrieval of the entire predicate from the knowledge base, whilst in reality the resolution set should be very small.

2.2. Partial Test Unification

Further refinement of the clauses which satisfy the first stage is provided by partial test unification using the second stage hardware (FS2). Using the clause references from the secondary index file, compiled clauses are extracted from the knowledge base. Facts and rule heads are compiled into pseudo in-line formats (PIF) ready for partial test unification. In the PIF format, an argument is represented by an 8 bit type tag followed by a 24 or 32 bit content field with an optional 32 bit extension. At present, 107 data types are supported under the PIF format, see appendix 1. The FS2 filter matches clause arguments in PIF against those of the query following a set algorithm. Five levels of matching have been investigated which depends on the depth of the two terms being compared:

- *Level 1* - type only.

- *Level 2* - type and content, ignoring complex structures.

- *Level 3* - type and content, catering for first level structures.

- *Level 4* - type and content, including full structures.

- *Level 5* - type, content with full structures and variable cross binding checks[†].

Since the cost and complexity of the matching hardware to cater for levels four and five are high, a level three partial test unification algorithm is being adopted. In addition to the original algorithm, variable cross binding checks have been incorporated. A simplified version of the matching algorithm is shown in figure 1. After the second stage, the percentage of false drops will be reduced significantly, resulting in a manageable clause set for full unification.

An independent software module, the Clause Retrieval Server (CRS), is being developed which links CLARE with the PDBM Prolog system. In practice, there will be four searching modes during a clause retrieval:

[†] A variable cross binding occurs when a database variable is bound to a query variable. Checking is essential to ensure that the cross binding relationship is consistent i.e. the variables are not instantiated to different terms. Referring to superimposed codeword index matching, cross binding is in fact an alternative form of shared variable and has the effect of creating undesirable false drops.

(a) By software only - the CRS performs all the search operations itself.

(b) Using FS1 only - the superimposed codeword hardware.

(c) Using FS2 only - the partial test unification hardware.

(d) Using both FS1 and FS2 - a two-stage hardware filter.

One of these modes will be selected depending on the nature of a query (e.g. whether it contains cross bound variables) and the knowledge base (e.g. whether it is rule or fact intensive). The CRS will also support simultaneous access by multiple clients which involves procedures for concurrency control and transaction handling.

At the hardware level, CLARE is incorporated in a SUN3/160 workstation. The communication between CLARE and the host takes place via the VMEbus interface. CLARE is memory mapped into the /dev/vme24d16, SUN's user space, using the mmap() system call [13]. Both filtering stages, FS1 and FS2, appear in the form of plug-in circuit boards. A common address space from ffff7e00(hex) to ffff7fff(hex) - 128k bytes in total - is shared by FS1 and FS2. The two filters are mutually exclusive. The selection between the two is governed by the third least significant bit, b_2, of an 8-bit control register - A 0 in b_2 selects FS1 and a 1 selects FS2.

3. The Second Stage Hardware (FS2)

Once a filtering stage is enabled, the setting of the first two significant bits of its control register determines the operation mode of the hardware. FS2 can be set to work in one of 4 operational modes :

Operational Mode	b0	b1
Read Result	0	0
Search	0	1
Microprogramming	1	0
Set Query	1	1

When a query is posed, it is translated into microprogram instructions. These instructions are loaded into the FS2 while it is set to Microprogramming mode. The FS2 is then switched to Set Query mode and all query arguments are written into the FS2 query memory. After performing the two operations, the FS2 is ready to perform a search. The DMA begin and end addresses of the disk transfer command block, where retrieved data will be placed, is specified to be the FS2 address space. A search is then initiated by setting the FS2 to Search mode. From then on the FS2 is, effectively, connected to the disk controller. At the end of the search, if a match has been found, the most significant bit (b_7) of the control register will be set. At this stage, in order to extract the potential answers to the query, the FS2 will be set to Read Result mode.

The overall architecture of the FS2 hardware is depicted in figure 2. It consists of four functional units. The Writable Control Store (WCS) provides the microprogram instructions to coordinate all the other units. Data streaming from the disk is retained in one of the two memory banks in the Double

Buffer (DB) while data stored previously in the other bank are subjected to partial test unification by the Test Unification Engine (TUE). The results of the test will decide which clause is to be captured in the Result Memory (RM).

3.1. The Writable Control Store (WCS)

The construction of the WCS, figure 3, is based extensively on AMD (Advanced Micro Devices, Inc) bit-slice components. The WCS consists of a bank of fast bipolar RAM which holds the microprogram instruction for coordinating the overall FS2 hardware during a query. A *one level pipeline based architecture* [14] is adopted by the WCS - the microprogram instruction appears one instruction ahead of the microprogram memory address. The RAM can hold a maximum of 2048 microprogram instructions, each 64 bits wide. Normally, the fast RAM is read only and is addressed by the Micro Program Controller (MPC). When the FS2 is operating in Microprogramming mode, the fast RAM is connected to the VMEbus. It will appear as normal memory to the SUN host and loading of microprograms is enabled. Two counters, one for the database input and one for the query, are used to keep track of the number of elements remaining during the matching of lists and structures. An 8 MHz clock is used to synchronise the various parts in the WCS.

At the beginning of a retrieval and after matching a clause, the MPC is engaged in a polling routine This routine repeatedly monitors the zeroth bit of the conditional code (CC) which is asserted when a new clause has been read into the Double Buffer and is ready to be examined. The output of the MPC which is the address in the fast RAM, can derive either from the MPC's internal counter or externally from the branch address field of the microprogram instructions when a branch or jump instruction occurs. Another external source comes from the output of the Map ROM. The Map ROM stores a list of jump vectors and its address port is connected to the db-data and Q-data bus from the Test Unification Engine. Only the type fields of the db-data and Q-data are effective. Depending on the combination of the type fields, different microprogram routines are invoked. The data types supported by the FS2 are classified into 3 categories (see appendix 1). Each category is handled differently :

Simple terms require simple matching.
Atoms, integers and floating point numbers are included in this category. Apart from the case of an integer constant (integer in-line) in which the content field is the value of the integer itself, the content fields of these data items are symbol table references. Equality is the testing condition when two arguments are compared against each other in this type.

Variable terms may require skipping, storing or fetch then match operation.
There are five variable types. An anonymous variable is effectively a don't care object and it causes a skip in the matching process. When an anonymous variable is encountered on either side during a match, the match will succeed immediately irrespective of the type of the other

side. The other variable types account for the origin of a variable - whether it occurs in a query (QV) or in a data/knowledge base (DV). QV and DV are further divided into two groups in order to record their modes of occurrence. For example, 1st-QV will be the type of a variable when it is being referred to in the first time during the partial test unification process; if the same variable occurs again in the same query, it will be typed as Sub-QV (subsequent query variable). At compile time, the subsequent occurrences and the first occurrence of a variable have the same content field which is a pointer to the internal memory of the Test Unification Engine. First occurrences of QVs and DVs will invoke an instantiation routine which stores, respectively, the database and the query argument terms in the Q-Memory and DB-Memory of the Test Unification Engine (see later). QVs and DVs which occurred subsequently are handled specially. It involves two microprogram instruction cycles : firstly, the location of the internal memory of the Test Unification Engine, referenced to by the content field of the variable, is read; and secondly, that value is subject to partial test unification.

Complex terms require repetitive matching
A complex term can be a list or a structure. In-line complex terms can contain one to 32 constituent terms. During the matching process, the arities of the in-line complex terms of both the database and query (which need to be the same) will be loaded into respective counters. The matching process will be performed upon each constituent term pair. At the end of a comparison, both counters are decremented. This process will be repeated until the counters reach zero. Structures and lists with arities greater than 32 are represented, respectively, by structure and list pointers. Comparison of these types is identical to simple term matching. As a subset of lists, unlimited lists are defined. They are lists which contain a tail variable, e.g. [a,b|Tail]. The arities of the terms being compared may not be equal in this case. The arities are loaded into two counters and matching is repetitively carried out until the value of either counter is zero.

3.2. The Double Buffer and the Result Memory

The Double Buffer is separated physically into two identical halves. Each half consists of a bank of memory and an output register. During a search, one half is selected for input while the other is selected for output, and these roles alternated whenever the input is filled. The half which is selected for input accepts the data streaming in from disk. The data from the output register is the clause stored in the corresponding memory in the previous cycle. The output data is fed into the Test Unification Engine for matching with the pre-loaded query data. Selection control is basically generated by a toggle flip flop. Both inverting and non-inverting outputs of the flip flop are utilised in order to produce two non-overlapping clocks. The clock period is variable and is equal to the time taken for the Double Buffer to read in 2 clauses.

The Result Memory has a capacity of 32K bytes which is large enough to contain all clause satisfiers of one disk track - the worst case of a single FS2 search call. While disk data is transferring to the Double Buffer, a copy of the data is written into the Result Memory in parallel. The address of the Result Memory is derived from the Address Generator. The Address Generator consists of two counters. One is 6 bits wide and contributes to the upper 6 bits of the Result Memory address (A_9-A_{14}). This counter is incremented whenever a clause satisfier is found. The value of this counter at the end of a retrieval indicates the number of clause satisfiers. The other counter is 9 bits wide and forms the lower 9 bits of the Result Memory address (A_0-A_8). The second counter is always reset to zero after a clause has been examined. The schematic block diagram depicting the Double Buffer and the Result Memory is shown in figure 4.

3.3. The Test Unification Engine (TUE)

The Test Unification Engine (TUE), figure 5, consists of two banks of memory (DB Memory & Query Memory) a comparator (Comp), three registers (Reg1-3) and 6 selectors (Sel1-6). The DB Memory is a dual port memory which is used for storing bindings of database variables at run time. It is reset to pointing to itself at the beginning of each clause input. The Query Memory is pre-loaded at query time and it contains the query argument terms. The Comparator (Comp) is a standard ALS 8-bit comparator which generates a 1-bit HIT signal according to the values of its A and B inputs. The A and B inputs correspond to the data/knowledge base and query argument terms respectively. HIT is fed into the conditional code register (CC) of the WCS which will select of the next microroutine. When the FS2 is in Set Query mode, only the Query Memory is enabled. The right hand branches of Sel4 are selected to provide, respectively, the data and address to the Query Memory. The Query Memory is directly connected to the VMEbus interface and appears to the host as ordinary memory.

While the FS2 is in Search mode, operation of the TUE is controlled by microcode. Depending on the types of the terms being compared, different microprogram routines are invoked. The main objective of the microprogram routines is to ensure that the right data appears at the memory and the comparator. This is done by selecting the appropriate paths of the six selectors and enabling the appropriate registers. Seven basic hardware operations are provided in realising the partial test unification algorithm listed in figure 1.

3.3.1. MATCH

This is the simplest operation which is applied when the data/knowledge base and the query arguments are integers, atoms, floating point numbers, structures or lists (corresponding to cases 1 to 4 in the algorithm shown in figure 1). The routes in which query and knowledge base terms are passed to the Comparator are shown by the thick dotted lines in figure 6. Whenever a hardware operation is invoked, data/knowledge base and query arguments travel in two separate routes in parallel. The routes taken during the MATCH operation are :

(1) The database route originates from the Double Buffer, along the In-bus, through the left branch of Sel1 and finally appears at the A-port of the Comparator. From the timing specifications of individual devices, the time taken for data to appear at the A-port is calculated to be 40ns (see bottom of figure 6).

(2) The query route starts from the left branch of Sel6, from which micro bits 13-20 provide the address of the Query Memory. Data derived from the Query Memory enters the right branch of Sel3 and ends up at the B-port. The estimated propagation time is 75ns.

It takes 30ns for the comparator to generate a result. Comparison can not take place until both A and B inputs are ready. Therefore, although information travels on both routes in parallel, the longest routing time of the two should be taken in calculating the execution time of the MATCH operation. This gives an execution time of 105ns (75+30).

3.3.2. DB_STORE

This operation is applied when the data/knowledge base argument's type is first occurrence variable (1st-DV) - corresponding to case 5a of figure 1. The aim is to store the query argument in the location of the DB Memory which is addressed by the content field of the data/knowledge base argument. Figure 7 shows the routes taken by the database and query arguments. On the database side, data is extracted from the Double Buffer; it streams via the In-bus to the left branch of Sel1. Travelling via the left branch of Sel2, the data appears on the A address port of the dual ported DB Memory. There is only one input port in the DB Memory and it is connected to the output of Reg3. The content of Reg3 is taken from the output of the Query Memory whose location is specified by the left branch of Sel6. The time taken to execute this operation is 95ns.

3.3.3. QUERY_STORE

This operation is applied when the query type is a first occurrence variable (1st-QV) - case 6a of figure 1. The objective is to store the data/knowledge base argument in the location of the Query Memory which is addressed by the content field of the query argument. Referring to figure 8, the database route travels from the Double Buffer through the left branch of Sel1, then through the right branch of Sel5 and passes the left branch of Sel4 to appear at the input port of the Query Memory. The route which the query data takes is derived from the left branch of Sel6 and terminates at the address port of the Query Memory. The total execution time for this operation is 115ns.

3.3.4. DB_FETCH

When a subsequently occurring data/knowledge base variable (Sub-DV) is encountered during a search - case 5b of figure 1, the DB Memory is accessed at the B-port in order to extract the binding of the variable for subsequent comparison. The routes taken by the data/knowledge base and the query arguments in this operation are depicted in figure 9. The database route starts from the Double Buffer which appears at the B address port of the DB Memory. The corresponding data is extracted from the DB Memory and it travels via the right branch of Sel1 to appear at the A-port of the Comparator. The query route is identical to the query route taken by the simple MATCH operation. The total execution time for this process is 105ns.

3.3.5. QUERY_FETCH

This operation is applied when the query type is a subsequently occurring variable (Sub-QV) - case 6b of figure 1. It is slightly more complicated to implement and requires two cycles for completion. In the first cycle, the query route (from the left branch of Sel6 → output of the Query Memory → right branch of Sel3 → right branch of Sel2 → A address port of DB Memory) provides the address to the A port of the DB Memory, figure 10. From the DB Memory the binding associated with the query variable is extracted and appears at the B-port of the Comparator via the left branch of Sel3 in cycle two. Running concurrently with the first and second cycles, the data/knowledge base argument is placed at the A-port of the Comparator. The time taken to execute this operation is 170ns.

3.3.6. DB_CROSS_BOUND_FETCH

DB_CROSS_BOUND_FETCH is required in situations when a data/knowledge base variable is initially bound to a query variable and the former is being used again in the same clause - cross binding (case 5c of figure 1). For example, it will be called for the second occurrence of the data/knowledge base variable A if the query f(X,a,b) is matched against the clause f(A,a,A). In the query side, data takes the simple route, i.e. ub13-20→left of Sel6→ output of Query Memory→right of Sel3→ A-port of Comp. Two cycles are required to establish the database route. In the first cycle, figure 11a, the data from the Double Buffer appears on the B address port of the DB Memory. From the DB Memory B data port, the reference to the cross bound variable is extracted and stored in Reg1. This reference is placed at the B address port in the second cycle, figure 11b. From the DB Memory the ultimate association is extracted and placed at the A-port of the Comparator via the right branch of Sel1. The total execution time is calculated to be 170ns.

3.3.7. QUERY_CROSS_BOUND_FETCH

The route taken by this operation is shown in figure 12. It is invoked when a query variable is initially bound to a data/knowledge base variable and the former is being used again in the same clause (case 6c of figure 1). This is the most complicated operation and requires 3 microprogram cycles. In the first cycle, the A-port of the Comparator is set up via the

database route (Double Buffer→left of Sel1) and concurrently, the A port of the DB Memory is addressed by the data presented on the query route (i.e. ub13-20→left of Sel6→Query Memory→right of Sel3→right of Sel2). In the second cycle the query variable binding is extracted from the DB Memory A data port. This binding is recycled and is put back at the A address port (via left of Sel2→right of Sel2). The ultimate value for comparison is routed to the B-port of the comparator (via left of Sel3). The time required to perform the operation is calculated to be 235ns.

4. Conclusion

A special purpose hardware engine, CLARE, is being developed which will provide Prolog with a rapid clause retrieval rate in dealing with large data sets. CLARE consists of two hardware components and together they form a 2-stage filtering architecture. The hardware is designed to be linked to a M68020 host, via the VMEbus interface, in a SUN3/160 workstation. The prototype of the first stage filter (FS1) hardware has been fully developed. It can search data at a rate of up to 4.5Mbyte/sec. The design of the second stage filter (FS2) is complete and the partial test unification algorithm has been verified. The construction of the FS2 is well under way. Once the CLARE hardware is fully developed, it will be subjected to benchmark tests similar to the ones devised in [7].

Execution times for the various FS2 hardware operations are calculated and they are summarised in table 1. From the table it can be seen that, QUERY_CROSS_BOUND_FETCH is the most time consuming operation which takes 235ns. This gives the worst case execution rate of the FS2 to be approximately 4.25Mbytes/second. The SUN3/160 workstation, the target platform of CLARE, can be mounted with either a SCSI based disk system, e.g. Micropolis 1325, or a SMD+ based disk system, e.g. Futjitsu M2351A. Even if the second type of disk (which offers a faster transfer rate) is used and it is tuned to operate at its peak rate (circa 2Mbytes/second), the FS2 hardware can still filter disk data at a faster rate than it can be delivered from the disk.

Acknowledgement

The material described herein is based on work carried out in the Prolog Database Machine project. This project, is a collaborative project involving the Department of Computer Science, Heriot-Watt University and International Computers Ltd (ICL, UK), and is funded by the Science and Engineering Research Council (SERC) and the Department of Trade and Industry (DTI) of the United Kingdom, under the Alvey initiative.

Reference

[1] Bocca, J., "EDUCE A Marriage of Convenience: Prolog and a Relational DBMS", Internal report KB-9, European Computer-Industry Research Centre, Munich, Sept.'85.

[2] Wong, K.F. & Williams, M.H. "Partial Matching Hardware for Clause Retrieval in Large Prolog Databases", Technical Report 88/2, Dept. of Computer Science, Heriot-Watt University, Edinburgh, Scotland, 1988.

[3] Li, D., A Prolog Database System, Research Studies Press, London 1984.

[4] Berra, P.B., Chung, S.M. & Hachem N.I., "Computer Architecture for a Surrogate File to a Very Large Data/Knowledge Base", IEEE Computer, pp25-32, March'87.

[5] Warren, D.H.D., "Logic Programming and Knowledge Bases", Proceedings of the Islamorada Workshop on Large Scale Knowledge Base and Reasoning Systems, pp69-72, Islamorada, Florida, February'85.

[6] Williams,M.H., Massey, P.A. & Crammond, J.A., "Benchmarks for Prolog from a Database Viewpoint", Proceedings of 2nd Alvey Workshop for SIGKME, ppC1-C8, Brunel University, England, 1987.

[7] Williams,M.H., Massey, P.A. & Crammond, J.A., "Benchmarking Prolog for Database Applications", Prolog and Databases: Implementations and New Directions, Ellis Horwood Series in AI, edited by P.M.D. Gray and R.J. Lucas, pp161-187, 1988.

[8] Williams, M.H., "The Design of a Prolog Database Machine", Proceedings of the 1st Workshop for SIGKME, ppL1-L5, Reading University, England, Jan'87.

[9] Clocksin, W.F., "Design and Simulation of a Sequential Prolog Machine", New Generation Computing, vol. 3, pp101-120, 1985.

[10] Wong, K.F. "Comment on A Comparison of Concatenate and Superimposed Code Word Surrogate Files For Very Large Data/Knowledge Bases", Technical Report 88/6, Dept. of CS, Heriot-Watt University, Edinburgh, Scotland, 1988.

[11] Ramamohanarao, K. & Shepherd, J. "A Superimposed Codeword Indexing Scheme for Very Large Prolog Database", Proceedings of 3rd International Logic Programming Conference, London, England, July'86.

[12] Wong, K.F. & M.H. Williams, "Design Considerations for a Prolog Database Engine", Proceedings of the 3rd International Conference on Data and Knowledge Bases, pp111-120, Jerusalem, Israel, 28-30 June'88.

[13] Sun Microsystems, Inc., "Writing Device Drivers for the Sun Workstations", Sun Workstation Manual, February'86.

[14] Advanced Micro Devices, Inc, "Architectures Using the 2910A", Bipolar Microprocessor and Logic Data Book, p(5)175 -177,1985.

Appendix I: Data Types Supported in the Pseudo In-line Format

Table A1: CLARE Data Type Scheme			
Items	Type Tag (1b)	Content (b/3b)	Extension (4b)
Variables:			
Anonymous Var	0010 0000 (0x20)	-	-
First Query Var	0010 0111 (0x27)	Variable Offset (b)	-
Subsequent Query Var	0010 0101 (0x25)	Variable Offset (b)	-
First DB Var	0010 0110 (0x26)	Variable Offset (b)	-
Subsequent DB Var	0010 0100 (0x24)	Variable Offset (b)	-
Simple Terms:			
Atom Pointer	0000 1000 (0x08)	Symbol Table Offset	-
Float Pointer	0000 1001 (0x09)	Symbol Table Offset	-
Integer In-line	0001 nnnn (0x1N)	Least Significant Value -	
	(nnnn = most significant nibble)		
Complex Terms:			
Structure In-line	011a aaaa	Functor Symbol Table Offset	-
	(aaaaa=arity, ≤31)	Structure Elements Follow	
Structure Pointer	010a aaaa	Functor Symbol Table Offset	Pointer to Structure
	(aaaaa=arity, ≤31)		
Terminated List In-line	111a aaaa	-	-
	(aaaaa=arity, ≤31)	List Elements Follow	
Unterminated List In-line	101a aaaa	-	-
	(aaaaa=arity, ≤31)	List Elements Follow	
Terminated List Pointer	110a aaaa	Pointer to List (4b)	-
	(aaaaa=arity, ≤31)	Only Use in DB Argument	
Unterminated List Pointer	100a aaaa	Pointer to a List (4b)	-
	(aaaaa=arity, ≤31)	Only Use in DB Argument	

1	**if** both types are integers **then**
	compare their contents (numbers)

2	**if** both types are atoms **OR** float **then**
	compare their contents (hashed values to the symbol table)

3	**if** both types are structures **then**
	compare their contents (functor names and arities &
	contents of top level elements)

4	**if** both types are lists **then**
	compare their contents (length of list and types &
	contents of top level elements)

5	**if** the database type is a variable **then**
	check for the existence of the clause variable
5a	**if** it does not exist **then**
	create a new entry in the DB variable store
	associate it with the query term

5b	**if** it exists **then**
	extract its association from the DB variable store
5c	**if** it is a variable itself **then**
	fetch the ultimate association from the DB store
	repeat the comparison operations again

6.	**if** the query type is a variable **then**
	check for the existence of the query variable
6a	**if** it does not exist **then**
	create a new entry in the Query variable store
	associate it with the database term
6b	**if** it exists **then**
	extract its association from the Query variable store
6c	**if** it is a variable itself **then**
	fetch the ultimate association from the DB store
	repeat the comparison operations again

Figure 1: The simplified partial test unification algorithm.

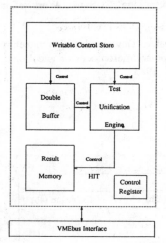

Figure 2: The overall architecture of the second stage filter hardware (FS2).

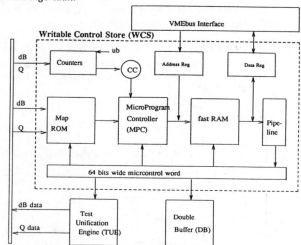

Figure 3: The Writable Control Store (WCS).

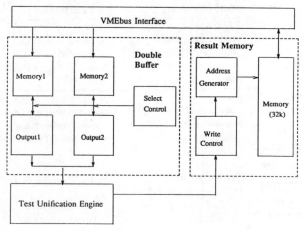

Figure 4: The Double Buffer and the Result Memory.

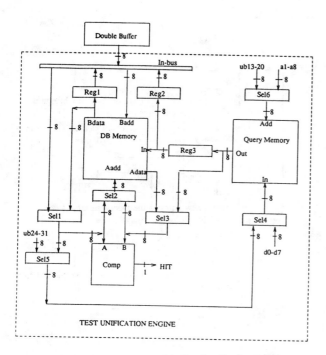

Figure 5: The Test Unification Engine.

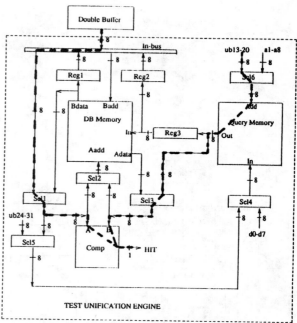

Timing Calculation for the MATCH Operation			
database route :	Double Buffer	Sel1	
	20	20	(=40)
query route :	Sel6 →	Query Memory →	Sel3
	20	35	20 (=75)
Comparison :	(=30)		

execution time = query route (75) + comparison (30) = 105ns.

Figure 6: The MATCH Operation

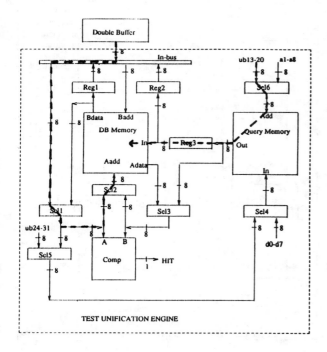

Timing Calculation for the DB_STORE Operation			
database route :	Double Buffer →	Sel1 →	Sel2
	20	20	20 (=60)
query route :	Sel6 →	Query Memory →	Reg3
	20	35	20 (=75)
DB Memory write :	(=20)		

execution time = query route + DB Memory write = 95ns

Figure 7: The DB_STORE Operation

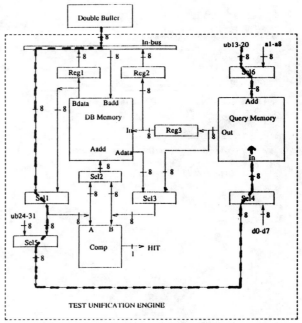

Timing Calculation for the QUERY_STORE Operation				
database route :	Double Buffer →	Sel1 →	Sel5 →	Sel4
	20	20	20	20 (=80)
query route :	Sel6			
	20			
Query Memory write :	(=25)			

execution time = database route + Query Memory write = 105ns

Figure 8: The QUERY_STORE Operation

219

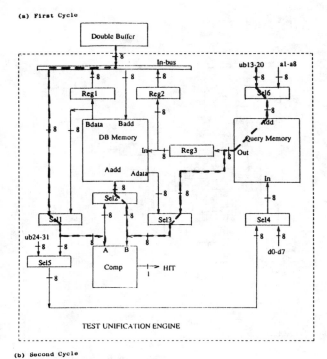

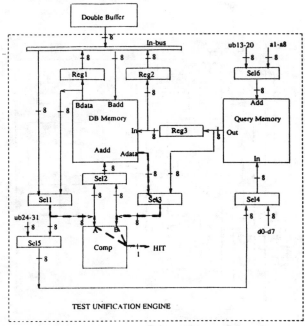

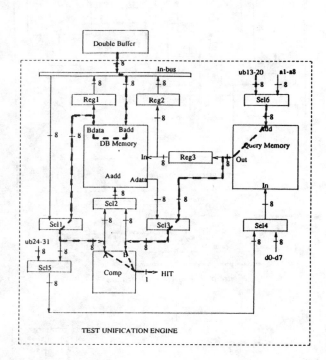

(b) Second Cycle

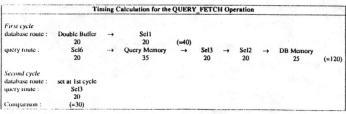

Timing Calculation for the DB_FETCH Operation				
database route :	Double Buffer	→	DB Memory	Sel1
	20		25	20 (=65)
query route :	Sel6	→	Query Memory	→ Sel3
	20		35	20 (=75)
comparison:	(=30)			

execution time = query route (75) + comparison (30) = 105ns.

Figure 9: The DB_FETCH Operation

Timing Calculation for the QUERY_FETCH Operation									
First cycle									
database route :	Double Buffer	→	Sel1						
	20		20	(=40)					
query route :	Sel6	→	Query Memory	→	Sel3	→	Sel2	→	DB Memory
	20		35		20		20		25 (=120)
Second cycle									
database route :	set at 1st cycle								
query route :	Sel3								
	20								
Comparison :	(=30)								

execution time = 1st cycle query route (120) + 2nd cycle query route (20) + comparison (30) = 170ns.

Figure 10: The QUERY_FETCH Operation

(a) First Cycle

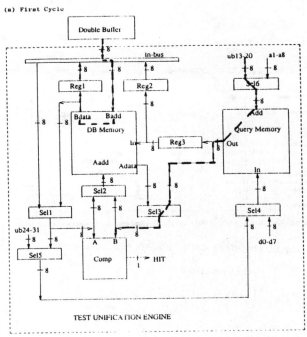

(a) First Cycle

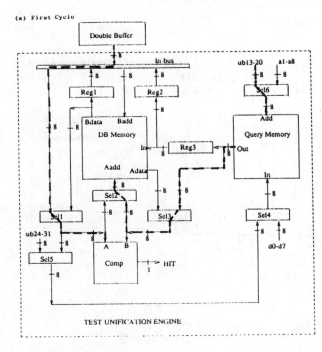

(b) Second Cycle

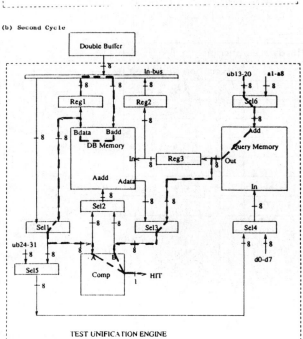

(b) Second Cycle

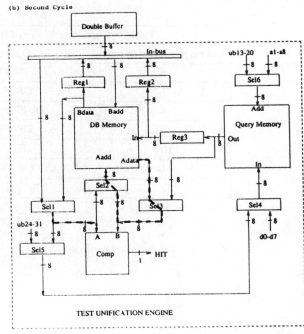

Timing Calculation for the DB_CROSS_BOUND_FETCH Operation				
First cycle				
database route :	Double Buffer	→	DB Memory	→	Reg1
	20		25		20	(=65)
query route :	Sel6	→	Query Memory	→	Sel3
	20		35		20	(=75)
Second Cycle				
database route :	Reg1	→	DB Memory	→	Sel1
	20		25		20	(=65)
query route :	set at 1st cycle			
comparison :			(=30)	

execution time = 1st cycle query route (75) + 2nd cycle database route (65) + comparison (30) = 170ns.

Figure 11: The DB_CROSS_BOUND_FETCH Operation

Figure 12: The QUERY_CROSS_BOUND_FETCH Operation

(c) Third Cycle

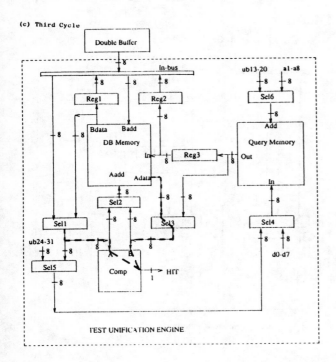

| Timing Calculation for the QUERY_CROSS_BOUND_FETCH Operation | | | | | | | | |

First cycle
database route :   Double Buffer → Sel1
                   20   20   (=40)
query route :   Sel6 → Query Memory → Sel3 → Sel2
                   20   35   20   20   (=95)

Second cycle
database route :   set in 1st cycle
query route :   DB Memory → Sel3 → Sel2
                   25   20   20   (=65)

Third cycle
database route :   set at 1st cycle
query route :   DB Memory → Sel3
                   25   20   (=45)
comparison :   (=30)

execution time = query routes of { 1st cycle (95) + 2nd cycle (65) + 3rd cycle (45) } + comparison (30) = 235ns

Figure 12: The QUERY_CROSS_BOUND_FETCH *Operation*

(Continuation)

Table 1: Execution Times of the FS2 Hardware Functions		
Corresponding Figure	**Operations**	**Execution times (ns)**
6	MATCH	105
7	DB_STORE	95
8	QUERY_STORE	115
9	DB_FETCH	105
10	QUERY_FETCH	170
11	DB_CROSS_BOUND_FETCH	170
12	QUERY_CROSS_BOUND_FETCH	235

Instruction Fetching

Comparing Software and Hardware Schemes
For Reducing the Cost of Branches

Wen-mei W. Hwu   Thomas M. Conte   Pohua P. Chang

Coordinated Science Laboratory
1101 W. Sprintfield Ave.
University of Illinois
Urbana, IL 61801

Abstract

Pipelining has become a common technique to increase throughput of the instruction fetch, instruction decode, and instruction execution portions of modern computers. Branch instructions disrupt the flow of instructions through the the pipeline, increasing the overall execution cost of branch instructions. Three schemes to reduce the cost of branches are presented in the context of a general pipeline model. Ten realistic Unix domain programs are used to directly compare the cost and performance of the three schemes and the results are in favor of the software-based scheme. For example, the software-based scheme has a cost of 1.65 cycles/branch vs. a cost of 1.68 cycles/branch of the best hardware scheme for a highly pipelined processor (11-stage pipeline). The results are 1.19 (software scheme) vs. 1.23 cycles/branch (best hardware scheme) for a moderately pipelined processor (5-stage pipeline).

1 Introduction

The pipelining of modern computer designs causes problems for the execution of branch instructions. Branches disrupt sequential instruction supply for pipelined processors and introduce non-productive instructions into the pipeline. However, approximately one out of every three to five instructions is a branch instruction[1][2]. A significant increase in the performance of pipelined computers can be achieved through special treatment of branch instructions[3][4][1].

There have been several schemes proposed to reduce the branch performance penalty. These schemes employ hardware or software techniques to predict the direction of

a branch, provide the target address of a branch, and supply the first few target instructions [3][4][1][5][6]. When the prediction is incorrect, the wrong instructions are introduced into the pipeline. After the branch instruction finishes execution and supplies the correct action to the instruction fetch unit, the incorrect instructions are flushed, or *squashed* from the pipeline [1]. These schemes rely on the assumption that the accuracy of the branch prediction scheme is high enough to mask the penalty of squashing. A small increase in the accuracy of a prediction scheme has a large effect on the performance of conditional branch instructions if the penalty for squashing an incorrectly predicted branch is large. Hence, highly accurate prediction schemes are desirable.

There have been many studies that investigate the effectiveness of solutions to the branch problem. Most of these studies focus on the accuracy of the branch prediction scheme employed [3][4][1][6][7]. Some studies also discuss hardware and software approaches to reducing the penalty of refilling the instruction fetch unit's pipeline [3][1][6].

Some schemes use static code analysis to predict branch behavior. One such scheme predicts all backward conditional branches as taken and all forward branches as not-taken. This is based on the assumption that backward branches are usually at the end of loops. In the study done by J. E. Smith [4], the average accuracy of this approach was 76.5%. However, in some cases this approach performed as poorly as only 35% accurate. Since the benchmarks used in the study were FORTRAN applications, which tend to be dominated by loop-structured code, the results may have been biased in favor of scientific workloads. Another study reported a 90% average accuracy for a static scheme, however the specific prediction mechanism was not reported nor was any additional statistical information besides the average [7].

Many architectures predict every conditional branch to either be all taken or all not-taken. In [1], this scheme is reported to be only 63% accurate if all branches are predicted taken. Similarly, [3] reports approximately 65±5%, [2] reports 67%, and [4] reports 76.7% of all branches are taken. Another static approach is to associate a prediction with the opcode of the branch instruction. This prediction is derived from performance studies and is stored

© 1989 ACM 0884-7495/89/0000/0224$01.50

in a ROM or with the branch's microcode. The accuracy of this scheme is reported to be 66.2% on-average in [3] and 86.7% in [4].

Several dynamic branch history-based prediction schemes are presented in [3] and [4]. Dynamic approaches to branch prediction usually include hardware support in the form of a specialized cache to store the prediction information. For example, some schemes calculate the autocorrelation of the history vector of a branch instruction to generate a prediction; however, there is high hardware overhead for this scheme. Another, less-expensive scheme uses an up/down counter for prediction. J. E. Smith reports an accuracy of 92.5% for a two-bit version of this counter scheme. He reports a slightly smaller accuracy for larger counter sizes, due to the "inertia" caused by large counter sizes.

Another method of reducing the cost of branches uses information gathered during profiling a program for compile-time branch prediction. Note that this is different from static techniques since it uses the observed dynamic behavior of the branches for prediction. It is also separate from the other dynamic approaches because it does not require a large amount of hardware support. Usually, the instruction set is modified to include a prediction bit in the branch instruction format. This bit is used by the compiler to specify the prediction (i.e., predicted taken or not-taken) to the hardware. For example, this approach is used in the MIPS architecture [1].

Some previous schemes provide special support to make up for inaccurate branch prediction schemes. A common approach uses condition codes and optional compare instructions [8][9]. A case for single-instruction conditional branches is given in [6]. When a compare instruction must be added, the two instructions must be placed far-enough apart to predict the branch's behavior. However, this may not always be possible. Also, conditional branches now take two instructions instead of a single instruction. In order to make up for this increase in the dynamic instruction count, a hardware mechanism was included in the CRISP project to dynamically absorb the actual branch instruction into its preceding instruction and store it in a partially-decoded form. After all these techniques were used, the compiler designers for CRISP later suggested that a compiler-supported prediction mechanism might be useful to further improve performance [7].

To mask the penalty of flushing the pipeline when the prediction is incorrect, some schemes provide the first few instructions of the branch's target path. Some hardware buffer approaches store these instructions along with the prediction information. Reduced instruction set computer architectures often use a delayed branch to mask this penalty. For example, delayed branches are used in the Stanford MIPS [1] and the Berkeley RISC I [10]. In this approach, the compiler fills the delay slots following the branch instruction with instructions before the branch. While the fetch of the target instruction is being performed, the instructions in the delay slots are executed. These schemes rely on the compilers ability to fill the delay slots. McFarling and Hennessy report that a single delay slot can be successfully filled by the compiler in approximately 70% of the branches. However, a second delay slot could be filled only approximately 25% of the time [1]. Therefore, it is hard to support moderately pipelined instruction fetch units using the delayed branch technique.

The issue of which branch prediction scheme to use for VLSI-implemented monolithic processors is a topic still open to debate. The CRISP processor used significant hardware support for a static compiler technique [7][8]. The MIPS processor used delayed branches with squashing for an architecture with a relatively shallow pipeline (five stages)[1]. Since the silicon real estate is expensive for such processors, schemes that address the branch problem for processors implemented in VLSI should use little or no hardware support and achieve high performance. As more and more systems of all classes are being designed with single-chip central processors, new solutions to the branch problem that match or exceed the performance of traditional approaches must be developed.

This paper investigates three (two hardware and one software) schemes to solve the branch problem. These three schemes are presented and compared in the context of a very general pipelined microarchitecture. An optimizing, profiling compiler assists the evaluation of the performance of the schemes using a substantial number of benchmarks taken from the Unix[1] domain [11]. The experiments are controlled to isolate the effects of pipelining the instruction fetch unit from those of pipelining the instruction decode and instruction execution units.

The remainder of this paper is organized into three sections. Section two provides a concise description of the three schemes used to solve the branch problem: a simple branch target buffer, a counter-based branch target buffer, and a software approach. Section three presents the experimental results used for evaluating the performance of the three schemes. Finally, section four offers concluding remarks and future directions.

2 Background

This section introduces the three architectures that are used for the investigation. The first two of these architectures use additional hardware to solve the branch problem. The third architecture uses a profiling-compiler-driven software approach. All three architectures share a common model of a pipelined microarchitecture. This microarchitecture is composed of four smaller pipelines, or *units*, connected in series: the instruction fetch unit, the instruction decode unit, the instruction execution unit, and the state update unit (see Figure 1).

2.1 Pipeline structure

The instruction fetch unit is divided into $k + 1$ stages, one stage to select the next address, and k stages to access the address. The next address selection logic takes

---

[1]Unix is a trademark of AT&T Bell Laboratories

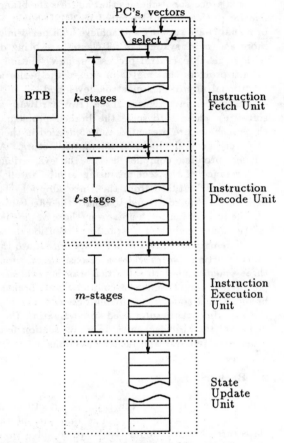

Figure 1: The pipelined microarchitecture.

various program counters and various interrupts and exception vectors to produce the address of the next instruction to fetch. Each branch instruction specifies a vector, or *branch target,* which is the address of the instruction to branch to. The subsequent k stages for instruction memory access take the instruction address generated and access the instruction memory hierarchy (i.e., instruction-buffer, instruction-cache, etc.).

The instruction decode unit is ℓ-stages in length. This stage decodes the instruction and calculates its actual operand values by decoding the operand the addressing modes and possibly accessing the register file or memory. Hence, the actual branch target and the branch action (for unconditional branches) is known at the end of this stage. This information is supplied through a feedback path to the selection logic of the instruction fetch unit.

The instruction execution unit is m-stages in length. The action of conditional branches is known when a branch reaches the end of the unit's pipeline. This information is supplied as a control signal in a feedback path to the selection logic of the instruction fetch unit. This pipeline may implement some form of interlocking, such as scoreboarding or the Tomasulo algorithm [12][13], or interlocking may be statically performed by the compiler. The effects of these interlocking strategies are parameterized to generalize the results (see below). It is assumed that comparisons are included in the semantics of the conditional branch instruction, as opposed to condition-code driven branch instructions. Finally, the state update unit is assumed to update memory, the register file, and/or the data cache with the results of executed instructions.

The issue of which instruction to fetch next is determined by the next address selection stage of the instruction fetch unit. In a simple next address selection stage, no special treatment is given to branches (i.e., branches are always predicted not-taken). If this prediction is incorrect, the wrong instructions will be introduced into the pipeline. These incorrectly-fetched instructions must be flushed from the pipeline when the actual branch behavior is determined. The instruction fetch unit's pipeline must always be flushed, and so must any incorrectly-fetched instructions in the instruction decode and instruction execution units' pipelines. A scheme should be provided for fast access to the k instructions following the branch target to hide the cost of flushing the instruction fetch unit.

Since on some machines the time to decode an instruction is not fixed but dependent on many factors (e.g., the complexity of the addressing modes used, the performance of the memory system, etc.), the penalty for flushing the pipeline of the instruction decode unit is treated as an average, $\bar{\ell}$, where $0 \leq \bar{\ell} \leq \ell$. Note that $\bar{\ell} = \ell$ for many RISC architectures. Due to interlocking, the number of instructions to flush from the instruction execution unit's pipeline may be determined by dependencies between instructions. Also, since unconditional branches are predicted with 100% accuracy, some branch instructions do not require any flush of the instruction execution unit. Hence, the penalty for flushing this unit's pipeline is also taken as an average, $\bar{m}$. For compiler-implemented static interlocking, $\bar{m} = f_{\text{cond}}m$, where f_{cond} is the fraction of branch instructions that are conditional branches. Therefore, it is assumed that on average, $k + \bar{\ell} + \bar{m}$ instructions must be flushed from the pipeline for each branch. This observation will be used in Section 2.3 in stating the general formula for branch cost.

2.2 Three branch cost-reduction schemes

A *Simple Branch Target Buffer,* or SBTB, is used to remember as many as possible of the taken branches that are encountered in the dynamic instruction stream. To mask the penalty of flushing the instruction fetch unit, the SBTB stores the first k instructions of a taken branch's target path. For this reason, any branch instruction not in the SBTB is predicted to be not-taken. If a branch instruction is predicted taken, but when executed it does not branch to a new location, the corresponding entry in the SBTB is deleted. The SBTB may be thought of as cache that uses the branch instruction's location in memory as its associative tag. When it is full, a replacement policy is used to select an entry to replace. The accuracy of the SBTB's predictions is expressed as A_{SBTB}, the probability of the prediction being correct. The SBTB in this paper is a 256-entry fully-associative SBTB with a least-recently-used replacement policy.

Like the SBTB, a *Counter-based Branch Target Buffer,* or CBTB, is also a type of cache. It remembers as many as possible of the branch instructions encountered in the dynamic instruction stream. As with the SBTB, the CBTB also stores the first k instructions of the target branch to mask the instruction fetch penalty. The CBTB implemented for this paper stores a counter used for prediction along with each branch instruction [4]. For each new entry in the CBTB, the n-bit counter, C, is initially set to a threshold, T, if the branch was taken, or $T-1$, if it was not taken. Subsequently if the branch is taken, the counter is incremented, else it is decremented. When $C = 2^n - 1$, it remains at this value, and when $C = 0$, it remains at zero. A branch is predicted taken when $C \geq T$, else the branch is predicted not-taken. Any branch instruction not already in the buffer is predicted not-taken. The accuracy of the CBTB's predictions is expressed as A_{CBTB}, the probability of the prediction being correct. The CBTB in this paper uses a 256-entry fully-associative CBTB with a least-recently-used replacement policy for its branch prediction hardware. The counters used for prediction are 2-bits long and $T = 2$.

The SBTB or CBTB are accessed using the address from the select stage of the instruction fetch unit for every instruction retrieved from memory. This access occurs in parallel with the actual memory access performed in the instruction fetch unit. If the location causes a SBTB/CBTB hit, it is then known that the instruction is a branch. If the SBTB/CBTB's predicts the branch as taken (the SBTB always predicts a hit as a taken branch), the first k instructions following the target are sequentially supplied to the instruction decode unit (see Figure 1).

The third approach to branch prediction, the *Forward Semantic,* uses an optimizing, profiling compiler to predict the direction of all branches in a program. The SBTB/CBTB hardware shown in Figure 1 is not used in this scheme. Instead, the program is first compiled into an executable intermediate form with probes inserted at the entry of each basic block. The program is then run once or several times for a representative input suit. During the recompilation, predictions are made for each branch and stored by setting or clearing a "likely-taken" bit in the instruction format of each branch instruction [11]. The accuracy of these predictions is again represented as a probability that the prediction is correct, A_{FS}. Based on the profiling information, groups of basic blocks that are virtually always executed together are then bundled into larger blocks called *traces* [11][14]. The result is that all conditional branches that are predicted taken are placed at the end of these traces. For each branch that is predicted taken, $k + \ell$ locations, or *forward slots,* following the branch instruction are reserved. The $k + \ell$ instructions from the target path of the branch are copied into these slots. During the execution, when the instruction is determined to be a branch instruction at the end of the instruction decode unit, the instructions in the forward slots will mask the penalty of incorrectly fetching the $k + \ell$ instructions following the branch. Hence, these instructions serve the same purpose as the k instructions stored with each entry in the SBTB or CBTB.

To fill the forward slots, the traces are sorted by execution weight. The following algorithm is then used to fill the slots, where there are N traces, trace[i] is the trace with the ith largest weight, trace[i]->next_trace is the target trace, target_addr[trace[i]] is the target address of the branch instruction at the end of trace trace[i], and trace[i]->offset_into_trace is the branch target address, expressed as an offset from the beginning of the target trace.

```
for i ← N downto 1 step -1 do
   next_trace ← trace->next_trace;
   offset ← trace->offset_into_trace;
   length ← size_of(next_trace) - offset;
   if (length ≥ k + ℓ) then
       Copy the next k + ℓ instructions
          of trace[i]->next_trace to
          the end of trace[i];
       target_addr[trace[i]] ←
          target_addr[trace[i]] + k + ℓ;
   else
       Copy the remaining instructions
          of next_trace to the
          end of trace[i];
       Fill the remaining forward slots
          with NO-OP's;
       target_addr[trace[i]] ←
          target_addr[trace[i]] + length;
   endif;
```

An example of the algorithm is shown in Figure 2. The branch instruction originally at location 5 is an unlikely branch. Therefore, it can be absorbed into the forward slots of the branch instruction at location 2. Note that the target for this branch is not altered when it is absorbed into the forward slots. The instructions in the forward slots at locations 3 and 4 of the altered program fragment execute using an alternate program counter register value which in the example will be set to location 7.

	1: I_1
1: I_1	2:beq $pc + 5$ *(likely)*
2:beq $pc + 3$ *(likely)*	3:beq $pc + 3$ *(unlikely)*
3: I_3	4: I_6
4: I_4	5: I_3
5:beq $pc + 3$ *(unlikely)*	6: I_4
6: I_6	7:beq $pc + 3$ *(unlikely)*
7: I_7	8: I_6
8: I_8	9: I_7
9: I_9	10: I_8
	11: I_9

Figure 2: An example of the Forward Semantic: original program fragment (*left*), and after application of the algorithm (*right*).

Note that the Forward Semantic is different from the "Delayed-Branch with Squashing" scheme presented in [1]. In that scheme, no branch instructions could be absorbed into the delay slots following the branch instruction. Also, the most-recently prefetched instruction and the instructions specified in the delay slots after the branch instruction were the instructions that would be squashed if the prediction was incorrect. However, in the Forward Semantic scheme, although $k + \ell + \bar{m}$ instructions are flushed from the pipeline, only $k + \ell$ forward slots following the branch are used. Hence, a Forward Semantic implementation for the architecture presented in [1] would have used only one forward slot following the branch instead of two, since $k = 0, \ell = 1, m = 2$ for MIPS-X.

2.3 Branch instruction cost

Whenever an incorrect prediction is made, the entire pipeline may potentially be flushed. This means the cost for an incorrect prediction for any of the three schemes is $k + \ell + \bar{m}$. When the prediction is correct, each of the three schemes successfully covers the flushing of the pipelines. Hence, the cost of executing a branch instruction for any of the three architectures is,

$$\text{cost} = A + (k + \bar{\ell} + \bar{m})(1 - A),$$

where $A = A_{SBTB}$, for the SBTB, $A = A_{CBTB}$, for the CBTB, and $A = A_{FS}$ for the Forward Semantic. This equation will be used in the remainder of this paper to calculate the cost of branches for the three architectures given the accuracy of the three prediction schemes. Assuming that time is measured in clock cycles, and each stage of the pipeline has a latency of one clock cycle,

3 Experimental Results

Table 1 summarizes several important characteristics of the benchmarks used for the experiments below. The *Lines* column shows the static code size of the C benchmark programs measured in the number of program lines. The *Runs* column gives the number of different inputs used in the profiling process. The *Inst.* column gives the dynamic code size of the benchmark programs, measured in number of compiler intermediate instructions. The *Control* column gives the percentage of dynamic conditional and unconditional branches executed during the profiling process. Both *Inst.* and *Control* are accumulated across all of the runs. Finally, the *Input description* column describes the nature of the inputs used in the profiling process. As reported in many other papers, the number of dynamic instructions between dynamic branches is small (about four).

The *Conditional* column of Table 2 confirms that on average 61% of the dynamic branches generated by the compiler are not-taken branches. When the SBTB or CBTB generates a miss for a given branch, the instruction fetch unit cannot fetch the target instructions in time, which forces the fetch unit to continue to fetch the next instruction. This is equivalent to predicting that the branch is not taken. Since the majority of the dynamic branches are not taken, the predictions made upon SBTB misses are actually accurate. Since only taken branches make their way into the SBTB, the low percentage of taken branches also reduces the number of entries needed in SBTB to achieve high prediction accuracy. Therefore, we can expect the SBTB performance reported below to be better than equivalent designs reported by the previous papers.

The *Known* column in Table 2 gives the percentage of availability of the target address for unconditional branches. Unconditional branches with known target address can be easily handled by all the three schemes as (extremely biased) likely branches. Branches with unknown target addresses (i.e., the address is generated as run-time data) pose a problem for all three schemes. Fortunately, almost all the unconditional branches for the benchmarks have known target addresses. Therefore, all the three schemes work well with the unconditional branches.

The performance of the benchmarks for the three architectures are presented in Table 3. The miss ratio for the SBTB, ρ_{SBTB}, is much larger than the miss ratio for the CBTB, ρ_{SBTB}. This is to be expected since only taken branches are saved in the SBTB, whereas all branches are eligible to be stored in the CBTB. Note also that the differences in prediction accuracy (i.e., A) between the three schemes increases with the complexity of the prediction mechanism used. A SBTB uses essentially information based on the most recent behavior of a branch instruction in the dynamic instruction stream. Since the counter used for the CBTB is 2-bits long, the CBTB bases its predictions on the four most-recent branches in the dynamic instruction stream. Hence, the CBTB predicts branch behavior slightly more accurately than does the SBTB. The most accurate scheme, the Forward Semantic, uses the behavior of the branch throughout the entire dynamic instruction stream for its predictions.

Observe that the accuracy values for all three architectures are very similar. However, if context switching had been simulated, one would expect the performance of the SBTB and the CBTB to be less impressive [3]. Note though that the prediction accuracy of the Forward Semantic would not have changed in the presence of context switching. Finally, both the SBTB and the CBTB are fully associative to provide the highest possible hit ratio. With 256 entries, it may not be feasible to implement full associativity. Hence, the results are biased slightly in favor of the two hardware approaches.

The values of $k = 1, 2, 4$, and 8 and the averages from Table 3 of A were used for the four graphs of branch cost versus $\bar{\ell} + \bar{m}$ in Figures 3 and 4, where SBTB cost is shown as a solid line, CBTB cost is a dashed line, and Forward Semantic cost is a dotted line. These figures show that as the length of the instruction fetch pipeline grows, the difference between the three architectures increases as does the overall branch cost. Increasing the length of the instruction decode and instruction execution pipeline also increases the difference between the three architectures.

Modern microprocessors have relatively shallow pipelines with a two-stage instruction fetch pipeline (e.g., $\bar{\ell} + \bar{m} \approx 2$, $k = 1$). Pipelining the on-chip cache memory system is a difficult task. Future increases in pipelining may therefore occur in the instruction decode unit. To see the effect of this possible design shift, the results for all benchmarks for $k + \bar{\ell} = 2$ and 3, and $\bar{m} = 1$ is presented in Table 4.

Note that the three schemes do have a slight increase in branch cost for the transition from $k + \bar{\ell} = 2$ to $k + \bar{\ell} = 3$ for each benchmark. The average percentage of increase in branch cost is 7.7%, 6.9%, and 5.3%, for the SBTB, the CBTB, and the Forward Semantic, respectively. Hence, the Forward Semantic reacts the best to scaling the degree of pipelining, the CBTB is next, and the SBTB is the least scalable.

Although the Forward Semantic has a slightly lower branch cost, code-size increases occur due to the copying of instructions into forward slots after each predicted-taken branch. Table 5 summarizes this effect. Because copying instructions into forward slots increases the spatial locality of the program, the expanded static code size does not translate linearly into increased miss ratios of instruction caches. Therefore, considering the saving of hardware over SBTB and CBTB, the Forward Semantic is definitely a favorable choice according to the benchmarks.

4   Conclusions

This paper introduced a software approach to reducing the cost of branches, the Forward Semantic, which is supported by a profiling, optimizing compiler and uncomplicated hardware. A model was presented for the cost of branches which is significantly more general than previous models. One of the main features of this model is the in-

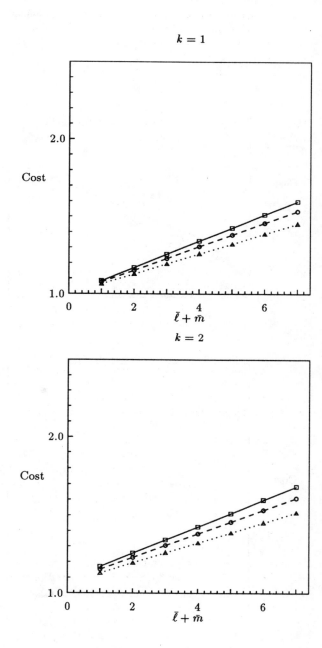

Figure 3: Branch cost vs. $\bar{\ell} + \bar{m}$ for $k = 1$ and $k = 2$.

dependent treatment of the instruction prefetch unit and the instruction execution unit.

The measurements performed for this paper were fair to all three architectures considered. The exact same benchmarks with the same inputs were used to derive the data for all three architectures, even though two architectures involved hardware schemes and one involved a software/compiler scheme. This provided a fair comparison between the Forward Semantic and the two hardware approaches.

The results of the performance study are encouraging. They indicate that the Forward Semantic compares favorably with the two other approaches. If context switching had been simulated, the Forward Semantic's performance would have remained the same, whereas the performance of the other two schemes would have suffered. The hardware needed for the Forward Semantic is considerably less complex than required for the other two schemes. Since the hardware schemes need to be accessed fast by the instruction prefetch pipeline, these schemes would have to be implemented on-chip in a microprocessor, using up valuable area. The Forward Semantic frees this area for other uses without sacrificing performance. Use of the Forward Semantic does cause an increase in code size, however. This additional code adds to the spatial locality of the program, since executing the instructions in forward slots often will cause the branch target's instructions to be in the instruction cache. For deep pipelines (e.g., $k + \ell = 4$), the Forward Semantic with its moderate 14.12% code-size increase seems to be more favorable than the the hardware of the SBTB/CBTB schemes, which increase linearly with k.

Acknowledgements

The authors would like to thank Sadun Anik, Scott Mahlke, Nancy Warter, and all members of the IMPACT research group for their support, comments and suggestions. This research has been supported by the National Science Fundation (NSF) under Grant MIP-8809478, a donation from NCR, the National Aeronautics and Space Administration (NASA) under Contract NASA NAG 1-613 in cooperation with the Illinois Computer laboratory for Aerospace Systems and Software (ICLASS), the Office of Naval Research under Contract N00014-88-K-0656, and the University of Illinois Campus Research Board.

References

[1] S. McFarling and J. L. Hennessy, "Reducing the cost of branches," in *Proc. 13th Annu. Symp. on Comput. Arch.*, (Tokyo, Japan), pp. 396–403, June 1986.

[2] J. S. Emer and D. W. Clark, "A characterization of processor performance in the VAX-11/780," in *Proc. 11th. Annu. Symp. on Comput. Arch.*, pp. 301–309, June 1984.

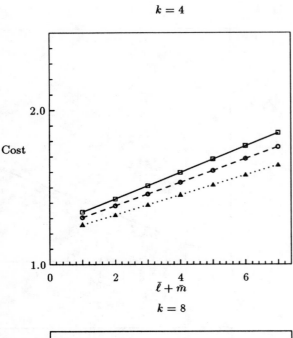

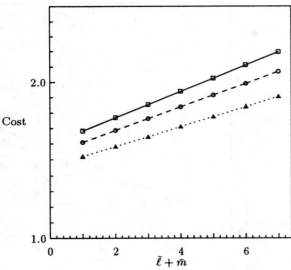

Figure 4: Branch cost vs. $\bar{\ell} + \bar{m}$ for $k = 4$ and $k = 8$.

[3] J. K. F. Lee and A. J. Smith, "Branch prediction strategies and branch target buffer design," *IEEE Computer*, Jan. 1984.

[4] J. E. Smith, "A study of branch predition strategies," in *Proc. 8th Annu. Symp. on Comput. Arch.*, pp. 135–148, June 1981.

[5] D. J. Lilja, "Reducing the branch penalty in pipelined processors," *IEEE Computer*, July 1988.

[6] J. A. DeRosa and H. M. Levy, "An evaluation of branch architectures," in *Proc. 15th. Annu. Symp. on Comput. Arch.*, pp. 10–16, June 1987.

[7] S. Bandyopadhyay, V. S. Begwani, and R. B. Murray, "Compiling for the CRISP microprocessor," in *Proc. 1987 Spring COMPCON*, pp. 86–90, 1987.

[8] D. R. Ditzel and H. R. McLellan, "Branch folding in the CRISP microprocessor: reducing branch delay to zero," in *Proc. 14th Annu. Symp. on Comput. Arch.*, pp. 2–9, June 1987.

[9] Digital Equipment Corp., *VAX11 Architecture Handbook*, 1979.

[10] D. A. Patterson and C. H. Sequin, "RISC I: a reduced instruction set VLSI computer," in *Proc. 8th Annu. Symp. on Comput. Arch.*, pp. 443–457, May 1981.

[11] W. W. Hwu and P. P. Chang, "Trace selection for compiling large C application programs to microcode," in *Proc. 21st Annu. Workshop on Microprogramming and Microarchitectures*, (San Diego, CA.), Nov. 1988.

[12] R. M. Tomasulo, "An efficient algorithm for exploiting multiple arithmetic units," *IBM Journal of Research and Development*, vol. 11, pp. 25–33, Jan. 1967.

[13] J. E. Thornton, "Parallel operation in the Control Data 6600," in *Proc. AFIPS FJCC*, pp. 33–40, 1964.

[14] J. A. Fisher, "Trace scheduling: A technique for global microcode compaction," *IEEE Trans. Comput.*, vol. c-30, no. 7, pp. 478–490, July 1981.

Table 1: Benchmark characteristics

Benchmark	Lines	Runs	Inst.	Control	Input description
cccp	4660	20	11.7M	19%	C progs (100-3000 lines)
cmp	371	16	2.2M	22%	similar/disimilar text files
compress	1941	20	19.6M	16%	same as cccp
grep	1302	20	47.1M	36%	exercised various options
lex	3251	4	3052.6M	37%	lexers (C, Lisp, awk, pic)
make	7043	20	152.6M	21%	makefiles
tee	1063	18	0.43M	40%	text files (100-3000 lines)
tar	3186	14	11M	14%	save/extract files
wc	345	20	7.8M	28%	same input as cccp
yacc	3333	8	313.4M	25%	grammar for C, etc.

Table 2: Benchmark branch statistics

Benchmark	Conditional		Unconditional	
	Taken	Not	Known	Unknown
cccp	31%	69%	81%	19%
cmp	20%	80%	100%	0%
compress	37%	63%	100%	0%
grep	5%	95%	100%	0%
lex	49%	51%	100%	0%
make	49%	51%	100%	0%
tar	89%	11%	100%	0%
tee	44%	56%	100%	0%
wc	24%	76%	100%	0%
yacc	47%	53%	100%	0%
Average	40%	61%	98%	1.9%

Table 3: Branch prediction performance of the benchmarks.

Benchmark	Branch prediction scheme				
	SBTB		CBTB		FS
	ρ_{SBTB}	A_{SBTB}	ρ_{CBTB}	A_{CBTB}	A_{FS}
cccp	0.57	90.7%	0.018	91.5%	89.6%
cmp	0.70	97.1%	0.0032	98.0%	98.6%
compress	0.49	87.8%	0.0053	86.1%	89.1%
grep	0.76	93.7%	0.0006	95.9%	96.0%
lex	0.36	98.2%	0.0002	97.7%	98.0%
make	0.42	90.5%	0.012	92.5%	94.4%
tar	0.11	97.9%	0.005	98.4%	98.7%
tee	0.39	84.4%	0.0058	88.7%	92.2%
wc	0.54	85.4%	0.0008	85.7%	90.4%
yacc	0.46	88.9%	0.0012	89.1%	88.3%
Average	0.48	91.5%	0.0053	92.4%	93.5%
Std. dev.	0.18	5.06%	0.0058	4.92%	4.13%

Table 4: Branch cost for $k + \bar{\ell} = 2$ and 3, and $\bar{m} = 1$

Benchmark	$k + \ell = 2$			$k + \ell = 3$		
	SBTB	CBTB	FS	SBTB	CBTB	FS
cccp	1.19	1.17	1.21	1.28	1.26	1.31
cmp	1.06	1.04	1.03	1.09	1.06	1.04
compress	1.24	1.28	1.22	1.37	1.42	1.33
grep	1.13	1.08	1.08	1.19	1.12	1.12
lex	1.04	1.06	1.04	1.06	1.07	1.06
make	1.19	1.15	1.11	1.29	1.23	1.17
tar	1.04	1.03	1.03	1.06	1.05	1.04
tee	1.31	1.23	1.16	1.47	1.34	1.23
wc	1.29	1.29	1.19	1.44	1.43	1.29
yacc	1.22	1.22	1.23	1.33	1.33	1.35
Average	1.17	1.15	1.13	1.26	1.23	1.19
Std. dev.	0.10	0.098	0.083	0.15	0.15	0.12

Table 5: Percentage of code-size increase as a function of k.

Benchmark	Percentage code-size increase			
	$k + \ell = 1$	$k + \ell = 2$	$k + \ell = 4$	$k + \ell = 8$
cccp	2.79%	5.80%	11.75%	29.57%
cmp	1.87%	3.74%	7.48%	14.96%
compress	2.10%	4.15%	8.82%	20.26%
eqn	3.50%	7.44%	14.87%	44.26%
espresso	4.19%	8.51%	17.82%	39.28%
grep	1.55%	3.36%	6.96%	15.81%
lex	5.68%	11.34%	24.08%	53.73%
make	3.93%	7.96%	16.35%	37.76%
tar	2.82%	5.89%	12.18%	27.17%
tee	1.29%	2.52%	5.34%	10.75%
wc	1.70%	3.41%	8.52%	19.00%
yacc	7.41%	15.43%	35.21%	82.92%
Average	3.24%	6.61%	14.12%	32.96%
Std. dev.	1.84%	3.83%	8.55%	20.52%

Improving Performance of Small On-Chip Instruction Caches

Matthew K. Farrens

Computer Sciences Department
University of Wisconsin-Madison
Madison, WI 53706

Andrew R. Pleszkun

Department of Electrical and
Computer Engineering
University of Colorado-Boulder
Boulder, CO 80309-0425

Abstract

Most current single-chip processors employ an on-chip instruction cache to improve performance. A miss in this instruction cache will cause an external memory reference which must compete with data references for access to the external memory, thus affecting the overall performance of the processor. One common way to reduce the number of off-chip instruction requests is to increase the size of the on-chip cache. An alternative approach is presented in this paper, in which a combination of an instruction cache, instruction queue and instruction queue buffer is used to achieve the same effect with a much smaller instruction cache size. Such an approach is significant for emerging technologies where high circuit densities are initially difficult to achieve yet a high level of performance is desired, or for more mature technologies where chip area can be used to provide more functionality. The viability of this approach is demonstrated by its implementation in an existing single-chip processor.

1. Introduction

In recent years, advances in VLSI technology have significantly increased the speed at which a single-chip processor (SCP) can be run. As was the case with the first mainframes, raw processing speed is now much greater than memory speed. Therefore, it behooves us to examine what the designers of the first high-performance computers did to minimize the negative impact of memory latency on processor performance and attempt to incorporate some of their methods with ours.

One important difference between the problems faced by mainframe designers and architects of single-chip processors is the adverse effect of off-chip bandwidth and pin limitations on SCP performance. Due to these limitations, certain mainframe approaches to reducing memory latency, such as a massive increase in the memory bandwidth, may not be available in the SCP environment. Other techniques, however, such as the incorporation of more pipelining in the processor, the use of queues between the processor and memory, and making wide use of caches, are still applicable.

Programs generate two different types of memory requests, requests for instructions (I-Fetches) and requests for data (D-Fetches). Both types of requests are competing for the same resource - memory. Mainframe designers developed techniques to

reduce the impact of this competition, such as supplying separate data and instruction caches, and allowing multiple outstanding memory requests. Due to physical space limitations in the SCP realm, it is not practical to supply separate *on*-chip data and instruction caches. Furthermore, supplying separate *off*-chip data and instruction caches would require extra I/O pins that may not be available. Therefore, given the inherent spatial and temporal locality exhibited by instructions, SCP on-chip caches are generally instruction caches, used to service I-Fetches. This permits the available off-chip bandwidth to be utilized for servicing D-Fetches. The use of an on-chip instruction cache has been suggested by others [PaSe80,SmGo85,Smit82], and has been already incorporated in several designs [ACHA87,BCDF87,KMOM87].

While a simple on-chip instruction cache will provide a significant increase in performance, some competition for external memory between I-Fetches and D-Fetches will still exist. This is because, even in mature technologies, physical limitations prevent extremely large on-chip caches. In addition, for new and emerging technologies that promise increased speed, the high densities needed to support even moderately sized caches are not available. In this paper we are interested in approaches that minimize the impact of this competition for external memory and provide performance equivalent to that provided by much larger instruction caches.

The remainder of this paper is divided into 6 sections. The next section presents a short discussion of I-fetch and its interaction with D-fetch. Section 3 gives a brief description of the PIPE processor which is used as a basis for our simulations. Next, we contrast the PIPE approach to I-fetch with a conventional instruction cache approach. In Section 5, simulation details are provided and in Section 6, a discussion of our simulation results is presented. Finally, Section 7 presents our summary and conclusions.

2. Instruction and Data Fetch Strategies

Most current processor designs assume the presence of a relatively large external cache, and that accessing that cache can be done quickly. An external cache access is typically associated with a stage of the pipeline and involves broadcasting a request off-chip and then latching the data item (in the case of read) when it is returned by the cache. Cleary, the off-chip communications and cache memory access activities associated with such a strategy can have a dramatic, limiting impact on a processor's performance. If a processor's design is too closely tied to the performance of the external cache, implementing the processor in a faster technology will not necessarily result in a faster system. Techniques to minimize this interdependence between processor and memory will now be presented.

2.1. Instruction Fetch

In the mid 1970's, Rau and Rossman [RaRo77] studied the instruction fetch strategies used by the IBM System/370 series, the

234

CDC 6600, and the Manchester University MU5. This study examined the use of Prefetch Buffers in conjunction with an Instruction Buffer (an instruction cache). In their model of instruction fetch, the decode logic takes instructions directly out of the Prefetch Buffers, which are loaded with as many sequential instructions as possible given the size of the buffers, the size of the instruction cache, and the speed of external memory. Their results showed that a reduction of up to 50% in average I-Fetch delay can be achieved by the use of these buffers. While the results indicated that, within certain bounds, better performance can be achieved by using more buffers, the results also indicated that increasing the number of Prefetch Buffers increases memory traffic. Since the penalty for going off-chip in an SCP environment is higher than in a mainframe, a balance must be struck between the number of Prefetch Buffers and the amount of off-chip accessing these buffers generate. A similar study by Grohoski and Patel [GrPa82] included the effect of operand accessing on program performance and found similar results.

The use of a Target Instruction Buffer (TIB) was also examined in both of the above studies, as well as one by Hill [Hill87]. A TIB can be used in place of or in addition to an instruction cache, and contains the n sequential instructions stored at a branch target address. (n is a function of the TIB size.) When a branch is taken, the n instructions are taken out of the TIB while the I-Fetch control logic issues requests for the instructions sequential to the ones in the TIB. If there are more instructions in the TIB than the number of clock cycles it takes to access external memory, the instruction stream will have no gaps in it. The AMD29000 [Adva87] uses such a TIB instead of an instruction cache. While the results of the studies indicate that a small TIB can provide better performance than a simple small instruction cache, the use of a TIB implies large amounts of off-chip accessing, which again can be a problem in SCP design.

2.2. Data Fetch

There are several ways to reduce the effective access time of data references. One technique is to treat the external memory as a functional unit, and schedule arrivals from memory. Some Load/Store architectures [HCSS87] employ a version of this technique by providing a delay slot after a load that can be filled with an instruction that will execute while the load is completing (in essence treating the external memory as a functional unit with access time of 2 clock cycles). The obvious drawback to this method is that the architecture is tied directly to external factors such as memory speed.

Another technique is to provide queues, either explicitly architectural or transparent to the user, that allow the machine to continue executing instructions while waiting for the memory request to be serviced. This method has the advantage of making the architecture independent of memory speed. The IBM 801 [Radi82], for example, provides what is in effect a single element transparent queue that allows instructions after a load that do not use the requested data to continue to issue. This machine only blocks issue when an instruction needs to use data that has not yet been returned from memory. However, since only a single element queue is used, even if memory is pipelined only one memory request can be outstanding at a time.

Making the queues part of the architecture and visible to the programmer permits the easy overlap of memory activities with program execution. If the memory is pipelined, several memory requests can be outstanding at the same time. In addition, the use of architectural queues allows requests generated by the instruction fetch unit to take precedence over data requests with a limited impact on performance. In a processor without queues, a data request is issued very near the time the data is required. If an instruction request interferes with this data request, the processor will lose cycles waiting for both the instruction request and the data request to finish. In processor designs incorporating queues, it is

assumed a data request has been issued some time before it is actually required, allowing an instruction request to interfere without necessarily causing the processor to block.

While both caches and queues are used to reduce the impact of memory latency on processor performance, there is a fundamental difference between these two strategies. Caches attempt to *eliminate* memory latency, while queues allow the processor to *tolerate* it. The proper combination of these two techniques can lead to significant increases in performance by eliminating the majority of the memory latency and allowing the processor to tolerate what remains. The PIPE architecture, described in the next section, achieves a high level of performance by combining the use of data and instruction queues with a relatively small on-chip instruction cache.

3. The PIPE Processor

The PIPE processor is a pipelined single-chip processor designed at the University of Wisconsin and is an outgrowth of the PIPE project. A more detailed description of the PIPE project is available elsewhere (GHLP85).

The PIPE processor features a simplified load/store instruction set, five stages of pipelining, an on-chip instruction cache with queues, both input and output data queues, and an extended version of a delayed branch. A block diagram of the processor is shown in Figure 1. The five pipeline stages consist of Instruction Fetch, Instruction Decode, Instruction Issue, ALU 1/Logical and ALU2. The use of queues throughout the processor is evident in the diagram. The following is a brief description of the architecture and the features most relevant to the instruction fetch studies to be presented later.

3.1. The PIPE Architecture

The PIPE architecture is a register to register type, and has much in common with the Cray and CDC architectures. The PIPE processor is a 32-bit processor with a 32-bit wide internal bus. PIPE uses sixteen 32-bit data registers, divided into a set of 8 foreground and 8 background registers to improve the speed of subroutine calling. PIPE is 16-bit word-addressable, has separate input and output busses, and a single-level interrupt. A barrel shifter is used to perform shifts and a standard ALU performs adds and subtracts as well as logic functions. There are also 8 Branch Registers, whose use will be described later.

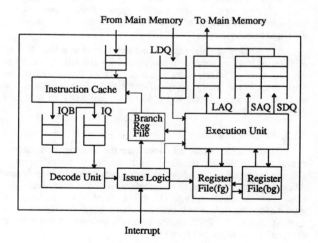

Figure 1. Block Diagram of the PIPE Processor

3.1.1. Instruction Set

PIPE instructions come in 2 forms, single parcel and two parcel, where a parcel is a 16-bit quantity (see Fig. 2). The position of the register fields is the same for all instructions, greatly simplifying the decode logic. The PIPE instruction set supports a basic repertoire of 3 operand instructions; addition, subtraction, logical operations, and shifts in their various forms are all provided. Due to the limited physical space available, PIPE does not support floating point numbers, nor is there any hardware support for multiplication or division.

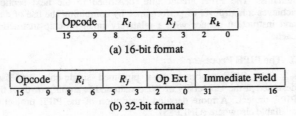

(a) 16-bit format

(b) 32-bit format

Figure 2. Instruction Format

3.1.2. Architectural Queues

As with the PIPE architecture, the PIPE processor provides both input and output queues which act as insulating buffers between external memory and the internal processing elements of the chip. These queues can be seen in Figure 1. This arrangement allows the on-chip clock rate to be determined solely by the timing delays through the processing elements that comprise the chip. The speed of the external memory has no effect on the processor's internal clock rate.

Since PIPE is a register-to-register type machine, all memory interactions occur through Load and Store instructions. A Load instruction generates a memory address and places it on the tail of the Load Address Queue (LAQ). Items in the LAQ are then sent to the memory system, which sometime later responds with the data item. The data item is not placed directly in a register, but on the *load queue* (LDQ) which acts as a buffer for data. The head of this input queue is visible to the programmer as a register (R7). By making this queue explicit in the architectural definition, a program can have multiple outstanding memory requests without forcing the issue logic to reserve a path into the register file for each request. By employing well known compiler optimization techniques, the load instructions are moved as far ahead of the instruction requiring the data as possible.

The writing of data items to memory occurs in a similar way. A store address is generated and placed on the tail of the Store Address Queue (SAQ). Data items are placed on the tail of the Store Data Queue (SDQ) by specifying register 7 as the destination operand. The items at the top of the SAQ and SDQ are sent as a pair to the memory.

3.1.3. Prepare to Branch

Branch instructions are notorious for causing performance degradation in heavily pipelined machines due to the difficulty in keeping the pipeline full of useful instructions while the branch condition is being evaluated. This problem has been extensively studied [DeLe87,McHe86,Smit81], and a number of methods for minimizing the impact of branches have been developed. The method used in the PIPE architecture is a generalized form of the delayed branch [HJBG82,Radi82].

In the delayed branch scheme, there are a fixed number of *delay slots* following a branch that are filled with instructions that are guaranteed to execute. Ideally the number of delay slots should be as large as possible to guarantee that the branch condition will

have been evaluated by the time the instructions complete, thus keeping the pipeline full. Studies of the delayed branch indicate that for many benchmark programs it is difficult to fill more than two delay slots, however. This means that the compiler has to either place null operations into the slots it is unable to fill, or the processor must have the ability to conditionally execute these instructions so that the compiler can place instructions into the delay slots that are *likely* to be executed.

Our experience with many scientific programs is slightly different. We have found that a compiler can easily generate code with an average of 4 instructions that can be unconditionally executed after a branch [YoGo84]. Therefore, PIPE uses an instruction called the prepare-to-branch (PBR) instruction which allows the compiler to specify the number of delay slots (between 0 and 7). Providing the ability to specify how many instructions are to be executed after a PBR instruction allows the PIPE architecture to *always* do as well as the more restrictive delayed branch scheme, while in some cases significantly out-performing it.

In order to support the PBR instruction, 8 Branch Registers were added to the architecture. These registers are not part of the general purpose registers, but a separate set of registers used to store branch target addresses. This allows the PBR instruction to be a single parcel instruction, and allows the compiler to load several branch target address at the beginning of a basic block.

3.2. The PIPE Cache

The PIPE instruction cache is direct mapped and composed of sixteen 4-word lines totaling 64 words, or 128 bytes. This is between 32 and 64 instructions, depending on the distribution of 1 and 2 parcel instructions. In addition to the cache there is an 8-byte Instruction Queue (IQ) and and an 8-byte Instruction Queue Buffer (IQB) that lie between the instruction cache and the decode logic. The only time the cache makes a request for a line from off-chip memory is if the line is guaranteed to contain at least one unconditionally executable instruction. In this paper, when we refer to the PIPE cache, we are actually referring to the physical cache, the IQ, the IQB, and the strategy we use to manage them. The PIPE cache has been explained in detail elsewhere [PlFa86].

This instruction cache, while relatively small, proves sufficient for our purposes. It allows us to verify the design of the control logic, and demonstrate that an I-Fetch strategy such as this need not adversely affect the clock rate. In addition, our simulation results indicate that if the IQ and IQB are used properly, larger instruction caches do not necessarily provide a significant improvement in performance.

3.3. The PIPE Chip

The PIPE chip was fabricated by the MOSIS fabrication facility in 3 micron NMOS with one layer of metallization, and contains just over 37,000 transistors. The chips have been tested and perform at a peak rate of slightly over 6 MIPS. While this number is not as impressive as the performance numbers quoted by several other existing processors, it is important to remember that PIPE was fabricated in a very restrictive technology. SPICE simulations of the PIPE processor using 2 micron NMOS parameters with low resist polysilicon interconnect indicate that if this less restrictive NMOS fabrication process were available to us, the PIPE performance rate would be over 18 MIPS. The availability of a second level of metallization would improve the performance even more. While such fabrication processes are currently being used by such companies as Intel, MOSIS does not support such processes in NMOS. (They do in CMOS, however.) A better comparison for PIPE would be with either RISC-II [Henn84] or MIPS [HJPR83], since both these processors were also manufactured in NMOS. PIPE is 2-3 times faster than either of these machines.

4. Contrasting PIPE and other Instruction Fetch Strategies

When an on-chip instruction cache is all that an SCP design uses to reduce off-chip memory traffic, choosing the correct cache prefetch strategy becomes critical. Hill [Hill87] used trace-driven simulations to compare a wide range of instruction cache configurations and instruction prefetch strategies. Among the many prefetch strategies he modeled were the ones used by the Berkeley SPUR processor, the MIPS-X processor, and a strategy he refers to as *Always*-prefetch. Throughout his study, the always-prefetch strategy consistently provided the best performance. We refer to a cache using this always-prefetch strategy as a *Conventional* cache. The following sections provide a detailed description of the PIPE approach and the approach used in the conventional cache.

4.1. The Conventional Cache

In the model used by Hill, a cache line is composed of a number of sub-blocks, each block with its own individual valid bit. A PC is presented to the cache at the beginning of each clock cycle and a tag lookup and cache array lookup of that PC can both be completed before the end of that cycle. The always-prefetch strategy prefetches an instruction from the next sequential location on each instruction reference, even if this address maps into the next cache line. Memory requests are made for only one instruction at a time, and a new one cannot begin until the previous one finishes. Data fetches have priority over both instruction fetches and prefetches, while instruction fetches have priority over prefetches.

As Hill points out, there are certain implementation problems with the always-prefetch scheme, such as the fact that two reads from the tag array per clock may be necessary. In spite of these problems, this is a very useful model since it consistently provided better performance than any other prefetch strategy studied by Hill.

4.2. The PIPE Instruction Fetch Logic

In the PIPE instruction fetch logic, there are two queues that lie between the instruction cache and the instruction register, the IQ and the IQB (see Fig. 1). Both these queues are the size of a cache line. The IQ, if not empty, is guaranteed to always contain at least one instruction to be executed. No such guarantee is made for the contents of the IQB.

When the IQ becomes empty, an attempt is made to fill it with the data contained in the IQB. If the IQB cannot provide the IQ with valid data, a cache lookup for a new line must be performed. If the line is not in the cache, then a request to memory is initiated.

When the IQB becomes empty, the next sequential line past the one in the IQ is prefetched from the on-chip cache. If that line is not in the cache, the off-chip request is blocked until the control logic can ensure that some portion of the requested line will be executed. The control logic determines whether to make an off-chip memory request based on a number of factors. Due to the encoding of the PIPE instruction set, the existence of a branch instruction is determined by a single bit of the opcode. This allows the cache control logic to easily scan the instructions in the IQ and determine if any are PBR instructions. If there are none, the next sequential line is guaranteed to contain at least one unconditionally executable instruction, and the control logic can initiate the appropriate fetch.

In addition, if there is a PBR instruction in execution, the control logic knows that a certain number of instructions past the PBR instruction will be unconditionally executed. (This number is provided in a 3-bit field of the PBR instruction.) Thus, the control logic can initiate cache lookups or fetches for these instructions to be unconditionally executed while the PBR instruction is being evaluated. Once all the instructions guaranteed to execute pass into the IQ and the result of the PBR instruction has been returned to the cache, the control logic can then start filling the IQB with the instructions stored at the branch target address. If the branch target address is in the cache, there will be no interruption in the supply of instructions and no wasted cycles. If the line is not on chip, having

an IQB allows the processor to begin fetching from external memory some number of clocks early. The implication of this is that if the number of delay slots can be made large enough no specific branch prediction strategies are necessary.

5. Simulation Details

For our benchmark programs we chose to use the first 14 Lawrence Livermore loops as defined in [McMa84]. There were two main reasons for this decision. First, we are assuming a scientific workstation environment and the Lawrence Livermore Loops are a well-established benchmark for numeric workloads. Secondly, and perhaps more importantly, we are interested in the interaction between instruction and data requests, and the Livermore Loops do generate a large number of data requests per inner loop, especially when an off-chip floating point unit is assumed. This high data request rate allows us to monitor the ability of the different prefetch schemes to interact with data requests, especially when the cache is small and large numbers of instruction requests are being generated.

The loops were compiled by the original PIPE compiler, and then revised by hand to reflect the slightly different architecture of the PIPE processor. No hand-optimization was done - the loops are not "tuned" to increase performance. The 14 loops were compiled as one large program, so that each loop would run until finished and then fall through to the next loop. This has the effect of flushing the cache every few thousand cycles, since it is guaranteed that at the beginning of each new loop no part of it will be in the cache. The sizes of the inner loops are listed in Table I. A total of 150,575 instructions are executed in a single run through the benchmark program.

Lawrence Livermore Loop sizes in bytes			
Loop #	Inner Loop Size	Loop #	Inner Loop Size
1	116	8	732
2	204	9	272
3	64	10	260
4	80	11	56
5	76	12	56
6	72	13	328
7	288	14	224

Table I. Inner Loops sizes

Memory is modeled as a large external cache that services both instruction and data requests. This cache is connected to the processor chip by a pair of busses, an input bus and an output bus (see Fig. 3). Only the cache deals directly with the large external main memory. The cache is assumed to be large enough to achieve a 100% hit rate in our simulations. The processor does not have an on-chip multiply unit, making an external floating point chip necessary. The floating point unit is addressed as a memory location, so that a pair of data stores to the appropriate locations will cause a

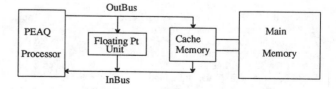

Figure 3. Simulation setup

237

multiply to occur. The number of clocks necessary to perform a floating point multiply is kept a constant, and is set to 4 clock cycles. Since both the cache and the floating point unit must share the return bus, some bus arbitration is necessary. The simulation model gives precedence to data and instruction loads and stores, followed by multiply results, with instruction prefetches having lowest priority.

Two versions of the PIPE simulator were created, one that used the PIPE cache and one that used the conventional cache. Simulation runs of the benchmark program were performed using both setups, and in the simulation runs performed, the following parameters were varied:

(1) instruction format
(2) instruction cache size
(3) the cache line size
(4) the speed of external memory
(5) the width of the input bus
(6) permitting a pipelined external memory
(7) the instruction queue (IQ) size
(8) the instruction queue buffer (IQB) size

The first parameter compares a fixed 32-bit instruction format to the 16 and 32-bit instruction formats used by PIPE. The second and third parameters are typically associated with cache studies and need no explanation. The next three parameters all deal with variations in effective memory speed. Parameters 4 and 5 specifically reflect technological variations. As a given design is built in a more aggressive technology, the processor may run at a faster speed than the memory. Varying the external memory speed will indicate which instruction fetch strategy can tolerate a relatively slower memory. The input bus width is related to the effective external memory speed since a wider bus will more easily allow prefetch of instructions and thereby make memory appear faster. The 6th parameter, pipelined memory, essentially permits multiple outstanding memory requests. If the memory is pipelined, it is assumed the memory system can accept a new request each clock cycle. The final 2 parameters are specific to the PIPE processor. The simulator was also able to select whether data or instructions have priority at the memory interface (since the PIPE processor uses queues).

Given the large number of parameters listed, it is impractical to include an exhaustive listing of all simulation results. We will therefore concentrate on the significant results and indicate when trends hold for other sets of parameters.

6. Discussion of Simulation Results

The goal of these simulation studies is to compare a conventional cache using the always-prefetch strategy with the PIPE instruction fetch strategy that is based on using an instruction cache, an instruction queue, and an instruction queue buffer. As described earlier, the IQ and IQB permit a type of *lookahead* into the instruction stream and are critical to an effective strategy for fetching off-chip instructions. The early detection of branches and instructions to be unconditionally executed relies on the existence and size of these buffers. In addition, the presence of the IQ makes the the instruction cache available for prefetch activities.

To begin, we compared the conventional cache against versions of the PIPE system with the parameter values listed in Table II. These parameter values were selected as representing a reasonable range of values that could be easily implemented. Notice that the IQ and IQB size track the line size of the cache, except in the case of the 32-byte line size. For this line size we simulated 2 different IQ sizes. For all the simulation results presented here, a fixed 32-bit instruction format was chosen in order to make comparisons to other machines that only have one instruction format more realistic. In addition, instructions requests are given priority over data requests at the memory interface.

Configuration	Line size	IQ size	IQB size
8-8	8 bytes	8 bytes	8 bytes
16-16	16 bytes	16 bytes	16 bytes
16-32	32 bytes	16 bytes	32 bytes
32-32	32 bytes	32 bytes	32 bytes

Table II. Simulated IQ and IQB configurations

Our simulation results indicate that one part of the I-Fetch strategy used by PIPE is non-optimal. As stated earlier, the PIPE processor is an outgrowth of the PIPE project which involved a tightly-coupled pair of processors sharing the same memory. In this environment, it was important to limit memory traffic as much as possible, and so the I-Fetch logic guarantees that some part of every line requested from off-chip will be executed. Our simulation results indicate that, for a single-chip processor on its own, a certain performance penalty is paid by using this strategy and not allowing true prefetch from off-chip. All simulation results presented in this paper assume that true prefetching from off-chip can be done. (The I-Fetch logic does not guarantee that some part of the line requested from off-chip will be executed.)

Our performance metric for these results is the total number of cycles needed to execute the 150,575 instructions. Our choice of this metric is due to the difficulty in computing an effective instruction access time when queues are involved and because the effective access time does not necessarily indicate the impact of the interaction of data and instruction requests upon performance. In the following graphs we plot the total number of cycles used on the vertical axis of our figures and cache size in bytes on the horizontal axis.

Figure 4 shows the performance of our 4 basic configurations and of the conventional cache in the case of a non-pipelined main memory with an access time of 1 clock cycle. (For a memory access time of 1 clock cycle, having a pipelined memory makes no difference.) This would correspond to a machine with a large, fast external cache. Figure 4a is for an input bus width of 4 bytes while in Figure 4b the bus width is 8 bytes. It is clear that the bus width can have a dramatic impact on performance for cache sizes less than 128 bytes. This effect is not unexpected if one considers that the underlying architecture can issue one instruction per cycle and that an instruction is 4 bytes long in these simulations. A bus only 4 bytes wide has difficulty supplying the processor with instructions faster than they are consumed, and cannot get ahead of the issue logic. A bus width of 8 bytes, however, allows the instructions to arrive from memory at twice the rate they are being consumed, thereby permitting the prefetch logic to stockpile instructions.

Looking at the curves in both graphs, an initial large performance improvement followed by a flattening of the curves is evident. The knee of the curve corresponds to the size of most of the inner loops of the benchmark program. In Table I, we see that half of the inner loops fit within a 128 byte cache. The performance improvement seen for an input bus width of 8 bytes is seen across all parameters and becomes more dramatic as the memory access time increases.

There are a couple of other interesting things to note in Figure 4. First, we see in Figure 4b that configurations 8-8 and 16-16 perform uniformly well for varying cache sizes with a bus width of 8 bytes. Thus, using a 16 or 32 byte cache with an IQ and IQB one can achieve close to the performance of a 512 byte cache. Second, as seen in Figure 4a, a memory access time of 1 clock cycle and a bus width of 4 bytes is the only case for which the conventional cache performs better than some PIPE configuration. For a memory access time larger than 1 clock cycle, *all* PIPE configurations *always* perform better than the conventional cache.

In Figure 5 we see the performance results for a bus width of 4 bytes and a bus width of 8 bytes when main memory has an access

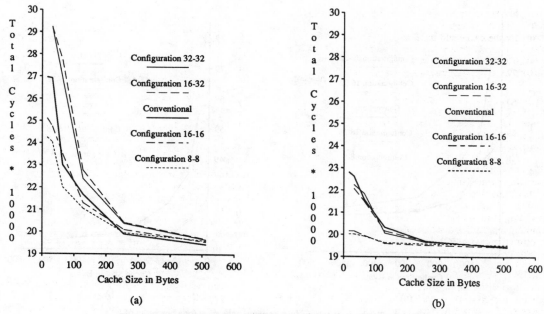

(a)   (b)

Figure 4. Total execution time with varying cache sizes for a non-pipelined
memory with a 1 cycle memory access time.
(a) bandwidth = 4 bytes. (b) bandwidth = 8 bytes.

time of 6 clock cycles and is not pipelined. (Notice that the scale for the total execution time axis has changed from that in Figure 4.) From Figure 5 we see that for small cache sizes and higher memory access times, the PIPE configurations are less sensitive to bus width than the conventional cache. (once the cache size·has grown to 256 bytes, the bus width does not make a significant difference.) Simulations with memory access times of 2 and 3 clock cycles showed similar results. Thus, if one is forced to use a bus width of 4 bytes due to technological constraints and memory access time is greater

than 1 clock cycle, the PIPE strategy will significantly outperform the conventional cache approach.

Figure 6 shows performance results for a system with a bus width of 8 bytes and a memory access time of 6 clock cycles. Figure 6a (which is the same as Figure 5b with a different scale) represents a non-pipelined memory and 6b represents a pipelined memory. Comparing Figures 6a and 6b, we see that while the shape of the curves is nearly the same, in Figure 6b the curves have shifted down and some compression has taken place. We again see that the

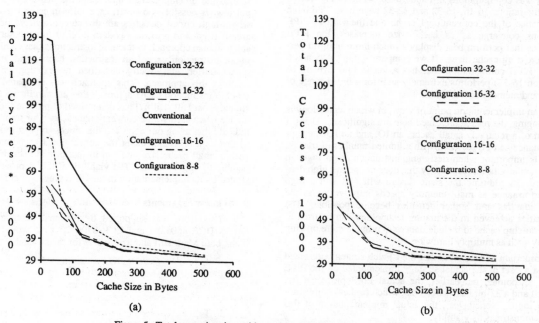

(a)   (b)

Figure 5. Total execution time with varying cache sizes for a non-pipelined
memory with a 6 cycle memory access time.
(a) bandwidth = 4 bytes. (b) bandwidth = 8 bytes.

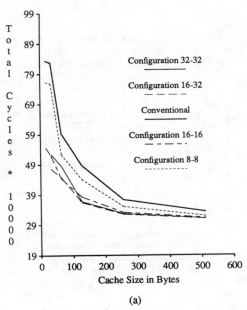

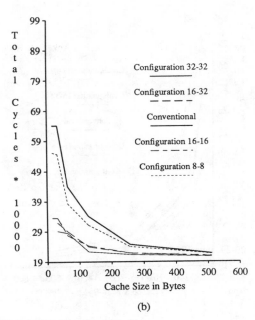

Figure 6. Total execution time with varying cache sizes for a bus width of 8
bytes and a 6 cycle memory access time.
(a) non-pipelined memory. (b) pipelined memory.

PIPE configurations always do better than the conventional cache configuration. In the case of a pipelined memory, some of the PIPE configurations perform substantially better. Figure 6 shows that the PIPE configurations providing the best performance have line sizes of 16 or 32 bytes, which is the reverse of the case shown in Figure 4. In Figure 4, a line size of 8 gave the best performance. Such a result is not completely unexpected and is confirmed by other cache studies [Smit82]. One thing to notice in these figures is the relative flatness of the configurations providing the best performance. In Figure 4b it was configurations 8-8 and 16-16, while in Figures 5b and 6b configurations 16-16, 16-32 and 32-32 were best. Although the performance of the conventional cache and the various PIPE configurations converge as as cache size increases, the PIPE configurations that perform best display a much more uniform performance across all cache sizes. If we compare Figures 4, 5 and 6 we see the PIPE configuration that has a cache line size of 16 (configuration 16-16) performs extremely well for a broad range of cache sizes and memory access times.

From an implementation point of view, in which technology is quickly changing, the results presented here are significant. Using a combination of a relatively small cache, an IQ, and an IQB, excellent performance can be achieved with a limited number of transistors. This is important when designing instruction fetch logic in newer, substantially faster technology that does not permit high density circuitry. In addition, the same design will maintain a high level of performance as main memory speeds improve, or as the technology matures and higher densities become possible. The higher densities achieved in the mature technology can be used to expand the on-chip cache to include data or to provide more on-chip functionality such as multiply hardware.

It is important to remember that the I-Fetch strategy presented here is for a subset of the actual strategy implemented on the PIPE processor. As pointed out earlier, the actual PIPE processor has both a 16-bit and a 32-bit instruction size, which further complicates the I-Fetch logic. Nonetheless, the actual implementation of this approach demonstrates its viability.

7. Summary and Conclusions

In this paper we have presented an evaluation of a set of instruction fetch strategies appropriate for single-chip processors. In most of today's approaches to instruction fetch, the single-chip processor is provided with a simple on-chip instruction cache. On a cache miss, a request is made to the external memory for instructions and these off-chip instruction requests compete with data references for access to the external memory. One way to reduce the number of off-chip instruction requests is to simply increase the size of the on-chip cache. Increasing the instruction cache size is not always possible, however, especially in emerging technologies where high circuit densities are difficult to achieve or where chip area is needed to provide a certain level of functionality. We have suggested an approach to fetching instructions that combines the use of an instruction cache, an instruction queue, and an instruction queue buffer, and briefly described an existing processor that employs this approach. This approach was compared to a simple on-chip instruction cache approach that uses an instruction prefetch strategy that Hill [Hill87] has determined to provide the best performance when used with a conventional cache. Our simulation results indicate that using our approach the processor performs up to twice as fast as a processor using the conventional cache-only approach with a small cache size and can in fact provide performance comparable to larger caches. The viability of this approach is demonstrated by its implementation in the PIPE processor chip.

8. Acknowledgements

This work was supported by National Science Foundation Grants DCR-8604224 and CCR-8706722. We would also like to thank both Mark Hill and Rob Joersz for their valuable assistance.

9. References

[ACHA87] A. Agarwal, P. Chow, M. Horowitz, J. Acken, A. Salz, and J. Hennessy, "On-chip Instruction Caches for High Performance Processors," *Proceedings of the Conference on Advanced Research in VLSI*, Stanford, pp. 1-24, March 1987.

[Adva87] "Advanced Micro Devices," AM29000 User's Manual (1987).

[BCDF87] A. D. Berenbaum, B. W. Colbry, D. R. Ditzel, R. D. Freeman, H. R. McLellan, and K. J. O'Conner, "CRISP: A Pipelined 32-bit Microprocessor with 13k-bit of Cache Memory," *IEEE Journal of Solid State Circuits*, vol. SC-22, pp. 776-782, October 1987.

[GHLP85] J. R. Goodman, J.-t. Hsieh, K. Liou, A. R. Pleszkun, P. B. Schechter, and H. C. Young, "PIPE: a VLSI Decoupled Architecture," *Proceedings of the Twelfth Annual Symposium on Computer Architecture*, pp. 20-27, June 1985.

[GrPa82] G. F. Grohoski and J. H. Patel, "A Performance Model for Instruction Prefetch in Pipelined Instruction" Units," *Proceedings of the Ninth International Symposium on Parallel Processing*, pp. 248-252, August 1982.

[HCSS87] M. Horowitz, P. Chow, D. Stark, R.T. Simoni, A. Salz, S. Przybylski, J. Hennessy, G. Gulak, A. Agarwal, and J.M. Acken, "MIPS-X: A 20-MIPS Peak, 32-bit Microprocessor with On-Chip Cache," *IEEE Journal of Solid-State Circuits*, vol. SC-22, pp.790-799, Oct. 1987

[Henn84] J. Hennessy, "VLSI Processor Architecture," *IEEE Transactions on Computers*, vol. C-33, No. 12, pp.1221-1246, Dec. 1984

[Hill87] M. D. Hill, *Aspects of Cache Memory and Instruction Buffer Performance*, Doctoral Thesis, Department of Computer Sciences, University of California, Berkeley, California.

[HJBG82] J. Hennessy, N. Jouppi, F. Baskett, T. Gross and J. Gill, "Hardware/Software Tradeoffs for Increased Performance," *Symposium on Architectural Support for Programming Languages and Operating Systems*, pp. 33-54, March 1983.

[HJPR83] J. Hennessy, N. Jouppi, S. Przybylski, C. Rowen, and T. Gross, "Design of a High Performance VLSI Processor," *Proceedings of the Third Caltech Conference on VLSI*, pp. 2-11, March 1982.

[KMOM87] H. Kadota, J. Miyake, I. Okabayashi, T. Maeda, T. Okamoto, M. Nakajima, and K. Kagawa, "A 32-bit CMOS Microprocessor with On-Chip Cache and TLB," *IEEE Journal of Solid-State Circuits*, vol. SC-22, pp.800-807, Oct. 1987

[McMa84] F. H. McMahon, "LLNL FORTRANS KERNELS: MFLOPS," Lawrence Livermore Laboratories, Livermore, CA, March 1984.

[PaSe80] D. A. Patterson and C. H. Sequin, "Design Considerations for Single-Chip Computers of the Future," *IEEE Transactions on Computers*, Vol. C-29, No. 2, February 1980.

[PlFa86] A. R. Pleszkun and M. K. Farrens, "An Instruction Cache Design for use with a Delayed Branch," *Advanced Research in VLSI: Proceedings of the Fourth MIT Conference*, April 1986.

[Radi82] G. Radin, "The 801 Minicomputer," *Symposium on Architectural Support for Programming Languages and Operating* Systems," pp. 39-47, March 1982.

[RaRo77] B. R. Rau and G. E. Rossman, "The Effect of Instruction Fetch Strategies upon the Performance of" Pipelined Instruction Units," *Proceedings of the Fourth Annual Symposium on Computer Architecture*, pp. 80-89, June 1977.

[Smit81] James E. Smith, "A Study of Branch Prediction Strategies", *Proceedings of the Eighth Annual Symposium on Computer Architecture*, pp. 135-148, May 1981.

[SmGo85] J. E. Smith and J. R. Goodman, "Instruction Cache Replacement Policies and Organizations," *IEEE Transactions on Computers*, Vol. C-34, No. 3, pp. 234-241, March 1985.

[Smit82] A. J. Smith, "Cache Memories," *ACM Computing Surveys*, Vol. 14, No. 3, September 1982.

[YoGo84] H. C. Young and J. R. Goodman, "A Simulation Study of Architectural Data Queues and Prepare-to-branch" Instruction," *Proceedings of the IEEE International Conference on Computer Design*, pp. 544-549, October 1984.

Achieving High Instruction Cache Performance
with an Optimizing Compiler

Wen-mei W. Hwu and Pohua P. Chang

Coordinated Science Laboratory
University of Illinois
Urbana, IL 61801
(217) 244-8270
hwu@bach.csg.uiuc.edu

Abstract

Increasing the execution power requires a high instruction issue bandwidth, and decreasing instruction encoding and applying some code improving techniques cause code expansion. Therefore, the instruction memory hierarchy performance has become an important factor of the system performance. An instruction placement algorithm has been implemented in the IMPACT-I (Illinois Microarchitecture Project using Advanced Compiler Technology - Stage I) C compiler to maximize the sequential and spatial localities, and to minimize mapping conflicts. This approach achieves low cache miss ratios and low memory traffic ratios for small, fast instruction caches with little hardware overhead. For ten realistic UNIX* programs, we report low miss ratios (average 0.5%) and low memory traffic ratios (average 8%) for a 2048-byte, direct-mapped instruction cache using 64-byte blocks. This result compares favorably with the fully associative cache results reported by other researchers. We also present the effect of cache size, block size, block sectoring, and partial loading on the cache performance. The code performance with instruction placement optimization is shown to be stable across architectures with different instruction encoding density.

Keywords : Cache, Memory hierarchy, Compiler optimization, Instruction placement, Data locality

* UNIX is a Trademark of Bell Laboratories

This research has been supported by the National Science Fundation (NSF) under Grant MIP-8809478, a donation from NCR, the National Aeronautics and Space Administration (NASA) under Contract NASA NAG 1-613 in cooperation with the Illinois Computer laboratory for Aerospace Systems and Software (ICLASS), the Office of Naval Research under Contract N00014-88-K-0656, and the University of Illinois Campus Research Board.

1. Introduction

1.1. Motivation

The instruction memory hierarchy has received only moderate attention because conventional machines typically have high microcycle count per instruction, and thus, demand low instruction bandwidth. For instance, it takes a VAX-11/780 10.5 microcycles to execute every 3.8 bytes of instructions[1]. An 8-byte instruction buffer that prefetches instructions during idle cache cycles provides enough instruction bandwidth for the VAX-11/780 microengine. In response to the increasing demand for processor speed, performance improving techniques such as pipelining have been widely used to implement processors that require much higher instruction bandwidth. For example, the VAX 8600 implementation requires 3.8 instruction bytes for every 6 microcycles. Futher reducing the number of microcycles per instruction increases the instruction memory bandwidth requirement and suggests the need for better instruction memory hierarchy designs.

Many processor architectures have adopted instruction formats and semantics which allow the instruction units to be efficiently pipelined[2-5]. To simplify instruction decoding, these processor architectures specify fixed instruction formats that prevent conventional encoding techniques from reducing program size. To simplify instruction sequencing, these processors prevent the use of powerful opcodes to encode sequences of microinstructions. Therefore, the instruction unit pipeline becomes more efficient and matches the speed of the execution pipeline. The cost is an increase in the dynamic code size and consequently an increase of the instruction bandwidth requirement.

Compiler code improvement techniques often increase code size. Inline expansion reduces function call overhead[6]. Loop unrolling increases code scheduling flexibility[7]. Trace scheduling extracts the program parallelism[7-8]. These techniques all increase code size and rely on the instruction memory hierarchy to absorb the code expansion cost. This adds further demand on the instruction memory hierarchy performance.

One conventional approach to improving the memory hierarchy performance is to increase the size and/or set-associativity of the top level cache memory[9-10]. For example, the MIPS-X processor uses an 2048-byte, 8-way set-associative instruction cache. This approach is limited by the fact that the cache cycle time increases as the size and set-associativity increase and the fact that only a limited amount of hardware is available[11-14]. To make it worse, if the compiler generates code with little spatial locality and/or many cache mapping conflicts, no cache of reasonable size and set-associativity can provide enough instruction bandwidth.

With advances in the compiler technology, an increasing number of microarchitecture design parameters have been exposed to the compiler. Examples of this trend include pipeline latency[15-16], parallel data paths[7-8,17], and register-file structure[18-20]. The advantage of exposing these microarchitecture details to the compiler is that the compiler can generate code to utilize these microarchitecture features without expensive hardware interlocking schemes. We believe that the instruction memory hierarchy should also be exposed to the compiler for improving the system performance.

1.2. Our Approach

In this paper, we present an instruction placement algorithm which improves the efficiency of caching in the instruction memory hierarchy. Based on dynamic profiling, this algorithm maximizes the sequential and spatial localities, and minimizes cache mapping conflicts of the instruction accesses. The instruction placement algorithm has been implemented in the IMPACT-I C Compiler and produced instruction placement for realistic C programs. The instruction placement for each program is based on the execution of millions of instructions using typical input files.

The instruction cache performance for each program, after applying the instruction placement algorithm, is measured by trace driven simulation. We demonstrate that the instruction layout algorithm can efficiently exploit small (about 2048B), direct-mapped instruction caches with large (about 64B) blocks. Direct mapped caches with large blocks are desirable due to their low control overhead (tag store and hit detection logic). The effect of varying the cache design parameters (cache size, block size, block sectoring, partial loading) is presented. We also demonstrate that direct mapped caches with instruction placement optimization compare favorable with fully associative caches without instruction placement optimization, and perform equally well for different code densities.

1.3. Organization of the Paper

This paper is organized into five sections. Section two describes related work in program optimization for memory system performance. Section three describes the IMPACT-I instruction placement algorithm. Section four presents measurement results of the instruction memory hierarchy performance using the IMPACT-I instruction layout algorithm. Section five concludes the paper and outlines the present research issues in the management and performance measurement of the instruction memory hierarchy. The Appendix gives an outline of the IMPACT-I instrcution placement algorithm.

2. Background

2.1. Previous Work

The problem of restructuring programs for memory system performance has been studied by various researchers. Ferrari examined the potential of restructuring programs to improve program paging behavior[21]. Data alignment methods based on data dependence analysis for highly iterative scientific

codes have been observed to improve the performance of cache and local memory organizations[22-24]. Hartley described a function-level program restructuring technique to improve the page-level locality of references and to reduce the number of page faults, using the call graph[25]. On the cache level, Przybylski showed that set associativity increases overall execution time if it increases the cycle time by more than a few nanoseconds[14]. McFarling showed that, by using profile information and excluding certain instructions from the instruction cache, his program restructuring algorithm significantly increased the performance of direct-mapped instruction caches[26].

2.2. Design Target

The goal of the IMPACT-I C Compiler instruction placement mechanism is to layout the target program to maximize the sequential and spatial localities, and to minimize the mapping conflict. To maximize the sequential locality, basic blocks are grouped into a trace if they tend to execute in a sequence. To maximize the spatial locality, instructions are mapped close to each other in the memory space if they are executed close to each other in time. Therefore, almost all the bytes in a memory block will be used when that block is brought in cache. Cache mapping conflicts are minimized by placing the functions with overlapping lifetime into memory locations which do not contend with each other in cache. With compile-time program restructuring, a direct-mapped instruction cache should compare favorably with a fully associative cache.

A.J. Smith has reported realistic values for the miss ratio as a function of cache size and line size[10,27-28]. Table 1 lists a small subset of the design target miss ratios reported by Smith for fully associative instruction cache[28]. Each column gives the expected miss ratios for a fixed block size and varying cache sizes. Each row presents the expected miss ratios for a fixed cache size and varying block sizes. For example, a 2048-byte fully instruction cache with 64-byte blocks is expected to give a 6.8% miss ratio. For another example, a 1024-byte fully associative instruction cache with 32-byte blocks is expected to give a 15.9% miss ratio. We will use the miss ratios in Table 1 as the basis for evaluating the effectiveness of our instruction placement optimization.

To minimize the effect of workload dependent and system dependent factors on the miss ratio, we use typical-size input data to generate traces and the entire execution traces are applied to the cache simulator. For small caches, the effect of context switch is not important. We also conduct a code scaling experiment to show that the instruction cache performance is not sensitive to the increase in the degree of instruction encoding.

3. Instruction Placement

IMPACT-I instruction placement is implemented in five major steps: execution profiling, function inline expansion, trace selection, function layout, and global layout.

Step 1. Execution profiling. In our C compiler, a program is represented by a weigthed call graph. A call graph is a directed graph where every node is a function and every arc is a function call. A weighted call graph is a call graph in which all the nodes and arcs are marked with their execution frequencies.

Each node of the weighted call graph is represented by a weighted control graph. A control graph for a function is a directed graph where every node is a basic block, and every arc is a branch path between two basic blocks. A weighted control graph is a control graph in which all the nodes and arcs are marked with their execution frequencies.

The IMPACT-I profiler translates each target C program into an equivalent C program with additional probe function calls. When the equivalent C program is executed, these probe function calls record the weights of nodes and arcs of the call graph for the entire program and the control graph for each function. It is critical that the inputs used for executing the equivalent C program be representative. Therefore, this approach is very suitable for characterizing realistic programs for which representative inputs can be easily collected. The IMPACT-I Profiler to C Compiler interface allows the profile information to be automatically used by the IMPACT-I C Compiler.

Step 2. Function inline expansion. The function calls (arcs in the weighted call graph) with high execution count are replaced with the function body if possible[6]. The goal is to transform all the important inter-function control transfers into intra-function control transfers. Inline expansion reduces the dynamic inter-function control transfers to a small percentage (about 1%) of all control transfers, which provides two major advantages. First, the spatial locality is increased in that almost all control transfers are within individual functions. Second, removing function calls also reduces potential cache mapping conflicts among functions.

Step 3. Trace* selection. For each function, basic blocks which tend to execute in sequence are grouped into traces. The traces are the basic units of instruction placement to maximize the sequential and spatial localities. A recent paper gave detailed description and evaluation of the trace selection algorithm of the IMPACT-I C Compiler[29]. Note that the inline expansion step provides large functions to enhance the size of the traces selected.

Step 4. Function layout. By carefully placing traces of each function in a sequential order, spatial locality can be further preserved. We start with the function entrance trace, and expand the placement by placing the most important descendent after it. We grow the placement until all the traces with non-zero execution count (profiled count) have all been placed. Traces with zero execution count (profiled count) are moved to the bottom of the function. This results in smaller effective function body, and allows more effective parts of functions to be packed into each page.

Step 5. Global layout. Each function is assumed to have two parts: the effective and non-executed parts. The goal of the global layout algorithm is to place functions which are executed close to each other in time into the same page, so that inter-function cache conflicts are further reduced (already reduced by inline expansion).

To evaluate the effectiveness of our code layout scheme, we randomly select one input for each benchmark to take the traces of dynamic instruction accesses. These dynamic traces include instruction accesses to both the user code and the library code; they do not include any access to the kernel code. In summary, the IMPACT-I instruction placement is based on profile information and the performance evaluation presented in this paper is based on trace driven simulation.

cache size (bytes)	Block Size (bytes)			
	16	32	64	128
512	23.0%	15.9%	11.9%	10.8%
1024	20.0%	13.4%	9.8%	8.4%
2048	15.0%	9.8%	6.8%	5.7%
4096	10.0%	6.3%	4.3%	3.2%

Table 1. Design Target Miss Ratio (Fully Associative)

4. Experimentation

Table 2 summarizes several important characteristics of our benchmarks. The *C lines* column shows the static code size of the C benchmark programs measured in the number of program lines. The *runs* column gives the number of different inputs used in the profiling process. The *instructions* column gives the dynamic code size of the benchmark programs, measured in number of dynamic instructions. The *control* column gives the dynamic count of control transfers other than function call/return executed during the profiling process. Both *instructions* and *control* are accumulated among all the runs. The *input description* describes the nature of the inputs used in the profiling process.

4.1. Basic Experiments

4.1.1. Inline Expansion Results

Table 3 offers the inline expansion results. The *code inc* column gives the percentage of increase in static code size due to inline expansion. The *call dec* column gives the percentage of dynamic function calls eliminated by the inline expansion. The *DI's per call* column gives the average number of dynamic instructions executed between dynamic function calls after inline expansion. The *CT's per call* column gives the average number of dynamic control transfers executed between dynamic function calls after inline expansion.

For most of the benchmark programs, the inline expansion mechanism successfully eliminates a large percentage of the dynamic function calls. For programs with infrequent function calls to begin with, the inline expansion mechanism does not eliminate large percentages of dynamic function calls. This is a desirable trait because the overall goal is to ensure infrequent function calls rather than to achieve high elimination percentages.

---

* The term *trace* here is used as in the *trace scheduling* for global microcode compaction. It is not used as in the *trace driven simulation*. In this paper, if the term *trace* is used as in the *trace driven simulation*, it will appear as *dynamic trace* whenever an ambiguity may occur.

name	C lines	runs	instructions	control	input description
cccp	4660	20	11.7M	2.2M	C programs (100-3000 lines)
cmp	371	16	2.2M	0.5M	similar/disimilar text files
compress	1941	20	19.6M	3.1M	same as cccp
grep	1302	20	47.1M	17.1M	exercised various options
lex	3251	4	3052.6M	1125.9M	lexers for C, Lisp, awk, and pic
make	7043	20	152.6M	32.4M	makefiles for cccp, compress, etc.
tee	1063	18	0.43M	0.17M	text files (100-3000 lines)
tar	3186	14	11M	1.5M	save/extract files
wc	345	20	7.8M	2.2M	same as cccp
yacc	3333	8	313.4M	78.7M	grammar for a C compiler, etc.

Table 2. Profile Results

name	code inc	call dec	DT's per call	CT's per call
cccp	17%	55%	506	95
cmp	3%	49%	265	58
compress	4%	91%	2324	368
grep	31%	99%	11214	4071
lex	23%	77%	7807	2880
make	34%	59%	388	82
tee	0%	0%	15	6
tar	16%	43%	983	127
wc	0%	0%	18310	5146
yacc	24%	80%	1205	303

Table 3. Inline Expansion Results

The program *tee* is a special case where data is copied from the input to the output by system calls (read, write), without much additional computation. Since system calls can not be inline expanded, the call frequency of *tee* is extremely high.

After inline expansion, the frequency of function calls is much smaller than the frequency of intra-function control transitions (branches). It is also observed that hundreds of dynamic instructions are executed per function call. The obvious gain is that register save and restore costs across function boundaries are greatly reduced. A more subtle advantage that directly affects the performance of our instruction placement algorithm is that the function inline expansion mechanism enlarges function bodies and reduces inter-function interactions. More sequential and spatial localities can be found in larger function bodies. Reducing inter-function interactions also removes potential cache mapping conflicts among interacting functions. The result is that most of the complexity in the global layout process can be shifted to the intra-function layout process (trace selection and placement) which is much simpler to implement. We have thus decided to implement a simple global layout process based on a variant of the depth-first-search algorithm (see appendix).

4.1.2. Trace Selection Results

Table 4 presents the trace selection results. The *neutral* column gives the percentage of control transfers from the end of a trace to the start of a trace. The average percentage (about 39%) for this category suggests that a careful selection of a linear ordering of traces could increase the spatial locality significantly. The *undesirable* column gives the percentage of control transfers which enter and/or exit traces at a non-terminal basic block. The *desirable* column gives the percentage of control transfers which go from a basic block to its successor in a trace. The small average percentage (about 3%) in the *undesirable* column and the large average percentage (about 58%) in the *desirable* column indicate that once the control is transferred into a trace, it is likely to remain through the end of that trace. This justifies our approach to use the traces as units of instruction placement. The *trace length* column gives the average number of basic blocks in each trace. On the average, each trace contains 3.4 basic blocks. Since each basic block in the IMPACT-I code contains about 4 machine instructions (4 bytes each), the unit of instruction placements contains about 54 bytes. Considering the spatial locality among traces, a reasonable prediction of a good instruction block size would be about 64 bytes.

We use trace-based analysis to evaluate the effectiveness of our code layout scheme. A trace is generated by feeding a randomly selected input (typical size) to each benchmark program. The entire execution traces are used. These dynamic traces include both user code and library code, but not kernel code. We do not simulate the effect of context swaps.

4.1.3. Memory Access Characteristics

Table 5 shows the instruction memory access characteristics of the benchmark programs and their corresponding dynamic traces. The *total static bytes* column gives the number of machine code bytes generated for each benchmark program. The *effective static bytes* column gives the number of machine code bytes which have non-trivial execution count. The *dynamic accesses* gives the number of dynamic instruction accesses recorded in each dynamic trace.

The effective static program size ranges from 2K to 34K whereas the total static program size ranges from 2.8K to 55K.

name	neutral	undesirable	desirable	trace length
cccp	55.23%	3.74%	41.05%	1.8
cmp	12.74%	4.23%	83.03%	6.9
compress	35.04%	3.15%	61.85%	2.8
grep	20.96%	1.80%	77.24%	4.7
lex	35.02%	1.79%	63.19%	2.8
make	53.93%	2.08%	43.99%	1.8
tar	86.85%	0.38%	12.77%	1.2
tee	24.77%	0.24%	75.00%	4.0
wc	15.09%	9.02%	75.88%	5.5
yacc	49.13%	4.62%	46.25%	2.0

Table 4. Trace Selection Results

name	total static bytes	effective static bytes	dynamic accesses
cccp	51.6K	29.6K	1.5M
cmp	2.8K	2.0K	0.3M
compress	15.6K	8.8K	2.8M
grep	11.1K	4.5K	0.1M
lex	40.4K	29.7K	51.9M
make	55.0K	34.1K	1.8M
tar	25.8K	15.7K	0.2M
tee	6.5K	3.4K	0.1M
wc	3.1K	2.6K	1.1M
yacc	35.7K	27.0K	3.3M

Table 5. Static and Dynamic Code Sizes of Benchmarks

Since the IMPACT-I compiler places the effective and ineffective parts of the program into different pages, only the effective part needs to be accomodated in the main and cache memories. As a result, when a page is transferred from the secondary memory to the main memory, all the bytes of that page are likely to be used.

4.2. Caching Experiments

The primary goal of the IMPACT-I instruction placement mechanism is to improve the cache performance and to reduce the cost of instruction memory hierarchy. For the instruction caches, the goal is to minimize the data storage size and the control overhead (set-associativity and tag storage) to obtain the desired cache hit ratio and memory traffic. Direct-mapped caches are used in all the measurements due to their minimal set-associativity overhead. The next two tables present the effectiveness of the instruction placement mechanism for minimizing the data storage and the tag storage.

4.2.1. Basic Organization

Table 6 shows the effect of varying cache size for a fixed block size (64 bytes). The *miss* columns give the cache miss ratios. The *traffic* columns give the ratios of the number of main memory accesses over the number of dynamic instruction accesses (memory traffic ratio). Note that for the block size of 64 bytes, a 2K-byte instruction cache provides a low miss ratio (average 0.5%) with a reasonable memory traffic ratio (average 8%). As a result, less than 1% of instruction accesses need to wait for the data from an outside cache or the main memory. Also, the bus to the outside cache and the main memory is only loaded by 8% of the instruction access traffic. Even a small instruction cache of 512 bytes provides a reasonable miss ratio (average 1.4%) with a moderate memory traffic ratio (average 22%). Comparing the cache sizes to the static program sizes reveals that the instruction placement algorithm is successful in mapping the programs into small caches.

Table 7 shows the effect of varying the block size for a fixed cache size of 2048 bytes. In general, the miss ratios decrease and the memory traffic ratios increase as the block size increases. The miss ratios decrease with the increase of the block size because each cache miss brings in more useful bytes for larger block sizes. The instruction placement algorithm maximizes this effect by placing the bytes which are accessed close in time in the same block. The traffic ratios increase with the increase of the block size because each cache miss brings in more useless bytes for large block sizes. The instruction placement mechanism minimizes this effect also by placing in the same block the bytes which are accessed close in time.

For a fixed cache size, the larger the block size, the smaller the number of tags that are required to manage the cache. For a 2K-byte instruction cache, the 64-byte block size provides a low miss ratio (average 0.5%) and reasonable memory traffic ratio (average 8%). The configuration requires only 16 tags, successfully minimizing the control overhead. Assuming 4 bytes of tag space for each block, we have a total of 64 bytes of tag space for the entire cache. The overhead is only (64-bytes / 2048-bytes) and is approximately 3% of the data store size.

Note that the memory traffic ratio is rather high for benchmarks *cccp* and *make*. Also, since the cache miss penalty increases with the block size, the effective cache access time may increase inspite of the decreased miss ratio. For some systems (especially multiprocessor systems), it is desirable to decrease the memory traffic ratio and the cache miss penalty at the cost of increasing the miss ratio.

We assume that the memory or secondary cache is interleaved and can deliver one data per cycle after the initial access

name	8K		4K		2K		1K		0.5K	
	miss	traffic	miss	traffic	miss	traffic	miss	traffic	miss	traffic
cccp	0.86%	13.79%	1.53%	24.40%	2.70%	43.13%	3.52%	56.32%	4.24%	67.87%
cmp	0.01%	0.15%	0.01%	0.15%	0.01%	0.15%	0.01%	0.15%	0.01%	0.17%
compress	0.00%	0.07%	0.00%	0.08%	0.01%	0.08%	0.01%	0.09%	3.54%	56.63%
grep	0.06%	0.88%	0.06%	0.91%	0.06%	0.87%	0.07%	1.11%	0.60%	9.62%
lex	0.01%	0.09%	0.01%	0.21%	0.03%	0.48%	0.06%	0.93%	0.31%	4.96%
make	0.32%	5.06%	0.69%	11.10%	1.35%	21.59%	2.03%	32.46%	2.44%	39.02%
tar	0.09%	1.51%	0.24%	3.88%	0.27%	4.27%	0.42%	6.76%	0.61%	9.79%
tee	0.06%	0.92%	0.06%	0.092	0.08%	1.2%	0.08%	1.28%	0.08%	1.33%
wc	0.00%	0.06%	0.00%	0.06%	0.00%	0.06%	0.00%	0.06%	0.00%	0.06%
yacc	0.02%	0.28%	0.23%	3.64%	0.49%	7.86%	1.17%	18.73%	1.99%	31.89%

Table 6. The Effect of Varying Cache Size

name	16B		32B		64B		128B	
	miss	traffic	miss	traffic	miss	traffic	miss	traffic
cccp	7.53%	30.10%	4.32%	34.58%	2.70%	43.13%	2.10%	67.33%
cmp	0.04%	0.15%	0.02%	0.15%	0.01%	0.15%	0.01%	0.16%
compress	0.02%	0.07%	0.01%	0.08%	0.01%	0.08%	0.00%	0.09%
grep	0.19%	0.76%	0.10%	0.82%	0.06%	0.91%	0.03%	1.01%
lex	0.08%	0.33%	0.05%	0.38%	0.03%	0.48%	0.02%	0.69%
make	4.24%	16.95%	2.40%	19.19%	1.35%	21.59%	0.95%	30.39%
tar	0.72%	2.90%	0.42%	3.32%	0.27%	4.27%	0.20%	6.37%
tee	0.25%	0.98%	0.13%	1.06%	0.08%	1.20%	0.04%	1.41%
wc	0.01%	0.06%	0.01%	0.06%	0.00%	0.06%	0.00%	0.06%
yacc	1.13%	4.53%	0.66%	5.25%	0.49%	7.86%	0.52%	16.78%

Table 7. The Effect of Varying the Block Size

delay. We also assume that the data for which the cache miss occurs is the first data delivered after the initial memory access delay (load forwarding). To furthur reduce the cache miss penalty, the processor resumes execution as soon as the accessed data comes back from main memory (early continuation). Subsequent instruction fetches after a cache miss, if sequential, can directly obtain the instructions from the memory bus as the cache block is being repaired (streaming). For a taken branch before the block is completely filled, the CPU is stalled until the block is completely transferred.

For a 64-byte block size and a 4-byte memory bus, 16 cycles are required after the initial memory access to complete the block transfer. Due to the large transfer size, the CPU may be stalled. Our layout algorithm does not guarantee that the data for which the repair sequence is incurred is positioned at the beginning of the cache block. Therefore, the CPU is stalled while repairing the part of the cache block in front of the data for which the miss is incurred. The average number of stalled cycles caused by each cache miss is about half of the block, assuming random access pattern. For a 64-byte block and a 4-byte memory bus, the CPU is stalled for about 8 cycles.

Including the initial memory access cost, the effective cache access time may increase although the miss ratio is lower than, for example, the 32 byte block size configuration.

4.2.2. Reducing Memory Traffic

One approach to decreasing the memory traffic ratio and the cache miss penalty while increasing the miss ratio is to partition each block into sectors and only bring in the accessed sector upon cache miss. The memory traffic ratio is reduced because the number of memory accesses caused by each cache miss is reduced to the size of each sector (rather than the size of each block), and thus fewer unused words are fetched. The miss ratio increases because the spatial locality is not fully exploited. Since the instructions placed into the same block are likely to be executed near each other in time, not bringing in the rest of a missing block can be expected to cause more cache misses.

The *sector* column in Table 8 presents the effect of dividing the 64B blocks into sectors of 8 bytes each for a 2048B cache. A comparison with the *64B* column in Table 7 shows that, for programs causing large memory traffic ratios, sectoring the blocks decreases the memory traffic ratio at the cost of increasing the miss ratio. The problem with this approach is that it increases the miss ratio to such a degree (e.g. cccp) that the average cache access time can actually increase.

An alternative scheme is to load only part of the missing block, from the accessed location to the end of that block or to a valid entry previously loaded in. The processor resumes execution as soon as the accessed location comes back from main memory.

The *partial* column in Table 8 presents the effect of loading only part of the missing block. The *avg.fetch* column shows the average transfer size (in 4-byte entities) for a cache miss. The *avg.exec* column indicates the average number of consecutive instructions (4-bytes each) used starting from a cache miss point to a taken branch or another cache miss. A comparison with the *64B* column shows that, for programs causing large memory traffic ratio, this approach can significantly reduce the memory traffic ratio at the cost of only slightly increasing the miss ratio. Note that for programs with extremely small miss ratio and memory traffic ratio, this scheme can actually increase both ratios. However, since the traffic ratios are so low for these programs that a slight increase does not have visible effect on the system performance.

4.2.3. Code Scaling Experiment

The code generated by the IMPACT-I C compiler very closely match the physical code of a fixed instruction format (32bits/instruction) RISC type processor. Different architectures have different code densities. To show that our result is more general, we will repeat the 2K, 64B block, partial loading experiment after code scaling. Code scaling simulates the effect of varying the degrees of instruction encoding. We scale the code to 0.5, 0.7 and 1.1 of its original size. The scaling affects the size of all basic blocks uniformly. The instruction size is still assumed to be 4 bytes, and therefore, the effect of code scaling is shown as changes in the number of instructions in basic blocks. For each basic block, the number of instructions is rounded to the nearest integer value.

The result, in Table 9, supports our claim that our compiler instruction layout optimization is generally applicable to many instruction sets and compilers with differing code improving ability. A richer instruction set may reduce the number of instructions to realize the intermediate form. Various code improving techniques can also change the code size. But the experiment result seems to indicate that the cache performance is rather stable.

4.2.4. Comparison with Previous Results

The effectiveness of the instruction placement optimization can be evaluated by comparing the numbers in Table 6 and Table 7 against the numbers in Table 1. To ensure that the comparison favors the conventional approach, we use the worst-case numbers in Table 6 and Table 7, the numbers for the *cccp* and the *make* programs. Our direct-mapped cache numbers are consistently better than the traditional fully associative cache numbers. In fact, the miss ratios are consistently less than half of the ones expected by Smith. If we take the average of the miss ratios across the 10 programs, the average miss ratio would be about 1/5 of Smith's design target miss ratios. The results are clearly in favor of the instruction placement optimization.

5. Conclusion

We have designed and implemented an instruction placement algorithm to improve the performance of the instruction memory hierarchy. Sequential and spatial localities are maxim-

name	sector		partial			
	miss	traffic	miss	traffic	avg.fetch	avg.exec
cccp	13.88%	27.76%	2.86%	33.78%	11.8	8.2
cmp	0.33%	0.65%	0.05%	0.66%	14.2	12.3
compress	0.47%	0.94%	0.07%	0.99%	13.9	12.0
grep	0.11%	0.21%	0.02%	0.24%	12.6	9.9
lex	0.18%	0.35%	0.04%	0.41%	11.1	7.8
make	8.82%	17.64%	1.52%	19.77%	13.0	10.1
tar	1.62%	3.25%	0.28%	3.55%	12.8	12.2
tee	1.31%	2.62%	0.21%	3.00%	14.0	9.9
wc	0.16%	0.33%	0.02%	0.33%	14.9	12.7
yacc	2.79%	5.57%	0.55%	7.13%	13.1	9.0

Table 8. Schemes to Reduce the Memory Traffic Ratio

name	0.5		0.7		1.0		1.1	
	miss	traffic	miss	traffic	miss	traffic	miss	traffic
cccp	2.60%	25.88%	3.02%	31.02%	2.86%	33.78%	3.21%	36.73%
cmp	0.06%	0.77%	0.05%	0.75%	0.05%	0.66%	0.05%	0.70%
compress	0.08%	1.05%	0.07%	1.00%	0.07%	0.99%	0.07%	1.02%
grep	0.03%	0.31%	0.02%	0.27%	0.02%	0.24%	0.02%	0.25%
lex	0.02%	0.21%	0.03%	0.32%	0.04%	0.41%	0.04%	0.41%
make	1.26%	13.75%	1.57%	18.22%	1.52%	19.77%	1.78%	23.10%
tar	0.32%	4.30%	0.27%	3.16%	0.28%	3.55%	0.32%	4.09%
tee	0.24%	2.97%	0.24%	2.99%	0.21%	3.00%	0.23%	2.95%
wc	0.02%	0.37%	0.02%	0.36%	0.02%	0.34%	0.02%	0.36%
yacc	0.65%	5.81%	0.64%	6.75%	0.55%	7.13%	0.42%	4.68%

Table 9. Effect of Code Scaling

248

ized by placing the instructions executed near each other in time into consecutive memory locations. Cache mapping conflicts are minimized by placing the functions with overlapping lifetime into memory locations which do not contend with each other in cache.

Using trace driven simulation, we have demonstrated that the instruction layout algorithm can efficiently exploit small, direct-mapped instruction caches with large blocks. The performance of an optimized direct-mapped instruction cache is better than Smith's target design miss ratio [28] using fully associative cache organization without code restructuring, for our ten benchmark programs. High instruction cache performance is achieved due to low miss ratio, low memory traffic ratio, and fast hardware. The effect of varying the cache design parameters (cache size, block size, block sectoring, and partial loading) has been presented. We have also measured the effect of varying the degree of instruction encoding on the instruction cache performance.

We are continuing this research in several directions. First, we are expanding the benchmark set to include more than 30 UNIX and CAD programs. This includes the programs, the library functions, and the representative input files. Second, we are conducting experiments on the instruction paging performance. The design parameters under investigation include working set size, page size, and page sectoring. Third, we are developing new performance measurement methods for the instruction memory hierarchy. With few mapping conflicts, performance measurements based on weighted call graphs could closely approximate the trace driven simulation. If the approximation proves to be accurate, we would be able to search the instruction memory hierarchy design space with billions of dynamic accesses.

References

1. J. Emer and D. Clark, "A Characterization of Processor Performance in the VAX-11/780," *Proceedings of the 11th Annual Symposium on Computer Architecture*, June 1984.

2. R. M. Russell, "The Cray-1 Computer System," *Comm. ACM*, vol. 21, no. 1, pp. 63-72, January 1978.

3. J. L. Hennessy , N. Jouppi, F. Baskett, and J. Gill, "MIPS: A VLSI Processor Architecture," *Proceedings of the CMU Conference on VLSI Systems and Computations*, October 1981.

4. P. Chow and M. Horowitz, "Architecture Tradeoffs in the Design of MIPS-X," *Proceedings of the 14th Annual International Symposium on Computer Architecture*, Pittsburgh, Pennsylvania, June 2-5, 1987.

5. D. A. Patterson and C. H. Sequin, "A VLSI RISC," *IEEE Computer*, pp. 8 - 21, September, 1982.

6. W. W. Hwu and P. P. Chang, "Inline Function Expansion for Compiling C Programs," *ACM SIGPLAN '89 Conference on Programming Language Design and Implementation*, Portland, Oregon, June 21-23, 1989.

7. J. R. Ellis, *Bulldog: A Compiler for VLIW Architectures*, The MIT Press, 1986.

8. J. A. Fisher, "Trace Scheduling: A Technique for Global Microcode Compaction," *IEEE Transactions on Computers*, vol. c-30, no.7, pp. 478-490, IEEE, July 1981.

9. A. J. Smith, "Cache Memories," *Computing Surveys*, vol. 14, no. 3, ACM, September 1982..

10. M. D. Hill and A. J. Smith, "Experimental Evaluation of On-Chip Cache Memories," *Proceedings of the 11th Annu. Symposium on Computer Architecture*, Boston, Massachusetts, June 17-19, 1985.

11. R. J. Eickenmeyer and J. H. Patel, "Performance Evaluation of On-chip Register and Cache Organizations," *Proceedings of the 15th International Symposium on Computer Architecture*, Honolulu, Hawaii, May 30 - June 2, 1988.

12. C. L. Mitchell and M. J. Flynn, "A Workbench for Computer Architects," *IEEE Design and Test of Computers*, IEEE, Feburary 1988.

13. D. B. Alpert and M. J. Flynn , "Performance Trade-offs for Microprocessor Cache Memories ," *IEEE MICRO* , pp. 44 - 54, IEEE , August 1988.

14. S. Przybylski, M. Horowitz, and J. L. Hennessy, "Performance Tradeoffs in Cache Design," *The 15th International Symposium on Computer Architecture Conference Proceedings*, pp. 290-298, Honolulu, Hawaii, May 30 - June 2, 1988.

15. J. L. Hennessy and T. Gross, "Postpass Code Optimization of Pipeline Constraints," *ACM Trans. on Programming Languages and Systems*, vol. 5, pp. 422-448, ACM, July 1983.

16. G. Radin, "The 801 Minicomputer," *Proceedings of the Symposium on Architectural Support for Programming Languages and Operating Systems*, pp. 39 - 47, March 1982.

17. R. P. Colwell, R. P. Nix, J.J. O'Donnell, D. B. Papworth, P. K. Rodman, "A VLIW Architecture for a Trace Scheduling Compiler," *Proceedings of the Second International Conference on Architectural Support for Programming Languages and Operating Systems*, pp. 105-111, ACM, Palo Alto, California, October 5-8, 1987.

18. G.J. Chaitin, "Register Allocation & Spilling Via Graph Coloring," *ACM SIGPLAN Notice*, vol. 17-6, pp. 201 - 207, June 1982.

19. F. Chow and J. Hennessy, "Register Allocation by Priority-bases Coloring," *Proceedings of the ACM SIGPLAN Symposium on Compiler Constructions*, pp. 222-232, June 17-22, 1984.

20. J. R. Goodman and W.-C. Hsu, "Code Scheduling and Register Allocation in Large Basic Blocks," *Proceedings of the 1988 International Conference on Supercomputing*, pp. 442-452, ACM, St. Malo, France, July 4-8, 1988.

21. Ferrari, D., "Improving Locality by Critical Working Sets," *CACM*, vol. 17, no. 11, November 1984.

22. Duncan H. Lawrie, "Access and Alignment of Data in an Array Processor," *IEEE Transactions on Computers*, vol. C-24, no. 12, December 1975.

23. Dennis Gannon, "Strategies for Cache and Local Memory Management by Global Program Transformation," *Journal of Parallel and Distributed Computing*, vol. 5, 1988.

24. Mauricio Breternitz Junior and John Paul Shen, "Organization of Array Data for Concurrent Memory Access," *Proceedings of the 21st Annual Workshop on Microprogramming and Microarchitecture*, November 30-December 2, 1988.

25. Stephen J. Hartley, "Compile-Time Program Restructuring in Multiprogrammed Virtual Memory Systems," *IEEE Transactions on Software Engineering*, vol. 14, no. 11, November 1988.

26. Scott McFarling, "Program Optimization for Instruction Caches," *Third International Conference on Architectural Support for Programming Languages and Operating Systems*, April 3-6, 1989.

27. A. J. Smith, "Cache Evaluation and the Impact of Workload Choice," *Proceedings of the 12th International Symposium on Computer Architecture*, Boston, Massachusetts, June 17-19, 1985.

28. Alan Jay Smith, "Line (Block) Size Choice for CPU Cache Memories," *IEEE Transactions on Computers*, vol. C-36, no. 9, pp. 1063-1074, September 1987.

29. P. P. Chang and W. W. Hwu, "Trace Selection for Compiling Large C Application Programs to Microcode," *Proceedings of the 21st Annual Workshop on Microprogramming and Microarchitectures*, San Diego, California, November 29 - December 2.

Appendix: The IMPACT-I Instruction Placement Algorithm

```
MIN_PROB = 0.7;

Algorithm TraceSelection {
  /** select the best immediate successor
  ** of the basic block, bb **/
  best_successor(bb) {
    ln = the outgoing arc with the highest execution count.
    if (weight(ln)==0) return 0;
    if (weight(ln)/weight(bb) < MIN_PROB) return 0;
    if (weight(ln)/weight(destination(ln)) < MIN_PROB)
      return 0;
    if (destination(ln) has been selected) return 0;
    return ln;
  }
  /** select the best immediate predecessor
  ** of the basic block, bb **/
  best_predecessor(bb) {
    ln = the incoming arc with the highest execution count.
    if (weight(ln)==0) return 0;
    if (weight(ln)/weight(bb) < MIN_PROB) return 0;
    if (weight(ln)/weight(source(ln)) < MIN_PROB) return 0;
    if (source(ln) has been selected) return 0;
    return ln;
  }
  trace_select(F) {
    int trace_id = 0;
    if (weight(F)==0) {
      /** for non-executed functions, each basic
      ** block forms a trace.
      **/
      for (all BBi in F) {
        trace_id = trace_id + 1;
        BBi.trace_id = trace_id;
      }
      return;      /** exit function **/
    }
    /** for non-zero weight functions. **/
    sort all BBi in F according to weight(BBi);
    mark all BBi in F not-selected;
    while (there are not-selected BB) {
      trace_id = trace_id + 1;
      seed = the not-selected BB with the highest
        execution count;
      seed.trace_id = trace_id;
      /** grow the trace forward **/
      current = seed;
      for (;;) {
        ln = best_successor(current);
        if ((ln==0) or (destination(ln)==ENTRY))
          break;      /** exit for loop **/
        s = destination(ln);
        s.trace_id = trace_id;
        current = s;
      }
      /** grow the trace backward **/
      current = seed;
      for (;;) {
        if (current==ENTRY)
          break;      /** exit for loop **/
        ln = best_predecessor(current);
        if (ln==0)
          break;      /** exit for loop **/
        s = source(ln);
        s.trace_id = trace_id;
        current = s;
      }
    }
  }
}

Algorithm FunctionBodyLayout {
  mark all traces un-visited;
  function space = 0;
  current = ENTRY trace;
L1 :
  while (current <> 0) {
    mark current visited;
    place the trace into the function space;
    /** try to find a connection to a trace header.
    ** we consider only non-zero weight traces.
    **/
    best = best trace connected to the current trace's
      tail. (terminal to terminal connection only)
    if (weight(best) <> 0) {
      current = best;
      continue;      /* goto L1 */
    }
    /** if there is no sequential locality at all,
    ** we will start from the most important not-visited
    ** trace.
    **/
    best = the most important trace among
      not-selected traces;
    if (best==0) /** all traces have been processed. **/
      break; /* goto L2 */
    current = best;
    continue;            /* goto L1 */
L2 :
}

Algorithm GlobalLayout {
  * assume a call graph is available.
  find all call sites (Fi, Fj) == Fi calls Fj;
  weight(Fi, Fj) = sum of all calls from Fi to Fj;
    except when Fi==Fj, weight(X,X) = 0.
  for each function Fi,
    determine the size of its active region.
```

determine the size of its non-active region.
```
/** apply depth-first-search, mark every node **/
Fi.visit = false for all Fi;
from functions Fi on top of the call graph
            hierarchy (e.g. "main")
  if (Fi.visit==false)
    Visit(Fi);
/** layout the function according to the depth-first order. **/
according to DFS order, layout the effective region of all
  functions.
according to the same DFS order, layout the
  non-active region of the functions.
}

Visit(F) {
  static int id=1;
  F.visit = true;
  F.id = id++;
  sort all subcalls from F by weight(F, Fj);
  /** from the most important to the
  ** least important call site. **/
  for all callees Fj in the sorted order
    if (Fj.visit==false)
      Visit(Fj);
}
```

The Impact of Code Density on Instruction Cache Performance

Peter Steenkiste*

Computer Systems Laboratory, Stanford University

Abstract

The widespread use of reduced-instruction-set computers has generated a lot of interest in the tradeoff between the density of an instruction set and the size of the instruction cache. In this paper we present and justify a method that predicts the cache performance for a wide range of architectures, based on the miss rate for a single architecture. When we apply the method to a number of cache organizations we find that changes in code density can have a dramatic impact on memory traffic, but that modest improvements in code density do not reduce program execution time significantly in a well-balanced system.

1. Introduction

Reduced-instruction-set architectures have a simple and regular instruction set that is easy to decode and implement. The advantages of such architectures to implementors and compiler writers are widely known, but a disadvantage is that RISC's often have a lower code density than more traditional architectures, requiring them to have larger instruction caches. The tradeoff between instruction set complexity and instruction cache size is even more pronounced for processors with on-chip instruction caches, since chip area is a limited resource [3, 13].

Several people have investigated the possibility of trading some of the simplicity of an architecture for a denser encoding. A comparison of the cache performance of three architectures in [4] shows that denser instruction sets have a significantly lower miss rate for small caches, but that this advantage disappears for larger caches; less dense architectures consistently generate more memory traffic, even for large caches. Mitchell [8, 6] compares the memory traffic generated by over 50 architectures for caches ranging from 512 to 16K bytes. He observes that less dense architectures pay the highest memory traffic penalty for intermediate cache sizes.

This paper evaluates the impact of code density on instruction cache performance. Unlike previous studies, we do not measure the cache behavior of several specific architectures, but we derive

The MIPS-X research project has been supported by the Defense Advanced Research Project Agency under contract # MDA903-83-C-0335

* Peter Steenkiste is currently with the School of Computer Science, Carnegie Mellon University, Pittsburgh PA 15213

results for a wide range of architectures from cache data for a single architecture. This approach is computationally attractive, and it gives interesting insights in the behavior of instruction caches. In Sections 2 and 3 we explain and justify our method. We then discuss the impact of code density on instruction cache performance both for on-chip caches (Sections 4 and 5) and off-chip caches (Section 6).

2. Code density and cache misses

Assume we have a program that is encoded using the instruction set of two different, but equally fast architectures T and S; the S encoding occupies twice as much memory as the T encoding (Figure 2-1). If the programs fit in the cache, only *first-time misses* [1] to load the program in the cache occur, and S will have twice as many misses as T. If the programs do not fit in the cache, the best general observation we can make is that S will have more than twice as many misses as T [8]: on S, twice as many memory lines are competing for the same number of cache lines, so active lines are knocked out of the cache faster, thus resulting in more *interference misses* [1] when lines are reused. In the remainder of this section we show how to estimate the miss rate for architectures with different code densities.

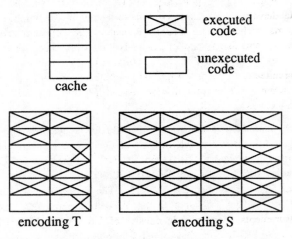

Figure 2-1: Two architectures with a different code density

2.1. Terminology and assumptions

A cache consisting of S *sets* [11] where each set contains D *lines* of size B is abbreviated as an S/D/B cache. D is called the *associativity*. The part of a line that is fetched on a miss is called a *sector*, and when sectors are equal to lines, the cache uses a line fetch strategy. Throughout this paper we will ignore instruction boundaries, and we will only consider how many instruction words (*I-words*) various architectures use. Our model of execution is that the decoder fetches I-words from the instruction cache as they are needed; each I-word can contain one, several, or part of, an instruction. By ignoring instruction boundaries, we hide details of the architecture that are not important for instruction cache behavior. For example, whether adding two words in memory takes two loads, an add and a store, or one memory-to-memory instruction is irrelevant; only the space occupied by the instruction sequence matters.

We define the *miss rate* as the ratio of the number of I-word misses to the number of I-word fetches. We define the *code density* ρ of an instruction set relative to a reference encoding as the ratio of the program size using the reference encoding to the program size using the target encoding. In Figure 2-1, the code density of T is twice the code density of S, independent of the reference encoding. The code density, i.e. a single number, is a coarse representation of the difference between two encodings:

- We defined the code density as a property of an architecture. In practice, the code density depends on how the program is compiled. Global optimization can substantially affect both the number of I-words fetched, and the static program size, so optimized and unoptimized code for the same architecture can have a different 'code density'.
- We silently assumed that changing the code density equally affects all program parts, independent of how often they are executed. We will call this the *uniformity condition*, and measurements by Mitchell [8] show that it is approximately fulfilled in practice. Note that the uniformity condition should not (and is not) valid for individual instructions; it only has to be valid for larger code segments such as extended basic blocks.

Two consequences of the uniformity condition are that the ratio of the static program size on two architectures (the 'static' code density) is roughly equal to the ratio of the number of I-words fetched during program execution (the 'dynamic' code density), and that the code density is program-independent. In order to be representative, the calculation of the code density of an architecture should be based on a significant code sample, and the same level of optimization should be used for different architectures.

The architectures studied by Mitchell have a code size ratio as high as 3.5, but in practice, code size ratios are lower, even when comparing typical 'RISC' and 'CISC' architectures. The Berkeley RISC I [10] and the MIPS R2000 [5] have code sizes about 50% larger than the VAX11. The code density of the Stanford MIPS [7] relative to the VAX11 is about 0.5. Our measurements show a code density of 1.6 for the MC68020 relative to SPARC; the density is 1.4 for optimized code.

2.2. Methodology

We would like to estimate the miss rate for one architecture, given the miss rate of another architecture and their relative code density. Changing the code density influences both the number of I-words fetches and the number of I-word misses. Assuming the uniformity condition is valid, the number of I-words fetched during program execution changes inverse-proportionally to the

code density. The change in the number of misses is harder to predict since it depends on how the memory lines interfere in the cache. Figure 2-2 suggests how the number of misses for an architecture T can be estimated based on measurements for an architecture S (example of Figure 2-1): we execute the program on architecture S using a cache with the same associativity and the same number of sets as the cache used by T, but with cache lines that are twice the size of the lines in the T cache. We expect the same number of misses as on architecture T because

1. in both cases, a cache line contains the same fraction of the program, so the same amount of information is fetched on a miss, and the two architecture/cache combinations have the same number of first time misses, and

2. in both cases, the same number of program lines are competing for the same number of cache lines so we can expect the same global replacement behavior, and the two architecture/cache combinations have the same number of interference misses.

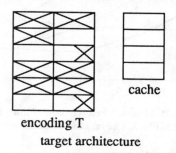

encoding T
target architecture

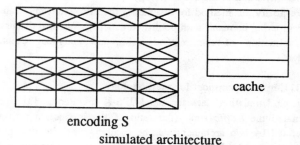

encoding S
simulated architecture

Figure 2-2: Two architecture/cache combinations with same number of instruction cache misses

More general, we want to estimate the miss rate m_T for a program on a *target architecture* T with code density ρ_T for a S/D/B cache. The *simulated architecture* S with code density ρ_S, using a $S/D/(\rho_T / \rho_S) \times B$ cache, will have the same number of misses as T, and since it fetches ρ_S / ρ_T as many I-words, we have

$$m_T = \frac{\rho_T}{\rho_S} \times m_S$$

Estimating the miss rate for arbitrary code densities requires the miss rate on the simulated architecture for caches with arbitrary line sizes. These miss rates can be obtained by interpolation on the miss rates for caches with line sizes that are a power of two (Figure 2-3). The thick curves connect caches with the same organization, but with varying line size. To simulate the effect of decreasing the code density, we increase the cache line size; this corresponds to moving down a thick curve. Similarly, increasing the code density corresponds to moving up. For a specific cache, the x-axis can be relabeled in code density, and after rescaling the y-axis, the miss rate for any code density can be read from the graph. Using this approach, data for one architecture allows us to estimate the miss rate for a wide range of code densities (architectures) and caches.

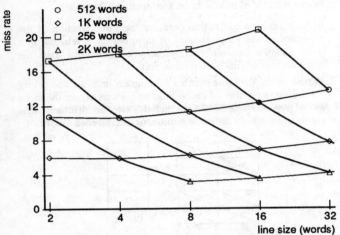

Figure 2-3: Miss rate as a function of line size
for MIPS-X-like on-chip cache (associativity 8)

2.3. Justification of the methodology

We justify our method for estimating the instruction miss rate by comparing its result with published data [8]. We also discuss the validation of the method using an analytical cache model [1, 2]

2.3.1. Empirical support for methodology

Using simulation data for the MIPS-X architecture [3], we estimated the *traffic ratio* (the ratio of the instruction traffic generated by two architecture/cache combinations) for the five programs used by Mitchell [8, 9]. Figure 2-4 compares our and Mitchell's [8, 6] estimated traffic ratios for the Fix32 relative to the OBI360, for 2-way set associative caches with a line size of four words. The Fix32 is a reduced-instruction-set processor. The OBI360 is a simplified version of the IBM360 with a static and dynamic code density, relative to the Fix32, of 1.42 and 1.52 respectively. Our results are based on the static, dynamic and mean code density. Our results and Mitchell's results are very similar. In general we expect estimates based on the dynamic code density to be applicable for small caches, and those based on the static density for larger caches. Differences in the compiler can have some effect on the results.

Figure 2-5 compares our estimated traffic ratio with Mitchell's results for several architectures; our estimates are based on the geometric mean of the static and the dynamic code density. There is a good match between our estimates and Mitchell's results, except for the Direct Correspondence Architecture (DCA3-16). The reason is that because DCAs are strongly optimized for space efficiency, the uniformity condition can be

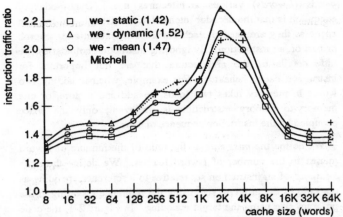

Figure 2-4: Memory traffic ratio for five Pascal programs -
comparing our results with Mitchell's results

completely invalid. This is the case for the DCA3-16: there is a big difference between the static and dynamic code density (1.54 versus 1.15).

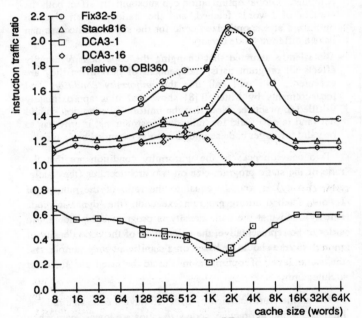

Figure 2-5: Memory traffic ratio for 5 Pascal programs -
our results (full) versus Mitchell's results (dots)

2.3.2. Justification using an analytical cache model

The analytical cache model presented in [1, 2] estimates the miss rate of a program using cache parameters and parameters extracted from an address trace. The miss rates predicted by the model closely approximate the results of trace-driven cache simulation. If our method for estimating the miss rate is correct, changing the trace parameters in the model to reflect a change in code density and changing the line size inverse-proportionally to the code density should leave the number of misses predicted by the model the same. This is correct, except for a term that results from the difference in instruction alignment in the target and the simulated architectures. We extended the cache model to account for alignment, and we found that for real architectures, the alignment term can be ignored. The reason is that architectures with a denser encoding usually have a finer instruction alignment (e.g. VAX11 instructions are byte-aligned, while MIPS-X instructions are word-aligned), so, in practice, the unit of alignment does approximately scale with code density.

Both our method and the cache model assume a line fetch strategy. For a cache with sectors, they estimate the *line miss rate*, the ratio of the number of line misses to the number of (word) fetches (a line miss is an access to a line that is not in the cache). An extension of the analytical cache model provides estimates for the ratio between the 'real' miss rate and the line miss rate, and using this ratio, our method can be used to estimate the miss rate for caches with sectors.

3. Assumptions and evaluation criteria

In the remainder of the paper we look at the cache behavior of a number of architectures. We use MIPS-X [3] as the basis for calculating the code density. Three architecture/cache combinations are involved in the analysis:

T   the target configuration: the architecture and cache we want to get performance results for.

S   the simulated configuration: the architecture and cache we have simulation results for; in our case, S is the MIPS-X [3] architecture (i.e. ρ_S is one) using the T cache with lines that are a factor ρ_T larger.

R   the reference configuration: the architecture and cache we want to compare T with; in this study R is an architecture with density one and with some cache that is of interest. The results can be applied to architectures with different code densities by rescaling the graphs.

We expect our results to be accurate for a wide range of architectures, with the exception of architectures that are heavily optimized for space efficiency. The only 'architectural variable' is code density, and we assume that all systems have the same execution time without instruction cache misses. Data misses are ignored since they are mostly unaffected by changes in code density; this amplifies the effect of code density since the execution time with data misses is larger. Our results do not apply to systems with a combined instruction and data cache. In such systems, the miss rate is often dominated by data misses, because data accesses have less locality.

For large changes in code density, "changing the code density" really means "changing the architecture", and even smaller changes (10%-30%) can have a considerable effect on an implementation. This study does not try to evaluate the impact of code density changes on the complexity, cost and performance of an implementation of an architecture. This effect depends strongly on the implementation.

A set of 17 programs is used in the study (see Appendix). Besides the miss rate, we also use the *memory traffic* and the *normalized execution time* to compare cache/architecture combinations:

$$\texttt{traffic} = \texttt{sector size} \times \texttt{miss rate} \times \texttt{I-words fetched}$$

$$\texttt{time} = 1 + \frac{\texttt{penalty} \times \texttt{miss rate} \times \texttt{words fetched}}{\texttt{execution time without misses}}$$

where the miss penalty depends on how many words are fetched on a miss. The relative memory traffic (traffic ratio), and the relative (normalized) execution time are averaged using the geometric mean.

4. Instruction caches with word fetching

On-chip instruction caches often have *small sectors* to avoid fetching unused words. The reason is that the penalty for a miss, not including the fetch time, is relatively low since the CPU and the cache are close together, so the higher miss rate that comes with small sectors is more attractive than the cost of fetching unused words. The extended analytical cache model shows that if the T and S architectures have a sector size equal to the alignment unit, the two architectures have the same miss rate. This result can also be derived intuitively. The simulated architecture S (density one) fetches ρ_T times as many I-words during program execution as T. Because of the choice of line size for S, both architectures have the same pattern of loading and invalidating lines in the cache. If the sector size is equal to the alignment unit, only used words are loaded in the cache, and S loads ρ_T times as many words in the cache as T, i.e. T and S have the same miss rate.

We present results for two-way set-associative caches, with four word lines and one word sectors. The fetch strategy used is the same as for MIPS-X: on a miss, the word that caused the miss, plus the dynamically consecutive word are fetched. Sizes for on-chip caches are limited to a small range, but we present results for a larger range (8 to 128K words) to show boundary effects. We concentrate on two architectures with code sizes that are 35% smaller (MIPS-Y) and 35% larger (MIPS-Z) than MIPS-X (densities 0.74 and 1.54).

4.1. Miss rate

Figure 4-1 gives the average miss rate for MIPS-X, MIPS-Y and MIPS-Z for various program groups. We can distinguish three areas on the graph:

- For caches larger than 32K words, the programs fit in the cache, and only first-time misses occur. In this area, MIPS-X, MIPS-Y and MIPS-Z have the same miss rate, as was also observed in [4]. This behavior was expected since both the number of I-word fetches and the number of misses change inverse-proportionally to the code density.

- For the 128 words to 32K word range, MIPS-Y has a lower miss rate than MIPS-X, which has a lower miss rate than MIPS-Z. This behavior was expected since the cache can contain more of the working set with the denser encoding. The miss rate for the group of small (large) programs is lower (higher) than the average miss rate for the whole group.

- For caches smaller than 128 words, the miss rates approaches its maximum value of 50%, and we observe that the miss rate for the group of small programs drops below the miss rate for large programs. The reason is that one of the large programs has a very low miss rate for small caches, and it illustrates how for small caches, short term locality is very important.

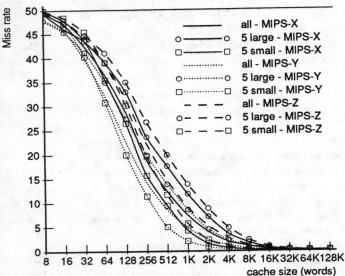

Figure 4-1: Miss rate for MIPS-X, MIPS-Y and MIPS-Z

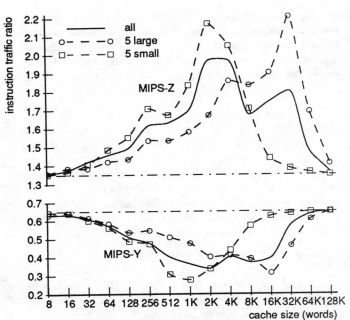

Figure 4-2: Memory traffic for MIPS-Y and MIPS-Z
relative to MIPS-X

4.2. Memory traffic

Figure 4-2 shows the instruction traffic ratios for the MIPS-Y and the MIPS-Z architectures relative to MIPS-X. For large (small) caches, the traffic ratio is equal to the ratio of the program sizes; this was expected since the number of misses is proportional to the static code size (number of I-words fetched). For intermediate cache sizes, the ratio is higher than the program size ratio, since with a denser encoding, a larger part of the working set fits in the cache [8]. Since different programs have different working sets, the curves for the different program groups peak for different cache sizes. The curve for the complete program set is smoother than the curves for the largest and smallest programs, because the programs with widely different working set sizes smooth each others peaks. The "MIPS-Z to MIPS-X" curve peaks at 2.2 (largest programs), and the "MIPS-Y to MIPS-X" curve has a minimum of 0.3 (smallest programs). Given a code size change of 35%, this is a substantial change in memory traffic.

The MIPS-Y and the MIPS-Z curves are very similar in shape, but they are not exactly each other's inverse: the MIPS-Y peak occurs for cache sizes that are about a factor of 2 smaller than the MIPS-Z peaks. This is no surprise: since MIPS-Y is twice as dense as MIPS-Z, we expect similar behavior of MIPS-Y, and of MIPS-Z with a cache that is twice as big. The two cases are not identical because they correspond to different cache organizations.

4.3. Execution time

Figure 4-3 shows the speedup that would result from reducing the MIPS-X code size by 35% or from increasing it by 35%; the MIPS-X fetch strategy is used, and the miss penalty is two cycles. For large caches, the speedup and slowdown converge to zero, i.e., first time misses have no impact on the overall execution time. For small caches, the miss penalty for MIPS-X,

MIPS-Y and MIPS-Z approaches its maximum value of 50%, and the speedup and slowdown converge to 17.5%; the number of I-word fetches changes by 35%, half of which are misses. In both cases, all program groups behave in the same way. The program groups behave differently in the intermediate range. For a 512-word cache, for example, the speedup of MIPS-Y ranges from 10.4% to 12.7%, for the 5 smallest and the 5 largest programs respectively; the slowdown of MIPS-Z ranges from 10.6% to 13.7%.

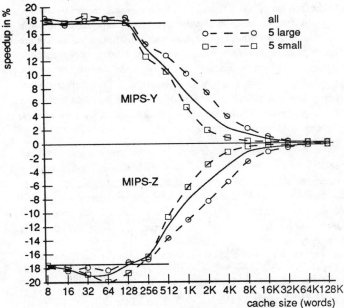

Figure 4-3: Speedup of MIPS-Y and MIPS-Z
relative to MIPS-X

An interesting result is that there is not much correlation between the 'performance' as it is measured by the memory traffic (Figure 4-2), and as it is measured by execution time (Figure 4-3). For example, for a 2 Kword cache, the cache size for which MIPS-Y offers a maximal 'memory traffic performance' benefit over MIPS-X, MIPS-Y is only 4% faster than MIPS-X. The reason for this discrepancy is that the traffic ratio gives no information about the absolute volume of memory traffic. Figures 4-2 and 4-3 show that the traffic ratio is highest for larger caches, where the contribution of cache misses to the program execution time is small.

5. An example: MIPS-X

In the previous section, we studied specific architectures and we let the cache size change. In this section we look at specific caches, and we let the code density vary. Figure 5-1 shows the speedup as a function of the density for three MIPS-X-like caches and for three program groups. The speedup is relative to MIPS-X using the same cache, and the maximum speedups possible (infinite code density) are also shown. The slopes of the speedup curves and the maximum speedups show that the impact of code density for small programs using a large cache is small because the programs spend little time handling cache misses, but that the impact for larger programs is much larger.

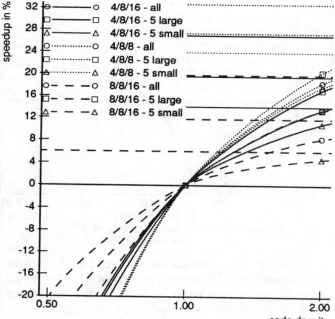

Figure 5-1: Speedup as a function of code density relative to MIPS-X

Figure 5-1 can be used to evaluate changes in the MIPS-X instruction encoding. One possible change is to eliminate the explicit no-ops in unused delay slots by extending the instruction set with versions of the load, store and branch instructions that wait for one or two cycles. For these 17 programs, 11.5% of the instructions executed are no-ops. Eliminating these instructions

would result in a code density of 1.13, and would give a speedup of 3%-4%.

In [6], changes to a RISC instruction set (for example MIPS-X) are considered. The authors first introduce an "RX" instruction format that allows one operand to reside in memory. This reduces the code size by 10%, giving a speedup of 3%. Adding a 16-bit register-to-register format would reduce the code size by another 30%. This would reduce memory traffic by almost a factor of two (this is consistent with the measurements in [6]), and it would give a speedup of 6%-10%. The architectural changes increase the complexity of the MIPS-X pipeline controller and decoder.

All results presented up to this point assume a miss penalty of 2 cycles, with two words fetched on a miss. Integrated circuit technology makes it possible to build faster and faster microprocessors, making off-chip communication relatively more expensive, and increasing the miss penalty for on-chip caches. Figure 5-2 show the effect of such change on the code density versus execution time tradeoff. The results are for the MIPS-X cache with the MIPS-X fetch back policy. As the miss penalty increases, decreasing the code density becomes more worthwhile. For a miss penalty of 8 cycles, for example, a code size decrease of 30% gives a speedup of 21%, versus 8% for a penalty of 2 cycles.

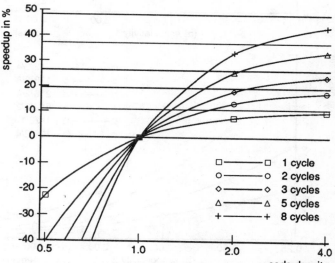

Figure 5-2: Speedup for different cache miss penalties relative to MIPS-X

6. Instruction caches with line fetching

Off-chip caches often use a line fetch strategy. The reason is that the cost of a miss is relatively high, while the incremental cost of fetching additional words on a miss (over a bus) is relatively low. As a result, reducing the miss rate by fetching lines is attractive, even if some of the fetched words are not used. The absence of sectors also makes the cache simpler and faster. With a line fetch strategy the miss rate is equal to the line miss rate predicted by our method. We look at 1K, 2K and 4K word caches, and the program set is reduced to the ten largest programs (see appendix). The code density changes between 0.25 and 4, and the miss penalty is ten cycles plus one cycle for every word transferred.

6.1. Miss rate

Figure 6-1 shows that the average miss rate decreases gradually as the code density increases. All curves have a similar exponential shape. The curves are rescaled copies of curves in the graph with the raw data (cf. 'thick' curves in Figure 2-3). For example, the curves for the 128/2/8 and 128/2/4 caches are both based on simulation results for programs coded in the MIPS-X instruction set, using 128/2/1 .. 128/2/32 caches.

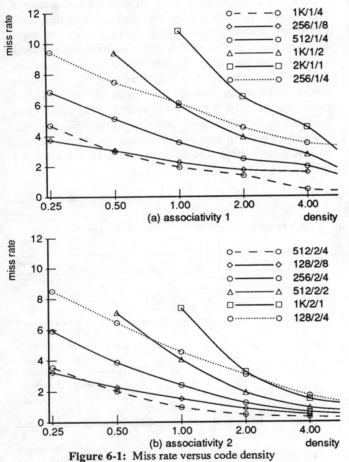

Figure 6-1: Miss rate versus code density

Unexpectedly, the miss rate does not always drop when the code density improves. When the code size is reduced by 50%, the number of misses usually goes down by more than 50% (Section 2), and the miss rate drops. But random interference in the cache, such as two frequently executed areas competing for the same set, can cause the number of misses to drop by less than a factor of two, thus resulting in an increased miss rate (even though the number of misses decreases). This effect explains the 'bulge' in the curves for associativity one (Figure 6-1a). These effects are less likely to have an impact in caches with associativity larger than one, or if the miss rate is high.

6.2. Memory traffic and execution time

Figure 6-2a shows that changing the code density has a dramatic impact on the instruction traffic; the traffic ratio is expressed relative to an architecture with code density one using the same cache. The curves are almost straight lines, and the angles of the curves are determined by the cache organization and size. The stipple line in Figure 6-2a corresponds to a reduction of the memory traffic equal to the code size reduction. For very small and very large caches, the curves coincides with the stipple line.

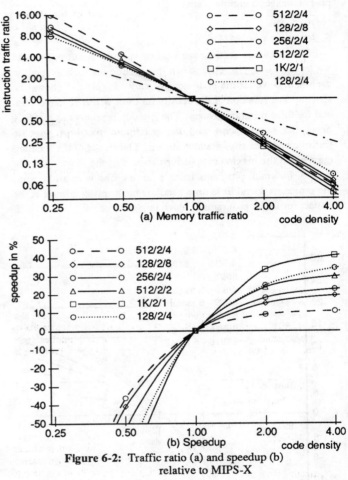

Figure 6-2: Traffic ratio (a) and speedup (b) relative to MIPS-X

Figure 6-2b shows the speedup resulting from changing the code density. For a 256/2/4 cache, a reduction in code size by a factor of two results in a speedup of about 18%. A code size reduction of 30% gives a speedup of 11%. For a 1K/2/1 cache, improving the code density gives spectacular speedups, but such a cache organization is not really realistic, at least not if the miss penalty is 11 cycles. This cache organization does illustrate that for an unbalanced system, i.e. a system that spends 50% of its time handling instruction misses, code density does have a strong impact on performance.

7. Conclusion

We presented a methodology to estimate the cache performance of various architectures based on measurements for a single architecture. The method ignores all architectural features except code density, and it is based on the assumption that code density changes more or less equally affect all parts of a program [8]. We confirmed earlier observations that relatively moderate changes in code density (e.g. 35%) can sometimes have a dramatic impact on instruction traffic (e.g. factor of 2-3), but we also observed that the impact of code density on the traffic ratio is most significant for larger caches, i.e. when the instruction traffic is low and when instruction cache misses contribute little to the program execution time.

Although code density can have a strong impact on instruction cache performance, no major benefits should be expected from small code density changes. When a cache is effective at reducing memory traffic, the impact of code density on execution time and instruction traffic is small, and when a system spends an excessive amount of time handling instruction cache misses, only major improvements in code density, i.e. major changes in the architecture, will solve the problem. With the current technology, how architectural features influence the cycle count and the complexity of the implementation is more important than how they affect code size.

Appendix: Details on programs

The following table shows the size and some miss rates for the programs used in the paper:

	object size (words)	line fetch (off-chip)		MIPS-X fetch (on-chip)	
		512/2/4	256/2/4	4/8/16	64/2/4
inter	2291	0.05	0.05	12.8	9.5
deduce	4323	0.12	0.70	11.7	12.5
dedgc	5309	0.09	0.47	5.5	7.3
rat	8271	0.60	2.37	24.3	22.4
comp	11847	1.00	1.99	16.6	14.9
opt	14474	0.29	0.62	5.5	7.9
frl	14226	1.30	3.61	23.2	20.7
simu	19384	1.41	3.95	13.4	13.2
dnfPO	12071	0.11	0.11	1.1	7.4
hopt	17441	0.23	0.85	11.7	11.2
bigfm	8771	0.03	0.04	9.6	9.5
upasm	62734	1.81	3.40	15.7	16.0
ccal	12120	1.25	3.33	17.1	15.9
comp	10629	0.01	0.20	4.3	3.6
pcomp	36324	1.20	2.62	12.6	13.2
pasm	12857	0.22	0.97	13.8	12.5
macro	34616	0.54	1.21	10.5	10.2

The first seven programs are written in LISP [12], while the others are written in Pascal. The last five programs were also used by Mitchell [8]. Following subsets are used to illustrate extreme or typical behavior:

1. five largest programs for on-chip caches (Sections 4 and 5): rat, frl, upasm, ccal, pcomp.
2. five smallest programs for on-chip caches (Sections 4 and 5): inter, deduce, deduce-gc, dnfPO, macro.
3. ten largest programs for off-chip caches (Section 6): rat, comp, opt, frl, simu, upasm, ccal, macro, pasm, pcomp.

Acknowledgements

I would like to thank John Hennessy and Anant Agarwal for their help and suggestions.

References

1. Agarwal, A., Horowitz, M., and Hennessy, J. An Analytical Cache Model. Tech. Rept. CSL 86-304, Stanford University, September, 1986.

2. Agarwal, A. *Analysis of Cache Performance for Operating System and Multi-tasking Workloads*. Ph.D. Th., Stanford University, May 1987.

3. Chow, P., and Horowitz, M. Architectural Tradeoffs in the Design of MIPS-X. 14th Annual International Symposium on Computer Architecture, IEEE, June, 1987, pp. 300-308.

4. Davidson, J., and Vaughan, R. The Effect of Instruction Set Complexity on Program Size and Memory Performance. Second International Conference on Architectural Support for Programming Languages and Operating Systems, ACM/IEEE, Palo Alto, October, 1987, pp. 60-64.

5. Ditzel, D, McLellan, H, and Berenbaum, A. Design Tradeoffs to Support the C Programming Language in the CRISP Microprocessor. Second International Conference on Architectural Support for Programming Languages and Operating Systems, ACM/IEEE, Palo Alto, October, 1987, pp. 158-163.

6. Flynn, M., Mitchell, C., and Mulder, H. "And now a Case for More Complex Instruction Sets". *IEEE Computer 20*, 9 (September 1987), 71-83.

7. Gross, T., Hennessy, J., Przybylski, S. and Rowen, C. "Measurement and Evaluation of the MIPS architecture and Processor". *ACM Transactions on Computer Systems 6*, 3 (August 1988), 229-257.

8. Mitchell, C. *Processor Architecture and Cache Performance*. Ph.D. Th., Stanford University, June 1986. Stanford Technical Report No. CSL-86-296.

9. Mitchell, C. Architecture and Simulation results for Individual Benchmarks. Tech. Rept. CSL-TN-86-289, Stanford University, December, 1986.

10. Patterson, D., and Sequin, C. A Reduced Instruction Set VLSI Computer. 8th Annual International Symposium on Computer Architecture, IEEE, Minneapolis, May, 1981, pp. 443-457.

11. A. Smith. "Cache Memories". *Computing Surveys 14*, 3 (September 1982), 473-530.

12. Steenkiste, P. *LISP on a Reduced-Instruction-Set Processor: Characterization and Optimization*. Ph.D. Th., Stanford University, March 1987.

13. Taylor, G.S., Hillfinger, P.N. Larus, J., et al. Evaluation of the SPUR Lisp Architecture. 13th Annual International Symposium on Computer Architecture, IEEE, Tokyo, June, 1986, pp. 444-452.

Parallel Architectures

Can dataflow subsume von Neumann computing?

Rishiyur S. Nikhil
Arvind

Massachusetts Institute of Technology
Laboratory for Computer Science
545 Technology Square, Cambridge, MA 02139, USA

Abstract: We explore the question: "What can a von Neumann processor borrow from dataflow to make it more suitable for a multiprocessor?" Starting with a simple, "RISC-like" instruction set, we show how to change the underlying processor organization to make it multithreaded. Then, we extend it with three instructions that give it a fine-grained, dataflow capability. We call the result P-RISC, for "Parallel RISC." Finally, we discuss memory support for such multiprocessors. We compare our approach to existing MIMD machines and to other dataflow machines.

Keywords and phrases: parallelism, MIMD, dataflow, multiprocessors, multithreaded architectures

1 Introduction

Dataflow architectures appear attractive for scalable multiprocessing because they have mechanisms (a) to tolerate increased latencies and (b) to handle greater synchronization requirements [1]. Unfortunately, these architectures have been sufficiently different that it has been difficult to substantiate or refute this claim objectively. In this paper, we sidestep this issue and continue a recent trend towards a synthesis of dataflow and von Neumann architectures. In [4, 3], Ekanadham and Buehrer explored the use of dataflow structures in a von Neumann architecture. Papadopoulos' Monsoon dataflow processor [13] uses directly-addressed frames instead of an associative wait-match memory, showing a similarity to von Neumann machines. Iannucci [9, 10] explored

a dataflow/von Neumann hybrid architecture. In this paper, we propose an architecture called P-RISC (for Parallel RISC). Not only can it exploit both conventional and dataflow compiling technology but, more so than its predecessors, it can be viewed as a dataflow machine that can achieve complete software compatibility with conventional von Neumann machines.

In Section 2, we describe the runtime storage model and the simple, RISC-like instructions on which we base our work. By RISC-like, our primary implication is that there are two categories of instructions—three-address instructions that operate entirely locally, *i.e.*, within a processing element, and load/store instructions to move data in and out of the processing element, without arithmetic [7, 14, 15, 18]. Further, the instructions are simple and regular, suitable for pipelining. Nevertheless, our storage model is unusual.

In Section 3, we change the underlying processor organization to make it multithreaded (*a la* HEP), itself an improvement for multiprocessors. In Section 4, we extend it with three instructions, giving it a fine-grained, dataflow capability, making it an even better building block for multiprocessors. Section 5 discusses memory support for such multiprocessors; Section 6 discusses some of the serious unresolved engineering issues, and Section 7 concludes with a comparision with other work. Our concern here is with asynchronous, MIMD models. This covers most current and proposed parallel machines, such as the HEP, BBN Butterfly, Intel Hypercube, IBM RP3, Cray YMP, IBM 3090, Sequent, Encore, *etc.*, and excludes machines like the Connection Machine, Warp, and VLIW machines.

2 The runtime model

2.1 Trees of frames, and heaps

Consider the following program:

© 1989 ACM 0884-7495/89/0000/0262$01.50

```
procedure h(x) ... ;

procedure g(y) ... h(e) ... ;

procedure M() ... g(e1) ... h(e2) ... ;
```

A sequential implementation uses a *stack* of *frames* (activation records) which goes through the configurations of Figure 1 (our stack grows upward). At each instant, only the code for the topmost frame is active—lower frames are dormant. In a parallel

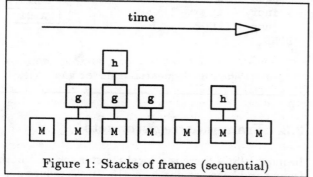

Figure 1: Stacks of frames (sequential)

implementation, however, M may call g and h concurrently, and g may call h concurrently as well, *i.e.*, all frames may exist concurrently. We must generalize the structure to a *tree* of frames (Figure 2). Further, at each instant, the code for any of the frames can be active, not just at the leaves.

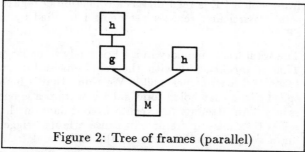

Figure 2: Tree of frames (parallel)

Another difference is in loops. Sequential loops normally use a single frame. In parallel loops, however, we need many frames in order that multiple iterations may run concurrently. Still, it is a tree structure: all frames for iterations of a loop have the same parent, and any procedure calls from the loop body are subtrees above the iteration frames. The set of paths to the root frame, in the parallel implementation's tree of frames, corresponds to the states of the sequential implementation's stack.

Of course, frames are not enough. In many modern programming languages, *e.g.*, Lisp, Smalltalk, ML, Id, *etc.*, it is possible for the lifetimes of data structures to differ from the the lifetimes of frames. Thus, data structures must be allocated on a global *heap*.

A pair of frames can share values in two ways. They may both refer to a common ancestor frame (by lex-

ical scoping), or they may both refer to a data structure in the heap. In this paper, we will only consider the latter mechanism, as lexical scoping of scalars can always be eliminated by "lambda-lifting" [11].

To summarize: our runtime model of storage consists of a tree of frames and a global heap memory, with frames containing pointers into the heap.

2.2 Processing Elements, Continuations and sequential "RISC" code

How is this abstract storage model mapped to a multiprocessor? We assume an interconnection of Processing Elements (PEs) and Heap Memory Elements (see Figure 3). Each PE has *local memory for code and frames*. Even though the memories may be physically distributed, we assume a single, *global address space* for all memories.

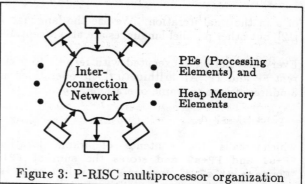

Figure 3: P-RISC multiprocessor organization

At each instant, a PE runs a *thread* of computation, which is completely described by an instruction pointer IP, and a frame pointer FP. The IP points into code in the PE, and the FP points at a frame in the PE (see Figure 4). We can regard this pair of pointers as a *continuation*, or "flyweight" process descriptor, and we use the notation <FP.IP>. They correspond exactly to the "tag" part of a token in the terminology of tagged-token dataflow. It is convenient for continuations to have the same size as other values, *e.g.*, integers and floats, so that continuations can be manipulated as values.

As a running example, we use the following procedure that computes the inner-product of two vectors A and B of size n:

```
def vip A B =
  { s = 0
  In {for i <- 1 to n do
      next s = s + A[i] * B[i]
      finally s}} ;
```

s is zero for the first iteration of the loop. For each subsequent iteration, s has the value from the previous iteration plus the product of two vector components. The value of the entire expression is the value

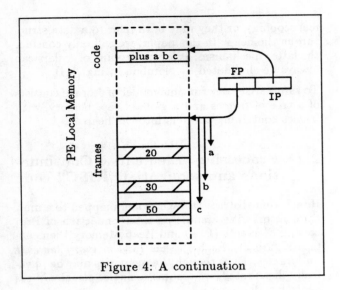

Figure 4: A continuation

```
load-immed   0  s
load-immed   1  i
LOOP:
   compare i  n      b
   jgt     b  DONE
   plus    A  i      aA
   load    aA Ai
   plus    B  i      aB
   load    aB Bi
   mult    Ai Bi     AiBi
   plus    s  AiBi   s
   incr    i  i
   jump    LOOP
DONE:
   ...
```

Frame
s
i
n
b
A
aA
Ai
B
aB
Bi
AiBi

Figure 5: Sequential code for vip

---

of **s** in the final iteration. We use the language Id [12], but other parallel languages are also acceptable.

Every instruction is executed with respect to a current **FP** and **IP**. All arithmetic/logic operations are 3-address frame-to-frame operations, *e.g.*:

   plus s1 s2 d

which reads the contents of frame locations **FP+s1** and **FP+s2** and stores the sum at **FP+d**. "Compare **s1 s2 d**" compares the values at **FP+s1** and **FP+s2** and stores a condition code at **FP+d**. A j*cond* instruction:

   j*cond* s IPt

(for various *cond*s) reads a condition code from **FP+s** and changes **IP** to **IP+1** or **IPt** accordingly. For computed jumps, a variation would be to pick up **IPt** from the frame.

"**Load a x**" and "**Store x a**" move data between frame location **FP+x** and the heap location whose address is in the frame at **FP+a**.

The instruction set is RISC-like in the following sense. All arithmetic operations are local to the PE. Load and **store** are the only instructions for moving data in and out of the PE, and they do not involve any arithmetic. Thus, instruction fetches and frame accesses involve local PE memory only, and no network traffic. Further, the arithmetic instructions are simple and regular so that they can be pipelined.

Sequential code for **vip** is shown in Figure 5 with the frame shown on the right (for expository reasons, we use more frame slots than necessary).

2.3 Frames as register sets

In most RISCs there is a local register set, and both frames and heap are non-local [15, 7]. To reduce non-local traffic, one can have more registers, have multiple register sets (as in the HEP and Berkeley RISC [14]), or provide instruction and data caches.

In P-RISC, we think of a frame as being local and synonymous with a register set. The collection of frames on a PE is regarded as a collection of register sets, a particular register set being identified by an **FP**.

The total frame memory in a PE is likely to be large. This is *inconsistent* with the requirement for two reads and a write per cycle. We think that a high-speed cache that holds some subset of frames is necessary. An attempt to execute a continuation that refers to a missing frame will cause a fault, triggering a swap of frames between the cache and frame memory. Such a cache implementation would perhaps be simplified if frames were of fixed size. The compiler may have to split large code blocks to meet this requirement.

2.4 Problems: memory latency and distributed memory

A major problem in our **vip** code is the latency of the **loads**. The round trip to heap memory can take significant time, especially in a multiprocessor. A cache may help, but even caches are less effective in multiprocessors. Thus, a processor may idle during a **load**, thereby reducing performance. In bus or circuit-switched networks, long-latency **loads** can also interfere mutually, also degrading performance. Ideally,

1. **Loads** should be *split-phase* transactions (request and response) so that the path to memory is not occupied during the entire transaction.
2. The processor should be able to issue multiple loads into the network before receiving a response, *i.e.*, the network should be a pipeline for memory requests and responses.
3. The processor should be able to accept responses in a different order from that in which requests were issued. This is especially true in a multiprocessor, where distances to memories may vary.
4. The processor should be able to switch to another thread of computation rather than idle.

Many previous processor designs address this issue to varying degrees. The Encore Multimax uses split-phase bus transactions but a particular PE can have only one outstanding load. The CDC 6600 [18], the Cray [16], and some RISCs can pipeline memory requests, but requests must come back in the same order. The IBM 360/91 could pipeline memory requests and receive them out of order, but there was a small limit to the number of such outstanding requests. Further, in all these cases there is significant added complexity in the processor circuits. A more detailed discussion of this issue is in [1]. An alternative is to make the processor multithreaded (*à la* HEP [17]).

3   Multithreaded RISC

Maintaining the same instruction set, we change the underlying processor organization to support fine-grained interleaving of multiple threads.

In most high-performance machines (including RISCs), the instruction pipeline is single-threaded, *i.e.*, consecutive entities in the pipeline are instructions from the same thread, from addresses IP, IP+1, IP+2, and so on. This introduces some extra complexity in the detection and resolution of inter-instruction hazards. Further, long latency instructions such as loads disrupt the pipeline and add complexity. The HEP's pipeline, on the other hand, was time-multiplexed among several threads [17]. On each clock, a different thread descriptor was inserted into the pipe. As they emerged from the end of the pipe, they were recirculated via a queue to the start of the pipe. Thus, there was no hazard between consecutive instructions in a particular thread. Further, when a thread encountered a load, it was taken aside into a separate pool of threads waiting for memory responses; thus, threads did not block execution of other threads during loads. Unfortunately, the number of threads that could be interleaved in the pipe and the number of threads that could be waiting for loads was limited.

For multithreaded RISC, we generalize the HEP approach to an *arbitrary* number of interleaved threads. The organization of the PE is shown in Figure 6. Recall that our thread descriptors (continuations) are <FP.IP> pairs. Since they are circulated in the processor, we also refer to them as *tokens*. Tokens reside in the token queue (like the HEP's PSW queue). On each clock, a token <FP.IP> dequeued and inserted into the pipeline, fetching the instruction at IP and executing it relative to the frame at FP. The pipeline consists of the traditional instruction fetch, operand fetch, execution and operand store stages. At the end of the pipe, tokens are produced specifying the continuation of the thread; these tokens are enqueued.

For arithmetic/logic instructions, the continuation is simply <FP.IP+1>. For the **jump** instruction, the continuation is simply <FP.IPt>. For j*cond* instructions, the continuation is either <FP.IP+1> or <FP.IPt>, depending on the condition code in FP+x.

The first interesting difference arises in the **load** instruction. A heap address *a* is fetched from frame location FP+a, and the following message is sent into the network:

    <READ,a,FP.IP+1,x>

There is *no continuation* inserted into the token queue! Meanwhile, the pipeline is free to process other tokens from the token queue. Some of them, in turn, may be **loads**, pumping more READ messages into the network.

The READ messages are processed by Heap Memory Elements, which respond with START messages:

    <START,v,FP.IP+1,x>

When such a message enters the PE, the value *v* is written into the location FP+x, and the token <FP.IP+1> is inserted into the token queue. Thus, the thread descriptor travels to the heap and back.

A **store** fetches a heap address *a* from frame location FP+a, and a value *v* from FP+x, and sends the message:

    <WRITE,a,v>

into the network. A Heap Memory Element receives this, and stores the value. Meanwhile, the token <FP.IP+1> emerges from the pipe and is inserted into the token queue.

3.1   Discussion

Notice that we have achieved our goals:

- loads are split-phase transactions,
- any number of loads can be pipelined into the communication network,
- responses can come back in any order

PE organization:

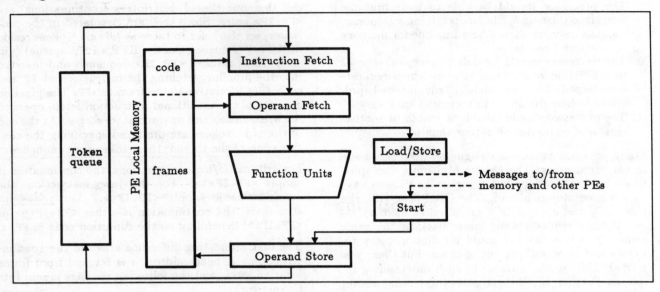

Instruction set summary:

Format	Frame operations	Continuations	Outgoing messages
Ordinary RISC-like instructions:			
op s1 s2 d	[FP+s1] op [FP+s2] → FP+d	<FP.IP+1>	—
jump IPt	—	<FP.IPt>	—
jcond x IPt	[FP+x] →	<FP.IPt> or <FP.IP+1> (depending on [FP+x])	—
load a x	[FP+a] →	none	<READ,[FP+a], FP.IP+1, x>
store x a	[FP+x],[FP+a] →	<FP.IP+1>	<WRITE,[FP+a], [FP+x]>
Incoming messages (from memory, other PEs):			
<START,v,FP.IP,y>	v → FP+y	<FP.IP>	—
P-RISC instructions (extensions for fine-grained parallelism):			
fork IPt	—	<FP.IP+1>, <FP.IPt>	—
join x	toggle [FP+x]	if [FP+x]: none / if ¬ [FP+x]: <FP.IP+1>	—
start v c d	[FP+v],[FP+c],[FP+d] →	none	<START,[FP+v], [FP+c], [FP+d]>
loadc a x IPr	[FP+a] →	<FP.IP+1>	<READ,[FP+a], FP.IPr x>

Figure 6: P-RISC Processing Element (PE) organization and instruction set summary

- The processor interleaves threads on a per-instruction basis, and is not blocked during loads. The number of threads it can support is the size of the token queue. Assuming enough tokens in the token queue, the pipeline can be kept full during memory loads—the processor never has to idle.

In the HEP, too, each thread could issue a load. The main difference is that the HEP had a small limit on the number of threads and outstanding loads. The HEP had another limitation shared by our multithreaded PE: even though there can be many outstanding loads from multiple computations, a *particular* computation can have no more than one outstanding load. We correct this situation next.

4 P-RISC: An extension for fine-grained parallelism

In any multithreaded system, there must be a way to initiate new threads and to synchronize two threads. Often, these involve operating system calls, traps, pseudo-instructions, *etc.* It is difficult to make this cheap and so one avoids fine-grained parallelism which, in turn, reduces the exploitable parallelism in programs.

We extend the multithreaded RISC to P-RISC with two instructions for thread initiation and synchronization. It is important that these are simple *instructions*—not operating system calls—that are executed entirely within the normal processor pipeline (again, please refer to Figure 6):

- Fork IPt is just like a jump, except that it produces *both* <FP,IPt> *and* <FP,IP+1> tokens as continuations.
- Join x toggles the contents of frame location FP+x. If it was zero (empty) it produces no continuation. If it was one (full) it produces <FP,IP+1>.

4.1 Inner-product revisited

Figure 7 shows, in outline, a new control flow in order to do the two loads concurrently. The corresponding code is shown in Figure 8 along with its frame. The frame has an additional location w used by the join, initialized to zero (empty) in the third statement.

The fork produces two continuations: <FP.LOADAi>, *i.e.*, the next instruction, and <FP.LOADBi>. Then, both address calculations and loads are executed concurrently. When the load in the LOADAi sequence is executed, it sends the continuation <FP.LOADAi+2> in its message to heap memory (LOADAi+2 points at the jump SYNCH instruction). When the response arrives, the value is written into frame location Ai, the

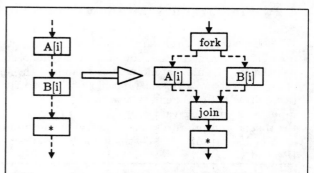

Figure 7: Sequential and parallel control flows for the two loads

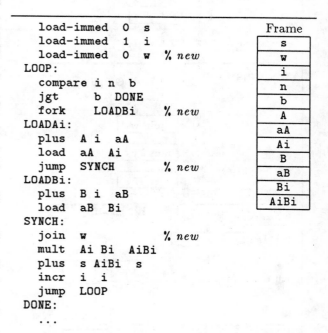

```
    load-immed   0  s
    load-immed   1  i
    load-immed   0  w      % new
LOOP:
    compare  i n  b
    jgt      b DONE
    fork     LOADBi        % new
LOADAi:
    plus  A i  aA
    load  aA  Ai
    jump  SYNCH            % new
LOADBi:
    plus  B i  aB
    load  aB  Bi
SYNCH:
    join  w                % new
    mult  Ai Bi  AiBi
    plus  s AiBi  s
    incr  i  i
    jump  LOOP
DONE:
    ...
```

Figure 8: Code for concurrent loads

Frame

s
w
i
n
b
A
aA
Ai
B
aB
Bi
AiBi

jump is taken, and join w is executed. When the LOADBi sequence is executed, it sends the continuation <FP.SYNCH> in its message to heap memory. When this response arrives, the value is written into frame location Bi and join w is executed.

Thus, join w is executed twice, once after the completion of each load. The first time, it toggles the location FP+w from empty to full and nothing further happens. The second time, it toggles it from full to empty and execution continues at the mult instruction. Note that the order in which the loads complete does not matter. Also, note that the location FP+w is ready for the next iteration as it has been reset to empty.

4.2   Fine-grained dataflow

With lightweight `fork` and `join` instructions, it is possible to simulate the fine-grained asynchronous parallelism of pure dataflow. For example, the top of Figure 9 shows a classical dataflow "+" instruction (at address IP0). When tokens t_l and t_r arrive on its input arcs carrying values, it "fires," *i.e.*, consumes the tokens and produces tokens carrying the sum on each of its output arcs, destined for instructions at IP1 and IP2.

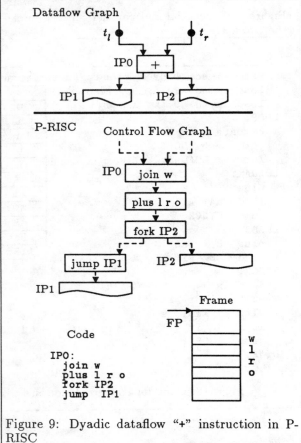

Figure 9:   Dyadic dataflow "+" instruction in P-RISC

The P-RISC control graph is shown next, followed by the P-RISC code and frame. The slots `l` and `r` are used to hold the left and right input values, respectively; the slot `o` is used to hold the output value, and the slot `w` is used for synchronization.

Corresponding to the dataflow graph producing t_l, there would be some P-RISC code that stores the left input value in `l` and inserts `<FP.IP0>` in the token queue. Similarly, some P-RISC code would store the right input value in `r` and insert an identical token `<FP.IP0>` in the token queue. Thus, getting past the `join` is a guarantee that both inputs are available. The last two instructions place the two tokens `<FP.IP1>` and `<FP.IP2>` in the token queue. With a little analysis, it is fairly easy to do better, *i.e.*, to have fewer `joins` than might be required by such a direct translation.

4.3   Extracting more parallelism

So far, the iterations of our inner-product program went sequentially, with just the two loads of each iteration proceeding concurrently. In principle, however, all $2n$ loads are independent, and all n multiplications are independent of each other. A loop compilation scheme that achieves this concurrency is described in [2, 19], along with optimizations permitting reuse of frames. Here, instead, we outline a recursive reformulation that is easier to describe:

```
def vip A B = vip_aux A B 1 ;

def vip_aux A B i =
    if i > n then 0
    else
        A[i]*B[i] + (vip_aux A B (i+1)) ;
```

The recursive call can be done concurrently with the two loads Further, the multiplication can be done before the recursive call has completed, as soon as both loads have completed (Figure 10). All $2n$ `loads` can

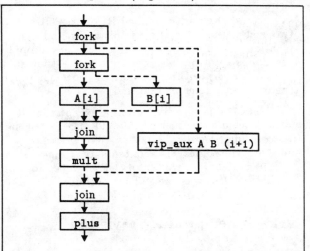

Figure 10:   Control graph for concurrent loads and iterations

be issued in parallel, the responses can come back in any order, and the multiplications are performed in an arbitrary order, automatically scheduling themselves as the load-responses arrive.

The additions in our program still proceed sequentially, and it would be easy to write a divide-and-conquer version where this is not so. However, the program as it stands dramatically illustrates that even in "apparently" sequential programs, there is much parallelism to be exploited by our architecture—all index calculations, loads and multiplications can be done in parallel.

4.4 Procedure call/return

There is no specific architectural support for procedure linkage— it is purely a compilation issue. In [2, 19], a mechanism is described that is capable of supporting the high degree of parallelism in nonstrict function calls. We summarize it here in P-RISC terms, keeping in mind that it is always possible to constrain it for less parallelism.

Suppose **g** calls **h** with n arguments. We can visualize this as storing n values into **h**'s frame and initiating n corresponding threads in **h**. Similarly, to return m results, we store m values in **g**'s frame and initiate m threads in **g**.[1] All this can be done asynchronously, *i.e.*, the n arguments and m results can be sent in any order. A fact often surprising to those unfamiliar with nonstrict functional languages is that it is possible to return results before all the arguments have been sent! For example, if **h** computes a vector-sum, it could allocate and return a pointer to the result vector even before it received the input vectors (assuming the size is known beforehand). This caller/callee overlap is a tremendous source of parallelism.

There is only one synchronization requirement—the j'th thread in **h** must not begin until the j'th argument has been stored in its frame (and similarly for returned results). For this we use a new instruction:

```
start dv dFPIP dd
```

which reads a value v from **FP+dv**, an **<FP.IP>** continuation from **FP+dFPIP** and an offset **d** from **FP+dd**, and sends the message:

```
<START,v,FP.IP,d>
```

to the destination PE. No continuation is placed in the token queue. We have already seen **START** messages (memory responses); when one arrives at a PE, it writes a value into a frame and initiates a thread.

A possible linkage convention is this. Let the first instruction in **h** be at **IPh**. Let **FPh** point at its frame. In **g**, we fork a thread for each argument. The j'th thread ends in a **start** instruction that sends:

```
<START,arg_j,FPh.IPh+j,j>
```

This deposits the argument into **FPh+j** and initiates a thread at **IPh+j**. Returned results are handled similarly. The only subtlety is that **g** needs to send extra arguments to **h** that describe its own slots and continuations that await the results.

---

[1]Of course, other threads may be active in **g** throughout.

The only remaining issue is frame allocation and deallocation. Since simple stack allocation will not do, **g** issues a call to a *frame manager* which returns a pointer to a frame allocated from a free list that it maintains in frame memory. The manager call is itself a split-phase transaction, so that other computations may proceed concurrently. The frame manager is not an ordinary procedure. It has a fixed, known context (frame), and is coded as a critical section, responding to requests in the order that they arrive. Requests that arrive while it is servicing a previous request are queued, possibly in I-structure memory. In a multiprocessor, there will typically be a frame manager on each PE, and these managers also perform load balancing to ensure that frames are evenly distributed across PEs.

After all results are received, **g** sends **FPh** back to the frame manager for deallocation. Many details are described in [2, 19], including automatic recirculation of frames and the generation of "self-cleaning" graphs to guarantee that a frame is not returned while there are still references to it. Frame allocation and deallocation does not need general garbage collection.

4.5 Discussion

Every **join** is fetched and executed twice. The first time, it introduces a bubble into the pipe because the thread dies. These bubbles correspond to the bubbles in the pipe of a Tagged-Token Dataflow Architecture when the wait-match operation fails (first token to arrive at a dyadic operator) [2, 5, 8].

Arithmetic instructions do two reads and one write into a frame. There is a potential hazard if two successive instructions in the pipe compete for the same frame location. To avoid this, many machines use reservation bits to stall the pipe. In a multithreaded machine, successive instructions can be from unrelated threads and are thus less likely to compete for the same location. This may mitigate, but not eliminate, the problem. In the HEP, an instruction was converted into a no-op and recirculated if it accessed an empty register.

If code is systematically and directly compiled from dataflow graphs (as in the "+" example in Section 4.2) we can, in fact, guarantee that, with one exception, such hazards will not arise—there will always be an adequate number of **join**s to prevent races between normal instructions. The exception is that there can still be a race between two **join** instructions. Each **join** reads a location, tests it, toggles it, and writes it back, and this must be atomic. If the next instruction in the pipe is a **join** for the same rendezvous location, the pipeline must be stalled.

We described a **join** as referring to an entire location, even though it needs only one bit. Several variations

269

are possible. The bits for all `join` locations in a frame could be packed into a few frame locations. Or, we could generalize it to an n-way synchronization: the frame location `x` is initialized to $n - 1$; a "`join x n`" instruction decrements it and dies if it is non-zero; if zero, it is reinitialized to n and the thread continues.

The `start` instruction and `START` message take three parameters: a value, a tag `<FP.IP>` and an offset `d`. An obvious variation is to combine the latter two: `<FPd.IP>`, where `FPd = FP+d`. The value is stored directly at `FPd` and the tag `<FPd.IP>` enqueued. The thread at IP can then adjust the frame pointer back to `FP` by subtracting `d`.

We can see that `loads` are frequently surrounded by `forks` and `jumps` to gain concurrency. It is thus useful to have the following "load and continue" instruction:

```
loadc a x IPr
```

It picks up a heap address a from `FP+a`, sends the message:

```
<READ,a,FP.IPr,x>
```

and continues at IP+1. Thus, it does an implicit fork. It simplifies the code of Figure 8:

```
LOOP:
    ...
    jgt    b    DONE
    plus   A    i   aA
    loadc  aA   Ai  SYNCH
    plus   B    i   aB
    load   aB   Bi
SYNCH:
    ...
```

5   Memory support for fine-grained parallelism

We have seen the following behavior for a Heap Memory Element. It receives two kinds of messages and responds with one kind of message. On receiving:

```
<READ,a,FP.IP,d>
```

it reads value v from location `a` and responds with:

```
<START,v,FP.IP,d>
```

On receiving:

```
<WRITE,a,v>
```

it writes the value v into address `a`.

However, this is inadequate, because it does not provide synchronization—a `READ` for a location may arrive from PE_0 before the corresponding `WRITE` from PE_1. To solve this, we extend the behavior of Heap Memory Elements in the direction of "I-Structures" [2]. Every location has additional presence bits that encode a state for that location.

For producer-consumer situations, we introduce two new types of messages. On receiving:

```
<I-READ,a,FP.IP,d>
```

if the location `a` is full, it behaves like an ordinary `READ`. If it is empty, the location contains a "deferred-list" (initially nil). Each list element contains the `(FP.IP,d)` information of a pending read. The information in the current `I-READ` message is added to the list. On receiving:

```
<I-WRITE,a,v>
```

if the location `a` is empty, for each `(FP.IP,d)` in the deferred list, the memory sends out a message:

```
<START,v,FP.IP,d>
```

and, finally, v is written into `a`. Thus, `I-READs` can safely arrive before the corresponding `I-WRITEs`. Of course, this assumes that the location is written only once; it may be possible to guarantee this at the language level and/or by compiler analysis (*e.g.*, it is easy in functional and logic languages).

There are, of course, other useful messages that can be processed by Heap Memory Elements, such as exchanges, test-and-sets, *etc.*

6   Implementation issues

Our development of P-RISC went as follows:

- Start with a RISC-like instruction set, *i.e.*, a `load`/`store` instruction set in which most instructions are simple, regular, 3-address frame-to-frame operations. Many variations on our instruction set are possible. In particular, it is possible to take the instruction set of an existing, commercial RISC and to generalize it in the direction of a P-RISC. This would facilitate a smooth transition for software development. One of the attractions of P-RISC is that it can use both conventional and dataflow compiling technology.

- Make it multithreaded, using a token queue and by circulating `<FP.IP>` tokens (thread descriptors) through the processor pipeline and token queue. `Loads` are split-phase—request to memory and response, so that the processor pipeline and the interconnection network are not blocked in the interim. Request and response messages are identified by the full continuation, so that the synchronization namespace is the full address space, network traffic can be pipelined, and responses may arrive in any order.

- Introduce **fork** and **join** instructions that are executed in the processor pipe, and a **start** instruction to communicate between frames on different PEs. The **loadc** instruction is a useful optimization.
- Introduce synchronization in the Heap Memory Elements using I-structure semantics.

Frames as register sets

This is perhaps the most serious implementation issue in P-RISC. Our dataflow experience indicates that total frame memory requirements are likely to be large. As mentioned earlier, the necessity for two reads and a write on each cycle will probably require an implementation that uses a cache for a subset of frames. With current technology, it should be possible to build a cache that can hold hundreds of frames. When a token referring to a missing frame is dequeued, it will trigger a fault that causes a frame to be swapped between the cache and the frame memory. It may be possible to continue executing other tokens during the swap. To avoid thrashing, the compiler/hardware would have to give preference to tokens in the token queue that refer to frames currently in the cache. Note that in P-RISC, a small number of frames can support a large number of concurrent threads, because of the fine-grained concurrency *within* a procedure activation or loop iteration.

Storage classes

We described four kinds of stores—code, token queues, frames and the global heap. For completeness, *e.g.*, for loading programs, debugging, garbage collection, *etc.*, additional instructions are necessary to read and write all stores. An interesting possibility would be to consider all local memory as a temporary copy taken from the global store.

Instruction scheduling

In our description, the processor pipe and the token queue formed a ring around which tokens were circulated. An alternative is this: as long as a thread does not die (due to **load** or **join**), continue executing the same thread, using the normal "IP+1" scheduling of a von Neumann processor; extract a token from the token queue only when a thread dies. This solution reintroduces the complexity of inter-instruction hazard detection and resolution, but it does allow adjacent instructions in a thread to communicate via a small set of named high-speed registers. Also, it could improve locality for a cache-based frame memory.

Compilation issues

Synchronization occurs in two places—in frames during a **join**, and in heap memory with I-structure operations. The former is more efficient because it needs no queueing—there is exactly one continuation. An I-structure write, on the other hand, can trigger an arbitrary number of continuations since it may have any number of consumers.

Compiler analysis of lifetimes and accessibility of variables can reveal additional information that can make use of the cheaper synchronization and better locality of frame storage by allocating data structures in frames instead of on the heap.

7 Comparison with other work

The work of Ekanadham and Buehrer was an important step in exploring the use of dataflow structures in a von Neumann architecture [4, 3]. Halstead and Fujita proposed a multithreaded processor architecture for Lisp [6].

Papadopoulos' Monsoon architecture [13] is a pure dataflow architecture in the sense that tokens not only schedule instructions but also carry data. Interprocessor tokens are identical to intra-processor tokens. Since tokens carry data, only one frame operation is required in each pass through the pipe, unlike P-RISC's three frame operations. While it is clear how to use dataflow compiling techniques for Monsoon, it is not clear how to use compiling techniques from conventional processors. Further, unlike P-RISC, it is not easy to imagine an implementation that uses the conventional "FP+1" instruction scheduling.

Closest to P-RISC is Iannucci's dataflow/von Neumann hybrid architecture [9, 10]. Every frame location has full/empty presence bits. A **load** instruction sends a request to memory along with the address of the destination frame location, and execution continues at the next instruction. An operation that tries to read an empty frame location traps, storing its process descriptor in that location and marking it "pending"; execution resumes at some other thread. When a response returns from memory to a pending frame location, the value is exchanged with the process descriptor residing there, and the process is re-enabled. Thus, Iannucci's architecture has split-phase loads, loads can be pipelined, responses can come in any order, and the namespace for waiting threads is the address space of local memory.

The primary difference between Iannucci's machine and P-RISC is that he has presence bits on every location in frame memory, and synchronization can occur in *any* instruction by using a synchronizing frame access operation. In P-RISC, frame memory does not have presence bits; instead, some locations are interpreted as full/empty synchronization locations. Synchronization occurs only at **join** instructions. Thus, P-RISC is a simpler architecture, but it may execute more instructions since synchronization is separated from arithmetic instructions.

These comparisons are by no means exhaustive, and much detailed design and experimentation remains to evaluate P-RISC. We hope this paper will stimulate research in this direction. The focus of current work at MIT is to take an existing RISC implementation and modify/extend it in the direction of P-RISC, while maintaining software compatibility with the original processor.

Acknowledgements: We thank current and past members of the Computation Structures Group at MIT, especially G.P. Papadopoulos and R.A. Iannucci, for an exciting and stimulating environment. We appreciate greatly the ideas and comments of K. Ekanadham of IBM, and the comments of S.L. Peyton Jones and K.J. Ottenstein. Funding for this work is provided in part by the Advanced Research Projects Agency of the Department of Defense under the Office of Naval Research contract N00014-84-K-0099.

References

[1] Arvind and R. A. Iannucci. Two Fundamental Issues in Multiprocessing. In *Proc. DFVLR Conf. 1987 on Parallel Processing in Science and Engineering, Bonn-Bad Godesberg, W. Germany, Springer-Verlag LNCS 295*, June 1987.

[2] Arvind and R. S. Nikhil. Executing a Program on the MIT Tagged-Token Dataflow Architecture. *IEEE Trans. on Computers*, 1989 (to appear). An earlier version appeared in *Proc. PARLE, Eindhoven, The Netherlands*, Springer-Verlag LNCS 259, June, 1987.

[3] R. Buehrer and K. Ekanadham. Incorporating Dataflow Ideas into von Neumann Processors for Parallel Execution. *IEEE Trans. on Computers*, C-36(12):1515–1522, Dec. 1987.

[4] K. Ekanadham. Multi-tasking on a dataflow-like architecture. Technical Report RC 12307 (55198), IBM T.J.Watson Res. Ctr., Yorktown Heights, NY, Nov. 1986.

[5] J. R. Gurd, C. Kirkham, and I. Watson. The Manchester Prototype Dataflow Computer. *Comm. of the ACM*, 28(1):34–52, Jan. 1985.

[6] R. H. Halstead, Jr. and T. Fujita. MASA: A Multithreaded Processor Architecture for Parallel Symbolic Computing. In *Proc. 15th. Annual Intl. Symp. on Comp. Arch., Honolulu, Hawaii*, June 1988.

[7] J. Hennessey. VLSI Processor Architecture. *IEEE Trans. on Computers*, C-33(12):1221–1246, Dec. 1984.

[8] K. Hiraki, S. Sekiguchi, and T. Shimada. System Architecture of a Dataflow Supercomputer. Technical report, Computer Systems Division, Electrotechnical Lab., 1-1-4 Umezono, Sakuramura, Niihari-gun, Ibaraki, 305, Japan, 1987.

[9] R. A. Iannucci. A Dataflow/von Neumann Hybrid Architecture. Technical Report TR-418, MIT Lab. for Computer Science, 545 Tech. Sq., Cambridge, MA 02139, May 1988.

[10] R. A. Iannucci. Toward a Dataflow/von Neumann Hybrid Architecture. In *Proc. 15th. Annual Intl. Symp. on Comp. Arch., Honolulu, Hawaii*, June 1988.

[11] T. Johnsson. Lambda Lifting: Transforming Programs to Recursive Equations. In *Proc. Func. Prog. Langs. and Comp. Arch., Nancy, France, Springer-Verlag LNCS 201*, Sept. 1985.

[12] R. S. Nikhil. Id (Version 88.1) Reference Manual. Technical Report CSG Memo 284, MIT Lab. for Computer Science, 545 Tech. Sq., Cambridge, MA 02139, Aug. 1988.

[13] G. M. Papadopoulos. Implementation of a General-Purpose Dataflow Multiprocessor. Technical Report TR-432, MIT Lab. for Computer Science, 545 Tech. Sq., Cambridge, MA 02139, Aug. 1988.

[14] D. Patterson. Reduced Instruction Set Computers. *Comm. of the ACM*, 28(1):9–21, Jan. 1985.

[15] G. Radin. The 801 Minicomputer. In *Proc. ACM Symp. on Arch. Support of Prog. Langs. and Op. Sys.*, pages 39–47, Mar. 1982.

[16] R. Russell. The CRAY-1 Computer System. *Comm. of the ACM*, 21(1):63–72, Jan. 1978.

[17] B. J. Smith. A Pipelined, Shared Resource MIMD Computer. In *Proc. 1978 Int'l Conf. on Parallel Processing*, pages 6–8, 1978.

[18] J. Thornton. Parallel Operations in the Control Data 6600. In *Proc. SJCC*, pages 33–39, 1964.

[19] K. R. Traub. A Compiler for the MIT Tagged-Token Dataflow Architecture. Technical Report LCS TR-370, MIT Lab. for Computer Science, 545 Tech. Sq., Cambridge, MA 02139, Aug. 1986.

Exploring the Benefits of Multiple Hardware Contexts in a Multiprocessor Architecture: Preliminary Results

Wolf-Dietrich Weber and **Anoop Gupta**
Computer Systems Laboratory
Stanford University
Stanford, CA 94305

Abstract

A fundamental problem that any scalable multiprocessor must address is the ability to tolerate high latency memory operations. This paper explores the extent to which multiple hardware contexts per processor can help to mitigate the negative effects of high latency. In particular, we evaluate the performance of a directory-based cache coherent multiprocessor using memory reference traces obtained from three parallel applications. We explore the case where there are a small fixed number (2-4) of hardware contexts per processor and the context switch overhead is low. In contrast to previously proposed approaches, we also use a very simple context switch criterion, namely a cache miss or a write-hit to shared data. Our results show that the effectiveness of multiple contexts depends on the nature of the applications, the context switch overhead, and the inherent latency of the machine architecture. Given reasonably low overhead hardware context switches, we show that two or four contexts can achieve substantial performance gains over a single context. For one application, the processor utilization increased by about 46% with two contexts and by about 80% with four contexts.

1 Introduction

As shared-memory multiprocessors are scaled (the number of processors is increased), there will invariably be an increase in the latency of memory operations. While local memory references need not have higher latency, remote memory operations will encounter higher latency because of the larger physical size of the machine, if not for any other reason. Consequently, there will always be times when a processor sits idle, waiting for some remote operation to complete [2,11]. If more than one context resides on each processor, and context switch overhead is low, this idle time can be used by additional contexts. Typically each context corresponds to a process from one parallel program.

In this paper, we evaluate the utility of multiple contexts per processor for a directory-based cache coherent multiprocessor [1]. While the idea of using multiple hardware contexts per processor is itself not new, we believe our scheme is simpler to implement than other proposals [4,8,11,19,21] (discussed in Section 5). In

our scheme, each processor contains a small fixed number (2-4) of hardware contexts with independent register sets to enable short context switch times. We use a very simple context switch criterion, which is to switch contexts on a cache miss or on a write-hit to read-shared data.[1] This simple scheme helps keep context switch overhead low, because the decision to switch can be made in a single cycle.

Our multiple context scheme is evaluated using multiprocessor memory-reference traces obtained from three applications [13,16,20]. The results indicate that multiple contexts can achieve substantial gains in processor utilization. In some cases processor utilization is increased by 46% with two contexts and by 80% with four contexts.

The rest of the paper is organized as follows. The next section presents the architecture and simulator used in this study. We also introduce the applications and the method employed to gather the reference traces. Section 3 gives general results for the three applications. After that we present a number of issues concerning multiple contexts. This section also gives the results of our simulations. Finally, we have the related work, discussion and conclusion sections.

2 Architectural Assumptions and Simulation Environment

In this section, we discuss the architectural assumptions that we made and describe the simulation environment that we used to obtain our results. We also describe the applications used in this study and the performance metric employed to evaluate the multiple context scheme.

2.1 Base Architecture and Simulator

Figure 1 shows the basic architecture that we assume in this paper. The architecture consists of several nodes linked together by an interconnection network. Each node has a processor, a physical cache, and its share of the global memory with the cache directory. It is connected to the network through the network interface. The processors may have one or more contexts. The caches are kept consistent using a directory-based cache coherence protocol as discussed in [1]. We study the performance as a function of several parameters such as the number of contexts, the context switch overhead, and the latency of the network. Performance results as a function of the above parameters are given in Section 4.

---

[1]To prevent starvation and deadlocks, we also introduce a watchdog timer that forces a context switch when it expires.

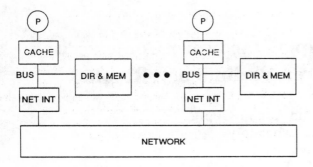

Figure 1: Architectural model.

We use a trace-driven simulator that emulates the above architecture to evaluate the effectiveness of multiple contexts. In the single context case, the simulator works as follows. Before starting the simulation, we first divide the interleaved reference stream generated by the tracing program into separate streams for individual processors. Then, one reference stream is assigned to each of the processors. At every simulated clock cycle, each active processor reads the next reference from its associated reference stream. This could be an ifetch, a read or a write reference. If the reference hits in the cache[2] the processor remains active and will issue another reference from the stream on the next clock tick. However, if it misses or a write to read-shared data occurs, it is marked idle. The cache sends a request over the network to fetch the missing line and/or update the state of the other caches in the system. During the period of time that the cache request is waiting to be satisfied, the processor remains in a suspended state and does not generate any more references.

In case of multiple contexts per processor, we have multiple memory reference streams associated with each processor — one for each context. At any given time only one of these contexts is active and the memory references come from that stream. However, when the active context enters the suspended state due to a cache miss or a write hit on read-shared data, a context switch occurs. The processor stays idle for the time required to perform the context switch. After that, memory references are issued from the newly activated context. If more than one context is ready when the active context blocks, a round-robin scheduling scheme decides which context is to be activated next.

The simulator that we use is quite detailed. It models the internal states of the caches, memory modules and directories, as well as contention for the local buses and interconnection network. It is possible to vary the delays associated with actions in each of the above modules. We use direct-mapped caches with line sizes of 16 bytes and an overall size of 64 Kbytes. We note that the interconnection network assumed in our simulations is a crossbar switch, but it could be any point-to-point network (e.g., grid [18], butterfly [3], omega [15]) depending on the number of processors we wished to interconnect. For the default parameters that we used (shown in Table 1), a remote read takes 26 cycles with no contention. If the processor and the memory are on the same node, no network transfer is required and the delay is only 18 cycles.

The simulator is driven by multiprocessor memory reference traces. Since the traces include 16 reference streams, we are limited to four processors if we wish to explore four contexts per processor. For runs with fewer than four contexts, only some of the reference streams were used. We model the scaling of the machine architecture to a larger number of processors by increasing the latency in

---

[2]For writes, the location has to be owned in addition to being present in the cache.

Table 1: Default Parameters for Simulator.

Operation	Time
miss detect, bus arbitration, dispatch message	7 cycles
network latency	4 cycles
directory lookup, memory read	5 cycles
bus arbitration, cache write	6 cycles

the underlying network (see Section 4.3). We also vary the context switch overhead and the number of contexts per processor. Section 4 presents the issues involved and the results obtained.

2.2 Traces and Applications

The multiprocessor traces used in our simulations were gathered on a VAX 8350, using a combined hardware/software scheme [5]. Basically, the tracing works as follows. We spawn as many processes as the application desires under the control of a master process. The master process then single steps the application processes in a round-robin manner. After each step, it records all references made by the application processes. For each reference, the number of the processor producing it, the address of the reference and its type (read/write/ifetch) are recorded. The traces that we use correspond to 16-processor runs.

The traces used were obtained from three applications: Locus-Route, MP3D and P-Thor. LocusRoute [16,17] is a standard cell global router. While the tasks spawned by it are quite coarse in granularity (each may execute around 100,000 instructions), its central data structure (a global cost array) is shared at a fine granularity. MP3D [13] is a 3-dimensional particle simulator that determines the shock waves generated by a body flying at high speed in the upper atmosphere. It uses distributed loops for parallelization (each loop executes around 250 instructions) and it is a typical example of parallel scientific code. P-Thor [20] is a parallel logic simulator that uses the Chandy-Misra distributed simulation algorithm. Each parallel subtask (a component evaluation) in P-Thor takes about 300 instructions to execute.

2.3 Performance Measure

The main figure of merit used in evaluating multiple contexts in this paper is *processor efficiency*. This is defined as the number of cycles spent doing useful work over the total number of cycles. Of course, the maximum is one reference per processor per cycle for 100% efficiency. The more time the processors spend idle, waiting for remote reads and writes, the lower the overall processor efficiency. In our simulations, we ran the system until one reference stream ran out of references, and then divided the total number of references by the elapsed time to get the efficiency.

3 General Results

In this section we present some general results obtained with the simulator. These results give an overall idea of the differences in behavior of the three applications. They also show the effect of increasing the network latency on the read and write latencies seen by the processors. The numbers are for a 4-processor system with one context per processor. The tables below give data about the run lengths and latencies for the three applications. Run length is defined as the number of simulator cycles between each cache miss.[3] Read and write latencies are the number of cycles required to satisfy the cache miss.

Results for network delays of 1 and 5 cycles are presented. A network delay of only one cycle is close to the minimum that can be achieved with any type of network. The network delay of five represents the latencies that might be expected in a larger multiprocessor.

Table 2: General application results with network delay of 1 cycle.

Application	Run Length	Read Ltncy	Write Ltncy
MP3D	16	32	42
P-Thor	50	25	55
LocusRoute	156	22	99

Table 3: General application results with network delay of 5 cycles.

Application	Run Length	Read Ltncy	Write Ltncy
MP3D	16	44	57
P-Thor	50	33	72
LocusRoute	154	29	128

MP3D has the shortest run-length and longest read latencies. There is a lot of global data traffic in MP3D and this leads to frequent misses, i.e., short run lengths. At the same time there is very little sharing of the global data. This leads to few invalidations per write and a low average write latency. LocusRoute, on the other hand, has very long run-lengths. The large size of the tasks and their relative independence allows for large portions of code that execute out of the cache without any misses. The read latencies are close to the minimum expected for this architecture. The shared data of LocusRoute is typically shared among many processes. This leads to a large number of invalidations per write and a large average write latency. P-Thor is somewhere in between the other two applications.

As the network delay increases, the read and write latencies grow as well. Writes are affected more because they frequently require extra network transactions for invalidations. As expected, run lengths are virtually unaffected by the increased network delay.

4 Issues and Results

We wish to explore several questions concerning the performance of multiple contexts:

- How many contexts are required to achieve good processor utilization?
- How does the context switch overhead affect the performance?
- What is the effect of increasing the network delay?
- What is the effect of cache interference?

- When should a context switch occur?
- How much does the performance vary with application?

This section explores all of these issues and presents results. We show graphs of processor efficiency. In each graph, we are plotting the processor efficiency against the network delay of the architecture. We show efficiencies for one, two and four contexts. Different context switch overheads are presented on different graphs. Figures 2–4 show results for MP3D, Figures 5–7 give results for P-Thor and Figures 8–10 show results for LocusRoute.

4.1 Number of Contexts

Depending on the single context processor efficiency, it may or may not be worthwhile to use two, four or more contexts. Note that the single-processor efficiency is basically a function of the cache miss rate and the read and write latency for the architecture. For LocusRoute (Figures 8–10) the processor efficiency is already close to 90% with a single context and little performance can be gained by adding more contexts. MP3D on the other hand (Figure 2), has single context performance near 38% and achieves substantial gains with more contexts (efficiency is 54% with 2, 65% with 4).

As expected, the graphs show diminishing marginal returns as the number of contexts is increased (see Figure 5 for example). In every case going from one to two contexts yields a greater benefit than going from two to four contexts. A small number of contexts is also preferable because it allows for simpler hardware. With a larger number of contexts, a penalty in the cycle time of the processor or an increase in context switch overhead may be inevitable. Also, a large number of contexts requires a large number of processes. Many applications may not be able to support such a large number of processes.

We note that if the context switch overhead is high, we actually lose performance by adding more contexts (see Figure 10). This is due to cache interference (see Section 4.4 below). With more contexts, the cache miss rate is increased. The cost of these misses cannot be hidden very well when the context switch overhead is high. Each context switch keeps the processor idle and so utilization drops.

4.2 Context Switch Overhead

The context switch overhead depends on the number of contexts kept in hardware, the amount of state kept for each context, and the amount of hardware dedicated to context switching. We explore context switch overheads of 1, 4 and 16 cycles. A single cycle overhead can be achieved by keeping multiple copies of the pipeline registers and being able to swap in the whole state in a single cycle. [4] If the pipeline has to be drained and filled, a 4-cycle overhead is reasonable. Both of these options require multiple register banks, one for each context. If we want to load and store the registers to some fast local memory, we have to allow at least 16 cycles. It is clear that the hardware is more complex if we require the context switch to be faster. Of course, beyond some overhead value, multiple contexts do not help any more, since a long latency operation will complete before the context switch is accomplished.

As expected, the results show that the effect of increasing the context switch overhead reduces the benefit achieved by having multiple contexts. Note that the single context graph line is identical for various context switch overheads (see Figures 2–4 for example), since there is no context switching in that case. When the

---

[3]Both here and in the rest of the paper, by *cache miss* we actually mean references that can not be satisfied by the cache alone and need to access the memory, or the network, or both. These include regular cache misses but also write-hits to read-shared data. In the latter case, the network needs to be accessed to invalidate that location from other caches and to gain ownership of that cache line.

[4]Alternatively multiplexors could be used to switch between multiple pipeline state copies.

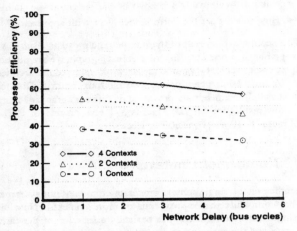

Figure 2: MP3D: Context Switch Overhead 1 Cycle.

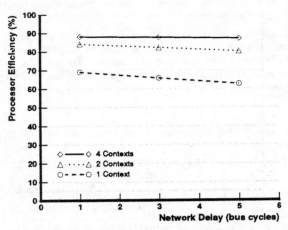

Figure 5: P-Thor: Context Switch Overhead 1 Cycle.

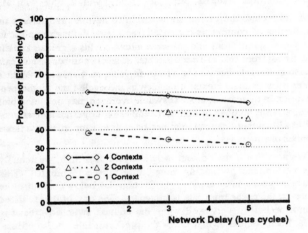

Figure 3: MP3D: Context Switch Overhead 4 Cycles.

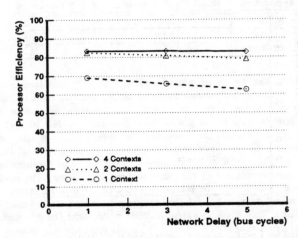

Figure 6: P-Thor: Context Switch Overhead 4 Cycles.

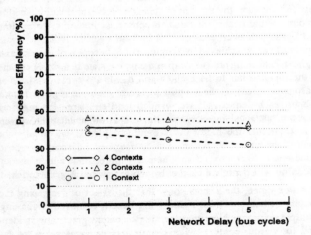

Figure 4: MP3D: Context Switch Overhead 16 Cycles.

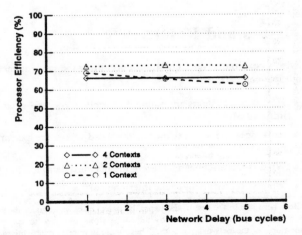

Figure 7: P-Thor: Context Switch Overhead 16 Cycles.

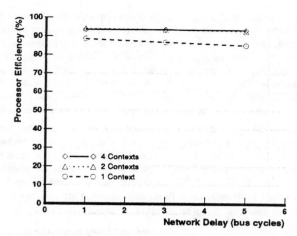

Figure 8: LocusRoute: Context Switch Overhead 1 Cycle.

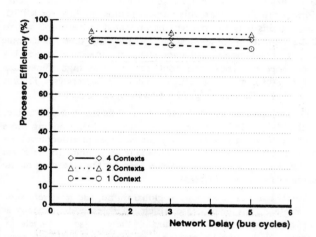

Figure 9: LocusRoute: Context Switch Overhead 4 Cycles.

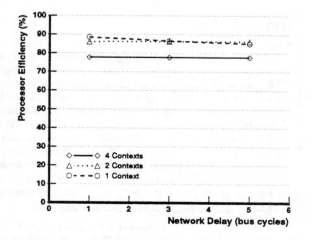

Figure 10: LocusRoute: Context Switch Overhead 16 Cycles.

context switch overhead is 16, none of the programs are gaining much processor efficiency with increased contexts. MP3D gains only 8% in efficiency with 4 contexts (Figure 4), while P-Thor loses 4% (Figure 7) and LocusRoute loses a full 12% (Figure 10). For multiple contexts to be useful, the context switch overhead will have to be kept low, preferably on the order of a few cycles.

4.3 Latency

The amount of latency incurred in remote operations is important for the effectiveness of processors with multiple contexts. With very low latencies, context switch overhead may be too large to allow multiple contexts to achieve any performance gain. As the latency increases, the single context processors do increasingly poorly because more and more processor time is spent idle. This is where multiple contexts can help. As seen in Figures 5–7, the relative value of multiple contexts increases as the latency increases. In other words, a processor with multiple contexts will suffer less efficiency degradation due to high latencies than a single context processor.

One reason for varying network latency in our evaluation of multiple contexts is to explore different types of architectures. A grid network, for example, is expected to have a much larger latency than a crossbar switch. At the same time the higher latencies can correspond to larger multiprocessors. As more processors are added to a parallel machine, the latencies increase due to deeper networks or more complex switches. Larger latencies present a greater opportunity for multiple contexts, because the single context efficiency is lower. At the same time we note that it is still possible to achieve very high efficiencies with just a few contexts. With a network delay of 5 cycles the processor efficiencies are still fairly high (56% for MP3D, 87% for P-Thor and 93% for LocusRoute). The point is that even as multiprocessors grow and latencies increase, processors with just a few contexts achieve good utilization.

4.4 Cache Interference

With several contexts working out of a single cache, there is potential for cache interference. This can be both positive or negative. Positive interference happens when one context serves to load the cache with code or data that is also needed by another context. It is performing a limited pre-fetch for the other context, and cache miss rates are lowered. On the other hand, the information cached by one context can knock out data needed by another context. This is negative interference and leads to a higher miss rate.

In all three of the applications used in this study, negative interference dominates over positive interference. In LocusRoute, the average cache miss rate increases from 0.55% to 1.22% as we go from one to four contexts with a 64 Kbyte cache. In P-Thor it increases from 1.6% to 2.2% and in MP3D it goes from 3.5% to 4.2%. The increased miss ratio is also reflected in decreased run-lengths (see Table 4).

Table 4: Effect of Cache Interference on Run Lengths.

Application	1 Context	2 Contexts	4 Contexts
MP3D	16	17	16
P-Thor	50	49	41
LocusRoute	156	75	56

Figures 11 and 12 show the effect of varying the cache size on processor performance. We do not present a graph for LocusRoute because the processor efficiencies are already very high and changing the cache size has little effect. We give results for 4-context processors and single context processors. For each one we use caches of 16 Kbyte, 64 Kbyte and 256 Kbyte size. Recall that the default cache size for all previous results was 64 Kbyte. For MP3D, the interference effect is drowned out by large miss rates due to frequent access of global shared data. This keeps efficiencies low overall, and the effect of varying the cache size is small (see Figure 11). For P-Thor, we see that the performance for four contexts degrades markedly as we move from a 64 Kbyte cache to a 16 Kbyte cache (Figure 12). This is because the smaller cache results in significantly larger interference. While the cache miss rate goes from 1.6% to 2.2% in the 64 Kbyte cache, it goes from 2.6% to 7.5% in the 16 Kbyte cache as we go from one to four contexts.

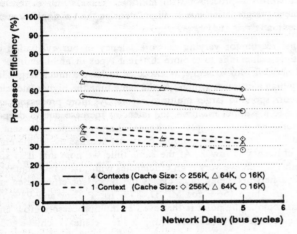

Figure 11: MP3D: Effect of Cache Size.

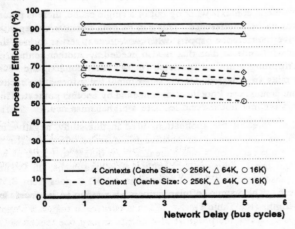

Figure 12: P-Thor: Effect of Cache Size.

4.5 When to Switch Contexts

Ideally, one would like to switch contexts whenever the context switch overhead is less than the latency of the operation being performed. Of course external operations may take longer or shorter depending on the congestion in the machine, and there is no easy way to predict how long a given operation will take. We thus choose the easiest context switch criterion: switch on any operation that requires a main memory access, either in the same node or remotely. Switching only on *remote* operations requires extra hardware, but is a feasible alternative if context switch overhead is relatively high. If a context switch takes 16 cycles, and local operations also take on the order of 16 cycles to complete, it does not make sense to initiate a context switch on every local operation.

Two of the applications had frequent memory accesses, but LocusRoute processes had long streaks of executing out of the cache. In order to prevent one context from hogging a particular processor we introduce a watchdog counter that pre-empts the current context after 1000 cycles.[5] This ensures that no context runs for longer than 1000 cycles at a time, thus allowing all contexts on a particular processor to make progress.

4.6 Applications

The three applications exhibited very different behavior. LocusRoute and P-Thor have relatively little global traffic, whereas MP3D has a lot. While 1.8% of LocusRoute instructions cause references to shared data, this number is close to 12% for MP3D. This explains why the run-lengths presented in Section 3 are so different for the three applications. At the same time LocusRoute has very good caching behavior and very little interference between processes. Thus LocusRoute achieves very high efficiencies (around 88%), even with single context processors (see Figures 8–10). Very little can be gained by adding extra contexts.

P-Thor achieves 60-70% utilization with single contexts (see Figures 5–7). This can be boosted effectively by adding more contexts. Not only is efficiency increased as more contexts are added, but the processors also become more immune to the effect of high latency operations. This is seen by the spreading of the curves as the latency increases.

MP3D has a large amount of global traffic, and relatively short run lengths. Thus the processor efficiency increases dramatically as more contexts are added. Unfortunately there is also more cache interference with several contexts per processor and this limits some of the gains, especially as misses become more expensive due to increased network delay. So in effect the increased resilience to network delay is cancelled by the increased cost of cache interference (see Figures 2–4).

5 Related Work

The idea of multiple hardware contexts per processor in itself is not new. In this section we discuss how our approach differs from earlier proposals and present some advantages and disadvantages. We begin with the Alto personal computer from Xerox [21] which provided multiple hardware microcode-level contexts, allowing the CPU to be shared between the instruction set interpreter and the I/O devices. The contexts were statically assigned to devices and were not available to general user processes. The aim of the multiple contexts was to make the power of the processor readily available for time critical I/O processing, a task that is frequently delegated to separate processors in more recent designs. The main motivation was not to hide memory latency from a very fast processor.

The HEP multiprocessor from Denelcor [19] also provided multiple hardware contexts per processor. Unlike the Alto, the contexts were available to arbitrary user processes. The processes shared a

---

[5]The counter value of 1000 was picked arbitrarily. The only constraint is that this value should be much larger than the context switch overhead.

large set of registers and on each cycle an instruction from a different process was executed. A minimum of 8 *active* processes (those processes that are not waiting for a memory reference to complete) were needed to keep the execution pipeline full. The HEP machine tolerated memory latency well, but its main drawback was that a single process could get at most 1/8 of the pipelined processor. In order to keep the pipeline full, a large number of processes were needed. This is in stark contrast to modern pipelined processors [6,14] where a single process almost fully utilizes the pipelined processor. Now the HEP scheme would not be a problem if all applications could be split into an arbitrarily large number of processes. However, this is often not possible in practice as there may not be enough intrinsic parallelism in the application [7], or because doing so greatly increases the amount of overhead.

More recently, Iannucci [11] has proposed using multiple contexts for his hybrid data-flow/von Neumann machine. Each processor consists of a hardware queue of enabled *continuations*. The continuations are very small in size (containing just the program counter and the frame base-register), and the hardware can switch between them in a single cycle. However, to make this single cycle switch possible, processor registers are not saved on a context switch. Consequently, the software is structured so that it does not rely on registers being valid between potential context switch points. The switch points are synchronizing references, where a read to a location tagged *empty* results in that continuation being suspended. In our view, the disadvantages of Iannucci's approach are the following. First, processes can not make full use of the register sets, given that the run-lengths (the number of instructions executed between switch points) are very small [11] and registers are not preserved in between. We believe that extensive use of registers is absolutely critical to the performance of modern processors [6]. Second, a processor that supports a large number of continuations (contexts) in hardware, keeps track of which ones are enabled and uses a complex criterion for deciding which continuation to issue the next instruction from [12], is very complicated. We believe such a processor will have a significantly more complex pipeline and much larger area than a simple RISC processor. Consequently, the cycle time of such a machine would be slower than that of modern RISC processors. Thus the hybrid machine has to make up the large factor that it loses over conventional microprocessors, before it becomes competitive. On the other hand, the scheme that we propose does not lose anything over modern RISC processors. In fact, it is possible to take multiple commercially available RISC processor chips (e.g., Motorola 88000 processor and cache chips) and connect them so as to simulate multiple contexts.

We now consider the MASA architecture proposed by Bert Halstead [8]. In this architecture each processor has a fixed number of hardware *task frames*. Each task frame is capable of storing a complete process context and consists of a set of auxiliary registers (like the program counter) and a set of general purpose registers. Since the number of processes may exceed the number of task frames, the process contexts are allowed to overflow into memory.[6] On each cycle, a context in the *enabled* or *ready* state may issue an instruction. However, once a process issues an instruction, it can not issue another instruction until the previous instruction has completed. Thus, in its current form, a process on MASA can get only 1/4 (inverse of pipeline depth) of the pipelined processor's performance. As discussed above for HEP, this is a major drawback. Halstead and group recognize it [8] and are exploring ways to remove this restriction.

We now discuss a more subtle but fundamental difference between the Iannucci and Halstead schemes and our scheme. In our scheme, the sole purpose of the multiple hardware contexts is to

mitigate the negative effects of memory latency. The number of hardware contexts needed for a particular machine is fixed and depends mainly on the expected cache hit ratio and the memory latency for that architecture. In the Iannucci and Halstead schemes, the context mechanism is instead made to serve two purposes at the same time. It is used to mask memory latency as in our scheme, but it is also used as a hardware task queue. Thus when a parallel subtask is created, it manifests itself as a new context that is then managed and scheduled by the hardware. Since the number of parallel subtasks can be arbitrarily large, mechanisms are needed and provided to handle overflow of contexts. Also, the number of contexts that are needed is large. In our scheme, the issue of subtask management is completely separated and is handled in software. This permits great flexibility, including the possibility to schedule tasks in a manner similar to the Iannucci and Halstead proposals, if a particular application so warrants.[7] Thus instead of using full/empty bits and hardware queuing in I-structure memory [10], we may simulate full/empty bits in software and switch to a different subtask if a piece of data is not ready. It is not obvious which scheme works better. We will be able to tell only by more in-depth analysis and/or prototyping.

6 Discussion

This section contains the discussion of several topics that relate to the evaluation of multiple contexts as presented in this paper.

One question that we must ask is, what are the real advantages of having multiple contexts? Since processors are cheap, why not simply have a larger number of processors in the multiprocessor? The fallacy in this argument is that, while CPU chips (e.g., MC68030 chips) are relatively cheap, a fast processor is not — a fast processor nowadays has a large amount of cache built out of expensive and fast SRAMs; in addition, there are expensive functional units such as floating point ALUs. Furthermore, each new processor needs an extra port to the network, or to the bus that it is placed on. The extra port increases the depth of the network, or the loading on the bus, thus increasing the latency. Several contexts per processor can share these expensive resources, thus making more efficient use of them.

Another question that arises is how the multiple contexts should be implemented. The options are to implement multiple contexts on the same chip, or to use multiple chips. In the case where the size of each processing node is small, on the order of a few chips [9], we need to have several contexts on a single chip using duplicated register sets. However, having to design a special processor for a given architecture makes that architecture less practical. So for larger processing nodes, for example where each processor occupies a whole board, it may be quite feasible to use separate processor chips for the different contexts. While simplifying the hardware design effort, this approach duplicates not just the register set but all of the data path and control as well.[8]

There are also some software issues that need to be resolved. In particular, how do you choose which processes to put on a single processor? Since the progress of contexts on any one processor is mutually exclusive, the correct placement of processes on processors may be important [22]. If a given program section requires several contexts to be active in order to make progress, it is best to place these on separate processors.

---

[6] Such overflow and underflow operations are quite expensive, and care must be taken to minimize them.

[7] We would normally expect there to be some sort of a distributed task queue to handle the scheduling of subtasks.

[8] An alternative to this scheme which uses multiple CPU chips for contexts is to let all these chips be active all the time, sharing and stalling on the cache as they proceed. We have, as yet, not done any performance evaluation for such a scheme.

7 Conclusions

In scalable multiprocessor architectures, processors with a small fixed number of contexts can achieve substantially greater efficiencies than single context processors. In some cases efficiencies increased 46% with two contexts and 80% with four contexts. Best improvements were found when: (i) the architecture had large read and write latencies; (ii) the context switch overhead was low; and (iii) the cache interference due to multiple contexts was small. High latency operations are to be expected in large-scale multiprocessors. Low context switch overheads can be achieved by having a small fixed number of contexts in hardware and by using a simple switch criterion: the cache miss. Cache interference is really a function of the parallel application. However, it can be kept low by having large caches.

One important difference between our context switch scheme and those proposed in [8,11,19] is that in our scheme the context switch mechanism is separated from the subtask management mechanism. This makes for simpler and faster hardware and allows greater flexibility and application-dependent performance tuning.

We are currently doing more in-depth evaluation of our multiple context scheme and looking further into the details of the implementation.

8 Acknowledgements

We would like to thank Truman Joe and Rich Simoni for allowing us to use the simulators for gathering the data for this paper. We also wish to thank Richard Sites at Digital Equipment Corporation, Hudson MA, for supporting Wolf-Dietrich Weber. Anoop Gupta is supported by DARPA contract N00014-87-K-0828 and by a faculty award from Digital Equipment Corporation. Thanks also to Helen Davis, Margaret Martonosi, Jonathan Rose, Rich Simoni, Larry Soule and Mike Smith for reviewing early versions of this paper.

References

[1] Anant Agarwal, Richard Simoni, John Hennessy, and Mark Horowitz. An Evaluation of Directory Schemes for Cache Coherence. In *15th International Symposium on Computer Architecture*, 1988.

[2] Arvind and R. A. Iannucci. A Critique of Multiprocessing von Neumann Style. In *10th International Symposium on Computer Architecture*, pages 426–436, 1983.

[3] W. Crowther, J. Goodhue, E. Starr, R. Thomas, W. Milliken, and T. Blackadar. Performance Measurements on a 128-node Butterfly Parallel Processor. In *Intl. Conf. on Parallel Processing*, pages 531–540, 1985.

[4] William J. Dally et al. Architecture of a Message-Driven Processor. *The 14th Annual International Symposium on Computer Architecture*, pages 189–196, June 1987.

[5] Stephen R. Goldschmidt. Simulating Multiprocessor Memory Traces. EE390 Report, Stanford University, December 1987.

[6] T. Gross, J. Hennessy, S. Przybylski, and C. Rowen. Measurement and Evaluation of the MIPS Architecture and Processor. *ACM TOCS*, 6, August 1988.

[7] Anoop Gupta et al. Parallel Implementation of OPS5 on the Encore Multiprocessor: Results and Analysis. *International Journal of Parallel Programming*, 17, 1988.

[8] R. H. Halstead and T. Fujita. MASA: A Multithreaded Processor Architecture for Parallel Symbolic Computing. In *15th International Symposium on Computer Architecture*, pages 443–451, 1988.

[9] J. P. Hayes et al. A Microprocessor Based Hybrid Supercomputer. *IEEE Micro*, 6, October 1986.

[10] S. K. Heller. An I-Structure Memory Controller (ISMC). Technical report, Massachusetts Institute of Technology, June 1983.

[11] R. A. Iannucci. Toward a Dataflow / von Neumann Hybrid Architecture. In *15th International Symposium on Computer Architecture*, pages 131–140, 1988.

[12] Robert A. Iannucci. *A Dataflow / von Neumann Hybrid Architecture*. PhD thesis, Massachusetts Institute of Technology, 1988.

[13] Jeffrey D. McDonald and Donald Baganoff. Vectorization of a Particle Simulation Method for Hypersonic Rarified Flow. In *AIAA Thermodynamics, Plasmadynamics and Lasers Conference*, June 1988.

[14] D. Patterson. Reduced Instruction Set Computers. *Comm. ACM*, 28, January 1985.

[15] G.F. Pfister, W.C. Brantley, et al. The IBM Research Parallel Processor Prototype (RP3): Introduction and Architecture. In *International Conference on Parallel Processing*. IEEE, 1985.

[16] Jonathan Rose. LocusRoute: A Parallel Global Router for Standard Cells. In *Design Automation Conference*, pages 189–195, June 1988.

[17] Jonathan Rose. The Parallel Decomposition and Implementation of an Integrated Circuit Global Router. In *Proc ACM SIGPLAN PPEALS*, pages 138–145, July 1988.

[18] Charles L. Seitz, William C. Athas, Charles M. Flaig, Alain J. Martin, Jakov Seizovic, Craig S. Steele, and Wen-King Su. The Architecture and Programming of the Ametek Series 2010 Multicomputer. In *Hypercube Concurrent Computers and Applications*, 1988.

[19] B. J. Smith. Architecture and applications of the HEP multiprocessor computer system. In *SPIE*, volume 298, pages 241–248, 1981.

[20] Larry Soule and Anoop Gupta. Characterization of Parallelism and Deadlocks in Distributed Digital Logic Simulation. In *26th Design Automation Conference*, June 1989.

[21] C. P. Thacker, E. M. McCreight, et al. Alto: A Personal Computer. In C. Gordon Bell Daniel P. Siewiorek and Allen Newell, editors, *Computer Structures: Principles and Examples*, pages 549–572. McGraw-Hill, 1982.

[22] Andrew Tucker and Anoop Gupta. Process Control and Scheduling Issues for Multiprogrammed Shared-Memory Multiprocessors. submitted for publication, March 1989.

Architectural and Organizational Tradeoffs in the Design of the MultiTitan CPU

Norman P. Jouppi

Digital Equipment Corporation Western Research Lab

100 Hamilton Ave., Palo Alto, CA 94301

Abstract

This paper describes the architectural and organizational tradeoffs made during the design of the MultiTitan, and provides data supporting the decisions made. These decisions covered the entire space of processor design, from the instruction set and virtual memory architecture through the pipeline and organization of the machine. In particular, some of the tradeoffs involved the use of an on-chip instruction cache with off-chip TLB and floating-point unit, the use of direct-mapped instead of associative caches, the use of a 64-bit vs. 32-bit data bus, and the implementation of hardware pipeline interlocks.

1. Introduction

The MultiTitan is a high-performance general-purpose 32-bit microprocessor developed at Digital Equipment Corporation's Western Research Lab (DECWRL). Each processor consists of three custom chips: the CPU, floating point coprocessor (FPU), and external cache controller (CCU). The CPU has been implemented in a 1.5u CMOS technology with 179,390 transistors and runs with a 40ns cycle time [6]. In this paper we will discuss architectural and organizational tradeoffs made in the design of the system.

Each processor of MultiTitan is similar in some respects to the DECWRL Titan [10]. The Titan was built from 100K ECL MSI parts, and was developed at the lab from 1982 to 1986. Like the ECL Titan, the MultiTitan is a very simple RISC machine with a branch delay of one. However, the MultiTitan is not object-code-compatible with the ECL Titan. Unlike the ECL Titan, the MultiTitan has hardware support for fine-grain parallel processing, unified vector/scalar floating point registers and operations, and a different pipeline and method for handling exceptions. Figure 1-1 is an overview of one MultiTitan processor.

The MultiTitan instruction set is very simple and has a regular encoding. The machine has a 4-stage pipeline: instruction fetch (IF), execute (EX), memory access (MEM), and write back (WB). The resources and timing of the pipeline are shown in Figure 1-2. The primary principle followed in the design of the the machine is:

Sustained performance must be maximized while the ratio of peak performance to sustained performance must be minimized. This is best accomplished by minimizing the latency of all operations as much as possible within a simple and regular framework.

Obviously sustained performance must be maximized, because that is what is delivered to the user. Peak performance should be minimized, since

Peak performance is meaningless except as an indicator of machine cost.

In other words, high peak performance requires high hardware cost. Thus to utilize the hardware most efficiently, the ratio of sustained performance to peak performance must be as close to 1 as possible.

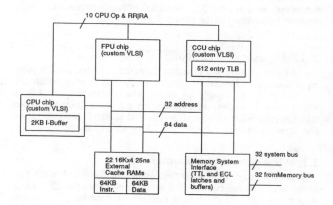

Figure 1-1: One MultiTitan processor

In general, the lowest possible latency provides the best possible performance. The latency of an operation is the time from its initiation until its completion. In contrast, bandwidth corresponds to the peak rate at which operations may be issued or retired but says nothing about how long each operation takes. Bandwidth is quoted when peak MFLOPS or the clock frequency of a microprocessor is given. By heavily pipelining a machine, the bandwidth of the pipeline is increased, but the latency of operations when measured in cycles is also increased. Latency is important because instruction-level parallelism is limited and data dependencies exist between instructions. If a large bandwidth is provided at high latency, data dependencies and limited parallelism will force the machine to stall waiting for the results of operations.

Finally, the latency must be minimized within a simple and regular framework. If the machine is made complex and irregular, the global machine control and overall machine organization can be adversely affected. This can slow down the basic cycle time or other operations in the machine, outweighing the result of the original speedup.

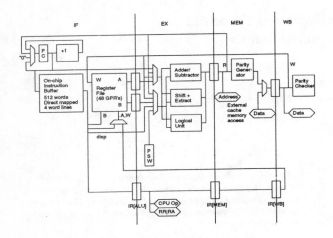

Figure 1-2: CPU pipeline and machine organization

This paper follows the structure of the MultiTitan pipeline. Section 2 discusses issues related to the IF pipestage such as the large on-chip instruction cache and hardware interlocks. The implementation of integer multiply and divide by the coprocessor and the use of a single adder in the CPU are discussed with other EX pipestage issues in Section 3. MEM pipestage issues such as the TLB and cache organization are the subject of Section 4. Issues involving the WB pipestage are presented in Section 5. Section 6 summarizes the major tradeoffs presented in the paper.

2. IF Pipestage Tradeoffs

In this section we describe how the primary design principle was applied to the IF pipestage. Excess latency before the execute stage is visible in stalls when branches are taken. Since about 1 in every 15 instructions are taken branches in our benchmarks, each extra cycle required to fetch an instruction can slow the machine down by 1/15, or about 7%.

2.1. What should be put on-chip?

At the level of integration available for the MultiTitan, several options are possible for what to place on the CPU chip. Along with the datapath and instruction decode, other recent machines have placed either the TLB on-chip [8, 11], the floating-point unit on-chip [3, 12], or an instruction cache on-chip [1, 5]. The choice of what to put on-chip in the MultiTitan was based on minimizing the average latency. The average latency of a particular operation must be weighted by the frequency of execution of that operation to obtain its effect on the overall machine performance. For example, in a RISC machine running at one cycle per instruction, an instruction must be fetched every cycle. Loads and stores usually account for around 30% of all instructions. Floating-point operations rarely account for more than 25% of all operations even in numeric applications.

If the instruction cache is placed on-chip and is a virtual instruction cache, then instruction accesses do not require address translation on a hit. Then the most frequent operation (instruction fetch every cycle) is on-chip, and the less frequent operations (load or store and their associated address translation) incur the increased latency of going off-chip. If a separate FPU chip has its own set of registers, then loads and stores to the FPU chip can take place directly from the data cache, with the same latency as an FPU on the CPU chip. Only when transfers between the floating-point registers and CPU registers are required is additional latency incurred. Luckily, transfers between CPU and FPU registers are rare, occurring only for conversions between integer and floating-point values and implicitly or explicitly when branches must be made on the result of floating-point compares. Our simulations showed transfers between CPU and FPU register sets or vice versa to be less than 3% of the instructions executed on the Livermore Loops (1-12), Whetstones, and other floating-point intensive benchmarks.

Of course this level of analysis is an oversimplification. Second-order effects, such as whether the instruction cache can be made large enough to have a good hit rate (and hence a low average latency) often dominate. Also, care must be taken to count additional latency only when it really affects the machine, such as counting instruction-fetch latency only during branches. Similar questions must be raised for the other possibilities as well. For example, could an on-chip TLB be made large enough to have a low average latency (i.e., high hit rate)? Similarly, would an on-chip FPU have enough transistors available to exploit potential parallelism in floating-point operations, such as a full multiplier array instead of an n-bit at a time algorithm?

Next the simplicity and regularity of the system must be considered. For example, if the TLB is put on-chip, will an off-chip backup TLB still be necessary? If so, then the on-chip TLB does not reduce the parts count on the board. If the instruction cache is on-chip, this will reduce the I/O requirements of the chip. If the instruction cache and data cache are both off-chip, then the data and address busses will either have to be time multiplexed (which is likely to add latency and impose an upper bound on performance), or separate busses must be provided (which implies a very high pin count). The signal integrity of high pin count packages is worse than that of low pincount packages, which further increases the latency of going off-chip. If the instruction cache is placed on-chip, and the external cache is a mixed cache, then an entire set of cache RAMs chips can be eliminated over the case where both the instruction and data caches are off-chip and are accessed with time-multiplexed busses. Finally, care must be taken not to add all sorts of mechanisms (e.g., branch target buffers) to decrease latency without verifying that they don't increase the latency of global control or other operations more than they have saved.

In the case of the MultiTitan, the chip area we had available was enough to build a TLB with a reasonable hit rate. However, this area was not enough for very high performance floating-point support. We decided to put the instruction cache on-chip instead of the TLB primarily to reduce chip pin I/O bandwidth requirements. By also reducing the requirement for two independent external caches to a single external cache, putting the instruction cache on chip eliminated more parts from the board than moving a TLB from a custom CCU chip on-chip or by eliminating the custom FPU chip. Thus, for the MultiTitan, we found that placing the instruction cache on the CPU chip would have a better effect on performance and simplify the system more than placing anything else on-chip.

2.2. Organization of the Instruction Cache

The decision to put an instruction cache on-chip is based on its hit rate which depends on its size and organization, so these decisions must be made concurrently. But given that an instruction cache was the best thing to put on-chip, what is the best organization of the cache? This was decided according to the primary design principle. In other words, we want to minimize the average instruction fetch latency. This is given by the sum of its hit latency and its miss latency times its miss rate (i.e., Equation 1).

$$\tau_{average} = \tau_{hit} + \rho_{miss} * \tau_{miss} \tag{1}$$

There are many contributors to latency in an instruction cache access. Three of these are extensively discussed in the literature: the hit rate, the cache line refill time, and the access time of the cache memory arrays. The hit rate of the cache itself depends on the overall size as well as the line size. The overall size of the cache was fixed by the space available on the die to 2K bytes. If the cache was made larger than this not only would the die size become prohibitively large, but the access time of a memory array twice as large is also longer than that of the smaller array. The line size is an important factor in determining the miss rate of an instruction cache. Since taken branches are about 1 in every 15 instructions, if we have just branched to a location the chances are very good that we will execute at least the next four instructions. Therefore, making the instruction cache refill fewer than 4 words on a miss is a bad idea since the machine will execute more instructions than that in a row on average. For example, a machine that fetched only one word on a miss would have four cache misses to execute 4 consecutive instructions, while a machine that fetched back four words on a miss would have only one or at most two misses. Although for a 2K byte cache an 8-word line would provide a better hit rate than a 4-word line, in the MultiTitan we chose a line size of four words. This brings up another observation:

Real caches are determined by the RAM sizes available and the system context and are intentionally non-optimal from the viewpoint of simulation studies.

In particular, three aspects of the MultiTitan system dictated the decision for a four-word line. First, the MultiTitan was targeted to run on the Titan memory and I/O system, and the Titan memory system returns four words on all accesses. If the off-chip mixed cache had a four-word line to match the memory system, then it would also be simpler and more regular for the on-chip cache to have a four-word line as well. Second, if the off-chip cache had an access time of one cycle, then the time lost on a miss to get the required instruction would be 2 cycles (IF fails from miss, fetch instruction, and IF succeeds). During this time 4 words could be fetched over a 64-bit data bus. Third, based on the aspect ratio of the available on-chip space and the RAM cell itself, 160 cells could be easily driven on one word line. This corresponds to four words plus a tag.

The cache associativity also affects latency. For example, by increasing the associativity the average access latency may be reduced a few percent due to a higher hit rate. However, a much more important effect is present in a direct mapped cache (see case *b* of Figure 2-1). In a direct-mapped cache where the data and tag stores are made of the same memory, the data is available at the same time as the tag. In many cases the tag comparison is a significant fraction of the cache access time. In a direct-mapped cache the processor can start using the data before hit or miss is computed. This reduces the latency of the cache access in the case of a hit to that of the RAM access time. In an associative organization (see case *a* in Figure 2-1), the machine does not know which data to use until the tag comparison and the multiplex between the sets is complete. The reduced latency provided by the direct-mapped cache organization far outweighs the small increase in average latency from its lower hit rate for the cache size of interest.

Another common organization of caches is a set of buffers with a set of corresponding associative tags, as in the CRAY-1 [2] or MIPS-X [1] (see case *c* and *d* of Figure 2-1 respectively). These organizations are just extreme cases of caches with very long lines and associativity equal to the number of lines in the cache. There are two cases to consider for this organization. These two cases differ based on the relationship between the buffer size and the size of the basic RAM building block used to construct the buffer. If the size of each buffer is greater than or equal to the basic building block used to build the buffer (e.g., 16-entry buffers made from 16x4 bit RAMs as in the case in the CRAY-1), the different buffers may be indexed immediately in parallel based on the low order bits

of the instruction address. This is because each chip stores data from at most one buffer, and all of the chips can be cycled in parallel. The tag comparison is also performed at the same time and can set up the multiplexors while the buffer access is still in progress. This method gives an access time for hits that is not much larger than that of the memory building block. However, the total number of tags available is limited to the total cache size divided by the size of each buffer. This limit on the number of tags (e.g., 4 in the CRAY-1) can have a significant negative impact on the hit rate. For example, three small code fragments that each cross a buffer address boundary would require two buffers each, for a total of six tags. In situations like this thrashing would result between the code fragments, and each of the large buffers would be poorly utilized. To circumvent this problem, the number of tags can be increased beyond the number of memory building blocks. Hence, data from several buffers will be stored in each RAM block. This was done in MIPS-X, where the cache is organized as 32 buffers of 16 words each. However, since the RAM itself only accesses four words in parallel, the tag comparison must be performed in order to generate the address of the block within the RAM to be accessed. This puts the tag comparison in series with the RAM access, and yields a latency about equal to that of the conventional associative case for a hit.

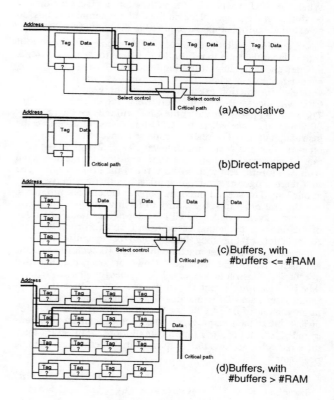

Figure 2-1: Effective latency of cache organizations

In summary, we have discussed four basic ways to organize a cache. Two methods put the latency of a tag comparison in series with the RAM access, while two put the tag comparison in parallel with the RAM access. Of the two parallel methods, one has a poorer hit rate than the other due to the limited number of tags available. For this reason, we chose a direct-mapped organization (method *b*) in the MultiTitan because its average latency is the lowest.

2.3. 64-bit Data Busses

As was mentioned in the previous section, the MultiTitan has a 64-bit data bus. This improves the performance of both double-precision floating-point benchmarks and machine performance during instruction cache misses. The costs and benefits of a 64-bit data bus for instruction cache refill will be quantified in this section.

The cost of a single 64-bit data bus and a 32-bit address bus shared by instructions and data is fairly low. It requires only 50% more pins than a 32-bit address and 32-bit data bus shared by instructions and data, and 25% fewer pins than separate 32-bit address and 32-bit data busses for both instruction and data references. The MultiTitan CPU is in a package with 140 signal pins and 36 power pins. Not all pins on the package are used since the die size is limited by the required perimeter of the bonding pads. The data bus also has byte parity, so together with the address bus they account for 102 of the 136 pins used. The remaining 34 pins are easily sufficient to handle all other I/O requirements of the chip.

Another cost of extra pins is increased power supply noise from simultaneously driving large numbers of outputs. In the case of the CPU chip, however, at most 32 outputs are driven at a time. (The CPU does not perform double-word stores.) When the CPU executes a store instruction, it places the data to be stored on the proper place on the 64-bit external data bus, so no external multiplexors are required in the path of the data.

Combined with the external 1-cycle cache, the 64-bit refill path reduces the time to refill a 16-byte line to 2 cycles. To get a better understanding of the implications of a two-cycle miss, consider the case where the CPU executes straight-line code with each instruction executed once and only once. Then the CPU will incur a 2-cycle miss on every line of code executed. The resulting performance of the CPU will only be degraded by 50% over the case where the CPU hits on every access to the instruction cache. For realistic code sequences that do not miss on every line, the cost is much lower. Table 2-1 gives the miss rate of six programs, and the time required to execute them with 32-bit refill and with 64-bit refill of the 16-byte line. The first three programs are large applications that are in use daily at our lab. The second three are popular benchmark programs. For the real programs, the ability to fetch instructions at a rate of two per cycle reduces the CPI (cycles per instruction) burden of the on-chip instruction cache from 0.168 CPI to 0.084 CPI. A reduction of this magnitude would be insignificant for a complex-instruction-set machine that took 10 cycles to execute an instruction on the average. However, on a machine that executes an instruction every 1.25 cycles on the average, a 0.084 CPI improvement is fairly important. Since the maximum issue rate of the machine is 1 instruction per cycle, an improvement of 0.084 CPI is a reduction of the stall cycles by 30%. Unlike the real programs, the three benchmark programs spend almost all of their time in small loops. This gives them miss rates that are two orders of magnitude better than the real programs.

benchmark	miss rate	Refill CPI burden 64-bit	Refill CPI burden 32-bit
ccom	5.4%	.108	.216
PCBroute	5.1%	.103	.206
TimingVerify	2.1%	.042	.083
real programs	4.2%	.084	.168
Linpack	0.03%	.0006	.0012
Livermore	0.05%	.0009	.0019
Stanford	0.01%	.0002	.0003
benchmark avg.	0.03%	.0006	.0011

Table 2-1: Performance improvement with 64-bit refill

One other possibility for reducing the CPI burden of instruction cache misses is a prefetch mechanism. For example, a machine that refilled cache misses over a 32-bit data bus might continue prefetching beyond the missed instruction until another miss occurred or the end of a very long cache line was reached. However, if the prefetcher only fetches 32 bits per cycle, the instruction fetch stage can easily becomed starved for instructions. This is because 30% of the instructions typically executed are loads or stores, and stores use the bus for two cycles (i.e., probe then write). Moreover, coprocessor ALU instructions (of which floating-point coprocessor arithmetic is the most important member) also use the address bus for one cycle when they are transferred between the CPU and the FPU. Thus, it is not uncommon for 50% of the bus cycles to be already occupied by instruction execution. Therefore even if the MultiTitan had a prefetch mechanism, a 64-bit bus would be necessary to allow the prefetcher to keep up with the instruction fetch stage, at least on the average.

2.4. Where did the Instruction Decode Stage Go?

In Section 2.2 a direct-mapped cache organization was chosen because it provided the data (at least provisionally, subject to the tag comparison registering a hit) faster than any other method. In the MultiTitan CPU many useful operations are overlapped with the instruction cache tag comparison. In fact, the entire contents of the instruction decode and register operand fetch stages of some machines are performed in parallel with the instruction cache tag comparison in the MultiTitan. This is possible because of the simplicity of the MultiTitan instruction set and the simplicity of the CPU organization. All control signals can be generated by the instruction decode using at most two levels of four-input logic and an inverter. A total of 74 gates are required in all of the instruction decode logic.

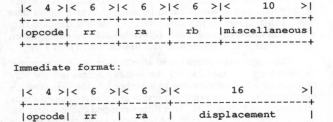

Figure 2-2: MultiTitan instruction formats

The MultiTitan instruction set consists of two instruction formats (see Figure 2-2). Registers to be fetched in the instruction fetch stage appear in the same place in both formats, so decoding of the format is not required before the access of the register file begins. For example, the register file always fetches the registers specified by the bits in the ra and rb positions, even if the instruction is in the immediate format. Similarly rr is always accessed in the WB pipestage, whether written for ALU operations and loads or read for stores. The encoding of the instruction fields was chosen to simplify decoding as much as possible. Although the opcode is four bits, many control functions can be determined by examining only a subset of the opcode bits. For example, all instructions in the immediate format have the most significant bit of their opcode equal to 1, while those in the register format have 0 as their most significant bit. All control information is decoded in the instruction fetch stage. Control bits that are used in later pipestages are delayed by shift registers until they are needed.

Table 2-2 shows the branch frequency for a number of programs. Since there is no instruction decode pipestage, one cycle is saved on every taken branch, or about 7% of the instructions. Assuming there is only one branch delay slot in the architecture, this improves the performance of the machine by approximately 7%. The improvements as a result of second-order factors, such as simpler resulting control logic or fewer PC queue entries are harder to quantify, but can be as significant. Although some machines have more than one branch delay slot, the second slot is not usually usefully filled without the use of branch "squashing" techniques [9], which add to the complexity of the machine.

| | percent of instr. executed | | | percent |
benchmark	uncond-itional	cond-itional	total taken	cond. taken
ccom	3.2	9.5	8.9	60%
PCBroute	3.7	9.7	8.2	46%
TimingVerify	3.5	7.7	7.3	50%
Linpack	0.1	2.3	1.7	69%
Livermore	0.0	4.7	4.4	94%
Stanford	2.6	13.1	12.9	79%
average	2.2	7.8	7.2	66%

Table 2-2: Frequency of branches

2.5. A Machine with Interlocked Pipeline Stages

In the Stanford MIPS project [4], it was decided to implement all interlocks in software by inserting NOPs in the code. Interlocks were implemented in software because hardware interlocks were thought to adversely affect machine performance due to added control complexity. As an experiment in the MultiTitan, all interlocks were put in hardware.

The four interlocks present in the CPU pipeline and detected by the MultiTitan are described below. In the following discussions, *store class instruction* will be used generically to refer to CPU->coprocessor transfer, coprocessor store, and CPU store, which all use an external bus in the WB stage. *Load class instruction* will be used to refer to CPU load, coprocessor load, coprocessor->CPU transfer, and coprocessor ALU instructions, which all use an external bus in the MEM pipestage. The FPU is responsible for stalling the machine if the result of a floating-point computation is requested before it is ready.

Load Interlock
If a CPU register is written by a load instruction, and used as a source in the next instruction, one cycle is lost. There is no delay required between a coprocessor load and the use of the load data by a coprocessor.

Store Interlock
If the instruction following a store class instruction is a load class or store class instruction, one cycle is lost.

Coprocessor->CPU Transfer Interlock
If a Coprocessor->CPU transfer instruction follows a coprocessor load or store, one cycle is lost.

CPU->Coprocessor Transfer Interlock
If a Coprocessor->CPU transfer instruction attempts to issue two cycles after a CPU->Coprocessor transfer, one cycle is lost. Note that if a CPU->Coprocessor transfer is followed immediately by a Coprocessor->CPU transfer, a store interlock will occur on the first attempted issue of the Coprocessor->CPU transfer, and then the CPU->Coprocessor transfer interlock will occur, increasing the spacing between the two transfers to three.

Table 2-3 gives the frequency of occurrence of these interlocks in several programs. Our three production programs are quite similar in their behavior, perhaps because they primarily use linked data structures. The numeric benchmarks in general make heavy use of array structures. The behavior of Linpack

and Livermore are quite similar except for store and transfer interlocks. The inner loop of this version of Linpack has two integer multiplies used for array addressing calculations. Each multiply requires two transfers to the coprocessor and one to return the result of the multiply. These transfers are a bottleneck and cause transfer interlocks between themselves. The Stanford benchmark suite contains a wide range of programs, and so the frequency of interlocks in it is between that of the numeric benchmarks and our production programs.

| | frequency of interlocks as a percent of all instructions executed | | |
benchmark	load	store & transfer	total
ccom	10.4	6.7	17.1
PCBroute	11.6	8.8	20.4
TimingVerify	12.7	8.6	21.3
Linpack	0.2	10.7	10.9
Livermore	0.6	1.0	1.6
Stanford	8.2	4.0	12.2
average	7.3	6.6	13.9

Table 2-3: Frequency of MultiTitan CPU interlocks

In the MultiTitan all interlocks are checked concurrently with the cache tag comparison. Since the instruction formats are so simple, the logic to detect interlocks is also very simple and fast. Like the instruction decode logic, at most two levels of logic and an inverter are required for interlock detection, with the exception of load interlocks which also require a pair of 6-bit register specifier comparators. Besides the comparators, there are only 22 gates and 5 latches required for detecting all interlocks in the CPU. This is about 18% of the total gate count of the control logic, which itself uses only 1.0% of the chip's transistors.

Based on the results from the MultiTitan, full hardware interlocks in a simple and regular machine provide a 14% improvement in code density for low cost. In particular, since interlock detection was performed in parallel with instruction decode, register fetch, cache parity checking, and cache tag comparison, interlock detection did not increase the cycle time of the machine. As a second-order effect, since the MultiTitan loses 8.4% of its cycles to instruction buffer refills, a code density improvement of 14% should result in approximately 1.2% fewer instruction cache miss refill cycles.

2.6. IF Pipestage Summary

During the design of the IF pipestage, we tried to follow our design principle as closely as possible. The timing of the resulting pipestage is summarized in Figure 2-3. It is hard to imagine an IF pipestage with an organization that results in lower latency.

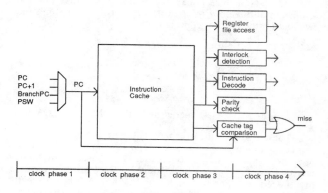

Figure 2-3: IF pipestage timing summary

3. EX Pipestage Tradeoffs

Several tradeoffs were made during the design of the MultiTitan regarding the execute pipestage. The two most important tradeoffs were the placement of EX operations in the pipeline, and the support provided for integer multiplication and division.

3.1. Where should the EX pipestage be?

To support memory refenences, after the instruction fetch pipestage we need a pipestage for address calculation and after that another to access the cache for loads or stores. Given this structure, the next decision to be made is where to execute ALU operations. Two reasonable choices exist.

The first option is that ALU operations could be performed in the same stage as addressing calculations (see Figure 3-1). If ALU operations are performed immediately after IF, the results of load instructions will not be available in time for an ALU operation that immediately follows the load. This results in a one cycle interlock in cases where another instruction can not be found to fill the load delay slot. This delay slot is not present for stores, since stores do not have a "result" accessible by ALU operations in a register-to-register machine. Similarly there is not an interlock for coprocessor loads and stores (e.g., floating-point loads and stores). This is because in the MultiTitan coprocessor ALU instructions are transferred to the coprocessor in the MEM pipestage over the address bus, and coprocessor operations begin execution in the CPU's WB pipestage. Coprocessor loads returning data at the end of the MEM pipestage then complete in time to begin a coprocessor ALU instruction in the WB pipestage. Thus if ALU operations are executed at the same time as address calculations, a 1 cycle interlock would occur between CPU load instructions and ALU operations that use the result of the load, but not for any other combinations of operations.

```
Load: IF    Ad/EX   MEM  *-+ WB
                          |
            IF     Ad/EX | MEM     WB
                          |
ALU:               IF   +>Ad/EX   MEM    WB
```

Figure 3-1: ALU operations in the address pipestage

As a second option ALU operations could be performed at the same time as memory references (see Figure 3-2). This has the advantage that there is no load delay cycle after CPU loads. However, the extra latency of addition and cache access (i.e., of memory reference instructions) versus that of an addition alone (i.e., for ALU instructions) appears in another place. If ALU operations are performed at the same time as cache accesses, then ALU operations that compute values used in a later address calculation cannot execute as the instruction before the instruction with the address calculation without a one cycle interlock. Note that unlike the first option, this restriction applies to all memory references, whether loads or stores, and whether for the CPU or coprocessor.

```
ALU: IF    Addr    MEM/EX+ WB
                       |
           IF     Addr | MEM/EX  WB
                       |
Load:             IF  +>Addr    MEM/EX  WB
```

Figure 3-2: ALU operations in the MEM pipestage

These two pipeline organizations are quite close in performance. Although the second option applies to all memory references, many address calculations are based on relatively constant values (e.g., the stack pointer is fixed for the execution of a procedure). For base addresses that have not been recently calculated this interlock does not occur. The first option, however, causes an interlock in a higher percentage of the cases

where it applies. This is because when a load is issued the data is usually required for another operation within a few cycles at most. To quantify the performance implications of both options, we ran a series of simulations of machines based on the two pipeline organizations (see Table 3-1).

| | frequency of interlocks | |
benchmark	load	address
ccom	11.6	13.1
PCBroute	10.4	7.4
TimingVerify	12.7	9.9
Linpack	0.19	0.34
Livermore	0.58	1.01
Stanford	8.2	7.9
average	7.3	6.6

Table 3-1: Load interlocks vs. address interlocks

Based on this table, it appears either executing ALU operations concurrent with addressing calculations or with memory references results in performance within 1% of each other. The next tradeoff to quantify are their relative implementation costs.

The big advantage of performing ALU operations at the same time as addressing calculations is that it allows the use of a single adder/subtractor for both. This is because in a load/store architecture ALU operations and addressing calculations are mutually exclusive. Besides performing address calculations and ALU operations, branch addresses can also be calculated in the same adder as well. This means that the machine only requires one adder/subtractor (and an incrementer for the program counter). Besides cutting down on the number of transistors and area required, the use of a single adder reduces the number of operand busses, bypass multiplexors, and control required in comparison to a machine with multiple adders. By reducing the area and complexity of the machine, we reduce the latency of communication across the machine for many different signals, both data and control. This means that the single adder machine should have a faster cycle time than a machine with multiple adders.

3.2. Where should integer multiplication and division be performed?

There are many different ways to provide support for integer multiplication and division. Some of the options we considered are listed in Figure 3-3. The most major choice is between performing the operations in the CPU itself versus in the FPU.

Integer multiplication:	cycles
In the CPU, 2 bits per cycle:	16
In the CPU, 4 bits per cycle:	8
In the CPU, 8 bits per cycle + 1 cycle:	5
In the FPU, transfer interlocks:	9
In the FPU, no transfer interlocks:	6
In the FPU, one constant operand, and no interlocks:	5

Integer division:	cycles
In the CPU, 1 bit per cycle:	32
In the CPU, 2 bits per cycle:	16
In the FPU, via reciprocal approx:	21

Figure 3-3: Integer multiplication & division tradeoffs

Performing integer operations in the FPU has the advantage that integer operations can use high-performance structures (e.g., a full multiplier array) already in place for the support of high-performance floating-point operations. These structures will have much better performance than any structure we could afford to place on the CPU. Although the FPU structures have lower latency, if integer operations are to be performed in another chip the time required to transfer operands and results between the chips must be added to the latency of the basic operations. If we perform these operations in the FPU with already-existing transfer and coprocessor ALU instructions, they add no hardware to the CPU. In contrast, if integer operations are performed in the CPU, the CPU datapath must be augmented with special hardware to support multiplication and division. Besides making the data path larger and slowing other operations down, this increases the design time of the CPU.

For these reasons in the MultiTitan we decided to support integer multiplication only in the coprocessor. The coprocessor provides an integer multiplication operation that returns the 64-bit product of two 32-bit integers in 3 cycles. Table 3-3 shows that the resulting integer multiplication times are equivalent to those available when performed in the CPU with a significant amount of hardware support (i.e., 4-8 bits per cycle). In many code situations the transfers to and from the coprocessor can be scheduled in order to avoid interlocks, resulting in an integer multiplication time of 6 cycles.

There is even less support for integer division in the MultiTitan than for integer multiplication. There is no integer division operation in the coprocessor, and no floating-point division operation either. Instead floating-point division is supported by a reciprocal approximation instruction followed by a series of Newton-step iteration instructions and floating-point multiplies. Integer division is performed by transferring the operands over to the coprocessor, converting them to floating-point values, performing a floating-point division via reciprocal approximation, converting the floating-point result back to an integer, and then transferring the result back to the CPU. Even with this long series of operations, performance between that of 1 bit per cycle and 2 bit per cycle CPU hardware is provided by the coprocessor. This performance is provided at no additional hardware cost over that required for floating-point operations.

4. MEM Pipestage Tradeoffs

In the MEM pipestage the MultiTitan performs a cache access for memory reference instructions. Two interesting tradeoffs made in the MEM pipestage during the design of the MultiTitan were the size of the external data bus and the size and organization of the external cache.

4.1. 64-bit external data busses

A 64-bit external data bus can dramatically improve the performance of double-precision floating-point applications at relatively low cost. (The implementation cost of 64-bit data busses was discussed in Section 2.3.) Table 4-1 shows the performance improvement in four programs derived simply from the ability to perform 64-bit coprocessor loads and stores. The four programs were chosen to cover a wide range of floating-point intensive applications. For each benchmark the percentage improvement obtained was estimated by increasing the execution time of the benchmarks on a MultiTitan with a 64-bit data bus by an additional cycle for each coprocessor load and by two additional cycles for each coprocessor store. This assumes that the two coprocessor stores required to store a 64-bit quantity will have a store interlock between them.

The MultiTitan FPU provides a simple vector capability [7]. Programs that use the vector hardware have increased needs for load/store bandwidth because computations can be effectively overlapped with loads and stores. The availability of vector operations reduces the inner loop of Linpack to not much else besides loads and stores. For the vector Linpack benchmark, the performance obtainable with 64-bit data busses is over 60% greater than that given 32-bit data busses. Scalar benchmarks vary in their load/store bandwidth requirements depending on whether their loops are unrolled by the compiler. For example, an unrolled version of the Livermore loops improves 46% when moving from 32-bit to 64-bit data busses, but the non-unrolled benchmark only improves by about 25%. Finally, some floating-point benchmarks such as Whetstones have a smaller percentage of floating-point loads and stores and benefit correspondingly less.

benchmark	%loads	%stores	%improved
vector Linpack	38.1	20.3	61.9
Livermore loops:			
unrolled scalar	23.2	19.6	46.1
rolled scalar	12.4	8.4	24.7
Whetstones	9.4	6.0	14.3
average	20.8	13.6	36.8

Table 4-1: Improvement from 64-bit loads and stores

4.2. Choosing the external cache size and organization

Just as was the case for the on-chip instruction cache in Section 2.2, the size and organization of the external cache was dictated primarily by the RAM sizes available and by the system context.

There are two ways to structure a cache with regard to writes: write-through and write-back. A write-through cache sends all writes on to the memory system. A write-back cache only writes to main memory when a dirty line is replaced or flushed. The external cache of the MultiTitan is a write-back cache. A write-back cache was chosen over a write-through cache for several reasons:

- A write-back cache is a simpler design than a write-through cache of similar performance. A write-through cache requires a write buffer and its associated control logic if good performance is to be maintained, while a write-back cache does not need a write buffer.

- A write-back cache generates less bus traffic than a write-through cache, which was important since the MultiTitan was targeted to be an 8-processor multiprocessor.

- We planned to use the Titan memory system. A write-back cache was used in the Titan, so the Titan memory system was tailored for operation with a write-back cache. Also, software to manage the write-back cache (e.g., flush I/O buffers to main memory) was already in place.

Since the external cache is a write-back cache, the cache must be probed (i.e., checked for a hit) before it can be written. This is because the cache contains a unique copy of some data, so we must probe it before we write the cache so that no unique data is lost. This read (i.e., probe) of the cache takes place in the MEM pipestage for stores, just as load instructions read the cache in the MEM pipestage. If the probe of a store is successful, then the write of the store is performed in the WB pipestage.

The external cache of the MultiTitan is a physically addressed cache. Since it appeared that a physically addressed cache was not any harder to implement in a system than a virtually addressed cache, we chose a physically addressed cache to make the software easier. In order to obtain the fastest possible cache access, the address mapping was performed in parallel with the cache access by a TLB. To allow pages to be placed in any page frame in main memory, we restricted ourselves to a cache organization that only indexed the cache with unmapped address bits (i.e., page offset bits). This allows the TLB map to proceed in parallel with the cache access (see Figure 4-1), but requires the page size to be as large as the cache.

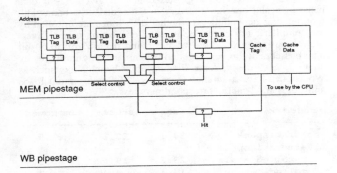

Figure 4-1: MEM pipestage timing summary

The TLB is implemented on the cache controller chip (CCU). The TLB has 512 entries, organized four-way-set associatively. With 64K byte pages this allows 32M bytes to be mapped at one time, which is much larger than most machines. For example, the WRL Titan TLB can map 4M bytes, and the R2000 [8, 11] TLB can map 256K bytes at one time. Unlike the direct-mapped nature of the caches, the TLB was made associative for several reasons. First, the TLB miss refill is performed in software. With our current software on the WRL Titan, this takes over 2,000 cycles, which is more than two orders of magnitude larger than a cache miss. Thus, while a program that uses two arrays of data that map to the same direct-mapped cache location might miss on every data reference and run up to 14 times slower, similar behavior with the TLB could result in programs running 2,000 times slower. A 4-way set associative organization allows the executing code fragment and three operands (e.g., A[i] := B[i] + C[i]) to overlap without thrashing in the TLB. Second, since the TLB and its comparators are on the same chip, and the custom TLB RAM access is faster than that of the external RAM parts, a four-way set-associative TLB can be built that operates in time for the comparison with the cache tag.

The MultiTitan external cache is a direct-mapped cache. Just as with the on-chip instruction cache, a direct-mapped organization was chosen because it has the shortest latency. In the external cache, the RAM access is performed in the MEM pipestage, but the tag comparison is not complete until well into to WB pipestage. By this time the data returned from a load instruction will have been written into the register file and possibly bypassed into an ALU operation which is almost complete. This allows the cycle time of the machine to be much closer to that of the fundamental RAM access time than if an associative organization was employed. Reduced cycle time is a very significant factor since it results in increased performance for all instructions, not just loads and stores.

In order for the cache latency to be as low as possible, we decided that only one row of 4-bit-wide RAM chips would be used for the cache. This minimized the capacitance of the address bus and improved the performance of the data bus relative to implementations with multiple chips per bit. The capacitance of the address bus can also account for a significant fraction of the cache access latency. By using 4-bit-wide chips, the loading on the address lines was cut to 1/4 that present if one-bit-wide memory chips were used. Since the largest fast static RAMs available when the MultiTitan was being designed were 16Kx4 20ns CMOS parts, this resulted in a 128K byte cache. (64 bits of data bus / 4 bits per chip = 16 chips for data, 16 chips x 8K bytes per chip = 128K bytes).

If the external cache were a mixed instruction and data cache, the resulting system would have 128K byte pages since the TLB map was in parallel with the cache indexing. This was judged to be a little too large, so the external cache was partitioned into a 64K byte instruction and a 64K byte data section. This partition required no extra chips: the high order address bit of the chips was merely connected to a pin on the CPU which specified whether an access was an on-chip instruction cache miss access or a data reference.

Table 4-2 gives the results of simulations of a split cache consisting of two 64K byte segments, versus a mixed 128K byte cache. The conventional wisdom on mixed versus split resources is that a single shared resource of a given size is always better than two private resources each of 1/2 size. This is the observed behavior for most programs, but the PC board router had better performance with a split cache than a mixed cache. This is because the external cache is a direct mapped cache, and providing separate instruction and data sections provides a measure of added associativity in the cache. In other words, with a split cache data references and instruction references that map onto each other can coexist in the cache, whereas they can thrash between each other in a mixed cache. However, for most programs, the mixed cache performed better than the split cache. This was especially true for the numeric benchmarks. These have large data sets and spend most of their time in small loops. For example, a 100x100 Linpack has an 80K byte array. This fits in a 128K byte mixed cache but does not fit in the 64K byte data side of a split cache, so its split performance is much worse than its mixed performance. Since the numeric programs spend much of their time in small loops, the external instruction cache is rarely used by the numeric benchmarks.

				Miss cost for all configurations is 14 cycles	
	split: two 64KB			mixed	split/
benchmark	instr	data	total	128KB	mixed
ccom	.208	.045	.253	.229	1.10
PCBroute	.039	.114	.153	.209	0.73
TimingVerify	.013	.020	.033	.020	1.65
Linpack	.0001	.192	.192	.031	6.19
Livermore	.0004	.095	.095	.020	4.75
Stanford	.001	.001	.002	.002	1.00
average	.044	.078	.121	.085	1.42

Table 4-2: Split vs. mixed external cache CPI burden

Although the mixed cache clearly performs better than the split cache, in the MultiTitan we implemented the split cache. This is because the overall difference between the two methods averaged over the six benchmarks above is only .036 CPI. At our design target of 25 Mhz, this means that the split cache machine is less than 1 MIP slower (i.e., 3.6%) than the machine with a mixed cache. It was felt that the reduction in page sizes would result in better net overall system performance even though the cache performance was somewhat lower.

5. WB Pipestage Tradeoffs

All MultiTitan instructions commit in the WB pipestage. For example, even though ALU operations are computed two pipestages before WB, they are not written into the register file until WB. By having all instructions commit in WB, the pipeline control of the machine becomes very regular and is simplified. Another implication of the uniform commit of instructions in WB is that instructions that enter the WB pipestage will write their result registers, even if the result is incorrect. For example, load instructions write the register file in the WB pipestage before it is known whether or not they will have a page fault. This means that in order to recover from page faults, the base register for a load cannot be the same as its target. If it is and a page fault occurs, the ability to calculate the address of the page fault will be lost. Floating-point operations also commit in the WB pipestage, even though they only begin execution the WB pipestage. Thus once a floating-point operation begins, it is guaranteed to complete no matter what types of interrupts may occur in the machine. Because the latency of all floating-point operations is three cycles, floating-point operations that abort will abort precisely relative to all other floating-point operations. Details of other floating-point tradeoffs are beyond the scope of this paper.

6. Conclusions

In this paper we presented some of the tradeoffs made during the design of the MultiTitan CPU. These tradeoffs were made to achieve the highest sustained performance with the lowest peak performance. In particular, many of the tradeoffs involved minimizing the latency of operations while simplifying the organization of the machine. Moreover, these tradeoffs were primarily driven by the available technology and system context.

The first IF pipestage tradeoff considered was the basic system partitioning of the design with regards to the CPU chip. By putting the instruction cache on-chip instead of the FPU or the TLB, we were able to maximize system performance while simplifying the system design. Second, a direct-mapped on-chip instruction cache organization was chosen because it had the lowest average latency when hit and miss latencies are combined with the probability of a miss. Third, by using a 64-bit bit data bus the refill latency was reduced by two cycles, improving the performance of the machine on our production programs by 8% at low cost. Fourth, by placing interlock detection, instruction decode, register fetch, and cache parity checking in parallel with the instruction cache tag comparison, the pipestage normally used for instruction decode in most machines could be eliminated. By eliminating this pipestage, the latency of branches is reduced, and hence the machine performance directly improves by 7% in machines with a single branch delay slot. The improvements as a result of second-order factors, such as simpler resulting control logic or fewer PC queue entries, are harder to quantify, but can be as significant.

The first tradeoff about the EX pipestage was where it should be in the machine. Based on simulations, placing it in the same pipestage as memory reference address calculations generates about the same number of interlock cycles as placing it concurrent with cache access. However, by combining the EX pipestage with the address calculation pipestage, the machine hardware was reduced by an adder and the bus, bypass, and control structure of the machine was simplified. Finally, in the MultiTitan we relied on high-performance hardware in the FPU for support of integer multiplication and division. This resulted in similar or better performance than methods with augmented CPU hardware but at negligible additional hardware cost.

Two MEM pipestage tradeoffs were discussed. First, the use of 64-bit busses were shown to dramatically improve double-precision floating-point performance by up to 60%. Second, the external cache was designed as a 128K byte direct-mapped cache, partitioned with 64K bytes for instructions and 64K bytes for data. This decision was driven primarily by the available static RAM technology and for the system desire to avoid 128K byte pages.

The most important feature of the WB pipestage is that it is when all instructions commit. This has implications for CPU load instructions (i.e., rr <> ra) and for floating-point operations. This regular commit framework helped permit a small, fast, and regular pipeline control structure to be designed.

7. Acknowledgements

Jeremy Dion was the first to simulate some of the cache and TLB tradeoffs, and was the chief designer of the CCU. Special thanks to David W. Wall for his help in providing the parameterizable MultiTitan simulator and code optimizer that was used for some of the tradeoffs in this paper. Many other people contributed in one form or another to the MultiTitan project, too many to list here. Jeremy Dion, John Ousterhout, Richard Swan, and David W. Wall provided many helpful comments on an early draft of this paper.

References

1. Chow, P., and Horowitz, M. Architectural Tradeoffs in the Design of MIPS-X. The 14th Annual Symposium on Computer Architecture, IEEE Computer Society Press, June, 1987, pp. 300-308.

2. Cray Research Inc. *The CRAY-1 Computing System Reference Manual.* Chippewa Falls, WI, 1976.

3. Dobbs, C., Reed, P., and Ng, T. "Supercomputing on Chip." *VLSI Systems Design* (May 1988), 24-33.

4. Hennessy, J., Jouppi, N., Baskett, F., Gross, T., and Gill, J. Hardware/Software Tradeoffs for Increased Performance. First International Conference on Architectural Support for Programming Languages and Operating Systems, IEEE Computer Society Press, March, 1982, pp. 2-11.

5. Hill, M., et. al. "Design Decisions in SPUR." *Computer* (November 1986), 8-22.

6. Jouppi, N. P., Tang, J. Y. F., and Dion, J. A 20 MIPS Sustained 32b CMOS Microprocessor with 64b Data Busses. The 36th International Solid-State Circuits Conference, IEEE Solid State Circuits Council and the University of Pennsylvania, February, 1989, pp. 84-85.

7. Jouppi, N. P., Bertoni, J., and Wall, D. W. A Unified Vector/Scalar Floating-Point Architecture. Third International Conference on Architectural Support for Programming Languages and Operating Systems, IEEE Computer Society Press, April, 1989, pp. .

8. Kane, G.. *MIPS R2000 RISC Architecture.* Prentice-Hall, 1987.

9. McFarling, S., and Hennessy, J. L. Reducing the Cost of Branches. The 13th Annual Symposium on Computer Architecture, IEEE Computer Society Press, May, 1986, pp. 396-403.

10. Nielsen, M. J. K. Titan System Manual. Tech. Rept. 86/1, Digital Equipment Corporation Western Research Lab, September, 1986.

11. Rowen, C., et. al. "RISC VLSI Design for System-Level Performance." *VLSI Systems Design* (March 1986), 81-88.

12. Sachs, H., and Hollingsworth, W. A High Performance 846,000 Transistor Unix Engine: The Fairchild Clipper. Proceedings IEEE International Conference on Computer Design: VLSI in Computers, IEEE Computer Society Press, October, 1985, pp. 342-346.

RUN-TIME CHECKING IN LISP
BY INTEGRATING MEMORY ADDRESSING AND RANGE CHECKING

Mitsuhisa Sato[*], Shuichi Ichikawa[*] and Eiichi Goto[* **]

[*] Research Development Corporation of Japan (JRDC),
5-6-4 Tsukiji, Chou-ku, Tokyo 104, Japan
[**] University of Tokyo, Department of Information Science,
7-3-1 Hongo, Bunkyo-ku, Tokyo 113, Japan

Abstract

This paper describes the BL addressing mode and the address tag in FLATS2 machine, which is a general-purpose MIMD computer now under construction. The BL addressing mode integrates memory accessing and range checking by hardware. Address tag is a bit in word, which indicates the capability for memory access. Combining them together, efficient memory protection is provided at run-time. It reduces the cost of run-time type checking in Lisp by checking the address tag and the address of a pointer against the range of the region associated to a type, in parallel with the memory access. The arithmetic instructions check the address tags of operands to support the generic arithmetic in Lisp. We can also make use of this scheme to check the number of arguments and multiple return values and to check array-bounds to support faster execution of Common Lisp program. These facilities are not specific to Lisp, so that they can be used more generally than other tagged architectures.

1. Introduction

Lisp includes a number of features that make Lisp programs difficult to execute efficiently on conventional machines. One of these features is *dynamic type checking*. Lisp associates type with values rather than identifiers. Dynamic type checking is implemented by adding to each data object a tag that encodes type information. Most of Lisp machines provide architectural support for tag manipulation, together with other works related to dynamic type checking and generic operations, to execute Lisp programs efficiently.

In this paper, we propose new architectural supports for run-time checking in Lisp, *BL addressing mode* and *address tag*, which can be used more generally than tagged architecture. BL addressing mode is integration of memory addressing and range checking. The effective address is checked against the specified pair of base and limit address in registers during memory access. An address tag is a bit in a word, which indicates whether the word is an address or not. It checks the

capability of memory access.

In Lisp, an object is represented as a pointer or an immediate value. Address tag distinguishes a pointer object, from an immediate data type such as fixnum. Generic arithmetic instructions check the address tag of operand to perform the operation according to the data type. By allocating the same type of objects in a segment, BL addressing mode checks the type of a pointer object during memory access by testing which segment the pointer points into. So, we can check the data type by the range checking instead of a tag. Like tag checking of tagged architecture, the range checking overlaps the memory access.

FLATS2 is an MIMD computer by cyclic pipeline architecture(CPA[9]), which exploits these features. It is a general-purpose computer, not lisp-specific one, because BL addressing mode and address tag are general architectural supports, not lisp-specific supports.

One of FLATS2's target languages is Common Lisp [13]. Common Lisp is an "industrial strength" dialect of Lisp providing a wide variety of data types and control structures. In this paper, we explain how FLATS2 supports faster execution of Common Lisp programs with BL addressing mode and address tag.

In Section 2, we describe the basic concept of BL addressing mode and address tag. Section 3 describes the basic architecture of FLATS2, and in Section 4, we explain the design of Common Lisp using our architectural support. In Section 5, we discuss BL addressing mode and address tag (compared to other tagged architectures) and their hardware implementation of FLATS2.

2. The concept of BL addressing mode and address tag

2.1 BL addressing mode

To access the memory, addressing modes locate operands in memory. In BL addressing mode, the effective address is checked by comparing the address with base address and limit address whenever the operand in memory is accessed. It allows memory access and range checking to be performed in parallel by hardware. If the effective address is not in the range between given base and limit, either a branch to a specified location or a trap occurs.

BL addressing modes are specified in the following form:

<BL> : <addressing mode>, <label>

where <addressing mode> is displacement(address) or index(address). (Displacement is a constant. Address and index may be a variable specified in a register.) <BL> gives the base and limit as a pair, which is called *BL pair*. <label> may be omitted and then a trap occurs instead of branching.

BL addressing mode provides memory protection on small domain at run-time. For example, BL addressing mode is used for array-bounds checking. It checks the indices to make sure that the reference is inside the given vector specified by BL pair. It is desirable to check array bounds to improve program reliability even in statically typed languages such as FORTRAN, PASCAL.

2.2 Run-time data type checking by BL-addressing mode

In dynamically typed languages such as Lisp, APL, and Icon, all data objects are allocated dynamically at run-time, and their types must be checked at run-time. Objects in memory are referenced indirectly through pointers. Each type of the objects can be allocated in the heap space associated with its type. We call a heap space corresponding to each type, *type segment*. The type of the pointer, then, can be checked by testing which type segment the pointer points into.

The compiler knows the expected data type and how to access the object in memory through the pointer. By using BL addressing mode with the BL pair of the type segment, the type can be checked in parallel with data access. For example in Figure 1, a cons cell in Lisp is represented by two words in the cons cell segment, where **BL-cons** indicates. The primitive operations **car**, **cdr** on a pointer **p** to the cons cell are performed by loading from memory with BL addressing mode respectively as follows:

car(p) := BL-cons : (p)
cdr(p) := BL-cons : 4(p)

Here the size of a word is 4 bytes. If **p** points outside of **BL-cons**, a trap occurs.

The predicate on list data type, **listp** is implemented simply by range checking on a pointer with the BL of cons cell segment.

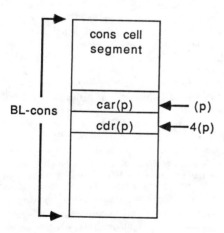

Figure 1. CAR/CDR operations by BL addressing mode

2.3 Address tag

Even though the address is the most fundamental property in computation, most of computers have no means to distinguish the address from just a data. In FLATS2, every data word on either memory or registers has one bit tag which indicates whether a word is an address or not.

Only *load effective address* instruction and memory access instructions can calculate an address, so that an address is defined in well-defined way. Both of base and limit of a BL pair must have address tags, as well as *address* in <addressing mode>. If a non-address word is used as an address entity in BL addressing mode, the exception occurs. The calculated effective address can never be outside of the range between given base and limit addresses.

At beginning of the execution of a program, the BL pair of the entire user's program space are given by the operating system. During the execution, no address outside of initial BL pair can be produced. So BL addressing mode and address tag work as memory protection mechanism on the single virtual space of FLATS2. We call this protection scheme *BL scheme*. Combining address tag and BL address checking can be thought as a kind of implementation of *capabilities* [16].

3. Basic architecture of FLATS2

In this section, we describe the basic architecture of FLATS2 briefly. The cyclic pipeline architecture of FLATS2 implements two instruction/data streams (virtual processors†) in one hardware. A more detail description is given in [7].

3.1 Memory and registers

FLATS2 provides the 32-bit single virtual space. The lower half of the address spaces is D space, which is used to store data. The upper half is divided into the space for instructions (I space) and the space for register-mapped memory (GV space). FLATS2 has 64 general purpose registers and four special purpose floating point registers. Each general purpose registers contain 33 bit word, 32 bits data and one bit for address tag. The general registers are divided into two groups: 32 global register and 32 local frame register. They are mapped on GV space by Global Frame Pointer (GFP) and Local Frame Pointer (CFP). Local frame registers are saved/restored by CALL/RETURN instruction to make function call faster. CALL instruction changes the local frame by incrementing CFP and saves the old processor status including CPF and the program counter (PC) in the new local frame. Floating point registers contain 64 bits floating point.

D space is byte-addressed. Each word (32 bit) word-aligned on memory has another bit for an address tag. The load/store operations transfer the entire 33 bit word between memory and registers.

3.2 Instructions

Most of instructions in FLATS2 are executed in one instruction cycle. Its basic formats is 64 bits in size, as shown in Figure 2. The fields *s1, s2, s3* specify the general purpose registers to be fetched. *GV-op* field specifies the operation between the general registers, and the addressing modes with the short displacement *d1, d2* form -128 to 127. The displacement can be extended to the long displacement (32 bit) in the following instruction word. The displacement field may be used as a immediate operand. *SP-op* field controls the

---

† This term *virtual processor* should not be confused with a virtual processor of the memory management in the operating system. In this paper, a virtual processor is a instruction/data stream in MIMD.

integer and floating points arithmetic unit, called *SP unit*.

The instructions without *SP-op* field perform address calculation, byte and short load/store, integer arithmetic operation, and a few of lisp specific operation. This set of instructions are basically load/store instruction set. These instructions use *SP-op* field for other purpose.

SP unit instructions (SP instruction) perform the floating and integer arithmetic operation between the general registers, floating point registers and memory operands, and store the result to either memory or registers. We can achieve full through-put of memory by the operation between memory operands in one instruction cycle.

The field *j1* specifies the relative jump location for in-word branching. It controls the exception of BL-addressing mode, as explained later.

Gv-op(14)	s1(6)	s2(6)	s3(6)

j1(8)	SP-op(8)	d1(8)	d2(8)

Figure 2. Basic instruction format of FLATS2

3.3 Variants of BL addressing mode

In addition to the basic BL addressing mode described in previous section, FLATS2 has some variants of BL addressing mode. FLATS2's addressing modes are listed in Table 1. The general purpose registers are used as either BL pair, index or address register. A BL pair is formed by an even/odd registers pair. The effective address is checked against BL pair in register, in any BL addressing modes.

Notation	Effective Address	Side Effect
#*xxx*	(Immediate)	
g*rn*, v*rn*, S*, P*	(Register)	
b:*disp*(p)	p + disp	
b:>*disp*(p)	p + disp	p += disp^1
b:<*disp*(p)	p	p += disp^2
b@i	b + i	
b@>i	b + i	b += i^1
b@<i	b	b += i^2
b@disp	b + disp	
b@>disp	b + disp	b += disp^1
b@<disp	b	b += disp^2
b@<disp(i)	b + i + disp	
b:disp(p)i	p + i + disp	

NOTE: *b* specifies odd/even register pair as BL. In effective address and side effect, *b* denotes the base register of BL. *i* specifies a register as index register. *p* specifies a register as address register. *disp* specifies a constant as displacement.

*) S,P are floating point registers. 1) pre-modify 2) post-modify

Table 1. BL addressing mode of FLATS2

BL-addressing modes can involve side effects, which are called *post-modify* and *pre-modify*. The side effect of post-modify (pre-modify) changes the base register or pointer register after (before) the effective address calculation according to the addressing modes. For example, the combination of index mode and post-modify specifies the base

address of BL pair as effective address and update the base register of BL pair incrementing by the index register. These side effects are used as post/pre-increment/decrement addressing mode, in conventional processors such as VAX or 68000, and each register can be modified by any displacement in both direction. When the modified address is outside of the range of BL pair, the address tag of the modified register is set to 0 and then cannot be used as an address any more.

The exception handling in BL-addressing mode is different from the definition described in previous section. Without specifying the jump target, the exception of BL addressing mode causes a trap. When the jump field is specified in BL addressing mode, this jump is executed if the memory access is completed successfully, otherwise the next instruction is executed. The following instructions handle the exception.

Since the pointer whose most significant bit is 1 points into the I space or GV space, it is a pointer to function code or local frame. Such a pointer is treated specially in BL addressing mode.

4. Design of Lisp on FLATS2

In this section, we describe how FLATS2 supports faster execution of Common Lisp program by using BL addressing mode and address tag.

4.1 Data formats and structures of Lisp

The formats and structures of data types are designed with BL addressing mode and address tag in mind, because the implementation of type checking depends on the data representation. Lisp objects are 33 bits long, 32 bits word and an address tag. A type is either an immediate type or a pointer type. An immediate type object has its address tag cleared. The type, fixnum is only an immediate type. The value of fixnum is stored in 32 bit word.

All data types except for fixnum are referenced through pointer objects. The word of a pointer object specifies a memory location where the data associated with the pointer object are stored: cons cells, symbols, ratio and floating point are represented in this way. These fixed length objects are allocated in *type segment* associated with a pointer type. The data of fixed-length objects are accessed through a pointer object by BL-addressing mode with constant offset and BL of its type segment.

For variable length object such as vector, array and string, the fixed-length header, which contains the descriptor of the variable length data, is stored in its type segment. The descriptor is a BL pair of variable length data in *data heap*. The BL pair of a vector is loaded from its header to access the elements of vector. BL addressing mode checks the accesses on the vector without overhead. Run time checking for vector access is rather natural usage for BL addressing mode.

4.2 Operations on list elements

Lists are one of the most frequently used data structure in Lisp. The basic operations required are **cons** to add an element to a list, and **car** and **cdr** to access the first element and tail of a list. Lists are sequences represented in the form of linked cells, called *cons cell*. Car and cdr are performed by load operation on a cons cell with BL addressing mode.

Car and **cdr** are defined in Common Lisp not only for a pointer to cons cell but also for a pointer to nil. In Common Lisp as in most Lisp dialects, the symbol nil is used to represent the empty list and the false value for boolean test. Nil is a special object which belongs to both list and symbol. Although it is a symbol like any other symbols, it appears to be treated as a variable when evaluated. The data structure of a symbol object consists of several words, including value cell, the function definition cell, property list, print name, package cell of a symbol and other attributes. The symbol structure is designed so that its value cell and function cell can be accessed by car and cdr operation as if it is a cons cell. The cons cell type segment adjoins the symbol type segment. The symbol nil is located on the intersection of both type segments. The BL pair used in car and cdr operation includes the nil symbol as shown in Figure 3. In case of nil symbol, its value cell and function definition cell are also nil.†

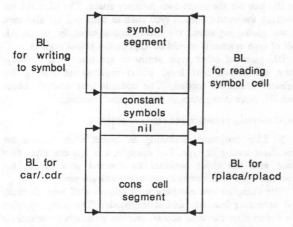

Figure 3. Cons cell segment and symbol segment

4.3 Constant symbols and read-only protection

Common lisp allows symbols to name a constant value by defconstant declaration. Once a name has been declared by defconstant as a constant, any further assignment to or binding of that named symbol is an error. In the interpreter, such binding can be detected by checking the attribute of symbols indicating the named constant with run-time overhead. The compiler can replace references to the name of a constant by its value of the constant in source level, and may also choose to issue warnings about bindings of the lexical variable of the same name.

However, even in compiled code, it is necessary to check the bindings to the system-supplied constant such as nil and t. Such read-only attributes of these objects can be implemented by selecting BL pair used in store operations. The shallow bindings to special variables modify the value cell of a symbol using BL pair of symbol type segment excluding read-only constants.

Rplaca and rplacd operations modify the list structures. Unlike car and cdr, these use BL excluding nil symbols to avoid modifying the value of nil.

---

† The value of nil symbol is defined as nil itself. This prevents nil symbol from being defined as a function name. Note that there is no description in [13] whether the function named "nil" is permitted to be defined or not. We may layout the internal structure as to use other cell instead of the function cell.

4.4 Explicit type operations

Type checking is required in checking operations specified at the source level, such as the function atom. The predicate for testing an individual primitive type is implemented by checking a object pointer against the BL pair of the associated type segment.

The data types defined in Common Lisp are arranged into a hierarchy defined by the subset relationship. For example, a type number includes integer, ratio, floating-point numbers and complex as its subtypes. The layout of type segments in memory is determined as to make it easy to test supertypes of basic data types (Figure 4). The type segments of subtypes are placed in the range of supertype. We can test the supertype by checking against the BL of the supertype. For example, the predicate function numberp tests the pointer object against BL pair including all subtype segment of number type.

We can implement the intersectional type of two types. Nil is an example of intersectional types of cons and symbol. The predicates endp and consp test against the BL excluding nil while the predicate listp uses the BL including nil as car and cdr.

The range checking for the pointer object is done by *load effective address* instruction with the pointer mode of BL addressing modes. This instruction branches by in-word jump field without delay.

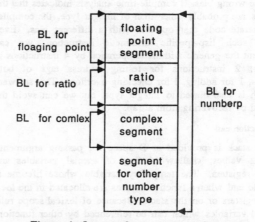

Figure 4. Layout of type segments for number

4.5 Generic arithmetic operations and Fixnums

Lisp generic functions must determine the types of their operands at run-time in order to perform the appropriate action.

For arithmetic operations, the most frequent type of operands is fixnum, which is the only type represented by an immediate type. To avoid testing the types of operands explicitly, the hardware performs an address tag check in parallel with arithmetic operations. FLATS2 has two kinds of arithmetic operation; *Lisp arithmetic* instructions checks address tags of both operands. Another kind of arithmetic instructions ignore address tags to perform the arithmetic operation on both value of data and produce non address result.

If both operands in Lisp arithmetic have no address tag, then arithmetic operation is completed just as conventional arithmetic operations. If either operand has an address tag, the instruction forces a trap to software. The software dispatches on the types of each operand to determine if both are numbers, coerces one of them if they have different types, and then perform the generic arithmetic operations by proper sequence of machine instructions. When the overflow condition is detected, a trap also occurs to extend the result to *bignum*.

There are two equality predicates used frequently in Common Lisp: EQ testing for the identical objects and EQL testing for identical objects or equality for numbers of the same type. The EQ test is performed simply by comparing the objects including address tags. The EQL comparison is more complicated because the pointer objects of numbers which have the same value may be located in different location. As Lisp generic arithmetic, Lisp compare instruction tests and traps to software if either operand has an address tag. If both operands are non-address words, then comparison is completed as conventional compare instruction.

This approach on generic arithmetic operation is similar to SPUR[14]. We use an address tag instead of SPUR's *fixnum* tag. This integer-biased generic arithmetic is based on the assumption that the integer is the most commonly used data type in arithmetic operations. This approach is very fast for the integer data types, but handling of other data types can be slow. Its performance depends on the treatment of a trap in the operating system and on how often integer operands are used. In the case of non-integer operands, rather large amount of time can be required for recovering from a trap.

In compile-time analysis, the type declaration and a sophisticated type inference can be used to reduce the cost of using the wrong bias. If compile-time analysis indicates that the operands are probably other than of integer type, the compiler can generate code that operates with a different bias. Even without such lisp-specific arithmetic instruction, we can implement the generic arithmetic operation by 4 instructions in software; 2 instructions for testing address tags of both operands, 1 for adding, 1 for checking overflow. This software approach is also biased to integer type, but we can avoid the overhead by recovering from a trap.

4.6 Function call

The stack is provided in D space for passing arguments, returning values, shallow binding of special variables and spilling registers. The temporary variable whose lifetime is known to end when a function returns are allocated in the local frame registers or on the stack. Because of lexical scope rule, the local variables which can be referenced by other functions must be allocated either on stack or in closure type segment. Switching the local frame registers by CALL/RETURN instructions avoids saving and restoring the temporaries of the calling function to make the function call faster.

The global registers are used to pass the arguments and return values. Common Lisp allows the variable number of arguments to be passed to functions, and provides a variety of specification on parameters. Called functions must check the number of arguments to take each argument according to the parameter specifier.

The calling function pushes the arguments onto the stack, and then uses the global register to pass the BL pair indicating high and low address of the arguments on stack instead of the number of arguments. The BL pair can be calculated from the stack pointer and the number of arguments in one instruction, called *make BL pair (mkbl)*. In order to setup the parameter variables, the arguments can be accessed by BL addressing mode in parallel with checking the number of arguments. The exceptions may cause a trap for an error, or move the default value to the parameter.

Common Lisp also allows the function to return the multiple values. Like passing argument, the called function pushes all the returned values on the stack and then returns the BL pair indicating high and low address of the return values. When control returns to the caller, it takes the return value through the returned BL pair to convert the values to the form required by the caller. Checking the number of the return value can be done during accessing the return value on the stack.

4.7 Global registers and system constants

FLATS2 has 32 global registers. The most frequently referenced system values are kept in global registers. These system values are the constant nil value, the stack pointer, and the BL pair for the entire own memory space. The BL pairs for checking the most common type such as cons cell are also kept in the global registers. We must choose carefully which BL pair of type segments should be kept in the global register.

BL pairs of other type segments are placed in memory. They are loaded into local frame registers or free global registers whenever needed. The compile-time analysis keeps such BL pairs in registers in the compiled function.

4.8 Combining predicate and access to object

In Lisp programs, accessing an object often follows the predicates testing its type. For example, **car** and **cdr** often take place after the check whether its operand is a list by the predicate **listp** or the complementary predicate **atom**.

The compiler can combine such sequence of type checking and accessing into BL addressing mode. The jump specifies the action after the data access, and the successive instructions execute the action after the type check is failed. The example of the program in **Appendix** uses this optimization.

This optimization is effective to implement the generic operation on *sequence*, which encompasses both lists and vectors. By checking on list data type first, we can do generic operations on the list sequence without overhead.

This technique is used also in FLATS1 [5], by using *error jump* facility of car/cdr instruction.

4.9 Array access

Bounds checking on array access is straightforward for BL addressing modes. The indices are checked against the bounds by index mode with BL pair of the array. When an array is accessed in loop, the compiler keeps the BL pair of its array in register as possible.

If an array has a fill pointer, it may be represented as an pointer instead of an index. Its elements are accessed through the BL pair of the array's base address and the fill pointer. If the access failed, the fill pointer is modified by a new address and then is accessed again. The element inside of the fill pointer can be accessed without overhead of checking against a fill pointer explicitly.

4.10 Floating point

FLATS2 supports single precisions (32 bits) and doule precisions (64 bits) of floating points numbers, which are basically compatible to the DEC floating points format [15]. In FLATS2, no immediate floating-point data types are used such as the single precision data type in Symbolics 3600 [8], because an immediate object represents only the fixnum data type. All floating point objects are represented through the pointer.

Most floating arithmetics are performed in one instruction cycle between memory operand and the floating point registers by SP instruction. Temporary results of floating points arithmetic can be kept either in the register or on the stack as two fixnum objects. For floating-point operands, the integer-biased generic arithmetic operation first have to dispatch on the types of their operands and then use the pointers to load the floating point numbers from memory to register. If either of the operands is known to be floating-point types at compile-time by the type declaration, the floating arithmetic instruction can access the operand on memory in parallel with type checking against the BL pair of floating point segment. When the operand is the pointer object of the floating type, we don't have to loose time for checking data types. If type check failed, the object is converted to the floating point data type and then arithmetic operation is done again.

4.11 Data allocation and storage management

Allocating storage for an object in a type segment is accomplished simply by incrementing the free pointer associated with that segment. For example, **cons** operation which allocates a cons cell, is accomplished by incrementing the free pointer associated with cons cell segment. When a free pointer for any space is incremented, a check must be made to see if the free space runs out. If so, the garbage collector is invoked.

The free area in a type segment is also managed as the BL pair of the free pointer and the limit pointer, which points the end of the free area. For *cons* operation, the special instruction is provided to store two words to the memory at the base of BL to increment the base pointer as side effect, and move the old base pointer to the target register as a newly created cons object. All these operations are executed in one instruction, called *allocate space (allocs)*. To allocate other types of objects, the side effect of BL addressing mode of store operation increments the base of BL pair pointing the free area. In either case, when the new base address runs over its limit address, the address tag of the base of BL pair is cleared to notify that the free space runs out. Next attempt for allocating the object will fail and cause a trap to reclaim memory. We minimize the time for the simple object allocations such as cons cell, floating-point by expanding it inline with a few instructions.

Storage is reclaimed with a stop-and-copy garbage collector by the following reasons:

— Copying improves paging performance because it compacts objects.

— If free space runs out, it is necessary to relocate the object in the segment into the other bigger segment in order to enlarge the size of free space. Copying makes it easy to implement the relocation of segments.

— We have no room for keeping extra bits in the pointer object for incremental GC.

Garbage collector needs to distinguish pointers from data. Address tags allow the pointers to be recognized by their tags.

As described in section 4.1, the data of variable-length data type is allocated in data heap. All free objects in data heap are managed by the free list.

5. Discussion

In this section, we discuss the feature of BL addressing mode compared to tagged architecture, and the hardware implementation of the BL addressing mode in FLATS2. It is difficult to evaluate the performance of Lisp on a specific architecture. Its performance depends on many factors including compiler quality and the operating system environment as well as the architectural support.

5.1 Full tagged architecture

Run-time type checking is implemented by adding a tag to each data object to encode the type of that object in either software or hardware. Most of Lisp machines such as Symbolics 3600 [8], TI Explorer [1], SPUR [14] and FLATS1 [8], adopt a tag architecture to execute Lisp programs efficiently. These machines provides a few of bits for the tag to represent the data types. We call such class of tag architecture *full tagged architecture*. The Lisp machines with tagged architecture support tag checking operations in parallel with other operations.

In addition to run-time checking, the tagged architecture offers several advantages. In most of Lisp machines except for SPUR, high-level instructions corresponding to Lisp primitive functions are micro-coded in firmware. Because micro-programming allows more parallelism, it could be faster than that of the software implementation on conventional machines. For example in TI Explorer VLSI processor [1], a tag dispatch table in chip is used by micro code to support generic arithmetic operations. If the test for the most common integer case failed, the micro-code dispatches on the type of operands. Further, language-specific instruction set designed by micro-program provides the high-level instructions easy to be compiled into, and compact codes, which increase code density. However, micro-code requires the additional hardware to control the sequence of micro-instructions. It would add on cycle time and decrease the total performance.

SPUR is a RISC processor, which incorporates tagged architecture into RISC. It has a few lisp-specific instructions for tag read/write, list access, integer-biased generic arithmetic. However, SPUR does not allow parallel checking on memory access other than list access, so tags except for list are checked by software.

FLATS2 provides only one bit tag indicating the capability for accessing the memory. The hardware related to the address tag is hard-wired. A valid address is created only from the effective address calculation by BL addressing modes. It enables the memory protection on small domains with BL addressing modes.

5.2 Run-time checking in full tagged architecture and BL addressing mode

Both of full tag checking and BL addressing modes provide dynamic type checking facility on the pointer object during address calculation.

In tag checking, the expected tag could be specified in a register, as an immediate, or in the opcode. The hardware testing is limited to a simple tag check, and is sufficient for list accessing. But for vector operation, array bounds checking would still have to be done in software or firmware.

In BL addressing mode of FLATS2, the BL pairs for type segments must be specified in registers. BLs for the type segments may change by relocation at run-time. But if a BL pair cannot be kept in the register, it takes more instructions to load it from memory. Some of the BL pairs which are used frequently, can be kept in global registers. The compile-time analysis can keep other BL pairs in registers during register allocation phase. The pair of registers occupy double registers, so BL addressing mode requires the large number of registers in order to make BL addressing mode work effectively.

As well as type checking at run-time, it can be effective in a number of situations, as described in the previous section. BL addressing mode provides more flexible checking mechanism at run-time than tag checking does.

The type checking on pointer objects is implemented by the address range checking in BL addressing mode. Type checking by BL-addressing mode requires objects of the same data type to be allocated in contiguous area on memory. Even in full tagged architecture, some Lisp systems allocates each objects in this way to make the storage management easier, so that it is not serious restriction on implementing Lisp system.

It is sometimes useful to dispatch on the type of the object like in a case statment. Such type checking is expensive in BL addressing mode. In full tagged architecture, it is easy to recognize data type from the object pointer simply by extracting the tag, because the tag in a object describes its data type. But in our approach, it is necessary to check the pointer address against BL pairs of all type-segments sequentially.† Sequential type checking can detect the most common type faster, but the detection on other data type can be slower. Fortunately, most of type checking in Lisp source program are performed by the predicate function of an individual data type. Dispathing on the data type is rarely used in compiled code.

5.3 The implementation of BL-addressing mode in FLATS2 CPC architecture

Steenkiste and Hennessy [11,12] studied on the cost of tag checking in respect of software and hardware support in RISC architecture. According to their results, run-time tag checking for primitive Lisp operations in software costs about 25 % of total execution time on average in Gabriel's benchmark programs[3]. By overlapping this tag checking and other operations in hardware, we can reduce this cost to obtain substantial speed up of execution.

Rather complicated instructions for type checking must be faster than a sequence of simpler instruction if they are to give performance improvement. The proposed hardware schemes must be evaluated not only for instruction count or convenience of software, but also for potential negative factor on the processor's cycle time.

In the case of FLATS2, BL addressing modes always take a BL pair as register operand, and jump field as an immediate, so rather long instruction is required. It may decrease code density and increase paging activity. Additional hardware required for BL addressing mode consists of two comparators for range checking and some logic for address tags. To read BL pair from register, an additional read port is required in register file. The BL range checking on effective address

overlaps load/store operation form/to memory. If such hardware is added to the critical path of execution, it would be negative impact on the cycle time.

FLATS2 has ten pipeline stages, and each stages are executed in 50 ns. Each instruction takes two successive slot in pipeline and the entire pipeline is shared by two instruction/data stream. Consequently, each instruction of a single virtual processor is executed in 200 ns. In the case of a conventional pipelined processor, branch dependences cause delays by a conditional branch such as the exceptional condition of BL addressing mode. Because each pipeline stages are shared by two virtual processor in FLATS2, a detection of branch targets can be determined by the next instruction fetch. In cyclic pipeline architecture, the total throughput can be achieved, though each program can take fixed of the total (a half of FLATS2).

Without cyclic pipeline architecture, BL addressing mode would be implemented with two instructions; The first instruction checks the pointers against the specified BL pair and jumps according to the result of the range checking, and the second instruction accesses the memory. With a "squashed delayed branch" in MIPS-X[2], these two instructions can be overlapped. The branch condition is calculated while the next instruction is fetched, and the effect of both instructions is canceled if the branch does occur.

The similar range checking instruction is proposed in [6] to support the range check of data values.

6. Conclusion

In this paper, we described the architectural support of the integration of memory addressing and range checking in FLATS2, and how it supports the efficient execution of Common Lisp program. It provides a variety of checking required at run-time, such as type checking, generic arithmetic, array-bounds checking, and the checking on the number the argument and multiple return value of functions. We can reduce the cost of run-time checking by BL addressing mode and address tag as by tagged architectures.

FLATS2 provides the large number of registers to check many types efficiently, because BL addressing mode requires the BL pair in registers to be checked. The compiler can optimize the register allocation for BL pairs to make use of the BL addressing modes.

In cyclic pipeline architecture of FLATS2, we implement BL addressing modes in one instruction cycle. In conventional computers, it would be implemented with two instructions.

As discussed in [4], incorporating tag architecture into a general-purpose computer might impose high-level language features that are essentially at odds with the computational model of statically typed languages. Our architectural support, however, is so primitive mechanism that it can be used also for array-bounds checking in FORTRAN, and the detection of illegal pointer usage in C [10].

FLATS2 is currently under construction. Its Lisp system is being developed in the instruction level simulator.

ACKNOWLEDGEMENTS

We are grateful to Norihiro Fukazawa, Paul Spee and the members of FLATS2 project for helpful discussions.

---

† If each type segment were allocated to make higher bits of the address indicate the type like the tag, we could do the same operation as the full tagged architecture.

REFERENCES

[1] Bosshart,P., Hewes,C., Chang, M., and Chau, K. "A553K-Transistor LISP Processor Chip". *Digest 1987 International Solid-State Circuits Conference*, IEEE, New York, February 1987.

[2] Chow,P.,and Horowitz,M. "Architectural Tradeoffs in the Design of MIPS-X". *Proceedings of the 14th Annual International Symposium on Computer Architecture*, ACM, June, 1987.

[3] Gabriel,R.P. *Computer Systems Series*. Volume: *Performance and evaluation of LISP systems*. The MIT Press, 1985.

[4] Gehringer, E.F. and Keedy, J.L. "Tagged Architecture: How Compelling Are its Advantage?". *Proceedings of the 12th Annual International Symposium on Computer Architecture*, ACM, June, 1985.

[5] Goto, E., Soma, T., Inada, N., Ida, T., Idesawa, M., Hiraki,. K., Suzuki, M., Shimizu, K., and Philipov, B. "Design of a Lisp Machine - FLATS2". *Conference Proceedings of 1982 ACM Sym. LISP and Functional Programming*, PittsPurgh, August 1982.

[6] Hill, D.D. "A hardware mechanism for supporting range checks". *Computer Architecture News*(ACM/SIGARCH), vol. 9, no. 4, pp. 15-21, June 1881.

[7] Ichikawa, S. "A study on the Cyclic Pipeline Computer: FLATS2". *MS Thesis*, February 1987, University of Tokyo.

[8] Moon,D.A. "Architecture of the Symbolics 3600". *Proceedings of the 12th Annual International Symposium on Computer Architecture*, ACM, June 1985.

[9] Shimizu, K., Goto, E. and Ichikawa, S. "CPC(Cyclic Pipeline Computer) - An Architecture Suited for Josephson Pipelined-Memory Machines". *Proceedings of 4th Riken Symposium on Josephson Electronics*, Wako-shi, March 1987 (to appear in IEEE Transactions on Computers).

[10] Spee, P. "Dynamic Type and Range Checking in C using a Tagged Architecture". Research and Development Corp. of Japan, 1988.

[11] Steenkiste, P. and Hennessy, J. "LISP on a Reduce-Instruction-set-Processor". *Proceedings of the 1986 Conference on LISP and Functional Programming*, ACM, Boston, August 1986.

[12] Steenkiste, P. and Hennessy, J. "Tags and Type Checking in LISP: Hardware and Software Approaches". *Proceedings of 2nd International Conference on Architectural Support for Programming Languages and Operating Systems*, Palo Alto, October 1987.

[13] Steele, Jr. G. *Common Lisp - The language*. Digital Equipment Corporation, 1984.

[14] Taylor, S.T., Hilfinger, P.N., Larus, J.R., Patterson, D.A. and Zorn, B.G. "Evaluation of the SPUR Lisp Architecture". *Proceedings of the 12th Annual International Symposium on Computer Architecture*, ACM, June 1986.

[15] *VAX Architecture Handbook*, Digital Equipment Corp., 1981.

[16] Wilkes, M.V. "Hardware Support for Memory Protection: Capability Implementations". *Proceedings of International Conference on Architectural Support for Programming Languages and Operating Systems*, Palo Alto, Ca., March 1982.

APPENDIX. An example of list append function

```
; source program of list append
;
;(defun append (x y)
;   (cond ((endp x) y)
;        (t (cons (car x) (append (cdr x) y)))))
;
; gr0-gr32 : global register
; vr0-vr32 : local frame register
; gr0/gr1  : BL for passing argument
;            and multiple return values
; gr10/gr11: BL for cons cell segment.
; gr12/gr13: BL for free area of cons cell segment.
; gr30/gr31: BL for entire space.

_Lappend:
    movw sp,fp              ; no local variable
                           ; on the stack
    movw gr10@0,vr1         ; move x to vr1.
    movw gr10@4,vr0         ; move y to vr0.
    movw.j gr10:(vr1),vr2,L1
                           ; load car(x) to vr2.
                           ; jump L1 if success.
    jmp L3                 ; if failed,
                           ; return y (vr0)
L1:
    movw gr10:4(vr1),vr3
                           ; load cdr(x) to vr3
    movw vr0,>-4(sp)       ; push y
    movw vr3,>-4(sp)       ; push cdr(x)
    mkbl (sp),4(sp),gr0    ; make BL to pass
                           ; the argument
                           ; base = sp,
                           ; limit = sp+4
    call _Lappend         ; call function
    lea  8(sp),sp          ; reset stack
    movw gr0@0,vr0         ; get return to vr0
L2:
    alloc.j gr12,vr2,vr0,#8,vr0,L3
        ; vr0 = cons(vr2,vr0)
        ; v2 and vr0 are stored to double word
        ; specified by the base of gr12,
        ; and gr12 is incremented by 8.
        ; if base > limit,
        ; then address tag of gr12 is cleared.
        ; and go to L3.
    trap #GC_TRAP         ; already address tag
                           ; of gr12 is cleared
                           ; call GC
    jmp  L2               ; again do cons
L3:
    movw vr0,>-4(sp)      ; push return value
    mkbl (sp),(sp),gr0    ; make BL for
                           ; return value on gr0
    movw fp,sp            ; reset stack
    ret                    ; return
```

Multiple vs Wide Shared Bus Multiprocessors

Andy Hopper, Alan Jones, Dimitris Lioupis

Olivetti Research Ltd.
Keynes House
24A Trumpington Street
Cambridge CB2 1QA
England

ABSTRACT

In this paper we compare the simulated performance of a family of multiprocessor architectures based on a global shared memory. The processors are connected to the memory through caches that snoop one or more shared buses in a crossbar arrangement.

We have simulated a number of configurations in order to assess the relative performance of multiple versus wide bus machines, with varying amounts of prefetch. Four programs, with widely differing characteristics, were run on each configuration. The configurations that gave the best all-round results were multiple narrow buses with 4 words of prefetch.

1. Introduction

Multiprocessors are used today to provide better performance at lower cost. Many commercially available systems are based on a shared memory, shared bus architecture. These machines have a relatively straightforward implementation since they are an extension of the uniprocessor bus system. Their globally shared memory and consistency mechanisms give a programming model that is very similar to systems of cooperating processes on uniprocessors. Commercial systems such as the Encore [ROS85] and Sequent [SEQ84] claim significant speed-ups at very low cost.

A major limitation of shared bus multiprocessors is the bandwidth of the bus, which limits the number of processors that can be connected to the same memory, and thus the performance of the system. To solve this problem we can increase the speed of the bus [DEC88], which is not always easy because of technology limitations, or we can use more wires to connect to the memory. For a given technology, more wires provide more bandwidth, but it is not obvious which is the best

way to connect the wires because of complications such as caches, code sharing and system complexity.

Wide buses are simpler to build but they provide only one path to memory. Multiple buses are more complex to implement but they reduce contention because of multiple paths to memory and more wires for control and addresses.

In this paper we study the effect of bus architecture on performance. Keeping the number of data wires constant, we found that multiple buses can provide better effective bandwidth to memory, and thus better performance. Multiple bus machines ran our sample programs from 0.9 to 3.5 times faster than wide bus machines.

The rest of the paper is organised as follows. In the next section we give a brief description of the proposed architecture and we compare it with existing designs. In section 3 we review the factors that may affect program performance to aid in understanding the results. Section 4 describes the simulator environment used to obtain the results included in section 5. We conclude with an overall analysis in section 6.

2. Architectural Description

Conventional multiprocessors (such as SPUR [HIL86], Firefly [THA87], and others) are connected to the shared memory by a single bus as shown in figure 1a.

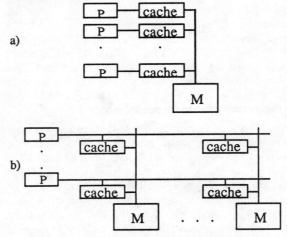

Figure 1 : Shared bus multiprocessors

To increase the bandwidth to memory, we use a multiple bus architecture. The resulting architecture shown in figure 1b, uses a grid of buses with a cache at each cross-point to connect to memory.

Each memory module contains a portion of the memory space and memory references are interleaved in cache block size intervals. If the cache block size is four words, then addresses 0 to 3 will reside in the first memory module, 4 to 7 in the second and so on. The caches implement the Berkeley protocol [KAT85] to maintain consistency on each memory bus by ownership and snooping. Because each portion of the address space (e.g. 0 to 3) is always mapped onto the same memory module, consistency can be maintained independently on each memory bus by the snooping mechanism in the corresponding caches.

The resulting architecture maintains the same programming model as conventional shared bus multiprocessors, whilst providing a higher bandwidth to memory. The number of memory buses is limited by the electrical load on the processor bus to about 4-8. We simulated up to 4 memory buses.

As we increase the number of memory buses, there is a linear increase in the number of cache chips, and in the number of buses. Many organisations, including Olivetti, are working on high density silicon-based interconnection technologies which could be used to implement such crossbar systems.

Recently many architectures have been proposed utilising both wide bus and multiple bus approaches. They all address the shared memory bottleneck problem by increasing the width of the data path to memory.

A multiprocessor with a 128 bit wide bus is under investigation by Olivetti. It is designed to accommodate up to 8 processors connected through a write back cache onto a pended bus. A processor issues a request, and releases the bus, then the corresponding memory module requests the bus when it has the reply ready. The bus operates at 20 MHz and can be extended by connecting two similar buses with a special interface. In our simulations we study a similar architecture which employs a write back cache, but with a different policy (Berkeley ownership). We use a master slave bus model which will behave differently to a pended model. Our multiple bus case however, shares the ability to have several transactions in progress at the same time, and these results may relate to the pended model.

The Wisconsin Multicube[GOO88], is a shared memory multiprocessor which uses a grid of buses to connect to memory. In this design there is a processor at each cross point resulting in a large number (up to 1024) of processors. We envisage a smaller number (up to 100) of processors connected to memory through caches at each cross point as shown in figure 1b. This simplifies the cache consistency mechanism which is a major problem in the Multicube. Consistency checks occur independently on the vertical memory buses, as in a conventional single bus multiprocessor.

Multiple buses are used on Aquarius as reported in [NGU88]. Processors are connected to memory buses through caches at each cross point. Aquarius is a multiprocessor designed for Prolog, which has a different model of execution to conventional languages, and imposes higher demands on the memory system. Due to the increased number of memory writes, separate buses are used to carry the invalidations to other caches. Its designers believe that multiple buses can provide enough bandwidth to meet these demands. We concentrate on the parallel execution of conventional languages and in particular programs written in C.

Factors Affecting the Performance of a Program.
This section discusses some of the factors that can affect the performance of multiprocessor systems. The different running times of a program on various configurations may not be directly related to the cache/memory bandwidth. The cache/memory parameters can subtly alter important factors such as load balance, synchronisation, or the detailed access pattern of the program. The programs that we use were chosen to depend differently on such factors.

As a concrete example for this section, we shall assume that 128 wires are used to carry the data on the memory bus, organised as a single transfer unit in the wide bus case, and as four independent 32-bit word units in the multiple bus case. The processor to cache bus is assumed to operate with 32-bit quantities.

On a cache miss, the wide bus case is assumed to transfer four sequential words, aligned on a four-word boundary. If these four words are not all useful to the processor during their time in the cache, then some of the extra bandwidth provided by the bus width is being wasted. However, other studies show that a few words of prefetch generally improve the cache hit rate, and that this outweighs any wasted data fetches [DEC88].

When an algorithm is designed to operate on a number of processors, it is often difficult to avoid one or two of the processors having to do more work than the others. In some cases this imbalance of workloads may be dependent on the data supplied for the run(e.g. quicksort). In others the imbalance may be inherent in the chosen implementation (e.g. a prime number sieve). In almost any parallel algorithm, there will be some computation that cannot be performed concurrently, and this will further upset the work distribution. Under these circumstances, some processors will become idle, leading to longer running times, but less bus traffic. Our program suite includes two such programs, but the amount of idle time is such that a 16 processor system still completes them faster than any less powerful machine.

In most programs, explicit synchronisation between processes occurs infrequently compared to the time spent in other computations [EGG88]. However, after processes have synchronised, they may for a time run together through the same data structures (e.g. a work queue) and this can lead to beneficial or detrimental interference until the processes move apart. Changing the memory parameters can subtly alter the amount of time that the processes are interfering, and this can have noticeable effects on performance.

Changes in the layout of data, or in the times that it is accessed during a computation, can drastically change the running time. The classic example of this occurs when scanning through matrices. If a cache block contains consecutive elements from the same row, then running through a row will take maximum advantage of the prefetch mechanism, whereas a column will only use one word per block.

3. Simulation

3.1. Simulator Details

We have developed a high-level event driven simulator to model various multiprocessor systems. Behavioural models of the individual chips and bus wires are written in Modula-2 [WIR82], and they accurately reflect the detailed timing of the external logic signals. For instance, the processor model fetches instructions from the memory model by driving signals in the same way as the real chip. The whole system is generated from a set of high-level parameters such as the number of processors, cache associativity and wire delays.

The underlying model is one of nodes (circuit elements) communicating by sending values (64 bits) across contacts. This allows us to pass 32-bit bus values in one event, and to display them in a meaningful way to the user (e.g. hexadecimal values). As the interpretation of these values is defined from outside the simulator, it can be tailored to the application, for instance, by disassembling instructions when the values on the data bus are displayed.

All the models register extensive debugging commands with the user interface. For example, breakpoints can be set on processor addresses to stop the simulator and allow register dumps or single stepping, the values stored in caches and memories can be read or written, and individual addresses can be monitored to trace all changes. When investigating the performance of some algorithms, it has proved particularly instructive to watch the accesses to a lock and the data items it protects.

To save time, the memory model can interpret loadable images, and initialise itself directly, removing the need for a loader and simulated input device. The processor modeled is the Acorn RISC Machine (ARM) [FUR87] with a cycle time of 200 ns and is connected by a bus translator chip to the caches. The caches are our own design, they are write back and communicate with the global shared memory over buses that implement the Berkeley consistency protocol.

Running on a Sun260 workstation, a simulated single processor machine runs at around 35 ips (instructions per second). Machines with larger numbers of processors impose a greater load on the simulator, keeping the aggregate instruction throughput at 15 to 30 ips. Our benchmark programs require around 1 million cycles to complete, and take between 8 and 24 hours for each run.

3.2. Programming Environment

The programs are written in C, with assembler libraries for booting, synchronisation and output. The main procedure takes two arguments representing the number of processors in the system, and the number of the processor that it is executing on. These numbers are computed by routines contained in the boot code. Each program can be linked for execution directly on the Archimedes workstation which compiles it, and debugged in single processor mode before being used in the simulation. After they have solved their particular problems, they use unimplemented instructions to signal the models to report statistics for that run, and they then proceed to verify that the results were correct. If the answers are correct, then a one line summary is entered in a collation file from which various performance graphs can be drawn. If the answers are incorrect, then the time is entered as zero to draw our attention to it, and the entry is ignored by subsequent tools. These checks have detected subtle errors in our C test programs, and faults in our simulated hardware that only rarely occur in particular configurations. The correct answers are obtained by running the programs on the real ARM in the Archimedes workstation.

3.3. Simulated Machines

We simulated four simple programs runs on three bus layouts to compare their performance:

1) Wide-bus: A 128 bit wide bus with 16 processors.
2) 2-bus: Two 64 bit wide buses with 16 processors.
3) 4-bus: Four 32 bit wide buses with 16 processors.

All systems use caches as shown in figure 1. The cache size is 1 kbyte per processor, which means that in the 4-bus case each cache is 256 bytes. It is small to correspond with the small size of our programs. The total system cache is also constant because we are using 16 processors. The buses use separate paths for addresses, data, and control, and the master keeps control of the bus until its request is satisfied. Arbitration for the bus takes 50 ns. and a memory fetch 400 ns. (plus 200ns. for each additional word).

The cache block size is important in a shared memory architecture because it influences the amount of traffic on the bus and thus contention. For each of the above bus configurations we performed three runs of each program to determine the effect of block size on our measurements.

Single Transfer

The cache block size is equal to the bus width. In this case, on a cache miss, a block will be transferred in one bus cycle.

Two-transfer

The block size is now twice the bus width. Whenever data has to be moved between cache and memory, one address is sent, followed by two cycles of data transfer.

Four-transfer

The block size is four times the bus width. Each block will be fetched in four sequential memory transfers. We gain some advantage by only presenting the address information once, and by using memories with fast page modes. In the *Wide-bus* case we are fetching 16 words, which may be advantageous for some programs, and not for others. The cache block sizes (also the data transfer sizes) for the nine runs are shown in table 1.

	Bus Width		
Transfers	1	2	4
1	1	2	4
2	2	4	8
4	4	8	16

Table 1: Cache block sizes (words)

4. Results

The results obtained are shown in the next four sections in bar chart form, one section for each program. Each bar represents the execution time of the program in microseconds (see figure 2). Thus a smaller bar represents a better processor performance. The text will refer to the bars by numbering them from the left, thus the wide-bus, 4-transfer case is bar 1, and the 4-bus, 1-transfer case is bar 9.

We also quote other statistics gathered from the simulations. Utilisation is given as the mean of the percentages of time that each individual bus is occupied by *any* processor. Average queue length is the mean number of processors that are requesting or have been granted the bus. We collect these statistics by observing the buses every 20ns., the period of the master clock from which all other clocks in the system are derived.

4.1. SOR

This program repeatedly computes the value of grid locations by taking the average of the four surrounding points. Eventually, this method converges to a solution of Laplace's equation for the given boundary values. Our grid consists of 32 rows of 9 elements each, and we

perform 25 iterations. For multiprocessor execution, we divide the grid equally into as many horizontal strips as there are processors. Each processor then updates every other element in its strip in turn, and increments its own iteration count. It then spins, waiting for its two neighbours to come to the same iteration number, then proceeds with the next wave of updates. At the edges of the strips, neighbouring processors are always trying to read the same locations, so the sharing overhead is high.

The running times for this program are shown in Figure 2..

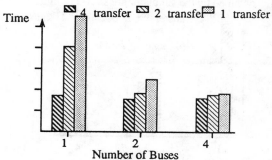

Figure 2 : Performance of SOR Program

Looking at bars 3, 6 and 9, the most striking feature of figure 2 is the very bad performance of the wide-bus machine with only one transfer per miss (bar 3). Normally, we would expect the prefetch given by a four-word block to enhance performance, but in this case it has dramatically reduced it. This is mainly due to the data for different processors being interleaved at one word grain in the regions where it is shared (a property of the software implementation). This leads to higher utilisation in the wide bus cases (greater block sizes): 99.8%, 89.7% and 41.6% for the 1, 2, and 4-bus cases respectively (bars 3, 6, and 9), leading to average queue lengths of 9.17, 3.49 and 0.88. The hit rates improve from around 90% on the narrow buses to 94% on the wide, not enough to overcome the effects of the much greater queue lengths.

The narrow bus machine with four transfers per miss (bar 7) does not suffer from this problem as it makes much better use of the memory (4 buses by 4 words = 16 words, transferred in 400 + 200 + 200 + 200 = 1000 ns.) than the wide bus with one transfer (bar 3, 4 words transferred in 400ns.). It also allows one processor to block its interfering neighbours for a longer period, but only on one bus, so the other buses become less congested, and other processors can proceed efficiently. Because the program causes a considerable amount of bus traffic, the buses become saturated if the memory is not used to best advantage, and we see 99.8% utilisation, 9.2 queue lengths for both the two- and single-transfer wide bus cases (bars 2 and 3). If we consider just the one-transfer cases, then we should see the effect of the greater prefetch as the buses become wider, as the time to satisfy a miss remains constant at 400ns.

303

4.2. Matrix Multiplication

The matrix multiplication program multiplies two matrices (16 x 16 elements) stored as global arrays to produce the result matrix. Each processor calculates a part of the resultant matrix determined by its number, which is used to index the resultant array. This means that eventually each processor will fetch all elements of the first matrix and a column of the second matrix. Write invalidations in the blocks that hold the result should influence the performance of this program. The results obtained by the simulator are shown in figure 3.

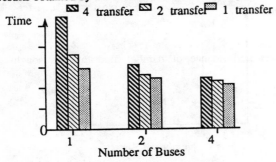

Figure 3 : Performance of Prod Program

There is a lot of read sharing in this algorithm, and fewer writes per instruction than the others, yet the average queue length in the wide bus case (single transfer, bar 3) was 6.45. This dropped to 1.93 and 0.92 in the 2-bus and 4-bus cases (bars 6 and 9). The main reason for the high contention on the wide bus is that each processor is responsible for computing every 16th element of the result. When one word is written, it invalidates the entire block, which contains the words being computed by three of the other processors, requiring extra bus transfers when they come to write their results. We therefore see this program being dominated by the effects of the wasted prefetch, with the smaller effect of the increased memory efficiency of multiple transfers playing a secondary role.

4.3. Quicksort

The quicksort algorithm has been rewritten for concurrent execution on the multiprocessor. It is still based on recursively dividing the input list into two lists with elements smaller than and greater than a pivot. The first element of the list is used as pivot. In the beginning only one processor starts executing and the rest spin on a lock. When the list is divided the processor keeps one half of the list and gives the other to the next processor by clearing its lock. This is repeated until there are no more processors, when the execution is reduced into normal recursive quicksort. The list is stored as a global array of random numbers in memory. The performance of this program depends heavily on the input list which determines the load balancing of processors. The program was run sorting 1000 random numbers and the results are

shown in figure 4.

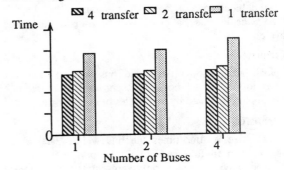

Figure 4 : Performance of Quicksort Program

Quicksort is the only program to take full advantage of the prefetch provided by the wide bus (bar 3), and runs slightly faster than with narrow buses in the single transfer mode (bar 9). When prefetch was added to the narrow bus case (bar 7), the program ran in only 70% of the time, outperforming the wide bus in all but the 4-transfer case (bar 1, 16 word blocks).

4.4. Sieve

This is a parallel implementation of the sieve of Eratosthenes. The main data structure is an array of 1024 integers, where the contents of array[i] indicate whether i is a prime or not. All processors start at the second element and move up the array looking for a zero. If they find one, they use a test-and-set instruction to mark the number as prime (a 1), and then proceed to mark all multiples as non-prime (a 2). When all processors have searched as far as the square root of the array size, the final processor scans the array, counting the number of primes (zeroes or ones).

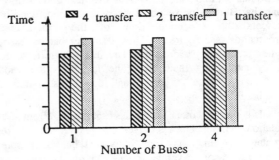

Figure 5 : Performance of the Sieve Program

Due to the restricted length of the sieve array, only eleven of the sixteen processors have any work to do, and after about 25% of the running time, the other five have found this and are idling. During the rest of the run, there can be considerable interference as processors rapidly mark off multiples of the remaining primes, so although the hit rate improves with prefetch, the invalidations also increase, leaving the running time largely unaltered. To show that bus bandwidth is indeed a bottleneck in this instance, we also show the mean

304

queue lengths on the buses in figure 6.

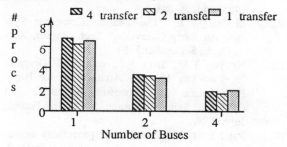

Figure 6 : Average Queue Lengths for the Sieve Program

Note that the queue length divided by the bus width remains roughly constant, so although the wide bus machines have greater latencies on a miss, their buses are transferring more data each time, and the overall performance becomes more a function of the efficiency of memory usage. We should therefore expect the multiple transfer machines to do much better (bars 1, 4, and 7), but due to the sparse nature of some of the accesses (e.g. marking every 29th element), the greater prefetch is sometimes wasted, and the improvement is not as great as might be hoped.

5. Discussion

Looking at the four sets of results together, we can try to find a machine configuration that is amongst the best for all programs. Single bus machines perform badly with the SOR program (1 and 2 transfer cases are bad), and with matrix multiplication in the 4-transfer case. Multiple bus machines with only single transfers perform badly for the highly sequential quicksort program. Thus we are left with the best all-round performers being a 4-bus machine with 2 or 4 single-word transfers on a miss, or a 2 bus machine with 2 dual-word transfers.

To help us to understand the factors influencing the running times; the processors, caches and memories gather detailed statistics about the bus accesses during the run. These are recorded in log files, and can be post-processed to display load balance, queue lengths, utilisations, hit rates, read/write ratios etc.

These programs represent only a few examples of the sort of behavior expected from the inner loops of parallel applications, but already some trends can be seen:

A large transfer unit is detrimental to programs that write shared data interleaved at a fine grain, as it can lead to unnecessary invalidations. An example would be updating items in a shared job queue or other list structure, where a change to one element could invalidate adjacent entries that were being worked on by other processors. This will lead to bad performance on wide bus machines with multiple transfers.

Buses with single transfers are not using the memory to best advantage (page modes, suppressed addressing of sequential blocks). Wide bus machines with single transfers are consistently slower than multiple bus machines with the same transfer unit. Compare the 1-bus 1-transfer, 2-bus 2-transfer, and 4-bus 4-transfer running times; all of these systems move data in four-word blocks, yet the 4-bus configuration is consistently faster.

From these observations, we expect that multiple bus machines will be worthwhile in environments where the very best performance of parallel algorithms is sought. They can provide high bandwidth to memory without the penalties of large transfer units, and with the added flexibility of concurrent transfers. When using wide bus machines for parallel applications, more care is required to make the best use of their potentially high bandwidth.

6. Conclusion

We have run a selection of parallel programs on nine variations of shared memory multiprocessor architectures. The results have been encouraging, as the special characteristics of each program have led to predictable differences in performance on the nine machines. Our original thesis, that multiple narrow buses offer a high bandwidth with more flexibility than single wide buses, has been borne out by the poor performances observed in some wide-bus runs.

Our simulations have all used small programs operating over a relatively small range of addresses. Whilst they cannot be taken as typical examples of complete multiprocessor applications, they are representative of the inner loops of compute-intensive programs. The instructions of such pieces of code are always cached, and often constitute the major part of the running time, but the data they access might not be cached. If they are writing to shared data, or are reading large amounts of data, then they will generate bus traffic similar to that seen on our simulated systems.

With current technologies, multiple bus machines of a significant size are not cost-effective. The crossbar interconnect of 32-bit buses, with high-speed cache elements at each intersection, proves very difficult to implement. As high-density interconnect systems become more widely used, the implementation of multiple buses will become easier, making such systems more attractive.

Wide-bus architectures, being more suitable for implementation on a conventional backplane, are now emerging in high-performance machines. It remains to be seen whether the unfavourable characteristics displayed by the SOR and matrix product programs can be avoided in practice.

Acknowledgements
The authors would like to express their thanks to James Kenney and Kami Sehat of Cambridge University Computer Laboratory for writing the processor and cache models; Stuart Wray and Mark Chopping of Olivetti Research Laboratory, Cambridge for their work during the development of the multiprocessor simulations and programs described in this paper.

References

[AGA88] Agarwal A. and A. Gupta, "Memory-Reference Characteristics of Multiprocessor Applications under MACH," Proceedings of ACM Sigmetrics 1988.

[ARC86] Archibald J. and J. Baer, "An Evaluation of Cache Coherence Solutions in Shared-Bus Multiprocessors," ACM Trans. on Computer Systems, 4,4, November 1986.

[BEL85] Bell C.G, "Multis: A New Class of Multiprocessor Computers," Science, 228, April 1985.

[CHE88] Cheriton D.R., A. Gupta, P.D Boyle and H.A Goosen, "The VMP Multiprocessor: Initial Experience, Refinements and Performance Evaluation," Proc. of 15th Intl. Symp. on Computer Architecture, Hawaii, June 1988.

[DAS85] Das C.R, and L.N. Bhuyan, "Computation Availability of Multiple-Bus Multiprocessors", U of Southwestern Louisiana, 1985.

[DEC88] Digital Equipment Corporation, "CVAX-based Systems", Digital Technical Journal no. 7, August 1988.

[EGG88] Eggers S. and R. Katz, "Characterization of Sharing in Parallel Programs and its Applicability to Coherency Protocol Evaluation," Proc. of 15th Intl. Symp. on Computer Architecture, Hawaii, June 1988.

[FUR87] Furber S. B and A. R Wilson,"The Acorn RISC machine - an architectural view", Electronics and Power, vol 33 no 6, pp 402-405 June 1987

[GOO83] Goodman J. "Using Cache Memories to Reduce Processor-Memory Traffic," Proc. of the 10th Intl Symp. on Computer Architecture, Stockholm June 1983.

[GOO88] Goodman J. and P.J. Woest, "The Wisconsin Multicube: A New Large-Scale Cache-Coherent Multiprocessor," Proc. of 15th Intl. Symp. on Computer Architecture, Hawaii, June 1988.

[GOT83] Gottlieb A., et. al. "The NYU Ultracomputer--Designing an MIMD Shared Memory Parallel Computer", IEEE Trans. on Computers, VolC-32, Feb 1983.

[HIL86] Hill M.D. et. al. "SPUR: A VLSI Multiprocessor Workstation," IEEE Computer, 19, 11 November 1986.

[KAT85] Katz R.H. et. al., "Implementing a Cache Consistency Protocol," 12th international Symposium on Computer Architecture, IEEE, 1985, pp. 276-283.

[MCR84] McCreight E, "The Dragon Computer System: An Early Overview," Tech. Report, Xerox Corp., September 1984.

[NGU88] Nguyen T.M, Srini V.P, and A.M. Despain, "A Two-Tier Memory Architecture for High-Performance Multiprocessor Systems", Intl Conf. on Supercomputing, St. Malo, France, July 1988.

[PAT81] Patel J. H, "Performance of processors-memory interconnections for multiprocessors", IEEE Trans on Computers, Oct 1981, pp 771-780.

[PAT82] Patterson D.A., Garrison P., Hill M.D., Lioupis D., Nyberg C., Sippel T.N. & Van Dyke K.S., "Architecture of a VLSI cache for a RISC", 10th Intl. Symp. on Computer Architecture, 1982.

[ROS85] Rose C.D, "Encore Eyes Multiprocessor Market," Electronics July 8, 1985.

[SAT80] Satyanarayanan M. "Commercial Multiprocessing Systems ," IEEE Computer, 13, 5, May 1980.

[SEQ84] Sequent Computer Systems, Inc. "Balance 8000" Technical Summary, Nov 1984.

[THA87] Thacker C. and L. Stewart, "Firefly: A Multiprocessor Workstation", 2nd Intl. Conference on Architectural Support for Programming Languages and Operating Systems, pp 164-172, ACM, October 1987.

[WIL87] Wilson A. W. Jr, "Hierarchical Cache/Bus Architecture for Shared Memory Multiprocessors," Proc of 14th Intl. Symp. on Computer Architecture, 1987.

[WIR82] Wirth N., "Programming in Modula-2," Springer Verlag, New York 1982.

Performance measurements on a commercial multiprocessor running parallel code

Marco Annaratone and Roland Rühl

Integrated Systems Laboratory
Swiss Federal Institute of Technology
8092 Zurich, Switzerland
(411) 256-5240

Abstract

The multiprocessor Sequent Symmetry was first delivered to customers with write-through caches. Later on each machine was upgraded with copy-back caches. Because all the other architectural parameters were unchanged (main memory, bus, cache organization and size, and so on), this made it possible to measure the performance of a multiprocessor with no caches, write-through caches, and copy-back caches. We also study the impact that the language (FORTRAN and C) has on the performance of the machine.

1. Introduction

The Sequent Symmetry S81 is a bus-connected multiprocessor. Our machine is configured with 12 processors, 64 Mbyte of two-way interleaved shared memory, and 1 Gbyte of mass storage. Each processor consists of an Intel 80386 CPU, a floating-point accelerator with Weitek chips, a 64K-byte instruction/data cache, and a custom VLSI chip for process synchronization and interrupt handling [1,2]. Sequent delivered to customers a Symmetry with write-through caches (model S81a), and upgraded it later on with copy-back caches (model S81b). Both caches are two-way set-associative; the line size is four, 32-bit words and LRU replacement policy is used. The S81a and S81b have identical memory and a bus with 53.4 Mbyte/s sustained transfer rate [3].

The goals of this study are (1) to measure the performance improvement on parallel code when write-through

This research was supported in part by ETH grant 0.330.066.23/4 and in part by the Mikrotechnik Kredit.

caches are replaced by copy-back caches, and (2) whether Symmetry users should write scientific code in FORTRAN or C. (Both languages have identical parallel extensions.)

The paper is organized as follows. First, we describe all the measurements performed and list the benchmarks used. Second, we explain how the algorithms have been parallelized. Then, the results of the cache comparison are presented and discussed. FORTRAN and C implementations are compared, and we explain the results obtained. Finally, speedup curves are presented to explain some of the results.

2. Measurements performed

Measurements have been performed for all combinations of the following parameters: parallelism (1, 5, 7, and 11 processors), language (FORTRAN and C), problem size of algorithm, and memory configuration (no caches, write-through caches, copy-back caches). We have run the following benchmarks:

- *Numerical programs.* Matrix multiplication, Gaussian elimination, generalized FFT, Householder transformation, QR iteration, Lanczos iteration. (All programs are running in double-precision floating-point.)
- *Non numerical programs.* PROLOG database interpreter, C parallel compilation, FORTRAN/C mix parallel compilation.

We report here only a subset of all possible parameter combinations, namely: write-through vs. copy-back cache comparison, FORTRAN vs. C comparison, and speedup curves with copy-back caches (FORTRAN code).

3. Mapping the numerical programs

Throughout the paper matrices are of size n^2, vectors are of size N, and p is the number of processors. The "parallelization grain-size" is the amount of data assigned to each processor after a microfork. It does not necessarily coincide with the total input size divided by the number of processors.

3.1 Matrix multiplication and Gaussian elimination

Matrix multiplication has the same number of multiplications and additions. Moreover, the data-set can be easily decomposed with almost no interaction among the processors. To achieve minimum synchronization overhead, we have parallelized the outermost loop [4]. The parallelization grain-size is $\frac{n^2}{p}$.

We used Gaussian elimination to compute the determinant of a real square matrix. Row storage is used. The outermost loop, the pivot search, and the row swap all run sequentially. After the row swap a microfork occurs: all processors in parallel perform row subtraction and matrix update. The average parallelization grain-size is $\frac{n^2}{2p}$.

3.2 Generalized FFT

The generalized FFT (GFFT) algorithm does not require the input data size N to be a power of 2. GFFT decomposes N into its $(a+1)$ prime factors q_i

$$N = \prod_{i=0}^{a} q_i .$$

$\mu \in 0 \ldots N-1$ can be uniquely represented by the ordered list $\{\mu_1 \ldots \mu_a\}$, with

$$
\begin{aligned}
\mu_1 &= \mu \bmod (q_1 q_2 \ldots q_a), \\
\mu_2 &= \mu \bmod (q_2 q_3 \ldots q_a), \\
&\vdots \\
\mu_a &= \mu \bmod q_a .
\end{aligned}
\tag{1}
$$

It follows that the Fourier terms y_μ

$$y_\mu = \sum_{i=0}^{N-1} \beta^{\mu i} x_i, \ \mu = 0 \ldots N-1, \ \beta = e^{-\frac{2\pi j}{N}} \tag{2}$$

($[x_0, \ldots, x_{N-1}]$ being the input, $[y_0, \ldots, y_{N-1}]$ being the output of a complex DFT) can be calculated as follows :

$$y_\mu = \sum_{\nu_0=0}^{q_0-1} \beta^{\nu_0 \mu_0 \eta_0} \sum_{\nu_1=0}^{q_1-1} \beta^{\nu_1 \mu_1 \eta_1} \ldots \sum_{\nu_a=0}^{q_a-1} \beta^{\nu_a \mu_a \eta_a} x_{k_a} , \tag{3}$$

$$
\begin{aligned}
\text{with} \quad & \mu_0 = \mu, \ \mu_i = \mu_{i-1} \bmod (q_i \ldots q_a), \\
& \eta_0 = 1, \ \eta_{i+1} = \eta_i q_i , \\
& k_{-1} = 0, \ k_i = k_{i-1} + \nu_i \eta_i .
\end{aligned}
$$

Computing each summation

$$\sum_{\nu_a=0}^{q_a-1} \beta^{\nu_a \mu_a \eta_a} x_{k_a}, \ \forall \mu_a, \eta_a \tag{4}$$

in equation (3) requires $N q_a$ multiplications and $N(q_a - 1)$ additions.

At each step the algorithm overwrites the input vector $\underline{x}$ with N partial sums (4). With the recursion

$$
\begin{aligned}
\underline{z}^{(a)} &= \underline{x}; \\
z^{(n-1)}_{k_{n-1}\frac{N}{\eta_n}+\mu_n} &= \sum_{\nu_n=0}^{q_n-1} \beta^{\nu_n \mu_n \eta_n} z^{(n)}_{k_n \frac{N}{\eta_{n+1}}+\mu_{n+1}} ,
\end{aligned}
\tag{5}
$$

after $(a+1)$ steps $(n = a, a-1, \ldots, 0)$ $\underline{z}^{(-1)} = \underline{y}$. Recursion (5) implements a generalized butterfly. For a proof of equations (3) and (5) see [5].

Implementation notes

GFFT consists of three nested loops:

1. Recursion (5) $(n = a, a-1, \ldots, 0)$.
2. N combinations of μ_n and η_n (4).
3. $\nu_n = 0, 1, \ldots, q_n - 1$ for the different n's.

We have parallelized the second loop. The parallelization grain-size is $\frac{N}{p} q_n$. For every recursion step (5), p processes are microforked, each of them executing $\frac{N}{p} q_n$ summations and multiplications before they join again.

3.3 Householder Transformation

The reduction to an upper Hessenberg matrix requires $n-2$ similarity transformations [6]

$$A_{r+1} = P_r A_r P_r , \ r = 1, \ldots, n-2$$

$A_1 \in \mathcal{R}^n \times \mathcal{R}^n$ being the input matrix. The orthogonal matrix P_r is of the form

$$P_r = I - u_r u_r^T / H_r ,$$

with

$$
\begin{aligned}
u_r^T &= [0, \ldots, 0, a_{r+1,r}^{(r)} \pm \sigma_r^{1/2}, a_{r+2,r}^{(r)}, \ldots, a_{n,r}^{(r)}] , \\
\sigma_r &= \sum_{i=r+1}^{n} (a_{i,r}^{(r)})^2 , \\
H_r &= \sigma_r \pm a_{r+1,r}^{(r)} \sigma_r^{1/2} .
\end{aligned}
$$

The computation of A_{r+1} takes place in two steps [6]:

$$
\begin{aligned}
B_{r+1} &= P_r A_r = A_r - u_r (u_r^T A_r)/H_r , \\
A_{r+1} &= B_{r+1} P_r = B_{r+1} - (B_{r+1} u_r / H_r) u_r^T .
\end{aligned}
\tag{6}
$$

Implementation notes

The two vector-matrix products and matrix subtractions shown in Equation (6) have been parallelized. The parallelization grain-size is $\frac{n^2}{p}$.

3.4 QR Iteration

The QR iteration requires the input matrix $A \in \mathcal{R}^n \times \mathcal{R}^n$ to be upper or lower Hessenberg, and can be written as [7]:

$$H_0 = A, \qquad (7)$$
$$H_i = R_i U_i + h_{n,n} I. \qquad (8)$$

$U_i R_i$ is a QR decomposition of $H_{i-1} - h_{n,n} I, i = 1, 2, \ldots$. H_i is upper/lower Hessenberg, is similar to A, and converges to an upper/lower triangular matrix. The *shift* $h_{n,n}$—if properly chosen—accelerates the convergence.

Some eigenvalues may be complex and hence the computation (8) is executed in $\mathcal{C}^n \times \mathcal{C}^n$. We have implemented the algorithm as proposed by Francis [8]. It executes two steps of (8) at once. The shifts are chosen so that H_i always stays real and converges to a matrix with scalars or submatrices of degree two on the diagonal and zero elements below. The average number of iterations per eigenvalue for random matrices is 1.8 [9].

Implementation notes

Each Francis step requires $n - 1$ similarity transformations [6]. Each of these Householder transformations eliminates three non-zero elements introduced by the previous transformation under the subdiagonal (*zero chasing*). This requires a row and column update. These updates run in parallel. Note that the average parallelization grain-size is $\frac{n}{2p}$, the smallest among all the algorithms implemented.

Because the convergence of QR depends on the eigenvalue spread of its input matrix, we show in Table I the minimum and maximum norm of the eigenvalues.

TABLE I

Eigenvalue spread in the random input matrices.

size	$\min_i \|\lambda_i\|$	$\max_i \|\lambda_i\|$
20	8.488e-02	1.022e+01
50	7.140e-02	2.483e+01
75	1.632e+00	1.878e+02
100	2.861e-01	4.977e+01
150	8.130e-02	7.464e+01
200	1.919e-01	9.969e+01
250	3.367e-01	1.254e+02
300	4.400e-01	1.500e+02

3.5 Lanczos Iteration

We have implemented the Lanczos iteration method to tridiagonalize an unsymmetric real matrix [7]. A simplified version of the algorithm operates on symmetric matrices, and is used to solve very large generalized eigenvalue problems [10]. These problems are typical of finite element methods applied for instance to structural mechanics [11].

Implementation notes

We parallelized this algorithm using parallel matrix $\times$ vector and vector $^T \times$ matrix, as was done for Householder transformation. The parallelization grain-size is $\frac{n^2}{p}$.

4. Measurements

All benchmarks have been compiled under the environment *Dynix V3.0.7*. No process migration occurred during the measurements. The machine was running single-user, and the same binary code has been used on both models (S81a and S81b).

4.1 Write-through cache vs. copy-back cache

A detailed description of write-through and copy-back caches can be found in a paper by Smith [12]. The only difference between write-through and copy-back caches is when the processor updates a cached value: a write-through cache always writes the updated value back to main memory (which is shared by all processors), while a copy-back cache updates main memory only when the entire line is replaced. Therefore, the main memory in a system with write-through caches always contains the correct, most recent values. When copy-back caches are used, the same variable, cached into different private memories, can have different values. This is known as the *cache coherency problem*. Several papers have presented different strategies to guarantee cache consistency and solve the coherency problem. The reader is referred to a paper by Bitar and Despain [13] and references therein for a general overview on this issue.

In a global bus multiprocessor, copy-back caches decrease the bus traffic because the main memory updates decrease. Note that if the number of main memory updates is comparable to the number of lines replaced write-through performs better. In order for this to happen, the number of stores shall be higher than the number of loads, and the code shall have poor temporal and spatial locality. Such an occurrence is generally rare, and of scarce importance in practical cases.

The protocol for keeping copy-back caches consistent in the S81b is described in some detail in a paper by Lovette and Thakkar [3]. There are four cache line states: INVALID, PRIVATE (the line has been read and does not exist in any other cache in the system), SHARED (the line has been read and may exist in another cache), MODIFIED (the line has been modified and does not exist in another cache in the system).

Figures 1,2, and 3 show cache speedups for the S81a and S81b systems over a Symmetry with no caches. We show the results for FORTRAN and C runs with 1, 5, and 11 processors. Each benchmark is represented by four bars: the speedup achieved with FORTRAN and write-through caches over the same code running with no caches (F/wt), the same with C code (C/wt), and with copy-back caches (F/cb and C/cb, respectively). Speedups are averaged over several problem sizes ($n = 50, 75, 100, 150, 200, 250, 300$; $N = 10000, 50000, 100000$). For this reason the standard deviation is also shown (dev).

The S81b has a performance improvement of 23.5% in C and 23.7% in FORTRAN (one processor), and of 34.4%

in C and 21.8% in FORTRAN (11 processors) over the S81a system. The different results of C and FORTRAN are explained in the next section.

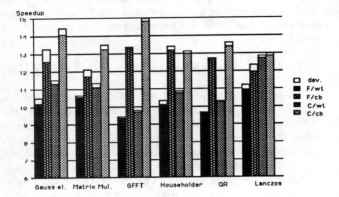

Figure 1. *Cache vs. no cache comparison, 1 processor.*

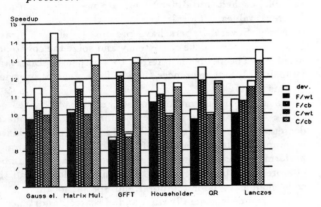

Figure 2. *Cache vs. no cache comparison, 5 processors.*

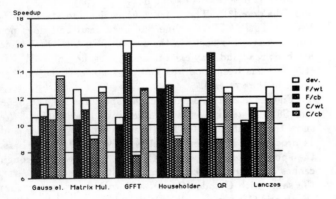

Figure 3. *Cache vs. no cache comparison, 11 processors.*

To summarize, we average the results of the C benchmarks over the problem size and the set of algorithms.

Comparing the machines with caches with an S81 booted without caches, write-through provides an 11-fold performance improvement on 1 processor and a 9.2-fold performance improvement on 11 processors. Copy-back provides a 13.5-fold performance improvement on 1 processor and a 12.3-fold performance improvement on 11 processors.

Not only does copy-back perform better than write-through on one processor but—as expected—copy-back increases the number of processors after which rapid performance degradation occurs due to the saturation of the bus bandwidth.

Note that Sequent claims that the positive influence of copy-back can be noticed when ten or more processors are running in parallel. Our measurements show a definite improvement for 5 and 7 processors as well.

Our measurements—to be interpreted correctly—shall be examined in view of the following considerations.

- *Limited number of processors.* Given a larger number of processors the difference between copy-back and write-through would have been more noticeable.

- *Characteristics of the code used.* All processors involved in the microforking start almost simultaneously to fetch lines from main memory. There is therefore the possibility of short-lived but severe bus contention at the beginning of the microforking. This affects both write-through and copy-back caches.

Scientific code differs from symbolic manipulation programs or supervisor code in two key aspects. First, it has high degree of locality. Second, the ratio between loads and stores is greater than in non-numerical code. These two facts combined explain the relatively small improvement of copy-back over write-through in the benchmarks presented so far.

Extrapolating from the results presented to reach more general conclusions is not justified. The results presented here could not be used to compare, for instance, copy-back and write-through in a multi-threaded environment.

TABLE II
Execution times (s) of single processor and parallel compilation runs (11 processors) for two example programs.

System	S81a	S81b	cacheless
F77P, parallel	64.2	48.4	588.1
F77P, single processor	190.3	141.8	1814.1
TRANS, parallel	12.6	12.0	121.6
TRANS, single processor	27.5	22.4	242.0

To show the effect that structurally different code can have on the comparison between write-through and copy-back caches we have also run three non numerical parallel benchmarks: two compiler programs (using the parallel "make" utility available on the Sequent), and a Prolog database application.

Two programs, F77P and TRANS, were compiled on both S81a and S81b on a single processor and in parallel on 11 processors. F77P implements a FORTRAN 77 parser, and consists of 9 files with a total of more than 3000 lines of C, C++, and YACC. TRANS solves a two-dimensional, steady-state, transonic small disturbance equation for fluid dynamics simulation. It consists of 8 files for a total of 1500 lines of FORTRAN and C code. Table II shows the execution times for the different compilations.

The PROLOG interpreter developed at the Laboratory [14] runs on a database containing the bus and tram network of the city of Zurich (VBZ). The database consists of 1000 facts of arity 3. The interpreter is written in C and finds the shortest tram connection between two stations in town. Because the structure of the database is highly unbalanced, such application parallelizes poorly. Table III shows the results for 1, 3, 6, and 9 processors. Note that the copy-back scheme still provides some reduction in the bus traffic—albeit small—compared with write-through.

TABLE III
*Execution time (s) of PROLOG interpreter running on
VBZ database.*

# proc.	S81a	S81b	cacheless
1	30.40	19.80	276.00
3	21.80	13.60	190.80
6	18.80	11.60	164.40
9	20.10	11.60	164.80

The S81b system is about 40% faster than the S81a system. A characteristic of this benchmark is the large number of memory updates. This, together with a good hit ratio due to the relatively small database, explains why copy-back performs better than in the numerical benchmarks.

It would be interesting at this point to compare our measures with what predicted by analytical models developed in recent years to compare write-through with copy-back. However, these models make architectural assumptions that do not correspond to the hardware characteristics of the Symmetry system. For instance, Patel assumes a cross-bar or delta network interconnection between processors and main memory [15].

The model developed by Dubois [16] assumes that the copy-back cache line has 3 states (Symmetry's has 4), the cache is fully associative (Symmetry's caches are two-way set-associatives), and memory contention does not represent a bottleneck (while the bus does). He then exercises the model on a successive-over-relaxation algorithm. This algorithm is known to parallelize well on distributed-memory parallel processors [17]: it requires almost no process synchronization, and —except for the values at the boundary of each decomposed domain—sharing of data is minimal. This makes it possible to write a parallel version of this code for shared-memory machines which requires very little process synchronization. Our benchmarks instead feature

larger synchronization overhead (except for matrix multiply).

Dubois' results are difficult to correlate with what we have measured, for the reasons mentioned above. He does not find any improvement of copy-back over write-through when the number of processors is relatively small (e.g., 16). We have measured clear improvements even for five processors. This can be explained by noting that a cache of 2K words (Symmetry's processors have 64 Kbyte caches) is assumed and the same paper shows that higher hit ratios favor copy-back more than write-through policies.

4.2 FORTRAN vs. C

The coding of the benchmarks followed strict guidelines to make the comparison between the two compilers as rigorous as possible. The only statement unique to either language is *while*, which is written in FORTRAN using a *GOTO* statement. Except for the already mentioned *while* statement, there is a one-to-one correspondence between C and FORTRAN statements. C programs do not use pointer arithmetic. The Sequent microforking extension is used in both languages, and both codings have the same portions of the program microforked and parallelized. FORTRAN code always involves static allocation; C performs dynamic allocation with pointer arrays for matrices. No I/O statement is present in the section of the code that has been benchmarked. Figures 4, 5, and 6 show the performance of the copy-back system S81b using either FORTRAN or C source with 1, 5, and 11 processors, respectively.

The serial FORTRAN implementation always performs better, apart from Householder. Different memory reference patterns (hence influencing the cache(s) hit ratio) do not explain this behavior. We obtained similar results for a cacheless machine, as shown in Table IV.

TABLE IV
*User times (s) for different algorithms without caches,
uniprocessor implementation*

Algorithm	size	C	FORTRAN
MatMul	250	2388.60	1357.00
Gauss	300	1420.00	925.50
GFFT	100000	2001.80	1581.50
Lanczos	250	3477.30	2809.50
Householder	250	7576.80	8170.90
QR	250	5815.90	4029.40

The performance difference between FORTRAN and C can be explained as follows:

1. FORTRAN allocates matrices column-wise, C allocates them row-wise.

2. The FORTRAN compiler allocates registers more efficiently.

Note that the way matrices are stored in memory does not justify by itself the difference in performance between the two languages. To prove this, we benchmark two small routines, namely matrix ×vector (Ax) and vector ^{T}× matrix ($x^T A$).

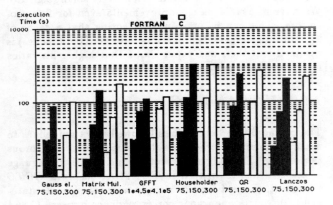

Figure 4. *C/FORTRAN Comparison, copy back, 1 processor.*

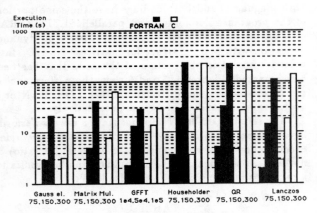

Figure 5. *C/FORTRAN Comparison, copy back, 5 processors.*

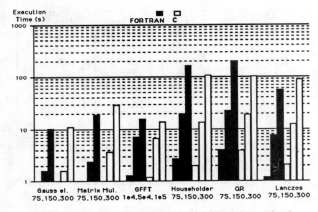

Figure 6. *C/FORTRAN Comparison, copy back, 11 processors.*

If the performance difference could be explained only in terms of storage mechanisms, C should run Ax more efficiently than FORTRAN, which should run more efficiently $x^T A$. Actually, FORTRAN performs better than C in both cases. If we now rewrite the C code so that registers are manually allocated, the two compilers produce code with similar performance. The execution times of the two routines on one processor cacheless Symmetry are ($n = 300$): 8.44s (C, Ax), 9.32s (C, $x^T A$), 6.59s (FORTRAN, Ax), 5.90s (FORTRAN, $x^T A$), 5.62s (C, Ax, manual register allocation).

The kernel of the Householder code features a sequence of six double nested loops, using all the same indeces. Such a program structure allowed us to parallelize the algorithm more efficiently. In this case the C compiler is able to allocate the indeces in registers.

A cross-examination of Figures 4, 5, and 6 shows that FORTRAN and C programs feature about the same speedup when running on 5 or 11 processors. An exception to this is the QR algorithm in which the C code parallelizes more efficiently than the equivalent FORTRAN code. In the QR C code it was possible to allocate only once the stack space used by local variables on the heap. This decreased the microfork overhead. This was not possible in FORTRAN: any time a microfork occurs a new large stack for each process has to be allocated.

4.3 Speedup

This section shows the maximum speedup achieved in the six numerical algorithms. Figures 7.a through 7.f show the results for FORTRAN code running on 5,7,and 11 processors of the S81b. All curves are actually linear interpolations of measurements taken for $n = 25, 50, 75, 100, 150, 200, 250, 300$ and $N = 10000, 50000, 100000$.

Gaussian elimination, Lanczos iteration, and Householder transformation achieve similar speedups. They have parallelization grain-size of the same order of magnitude. The QR iteration behaves much worse, because of the larger synchronization overhead due to smaller grain-size. The parallelization grain-size of GFFT is proportional to the size of the input vector; this explains why for large N's the achieved speedup is comparable to that of Gaussian elimination, Lanczos iteration, and Householder transformation.

As expected, matrix multiplication parallelized almost perfectly. Because of the (prime) number of processors, some load imbalance occurs when the remainder of $\frac{n^2}{p}$ is large This effect is noticeable in the 11 processor curve of Figure 7.a (e.g., when $n = 100$).

5. Conclusions

In the introduction we stated the goals of this study: (1) to quantify the performance improvement of copy-back over write-through caches in the Symmetry multiprocessor, and (2) to evaluate the performance of the same algorithms written in FORTRAN and C.

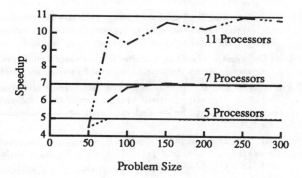

Figure 7.a *Speedup over problem size, FOR-TRAN code, copy-back caches, matrix multiplication.*

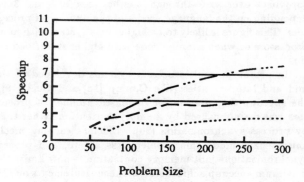

Figure 7.b *Speedup over problem size, FOR-TRAN code, copy-back caches, Gaussian elimination.*

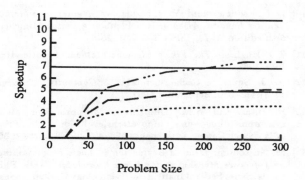

Figure 7.c *Speedup over problem size, FOR-TRAN code, copy-back caches, Lanczos iteration.*

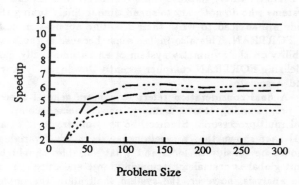

Figure 7.d *Speedup over problem size, FOR-TRAN code, copy-back caches, Householder transformation.*

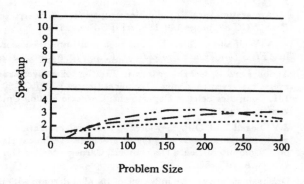

Figure 7.e *Speedup over problem size, FOR-TRAN code, copy-back caches, QR iteration.*

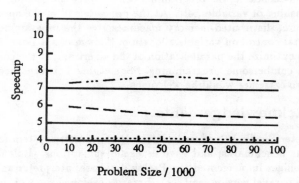

Figure 7.f *Speedup over problem size, FORTRAN code, copy-back caches, GFFT.*

313

The performance improvement on numerical codes of copy-back over write-through was between 20% and 30%, depending on the language used and the number of processors. This figure is likely to be higher on a system with more processors or when running code with higher store/load ratio.

In prototype multiprocessor systems developed in the mid and late seventies (like C.mmp [18] and Cm* [19]), the speedup degradation for increased number of processors was mainly caused by memory contention rather than by process synchronization [20]. Efficient caching mechanisms have made this problem less severe, and process synchronization—not memory contention— now limits the maximum speedup achievable, as our measurements on QR have shown.

The results from FORTRAN vs. C comparison are to be interpreted as related to the Sequent system. Generalizations are not possible. Better register allocation in the C compiler would improve the situation. Users of Sequent systems who do not want to spend time in finely tuning the code are adviced to write their scientific application code in FORTRAN. This also makes sense because of the availability on the Symmetry system of an automatically parallelizing FORTRAN compiler recently developed by Kuck and Associates.

A final consideration refers to a more general aspect of programming shared-memory, bus-connected commercial multiprocessors. Studies like that of Vrsalovic et al. [21] have shown that a careful analysis of what variables should be considered local and what variables should be kept global is crucial for achieving large speedups. After the analysis, however, the system shall allow the implementation of the chosen storage strategy. Most commercial multiprocessors—and Symmetry is among them—make any manual variable allocation quite difficult, if not all together impossible. Data cannot be defined as cacheable or non-cacheable, the programmer cannot force the caching or flushing of variables, etc. At the opposite end of the spectrum, distributed-memory machines give the programmer total control on variable allocation. This makes it possible to optimize the parallelization of the algorithm, at the cost of cumbersome programming. Something between these two extremes would be welcomed.

Acknowledgements

Peter Beadle helped us to set up the Symmetry system for our benchmarks, and gave us useful suggestions. Roland Holliger implemented the Prolog database interpreter and its parallel version, and Raja Prasad developed some of the FORTRAN code.

References

[1] B. Beck, B. Kasten, and S. Thakkar. VLSI assist for a multiprocessor. In *Proc. ASPLOS II*, pages 10–20, IEEE, October 1987.

[2] T. Manuel. How Sequent's new model outruns most mainframes. *Electronics*, 76–78, may 28 1987.

[3] T. Lovett and S. Thakkar. *The Symmetry Multiprocessor System*. Technical Report, Sequent Computer Systems, 15450 SW KOLL Parkway, Beaverton, Oregon, 1988.

[4] A. Osterhaug. *Guide to Parallel Programming on Sequent Computer Systems*. Sequent Computer Systems, Inc., 1986.

[5] I. Meyer and R. Rühl. *Software zur Wignerverteilung*. Technical Report, Institut für Signal- und Informationsverarbeitung, Swiss Federal Institute of Technology Zürich, 1987.

[6] J. H. Wilkinson and C. Reinsch. *Handbook for Automatic Computation – Linear Algebra*. Volume 2, Springer Verlag, 1971. ISBN 0-387-05414-6.

[7] G. H. Golub and C. F. Van Loan. *Matrix Computations*. Johns Hopkins, 1983. ISBN 0-8018-3010-9.

[8] J. C. F. Francis. The QR transformation – a unitary analogue to the LR transformation. *Comput. J.*, 4:265–271, 332–345, 1961/62.

[9] W. H. Press, B. P. Flannery, S. A. Teukolsky, and W. T. Vetterling. *Numerical Recipes*. Cambridge University Press, 1986. ISBN 0 521 30811 9.

[10] D. K. Faddejew and W. N. Faddejewa. *Numerische Methoden der linearen Algebra*. R. Oldenbourg Verlag München, 5-th edition, 1979. ISBN 3-486-31125-5.

[11] T.J. Hughes. *The Finite Element Method*. Prentice-Hall Inc., 1987.

[12] A. J. Smith. Cache memories. *Computing Surveys*, 14(3):473–530, September 1982.

[13] P. Bitar and A.M. Despain. Multiprocessor cache synchronization–issues, innovations,evolution. In *Proc. 13th Symp. Comp. Arch.*, pages 424–433, IEEE, June 1986.

[14] M. Nussbaum. *Delayed Evaluation in Logic Programming: an Inference Mechanism for Large Knowledge Bases*. PhD thesis, Swiss Federal Institute of Technology Zürich, August 1988. Diss. ETH Nr. 8542.

[15] J.H. Patel. Analysis of multiprocessors with private cache memories. *IEEE Trans. on Computers*, C-31(4):296–304, April 1982.

[16] M. Dubois. Throughput analysis of cache-based multiprocessors with multiple busses. *IEEE Trans. on Computers*, C-37(1):58–70, January 1988.

[17] M. Annaratone et al. Applications experience on Warp. In *Proc. NCC 87*, pages 149–158, AFIPS Press, 1987.

[18] W.A. Wulf and C.G. Bell. C.mmp: a multi-miniprocessor. In *AFIPS Conference Proceedings, FJJC '72*, AFIPS, 1972.

[19] A. Jones and E. Gehringer (eds.). *The Cm* multiprocessor project: a research review*. Technical Report CMU-CS-80-131, Computer Science Department, Carnegie Mellon University, July 1980.

[20] Z.V. Segall and D.P. Siewiorek. *Practical evaluation of multiprocessors across a range of problems*. Technical Report, Computer Science Department, Carnegie Mellon University, April 1985.

[21] D. Vrsalovic et al. The influence of parallel decomposition strategies on the performance of multiprocessor systems. In *Proc. 12th Symp. Comp. Arch.*, pages 396–405, IEEE, June 1985.

Interprocessor Communication Speed and
Performance in Distributed-memory Parallel Processors

Marco Annaratone, Claude Pommerell, and Roland Rühl

Integrated Systems Laboratory
Swiss Federal Institute of Technology
8092 Zurich, Switzerland
(411) 256-5240

Abstract

We have simulated several numerical and non-numerical algorithms on five distributed-memory parallel processors (DMPPs). All five DMPPs have the same topology (a torus), and the same number of nodes. The architectures differ only in the communication speed between neighboring nodes, while the computation unit is kept unchanged. The goal of the paper is to quantify the effect that interprocessor communication speed and synchronization overhead have on the performance of the DMPPs. After introducing the rationale for this study and reviewing related work, we present and discuss the results of the simulations.

1. Introduction

We have simulated five different distributed-memory parallel processors (DMPPs) with neighbor-to-neighbor connection. These five architectures are identical: same local memory, computation unit, number of processing elements (PEs), and topology (a torus). The five architectures differ in one key aspect, i.e., the time for each PE to send or receive data to or from a neighboring PE. We define the PE communication/computation ratio q as follows:

$$q = \frac{io_t}{c_t}, \qquad (1)$$

where io_t is the time for a PE to send or receive a double-precision quantity to or from a neighbor processor, and c_t is the time to perform a double-precision multiply-add operation as in DAXPY [1]. We have

$$io_t = \frac{io_{oh} + io_{dp}M}{M}, \qquad (2)$$

where io_{oh} is the fixed overhead to construct a message and set up the appropriate communication mechanism, io_{dp} is the time to send a double-precision number, and M is the message length in double-precision numbers. Table I reports io_{oh}, io_{dp}, and c_t for some commercial or announced (iWarp) DMPPs[1].

TABLE I
Communication and computation parameters for various computers.

Model	io_{oh} (μs)	io_{dp} (μs/dbl)	c_t (μs/flop)
NCUBE	384	10.4	35
iPSC/2-SX	900	3.0	$12.5 \div 3.3$
iPSC/2-VX	900	3.0	$14.3 \div 0.38$
Warp	0	0.4	$1.0 \div 0.2$
iWarp	0	0.2	0.4
T800-20	0.95	4.6	1.35

The values of q computed from Table 1 range from 0.5 to almost 3000. Values greater than about 200 come from unrealistic situations. (For instance, using c_t for infinitely long vectors on the iPSC/2-VX and assuming that messages contain only one double-precision quantity.) q has been varied in our simulations in the interval [0.5; 256].

The goal of this paper is to *quantify* the effect that slow interprocessor communication has on performance. Besides studying the relationship between execution time and interprocessor communication speed, we want to analyze the behavior of the synchronization overhead associated with each architecture, and how it varies when neighboring PEs communicate at slower speed. We call the synchronization overhead *idle time* (t_{idle}) in this paper, because during this time a PE is neither computing nor actively communicating with one of its neighbors. Idle times occur when a PE wants to receive from an empty queue or wants to write to a full queue. The latter case never happens in our simulations

This research was supported in part by ETH grant 0.330.066.23/4 and in part by a Mikrotechnik Kredit.

[1]The numbers for the iPSC/2 have been taken from Intel documents [2,3] and from the work by Dunigan [4], the NCUBE numbers have been taken from a study by Heath and Romine [5] and are consistent with those presented by Gustafson et al. [6], the T800 transputer numbers have been taken from an INMOS document [7]. Warp and iWarp numbers come from [8] and [9], respectively. Maximum and minimum c_t's for the iPSC and Warp depend on the vector length (one/infinity and one/seven or more, respectively). Warp's parameters refer to single- rather than double-precision quantities.

because the queues are deep enough to prevent "blocking-on-write." We define the t_{idle} of an algorithm mapped on a p processor DMPP as

$$t_{idle} = t - \frac{\sum_{i=1}^{p}(t_c^{(i)} + t_{io}^{(i)})}{p}. \qquad (3)$$

t is the execution time, $t_{io}^{(i)}$ is the time that the i-th PE spends actively communicating with its neighbors, and $t_c^{(i)}$ is the time that the i-th PE spends doing local computation. The above parameters are computed from the output of our simulator.

The paper is organized as follows. After giving the motivations for this study, we justify the choice of a torus as an appropriate topology for our work. Then, we describe the simulation scenario, together with some important remarks. We present the numerical and non-numerical algorithms implemented, and for each of them we show the simulation results obtained. Finally, a discussion of the results follows.

2. Motivations for the study

Many hypercube users map their algorithms on grid-like structures [10,11,12,13,14,15]. By doing this, they do not exploit the positive characteristics of such machines—i.e., rich interconnectivity and powerful message-passing with transparent routing—and instead suffer from the inevitable drawback of slow interprocessor communication, as Table I shows. *Is using a hypercube as a mesh-connected DMPP justifiable? What is the impact on performance when such mapping is implemented?*

Architects of DMPPs need to know whether the significant effort in building fast channels connecting adjacent PEs is justified. The design of fast channels between neighboring PEs is both time-consuming and expensive. On Warp [8], channels take about 10% of the total board area, but their design is very simple. On the iWarp [9] single-chip, where channels are much more sophisticated, they alone take about half the total pin-count and a sizeable portion of the silicon area. *How fast should each communication channel connecting two neighboring PEs be to minimize the hardware costs and maximize the computing power of the DMPP?*

Theoretical studies on computation vs. communication have been carried out in recent years, like those by Johnsson [16] and H.T. Kung [17]. These studies ignore the synchronization overhead because it is analytically intractable and impossible to quantify, being strongly algorithm dependent. They also assume the parallelization grain-size as going toward infinity. Our measures will quantify the impact of synchronization overhead on the total execution time, and assume realistic parallelization grain-sizes. *How realistic are those studies which disregard the impact of the synchronization overhead?*

It is generally assumed that slower interprocessor communication speed does not decrease processor utilization if we increase the parallelization grain-size in the DMPP. This can be done by increasing the problem size keeping the number of PEs constant, or by decreasing the number of PEs keeping the problem size constant. However, no detailed study has been done on how the synchronization overhead varies when both computation grain-size and interprocessor communication time increase. *Can we keep the PE utilization constant by increasing the computation grain-size when the communication between neighboring PEs is slowed down?*

PEs in DMPPs can communicate through two different mechanisms: blocking and spinning. On receiving from an empty queue, a PE will freeze (block) until some data have arrived. This method is implemented in Warp and iWarp. Pure spinning is implemented only in Transputer-based machines such as the Computing Surface from Meiko [18]: when the computing process receives from an empty queue it may perform a task switch serving a different process rather than staying blocked on that empty queue. Hypercubes implement a somewhat different scheme. On the iPSC/2, there are both blocking and non-blocking receives. The *crecv* routine implements a blocking receive, while the *irecv* routine is non-blocking. On the NCUBE, the receive routine *nread* blocks when the message is not present. Because of the availability of non-blocking receives, spinning could be implemented (in software) on the iPSC/2. Spinning makes sense only when the PE utilization rate is small compared to its total execution time, i.e., for large t_{idle}'s. *When synchronization overhead is taken into account, is spinning a sound architectural choice?*

A study similar to that reported here was performed by Adams and Crockett [19]. They simulated different configurations of the Finite Element Machine, varying the speed of the communication between neighbor processors, and including the synchronization overhead in their simulation model. The study considered a single algorithm (conjugate gradients) on a small problem (1536 variables). They concluded that for two values of q, namely 1 and 10, and more than 64 processors, communication dominates. For $q = 10$ adding more processors results in an *increase* of the execution time.

3. Why a torus

Recent studies—namely those by Dally, Vitányi, and Johnsson —justify the choice of a torus.

Dally [20] makes the assumptions that (1) the network has to be laid out on a plane in a regular way, (2) wormhole routing is used to transmit a uniform distribution of messages, and (3) the channel delay is constant, or depends logarithmically or linearly on the wire length. k-ary n-cube networks are analyzed. These include rings, tori, and hypercubes. Networks with the same number of nodes $N = k^n$ are compared for constant wire density. It is shown that the network latency is generally minimal for small n. In particular, for $N = 256$, $n = 2$ is optimal.

Vitányi [21] derives hard lower bounds on the total wire length of several graph topologies, under the assumption that they have to be embedded in physical, three-dimensional space. He concludes that mesh-connected architectures are the most cost-effective.

Johnsson compares the number of communication steps required to calculate the transpose of a $2^n \times 2^n$ matrix (1) stored in a $2^k \times 2^k$ array embedded in a boolean cube and (2) blockallocated in a torus with $2^k \times 2^k$ processing elements [16]. The torus outperforms the hypercube if the number of PEs is 64 or less.

4. Remarks

Goal of this study is not to compare commercial DMPPs. Hypercubes and systolic computers, for instance, require a very different programming style. Because of the overhead associated with the message construction, hypercube programmers tend to cluster several data together before shipping them to the receiving node. We do not cluster data together, and in fact we always send single values (either doubles or integers) as soon as they are computed.

We have also used the same domain decomposition and algorithm implementation on all architectures. Knowing that the interprocessor communication is slow, a programmer can choose an algorithm mapping with greater local computation but lower interprocessor communication.

Finally, our model does not support overlapping of computation and communication. Data flowing through PEs to reach their final destination stop the local computation on each PE traversed because the computing engine handles the communication as well. This model describes accurately the actual behavior of Warp. Transputer-based machines and hypercubes support overlapping of computation and communication, and the latter architectures have transparent forwarding of messages. In order to make the results of our simulations applicable to different architectures, we have chosen a set of algorithms that—when mapped efficiently on a torus—have either one of the following characteristics:

- The algorithm requires neighbor-to-neighbor communication.

- The algorithm requires communication between distant processors, but data traversing each processor is also utilized by it (see, for instance, conjugate gradients on localities A and B).

The sorting algorithm presented below is the only exception; here, however, neighbor-to-neighbor communication represents about 50% of the total communication, and non-local communication traverses one processor.

5. Simulation scenario

The algorithms have been implemented on two topologies: torus and ring. PEs communicate via *send* and *receive* statements. Five architectures have been simulated. They have PEs with identical c_t but different io_t's. The five architectures, labeled **A1** (the one with the lowest io_t) through **A5** (the one with the highest io_t), are characterized by the following q's (see Equation (1)): 0.5, 8, 16, 64, and 256. Finally, the io_t for 32-bit integers is half of that for double-precision numbers.

The simulator we used is called K9 and has been developed at the Laboratory. K9 is written in C++ and runs on a multiprocessor Sequent Symmetry and on SUN workstations. K9 allows the user to define a topology, which can be either regular—e.g., linear array, torus, hypercube— or irregular—e.g., semantic and neural networks. Each PE has associated timing information at the instruction level. Programs are written in C++ with *send* and *receive* statements. The simulator does not simulate any disk I/O activity and therefore all the results refer to "input data decomposed in the array – output results decomposed in the array."

The processor model used in the simulator is that of an AMD 29000 microprocessor with floating-point coprocessor. This model has been finely tuned to match the performance of the actual chip. We have compared the results of the AMD 29000 instruction-set simulator with the K9 model and noticed a discrepancy of $\pm 7\%$. The instruction-set simulator models the local memory as well, with single access taking five cycles (the cycle time is 40ns).

6. Description of the algorithms and simulation results

The algorithms simulated are both numerical and non-numerical. They are:

- *Linear Algebra.* Gaussian elimination with partial pivoting, BLAS 2 routines, Householder transformation.

- *Finite difference methods.* Analysis of airflow around airfoil in transonic regime.

- *Sparse matrix computation.* Conjugate gradients and derivatives.

- *Non-numerical algorithms.* Bitonic sorting, dynamic message routing, and static message routing.

The results are presented with bar graphs. For each algorithm we show the relative execution time and the relative idle time for the five architectures. The relative idle time is averaged over all PEs. For each problem the execution time of the slowest simulation on A5 is equal to 100%. The execution time on the other architectures is given relative to that of A5, unless specified o A5, unless specified otherwise. The idle time is given as percentage of the execution time; an idle time of 30% means that, on the average, each processor was idle 30% of the time. Execution times are shown in the left half of the figure, idle times in the right half. Bars are clustered in groups of five, one bar for each of the five architectures considered. The leftmost bar refers to A1, the rightmost bar (the fifth) refers to A5.

Householder could only be simulated on a 4×4 torus, because of limitations in the simulator. The other algorithms have been simulated on 64 or more processors. Finally, some algorithms have been also mapped on a linear array, being this topology embedded in the torus.

6.1 Gaussian elimination with partial pivoting

Gaussian elimination solves a linear system $Ax = b$. We have implemented Gaussian elimination with partial pivoting on a linear array with 64 processors. Column-storage has been used: contiguous columns of A are stored onto each processor. This has been shown by Ipsen et al. [22] to be an efficient storage scheme on linear arrays when pivoting is carried out.

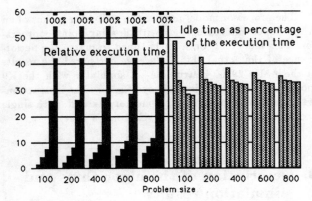

Figure 1. *Gaussian elimination with partial pivoting for different problem sizes. Relative execution times (black) and percentage of idle times (grey) are shown for models A1 through A5; 64-processor linear array.*

Figure 1 shows the results for a 64-processor linear array. On small problems, A2, A3, and A4 are two to three, four to five, and fifteen times slower than A1, respectively. On large problems, A4 is ten times slower than A1. A5 always performs much worse than A1, even on large problem sizes.

Note the interesting behavior of the idle times. On A1, idle times decrease with the increase of the problem size, while on A5 idle times increase with the increase of the problem size. One would normally expect to see the idle times decrease with the increase of the problem size independently of the interprocessor communication speed, because more local computation is carried out. The idle times showed in figure 1 seem to exhibit a monotonically decreasing or increasing behavior. In fact, this monotonicity is simply caused by the limited range of problem sizes we studied. Had we considered much smaller or larger problem sizes, all idle time curves would have shown a "bell-shaped" behavior, with maximum values centered at different problem sizes depending on the interprocessor communication speed.

6.2 BLAS 2 routines

We have implemented the BLAS 2 (Basic Linear Algebra Subroutines) routines [23] for double-precision real data structures. All implementations assume a torus with p processors. Matrices are mapped onto the torus with two allocation strategies:

Block allocation. Each processor contains a square submatrix.

Row allocation. Each processor contains an equal number of rows.

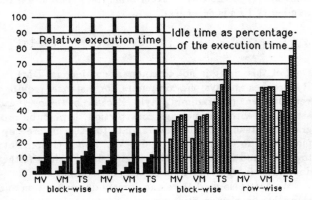

Figure 2. *Three BLAS 2 routines mapped on an 8×8 processor torus with two storage allocation schemes. Relative execution times (black) and percentage of idle times (grey) are shown for models A1 through A5. Problem size is 200.*

We have benchmarked the following three routines: matrix × vector (MV), vector ^{T} × matrix (VM), and the solution of a triangular system (TS). The results for an 8×8 torus, and for the two storage allocation schemes are shown in figure 2. The problem size is 200.

As expected, MV and VM produce the same execution and idle times since block allocation is symmetric. MV for row-wise allocation shows no idle time; the calculation of p parts of the product is done with no communication at all. Then each processor broadcasts its part of the result to the other processors. All processors communicate with total synchronicity; no idle time occurs.

6.3 Householder transformation

The Householder transformation reduces a general real matrix $A_1 \in \mathcal{R}^n \times \mathcal{R}^n$ to an upper Hessenberg matrix applying $n - 2$ similarity transformations [24]

$$A_{r+1} = P_r A_r P_r, \quad r = 1, \ldots, n - 2.$$

The orthogonal matrix P_r is of the form

$$P_r = I - u_r u_r^T / H_r,$$

with

$$u_r^T = [0, \ldots, 0, a_{r+1,r}^{(r)} \pm \sigma_r^{1/2}, a_{r+2,r}^{(r)}, \ldots, a_{n,r}^{(r)}], \quad (4)$$

$$\sigma_r = \sum_{i=r+1}^{n} (a_{i,r}^{(r)})^2, \quad (5)$$

$$H_r = \sigma_r \pm a_{r+1,r}^{(r)} \sigma_r^{1/2}. \quad (6)$$

Each iteration consists of the following two steps:

$$B_{r+1} = P_r A_r = A_r - u_r (u_r^T A_r) / H_r,$$
$$A_{r+1} = B_{r+1} P_r = B_{r+1} - (B_{r+1} u_r / H_r) u_r^T.$$

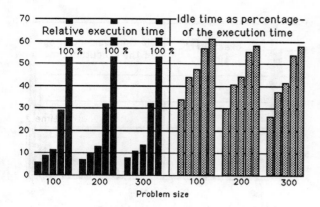

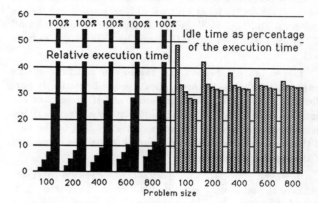

Figure 3. *Householder on a 4×4 torus for different problem sizes. Relative execution times (black) and percentage of idle times (grey) are shown for models A1 through A5.*

The two subroutines MV and VM are called in each iteration. In addition, two matrix subtractions and two vector^T × vector products are performed. The serial part of the algorithm—i.e., the computation and broadcast of H_r (6)—resynchronizes the torus at each iteration step. Execution and idle times of Householder reflect the behavior of MV and VM.

6.4 Fluid dynamics problem

The analysis of the behavior of airfoils in subsonic, transonic, and supersonic regime is carried out by using the method developed by Murman and Cole [25]. This method was adapted by Jameson and Caughey [26] for three-dimensional analysis. The program solves a two-dimensional, steady-state transonic small disturbance equation. More details can be found in any textbook on aerodynamics; see for instance that by Moran [27].

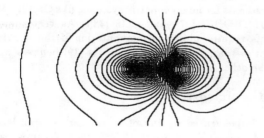

Figure 4. *Isomach lines for airfoil with elliptical section at Mach = 0.9. Direction of flight is from right to left.*

A finite difference method is used to solve the problem iteratively. The plane on which the airfoil section lies is discretized with a 200 × 400 point grid. The gradient of the velocity potential is determined simultaneously on each successive vertical grid-line marching in streamwise direction, by a relaxation method for the subsonic flow, and by

an implicit scheme for the wave equation in the supersonic zone. The result is a set of isomach lines surrounding the airfoil section as shown in figure 4 for a wing with elliptical section at Mach 0.9. The direction of flight is from right to left, and it is possible to notice the onset of the shock wave.

Figure 5. *Fluid dynamics problem on a 100-processor ring and on a 10 × 10 torus. Relative execution times (black, normalized on torus with architecture A5) and percentage of idle times (grey) are shown for models A1 through A5.*

The algorithm is iterative; the number of iterations for convergence in transonic flow is large enough (2000 or more iterations) that long linear arrays of processors can be used. Their large start-up latency has no effect on the overall performance. Performance is independent of the shape of the wing section.

The program has been executed on two topologies: a 100-processor linear array and a 10 × 10 torus. This application is particularly compute-intensive: using the same grid size, one iteration takes about 3.62s on a Vax 8650 with floating-point accelerator and about 40ms on a 10-processor Warp.

The results are presented in figure 5. The problem mapped on the ring has perfectly matching sends and receives: $t_{idle} = 0$ for all five architectures. When the problem is mapped on a torus, the tridiagonal system to be solved for the grid points in the vertical direction is partitioned across a column of processors. Its solution proceeds almost serially, therefore. This affects the total execution time and also results in large idle times. The ring mapping performs about three times faster than the torus mapping for architectures A1 through A3.

6.5 Conjugate gradients and derivatives

We use the conjugate gradient algorithm [28] to solve a sparse system $Ax = b$, where A is an $n \times n$ matrix with m nonzero entries ($n \leq m \ll n^2$). At each iteration, the basic algorithm involves one multiplication of the sparse matrix A by a vector, two vector dot products, three multiplications of a vector by a scalar, three additions of vectors, two scalar divisions, and a test for convergence.

The divisions and some flow control (including the convergence test) form the serial part of the algorithm. The linear operations on vectors and the scalar multiplications inside the vector dot product can be perfectly parallelized on p processors when each processor owns $\frac{n}{p}$ elements of each vector.

Each processor needs $\frac{n}{p} - 1$ additions to complete the dot product on its local vectors. These partial results are added up globally, and the result is made available to all the processors. This operation can be parallelized only in part.

The m multiplications and the $m - n$ additions in the sparse matrix by vector multiplication can be perfectly parallelized if A is partitioned row-wise and if these rows are distributed in a way to balance equally the nonzero entries. Every processor gets all the rows corresponding to the part of the vectors it owns, thus producing again the same part of the resulting vector.

However, processors need to access some non-local elements of the operand vector, depending on the sparsity pattern of the local rows. The sparsity structure of A defines a graph stemming from the physical discretization of partial differential equations. This graph can often be mapped onto the topology in a way that only local communication is required. While for finite difference graphs this is easy to accomplish, mapping more complex structures optimally—like finite element graphs—is NP-complete [29]. If the graph cannot be mapped efficiently, the whole vector has to be sent to all processors.

In our simulations, we exploited the locality in four different ways:

A Every processor performs $n - \frac{n}{p}$ sends and receives to get the whole vector. This is the worst case, when the problem graph is mapped randomly.

B Every processor performs $\frac{n}{p}$ sends and receives to and from its 8 nearest neighbors.

C Every processor performs $\frac{n}{p}$ sends and receives to and from its 4 direct neighbors.

D Every processor performs $\sqrt{\frac{n}{p}}$ sends and receives to and from its 4 direct neighbors. This is the best case [30], achievable only on five-point stencil finite difference schemes.

Idle times come from two different sources: (a) imbalance in the computation load for the matrix-vector product, because some rows of the matrix are more sparse than others, and (b) synchronization during the global summation in the vector dot products.

Figure 6 shows the execution and idle times for the five architectures and the four locality models. All execution times are relative to that of architecture A1 with locality **A**. The matrix A is 4096×4096 with 0.12% density. The same matrix structure has been used by Hageman and Young [31] to compare different iterative methods.

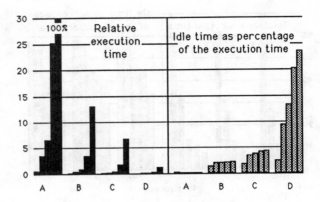

Figure 6. *Conjugate gradients with different degrees of locality. Relative execution times (black, normalized on model A5 for locality A) and percentage of idle times (grey) are shown for models A1 through A5.*

The number of sends and receives could be reduced in the matrix-vector product by exploiting locality. A further improvement in the execution time could come from reducing the idle time. This reduction is of little effect in architectures with fast communication channels like A1, where the idle time is always below 2.5% of the total execution time. The idle time in A5, however, represents 24% of the total execution time (locality D): the vector dot product is dominating. This effect was already noticed by iPSC users [32,33]. Aykanat and Ozguner [34] propose to overcome this bottleneck by increasing the granularity of the problem and decreasing the communication overhead. A similar approach for successive over-relaxation is taken by Saltz et al. [35], who reduce the total number of convergence checks. Although the computation time increases, these methods speed up the execution time because of the slow interprocessor communication.

We obtained similar results for some variants of conjugate gradients for nonsymmetric systems, like ORTHOMIN [36], ORTHODIR [37], and CGS [38]. As vector-matrix products require additional computation if the matrix is stored row-wise, biconjugate gradients [39] behaves worse than the other methods.

6.6 Bitonic sorting

We implemented sorting of an integer array of length $N = 64n$ on an 8×8 torus. The integer array is partitioned into 64 subvectors of length n; each subvector is allocated on a different PE. The algorithm works as follows: first, the subvectors are locally sorted using heapsort; second, the sorted subvectors are merged together following the arcs in a bitonic tree [40]. The mapping of subvectors onto PEs is shown in figure 7. With such a mapping, the maximum distance of the communication is two, and the two communication steps used most often are those between neighboring PEs. We have also implemented local quicksort, obtaining similar results. Those presented here refer to the implementation based on heapsort.

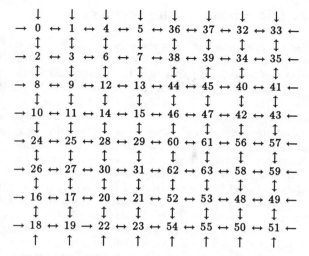

Figure 7. *Bitonic sorting. Mapping of the 64 subvectors onto the 64-processor torus.*

The results are shown in figure 8 for different sizes of the integer array to be sorted. The computation/communication ratio is here proportional to the logarithm of the problem size; in the previous numerical algorithms this figure was proportional to the problem size. Therefore, the performance of sorting on tori degrades quickly when the interprocessor communication is slowed down.

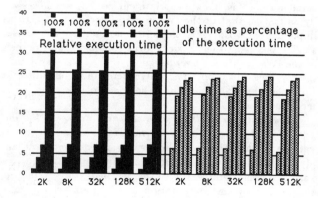

Figure 8. *Sorting of different integer array size on an 8×8 torus. Relative execution times (black) and percentage of idle times (grey) are shown for models A1 through A5.*

Idle times are about constant for each architecture examined, and do not depend on the problem size. Note however that the difference in idle times between A1 and A5 is much more pronounced than that of all the other algorithms discussed, with the exception of conjugate gradients on locality D.

6.7 Dynamic message routing

The algorithm discussed in this section implements a simple but realistic message-passing. That is, messages have source, destination, and body. Destinations are determined locally at run-time.

Similar algorithms have been used to compare interconnection topologies [20,21,41], or to show the performance of a message scheme [42]. Applications of dynamic message routing include data redistribution after reordering, or localization in sparse iterative solvers, neural network simulators, etc.

We have simulated the following scenario: at the beginning, n objects are distributed uniformly over the p processors. These objects have to be redistributed in a random way, i.e., each processor randomly selects the destination processors for each of its $\frac{n}{p}$ objects.

Every processor examines the state of the connections before considering the next local object and sending it as a body of a message. If it finds a message on a connection, it checks its destination and then forwards it or locally stores the contents of the body. After shipping all its objects, the processor simply waits for incoming messages to store or to reroute. A special token message is sent around to inform all processors that the message-passing has been completed.

The dynamic message routing algorithm was simulated with $n = 128000$ short messages (20 bytes), on five different torus sizes. Figure 9 shows the execution times relative to the A5 model on an 8×8 torus.

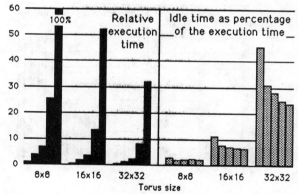

Figure 9. *Dynamic message-routing for 128000 messages on five tori. Relative execution times (black, normalized on model A5 for an 8×8 torus) and percentage of idle times (grey) are shown for models A1 through A5.*

6.8 Static message routing

This algorithm is part of an automatically parallelizing FORTRAN compiler for DMPPs currently under development at the Laboratory. The compiler itself runs in parallel on a DMPP torus. A binary directed graph represents the data dependency graph of a given serial FORTRAN source with a fixed number of loop instances. Each node of the graph represents a variable or an array member. Each directed arc represents a data-dependency.

A direct mapping of the data-dependency graph on the DMPP will result in dependencies connecting non-neighboring processors. The static message routing (SMR) eliminates these dependencies by generating a semantically equivalent graph which contains only dependencies between adjacent nodes. This is accomplished by the insertion of dummy dependencies so that the (hyper)graph is flattened on a two-dimensional surface, with dependencies between neighboring nodes being consistent with a Manhattan routing scheme.

During the execution each processor manages a message queue. A message contains 30 bytes. Each processor repeatedly retrieves an element from its message queue, sends it to one of its neighbors, and receives a message from one of its neighbors. The message size is comparable to that used in the dynamic message routing. The SMR differs from the latter in the following aspects:

- The idle time is caused by blocking when receiving from empty queues, as happens with all other algorithms simulated so far. In the dynamic message routing, idle times were caused by polling on the queues.

- No message can be appended to the message queue at run time. The message routes are defined at the beginning of the algorithm (Manhattan routing).

- SMR always works in "store and forward" mode, while the dynamic message routing performs either "store" or "forward."

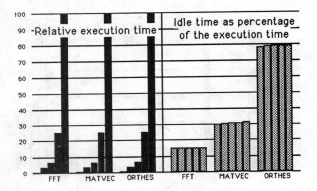

Figure 10. *Static message routing on an 8 × 8 torus for data-dependency graphs from three algorithms: MATVEC, FFT, and ORTHES. Relative execution times (black) and percentage of idle times (grey) are shown for models A1 through A5.*

We simulated the algorithm on an 8 × 8 torus using as input three data-dependency graphs generated by the compilation of FORTRAN programs: matrix×vector multiply (MATVEC), fast Fourier transform (FFT), and Householder transformation (ORTHES). Figure 10 shows the execution and idle times relative to the execution time on architecture A5.

From figure 10 one can notice that the execution and idle times strongly depend on the FORTRAN source code. If the compiled FORTRAN code results in a graph which maps poorly on the torus (such as in the case of ORTHES), communication congestion and high idle times on some PEs occur.

The execution time is very sensitive to communication slow-down, while idle times are independent of the communication speed.

7. Discussion of the results

We have listed in Section 2 some questions that our study aimed to answer. In this section we summarize the results obtained by giving an answer to the questions in Section 2.

Is using a hypercube as a mesh-connected DMPP justifiable? The algorithms we have simulated show that slower communication speed only marginally affects the total execution time, for small q's. DMPPs with PEs with $q = 16$ are on the average 4.77 slower than DMPPs with PEs with $q = 0.5$ on the 32 simulations carried out. For larger q's performance degrades fairly quickly, reaching up to two orders of magnitude like in some BLAS 2 routines, conjugate gradients (locality A), and bitonic sorting. Hypercube systems have q's between 11 (NCUBE) and 70 (iPSC-2/VX) for $M = 1$. Achieving high-performance from a "mesh-connected hypercube" can be non-trivial, therefore. Clustering data before shipping them reduces q but will undoubtedly increase t_{idle}. Careful profiling of the program can determine if clustering can be advantageous. If mesh-connected topologies are used most of the time, a user should obviously choose for his or her applications a mesh-connected processor with very fast channels and no sophisticated message passing schemes.

How fast should each communication channel connecting two neighboring PEs be to minimize the hardware costs and maximize the computing power of the DMPP? A q smaller than 8 is the appropriate choice, but not necessarily as fast as that of the iWarp chip ($q = 0.5$). If a torus implemented with iWarp chips runs normally in single-user single-task using the physical torus topology, the channels of the iWarp chip are overdesigned. If the iWarp system is mostly used to support (virtual) interconnections different from the physical torus, then the speed of the channels is more justified.

How realistic are those studies which disregard the impact of the synchronization overhead? We have some reservations on the validity of the conclusions derived from analytical studies that disregard idle times. In fact, idle times vary in a non-trivial way with the parallelization grain-size, the ratio between computation and communication, and the number of processors. One would expect idle times to decrease—as percentage of the execution time—for larger computation grain-sizes or decreasing number of processors. The analysis of our results shows indeed this: Gaussian elimination (figure 1) and Householder (figure 3) display this behavior. However, a more careful analysis of figure 1 shows that the decrease in idle times tends asymptotically to 30%.

The behavior of the idle time is not influenced by the interprocessor communication in an obvious way. It increases with the decrease in communications speed in most BLAS 2 routines, Householder, and conjugate gradients. It decreases with the decrease in communication speed in the fluid dynamics problem, Gaussian elimination, dynamic message routing, and the static message routing.

Finally, some algorithms involve communication-intensive routines, and the overall performance reflects the performance of these routines. This happens with Householder, the fluid dynamics problem, and conjugate gradients.

We can conclude that the behavior of idle times for larger parallelization grain-sizes and/or slower interprocessor communication is *generally* unpredictable.

Can we keep the PE utilization constant by increasing the computation grain-size when the communication between neighboring PEs is slowed down? A common assumption in parallel processing is that we can trade local memory for interprocessor communication. This means that we can design slower channels but have the same PE utilization rate if we increase enough the problem size. A typical example of this is Householder: the idle time of the A2 model on a 200×200 problem is about the same of the idle time of the A3 model on a 300×300 problem. The dynamic message routing displays the opposite behavior, however, and Householder shows that we would have to increase the problem size unrealistically for A2 to have the same idle time of A1 on a 100×100 problem.

When synchronization overhead is taken into account, is spinning a sound architectural choice? Our results are not sufficient to answer this question, but few comments based on our simulations can be made. Large idle times (e.g., 30% of the execution time or more) are at least an indication that spinning should be included, especially now that PEs able to perform fast process switch are available [7] or have been proposed [43]. Large idle times are not necessarily related to slow interprocessor communication: Householder shows different behavior from the fluid dynamics problem on a torus, the static message routing, and the dynamic message routing, in this respect. The assumption that DMPPs with relatively slow interprocessor communication benefit from spinning is not totally justified: the first three locality models (A, B, and C) in the conjugate gradient example and the dynamic message routing on an 8×8 torus show that idle times can be very small even for large q's.

A final comment has to do with the algorithms chosen in our simulations. Besides bitonic sorting and dynamic and static message routing, all the others are typical of scientific computation, and characterized by having many operations performed on each received value. This explains why the execution time does not drastically increase when we slow down the interprocessor communication speed. Had we simulated algorithms from signal or low-level vision processing, the difference in performance between A1 and A5 would have been more significant.

8. Conclusions

The main consideration we can make after this study is that idle times must be included in any theoretical performance evaluation or architectural study of DMPPs. We also show how unpredictable they are: even considering the simplest case—i.e., the asymptotic behavior—idle times are difficult to determine without simulating the algorithm.

Our initial skepticism on the results coming from analytical formulations of such a complex problem like the interaction among computation grain-size, interprocessor communication speed, algorithm mapping, and final performance has not been dispelled by our measurements. On the contrary, we believe that unless the algorithm is trivial (e.g., matrix multiplication or tridiagonalization), and therefore of scarce practical interest, analytical approaches are likely to produce models that oversimplify this complex problem. The conclusions derived from analytical formulations should be supported by simulations or measurements, therefore.

Acknowledgements

Peter Beadle developed the K9 simulator and helped us considerably during our simulations. Kyoshi Nakabayashi developed the AMD 29000 model for the K9 simulator, and designed the 29000-based node to assess how fast the channels could be designed.

References

[1] C. L. Lawson, R. J. Hanson, D. R. Kincaid, and F. T. Krogh. Basic linear algebra subprograms for Fortran usage. *ACM Transactions on Math. Softw.*, 5(3):308–323, September 1979.

[2] P. Close. The iPSC/2 node architecture. In *Concurrent Supercomputing*, pages 43–49, Intel Scientific Computers, 1988.

[3] S.F. Nugent. The iPSC/2 direct-connect communication technology. In *Concurrent Supercomputing*, pages 59–67, Intel Scientific Computers, 1988.

[4] T.H. Dunigan. *Performance of a second generation hypercube*. Technical Report ORNL TM-10881, Oak Ridge National Laboratory, November 1988.

[5] M. T. Heath and C.H. Romine. Parallel solution of triangular systems on distributed-memory multiprocessors. *SIAM J. Sci. Stat. Comput.*, 9(3):558–588, May 1988.

[6] J.L. Gustafson, G.R. Montry, and R.E. Benner. Development of parallel methods for a 1024-processor hypercube. *SIAM J. Sci. Stat. Comput.*, 9(4):609–638, July 1988.

[7] INMOS Limited. *Transputer Reference Manual*. Prentice Hall, 1988.

[8] M. Annaratone et al. The Warp Computer: Architecture, Implementation, and Performance. *IEEE Trans. on Computers*, December 1987.

[9] S. Borkar et al. iWarp: an integrated solution to high-speed parallel computation. In *Proc. Supercomputing 88*, November 1988.

[10] V. Cherkassy and R. Smith. Efficient mapping and implementation of matrix algorithms on a hypercube. *The Journal of Supercomputing*, 2(1):7–27, September 1988.

[11] P. Sadayappan and F. Ercal. Nearest-neighbor mapping of finite element graphs onto processor meshes. *IEEE Transactions on Computers*, C-36(12):1408–1424, December 1987.

[12] J. L. Gustafson, G. R. Montry, and R. E. Benner. Development of parallel methods for a 1024-processor hypercube. *SIAM J. Sci. Stat. Comput.*, 9(4):609–638, July 1988.

[13] T. Priol and K. Bouatouch. *Experimenting with a Parallel Ray-Tracing Algorithm on a Hypercube Machine*. Publication Interne 405, Institut de Recherche en Informatique et Systèmes Aléatoires, Campus Universitaire de Beaulieu, 35042 - Rennes Cédex, France, Avril 1988.

[14] S. C. Eisenstat, M. T. Heath, C. S. Henkel, and C. H. Romine. Modified cyclic algorithms for solving triangular systems on distributed-memory multiprocessor. *SIAM J. Sci. Stat. Comput.*, 9(3):589–600, May 1988.

[15] D. M. Nicol and F. H. Willard. Problem size, parallel architecture, and optimal speedup. *Journal of Parallel and Distributed Computing*, 5:404–420, 1988.

[16] S. L. Johnsson. Communication efficient basic linear algebra computations on hypercube architectures. *J. of Parallel and Distributed Processing*, 4(2):133–172, April 1987.

[17] H.T. Kung. Memory requirements for balanced computer architectures. In *Proc. 13th Computer Architecture Symposium*, pages 49–54, June 1986.

[18] Meiko Inc. The Meiko Computing Surface. 1988.

[19] L. M. Adams and T. W. Crockett. Modeling algorithm execution time on processor arrays. *IEEE Computer*, 38–43, July 1984.

[20] W. J. Dally. *Wire-Efficient VLSI Multiprocessor Communication Networks*. VLSI Memo 86-345, Massachusetts Institute of Technology, Cambridge, Massachusetts, October 1986.

[21] P. M. B. Vitányi. Locality, communication, and interconnect length in multicomputers. *SIAM J. Comput.*, 17(4):659–672, August 1988.

[22] I.C. Ipsen, Y. Saad, and M.H. Schultz. Complexity of dense-linear system solution on a multiprocessor-ring. *Linear Algebra and its applications*, 77:205–239, May 1986.

[23] C. L. Lawson, J. D. Croz, S. Hammarting, and R. J. Hanson. A proposal for an extended set of fortran basic linear algebra subprograms. *SIGNUM Newsletter*, 20(1):2–18, September 1985.

[24] J.H. Wilkinson and C. Reinsch. *Linear Algebra*. Springer-Verlag, 1971.

[25] E. M. Murman and J. D. Cole. *Calculation of plane steady transonic flows*. Technical Report 1D-82-0943, Boeing Scientific Research Laboratories, 1970.

[26] Jameson and Caughney. *Numerical calculation of transonic flow past a swept wing*. ERDA Report C00-3077-140, New York University, 1977.

[27] J. Moran. *An Introduction to Theoretical and Computational Aerodynamics*. John Wiley & Sons, 1984.

[28] M. R. Hestenes and E. Stiefel. Methods of conjugate gradients for solving linear systems. *J. Res. Nat. Bur. Stand.*, 49:409–436, 1952.

[29] M. R. Garey and D. S. Johnson. *Computers and Intractability, A Guide to the Theory of NP-Completeness*. W. H. Freeman and Company, New York, 1979.

[30] D. A. Reed, L. M. Adams, and M. L. Patrick. Stencils and problem partitionings: their influence on the performance of multiple processor systems. *IEEE Transactions on Computers*, C-36(7):845–858, July 1987.

[31] L. A. Hageman and D. M. Young. *Applied Iterative Methods. Computer Science and Applied Mathematics*, Academic Press, 1981.

[32] C. Aykanat and F. Ozguner. Large grain parallel conjugate gradient algorithms on a hypercube multiprocessor. In S. K. Sahni, editor, *Proceedings of the 1987 International Conference on Parallel Processing*, pages 641–644, August 1987.

[33] O. A. McBryan and E. F. van de Velde. Hypercube algorithms and implementations. *SIAM J. Sci. Stat. Comput.*, 8(2):s227–s287, March 1987.

[34] C. Aykanat, F. Özgüner, F. Ercal, and P. Sadayappan. Iterative algorithms for solution of large sparse systems of linear equations on hypercubes. *IEEE Transactions on Computers*, C-37(12):1554–1568, December 1988.

[35] J. H. Saltz, V. K. Naik, and D. M. Nicol. Reduction of the effects of the communication delays in scientific algorithms on message passing MIMD architectures. *SIAM J. Sci. Stat. Comput.*, 8(1):s118–s134, January 1988.

[36] P. K. W. Vinsome. ORTHOMIN – an iterative method for solving sparse sets of simultaneous linear equations. In *Proc. Fourth SPE Symposium on Reservoir Simulation*, pages 149–160, Society of Petroleum Engineers, Los Angeles, February 1976. Paper SPE 5739.

[37] D. M. Young and K. C. Jea. Generalized conjugate-gradient acceleration of nonsymmetric iterative methods. *Linear Algebra and its Applications*, 34:159–194, 1980.

[38] P. Sonneveld. *CGS, a fast Lanczos-type solver for non-symmetric linear systems*. Technical Report 84-16, Delft University, Dept. of Math., Delft, The Netherlands, 1984.

[39] R. Fletcher. Conjugate gradient methods for indefinite systems. In G. A. Watson, editor, *Proc. of the Dundee Biennal Conference on Numerical Analysis*, Springer-Verlag, New York, 1975.

[40] D. E. Knuth. *The Art of Computer Programming - Sorting and Searching*. Addison-Wesley, Reading, MA, 1973.

[41] D. A. Reed and H. D. Schwetman. Cost-performance bounds for multimicrocomputer networks. *IEEE Transactions on Computers*, C-32(1):83–95, January 1983.

[42] Thinking Machines Corporation. *Connection Machine Model CM-2 Technical Summary*. Technical Report HA87-4, Thinking Machines Corporation, April 1987.

[43] W.J. Dally et al. Architecture of a message-driven processor. In *14th Ann. Intl. Symp. on Computer Architecture*, pages 189–196, IEEE Computer Society, June 1987.

Analysis of Computation-Communication Issues in
Dynamic Dataflow Architectures

Dipak Ghosal and Satish K. Tripathi
Institute for Advanced Computer Studies
University of Maryland
College Park, MD 20742

Laxmi N. Bhuyan and Hong Jiang
The Center for Advanced Computer Studies
University of Southwestern Louisiana
Lafayette, LA 70504-4330.

Abstract

This paper presents analytical results of computation-communication issues in dynamic dataflow architectures. The study is based on a generalized architecture which encompasses all the features of the proposed dynamic dataflow architectures. Based on the idea of characterizing dataflow graphs by their average parallelism, a queueing network model of the architecture is developed. Since the queueing network violates properties required for product form solution, a few approximations have been used. These approximations yield a multi-chain closed queueing network in which the population of each chain is related to the average parallelism of the dataflow graph executed in the architecture. Based on the model, we are able to study the effect on the performance of the system due to factors such as scalability, coarse grain vs. fine grain parallelism, degree of decentralized scheduling of dataflow instructions, and locality.

1. Introduction

The dataflow model of computation is significantly different from the von Neumann model of computation [3, 24]. In this model the program parallelism is expressed in terms of a directed graph, in which the nodes describe the operation to be performed and the arcs represent the data dependencies among the operations [5]. Execution of the directed graph is data driven in the sense that the execution of a node does not proceed until the availability of the data at the input of the node. The node executes by consuming the data values from the input arc and subsequently produces the output data value(s) on the output arc(s).

The two characteristics which distinguish the dataflow model of computation from the von Neumann model are the absence of both the program counter and the global updatable memory. The dataflow model deals only with values in the sense that an operator produces value(s) which is (are) needed by other operator(s). Thus, the model does not have a built-in notion of an updatable memory cell.

Based on the node firing rules, the dataflow model of computation is classified into two types [3, 6, 17]. In the first approach, called the static model, the firing rule restricts the number of data items on any arc at any time to one. As a result, the node fires if all the input data are available and there is no data on the output arc. In the second approach, called the dynamic model, infinite storage is allowed on each arc. Since data values for a particular instantiation of the operator have to be identified, tags are assigned to the data token(s) [2]. For this reason the second scheme is often referred to as the *tagged-token* approach. The node firing rule in the dynamic dataflow model is thus : a node is executed when and only when all the inputs are available. The condition for availability of all input data items is determined by matching the tags of the data items on each of the input arcs. A token in the dynamic dataflow model of computation refers to the packet carrying a data item. Other than serving as a place holder for the data item, the token also carries, among other information, the destination instruction address (also referred to as the tag) which uses the data as an operand. The two well known architectural realization of the dynamic dataflow models are known as the MIT tagged token dataflow architecture [3] and the Manchester dataflow computer [14].

A number of dynamic dataflow architectures have been proposed [14, 3, 4]. In this paper we address some computation-communication issues that pertain to these architectures. The first and the most important issue is the number of (PEs) on which a dataflow graph should be executed. The delay through the interconnection network (IN) connecting the PEs poses a limit on the size of the system. The second issue relates to the question of fine grain vs. coarse grain parallelism. The dataflow model of computation exploits fine grain parallelism as a result of which the degree of parallelism exposed is maximum. However, this advantage is counteracted by a high overall communication requirement. Operating at a coarse grain parallelism results in lower communication requirement but reduces the exploitable parallelism. Thus, for a given underlying architecture, a trade-off exists between the execution time of the algorithm and the granularity of computation. The third issue relates to the degree of centralization of scheduling of the dataflow instructions. In the dataflow model of computation, an instruction is initiated when and only when the data is available at its input. This implies that the scheduling is fully decentralized. At the hardware level, this scheduling is carried out by a matching unit. Providing full decentralization at the hardware level would require a large number of processing elements (PEs) and matching units connected through an interconnection network (IN). This would result in a large delay in the network. Centralization can be incorporated by assigning one matching unit to a number of dataflow PEs. This would reduce the size of the IN and the corresponding network delay, but at the same time it would require a higher rate to perform the matching. Thus, given a dataflow graph, there exists a trade-off between the execution time of the dataflow graph and the degree of decentralized scheduling. Finally, there is the issue of locality which means assigning dataflow instructions to PEs where their predecessors were executed. This would mean that most of the data tokens would stay in the same PE without any communication delay in the IN. However, the compiling/allocating time increases exponentially under this constraint.

All the above issues are highly inter-related and in order to study them, one needs a mathematical model so that various results can be obtained by changing the input parameters. On the architecture side, different implementation have been suggested [3, 15]. If a generalized model for dynamic dataflow architectures can be developed, performance on different architectures can be obtained from the analytical model by appropriately changing the parameters. In this paper, we develop such a generalized model for dynamic dataflow architectures based on packet switched multistage interconnection network (MIN). The dataflow graph executed in the architecture is characterized by its average parallelism [14, 11, 9]. Based on this characterization, a queueing network model of the generalized dynamic dataflow architecture is developed. The queueing network model violates the condition necessary for product form solution [19, 16] on two accounts; 1) due to concurrency in the dataflow graph and 2) due to the fixed service time of the switches in the MIN. The non-product form network is solved in two steps. First by incorporating fictitious servers into the network [16, 1] and appropriately modifying the population size we take care of the concurrency in the dataflow graph. In the second step an approximate Mean Value Analysis (MVA) algorithm [22] is used to account for the fixed service time of the switches in the MIN and the batch arrival due to the concurrency in the dataflow graph. The final approximate network consists of four chains, with their respective population related to the average population of the dataflow graph and the percentage of the dyadic instructions. Through the queueing model, we are able to carry an in-depth study of the scalability and the trade-off issues in dynamic dataflow architectures.

This paper is organized as follows. The next section of this paper describes the proposed generalized tagged token dataflow architecture. The MIT tagged token dataflow architecture [3], the

Manchester dataflow computer [14], and the Multi-ring dataflow computer [4] are shown to be particular cases of this generalized architecture. The queueing model and the assumptions are discussed in Section 3. The analysis and the modification of the MVA algorithm to solve the multi-chain closed queueing network are briefly discussed in Section 4. The results are discussed in Section 5. Finally, Section 6 concludes the paper.

2. Description of the Generalized Dataflow Architecture

The overall organization of the tagged token dataflow architecture is shown in Fig.1a. It consist of several processing elements (PEs) interconnected via a packet switched interconnection network (IN). A processing element consists of a matching store unit (MU), a instruction fetch unit (IFU), a processing unit (PU), and an output unit (OU). The organization of a PE is shown in Fig.1b. The matching unit (MU) is typically a pseudo-associative store implemented using hardware hashing scheme [14]. If a token arriving at the matching unit completes all the input requirements for the execution of an instruction, a group token is formed with all the input data and is sent to the code fetch unit. Otherwise, the token is added into the the pseudo-associative store with the tokens already gathered for the instruction.

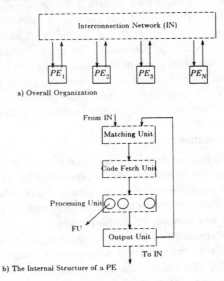

a) Overall Organization

b) The Internal Structure of a PE

Fig.1 : The generalized tagged token dataflow architecture.

When the instruction fetch unit (IFU) receives a packet with all the data for a particular instruction, the corresponding instruction is fetched. The instruction along with the data then forms an executable packet which is sent to the processing unit (PU) as shown in Fig.1b. The PU contains a number of functional units (FUs) which can perform the dataflow operations in parallel. The result generated by the PU is sent to the next box which is called the output unit (OU). The main function of the OU is to form the tokens from the result generated by the PU. Further, the OU unit also evaluates the assignment function to determine the physical address of the PE to which the token needs to be sent. Depending on the physical address of the destination PE, the token from the OU can be either sent to the MU of the same PE via the feedback path or to the MU of another PE via the IN.

In the above architectural description, we have not considered a separate I-structure store (IS) unit [3, 15]. The IS unit is a special memory module with a hardware controller which provides read-write synchronization without the risk of races [3]. In very simple term, the I-structures can be viewed as an array of slots which are initially empty and which can be written at most once. Essentially, a presence bit is associated with each memory location which is used to synchronize accesses to the memory location in a way such that the determinacy property of the dataflow model of computation is preserved. The primary function of the I-structure store is to implement common data structure such as arrays, records, etc. In this paper, we consider the common data structures to be stored in the MU and that accesses to the data structure elements are controlled by special matching functions to ensure proper synchronization.

As in any other parallel processing system, the IN which interconnects the different PEs in the dataflow architecture has a major influence on the performance of the entire system. Various types of interconnection schemes have been proposed for multiprocessing systems and as such these are also applicable for the dynamic dataflow architectures [2, 10, 13]. In this paper, we have considered a packet switched MIN [7, 17] the structure of which is shown in Fig.2a. It is a Delta network [21], which consists of $logN$ stages of 2×2 buffered crossbar switches with $N/2$ such switches per stage. The model of a 2×2 buffered switch is shown in Fig.2b. The packet arriving at any switching element is buffered and sent out through the output link to the next stage in an FCFS queueing discipline.

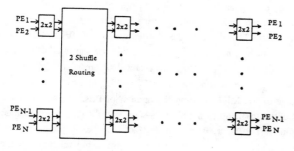

Figure 2a A packet switched MIN.

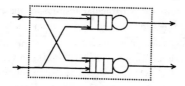

Figure 2b Model of a 2*2 buffered switching element.

Fig.2 : The packet switched Multistage Interconnection Network (MIN).

The above architecture is a generalization of the multi-ring Manchester dataflow (MMD) computer [4] and the MIT tagged

token dataflow architecture [3]. The difference between the above architecture and the MMD relates to the feedback path from the OU to the MU in each PE. This path is not present in the organization of the MMD [4]. On the other hand, in the MIT tagged token dataflow architecture the PU consists of a single FU unit while in the architecture considered in this paper, the PU can have more than one FU. The Manchester dataflow computer [14] is basically a single ring machine with number of PE's equal to 1. Although the above differences may appear minor in nature, these can have, as will be shown later, significant impact on the overall performance of the system.

3. The Model and the Assumptions

Our intent is to develop a queueing network model of the generalized dataflow architecture executing an arbitrary dataflow graph G. The development of such a model is significantly difficult since the dataflow graph can have arbitrary form. Thus, we consider characterizing the dataflow graph by some of its intrinsic properties. For this study, we use the average parallelism of the dataflow graphs [14, 11, 9] as the characterizing feature. The average parallelism of the dataflow graph, π_{av}, is defined as

$$\pi_{av} = \frac{T_1}{T_\infty} \, ,$$

where, T_1 and T_∞ are the execution time of the dataflow graph with one and unbounded number of processors, respectively, and assuming ideal machine organization with no overhead. Essentially, given the dataflow graph G, shown in Fig.3, we construct a rectangular dataflow graph G', shown in Fig.4, whose width is equal to average parallelism of G. Note that we consider dataflow graph with instructions which have only monadic and dyadic input/output dependencies. This is not a severe restriction [14]. The fraction of dyadic instructions in the dataflow graph is denoted by p_d. Further, in constructing the rectangular dataflow graph, we maintain the fraction of dyadic instructions at each level equal to p_d. The above characterization of the dataflow graph has been shown to be reasonably accurate in predicting the performance of an algorithm when executed on a dataflow architecture [11].

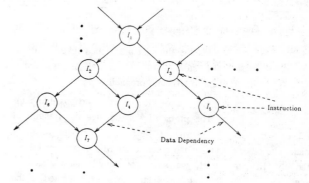

Fig.3 : A portion of an arbitrary dataflow graph G.

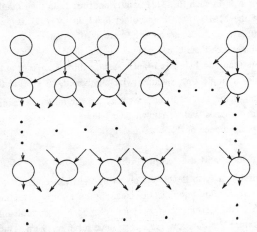

Fig.4 : A rectangular dataflow graph G' with width equal to average parallelism of G.

The generalized dataflow architecture is modeled as a network of queues as shown in Fig.5. The model of each PE is similar to the model of the dataflow architecture reported in [11]. The matching unit (MU), the instruction fetch unit (IFU), the processing unit (PU), and the output unit (OU) are the various service centers in each PE. Each service center has a queue associated with it as shown in the figure. The switching elements in the IN are modeled as queues with an associated server as was shown in Fig.2b. The delay unit (DU) is required for the dyadic

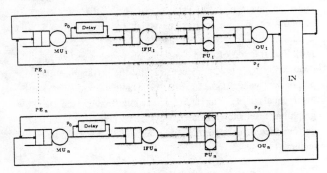

Fig.5 : The dataflow architecture as a network of queues.

instructions and denotes the time an unmatched token waits in the pseudo-associative store until the arrival of its partner token(s). A token waits in DU with probability p_0.

The tokens at the output of the OU have two possible paths as shown in Fig.5. The probability p_f denotes the fraction of tokens sent back to the MU of the same PE via the feedback path. The other path takes the token to the MU of another PE via the IN. In our model, we have considered static allocation schemes, i.e., the the dataflow instructions are allocated to the various PEs by a mapping function determined at compile time. The probability p_f depends on the allocation scheme and affects

the load on the communication network. For example, if random and uniform allocation is adopted, p_f will be equal to $1/N$, N being the number of PEs. The value of p_f can be increased if more complex allocation policy is used. This will reduce inter-PE communication but would require higher compiling/allocation cost. The effect of p_f on the performance is discussed in Section 5.

Next we state the following assumptions.

Assumption 1 : A sequence of dataflow graphs each with the same average parallelism is executed in the dataflow architecture and it is assumed that the machine is never idle.

Assumption 2 : We assume that each service center in the PE has a service time which is exponentially distributed while those corresponding to the IN have fixed service times.

Assumption 3 : The queue associated with each service center has infinite buffer length and the queueing discipline is FCFS (first come first served).

Assumption 1 essentially means that we are considering steady state analysis of the system. The fixed service time distribution assumption for the switches in the IN realistically models the packet switched MIN. The infinite buffer length of the switches is not a very unreasonable as previous studies [7, 18] show that the difference in performance between finite buffer and infinite buffer cases is not significant when the buffer size is greater than a few. The other assumptions are typical of queueing theoretic based models and reasonably approximate the real environment.

4. Analysis

We need to find the population of the network for the execution of the rectangular dataflow graph G'. In the following discussion, the term job will generically refer to tokens in the IN, MUs, and DUs, and to the instructions in the IFUs, PUs, and OUs. Let $n_{1,i}$, $n_{2,i}$, $n_{3,i}$, $n_{4,i}$, $n_{5,i}$, and $n_{6,i,j}$ be the number of jobs in MU_i, DU_i, IFU_i, PU_i, OU_i, and $IN_{i,j}$, respectively, where, $i = 1,...,N$, $j = 1,...,logN$, and $IN_{i,j}$ is the ith switch in the jth stage of the MIN, N being the number of PEs. The switches are counted from top to bottom in a stage and the stages are counted from left to right. Based on the fact that the dataflow graph is rectangular, it can be shown that the following relations on the number of jobs in the various service centers of the system is satisfied.

$$\frac{(1 - p_1)(\sum_{i=1}^{N} n_{1,i} + \sum_{i=1}^{N}\sum_{j=1}^{logN} n_{6,i,j}) + \sum_{i=1}^{N} n_{2,i}}{2} + \sum_{i=1}^{N} n_{3,i} \quad (1)$$

$$+ \sum_{i=1}^{N} n_{5,i} + \sum_{i=1}^{N} n_{4,i} + p_1(\sum_{i=1}^{N} n_{1,i} + \sum_{i=1}^{N}\sum_{j=1}^{logN} n_{6,i,j}) = \pi_{av} .$$

Also,

$$Max(\sum_{i=1}^{N} n_{1,i} + \sum_{i=1}^{N}\sum_{j=1}^{logN} n_{4,i,j}) = (1 + p_d)\pi_{av} , \quad Max(\sum_{i=1}^{N} n_{3,i}) = \pi_{av} . \quad (2)$$

In Eq.(1), p_1 correspond to the fraction of jobs in the IN, OUs and MUs that correspond to monadic instructions. It can be easily shown that [12]

$$p_1 = \frac{1 - p_d}{1 + p_d}, \qquad (3)$$

where p_d is the percentage of the dyadic instructions. Although Eq.(1) can be obtained from explicit enumeration of the state space, one can intuitively argue it out by noting that the fraction of the jobs in the MUs, the DUs, and in the IN which correspond to dyadic instructions contribute to half an instruction while the jobs in the IFUs, PUs, and OUs correspond to one instruction.

The queueing network violate conditions required for product from solution due to 1) the concurrency, and 2) the fixed service time of the switches in the IN. The concurrency result in the addition and removal of jobs from the network and in the bulk arrival in certain queues in the network. The removal of jobs from the network occurs after a successful match at the MU, while jobs are added into the network when the OU produces two copies of a result which are destined to two different instructions. We take care of of these issues in two steps. In the first step, we incorporate fictitious servers in the network to model the loss and gain of jobs [16, 1] while in the second step we modify the Mean Value Analysis (MVA) algorithm [19, 23] to account for the bulk arrival and the fixed service time of the switches.

The incorporation of the fictitious server can be formally obtained by rewriting Eq.(1) as

$$\sum_{i=1}^{N} n_{1,i} + \sum_{i=1}^{N} n_{2,i} + \sum_{i=1}^{N} \sum_{j=1}^{logN} n_{6,i,j} + 2(\sum_{i=1}^{N} n_{3,i} \qquad (4)$$

$$+ \sum_{i=1}^{N} n_{4,i} + \sum_{i=1}^{N} n_5) + p_1(\sum_{i=1}^{N} n_{1,i} + \sum_{i=1}^{N} \sum_{j=1}^{logN} n_{6,i,j}) = 2\pi_{av}.$$

The above Eq.(4) suggests the network shown in Fig.6 which is obtained from Fig.5 by inserting fictitious servers. The fictitious server FPU_i, $FIFU_i$ and FOU_i put in parallel to PU_i, IFU_i and OU_i in PE_i, $i = 1,...,N$ models the loss and gain of jobs in the queueing network. This is because the mean time between the instant a job is lost from the system (due to a successful match) until the time it is injected back into the network (as a result of the OU forming two tokens for those results which are destined to two destination instructions) is the same as the sum of the response time of the PU_i, IFU_i, and OU_i. The fictitious server FMU_i in PE_i, $i = 1,...,N$, provides a path to route the extra tokens corresponding to the monadic instructions that have been added as a result of increasing the population to $2\pi_{av}$. Note that the service time of DU_i is not known a priori and must be obtained from the solution of the network. Because of Eq. (2), the above network must be solved as consisting of four chains with the sum of the population in the chains equal to $2\pi_{av}$. The service centers in each chain and their population are shown below.

1. Chain 1 has population $p_d\pi_{av}$ and consists of centers MU_i, DU_i, IFU_i, PU_i, OU_i, and $IN_{i,j}$, $i = 1,..,N$, $j = 1,..,logN$.

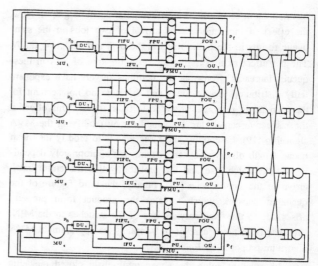

Fig.6 : The transformed network for a 4-PE generalized dynamic dataflow architecture

2. Chain 2 has population $p_d\pi_{av}$ and consists of centers MU_i, DU_i, $FIFU_i$, FPU_i, FOU_i, and $IN_{i,j}$, $i = 1,..,N$, $j = 1,..,logN$.

3. Chain 3 has population $(1 - p_d)\pi_{av}$ and consists of service centers MU_i, IFU_i, PU_i, OU_i, and $IN_{i,j}$, $i = 1,..,N$, $j = 1,..,logN$.

4. Chain 4 has population $(1 - p_d)\pi_{av}$ and consists of service centers FMU_i, $FIFU_i$, FPU_i and FOU_i, $i = 1,..,N$.

It should be noted that Chains 1 and 2 relate to the routing behavior of the dyadic instructions whereas Chains 3 and 4 represent the service centers visited by the monadic instructions. Chain 4 represents the routing of the extra $((1 - p_d)\pi_{av})$ monadic instructions.

The addition of fictitious servers account for the addition and removal of jobs from the network and results in a multi-chain closed queueing network. However, as pointed out before, there are two features that lead to the non-product from nature of the closed queueing network. First, is the bulk arrival process in the first stage of the IN and the MUs. To understand this phenomena, consider the instant the OU_i receives a result token from PU_i. If the result token is destined to two instructions, the OU_i creates two result tokens with different destination addresses. Now, the probability that both these jobs are destined to the same queue in the first stage of the IN or MU_i in PE_i will depend on the probability p_f, i.e., on the allocation policy. Specifically, the probability $p_{IN_{i,1}}$, that both jobs visit the same queue in the IN is given by

$$p_{IN_{i,1}} = \frac{1}{2} p_d (1 - p_f)^2 . \qquad (5)$$

Similarly, the probability p_{MU_i} is given by

$$p_{MU_i} = p_d p_f^2 \qquad (6)$$

where, p_d is the probability that the instruction completed in PU_i produces two jobs. This is equivalent to the fraction of dyadic instructions in each row of the rectangular dataflow graph. Now, the effect of the simultaneous arrival of two jobs in the same queue results in the bulk arrival at the $IN_{i,1}$ and MU_i, $i = 1,...,N$. The net effect of this is that the response time of jobs in these queues increases. Note that the fictitious servers have exponentially distributed service times and therefore do not account for the increase in response time due to bulk arrival. This effect at the respective centers are accounted for by modifying the MVA algorithm [19]. Essentially, the basic idea is to modify the mean queue length observed by an arriving job appropriately depending on the batch size and the probability that the entire batch arrive in the same queue [12]. Finally, the third feature of the queueing network which violates the product form property arises due to the fixed service time of the switches in the MIN. This has been taken care of by adopting the approximate MVA algorithm proposed by Reiser [22].

In order to solve the above multi-chain closed queueing network using MVA algorithm, the following issues must be addressed, namely, 1) derivation of the service demands of the various service centers, and 2) the derivation of the DU service time. Since our main intent of this paper is to study the trade-off issues, we will not include the detail derivation of these quantities rather we will briefly outline the method that has been adopted. Details related to these are reported in [12].

The service demand of a customer in a queueing center in a particular chain depends on the visit count of a customer in that chain to the service center and the service requirement per visit. The service requirement per visit is equal to the service time of the center and is known for all the centers except the DUs. The visit count can be obtained by finding the ratio of the number of completions at the center to the overall system completions for that chain.

The service time of the DUs represents the synchronization time and this, in general, is a difficult problem [8, 20]. The complexity of the problem is further increased by the distributed matching process that is considered in this paper. We use an iterative method to obtain the service time of the DU. Note that the time a job wait in the DU depends on the response time of the other service centers in the network. The basic idea is to obtain an approximate expression of the service time of the DU as a function of the response time of the other centers in the network and then use a iterative solution technique [1, 16, 12].

We would like to point out here, that much of the details of the analysis has been omitted primarily to keep the paper short and readable. Also, the main thrust of the paper is to study the computation-communication issues that relate to the dynamic dataflow architectures and not the mathematical issues involved in the development of the model. Finally, we would like to point out that we have done simulation to validate the results that have been obtained from the analytical model.

5. Results and Discussions

The multi-chain closed queueing network model of the gen-eralized dynamic dataflow architecture is solved using a modified MVA algorithm. The solution of the queueing network for a given set of parameters provides different performance metrics. In this study we have primarily focussed on two different performance metrics, namely, 1) processing power, i.e., the sum of the utilization of the PUs and 2) the system response time. The later quantity is defined as

$$R_{sys} = R_{IFU} + R_{PU} + R_{OU} + (1 - p_f)R_{IN} + R_{MU} + p_0 R_{DU},$$

where p_f and p_0 correspond to the feedback probability and the probability of waiting in the DU, respectively, p_d is the fraction of dyadic instructions and R_i's are the mean response time of the appropriate queues. Note that R_{sys} is the average cycle time of an instruction and hence the execution time of the dataflow graph is the product of R_{sys} and the number of instruction in the critical path.

The parameters of the model include the service times of the various service centers, the average parallelism, π_{av}, the system size, N, i.e., the number of PEs, the number of FUs in each PU (will be denoted as number of servers), the feedback probability, p_f, and the percentage of dyadic instructions, p_d. With so many parameters, it is difficult to make an exhaustive analysis of the computation-communication issues as a function of these parameters. As a result, we have fixed some of the parameters based on the data available in the literature. With respect to the dataflow graphs, we consider the fraction of dyadic instruction, p_d to be 0.4. This is based on the results published in [14] which shows that for a large number of benchmark applications, the percentage of monadic instructions varied from 0.55 to 0.71. The matching unit is assumed to process at the rate of 2.14 million tokens per second. This is based on the prototype Manchester dataflow computer [14]. The IFU and the OU service 2 million packets per second. Finally, each switching element can forward 1 million packets per second. Unless otherwise stated, these parameters are assumed to be fixed for all the results reported in the following paragraphs.

The first experiment pertains to the performance of the architecture as a function of the system size. Fig.7 plots the processing power as a function of the number of PEs. In this experiment, each PU contains four servers (i.e., four FUs) which can execute instructions concurrently. Also, the feedback probability is assumed to be $1/N$, N being the number of PEs. Note that this corresponds to a random and uniform allocation of the instructions among the PEs. From the figure it is observed that for an average parallelism of 64 the utilization is very poor and even when the average parallelism is increased to 256, for N equal to 64 we get only 50 percent utilization. For low value of average parallelism, the low utilization is not due to any bottleneck rather it is due to the lack of parallelism. For average parallelism equal 64 all the processors cannot be kept busy all the time, i.e., there are not enough instructions to keep the pipeline filled up. Note that the total hardware parallelism is four times the number of PEs since each PU contains 4 FUs. From the above figure we observe that we can get 80 percent utilization with software

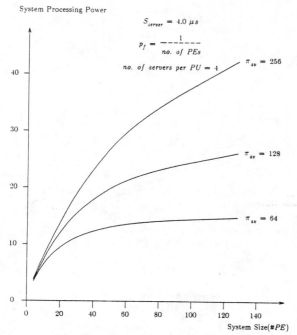

Fig.7 : System processing power as a function of system size.

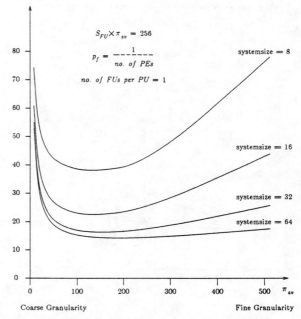

Fig.8 : System response time as a function of granularity.

parallelism four times as much as the hardware parallelism. With twice as much software parallelism, the utilization falls of to less than 70 percent and finally when the hardware parallelism is equal to the software parallelism only 50 percent utilization is achieved. Similar results were reported in [15].

The second experiment deals with the effect of granularity on the system response time. The way we model the variation of granularity is as follows. Given the rectangular dataflow graph G', shown in Fig.5, with certain average parallelism and service requirement of each instruction, we define the software computation requirement of each row to be the product of the average parallelism and the service time of each instruction. By grouping instructions together, we can increase the service time of each instruction and reduce the average parallelism so as to keep the total software computation requirement constant. For this experiment we assume that even with the grouping of the instructions, the proportion of monadic and dyadic instructions is the same as in the original dataflow graph. For the results shown in Fig.8, the software computation requirement of each row is assumed to be 256 time units. As in the previous study, the feedback probability, p_f is assumed to be $1/N$, N being the number of PEs. Also, the number of servers per PU is assumed to be equal to 1. From the figure it is observed that for a given system size, decreasing the granularity (i.e., changing the granularity from coarse to fine) at first results in significant decrease in the response time but subsequently it increases with finer granularity. Essentially, the decrease in the response time due to increase in concurrency is counteracted by increase in the network delay due to large number of jobs corresponding to fine granularity of parallelism. For all system sizes, the increase in the response time at fine

Table 1. Queue lengths at the service centers as a function of granularity. $S_{PU} * \pi_{av} = 256$ *time units, no. of servers per PU = 1* and $p_f = 1/no.$ *of PEs.*

Average Parallelism	System Size = 16			System Size = 64		
	PU	MU	IN	PU	MU	IN
8	0.377	0.007	0.041	0.087	0.002	0.018
16	0.701	0.026	0.130	0.010	0.006	0.061
32	1.273	0.094	0.36	0.240	0.018	0.184
64	2.188	0.327	0.957	0.341	0.051	0.507
128	3.310	0.993	2.732	0.420	0.126	1.273
256	2.182	1.310	10.95	0.419	0.251	2.97
512	0.624	0.749	28.57	0.315	0.377	6.54
1024	0.250	0.602	60.25	0.185	0.444	13.94

granularity is due to the IN becoming a bottleneck center as can be observed from the queue lengths shown in Table 1. In general, for a given system size, there is an optimum level of granularity which yields the minimum response time.

As mentioned before, the dataflow model of computation purports a fully decentralized scheduling of the dataflow instructions. This scheduling in the dynamic dataflow architectures is carried out by the MU. An architectural model supporting full decentralized scheduling would thus correspond to one MU serving a PU with one FU. Centralization can be achieved by incorporating more number of servers in each PU. Fig.9 shows the effect of centralization on the system response time. For this study we define the total hardware computing power to be the product of the number of PEs and the number of server in each

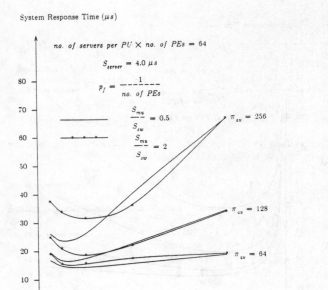

System Response Time

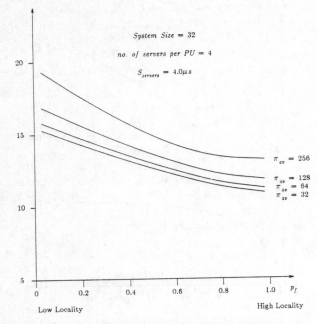

Fig.10 : System response time as a function of locality.

Fig.9 : System response time as a function of degree of centralization.

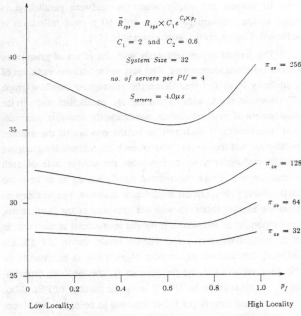

Fig.11 : System response time weighted with scheduling cost as a function of locality.

PU. By putting more of servers in each PU and reducing the number of PEs so as to keep the total hardware computing power constant, we increase the degree of centralized scheduling.

Fig.9 shows the effect of centralization on the system response time for different values of average parallelism. For this experiment, the total hardware computing power is set equal to 64. Again, the feedback probability, p_f, is assumed to be $1/N$, N being the number of PEs. The two sets of curves correspond to two different ratios of the MU service time to the service time of the switches in the IN. From the figure it is observed that, for the particular set of parameters, there is an optimum level of centralization that yields the minimum system response time. For fully decentralized scheduling, the IN is large resulting in a large network delay. At higher degree of decentralized scheduling, the response time increases due to the bottleneck in the MU. It also depends on the ratio of the service time of the switching element and MU as shown in the figure.

The final experiment deals with the effect of locality on the system performance. The effect of locality can be studied by changing the value of p_f. Fig.10 plots the system response time as a function of p_f. Consistent with our intuition, we observe that increasing the value of p_f results in a decrease in the system response time. As already mentioned before, increasing p_f requires higher compiling/allocating cost and it is commonly known that the cost increases exponentially. In order to study the cost effectiveness of exploiting locality, we considered the weighted system response time, $\overline{R}_{sys}$, which is defined as

$$\overline{R}_{sys} = R_{sys} C_1 e^{C_2 * p_f}$$

where C_1 and C_2 are some positive constants. Note that the second term in the right hand expression is an exponentially increasing cost function which correspond to the compilation/allocation cost as a function of p_f. The constants, C_1 and C_2, for the results shown in Fig.11 are taken as 2 and 0.6, respectively. We studied the system for other sets of constants. For some values, $\bar{R}_{sys}$ decreased monotonically, for some it increased monotonically, and for some we obtain the types of curves shown in Fig.11 with distinct minimum values of $\bar{R}_{sys}$ for a particular p_f. The point of the experiment is that given the constants, C_1 and C_2, obtained based on software engineering concepts, one can obtain the degree of locality that is most cost-effective.

6. Conclusion

This paper deals with the study of various computation-communication related issues in dynamic dataflow architectures. In order to address these issues, we developed a generalized model of dynamic dataflow architectures which encompassed all the basic features of the proposed architectures. The execution of the dataflow graph in the dynamic dataflow architecture is modeled by characterizing the dataflow graph by its average parallelism. Since the analytical queueing network model of the architecture does not have the properties required for product form solution, approximate methods were developed.

Based on the queueing network model, we carried out an extensive study of the various computation communication issues in dynamic dataflow architectures. From the results it was observed that in order to obtain high utilization, the parallelism in the dataflow graph must be greater than the hardware parallelism by a factor of four times or greater. With respect to the question of granularity, we observed that going for fine granularity is advantageous only upto a certain point. The increase in the communication at fine granularity can dominate over the decrease in the response time due to increased parallelism. We also studied the effect of centralization in the scheduling of the dataflow instructions on the response time of the system and observed the associated trade-off. Finally, we addressed the issue of locality and attempted to bring in a cost factor to quantify the level of locality that can be exploited in a cost-effective manner. In conclusion it should be pointed out that the study reported here is not an exhaustive one with respect to the various parameters of the model. The main contribution of this paper is that it provides the designer of the dataflow architecture with a simple and fast analytical tool to make certain design decisions associated with the computation-communication issues.

References

[1] Agrawal, S. C., *Metamodelling : A Study of Approximation in Queueing Models*. Computer System Series, The MIT Press, 1985.

[2] Arvind and Kathail, V., "A multiple processor dataflow machine that supports generalized procedures", *Proc. 8th Ann. Symp. Comput. Arch.*, May 1981, pp. 291-302.

[3] Arvind and Culler, D. E., "Dataflow Architectures", *MIT/LCS/TM-294*, Laboratory for Computer Science, MIT, Feb. 1986.

[4] Barahona, P. M. C. C., and Gurd, J. R., "Processor Allocation in a Multi-ring Dataflow Machine," *Journal of Parallel and Distributed Computing*, Vol. 3, 1986, pp. 305-327.

[5] Davis, A. L., and Keller, R. M., "Dataflow program graphs", *IEEE Computer*, vol. 15, no. 2, Feb. 1982, pp. 26-41.

[6] Dennis, J. B., "Dataflow Supercomputers", *IEEE Computer*, vol. 13, no. 11, Nov. 1980, pp. 362-376.

[7] Dias, D. M., and Jump, J. R., "Analysis and simulation of buffered delta networks", *IEEE Trans. on Comput.*, vol. c-30, April 1981, pp. 273-282.

[8] Duda, A. and Tadeusz, C., "Performance Evaluation of Fork and Join Synchronization Primitives," *Acta Informatica*, Vol. 24, 1987, pp. 525-553.

[9] Eager, D. L., Zahorjan, J., and Lazowska, E. D. "Speedup Versus Efficiency in Parallel Systems," *IEEE Trans. on Comput.*, Vol. C-38, no. 3, March. 1989, pp. 408-423.

[10] Gaudiot, J. L., and Ercegovac, M. D., "Performance Evaluation of a Simulated Data-Flow Computer with Low Resolution Actors* ", *Journal of Parallel and Distributed Computing*, Vol.2, Feb. 1985, pp. 321-351.

[11] Ghosal, D., and Bhuyan, L. N., "Analytical Modeling and Architectural Modification of a Dataflow Architecture", *14th Ann. Intl. Symp. Comput. Arch.*, June 1987.

[12] Ghosal, D., "A Unified Approach to Performance Evaluation of Dataflow and Multiprocessing Architectures," *Ph.D Dissertation*, The Center for Advanced Computer Studies, Univ. of Southwestern Louisiana, 1988.

[13] Gostelow, K. P., and Thomas R. E., "Performance of simulated dataflow computer", *IEEE Trans. on Comput.*, vol. c-29, no. 10, Oct. 1980, pp. 905-919.

[14] Gurd, J. R., Watson, I., and Kirkham, C. C., "The Manchester prototype dataflow computer", *Commun. Ass. Comput. Mach.*, vol. 28, Jan. 1985, pp. 34-52.

[15] Gurd, J. R., and Kirkham, C. C., "Dataflow: Achievements and Prospects", *Information Processing*, North-Holland, 1986, pp. 61-68.

[16] Heidelberger, P., and Trivedi, K. S., "Analytic Queueing Models for Programs with Internal Concurrency," *IEEE Trans. on Comput.*, vol. C-32, no. 1, Jan. 1983, pp. 73-82.

[17] Hwang, K., and Briggs, F. A., *Parallel Processing and Computer Architecture*. McGraw-Hill, New York, Apr. 1984.

[18] Kruskal, C. P., and Snir, M., "The performance of multistage interconnection networks for multiprocessors", *IEEE Trans. on Comput.*, vol. c-32, No. 12, Dec. 1983, pp. 1091-1098.

[19] Lazowska, E.D., Zahorjan, J., Graham, S. G., and Sevcik, K. C., *Quantitative System Performance : Computer System Analysis using Queueing Network Models*. NJ : Prentice-Hall Inc., 1984.

[20] Nelson, R., Towsely, D., and Tantawi, A. N., "Performance Analysis of Parallel Processing Systems," *IEEE Trans. on Software Engg.*, Vol. 14, No. 4, April 1988, pp. 532-540.

[21] Patel, J. H., "Performance of Processor Memory Interconnections for Multiprocessors," *IEEE Trans. on Comput.*, vol. c-30, no. 10, Oct. 1981, pp. 771-780.

[22] Reiser, M., "A Queueing Network Analysis of Computer Communication Networks with Window Flow Control," *IEEE Trans. on Commun.*, vol. COM-27, No. 8, Aug. 1979, pp. 1199-1209.

[23] Sauer, C. H., and Chandy, K. M., *Computer Systems Performance Modeling*. Prentice-Hall, Inc. NJ, 1981.

[24] Treleaven, P. C., David, B. R., and Hopkins, P. R., "Data driven and demand driven computer architecture", *Computing Surveys*, vol. 14, pp. 93-143, Mar. 1982.

Logic Simulation on Massively Parallel Architectures

Saul A. Kravitz, Randal E. Bryant, and Rob A. Rutenbar

Department of Electrical and Computer Engineering
Carnegie Mellon University
Pittsburgh, Pennsylvania 15213

Abstract

This work examines the mapping of logic simulation onto massively parallel computer architectures. We discuss alternative communication primitives for a massively parallel instruction set architecture and the impact of the choice of communication primitives on logic simulation. We have developed compilation tools to automatically map the simulation of an MOS transistor circuit onto a massively parallel computer. We analyze the efficiency of this mapping as a function of the available communication primitives. The compilation process is illustrated by describing our pilot implementation on a 32k processor Connection Machine.

1. Introduction

Simulation provides an important tool for establishing the correctness of a digital system prior to construction. The time consuming and critical nature of the simulation task has motivated many attempts to provide faster simulation by mapping simulation algorithms onto special-purpose hardware accelerators and general-purpose parallel machines. Previous work on accelerating logic simulation has focused on the application of limited amounts of parallelism to the simulation task ([Smith 86], [Frank 86], [Denneau 82], [Agrawal 87]). This work explores the feasibility of mapping logic simulation onto computers with thousands of processors, or so-called *massively parallel* machines.

The focus of our work is the COSMOS switch-level logic simulator [Bryant 87]. COSMOS preprocesses a MOS circuit into an equivalent Boolean model by performing a symbolic analysis of the circuit structure. The run time activity of the COSMOS simulator involves evaluating the Boolean formulas comprising the model for a given circuit. This paper presents and analyzes techniques for mapping this runtime Boolean evaluation activity onto massively parallel computer architectures. The work is therefore applicable not only to COSMOS in particular, but to logic simulation in general.

Logic simulation is a particularly difficult application to map onto a parallel computer due to its extremely fine grain of computation, and its high communication requirements. Logic simulation typically utilizes the simplest and fastest instructions, namely those for evaluating simple Boolean operations, and the most complex communication, namely transfers of data among processors connected in an arbitrary topology. Typically the ratio of communication operations to Boolean evaluations is about 1:1. Most parallel machines are not designed to effectively support this high ratio of communication to computation. Performance of parallel logic simulation, as a result, is limited by communication speed. To date, the application of parallel hardware to the logic simulation task has met with limited success.

Although previous work has claimed that only extremely limited parallelism exists in logic simulation([Bailey 88], [Wong 86], [Frank 86]), we will show that thousand-fold parallelism exists in the Boolean formulas derived by COSMOS for actual circuits. Previous work was burdened with the unwarranted assumption that any parallel implementation would closely follow conventional serial implementations. In contrast, our work starts from the ground up and involves a substantial restructuring of the simulation algorithm to expose parallelism.

The selection of communication primitives provided by a massively parallel instruction set architecture (ISA) has a critical impact on the mapping process. We present three alternative communication schemes and analyze the impact of the available primitives on logic simulation. The choice of communication primitives affects the ease of implementation and the runtime performance of the parallel simulator in much the same as the ISA of a serial computer affects the difficulty of writing a code generator and the efficiency of the resulting code. We have developed compilation tools which automatically map the simulation of an MOS transistor circuit onto a massively parallel computer architecture. We analyze the efficiency of this mapping generated by our compilation tools as a function of the available communication primitives. The compilation process is illustrated by describing our pilot implementation on a Thinking Machines Corporation Connection Machine System (CM).

2. Simulation Algorithm

The COSMOS (COmpiled Simulator for MOS) simulator provides fast and accurate switch level modeling of digital MOS circuits. It attains high performance by preprocessing a transistor network into a functionally equivalent Boolean representation. The preprocessor reads a transistor-level description of a circuit's structure and creates a Boolean representation of its behavior. This Boolean representation captures all details of the switch-level model, including bidirectional transistor operation, different signal strengths, the effects of stored charge, and the effect of indeterminate (X) values. Following this preprocessing, a switch-level simulator can operate by simply evaluating the operations in the Boolean representation.

The COSMOS preprocessor partitions a transistor circuit into subnetworks and generates a Boolean description for each subnetwork. Each of these descriptions is essentially a logic gate network. Figure 1 shows a small CMOS shifter cell, with each subnetwork outlined with a shaded box. The essential aspect of COSMOS for this paper is the evaluation of the collection of Boolean descriptions which constitutes the simulation model.

COSMOS supports a 3-valued logic, where each node has state 1, 0, or X (indeterminate). To facilitate the use of a Boolean behavioral model, the state of each circuit node is represented by a pair of Boolean values. Table 1 illustrates this encoding. Note that no inverters are required to implement the Boolean simulation model, because inverting a node S involves merely swapping S.L and S.H.

S	S.L	S.H
0	1	0
1	0	1
X	1	1

Table 1: Boolean Encoding of Node State

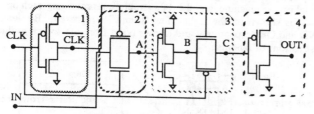

Figure 1 – Example Circuit

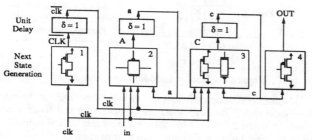

Figure 2 – Circuit Model

COSMOS identifies and analyzes all of the unique subnetworks in the circuit. For each unique subnetwork, Boolean formulas are generated for each circuit node controlled by the subnetwork. The resulting Boolean model behaves like a Finite State Machine, generating new values for the subnetwork outputs as a function of its inputs and the previous state of the outputs. Each time an input changes, the Boolean model is repeatedly evaluated until a stable state is reached. Figure 2 shows the Boolean model for the example circuit. Note that in this circuit, a change to one of the inputs (CLK or IN) requires several evaluations of the model before all of the nodes stabilize. A simulation *step* is the process of generating new values of the nodes and checking for stability.

In mapping the simulator onto a massively parallel machine, our starting point is the set of Boolean descriptions of a circuit's subnetworks, and a description of their interconnection. We conceptually merge the individual subnetwork descriptions into a single large Boolean simulation model, and map this model onto the parallel machine. Note that only binary AND and OR operators are required to evaluate the model.

The massively parallel implementation of COSMOS does not use an event list. Instead, all of the Boolean descriptions are computed on each step. This allows us to fully exploit the parallelism in the circuit model, at the cost of performing some redundant computation. We expect that the high degree of parallelism in the circuit model will more than compensate for the wasted computation. This approach has been used with success in more modestly parallel machines [Denneau 82] and will be discussed in Section 7.

3. Abstract Massively Parallel Computer

By massively parallel, we mean a machine having thousands of processors. Such a machine will most likely be of Single Instruction Multiple Data (SIMD) design, meaning that all proces-

sors execute from a single thread of control, with each processor operating on its own distinct data. The ISA of such a computer has a critical impact on both our ability to map logic simulation onto the computer, and the efficiency of the mapping. In this section we discuss the instruction types required by the COSMOS simulator and we describe two alternative interprocessor communication primitives which could provide a basis set on which to implement the simulator. We view the mapping of the simulator onto the massively parallel architecture as a compilation problem. As such a tradeoff exists between the power of the available communication primitives, and both the complexity of the compilation problem and the performance of the resulting parallel simulator. We will examine both of these tradeoffs later in the paper.

To provide a platform for the COSMOS simulator a massively parallel architecture must provide the following minimal instruction types:

- Boolean operators: 2 input AND and OR operators
- Select/Disable Processors
- Equality Testing
- Communication Operations
- Interface to Sequential Host

The Boolean operators and the ability to select and disable processors are required to evaluate the operators in the Boolean model. Equality testing is required to test for convergence. After each *step*, the values generated by the current *step* are compared to the values generated by the previous *step*. If no change has occurred in nodes with fanout, then stability has been achieved. The interface to the sequential host is required to support downloading the model, providing stimulus, and to support the sequential aspects of the simulator. With the exception of the required communication operations, the other required aspects of the ISA are relatively standard.

Let us now consider a range of possible instructions for transferring data in the machine. There is a private RAM associated with each processor. We refer to a memory location on a given processor by (p,a), where p is a processor number and a is a location within the processor's memory. First, the processors can copy values from one location to another, with all processors using the same source and destination addresses. This is the simplest data movement, or communication instruction, and we refer to it as MOVE (see figure 3a). Alternately, addressing could be done indirectly, with each processor using a locally stored address as the destination address for the move. We refer to this as an indirect move, or IMOVE (see figure 3b).

Communication operators for interprocessor communication can span a wide range of complexity and sophistication. One simple form is an operator supporting communication patterns where the interconnection pattern forms a permutation. In other words data at location (SP_i,s) is moved to location (DP_i,d), where $DP_i = \Pi(SP_i)$, for some permutation Π (see figure 3c).

A more general communication operator is one capable of storing a value from a location in each processor's memory into an arbitrary memory location on an arbitrary processor. In other words, data at location (SP_i,SA) is stored at location (DP_i,DA_i), where the relations between DP_i and SP_i, and DA_i and SA are arbitrary. We will refer to this complex operator as a STORE (see figure 3d). Note that a single STORE can cause values to be stored into multiple locations on a single processor. Thus, a STORE operation is not equivalent to a PERMUTE followed by an IMOVE. A processor receives at most a single value as a result of a PERMUTE operation, and the data is stored at the same address on all processors.

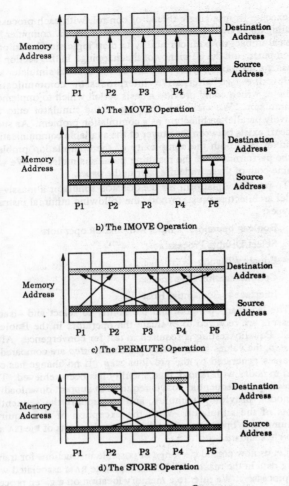

a) The MOVE Operation

b) The IMOVE Operation

c) The PERMUTE Operation

d) The STORE Operation

Figure 3 – Data Movement Operators

A key point is that although the communication operations required by logic simulation may be complex, the communication patterns are not data dependent. Therefore, a massively parallel machine for logic simulation need not support dynamic message routing, since all routing patterns are known in advance.

Either PERMUTE or STORE used in conjunction with either MOVE or IMOVE provides a sufficient basis from which to implement COSMOS on a massively parallel computer. However, the exact communication ISA has a significant impact on both the compilation process and the runtime performance.

Our work does not assume any particular network topology, and therefore should be applicable to any machine providing the limited programming model described above. We have made an implicit assumption that the cost of a communication operation is roughly independent of the pattern of communication. The irregular nature of communication found in logic simulation is very difficult to efficiently map onto communication topologies in order to achieve a topology-dependent acceleration. As such, the fast neighbor communications found in a grid-based machine [Batcher 80] or hypercube-based machines such as the CM are not of much use. Both of these machine classes are capable of supporting our model of computation, with the hypercube-based machines providing $O(\log N)$ time permutations and the grid-based machines $O(\sqrt{N})$, where N is the size of the machine.

4. Implementation of COSMOS on a Massively Parallel Machine

Our starting point is the set of Boolean descriptions of a cir-

cuit's subnetworks, and a description of their interconnection generated by the COSMOS preprocessor. Conceptually, we merge the subnetwork descriptions into a single Boolean model, and map this model onto the parallel machine. Unlike the sequential version of COSMOS, the computation is no longer event driven. Each simulation step takes equal time, independent of circuit activity.

The massively parallel machine is used in much the same fashion as the Yorktown Simulation Engine (YSE)[Denneau 82]. The Boolean model is represented by operator records in the processor memories. Each processor memory is loaded with an array of operators. Figure 4 shows the arrangement of the Boolean model on the machine and the data structure representing each operator is shown on the right. The 'x' and '+' represent Boolean AND and OR respectively and arrows point from the source to the destinations of fanouts.

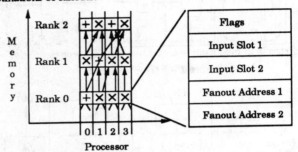

Figure 4 – Boolean Model Data Structures

Boolean operations are arranged in levels, or *ranks* in the processor memories. Evaluating a rank of operators and fanning out the results to the 2 fanout addresses is the atomic unit of computation in the simulation algorithm. Communication occurs after the evaluation of each rank of operators in order to distribute the results to succeeding ranks, and will most likely require far more time than our simple Boolean computations. To evaluate the Boolean model, the ranks of operators are evaluated in ascending order starting with rank 0. The Boolean model is levelized before mapping it onto the processors, so that successively evaluating the ranks of operators corresponds to evaluating the model in rank order.

Evaluating a *step* in the COSMOS simulator is a three stage process. First, the inputs to the Boolean model must be loaded into the input slots of all operators that require them. We refer to this as the *global fanout* stage. Second, the Boolean model is evaluated as described above, producing new values of the outputs. Finally, the new values of the outputs are compared with the old values, to determine whether a stable state has been reached. To evaluate the circuit's response to an input change, the program performs a series of these *steps* until the network reaches a stable state.

5. Compilation Issues

We exploit the two level hierarchy produced by the COSMOS preprocessor. The Boolean model for each unique subnetwork is mapped onto a *processor-time rectangle* — a rectangle of operators with one dimension being ranks and the other processors. The complete simulation model is then created by packing the rectangles in a manner that utilizes as many processors as possible to minimize overall rank. Although we could undoubtedly obtain a denser packing by treating the entire collection of Boolean models as a flattened network of Boolean operators, our approach requires far less time and space. In addition, the time to build and download the simulation model is reduced, because we can exploit hierarchy to speed incremental compilation.

Throughout the remainder of the paper we use the following terms:

- **Circuit**- The entire transistor circuit.

- **Subnetwork**- A DC connected component of the circuit.
- **Boolean module (or module)**- Boolean formulas derived for a single subnetwork.
- **Simulation model**- The set of modules comprising the model for the entire circuit.

5.1 Module Compilation

The module compilation process takes a Boolean module and maps it onto a *processor-time* rectangle. A clear objective of the compilation process is to map the module onto the smallest rectangle possible, since empty space inside the rectangle implies a reduction in processing power due to idle processors. In addition, the time required to evaluate the module is proportional to its height, since the height corresponds to the number of ranks of operators needed to evaluate the module.

There are two steps involved in compiling a module. The first step is to assign each operator in the module to a rank, and the second step is to bind each operator to a specific processor within the rank. The assignment of an operator to a rank is constrained by data dependencies. That is, an operator must be assigned to a rank greater than that of the operators producing its inputs, and less than that of all operators consuming its output. The ISA of the target machine constrains both rank assignment and processor binding.

Some operators have fanout greater than one. On a SIMD machine, the speed of the communication step at a given rank will be related to the maximum number of fanouts of an operator at that rank. We want to execute only a small fixed number of communication operators per rank. Therefore, we restrict each operator to having two fanouts, and add fanout trees for operators with higher fanout.

Since each operator has at most fanout two, clearly we need at least two data movement operations for each rank. If two STOREs are used to perform this fanout, a significant amount of flexibility is gained in both assigning each operator to a rank, and binding it to a processor. This flexibility can be used to produce a *processor-time* rectangle with smaller area by *stretching* the rectangle, increasing the number of ranks to decrease the total area. Another alternative is to perform the fanout using PERMUTEs, but this imposes significant constraints. The most important constraint concerns what to do in the case of an operator at rank i whose output is not consumed until rank j, where $j > i+1$. With the STORE primitive, each processor STOREs its results, to wherever they are to be consumed. So, outputs of operators in a given rank can be sent to any operator in any of the succeeding ranks. With the PERMUTE primitive, all processors send to a single rank. To send to m distinct ranks requires m PERMUTE operations, each of which deposits data in a distinct, separate rank. At the very minimum, the results of some of the operators at rank i will be consumed at rank $i+1$. If we impose the constraint that only PERMUTEs which advance the outputs of rank i to the inputs of rank $i+1$ are permitted, values which are produced at rank i, but not consumed until ranks beyond $i+1$, must be must be buffered by inserting a chain of identity operations. A middle ground between STORE and PERMUTE is using PERMUTE in conjunction with IMOVE. The use of the IMOVE instruction can significantly reduce the need for chains of identity operations.

The module compilation process is illustrated in Figure 5. Shown are the *processor-time rectangles* resulting from the compilation of a single module using the STORE (5a and 5b) and PERMUTE (5c) primitives. For the module shown, the result of compilation for using PERMUTE and IMOVE is the same as the result using STOREs, although this is not usually the case. Each circle represents an operation, with 'x' and '+' representing Boolean AND and OR, respectively. Empty circles represent identity operators required when using the PERMUTE primitive. Arrows represent the flow of data from one operator to another. Arrows which do not originate

at an operator are inputs to the module.

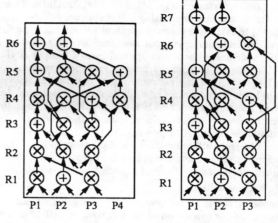

(a) STORE Schedule
(4 processors x 6 ranks)

(b) Stretched STORE Schedule
(3 processors x 7 ranks)

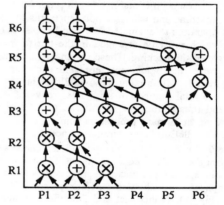

c) PERMUTE Schedule
(6 Processors x 6 Ranks)

Figure 5 – Module Compilation

Figure 5a shows the result of compiling the module using STORE primitives with the constraint that the number of ranks be minimal. If this constraint is relaxed, the module can be compiled for evaluation in 7 ranks instead of 6 as shown in Figure 5b, resulting in a more efficient *processor-time* rectangle. The STORE primitive provides the flexibility for stretching the module since communication can traverse an arbitrary number of ranks. When the module is compiled using the PERMUTE primitive, as shown in Figure 5c, the width of the resulting *processor-time* rectangle expands from 4 to 6. This expansion results because identity operators (empty circles) must be introduced to transport the results of operators which must traverse several ranks before being consumed. An advantage of compilation for the PERMUTE primitive is that the operations can always be arranged so that one fanout of an operator is on the same processor. This allows the fanout to be performed using one PERMUTE and one MOVE, in contrast to compilation using STOREs which always requires two STOREs. Compilation with PERMUTE/IMOVE requires three communication operations per rank: two PERMUTEs and one IMOVE. So although PERMUTE scheduling is the least space-efficient, it is by far the fastest, requiring only one communication instruction per rank.

To maximize parallelism we must transform the Boolean formulas produced by the COSMOS preprocessor into a form better suited for parallel evaluation. In particular, this means reducing the rank depth of the formulas, since we would prefer a *processor-time* rectangle which requires more processors and fewer ranks. We perform two transformations to reduce the rank depth of Boolean modules. Both transformations identify tree structures in the formulas, and restructure them using a Huffman coding technique [Huffman 52] to minimize the rank depth of the module. The first transformation finds multiple input Boolean gates (e.g., a 4-input AND gate implemented as a non-optimal tree of 2-input ANDs) and rebuilds them as unbalanced trees whose root has minimum rank. In large modules, the restructuring of multi-input Boolean gates often leads to reductions of rank depth by a factor of two. The second transformation builds unbalanced fanout trees that have minimal impact on the critical path of the module. This transformation is essential to prevent the introduction of fanout trees from adversely affecting the rank depth of modules. Using this transformation, we have found that the introduction of fanout trees typically increases the depth of a module by at most 10-20%.

5.2 Module Composition

Composing the modules conceptually merges them into the simulation model for evaluation on the massively parallel machine. The network composition problem is an instance of the two-dimensional bin-packing problem [Coffman 80]. We have a bin whose width represents the total number of processors available on our parallel machine and whose height represents time, measured in ranks of operators to evaluate. We also have a set of oriented rectangles which must be arranged in the bin to minimize the overall height of the packing. These rectangles are the individual *processor-time* rectangles that represent each module in the simulation model. Minimizing the overall height of the packing minimizes the total number of sequential ranks of operators to evaluate, and thus minimizes simulation time. An inefficient packing will result in many processors being idle, and thus reduce the effective parallelism in the simulation model.

Figure 6 illustrates module composition. The shaded rectangles represent the modules constituting the simulation model for a circuit. White space represents idle processors. The modules are shown composed for evaluation on 15 processors (Fig 6a) and 30 processors (Fig 6b). Notice that as the number of processors is increased, the number of ranks required to evaluate the model decreases. However, the model cannot be evaluated in fewer than 12 ranks, as shown in Fig 6b., since that is the number of ranks in the tallest module.

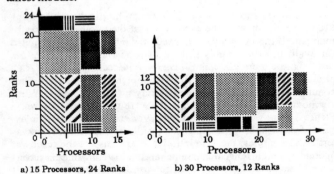

a) 15 Processors, 24 Ranks   b) 30 Processors, 12 Ranks

Figure 6 – Module Composition

6. Parallelism in Benchmark Circuits

Several studies of potential parallelism in logic simulation ([Bailey 88], [Wong 86], [Frank 86]) have indicated only low degrees of dynamically measured concurrency (e.g., 5-30). They concluded that only limited speedup can be achieved by exploiting parallelism in logic simulation algorithms.

An implicit and, we argue, unwarranted assumption of previous studies is that any implementation of parallel logic simulation would follow a conventional approach using fine-grain, event-driven parallelism. In contrast, we assume that a parallel imple-

mentation will require a complete restructuring of the simulation algorithm. The same tricks that help make serial simulators fast will not necessarily apply to parallel simulators. To exploit massive parallelism we must expose parallelism at every level of the simulation algorithm, and eliminate serial computation. Furthermore, the benchmarks these researchers used were small by VLSI standards.

Our work differs substantially from previous work in several ways. First of all, the COSMOS simulator employs a completely different approach to node evaluation than the simulators previously studied, an approach which offers more exposed parallelism. Second, we make no assumptions about the structure of a parallel implementation of the simulator; i.e., we do not simply assume that an event driven implementation is the best approach in the presence of massively parallel computational resources. In fact, we argue that this is precisely the wrong approach for massively parallel simulation. Our approach exposes all of the parallelism in the circuit model by eliminating the event list, and evaluating the entire circuit model each simulation step. The network compilation process exposes the parallelism within each Boolean module, and the network composition process exposes parallelism among the modules.

	Nodes	Trans-istors	Subnetworks		Booleans
			Total	Unique	
CktA	17731	43004	6390	429	139,015
CktB	7587	20167	2337	81	99,698

Table 2 – Benchmark Circuits

This section presents the results of the application of the module compilation and composition techniques described in the previous section to two real circuits. Table 2 shows the important characteristics of both circuits. The two circuits represent two distinct data points in the design space. CktA is an industrial bus controller, constructed from a library of standard cells and PLAs. CktB is a full custom data path circuit designed at Carnegie Mellon. Although the two circuits differ by less than a factor of two in total numbers of transistors, nodes and operators in their simulation models, they differ substantially in character. CktB has a shifter subnetwork with a large Boolean module containing over 30,000 operators. CktA has a relatively homogeneous mix of module sizes, but no module has more than 1000 Boolean operators. We will see later in this paper that circuits having a small number of extremely large subnetworks present some particular difficulties to our approach.

One of the important questions to be addressed by our work is how much parallelism is available in the simulation model, and how much of this parallelism can be successfully exposed using our circuit compilation techniques. The degree to which parallelism can be exposed depends on the circuit model, the number of processors, and on the communication model.

Figures 7-8 illustrate the results of compiling our three example circuits for different numbers of processors, using PERMUTE, PERMUTE/IMOVE and STORE primitives. Each graph shows the effective parallelism achieved when the given circuit is scheduled with the different communication primitives, for different numbers of processors. We measure the effective parallelism by dividing the total number of Boolean operators by the number of ranks of operators in the schedule for a given number of processors. The Boolean utilization of a circuit compiled for a given communication model is defined to be the effective parallelism expressed as a percentage of the number of processors used. This is a good measure of the efficiency of compilation with a given communication model.

As described in the previous section, the ISA of the target machine has a significant impact on the network compilation process. In particular, large, deep modules compiled using the PERMUTE primitive will require a much wider *processor-time* rectangle, since many operators must be allocated for buffering. Use of the STORE primitive leads to the highest Boolean utilization for both circuits. Using STOREs completely eliminates the need for buffer operators, and reduces the amount of internal empty space be permitting flexibility in module shapes, i.e., the *processor-time* rectangle for each module can be reshaped to facilitate higher utilization. Scheduling using the PERMUTE primitive is the least efficient, with PERMUTE/IMOVE representing a middle ground. Compared to using PERMUTE, the use of the STORE primitive reduces the number of processors required to achieve maximum parallelism by a factor of 3 for CktA, and almost a factor of 10 for CktB. Scheduling with PERMUTE/IMOVE typically requires only 1.5 times as many processors to achieve the same effective parallelism as a STORE schedule.

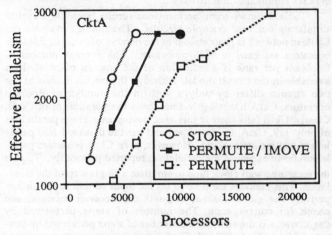

Figure 7 - Effective Parallelism in CktA

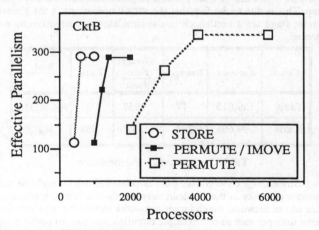

Figure 8: Effective Parallelism in CktB

Little external empty space is introduced by our two-dimensional composition of the Boolean modules, except in the case where the simulation model has been scheduled at or near minimum depth (maximum parallelism). The curves of Effective Parallelism versus Processors follow the expected hyperbolic shape, since if we ignore the discrete nature of the packing, the area of the *processor-time* rectangle for a given model is a constant, independent of the number of processors. This means that to a large extent, we can smoothly increase performance as we map the circuit model onto additional processors. All of the graphs clearly

show that there is an upper bound on how much parallelism we can extract from a given circuit model, since performance will be limited by the depth of the formulas for the deepest subnetwork.

The Boolean network for CktA clearly has the thousand-fold parallelism we require. CktB, with its large deep modules has far more limited parallelism, and can effectively utilize only about 500 processors using STOREs. The structure of CktB introduces several difficulties. CktB contains a large shift network for which the COSMOS preprocessor derives large, deep Boolean formulas. The extreme depth of the module results in a huge proliferation of buffer operators when using PERMUTEs, increasing the width of the *processor-time* rectangle for this module by a factor of 10. The large discrepancy in size between these large Boolean modules and the other modules in the circuit results in a poor two-dimensional packing efficiency. CktB points out how critical the communication model is to scheduling efficiency, and the importance of manipulating the formulas produced by the COSMOS preprocessor to minimize the depth of expressions.

In summary, the communication model has a strong impact on circuit compilation. Boolean utilization of 50% is achievable using STOREs, and 15 to 20% using PERMUTEs. PERMUTE/IMOVE represents a middle ground, with utilization in the range of 30-40%. Circuits with Boolean modules that are very deep, and narrow present problems that point to the need to manipulate the formulas to minimize depth. The two dimensional packing algorithm employed for network composition works well, and introduces little wasted space. Clearly parallelism is available that is far in excess of that reported in previous work.

7. The Event Driven Simulation Tradeoff

Although we have exposed thousand-fold parallelism in the Boolean model, this by no means guarantees significant speedups when simulations are run on massively parallel hardware. One factor which must be considered is how the static parallelism identified above relates to the actual dynamic level of activity in the circuit. Serial simulators exploit latency in the circuit by evaluating only active portions of the circuit model using an event-driven approach. We have exposed parallelism at the expense of eliminating the event list from the simulator. A key question posed by this research is whether the tradeoff of finding additional parallelism at the expense of simulating latent portions of the circuit model is an attractive one.

It is important to remember that evaluating as few gates as possible will not necessarily result in the fastest simulator. Event scheduling is not without its costs. As the grain of event scheduling becomes finer, less Boolean computation will be performed, at the cost of sharply increased scheduling costs. To maximize speed, the simulator must minimize the sum of the costs of Boolean evaluation and event scheduling. The appropriate grain of event scheduling depends on the relative costs of Boolean evaluation and event scheduling. Event scheduling becomes costly relative to Boolean evaluation when parallel resources are available to perform the Boolean evaluation. In that case, it is of greatest importance to minimize serial components of the computation such as event scheduling.

We have instrumented the COSMOS simulator to help analyze the event-driven simulation tradeoff. A complete discussion of this issue will appear elsewhere [Kravitz 89], and only a summary will appear here. Without event scheduling, the amount of Boolean computation performed by COSMOS increases by a factor of 4 for circuits similar to CktB, and by a factor of 20 for circuits similar to CktA. Our measurements of COSMOS indicate that only 1-10% of computation time is consumed by actual Boolean computation, and the rest by scheduling and evaluation overhead. However, circuits for which event scheduling provides the greatest reduction in Boolean computation, tend to spend the least time doing Boolean computation. In other words, for these circuits, even the serial simulator would benefit from a coarser level of event scheduling.

The implementation strategy of the parallel simulator is to sharply reduce the scheduling and evaluation overhead and apply parallelism to Boolean evaluation, at the expense of increasing the amount of Boolean evaluation. This represents a tradeoff of serial computation for parallel computation. The additional Boolean evaluation represents the cost of exposing parallelism. By applying massive parallelism to the simulation task, we hope to quickly recoup this investment.

8. Prototype Implementation

We have constructed a prototype implementation of our massively parallel COSMOS simulator, called CM_COSMOS, on the Connection Machine System(CM)[Hillis 86]. The CM is a SIMD machine with up to 64k single bit processors. The processors support a relatively large instruction set, including the Boolean AND and OR, and the data movement instructions required by our application. The CM supports both the PERMUTE and STORE communication primitives using a dynamically scheduled routing network, as well as the MOVE and IMOVE data movement primitives. Although some work on electrical circuit simulation on the CM has been reported[Webber 87], to our knowledge this is the first use of the CM for switch-level logic simulation.

The CM is a general purpose machine intended for a broad variety of applications. The general purpose nature of the CM requires that its ISA be far richer than required by our application. For example, the CM provides dynamic message routing in order to support data dependent communication. The communication in our application is static and could potentially be supported with a much simpler and faster communication network. However, the CM is an ideal testbed for our compilation ideas, since we can emulate a number of different communication ISAs without designing or building any hardware.

CM_COSMOS is a complete implementation of the COSMOS logic simulator on the CM, including both a circuit compiler, and a simulation kernel. The circuit compiler incorporates the network compilation and network composition algorithms discussed in section 3. CM_COSMOS has the same user interface and command set as the COSMOS simulator, and has been successfully run on several circuits. CM_COSMOS is written in C/PARIS (v4.3) and runs on a 32k processor CM -2 with a VAX8800 front end.

CM_COSMOS is *not* an implementation of COSMOS specifically designed for the CM, and fully exploiting the CM's features. Our programming model for the CM (see figure 4) is in sharp philosophical and practical conflict with the programming model envisioned for the CM [Hillis 86a]. CM_COSMOS makes extremely limited use of SCAN operations [Blelloch 88], and no use of the CM's virtual processor mechanism. This is not an oversight on our part, but a conscious effort to use the CM as a hardware emulator for a larger class of massively parallel architectures. Many improvements in implementation, and thus performance, could be made to CM_COSMOS to more effectively exploit the CM's strengths and avoid its weaknesses. We are currently implementing a new version of CM_COSMOS which will address these issues.

The performance of the routing network of the CM is data dependent, that is, the time to perform a STORE or PERMUTE is related to the particular communication pattern being used and the number of active processors. A complex communication instruction, involving many active processors or a complex pattern of communication, may require significantly more time than a simple version of the same instruction. Instruction times for operations which do not utilize the routing network are data independent.

As we showed in section 4, compiling networks using the STORE primitive results in a much higher utilization of the processors for Boolean computation. Compilation is also more straightforward using the STORE primitive. For these reasons, we initially implemented the simulator using STORE operators. However, performance was extremely disappointing. The STORE primitive is a costly operation on the CM. Although the times for simple STOREs and PERMUTEs do not differ dramatically, the times for complex STOREs can exceed the times for a complex PERMUTE by a factor of 1000. We encountered STOREs in our application which required as much as .25s to complete. Therefore, our current implementation uses only PERMUTE operators for evaluating the Boolean network. STORE instructions are still used in the global fanout stage. Although the communication pattern in CM_COSMOS is static, the CM implements communication instructions with a dynamic routing network. Therefore, traffic reduction can lead to performance improvement. We achieved almost a 5x improvement in performance when we made all communication *activity-driven*. That is, only values which have changed are communicated using the CM's communication network.

Table 3 shows some performance results from CM_COSMOS simulating our two example circuits. The time to evaluate the Boolean network is proportional to the number of ranks of Boolean operators assigned to each processor. The average number of Booleans per rank is a reflection of the amount of parallelism available in the circuit model. Although the circuit models of the two circuits differ by only a 40% in the number of Boolean operators, CktA has roughly four times the parallelism of CktB. Clearly, CktB falls short in this area, having an average parallelism of only 339. CktA, on the other hand has the thousand-fold parallelism that we are seeking. However, even CktB possesses parallelism far in excess of the parallelism reported previously. T_{step} is the measured wall clock time to simulate a single step of the simulation. This includes the time to set the input stimuli to the circuit, perform the global fanout, evaluate the Boolean network, and check for convergence. The number of *steps* performed by CM_COSMOS is the same as the number of *steps* performed by COSMOS. Notice that although CktA has one sixth as many ranks of Boolean operators as CktB, it still requires one half the time per step. This is due to the fact that the STORE operations in the global fanout stage are a bottleneck in the simulator as currently implemented.

Circuit	Booleans	Ranks	Average Bools Rank	T step	Bools s
CktA	139,015	47	2957	.03s	4,638,333
CktB	99,698	294	339	.08s	1,246,225

Table 3: CM_COSMOS Performance

Since CM_COSMOS' run time is related more strongly to the number of ranks in the Boolean network than it is to the absolute size of the network, much larger networks should run at about the same time per step as our example circuits. The current capacity of the simulator is about 100 million operations on a 32k CM -2 with 64k bits of memory per processor. Even assuming 10% utilization, we still have a capacity of 10 million Boolean operators, or about 20-50 times the size of our example circuits.

9. Conclusions

We set out to examine whether the emerging class of massively parallel computers would prove to be suitable hosts for the switch-level logic simulation of large VLSI circuits. We have described a mapping of the COSMOS switch-level logic simulator onto this class of machines. Parallelism has been identified and exposed at two levels in the Boolean simulation model: fine-grain parallelism within each Boolean module and coarse-grain parallelism among the modules. Compilation tools have been developed to automatically map the simulation of a circuit onto a massively parallel machine for three different communication schemes. A prototype simulator designed to study compilation issues and examine the utility of different communication schemes has been implemented on a Connection Machine System.

Clearly, the simulation models of large circuits have the thousand-fold parallelism that we sought. Previous studies have failed to identify this parallelism due to unwarranted assumptions about the structure of parallel simulators, and the choice of relatively small benchmark circuits. The simulation models of the midsized benchmark circuits examined in this paper have parallelism far exceeding that previously reported.

Although event scheduling may reduce the amount of Boolean evaluation by a factor of 4-20, it is not the case that the fastest simulator evaluates the fewest Boolean operations. In fact, the choice of event-scheduling granularity depends on the relative cost of Boolean evaluation and event-scheduling. In the presence of massively parallel computational resources which can be applied to Boolean evaluation, event scheduling is no longer an appropriate implementation choice. Serial simulators spend only 1-10% of their computation time engaged in actual Boolean evaluation. Parallel simulation can eliminate event-scheduling overhead and sharply reduce evaluation overhead at the expense of increased Boolean evaluation. This represents an attractive tradeoff if sufficient parallelism can be exposed in the simulation model, and exploited by parallel hardware.

We regard it as surprising that our experimental measurements and analyses suggest that even a CM-2 can provide simulation performance in the range of millions of Boolean gate evaluations per second for our midsized benchmark circuits. We expect future generations of massively parallel machines to provide both faster clock rates and better communication performance. Although the current generation of CMs are not ideal logic simulation engines, our prototype CM_COSMOS implementation has served several important purposes. In particular, we have demonstrated the potential for exploiting thousand-fold parallelism in many circuits, especially those large circuits which require the simulation speed provided by special purpose hardware accelerators such as the YSE. By constructing a working circuit compiler and simulation kernel, we have demonstrated that the problem of mapping logic simulation onto massively parallel machines with even a limited communication model (only PERMUTE) is a tractable one.

Our experience compiling the circuits presented in this paper shows that a circuit compiled using STORE primitives requires three to ten times fewer processors than if compiled using PERMUTE and MOVE primitives, to achieve the same degree of effective parallelism. Compilation using PERMUTE and IMOVE primitives is nearly as efficient as compilation using STOREs. The combination of PERMUTE and MOVE is the least efficient in terms of Boolean utilization, but the fastest at runtime, since only a single communication operation is required per rank of operators. With respect to matching a machine architecture to our application, given the tradeoff of a larger machine with only the PERMUTE and MOVE primitives or a smaller machine with a either an IMOVE primitive or a fast implementation of STORE, we would suggest the latter.

For the mapping that we have described, the speed of simulation of large circuits on massively parallel architectures is limited more by the depth of the deepest Boolean module in the circuit's simulation model, than by the sheer size of the model. This suggests the importance of two avenues for future work. The rank order depth of the simulation model can be reduced somewhat by manipulation of the formulas produced by the COSMOS preprocessor. An additional way to reduce network depth is to increase the granularity of each rank of operators. That is, evaluating more than a single two-input Boolean operation at each rank. Taken together, these two techniques may reduce the depth of the large modules such as those in CktB by as much as a factor of 5-10.

Our prototype simulator on the CM, CM_COSMOS, was designed as a research tool to ground our research on compilation issues in reality and was based on our abstract machine model. Any implementation on a real machine will benefit from tuning to take advantage of machine-specific features. We are currently developing a new, tuned implementation of CM_COSMOS[Kravitz 89a].

Acknowledgements

This work was supported in part by the Semiconductor Research Corporation, and by the Defense Advanced Research Projects Agency, ARPA contract 4976. Connection Machine time was provided by the Northeast Parallel Architecture Center at Syracuse University. Example circuits were provided by Allan Fisher at Carnegie Mellon, and George Cox at Intel.

References

[Agrawal 87] P. Agrawal, et al, *MARS: A Multiprocessor-Based Programmable Accelerator*, IEEE Design and Test of Computers, V4 (1987).

[Bailey 88] M.L. Bailey, et al, *An Empirical Study of On-Chip Parallelism*, Design Automation Conf., 1988.

[Batcher 80] K.E. Batcher, *Design of a Massively Parallel Processor*, IEEE Trans. Comp., Vol C29, Sept. 1980.

[Blelloch 88] G. Blelloch, *Scans as Primittive Parallel Operations*, Int'l Conference on Parallel Processing, 1986.

[Bryant 87] R.E. Bryant, et al, COSMOS : *a Compiled Simulator for MOS Circuits*, Design Automation Conference, 1987.

[Coffman 80] E. Coffman, Jr.et al,*Performance Bounds for Level-Oriented Two-Dimensional Packing Algorithms*, SIAM J. Computing, V9 (1980), pp. 808-826.

[Denneau 82] M. Denneau, *The Yorktown Simulation Engine*, Design Automation Conference, 1982.

[Frank 86] E. Frank, *Exploiting Parallelism in a Switch Level Simulation Machine*, 13th Int'l Symposium on Computer Architecture, 1986.

[Hillis 86] W. D. Hillis, *The Connection Machine*. Cambridge, Mass: The MIT Press, 1986.

[Hillis 86a] W. D. Hillis et al, *Data Parallel Algorithms*, CACM, pp. 1170-1183, Dec. 1986.

Huffman 52] D.A. Huffman, *A Method for Construction of Minimum Longest Common Subsequences*, CACM 20:5, 1952.

[Kravitz 89] S. Kravitz, *Massively Parallel Switch-Level Simulation: a Feasibility Study*, to appear at Design Automation Conference, 1989.

[Kravitz 89a] S. Kravitz, et al, *Massively Parallel Switch-Level Simulation: a Feasibility Study*, PhD Thesis, *in preparation*.

[Smith 86] R. Smith, Jr., *Fundamentals of Parallel Logic Simulation*, Design Automation Conference, 1986.

[Webber 87] D. M. Webber, et al, *Circuit Simulation on the Connection Machine*, Design Automation Conference, 1987.

[Wong 86] K.F. Wong, et al, *Statistics on Logic Simulation*, Design Automation Conference, 1986.

R256: A Research Parallel Processor for Scientific Computation

Tomoo Fukazawa, Takashi Kimura, Masaaki Tomizawa

Kazumitsu Takeda and †Yoshitaka Itoh

NTT LSI Laboratories, †NTT Electronics Technology Co.

3-1 Wakamiya, Morinosato, Atsugi City, JAPAN

+81 462 40 2125

Abstract

A scientific parallel processor called the R256 has been developed. The R256 is composed of 16×16 processing elements, and has the outstanding features of a " distributed parallel network " as well as on IEEE 80-bit extended floating point computation ability. The computation accuracy, required by an exhaustive number of iterations in scientific computations, is resolved by the dedicated 80-bit VLSI processor, which was developed here for the R256. The innovative distributed parallel network was designed so as to effectively resolve heavy communication problems, which are found in applications based on the Monte Carlo simulation technique. The R256 network was very economical at a hardware cost of $\sqrt{N}$-folds (16 folds in this case) to that of an ideal full-crossbar switch, at the same time keeping the rates comparable to that of an ideal switch. The R256 demonstrates high performance of 2-GB/s data transfer rates and 500-MFLOPS computation rates on a semiconductor device simulation application.

Keywords: *Parallel Processor, Distributed Parallel Network, VLSI 80-bit Floating Point Processor, Monte Carlo Simulation, Device Simulation*

1   Introduction

1.1   Background

Parallel processors have proved to have enormous potential for the growth of computation power. Current parallel computers can attain operational speeds from several hundreds MFLOPS [1] [2][3][4] up to 10 GFLOPS [5]. The efficiency of parallelism, is not fully exploited, however, because the interconnection network (e.g., widely used Hyper cube network), cannot provide the efficient bandwidth for

the data transfer. Especially, in a semiconductor device simulation based on the Monte Carlo method, an extreme case of an intercommunication is required. That is, every processing element (PE) requires to send data to every other PEs almost at the same time, which is a heavy communication load for the conventional parallel processor.

In this paper, a new configuration of multiple multistage networks, called here a *distributed parallel network* and an array processor equipped with the network is proposed to solve the problem of the heavy communication load. With this architecture, efficient control is the key, and is also proposed.

1.2   Device Simulation and Communication Problem

In the device simulation, motion of individual particles, which are assumed to be holes or electrons moving in the electric field, is computed by solving a differential equation associated with the electric field. To get precise physical characteristics, a larger number of particles, more than 10^5, are required to be handled. By counting the number of the particles, which reach the opposite electrode, I-V characteristics of the device is obtained as a result.

For the semiconductor device simulation, an array processor can be chosen as a simple architecture. The electric field to be solved can be understood with ease by mapping the two or three dimensional space of the device onto the orthogonal array.

The computation is iteratively executed on each particle motion and the resultant quasi-static potential field. Both particle motion and potential field are altered by each other. In the quasi-static potential field, a pseudo random fluctuation on these particles are induced to attain a rapid conversion. The exhaustive calculation is expected to be settled by making the particle distribution so unified as to be carried out in parallel fashion. In the stage of particle redistribution among each time step, on the other hand, a heavy communication problem caused the crucial overhead on the parallelism. This heavy communication arises simultaneously from almost all PEs and every PE requires to send data to every other PE.

Thus, a purpose of the present study is to resolve a heavy communication overhead inherent to a large scale

344

parallel computation such as device simulation. A research parallel processor, the R256, has been developed based on the distributed parallel network to perform the heavy intercommunication. Furthermore, highly accurate scientific calculation inherent in the device simulation is achieved by developing a dedicated CPU VLSI processor for each PE.

2   Distributed Parallel Network for an Array Processor

2.1   Distributed Parallel Network

The distributed parallel network is shown in the Fig. 1. The distributed parallel network, proposed here is a set of multiple switching units placed in every row and column of the PE array. So, the distributed parallel network basically consists of $2N$ switching units so the PE array is N × N.

The distributed parallel network is controlled in a hierarchical fashion. That is, switching units in the i-th column and in the i-th row are controlled by a local control unit, and N local control units are controlled by a main control unit. Local control units set the switching units in an adequate state in response to a connecting request from the PE. The parallel control of the switching units by the local control units can make the control overhead smaller.

Data transfer using the distributed parallel network is generally accomplished in 2 steps. First, data is transferred in either row or column direction, and then in the other

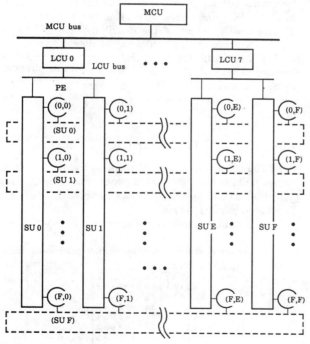

MCU : Main Control Unit

LCU i : Local Control Unit

PE   : Processing Element

SU i : Switching Unit of Distributed Parallel Network

Figure 1: R256 Architecture

direction. As this transfer goes in a parallel fashion , the heavy load of the data transfer, inevitable in the device simulation, is carried out with small overhead. The data transfer in each step is carried out after the PEs in the row or column synchronize themselves. Each PE having data to be transferred, makes a synchronize request to a local control unit. After the local control unit receives all signals of requesting PEs connected to the local control unit, the local control unit sets the switching unit of the distributed network in one of the switching patterns , and it broadcasts the acknowledge signal back to the requesting PEs. After getting the signal, each PE starts to transfer data.

The switching unit is basically designed to have the function of an N-I/O multi-stage switching network. Multistage networks, such as baseline network, omega network, banyan network(S = F = 2), etc. have been proved to be topologically equal[7]. Figure 2-(a) shows the 16-I/O baseline network. It is restructured with a lower order multistage network[6], i.e. 4-I/O multi-stage network as shown in Fig. 2-(b), which is more suitable for hardware implementation because of its hierarchical modularity. The switching unit is characterized by two stages of four 4 × 4 crossbar switches, as shown in Fig. 3, where the identifiers of the input and output ports specifies the corresponding PE. When the switching unit is used in a row direction, each identifier corresponds to a column number of the PE and when used in a column direction , it corresponds to a row number of the PE. These are numbered so that the same identifier of the input and output is connected when the switching state is straight.

The 4 × 4 crossbar switch has four 4 to 1 selectors, or 32 selectors that are controlled dynamically by the local control units. To reduce the control line and simplify the control of the switching unit, a preloaded memory is used. That is, patterns to control selectors are loaded in the memory and switching control is carried out by specifying the address of the preloaded memory. Broadcasting from any PE to all other PEs is also accomplished by selecting one of the switching patterns.

2.2   Control Scheme

The heavy Data transfer that every PE sends data to all the other PE simultaneously is carried out as follows using the distributed parallel network. First, for instance, data transfer is taking place in the column direction in a parallel fashion as shown in the Fig. 4-(a). In this phase, all PEs in the same column synchronize themselves by the local control unit. After synchronization, the local control unit sets the state of the switching unit, in which each PE connects to some other PE and the local control unit sends acknowledge to PEs. Data is sent from every PE to its connected PE, which is the pivot of the source PE and the destination PE. Then, PEs synchronize themselves again and the local control unit sets the switching unit in another state. 15 states are necessary for the switching unit so that every PE connects to all the other PE in the same column. After 15 iteration of the synchronization, switching and transfer, there are no data to be transferred

345

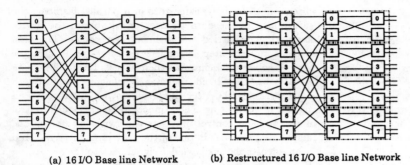

(a) 16 I/O Base line Network   (b) Restructured 16 I/O Base line Network

Figure 2: 16-I/O Multi-Stage Switching Network

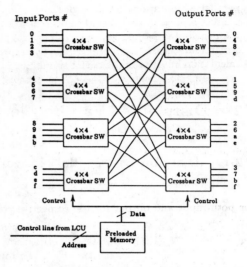

Figure 3: 16-I/O Switching Unit

in the column direction. At this time, all local control units synchronize themselves using the main control unit and set the switching units to be used in the row direction. Second, row directional transfer is taking place as shown in the Fig. 4-(b). All transfer is finished after 15 iteration of synchronization and data transfer in the same way as in the first phase. As a whole, 30 iteration of synchronization, switching and parallel data transfer complete the all data transfer request.

An example of 15 states of the switching unit is shown in Table 1. In this table, input port numbers of the switching unit connected to the corresponding output port in each state are shown. As every output port is connected to every other input port in a certain state, the connection patterns give a perfect permutation for the global transfer described above.

Permutation function in this table is generally introduced as follows using binary representation of the port number. Let $(o_{n-1} \cdots o_0)$ and $(i_{n-1} \cdots i_0)$ be binary representations of output port number and input port number of the switching unit respectively. An elementary permutation function $\sigma_i (0 \le i \le n-1)$ is defined as follows, which is well known as a hyper cube connection.

$$\sigma_i : (o_{n-1} \cdots o_i \cdots o_0) = (i_{n-1} \cdots \overline{i_i} \cdots i_0),$$

where $\overline{i_i}$ is the reverse value of o_i (0 or 1).

All possible composition of the elementary function σ_i gives the permutation rule shown in Table 1. The connection patterns in the table are loaded in the preloaded memory of the switching unit.

3 Architecture and Implementation

3.1 Design Concept

A scientific processor the R256, composed of 16×16 PE array, was designed on the basis of MIMD (Multiple Instruction and Multiple Data stream) control scheme, and the distributed parallel network. Concerning the design of the R256, following points were taken into account.
(1) The hardware cost of the distributed network is reduced in keeping the high efficiency of the data transfer.
(2) For a scientific computation, enough computational precision is assured while the scale is kept small.
(3) Simple and efficient control mechanism of the R256 including software programming and debugging environment.

3.2 Overall Hardware Architecture

The R256 consists of a main control unit (MCU), 8 local control units (LCU), a 16×16 processing element array (256 PEs) and 16 switching units (SU) realizing here the distributed parallel network.

The distributed parallel network of the R256 is com-

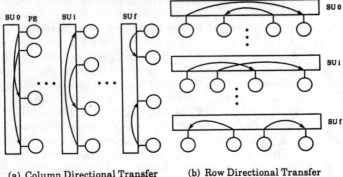

(a) Column Directional Transfer   (b) Row Directional Transfer

Figure 4: Global Transfer Scheme

Table 1: An example of switching pattern

Output port #	0 1 2 3 4 5 6 7 8 9 a b c d e f	function	state #
Input port #	1 0 3 2 5 4 7 6 9 8 b a d c f e	σ_0	1
	2 3 0 1 6 7 4 5 a b 8 9 e f c d	σ_1	2
	3 2 1 0 7 6 5 4 b a 9 8 f e d c	$\sigma_0 \circ \sigma_1$	3
	4 5 6 7 0 1 2 3 c d e f 8 9 a b	σ_2	4
	5 4 7 6 1 0 3 2 d c f e 9 8 b a	$\sigma_0 \circ \sigma_2$	5
	6 7 4 5 2 3 0 1 e f c d a b 8 9	$\sigma_1 \circ \sigma_2$	6
	7 6 5 4 3 2 1 0 f e d c b a 9 8	$\sigma_0 \circ \sigma_1 \circ \sigma_2$	7
	8 9 a b c d e f 0 1 2 3 4 5 6 7	σ_3	8
	9 8 b a d c f e 1 0 3 2 5 4 7 6	$\sigma_0 \circ \sigma_3$	9
	a b 8 9 e f c d 2 3 0 1 6 7 4 5	$\sigma_1 \circ \sigma_3$	10
	b a 9 8 f e d c 3 2 1 0 7 6 5 4	$\sigma_0 \circ \sigma_1 \circ \sigma_3$	11
	c d e f 8 9 a b 4 5 6 7 0 1 2 3	$\sigma_2 \circ \sigma_3$	12
	d c f e 9 8 b a 5 4 7 6 1 0 3 2	$\sigma_0 \circ \sigma_2 \circ \sigma_3$	13
	e f c d a b 8 9 6 7 4 5 2 3 0 1	$\sigma_1 \circ \sigma_2 \circ \sigma_3$	14
	f e d c b a 9 8 7 6 5 4 3 2 1 0	$\sigma_0 \circ \sigma_1 \circ \sigma_2 \circ \sigma_3$	15

346

posed of 16 switching units (SU). Each switching unit is connected to 16 PEs in a row direction or column direction according to the state indicated by its control LCU so as to reduce hardware cost by sharing the row and the column function of the switching unit. Furthermore, this switching unit supports communication between an LCU and a single PE, as well as broadcast from an LCU to all or a select set of PEs.

A dedicated 80-bit floating point VLSI processor is introduced into each processing element. The VLSI contains data transfer facility of two 12-bit serial ports to make PE simple and small, which enables installing a large number of PEs. Every PE in the R256 is not only connected to the switching unit but also four adjacent interconnection paths in a torus configuration. Each PE has 12-bit ports for both input and output for the respective connection. The control scheme is based on the MIMD scheme and every PE has 1.25-MByte local memory, in which program running on the PE is stored.

MCU and LCUs are constructed hierarchically and are connected via an MCU bus. An MCU bus is used with a VME bus and this interface makes it possible for the R256 to be used as a floating point computation accelerator for a general workstation. By using a general workstation as the MCU, the programming environment is provided on the UNIX system.

3.3   Local Control Unit

The R256 has 8 local control units (LCU) parallelled to distribute and alleviate control overhead. They are connected via the standard VME bus.

The LCU mainly consists of a local control processor and local memory, as shown in Fig. 5. The local control processor is a state-of-the-art 32b micro processor, and the local memory is a dual port memory of 2-MByte. The dual

port memory as shown in Fig. 5 enables a data transfer between the MCU and the LCUs in a pipelined manner. That is, local memories are shared with MCU and their corresponding LCUs.

Command registers in both directions from LCU to MCU and from MCU to LCU are provided to pass the control message by hardware, to efficiently exchange the status and command. A program running on an LCU is loaded from the MCU into the local memory, and is started by the command received via the command register. Any status or return value of the command is also transferred via the command register.

The LCU is designed to have its own individual bus (LCU bus) to control two switching units of the distributed parallel network and transfer 80 bit IEEE format data to and from the PEs. Control lines and data lines to and from the switching networks are mapped onto the LCU memory space.

The synchronization request lines from each PE and corresponding acknowledge lines are also mapped onto the specific address spaces of the LCU bus. When any of these synchronization/acknowledge lines are activated, 8 bit status or command can be transferred to and from PEs using 8 bit of the serial data lines.

3.4   VLSI processor and PE

The VLSI CPU was designed to integrate the function of serial/parallel data conversion and the synchronization control for inter-PE communication to make the PE simple as shown in Fig. 6. The PE contains only one VLSI CPU, its memory, and I/O multiplexor.

A block diagram of the 80-bit floating point VLSI is shown in Fig. 7. This PE LSI contains two main functional units: an 80-bit floating-point operation unit and a 32-bit fixed-point operation unit.

The floating-point operation unit is composed of a 32-w × 80-bit register file, an 8-w × 86-bit work register for internal microprogram, an 86-bit ALU, an 86-bit barrel shifter, a 70-bit × 36-bit multiplier, and a format converter. The format converter changes the data format from IBM to IEEE formats, from fixed-point to floating-point formats, and from 32-bit or 64-bit to 80-bit formats and vice-versa. Microprogram memory ROM (2 kw × 48 bit) for sequence control is also included. To guarantee the precision of IEEE 80-bit floating-point calculations, 6 extra bits have been added as guard bits to the datapath. The fixed point operation unit has a 32-w × 32-bit register file, a 32-bit ALU, a 32-bit barrel shifter, a microprogram memory (1 kw × 32 bit) , and parallel to serial, serial to parallel data transfer blocks.

For memory interface, the LSI supports an 80-bit data bus, a 23-bit address bus and a couple of SRAM control lines. Memory is accessed in both the 40-bit and 80-bit format. For addressing the memory, 40 bit is handled as one word.

Individual 10-bit serial lines of input and output respectively are also supported in the LSI for data transfer between an LCU and another PE. Two additional lines

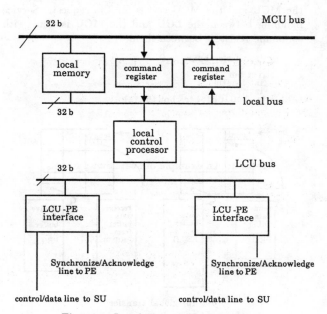

Figure 5: Local Control Unit (LCU)

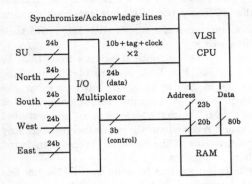

Figure 6: Processing Element (PE)

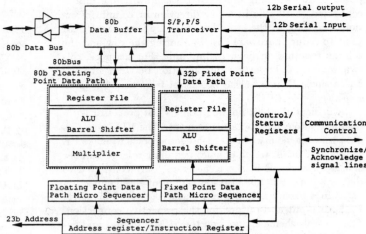

Figure 7: VLSI CPU Block Diagram

are provided, one for clock and one for tag. With these serial lines, 2 word data (80 bit) is transferred in 2.5 μs (4 MByte/s) for both directions simultaneously. The value of the transfer rate includes control overhead and memory access.

In order to accomplish synchronization of PEs, this VLSI is equipped with 5 pairs of synchronize/acknowledge lines. With these lines, command or status is also transferred to and from an external controller. That is, when any of these synchronize lines are activated, status stored internal F/F is sent on the output serial lines described above. On the other hand, when any of these acknowledge lines are activated, data on the input serial lines are read into input internal status F/F.

Data transfer and synchronization associated with these status F/F are handled by the respective machine instruction.

Every instruction is designed to be executed in a single word to speed up instruction fetch and to simplify the sequencer of the VLSI. This VLSI processor is designed on the basis of the CISC design concept. The number of instructions is 79 for fixed-point operations including control, data transfer and synchronize operation and 144 for floating-point operations which covers several basic math-

ematical functions. The mathematical functions are executed by self-contained micro program control.

3.5 Software

The programming environment is provided on the UNIX system. The utilities of cross compiler, cross assembler, linker, loader, etc. for the dedicated PE VLSI are provided on the UNIX system.

For application programming, C language and the library of system subroutines shown in Table 2 are provided. When the library is invoked by the application program, the PE makes a service request to the LCU if necessary. The service request from the PE to the LCU is handled by a pair of synchronize/acknowledge lines associated with status. The status indicates a kind of service. If the LCU needs help from the MCU, it makes a service request to the MCU and the MCU serves for the request. Service handling between the LCU and the MCU is done with command registers between them.

```
g__transfer(s__bpt,r__bpt)
  struct buf__p {
      int length;
      int *buf;
  } *s__bpt[16][16],*r__bpt[16][16];
```

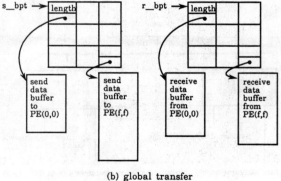

```
transfer(dest,s__bp,r__bp)
  int dest;
  struct buf__p {
      int  length;
      int *buf;
  } *s__bp,*r__bp;

  dest: Destination PE id.
```

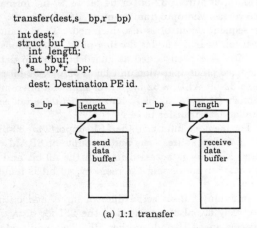

(a) 1:1 transfer

(b) global transfer

Figure 8: System Library for Data Transfer

348

Table 2: System Library

Subroutine Name	function
printf scanf	formatted I/O
fopen fclose	open file close file
read write	read from file write to file
transfer g_transfer	1:1 data transfer global data transfer
synch	synchronization
exit	exit program

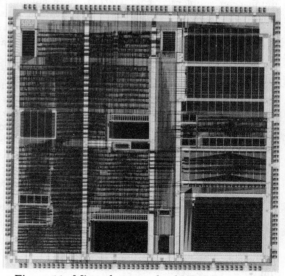

Figure 9: R256 External View

The parallelism of multiple PEs is described explicitly. For inter PE communication, function *transfer* and *g-transfer* are supported. The function *transfer* is designed to support one to one communication and the function *g-transfer* is designed to handle such heavy communication as every PE requests to send data to all the other PEs simultaneously. C interface of the *transfer* and the *g-transfer* for PE programmer is illustrated in the Fig. 8. The function *transfer* has three parameters, destination PE identifier, and two structures that specify send buffer and receive buffer. The receive buffer is allocated by the system. The function *g-transfer* has two parameters. One is a pointer to 16×16 matrix of length and pointer to the send buffer. The index of the matrix corresponds to the destination PE identifier. The other parameter is a pointer to a matrix points to the receive buffer in the same way.

One to one communication is realized in a hierarchical way using the switching network and the local memory of LCU. The switching unit is controlled by the LCU at the request of the PE and the data transfer between the

local memory of the LCU is performed by the MCU at the request of LCU.

g-transfer is realized using the distributed parallel network efficiently as described in paragraph 2.2.

3.6 Implementation

An external view of the R256 is shown in Fig. 9. The rack size is 3280W × 1780H × 760D (mm) including power supplies and air cooling units. The total power consumption is approximately 10 KVA.

The R256 is designed with 176 A3 boards on which 45,200 conventional TTL ICs and 80-bit floating-point VLSI processors of 256 are implemented. Among the 176 boards, 128 are PE boards, 16 are switching unit boards for the distributed parallel network, 8 are LCU boards and the other 24 are interface boards. Thus, the distributed network occupies less than 10% of the total hardware size.

Figure 10: PE Board

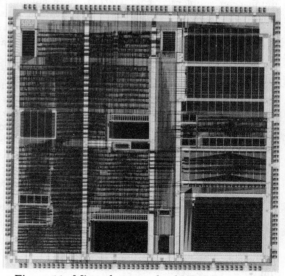

Figure 11: Microphotograph of VLSI Processor

The number of elements	~500 k transistors logic : ~90 k Gates ROM : ~140 kb
Supply voltage	5.0 V
Power consumption	1 W
Clock rate	33.3 MHz
Process	1.2 μ CMOS
Die size	13.9mm × 14.1mm
Pin counts/Package	208 PGA

The MCU resides outside the rack where a single board computer for channel interface to the mainframe is implemented. A workstation is connected via the electrically extended VME bus, as a service processor and a graphic station. The LCUs are state-of-the-art 32-bit microprocessors.

Each PE consists of a single dedicated PE VLSI, 1.25-MByte (256 kw) memory and I/O buffers. Two PEs are implemented on an A3 board, as shown in Fig. 10. In the PE array, 320 MByte of memory are provided overall. The PE LSI has been developed with 1.2-μm CMOS process technology. A photograph of the LSI is shown in Fig. 11. More than 500-k transistors are integrated in a 14 mm × 14 mm chip area. The clock cycle is 33 MHz. These features are summarized in Table 3.

4 Evaluations and Discussion

The performance of the R256 having a distributed parallel network is evaluated in comparison with other processors having representative networks: Hyper Cube [8], crossbar switch networks and an array processor.

A crucial communication problem—a semiconductor device simulation based on Monte Carlo simulation—is evaluated on these processors having representative interconnection networks, and an array processor. The communication problem is characterized by a simple model that requires all processing elements to send a considerable amount of data to all the other PEs simultaneously. The total number of steps to complete the data transfer are evaluated as follows.

We assume each PE has the ability to send and receive data simultaneously. With this assumption, it is possible for the representative processors mentioned to schedule their networks not to conflict while all PEs receive and send simultaneously and every data takes the shortest path. therefore, if one step is counted for a data transfer from one PE to another PE, total steps for data transfer is approximately obtained by multiplying of the average distance between PEs and the average number of data that are transferred from each PE to all other PEs.

Suppose $\overline{n}$ is the average number of data in a PE that are transferred to all other PEs. The R256 distributed parallel network takes $2\overline{n}$ steps to accomplish all of the transfers. The array network takes $\frac{\sqrt{N}}{2}\overline{n}$, where N is the number of PEs in an array processor. The number of data transfer steps for hyper cube and the crossbar switch are $\frac{\log_2 N}{2}\overline{n}$ and $\overline{n}$, respectively. The formulation can be simply understood as follows.

The array network carries out adjacent transfers simultaneously and repeatedly in the row and column directions. The maximum distance is the length between two PEs located at the two opposite edges in a two-dimensional array, which is equal to $2\sqrt{N}$. Obviously, the minimum distance is 1. Thus, the average distance is given by $\sqrt{N}$, when N is large. The torus interconnection and transfer in both directions (right/left or upward/downward) reduces the maximum length to one half. Therefore, $\frac{\sqrt{N}}{2}$ is the average distance. The hyper cube network has the characteristics that the maximum distance of N PEs is $\log_2 N$ and the minimum distance is 1. Thus, average distance is approximately $\frac{\log_2 N}{2}$.

On the other hand, every data transfer in the distributed network is carried out by 2 steps at most. In the full crossbar network, every data are sent to their destination in 1 step via the switching network and this is the ideal case. The analytical modeling suggests that the distributed parallel network of the R256 enables highly efficient data transfer comparable to an ideal full-crossbar switch. The transfer steps do not exceed twice that of the ideal network.

The advantage of the distributed parallel network compared to the full-crossbar network lies in its hardware cost. In implementing the full-crossbar network, N^2 switching nodes are necessary, while N switching nodes are sufficient for one switching unit of the distributed parallel network, even if the switching unit is used with the crossbar type. Since the distributed network consists of $\sqrt{N}$ switching units , the total switching nodes in the distributed parallel network comes to $N\sqrt{N}$. Thus, the hardware cost can be reduced by a factor of $\sqrt{N}$-fold compared to the full-crossbar network.

A semiconductor device simulation based on the Monte Carlo simulation technique is demonstrated on the R256. A principal computation flow of the device simulation is shown in Fig. 12. The computation under the R256 is carried out by parallelizing the local potential field computation on the 16 × 16 PEs, to which the physical device area is divided and mapped. It is also done by preassigning a set of particles on each PE to handle the particle

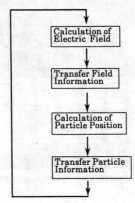

Figure 12: General Flow Chart of Device Simulation

motion. Between the two calculation steps of particle motion and the local potential, the physical parameters associated with each particle are redistributed over the 256 PE. The simulation of 250,000 particles in an FET device is done in more than 1,200 minutes using a currently available 15MIPS mainframe computer.

From this computation, we extracted typical distribution of particles and evaluated data transfer overhead on several kinds of architecture. The number of steps to transfer data along the number of PE is shown in Fig. 13. In this figure, the number of steps is normalized by the average number of data each PE contains. As this figure shows, on the distributed parallel network, the steps to transfer data doesn't increase along with the increase in the number of PEs.

The computation time for each iteration of the flow shown in Fig. 12 is estimated as follows. For the calculation of electric field and particle position, $\sim 1.0s$ is taken respectively. It is pure processing time without communication with other PEs. For the data transfer of field information and particle information, there arise 10,000 of 80bit data transfer from every PE in each transfer phase. It takes $\sim 75ms$ for respective transfer. Thus, less than 10% of the pure processing time is the overhead for data transfer. For the synchronization, it takes $\sim 10\mu s$ for 1 synchronization including switching the state of the network. As 30 times of synchronization are necessary to complete the data transfer, the synchronization overhead is $\sim 300\mu s$. It is less than 5% of the total data transfer overhead and is negligible compared to processing time.

For 1,000 iteration of the particle simulation, the computation time resulted in approximately 36 minutes using the R256 while 1200 minutes using the conventional 15MIPS mainframe computer. Thus, the R256 fully exploits the parallelism in the application with fairly small overhead of data transfer, which would be a heavy load for conventional parallel processors. Consequently, the R256 is able to sustain 500 MFLOPS, despite the apparent data transfer overhead and is expected to execute larger scale problems with more accurate simulation.

5 Conclusion

A scientific parallel processor called the R256 has been developed. The innovative network architecture is confirmed to demonstrate highly efficient data transfer and to reduce the overhead in the parallel calculation. Furthermore, the hardware scale of the network is quite practical because the size is minimized by $\sqrt{N}$-fold compared with a crossbar switch network.

A dedicated 80-bit floating-point CMOS VLSI processor has also been developed. The extended IEEE floating-point data execution, which the LSI supports, can be widely applied in large-scale scientific calculations.

The performance of the 256 PEs reaches 500 MFLOPS, a value which includes the small overhead of data transfer operations of less than 10%. This is derived from 2-GByte/s high-speed data transfer rates and the distributed parallel network.

The implementation of the R256 described in the present study has been made on the basis of conventional TTL technology. The scale of the machine, therefore, fills a room. The size could be cut in half, however, by using state-of-the-art LSI technology. We believe the R256 architecture has potential for going far beyond GFLOP speeds while still maintaining a highly efficient data-transfer rate.

Acknowledgments

The development of the R256 is owed to many people who have contributed to the long-term project. Particularly, the authors wish to thank Dr. Sudo for leading and encouraging this project. Drs. A. Yoshii, N.Nakashima, K. Horiguchi and N. Miyahara are acknowledged for their helpful discussions. The project has been accomplished by the support of T.Okamoto and his colleagues in NTT LSI Lab., K. Ishikawa and his colleagues in NTT Electronics Technology Co., and Y. Hoshino and her colleagues in Nippon Telecommunication Consulting Co.

References

[1] Rattner, J. , "Concurrent Processing:A New Direction in Scientific Computing," Proc. of Nat'l Computer Conf., 1985, pp.158-166.

[2] Jurasek, D. , Richardson, W. , Wilde, D. , "A Multiprocessor Design in Custom VLSI," VLSI SYSTEM DESIGN, Jun. , 1986, pp. 26-30.

[3] Hoshino, T. ,et al. , "Highly Parallel Processor Array 'PAX' for Wide Scientific Applications," Proc. of the ICPP, Aug. 1983, pp. 95-103.

[4] Pfester, G. F. , Brantley, W. C. , George, D. A. , et al. , "The IBM Research Parallel Processor Prototype (RP3): Introduction and Architecture," Proc. of the 1985 Int'l Conference on Parallel Processing, 1985, pp. 764-769.

[5] Beeten, J. , Dennau, M. and Weigaren, D. , "The GF11 Super Computer," Proc. of the 12th Int'l Symposium on Computer Architecture, 1985, pp. 108-115.

[6] Andresen,S.,"The Looping Algorithm Extended to Base 2^t Rearrangeable Switching Networks,"IEEE,Trans. on Comm., Vol.COM-25.No.10,Oct. 1977,pp.1057-1063.

[7] Wu,C. and Feng,T. "On a Class of Multistage Interconnection Networks",IEEE, Trans. on Comput.,Vol.C-29,No.8,Aug.1980,pp.694-702.

[8] Seitz, C. L. , "The Cosmic Cube," Communications of the ACM, Vol. 28, No. 1, Jan. 1985, pp. 22-33.

[9] Tomizawa, M. ,et al. , "Modeling for an AlGaAs/GaAs Heterostructure Device Using Monte Carlo Simulation," IEEE Electron Device Letters, Vol. EDL-6, No. 7, July 1985, pp. 332-334.

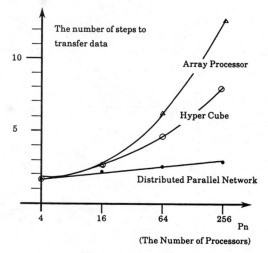

Figure 13: Evaluation

Special Purpose Architectures
Chair: S. Ruhman, Weizmann Institute

A THREE-PORT / THREE-ACCESS REGISTER FILE
FOR CONCURRENT PROCESSSING AND I/O COMMUNICATION
IN A RISC-LIKE GRAPHICS ENGINE

M. L. Anido, D. J. Allerton and E. J. Zaluska

Dept. of Electronics and Computer Science
University of Southampton, SO9 5NH, U. K.

ABSTRACT

A novel method that provides extremely fast Input/Output (I/O) data transfer to a RISC-like graphics engine is presented. This method employs a combined two-port / two-access and a three-port / three-access register file used for concurrent processing and I/O data transfer. The three-port cell employed is only 25 % larger than the two-port cell, offering considerable advantages over alternative approaches, such as FIFOs or register banks.

This paper discusses some methods that can provide highly fast I/O data transfer in parallel with execution and focuses on the design and implementation of the CMOS-2um register file employed.

Index Terms - Computer Architecture, Reduced Instruction Set Computers, VLSI Design, Computer Image Generation, Interprocessor Communication.

I. INTRODUCTION

A RISC for Image Generation termed RIG, designed to perform Geometric Computations [01] concurrently with other similar processors was implemented using proprietary LSI and MSI chips and its internal architecture is depicted in figure 2. Figure 1 depicts the MIGS (Multiprocessor Image Generation System) system that employs several RIG processors running in parallel.

Each RIG processor executes the Geometric Procedures approximately fifteen times faster than a 12Mhz MC68000 microprocessor and a CMOS-2um version is under development [02][03]. This graphics engine receives 3-D input polygon co-ordinates from an external memory (input data) and generates 2-D output co-ordinates (output data), corresponding to the vertices of polygons to be depicted on the screen.

As illustrated in figure 1, the Host Computer, the Geometric Computations System, the Scan Conversion System and the Image Enhancements System are organised in pipeline. This organisation is essential to provide a level of parallelism required to render polygons in real-time.

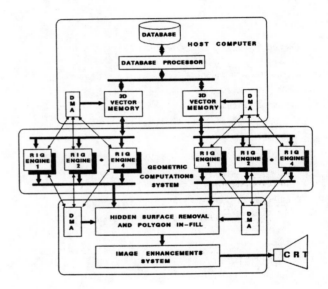

Fig. 1. MIGS - A Multiprocessor Image Generation System

The Geometric Computations problem allows straightforward partitioning of the workload, thus several RIG processors can operate concurrently in a MIMD arrangement, as depicted in figure 1. Among the main issues of this system are: fast processing, extremely fast I/O data transfer, simple interface with the parallel processing system and minimal external circuitry.

Another fundamental issue is that each RIG processor deals with the co-ordinates of one polygon at a time and such data is sufficiently small to be stored in the 128 internal registers. The RIG processor requires 48 registers (three-port registers) for I/O data storage and the remaining 80 registers (two-port registers) are used to store polygon data, local and global variables and are also used as working registers.

The rationale for the extremely fast I/O communication requirement is that processing time is of the same order of magnitude as the data transfer time. Therefore, Direct Memory Access (DMA) is employed to minimise the data transfer time. Data is trasferred in DMA burst mode directly into processor internal registers. In order to minimise the overall time (processing time plus I/O data transfer time), processing is performed concurrently with I/O data transfer, by using three-port / three-access register cells.

The processor does not have to perform memory data access. Data is ready to be processed in the G.P. registers. Therefore, there is no delay in the internal pipeline, simplifying processor architecture and improving overall system performance.

The three-port register file was essential to provide a continuous flow of polygons into and out of each RIG processor, keeping the system pipeline busy. Any delay in the system pipeline reduces real-time speed.

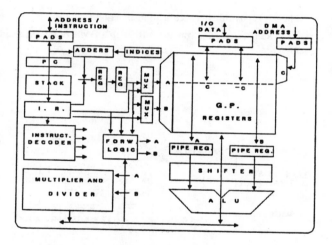

Fig. 2. RIG Internal Architecture

II. SOME OPTIONS TO PROVIDE FAST DATA TRANSFER IN PARALLEL WITH PROCESSING

Some architecture options to provide fast data transfer in parallel with processing are analysed. The emphasis is on area, regularity and complexity. Additional logic on critical paths can slow down the processor cycle and has to be considered and, if possible, avoided. In order to compare equivalent designs, all options have to allow fast data transfer (such as DMA transfer) and concurrency between processing and I/O operations. Because of pin limitation input and output operations share the same data bus, therefore they cannot occur simultaneously.

We start by considering the use of two FIFOs (internal to the CPU), to connect the processor to the external environment (Host Processor or Scan Conversion System). One FIFO is written by the CPU and read by the external DMA controller and the other FIFO operates in the opposite direction, as depicted on figure 3. The CPU has to read data from the FIFO and write into the G.P. registers before processing and conversely write data into the FIFO after processing. The disadvantages of the FIFO approach, when compared with the schemes that will be shown are:

- The CPU spends time reading and writing data into the FIFOs, slowing down overall speed.
- Data is replicated in the FIFO and G.P. registers, wasting silicon area.
- Additional buses are required to connect the CPU to the FIFOs.
- Complex control is required in comparison with the foreseen schemes.

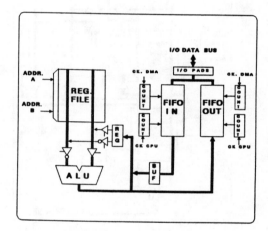

Fig. 3. Using FIFOs for I/O Data Transfer

A second option is the use of two register banks composed of the registers employed for I/O data transfer (see figure 4). This method operates by switching the register banks after an Input or Output operation has been completed. While the CPU uses one register bank, input or output data transfer occurs between the other register bank and the external environment. Accordingly, register banks are used not only for I/O but also for processing. A positive aspect of this approach, when compared with the three-port register file to be shown, is the use of standard two-port register cells. However, the main problems with this approach are the additional logic and bus buffers (which increase register access time), together with the extra buses required.

A third option, which offers more flexibility than the register bank approach, is to use a linear addressing range for the Input/Output registers and for the General Purpose registers. This requires an increase in the operand field addressing range, which may be possible or not depending on pin limitation. This option may be further enhanced if the register file employs a three-port cell, such as shown in figure 8. This cell allows read operations on the A and B ports to be concurrent with write operations on the C port. (It does not allow read/write operations on the C port, such as the Three-Port cell to be discussed). Again, the major disadvantages of this approach are the bus buffers required to separate the I/O sections of the register file from the General-Purpose (commonly used) registers, together with the necessary additional buses.

A three-port / three-access register file, allowing read/write operations on the third port, affords most advantages in terms of silicon regularity, the number of buses and control simplicity. It is depicted in figure 5. The issue of silicon area is not obvious and it will be shown in section three that a three-port cell is also attractive in terms of size. A similar or even larger area would probably be required by the alternative solutions discussed, but providing less silicon regularity.

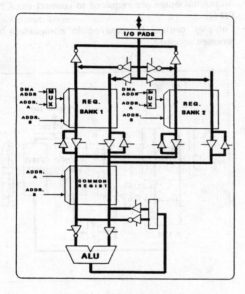

Fig. 4 - Using Register Banks

III. RIG REGISTER FILE

RIG Register File is composed of two-port / two-access and three-port / three-access cells, as indicated in figure 5. The *A* and *B* decoders decode addresses provided by the *sc1*, *sc2* or *dst* fields of the Instruction Register. The *C* decoder decodes addresses provided by the external DMA controller.

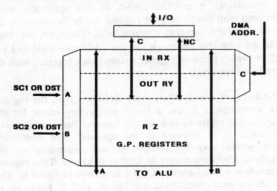

Fig. 5 - RIG Register File

Operands / data are accessed via the *A* and *B* buses with both buses connected to all the cells. Results are written into the register file using the same *A* and *B* buses. Data to be written is inserted into the *A* bus and its complement into the *B* bus. Then, the destination cells are selected and data is written. The *C* and *NC* buses connect the three-port cells to the Host Processor, via the I/O data bus. In order to avoid access conflict to three-port cells during write operations, a software protocol and a hardware mechanism are employed. If a programming error occurs, the hardware mechanism prevents simultaneous accesses from writing into three-port cells. When the CPU is writing to a three-port register it inhibits the corresponding *C* address, thus preventing an erroneous write operation to that register.

Concurrence between processing and I/O data transfer is illustrated in figure 6. *Rx*, *Ry* and *Rz* are generic groups of registers which indicate:

- *Rx* - group of three-port registers used for Input and processing;
- *Ry* - group of three-port registers used for Output and processing;
- *Rz* - group of two-port General-Purpose Registers.

Thus, it is possible to execute an instruction such as:

ADD Rx56 , Rz1 , Rz2 concurrently with a DMA read operation on *Ry32*.

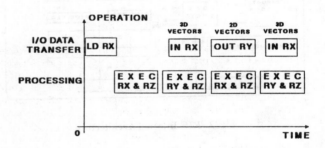

Fig. 6 - Concurrence between Processing and I/O Data Transfer

IV. MULTIPLE-PORT / MULTIPLE-ACCESS CELLS

RISCs using three-address instruction types usually rely on two-port register files to enhance their performance [4][5][6]. A basic three-address instruction such as:
ADD ra, rb, rc simultaneously reads the *ra* and *rb* registers, executes the instruction and writes back the result in the same cycle or in the next cycle. Several two-port / two-access [6][7][8][9] and three-port / three-access [10] static register cells have been reported in the literature.

Sherburne *et al* [7] describe the design of a two-port 6-T NMOS cell employed in the Berkeley RISC chip, which uses both bit lines to read and write. The Berkeley RISC cell is depicted in figure 7. A read operation to both ports can be performed on the same cell (or on different cells) by activating the appropriated word select lines. By precharging the bit lines to ONE, only N-type transistors are necessary to access the cell, otherwise transmission gates and complementary word select lines would be required, increasing cell size. Moreover, only the N-type pull-down transistor has to be large enough to drive the long bit lines. The pull-up P-type transistor can be small, because it only has to replenish cell leakage. One of the bit lines operates with data in complemented mode and has to be subsequently inverted after reading. In order to write into the cell, the data to be written is first inserted into the bit lines, one bit line being the one's complement of the other, and the selected cell is then addressed via the word select lines.

The major advantage of this method, when compared with other access mechanisms [10] is that it eliminates the extra bit and word select lines that are usually required for the write operation. The penalties in using this approach are that no simultaneous write operations can occur and also bit lines have to be time-multiplexed to accomplish read and write operations.

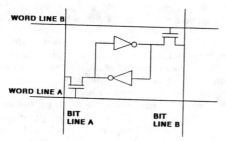

Fig. 7 - Berkeley RISC cell

A three-port / three-access CMOS cell using a *weak* inverter and two additional lines (one write bit line and one write word line) has been reported by Tago *et al* [10] and is depicted in figure 8. The major advantage of this cell is that it allows simultaneous and asynchronous read/write operations on the register file. However, the ALU execution time is normally larger than the register file access time in ordinary RISCs (a factor of two is a good estimate). This makes it possible to write the result of the previous operation and read the next operands during the ALU execution interval, making simultaneous read and write operations unnecessary.

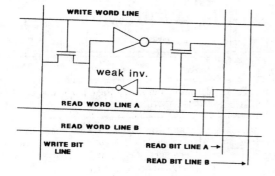

Fig. 8 - Tago's three-port cell

The Stanford MIPS-X project described by Horowitz *et al* [6] used a CMOS version of the six-transistor RAM cell described by Sherburne [7]. Precharged bit lines and self-timed write were used in the design of the cell. Fig. 10 shows the CMOS cell employed in the MIPS-X project. Self-timed precharge and self-timed write operations will be discussed in sections six and seven.

A new type of CMOS 6-T two-port memory cell has been presented by O'Connor [8], claiming read access to one cell and concurrent read/write operations to separate cells. This cell is depicted in figure 9 and it uses two pass transistors (a P-type and a N-type) connected to a common node. Two bit lines (one precharged low (*BLpl*) and another precharged high (*BLph*)) are used to read/write the cell. Word select lines are used with complementary logic. However, read operations on one cell concurrently with write operations on another cell are only possible if they are synchronized and most important of all, the value to be written (ZERO or ONE) determines which bit line will have to be used to write into the cell, forcing the simultaneous read operation on the other cell to use the alternative bit line. For example, if a ZERO is to be written into cell *a*, cell *b* has to be read using bit line *BLpl* (via the P-type pass transistor), leaving bit line *BLph* free for the write operation (the N-type pass transistor propagates a ZERO level better than a ONE level).

Thus, the additional complexity of the write operation, together with the need for complementary word select lines has to be carefully contrasted with its advantages. Moreover, the graphics system under analysis requires asynchronous read/write operations on diferent cells, eliminating this option.

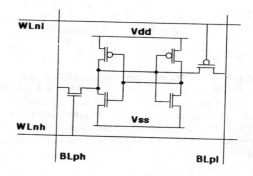

Fig. 9 - O'Connor's cell

V. RIG TWO-PORT AND THREE-PORT CELLS

The RIG register file employs the 6-T two-port CMOS cell illustrated in figure 10 for those registers used only for processing. As already said, the three-port / three-access cell is employed in those registers used to read/write data via the I/O channel and also for processing. It is based on the two-port cell and is depicted in figure 11.

It is evident from figure 11 that the three-port cell uses three additional lines (one word select line and two bit lines). The operation is identical to the two-port cell already described. The inclusion of the third port (port *C*) allows access on the *A* and *B* ports to be concurrent and asynchronous with read/write operations on the *C* port, on different cells.

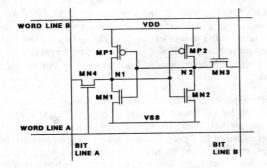

Fig. 10 - Two-Port Static Cell

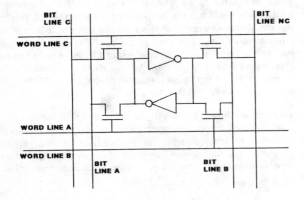

Fig. 11 - Three-Port / Three-access Cell

5.1 - Design Criteria

In order to combine reliability with small size, some design criteria will be reviewed. The P-load transistor in figure 10 can be minimum size, as it only has to counteract the effects of leakage in the drain of the N-type pull-down and pass-transistors. The P-load transistor also does not have to pull the bit lines up because this is done by the precharge circuit.

The effective series ratio of the pass-transistor and the pull-down transistor determines the pull-down speed of the bit line. This ratio also affects the write operation - a small pass transistor slows down the write operation into the cell. On the other hand, the larger the pass transitor, the larger the load on the word line, slowing down the cell and possibly increasing cell area. This effect can be compensated by increasing the word line driver.

a. Static Read Operation

The cell must be operated in such a way that the voltage at node N1 (or N2) must be kept below the inverter switching point formed by MN2 and MP2 (or MN1 and MP1). Transistor MN1 must always operate in the linear region to maintain cell stability. The pass to pull-down *Beta* ratio has to be such that the pull-down is able to clamp the stored *low* level to well below the inverter switching point.

b. Static Write Operation

Because write operation is performed by writing data and its complement into the bit lines, only one of the N-type pass transistors is involved in the write operation (the one that has to write a ZERO). Considering figure 10, transistors MN4 and MP1 are involved in switching node N1 from the ONE to the ZERO state.

The MN4 to MP1 *Beta* ratio has to be selected to guarantee cell switching, that is, when BIT line *A* is at ZERO (and Word Line *A* is at ONE), the voltage drop at N1 has to be sufficient to turn transistor MP2 *ON*. Thus the MN4 to MP1 *Beta* ratio has to be such that the voltage at node N1 is lower than the threshold voltage of MP2 (approx. 2/3 Vdd). Simultaneously N2 rises, providing positive feedback to switch the cell even faster.

c. Dynamic Operation

Charge sharing due to the ratio of the bit line capacitances to the internal cell capacitances affects the dynamic operation of the cell, making transitions between states slower. This effect can be minimised by making cell pull-down and pass-transistors bigger, but the area will increase and a compromise solution has to be found.

Several transistor configurations were tested and a compromise solution was found for Wpu = 4u, Wpass = 6u and Wpd = 8u. Figure 12 illustrates the circuit employed to simulate cell behaviour. Simulations were carried out using the SPICE2-G and SPICE3 electrical simulators, estimating a bit line capacitance of 1.0 pF and worst case voltage of 4.5V. Worst case transistor parameters were also used . Figure 13 depicts the results of the electrical simulation of the cell, for write, precharge and read operations. Considering a bit line capacitance of 1.0 pF, it is possible to write and precharge the cell or to read it in less than 15ns.

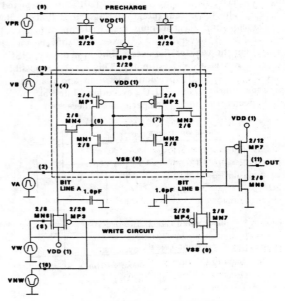

Fig. 12 - Circuit used to simulate the cell

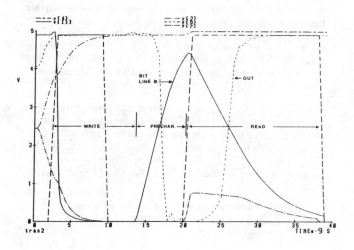

Fig. 13 - SPICE results

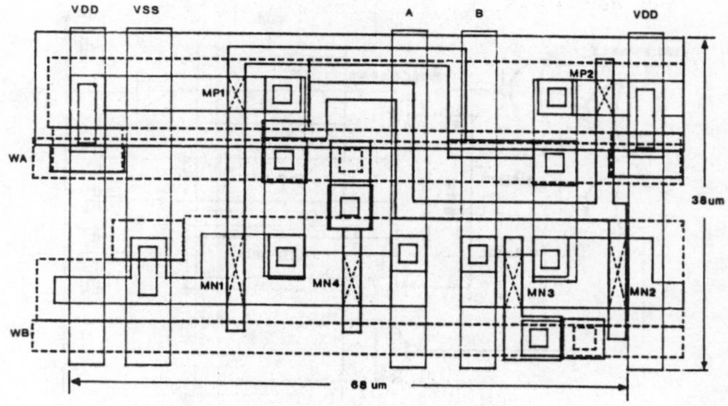

Fig. 14 - Two-port Cell Layout

5.2. Layout of the Two-port and Three-port cells

The layouts illustrated in figures 14 and 15 were developed using an in-house CMOS mask editor and DRC. One of the most important issues about cell layout is area, which had to be minimised because of the large number of cells required. Another important topic was the minimisation of the bit lines lenght (which run in *metal 1*), so that bit line capacitances are minimised. This affects the cell aspect ratio. Separating the bit lines in the cell does not cause any problem to the ALU layout because the ALU bit pitch is normally larger than that of the register file. Word lines run in *metal 2* to provide fast access, because they have lower capacitance and less resistance than polysilicon.

The two additional transistors required for the implementation of the three-port cell do not contribute to increase the cell area because they run under metal. Only the two extra bit lines contribute to increase the area of the three-port cell, which is only 25 % larger than the area of the two-port cell. This area increase seems a reasonable price to pay in view of the inherent advantages of the approach when compared with the options discussed in section two.

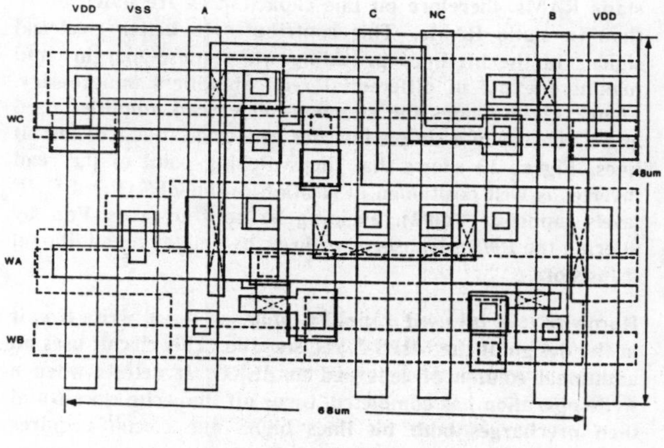

Fig. 15 - Three-port Cell Layout

VI. SELF-TIMED PRECHARGE CIRCUIT

Before a read operation is effected, the bit lines have to be precharged to ONE and this has to be performed very quickly so that the read operation is not delayed. The bit lines only have to be precharged sufficiently HIGH to activate the read circuit and account for a safe noise error margin.

In order to accomplish a reliable precharge operation and also improve speed, a self-timed precharge circuit is employed [11][12][13]. The register file cycle time is subdivided into two halves. During the first half, a write operation is enabled (write may occur or not) together with the precharge of the bit lines. During the second half, a read operation takes place.

Figure 16 illustrates the self-timed precharge circuit used. At the end of the write enable signal, the flip-flop is toggled, generating a signal that disables all row decoders. Only when all row decoder lines are at ZERO (isolating all the cells) the precharge line is activated LOW, making the P-type transistors precharge the bit lines to ONE. When the bit lines have crossed HIGH by a sufficient margin to switch the NAND gate, the flip-flop is reset, enabling the row decoder to be activated again. The additional P-type transistor on the precharge circuit interconnecting the two bit lines balances the high level, minimising the possibility of a destructive read operation due to unbalanced bit lines. P-type transistors are used in the precharge circuit because they propagate HIGH level better than N-type transistors.

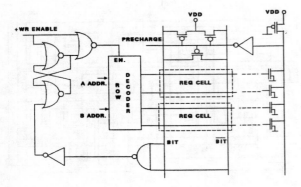

Fig. 16 - Self-Timed Precharge Circuit

VII. READ AND WRITE CIRCUITS

The register file under analysis uses less cells than commercial static RAMs, therefore bit line capacitances are much lower than in static RAMs. This contributes to better electrical signals in the bit lines providing wider noise margins and making the use of differential read amplifiers unnecessary. Figure 12 illustrates the common-mode read amplifier used and it consists of a simple inverter connected to one of the bit lines. Figure 13 shows that the switching point of the read inverter is well positioned in relation to the ZERO and ONE levels (approx. Vdd/2), avoiding its shift towards Vdd by altering the *Bp/Bn* transistor ratio or by employing additional transistors.

Horowitz *et al* [6] used a sophisticated self-timed write circuit in the design of the MIPS-X register file. This circuit uses an additional column of cells tied to ZERO. It detects when a write operation has completed, turns off the write circuit and then precharges both bit lines high. The circuit requires careful design to avoid oscillation.

A more conservative approach was employed in the design of the write circuit of the RIG processor. Write operation timing is derived from the processor clock.

VIII. ROW DECODER

There are several options of decoders in the open literature [14][15][16]. In order to employ a suitable decoder, we persued the following commonly used guidelines:

- pre-decoding minimises logic and enhances decoder speed.
- pass-transistors slow down decoding time and their use should be kept to a minimum.
- decoder layout should match register cell layout.
- low power consumption is an important issue.
- the layout structure of the address lines and the decoded lines affects decoder regularity and compactness.

Based on these guidelines and having in mind that a very fast decoder disable mechanism was essential to provide fast bit line precharge, the decoder shown on figure 17 was chosen. It uses a fast NOR gate decoder together with a special latch at the output stage. Instead of a static NOR with slow pull-ups or a dynamic NOR with its associated discharge susceptibility and low frequency limit operation, we opted for a latch composed of the row buffer and a *weak* inverter as shown in figure 17.

The ROW ENABLE signal is activated when the address lines are stable and when a read or write operation takes place. During the precharge of the bit lines, this signal is OFF. This decoder is able to decode the address lines in less than 3ns, for worst case transistor characteristics. Total decode time, including address line buffers delay (for 1.0 pf capacitance) is under 5ns.

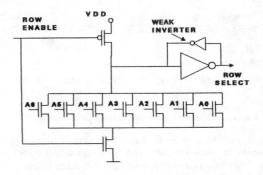

Fig. 17 - Row Decoder Circuit

IX. CONCLUSIONS

A new and extremely fast method to transfer data to a processor has been presented. Data is transferred (in DMA burst mode) directly into the processor internal registers, in parallel with processing. The presented solution proved to be very efficient to perform Geometric Computations, but may also be very attractive in other applications where the processing time is of the same order of magnitude as I/O data transfer time and where the amount of data to be stored (per operation) is commensurate with the number of processor internal registers.

This paper also shows that Three-port / Three-access register cells can be very attractive in terms of silicon area and regularity, when compared with other memory structures, such as FIFOs or Register Banks, provided simultaneous write operations to commonly used cells are not required. The Three-port cell presented is only 25 % larger than a standard two-port cell, which compensates for the area that would probably be required if FIFOs or Register Banks had to be used. It also provides a highly regular and fast memory structure.

ACKNOWLEDGEMENTS

We acknowledge the financial support provided by the Brazilian organasation CNPQ, the Federal University of Rio de Janeiro and the ORS Award Scheme (U.K) for the research of M.L. Anido at the University of Southampton.

REFERENCES

[01] Foley, J.D. and Van Dam, A., "Fundamentals of Interactive Computer Graphics", Addison Wesley, Reading, Mass., 1980.

[02] Anido, M.L., Allerton, D.J. and Zaluska, E.J., "The Architecture of RIG: A RISC for Image Generation in a Multi-Microprocessor Environment", Proc. EUROMICRO 88 - Zurich, North-Holland Publish., pp. 581-588.

[03] Anido, M.L., Allerton, D.J. and Zaluska, E.J., "MIGS - A Multiprocessor Image Generation System using RISC-like Microprocessors", proc. Computer Graphics International 1989 - CGI'89, June, Leeds - U.K. To be published by Springer Verlag.

[04] Patterson, D.A. and Sequin, C.H., "A VLSI RISC", Computer, September, 1982, pp. 8-22.

[05] Hennessy, J.L., Joupi, N. et al, "Design of a High Performance VLSI Processor", 3rd. Very Large Scale Integration Conf., Caltech, Pasadena, 1983, pp. 33-54.

[06] Horowitz, M., Chow, P., Stark, D. et al., "MIPS-X: a 20-MIPS Peak, 32-bit Microprocessor with On-Chip Cache", IEEE Journal of Solid-State Circuits, Vol. sc-22, No. 5, October 1987, pp. 790-799.

[07] Sherburne, R.W., Katevenis, M.G.H., et al, "Datapath Design for RISC", Conf. on Advanced Research in VLSI, M.I.T., 1982, pp 53-63.

[08] O'Connor, K.J., "The Twin-Port Memory Cell", IEEE Journal of Solid State Circuits, Vo. sc-22, No. 5, October, 1987, pp. 712-720.

[09] Barber, F.E., Eisenberg, D.J., et al, "A 2Kx9 Dual Port Memory", IEEE ISSCC, Feb. 1985, pp. 44-45.

[10] Tago, H., Shiochi, M., Takada, T. et al, "A CMOS Array with easily testable three-port RAMs", Proc. IEEE Internaltional Conference on Computer Design: VLSI in Computers, ICCD'84, New York, pp. 424-427.

[11] Glasser, L.A. and Dobberphul, D.W., "The Design and Analysis of VLSI Circuits", Addison Wesley Publ., 1985.

[12] Rushton, A. J., "A General Purpose Parallel Computer", Ph. D. Thesis, Dept. of Electronics and Comput. Sc., Southampton University, 1987, UK.

[13] Mead, C. and Conway, L.,"Introduction to VLSI Systems", Addison Wesley Publ., 1980.

[14] Weste, N. and Eshraghian, K., "Principles of CMOS VLSI Design", Addison Wesley Publ., 1985.

[15] Mukherjee, A., "Introduction to NMOS and CMOS VLSI Systems Design", Prentice Hall Publ., 1986.

[16] Lyon, R. and Schediwy, R.R., "CMOS Static Memory with a New Four-Transistor Cell", Losleben, Proc. Conf. Adv. Research in VLSI, MIT Press, 1987 pp. 111-132.

An Architecture Framework for Application-Specific and Scalable Architectures

J.M. Mulder, R.J. Portier, A. Srivastava, R. in 't Velt

Section Digital Systems and Computer Architecture

Department of Electrical Engineering

Delft University of Technology

POBox 5031, 2600 AG Delft, The Netherlands

duteca!hansm@uunet.uu.net

Ph: +31 (0)15 785021

Abstract

Two major limitations concerning the design of cost-effective application-specific architectures are the recurrent costs of system-software development and hardware implementation, in particular VLSI implementation, for each architecture.

The SCalable ARChitecture Experiment (SCARCE) aims to provide a framework for application-specific processor design. The framework allows scaling of functionality, implementation complexity, and performance. The SCARCE framework consists and will consist of: an architecture framework defining the constraints for the design of application-specific architectures; tools for synthesizing architectures from application or application-area; VLSI cell libraries and tools for quick generation of application-specific processors; a system-software platform which can be retargeted quickly to fit the application-specific architecture;

This paper concentrates primarily on the architecture framework of SCARCE, but also presents briefly some software issues and outlines the process of generating VLSI processors.

1 Introduction

Developments in computer-aided VLSI design and integration technology have made the design of integrated application-specific processors a technological reality. The cost of both system-software development and (VLSI) processor design, however, hampers the application of this technology on a large scale. Ideally, one requires a system that analyzes an application and generates the appropriate system software and processor hardware. Proximities of such a system are the IDAS and the FLEX system [1,2].

However, the characteristics of a large application space –and associated implementation space– are too diverse to allow automatic generation of efficient but arbitrary system-software and VLSI-processor designs. The only way to achieve efficient processor and software generation is to define a set of constraints under which application-specific processors can be designed. These constraints, however, need to be defined very carefully to avoid creating a system which leaves insufficient space for the definition of application specificity or imposes to many requirements on low-end implementations.

In this paper we give a brief overview of a framework for the design of application-specific processors (the SCARCE[1] framework). The framework consists of four parts: the architecture framework, the application analysis and architecture synthesis tools, the processor generator, and the system software generator. This paper discusses only the architectural features of the framework (called the SCARCE architecture framework) in detail.

2 Overview of the SCARCE framework

The goals of the SCARCE framework are: scalability in architecture, implementation complexity, and performance. The essence of achieving the goals is the definition of an architecture framework which provides the three forms of scalability. The following two subsections introduce scalability and architecture framework; a discussion on architecture analysis, system-software generation, and processor generation can be found in Sections 7, 9, and 8 respectively.

2.1 Three-way scalability

The foundation of the framework is scalability:

in functionality: the ability to customize the architecture towards a particular (class of) application(s). Most of the architecture framework is dedicated towards this goal.

in implementation complexity: the ability to reduce hardware complexity without modifying the processor architec-

---

[1]SCalable ARChitecture Experiment

ture. The emulation facility of the architecture framework is dedicated towards this goal [3]. Scalability of implementation complexity is an important feature when implementation constraints disallow integration of the whole architectural functionality. A typical example is a move from high-density technology (e.g. CMOS) to a low-density technology (e.g. GaAs). Another example is integration of multiple functions on chip (e.g. memory, I/O, co-processors) reducing the available area for the CPU. Scalability in implementation guarantees object code compatibility among all implementations of a particular architecture. An additional advantage is the possibility of quick prototyping of application-specific architectures and software.

in performance: the ability to control performance according to cost and the availability of low-level parallelism. The VLIW extension of the architecture framework is dedicated to this goal. The VLIW extension (called VSCARCE) will not be discussed in this paper[2].

2.2 Architecture framework

The architecture framework builds on a base architecture with minimal functionality. The base architecture, however, contains sufficient *hooks* which allow the three forms of scalability. The architecture and *hooks* can be viewed as follows:

core set / function units	co-processor support	short instruction support	trap, emulation, + interrupt support	virtual-memory support	VLIW support
VLSI processor framework					

The *hooks* can be classified into four groups:

functional: function units and co-processor interfacing; see Section 4.

format optimizing: the use of 16-bit instruction formats to increase code density; see Section 5.

exception support: the handling of interrupts, traps, operation exceptions, and unimplemented instructions; see Section 6.

virtual-memory support: the ability to address many large virtual spaces; virtual-memory support will not be discussed in this paper.

performance: the ability to operate multiple processor in lock step.

After discussing the base architecture in the following section, subsequent sections present the architecture *hooks*.

---

[2]A draft of a VSCARCE description is available from the authors.

3 The base architecture

The base architecture constitutes the foundation of the architecture framework. In itself it is not a complete architecture because it specifies no data transformations or conditional control transfers, only data transfers and explicit control transfers. In the following three subsections we define the instructions and register organization of the architecture, the architectural visibility of the execution pipeline, and present a processor organization based on the architecture. In subsequent sections, extensions to the processor organization will illustrate the architecture *hooks* of the base architecture.

3.1 Instructions and register organization

The base architecture is a 32-bits load-store architecture in its barest form. Table 1 shows the division of the architecture in two instruction groups: memory and control. The *memory* group

Table 1: architecture framework, base architecture.		
group	subgroup	operation[a]
memory	load	$R := M[R + O_{14b}]$
	store	$M[R + O_{14b}] := R$
	load imm.	$R := Imm_{21b}$
control	jump	$PC := R + O_{19b}$
	link	$R := PC; PC := R + O_{16b}$

[a]R=register, M[ ]=memory operand, O_{xb}=signed offset of x-bit, Imm_{xb}=signed x-bit immediate, PC=program counter.

implements the data transfers with the outside world. Data-memory loads and stores operate solely on 32-bit objects. The addresses calculated are, however, only 30 bits wide. An address stored in a 32-bit container (memory or register) always takes the upper 30 bits. The immediate field in the load immediate is stored in the lower 21 bits and is sign extended.

The *control* group implements control transfers to non-sequential instructions. Instructions are always 32 bits wide and an instruction pointer is always 30 bits.

The architecture defines a maximum of 32 32-bit visible registers. As we will show in Section 6, the exception architecture allows a second set of registers to (partly) overlay the first set.

3.2 Pipeline

With respect to performance, implementation independence and implementation efficiency are adversary features. A typical example concerning RISCs is the visibility of the pipeline in the architecture.

Efficiency: We sacrificed implementation independence by making two branch-delay slots visible, which implies that a control transfer does not take effect until the completion of the second instruction after the jump or link. Note that, given the base architecture, a single delay slot would be sufficient; two-slots were chosen instead to unify control-transfer delay of jumps and links with conditional transfers (Section 4.1) and traps (Section 6).

Independence: We sacrificed implementation efficiency for additional implementation complexity by defining data-dependency interlocks to be resolved in hardware. Data dependencies in RISC machines can be detected and resolved in software [4], in hardware, or in both. Using hardware to resolve data-dependencies requires a hardware investment with respect to both detection and resolution. A typical SCARCE processor, however, already implements dependency detection to allow bypassing of ALU results to ALU operands, and implements an interlock mechanism for synchronization of CPU and external circuits (e.g. caches or co-processors); the additional hardware investment for detection and resolution of all data dependencies will be very small. SCARCE, therefore, resolves data-dependencies in hardware. It is worth noting, however, that dependency resolution in hardware does not exclude the potential advantage of software reorganization – in fact it is advisable to make use of it.

3.3 Processor organization

The processor organization as shown in Figure 1 does not add to the architecture definition, but, will in subsequent sections, illustrate how functionality can be added by means of the architecture *hooks*.

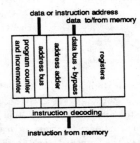

Figure 1: Processor organization based on the base architecture.

The figure shows five abutted subsystems, communicating with each other horizontally, and communicating with the outside world vertically. The processor generator (Section 8 actually uses the organization in Figure 1 as base floor-plan[3].

4 Scalability in functionality

Function scalability is an essential feature when defining application-specific architectures. However, to reduce recurrent architecture-, software-, and hardware-development costs, it is important to constrain this form of scalability. The architecture framework includes two forms of constrained function scalability: function units (FUs) and co-processors. Function units are integrated in the processor data-path and affect the processor state. Co-processors are removed from the processor, operate on their own state, and cannot alter the processor control flow directly. After presenting FU and co-processor support, the processor or-

---

[3]The proportions of subsystem sizes shown Figure 1 have no relation with the proportions of the actual VLSI-cell sizes.

ganization introduced in Figure 1 is extended to include scalable functionality.

4.1 Function units

Function units can alter the control flow and operate directly on the processor registers. The FU instruction format and basic operation are simple: they take two operands and, depending on the operation, yield a result or cause a PC-relative branch. The following two subsections discuss the FU formats and operation side effects, and a core set of FUs.

FU operations and side effects:

Since FUs can alter the control flow by instructing the program-counter circuit to perform PC-relative branches, FUs have delay slots too. Because statistics [5] suggest that the second delay slot is frequently unused, the architecture framework defines delay slot squashing [4]. Because the architecture framework does not distinguish between register-to-register operations and branches is not very clear in the architecture framework, all function units are capable of squashing one or both subsequent instructions depending on the operation and its result. Table 2 illustrates this capability by showing how an FU instruction affects the following three instructions. The operation functionality of FUs is basically unrestricted; only the total number of operations is limited by the instruction format (512 operations). The instruction format restricts the number and use of operands. Besides typical ALU operations (as shown in the next section), FUs are used for system support (Section 6) and implementation of VLIW functionality.

As will be clear in Section 6, many important FUs will not be able to operate without FU-internal state. Depending on the possible implementation of exception handling and the state operations, some FU state may, however, require a similar pipelined-write and bypassing mechanism as the register file.

Core function-unit set

In the process of defining the architecture framework, we have defined a set of FUs (the core set). This core set together with the base architecture currently forms the architecture basis for system-software development. The core set must have enough functionality to support common languages and must be able to support emulation of arbitrary (more complex) function units. The design of the core units centers around the trade-off of finding the balance between reduced functionality and emulation efficiency.

As shown in table 3, the only sacrifice with respect to the requirement of minimal functionality is the existence of one- and two-bits rotate instruction (see Table 3). Rotates are not frequent operations in general-purpose computations [6]. The core set, however, does include a rotate to allow quick access to the upper data bits, for efficient emulation of, for example, multiply, divide, double-word arithmetic, and upper-bit tag decodes.

Table 2: architecture framework, function units.

group	subgroup	effect[a] on instructions in sequence			
		operation	I_{+1}	I_{+2}	I_{+3}
function	data	R := R op R	I_{+1}/nop	I_{+2}/nop	I_{+3}
	branch	R rop R	I_{+1}/nop	I_{+2}/nop	$I_{+3}/I_{PC+O_{10b}}$
function	data	R := R op Imm$_{5b}$	I_{+1}/nop	I_{+2}/nop	I_{+3}
	branch	R rop Imm$_{5b}$	I_{+1}/nop	I_{+2}/nop	$I_{+3}/I_{PC+O_{10b}}$

[a]R=register, Imm$_{5b}$= 5-bits unsigned immediate, nop=no operation, I=instruction, PC=program counter, O_{10b}=10-bits signed offset.

Table 3: architecture framework, core function units.

group	subgroup	operation[a]	field specification
function	arithmetic	R := R op RI$_{5b}$	$op \in \{+, -, negate\}$
	logical	R := R op RI$_{5b}$	$op \in \{|, \&, \oplus\}$
	shift	R := (R $\ll_a$ C) + RI$_{5b}$	$C \in [-2,-1,1,2]$
	shift	R := (R $\ll_l$ C)	RI$_{5b}$	$C \in [-2,-1,1,2]$
	rotate	R := (R $\ll_r$ C) & RI$_{5b}$	$C \in [-2,-1,1,2]$
function	branch	if R rop RImm$_{5b}$ then PC := PC+O$_{10b}$	$rop \in \{<, \leq, =, <_u, \not<, \not\leq, \neq, \not<_u\}$

[a]R=register, RImm$_{5b}$=register or 5-bit unsigned immediate, C=constant shift amount, a=arithmetic, l=logical, r=rotate, u=unsigned, PC=program counter, O_{10b}=10-bit signed offset.

4.2 Co-processor instructions

We distinguish two sets of co-processor related instructions. The first set specifies the co-processor interface. This set aims at efficient communication between CPU, memory, and co-processor. Specially the memory-co-processor interface allows reduced co-processor complexity, because memory-addressing functionality in the co-processor is unnecessary (see Table 4). Note that architecture framework does not actually specify the existence or the number of co-processor registers; the interpretation of the 5-bits register identifier is up to the co-processor itself. With the

Table 4: architecture framework, co-processors.

group	subgroup	operation[a]
memory	move to	CR$_{id}$:= R
		CR$_{id}$:= M[R+O$_{12b}$]
	move from	R := CR$_{id}$
		M[R+O$_{12b}$] := CR$_{id}$
	operation	Cop[id] $\leftarrow$ F$_{23b}$

[a]R=register, CR$_{id}$=register R of co-processor id, id=co-processor identification ($id \in [0,7]$), O_{12b}=12-bit signed offset M[ ]=memory operand, Cop[id]=co-processor id, F$_{23b}$=23-bit operation specification.

second set one may specify the architecture of the co-processor. This set is left unrestricted except for the maximum number of operations (see Table 4).

Although not discussed any further in this paper, co-processors are very important in implementing application-specificity. We are in the process of developing co-processor architecture frameworks for different applications; frameworks with a structure similar to the one of the architecture framework.

4.3 Processor organization

When compared with Figure 1, Figure 2 shows three changes. First, a complex of function units interconnected by a bus (FU

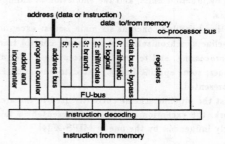

Figure 2: Processor organization with FUs and co-processor interface

bus) replaces the address adder used for most *memory* and *control* instructions. The FU bus provides the possibility, for example, to select FUs, to signal FU exceptions, to squash subsequent instructions, and to signal the PC circuit to branch. Second, an adder in the PC circuit calculates PC-relative addresses when signaled by a FU to do so. Third, the co-processor bus, together with the data bus, forms the interface with the processor for up to eight co-processors.

5 16-bits instruction formats

Applications requiring dense static and dynamic code size may profit significantly from 16-bit instructions [7]. Because every application-specific architecture profits from a different set of 16-bit instructions, the architecture framework leaves the format completely open. Our measurements indicate that allowing application-specific 16-bit formats yield an approximate reduction of 35% in static and dynamic code size (fairly independent of applications). Note that this feature is incorporated specifically to increase the efficiency of the use of on-chip instruction memory.

Every 16-bit instruction is required to have a 32-bit equivalent

Table 5: architecture framework, 16-bit formats.

group	general format	set of operations	max. set size
16-bit	unrestricted	$\in \{I_{32bit}\}$	2^{15}

(see Table 5). This requirement limits the impact of introducing 16-bit instructions to the instruction-decoder circuit in the VLSI core (see Section 9). Decoding of 16-bits instructions can be implemented by means of expansion into 32-bit instructions. The architecture framework requires 16-bit instructions to occur in pairs, because it can not address 16-bit quantities.

6 Exception support

Except for a reset, processors based on the base architecture combined with function units (FUs) cannot synchronize with external or internal events which require instant control-flow changes. This section presents the *hooks* in the base architecture that allow the processing of interrupts (from outside the processor), errors detected by function units, and the emulation of unimplemented operations.

Exception handling concerns six main issues: exception detection, pipeline synchronization, state freeze, control transfer, exception processing, and return from exception. After discussing these issues, some specific issues related to operation emulation will be presented.

Just ast the pipeline scheme currently used in the architecture framework, the exception architecture presented in this section is strongly influenced by the one in MIPS-X [4].

6.1 Exception detection

Detection depends on the type of exception. The exception architecture in the framework distinguishes two classes of exceptions: external or internal.

External exceptions (interrupts) are generated outside the processor. Detection requires an exception FU, providing an interrupt line for the outside world. Because interrupt detection is done by means of an FU, the interrupt structure (e.g. number of lines, priorities, etc.) can be application specific.

Internal exceptions (FU-related errors, unimplemented instructions, and trap instructions) are all generated inside the processor and broadcasted over the FU bus. Detection requires an exception FU, which monitors the FU bus. Because trap detection is done by means of an FU, the trap structure can be determined by the application.

6.2 Pipeline synchronization

Before performing the actual control-flow change, the pipeline has to be brought in a state which allows a restart of the pipeline after completion of the exception processing. The pipeline scheme currently used in the architecture framework has five stages: IF, instruction fetch; RF, register fetch; EX, execute; MEM, memory access; WB, write result into register file. Synchronization of the pipeline depends on the type of exception and is done by the exception FU.

All external events are classified as imprecise. An imprecise exception requires abortion of all instructions in the pipeline except for the one in the last stage, which is side-effect free. Because of the two delay slots, three instructions need to be restarted; in this case the ones interrupted in RF, EX, and MEM.

All internal events are classified as precise, because the pipeline stage causing the exception is precisely known. A precise exception requires completion of all instructions before the one causing the exception and abortion of this instruction and all subsequent ones. In the current scheme detection of all internal exceptions occurs in the EX stage; the MEM and WB stages, therefore, complete execution, and the IF, RF, and EX stages abort execution. Depending on the exception, the instructions aborted in IF and RF, and, in some cases EX, need to be restarted after exception processing.

6.3 Freezing state

The essence of restarting an interrupted instruction stream after processing an exception is restoring the processor state to the state which existed just before the exception occurred. As indicated in the previous subsection, two or three instructions need to be restarted, which implies that the program counters of three instructions need to be saved.

Program-counter chain: To be able to save the state at any time, a chain of three program counters is added to the program-counter circuit. These three counters always contain the addresses of the instructions in the RF, EX, and MEM stage respectively. The chain shifts concurrently with the instructions in the pipe. Saving the state now simply involves freezing the chain and disallowing subsequent exceptions.

When a particular application requires nested exceptions, architecture support is needed for reading from and writing to the chain (Table 6), and for explicitly enabling chain shifting.

Table 6: architecture framework, exception support.

group	subgroup	operation[a]
control	pc	$XPC_{rf} := R$
		$R := XPC_{mem}$
function	psw	$DPSW := R$
		$R := DPSW$

[a]PC=program counter, XPC_x is the program counter of an instruction interrupted in stage x, DPSW=distributed processor status word.

The shift-enable bit is a part of the processor status word (PSW), but is located as local state in the exception FU. In subsequent sections, more bits will be defined which are part of the PSW, but are distributed over different FUs. To be able to save and restore the PSW, the FU bus allows access to all distributed state bits in a single instruction (Table 6).

6.4 Control transfer

Control transfers occur similar to jumps and links, and are identical for both internal and external exceptions. The exception

FUs take care of the transfer by placing the starting address of the exception handler on the FU-result bus and signaling the program counter that a new instruction address has been generated in the data-path. Because the FUs determine the address, dispatch to a particular interrupt trap, or emulation routine can occur instantaneously.

The emulation FU implemented in a currently designed processor, dispatches without penalty to any of the 512 emulation routines, while the interrupt/trap FU dispatches immediately to four interrupt routines and one trap routine.

6.5 Exception handling

Although the handling of an exception is, of course, exception dependent, two support issues are architecturally defined; the use of privilege levels and immediate provision of working registers.

Privilege levels: Systems requiring a strict separation between resources for common and restricted access need (at least) two processor-operation modes to implement this separation. Within the exception architecture we have defined two modes, restricted and unrestricted, together with their transitions.

The processor always starts up in unrestricted mode and can be changed to restricted mode explicitly under program control, or implicitly by a return from exception. The transfer from restricted to unrestricted is a system trap in the form of an FU instruction. The bit indicating which mode the processor is in resides in the PSW. The operation mode is also made available to all FUs (over the FU bus) to allow definition of restricted/unrestricted FU operations.

Working registers: Handling of exceptions always requires some initial state in the general purpose registers (e.g. stack pointer). To allow quick exception handling (e.g. a TLB miss), the architecture framework allows definition of up to 32 alternate registers which overlay the general registers. Exception handlers, therefore, can have working registers at their disposal immediately. The bit indicating which of the register sets is up front resides in the PSW-FU. A change to unrestricted mode always causes a switch to the alternate registers. A return from exception only switches the registers if control returns into restricted mode.

6.6 Return from exception

Table 7: architecture framework, exception return.

group	subgroup	operation[a]
control	return	$PC := XPC_{mem}$, restore PSW
		$PC := XPC_{ex}$
		$PC := XPC_{rf}$

[a]PC=program counter, PC_x is the program counter of an instruction interrupted in stage x, PSW=processor status word.

By means of the mechanism and instructions described in the section on saving processor state, the program counters of the

two or three instructions which need to be restarted reside in the frozen counter chain. Restoring the state requires restarting the interrupted instruction stream and restoring the PSW-FU bits to the state as existed at the time of the exception. Restarting the interrupted instruction stream now requires three jumps (or two jumps and a no-op) to the addresses saved in the PC chain. PSW restoration occurs by copying bits saved at the time of the exception back into the PSW. Both *current* and *saved* PSW bits are implemented in the same (distributed) register; reading the PSW, therefore, yields both sets.

6.7 Emulation-specific issues

Emulation of unimplemented FU operations deviates slightly from general exception handling. First, for emulation and interrupt efficiency, emulations should be continuously interruptible without the overhead of saving the state in registers or memory [3]. Second, control-transfer to the appropriate emulation routine should be immediate. Third, for emulation efficiency it should be possible to recover the two operands quickly. Fourth, it should be possible to recover the result of the emulation in the destination register which was specified in the emulated instruction. These four issues and a quantification of their efficiency will be discussed next.

Interrupted emulations To allow interrupted emulations, the exception architecture provides two identical exception structures. All exception-related instructions (Table 6 and 7) now select the structure to operate upon: EPC (Emulation Program Counters) or XPC (eXception Program Counters).

Dispatch Immediate dispatch to the appropriate emulation routine in the emulation architecture occurs by calculating the address by means of the opcode and FU identification of the unimplemented FU. By padding the address with six zeros on the least-significant side, every operation has an emulation space of 64 instructions. The emulation FU contains a base address for all emulation routines (EBAR, see Table 8).

Table 8: architecture framework, emulation support.

group	subgroup	operation[a]
function	recover	$R := OS_1$
		$R := OS_2$
	restore	$OS_1 := R, OS_2 := R$
	vector	$EBAR := R$
		$R := EBAR$
control	return	$PC := EPC_{mem}, R_{dest} := R$

[a]R=register, OS=operand shadow registers, EBAR=Emulation Base Address, EPC=emulation program counter.

Operand recovery The emulation architecture (implemented in an FU) defines two FU registers (Operand Shadows, OS_1 and OS_2). Upon detection of an unimplemented operation the FU reads the two operands for this operation into the shadows. Table 8 shows the FU instructions operating on these registers.

Result recovery Result recovery occurs during the first instruction of the return sequence by moving the contents from an operand register specified in the return instruction to the destination register specified in the emulated instruction (see Table 8). The destination identifier is saved at the time of the emulation trap in the emulation FU.

Table 9: Emulation overhead in instructions.

mechanism	trap	disp.	op. rec.	return	res. rec.	Σ
trap[a]	7	10	10	7	5	39
emulation[b]	3	0	2	3	0	8

[a]Interrupt re-enabled immediate after trap.
[b]Fully interruptable.

Quantification of emulation efficiency Table 9 shows the resulting emulation overhead compared with the overhead when emulation occurs through the exception mechanism (Section 4.1). The overhead reduces from $\approx$ 39 instructions to 8.

6.8 Processor organization

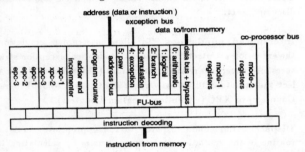

Figure 3: Processor organization including exception and emulation support.

As shown in Figure 3, exception and emulation support possibly adds four parts to Figure 2: two program-counter chain(s); exception and emulation function units; and a second register file.

7 Application analysis and architecture synthesis

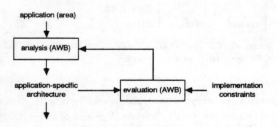

Figure 4: Application analysis by means of the Architect's Workbench.

Currently, the analysis tools used are those of the Architect's Workbench [9] (see Figure 4). The AWB allows extraction of run-time characteristics of arbitrary Pascal/Fortran/C programs. Characteristics are procedure profiles, instruction frequencies, instruction density, referencing behavior, and potential cache performance. Current developments concern AWB tools specifically for analysis and synthesis of architectures in the SCARCE framework.

8 Processor generation

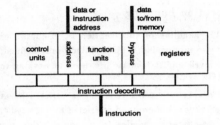

Figure 5: Processor system architecture and layout.

Generation of processor layout is basically a matter of cell selection, placement, and routing. The organization shown in Figure 5 indicates the basic cell types from which selection is made; the decoder is (functionally) the same for all implementations[4]; the application-specific architecture guides the selection of control cells, FU cells, and register cells; in addition, VLIW SCARCE processors require non-standard address busses and bypass/data-bus logic.

The tools used to develop the VLSI part of the SCARCE framework are those from the Nelsis project [10]. Processors are generated by specifying (currently by hand) cell configurations in LDMC [11] and routing them with the Nelsis router [12].

9 System-software generation

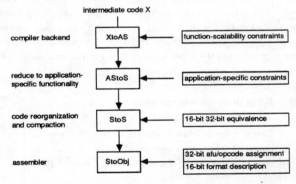

Figure 6: Generation of application-specific code.

Figure 6 shows the essential parts of the retargetable system software. The first part translates from an arbitrary intermediate

---

[4]We are currently implementing a decoder generator for both 32-bit and (arbitrary) 16-bit instructions, with adaptable aspect ratio.

language to Abstract SCARCE (AS). This part takes care of mapping any virtual machine into a machine which is limited only by the constraints of the architecture framework.

The second part translates AS into SCARCE assembler; AS functionality not available in the application-specific architecture expands in available functionality. SCARCE assembler is the assembler of the application-specific architecture.

The third part, converting SCARCE assembler into SCARCE assembler, consists of two stages: first, instruction reorganization [13] to reduce the number of unused branch-delay slots and to avoid potential data-dependency interlock penalties; second, code compaction by means of pairs of 16-bit instructions (when appropriate). Evidently, this stage requires the subset relation between 16-bit and 32-bit instructions. The last part transforms SCARCE assembler into object code and requires the bit-field encoding of both FUs and 16-bit instructions.

The SCARCE system software is currently driven by the Amsterdam Compiler Kit [14] and the Stanford U-code system [15]. The system software in turn generates code for a SCARCE interpreter and a mixed-level simulator of the Nelsis VLSI-design software [10]. Although, code generation and execution can take place, the system-software complex is still in an incomplete state.

10 Conclusion and project status

A framework for easy definition and quick implementation of application-specific architectures is desirable for the automatic generation of cost-effective application-specific processors and system software.

In this paper we have presented the SCARCE framework for application-specific processor design, and have specifically emphasized the architecture framework which allows expression of application specificity.

Currently most advances have been made in the definition of the architecture framework, the generation of processors and system software. Processor generation currently is hampered by insufficient laid out VLSI cells and the availability of only a 3-micron process. Processor generation will, on short term, occur in a 1.6 micron technology. Although, the system-software includes some advanced U-code tools (e.g. optimization and interprocedural register allocation), code reorganization for exploitation of delay slots and avoidance of data-dependency interlocks has not yet been implemented. Except for the existing AWB tools, no architecture analysis and synthesis tools have been designed yet.

Currently, one of the most important activities within the SCARCE project is the development of application-specific processors. Currently paper development is being done on a prolog processor, a graphics-list processor, a real-time heart-image processor, and a general-purpose VLIW.

References

[1] *Integrated Design Automation System, IDAS, Product Description Summary.* JRS Research Laboratories Inc, 1988.

[2] A. Wolfe and J.P. Shen. Flexible Processors: A Promising Application-specific Processor Design Approach. In *Proceedings of the 21st annual workshop on microprogramming and microarchitecture*, pages 30–39, November 1988.

[3] J.M. Mulder, R.J. Portier, A. Srivastava, and R. in't Velt. Efficient macro-code emulation in hardwired pipelined processors. In *Conference Proceedings of the IEEE Micro-21*, November 1988.

[4] Paul Chow and Mark Horowitz. Architectural tradeoffs in the design of the mips-x. In *Proceedings, 14th Annual International Symposium on Computer Architecture*, June 1987.

[5] Scott McFarling and John Hennessey. Reducing the cost of branches. In *Proceedings, 13th Symposium on Computer Architecture*, pages 396–403, June 1986.

[6] Manolis G.H. Katevenis. *Reduced Instruction Set Computer Architectures for VLSI.* PhD thesis, University of California Berkeley, October 1983.

[7] M.J. Flynn, C.L. Mitchell, and J.M. Mulder. And now a case for more complex instruction sets. *IEEE Computer*, September 1987.

[8] *Hewlett-Packard Precision Architecture Handbook, Precision Architecture and Instruction Reference Manual.* Hewlett-Packard Company, 1987.

[9] J. Torrellay, B. Bray, K. Cuderman, S. Goldschmidt, A. Kobrin, and A. Zimmerman. *Introductory User's Guide to the Architect's Workbench Tools.* Technical Report CSL-TR-88-355, Stanford University, Stanford, California 94305, May 1988.

[10] O.E. Herrmann and B.J.F. van Beijnum. *Lecture Notes of the Nelsis-Project.* Technical University Twente, Enschede, The Netherlands, 1988.

[11] N.P. van der Meijs. *LDMC User's Manual.* Delft University of Technology, The Netherlands, March 1987.

[12] Hong Cai and Patrick Groenveld. *Delft Placement and Routing User's Manual.* Delft University of Technology, The Netherlands, September 1988.

[13] Thomas Gross. *Code Optimization of Pipeline Constraints.* PhD thesis, Stanford University, December 1983. Available as Stanford University CSL Technical Report 83–255.

[14] A. Tanenbaum, H. van Staveren, E. Keizer, and J. Stevenson. A practical tool kit for making portable compilers. *Comm. ACM*, 26(9):654–660, September 1983.

[15] Peter Nye. *U-Code An Intermediate Language for Pascal* and Fortran.* S-1 Document PAIL-8, Stanford University, May 1982.

Perfect Latin Squares and Parallel Array Access

Kichul Kim and V. K. Prasanna Kumar

Department of Electrical Engineering-Systems

University of Southern California

Los Angeles, CA 90089-0781

Abstract

A new nonlinear skewing scheme is proposed for parallel array access. We introduce a new Latin square(perfect Latin square) which has several properties useful for parallel array access. A sufficient condition for the existence of perfect Latin squares and a simple construction method for perfect Latin squares are presented. The resulting skewing scheme provides conflict free access to various subsets of an $N \times N$ array using N memory modules. When the number of memory modules is an even power of two, address generation is performed in constant time using a simple circuit. This scheme is the first memory scheme that achieves constant time access to rows, columns, diagonals, and $N^{1/2} \times N^{1/2}$ subarrays of an $N \times N$ array using the minimum number of memory modules.

1 Introduction

One of the well known but not yet well solved problems in parallel processing is how to store an $N \times N$ array into memory modules such that no memory conflict occurs when various subsets of the array(rows, columns, diagonals and subarrays) are accessed[2,12]. The importance of the problem is well understood in terms of effective memory bandwidth. High performance pipelined computers and parallel computers use multiple memory modules to overcome the effect of memory cycle time on the performance of the system. However, the effective bandwidth of the memory system depends not only on the speed and the number of memory modules but also on the memory conflict which occurs when more than one request is given to the same memory during a memory cycle. In the extreme case, if all the data needed are in the same module, the effective bandwidth is same as using only one memory module irrespective of the number of memory modules in the memory system. Hence, special attention should be given to design memory system to avoid memory conflicts.

A skewing scheme is a mapping function of array elements into memory modules to provide conflict free access to various subsets of the array. Figure 1a shows a naive skewing scheme in which elements of a 4×4 array are stored into 4 memory modules in row major order. The number below $a_{i,j}$ represents the number of the memory module in which $a_{i,j}$ is stored. It is easy to see that, if any column is to be accessed, four memory cycles are needed. On

$a_{0,0}$ 0	$a_{0,1}$ 1	$a_{0,2}$ 2	$a_{0,3}$ 3
$a_{1,0}$ 0	$a_{1,1}$ 1	$a_{1,2}$ 2	$a_{1,3}$ 3
$a_{2,0}$ 0	$a_{2,1}$ 1	$a_{2,2}$ 2	$a_{2,3}$ 3
$a_{3,0}$ 0	$a_{3,1}$ 1	$a_{3,2}$ 2	$a_{3,3}$ 3

(a)

$a_{0,0}$ 0	$a_{0,1}$ 1	$a_{0,2}$ 2	$a_{0,3}$ 3
$a_{1,0}$ 1	$a_{1,1}$ 2	$a_{1,2}$ 3	$a_{1,3}$ 0
$a_{2,0}$ 2	$a_{2,1}$ 3	$a_{2,2}$ 0	$a_{2,3}$ 1
$a_{3,0}$ 3	$a_{3,1}$ 0	$a_{3,2}$ 1	$a_{3,3}$ 2

(b)

Figure 1: Two skewing schemes.

the other hand, figure 1b shows another skewing scheme which provides conflict free access to rows and columns. A skewing scheme S is called linear if it assigns the array element $a_{i,j}$ to the memory module $pi + qj \pmod{N}$ for some fixed integers p and q[20]. If a skewing scheme S is not linear, then it is called a nonlinear skewing scheme.

The evaluation of a skewing scheme must include three factors. One is the class of subsets that can be accessed without memory conflicts. Of most importance are rows, columns, diagonals and subarrays that partition the array, since they are needed heavily in matrix computations. Another aspect is the feasibility of address generation. A skewing scheme is not considered to be good if it needs a complicated circuit and much time to generate the memory module address and the local addresses within each memory module. The other important aspect to be considered is the number of memory modules used. If N^2 memory modules are used to store an $N \times N$ array, there is a trivial skewing scheme to provide conflict free access to any subset of data. However, the utilization of the memory modules will be very low.

Many researchers have investigated the problem of efficient storage of arrays[1-3,6,10,12-14,16-21]. Budnik and Kuck[2,10] introduced linear skewing scheme and prime memory system which allows conflict free access to rows, columns, diagonals and $N^{1/2} \times N^{1/2}$ subarrays of an $N \times N$ array, in which the number of memory modules is a prime number greater than N. However, their method needs modulo operation of a prime number in address generation, which can not be performed in constant time with a reasonable amount of circuitry. Lawrie[12] generalized the linear skewing scheme and proposed an array storage scheme with a simple address generation. His scheme provides conflict free access to rows, columns, diagonals and $N^{1/2} \times N^{1/2}$ subarrays of an $N \times N$ array using $2N$ memory modules. He also introduced the omega network to perform data routing and data alignment. However, his scheme suffers from low utilization of memory modules. Only half of the memory modules are used in a memory fetch. Wijshoff and Leeuwen[19,20] developed a theory of linear skewing schemes. Lee[14] presented a non-

linear skewing scheme(scrambled storage) and a new network which allow conflict free access to rows, columns, square blocks and distributed blocks. The scrambled storage scheme does not need modulo operations for address generation. However, it can not provide efficient access to diagonals. In section 3, it will be shown that the scrambled storage scheme is a special case of ours and it can provide memory conflict free access to more subsets of interest than shown in [14]. Balakrishnan et al. showed a nonlinear skewing scheme to provide conflict free access to rows, columns and diagonals using N memory modules when N is a power of two[1]. A general construction scheme for such storage patterns can be found in [5].

To achieve conflict free access to various subsets of data, we propose to use Latin squares which are well known combinatorial objects for centuries[4]. We introduce a new Latin square(perfect Latin square) which has properties useful for parallel array access. We show a sufficient condition for the existence of perfect Latin squares and a simple construction method for perfect Latin squares. Using perfect Latin squares, many interesting subsets of an array(rows, columns, diagonals, subsquares and same positions) can be accessed without memory conflicts. Furthermore, the address generation can be performed in constant time with a simple circuit when the number of memory module is an even power of two. The efficient skewing scheme and the constant time address generation provide constant time access to many subsets of an array needed in matrix computations.

The next section includes some basic definitions. Section 3 shows a sufficient condition for the existence of perfect Latin squares and a simple construction method for perfect Latin squares. Section 4 shows how the address generation for perfect Latin square can be performed in constant time with a simple circuit. Section 5 concludes the paper.

2   Definitions

A *Latin square* of order n is an $n \times n$ square composed with symbols from 0 to $n-1$ such that no symbol appears more than once in any row or in any column[4]. The rows are numbered from 0 to $n-1$, top to bottom. The columns are also numbered from 0 to $n-1$, left to right. The squares A and B shown below are examples of Latin squares of order 4.

$$A = \begin{bmatrix} 0 & 1 & 2 & 3 \\ 1 & 2 & 3 & 0 \\ 2 & 3 & 0 & 1 \\ 3 & 0 & 1 & 2 \end{bmatrix} \qquad B = \begin{bmatrix} 0 & 1 & 2 & 3 \\ 2 & 3 & 0 & 1 \\ 3 & 2 & 1 & 0 \\ 1 & 0 & 3 & 2 \end{bmatrix}$$

A *transversal* of a Latin square of order n is a set of n cells, no two in a same row, no two in a same column and no two have a same symbol. A *diagonal Latin square* of order n is a Latin square such that no symbol appears more than once in any of it's two main diagonals. A simple construction method is known for diagonal Latin squares of order n when n is a power of two[4]. Gergely showed a general method to construct diagonal Latin squares of any order n[5]. The square B shown above is an example of a diagonal Latin square of order 4. Two Latin squares C and D of order n are *orthogonal* to each other if the set of ordered pairs $CD = \{(c_{i,j}, d_{i,j}), 0 \leq i, j \leq n-1\}$ is equal to the set of all possible ordered pairs $(i, j), 0 \leq i, j \leq n-1$. The squares C and D shown below are orthogonal to each other.

$$C = \begin{bmatrix} 0 & 1 & 2 \\ 1 & 2 & 0 \\ 2 & 0 & 1 \end{bmatrix} \qquad D = \begin{bmatrix} 0 & 1 & 2 \\ 2 & 0 & 1 \\ 1 & 2 & 0 \end{bmatrix}$$

A *self-orthogonal Latin square* is a Latin square orthogonal to its transpose. We define a *doubly self-orthogonal Latin square* as a Latin square orthogonal to its transpose and to its antitranspose. Notice that a doubly self-orthogonal Latin square is also a diagonal Latin square. The square B shown above is also an example of a doubly self-orthogonal Latin square. We define a *subsquare* $S_{i,j}$ of a Latin square of order n^2 as an $n \times n$ square whose top left cell has the coordinate (i, j). When $i \equiv 0 \bmod n$ and $j \equiv 0 \bmod n$, the subsquare $S_{i,j}$ is called a *main subsquare*. Subsquare $S_{0,1}$ of the square B is $\begin{bmatrix} 1 & 2 \\ 3 & 0 \end{bmatrix}$ and main subsquare $S_{2,0}$ of the square B is $\begin{bmatrix} 3 & 2 \\ 1 & 0 \end{bmatrix}$. We define a *perfect Latin square* of order n^2 as a diagonal Latin square of order n^2 such that

no symbol appears more than once in any main subsquare. Hence, in a perfect Latin square, no symbol appears more than once in any row, in any column, in any diagonal or in any main subsquare. The square E shown below is a perfect Latin square of order 9.

$$E = \left[\begin{array}{ccc|ccc|ccc} 0 & 3 & 6 & 1 & 4 & 7 & 2 & 5 & 8 \\ 2 & 5 & 8 & 0 & 3 & 6 & 1 & 4 & 7 \\ 1 & 4 & 7 & 2 & 5 & 8 & 0 & 3 & 6 \\ \hline 3 & 6 & 0 & 4 & 7 & 1 & 5 & 8 & 2 \\ 5 & 8 & 2 & 3 & 6 & 0 & 4 & 7 & 1 \\ 4 & 7 & 1 & 5 & 8 & 2 & 3 & 6 & 0 \\ \hline 6 & 0 & 3 & 7 & 1 & 4 & 8 & 2 & 5 \\ 8 & 2 & 5 & 6 & 0 & 3 & 7 & 1 & 4 \\ 7 & 1 & 4 & 8 & 2 & 5 & 6 & 0 & 3 \end{array}\right]$$

It is clear, from the definition, that rows, columns, diagonals and main subsquares are accessible without memory conflicts if perfect Latin squares are used as the skewing scheme.

3 Perfect Latin Squares for Array Access

In this section, we show a sufficient condition for the existence of perfect Latin squares and a simple construction method for Latin squares of order n^2 where n is odd, n is a power of two or $n = 2^l m^2$, $l \in \{2, 3, 4 \ldots\}$, m is odd. We also show that the perfect Latin squares built from our method have several properties useful for parallel array access.

A sufficient condition for the existence of a perfect Latin square is given in the following theorem.

Theorem 3.1 *If there exist two Latin squares A and B of order n such that A is orthogonal to the transpose of B and to the antitranspose of B, then there exists a perfect Latin square P of order n^2. Furthermore, P is also a doubly self-orthogonal Latin square.*

Proof: From Latin squares A and B, we construct a Latin square C of order n^2 with the following rule:

$$c_{i,j} = n \times a_{[i/n],[j/n]} + b_{i \bmod n, j \bmod n}, \quad 0 \leq i, j \leq n^2 - 1$$

where $[i/n]$ represents the largest integer not exceeding i/n and $i \bmod n$ represents the non-negative remainder of i/n. The construction of C can be viewed as follows:

1. Construct a square of order n^2 using n^2 B's. Let $B_{i,j}$ be the square B whose position is $i+1$ from top and $j+1$ from left.

2. Add $n \times a_{i,j}$ to the all members of $B_{i,j}$.

From C, we construct another Latin square P of order n^2 using the following row exchange rule:

$$p_{i,j} = c_{n \times i \bmod n + [i/n], j}$$

An example is shown for $n = 3$. Notice that A is orthogonal to the transpose of B and to the antitranspose of B.

$$A = \begin{bmatrix} 0 & 1 & 2 \\ 1 & 2 & 0 \\ 2 & 0 & 1 \end{bmatrix} \qquad B = \begin{bmatrix} 0 & 1 & 2 \\ 2 & 0 & 1 \\ 1 & 2 & 0 \end{bmatrix}$$

$$C = \left[\begin{array}{ccc|ccc|ccc} 0 & 1 & 2 & 3 & 4 & 5 & 6 & 7 & 8 \\ 2 & 0 & 1 & 5 & 3 & 4 & 8 & 6 & 7 \\ 1 & 2 & 0 & 4 & 5 & 3 & 7 & 8 & 6 \\ \hline 3 & 4 & 5 & 6 & 7 & 8 & 0 & 1 & 2 \\ 5 & 3 & 4 & 8 & 6 & 7 & 2 & 0 & 1 \\ 4 & 5 & 3 & 7 & 8 & 6 & 1 & 2 & 0 \\ \hline 6 & 7 & 8 & 0 & 1 & 2 & 3 & 4 & 5 \\ 8 & 6 & 7 & 2 & 0 & 1 & 5 & 3 & 4 \\ 7 & 8 & 6 & 1 & 2 & 0 & 4 & 5 & 3 \end{array} \right]$$

$$P = \left[\begin{array}{ccc|ccc|ccc} 0 & 1 & 2 & 3 & 4 & 5 & 6 & 7 & 8 \\ 3 & 4 & 5 & 6 & 7 & 8 & 0 & 1 & 2 \\ 6 & 7 & 8 & 0 & 1 & 2 & 3 & 4 & 5 \\ \hline 2 & 0 & 1 & 5 & 3 & 4 & 8 & 6 & 7 \\ 5 & 3 & 4 & 8 & 6 & 7 & 2 & 0 & 1 \\ 8 & 6 & 7 & 2 & 0 & 1 & 5 & 3 & 4 \\ \hline 1 & 2 & 0 & 4 & 5 & 3 & 7 & 8 & 6 \\ 4 & 5 & 3 & 7 & 8 & 6 & 1 & 2 & 0 \\ 7 & 8 & 6 & 1 & 2 & 0 & 4 & 5 & 3 \end{array} \right]$$

From the construction, it is clear that, in square P, no symbol appears more than once in any row, in any column or in any main subsquare. Suppose P is not orthogonal to its transpose. There should be i, j, k and l, $i \neq k$ or $j \neq l$, such that $p_{i,j} = p_{k,l}$ and $p_{j,i} = p_{l,k}$. From the construction, $p_{i,j}$, $0 \leq i, j \leq n^2 - 1$, can be expressed as

$$p_{i,j} = n \times a_{i \bmod n, [j/n]} + b_{[i/n], j \bmod n}$$

Since $0 \leq a_{i,j}, b_{i,j} \leq n - 1, 0 \leq i, j \leq n - 1$, from $p_{i,j} = p_{k,l}$, we have

$$a_{[i/n], j \bmod n} = a_{[k/n], l \bmod n} \text{ and } b_{i \bmod n, [j/n]} = b_{k \bmod n, [l/n]} \quad (1)$$

From $p_{j,i} = p_{l,k}$, we have

$$a_{[j/n], i \bmod n} = a_{[l/n], k \bmod n} \text{ and } b_{j \bmod n, [i/n]} = b_{l \bmod n, [k/n]} \quad (2)$$

(1) and (2) contradict the assumption that A and the transpose of B are orthogonal. Hence P is orthogonal to its transpose. The same argument can be applied to P and its antitranspose. Hence, P is a doubly self-orthogonal Latin square and no symbol appears more than once in any of its two main diagonals. $\square$

From the above theorem and the definition of a doubly self-orthogonal Latin square, we get the following corollary.

Corollary 3.1 *If there exists a doubly self-orthogonal Latin square of order n, then there exists a perfect Latin square of order n^2, which is also a doubly self-orthogonal Latin square.*

Since the resulting perfect Latin squares from theorem 3.1 and corollary 3.1 are doubly self-orthogonal Latin squares, by applying the construction method recursively, we have an infinite set of perfect Latin squares. Thus, we have the following theorem.

Theorem 3.2 *If there exist two Latin squares A and B of order n such that A is orthogonal to the transpose of B and to the antitranspose of B, or there exists a doubly self-orthogonal Latin square of order n, then there exists an infinite set $S = \{$perfect Latin square of order $n^{2^k}, k \in \{1, 2, 3, \ldots\}\}$.*

The following theorem shows the construction of perfect Latin squares of order n^2, when n is odd.

Theorem 3.3 *For all odd n, there exists a perfect Latin square of order n^2, which is also a doubly self-orthogonal Latin square.*

Proof: A cyclic Latin square C_n of odd order n is composed of n distinct transversals, one of them being a main diagonal and others being broken diagonals. We fill a transversal with a same symbol, but using distinct symbols for distinct transversals. The resulting square is a Latin square D_n orthogonal to C_n. The transpose of D_n is a symbol permutation of D_n which is also orthogonal to C_n. The antitranspose of D_n is identical to D_n, therefore, orthogonal to C_n. An example is shown below for $n = 5$. Hence, by theorem 3.1, there exists a perfect Latin square of order n^2 for all odd n. □

$$C_5 = \begin{bmatrix} 0 & 1 & 2 & 3 & 4 \\ 1 & 2 & 3 & 4 & 0 \\ 2 & 3 & 4 & 0 & 1 \\ 3 & 4 & 0 & 1 & 2 \\ 4 & 0 & 1 & 2 & 3 \end{bmatrix} \quad D_5 = \begin{bmatrix} 0 & 1 & 2 & 3 & 4 \\ 4 & 0 & 1 & 2 & 3 \\ 3 & 4 & 0 & 1 & 2 \\ 2 & 3 & 4 & 0 & 1 \\ 1 & 2 & 3 & 4 & 0 \end{bmatrix}$$

For the construction of perfect Latin squares of order n^2, where n is a power of two, we start with the following lemma.

Lemma 3.1 *If there exist two doubly self-orthogonal Latin squares A of order m and B of order n, then there exists a doubly self-orthogonal Latin square C of order mn.*

Proof: We construct C with the following rule:

$$c_{i,j} = n \times a_{[i/n],[j/n]} + b_{i\bmod n, j\bmod n}, \quad 0 \le i, j \le mn - 1$$

Notice that the construction method is same as the method for C shown in theorem 3.1. From the construction, it is clear that C is a Latin square. Suppose C is not orthogonal to its transpose. There should exist i, j, k and l, $i \ne k$ or $j \ne l$, such that $c_{i,j} = c_{k,l}$ and $c_{j,i} = c_{l,k}$. Since $0 \le a_{p,q} \le m - 1$, $0 \le p, q \le m - 1$, and $0 \le b_{r,s} \le m - 1$, $0 \le r, s \le m - 1$, from $c_{i,j} = c_{k,l}$, we have

$$a_{[i/n],[j/n]} = a_{[k/n],[l/n]} \text{ and } b_{i\bmod n, j\bmod n} = b_{k\bmod n, l\bmod n} \quad (3)$$

From $c_{j,i} = c_{l,k}$, we have

$$a_{[j/n],[i/n]} = a_{[l/n],[k/n]} \text{ and } b_{j\bmod n, i\bmod n} = b_{l\bmod n, k\bmod n} \quad (4)$$

(3) and (4) contradict the assumption that A and B are doubly self-orthogonal Latin squares. Hence, C is orthogonal to its transpose. The same argument can be applied to C and its antitranspose. Therefore, C is a doubly self-orthogonal Latin square. □

Now, we are ready for the following lemma.

Lemma 3.2 *For all $k \in \{2, 3, 4, \ldots\}$, there exists a doubly self-orthogonal Latin square D^k of order 2^k.*

Proof: We use induction on k.
Bases: For $k = 2$ and $k = 3$, the following squares are doubly self-orthogonal Latin squares of order 2^2 and 2^3. D^3 can be found in [1].

$$D^2 = \begin{bmatrix} 0 & 1 & 2 & 3 \\ 2 & 3 & 0 & 1 \\ 3 & 2 & 1 & 0 \\ 1 & 0 & 3 & 2 \end{bmatrix} \quad D^3 = \begin{bmatrix} 2 & 3 & 0 & 1 & 7 & 6 & 5 & 4 \\ 0 & 1 & 2 & 3 & 5 & 4 & 7 & 6 \\ 6 & 7 & 4 & 5 & 3 & 2 & 1 & 0 \\ 4 & 5 & 6 & 7 & 1 & 0 & 3 & 2 \\ 3 & 2 & 1 & 0 & 6 & 7 & 4 & 5 \\ 1 & 0 & 3 & 2 & 4 & 5 & 6 & 7 \\ 7 & 6 & 5 & 4 & 2 & 3 & 0 & 1 \\ 5 & 4 & 7 & 6 & 0 & 1 & 2 & 3 \end{bmatrix}$$

Hypothesis: There exists a doubly self-orthogonal Latin square D^k of order 2^k.
Induction Step: We construct a Latin square D^{k+2} of order 2^{k+2}, using D^2 and D^k whose existence is proven in the previous lemma. □

Notice that D^2 in the above lemma is also a perfect Latin square. From the above lemma and corollary 3.1, we have the following theorem.

Theorem 3.4 *For all $k \in \{1, 2, 3, \ldots\}$, there exists a perfect Latin square P^{2k} of order 2^{2k}, which is also a doubly self-orthogonal Latin square.*

Since the perfect Latin squares built from theorem 3.1 is also a doubly self-orthogonal Latin square, we have the following theorem.

Theorem 3.5 *For all $n = 2^k m^2, k \in \{2, 3, 4 \ldots\}, m$ is odd, there exists a perfect Latin square of order n^2, which is also a doubly self-orthogonal Latin square.*

As mentioned earlier, the usefulness of perfect Latin squares as a skewing scheme is obvious from the definition. Furthermore, there are more properties useful for parallel array access in the perfect Latin squares built from our construction method.

It is easy to check the following lemma applies to the

perfect Latin square A of order n^2 built from theorem 3.1.

Lemma 3.3 *No symbol appears more than once in a subsquare $S_{i,j}$ such that $i \equiv 0 \bmod n$ or $j \equiv 0 \bmod n$.*

The above lemma shows a subsquare in the horizontal or vertical strip of width n are accessible without memory conflict as well as main subsquares.

It is easy to see that there does not exist a skewing scheme to store an $N \times N$ array in N memory modules such that rows, columns, and all $N^{1/2} \times N^{1/2}$ subarrays can be accessed without memory conflict. However, we have the following lemma which assures that the maximum degree of memory conflict is two when an arbitrary subsquare is accessed.

Lemma 3.4 *No symbol appears more than two times in any subsquare $S_{i,j}$.*

The above lemma is a direct result of lemma 3.3 because every subsquare can be partitioned into two parts such that each part belongs to a subsquare on a strip of width n.

Another set of possible interest is the set of elements whose coordinates are the same within each main subsquare. Let a *same position $SP_{i,j}$* of a perfect Latin square A of order n^2 be defined as follows:

$$SP_{i,j} = \{a_{k,l} \mid k \equiv i \bmod n, l \equiv j \bmod n\}, \ \ 0 \le i, j \le n-1$$

Now, we have the following lemma which shows no memory conflict occurs when a same position is accessed.

Lemma 3.5 *No symbol appears more than once in any $SP_{i,j}$.*

It is noteworthy that Lee's skewing scheme[14] is a special case of our construction method. If we use the following squares G^2 and G^3 instead of D^2 and D^3 in lemma 3.2 respectively, the construction method in theorem 3.1 will result in Lee's skewing scheme. Notice that G^2 and G^3 are not doubly self-orthogonal Latin squares; thus the scheme in [14] can not provide conflict free access to diagonals. However, it can be shown that the scheme has the properties in lemma 3.3 and lemma 3.4.

$$G^2 = \begin{bmatrix} 0 & 1 & 2 & 3 \\ 1 & 0 & 3 & 2 \\ 2 & 3 & 0 & 1 \\ 3 & 2 & 1 & 0 \end{bmatrix} \quad G^3 = \begin{bmatrix} 0 & 1 & 2 & 3 & 4 & 5 & 6 & 7 \\ 1 & 0 & 3 & 2 & 5 & 4 & 7 & 6 \\ 2 & 3 & 0 & 1 & 6 & 7 & 4 & 5 \\ 3 & 2 & 1 & 0 & 7 & 6 & 5 & 4 \\ 4 & 5 & 6 & 7 & 0 & 1 & 2 & 3 \\ 5 & 4 & 7 & 6 & 1 & 0 & 3 & 2 \\ 6 & 7 & 4 & 5 & 2 & 3 & 0 & 1 \\ 7 & 6 & 5 & 4 & 3 & 2 & 1 & 0 \end{bmatrix}$$

One related problem is how to store an $N \times N$ array into M memory modules, when N is much larger than M. The importance of this problem is clear considering that the number of memory modules in a computer is fixed and the size of the array varies in each application.

Suppose we are storing $N \times N$ array A in 2^{2k} memory modules, where N is a multiple of 2^{2k}. We employ a simple method that the array element $a_{i,j}$ is stored in the local address $i + 2^{\lceil \log N \rceil} \times \lfloor j/2^{2k} \rfloor$ of the memory module $P^{2k}_{i \bmod 2^{2k}, j \bmod 2^{2k}}$, where $\lceil k \rceil$ represents the smallest integer not less than k. It is easy to see that row vectors and column vectors of length 2^{2k} and $2^k \times 2^k$ subarrays of array A are accessible in constant time. Diagonals of array A are accessible in $N/2^{2k}$ time which is the minimum possible. As shown in the next section, the address generation for memory modules can be performed in constant time and no logical operation is needed for the local address generation. The first $\lceil \log N \rceil - 2k$ most significant bits of j and entire bits of i are used for the local address. This method has a draw back that some address space is not used for array elements when N is not a power of two.

4 Address Generation

The previous section mainly showed the skewing scheme that guarantees conflict free access to various subsets of an array. Even if a skew function provides a conflict free assignment of memory modules, the memory system can not provide an efficient memory access unless the address generation is simple and fast. In this section, we show that the address generation for perfect Latin square P^{2k} of order

2^{2k} can be done in constant time. The importance of the case when the number of memory modules is an even power of two is clear from the viewpoint of address generation, utilization of address space and interconnection network. Notice that we are storing an $n^2 \times n^2$ array in n^2 memory modules.

From lemma 3.2, we can build a doubly self-orthogonal Latin square D^k of order 2^k from D^2 and D^3. We can express $d_{i,j}^k$ as follows,

$$d_{i,j}^k = 2^{k-2} d_{[i/2^{k-2}],[j/2^{k-2}]}^2 + d_{i \bmod 2^{k-2}, j \bmod 2^{k-2}}^{k-2}$$

Since $0 \le d_{i,j}^k \le 2^k - 1$, $0 \le i, j \le 2^k - 1$, the first two most significant bits of $d_{i,j}^k$ are determined by the first two most significant bits of i and the first two most significant bits of j. The rest bits of $d_{i,j}^k$ can be determined using the above relation recursively.

Let $d_{k-1}^k d_{k-2}^k d_{k-3}^k \ldots d_0^\kappa$ be the binary representation of $d_{i,j}^k$. Also, let $i_{k-1} i_{k-2} i_{k-3} \ldots i_0$ and $j_{k-1} j_{k-2} j_{k-3} \ldots j_0$ be the binary representations of i and j respectively. From the doubly self-orthogonal Latin squares D^2 and D^3, we get the following relations.

$$d_0^2 = i_1 \oplus j_0$$
$$d_1^2 = i_0 \oplus i_1 \oplus j_1$$
$$d_0^3 = i_2 \oplus j_0 \oplus j_2$$
$$d_1^3 = i_0 \oplus \bar{j_1}$$
$$d_2^3 = i_1 \oplus j_2$$

From the above relations, we get:
(1) when k is even, for all m, $0 \le m \le k - 1$,

$$d_m^k = \begin{cases} i_{m+1} \oplus j_m & \text{when } m \text{ is even} \\ i_{m-1} \oplus i_m \oplus j_m & \text{otherwise} \end{cases}$$

(2) when k is odd, we have

$$d_0^k = i_2 \oplus j_0 \oplus j_2$$
$$d_1^k = i_0 \oplus \bar{j_1}$$
$$d_2^k = i_1 \oplus j_2$$

and for all m, $3 \le m \le k - 1$,

$$d_m^k = \begin{cases} i_{m+1} \oplus j_m & \text{when } m \text{ is odd} \\ i_{m-1} \oplus i_m \oplus j_m & \text{otherwise} \end{cases}$$

The address of the perfect Latin square P^{2k} can be easily obtained from the address of the doubly self-orthogonal Latin square D^k. The perfect Latin square P^{2k} is obtained from D^k using the following relation:

$$p_{i,j}^{2k} = 2^k \times d_{i \bmod 2^k, [j/2^k]}^k + d_{[i/2^k], j \bmod 2^k}^k$$

From the above relation, we can see that the first k most significant bits of $p_{i,j}^{2k}$ are determined from the k least significant bits of i and the first k most significant bits of j. The first k least significant bits of $p_{i,j}^{2k}$ are determined from the first k most significant bits of i and the first k least significant bits of j. In figure 2, an example of memory module address generation is shown for the perfect Latin square P^8. The only logic element used in the circuit has four inputs and two outs, i.e., $f = d_1^2 = i_0 \oplus i_1 \oplus j_1$ and $g = d_0^2 = i_1 \oplus j_0$. Note that memory module address generation can be performed in constant time.

For the local address generation within each memory module, we adapt a simple scheme that the array element $A(i,j)$ is stored in the local address i of the memory module $P_{i,j}^{2k}$. Notice that we do not need any hardware for the local address generation.

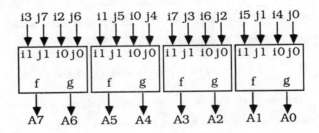

Figure 2: The address generation circuit for P^8.

5 Conclusion

An efficient memory system is proposed for parallel array access in this paper. A new Latin square(perfect Latin square) is introduced to be used as the nonlinear skewing scheme of the memory system. Using perfect Latin squares of order n^2 as the skewing scheme, many subsets of an $n^2 \times n^2$ array(rows, columns, diagonals, main subsquares, subsquares on the strip of width n, and same positions) are accessible without any memory conflict using n^2 memory modules. Furthermore, the maximum degree of memory conflict is two when an arbitrary subarray is accessed.

The address generation for memory modules is performed in constant time using a simple circuit when n is a power of two. The address generation of the local addresses within each memory module does not need any hardware.

The efficient skewing scheme along with the constant time address generation provides constant time access to many subsets of an array needed in matrix computations. This memory system is the first that achieves this goal with the minimum number of memory modules.

*Acknowledgements:*This research was supported in part by the National Science Foundation under grant IRI-8710836 and in part by AFOSR under grant AFOSR-89-0032.

References

[1] M. Balakrishnan, R. Jain and C. S. Raghavendra, "On Array Storage For Conflict-Free Memory Access For Parallel Processors," *Proc. Intl. Conf. Parallel Processing*, vol. 1, pp. 103-107, 1988.

[2] P. Budnik and D. J. Kuck, "The Organization and Use of Parallel Memories," *IEEE Trans. Comput.*, vol. C-20, pp. 1566-1569, 1971.

[3] A. Deb, "Conflict-free Access of Arrays-A counter Example," *Inf. Proc. Letters*, vol. 10, No. 1, pp. 20, 1980.

[4] J. Denes and A. D. Keedwell, *Latin Squares and Their Applications*, Academic Press, New York, 1974.

[5] E. Gergely, "A Simple Method for Constructing Doubly Diagonalized Latin Squares," *J. Combinatorial Theory*, A 16, pp. 266-272, 1974.

[6] D. T. Harper III and J. R. Jump, "Vector Access Performance in Parallel Memories Using a Skewed Storage Scheme," *IEEE Trans. Comput.*, vol. C-36, pp. 1440-1449, 1987.

[7] A. Hedayat, "A Complete Solution to the Existence and Nonexistence of Knut Vik Designs and Orthogonal Knut Vik Designs," *J. Combinatorial Theory*, A 22, pp. 331-337, 1977.

[8] F. K. Hwang, "Criscross Latin Squares," *J. Combinatorial Theory*, A 27, pp. 371-375, 1979.

[9] K. Hwang and F. A. Briggs, *Computer Architecture and Parallel Processing*, McGraw-Hill, 1984.

[10] D. J. Kuck, "ILLIAC IV Software and Application Programming," *IEEE Trans. Comput.*, vol. C-17, pp. 758-770, 1968.

[11] S. Y. Kung, *VLSI Array Processors*, Prentice Hall, 1988.

[12] D. H. Lawrie, "Access and Alignment of Data in an Array Processor," *IEEE Trans. Comput.*, vol. C-24, pp. 1145-1155, 1975.

[13] D. H. Lawrie and C. R. Vora, "The Prime Memory System for Array Access," *IEEE Trans. Comput.*, vol. C-31, pp. 435-442, 1982.

[14] D. Lee, "Scrambled Storage for Parallel Memory Systems," *Intl. Symp. Computer Architecture*, pp. 232-239, 1988.

[15] J. N. Navarro, J. M. Llaberia and M. Valero, "Partitioning: an essential step in mapping algorithms into systolic array processors," *IEEE Computer*, pp. 77-89, July 1987.

[16] J. W. Park, "An Efficient Memory System for Image Processing," *IEEE Trans. Comput.*, vol. C-35, pp. 669-674, 1986.

[17] H. D. Shapiro, "Theoretical Limitations on the Efficient Use of Parallel Memories," *IEEE Trans. Comput.*, vol. C-27, pp. 421-428, 1978.

[18] D. C. V. Voorhis and T. H. Morrin, "Memory Systems for Image Processing," *IEEE Trans. Comput.*, vol. C-27, pp. 113-125, 1978.

[19] H. A. G. Wijshoff and J. V. Leeuwen, "The Structure of Periodic Storage Schemes for Parallel Memories," *IEEE Trans. Comput.*, vol. C-34, pp. 501-505, 1985.

[20] H. A. G. Wijshoff and J. V. Leeuwen, "On Linear Skewing Schemes and $d-$Ordered Vectors," *IEEE Trans. Comput.*, vol. C-36, pp. 233-239, 1987.

[21] W. Oed and O. Lange, "On the Effective Bandwidth of Interleaved Memories in Vector Processor Systems," *IEEE Trans. Comput.*, vol. C-34, pp. 949-957, 1985.

An Aperiodic Storage Scheme to Reduce Memory Conflicts in Vector Processors

Shlomo Weiss

Department of Computer Science
University of Maryland – BC
Baltimore, MD 21228
and
Institute for Advanced Computer Studies
University of Maryland – CP
College Park, MD 20742

Abstract

One of the most noticeable differences between the CRAY-2 and its predecessors, the CRAY-1 and the CRAY X-MP, is a significantly longer memory path. This is a consequence of increasing the size of the memory at the expense of the bank access time. With a longer memory path, the impact of bank conflicts becomes more apparent. In this paper we study a storage strategy for vector processors that has the following properties: (1) it is aperiodic, (2) it tends to distribute references more uniformly over the memory banks, (3) the implementation of the addressing hardware is straightforward, and (4) the delay added to the memory path is minimal. The first two properties help in reducing the frequency of bank conflicts.

1 Introduction

Device densities have increased to the point where modern supercomputers can afford main memories as large as 256 million 64-bit words. Future generations will have, in all likelihood, even larger memories. This, however, comes at the cost of an increased disparity in speed between the CPU cycle time and the main memory cycle time. As an example, the memory path in the CRAY-2 is over 50 clock cycles, several times as long as the 11 clock cycle memory path in the CRAY-1.

While it seems obvious that a longer memory path should have a negative impact on scalar performance, recent studies [BAIL87] show that the vector performance is also reduced substantially. The major factor that affects vector performance is bank conflicts. Bank conflicts may occur when a request is made to a busy bank, or when simultaneous requests are made to the same bank in a system that supports multiple vector streams. Among the factors that have an effect on the frequency of bank conflicts one can count the following: the number of banks, the organization of the memory system, and the stride. The *stride* is the distance (in memory words) between two successive vector items. The duration of a bank conflict is determined by the bank busy time.

When the stride and the number of banks are relatively prime, then all accesses are conflict free [BUDN71]. This result was used in the BSP [KUCK82], whose memory system consists of a prime number (17) of banks. One difficulty in using a number of banks that is not a power of two is the need to do integer division in the addressing hardware [LAWR82]. Furthermore, if the stride is a multiple of the number of banks, then all the memory references are directed to the same bank and the memory bandwidth is reduced to the access time of a single bank.

In memory systems where the number of banks is a power of two, as in most present-day supercomputers, vector references with odd strides can access the memory at the maximum rate. Accesses with other strides may be penalized, depending on the bank busy time. The CRAY-1, for example, has 16 banks and the bank busy time is 4 cycles. Vector accesses with strides 2 and 4 are free of conflict, but the memory bandwidth is reduced to one half for strides that are odd multiples of 8, and to one fourth for strides that are multiples of 16. In the CRAY-2 the problem of bank conflicts is aggravated because of the longer bank access time.

1.1 Storage Strategies

So far we have assumed that the vector elements are stored consecutively in the memory banks. This method is commonly termed *interleaving* in the literature [KOGG81]. Budnik and Kuck [BUDN71] indicate that important access patterns in matrices include rows, columns, diagonals and square submatrices. Hence, in the context of scientific computing, a "good" storage strategy would allow conflict-free access to these matrix references. This problem (commonly named *skewing*) has been studied extensively [BUDN71, SHAP78, LAWR82, HOSS83, WIJS85, HARP87]. A skewing scheme maps a set of addresses to a set of banks. Essentially, a skewing scheme is a storage map for all the addresses in the address space.

A skewing scheme is shown in Fig. 2 for a memory system with eight banks. In this example, each row of addresses is right shifted by one bank relative to the row above it, The shifting is done modulo the number of banks. Fig. 1 shows a storage scheme without skewing, in which vector elements are

Bank Number

0	1	2	3	4	5	6	7
0	1	2	3	4	5	6	7
8	9	10	11	12	13	*14*	15
16	17	18	19	20	*21*	22	23
24	25	26	27	*28*	29	30	31
32	33	34	*35*	36	37	38	39
40	41	*42*	43	44	45	46	47
48	*49*	50	51	52	53	54	55
56	57	58	59	60	61	62	63

Fig. 1. Simple storage scheme.

Bank Number

0	1	2	3	4	5	6	7
0	1	2	3	4	5	6	7
15	**8**	9	10	11	12	13	*14*
22	23	**16**	17	18	19	20	*21*
29	30	31	**24**	25	26	27	*28*
36	37	38	39	**32**	33	34	*35*
43	44	45	46	47	**40**	41	*42*
50	51	52	53	54	55	**48**	*49*
57	58	59	60	61	62	63	**56**

Fig. 2. Skewed storage scheme.

stored consecutively in banks. In this simple storage scheme, vectors with stride 8 are always stored in the same bank. Referring to Fig. 2, we see that vectors with stride 8 are distributed uniformly over the banks. But now some other strides become problematic. For example, if bank number 7 is the one accessed first, then the next seven accesses with stride 7 request again the same bank.

This impediment is inherent in linear skewing schemes. In [SHAP78], Shapiro studies two categories of skewing schemes that he considers of practical interest: *periodic* skewing and *linear* skewing. A linear skewing scheme is also periodic. In a periodic skewing scheme vector accesses with strides that are multiples of the period will access only one bank.

Most of the research in linear skewing schemes has been done for parallel array SIMD processors (e.g. the BSP). In such an architecture, banks are accessed in parallel and maximum throughput is possible if the access is conflict free. Most of the papers in this area [BUDN71, SHAP78, LAWR82, HOSS83, WIJS85] deal with conflict-free access as a function of the number of banks and the stride.

In a pipelined vector processor, such as the CRAY-1, the access to memory is done one bank at a time, in a pipelined fashion. In a recent work [HARP87], Harper and Jump demonstrate that in a pipelined vector processor maximum throughput may be obtained even if access is not conflict free. They propose a memory architecture in which buffers tend to smooth out temporary nonuniformity of requests across the memory banks. In their skewing scheme, the memory module number is determined by the expression

$$\left(A + \left\lfloor \frac{A}{m} \right\rfloor \right) \bmod m$$

where A is the address and m is the number of banks.

Skewing storage can be also implemented by logical manipulation of address bits. An early reference to the idea of implementing skewing storage using exclusive-or logic is [BATC77] (also called *scrambled* storage). More recently, Frailong et al. [FRAI85] propose using bitwise XOR operations to implement linear skewing schemes, and demonstrate that parallel access may be obtained simultaneously to various structures of interest.

In a recent paper [LEE88], Lee proposes a scrambled storage scheme that allows conflict-free access to rows, columns, square blocks and distributed blocks. The addressing hardware in this scheme can be implemented with only n exclusive-or gates for a parallel memory system with 2^n modules. In his paper, Lee studies some of the important properties of the suggested scramble/unscramble scheme.

The permutation-based interleaving (PBI) scheme proposed by Sohi [SOHI88] can be implemented with a small amount of additional hardware, using exclusive-or logic, and the overhead added to the memory access time is minimal. In this scheme, all the address bits may potentially be used to compute the bank number. Sohi performed a simulation study of an example permutation-based interleaving system and compared it with conventional interleaving and with a skewing scheme similar to the one in [HARP87]. He reports that the PBI scheme leads to higher memory throughput.

1.2 Paper Overview

In this paper we develop a storage scheme that is aperiodic. As the discussion in section 2.2 indicates, the addressing hardware has little effect on the length of the memory path and its implementation is straightforward. We begin in the next section with an example. The rest of the section contains analytical results that highlight the main properties of the proposed storage technique. Section 3 begins with a performance comparison to a commonly used storage scheme in vector processors, and contains a study of the sensitivity of memory efficiency to queue lengths and to the bank busy time.

2 Storage Scheme Overview and Analysis

Fig. 3 shows an example of the proposed storage technique. In this figure, the assignment of addresses to banks appears to be less regular than in figures 1 and 2. It is this lack of regularity that tends to distribute references more evenly over the memory banks. In the rest of this section we analyze this storage strategy.

We assume an m-way interleaved memory system with $m = 2^M$ banks. Given a word with an address A, a simple way to store this word in memory is by placing it in the bank whose address is $A \bmod m$. Now consider a storage scheme in which some of the M least significant bits of A are modified by performing certain bitwise exclusive-or operations. This is done by a function f that is defined more precisely below. The address of the bank is determined by $f(A) \bmod m$. That is, a word with address A is placed in the bank $f(A) \bmod m$, which may be different than $A \bmod m$.

Bank Number

0	1	2	3	4	5	6	7
0	5	3	6	4	1	7	2
13	**8**	*14*	11	9	12	10	15
23	18	20	17	19	22	**16**	*21*
26	31	25	*28*	30	27	29	**24**
35	38	**32**	37	39	34	36	33
46	43	45	**40**	*42*	47	41	44
52	*49*	55	50	**48**	53	51	54
57	60	58	63	61	**56**	62	59

Fig. 3. An example of the proposed storage scheme.

We initially look at some simple functions that only change exactly one bit in A. These simple functions are our building blocks for more complex mappings, in which potentially all the M bits that determine the bank address could be altered. What follows is a more detailed and somewhat more formal description of this idea.

The address space $\mathcal{N} = \{0 \ldots 2^N - 1\}$ is the set of all N-bit integers, and an address $A \in \mathcal{N}$ in its binary representation is a vector of N bits $A[N-1]\, A[N-2] \ldots A[0]$. The notation $A[i]$ refers to bit i of A.

Definition 1: For all $A \in \mathcal{N}$, a function $f : \mathcal{N} \longrightarrow \mathcal{N}$ is defined as follows:

$$f_{(i,i_0,i_1,\ldots i_n)}(A) = A[N-1]\, A[N-2] \ldots A'[i] \ldots A[0]$$

where

$$i \in \{0 \ldots M-1\}$$
$$\{i_0, i_1, \ldots i_n\} \subseteq \{0 \ldots N-1\}$$
$$i_0 \neq i_1 \neq \ldots \neq i_n$$
$$A'[i] = A[i_0] \oplus A[i_1] \oplus \ldots \oplus A[i_n]$$

The symbol $\oplus$ denotes exclusive or. We shall occasionally use the shorter notation $f_i(A)$ instead of $f_{(i,i_0,i_1,\ldots i_n)}(A)$. $f_i(A)$ may be different than A in only one bit: bit i. This bit is one of the least significant M bits that determine the bank number, so $f_i(A)$ can be in a different bank than A. Bit i of $f_i(A)$ is determined by the exclusive-or of some subset of bits from A.

At this point, a rather important constraint on our mapping scheme should be considered. To be useful, this mapping must be one-to-one; otherwise, two different addresses generated by the processor will map to the same memory cell.

Definition 2: A function f is *one-to-one* if for any two addresses $A \in \mathcal{N}$ and $B \in \mathcal{N}$ if $A \neq B$ then $f(A) \neq f(B)$.

The following theorem states a sufficient and necessary condition for a function f to perform a one-to-one mapping.

Theorem 1: A function $f_{(i,i_0,i_1,\ldots i_n)} : \mathcal{N} \longrightarrow \mathcal{N}$ is one-to-one if and only if $i \in \{i_0, i_1, \ldots i_n\}$.

Proof: We first assume that $i \in \{i_0, i_1, \ldots i_n\}$. A function f_i only affects bit i of an address, so if two addresses A and B are different in some bits other than i, then we also get $f_i(A) \neq f_i(B)$.

Let's now assume that A and B are identical in all their bits other than bit i, so we have $A[i] \neq B[i]$.

By definition 1 we have

$$f_i(A)[i] = A[i_0] \oplus A[i_1] \oplus \ldots \oplus A[i_n] \tag{1}$$

$$f_i(B)[i] = B[i_0] \oplus B[i_1] \oplus \ldots \oplus B[i_n] \tag{2}$$

Using the assumption that $i \in \{i_0, i_1, \ldots i_n\}$ we have

$$f_i(A)[i] = A[i_0] \oplus A[i_1] \oplus \ldots \oplus A[i] \oplus \ldots \oplus A[i_n] \tag{3}$$

$$f_i(B)[i] = B[i_0] \oplus B[i_1] \oplus \ldots \oplus B[i] \oplus \ldots \oplus B[i_n] \tag{4}$$

But the exclusive-or expressions in (3) and (4) are different in exactly one bit: bit i. Hence we have $f_i(A)[i] \neq f_i(B)[i]$ and therefore $f_i(A) \neq f_i(B)$. This shows that $i \in \{i_0, i_1, \ldots i_n\}$ is a sufficient condition to get a one-to-one mapping.

To demonstrate that it is also a necessary condition, we observe that if $i \notin \{i_0, i_1, \ldots i_n\}$ then any two addresses that are only different in bit i will map to the same address. $\square$

We now consider the composition of two functions. For all $A \in \mathcal{N}$, the *composition* of two functions f_i and f_j is defined by

$$f_i \circ f_j = f_{(i,i_0,i_1,\ldots i_n)}(f_{(j,j_0,j_1,\ldots j_p)}(A)) \tag{5}$$

Theorem 2: If $j \notin \{i_0, i_1, \ldots i_n\}$, $i \notin \{j_0, j_1, \ldots j_p\}$, and $i \neq j$ then $f_i \circ f_j = f_j \circ f_i$.

Proof: We shall use $f_i(A)$ for $f_{(i,i_0,i_1,\ldots i_n)}(A)$ and $f_j(A)$ for $f_{(j,j_0,j_1,\ldots j_p)}(A)$. From definition 1:

$$f_i(f_j(A))[k] = \begin{cases} f_j(A)[k] & \text{for } k \neq i \\ f_j(A)[i_0] \oplus f_j(A)[i_1] \oplus \ldots \oplus f_j(A)[i_n] & \text{for } k = i \end{cases}$$

If $j \notin \{i_0, i_1, \ldots i_n\}$ then:

$$f_i(f_j(A))[k] = \begin{cases} f_j(A)[k] & \text{for } k \neq i \\ A[i_0] \oplus A[i_1] \oplus \ldots \oplus A[i_n] & \text{for } k = i \end{cases} \tag{6}$$

But

$$f_j(A)[k] = \begin{cases} A[k] & \text{for } k \neq j \\ A[j_0] \oplus A[j_1] \oplus \ldots \oplus A[j_p] & \text{for } k = j \end{cases} \tag{7}$$

Substituting $f_j(A)[k]$ in (6) with the expression in (7):

$$f_i(f_j(A))[k] = \begin{cases} A[k] & \text{for } k \neq i \text{ and } k \neq j \\ A[i_0] \oplus A[i_1] \oplus \ldots \oplus A[i_n] & \text{for } k = i \\ A[j_0] \oplus A[j_1] \oplus \ldots \oplus A[j_p] & \text{for } k = j \end{cases} \tag{8}$$

If $i \notin \{j_0, j_1, \ldots j_p\}$ then we get the same expression for $f_j(f_i(A))$. $\square$

We now consider the composition of M functions. In the rest of this paper we shall assume that $M|N$ and define $Q = N/M$. Our results can be easily extended to the case that $N \bmod M \neq 0$.

Definition 3: For all $A \in \mathcal{N}$, a function $F : \mathcal{N} \longrightarrow \mathcal{N}$ is a composition of M functions

$$F(A) = f_{(M-1,m_0,m_1,\dots m_{Q-1})} \cdots (f_{(1,j_0,j_1,\dots j_{Q-1})}(f_{(0,i_0,i_1,\dots i_{Q-1})}(A)))$$

with the following properties:

$$i_0 = 0, j_0 = 1, \dots m_0 = M - 1$$
$$\{i_1, j_1, \dots m_1\} = \{M, M+1, \dots 2M-1\}$$
$$\{i_2, j_2, \dots m_2\} = \{2M, 2M+1, \dots 3M-1\}$$
$$\vdots$$
$$\{i_{Q-1}, j_{Q-1}, \dots m_{Q-1}\} = \{(Q-1)M, (Q-1)M+1, \dots QM-1\}$$

This definition implies that the set

$$\mathcal{S} = \{\{i_0, i_1, \dots i_{Q-1}\}, \{j_0, j_1, \dots j_{Q-1}\}, \dots \{m_0, m_1, \dots m_{Q-1}\}\} \tag{9}$$

is a partition of the set $\{0 \dots N\text{-}1\}$. Following theorem 1, each one of the functions $f_0, f_1 \dots f_{M-1}$ is one-to-one, and therefore $F : \mathcal{N} \longrightarrow \mathcal{N}$ is also one-to-one. Following theorem 2, the composition order of the M functions is not important.

We shall consider now the issue of periodicity. When dealing with a finite address space, as we do in this section, we find ourselves in the awkward position that the period P can be as large as the largest address in the address space. Intuitively, the concept of periodicity is meaningless for periods of this size, since multiples of P (other than 0 and 1 multiples) will exceed the address space. This problem can be avoided by making the address space infinite. Instead, we shall limit the period P such that $P < 2^{N-M}$. This choice is necessary to formulate a rigorous proof for the next theorem. If the address space is infinite, the same proof carries over without any limitations on P. Notice that in typical implementations, N is significantly larger than M (for example, on the CRAY-2 N and M would be 32 and 7 respectively). Periods larger than 2^{N-M} are of little practical interest, since strides of this size are rather unusual.

Definition 4: A function $f : \mathcal{N} \longrightarrow \mathcal{N}$ is periodic with a period $P \in \{1 \dots 2^{N-M} - 1\}$ if for all $A \in \{0 \dots 2^N - P - 1\}$ we have $f(A+P) \equiv f(A) \pmod{m}$.

Theorem 3: $F : \mathcal{N} \longrightarrow \mathcal{N}$ is aperiodic.

Proof: Assume to the contrary that F has period P and let p_r be the most significant bit of P. Since $p_r \in \{0 \dots N-1\}$, and the set $\mathcal{S}$ as defined in (9) is a partition of the set $\{0 \dots N-1\}$, we must have $p_r \in \mathcal{S}$. Let $\mathcal{J} = \{j_0, j_1, \dots j_{Q-1}\}$ be one of the sets in $\mathcal{S}$, and without loss of generality, we assume that $p_r \in \mathcal{J}$.

We can partition $\mathcal{J}$ into two sets $\mathcal{J}_1 = \{j_0, j_1, \dots j_{s-1}\}$ and $\mathcal{J}_2 = \{j_s, j_{s+1} \dots j_{Q-1}\}$ such that $j_{s-1} = p_r$ and $j_s > p_r$. Since $P < 2^{N-M}$ we have $p_r < N - M$. Substituting $N = MQ$ we

get $p_r < (Q-1)M$. From definition 3 $j_{Q-1} \in \{(Q-1)M, (Q-1)M+1, \dots QM-1\}$ hence $j_{Q-1} \geq (Q-1)M$. It follows that $j_{Q-1} > p_r$, and therefore the set $\mathcal{J}_2$ must contain at least one element: j_{Q-1}. Hence

$$\mathcal{J}_2 \neq \emptyset \tag{10}$$

We shall use the following notation. Given some $X \in \mathcal{N}$ in its binary representation, then

$$\mathcal{X}^1 = \{X[i] \mid X[i] = 1\}$$
$$\mathcal{X}^1_J = \{X[i] \mid X[i] = 1 \text{ and } i \in \mathcal{J}\}$$

The rest of this proof consists of two parts.

Part A: Assume

$$|\mathcal{P}^1_J| \bmod 2 = 1 \tag{11}$$

Let $A = 2^{j_s}$. We can always assign such a value to A since in (10) we have shown that $\mathcal{J}_2 \neq \emptyset$. Then $\mathcal{A}^1_J = \{j_s\}$ and

$$|\mathcal{A}^1_J| = 1 \tag{12}$$

From definitions 3 and 1:

$$F(A)[j] = |\mathcal{A}^1_J| \bmod 2 = 1 \tag{13}$$

We have chosen A such that $\mathcal{A}^1 \cap \mathcal{P}^1 = \emptyset$. It follows that $\mathcal{A}^1_J \cap \mathcal{P}^1_J = \emptyset$ and that

$$F(A+P)[j] = (|\mathcal{A}^1_J| + |\mathcal{P}^1_J|) \bmod 2 \tag{14}$$

From (11), (12), and (14) we have:

$$F(A+P)[j] = 0 \tag{15}$$

Comparing (13) with (15) we see that $F(A)[j] \neq F(A+P)[j]$ and therefore $F(A) \neq F(A+P)$.

Part B: Now assume

$$|\mathcal{P}^1_J| \bmod 2 = 0 \tag{16}$$

Let $A = 2^{j_s} - 2^{p_r}$. Then $\mathcal{A}^1_J = \{p_r\}$ and

$$|\mathcal{A}^1_J| = 1 \tag{17}$$

From definitions 3 and 1:

$$F(A)[j] = |\mathcal{A}^1_J| \bmod 2 = 1 \tag{18}$$

Substituting the value chosen for A we have

$$A + P = 2^{j_s} - 2^{p_r} + P = R + 2^{j_s}$$

where $R = P - 2^{p_r}$. From here

$$F(A+P)[j] = (|\mathcal{R}^1_J| + 1) \bmod 2$$

But $|\mathcal{R}^1_J| = |\mathcal{P}^1_J| - 1$ and therefore

$$F(A+P)[j] = |\mathcal{P}^1_J| \bmod 2 \tag{19}$$

From this and (16) we have

$$F(A+P)[j] = 0 \tag{20}$$

Comparing (18) with (20) we see that $F(A)[j] \neq F(A+P)[j]$ and therefore $F(A) \neq F(A+P)$. $\qquad\square$

2.1 Example

In Fig. 3, the assignment of addresses to banks was done by the function

$$\text{bank number} = f_{(2,4,3,2,0)}(f_{(1,5,4,1)}(f_{(0,3,1,0)}(A))) \bmod 8$$

and the address A was varied from 0 to 63. For the 8 banks in this example, three functions are needed, one function for each one of the three least significant bits of the address. These are the bits that determine the bank address.

Since in this example we were interested in the address range 0 to 63, we have only used the rightmost 6 bits of the address as indices in the above functions. The pattern shown in Fig. 3 will repeat itself for addresses larger than 63. As shown in the previous section, this mapping scheme can be made aperiodic for an arbitrarily large address space.

2.2 Addressing Hardware

To make the analysis in section 2 feasible, we defined the mapping scheme to be a sequence of several functions, each function being applied to one of the M least significant bits in the address. Once the mapping scheme has been determined, we can easily derive, for each one of the M bits, a boolean expression that depends directly on the address bits. This boolean expression is simply the exclusive-or of some subset of the N address bits. In this section we consider the effect of the addressing hardware on the memory path length.

If the technology available is 2-input logic gates, then the implementation of the above exclusive-or expression will take at most $\lceil \log_2 N \rceil$ levels of 2-input exclusive-or gates. This is a worst case scenario, since typically only a subset of the N bits will be used. It takes 3 levels of conventional logic gates to implement a 2-input exclusive-or gate (including inverters), so the addressing hardware needs at most $3\lceil \log_2 N \rceil$ logic levels.

As an example, we assume an implementation with pipelining to the same degree as the CRAY-1. If N is 32 bits, then the addressing hardware will consists of at most 15 logic levels. In the CRAY-1 there are 8 logic levels in each stage in the pipeline, which means that the addressing hardware will add at most two stages to the memory "pipeline". Therefore, the memory path may become two cycles longer – a minimal delay compared to the memory path length in a modern supercomputer as the CRAY-2.

3 Performance Study

The performance measure that we are interested in is the memory system efficiency, which we define as the number of memory access cycles divided by the total number of cycles. The total number of cycles includes wait cycles introduced by bank conflicts. The memory efficiency depends on the stride, and, for the examples shown, we consider strides in the range 1 to 16. These figures are reduced to one number, the *aggregate* memory efficiency, which is the ratio of access cycles (for all the strides considered) to the total number of cycles. The aggregate performance is a more accurate measure than the arithmetic mean [SMIT88].

Stride	Memory Efficiency (percent)			
	Storage as in Fig. 1		$F_0(A) \bmod 8$	
	no queue	queue = 4	no queue	queue = 4
1	100.00	100.00	71.91	100.00
2	51.61	51.61	68.09	100.00
3	100.00	100.00	35.36	74.42
4	25.60	25.60	65.31	100.00
5	100.00	100.00	33.33	68.82
6	51.61	51.61	35.56	62.75
7	100.00	100.00	46.72	68.82
8	12.67	12.67	79.01	100.00
9	100.00	100.00	41.29	73.56
10	51.61	51.61	32.65	73.56
11	100.00	100.00	28.32	50.00
12	25.60	25.60	43.24	72.73
13	100.00	100.00	26.34	47.76
14	51.61	51.61	47.76	80.00
15	100.00	100.00	41.56	77.11
16	12.67	12.67	66.67	100.00
Aggregate	40.67	40.67	42.60	74.10

Table 1. Memory efficiency for two storage schemes.

In this section the storage scheme used is given by the function

$$F_0(A) = f_{(2,11,9,8,7,6,4,3,2,0)}(f_{(1,10,9,7,5,4,1)}(f_{(0,9,8,7,6,3,1,0)}(A)))$$

and the bank number is $F_0(A) \bmod 8$. This particular function was chosen experimentally. We assume an interleaved memory system with 8 banks and, except were pointed out otherwise, the bank busy time is 8 cycles. The vector length is 64, as in the CRAY computers.

Recent proposals of high performance memories [HARP87, JEGO86] suggest increasing the throughput by including buffers in the memory system. For the purpose of the study in this section, we assume a similar memory system in which there is a queue associated with each bank. If the number of banks is large, the memory may be partitioned into sections, and queues attached to each section rather than to each bank. The CRAY-2 [CRAY85] is an example of such an implementation. In a buffered memory system, a mechanism is needed to ensure that requests return in the same order as submitted. We shall not consider this problem further, as it has been already addressed elsewhere [HARP87, JEGO86].

Table 1 compares the memory efficiency for the common storage strategy illustrated in Fig. 1 and the storage scheme given by $F_0(A) \bmod 8$. In the rest of this section we shall refer to these two storage schemes as C-storage and F_0-storage respectively. Consider the C-storage scheme. Any odd vector stride and the number of banks are relatively prime, and therefore vector accesses with odd strides are guaranteed to be conflict free. The performance of even strides is lower, the worst case being strides that are multiples of 8. When the stride is even, but not a multiple of four, the memory efficiency is somewhat higher than 50%. This reflects the transient situation for the first four accesses, which are conflict free since the banks are not busy. The presence of a queue makes no difference for this storage scheme.

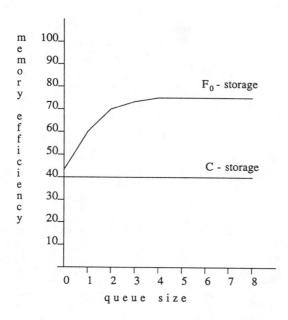

Fig. 4. Memory efficiency versus queue length.

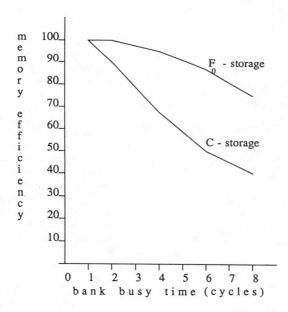

Fig. 5. Memory efficiency versus bank busy time.

The figures for the F_0-storage scheme in Table 1 indicate that the memory efficiency varies less than in the C-storage scheme. The more uniform distribution of references over the banks leads to higher aggregate memory efficiency, when the queue length is four. As indicated in fig. 4, longer queues do not increase the performance.

Referring again to Table 1 (F_0-storage), we see that with a queue length of 4, strides that are a power of 2 access the memory at the maximum rate. The need for a buffer is apparent from fig. 3. If we begin a vector stream with stride 2 from bank 0, for example, then the first 8 references access all the 8 banks. The next sequence of 8 references, however, does not begin from bank 0, but from bank 6. For stride 2, the average frequency of access is the same for all the banks, and with a queue of size 4 the memory efficiency rises to 100%.

4 Conclusions

In this paper we have studied an aperiodic storage scheme that can be implemented efficiently. Assuming a 32 bit address space and pipelining to the same degree as in the CRAY-1, the addressing hardware adds at most two cycles to the memory path. A comparison with the simple storage strategy used in most vector processors demonstrates a significant increase in the efficiency of the parallel memory system. This increase is mainly attributed to a more even distribution of references over the memory banks. The difference between the two storage strategies is more apparent when the bank busy time is longer. The simulations also show that the higher performance of the proposed storage scheme depends on the presence of queues in the memory system. For the parameters studied, no performance improvement has been observed for queues longer than 4 stages.

5 Acknowledgement

The author wishes to thank Leonid Stern for helpful discussions on this topic.

References

[BAIL87] D. H. Bailey, "Vector computer memory bank contention", *IEEE Transactions on Computers*, vol. C-36, no. 3, March 1987.

[BATC77] D. E. Batcher, "The Multidimensional Access Memory in STARAN", *IEEE Transactions on Computers*, vol. C-26, no. 2, Feb. 1977.

[BUDN71] P. Budnik and D. J. Kuck, "The organization and use of parallel memories", *IEEE Transactions on Computers*, vol. C-20, Dec. 1971.

[CRAY85] Cray Research Inc. "CRAY-2 Computer System Functional Description", HR-2000, Nov. 1985.

[FRAI85] J. M. Frailong, W. Jalby, and J. Lenfant, "XOR-Schemes: A Flexible Data Organization in Parallel Memories", *Proceedings 1985 International Conference on Parallel Memories*, Aug. 1985.

[HARP87] D. T. Harper and J. R. Jump, "Vector access performance in parallel memories using a skewed storage scheme", *IEEE Transactions on Computers*, vol. C-36, no. 12, Dec. 1987.

[HOSS83] F. Hossfeld and P. Weidner, "Parallele Algorithmen", *Inf. Spektr.*, vol. 6, pp. 142-154, 1983.

[JEGO86] Y. Jégou and A. Seznec, "Data Synchronized Pipeline Architecture: Pipelining in Multiprocessor Environments", *Journal of Parallel and Distributed Computing*, 3, pp. 527-552, 1986.

[KOGG81] P. M. Kogge, "The Architecture of Pipeline Computers", Hemisphere Publishing Corp., New York, 1981.

[KUCK82] D. J. Kuck and R. A. Stokes, "The Burroughs Scientific Processor (BSP)", *IEEE Transactions on Computers*, vol. C-31, no. 5, May 1982.

[LAWR82] D. H. Lawrie and C. R. Vora, "The prime memory system for array storage", *IEEE Transactions on Computers*, vol. C-31, no. 5, May 1982.

[LEE88]   D. Lee, "Scrambled Storage for Parallel Memory Systems", *The 15th Annual International Symposium on Computer Architecture"*, May 1988.

[SHAP78] H. D. Shapiro, "Theoretical limitations on the efficient use of parallel memories", *IEEE Transactions on Computers*, vol. C-27, no. 5, May 1978.

[SMIT88] J. E. Smith, "Characterizing computer performance with a single number", *Communications of the ACM*, vol. 31, no. 10, Oct. 1988.

[SOHI88] G. S. Sohi, "High-Bandwidth Interleaved Memories for Vector Processors - a Simulation Study", Tech. Report 790, Computer Sciences Dept., University of Wisconsin-Madison, Sept. 1988.

[WIJS85] H. A. G. Wijshoff and J. van Leeuwen, "The structure of periodic storage schemes for parallel memories", *IEEE Transactions on Computers*, vol. C-34, no. 6, June 1985.

ANALYSIS OF VECTOR ACCESS PERFORMANCE ON SKEWED INTERLEAVED MEMORY

Chuen–Liang Chen

Department of Computer Science
and Information Engineering
National Taiwan University
Taipei, Taiwan, R.O.C.

Chung–Kai Liao

Institute of Electrical Engineering
National Taiwan University
Taipei, Taiwan, R.O.C.

Abstract

Memory interleaving and memory skewing are two hardware approaches to reduce memory access conflict for many advanced computer architectures, while pipelined vector computer covers many commercially available supercomputers. The goal of this paper is to study the vector accessing behavior on skewed interleaved memory under pipelined processing environment.

We establish a criterion, called average time delay, to indicate the performance of a vector access; and a criterion, called aggregate average time delay to indicate the performance of a given memory system. Under these criteria, we analyze some memory design problems. These problems centralize how to design a memory system which is cost–effective and has less conflicts for vector accesses.

We also propose a software approach to reduce memory access conflict, called dimension extension strategy. This strategy performs very well under our analysis.

§1 Introduction

Due to the high–speed computational requirement for many practical calculations, many computer scientists have paid their attention upon the design and manufacture of advanced computer architectures. Of course, a powerful CPU is the kernel of a successful architecture. However, it is not the whole. Usually, a proper memory system is another major consideration. For the design of advanced computer architecture, memory interleaving [1] and memory skewing [2] are two widely–used techniques to enhance memory bandwidth. On the other hand, among the proposed advanced computer architectures, pipelined vector computer [3] is a major approach. Many commercially available supercomputers can be classified into it. The goal of this paper is to analyze the performance of skewed interleaved memory for pipelined vector computers.

This work is supported in part by the National Science Council of Republic of China, under contract number NSC77–0408–E002–07.

Pipelined computer is a machine which utilizes the pipeline technique and is very attractive for vector processing. So, almost all of today's pipelined computers support many vector instructions. But, usually the allowable vector operations must satisfy the *vector operand identification constraint*. The vector operand identification is used to specify the addresses sequence of a vector operand. It is very impractical and impossible to explicitly write down the whole addresses sequence on an instruction. In order to avoid the explicit specification, almost all of today's pipelined computers adopt the following three parameters to simplify the specifications: 1) the initial address of the sequence, 2) the constant increment (or named *stride*) between two consecutive elements on the sequence and 3) the length of the sequence. In this paper, we discuss how to fetch such a vector operand from the memory.

In a parallel processing environment, main memory is normally shared by all processors or independent units of a pipelined processor. In order to avoid that two or more processors simultaneously attempt to access the memory system and then result in memory interference, usually the main memory is partitioned into several independent memory modules and the addresses are distributed across these modules. This scheme is called *memory interleaving* [1]. The interleaving of addresses among N modules is called *N–way interleaved*. For an N–way interleaved memory system, address A is located at module *A mod N*.

Many researchers had studied the behavior of interleaved memory [4–11]. Most of them [4–8] were under the SIMD or MIMD environment and considered that more than one processors access the memory simultaneously. Under this situation, the accessed addresses sequence is random in some sense. This is different from our discussions. Lawrie and Vora [9] discussed the memory design of BSP system. BSP is also an SIMD machine. It has 16 processing elements and 17 memory modules. The selection of 16 and 17 is due to that 16 and 17 are relatively prime. This is a major result of [9]. The other two articles [10–11] discussed multiple vector accesses for pipelined vector computers. This point is more general than ours. However, they did not consider the case of memory skewing and they only consider how to make a specific system (Cray X–MP) have less memory access conflict. These two points are less general than ours.

Memory skewing scheme [2] is to skew the address distribution. Table 1 is an illustration of 2–way skewed 5–way interleaved memory system. The first round of address distribution (0 to 4) starts from module 0; the second round of address distribution (5 to 9) starts from module 2 because "2" is skewed from "0" with 2 steps; the third round of address distribution (10 to 14) starts from module 4 because "4" is skewed from "2" with 2 steps; and so on. In general, for a K–way skewed N–way interleaved memory system, address A is located at module $A+K\left\lfloor\dfrac{A}{N}\right\rfloor \bmod N$.

M_0	M_1	M_2	M_3	M_4
0	1	2	3	4
8	9	5	6	7
11	12	13	14	10
⋮				

Table 1: Illustration of memory skewing

There were some articles which discussed the performance of memory skewing [12–13]. The model adopted by Harper and Jump [13] is very similar with ours. But, they just considered 1–way skewed scheme. Their result is that 1–way skewed scheme is better than non–skewed scheme.

The organization of this paper is described as follows. In Section 2, we propose a model to describe the operations of skewed interleaved memory system. We also give a criterion, called average time delay, to indicate the performance for a vector access on a skewed interleaved memory. Then, we develop a method to evaluate this criterion in Section 3. In Section 4, we give another criterion, called aggregate average time delay, to indicate the performance for all vector accesses on a skewed interleaved memory. Then, in Sections 5 to 7, we answer some interesting problems about how to design a good memory system. We have some surprising results. Finally, Section 8 is a conclusion.

§2 The Memory Model

The proposed memory model is shown in Figure 1. When a pipelined processor issues a vector instruction, it uses Initial address (I), Stride (S) and Length (L) to specify the vector operand. This request is sent to the *address generator* which will generate a stream of addresses to be referenced. This stream is sent to the *address dispatcher* in a pipeline manner. Then, the address dispatcher depends on the configuration of the memory system, i.e., K–way skewed and N–way interleaved, to dispatch the addresses to the proper memory modules. Then, the memory accesses can be performed. The address dispatcher hardware can be constructed by a similar method as shown in [13]. Furthermore, we assume that the ratio of the memory access time to the pipeline clock time is T. For the sake of simplicity, we shall treat pipeline clock time as unit time, and call T as *memory cycle time*. If there is a conflict in a module, all of the remaining accesses will be hold until the conflicted module is released from the previous access.

DEFINITION 1: For a given vector operand specification with initial address I and stride S, the *address sequence*, denoted as Aseq(S,I), is the sequence produced by the address generator; i.e., I, I+S, I+2S, ⋯ . □

In the remaining discussions, we only concern the convergent properties, i.e., we imagine that we have an infinite length vector operand, hence we get rid of the operand length L from our definition.

For the sake of convenience, we enumerate Aseq(S,I) from 0. That is, we shall treat I as the 0–th element, I+S as the first element, and so on. It is also true for other sequences defined below.

DEFINITION 2: For a given Aseq(S,I) on a K–way skewed N–way interleaved memory, the *module sequence*, denoted as Mseq(N,K,S,I), is the sequence of module

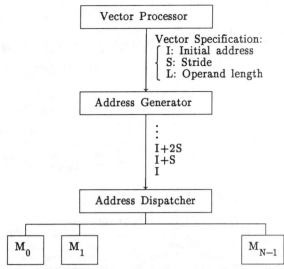

Figure 1: The Memory Model

numbers to which address dispatcher distributes the Aseq(S,I). Furthermore, let Mseq(N,K,S,I;j) denote the j–th element of Mseq(N,K,S,I) for $j\geq 0$. □

According to the properties of memory skewing and memory interleaving we can derive that
$$Mseq(N,K,S,I;j) = (I+jS+K\left\lfloor\dfrac{I+jS}{N}\right\rfloor) \bmod N.$$

DEFINITION 3: For a given Mseq(N,K,S,I) and a given memory cycle time T, the *delay sequence*, denoted as Dseq(T,N,K,S,I), is the sequence of time delays which are added before each memory access in order to resolve the conflict with a previous memory access. Furthermore, let Dseq(T,N,K,S,I;j) denote the j–th element of Dseq(T,N,K,S,I) for $j\geq 0$. □

In general, Dseq(T,N,K,S,I;j) is not easy to be determined; it depends on the previous memory accesses and the previous added time delays. We use the following example to explain that.

EXAMPLE 1: Consider the memory system with parameters T=8, N=8 and K=1. If this system is asked to access a vector operand with parameters S=3 and I=1000, the associated sequences are listed in Table 2. The memory system will add 3 delays before the 5–th access. Because, the 0–th and the 5–th accesses use the same memory module and the time between these two accesses is only 5 so 3 extra delays are needed to make the time between these two accesses becomes 8 (the memory cycle time).

With a similar reason, the memory system will add 1 delay before the 12–th access. Then, it will add 2 delays before 13–th access. The reason of the insertion of 2 delays is described below. Originally, the 8–th and the 13–th accesses use the same memory module so there must be 3 delays between these two accesses. However, the system had added 1 delay before the 12–th access so it just needs to add 2 additional delays before the 13–th access. □

After establishing the model to describe a vector access on a skewed interleaved memory, we give a criterion to represent the performance of such a vector access.

DEFINITION 4: The *average time delay* for a vector access with parameters T, N, K, S and I is defined as:

$$ATD(T,N,K,S,I) = \lim_{p\to\infty}\sum_{j=0}^{P}\dfrac{Dseq(T,N,K,S,I;j)}{p+1}$$ □

As for the method to find this criterion, we show it in the next section.

j	Address Sequence	Module Sequence	Delay Sequence
0	1000	5	0
1	1003	0	0
2	1006	3	0
3	1009	7	0
4	1012	2	0
5	1015	5	+3
6	1018	1	0
7	1021	4	0
8	1024	0	0
9	1027	3	0
10	1030	6	0
11	1033	2	0
12	1036	5	+1
13	1039	0	+2
14	1042	4	0
15	1045	7	0
⋮	⋮	⋮	⋮

Table 2: The example sequences

§3 Average Time Delay Evaluation

First, we need a property about module sequence.

THEOREM 1: For any $Mseq(N,K,S,I)$, $Mseq(N,K,S,I;j) = Mseq(N,K,S,I;j+nP_m)$ for any integer n, where $P_m = \dfrac{N^2}{gcd(K,N) \; gcd\left(S, \dfrac{N^2}{gcd(K,N)}\right)}$.

PROOF: First, notice that $P_m S = \dfrac{N}{gcd(K,N)} \times \dfrac{S}{gcd\left(S, \dfrac{N^2}{gcd(K,N)}\right)} \times N$. Let $C_1 = \dfrac{N}{gcd(K,N)}$ and $C_2 = \dfrac{S}{gcd\left(S, \dfrac{N^2}{gcd(K,N)}\right)}$. According to the primary property of *gcd*, we know that both of C_1 and C_2 are integers. Then, we have:

$Mseq(N,K,S,I;j+nP_m)$

$= (I+(j+nP_m)S+K \left\lfloor \dfrac{I+(j+nP_m)S}{N} \right\rfloor) \bmod N$

$= (I+jS+nC_1C_2N+K \left\lfloor \dfrac{I+jS+nC_1C_2N}{N} \right\rfloor) \bmod N$

$= (I+jS+nC_1C_2N+nC_1C_2K+K \left\lfloor \dfrac{I+jS}{N} \right\rfloor) \bmod N$

$= (I+jS+nC_1C_2N+nC_2 \dfrac{K}{gcd(K,N)}N+K \left\lfloor \dfrac{I+jS}{N} \right\rfloor) \bmod N$

$= (I+jS+K \left\lfloor \dfrac{I+jS}{N} \right\rfloor) \bmod N = Mseq(N,K,S,I;j)$.

In the above derivation, notice that $\dfrac{K}{gcd(K,N)}$ is an integer. □

THEOREM 2: P_m is the minimal period.

PROOF: Due to the long derivation, we omit it here. □

For a memory system with memory cycle time T, we observe that only the events occurring within the previous T−1 clocks can affect the current access, because the accesses, which happened at T or more clocks before, should have been finished. So, we define the state of an access as follow:

DEFINITION 5: The *memory access state*, exactly before accessing j–th element of a vector with initial address I and stride S from a memory system with parameters T, N and K, is denoted as:

$STATE(T,N,K,S,I;j) = (C_1,C_2,...,C_{T-1})$

where $C_i \in \{0,1,...,N-1\} \cup \{-\}$. C_i="−" means that the

memory system has inserted a delay at i clock before. C_i=p means that the p-th module has been initiated an access at i clocks before. □

EXAMPLE 2: For a vector access with parameters T=4, N=4, K=1 ,S=1 and I=0, the corresponding module sequence $Mseq(4,1,1,0)$ is 0,1,2,3,1,2,3,0,2,3,0,1,3, 0,1,2,0,1,2,3,⋯. Because the memory cycle time is 4, the memory system will insert a delay before the 4–th, 8–th, 12–th, ⋯ accesses. So the memory access states are:

$$STATE(4,4,1,1,0;0)=(-,-,-)$$
$$STATE(4,4,1,1,0;1)=(0,-,-)$$
$$STATE(4,4,1,1,0;2)=(1,0,-)$$
$$STATE(4,4,1,1,0;3)=(2,1,0)$$
$$STATE(4,4,1,1,0;4)=(-,3,2)$$
$$STATE(4,4,1,1,0;5)=(1,-,3)$$
$$STATE(4,4,1,1,0;6)=(2,1,-)$$
$$\vdots$$
$$STATE(4,4,1,1,0;17)=(0,-,2)$$
$$STATE(4,4,1,1,0;18)=(1,0,-)$$

For example, the state exactly before accessing the third element is (2,1,0). After accessing the third element, the state will become (3,2,1). The next access will use memory module 1 which is still used, therefore one delay will be inserted and the state will become (−,3,2). This is the state exactly before accessing the fourth element. □

The key point of the evaluation is how to eliminate the *lim* operation from the ATD expression. We need the following definition and theorems.

DEFINITION 6: For a vector access with parameters T, N, K, S and I, if $STATE(T,N,K,S,I;j) = STATE(T,N,K,S,I;j+qP_m)$ for some q≥1 then we call that $STATE(T,N,K,S,I;j)$ is a *steady state* with period qP_m. □

EXAMPLE 3: (Continued from Example 2) For this case, the corresponding P_m=16. We find that $STATE(4,4,1,1,0;2) = STATE(4,4,1,1,0;2+16)$, so we say that $STATE(4,4,1,1,0;2)$ is a steady state. □

THEOREM 3: For any vector access with parameters T, N, K, S and I, there always exists a steady state.

PROOF: From Definition 5, we know that the total number of possible states is $(N+1)^{T-1}$. Consider the set of states $\{STATE(T,N,K,S,I;j+iP_m) \mid 0 \le i \le (N+1)^{T-1}\}$. This set has $(N+1)^{T-1}+1$ states, therefore at least two states in this set are the same, i.e., there is a steady state. □

THEOREM 4: For a vector access with parameters T, N, K, S and I, if $STATE(T,N,K,S,I;j)$ is a steady state with period qP_m then, for all r≥0:

$$STATE(T,N,K,S,I;j+r)=STATE(T,N,K,S,I;j+r+qP_m)$$

and $Dseq(T,N,K,S,I;j+r)=Dseq(T,N,K,S,I;j+r+qP_m)$.

PROOF: From Theorem 2, P_m is the minimal period of module sequence, hence $Mseq(N,K,S,I;j) = Mseq(N,K,S,I;j+qP_m)$. Because the states which are exactly before j–th and $(j+qP_m)$–th accesses are the same, these two accesses will induce the same state and delay sequence, that is,

$STATE(T,N,K,S,I;j+1)=STATE(T,N,K,S,I;j+1+qP_m)$ and $Dseq(T,N,K,S,I;j+1)=Dseq(T,N,K,S,I;j+1+qP_m)$. Then, by induction, we can prove this theorem. □

COROLLARY: For a vector access with parameters T, N, K, S and I, if $STATE(T,N,K,S,I;j)$ is a steady state with period qP_m then, for any $n_1, n_2 \ge 0$:

$$\sum_{\ell=j+n_1qP_m+1}^{j+(n_1+1)qP_m} Dseq(T,N,K,S,I;\ell)$$

$$= \sum_{\ell=j+n_2qP_m+1}^{j+(n_2+1)qP_m} Dseq(T,N,K,S,I;\ell). \qquad \square$$

Now, we are ready to show that the ATD can be calculated on a period only.

THEOREM 5: For a vector access with parameters T, N, K, S and I, if STATE(T,N,K,S,I;j) is a steady state with period qP_m then

$$ATD(T,N,K,S,I) = \sum_{\ell=j+1}^{j+qP_m} \frac{Dseq(T,N,K,S,I;\ell)}{qP_m}.$$

PROOF: Let $D_0 = \sum_{\ell=0}^{j} Dseq(T,N,K,S,I;\ell)$ and $D = \sum_{\ell=j+1}^{j+qP_m} Dseq(T,N,K,S,I;\ell)$. Then, we have the following derivations:

$$ATD(T,N,K,S,I) = \lim_{p\to\infty} \sum_{\ell=0}^{p} \frac{Dseq(T,N,K,S,I;\ell)}{p+1}$$

$$= \lim_{p'\to\infty} \frac{D_0+p'D}{j+1+p'qP_m} = \frac{D}{qP_m}$$

$$= \sum_{\ell=j+1}^{j+qP_m} \frac{Dseq(T,N,K,S,I;\ell)}{qP_m} \qquad \square$$

This theorem shows that the evaluation of ATD is no longer evaluating a limit value of an infinite sum. We can evaluate it just on a period qP_m. So, we just need to reach a steady state, sum up delays in the period and divide the summation by the period.

EXAMPLE 4: (Continued from Example 3) We know that STATE(4,4,1,1,0;2) is a steady state with period 16, so

$$ATD(4,4,1,1,0) = \sum_{\ell=2+1}^{2+16} \frac{Dseq(4,4,1,1,0;\ell)}{16} = \frac{4}{16} = 0.25. \quad \square$$

§4 Aggregate Average Time Delay

In the next three sections, we plan to use average time delay as a tool to analyze some problems. These problems centralize how to design a memory system which has less conflicts for vector accesses. But, in the model defined in Section 2, a memory system has 3 characteristics (T, N and K), while the average time delay for a vector access has 5 parameters (T, N, K, S and I). The objective of this section is to give a time delay measurement for the whole memory system, i.e., with parameters T, N and K only.

We start from the periodic property of average time delay.

THEOREM 6 : For any Mseq(N,K,S,I), Mseq(N,K,S,I) = Mseq(N,K,S+nP_s,I) for any integer n, where $P_s = \frac{N^2}{\gcd(K,N)}$.

PROOF: We need to show that $Mseq(N,K,S+nP_s,I;j) = Mseq(N,K,S,I;j)$ for all j. We have the following derivations:

$$Mseq(N,K,S+nP_s,I;j)$$

$$= (I+jS+njP_s+K\left\lfloor\frac{I+jS+njP_s}{N}\right\rfloor) \bmod N$$

$$= (I+jS+nj\frac{N^2}{\gcd(K,N)}+K\left\lfloor\frac{I+jS+nj\frac{N^2}{\gcd(K,N)}}{N}\right\rfloor) \bmod N$$

$$= (I+jS+nj\frac{N}{\gcd(K,N)}N+K\left\lfloor\frac{I+jS}{N}\right\rfloor+nj\frac{K}{\gcd(K,N)}N) \bmod N$$

$$= (I+jS+K\left\lfloor\frac{I+jS}{N}\right\rfloor) \bmod N$$

$$= Mseq(N,K,S,I;j)$$

In the above derivation, notice that $\frac{N}{\gcd(K,N)}$ and

$\frac{K}{\gcd(K,N)}$ are integers. $\qquad \square$

THEOREM 7: For any vector access with parameters T, N, K, S and I, ATD(T,N,K,S,I) = ATD(T,N,K,S mod P_s,I).

PROOF: Because the associated module sequences are the same, these two average time delay must be the same. $\qquad \square$

In Section 2, we define the average time delay as a function of 5 parameters (T, N, K, S and I). We strongly conjecture that this function is independent of the starting address I. Hence, we will set I to 0 in the remaining of this paper. And, we use ATD(T,N,K,S) to represent ATD(T,N,K,S,0). Then, for a given memory system with parameters T, N and K, in order to give a single measurement of time delay, we define the aggregate average time delay as follow:

DEFINITION 7: For a memory system with parameters T, N and K, the *aggregate average time delay*, denoted as G(T,N,K), is defined as:

$$G(T,N,K) = \frac{\sum_{s=0}^{P_s-1} ATD(T,N,K,s)}{P_s} \qquad \square$$

In this definition, we just consider the stride varying on a period P_s because of Theorem 7.

EXAMPLE 5: Consider the memory system with parameters T=4, N=6 and K=1. Its stride period $P_s = \frac{6^2}{\gcd(1,6)} = 36$. The associated average time delay on strides from 0 to P_s-1 is listed in Table 3. So, its aggregate average time delay is $\frac{23}{36} = 0.64$. The number 23 is the summation of all average time delays listed in Table 3. $\qquad \square$

S	ATD(4,6,1,S)	S	ATD(4,6,1,S)
0	3.00	18	1.00
1	0.00	19	0.17
2	0.00	20	1.00
3	0.00	21	1.50
4	0.00	22	0.00
5	2.50	23	0.67
6	0.00	24	0.33
7	0.17	25	0.50
8	0.67	26	2.00
9	0.00	27	0.00
10	2.00	28	0.67
11	0.50	29	0.17
12	0.33	30	0.00
13	0.67	31	2.50
14	0.00	32	0.00
15	1.50	33	0.00
16	1.00	34	0.00
17	0.17	35	0.00

Table 3: ATD(4,6,1,S)

This is a simple criterion to indicate the performance for the whole memory system under accessing vectors with different strides. However, this criterion has a drawback, that is, we treat the probabilities of the occurrences of each stride are the same. In fact, for the algorithms running on a pipelined vector computer, some strides are more frequently used than others, e.g., the power of 2. So, we define weighted aggregate average time delay as follow:

DEFINITION 8: For a memory system with parameters T, N and K, the *weighted aggregate average time delay*, denoted as WG(T,N,K), is defined as:

$$WG(T,N,K) = \frac{\sum_{s=0}^{P_s-1} ATD(T,N,K,s) \times W(s)}{\sum_{s=0}^{P_s-1} W(s)},$$

where $W(s) = 1 + \sum_{j=0}^{20} u(s,j)$ and $u(s,j)$ are:

$$u(s,j) = \begin{cases} 4 & \text{if } 0 \le j \le 10 \text{ and } 2^j \bmod P_s = s \\ 2 & \text{if } 11 \le j \le 20 \text{ and } 2^j \bmod P_s = s \\ 0 & \text{otherwise} \end{cases} \qquad \square$$

The reason of weight selection is described as follows. Our original motivation is to highlight the power of 2 strides. We add a weight 4 for each stride 2^j with $0 \le j \le 10$, and a weight 2 for each stride 2^j with $11 \le j \le 20$. The different selection of 2 or 4 is based on the observation that the shorter strides are used more frequently than the longer strides in practical applications. Furthermore, because we just consider strides from 0 to P_s-1, we have "$2^j \bmod P_s = s$" condition after applying Theorem 6.

EXAMPLE 6: (Continued from Example 5)
Because of:

$2^0 \bmod 36 = 1$,	$2^1 \bmod 36 = 2$,	$2^2 \bmod 36 = 4$,
$2^3 \bmod 36 = 8$,	$2^4 \bmod 36 = 16$,	$2^5 \bmod 36 = 32$,
$2^6 \bmod 36 = 28$,	$2^7 \bmod 36 = 20$,	$2^8 \bmod 36 = 4$,
$2^9 \bmod 36 = 8$,	$2^{10} \bmod 36 = 16$,	$2^{11} \bmod 36 = 32$,
$2^{12} \bmod 36 = 28$,	$2^{13} \bmod 36 = 20$,	$2^{14} \bmod 36 = 4$,
$2^{15} \bmod 36 = 8$,	$2^{16} \bmod 36 = 16$,	$2^{17} \bmod 36 = 32$,
$2^{18} \bmod 36 = 28$,	$2^{19} \bmod 36 = 20$,	$2^{20} \bmod 36 = 4$,

we have $u(1,0) = u(2,1) = u(4,2) = u(8,3) = u(16,4) = u(32,5) = u(28,6) = u(20,7) = u(4,8) = u(8,9) = u(16,10) = 4$; $u(32,11) = u(28,12) = u(20,13) = u(4,14) = u(8,15) = u(16,16) = u(32,17) = u(28,18) = u(20,19) = u(4,20) = 2$; and other $u(i,j) = 0$. Hence, the $W(s)$ are as listed in Table 4. For example, $W(4) = 1 + u(4,2) + u(4,8) + u(4,14) + u(4,20) = 13$. Then,

$$WG(4,6,1) = \frac{3.00 \times 1 + 0.00 \times 5 + \cdots + 0.00 \times 1}{1 + 5 + \cdots + 1} = 0.53 \quad \square$$

S	W(s)	S	W(s)
0	1	18	1
1	5	19	1
2	5	20	9
3	1	21	1
4	13	22	1
5	1	23	1
6	1	24	1
7	1	25	1
8	11	26	1
9	1	27	1
10	1	28	9
11	1	29	1
12	1	30	1
13	1	31	1
14	1	32	9
15	1	33	1
16	11	34	1
17	1	35	1

Table 4: W(S) for N=6, K=1

§5 How about Dimension Extension ?

Now, we are ready to examine some interesting problems about how to resolve memory conflicts when accessing a vector. The approach that we consider in this section is by software. We describe the idea of our software approach first.

Assume that we are given a memory system with parameters T=4, N=6 and K=1. Its associated average

time delay can be found from Table 3. And assume that we have a 2-dimensional array with dimension [5,100] stored in row-major form. If we want to fetch a column from this array, we encounter a vector access with stride 5. From Table 3, we know that this vector access will induce serious time delays. Also, we know that the vector access with stride 6 has no time delay. If such a column access is used frequently, why don't we extend the dimension of this array to [6,100]? Of course, this approach waste some storage but has faster access speed.

This task can be achieved by a compiler or a language preprocessor. Such a compiler needs to know the average time delay for each different stride. This information can be pre-calculated and stored in a table. And, such a compiler need have the ability to decide whether the dimension extension is beneficial. For example, if we do not fetch any column from the array explained above, then the extension is useless. Or, for example, what do we do if we frequently fetch either a column or a diagonal from this array? This is a big problem and needs many efforts to construct such a compiler. But, is it worthwhile to pay these efforts? The goal of this section is to answer this problem.

DEFINITION 9: For a memory system with parameters T, N and K, the *aggregate average time delay with extension e*, denoted as $G^e(T,N,K)$, is defined as:

$$G^e(T,N,K) = \frac{\sum_{s=0}^{P_s-1} \min_{s \le s' \le s+e} ATD(T,N,K,s')}{P_s} \qquad \square$$

DEFINITION 10: For a memory system with parameters T, N and K, the *weighted aggregate average time delay with extension e*, denotes as $WG^e(T,N,K)$ is defined as:

$$WG^e(T,N,K) = \frac{\sum_{s=0}^{P_s-1} \left[\min_{s \le s' \le s+e} ATD(T,N,K,s') \right] \times W(s)}{\sum_{s=0}^{P_s-1} W(s)} \qquad \square$$

These definitions are modified from Definitions 7 and 8. In fact, the $G(T,N,K)$ and $WG(T,N,K)$ defined previously are exactly the $G^0(T,N,K)$ and $WG^0(T,N,K)$ defined now, respectively. The extension e specifies that we can extend a vector access with stride S to that with stride at most S+e and we always choose the best.

EXAMPLE 7: (Continued from Example 6) Let us consider the case with extension 2. Let $ATD^e(T,N,K,S)$ denote $\min_{s \le s' \le s+e} ATD(T,N,K,s')$. The associated ATD^2 is listed in Table 5. For example, because $ATD(4,6,1,9)$ is the smallest among $ATD(4,6,1,7)$, $ATD(4,6,1,8)$ and $ATD(4,6,1,9)$, $ATD^2(4,6,1,7) = ATD(4,6,1,9) = 0.00$. Then, we can calculate out that $G^2(4,6,1) = \frac{2.17}{36}$. The number 2.17 is the summation of all average time delay with extension 2 listed in Table 5. Furthermore, we have $WG^2(4,6,1) = \frac{3.87}{100}$. $\square$

A large extension will waste more storage than a small extension. We can expect that it is no sense to make an infinite extension. We also try to find the suitable extension in the section.

For the sake of analysis, we have evaluated G^e and WG^e, $0 \le e \le 4$, for 290 cases. These cases are combinations of $6 \le N \le 10$, $2 \le T \le N$ and $0 \le K \le N-1$. Table 6 lists the average ratio of G^e to G^0 and WG^e to WG^0, for $1 \le e \le 4$, over these 290 cases. We find that only 22%

S	ATD^2(4,6,1,S)	S	ATD^2(4,6,1,S)
0	0.00	18	0.17
1	0.00	19	0.17
2	0.00	20	0.00
3	0.00	21	0.00
4	0.00	22	0.00
5	0.00	23	0.33
6	0.00	24	0.33
7	0.00	25	0.00
8	0.00	26	0.00
9	0.00	27	0.00
10	0.33	28	0.00
11	0.33	29	0.00
12	0.00	30	0.00
13	0.00	31	0.00
14	0.00	32	0.00
15	0.17	33	0.00
16	0.17	34	0.00
17	0.17	35	0.00

Table 5: ATD^2(4,6,1,S)

delays are left if extension 1 strategy is applied and only 11% if extension 2 strategy is applied either from points of view of aggregate average time delay or weighted aggregate average time delay. We have the following conclusions.

1) It is worthwhile for dimension extension strategy.

2) The strategy with extension 1 or 2 is good enough.

e	1	2	3	4
G^e/G^0	0.224	0.113	0.066	0.047
WG^e/WG^0	0.221	0.118	0.060	0.045

Table 6: Average ratio of G^e to G^0 and WG^e to WG^0

§6 What is the Suitable Skew ?

The second problem is, for given memory cycle time T and number of memory modules N, how to select the skew K.

We do the analysis with 4 criteria G^0, G^1, WG^0 and WG^1. From the 290 cases, the information about the best K for each combination of T and N is collected in Table 7. For example, for T=3 and N=8, all of G^0(3,8,1), G^0(3,8,3), G^0(3,8,5) and G^0(3,8,7) are the minimal. So in row T=3 and N=8, we mark a "1" in the second column to indicate that K=1 will result the best performance and a "3" in the third column to indicate that 3 possible K, which are greater than 1 and are relatively prime to N, will result the best performance.

We have the following observations:

1) It seems that the parameter T is not sensitive in selection K.

2) When not applying dimension extension strategy, we frequently find that K=1 is the best when N is a power of 2, K=0 is the best for many other cases and other K are seldom the best.

3) When applying dimension extension strategy, K=0 is always the best and K=1 is always not the best for all the cases that we have tried. What a surprise!

From previous research results, we have an impression that skewing scheme is a good approach to avoid memory conflict. Maybe, it is true for other architec-

The Best T	N	G^0				G^1				WG^0				WG^1			
		α	β	γ	δ	α	β	γ	δ	α	β	γ	δ	α	β	γ	δ
2	6	1	1	1	3	1			3	1				1			3
3	6	1	1	1		1			1	1				1			1
4	6	1	1			1				1				1			
5	6	1	1			1				1		1		1			
6	6	1	1			1				1			1	1			
2	7	1	1	5		1		4		1				1		4	
3	7	1				1		2		1				1		2	
4	7	1				1				1				1			
5	7	1				1				1				1			
6	7	1				1				1				1			
7	7	1				1				1				1			
2	8	1	1	3	3	1		2	3	1			3	1		2	3
3	8		1	3			1		1		1	3			1		1
4	8		1	3			1		1		1	2			1		1
5	8		1	3			1				1	1			1		
6	8		1	3			1				1	1			1		
7	8		1	3			1				1				1		
8	8		1	3			1				1				1		
2	9	1	1	5	2	1		4	2	1				1		4	2
3	9	1				1		2	2	1				1		2	2
4	9	1				1				1				1			
5	9	1				1				1				1			
6	9	1				1				1				1			
7	9	1				1				1				1			
8	9	1				1				1				1			
9	9	1				1				1				1			
2	10	1	1	3	5	1		2	5	1				1		2	5
3	10	1				1		2	1	1				1		2	1
4	10	1				1		1	1	1			1	1		1	1
5	10	1				1		1	1	1			1	1		1	1
6	10	1				1				1				1			
7	10	1				1				1				1			
8	10	1				1				1				1			
9	10	1				1				1				1			
10	10	1				1				1				1			

α: K=0   β: K=1
γ: K>1 and relatively prime to N
δ: K>1 and not relatively prime to N

Table 7: The analyses of best skew K

tures, e.g., SIMD. But, it is not true for pipelined vector computers, especially after applying dimension extension strategy.

§7 How Many Memory Modules are Sufficient ?

The third problem is, for a given memory cycle time T, how to determine the number of memory modules N.

We have analyzed the cases of $2 \le T \le 10$. For each case, we plot 8 functions by varying N from 1 to 32. These 8 functions are $G^0(T,N,0)$, $G^1(T,N,0)$, $WG^0(T,N,0)$, $WG^1(T,N,0)$, $\min_{0 \le K \le N-1} G^0(T,N,K)$, $\min_{0 \le K \le N-1} G^1(T,N,K)$, $\min_{0 \le K \le N-1} WG^0(T,N,K)$ and $\min_{0 \le K \le N-1} WG^1(T,N,K)$. The first four functions are under not applying skewing scheme, while the last four functions are under applying the best skewing scheme.

We just show the cases of T=2 and T=10 here (Figures 2 and 3).

We have the following observations:

1) We find that these figures are very similar except the scale. This means that the skewing scheme does not make big difference. This result matches that got in the previous sections.

2) It is poor when N is a power of 2. This is within our expectation.

3) It is not good enough when N is a multiplicity of 6, e.g., 6, 12, 18 and 24, with respect to the neighboring N. We guess that this is due to that 6 can be factorized into primes 2 and 3. Hence, multiplicity of 6 is very easy to have a common factor with other numbers.

4) Under not applying dimension extension strategy, the improvement on time delay is not significant if we increase N over T.

5) Under applying dimension extension strategy, in general, it is good enough to let N be the same as T. Furthermore, there is nearly no time delay.

Summarily, we have three conclusions.

1) It is a good strategy to let N be a prime number, e.g. 17 of BSP [9].

2) It makes no sense to let N much greater than T.

3) From this analysis, it also shows that the dimension extension is a worthwhile strategy.

§8 Conclusion

We had studied the vector accessing behavior on skewed interleaved memory under pipelined vector processing environment. We gave criteria to indicate the performance of a given memory system. And, we used them to analyze and answer some problems about how to design a good memory system. The word "good" means that the memory system not only has less conflicts but also is cost-effective.

The major results of the analyses are :

1) From the previous research results, we had an impression that 1-way skewed scheme is a good approach to resolve memory access conflict. But, from our analyses, we find that non-skewed scheme often has the best performance. Hence, we do not suggest applying skewing scheme for pipelined vector processing.

2) When the number of memory modules is greater than the ratio of memory access time to pipeline clock time, it has not significant improvement to resolve memory access conflict.

3) When the number of memory modules is a

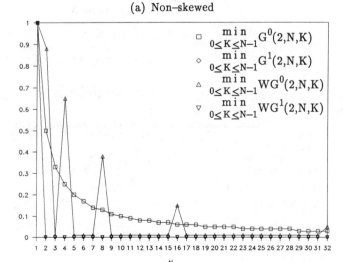

(a) Non-skewed

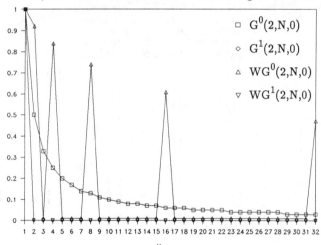

(b) Skewed

Figure 2: The analysis of suitable N for T=2

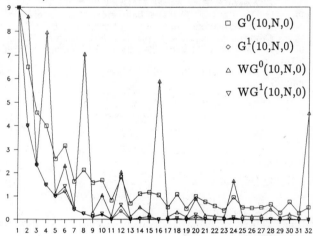

(a) Non-skewed

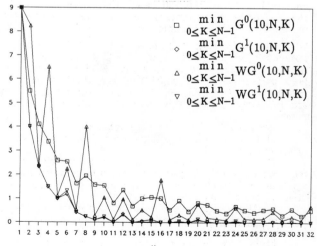

(b) Skewed

Figure 3: The analysis of suitable N for T=10

prime number, the system frequently performs well. Hence, we suggest that it is a good decision to let N be the smallest prime number greater than T. This result is similar with [9].

4) In general, the dimension extension strategy is a good approach to resolve memory access conflict. This strategy was also proposed in this paper.

As for the further research, there are some directions:

1) Extend the result to multi-port memory system as [10-11].

2) Extend the result to pipelined multiprocessor environment. Today, many state-of-the-art super-computers are pipelined multiprocessor system.

3) Detailedly study and implement the dimension extension strategy.

References

[1] G. J. Burnett and E. G. Coffman, Jr, "A study of interleaved memory systems," in *Proc. Spring Joint Computer Conference*, vol. 36, 1970, pp. 467–474.

[2] D. J. Kuck, "Illiac IV software and application programming," *IEEE Trans. Computers*, vol. C–17, pp. 758–770, August 1968.

[3] P. M. Kogge, *The Architecture of Pipelined Computers*, New York: McGraw–Hill, 1981.

[4] C. V. Ravi, " On the bandwidth and interference in interleaved memory system," *IEEE Trans. Computers*, vol. C–21, pp. 899–901, August 1972.

[5] D. P. Bhandarkar, "Analysis of memory inter-ference in multiprocessors," *IEEE Trans. Computers*, vol. C–24, pp. 897–908, September 1975.

[6] F. A. Briggs and E. S. Davidson, "Organization of semiconductor memories for parallel–pipelined processors," *IEEE Trans. Computers*, vol. C–26, pp. 162–169, February 1977.

[7] D. Y. Chang, D. J. Kuck and D. H. Lawrie, "On the effective bandwidth of parallel memories," *IEEE Trans. Computers*, vol. C–26, pp. 480–490, May 1977.

[8] D. H. Bailey, "Vector computer memory bank contention," *IEEE Trans. Computers*, vol. C–36, pp. 293–298, March 1987.

[9] D. H. Lawrie and C. R. Vora, "The prime memory system for array access," *IEEE Trans. Computers*, vol. C–31, pp. 435–442, May 1982.

[10] W. Oed and O. Lange, " On the effective band-width of interleaved memories in vector processing systems," *IEEE Trans. Computers*, vol. C–34, pp. 949–957, October 1985.

[11] T. Cheung and J. E. Smith, "A simulation study of the Cray X–MP memory system," *IEEE Trans. Computers*, vol. C–35, pp. 613–622, July 1986.

[12] P. Budnik and D. J. Kuck, "The organization and use of parallel memories," *IEEE Trans. Computers*, vol. C–20, pp. 1566–1569, December 1971.

[13] D. T. Harper III and J. R. Jump, "Vector access performance in parallel memories using a skewed storage scheme," *IEEE Trans. Computers*, vol. C–36, pp. 1440–1449, December 1987.

Cache Coherence and Synchronization II
Chair: J. Goodman, University of Wisconsin, Madison

Adaptive Backoff Synchronization Techniques

Anant Agarwal and Mathews Cherian

Laboratory for Computer Science

Massachusetts Institute of Technology

Cambridge, MA 02139

Abstract

Shared-memory multiprocessors commonly use shared variables for synchronization. Our simulations of real parallel applications show that large-scale cache-coherent multiprocessors suffer significant amounts of invalidation traffic due to synchronization. Large multiprocessors that do not cache synchronization variables are often more severely impacted. If this synchronization traffic is not reduced or managed adequately, synchronization references can cause severe congestion in the network. We propose a class of adaptive backoff methods that do not use any extra hardware and can significantly reduce the memory traffic to synchronization variables. These methods use synchronization state to reduce polling of synchronization variables. Our simulations show that when the number of processors participating in a barrier synchronization is small compared to the time of arrival of the processors, reductions of 20 percent to over 95 percent in synchronization traffic can be achieved at no extra cost. In other situations adaptive backoff techniques result in a tradeoff between reduced network accesses and increased processor idle time.

1 Introduction

Processor self-scheduling schemes in shared-memory multiprocessors commonly use shared variables to synchronize activities among processors [7, 22, 15]. This use of synchronization variables often leads to widespread sharing among processors. Our trace-driven simulations of parallel applications show that these widely shared synchronization variables adversely impact the performance of large-scale multiprocessors, cache-coherent or otherwise.

In systems without hardware support for cache coherence, such as the IBM RP3 [18], Ultracomputer [9], Cedar [8], these references to shared variables must traverse the interconnection network. Not only do synchronization references consume a significant fraction of the network bandwidth, but more important, a widely-shared synchronization variable (such as in a barrier synchronization) will result in heavy traffic to the same location in memory and cause hot-spot contention problems [19].

On the other hand, in systems that use directory schemes to maintain cache coherence, we show that synchronization variables result in excessive invalidation traffic when the number of pointers in the cache directory is limited. A potential solution for cache directories would be to implement software combining trees [24] for synchronization variables. As long as the degree of the nodes in the combining tree is less than the number of pointers in the cache-directory, then synchronization variables will not result in extra invalidation traffic. We are currently investigating this approach and will not address it here. An alternate method is to disallow caching of synchronization variables.

In this paper we consider software schemes to reduce the number of synchronization spins in multiprocessors that do not cache their synchronization variables. We propose a set of adaptive backoff techniques which make use of available synchronization state information in order to "back off" and postpone polling a synchronization variable.

The general idea of backoff has been used in one form or another in a number of applications. The approach was first used in Aloha [1], a radio-based, packet-switching network. If a collision occurred in the network, each source would backoff for a random interval before attempting to retransmit. The Ethernet [16] went one step further and used a random retransmission interval in which collision history influenced the choice of the mean of the random intervals. Adaptive control schemes for multiple access communications networks have been analyzed in [13, 12, 14].

We evaluate the performance of adaptive backoff synchronization techniques by applying them to the *barrier* synchronization. Barrier synchronizations are commonly used in applications to guarantee that all processors have reached a point in a program before proceeding.

This paper focuses on barriers implemented using two shared variables with busy waiting on synchronization variables [22] (described in detail below). Alternate barrier implementations might use a scheme where processors arriving at a barrier are put to sleep until the last processor arrives. This method avoids the extra network traffic of polling a barrier flag, but incurs the potentially high overhead of enqueuing a process on a condition variable. Often, the choice of busy waiting or blocking cannot be made at compile time due to uncertainty in execution times of processes. In such cases, our adaptive methods can be used to decide when it might be best to put to sleep a busy-waiting process as explained in a later section.

Hardware support for barriers has also been proposed in several forms. The RP3 [18] proposed a combining network in which switches contain special hardware to combine simultaneous data accesses destined to the same memory location and forward one request. This would eliminate contention in the network and at the memory modules, but RP3 cost estimates predict that the switches are expensive and slow [19]. Several cache-coherent multiprocessors allow simultaneous invalidates of all cached copies of a block. In such systems all repeat accesses of a synchronization variable can be satisfied by the cache. However, the need to rely on resources that can support broadcast invalidates, such as a shared bus, limits the scalability of such systems. The PAX computer [10] uses special global-synchronization logic implemented in hardware to allow low-latency, low-cost barrier synchronization. Issues which arise with this approach concern flexibility in allowing multiple numbers of barriers to execute simultaneously with varying numbers of processors.

Our results show that backoff techniques applied to barriers yield reductions in synchronization traffic by 20 percent to over 95 percent in cases where the number of processors involved in the barrier is small compared to the time of arrival between processors. In other situations, these schemes provide a tradeoff between cost (in terms of processor idle time) and performance - a tradeoff that can be determined by the user's needs.

The rest of this paper is organized as follows. We first present results from our trace-driven simulations describing how synchronization impacts large-scale multiprocessors. We then describe the network model that we assume for this study. Section 4 presents the adaptive backoff synchronizations techniques as they apply to barriers. We then discuss the barrier evaluation model and our simulation methodology. We evaluate these ideas and discuss the tradeoffs involved in their implementation using a simple analytical model and through simulations in Sections 6 and 7. Sections 8 and 9 suggest extensions to our work and summarize our findings.

2 The Synchronization Problem

In this section we present data from trace-driven multiprocessor simulations of the FFT [5], SIMPLE [6], and WEATHER [11] applications[1] and use the example of a barrier to explain why synchronization is a problem in large-scale systems.

A common implementation of a barrier splits the barrier into two shared variables [22]: an incrementing variable (henceforth called the barrier variable) initially set to zero, and a barrier flag variable also initially reset. An arriving processor increments the barrier variable. If the variable's value is less than N, the processor polls the barrier flag which is set by the last processor to reach the barrier. This scheme requires that the last processor reaching the barrier compete with the N-1 processors testing the barrier flag when it tries to set the flag. More importantly, however,

---

[1]See Appendix for a description of the applications, the tracing technique, and multiprocessor simulation methodology.

the shared variables involved are necessarily shared among all processors in the system. It is precisely this widespread sharing that impacts performance when scaling to large systems.

2.1 Synchronization References and Scalability

The widespread sharing that occurs with synchronization variables is not a problem when used in bus-based snoopy-cache multiprocessors. Because snoopy-cache-based protocols perform broadcast invalidates or updates, a variable shared among all processors generates no more traffic on the shared bus than a variable shared among only two processors. The limitation of snoopy-based schemes, however, is that they do not scale to large multiprocessor systems. Since these schemes require low latency broadcasts for cache coherence, as well as the ability to "watch" all bus transactions, they must use a shared bus for communication. A single bus cannot offer the bandwidth demanded by large-scale shared-memory multiprocessors.

Unfortunately, widespread sharing of synchronization variables can drastically impair performance in large-scale multiprocessors, cache-coherent or otherwise. First, let us consider multiprocessors with coherent caches, where a directory is used to keep track of cached copies of shared blocks. In general, for every memory block, a directory must store as many pointers as the number of processors (say N) in the system [4]. Such a scheme is termed $Dir_N NB$, for N-pointers-No-Broadcast in [3]. In practice, it is possible to maintain just i pointers ($i < N$) to yield the $Dir_i NB$ scheme [3]. Invalidations are forced to limit the cached copies of a block to i, or to gain exclusive ownership on a write. Results in [3] showed that during an invalidation situation, few invalidations were actually necessary. Results from our trace-driven simulations of 64-processor systems discussed below as well as the results in [23] corroborate the findings in [3]. In our 64 processor simulations, over 99% of writes to previously clean blocks resulted in invalidations from less than four caches. (See [2] for details.)

Why do synchronization references hurt performance? Our simulations revealed that synchronization variables were largely responsible for the cases in which more than four caches were invalidated. Synchronization references are even more damaging when the effect of simultaneous read sharing is considered. Recall that using i pointers limits simultaneous read sharing of a block to only i copies, and invalidations must occur to enforce this rule. For synchronizations like barriers, active sharing might occur among all processors involved, resulting in a high invalidation rate in directory-based schemes.

Table 1 shows the fraction of synchronization references out of the total number of synchronization references which resulted in an invalidation. The percentage is far higher than the corresponding fraction for non-synchronization data references.

It is clear that invalidation traffic due to synchronizations can be deleterious to the performance of cache-coherent multiprocessors. One solution is to use software combining

Ptrs	SIMPLE		WEATHER		FFT	
	NS	S	NS	S	NS	S
2	8.5	93.5	1.9	99.9	6.7	99.0
3	7.1	81.3	1.7	99.9	5.0	99.0
4	6.0	81.1	1.5	99.9	3.5	98.9
5	5.2	99.9	1.5	99.9	3.5	98.8
64	.53	1.2	1.2	.03	3.5	3.5

Table 1: Percentage of non-synchronization (NS) and synchronization (S) references that cause invalidations in directory schemes with 2, 3, 4, 5, and 64 pointers in a 64 processor system. Synchronization references comprised 0.2%, 7.9%, and 5.3% of the data references in FFT, WEATHER, and SIMPLE respectively.

Ptrs	SIMPLE	WEATHER	FFT
	Traf. (%)	Traf. (%)	Traf. (%)
2	22.0	55.4	1.3
3	23.5	56.3	1.4
4	24.6	57.4	1.5
5	25.6	57.6	1.5
64	35.3	59.9	1.5

Table 2: Synchronization traffic to main memory as a percentage of the total traffic when the synchronization variables are not cached. Block size is 16 bytes and cache size is 256KBytes. The non-synchronization blocks are cached and coherence is maintained using directory schemes with 2, 3, 4, 5, and 64 pointers in a 64 processor system.

trees. Alternatively, one can disallow caching synchronization variables.

2.2 Disallowing Caching of Synchronization Variables

If most synchronization accesses cause invalidations that involve multiword transfers, then why cache synchronization variables? The problems with this approach are similar to those in multiprocessors that make all shared locations uncacheable: increased network traffic and potential hotspot contention. Synchronization references are often to the same location in memory, and even a small fraction of all data accesses to the same "hot" module can cause tree saturation [19] in the interconnection network and a corresponding severe drop in the effective memory bandwidth.

Table 2 shows that the percentage of uncached synchronization traffic to memory out of the total data traffic can be large. We compute traffic to memory by summing the total number of network transactions generated by references. For example, in the case of a cache miss, two network transactions are generated: one to send the requested address to memory and one to send the requested data from memory to the processor.

The reason SIMPLE and WEATHER generate far more synchronization traffic than FFT is that their load balancing is not as good as in FFT (see Section A for details), resulting in more synchronization accesses at loop barriers as processors wait for all processors to arrive. The slight relative increase of synchronization overhead in all cases when going from two to five pointers is because synchronization traffic remained constant while invalidation traffic (part of total memory traffic) decreased as more pointers were available for sharing of blocks.

Therefore, if we are to scale multiprocessors, network traffic due to synchronization must be rigorously minimized.

In large-scale shared-memory multiprocessors, such as the RP3, Ultracomputer, Cedar, all traffic to shared variables must go over the network[2], and the relative fraction of network accesses attributable to synchronization is slightly smaller. We measured memory traffic when shared variables

---
[2] Although temporary caching of shared locations with compiler inserted cache flush directives can help relieve network load.

were not cached and found that synchronization traffic accounted for 25.5%, 49.2%, and 1.47% of the total traffic in SIMPLE, WEATHER, and FFT, respectively, in 64 processor simulations. Our motivation for reducing the network traffic, especially traffic that is partial to a specific memory location, still remains.

3 The Network Model

The network model we assume is the following: processors can access any memory over the network in one network cycle. We do not model network contention, but do model contention for the barrier variable and flag. We also assume that the barrier variable and flag are in different memory modules, so simultaneous requests to the two by different processors can be satisfied. We assume that in a network cycle only one processor can access the barrier variable or the barrier flag. If a processor is denied access to the variable in a network cycle it repeats the access to the variable in the next network cycle. This model might correspond to a crossbar switch where the only contention is for the end memory modules that have the barrier variable and flag. It also roughly approximates the performance of a circuit-switched multistage interconnection network, where the network cycle time can be the round-trip time over the network. In the latter case the contention at intermediate network nodes is not included.

The network traffic rates computed using our barrier scheme might also be input into a more complex model of a multistage interconnection network such as that proposed by Patel [17] if network contention results are desired. Unfortunately Patel's model does not account for hot-spot contention. We are also using large parallel traces of real applications derived using various synchronization schemes to drive network models to obtain performance estimates in the presence of hot-spots caused by barrier traffic and when the barrier traffic is reduced using our techniques.

4 Adaptive Backoff Barrier Synchronization

The basic idea behind adaptive backoff methods is simple. An adaptive backoff barrier technique makes use of available information in deciding how long to wait before trying to read a barrier flag rather than continuously polling the flag.

We will assume barriers implemented using a separate barrier variable and a barrier flag as described earlier. If the barrier variable and flag are one and the same object, the relative advantage of using adaptive backoff techniques will be even greater.

4.1 Backoff on the barrier variable

The first method, called *backoff on the barrier variable*, is the simplest and attempts to make use of the state of the barrier variable to reduce unnecessary network accesses on the barrier flag. The barrier variable value reveals the number of processors waiting at the barrier. Let there be N processors that must arrive at the barrier, and let the average memory access time over the network be 1 cycle as mentioned earlier. If i processors have reached the barrier, then an arriving processor can start polling the barrier flag at least (N-i) cycles after reaching the barrier variable A.

4.2 Backoff on the barrier flag

Backoff on the barrier flag is another method that tries to reduce the number of spins on the barrier flag. Processors can remember the number of times they have polled the barrier flag and correspondingly backoff by a linear or exponential amount the longer they have waited. This code can be part of the barrier implementation in software and needs no hardware support. In discussing the performance of these latter methods, we assume that backoff on the barrier variable is also applied.

In backoff on the barrier variable, if the interarrival times of processors are very large, then a processor might wait its N-i cycles and start polling the barrier flag long before the last processor arrives at the barrier. In these situations, we might wait longer before polling the flag, say (N-i)+C or (N-i)*C, where C is some positive integer. While this might reduce the number of unnecessary network accesses, it might also cause the processor to remain idle and miss accessing the barrier at the earliest it becomes available. We suggest some methods of choosing appropriate backoff parameters in Section 8.

In backoff on the barrier flag, there exists a danger of backing off much more than necessary. Clearly there is a tradeoff between network access reduction and cpu idle time. If only a small fraction of the processors are involved in a barrier synchronization, then to reduce the hot-spot contention problem, one might prefer to take the hit in cpu idle time for these contending processors so that the remaining processors in the system can perform unhindered. As mentioned before, even a small percentage of memory references to the same "hot" memory module can result in severe congestion in the interconnection network, thereby reducing all processors' utilization [19]. Of course, if all processors in a system are involved in a barrier synchronization, then the cpu idle time becomes an important consideration.

Backoff decisions are made only when a process has just updated the barrier variable, and when the process has read

```
Execution     Bar. Execution     Bar.
|-------------|----|-------------|----|-----
       E         A        E         A
```

Figure 1: Intervals of execution and synchronization.

the barrier flag and the flag is not set. So, once a processor initiates a barrier read request, the network controller for that processor attempts to read the barrier. If contention thwarts this attempt, the access is repeated until the flag is read. We propose some other schemes where the network controller can back off if network congestion is high.

For software-tree based implementations of barriers on non-cache-coherent multiprocessor as suggested by Yew, Tzeng, and Lawrie [24], our methods can still be used to reduce the spins on the intermediate nodes of the tree.

We evaluate these ideas using a barrier model through analysis and simulations and discuss the tradeoffs between reduced synchronization accesses and wasted cpu cycles.

5 A Barrier Model

We first describe the model that we use to evaluate barriers. We use two metrics: (1) the number of network accesses per process in accessing the barrier variable and barrier flag; and (2) the number of cycles that an average process spends from the time it arrives at the barrier to the time it is allowed to proceed from the barrier.

Overall performance is impacted by the total network traffic, which includes the regular non-barrier traffic and the barrier traffic. Because we currently do not model hot-spot traffic contention in the network, we preferred to present the numbers for the barrier traffic alone, as average numbers for overall traffic might be misleading in terms of the adverse effect of the barrier traffic focused on one memory module.

Let us define A to be the time interval during which processes can arrive at the barrier. A is the time from the first processor's arrival at the barrier variable to the last processor's arrival. The complementary interval between these two events we call E, i.e., the time between barriers in an application. If we were to follow an application's execution through time, E and A would appear as shown in Figure 1.

Table 3 measures A for our applications. A is defined to be the number of cpu cycles from the time the first processor starts polling the barrier flag to the time the last processor sets the barrier flag. Interestingly the average A for SIMPLE and WEATHER did not increase as greatly as for FFT when going from 16 to 64 processors. For highly uniform and load-balanced applications such as FFT the spread among arrivals is primarily due to the serialization which takes place at the loop index assignment. Thus, FFT was relatively more affected than the other applications when the number of processors increased.

E and A for SIMPLE and WEATHER with 64 processors are similarly sized because the applications were not perfectly load-balanced: Not all the parallel loops contained a

Application	Processors	A	E
SIMPLE	16	7021	42007
	64	7068	6195
WEATHER	16	82754	495298
	64	82787	82716
FFT	16	237	228073
	64	285	57997

Table 3: Average number of cycles, A, between first and last arrivals at waits and barriers. E is the average number of cycles between the last arrival at the previous barrier (or wait) and the first arrival at the next barrier (or wait), i.e. it is the average time between barriers or waits.

nice multiple of iterations which could be distributed evenly among all processors. The few processors without work proceeded directly to the barrier.

The barrier model we use for our analysis and simulations is actually slightly different from the A we measured, and allows us to model a varying number of synchronizing processors for a given value of A. Our measurements of A from the applications were for a relatively large number of processors and this measurement yields an indication of the maximum time span between the first and last arrival at a synchronization point in that application. It is likely that a smaller number of processors can have an actual value of A much smaller than this maximum span. Therefore, we now define A to be the interval during which processors *may* arrive at the barrier, and N to be the number of synchronizing processors. We further assume that each processor has a uniform probability of appearing at any time instant during the interval A. From the uniform probability of arrival during the interval A we must compute the average time span between the first and last arrivals out of a total of N arrivals. This span must tend to A as N becomes large.

To determine whether our assumption of uniform probability of arrival within A was reasonable we measured the arrival times in our applications. We found that the distribution is roughly uniform for FFT but is skewed towards the beginning and the end of the interval for SIMPLE. This skewing occurs because of uneven load-balancing. We observed, however, in the last peak that processor arrivals were still uniform over the last 200 references [2]. There seems to be no real pattern and our assumption of a uniform distribution is not expected to significantly change our results for minor variations in the arrivals. We also present additional validation of this model by comparing the predictions obtained through simulations using the model and through measurements using the actual traces in Section 7.1.

5.1 Analytically Estimating Barrier Performance

We first present some simple calculations for extreme cases of A to determine the bounds on the possible savings and to provide insight into our simulations.

When all processors arrive simultaneously $(A = 0)$ and no backoff, a processor will make on average $N + N + N/2$ syn-

chronization references. Each processor makes $N/2$ barrier variable references, polls the barrier flag $N/2$ times before the last processor gets through the barrier variable, continues polling the barrier flag N times until the last processor sets the flag, and finally leaves after $N/2$ references, on average. We denote this model that assumes simultaneous arrival as Model 1.

If $A \gg N$, there is practically no contention to get the barrier variable. In this case we assume that processors appear at the barrier at a given time instant within the time interval A with uniform probability. Let us first compute the average time span τ between the first and the last arrival within the interval A given N processors. The average time from the beginning of the interval to the first arrival can be shown to be $A/(N+1)$, and the average time from the last arrival to the end of the interval to be $AN/(N+1)$. The required time span τ is the difference of the two, or

$$\tau = A\frac{N-1}{N+1} \qquad (1)$$

Observe that τ approaches A as N becomes large. Thus, each processor make on average $\tau/2 + N + N/2$ network accesses during the synchronization phase. This is Model 2.

Let us now consider backoff on the barrier variable, where we backoff an amount proportional to the the barrier variable value. If i is the value of the barrier variable upon a processor's arrival, then the processor can wait $N - i$ cycles before beginning to poll the barrier flag. When $A = 0$, the average number of synchronization accesses becomes $N/2 + N + N/2$ cycles because the processor does not start polling the flag until the last processor gets through the barrier. A similar savings of N/2 is made for $A \gg N$. With backoff only on the barrier variable, the potential savings get smaller as A gets larger because the savings is a constant $N/2$ no matter what A is.

Backoff on the barrier flag uses the number of times the flag has been polled. Rather than continuously polling the barrier flag until it is set, we backoff by some function of the number of times we have already read the shared variable. From Model 2 for $A \gg N$, the potential savings in network accesses can be as large as $log_b(\tau/2)$ for exponential backoff, where b is the basis of the exponential backoff algorithm used. In addition we reduce interference with the final processor write request that will release the processes waiting on the flag. The backoff on the barrier flag can also incur a high penalty – we might backoff too far and waste cpu cycles. This idea is tested out in simulations discussed in the next section.

Finally, we present some network access rates for barriers on multiprocessors with hardware support for barrier synchronization to provide a basis for comparison with the backoff schemes. Examples of such hardware support are a bus to allow either global invalidations, or global updates, of cache entries, a directory with a full pointer map, and special logic to implement a global synchronization gate as suggested by Hoshino [10]. If there are N processors the invalidating bus incurs $3n + 1$ accesses for a barrier: n fetches of the barrier variable, n invalidations for n writes of the barrier variable, n fetches of the flag, and the final global invalidation caused by the write into the barrier flag, yielding roughly 3 accesses per processor per barrier operation. The updating bus uses roughly 2 bus accesses per processor. The same number of accesses applies to an invalidating scheme that can detect a fetch with intent to write. Like the bus, the directory scheme incurs $3n$ on barrier variable accesses and invalidations, and flag accesses, but lacking a global broadcast must incur an additional n for the individual invalidates on the final write to the barrier flag, yielding 4 on average per processor per barrier operation. The Hoshino scheme uses n accesses to the global synchronization gate and the final single broadcast message to the participants to inform them to proceed, for a per-processor average of 1.

5.2 Simulation Methodology

We also use simulations to predict barrier performance with and without backoff. The barrier and network models are the same as described previously. Our simulation methodology is described here.

In our simulations, processors arrive with uniform probability during the interval of size A. Each processor first increments the barrier variable and then spins on the barrier flag until it is set by the last arriving processor. Our previous data in Table 3 showed that for three applications the value of E was between 6195 and 495298 cycles on average and the value of A was between 237 and 82787 cycles. While we simulated a wide range of A values, we show the results for $A = 0$, 100, and 1000 for brevity because it is only the relative size of the interval with respect to the number of processors involved in the barrier that is important; larger values of A yielded no additional insight.

Each simulation run measured the average number of network accesses made by a process from the time it arrived at the barrier variable to the time it proceeded from the barrier flag after having successfully tested the flag and observing a true value. As mentioned before, the number of network accesses includes contention for the barrier. We also measured the average time each process spent from the time it arrived at the barrier to the time it left.

6 Evaluation

We evaluate the backoff methods using the models just described. This section first compares the predictions of the model with simulations. We then estimate the potential savings in network traffic using backoff techniques and discuss the tradeoffs involved in choosing the right parameters for the backoff algorithm.

6.1 Estimating the Potential Reduction in Traffic

We will first analyze the accuracy of our simple model in predicting the behavior of the barrier synchronization under various load conditions. The model will indicate the range of performance gains that we might expect using the backoff techniques and give insight into our simulation numbers.

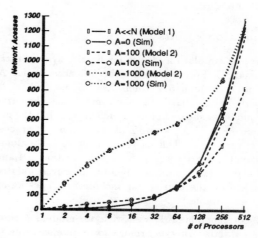

Figure 2:   Comparing the predictions of the analytical model and predictions of barrier performance.

Figure 2 compares model predictions of network accesses with simulation results for $A = 0$, $A = 100$, and $A = 1000$, without backoff. The model can be modified to predict the performance of the backoff schemes, but for certain cases it can get quite complicated. We will, however, mention what terms in the model equations get impacted by the various schemes.

The network accesses for $A = 0$, $A = 100$ do not differ much overall, but the way in which they differ is significant. For $N < 32$, $A = 0$ results in fewer accesses than $A = 100$ because when $A = 0$ processes do not have to wait for the last processor to arrive at the barrier. For larger N, however, $A = 100$ starts performing better because when the arrivals are spread out slightly, there is less contention in accessing the barrier. We observe a similar behavior for $A = 1000$ as N approaches A. When N is small, $A = 1000$ makes far more accesses than $A = 0$ or $A = 100$.

The model is accurate as the figure shows. Model 1, as expected, matches the curves for the $A << N$ cases. In particular, Model 1 closely approximates the $A = 0$ case, and yields a good match with the $A = 100$ curve for $N > 16$.

Model 2 matches all the cases where $A >> N$. Specifically, the Model 2 curve for $A = 1000$ provides a near perfect match with the corresponding simulation curve for all the values of N shown. The Model 2 curve for $A = 100$ matches the simulation $A = 100$ curve for $N < 128$. When N is greater than 128, the model begins to underestimate the contention in accessing the barrier variable. In general, the maximum of the predictions of the two models yields a good fit with simulation in all ranges.

Where $N > A$, the model implies that the potential reduction in network traffic is 20%. When $A > N$, the potential gains are much more significant. If an exponential backoff method is used with base b, then if the network accesses of the flag were M, with backoff these accesses can be reduced to the order of $log_b(M)$. Because the waiting processes are not busily accessing the flag, the final process that must set the flag can usually proceed to update the flag without interference.

6.2 Simulation results

We now present simulation results for barrier synchronization performance. Figure 3 shows the net accesses for N ranging from 2 through 512 when $A = 0$, i.e., when all processes arrive at the barrier at the same time. The curve follows the model as shown before, which means that the net accesses increase as $5N/2$, where N is the number of processors. The curves for backoff on the barrier variable alone, and backoff on the barrier flag with backoff constant 2, 4, and 8 are also shown (as mentioned before, all our simulated cases of backoff on the barrier flag include first backing-off on the barrier variable.)

Figure 3 corresponds fairly well with our model's prediction of the reduction in synchronization references due to backing off on the barrier variable. Backoff on the barrier variable reduced the number of network accesses from 160 to 132, a 15% reduction. Not surprisingly, backoff on the barrier flag made no difference because everyone reaches the barrier at the same time when $A = 0$.

Backoff with $A = 1000$ often has a savings greater than the log of the time interval of arrival at the barrier because of reduced interference with the final write request into the flag. This phenomenon also explains the fewer network accesses for backoff with base 8 at A=1000 than at A=0 for 32 processors. However, this savings often comes at the expense of increased processor waiting times.

Figures 4 and 5 correspond to the network accesses by a process for $A = 100$ and $A = 1000$ respectively. In Figure 4 for the backoff on the barrier variable we see similar savings as in Figure 3 with $A = 0$ because the interval A is still not very big compared to the number of processors. Note, however, the big reductions that the exponential backoffs on the barrier flag gave. With $A = 100$, not everyone reaches the barrier flag simultaneously, so the ones who arrive early backoff by a large value. For example, with 16 processors and a base 4 backoff on the barrier flag, we see a savings of over 90% in network accesses. For 64 processors, base 8 backoff yields savings of about 60%.

The proportional benefit due to backoff decreases as N increases because contention in the network to access the barrier flag becomes a sizable portion of the network accesses. Recall that an unsuccessful network access in accessing the barrier flag is still counted as a network access. (To reduce these unsuccessful accesses one might use backoff techniques in the network accessing as discussed later.) For example, when $A = 100$ and $N = 512$, base 8 backoff yields less than a 30% reduction in network accesses.

Backoff on the barrier variable alone, for $A = 1000$, offers only modest savings. Interestingly this scheme offers virtually no savings for up to 32 processors, because few processors contend for the barrier flag, but the savings become more significant as the number of processors increases. For 256 processors, for example, backoff on the barrier variable yields about a 15% improvement.

The savings due to exponential backoff on the barrier flag with $A = 1000$, however, are quite dramatic. Since the pro-

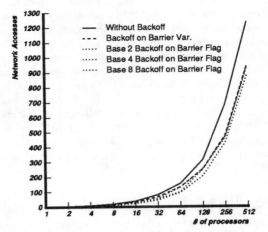

Figure 3: Performance of backoff algorithms for $A = 0$.

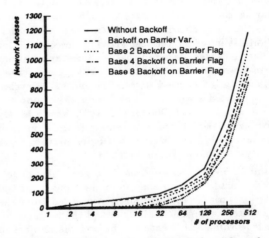

Figure 4: Performance of backoff algorithms for $A = 100$.

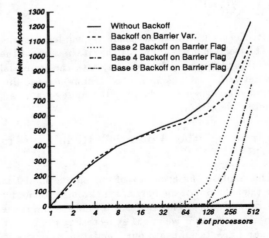

Figure 5: Performance of backoff algorithms for $A = 1000$.

cessors potentially have a large interval to poll the barrier flag before everyone arrives, over 95% savings in network accesses results with binary backoff on the barrier flag with 16 processors. The 64 processor case offers a similar improvement.

The small number of network accesses with backoff on the barrier flag for the cases $A = 0$ and $N < 8$, $A = 100$ and $N < 32$, and $A = 1000$ and $N < 128$, compares reasonably with the network accesses in the bus-based schemes, the broadcast based schemes, or the Hoshino scheme, with no extra hardware or the broadcast requirement. However, when A is smaller or N is larger, the backoff schemes tend to do much worse than the schemes that have special hardware support for synchronization.

It is clear that backoff on the barrier flag is potentially much more beneficial for large A because most of the network accesses that happen while the processes await the remaining processes to arrive at the barrier can be obviated. These accesses correspond to the first term in the Model 2 equation. Backoff on the barrier variable alone does not impact performance significantly when N is small compared to A, but can yield up to a 20% improvement when N is large.

It is interesting to see that the network accesses increase dramatically for $N = 128$ ($A = 1000$). It seems that the backoff techniques are not as useful in this case (improvement is less than about 30% for $N = 256$ and backoff with base 2), although for these cases barrier synchronization is probably inappropriate anyway without some form of distributed software combining [24]. Our backoff methods can still be used on the intermediate nodes of the combining tree. The reason for the sharp increase can be described as follows: When the number of processors is small compared to A, a process can get access to the barrier flag usually within one network access. However, when the number of processors is not small compared to A, then a process will suffer contention in trying to access the barrier flag, and contention shows up as repeated network accesses.

In both cases the network accesses can be dramatically reduced for $N < 128$. For larger N, when the contention due to multiple processors simultaneously accessing the barrier increases, the relative benefit decreases. Recall, we do nothing about these contention accesses. A method described in the next section can help reduce this problem.

Our simulations show that using a backoff method on both the barrier variable and the barrier flag can yield savings from 20% to over 95% of the network accesses. However, the reduction in network traffic using the backoff methods does not always come for free. Because a backoff method can cause unnecessary processor idle time, we must carefully analyze the delays that these techniques can introduce. The occurrence of delays alone might not be a major cause for alarm, because these delays correspond to the delays suffered by the synchronizing processes alone, and do not affect other processes. The next section addresses these issues.

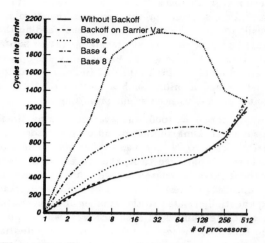

Figure 6: Processor waiting times for backoff algorithms for $A = 1000$.

7   Discussion of Tradeoffs

An appropriate backoff constant must be determined by trading off the reduction in network accesses with the potential increase in the number of cycles the cpu spends idling during backoff.

We determined from our simulations the average waiting times per processor when $A = 0$, 100 and 1000 for four cases: without backoff, with backoff on the barrier variable and with exponential backoff on the barrier flag with bases 2, 4 and 8. The waiting time for a process is computed as the number of cycles between first arriving at the barrier to when the process finds the barrier flag set.

For $A = 0$, and $A = 100$, we found that the waiting times for all the four curves are similar because the opportunity for a large backoff time is rare given that all the processes arrive within a 100 cycles of each other. The waiting time in these cases is proportional to the number of network accesses, as it is precisely these network accesses that give rise to the delays at the barrier.

We found that in all cases binary backoff provides a favorable tradeoff between large reductions in synchronization references and contained increases in wasted cpu cycles. Consider, Figure 6, which shows average processor waiting times for $A = 1000$. For 64 processors, binary backoff decreased synchronization accesses by 97% while increasing the time spent at the barrier by only 16%.

However, the average time spent idling can increase dramatically when both A and the base of the backoff algorithm are large because of the possibility of large backoff times. As an example, for 64 processors and $A = 1000$, the waiting times without backoff and with base 8 exponential backoff on the flag are 576 and 2048 respectively – depicting an increase of over 350% due to backoff. Even in this case, one important benefit is that the barrier accesses are both reduced and spread out uniformly over time.

When the arrival interval A is much larger than the number of processors, and a high processor utilization is important, one can modify the backoff algorithm as follows. If the backoff amount crosses some preset threshold, then it might be worthwhile to place the process on a queue pending the arrival of the last process. The enqueuing operation incurs a constant overhead that might be unnecessary should the processes arrive within a small interval. Because A cannot often be determined a priori, such a method of deciding when to put a process to sleep seems promising.

Interestingly, for $A = 1000$, the average waiting times per processor reach a maximum around 64 processors and then actually decline as N increases. When the number of processors is small compared to A, the processors can test the flag without excessive contention with other processors. After each unsuccessful test, they back off, and the backoff time is exponentially related to the number of unsuccessful tests. Because the number of such accesses can be quite large when contention is low and A is large, the potential for overshooting the point where the flag is set arises. Conversely, when the number of processors is comparable to A (or greater than A), the number of times a process manages to access the barrier flag is small due to contention with other processes. In such cases, the network access count increases, but the average waiting time per processor decreases. Referring to Figures 5 and 6 the decrease in the waiting time for the backoff curves closely corresponds to the increase in network accesses.

7.1 Summary

A few general observations can be made at this point. When the number of processors participating in the barrier synchronization is small compared to the time of arrival of the processors, significant reduction in network accesses can be achieved without compromising processor utilization due to backoff waiting for a small backoff base. In such cases, the number of synchronization network accesses is similar to those made in schemes that use special hardware support such as synchronization buses, broadcasts, or global synchronization logic. When the number of processors is large, and if they arrive within a relatively small interval of time, a penalty in either network accesses or processor idle time must be paid. However, depending on the situation, one can be traded for the other.

Our discussion thus far focused on the traffic and the waiting time *during* the execution of the barrier. We can also look at the effect on average traffic with the caveat that such smoothing might tend to make barrier accesses seem less disruptive. We measured the average network data traffic per processor in FFT (assuming separate packet-switched networks for the request and response), excluding synchronization references, to be 0.133 network accesses per cycle. Using results from our simulations of the barriers with $A = 100$ (roughly approximating the barrier interval A in FFT with 64 processors) we compute the extra traffic due to barriers when the barrier variable and the barrier flag are not cached. Adding these synchronization references to our base network traffic, the average traffic increases to 0.136 network accesses per cycle (assuming that the base traffic in A is also 0.133). Now, with a base 8 exponential backoff we find that the average network traffic drops to 0.134. This

decrease is significant considering that these savings come from reductions in synchronization references which are effectively hot-spot references. Moreover, we observe in this case that the base 8 exponential backoff also results in a 10 percent decrease in waiting time at the barrier. Both average network traffic and waiting time at synchronizations are reduced using backoff methods for our FFT application.

As a validation of our barrier simulation model, we also compared the average network traffic in FFT when synchronization references are not cached with the average network traffic predicted by our barrier model simulations. The numbers correlated well, with barrier simulations predicting 0.136 net accesses per cycle per processor, while measurements from FFT yielded 0.135.

We analyzed the tradeoff between network accesses and processor idle time due to backoff. In general, reducing the number of network accesses might be more important than reducing the processor idle time because reducing the number of network accesses also reduces the processor idle time because of the reduced contention in the network, and because of decreased competition with the regular network activities of the other processors not involved in the barrier.

8 Optimizations and Extensions

Adaptive backoff techniques have several other applications. For example, this technique can be applied to processors waiting on a resource that requires mutually exclusive access. Instead of spinning on the resource lock, the processors can backoff testing the lock by an amount proportional to the number of waiting processors. Adaptive techniques are more suited to this situation than barrier synchronization because the waiting time is proportional to the number of processors (the constant of the proportion is the average time the resource is held by each processor).

An adaptive backoff method can be used to reduce contention in unbuffered circuit-switched networks. If a network access suffers a collision, instead of resubmitting the request immediately, one can backoff some amount first. We are investigating such schemes in a large-scale multiprocessor project called ALEWIFE – a joint effort with Tom Knight at MIT. The backoff amount can be determined in one of several ways:

- The backoff amount can be proportional to the network depth traversed by the message, which is determined by a network supplied status byte indicating the stage at which the collision occurred. The rationale for this choice is that the deeper a message travels, the greater the network resource that it ties up in its unsuccessful attempt. Conversely, if a collision occurs within a few stages of travel into the network, the access can be resubmitted sooner as the network resources tied up will be smaller.

- An argument for making the backoff amount *inversely* proportional to the network depth traversed can also be made. The deeper a message travels before colliding, the less congested the network is expected to be, and so the access can be retried sooner. Simulations can be used to study the tradeoffs involved in these two opposing arguments and suggest a practical back-off algorithm.

- A colliding network access might wait some constant time proportional to the average round trip time through the network before retrying.

- The number of previous unsuccessful tries can be used as a parameter to an exponential backoff algorithm.

- In a packet-switched network, Scott and Sohi [20] make use of state information in the memory module queues to signal processors to hold back requests in congested situations. This state information could also be used to have the processors backoff sending requests by some time proportional to the length of the queue.

As we mentioned before, the adaptive backoff techniques that we evaluated do not require special hardware support. The synchronization software that determines which back-off method is used can be designed in one of several ways. One can be conservative and use a simple adaptive backoff on the barrier variable and a binary backoff on the barrier flag. The programmer can write the algorithms into the synchronization macros or routines from a knowledge of the application. The compiler can determine appropriate code sequences for the barrier synchronizations based on expected behavior of loops and the amount of visible parallelism. A more venturesome method might use profiling to determine the temporal behavior of the application and the number of processors participating in the synchronization and pass this information on to the compiler for further optimization. One case where such information might be useful is in determining when to (or whether to) queue a process to await a signal when the barrier flag is set rather than spinning on the network.

9 Conclusions

Network bandwidth is a precious resource in large-scale shared memory multiprocessors. This paper presents a group of adaptive backoff techniques aimed at reducing the number of network accesses due to synchronizations. We model adaptive techniques for barrier synchronizations and show that in many cases these techniques can achieve dramatic savings at minimal extra cost, while in other situations network accesses can be reduced while trading-off utilization of synchronizing processors. These techniques are implemented in software, and they can be optimized for varying applications.

The central idea behind an adaptive synchronization technique is to use synchronization state information and past history to reduce the number of idle synchronization spins. The general technique has many applications, such as reducing network accesses in barrier synchronizations, minimizing spin-lock accesses of processors waiting on a shared resource, and reducing contention in unbuffered circuit-switched networks.

10 Acknowledgements

We thank Kimming So, Harold Stone, and Prabhakar Raghavan for their insights contributed during discussions on many of the ideas presented in this paper. Kimming So aided us greatly in obtaining traces from PSIMUL. We also thank Pat Teller from NYU for providing the parallel SIMPLE and WEATHER programs. This research was funded by the Defense Advanced Research Projects Agency under contract # N00014-87-K-0825, and by IBM under a joint research program.

A Tracing Methodology

Our multiprocessor traces were generated using a "post-mortem scheduling" technique in which a multiprocessor trace is created from a memory reference trace of the uniprocessor execution of a parallel application. The uniprocessor trace is produced by PSIMUL [21], a multiprocessor simulator. Using the record of synchronization events contained in the uniprocessor execution trace, a postprocessor can schedule tasks from the uniprocessor execution trace into a multiprocessor trace in which the synchronization sections are simulated assuming some model of synchronization. The scheduler simulates processors generating the requests in a round-robin fashion.

This methodology can be used for a variety of programming paradigms. The three applications we traced were written in EPEX/FORTRAN using the Single-Program-Multiple-Data (SPMD) computational model [7]. In this model all processes are created at the beginning of the program and execute the same program. Though all processes are executing the same program, synchronization constructs embedded in the code dynamically determine which sections of the program processors execute. The SPMD model for Epex/Fortran contains serial and parallel sections along with replicate sections, which are executed by all processors.

The post-mortem simulates synchronization events in the application using some prescribed synchronization implementation. We simulate fetch-and-adds (F&A), a synchronization primitive used to exclusively update a location in memory, with an atomic read-modify-write operation. In EPEX/FORTRAN, synchronization constructs at the beginning of parallel and serial sections perform F&As on shared variables to determine task assignments to processes. Barriers and waits at the end of loops and serial sections are simulated by arriving processors first incrementing a shared variable through a F&A and then polling a barrier flag until it is set by the last arriving processor.

The Fast Fourier Transform (FFT) application, written at IBM, is a parallelized version of a Radix-2 FFT computation in two variables on a random array of complex numbers. Since we used a problem size of 128, the parallel loops working on the 128x128 matrix contained 128-way parallelism, providing for an even distribution of work to the 64 processors in our simulations.

The SIMPLE code models hydrodynamic and thermal behavior of fluids in two dimensions. Finite difference methods are used to solve the equations of inviscid compressible hydrodynamics and simple heat conduction on an N x N mesh. Once again, we used a problem size of 128, but several parallel sections do not contain fully 128-way parallelism resulting in an uneven distribution of work among the 64 processors in our simulations. SIMPLE is representative of an application with neither worst-case, nor best-case performance in the SPMD computational model.

The WEATHER code forecasts the weather by modeling the state of the atmosphere. The algorithm breaks the atmosphere down into a three-dimensional grid (108 x 72 X 9 in our case) encircling the globe and computes the value of several inter-related state variables using finite difference methods. WEATHER was the most poorly load-balanced application of the three we traced. Fifty-four processors (we used 64) would be the preferred number of processors to execute this application for the problem size used. Thus the load balancing in our three applications showed a wide range.

References

[1] Norman Abramson. The ALOHA System – Another alternative for computer communications. In *Proc. Fall Joint Computer Conf.*, pages 281–285, 1977.

[2] Anant Agarwal and Mathews Cherian. *Adaptive Back-off Synchronization Techniques*. MIT VLSI Memo, April 1989.

[3] Anant Agarwal, Richard Simoni, John Hennessy, and Mark Horowitz. An Evaluation of Directory Schemes for Cache Coherence. In *Proc. 15th Intl. Symp. on Computer Architecture*, IEEE, New York, June 1988.

[4] Lucien M. Censier and Paul Feautrier. A New Solution to Coherence Problems in Multicache Systems. *IEEE Trans. on Computers*, C-27(12):1112–1118, December 1978.

[5] J. W. Cooley and J. W. Tukey. An Algorithm for the Machine Calculation of Complex Fourier Series. *Math. Comput.*, 19:297–301, April 1965.

[6] W. P. Crowley and C. P. Hendrickson and T. E. Rudy. *The Simple Code*. Lawrence Livermore Laboratory TR, February 1978.

[7] F. Darema-Rogers, D. A. George, V. A. Norton, and G. F. Pfister. *Single-Program-Multiple-Data Computational Model for EPEX/FORTRAN*. TR RC 11552 (55212), IBM T. J. Watson Research Center, Yorktown Heights, November 1986.

[8] Daniel Gajski, David Kuck, Duncan Lawrie, and Ahmed Saleh. Cedar – A Large Scale Multiprocessor. In *Proc. ICPP*, pages 524–529, August 1983.

[9] A. Gottlieb, R. Grishman, C. P. Kruskal, K. P. McAuliffe, L. Rudolph, and M. Snir. The NYU Ultracomputer – Designing a MIMD Shared-Memory Parallel Machine. *IEEE Trans. on Computers*, C-32(2):175–189, February 1983.

[10] Tsutomu Hoshino. *PAX Computer. High-Speed Parallel Processing and Scientific Computing*. Addison Wesley, Reading Mass., 1989. Harold S. Stone, Editor.

[11] Eugenia Kalnay-Rivas and David Hoitsma. *Documentation of the Fourth Order Band Model*. Technical Report, NASA Modeling and Simulation Facility Laboratory for Atmospheric Science, NASA/Goddard Space Flight Center, Greenbelt, MD, 1979.

[12] L. Kleinrock and Y. Yemini. An Optimal Adaptive Scheme for Multiple Acess Broadcast Communication. *Proc. ICC*, pages 7.2.1–7.2.5, June 1978.

[13] S. S. Lam. A Carrier Sense Multiple Access Protocol for Local Networks. *Computer Networks*, 4(1):21-32, Jan. 1980.

[14] S. S. Lam and L. Kleinrock. Packet Switching in a Multiaccess Broadcast Channel: Dynamic Control Procedures. *IEEE Trans. on Computers*, C-23, Sept. 1975.

[15] E. L. Lusk and R. A. Overbeek. *Implementation of Monitors with Macros: A Programming Aid for the HEP and other Parallel Processors*. TR ANL-83-97, Argonne National Laboratory, Argonne, Illinois, December 1983.

[16] R. Metcalfe and D. Boggs. Ethernet: Distributed Packet Switching for Local Computer Networks. *Communications of the ACM*, 19(7), July 1976.

[17] Janak H. Patel. Analysis of Multiprocessors with Private Cache Memories. *IEEE Trans. on Computers*, C-31(4):296–304, April 1982.

[18] G. F. Pfister, W. C. Brantley, D. A. George, S. L. Harvey, W. J. Kleinfelder, K. P. McAuliffe, E. A. Melton, A. Norton, and J. Weiss. The IBM Research Parallel Processor Prototype (RP3): Introduction and Architecture. In *Proc. ICPP*, pages 764–771, August 1985.

[19] G. F. Pfister and V. A. Norton. 'Hotspot' Contention and Combining in Multistage Interconnection Networks. *IEEE Trans. on Computers*, C-34(10), October 1985.

[20] Steven Scott and Gurindar Sohi. Using Feedback to Control Tree Saturation In Multistage Interconnection Networks. In *Proc. 16th Annual Int. Symp. on Computer Architecture*, June 1989.

[21] K. So, F. Darema-Rogers, D. A. George, V. A. Norton, and G. F. Pfister. *PSIMUL - A System for Parallel Simulation of Parallel Systems*. Technical Report RC 11674 (58502), IBM T. J. Watson Research Center, Yorktown Heights, November 1987.

[22] Peiyi Tang and Pen-Chung Yew. Processor Self-scheduling for Multiple-Nested Parallel Loops. In *Proc. ICPP*, pages 528–535, August 1986.

[23] Wolf-Dietrich Weber and Anoop Gupta. Analysis of Cache Invalidation Patterns in Multiprocessors. In *Proc. ASPLOS III*, April 1989.

[24] P.-C. Yew, N.-F. Tzeng, and D. H. Lawrie. Distributed Hot-Spot Addressing in Large-Scale Multiprocessors. *IEEE Trans. on Computers*, C-36(14):388–395, April 1987.

A Cache Consistency Protocol for Multiprocessors with Multistage Networks

Per Stenström

Department of Computer Engineering, Lund University
P.O. Box 118, S-221 00 Lund, Sweden

Abstract

A hardware based cache consistency protocol for multiprocessors with multistage networks is proposed. Consistency traffic is restricted to the set of caches which have a copy of a shared block. State information is distributed to the caches and the memory modules need not be consulted for consistency actions.

The protocol provides two operating modes: distributed write and global read. Distribution of writes calls for efficient multicast methods. Communication cost for multicasting is analyzed and a novel scheme is proposed.

Finally, communication cost for the protocol is compared to other protocols. The two-mode approach limits the upper-bound for the communication cost to a value considerably lower than that for other protocols.

1   Introduction

One of the main problems of shared-memory multiprocessors is the network traffic caused by several processors accessing the global shared memory [14]. In order to increase the memory bandwidth, different interconnection networks can be used. One alternative for large-scale multiprocessors is to use a *multistage network* (e.g. as used by the RP3 [10], or by the Butterfly [3] multiprocessors). However, private caches are needed to reduce the network traffic as shown in Figure 1.

Private caches in a shared-memory multiprocessor introduce the *cache consistency* or *cache coherence problem* because of the existence of copies of a memory block.

The cache consistency problem has been extensively studied over the past years. There are two main approaches to attack the cache consistency problem: software and hardware methods.

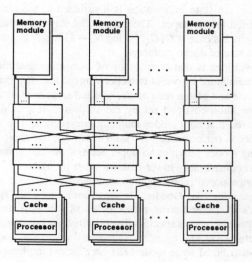

Figure 1: An example multiprocessor with private caches and a multistage interconnection network.

In the software approach, memory blocks are tagged as cacheable or noncacheable depending on the access pattern to shared data. Read-only or non-shared data structures can always be cached because cache consistency is only an issue for shared read-write data structures. Several software schemes have been proposed [13,4,6]. They all suffer from high cache miss ratio for shared read-write data structures simultaneously accessed by several processors. Another disadvantage is that the cache system as viewed by the software is not coherent; the user (or compiler) is responsible for tagging data with respect to cacheability.

In the hardware approach, consistency is maintained by a hardware implemented *cache consistency protocol* resulting in a coherent software view of the memory system.

Several cache consistency protocols for bus-oriented architectures have been proposed and are evaluated in [2]. These are called *snoopy cache protocols* because modifications of the state of a cached block are *broadcast* to all caches and each cache monitors the bus for consistency actions (typically invalidations or distributed writes).

Broadcast operations are too expensive to make snoopy cache protocols feasible for multistage networks; consistency traffic should be restricted to caches that have a copy of a block. In protocols based on this approach [5,16], a directory is typically stored at the memory level with one entry for each memory block. It contains state information for the block and a vector with one bit for each cache indicating which caches have a copy of the memory block.

Reduction of network traffic is paid for by the size of the memory storing the state information, which equals $O(NM)$, where N equals the number of caches and M equals the size of main memory. Another disadvantage is that the state information is not stored close to the caches which increases the network traffic.

A cache consistency protocol based on the same approach but where the state information is distributed to the caches is proposed in this paper. The size of the state information memory in this case is $O(C(N + \log N) + M \log(N))$, where C is the size of cache memory.

A novel idea is that consistency of each individual block can be maintained by one of two operating modes: *distributed write mode* and *global read mode*, selected so as to minimize communication cost and set by the software. It should be emphasized that both modes maintain consistency. The sole difference is performance. We shall show that our choice of operating modes provides an upper limit of the communication cost considerably lower than for other protocols.

Other proposed protocols are either tuned to specific program behavior like Goodman's write-once protocol [7] or Dragon's distributed write protocol [9]. Other approaches are adaptive protocols specifically optimized for bus-oriented architectures [11,1].

The distributed write mode calls for efficient implementation of multicast operations in multistage networks. The network traffic caused by multicasting is analyzed and a novel scheme is proposed. Finally, the communication cost for the cache consistency protocol is evaluated and compared to other protocols.

2 The Cache Consistency Protocol

2.1 Definitions and Basic Mechanisms

Cache memories are interconnected with each other by an $N \times N$ multistage network, given N caches, providing a path between every cache pair. The network also provides a path between each cache and memory module.

A *block* is a logical unit of memory consisting of a number of words and with an identification. Each memory module stores a number of blocks.

Copies of a block can reside in more than one cache. At most one cache *owns* the block. The owner is the only one allowed to modify the block.

Consistency of each individual block can be maintained in two ways, controlled by the owner. In *distributed write mode*, all writes are distributed to the caches that have a copy of the block. In *global read mode*, only one copy, the owner's copy, is allowed. If a block is referenced by another processor than the one attached to the cache that owns the block, the data

is read globally from the owner instead of loading a copy of the block.

The protocol is supported by the following states of a cached block: **Invalid**, **UnOwned**, **Owned Exclusively Distributed Write**, **Owned Exclusively Global Read**, **Owned NonExclusively Distributed Write** and **Owned NonExclusively Global Read**. All Owned states have an attribute **Modified** which determines whether the copy is consistent with the memory copy and eventually has to be written back.

Invalid means that the cache line does not contain a valid copy and the requested data has to be retrieved globally. **UnOwned** means that the cache contains a valid copy of the requested block. However, the block is not allowed to be modified. It also means that there exist other copies of the same block. If the copy is in one of the states denoted owned, it is allowed to be modified. State **Owned Exclusively Distributed Write**, means that there is no other copy and the write can proceed locally. State **Owned NonExclusively Distributed Write** means that the cache owns the copy but there exist other copies in the system which are updated if the block is modified. **Owned Exclusively or NonExclusively Global Read** means that there is only one copy, the owner's copy. If a cache needs to load a copy, the owner will prevent it to do so by responding only with the data requested.

Each cache contains a table consisting of a number of *cache entries*, each containing a data portion, a tag field, and a state field. The data portion holds the copy of a block. The tag field holds the identification of the block that currently occupies the cache entry. The state field holds information used by the cache consistency protocol and which determines the action to be taken.

In order for the cache controller to keep track of the state, the state field contains the following entities: A Valid bit (V) indicating whether the copy of the block is valid, an Ownership bit (O) indicating whether the block is owned, a Modified bit (M) indicating whether the copy is consistent with the copy in main memory, a Distributed Write bit (DW) which determines the operating mode, a vector of Present flags ($P_1 P_2 \ldots P_N$), one flag for each cache, indicating which caches (if any) have a copy of the block (in distributed write mode) or which caches have invalid copies of the block (in global read mode), and finally an owner identification (OWNER) occupying $\log_2 N$ bits.

The present flag vector and the modified and distributed write bit are used only by the owner. The owner identification is used only if the state of the block is invalid and determines where to retrieve the block.

The possible states for the copies and their meaning together with the content of the state field are summarized in Table 1.

Each memory module keeps track of the owner for each of its cached blocks by means of a data structure called *block store* containing one entry for each block. Each entry contains a valid bit (V) and an ID-field containing $\log_2 N$ bits storing the identification of the owner for the block.

In Figure 2, we show a situation where four private caches are used. Two copies of a block (block identification X)

State	Description	State field
Invalid	does not contain a valid copy.	$V = 0$
UnOwned	contains a valid copy which is not allowed to be modified. There exist other copies.	$V = 1, O = 0$
Owned Exclusively Distributed Write	The copy is owned and the only copy in the system. Copies are allowed.	$V = 1, O = 1, DW = 1,$ $P_i = 1, \ P_j = 0 \ \forall j \neq i$
Owned Exclusively Global Read	The copy is owned and the only copy in the system. Copies are **not** allowed	$V = 1, O = 1, DW = 0,$ $P_i = 1, P_j = 0 \ \forall j \neq i$
Owned NonExclusively Distributed Write	The copy is owned and there exist other **valid copies**	$V = 1, O = 1, DW = 1,$ $P_i = 1, P_j = 1$ for any $j \neq i$
Owned NonExclusively Global Read	The copy is owned and there exist other **invalid** copies	$V = 1, O = 1, DW = 0,$ $P_i = 1, P_j = 1$ for any $j \neq i$

Table 1: States for cached blocks, their meaning, and the content of the state field for cache i.

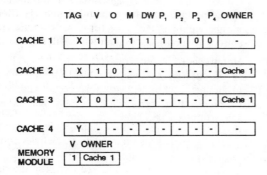

Figure 2: An example of how status information is distributed among caches and the memory controller.

are resident in cache 1 and 2. Cache 1 is the owner which means that its identification is stored in the block store. The content of the state field of cache 1 indicates that the copy is modified (i.e. inconsistent with the memory copy). The operating mode for this block is distributed write. The present flag vector indicates that cache 2 has a copy. Cache 3 has an invalid copy (the valid bit is 0) and cache 4 has no copy of block X (indicated by block identification Y occupying the cache entry). The OWNER field for cache 2 and 3 indicates that cache 1 is the owner creating a bypass directly to cache 1 instead of communicating through the memory module.

All actions taken by the protocol are a result of a memory read or a write operation issued by a processor. Therefore, the behavior of the protocol is described by making clear the actions taken (and state transitions) on the four results of a read or write operation, namely read hit, read miss, write hit, and write miss. We also make clear the actions taken when the operating mode for a block is changed.

2.2 Protocol Behavior

The following actions are taken depending on the result of a processor read or write operation. With hit we mean that the copy is valid. With miss we mean that the copy is either invalid or nonexistent in the cache.

1. *Read hit.* The copy is consistent and the read operation can be carried out locally in the cache.

2. *Read miss.*

   Copy is nonexistent

   A load request is sent to the memory module. Two cases are possible:

   (a) *There is no other copy.* The block is loaded into the cache from the memory and the state for this block is set to Owned Exclusively Global Read. The identification of this cache is marked in the block store.

   (b) *There are other copies.* The memory controller sends the load request to the owner (consulting the block store). The owner sets the present flag for the requesting cache. Two cases are possible:

      i. *Mode=distributed write.* The owner sends a copy of the block to the requesting cache. The state of the owner's copy is set to Owned NonExclusively Distributed Write and the state of the requested copy is set to Un-Owned.

      ii. *Mode=global read.* The owner sends only the requested datum and the owner identification. The requesting cache reserves a cache entry initialized to Invalid and sets the OWNER field to the owner's identification. The state of the owner's copy is set to Owned NonExclusively Global Read.

State=Invalid

The load request is sent directly to the owner by using the OWNER field. Two cases are possible:

(a) *Mode=distributed write*. The owner sends a copy to the requesting cache and the state for this is set to UnOwned. The final state of the owner's copy is Owned NonExclusively Distributed Write.

(b) *Mode=global read*. The owner sends only the requested datum. The final state of the owner's copy is Owned NonExclusively Global Read.

Possibly, a block must be replaced with the one that was loaded. Block replacement involves some protocol actions that are specified later.

3. *Write hit*. Four cases are possible depending on the state of the copy:

(a) *State=Owned Exclusively (Distributed Write or Global Read)*. Since this is the only copy, the write operation is carried out locally in the cache. The modified bit is set.

(b) *State=Owned NonExclusively Distributed Write*. The write operation is distributed to all caches which have a copy of the block (defined by the present flag vector). The modified bit is set.

(c) *State=Owned NonExclusively Global Read*. Since no copies are allowed in global read mode, the write operation is carried out locally. The modified bit is set.

(d) *State=UnOwned*. The block is not allowed to be modified and an ownership request is sent to the memory module. The memory module sends the request to the owner (consulting the block store). It also changes the corresponding entry in the block store to indicate the new owner. Two cases are possible:

    i. *Mode=distributed write*. The old owner sends the content of the state field to the new owner. It changes the state of the block to UnOwned.

    ii. *Mode=global read*. The old owner sends a copy and the state field to the new owner. It distributes the new owner identification to all caches which have an invalid copy and invalidates its own copy.

The subsequent actions of the write operation are carried out in the way specified for the Owned states above.

4. *Write miss*. A load with ownership request is sent to the memory module. Two cases are possible:

(a) *There is no other copy*. The block is loaded from memory and set to state Owned Exclusively Global Read. The write operation is then carried out locally and the modified bit is set.

(b) *There are other copies or state=Invalid*.

The request is sent to the owner via the memory module, which changes the corresponding entry in the block store to indicate the new owner. The old owner sets the present flag for the new owner. It also sends the copy and the state field to the new owner. If

    i. *Mode=distributed write*. The state of the owner's copy is set to UnOwned.

    ii. *Mode=global read*. The old owner distributes the new owner identification to all invalid copies and invalidates its own copy.

The subsequent actions of the write operation are carried out in the way specified for write hit for the Owned states.

5. *Block replacement*. Three cases are possible depending on the state of the block to be replaced:

(a) *State=Owned Exclusively (Distributed Write or Global Read)*. A message is sent to the memory module excluding it from the block store by clearing the valid bit. If the modified bit is set then the copy is written back to memory.

(b) *State=Owned NonExclusively (Distributed Write or Global Read)*. Ownership has to be transferred to another cache. An arbitrary cache marked in the present flag vector can be chosen. A request is sent to this cache. Upon reception, this cache either sends an acknowledgement back if it still has a copy or a negative acknowledgement if it has replaced this block in the mean time. If the cache accepts the ownership, it requests the ownership according to the protocol described above. If the cache does not accept to receive ownership, then the old owner has to try another cache.

(c) *State=UnOwned or Invalid*. A request is sent to the memory module which retransmits the request to the owner. Upon reception, the owner clears the corresponding bit in the Present flag vector.

6. *Set mode=distributed write*. This operation involves acquiring ownership which is done according to the actions described above. The DW bit is then set.

7. *Set mode=global read*. This operation also involves acquiring ownership and clearing DW. In addition, if state is Owned NonExclusively Distributed Write, an invalidation to be is sent to all caches and the DW bit is cleared.

3 Multicast Schemes

Network traffic for the proposed protocol is mainly caused by distributing writes to all caches that have a copy of the block in distributed write mode. We shall therefore investigate the communication cost for some multicast schemes for multistage networks.

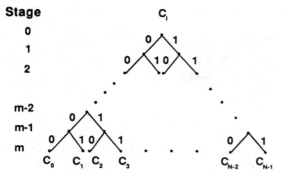

Figure 3: Paths from one node to all other nodes in an $N \times N$ omega network composed of 2×2 switches.

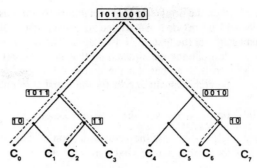

Figure 4: An example of how a message is routed using scheme 2 and an omega network interconnecting $N = 8$ caches.

A multistage network consists of a number of stages of switches. Given an $N \times N$ network composed of $a \times a$ switches, the number of stages is $m = \log_a N$ and the number of switches in each stage is N/a. Several topologies of multistage interconnection networks have been proposed [12]. For the sake of simplicity, we shall restrict the discussion of possible multicast schemes to omega networks composed of 2×2 switches even if the results can be generalized to other topologies of multistage networks with other switches.

In an omega network [8] composed of 2×2 switches, paths from a particular source to all destinations can be viewed as a binary tree (see Figure 3), where nodes represent switches, branches represent links, and leaves represent destinations. Stages are numbered $i = 0, 1, \ldots, m$, $m = \log_2 N$, where stage m denotes the destinations. Each switch has two outputs denoted 0 and 1 in Figure 3.

We will use a metric for network traffic that is as implementation independent of the network as possible. The metric to be used, which we call *communication cost*, is the amount of information that has to pass each link summed over all links. Let L_i be the amount of information that passes links to stage i, then the communication cost CC is

$$CC = \sum_{i=0}^{m} L_i \tag{1}$$

3.1 Scheme 1

A routing scheme for omega networks has been proposed [8] which works in the following way. Let the destination address be $D = <d_0 d_1 \ldots d_{m-1}>$. At stage i the output is determined by d_i; if $d_i = 0$ then the message is sent to output 0, and if $d_i = 1$ the message is sent to output 1. One bit is stripped off the routing tag at each stage.

Assume that we want to send a message containing M bits to $n = 2^k$ destinations, then the communication cost for these n messages is calculated by summing up the amount of information that passes each link in one path and multiply this by n. Hence

$$CC_1 = n \sum_{i=0}^{m} (m - i + M) = n(m+1)(M + m/2) =$$

$$n(\log N + 1)(2M + \log N)/2 \tag{2}$$

The communication cost is proportional to the number of destinations. This scheme does not take advantage of that there might exist common links in the paths to the destinations. This could be utilized by sending the message only once over common links. We shall investigate a *new* scheme that takes this into account and examine its communication cost.

3.2 Scheme 2

In this scheme, the present flag vector is used as a routing tag and it works in the following way. The vector $V = <v_0 v_1 \ldots v_{N-1}>$ contains one bit for each destination. Destination x receives a message iff $v_x = 1$.

Consider switches at stage i and let $y = 2^{m-i}$. The following operations then take place in each switch i, $i = 0, 1, \ldots, m-1$.

1. The destination vector $C = <c_0 c_1 \ldots c_{y-1}>$ is received from previous stage;

2. C is divided into two subvectors $A = <c_0 c_1 \ldots c_{\frac{y}{2}-1}>$ and $B = <c_{\frac{y}{2}} c_{\frac{y}{2}+1} \ldots c_{y-1}>$;

3. A is sent to output 0 iff there is at least one vector element $c_j = 1$, $j \in \{0, 1, \ldots \frac{y}{2} - 1\}$;

4. B is sent to output 1 iff there is at least one vector element $c_j = 1$, $j \in \{\frac{y}{2}, \frac{y}{2}+1, \ldots, y-1\}$.

In Figure 4 we show how a message is routed from an arbitrary source to destinations 0, 2, 3, and 6, given an omega network interconnecting $N = 8$ caches.

Let us derive an expression for the communication cost. It should be clear that the communication cost very much depends on where the destinations are situated. The *best case* occurs when the destinations are neighbors. In this case, the vector will be divided and passed to one switch in the subsequent stage for the first $m-k+1$ stages. The *worst case* is when the destinations are situated so that the destination vector is sent to both outputs for the first $k+1$ stages. We shall derive the communication cost for the worst case only:

Communication cost for scheme 2 (worst case):

In the table below we show the communication cost associated with links to each stage. Given $n = 2^k$ and $N = 2^m$ we get

Stage	Communication cost
0	$M + N$
1	$2(M + N/2)$
.	.
k	$2^k(M + N/2^k)$
$k+1$	$2^k(M + N/2^{k+1})$
.	.
m	$2^k(M + N/2^m)$

and hence

$$CC_2 = \sum_{i=0}^{k} 2^i(M + N/2^i) + \sum_{i=k+1}^{m} 2^k(M + N/2^i)$$

and if we replace m and k with their definitions we get

$$CC_2 = N(\log n + 1) + M(2n - 1) +$$
$$nM(\log N - \log n) + N - n$$

which after reduction leads to

$$CC_2 = n(M \log N - M \log n + 2M - 1) +$$
$$N(\log n + 2) - M \tag{3}$$

Let's compare the communication cost for scheme 1 and scheme 2.

$$CC_2 - CC_1 = n(M(1 - \log n) -$$
$$\log N(1 + \log N)/2 - 1) + N(\log n + 2) - M \tag{4}$$

From equation 4 the following can be proved.

- There exists an $n \le N$ such that scheme 2 results in less communication cost than scheme 1, for $N \ge 4$. We call this number *break-even* between scheme 1 and 2.

- Break-even will decrease when the message size (M) increases.

- Break-even will increase when the number of caches (N) increases.

In Figure 5, we show the communication cost for scheme 1 and scheme 2 versus n for a multiprocessor containing 1024 caches (m is 10) and the message size 20 (M is 20). In this case, break-even occurs when n is a small fraction of N. In Table 2 we can see break-even for the two schemes and how it is affected by the message size (M) and the number of caches (N).

	$M = 0$	$M = 40$	$M = 100$
$N = 64$	16	1	1
$N = 128$	32	4	1
$N = 256$	32	8	4
$N = 512$	64	16	8
$N = 1024$	128	32	16

Table 2: Break-even for scheme 1 and 2 and how it is affected by the message size (M) and the number of caches (N).

3.3 Scheme 3

Scheme 1 and 2 have the main advantage that we can route messages to an arbitrary set of destinations. There exists, however, another multicast scheme, proposed in [15] that has the restriction that the number of destinations must equal a multiple of 2, that is, $n_1 = 2^l$, $l = 0, 1, \ldots, m$ and the hamming distance of the destination addresses must be less than or equal to l.

The routing tag, denoted $b_0 b_1 \ldots b_{m-1} d_0 d_1 \ldots d_{m-1}$, consists of $2m$ bits and is used in the following way. Bits b_i and d_i are used by stage i; if b_i is 1 then the message is sent to both outputs (broadcast). Otherwise it is routed the same way as by scheme 1, that is, the message is sent to the output specified by d_i. b_i and d_i are stripped off at stage i.

We shall investigate the communication cost for this scheme given that the destinations are neighbors. In fact this is interesting if tasks that share a data structure are allocated to adjacent processors.

Assuming $n_1 = 2^l$, the communication cost at links to each stage is

Stage	Communication cost
0	$M + 2m$
1	$M + 2(m - 1)$
.	.
$m - l$	$M + 2(m - (m - l))$
$m - l + 1$	$2(M + 2(l - 1))$
.	.
m	$2^l M$

and hence

$$CC_3 = \sum_{i=0}^{m-l}(M + 2(m - i)) + \sum_{i=0}^{l-1} 2^{i+1}(M + 2(l - 1 -$$

and if m and l are replaced by their definitions we get

$$CC_3 = (\log N - \log n_1 + 1)(\log N + \log n_1 + M) +$$
$$2(M + 2(\log n_1 - 1))(n_1 - 1) - 4(2 + n_1(\log n_1 - 2))$$

and hence

$$CC_3 = n_1(2M + 4) - \log n_1(\log n_1 + M + 3) +$$
$$\log N(\log N + M + 1) - M - 4 \tag{5}$$

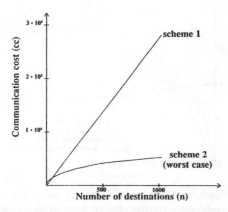

Figure 5: Communication cost vs. number of destinations for scheme 1 and scheme 2 (worst case).

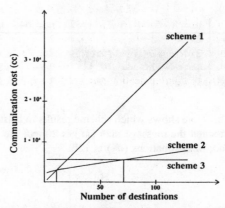

Figure 6: Communication cost vs. number of destinations for scheme 1, 2, and 3 for $N = 1024$, $n_1 = 128$, and $M = 20$.

	$n = 4$	$n = 8$	$n = 16$	$n = 64$	$n = 128$
$M = 0$	1	1	3	3	3
$M = 20$	1	1	2	2	3
$M = 40$	1	2	2	2	3
$M = 60$	1	2	2	2	3

Table 3: This table shows which scheme results in least communication cost for 1024 caches when the maximum number of destinations (n_1) equals 128. 1=scheme 1, 2=scheme 2, and 3=scheme 3.

3.4 A Combined Scheme

Let's assume that the maximum number of tasks in a parallel application is $n_1 = 2^l$, where $n_1 \leq N$, and that they are allocated on adjacently placed processors. At a given moment, an arbitrary subset, say $n \leq n_1$, of these processors will have a cached copy of a block of the shared data structure. Our question is which of the schemes results in least communication cost.

If scheme 2 is used, the worst case is no longer that of equation 3 because the destinations are among n_1 adjacently placed destinations. The worst case is now given by

$$CC_2' = \sum_{i=0}^{m-l-1} (M + N/2^i) +$$

$$\sum_{i=m-l}^{m-l+k} 2^{i-(m-l)}(M + N/2^i) + \sum_{i=m-l+k+1}^{m} 2^k(M + N/2^i)$$

which can be reduced to

$$CC_2' = n(M \log n_1 - M \log n + 2M - 1) + n_1 \log n +$$

$$M(\log N - \log n_1 - 1) + 2N \qquad (6)$$

It can easily be shown that there exists a break-even between scheme 1 and scheme 2 (CC_2' according to equation 6) which has the same properties as before. We shall investigate break-even between scheme 2 and 3.

We get

$$CC_3 - CC_2' = M(2(n_1 - n) + n(\log n - \log n_1)) +$$

$$n_1(4 - \log n) - \log n_1(\log n_1 + 3) +$$

$$\log N(\log N + 1) + n - 2N - 4 \qquad (7)$$

The following can be proved from equation 7.

- There exists an $n \leq n_1$ such that scheme 3 results in less communication cost than scheme 2.

- Break-even between scheme 2 and 3 will increase when the message size (M) increases.

- Break-even will decrease when the number of caches (N) increases.

These observations are exemplified in Tables 3 and 4. Now, assume that N is 1024, n_1 is 128, and M is 20 and let's investigate the communication cost for scheme 1, scheme 2, and scheme 3. In Figure 6 we show the communication cost versus the number of destinations according to equations 2, 5, and 6.

Scheme 1 is favorable for a small number of destinations, and scheme 2 for a moderate number and scheme 3 for a large number of destinations. We propose a combined scheme for which the communication cost is

$$CC_4 = \min(CC_1, CC_2', CC_3) \qquad (8)$$

In the last section, we shall discuss how to choose the scheme with least communication cost.

4 Performance Evaluation

Consider a parallel application where n tasks access a shared read-write data structure. For each block in the data structure we assume that exactly one task modifies it and all other tasks access it. The fraction of writes to the block is w.

413

	$n = 8$	$n = 16$	$n = 32$	$n = 64$	$n = 128$
$N = 256$	2	2	2	2	3
$N = 512$	2	2	2	2	3
$N = 1024$	1	2	2	2	3
$N = 2048$	1	1	3	3	3

Table 4: This table shows which scheme results in least communication when the message size (M) is 20 and the maximum number of destinations (n_1) is 128.

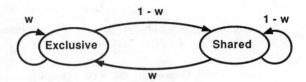

Figure 7: State transition probabilities for write-once.

We shall compare the average communication cost for each reference to the block if the block is stored at memory with the communication cost for some classical cache consistency protocols. We make the simplified assumption that the communication cost for a read is twice of that for a write. We will only take into account the consistency related network traffic (the cache is big enough for the data structure).

In case the block is stored at memory, the mean communication cost for each reference to this block is

$$CC_{NC} = (1 - w)2CC_1 + wCC_1 \qquad (9)$$

where CC_1 is defined in equation 2 with $n = 1$.

We now consider the *write-once protocol* [7]. Each cache resident block can be in one of two global states; *exclusive* or *shared*, according to Figure 7.

If the block is exclusive (only one copy), it will be shared if the next memory reference is a read operation. If the block is shared, it will be exclusive if the next reference is a write operation which leads to an invalidation sent to all caches. We model the global memory reference string as a Marcov process. Given that the probability of a write is w, we get the transition probabilities according to Figure 7.

From the state transition diagram, we can derive an expression of the mean communication cost per memory reference as

$$CC_{WO} = w(1 - w)(CC_4(n) + 2CC_1) \leq$$
$$w(1 - w)(n + 2)CC_1 \qquad (10)$$

where CC_4 is defined in equation 8, since an invalidation has to be multicast to n caches on each transition from shared to exclusive, and the block has to be loaded on each transition from exclusive to shared.

Next protocol we consider is the *distributed write protocol*. In this case we get

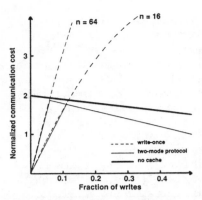

Figure 8: Normalized communication cost versus fraction of writes, for write-once (dashed lines), the two-mode protocol (solid lines). The normalized communication cost when the block is stored at memory is shown as a reference (bold).

$$CC_{DW} = wCC_4(n) \leq wnCC_1 \qquad (11)$$

because all read operations are local.

Finally, if consistency of the block is controlled by *global read*, the mean communication cost per memory reference is

$$CC_{GR} = (1 - w)2CC_1 \qquad (12)$$

because all read operations have to traverse the network twice.

For simplicity reasons we assume that multicast scheme 1 is used. From equations 9, 10, 11, and 12 we can prove that if distributed write mode is used when $w \leq w_1 = 2/(n + 2)$ and else global read then the average communication cost per reference is

- less than the communication cost without a cache, and

- the communication cost for write-once.

In Figure 8, we show the normalized communication cost (communication cost divided by CC_1) per memory reference for the different protocols.

5 Discussion of Results

A cache consistency protocol for multiprocessors with multistage networks has been proposed in this paper. One of its advantages over previously proposed protocols is that state information is distributed to the caches, restricting the size of the state memory to be proportional mainly to the size of the cache memory. The state memory can be further reduced by a split-cache organization, where only parts of the available cache supports shared read-write data structures.

Since the present flag vector is used only by the owner, we could separate parts of the state memory from the cache directory and select an entry in the state memory using an associative memory scheme. The size of the state memory could then be reduced.

The protocol is a type of ownership-protocol; a block must be owned before it is modified. For any application where each block of its shared data structure is modified by at most one task, ownership will not change. This is true for many supercomputing applications such as algorithms based on matrix operations. However, for applications where several tasks can modify a block, or when tasks can migrate, ownership will change which increases the network traffic.

We also analyzed some multicast schemes for multistage networks and found that communication cost can be reduced considerably if tasks are allocated on adjacently placed processors, employing different schemes depending on the number of tasks as proposed in the combined scheme of equation 8. In that scheme, break-even between scheme 1, 2, and 3 only depends on the number of caches (N), the maximum number of tasks (n_1) and the message size (M). It should be possible for the compiler to determine both the message size and the maximum number of tasks and consequently break-even. Break-even for a whole data structure could be stored in some registers. Hardware mechanisms could then use the contents of these registers together with the number of present flag bits that are set to determine which of the schemes to use.

We also found that the upper-bound for the communication cost could be reduced considerably using the two-mode protocol. We modeled the global reference string as a Markov process. This is justified for many algorithms based on matrix operations. However, communication cost for write-once can be much lower given locality in write operations. The point here was to show that write-once and distributed write can result in huge network traffic. By employing the two-mode scheme we can limit the upper-bound of the communication cost to a value lower than that without a cache. This is important if the multiprocessor is to support general-purpose applications.

By measuring the fraction of writes in the distributed write mode and the fraction of reads in the global read mode it should be possible to choose the mode with least communication cost. This could be done by using two counters; one counter counts all memory references to a block, and the other all reads to this block in global read mode. The present flag vector reflects the number of tasks if the cache is assumed to have space for the whole data structure. Consequently, w_1 can be specified and the mode could be selected from these measurements.

Acknowledgments

I remain indebted to Professor Lars Philipson for his advice and continuing support of my work. This research was supported by the Swedish National Board for Technical Development (STU) under contract numbers 80-3962, 83-3647, and 85-3899.

References

[1] J. Archibald. A Cache Coherence Approach for Large Multiprocessor Systems. In *Proc of 1988 International Conference on Supercomputing*, pages 337–345, 1988.

[2] J. Archibald and J-L. Baer. Cache Coherence Protocols: Evaluation Using a Multiprocessor Simulation Model. *ACM Transactions on Computer Systems*, 4(4):273–298, Nov 1986.

[3] BBN. Butterfly Parallel Processor Overview. Technical report, BBN Laboratories Incorporated, March 1986.

[4] W. C. Brantley, K. P. McAuliffe, and J. Weiss. RP3 Processor-Memory Element. In *Proc of the 1985 International Conference on Parallel Processing*, pages 782–789, Oct 1985.

[5] L. M. Censier and P. Feautrier. A New Solution to Coherence Problems in Multicache Systems. *IEEE Transactions on Computers*, C-27(12):1112–1118, 1978.

[6] J. Edler, A. Gottlieb, C. P. Kruskal, K. McAuliffe, L. Rudolph, M. Snir, P. Teller, and J. Wilson. Issues Related to MIMD Shared-memory Computers: the NYU Ultracomputer Approach. In *Proc of 12'th International Symposium on Computer Architecture*, pages 126–135, 1985.

[7] J. R. Goodman. Using Cache Memory to Reduce Processor-Memory Traffic. In *Proc of 10th Annual International Symposium on Computer Architecture*, pages 124–131, 1983.

[8] D. Lawrie. Access and Alignment of Data in an Array Processor. *IEEE Transactions on Computers*, C-24(12):1145–1155, 1975.

[9] L. Monier and P. Sindhu. The Architecture of the Dragon. In *Proc of 30th IEEE Computer Society International Conference*, pages 118–121, 1985.

[10] G. F. Pfister, W. C. Brantley, D. A. George, S. L. Harvey, W. J. Kleinfelder, K. P. McAuliffe, E. A. Melton, V. A. Norton, and J. Weiss. The IBM Research Parallel Processor Prototype (RP3): Introduction and Architecture. In *Proc of the 1985 International Conference on Parallel Processing*, pages 764–771, Oct 1985.

[11] L. Rudolph and Z. Segall. Dynamic Decentralized Cache Schemes for MIMD Parallel Architectures. In *Proc of 11th Annual International Symposium on Computer Architecture*, pages 340–347, 1984.

[12] H. J. Siegel. *Interconnection Networks for Large-Scale Parallel Processing*, pages 113–174. Lexington Books, 1985.

[13] A. J. Smith. CPU Cache Consistency with Software Support Using One-Time Identifiers. In *Pacific Computer Communication Symposium*, pages 153–161, 1985.

[14] P. Stenström. Reducing Contention in Shared-Memory Multiprocessors. *IEEE Computer*, (Nov):26–37, 1988.

[15] K. Y. Wen. *Interprocessor Connections – Capabilities, Exploitation, and Effectiveness*. PhD thesis, CSD University of Illinois at Urbana, 1976.

[16] W. C. Yen, D. W. L. Yen, and K. Fu. Data Coherence Problem in a Multicache System. *IEEE Transactions on Computers*, C-34(1):56–65, 1985.

On Data Synchronization for Multiprocessors

Hong–Men Su   Pen–Chung Yew

Center for Supercomputing Research and Development
University of Illinois at Urbana–Champaign
Urbana, Illinois 61801

Abstract

As the grain size becomes smaller, more parallelism can be found in most programs. However, to exploit smaller grain parallelism, more efficient synchronization primitives are needed to reduce the increased synchronization overhead. The granularity of parallelism that can be exploited on a multiprocessor system depends heavily on the type and the efficiency of the synchronization supported by the system. For medium–grain parallelism, ordered dependences such as data dependences and control dependences need to be enforced in order to guarantee the correctness of the parallel execution. Hence, data synchronization is one of the major sources of synchronization overhead in the program execution.

In this paper, we classify the synchronization schemes based on how synchronization variables are used. A new scheme, the **process–oriented scheme**, is proposed. This scheme requires a very small number of synchronization variables and can be supported very efficiently by simple hardware in the system.

Keywords: data dependences, data synchronization and parallelizing compilers.

1. Introduction

In shared–memory multiprocessor systems such as the Cray X–MP, the Alliant FX/8, the IBM 3090, the Cedar system [15] and the RP3 [21], speeding up the execution of a single job (as opposed to the improvement of system throughput) is of primary concern. In many scientific applications, getting good performance out of these systems has proven to be a nontrivial task. It requires exploiting all levels of parallelism in algorithm, program and machine architecture. It has been known for many years through Amdahl's Law that a small portion of serial code in a program can severely limit the speedup that can be obtained from parallel processing. Blindly adding more processors to a system without considering software issues will contribute very little to the system performance, and may actually be harmful due to the requirement of bulky interconnection schemes.

Exploring parallelism in algorithms and user programs has become a major thrust in parallel processing. Many compiler techniques have been developed to detect and enhance parallelism. Several successful parallelizing compilers such as VAST from Pacific Sierra, KAP from Kuck and Associates, Inc., University of Illinois' Parafrase [13], Rice University's PFC [2], IBM's PTRAN [1], to name a few, have been developed over the years. Empirical data have shown that parallelism can be exploited quite successfully in many applications on multiprocessor systems [14,16]. It has also been found that as the granularity of the parallelism becomes smaller, more parallelism can be found in most of the programs.

The trend of exploiting lower–level parallelism can be witnessed by Cray's moving away from large–grain macrotasking to support medium–grain microtasking in the Cray X–MP. However, as lower–level parallelism increases, more synchronizations become necessary. The overhead of these synchronizations determines the granularity of parallelism that can be exploited effectively. The more efficiently a system can support these synchronizations, the smaller the granularity (and hence, the more parallelism) can be exploited on the system. The data–flow computation model represents one extreme in which the granularity of parallelism is exploited down to the individual arithmetic operation level. Drastic architectural change is needed to support such systems.

In most scientific applications, loops (such as DO loops in Fortran) usually contain most of the computation in a program and are the most important source of parallelism [14]. Each loop often contains a large number of iterations with comparable running time in each iteration. The structure of these loops is very well defined, making it relatively easy to schedule them on a large number of processors.

Very often, the iterations of a loop are independent of each other and no interaction is needed when they are executed on different processes (they are called **Doall** loops in [25]). Many techniques have been developed to identify parallel loops and to transform a serial loop into a parallel loop [25]. However, even more prevalent is the case where the result produced in one iteration is used in a later iteration, or data fetched in one iteration is updated later in another itera-

This work is supported in part by National Science Foundation under Grant No.US NSF MIP–8410110, NASA NCC 2–559, the U.S. Department of Energy under Grant No. US DOE DE–FG02–85ER25001, and IBM Corporation.

tion (see Fig.2.1.a). This data access order is called data dependence [13]. Data dependence has to be enforced in order to preserve the semantics of a program. One way to enforce data dependences is to execute the loop sequentially which, of course, is very undesirable. However, if synchronization schemes are provided to allow those data dependences to be enforced among processes, all of the loop iterations can be executed concurrently (such loops are called **Doacross** loops in [8]). Of course, depending on the amount of time a processor has to wait for another processor to satisfy the data dependence, it may not be desirable to run a loop concurrently. A compiler is required to perform thorough data dependence analysis on the loop to determine which loop should be a Doacross loop. These issues have been studied quite extensively [1,4,8,25] and are beyond the scope of this paper.

Recognizing the importance of these low–level synchronizations in the exploitation of medium–grain parallelism, many recent multiprocessor systems are beginning to provide architectural support for such functions. The Cray X–MP has a set of shared semaphore registers [17], the HEP has a full/empty bit associated with each memory word [22], the Alliant FX/8 has a concurrency control bus and a set of synchronization instructions [3], and the Cedar system has a key/data scheme and a synchronization processor in each global memory module [26], etc.

In this paper, we first examine the issue of data dependences in section 2. In section 3, the existing synchronization schemes for enforcing data dependences are classified based on how synchronization variables are used. The advantages and the disadvantages of these schemes are also discussed. We then propose in section 4 a new synchronization scheme to eliminate most of the shortfalls discussed in section 3. Several examples of how to use this new scheme to exploit parallelism in programs are shown in section 5. In section 6, the hardware support needed to implement such a synchronization scheme is described. Section 7 contains our conclusions.

2. Dependences and Synchronization

2.1. Data Dependence

The dependences of programs consist of data and control dependences. Control dependence is caused by conditional branches. It can be handled by the methods similar to those for data dependences [18,26]; hence, we will only concentrate on data dependence here.

Data dependence includes (1) **flow dependence** (read–after–write), (2) **anti–dependence** (write–after–read); and (3) **output dependence** (write–after–write). These data dependences are extremely important in detecting parallelism and program restructuring. They imply a sequential order on accessing a data element, and need to be enforced in that order for correct data values. Hence, they can limit the amount of parallelism in a program.

According to their effects on program execution, the dependence relations can be categorized into two types [20]: the **ordered dependence** and the **access dependence** (or the **unordered dependence**). An **access dependence** occurs when several processes are trying to access a critical region. Each time only one process is allowed in the critical region. However, the order that those processes can enter the critical region is not restricted. It appears in many transaction–type operations and in barrier synchronization. Monitors [12], Fetch&Add [10], P's and V's operations or the

like can be used effectively for this type of synchronization. Since maintaining access dependence only needs mutual exclusion, a hardware cache coherent scheme can be easily extended to enforce it [5]. Most synchronization research of the past has concentrated on enforcing this type of dependence.

In this paper, we focus on the **ordered dependence** which occurs most frequently in numerical programs, and which often determines the amount of parallelism that can be exploited. An ordered dependence exists when the order of the accesses to an object is to be enforced. A data dependence analysis can be performed on a program to obtain a **data dependence graph** using any of the schemes proposed in [2,4,25]. A data dependence graph is a directed graph. Each node in the data dependence graph is an executable statement, and each arc represents a data dependence between two nodes. The node at the tail of the arc is the *source*, and the node at the head of the arc is the *sink* of the data dependence. Since all three types of data dependences specify some kind of access order, there is no need to differentiate them when we are just trying to enforce the access order.

To simplify our discussion, we will assume that only one level of nested DO loops is to be executed in parallel. Each iteration of the loop is a **process** which can be scheduled on a processor. The idea can be extended to multiply–nested loops as well. In Fig.2.1.a, there is a loop with 4 statements: S1, S2, S3, S4 and S5. Its data dependence graph is in Fig.2.1.b. There are flow dependences S1→S2, S1→S3 and S4→S5; anti–dependences S2→S4 and S3→S4; and the output dependence S1→S4. Notice that by enforcing dependences S1→S3 and S3→S4, the dependence S1→S4 can be covered. In Fig.2.1.c, we expand the loop to show data dependences which are to be enforced between loop iterations. Each iteration is a process scheduled on a processor, and synchronization instructions are needed when these processes are accessing data elements of the array A. We call this type of synchronization **data synchronization**.

Data dependence distance is a very useful concept in data synchronization. In Fig.2.1.c, the flow dependence S1→S2 occurs in processes two iterations apart, i.e., the result stored in S1 of iteration i is used in S2 of iteration $i+2$. The data dependence distance between S1 and S2 is thus 2, and is shown next to the corresponding dependence arc in Fig.2.1.b. This data dependence distance can be easily computed by subtracting the subscript expressions of the two array references. The rest of the data dependence distances are shown in

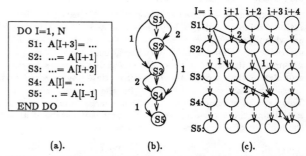

(a).   (b).   (c).

Fig.2.1 (a) A loop with ordered dependences. (b) Its dependence graph. (c) Its expanded dependence graph showing only dependences around *A[i+3]*. (*Dashed lines*: execution order within iterations; *Solid lines*: cross–iteration dependences.)

Fig.2.1.b. All of the data dependences in Fig.2.1.a have a constant distance.

2.2. Data Synchronization

All data dependences must be enforced by synchronizing processes when they are accessing those shared data items. As shown in Fig.2.1, one statement can be the source or the sink of several data dependences. The following requirements must be met in order to perform correct data synchronization:

(1) The process which executes the source statement of a data dependence can signal the completion of its execution to the process which executes the sink of the data dependence only after the effect of its execution can be observed by that process. For example, in a flow dependence, the process which updates a value in its private cache must wait until the updated value is reflected in the shared memory, or reflected in a coherent cache state before it can signal the completion of its execution [9].

(2) A process executing a statement which is the sink of several data dependences (e.g. S4 in Fig.2.1.c) must wait until all of the source statements have completed before it can proceed.

Any synchronization requires some information to be transmitted between synchronizing processes. In data synchronization, this information can be stored in full/empty bits in the HEP, the synchronization registers in the Cray X–MP and in the Alliant FX/8, or the key/data pair in the shared global memory of the Cedar system. To facilitate our discussion, we use synchronization variables to represent this information. Different data synchronization schemes can incur different amount of overhead. Schemes such as HEP's full/empty bits, or Cedar's key/data pair require large amount of storage for synchronization variables in shared global memory. They are suitable for large scale multiprocessor systems. In this paper, we propose a scheme which requires smaller amount of storage for synchronization variables and is more suitable for small scale multiprocessor systems such as the Cray X–MP, the Alliant FX/8, the Encore Multimax, etc.

3. Data Synchronization Schemes

Constant–distance dependence occurs very frequently in numerical programs [25] and, due to its fixed dependence distance, can be enforced by very efficient mechanisms. Various data synchronization schemes can be characterized by the way synchronization variables are used.

3.1. Data–Oriented Schemes

In this type of schemes, at least one dedicated synchronization variable (called a key) is associated with each datum on which access order is to be enforced. A datum can be a scalar or an element of a structure, such as an array. A datum and its key(s) are usually stored in the same memory module, so that a data access and its related synchronization operation can be done efficiently by the memory controller. This type of scheme usually requires a large number of keys. Initializing these keys can result in significant overhead unless the number of processors in the system is large.

Based on different programming models, two types of schemes have been proposed: the reference–based schemes, and the instance–based schemes. We use the program in Fig.2.1 as an example to illustrate these schemes. Fig.3.1 shows how accessing array element A[i+3] is synchronized among processes using these schemes.

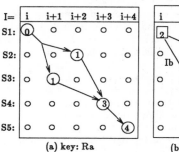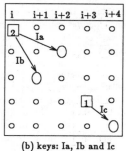

(a) key: Ra   (b) keys: Ia, Ib and Ic

synchronization operations:

$\boxed{N}$: write N copies of data; set all keys to full.

$\widehat{N}$: wait until key$\geq$N; read/write data; ++key.

$\bigcirc$: wait until key=full; read data.

Fig.3.1 Synchronization activities of Fig.2.1 under (a) The reference–based scheme (b) The instance–based scheme.

●**Reference–Based Schemes.** Each data element is associated with a key. In Fig.3.1.a, each number in the circles indicates the **access order** which is to be compared with the key when accessing the data element. The key is initialized to 0, and after each access the key is incremented (see the instruction in Fig.3.1.a). The way the access order is checked in Fig.3.1.a allows data fetches in S2 and S3 to be performed in any order. Cedar synchronization instructions can be used to perform these operations very efficiently in a global memory module [26].

●**Instance–Based Schemes.** Each updated value of a data element is assigned a different memory location and a different key to allow read operations after the update to proceed in parallel (see Fig.3.1.b). It is similar to the single-assignment rule in the functional languages, where no output dependences and anti–dependences exist in the program. The full/empty bit in Denelcor's HEP machine [22], where each key only assumes two values (0 for empty and 1 for full), is very suitable for this scheme. **Variable renaming** is needed during compile time to remove output and anti– dependences. Multiple copies of an updated value are also needed if there are multiple reads for the updated value.

3.2. Statement–Oriented Schemes

In this class of schemes [3,18], each statement Sa is assigned a synchronization variable sc (called **statement counter** or **SC**) shared among all instances of data dependences in which Sa is the source (Fig.3.2.b). It enforces a sequential order such that, after process i completes its execution of Sa, it waits until $sc=i-1$ before it increments sc to i. Hence, when $sc=i$, all of the process j, $j\leq i$, must have completed the execution of Sa. Initially, sc is set to k–1 if the first iteration is k. For process i to execute a sink statement Sb (Fig.3.2.a), it has to check if each of its corresponding sources has completed, i.e., for each Sa with $Sa \rightarrow Sb$, it checks if $sc \geq i-D$, where D is the distance of $Sa \rightarrow Sb$. If a statement is both a source and a sink, it must behave as a sink first. The Alliant FX/8 uses this scheme to execute Doacross loops with the support of a concurrency control bus and Advance/Await instructions [3]. Statement–oriented schemes are fairly simple to implement, but they force the updating of the SC associ-

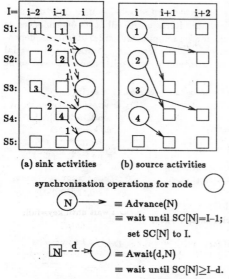

Fig.3.2 The statement–oriented scheme for Fig.2.1.

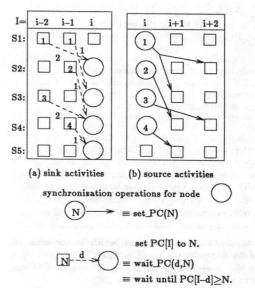

Fig.4.1 The process–oriented scheme for Fig.2.1.

ated with each source statement to a sequential order, resulting in some loss of parallelism. For loops with many data dependences, statement–oriented schemes are also not suitable (see Example 1 in section 5).

4. A Process–Oriented Scheme

In this section, we propose a new scheme which only requires a small number of synchronization variables. There exists a **duality** between this scheme and the statement–oriented scheme. The main idea is that, instead of assigning one synchronization variable to each datum or each statement, each process (i.e., each iteration) is assigned one synchronization variable, called a **process counter (PC)**. The PC can only be updated by the process itself. A PC can be viewed as part of the state of a process which contains two pieces of information: the *process id* and the *step*. The step of a PC is updated after the completion of each source statement (see Fig.4.1). The maximum step for a PC is the total number of the source statements in each iteration. The execution of a sink statement requires it to check the PC's of all of its corresponding source statements (see Fig.4.1).

The number of iterations in a loop is usually very large. Assume we only have **X** PC's in the system. The loop needs to be **folded** to share X PC's, and each process needs to acquire a PC before it can update the PC. The process id of a PC is thus used to designate the *owner* of the PC. PC's can be arranged so that processes i, X+i, 2X+i, ..., etc. share the same process counter PC[i], where $1 \leq i \leq X$. Process X+i can update PC[i] only after process i releases it (by executing release_PC as explained later in Fig.4.2.a). However, a process can start its execution without obtaining a PC as long as it need not update the PC. Note that initially PC[i] should be assigned to process i, where $1 \leq i \leq X$.

Several useful primitives are needed in the process–oriented scheme (please refer to Fig.4.2.a): (1) **set_PC** which updates the step of the PC after the completion of a source statement (except the last one); (2) **release_PC** which gives the PC to the next process after the completion of the last

i: the number of the iteration being executed.
X: number of process counters used.
mod: modulus operation.
PC's format: <owner, step>, and
$\quad$ <w,x> $\geq$ <y,z> iff w>y, or w=y and x$\geq$z.
Initially, PC[i]=<i,0>, $1 \leq i \leq X$.

- **set_PC**(*current_step*): /* update PC to current step. */
$\quad$ PC[i mod X].step $\leftarrow$ *current_step*.
- **release_PC**(): /* release PC for process i+X to use. */
$\quad$ PC[i mod X] $\leftarrow$ <i+X, 0>.
- **wait_PC**(*dist, step*): /* i−*dist*: pid of the source. */
$\quad$ while(PC[(i−*dist*) mod X] $<$ <i−*dist*, step>).
- **get_PC**(): /* get the ownership of PC. */
$\quad$ wait_PC(0, 0). $\qquad$ — (a) —

```
doacross i=1, N
  S1(i);
  get_PC(); /* wait for the PC to be available. */
  set_PC(1); /* completion of source 1. */
  wait_PC(2, 1); /* until process i−2 completes source 1.*/
  S2(i);
  set_PC(2);
  wait_PC(1, 1);
  S3(i);
  set_PC(3);
  wait_PC(1, 2);
  wait_PC(2, 3);
  S4(i);
  release_PC(); /* complete last source and release PC. */
  wait_PC(1,4);
  S5(i);
end doacross                              — (b) —
```

Fig.4.2 (a) The primitives for the process–oriented scheme.
(b) The Doacross loop transformed from the loop in Fig.2.1.

source statment; (3) **wait_PC** which, before execution of a sink statement, spin waits until the corresponding source is completed; and (4) **get_PC** which waits for acquiring the ownership of a proper PC. Fig.4.2.b shows the code needed to syn-

myPC: the index to the owned PC.
owned: a flag denoting if a process has got its PC.
•wait_PC, get_PC, set_PC, release_PC: same as before.

•load_index(*pid*):
   myPC ← *pid*;   /* use pid as index to PC. */
   owned= FALSE.   /* Initially, PC is not owned. */
•mark_PC(*current_step*):
   if(not owned and PC[myPC mod X].owner < myPC)
   /* not previously owned and not transferred, don't change PC. */
      return;
   set_PC(*current_step*);
   owned= TRUE.
•transfer_PC():
   if(not owned) get_PC();
   release_PC().   /* give ownership to next process. */

Fig.4.3 The improved primitives for the process–oriented scheme.

chronize the loop in Fig.2.1. The transfer of the ownership is accomplished by process i executing **release_PC** on the completion of its last source statement, and by process X+i executing **get_PC** before it first updates the PC.

Notice that in the statement–oriented scheme, the ownership of a SC is shared in turn by all instances of the same source statement. Since different instances of the same source statement very often can be executed simultaneously as in Fig.2.1, such "horizontal" sharing introduces unnecessary delay due to waiting for ownership. In other words, the process i must wait for process i–1 to release the ownership of each SC, implying that process i must wait for the completion of all the processes before it. If for some reason one process delays its release of the SC (e.g. executing a longer branch), all later processes will be affected. In the process–oriented scheme, a PC is shared by all source statements in the same process. Since statements are assumed to execute sequentially within a process, this "vertical" sharing of a PC can never result in such delay. In the folded version, the delay due to waiting for ownership of a PC currently belonging to process i can happen only in processes X+i, 2X+i, ..., etc. However, this occurs less frequently than in the statement–oriented scheme if X is large enough.

Actually, if we study it more carefully, the requirement of acquiring a PC before executing the first source statement as in Fig.4.2.b can be further relaxed. We can have an improved scheme based on the new primitives in Fig.4.3. On completion of each source statement (except the last one), a process tests the ownership of the PC. If it owns the PC, then a new state is marked; otherwise, it proceeds without waiting for the availability of the PC. This is done by executing **mark_PC**. However, to signal the completion of all its source statements and to transfer the ownership of the PC to the next process, it must execute **transfer_PC** after the completion of the last source statement. Executing **transfer_PC** guarantees that a process has owned a PC and has the right to transfer the PC to the next owner. In Fig.4.3, another primitive **load_index** is also introduced. It saves the index of a PC in an internal variable *myPC* to be used by others primitives and resets the flag *owned*. In the improved scheme, the new primitives **mark_PC** and **transfer_PC** replace the **set_PC** and the **release_PC**, respectively; while the **load_index** can substitute the **get_PC**. (In fact, load_index can be the first statement of the loop body.)

5. Applications

Because the process–oriented scheme uses only one synchronization variable per iteration for all of its dependences, it can handle much more complicated cross–iteration dependences, especially when a Doacross loop contains other serial loops or procedure calls, and when loop boundaries need to be considered.

•**Example 1.** a Doacross loop enclosing a serial loop:

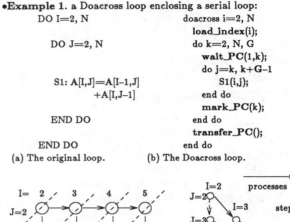

(a) The original loop.   (b) The Doacross loop.

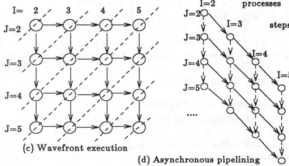

(c) Wavefront execution

(d) Asynchronous pipelining

Fig.5.1 Synchronizing a Doacross loop enclosing a serial loop.

Fig.5.1.a is a simplified four–point relaxation code. Fig.5.1.c depicts the well known **wavefront** method which requires loop index transformation. A barrier synchronization is needed between two consecutive wavefronts. However, the execution of a barrier requires that processors be busy–waiting at the barrier until all of the processors arrive. An alternative is to use an **asynchronous pipelined** method as shown in Fig.5.1.d, in which we serialize the inner loop as a process and execute the outer loop as a Doacross loop. The two methods will have the same number of parallel steps; however, the efficiency and the processor utilization is much better in the asynchronous pipelined method.

Since there are N–1 synchronization points between two consecutive processes (Fig.5.1.d), this implies that N–1 SC's are needed to get the maximum parallelism if we use the statement–oriented scheme. However, in practice, N is very large which makes the statement–oriented scheme perform poorly when the number of SC's is limited. By using the process–oriented scheme, we are able not only to synchronize the loop with a small number of PC's, but also to exploit the parallelism very effectively. We can also reduce the amount of synchronization needed between successive iterations of I by grouping **G** iterations in the J loop as shown in Fig.5.1.c. (Assume (N–1)/G is an integer.) Some extra delay will be incurred between the successive iterations of the I loop; however, the amount of synchronization can be reduced significantly due to the increase of granularity.

•**Example 2.** A multiply–nested Doacross loop:

```
DO I=1, N                    doacross i=1, N
    DO J=1, M                    doacross j=1, M
                                     load_index((i−1)*M+j);
S1: A[I,J]= ...                      s1(i,j);
                                     mark_PC(1);
                                     wait_PC(1,1);
S2: B[I,J]= A[I,J−1] ...             s2(i,j);
                                     transfer_PC();
                                     wait_PC(M+1,2);
S3: ... = B[I−1,J−1]                 s3(i,j);
    END DO                       end do
END DO                       end do
(a) The original loop        (b) The Doacross loop
```

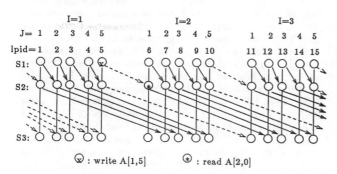

: write A[1,5]   : read A[2,0]

(c) The expanded dependence graph with M=5.

Fig.5.2 Synchronizing a multiply–nested Doacross loop.

One of the major problems in data–oriented schemes is that they are quite awkward in handling loop boundaries when there are multiple loop nestings. As shown in Fig.5.2.c, at loop boundaries (when J=1), A[I,J−1] in S2 and B[I−1,J−2] in S3 do not depend on any source as shown by dashed lines. Whereas, in the rest of the iterations, A[I,J−1] in S2 depends on A[I,J] in S1, and B[I−1,J−2] in S3 depends on B[I,J] in S2 as shown by solid lines. These boundaries need to be handled explicitly by a lot of extra code and overhead.

Using the process–oriented scheme, these loop nestings can be implicitly coalesced to obtain a **linearized process id** (*lpid*) as the index to the PC. When loop index set is equal to (i,j), the *lpid* is *(i−1)*M+j*. After that, the loop can be executed as a singly–nested loop without worrying about loop boundaries (Fig.5.2.b). However, implicit coalescing can introduce extra dependences (shown as dashed lines in Fig.5.2). Some parallelism may be lost from these extra dependences, but the complexity of detecting boundaries is avoided. That overhead can be $O(r^2d)$ per iteration, where *r* is the number of occurrences of an array variable and *d* is the depth of the nested loop [24].

Note that data–oriented schemes still have the boundary problem even after the loop is linearized. This is because, in those schemes, synchronizations are done on each data element. The number of times each data element is accessed (or synchronized) in a loop is fixed, and may be different for those data elements referenced at the loop boundaries. Linearization cannot change the number of times a data element is accessed. Furthermore, introducing extra accesses for those data elements at the boundaries to make the number of syn-

chronizations the same for all data elements requires the testing of boundaries anyway. It is not as easy as in our process–oriented scheme.

•**Example 3.** Dependence sources in branches:

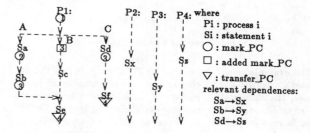

Fig.5.3 Synchronizing dependences with sources in branches.

When there are conditional branches, some of the data dependences may not exist because a branch may not be taken. One solution is as follows: if a synchronization primitive changes a synchronization variable in one path, the synchronization variable must also be changed in all other paths to allow the effect to be the same no matter which branch was taken.

In Fig.5.3, P1 executes **transfer_PC** before it completes its execution. Every sink of P1 eventually can proceed. However, P1 should inform the sinks to proceed as soon as possible. So in Fig.5.3, after Sd in branch C, **mark_PC(3)** is executed instead of **mark_PC(2)**; and **mark_PC(3)**, though not required, is added as the first statement in branch B.

•**Example 4.** Implementing a butterfly barrier:

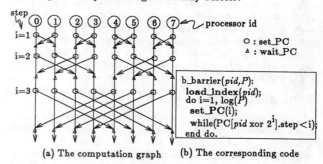

(a) The computation graph   (b) The corresponding code

Fig.5.4 Implementing a butterfly barrier.

A butterfly barrier (Fig.5.4.a), which can remove the hot–spot effect, performs better than a counter–based barrier even in a small bus–based system [6], and it needs no atomic operation. Using the process–oriented scheme, it requires fewer synchronization variables and operations than those needed in [6]. Procedure b_barrier() in Fig.5.4.b is called by each processor with different *pid*, where P, the number of processors, is a power of 2 and xor is a bitwise exclusive–or operation. Since each process corresponds to a processor in this case, no folding is needed. Thus the computation involved in obtaining the ownership can be eliminated. The *while* statement in Fig.5.4.b is a modified version of **wait_PC**. Note that with a minor modification, b_barrier() can work even when P is not a power of 2 [11].

●Example 5. Executing phases of computation with local
communication:

```
fft(pid, P):        /* pid, P: same as in b_barrier(). */
    load_index(pid);
    do i=1, log(P)
        BASIC_FFT(pid, i, P);
        set_PC(i);
        while( PC[pid xor 2ⁱ].step < i );
    end do.
```

The example shown here is an FFT. If we partition the data
used in the FFT into chunks equal to the number of processors, the computation pattern is the same as a butterfly barrier in Example 4, except that an additional BASIC_FFT() is
performed in each stage. However, since communication only
takes place between two processors in each stage, there is no
need for a global barrier as in [7]. Instead, in each stage, after
each processor completes its computation in BASIC_FFT(), it
only waits for another processor with which it exchanges data.
Procedure fft() is intended to be called in the same way as
b_barrier() in Example 4. In fact, the process-oriented scheme
is very suitable for code with many phases of computation.
After each phase, a limited amount of communication is
needed in each sub-group. Another example is the discretization method for solving partial differential equations [19], in
which a process only needs to synchronize with processes computing its neighboring regions.

Several comments can be made about the process-
oriented synchronization scheme. First, it can be incorporated
into a concurrentizing compiler using algorithms similar to
[18]. Second, it can also be used as a new paradigm in parallel
programming. Only one synchronization variable is needed in
each process to handle all ordered dependences. Third, it fits
very well in dynamic scheduling schemes such as processor
self-scheduling [24], where better load balancing among processors can be achieved. As a matter of fact, dynamic scheduling is assumed in all of the examples shown above.

6. Hardware Considerations

Notice that because we are trying to support medium-
grain parallelism, it is not efficient to use context switching
whenever a synchronization operation needs to wait. **Busy-
waiting** is more appropriate in this case. A good scheduling
policy such as proposed in [23] can reduce such busy-waiting
even further.

Excluding busy-waiting, each access to the source or the
sink of a data dependence requires only one extra access to its
corresponding PC. The extra traffic incurred is small, but the
parallelism obtained can be very significant. The PC's could
be incorporated in a hardware-maintained coherent cache system, even though they may be purged out of a cache.

To reduce the access time of a PC and the impact of
busy-waiting traffic, we can use a dedicated synchronization
bus and some synchronization registers to store the PC's as in
Alliant FX/8. Each processor keeps an image of all PC's in its
local synchronization registers. Whenever a PC is updated in
one processor, the new value is broadcast via the bus to all of
the other processors so that the local image of the PC in each
processor can be updated. Notice that, since a PC needs to be
updated only after the source statement is completed, the
amount of such traffic is no worse than that in the main data
bus. Busy-waiting operations can then be performed on the
local copies of the PC's without introducing extra traffic to

the synchronization bus. Also, since the process id is used
quite frequently in our synchronization primitives, a special
register **myPC** for each processor can be used to store its
value. A local status bit **owned** is also helpful to indicate if it
has already owned its corresponding PC. **Owned** is set when
a process updates its PC in mark_PC, and is reset in
load_index. The proposed scheme works best if the number of
PC's (i.e., X) equals to a power of 2 and is a small multiple of
the number of processors. The modulus operation needed in
computing the index of a PC can then be done easily by taking
the lower bits of a process id.

It is worth noting that the primitives need **not** be
atomic, because each PC is monotonically incremented by
only one processor at any time and wait_PC waits for the PC
to exceed (not stay at) a certain value. This makes the primitives much easier to implement. Also, the two fields in a PC,
i.e., **owner** and **step**, need not be updated simultaneously
(this can reduce the bus width). There are two reasons for
this. First, in our scheme, it is impossible for two processes to
update the same PC at the same time. Second, the read of a
local PC (by wait_PC) and the update of the PC (by a
mark_PC or transfer_PC) can proceed in any order without
changing the desired synchronization behavior. Assume the
value of the PC is $<i,j1>$. An update will change it to either
$<i,j2>$ where $j2>j1$ (by a mark_PC), or $<i+X,0>$ (by
transfer_PC). In the former case, a read either gets $<i,j1>$ or
$<i,j2>$. If retried, it will eventually get the value $<i,j2>$.
In the latter case, if **step** is updated first, then the transition
of the PC's values is $<i,j1> \rightarrow <i,0> \rightarrow <i+X,0>$ which
again will not cause any undesired side effect.

Further reduction in the broadcast transactions (i.e.,
writes) is possible because a PC is updated by the sequence of
mark_PC(1), mark_PC(2), ..., and transfer_PC from the same
process. Each later write covers all previous ones. However,
individual information should be provided as soon as possible.
As seen in section 4, a mark_PC need not update the PC if the
ownership has not been obtained. However, its ownership is
guaranteed by the final transfer_PC in each process. This can
reduce the number of global synchronization operations and
unnecessary waiting. A similar improvement can also be
applied to hardware. For example, an issued write need not
be sent out if a second write to the same PC arrives before the
former has gained the bus access, thus avoid the extra bus
traffic.

The above proposed implementation is similar to the
concurrency control bus in the Alliant FX/8. However, by
allowing a synchronization variable (PC) to be indexed by a
variable[1] (i.e., **pid** needed in the primitives is stored in register **myPC**), it significantly improves the functionality of our
proposed primitives. Hardware and software reduction of synchronization and waiting operations also become easier in our
scheme.

The advantages of the process-oriented scheme can be
summarized as follows: (1) It eliminates the use of barrier synchronization to implicitly enforce data dependences when the
latter is not suitable (Example 5). Memory contentions (i.e.,
the hot-spot effect) and the inefficiency caused by waiting for
the last processor to complete in a barrier synchronization can
be avoided; (2) Compared to the statement-oriented scheme,
it eliminates unnecessary serialization of consecutive iterations

---

[1] The index to a synchronization register accessed by Alliant's Advance and
Await must be a constant.

and can handle loops with many dependences more efficiently (Example 1); and (3) It can handle multiply–nested loops without the overhead of checking loop boundaries as needed in data–oriented schemes (Example 2). It also reduces the number of synchronization variables and the overhead associated with initializing these variables very substantially.

7. Conclusions

In exploring low–level parallelism, efficient synchronization schemes are needed. Ordered dependences are very important in exploring medium–grain parallelism. They require synchronization mechanisms which are very different from the transaction–type of synchronization such as maintaining the exclusive usage of a critical region. To enforce ordered dependences, efficient data synchronization is essential.

We have identified issues which are important in data synchronization. By the method of exchanging synchronization information, several synchronization schemes are categorized and compared. A new process–oriented scheme which requires only a small number of synchronization variables is proposed. It can be supported by very simple hardware in the system. Several applications of this scheme are presented to show its advantages over the previously proposed schemes.

References:

[1]. F. Allen, M. Burke, P. Charles, R. Cytron and J. Ferrante. *An Overview of the PTRAN Analysis System for Multiprocessing*. Int. Conf. on Supercomputing (June 1987).

[2]. R. Allen and K. Kennedy. "PFC: A Program to Convert Fortran to Parallel Forms", Rep. MASC–TR82–6, Rice Univ., 1982.

[3]. Alliant. *FX/Series Architecture Manual*. Alliant Computer Systems Corp., 1986.

[4]. U. Banerjee. "Speedup of Ordinary Programs", Ph.D. Thesis, Univ. of Illinois at Urbana–Champaign, DCS Report No. UIUCDCS-R-79-989, 1979.

[5]. Bitar and A. Despain. *Multiprocessor Cache Synchronization: Issues, Innovations, Evolution*. Int. Symp. on Computer Architecture (June 1986) pp. 424–433.

[6]. E.D.Brooks III. *The Butterfly Barrier*. Int J. of Parallel Programming (1986) vol. 15–4, pp. 295–307.

[7]. Z.Cvetanovic. *Performance Analysis of the FFT Algorithm on a Shared–Memory Parallel Architecture*. IBM J. Res. Develop. (July 1987) pp. 435–451.

[8]. Ron Cytron. *Doacross: Beyond Vectorization for Multiprocessors*. 1986 Int. Conf. on Parallel Processing (Aug. 1986) pp. 836–845.

[9]. M. Dubois, C. Scheurich and F. Briggs. *Synchronization, Coherence, and Event Ordering in Multiprocessors*. Computer (Feb. 1988) pp. 9–21.

[10]. A. Gottlieb, R. Grishman, C. Kruskal, K. McAuliffe, L. Rudolph and M. Snir. *The NYU Ultracomputer -- Designing an MIMD Shared Memory Parallel Computer*. IEEE Trans. Comput. (Feb. 1983) pp. 175–189.

[11]. D. Hensgen, R. Finkel and U. Manber. *Two Algorithms for Barrier Synchronization*. Int. J. of Parallel Programming (1988) vol. 17–1, pp. 1–17.

[12]. C.A.R Hoare. *Monitors: An Operating System Structuring Concept*. CACM (Oct. 1974) pp. 549–557.

[13]. D. Kuck, R. Kuhn, D. Padua, B. Leasure and M. Wolfe. *Dependence Graphs and Compiler Optimizations*. ACM Symp. on Principles of Programming Languages (July 1981).

[14]. D. Kuck, A. Sameh, R. Cytron, A. Veidenbaum, C. Polychronopoulos, G. Lee, T. McDaniel, B. Leasure, C. Beckman, J. Davies and C. Kruskal. *The Effects of Program Restructuring, Algorithm Change, and Architecture Choice on Program Performance*. 1984 Int. Conf. on Parallel Processing (Aug. 1984).

[15]. D. Kuck, E. Davidson, D. Lawrie and A. Sameh. *Parallel Supercomputing Today and the Cedar Approach*. Science (Feb. 1986) vol. 231, pp. 967–974.

[16]. M. Kumar. *Effect of Storage Allocation/Reclamation Methods on Parallelism and Storage Requirements*. Int. Symp. on Computer Architecture (June 1987) pp. 197–205.

[17]. J. Larson. *Multitasking on the Cray X-MP-2 Multiprocessor*. Computer (July 1984) pp. 62–69.

[18]. Samuel Midkiff and David Padua. *Compiler Algorithms for Synchronization*. IEEE Trans. Comput. (Dec. 1987) pp. 1485–1495.

[19]. D.M.Nicol and F.H.Willard. *Problem Size, Parallel Architecture, and Optimal Speedup*. Int Conf. Parallel Processing (Aug. 1987) pp. 347–354.

[20]. Anita Osterhaug. *Guide to Parallel Programming on Sequent Computer Systems*. Sequent Computer Systems, Inc., 1986.

[21]. G. Pfister, W. Brantley, D. George, S. Harvey, W. Kleinfelder, K. McAuliffe, E. Melton, V. Norton and J. Weiss. *The IBM Research Parallel Processor Prototype (RP3): Introduction and Architecture*. 1985 Int. Conf. on Parallel Processing (Aug. 1985) pp. 764–771.

[22]. B. J. Smith. *A Pipelined, Shared resource MIMD Computer*. 1978 Int. Conf. on Parallel Processing (Aug. 1978) pp. 6–8.

[23]. P. Tang, P. C. Yew and C. Q. Zhu. *Impact of Self-Scheduling Order on Performance of Multiprocessor Systems*. 1988 Int. Conf. on Supercomputing (July 1988) pp. 593–603.

[24]. Peiyi Tang. "Self-Scheduling, Data Synchronization and Program Transformations for Multiprocessor Supercomputers", Ph.D. Thesis, CSRD Report #809, Univ. of Illinois, Urbana–Champaign., 1988.

[25]. M. Wolfe. "Optimizing Supercompiler for Supercomputers", Ph.D. thesis, Rep.82–1105, DCS, Univ. of Illinois at Urbana–Champaign, 1982.

[26]. Chuan Qi Zhu and Pen–Chung Yew. *A Scheme to Enforce Data Dependence on Large Multiprocessor Systems*. IEEE Trans. Software Eng. (June 1987) pp. 726–739.

Author Index

Agarwal, A. 396
Allerton, D.J. 354
Anido, M.L. 354
Annaratone, M. 307, 315
Arvind, ... 262
Baer, J.-L. 140, 158
Bandoh, T. 203
Beacco, J.M. 186
Ben-Asher, Y. 88
Benker, H. 186
Bescos, S. 186
Bhuyan, L.N. 325
Boyle, P.D. 16
Bryant, R.E. 336
Chang, P.P. 224, 242
Chen, C.-L. 387
Chen, M.-S. 105
Cherian, M. 396
Cheriton, D.R. 16
Conte, T.M. 224
Davidson, G.S. 36
Dorochevsky, M. 186
Eggers, S.J. 2
Egozi, D. 88
Ezhilchelvan, P.D., ... 177
Farrens, M.K. 234
Fukazawa, T. 344
Ghosal, D. 325
Goosen, H.A. 16
Goto, A. 25
Goto, E. 290
Grafe, V.G. 36
Gupta, A. 273
Harper, D.T. III 72
Hennessy, J. 114
Hill, M.D. 131
Hiraki, K. 46
Hoch, J.E. 36
Holmes, V.P. 36
Hopkins, T.M. 64
Hopper, A. 300
Horowitz, M. 114
Hwu, W.W. 224, 242
Ibbett, R.N. 64
Ichikawa, S. 290
in 't Velt, R. 362
Irie, N. 78
Itoh, Y. 344
Jeffré, Th. 186
Jesshope, C.R. 150
Jiang, H. 325

Jones, A. 300
Jooss, R. 131
Jouppi, N.P. 281
Katz, R.H. 2, 122
Kessler, R.E. 131
Kim, K. 372
Kimura, T. 344
Kodama, Y. 46
Kravitz, S.A. 336
Kuga, M. 78
Lazowska, E.D. 158
Lebeck, A. 131
Levy, H.M.. 140
Liao, C.-K. 387
Linebarger, D.A. 72
Lioupis, D. 300
Llaberia, J.M. 96
Matsumoto, A. 25
McKinnon, K.I.M. 64
Miller, P.R. 150
Mizrahi, H.E. 158
Morioka, M. 203
Mulder, J.M. 362
Murakami, K. 78
Navarro, J.J. 96
Nikhil, R.S. 262
Nitezki, P. 54
Noyé, J. 186
Patt, Y.N. 195
Pleszkun, A.R. 234
Pommerell, C. 315
Portier, R.J. 362
Poterie, B. 186
Prasanna Kumar, V.K. 372
Przybylski, S. 114
Pöhlmann, A. 186
Rühl, R. 307, 315
Rutenbar, R.A. 336
Sakai, S. 46
Sato, M. 290
Schuster, A. 88
Scott, S.L. 167
Sexton, A. 186
Shin, K.G. 105
Shrivastava, S.K. 177
Singhal, A. 195
Sohi, G.S. 167
Srivastava, A. 362
Steenkiste, P. 252
Stenström, P. 407
Su, H.-M. 416

Syre, J.C. 186
Takeda, K. 344
Thibault, O. 186
Tick, E. 25
Tomita, S. 78
Tomizawa, M. 344
Tripathi, S.K. 325
Tully, A. 177
Valero, M. 96
Valero-Garcia, M. 96
Wang, W.-H. 140

Watzlawik, G. 186
Weber, W.-D. 273
Weiss, S. 380
Williams, M.H. 211
Wong, K.-F. 211
Wood, D.A. 122
Yamaguchi, S. 203
Yamaguchi, Y. 46
Yantchev, J.T. 150
Yew, P.-C. 416
Yuba, T. 46